Apocalypticism
in the Mediterranean World
and the Near East

Proceedings of the International Colloquium
on Apocalypticism
Uppsala, August 12–17, 1979

edited by

DAVID HELLHOLM

2nd edition
enlarged by Supplementary Bibliography

1989

J. C. B. Mohr (Paul Siebeck) Tübingen

Sponsors of the Colloquium

THE ROYAL ACADEMY OF LETTERS, HISTORY AND ANTIQUITIES
Professor Torgny Säve-Söderbergh, President

THE FACULTY OF THEOLOGY AT THE UNIVERSITY OF UPPSALA
Professor Thorvald Källstad, Dean

Organizing Committee

Professor GEO WIDENGREN, Royal Academy of Letters,
History and Antiquities (Chairman)

Professor JAN BERGMAN, University of Uppsala

Professor HANS DIETER BETZ, University of Chicago

Professor LARS HARTMAN, University of Uppsala

Professor THORVALD KÄLLSTAD, University of Uppsala,
Dean of the Faculty of Theology

Professor EVALD LÖVESTAM, University of Lund,
Dean of the Faculty of Theology

Professor HELMER RINGGREN, University of Uppsala

Professor TORGNY SÄVE-SÖDERBERGH, University of Uppsala,
President of the Royal Academy

Docent DAVID HELLHOLM, University of Uppsala (Secretary)

Published with support from

Kungl. Vitterhets Historie och Antikvitets Akademien
Villagatan 3, S-114 32 Stockholm

Förderungs- und Beihilfefonds Wissenschaft der VG Wort GmbH
Goethestrasse 49, D-8000 München 2

CIP-Titelaufnahme der Deutschen Bibliothek

Apocalypticism in the Mediterranean world and the Near East: proceedings of the
Internat. Colloquium on Apocalypticism, Uppsala, August 12–17, 1979 / ed. by
David Hellholm. [Sponsors of the colloquium the Royal Academy of Letters,
History and Antiquities; the Fac. of Theology at the Univ. of Uppsala]. – 2. ed.,
enlarged by supplementary bibliography. – Tübingen: Mohr, 1989
ISBN 3-16-145386-7
NE: Hellholm, David [Hrsg.]; International Colloquium on Apocalypticism
(1979, Uppsala)

Ph. Vielhauer

In Memoriam

PHILIPP VIELHAUER

★ 3. 12. 1914 − † 23. 12. 1977

Editor's Foreword

With the appearance of this volume of proceedings from the International Colloquium on Apocalypticism (Uppsala, August 1979) a work which began in the spring of 1977 is brought to its completion.

As the list of members of the Organizing Committee, the list of contributors to the volume, and persons and institutions mentioned in this foreword indicate, many people have been involved in this extensive and – as I hope – rewarding enterprise.

Firstly, I want to express a word of sincere gratitude to those with whom I have had the privilege to co-operate in planning and implimenting the Colloquium as well as in publishing the present volume:

(a) This holds first of all for the members of the Organizing Committee for their steadfast and continuous support and for the authors for their unfailing collaboration. The arrangement of the Colloquium was made possible by support from Kungl. Vitterhets, Historie och Antikvitets Akademien (Stockholm), The University of Uppsala and its Faculty of Theology (Uppsala), and Magn. Bergvalls Stiftelse (Stockholm).

(b) Due to the initiative of Prof. Martin Hengel the publisher Mr. Georg Siebeck of J. C. B. Mohr (Paul Siebeck) (Tübingen) graciously offered to publish this large volume of proceedings. The publication was made possible by substantial grants from Kungl. Vitterhets, Historie och Antikvitets Akademien (Stockholm) and Förderungs- und Beihilfefonds Wissenschaft der VG Wort GmbH (Munich).

(c) During the process of seeing the volume through the press I have received excellent help from members of the Organizing Committee, from my colleague at Emory University (Atlanta, Ga.), Prof. John H. Hayes, and – as far as corrections and proof-reading of the English essays are concerned – from Mr. Michael R. Cosby and Mr. J. Lee Magness, also from Emory University, as well as Mr. Bruce C. Johanson from the University of Uppsala. Most of all, however, my thanks are due to my wife, Mrs. Berit Hellholm, who has supported this undertaking not only in various ways during the meeting itself but also in typing and correcting manuscripts and in proof-reading the German essays during the process of publication.

Secondly, a word regarding the dedication. The participants of the Colloquium decided unanimously to dedicate the volume of proceedings to the memory of the late Professor Philipp Vielhauer. When visiting Dr. Vielhauer in his home in Bonn in June 1977, I invited him to present a paper at the Colloquium on "Early Christian Apocalypses", an offer which he accepted with great delight.

Only a few months later I learned with deep sorrow about his premature death, which was not only a personal loss for all his friends but also a severe loss for New Testament scholarship and Apocalyptic research. The present volume affirms throughout the appraisal given by Prof. Wilhelm Schneemelcher in his memorial address: ". . . man vergleiche einmal die ausgezeichnete Darstellung, die Vielhauer der urchristlichen Apokalyptik . . . gewidmet hat, mit den vielen neueren Arbeiten auf diesem Gebiet. Dann wird deutlich, daß zwar in vielen Punkten inzwischen neue Einsichten gewonnen sind, daß aber auch die neueren Arbeiten aufbauen auf dem Fundament, das eine frühere Generation gelegt hat" (*In Memoriam Philipp Vielhauer* [Schriften der Universität Bonn: Reihe 3, Alma Mater. Beiträge zur Geschichte der Universität 44], Bonn: Bouvier 1978, 11).

Uppsala/Linköping, October 1982   DAVID HELLHOLM

Contents

THE PHENOMENON OF APOCALYPTICISM
DIE VORSTELLUNGSWELT DER APOKALYPTIK
LE PHÉNOMÈNE DE L'APOCALYPTIQUE

THE LITERARY GENRE OF APOCALYPSES
DIE LITERATURGATTUNG APOKALYPSE
LE GENRE LITTÉRAIRE DES APOCALYPSES

THE SOCIOLOGY OF APOCALYPTICISM AND THE
"SITZ IM LEBEN" OF APOCALYPSES
DIE SOZIOLOGIE DER APOKALYPTIK UND DER
SITZ IM LEBEN DER APOKALYPSEN
LA SOCIOLOGIE DE L'APOCALYPTIQUE ET LE
"SITZ IM LEBEN" DES APOCALYPSES

CONCLUSION AND EVALUATION
ZUSAMMENFASSUNG UND AUSWERTUNG
BILAN ET PERSPECTIVES

Introduction

David Hellholm

In my brief introduction I will refrain from summarizing or evaluating the contributions to this volume. This task has been undertaken by Prof. Kurt Rudolph in his concluding article. My duty is merely to describe the origin of the Colloquium, its intended purpose and the structure of the program and consequently also of this volume.

1. Origin and Planning of the Colloquium

The first plans for an International Colloquium on Apocalypticism were drawn up in a conversation between Prof. Geo Widengren, Prof. Hans Dieter Betz and the present writer in May of 1977.

Kungliga Vitterhets, Historie och Antikvitets Akademien (The Royal Academy of Letters, History and Antiquities, Stockholm) with its President, Prof. Torgny Säve-Söderbergh, and the Faculty of Theology at the University of Uppsala with its Dean, Prof. Thorvald Källstad, declared themselves willing to support the idea of such an international conference on Apocalypticism and to serve as sponsors of the Colloquium. They also appointed an *Organizing Committee* consisting of the following members:

Professor Geo Widengren, Royal Academy of Letters, History and Antiquities (Chairman)

Professor Jan Bergman, University of Uppsala (Treasurer)

Professor Hans Dieter Betz, University of Chicago

Professor Lars Hartman, University of Uppsala

Professor Thorvald Källstad, University of Uppsala (Dean of the Faculty of Theology)

Professor Evald Lövestam, University of Lund (Dean of the Faculty of Theology)

Professor Helmer Ringgren, University of Uppsala (Vice-chairman)

Professor Torgny Säve-Söderbergh, Royal Academy of Letters, History and Antiquities (President of the Academy; Adjunct member of the Committee)

Docent (*nunc*) David Hellholm, Universities of Uppsala/Linköping (Secretary and editor of the volume of proceedings)

The Organizing Committee decided to invite thirty-three scholars from different countries and continents to deliver papers in their own fields of expertise. In addition to the lecturers a number of scholars were invited to take part in the discussions and/or to preside over the sessions. With great regret we had to acknowledge that a few invited scholars were prevented from participation due to either professional, political or personal reasons, to illness and even decease.

2. The Purpose of the Colloquium

The positive experience of the *Colloquium on Gnosticism* held in Stockholm in 1973, which also was sponsored by the Royal Academy, resulted in a desire to accomplish for Apocalypticism what had been achieved for Gnosticism in Messina and Stockholm.[1]

The purpose of the conference was laid down by the Organizing Committee in the following words of the Program:[2]

> *The purpose of the Colloquium is to give a survey of the present situation in apocalyptic research, to point out new thoughts and methods, and to stimulate further research in this field.*

In the planning of the Colloquium this intended purpose was the model according to which scholars were selected and the structure of the program was conceived.

Contrary to the Messina conference[3] no agreement upon a definition of Apocalypticism could be reached during the conference. In spite of several attempts at a definition, there seemed to be a consensus that for the time being *"contra definitionem, pro descriptione"* (Assmann) would be the appropriate way to pursue investigations in the field of Apocalypticism. And yet one can see that most contributors have in one way or another reflected upon the question of definition in their contributions and even stipulated their own definitions as a starting point for their investigations. This state of affairs is, in fact, a clear indication of the necessity for a hermeneutic mediation between *inductive* and *deductive* methods also in the area of apocalyptic research.[3a]

---

[1] Cf. the proceedings of these conferences: Ugo Bianchi (ed) 1967; Geo Widengren/David Hellholm (eds) 1977.

[2] Program page 5.

[3] Bianchi (ed) 1967, XX–XXXII.

[3a] See Hellholm 1980, 66, 96; *idem* 1982, § 3.3.3. and § 4.2.1.3.4. # (b).

3. The Structure of the Program and the Publication of Proceedings

Since "Apocalypticism"[4] is such a broad signeme *extensionally* as well as *intensionally*,[5] the Organizing Committee decided with regard to the former aspect to limit the topic to

Apocalypticism in the Mediterranean World and the Near East in Antiquity with certain emphasis on the Jewish and Christian religions.[6]

However regrettable from a scientific point of view, this temporal and local limitation was an absolute necessity from a practical perspective. Inevitably such a restriction resulted in the exclusion of other areas of equal significance to Apocalypticism in general.[7]

With regard to the intensional aspect, the program was devided into four sections:[8]

I. *The Phenomenon of Apocalypticism (Vorstellungswelt);*
II. *The Literary Genre of Apocalypses (Literaturgattung);*
III. *Sociology of Apocalypticism and "Sitz im Leben" of Apocalypses;*
IV. *The Function of Apocalypticism (in its Historical Setting).*

In the present volume, however, the last section has been subsumed into section III. and replaced by *IV. Conclusion and Evaluation* which heads Prof. Rudolph's discussion of the contributions to the present volume. These intensional significations of the lexeme "Apocalypticism" correspond to the form-critical program of content, form and "Sitz im Leben"[9] as well as to the text-semiotic dimensions of text-semantics, text-syntactics and text-pragmatics.[10]

The integration of the intensional and extensional aspects was attained by means of subsuming the extensional treatment of the various religions

---

[4] The lexeme "Apocalypticism" in the title of this volume and in this introduction is used in a broad sense (like the German term "Apokalyptik") including the conceptual significations (cf. Kurt Baldinger 1980, 110) referred to *infra*. A different and more narrow usage of "Apocalypticism" is found, *e.g.*, in Paul D. Hanson 1976, 30, James A. Brashler 1977, 71 ff., esp. 72 f. note 5, and in various contributions to this volume.

[5] For these semantic terms cf. Albert Menne 1973, 25, 75; Jens Allwood et alii 1977, 125 ff.; Dieter Wunderlich 1979, 205 ff. and esp. Hartmut Kubczak 1975.

[6] Program page 5.

[7] Cf. Kurt Rudolph's remarks in his contribution *infra* § 1.

[8] Program page 5.

[9] Cf. Hermann Gunkel 1925, 283 f.: "Genres I establish a) according to the common store of thoughts and moods, b) according to the similar 'Sitz im Leben', c) according to the constant forms of expression"; *idem* 1924, 183: "Only where we have all three criteria preserved together . . . have we the right to speak of a genre"; Philipp Vielhauer 1965: Literary Character – Literary Genre (582 ff.), The World of Ideas – Contents (587 ff.), Origin of Apocalyptic – 'Sitz im Leben' of Apocalypses (594 ff.); *idem* 1975, 487–493; Hanson 1976, 29 ff.

[10] Cf. Hellholm 1980, *passim*, esp. the summary on pp. 72–74; *idem* 1982, §§ 1.–4.1.

in Antiquity into the four intensionally defined sections referred to above. Apart from the just mentioned exception this structuration has been kept in publishing the contributions from the Colloquium in this volume of proceedings.

The advantage of such an integration is obvious: (a) on the one hand it enables the reader to recognize the presence or (possible) absence and – in case of occurrence – the type(s) of apocalyptic conceptions, the literary genre Apocalypse and the historical and sociological presupposition(s) together with the communicative function(s) within locally and temporally pre-determined religious and cultural areas; (b) on the other hand it allows the reader to study the same religion from different perspectives such as content, form and "Sitz im Leben"/function. This enables the reader to establish the presence or absence and – in case of occurrence – the characteristic features of one, several or all of the intensionally defined dimensions in each of the extensionally pre-determined areas. This, however, is at the most an ideal for a Handbook and the present volume can only to a certain degree realize this goal, since it would have required a much stronger piloting on the part of the Organizing Commitee. Except for the broad intensional structuring of the program and the extensional assignments to certain different religions no restrictions were imposed on the contributers. This combination of assignments and freedom within the limits just mentioned had a two-fold consequence: (a) a certain degree of uniformity and (b) a diversity of methods, approaches, insights, and materials analyzed. As a result this collection of essays has the character of a systematized volume of proceedings without the strictly enforced structure of a regular Handbook.

In order to do justice to the first purpose set for the meeting, *viz.* to survey the present situation in apocalyptic research, the first paper in each section was to give a survey of the scholarly achievments for each of the three dimensions. Due to unfortunate circumstances there is – even in this volume[11] – no survey article introducing the last section, a fact which is all the more regrettable, since this dimension played a significant rôle in early form-critical investigations and has been in the focus of scholarly research in Apocalypticism as well as in other areas during the last decade.

In a number of papers dealing primarily with other aspects, however, matters pertaining to the social background of Apocalypticism and "Sitz im Leben" of Apocalypses have been deliberated upon more or less extensively as is the case in the contributions by, *e.g.,* H. Cancik, B.

---

[11] In contrast to the editorial freedom when editing a pre-conceived Handbook, the editor when bringing out a volume of proceedings reflecting the actual events at the Colloquium was prevented from filling in such a severe gap.

Gladigow, A. Hultgård, J. C. H. Lebram, T. Olsson, E. P. Sanders and M. Smith. This state of affairs is worthwhile recognizing particularly in view of the relatively small number of contributions to this section.

In this volume five changes over against the original program have been made: most contributers have updated and expanded their papers quite considerably; Prof. Morton Smith's paper has been placed at the beginning of section one instead of in section three, where it originally belonged; the contribution by Prof. Adela Yarbro Collins now precedes that by Prof. Hans G. Kippenberg due to the subsumption of section IV of the program into section III as indicated above; Prof. Helmer Ringgren kindly accepted to contribute the final paper on "Akkadian Apocalypses"; this task originally was assigned to and carried out by Prof. Åke Sjöberg, Philadelphia, Penn. at the Colloquium; Prof. Geo Widengren's brief opening address has – at the request of the editor – been expanded into a substantial article on "Leading Ideas and Sources of Iranian Apocalypticism".

It is the hope of the editor that this volume of proceedings from a highly productive conference will accomplish what the Organizing Committee set forth as the two remaining goals for the Colloquium, *viz.* to point out new thoughts and methods, and to stimulate further research in the broad field of apocalyptic investigations within the world-wide community of scholarship.[12]

Bibliography

Allwood et alii [Allwood, J./Andersson, L. G./Dahl, Ö.] 1977: *Logic in linguistics* (CTbL), Cambridge 1977.

Baldinger, K. 1980: *Semantic Theory*. Towards a modern Semantics, Oxford–New York 1980.

Bianchi, U. (ed) 1967: *Le Origini dello Gnosticismo*. Colloquio di Messina 13–18 Aprile 1966. Tessi e discussioni (NumenSup XII), Leiden 1967 [2nd edition 1970].

Brashler, J. A. 1977: *The Coptic Apocalypse of Peter. A Genre Analysis and Interpretation*, PhD Diss., Claremont, Calif. 1977.

Gunkel, H. 1924: "Jesaia 33, eine prophetische Liturgie. Ein Vortrag", in: *ZAW* 42 (1924) 177–208.

– 1925: "Letter from Hermann Gunkel to Adolf Jülicher from 8 September 1925", in: H. Rollmann, "Zwei Briefe Hermann Gunkels an Adolf Jülicher zur religionsgeschichtlichen und formgeschichtlichen Methode", in: *ZThK* 78 (1981) 276–288, here 281–286.

Hanson, P. D. 1976: "Apocalypticism", in: *IDBSup*, Nashville, Tenn. 1976, 28–34.

Hellholm, D. 1980: *Das Visionenbuch des Hermas als Apokalypse*. Formgeschichtliche und texttheoretische Studien zu einer literarischen Gattung. Vol. I: Methodologische Vorüberlegungen und makrostrukturelle Textanalyse (CB.NT 13:1), Lund 1980.

---

[12] In addition to other collections of essays on Apocalypticism referred to throughout this volume cf. now also the recent publication of earlier contributions (1843–1971) in Koch/Schmidt (eds) 1982.

– 1982: "The Problem of Apocalyptic Genre and the Apocalypse of John", in: K. H. Richards
    (ed), *SBL Seminar Papers, 21, 1982,* Chico, Calif. 1982, 157–198.
Koch, K./Schmidt, J. M. (eds) 1982: *Apokalyptik* (WdF 365), Darmstadt 1982.
Kubczak, H. 1975: *Das Verhältnis von Intension und Extension als sprachwissenschaftliches Problem*
    (FbIdS 23), Tübingen 1975.
Menne, A. 1973: *Einführung in die Logik* (UTB 34), 2nd edition, Munich 1973.
Vielhauer, P. 1965: "Apocalypses and Related Subjects: Introduction", in: E. Hennecke/W.
    Schneemelcher/R. McL. Wilson (eds), *New Testament Apocrypha,* Vol. II, Philadelphia,
    Penn. – London 1965, 581–607.
– 1975: *Geschichte der urchristlichen Literatur.* Einleitung in das Neue Testament, die Apokry-
    phen und die Apostolischen Väter (GLB), Berlin–New York 1975.
Widengren, G./Hellholm, D. (eds) 1977: *Proceedings of the International Colloquium on Gnosti-
    cism. Stockholm August 20–25 1973* (KVHAAH.FFS 17), Stockholm 1977.
Wunderlich, D. 1979: *Foundations of Linguistics* (CStL 22), Cambridge 1979.

The Phenomenon of Apocalypticism
Die Vorstellungswelt der Apokalyptik
Le phénomène de l'Apocalyptique

On the History of *ΑΠΟΚΑΛΥΠΤΩ* and *ΑΠΟΚΑΛΥΨΙΣ*

Morton Smith

As a first step towards discussing "the apocalyptic movement" in antiquity it seems necessary to find out who then used the terms "apocalyptic" and "apocalypse", and what they used them for.

1. *ΑΠΟΚΑΛΥΠΤΙΚΟΣ*

So far as I know, *ἀποκαλυπτικός* never occurs in classical Greek. Lampe's *Patristic Greek Lexicon*[1] cites it first from Clement of Alexandria (*Paedagogus* I.1) as meaning "revealing"; the divine Word, Clement says, when engaged in intellectual teaching – as in his former work, the *Protreptic* – is "clarifying and revealing" (*δηλωτικὸς καὶ ἀποκαλυπτικός*), whereas in his present work its concern will be moral reformation. Here the adjective has nothing to do with what we should call apocalypses. From Lampe's brief entry, I suppose it never did. It seems to have been a comparatively rare word even in the Christian vocabulary. Christians of the patristic period were undoubtedly aware of "the apocalypse" as a literary form; they used the noun to describe many works; but apparently they never used this adjective for that purpose.

2. *ΑΠΟΚΑΛΥΠΤΩ* and *ΑΠΟΚΑΛΥΨΙΣ*

2.1. From the adjective, therefore, we turn to the noun and the verb, both of which were masterfully mishandeled by Oepke in his *ThWNT* article on *καλύπτω κτλ.*[2]

2.1.1. Oepke did, however, correctly observe that *ἀποκαλύπτω* is a comparatively rare word, and for *ἀποκάλυψις* he appositely cited Jerome: *proprie scripturarum est ... a nullo sapientium saeculi apud Graecos usurpatum (Ad Galatas 1:11f.)*[3]. Jerome went on to argue from this that the translators of the Septuagint, to indicate that the true, Israelite revelation was like

---

[1] Lampe 1968, 194, s.v.
[2] Oepke 1938, esp. 565–597.   [3] *Ibid.*, 573; ed. Vallarsi, VII, 1, 387.

nothing in the pagan world, had created peculiar terms to describe it, *nova novis rebus verba fingentes*. Oepke happily followed this lead. Having collected a few late examples of ἀποκαλύπτω and ἀποκάλυψις used with reference to things divine, he concluded from no substantial evidence that they were not native to Greek but imported from the east and probably from the Septuagint. Hence he took off in a eulogy of the unique character of Old Testament revelation. When he finally came down to the data (pp. 579 f.) he had to recognize that the Septuagint never uses ἀποκάλυψις of matters divine,[4] and more often than not uses ἀποκαλύπτω of matters human. In fact, there are about a dozen uses in equivalents of the idiom "uncover the shame", half a dozen of the idiom "uncover the ear", and more than two dozen of miscellaneous uses for human matters, against only two dozen in which God is explicitly the subject of the verb. Moreover, even when God is the subject, there is commonly no apocalyptic implication. When he "uncovers the ear" of Samuel or "uncovers the backside" of the wicked city (Jer 13:26; Nah 3:5 LXX), the act is no doubt revelatory, but so is that of a strip-tease artist, and a revelation does not become "apocalyptic" (in the modern sense) whenever it is described by a common verb meaning "uncover".

2.1.2. (Another slip that may be mentioned in passing is Oepke's statement, p. 579, that when ἀποκαλύπτω is used of God's giving knowledge it refers not to factual information, but to "intuitive contact with that which is yet hidden in the Transcendent." To the contrary we have 1 Sam 9:15 f.:

"And Yahweh uncovered the ear of Samuel one day before Saul came, saying, 'About this time to-morrow I shall send you a man from the territory of Benjamin, and you are to anoint him to be the leader of my people Israel.'"

These are specific facts).

2.2. The main points to be noted, however, are that the Septuagint does not use ἀποκάλυψις to refer to what we should call "an apocalypse" nor, in fact, to any sort of divine revelation; it does not use ἀποκαλύπτω *in the main* for divine revelations, and when it does so use the verb, the revelations referred to are never of what we should call the apocalyptic sort. Consequently the use of these terms for what are commonly called apocalyptic works cannot be derived directly from the Septuagint. It is rather a development of common usage, of which usage the Septuagint is the richest example – richest in large part because it had to translate literally the common Hebrew idioms mentioned above.

2.3. When we look in pagan authors for other evidence of the common usage we find the literal sense of ἀποκαλύπτω "uncover", already in

---

[4] Oepke's list of the instances omits 1 Kgs 20:30.

Herodotus (I.119), the figurative, for uncovering one's opinion or abilities, in Plato.[5]

Ἀποκάλυψις, the noun, is almost as rare as Jerome thought, but it does appear at last in Philodemus[6] with reference to uncovering the head; thereafter come other non-religious uses, both literal and figurative. Both words are rare, and surprisingly so in the papyri,[7] which suggests that their survival was probably due to lower class Greek usage rather than near-eastern influence. On the other hand, the question of subject matter is important in evaluating the evidence of such documents. We know from literary evidence that ἀποκαλύπτω/ἀποκάλυψις were important in Greek speaking Jewish and Christian circles, but they do not appear in the *Corpus Papyrorum Judaicarum*[8] and I have not found either in the collection of Jewish inscriptions appended to *CPJ* nor in the *Corpus Inscriptionum Iudaicarum*.[9] Neither appears in the volume of Greek inscriptions from Beth She'arim, nor in Naldini's collection of Christian letters on papyri.[10] In the Cairo Museum's great collection of Byzantine papyri ἀποκαλύπτω appears only once – in a promise that evidence will be revealed to a court, and this promise was written by a literary man.[11] Admittedly these collections are far from being sufficient for a complete search, but I think they do suffice to show that matters of considerable importance in the religious life of a community may leave little or no trace in its public and private documents, as distinct from its literary works. Hence the rarity of ἀποκαλύπτω/ἀποκάλυψις in pagan inscriptions and papyri may not justify the conclusion that there were no apocalypses in the pagan literature now lost.

2.3.1. In all such efforts to trace rare words we are terribly at the mercy of the accidents of preservation, not to mention the catastrophies of inadequate indexing. The *Thesaurus*, when readily accessible, should begin a new era for studies of this sort. While awaiting that dayspring from on high, in the darkness of the present dispensation (made doubly dark by the loss of so much hellenistic material) the report of what a fairly thorough search has yielded may prove misleading. For better or worse, however, by searching most of the indexed literary works and the major papyrological and epigraphic collections covering the hellenistic and early Roman

---

[5] *Protagoras* 352a; *Gorgias* 455d.

[6] *Peri kakion* XXII, 15.

[7] Except for the technical term γῆ ἀποκεκαλυμμένη, "land left exposed" (by the recession of the Nile's flood waters), which is frequent after the first century A.D.

[8] Tcherikover/Fuks 1957–1964.

[9] Frey 1936/1952.

[10] Naldini 1968.

[11] Maspero 1916, no. 67295, col. II line 8. The document is a VI century copy of a late V century letter by the pagan philosopher Horapollo, author of the *Hieroglyphics*, who eventually became a Christian.

periods, I have found only very few instances of ἀποκαλύπτω and none of ἀποκάλυψις in the hellenistic period prior to Philodemus, who used both. He was born in Gadara about 110 B.C. and died shortly after 40 B.C. in Herculaneum, where he had been installed by his Roman patron, L. Calpurnius Piso Caesonius, consul in 58, sometime father-in-law to Julius Caesar, and one of the leading figures of the Epicurean circle that had Philodemus among its influential teachers and Lucretius, the young Vergil, and, later on, the younger Horace among its more influential pupils.[12] After Philodemus' time, ἀποκαλύπτω appears fairly often in pagan writers, and ἀποκάλυψις occasionally; the citations in Liddell-Scott-Jones[13] adequately reflect the distribution. I hope this statement of the facts will not be taken to imply that I think Philodemus had anything substantial to do with the popularization of ἀποκαλύπτω/ἀποκάλυψις; I see no reason to think he did. He simply happens to be the first pagan author in whose works we find evidence of their increasing popularity. Why ἀποκαλύπτω which was in good usage in the fifth and fourth centuries B.C., drops almost out of sight in the third, and then slowly begins a resurgence that will eventually place its derivatives among the most important religious terms of the western world, is uncertain. One thing seems clear: its success was not due to its suitability to the type of revelation it and its derivatives were eventually used to describe. Apocalyptic revelations are not customarily effected by removing a cover; the heavens are not stripped away, nor the lid of the earth taken off; even the old folkloristic notion of taking a cover off the eyes, so that they can see spiritual beings (for which ἀποκαλύπτω was used in the story of Balaam, Num 22:31) is not developed, in spite of the increasing popularity of the words (which would favor the development). Perhaps, however, I may now advance a conjecture suggested to me by the evidence that will follow. I conjecture that the actual course of events went like this: In the last centuries B.C. ἀποκαλύπτω came to be commonly used of revealing secrets. At about the same time began a great increase of the belief that the god(s) had very important secrets to reveal, secrets about the structure and future of the world that would enable those who knew them to escape impending disaster. In the lower-middle-class, eastern Mediterranean milieux where these ideas first caught hold, ἀποκαλύπτω was already the common word for revealing secrets, so it eventually came to be used for revealing these, and their ultimate success carried it with them, in spite of the inappropriateness of its root meaning for its new role.

---

[12] Caesar was sometime backer of C. Memmius; Memmius was patron of Lucretius, Catullus, and Cinna; their friend C. Asinius Pollio became an elder friend of Horace and Vergil.

[13] *LSJ* 1940; *LSJSup* 1968 gives no additional references.

2.3.2. Before leaving Philodemus, let me add that he is a figure who tempts speculation, the more so because his fellow Gadarene, Meleager, the famous collector of epigrams, bragged in his epigrammatic epitaph of being able to speak to Syrians and Phoenicians, as well as to Greeks, in their native languages.[14] Meleager's floruit was within a decade or so of Philodemus' birth, and Meleager was then already in Tyre, so there is no likelihood of direct influence. However, the two authors may be taken as evidence that Gadara was both a center of Greek culture and a city where men acquainted with Greek literature might also be acquainted with the language of the Semitic world around them. It is not impossible that Philodemus may have known Semitic languages well enough to amuse himself by reading the Aramaic and Hebrew prophecies that probably circulated in his time both in the Decapolis and in Italy.

2.3.3. Let me indulge in one more aside, on the role of ancient prophecy as a form of entertainment. Ezekiel complains that men come to hear him as a singer, rather than a prophet (33:32). A century before Philodemus, a Syrian named Eunus was enslaved in Sicily. He was a prophet of the Syrian goddess, who had promised to make him king. His master used to have him brought in after dinner to amuse the guests by prophesying in her name; they sometimes gave him tidbits and asked him to remember them when he came into his kingdom. He later led the great slave revolt of 135 B.C. which his master probably found less amusing.[15] Just about the time of Philodemus' death Vergil chose to parody such prophecies in his delightful nonsense poem for a child's birthday, the fourth *Eclogue*. Some of the nonsense, it is true, may come from the prophetic original, but the fact that Vergil perceived it as nonsense, and used it deliberately to amuse, is proved not only by the absurdity of the opposite supposition – to suggest that he took it seriously would equate him in stupidity with his interpreters – but also by the poem's conclusion (IV, 66–70):

> *Incipe, parve puer, risu cognoscere matrem...*
> *Incipe, parve puer; qui non risere parenti*
> *Nec deus hunc mensa, dea nec dignata cubili est.*

2.4. Now back to our muttons: Evidence of the revival of ἀποκαλύπτω/ἀποκάλυψις by literary circles in the eastern Mediterranean began with the Septuagint, of which the evidence has already been reviewed. The Septuagint probably covers a span of about a century and a half; its earliest element, the Pentateuch, may have been translated shortly after 275, its latest may be the preface written by Ben Sira's grandson in 117 B.C. "Aristeas" used the verb of uncovering a physical object (177); Josephus

---

[14] *Anthologia Palatina* VII, 419.
[15] Diodorus XXXIV/XXXV, 2,8.

twice in that sense, and twice of revealing human secrets[15a]. Otherwise I have not found the words in the Jewish historians. They do not occur in the Jewish imitations of classical poetry (including *Sibyllines* III). As to their use in what are commonly called "the pseudepigrapha", it is difficult to judge because so few of these texts have been preserved in Greek and the Greek texts of those few are commonly late and interpolated. *The Testaments of the Twelve Patriarchs* use the verb eight times, five of these in references to revealing secrets. In two instances it is God who reveals the secret – Reuben's adultery and Potiphar's wife's plan to poison Joseph – he also reveals Levi's imminent death. Levi is made to prophesy the coming of "a new priest, to whom all the words of the Lord will be revealed." What seems a Christian interpolation says that God will reveal his salvation to all the gentiles.[16] In *Joseph and Aseneth* there are three uses of the verb: Aseneth reveals her sins in confession to God (12:4); consequently an angel is sent to read her a lecture, give her a piece of heavenly honeycomb, and assure her that the secrets of God have been revealed to her (16:7); later, when she makes friends with Levi, he reads things written in heaven and reveals them to her in secret (22:9).

2.5. Remarkable is the rarity of the words in works now commonly called "apocalypses." I do not know any such text prior to the New Testament Apocalypse which either describes itself or the proceedings in it as ἀποκαλύψεις or even uses the verb ἀποκαλύπτω for the whole of the revelation. A number of such works are referred to by partistic writers as "apocalypses", but such references pose a problem to be considered later.

2.5.1. The immediate problem is that of the use of the words in the New Testament. They are rare in the Gospels – ἀποκάλυψις only once, in Luke's reference to Jesus as "a light for enlightenment (?) of the Gentiles" (2:32 – a unique usage). Ἀποκαλύπτω appears in four items about revealing secrets and two about revealing God,[17] in John's quotation of Isa 53:1, "To whom has the arm of the Lord been revealed?" (12:38), and – at last! – in a single "apocalyptic" passage, of "the day when the Son of Man shall be revealed" (Luke 17:30). The references to revealing secrets continue the usage we have just noticed in Josephus, *Joseph and Aseneth*, and *Testaments of the Twelve Patriarchs*; it is even more conspicuous in ben Sira who has a dozen uses with this reference against three or four with others. All in all, the gospel usage can hardly be made into evidence of a major theme, or of

---

[15a] Josephus: *Bell* 1, 297; 5,350; *Ant.* 12,90; 14,406.

[16] Secrets: *Reuben* 3:15; *Judah* 16:4 (*ter*); *Joseph* 6:6, of these the first and last are revealed by God. Levi's death: *Levi* 1:2. Salvation for the gentiles: *Benjamin* 10:5 (the ἕως clause seems a Christian attempt to void the initial command; notice the change from θεός to κύριος). The new priest: *Levi* 18:2. See below, notes 25 ff., for similar Christian changes in other texts.

[17] Secrets: Matt 10:26/Luke 12:2; Matt 11:25/Luke 10:21; Matt 16:17; Luke 2:35; God: Matt 11:27/Luke 10:22.

clear connection with Palestine, two of the nine instances being peculiar to Luke, one Johannine, and four from the peculiar "Johannine" pericope of Q. Outside the Gospels, the words are *exclusively* Pauline and deutero-Pauline (*i.e.* in Ephesians and I Peter), except for the solitary use as the first word of the Apocalypse. (Was it part of a title? If so, was the title secondary? Who knows?)

2.5.2. For Paul, as we know him in his letters, ἀποκάλυψις is the core of his life, but this ἀποκάλυψις means "revelation", not "apocalypse", and this revelation has nothing to do with "uncovering". Paul's choice of the word can be explained neither by its root meaning, nor by its later connection with the apocalypses. The explanation must lie in some aspect of its previous usage, most likely in that for revealing secrets, but the connection is not clear and the data are puzzling. What is clear is that the center of Paul's concern is not any revelation to Paul, but the revelation *in* Paul. Gal 1:12, where he insists that "I did not receive" my gospel "from men ... but by revelation of Jesus Christ" is explained by the following reference in 1:15f. to God who "was pleased ... to reveal his Son *in* me, that I might proclaim him", and this "in" cannot be read as "by" – it is used in preparation for Paul's clinching argument in the dispute with Peter to which this section of the letter is leading, "I live no longer I, but Christ lives in me" (2:20), where even the most ardent advocate of "ἐν instrumental" would not dare to use "by". Paul's notion that he is the living revelation of Jesus is spelled out fully in 2 Cor 3–5 and Rom 6–8, which make clear that the revelation is conceived not as vision, but as possession and progressive transformation, and is extended, by Paul's preaching, the rite of baptism, and the gift of the spirit (which is Jesus, 2 Cor 3:17), to his converts. Moreover, it is not a single event, but a continuing process, the acts and powers of the spirit being the constant witness in the believers that they are continually "receiving the revelation of our Lord Jesus Christ" (1 Cor 1:7).

2.5.2.1. This revelation, as expressed in Paul's gospel, is not only of the immediate powers of God, but also of his future purposes; it reveals his wrath to the wicked, to the righteous his justice (Rom 1:17f.) and the things he has prepared fot them (1 Cor 2:10); it is thus a revelation of the long-secret mystery of his will (Rom 16:25). Because continuing, it is not yet complete – more will be revealed at the end, first the Antichrist (2 Thess 2:3; 6:8), then the heavenly return of Jesus with the angels (2 Thess 1:7), the fiery test of what each man has done (1 Cor 3:13), the just judgment of God against the wicked (Rom 2:5), and the destined glory of the saints (Rom 8:18f.).

2.5.2.2. While awaiting these final revelations, Paul and the other saints enjoyed frequent specific revelations from the spirit that dwelt in them, and these revelations were often of secrets. This accords with the usage of ἀποκαλύπτω for revealing secrets, as we saw it in the Gospels and in earlier Jewish works. The secrets revealed by God might, in human terms, be answers to particular questions. Jews and Christians used their deity as pagans used the oracles of their gods and modern believers in alien wisdom use the columnists and television seers who live by telling people what to do. Thus Paul claims that his second trip to Jerusalem after his conversion was dictated by revelation (Gal 2:2); he promises the Philippians that God will reveal to them the truth of competing opinions (3:15).

2.5.2.3. The meetings of the Pauline congregations seem often to have been devoted to encounters with the spirit, which expressed itself in different oral forms. I Cor 14:6 opposes speaking with tongues to several forms of rational speech – revelation, "knowlege" (proverbs?), prophecy, and teaching. Here, as in the preceding passages, the word translated "revelation" is ἀποκάλυψις and a reader unaware of its meaning elsewhere in Paul might be tempted to translate it by "apocalypse" and take it to mean "a report of a vision of the sort described in the literary apocalypses". But we have found no evidence that at Paul's time the literary apocalypses were called "apocalypses", and Paul clarifies his meaning here by his argument later in the chapter (vss. 23 ff.):

> "If the whole church is assembled and everybody speaks with tongues, and some who are uninitiated or unbelieving come in, won't they say you are mad? But if everybody prophesies and some unbeliever or uninitiate comes in, his vices will be exposed by everybody, he will be judged by everybody, his hidden thoughts will be laid open, and consequently, prostrating himself, he will worship God. ... So what is (to be done), brethren? When you come together (and) each has a psalm, a teaching, a revelation, a 'tongue', an interpretation, arrange everything so (that the proceedings will be) edifying."

Clearly, "prophecy" here refers not to foretelling eschatological events, but to revealing the thoughts and characters of persons present – a remarkable gift of Old Testament prophets, as Gehazi learned to his grief (2 Kgs 5:26 f.). By analogy with this use of prophecy, and in the light of the previous passages, I think "revelation" here probably means "answer to some question", whether practical ("Should Paul go up to Jerusalem?") or dogmatic ("What is to be thought of Peter's teaching?"), or the like.

2.5.2.4. The same meaning is indicated in 2 Cor 12:1 ff. where Paul is forced to boast of his "visions and revelations given by the Lord." He boasts first of the visions (ὀπτασίαι) especially of a former experience, perhaps his own, more likely that of Jesus who now lives in him and of whom alone, he has said, he will boast.[18] This experience was an ascent to the third heaven, where things ineffable were heard. Next he goes on to his own present condition: he will (after all) boast of his illness, since it was

---

[18] Cf. 12:5 and 10:17.

given him as a humiliation lest he should think too highly of himself because of "the excess" (ὑπερβολή) of his revelations. The text here (12:6–7) is notoriously corrupt and "excess" certainly refers to quality as well as number, but there is clear contrast between these plural, excessive, evidently current ἀποκαλύψεις and the one great ὀπτασία for which Paul has to go back fourteen years and more, and which he describes in such a way as to suggest it was not his own. Ὀπτασία, moreover, is a good translation of the Hebrew *mar'eh*, the chief term for the visions in Daniel 8, 9 and 10; it was thus appropriate for the first experience Paul described. Accordingly we should not suppose the content of the former vision was identical with that of the present revelations, nor think that Paul was constantly commuting to the third heaven. Rather, the boasting here and the connection of the revelations with his illness recall 10:8, where he said that he would boast of his authority over the churches, and 11:28 ff., where he speaks of his direction of the churches as the climactic item in a list of his burdens as servant of Christ, from which he goes directly to his (consequent?) illness as something to boast of. These connections suggest that his administrative and political decisions entailed not only the anguish often expressed in his letters, but also psychosomatic disturbances which produced both the physical symptoms he left undescribed and the frequent revelations by which the Lord settled difficult problems as Paul wanted them to be settled.

2.5.2.5. The deutero-Pauline uses of ἀποκαλύπτω and ἀποκάλυψις testify to the importance of the terms in Paul's work, and slightly extend their meanings, along Pauline lines.[19] Ignatius, as usual, is close to the deutero-Paulines.[20] 1 Clement, like John, uses only ἀποκαλύπτω (16:3) and that only in a quotation of Isa 53:1. In sum, down to Domitian's time, or perhaps well thereafter (if we reject the traditional date of the canonical Apocalypse), the preserved Christian uses of ἀποκαλύπτω and ἀποκάλυψις are, with few exceptions, not apocalyptic.

2.5.2.6. This fact brings into focus the inconsistency latent in Paul. The revelation from within, by Jesus living in and working through the believer, which is Paul's main concern, differs markedly from the final revelation to be given by external events – the Antichrist, the external Jesus and his angels, etc. As is well known, the clearest Pauline references to these events are concentrated in 2 Thess and have led many to think it spurious. For our present purpose that question can be left aside; the important thing is that in the Pauline corpus this final, external revelation

---

[19] Revelations as means of solving present and past church problems: Eph 1:7; 3:3 ff.; 1 Pet 1:12. Revelation of Christ in the believers: 1 Pet 1:7,13 (?). Revelations of Jesus, glory, and salvation, to be given in the End: 1 Pet 4:13; 5:1; 1:5.

[20] Ign. *Eph.* 20:1, he hopes for further revelations of the nature of his life in Christ.

appears as a different sort of thing from the internal revelation that was Paul's main concern. The external revelation has of course much cognate material in the Old Testament, pseudepigrapha, and Gospels; but for this material, so far as can be judged from the preserved evidence, the term ἀποκάλυψις had not hitherto been used and would not have been the most likely choice, since the material is commonly presented as visions, with terms like *mar'eh* and *ḥizzayon,* which ἀποκάλυψις does not render accurately. The first vision of this sort to carry the Pauline title ἀποκάλυψις is now the canonical Apocalypse. Should we therefore think the title came from Pauline circles? Little else in the work seems to be Pauline; in particular Paul's essential notion of internal revelation is hard to find there. But if its title did not come from Paul, what was the source from which both it and Paul derived this somewhat unlikely term for such material? Are we dealing with the literary Greek of Palestine and Jewish circles in Alexandria, or with the lower-middle-class Greek of Corinth and of the cities of Asia Minor? For want of evidence, the questions are open.

2.5.3. We have much better evidence for the great success of the term ἀποκάλυψις for this type of work in the second century and thereafter. The canonical Apocalypse is closely followed by that of Hermas (in the lower-middle-class Greek of Rome). From then on, as Lewis Carroll said, "Thick and fast they came at last, and more, and more, and more."[21] This suggests a problem that should be investigated: If literary works of the class now called "apocalypses" were first commonly so named by the Church fathers, which fathers did most to extend this nomenclature? Which circles took it up, and why? But here again, caution is in order. Because we have and hear of Christian and cognate apocalypses, we are apt to think of this epidemic as traceable within the Christian tradition – at least if "Christian" be used in its larger sense, to include the so-called "gnostics".

However, by the end of the third century Iamblichus was using the same terminology, and *he* is not likely to have taken it over from the Christians.[22] In the late fourth century Synesius as a young man wrote to his brother, from Alexandria, "We have had a swarm, of both private individuals and priests, forging dreams which they call 'apocalypses'; they would make my waking life a nightmare were I not soon to get away to holy Athens."[23] The priests were presumably pagans. Synesius had been studying Platonism with Hypatia, whose relations with the Christians were somewhat cool. The lateness of this evidence prohibits any conclusion about the early period, but its mere existence suggests that pagan circles may have contributed to the spead of the terminology.

---

[21] *Through the Looking Glass,* ch. IV.
[22] *De Mysteriis,* VI,7 (248), for revelations that would destroy the world.
[23] *Epistulae,* 54.

2.6. One consequence of the spread was the introduction of ἀποκαλύπτω/ἀποκάλυψις into earlier Jewish texts about revelations. Theodotion, for instance, in his second century A.D. (?) revision of the Septuagint, used ἀποκαλύπτω in half a dozen passages of Daniel where the earlier Greek had other verbs; he thus first gave the vision of chapter 10 a linguistic claim to be an apocalypse.[24] Similarly, the words were not in the oldest text of *The Lives of the Prophets*, but were twice introduced in later expansions;[25] they were not in the oldest text of the *Testament of Solomon*, but appear twice in later versions;[26] they were not in the *Greek Apocalypse of Baruch*, but appear now in the Christian title and introduction, and in a Christian interpolation;[27] they were not in the original *Martyrdom of Isaiah*, but *revelatio* (for ἀποκάλυψις?) was used in the Christian addition, the *Ascension* (6:14). We have already noticed a use of ἀποκαλύπτω in what seems to be a Christian addition to the *Testament of Benjamin*.[28] The *Testament of Abraham* never uses either word, but was probably described by Epiphanius as an "apocalypse";[29] he says the Sethians already called it so. To the best of my knowledge, all other pseudepigraphic apocalypses of the last centuries B.C. and the first A.D. which are commonly listed as evidence of "the apocalyptic movement" owe their apocalyptic titles either to patristic references, or to late manuscripts, or to modern scholars – and none of these sources is reliable.

2.7. In sum, as far as the preserved evidence goes, we must say that the literary form we call an apocalypse carries that title for the first time in the very late first or early second century A.D. From then on, both title and form are fashionable, at least to the end of the classical period. Their fashionableness is part of the well known growth of superstition and of claims to special revelations and to occult knowledge, complementary characteristics of the later Roman Empire which forms their fairly familiar social background.

---

[24] Cf. Theodotion and LXX for Dan 2:19,22,28,29,30,47; 10:1; 11:35.

[25] *Epiphanii recensio prior* 19; *Dorothei recensio*, ed. Schermann 1907, 38.

[26] Ed. McCown 1922, 8* line 8; 87* line 7.

[27] The whole conclusion of ch. 4, at least from f. 176 on, is a Christian interpolation; it breaks the connection of 175b with ch. 5. Ἀποκαλύπτω appears twice in 4:13f.

[28] Above, n. 16 on paragraph 2.4.

[29] *Panarion* 39:5, if our text be that of which he is speaking.

Bibliography

Frey, J. B. 1936/1952: *Corpus Inscriptionum Iudaicarum*, Vol. I–II, Rome 1936/1952.

Lampe, G. W. H. 1968: *A Patristic Greek Lexicon*, Oxford 1968.

Liddell, H. G./Scott, R./Jones, H. S. 1940: *A Greek-English Lexicon*, Oxford 1940.

Liddell, H. G./Scott, R./Jones, H. S./Barber, E. A. 1968: *A Greek-English Lexicon. A Supplement*, Oxford 1968.

Maspero, J. 1916: *Papyrus grecs d'époque byzantine*, Vol. III, Cairo 1916.

McCown, C. C. 1922: *The Testament of Salomon..., with Introduction* (UNT 9), Leipzig 1922.

Naldini, M. 1968: *Il Cristianesimo in Egitto*, Florence 1968.

Oepke, A. 1938: "καλύπτω κτλ.", in: *ThWNT* III (1938), 558–597.

Schermann, Th. 1907: *Prophetarum vitae fabulosae, Indices apostolorum discipulorumque Domini* (BiTeu), Leipzig 1907.

Tcherikover, V. A./Fuks, A. 1957–1964: *Corpus Papyrorum Judaicarum*, Vol. I–III, Cambridge/Mass. 1957–1964.

The Apocalyptic Activity. The Case of J̌āmāsp Nāmag.

TORD OLSSON

The title of this paper has a double meaning. It refers to the activity which the rediscovery of apocalypticism[1] has provoked among scholars of religions and to apocalypticism itself, which I will consider as a type of speculative and verbal activity illustrated by taking the Middle Iranian apocalypse *J̌āmāsp Nāmag* as a test case in the second part of the article.

1. Approaches to Apocalypticism

1.1. The Ambiguity in the Use of Terminology

1.1.1. The terms apocalyptic and apocalypticism have been used to designate a type of literature consisting of revelatory writings which disclose the secrets of the beyond and especially of the end of time, but also to designate the realm of ideas or the type of religion usually expressed in this literature. The terms are derived from the Greek verb ἀποκαλύπτειν "to unveil, reveal". Since the word ἀποκάλυψις is used as a self-designation in the New Testament Apocalypse of John (Rev 1:1), the term has become a literary title and a designation of a number of related scriptures, though it is usually not employed as an original self-designation in these scriptures themselves.[1a]

1.1.2. As technical terms, "apocalypse", "apocalypticism" and "apocalyptic literature" have been used rather ambiguously in scholarly literature. One reason is apparently that the number of phenomena which they denote has been successively increased on a principle of resemblance. Space does not allow for a detailed account of this process, so for the sake of brevity I will try to sum it up in the following theoretical terms: Consider that "apocalypticism" and related terms designate the phenomena A, B, C and D, and that these phenomena have the characteristics a, b, c, d, e, and f according to the model below,

---

[1] Koch 1972; Koch 1970.

[1a] Vielhauer 1965, 582.

"apocalypticism" etc.

A	B	C	D
a	b	c	d
b	c	d	e
c	d	e	f

Suppose that A is the phenomenon first explored and originally designated by the term "apocalypticism", and that B, C, and D have been
successively explored. "Apocalypticism" may now be a convenient term
for B because of the characteristics b and c in common with A but also for
C, because A and C have c in common, and B and C have c and d in
common. When later the phenomenon D is explored, it may be suggested
that "apocalypticism" is a convenient term also in this case, because D has d
in common with B and C, and d and e with C, although D has no
characteristics at all in common with A! If this interpretation is correct, we
cannot escape the impression that much of the theoretical discussion on
apocalypticism is based on a naturalistic fallacy. What has been called
"apocalypticism" is apparently not an autonomous institution, not a
species in the realm of religion, like a flower in the field, but a *mixtum
compositum* which scholars have arbitrarily blended. But since there seems
to exist a sort of family resemblance between these phenomena (as Wittgenstein would have said), this may possibly serve as a justification for
using a common lable for all of them. Of course this state of affairs is far
from satisfactory, but since we cannot do without such "umbrella terms"
as "apocalypticism" once they have been adopted in the scholarly language,
we should at least try to produce tentative definitions which may help us to
refocus the discussion of apocalypticism on the ancient and modern texts
themselves and upon the social and historical situations in which these texts
have taken form.

1.2. The First Comprehensive Work

Friedrich Lücke's "Versuch einer vollständigen Einleitung in die Offenbarung Johannis und die gesammte apokalyptische Litteratur", published
in 1832, was the first comprehensive work on this topic. The book is of
great interest not only because it represents pioneer work, but it also raises
methodological and theoretical problems which, since published, have
triggered the scholarly debate. Lücke considered apocalypticism as a special
form of the more general phenomenon of (biblical) prophecy and its chief
motif, eschatology. Thus two problems were raised which are still on the
agenda of scholarly debate: the relation of apocalypticism to prophecy and
to eschatology. What today seems still more important is his emphasis on a
particular conception of history as the essential basis of apocalypticism and
from which its other characteristics can be generated: visionary form and

symbolism, apocalyptic time measuring, pseudonymity, its learned and artificial style, and the conception of an *angelus interpres*.

1.3. Types of Definitions and Approaches

1.3.1. Among the numerous studies devoted to apocalypticism in recent research, it is, generally speaking, possible to distinguish certain main types of definitions. Although they are partly overlapping, emphasis is placed differently, reflecting different scholarly approaches and interests.

(a) Criteria according to the content of the revelation

The etymology of the word "apocalypticism" seems to be relevant so far as it raises the question of the content of revelation; if something is revealed or uncovered, it must, of course, be a revelation of things that have been previously hidden, *i.e.* secrets. Opinions differ, however, concerning the nature of the secrets revealed. Apocalypticism is thus defined as revelation of the secrets of the cosmos and/or the invisible, divine world,[2] or as revelation about the end of the world,[2a] or as revelation concerning the course of the world's history from creation till the end of time according to a fixed chronological framework, arranging history in particular periods though concentrating on the final phase.[3]

(b) Additional formal criteria

A more narrow approach is developed from definitions of type (a), in that stylistic or formal features are included in the definition. The character of apocalypticism as revelation of secrets is supposed to be reflected in the stylistic and formal features of apocalyptic texts. Thus Bright speaks about "eschatological language",[4] and Stuhlmüller of "symbolic form".[5] Frost[6] and, quoting him, Vawter[7] define apocalypticism as the "mythologizing of eschatology". Ringgren defines apocalypticism as "eine Spekulation, die – gern in allegorischer Form ... den Weltlauf deuten und das Weltende enthüllen will".[8] He further emphasises features such as secret wisdom, the forms of dreams and visions, similes, and symbolism in the Jewish apocalypticism.[9]

---

[2] Baldensperger 1903, 176, 188; Frey 1928, 327; Kaufmann 1928, 1142; Volz 1934, 5; Ladd 1957, 129.

[2a] Betz 1966, 392; Bright 1966, 490; Stuhlmüller 1968, 343; Eybers 1971, 15.

[3] Ringgren 1957a, 463; 1957b, 464; Widengren 1969, 440, 456; cf. already Bousset 1903, 18; cf. also S. S. Hartman 1976, 1 and in this volume § 1.2.

[4] Bright 1966, 490.   [5] Stuhlmüller 1968, 343.

[6] Frost 1952, 33.   [7] Vawter 1960, 36.   [8] Ringgren 1957a, 463.

[9] Ringgren 1957b, 465; cf. also Sickenberger 1950, 504, and Vielhauer 1965; Schreiner 1969a, 1969b.

(c) Form-critical approach and the apocalyptic genre

The difficulties of finding a constructive element of content as a basic criterion characterizing apocalyptic scriptures may well be considered a relevant reason for giving priority to a formal approach. Instead of taking a "theologisch-weltanschauliches Phänomen" as the starting-point for research, G. von Rad maintains that apocalypticism should first be studied as a literary phenomenon;[10] and in his criticism of the situation of research in 1970, Koch suggests that "den Maßstab für das, was apokalyptisch ist, eher enger zu fassen als weiter und auf einer strikt formgeschichtlichen Ausgangsbasis zu bestehen".[11] A genre-analysis on a formal basis is thus considered as a necessary precondition for the characterization of a certain text as "apocalyptic". Dexinger, referring to the opinion just mentioned, states in his recently published book: "Hier liegt praktisch noch forschungsmäßiges Neuland",[12] and adds: "Erst nach einer formgeschichtlichen Analyse läßt sich 'Sitz im Leben' ermitteln."[13] The most comprehensive attempt in this direction so far is presented by Collins and his colleagues in a special issue of Semeia (No. 14, 1979), entitled "Apocalypse: The Morphology of a Genre". The studies are here carried out on a phenomenological and comparative basis and are not concerned with historical derivation or social setting.

(d) Apocalypticism restricted to a text-corpus

A quite narrow approach is suggested by scholars in the fields of Jewish and Christian apocalypticism who tend to restrict the phenomenon to a corpus of certain texts. In recent studies this bias is shown by Ladd, who speaks of "a body of literature"[14] and L. Hartman: "a number of texts".[15] Dexinger also understands "apocalypticism" in an almost statistical sense as a "Sammelbezeichnung für eine Anzahl von Büchern".[16]

(e) Social factors considered

A fairly recent approach is represented by scholars who deal with apocalypticism in terms of social function and as systems of thought which are conditioned by social factors. (I shall try to sketch a possible approach along similar lines below.) This trend is represented by scholars like Plöger,[17] Hengel,[18] Isenberg,[19] Hanson,[20] and, in their contributions to this Colloquium, by Nickelsburg and Sanders. I refer to their presentation and

---

[10] G. von Rad 1961, 314, though it does not represent a literary genre (cf. the criticism by Collins 1979a, 3).

[11] Koch 1970, 33.

[12] Dexinger 1977, 11.   [13] *Loc. cit.*   [14] Ladd 1957, 192.

[15] L. Hartman 1966, 17.   [16] Dexinger 1977, 13.   [17] Plöger 1959.

[18] Hengel 1969.   [19] Isenberg 1974.   [20] Hanson 1975; 1976.

discussion and restrict myself here to quote a definition proposed by Hanson: "Apocalypticism refers to the symbolic universe in which an apocalyptic movement codifies its identity and interpretation of reality."[21] Though not stated by Hanson, his terminology strongly reminds one of categories employed by Berger and Luckmann in their sociology of knowledge.[22]

1.3.2. I have ranged the diverse definitions under these major types, first, because it serves to illustrate how these stipulations reflect variant approaches in the study of apocalypticism, and it is certainly not by chance that these approaches broadly coincide with the major divisions of this Colloquium. Second, we can see how loosely the word "apocalypticism" is used, and that it frequently is interchanged with the related terms "apocalyptic", "apocalypse" or "apocalyptic literature".

It is obvious that the types of definitions and corresponding approaches listed above rely upon certain presuppositions maintained by individual scholars, such as their research-guiding interests, ideals of research, and the scholarly tradition in which they have been educated. So far it is clear that the cited definitions have been suggested mainly by scholars of biblical research. Thus when "apocalypticism" is defined by them, it is therefore reasonable to assume that they have its particular Jewish or Christian forms in mind. This also seems to be a natural approach in view of the fact that the bulk of apocalyptic documents stems from Palestine, the Jewish diaspora, and from early Christian circles at about the turn of the era.

But this position appears problematic as soon as we take historical and social dimensions into consideration, and particularly if we claim that a methodologically reliable approach should serve the nomothetical research interests of a comparative or phenomenological study of apocalyptic evidence, as it is found in diverse cultural climates and ethnic groups.

1.4. Jewish Apocalypticism and its Historical Origins

1.4.1. A great deal of the extensive literature on Jewish apocalypticism has in fact been concerned with its historical origins. Though the problem has indeed given rise to a bewildering number of scholarly opinions, it is possible to identify a few major trends. Biblical scholars have tended to explain it as a development either from OT prophecy or from OT

---

[21] Hanson 1976, 30.

[22] Berger-Luckmann 1967, *e.g.* 95: "Symbolic universes ... are bodies of theoretical tradition that integrate different provinces of meaning and encompass the institutional order in a symbolic totality."

wisdom, while historians of religion have given prominence to foreign, and particularly Iranian, influence.[23]

1.4.1.1. The first of these opinions, that Jewish apocalypticism is a continuation of OT prophecy, which was proposed already by Lücke and advanced by Rowley in 1944, still seems to dominate the discussion carried on by biblical scholars (Hanson and others), while G. von Rad's attempt to derive apocalypticism from OT wisdom[24] has received fierce criticism from P. von der Osten-Sacken[25], and more recently from P. D. Hanson,[26] and J. J. Collins.[27] As Collins rightly remarks, the discussion is to a great extent confused by the failure of making a distinction between proverbial wisdom and mantic wisdom. Chief exponents of the theory of Iranian influence on Jewish apocalypticism include Bousset,[28] Reitzenstein,[29] Otto,[30] and the participants in this colloquium Widengren[31] and S. S. Hartman.[32]

1.4.1.2. The historical dilemma is particularly highlighted in the energetic discussion about direct or indirect Iranian influences on Jewish and Christian apocalypticism. The dispute has concerned apocalyptic patterns and motifs in the Enoch literature and Qumran texts, but especially the relation between the Pahlavi Bahman Yašt and the Book of Daniel. The main reason is, of course, that both texts employ the well-known allegory of four metals which symbolize four dynasties. Scholars[33] who have denied Iranian influence on Daniel have argued that Bahman Yašt is a very late scripture and that the 4-metal scheme in Daniel derives from Greek sources (Hesiod).[34]

Those who postulate Iranian influence on Daniel by way of ideas, as these ideas are retained in the Bahman Yašt in its present form, argue as follows:

(1) Iranian speculations about the ages of the world and the periodization of history are older than the Book of Daniel. Plutarch's account of these speculations refers to the writing of Theopomp, and the latter was a contemporary to Alexander the Great.[35]

(2) Parallels between the Oracles of Hystaspes and Bahman Yašt prove

---

[23] Cf. the reviews and references in Schmidt 1969; Schreiner 1969b, 165–177; Hanson 1976; Dexinger 1977, 23–57.

[24] von Rad 1961, 314ff.   [25] von der Osten-Sacken 1969, 9–12.
[26] Hanson 1975, 5, 8.   [27] Collins 1975, 232.
[28] Bousset 1906.   [29] Reitzenstein 1921.
[30] Otto 1934.   [31] Widengren 1966; 1969, 470ff.
[32] S. S. Hartman 1973; 1976 and in this volume.
[33] For the following see S. S. Hartman 1973.
[34] Moulton 1902, 988ff.; Scheftelowitz 1920, 220f.; Duchesne-Guillemin 1953, 78f.; Glasson 1961, 2f.; cf. Collins 1979c, 207f.
[35] Bousset 1906, 547 note 2; Widengren 1969, 471f. and note 52, and in this volume § 5.

that certain apocalyptic ideas which have been retained in the latter work were spread about 100 BCE.[36]

(3) In its present form Bahman Yašt is admittedly a late work, but it draws upon an older source, which, in view of linguistic evidence, was probably written in Avestan.[37]

(4) The apocalypticism of the Book of Daniel is an extraneous element in the OT.[38]

(5) Daniel's highly selective and artificial interpretation of the historical progression of rule in the East – Assyria, Media, Persia, Macedonia – conforms exactly with the account given by Roman writers before 171 BCE, that is, before the redaction of Daniel, and such a sequence must derive from Persian sources.[39]

(6) The language in Daniel 2–6 is Aramaic, which was the language of administration in the Persian empire, and also contains a number of Iranian loan words.[40]

1.4.2. I have reviewed this discussion not only because of the historical problems involved, but also because it again reflects tacit assumptions concerning apocalypticism and its relation to apocalyptic ideas and texts. It is obvious that historians of religion, to a great extent, have viewed apocalypticism from the standpoint of Iranian evidence, and that this perspective is reflected in the above (§ 1.3.1.) suggested definitions.

1.4.2.1. Recalling these definitions, we can see first that they all emphasize criteria of content. The definitions concern apocalyptic ideas, or thought patterns, and consider very little formal or structural features of apocalyptic discourses.

Second, these criteria concern ideas or thought patterns which constitute prominent features of *Iranian* apocalypticism and *Iranian* views of history. However, if the bulk of apocalypses stems from Jewish circles, and if this literature draws on Iranian sources, then any definition of apocalypticism should seriously take the Iranian evidence into account.

1.4.2.2. Much of the discussion of historical influences on Jewish apocalypticism is confused by the failure to distinguish between apocalypticism and related phenomena. It would thus be convenient to make distinctions between

(1) *apocalypticism* as a speculative and verbal activity comprising more or less coherent systems of apocalyptic ideas,

---

[36] Eddy 1961, 16, 18, 32 ff.; Widengren 1961, 222–225; 1965, 199–207; 1966, 144 and note 5, and in this volume § 4.3.2.

[37] West in SBE V, LIII; Eddy 1961, 16; Winston 1966, 190 f. and note 19; Widengren 1966, 144 f.; 1969, 471, note 51, and in this volume § 4.

[38] Widengren 1966, 149 f.

[39] Swain 1940, in particular 10 f.; Eddy 1961, 16; Winston 1966, 189 f.; Ginsberg 1948, 5.

[40] Widengren 1966, 140 f.

(2) *apocalyptic ideas* which constitute the above systems but are also found in other contexts than apocalypticism, and

(3) *apocalypse* as a literary type in which apocalyptic ideas or systems of ideas are expressed. It should be noted, however, that apocalyptic ideas and systems of ideas are also communicated in media other than that of the apocalypse.

The distinctions are relevant for the question of historical influence since it implies that the presence and the spread of apocalyptic ideas are neither restricted to apocalypticism, nor to apocalypses, and, furthermore, that the presence and spread of apocalyptic systems of ideas are not confined to apocalypses. In any case the question of historiacl influence should not primarily be viewed as a relation between individual apocalyptic texts.

1.5. Phenomenological Parallels from Other Cultures

1.5.1. Though the historical dimension must be taken into account, it is but one aspect of the problems we have to face when approaching apocalypticism; if we attempt to identify, understand, and explain this phenomenon, we cannot, of course, reduce the problem to a question of "origins". The Near East and Mediterranean types of apocalypticism are certainly the most literarily elaborated, and from this point of view it is perfectly justified to confine the topic of the Colloquium to these particular types. However, if we widen our scope, we will find striking phenomenological parallels in the cultures of the Americas, Africa and Oceania, which can hardly be explained with reference to early historical connections with the above area, or by way of diffusion.

1.5.2. Phenomenological parallels to the well-known notion of the 4 periods represented by the 4-metal scheme in Hesiod, Bahman Yašt, and the Book of Daniel are found among the ancient cultures of Mexico, the Mayas and the Aztecs. In the Aztec sources the four eras are represented by different "suns". Although the sequence followed by the various texts differs greatly, there are the periods of: The Earth Sun, The Fire Sun, The Air Sun and The Water Sun, which precede the present Era. Each of these cosmic cycles was terminated by a universal cataclysm, and the Aztecs looked forward with fear to the end of the present period.

> The Earth Sun was terminated by famine,
> The Fire Sun was terminated by conflagration,
> The Air Sun by a hurricane, and
> The Water Sun by a flood.[41]

---

[41] Gray 1925.

In this chronological framework a dualistic system is involved which seems to represent the positive and negative aspects of the different 'Suns'. In the present Era there was a period when *Quetzalcoatl* – associated with the year *Ce Acatl* – was a king among men and the world prospered, but this period came to its end with the advent of the Europeans and was introduced by a new incarnation of *Quetzalcoatl* – in the Person of Cortéz. The year was 1519: *Ce Acatl*.[42] Such ideas were actualized in Montezuma's visions during these years, and "he saw the heavens change, and there was a vision of strangely armed men approaching to destroy Mexico and himself and the gods."[43]

1.5.3. However striking, it is not the external analogy between elements of content – the 4-period scheme – which is the most important factor in this comparison. If we extended our collection of parallels to similar instances among millenarian and related movements of the third world, we would find a more fundamental correspondance which consists of a certain method of interpreting reality with reference to cultural heritage. This activity is conditioned by certain social and ideological determinants.

The revitalization of mythic material and its reinterpretation with reference to the contemporaneous situation is a recurrent feature in these movements.[44] The characterization of the rebellion and migration movements among the Tupi-Guaraní as "responses to new situations in terms of a pre-existing mythology"[45] could well be generalized to include other cases. Since the study of these phenomena began, anthropologists have explained them in terms of their social preconditions. For instance, already Kroeber considered the cult millenialist movements among North American Indians as responses to the impending destruction of the native way of life,[46] and Nash proposed that "Nativistic cults arise among deprived groups. They follow a shift in the value pattern, due to suppression and domination, and are movements to restore the original value pattern which they do by the construction of a fantasy situation."[47] As to the ideological preconditions involved, these consist of the actualization of a particular perspective on reality which I refer to in the following as the "revelatory world-view".

---

[42] Burland 1967, 141; Hvidtfeldt 1968, 309; Gray 1925, 183.
[43] Burland 1967, 65.
[44] Wilson 1973, 199 ff. *et passim;* Worsley 1970, 244 f. *et passim.*
[45] Wilson 1973, 209.
[46] Kroeber 1925; cf. Wilson 1973, 288.
[47] Nash 1937, 377; cf. the discussion in Wilson 1973, 288 ff.

1.6. Apocalypticism as a Universal Phenomenon

1.6.1. If we claim that a universally valid definition of apocalypticism should be useful in explanatory reasoning, whether it concerns its historical, ideological, social or verbal dimensions, then it would be tactical to take such dimensions into account already at the stipulation of the definition. This also implies that we should not rely exclusively on a number of general characteristics collected from more or less restricted areas but on what we from cross-cultural studies can appreciate as its generic features. Simultaneously with this procedure, we should be able to identify its individual and local forms by their culturally and historically patterned features. As a starting-point for research into apocalypticism seen as a universal phenomenon, it would be wise to view it basically in the light of its social and ideological preconditions.

1.6.2. After considering the rich evidence from the fields of social anthropology, comparative religion and biblical research, I would suggest that a general approach could be possible along the following lines:[48] Apocalypticism in its various aspects is related to a type of *world-view* which contains ideological premises for belief in the possibility of communication between man and the supramundane world, *i.e.* that divine secrets or plans relative to the mundane world in the present, past or future, can be revealed to a human recipient. These revealed secrets may then refer to such diverse matters as the course of world history from beginning to end, certain epochs in history, eschatological events, and existential problems of human life.

This type of world-view is in no way restricted to apocalyptic phenomena; it is reflected as well in other ill-defined complexes such as shamanism, prophecy, oracles, mantic wisdom, gnosis, jñāna, mysticism, astrology and various deterministic beliefs. Instead of calling it an apocalyptic world-view, I would prefer then to speak of a *revelatory world-view* which is embraced by apocalyptists but also by others.[49]

If we consider the data from the fields of social anthropology[50] and comparative religion, we can observe that revelatory world-views are

---

[48] For reviews of data, references and theoretical discussions relative to the following cf. Wilson 1973; Worsley 1970; Burridge 1969; Betz 1966; Lebram 1970, 519; Schreiner 1973, 237 ff.; Müller 1973; Steinschneider 1874 (on late Arabic and Hebrew texts); Plöger 1959; Hengel 1969; Isenberg 1974; Smith 1975; Hanson 1975 and 1976; Stone 1976. Cf. also the contributions to this Colloquium by Sanders and Nickelsburg. For further references cf. Instituto Fe y Secularidad 1975 § 5.1.3.3.

[49] I find Hanson's suggestions on "apocalyptic eschatology" highly illuminating (Hanson 1976, 29 f., 32). "Apocalyptic eschatology", however, should not be identified with the wider concept "revelatory world-view" used here.

[50] For reviews and references see note 48.

regularly actualized in situations of conflict or crisis, real or imagined, or in the context of fear of such situations. One type of situation emerges when the social organization, including access to central power, has been affected by a decrease in intra-system communication so that the cultural integration of a certain group is jeopardized. This decrease is no doubt the operating factor in the change process in which a group is forced into an organizational and cultural niche. Another type of situation arises when the cultural integrity of a community or group is exposed to external influence, e.g. in the form of war, colonialism, and political or religious propaganda.

1.6.3. I propose, therefore, that *apocalypticism* should be defined as the speculative and verbal activity which emerges when communities or groups are involved or perceive themselves involved in such types of situations mentioned above. These communities or groups tend to codify or restore their cultural identities or traditional value-systems in opposition to rival communities or groups through revelatory systems of ideas, which verbally manifest themselves by way of actualizing and reinterpreting traditional values, motifs or themes from religious literature or ritual with reference to the contemporaneous situation.

Since this activity, including the apocalyptic systems of ideas, is culturally patterned, it is not possible to give a universally valid definition which takes into account features of manifest content. Therefore, instead of listing a number of more or less recurrent motifs, I have chosen to illustrate the general outline above by means of a case-study of a particular text, the Pahlavi *Jāmāsp Nāmag*.

2. The Case of Jāmāsp Nāmag

2.1. Iranian apocalyptic texts[51] often allude to legends about the *Pēšdāds*, the early rulers of Iran, who founded civilization in constant struggle with peoples which Ahriman sent against the Iranians. Of these hostile peoples it was the Turanians and their king *Frāsyāp* who caused the most serious trouble until they were beaten by the second Iranian dynasty, the Kayanians.[52] We will see how some of these conflict motifs are still used as models in one of the Middle Iranian apocalypses, the *Jāmāsp Nāmag*. In this type of literature legendary motifs are thus actualized, and reinterpreted,

---

[51] For the editions of the principal texts see Tavadia 1956, ch. 13; cf. further *e.g.* Abegg 1928, 203–240; Widengren 1961, 181–214, 222–225; 1965, 102–108, 199–214; 1969, 459 ff.; 1966; S. S. Hartman 1976. For reviews and references see Czeglédy 1958; Kippenberg 1978; Collins 1979c. Cf. also above notes 28–40 and the contributions by S. S. Hartman, Hultgård and Widengren in this volume.

[52] Cf. Klíma 1968, 42; Christensen 1917, 136 *et passim* and 1932.

often in political terms with reference to the contemporaneous situation or confused with accounts of recent conflicts with the Arabs and other peoples. Basically, the apocalypses and legends thus deal with the same essential problem – the fundamentals of Iranian civilization, culture, and religion.

2.2. *Ĵāmāsp Nāmag* (ĴN) is preserved in Pazand, Pahlavi, and Persian versions[53] and contained as chapter XVI in *Ayādgār ī Ĵāmāspīg* (AĴ).[54] The apocalypse is presented as a vaticination delivered by *Ĵāmāsp,* a pseudonymic sage of the past. In the Pazand text introducing the AĴ it is stated[55] that the book was written when king *Wištāsp* ruled. For consultation he invited Ĵāmāsp, who had received the gift of omniscience from Zoroaster on the command of Ōhrmazd.[56]

The tradition of the visionary qualities transmitted by Zoroaster to Ĵāmāsp is retained in the late Pahlavi tractate *Wizīrkard ī Dēnīg* 19. After performing the *drōn*-ceremony and having invoked the Creator, Zoroaster gave to Ĵāmāsp the flower of visionary knowledge:

ud gul⟨ī yašt⟩pad ō ī dastwar Ĵāmāsp dād kē az ast ud būd ud bawēd hamāg dīdāragān (ī) āgāhēnēd.
And he gave the flower dastwar to Ĵāmāsp, who became aware, through visions, of all that is, was, and will be.[57]

Still in the Persian Zardušt-nāmah of Zardušt Bahrām, it is said that Ĵāmāsp acquired the power of foretelling by smelling the flower which Zoroaster had consecrated in the *drōn*-ceremony.[58]

be Ĵāmāsp dādaš azān yašte bōy // hame ilmhā gašt roušan be dōy
be dānist čīzīke bāyad šodan // va tā rastxīz ānče xāhad bodan.
He gave to Ĵâmâsp some of the consecrated perfume, and all sciences became intelligible to him. He knew all things that were to happen and all that was to happen, up to the day of Resurrection.[59]

The divine knowledge that Zoroaster received in his dialogues with Ōhrmazd has thus been transmitted to Ĵāmāsp and is further revealed by the latter in his dialogue with Wištāsp. Besides this alleged setting of the tractate in the early Zoroastrian community and the allusions to Avestan traditions, its alleged antiquity is occasionally strengthened by certain stylistic or syntactic features such as the use of Avestan word order, placing

---

[53] Ed. Modi 1903. This edition is used here. Cf. also the transcriptions and translations by Bailey 1930; 1931; Benveniste 1932; Messina 1939. When not stated otherwise I employ the paragraphing in Bailey 1930 + 1931. For the transcription of the Pahlavi I have adopted the phonemic system suggested by MacKenzie 1967 and 1971.

[54] Ed. Messina 1939.

[55] Pazand text in Modi 1903, 58.

[56] Pazand text *ibid.,* 58 ff.

[57] Cf. text and translation in Molé 1967, 13 ff.

[58] Modi 1903, xxxiv.

[59] Text and translation *loc. cit.*

the verb first in the sentence, and subject, object etc. after (as in JN 1, 58, 84, 100).[60] Though I am not concerned here with problems of redaction concerning the relation between JN and AJ, or the literary background of the extant texts, it should be pointed out that the general form of question and answer which is typical for the whole of AJ is also specific for JN. The Pahlavi text of JN, as it now stands, is presented in the following form:

(1) A short introduction consisting of a question put by Wištāsp:

pursīd Wištāsp šāh kū ēn dēn ī abēzag sāl rawāg bawēd ud pas az ān čē āwām ud zamānag rasēd.
King Wištāsp asked: This pure religion, how many years will it endure, and afterwards, which age, period, will come? (1)

(2) The rest of the text consists of an extensive answer in the form of a prophecy (2–106) delivered by Jāmāsp, beginning as follows:

guft-aš Jāmāsp ī bīdaxš kū ēn hazār sāl rawāg bawēd. pas awēšān mardōmān ī andar ān āwām bawēnd hamāg ō mihrādrūjīh ēstēnd.
Jāmāsp, the bīdaxš[61] (minister), said: It will endure 1,000 years. Then those men at that age will all become breakers of Faith (2–3).

(3) After this introduction, which refers to the above mentioned dialogue situation in which Jāmāsp communicates the revealed knowledge to the king, the reader is only occasionally reminded of the general form by insertions such as: *u-t ēn-iz gōwam kū...* = And this, too, I will tell you... *viz.* that Jāmāsp is addressing Wištāsp (63 and 70); and by the expression *(ud bē āyēd) Pēšyōtan ī ašmā pus,* where *Pēšyōtan* is followed by the gloss *ī ašmā pus* 'your son' (99 and 100); and by the inserted vocative form *tō Wištāsp* 'You, O Wištāsp' (96).

2.3. Looking at the composition of the discourse as a whole, we can distinguish four main sequences which correspond to four courses of events vaticinated by the sage. These will affect the Iranian nation politically and culturally.

(1) In the most elaborated sequence (2–58) the disasters following the advent of the Arabs (*Tāzīgān*) are described as a national catastrophe. Disintegration and decadence will involve all aspects of the society, and even the normal course of nature will be disturbed. Untimely deaths will abound (11), death will seem sweet (16) and will be held as a refuge (57), the rich will deem the poor fortunate (14), son will strike father and mother (18), the younger brother will strike the elder brother (19), "the insignificant and undistinguished will come into notice" (21),[62] the childless will be

---

[60] On Avestan syntax in Pahlavi writings see Widengren 1967 (examples from Zātspram and Bundahišn) and his contribution to this volume § 4., and Nyberg 1974, 284.

[61] For this title see Asmussen 1965, 106, note 134 with references.

[62] *ud xʷurdag ⟨ud⟩ apaydāg mardōm ō paydāgīh rasēd.* For *xʷurdag* Bailey 1930, 57 reads *avarīk* ['wlyk], and Messina 1939, 67 *anarīk* ['nlyk]. I prefer *xʷurdag* [hwldk] as in 58 (cf. MacKenzie 1974, 280).

deemed as fortunate, and the reverse (24), a horseman will become a man on foot, and the reverse (35), bad deeds will be held as a source of joy (41), the contentious and greedy and violent man will be deemed good, but wise men of good faith will be held as *dēw*s (44), mockery and defilement will be an ornament (47), etc.

As a literary form this passage can be classed as a *descriptio mundi inversi,* as I propose to call it. This recurrent form in apocalyptic literature[62a] is well worthy of systematic investigation in relation to social value sytems. The inversion of the ideal social values is in ĴN explicitly connected with the advent of the Arabs (5). According to the general conflict perspective of the apocalyptist, the Iranian nation and its distinctive cultural character is seen in sharp contrast to foreign peoples and their habits. By the transgression of ethnic and culturally defined limits, the catastrophe is a fact and consists in the disintegration of cultural identity.

In other words, the author of the text relates a profound process of acculturation seen from an ethnocentric perspective in which the Iranian and the non-Iranian are opposed:

ud hamāg Ērān šahr ō dast ī awēšān dušmanān rasēd (12) ud Anērān ud Ērān gumēzihēnd ēdōn kū ērīh az anērīh paydāg nē bawēd, ān ī ēr abāz anērīh ēstēnd (13)

And all Ērān šahr will fall into the hands of these enemies (12). And Anērān and Ērān will be confounded, so that the Iranians will not be distinguished from the non-Iranian. Those who are Iranians will turn back to non-Iranian ways. (13)

The proceeding sequences of the apocalypse correspond to three episodes of rulers who will appear in Ērān.

(2) In the land of X^uarāsān will emerge a false pretender, "an insignificant and undistinguished man" (x^uurdag ud apaydāg mardē) (58). He will conquer the land by violence and military force, but in the middle of his reign he will disappear, whereupon sovereignty will pass from the men of Ērān and go to foreigners (Anērān) (60), "and religions and laws and manners of life will abound" (ud was kēš ud dād ud rawišn bawēnd) (61). The result is again a corrupt and inverse world where the killing of a man will be considered a merit (62), and the sovereigns will deal tyrannically and unlawfully (stambag ⟨ud⟩ apēdād) with the men of Ērān šahr (65). "In that evil time loyalty and reverence will not exist" (andar ān wad āwām mihr ud āzarm nē bawēnd) (68); "among them the superior will not be distinct from the inferior, nor the inferior from the superior, and they will not assist one another" (u-šān meh az keh ud keh az meh nē paydāg, u-šān hampuštīh nē bawēnd) (69). It is better not to be born, or to die, than to see so much evil and oppression that will come (70). The future misery of Ērān is again put in connection with the invasion of the Arabs and other foreign peoples:

[62a] Compare *e.g.* the 18th Book of Right Ginza (Lidzbarski 1925).

"Those Arabs will intermingle with Romans (Byzantines) and Turks, and they will ravage the world" (*awēšān Tāzīgān abāg Hrōmīgān ud Turkān andar gumēzēnd ud kišwar bē wišōbēnd*) (73). This conflict between Ērān and the foreign nations, which is described in socio-political and cultural terms, has a mythological duplicate in the interfoliated passages about the great eschatological conflict between *Mihr* and *Xēšm* that will take place at the end of the millenium. The vague allusions in 77 to "that conflict" in which Mihr and Xēšm will fight together is typical for the apocalyptic style of JN. It refers to a well-known conflict described in Bahman Yašt.[62b]

The motif of a *mundus inversus,* which we have met in terms of social and cultural rules and values, gets a pregnant mythological expression in the words of *Spandarmad,* the goddess of the earth, who complains to Ōhrmazd: "I am turned upside down and I turn mankind here upside down" (*azadar azabar bē man bawam ud ēn mardōm azabar azadar bē kunam*) (75).

(3) There follows a short sequence (84–87) which again speaks about a false pretender who will emerge from *Kust ī Nēmrōz* and seize power by violence. He will cause much bloodshed, will flee from his enemies to Zāwul, but will return with a great army and cause much misery to Ērān. Superior and inferior will seek a refuge for their souls.

(4) The next passage (88–106), which I will deal with more closely below, relates how the King of *Padašx"ārgar,* exhorted by the messenger of *Mihr Yazd,* revolts against his oppressor and against the Arabs, Turks, and Romans (Byzantines). The account of this conflict again reflects old legendary motifs. The passage is completed by an account of the eschatological hero of the millenium, *Pēšyōtan.*

2.3.1. The very composition of the discourse thus shows a tendency to

---

[62b] Bahman Yašt VII, 32–35 (III, 34–35) (Text: Anklesaria 1957, 66–67):

32. *pas Mihr ī frāx"-goyōd wāng kunēd kū ēn 9000 sāl paštē ī-š kard tā nūn Dahāg ī duš-dēn ud Frāsyāp ī Tūr ud Alaksandar ī Hrōmāyīg ud awēšān dawāl-kustīgān dēwān ī wizārd-wars 1000 sālān āwām wēš az paymān x"adāyīh kard.*

33. *stard bawēd ān druwand Ganāg Mēnōg ka ēdōn ašnūd.*

34. *Mihr ī frax"-goyōd be zanēd Xēšm ī xurdruš* [= DH; K 20: xlwdlpš], *pad stowīh dwārēd.*

35. *ān druwand Ganāg Mēnōg abāg wišūdagān wad-tōhmagān abāz ō tār ud tom ī duš-ax" dwārēd.*

32. Then Mihr of wide pastures will cry out: This 9000 years' Compact which was made, until now Dahāg of evil faith and Frāsyāp the Tūr and Alexander the Roman and those with leather belts and the dēws with dishevelled hair have held dominion a period of 1000 years beyond the treaty.

33. That wicked Ganāg Mēnōg will be confounded when he has heard that.

34. Mihr of wide pastures will smite Xēšm of the bloody club. In distress he will flee.

35. That wicked Ganāg Mēnōg will flee with the misbegotten ones of evil seed back to the darkness and gloom of the evil existence.

Syntactic features suggest that the text is in part a translation from Avestan (Bailey 1931, 588; Widengren in this volume § 4.2.1. and § 4.2.1.1.).

structure the course of events of the 4th millenium into periods. This periodization of history is a distinctive feature of a main type of apocalypses such as Bahman Yašt I, III (I, II)[63] the apocalyptic sections of Bundahišn (ch. XXXIII, BdA 211,3–220,15); the book of Daniel 2; 7–12; the Animal Apocalypse (1 Enoch 85–90); the Apocalypse of Weeks (1 Enoch 93:1–10; 91:12–17); Jub. 23; 4 Ezra; 2 Apoc. Bar.; 2 Enoch 22–38; The Apoc. of Abraham 24–27, and in particular 28; Test. of Abraham 9–11; Jacob's Ladder 4–8; Sib. Or. 1–2, 4, 8; the Coptic Apoc. of Elijah 2:2–45; the Hebrew Apoc. of Elijah; Sefer Hekalot (3 Enoch); the Apoc. Adam CG V, 5, the 18th Book of Right Ginza,[63a] Haran Gawaita 18–21,[63b] and later tractates such as the Apocalypse of the angel Metatron to Simon ben Jochai.[64] Apocalypses of this type seem to be the most widely recognized,[65] particularly by historians of religion for whom the notion of the periodization of history often constitutes the basis for classifying a text or a complex of ideas as apocalyptic.

In the JN this feature is combined with a spatial structure. The four episodes are presented according to a geographical model in which each episode corresponds to one of the four directions.

(1) The Arabs, who are described as allied with the Romans and Turks, are vaguely seen as enemies from the West.[65a]

(2) The "insignificant and obscure" pretender arises in the land of X^uarāsān, which is the East (x^uarāsān zamīg = 'the land of sunrise').

(3) The following pretender will emerge "from the direction of the South" (az kust ī nēmrōz) (84), if we translate the phrase literally, or, from Kust i Nēmrōz, taking the compound as the proper designation = 'The Southern District'.

(4) The episode that concerns the last pretender and his oppressor is initially located in Padašx^uārgar, which is the mountain range (gar) south of the Caspian Sea, or the region Tabaristān that is in the North.

2.3.2. Despite these temporal and spatial structures being combined, we do not find elaborated symbolism as in the well-known vision in Bahman Yašt (I)[66] and in much of apocalyptic literature.[67] The JN contains a number

---

[63] Ed. Anklesaria 1957. The division of West in SBE V is given in parenthesis. For the following texts cf. Semeia 14 (1979).

[63a] Lidzbarski 1925.

[63b] Drower 1953.

[64] Steinschneider 1874, 635 ff.; cf. ibid. for other late Hebrew, Persian, and Arabic apocalypses.

[65] Cf. Collins 1979a, 14; 1979b, 23.

[65a] The early contacts between Zoroastrians and Arabs took place mainly in the SW of Iran. For Arabic sources (Balādurī 388; Tabarī I, 2696) see Wikander 1946; for the confused accounts in Šāhnāmah see Monchi-Zādeh 1975.

[66] Ed. Anklesaria 1957, text 2–4 (2–5), translation 101–102.

[67] See Semeia 14 (1979).

of vague allusions to mythical, legendary and ritual topics – and this is one of its most outstanding stylistic features – but there are no obscure symbols or allegories which need interpretation, and there is nothing like an *angelus interpres*. The tenor of the apocalypse concerns situations of political and ethnic conflicts in which the cultural identity of the Iranians is threatened, but the text ends up with the conviction of a positive solution to these conflicts. The hope is tied to a King of the future who will defeat the enemies by military force and by support of the traditional gods of Ērān. Religion will be reestablished through a ritual act performed by Pēšyōtan, and peace will reign.

The JN thus deals broadly with the same subject as, for instance, Dēnkard VII, 8, which concerns

[1] 'the miracles, which, it is revealed, will be manifested after the ending of Iranian rule in Eranshahr and until the end of the millenium (of Zoroaster) and the coming of Ushetar' and especially what is 'revealed in the Avesta concerning the 9th and 10th centuries.'[68]

The text of Dēnkard continues to describe the acculturation process in political and social terms:

[2] That state of affairs now evident is indicative of how Iranian rule has come to an end in Ērān šahr, and of the destruction of justice and customs and classes, and of the rule of those with dishevelled hair (Arabs) and the *haughty (Turks) and the churchmen (Byzantines).

[3] And of the mixing together and combining of all three of them, of the being trusted and attaining the highest station with them of the inferior, the petty, the transient and the undistinguished of the age, and the destruction and downfall of excellent and notable men in their time.[69]

And near the end of the millenium the act of restoration will be performed by Pēšyōtan and his disciples as it is described according to Dēnkard 190.7–190.13 (ed. Madan 1911):

– – – *ud tabāhīh wirānīh az ābān ataxšān zamīgān abārīg weh dahišnān andar Ērān dehān, pad abāz paywastan amāwandīh ud pērōzgarīh ī ō ān ī Ōhrmazd dēn Zarduštān hazangrōzim nazd frazāmīh abar Čisrōgmēnāg ī ahlaw kē pad any nām Pēšyōtan-iz x"ānēd ī Wištāsp pus x"ad ud 150 ī ōy hāwišt abzārīh bawēd, pad dādār kām ud framām.*

– – – the restoration of the destruction of the waters, the fires, the earths, and other good creatures in the countries of Ērān, reuniting the power and victory of the religion of Ōhrmazd, near the end of the Zoroastrian millenium, will become the work of the righteous Čisrōgmēnāg, who with another name is also called Pēšyōtan, Wištāsp's own son, and 150 of his disciples, according to the will and command of the Creator.

---

[68] Translation MacKenzie 1974, 279f.

[69] [2] *ān ī nūn wēnābdāg ēdōnīh nimūdār ast čiyōn hanǰāfišn ī Ērān-x"adāyīh az Ērān šahr, ud wišōbišn ī dād ud ēwēn ud ristag, ud pādixšāyīh ī wizārd-wars ud buland-pēšag ud *kilīsāyīg.*
[3] *ud āgenēn āmēxtagīh ud paywandīh-iz ī awēšān har*3, wābarīhistan ud ō abardar pāyag madan abāg-sān ī nigūnān, x"urdagān, wideragān ud apaydāgān ī āwām, ud wišōbīhistan ud nigūnīhistan ī bowandag ud paydāg mardōm andar ān ī awēšān zamānag.*
Reading and translation according to MacKenzie 1974, 280 with some minute alterations.

2.4. The method of revitalizing old conflict motifs or patterns taken from traditional religious literature or ritual is manifested in recognizable patterns and modes of expression in the apocalyptic texts. Considering formal features, the apocalyptic discourse-unit can thus be modelled on the structure of a certain episode in a religious tradition. Furthermore, as to content, elements from the realms of myth, ritual and legendary history can be actualized and reinterpreted as future events which are vaticinated by a pseudonymic visionary of the past. In the apocalyptic discourse such patterns and components may serve simultaneously as models for the interpretation of social and political situations in which the text has been composed, redacted or actualized. In the JN such features are especially salient in the 4th sequence which is worth quoting *in extenso.*

JN 88–106 (Text: Modi 1903, 6, 1.12–8, 1.7):

88. *ud pas az ān Padašx"ārgar az nazdīkīh ī drayāb bār mard Mihr Yazd be wēnēd.*

89. *ud Mihr Yazd was rāz ⟨ī⟩ nihān ō ān mard gōwēd.*

90. *pad paygām ō Padašx"ārgar šāh frēstēd kū ēn x"adāy karr ud kōr[70] čim dārēh. ud tō-č x"adāyīh ēdōn kun čiyōn pidarān ud niyāgān ⟨ī⟩ tō ud ašmā kard.*

91. *ōy ⟨ī⟩ mard gōwēd kū man ēn x"adāyīh čiyōn šāyēm kardan ka-m ān gund ud spāh ud ganj ud spāh-sardār nēst čiyōn pidarān ud niyāgān ⟨ī⟩ man būd.*

92. *ān paygāmbar gōwēd kū be awar tā-t ganj ud x"āstag ī pidarān ud niyāgān ⟨ī⟩ tō awiš abespāram.*

93. *u-š ganj ī wuzurg ⟨ī⟩ Frāsyāp awis nimāyēd.*

94. *čiyōn ganj ō dast āwarēd, spāh ud gund ⟨ī⟩ Zāwul ārāyēd ō dušmanān šawēd.*

95. *ud ka ⟨ō⟩ dušmanān āgāhīh rasēd Turk ud Tāzīg ud Hrōmīg ō ham āyend kū gīram Padašx"ārgar šāh ud stānam aň ganj ⟨ud⟩ x"āstag az ōy mard.*

96. *ud pas ōy mard ka-š ān āgāhīh āšnawēd abāg was spāh ud gund ⟨ī⟩ Zāwul ō mayān ī Ērān šahr āyēd ud abāg awēšān mardōmān pad ān dašt ī tō Wištāsp abāg spēd ⟨ī⟩ Xiōnān pad Spēd-Razūr kard abāg Padašx"ārgar šāh kōxšišn ud kārezār frāz kunēnd.*

97. *ud pad nērōg ī yazdān ī Ērān ⟨ud⟩ kayān (ud) x"arrah ⟨ud⟩ dēn ⟨ī⟩ māzdēsnān ud x"arrah ī Padašx"ārgar ud Mihr ud Srōš ud Rašn ud Ābān ud Ādurān ud Ātaxšān abēr škoft kārezār kunēnd.*

98. *ud az awēšān wēh āyēd, az dušmanān čand be ōzanēd kē marag nē tuwān grift.*

99. *ud pas Srōš ud Nēryōsang Pēšyōtan ⟨ī⟩ ašmā pus az framān ī dādār Ōhrmazd az Kangdiz ī kayān be hangēzēnd.*

100. *ud bē āyēd Pēšyōtan ī ašmā pus abāg 150 hāwišt [hwwšt] kē-šān paymōzan ī spēd (ī) ⟨ud⟩ syā.*

101. *⟨ud⟩ dast ⟨ī⟩ man pad drafš tā Pārs ō ānōh kū ātaxš ⟨ud⟩ ābān nišāst ēstēd.*

102. *ānōh yašt kunēd.*

103. *ka yašt sar bawēd, zōhr ō āb rēzēnd ud ⟨ō⟩ ān ātaxš zōhr dahēnd.*

104. *ud druwandān ud dēw-ēsnān[71] ēdōn be abesīhēnd čiyōn pad zamestān ⟨ī⟩ sard warg ī draxtān be hōšēnd.*

105. *ud gurg āwām be šawēd ud mēš āwām andar āyēd.*

106. *ud Hušēdar ⟨ī⟩ Zarduxštān pad dēn nimūdārīh ō paydāgīh āyēd ud anāgīh ud *drōšag sar āyēd,[72] rāmišn ud šādīh ⟨ud⟩ hurāmīh be bawēd.*

88. Afterwards in Padašx"argar near the seashore a man will see Mihr Yazd.

89. And Mihr Yazd will tell that man many hidden secrets.

---

[70] For the expression *karr ud kōr* see Bailey 1931, 591.

[71] For my reading *dēw-ēsnān* < Av. *daēva-yasna*, compare its opposite *mazdēsnān;* Bailey 1931, 586 has *dēv ut xyōnān* = "the *dēvs* and the *Hyōns*". Cf. also Benveniste 1932, 346, 358, reading as Bailey *loc. cit.*

90. He will send him with a message to the King of Padašx^uārgar, saying: Why do you support this ruler, deaf and blind? And you shall exercise dominion just as your fathers and your forefathers have done!

91. This man will say: How should I be able to exercise dominion, since I have not the troops and army and treasure and generals such as my fathers and forefathers had?

92. The messenger will say: Come, that I may entrust you with the treasure and wealth of your fathers and forefathers.

93. And he will show him the great treasure of Frāsyāp.

94. When he brings the treasure into his hand, he prepares the army and troops of Zāwul and advances against his enemies.

95. When the news reaches his enemies, Turk and Arab and Roman will come together, saying: I will seize the King of Padašx^uārgar and take that treasure and wealth from that man.

96. And then that man, when he hears the news, with a large army and troops of Zāwul will come to the centre of Ērān šahr and with those men on that plain, where you, O Wištāsp, (fought) with the White Xionites in the White Forest, they will struggle in battle with the King of Padašx^uārgar.

97. By the might of the gods of Ērān and the Kayānian Glory and the Faith of the Mazda-worshippers and the Glory of Padašx^uārgar, and Mihr and Srōš and Rašn and the Waters and the Sacred and Domestic Fires they will wage a very hard battle.

98. And he will prove better than them; he will kill so many of the enemies that their number cannot be counted.

99. Then Srōš and Nēryōsang will stir up your son Pēšyōtan, by command of Ōhrmazd the Creator, from the Kang fortress of the Kayān.

100. And your son Pēšyōtan will come with 150 disciples, whose raiment is white and black.

101. And my hand will hold the banner as far as Pārs to the place where the fire(s) and waters are established.

102. There he will perform the yasna ritual.[72a]

103. When the yasna ritual is finished, they will pour the libation into the water and will give the libation to that fire.

104. And the wicked and the dēw-worshippers will be annihilated as when in a cold winter the leaves of trees wither.

105. And the time of the wolf will pass away and the time of the sheep will enter.

106. And Hušēdar son of Zoroaster will appear to reveal the faith, and evil and *desolation will come to an end; joy and happiness and gladness will have come.

2.4.1. Already Benveniste suggested that the apocalypse here has con-served traits of the old legend about the conflict between *Mānuščihr* and *Frāsyāp*, though representing a variant of the legend that is not usually found in the Pahlavi books.[73]

"Dans la tradition acceptée par la plupart des livres pehlevis, c'est la conclusion d'un traité, scellé sous les auspices de Spandarmad, qui remet Manuščihr en possession de son royaume.

---

[72] I read *ud* **drōšag sar āyēd;* cf. Messina 1939, 74. Bailey, however, has *tāk sar āyet!* (*loc. cit.*), but in his notes *ibid.,* 594 f. deals with Av. *draoša* > Pahl. *drōš.* Cf. further Benveniste *loc. cit.:* *pat sar āyēt!*

[72a] *yašt kardan* is a technical term for performing the yasna ritual; cf. Bahman Yašt (K 43, fol. 270v, 4) *kē-š yašt kard ēstēd.* Cf. Kanga 1974, 254 note 1 for passages in Vendidad IX. 32 (gloss) and Epistle I, ch. 6,1 of Manuščihr.

[73] Benveniste 1932, 368 ff.; 1932–33, 199.

Ici le messager d'un dieu lui apporte des encouragements, et, par son appui positif, le
détermine à prendre les armes."[74]

These observations and the brilliant analysis carried out by Benveniste
are indeed convincing. I would, however, refrain from his tendency to
consider the ǰN-episode as simply a variant of the legend. His analysis
concerns "l'authenticité el l'antiquité de la narration du Žāmāsp-Nāmak"[75]
and does not consider such dimensions as the author's or redactor's
intensions, the episode's apocalyptic character, its contextual relation,
particularly to the eschatological events of the millenium, or its reference to
recent political conditions.

Benveniste has been criticized by Messina and Czeglédy, but since they
too have disregarded such communication aspects and the interpretative
character of apocalyptic texts, their criticism totally misses the point.
According to Messina[76] and Czeglédy,[77] the most important argument
against the "assumption of Beneveniste" is that "the *Žāmāsp nāmak* speaks
of the eschatological events of Zoroaster's Millenium, while Manōščihr is a
figure of the Third Millenium".[78] Of course, it is true that the traditional
periodization, as found in Bundahišn, assigns the conflict between Mānuščihr and Frāsyāp to the 3rd millenium (= 9th millenium according to the
12-millenium scheme),[79] and that ǰN relates the events of the 4th (the
Zoroastrian) millenium (= the 10th, respectively, see the synopsis); the
dialogue of the apocalypse between Wištāsp and ǰāmāsp takes place in the
beginning of the 4th era and ǰāmāsp prophesies the events up to the
appearance of Hušēdar at the end of the millenium.

The apparent paradox would be that ǰāmāsp vaticinates the events of the
era that preceded his own. Provided that the apocalyptist was acquainted
with the legendary history of Iran, he would therefore hardly have
considered the passage 88 ff. as simply an account of the conflict between
Mānuščihr and Frāsyāp, nor would he have expected this from his audience. His intention was certainly different. The passage is part of an
apocalyptic discourse and should be dealt with accordingly, and not only as
a variant of a legend. For this reason the criticism is totally misleading
because we are not concerned here with problems of proper transmission
and historical authenticity or the logical coherence of legendary history but
with a process of literary creation which is typical for apocalyptic texts.
Thus if we consider the genres of the respective texts, it is evident that the
compositional elements that originally belong to myth or legend convey a

---

[74] Benveniste 1932, 369.

[75] *Ibid.*, 370.   [76] Messina 1939, 116 note 2.

[77] Czeglédy 1958, 33.   [78] *Loc. cit.*

[79] BdA 211, 14; on the chronological frame and the advent of the Arabs cf. BdA
238.6–240.8.

Millenium ĬN	Great Bundahišn XXXIII
III/IX	Mānuščihr is born. Afrāsyāp/Frāsyāp emerges and drives away (spōxt) Mānuščihr with the Iranians to Padašxᵘārgar, and causes distress (sēĵ), misery (niyāz) and much death (was margīh) among them. (BdA 211,13–212,1). Kay Xusraw kills Frāsyāp in this millenium. (BdA 213,13–14). After King Wištāsp has reigned 30 years the millenium is at an end. (BdA 213,15–214,1).

| IV/X | Ĵāmāsp delivers a prophecy to Wištāsp: the pure religion will endure a thousand years, then all will become covenant-breakers (1–3). The country will be delivered up to the Arabs (Tazīgān). Lawlessness, untimely deaths; social, moral, cultural, and economic dissolution. Ērān and Anērān will be confounded (4–57). Appearance of 3 pretenders in Xᵘarāsān, Nēmrōz and Padašxᵘārgar. The king of P., without army, troops, and treasure, is forced to support a king who is "deaf and blind". The servant of Mihr Yazd delivers the treasure of Frāsyāp to the King of P. who defeats the evil forces (Turks [Turk], Arabs [Tazīgān] Roman [Hrōmīg] are mentioned). Pēšyōtan comes from Kangdiz with 150 disciples and ritually performs the final restitution (58–104). The wicked and the dēw-worshippers will perish (104). | The 4th millenium begins., Zoroaster receives the religion from Ōhrmazd and Wištāsp disseminates it. Many wars between Ērān and Anērān. (BdA 214,1–214,4). Conflicts with Byzantine empire (Hrōm), Arabs (Tazīgān), Hephtalites (Hēftālān), Xionites (Xiōn), and Turks (Turk) (BdA 214,8–217,10). In a future period, when the Romans (Rōmīg) have exercised dominion during one year, Kay Wahrām, with the glory of the family of gods (xᵘarrah pad-aš az dūdag ī bayān) will reestablish Iranian sovereignty and Zoroastrian religion. Pēšyōtan will come from Kangdiz with 150 righteous men and ritually perform the final restitution (BdA 217,10–218,5). |

| V/XI | Hušēdar's millenium begins (106). | Hušēdar's millenium begins. |

different or additional meaning when adopted as components of the apocalypse. The relative vagueness of the allusions of the apocalyptic text serves this purpose, while an overtly obvious reference to the traditional motifs would have restricted the connotational range of these components.

The passage (88–93) quoted above concerns a power relation between two kings. The king of Padašxᵘārgar is deprived of authority and forced to support another king who is "deaf and blind". A messenger of Mihr Yazd is sent to the king of Padašxᵘārgar, calling his attention to the dishonourable situation and his royal dignity. He exhorts him to seize power and shows him the treasure of Frāsyāp. None of the *dramatis personae* is thus directly mentioned by name except the god Mihr Yazd who reveals the concealed secrets, *rāz ī nihān,* to the messenger.[80] The subsequent passage (94–98) deals with the King's victory over his enemies. Equipped with the royal treasure he prepares the army of Zāwul and defeats his enemies; the joined forces of the Turks, Arabs, and Romans (Byzantines) are mentioned. There follows the reestablishment of religion through a ritual act performed by Pēšyōtan, the immortal son of Zoroaster. The wicked and the dew-worshippers will perish, and the happy millenium of Hušēdar will begin (99–106). Since the external discourse pattern is guided by a principle of temporal and spatial contiguity which unites the constituents of the text, the King of Padašxᵘārgar is metonymically connected with the mentioned enemies and the eschatological events of the millenium. The tenor of the text thus concerns a Savior King of the future, and he is portrayed as a political liberator who will defeat the hostile foreign nations by military force. His eschatological victory is won with the help of the divine forces of Ērān and has a ritual correlate in Pēšyōtan, who reestablishes religion by performing the yasna ritual and the libation sacrifices to the water (*āb*) and to the fire (*ātaxš*) (102–103). The apocalyptist would consequently not have claimed simply to relate a variant of the legend of Mānuščihr and Frāsyāp.

2.4.2. Nevertheless, the apocalypse is *modelled* on the legend. Not only do the names Padašxᵘārgar and Frāsyāp recur in the apocalyptic text, there is also a structural correspondance to a main type of the legend. On the basis of the information about the *dramatis personae* and their relations given in the Avesta, the Pahlavi books, and the accounts by Syriac and Arabic writers,[81] we can conclude that there must have existed at least two main

---

[80] The Word *rāz* here is the current technical term for the secrets revealed in apocalypses and also when used as a loan-word in Jewish and Mandean texts.

[81] Yasna 11, 7 (20) = Darmesteter 1892 I, 111.
Yt 5:41–42; Yt 8:6–7, 37–38; Yt 9:18, 22; Yt 13:131; Yt 17:38, 42; Yt 19:56–64, 77, 82, 93 (transl. Lommel 1927);
Bundahišn XX, 34; XXIX, 5; XXXI, 20–22 (SBE, V, 82, 117, 135 f.); BdA, 211–213;
Dēnkard VII, 1, 30 f. (ed. Molé 1967, 8 [text] 9 [transl.]; Dēnkard VII, 11,3 (ed. Molé 1967, 102 [text], 103 [transl.]);
Zātspram XII, 3 (SBE, XLVII, 134);
Dādestān ī Dēnig LXX, 3 (SBE, XVIII, 213 f.); XC, 3–4 (*ibid.,* 257);
Mēnōg ī Xrad 27:41–44, 59 (Pahlavi text TD 2 ed. Molé 1963, 430 [text], 432 [transl.]);
Mēnōg ī Xrad 62:31–36 (Pahlavi text K 43, fol. 175v, 15–176r, 3; Pazand text and transl. ed. West 1871, 56 and 186.);
Šāyest nē Šāyest X, 28 (SBE, V, 228 f.);
Šahrīhā ī Ērān § 38 (ed. Markwart 1931, 18, text and transl.);
Theodor bar Kōnai (Pognon 1898/1899, 112 [text]). The text has the metathesis *prysg,* read *prsyg* = Frāsiyāg (cf. Markwart 1938, 15, note 5; Benveniste 1932, 194; transl. Pognon, 161);
Hamza al-Iṣfahānī, 34 (ed. Gottwaldt 1848; text);

types of the legend with regard to how the initial situation is dissolved. At different times and in different local traditions, motifs have been combined syntagmatically into a number of variants. However, certain motifs are mutually exclusive in the same variant; that is, they can not be syntagmatically combined in the same plot. It is sufficient to note here that the solution of the initial conflict either by the Servant of a god or gods, or by an Archer's shot, are mutually exclusive motifs in the same plot, and therefore constitute distinctive features of two incompatible morphological types. Let us call them Type I and Type II respectively. Since the Archer's shot is not mentioned in the apocalypse, but rather that the initial conflict situation between the two kings is solved by the Servant of Mihr Yazd, the apocalypse corresponds to Type I of the legend.

The Servant thus plays a prominent role in this type, as represented by Great Bundahišn XXXI (BdA 231,5–11):

ud az Ayrērad Gōbedšāh [gwkptšh] zād. ka Frāsyāp Mānuščihr abāg Ērānagān andar gar ī Padašx^uārgar-kōf tar kard, sēj ud *niyāz[82] abar hišt. Ayrērad az yazdān āyaft x^uāst, u-š ān nēwagīh windād kū-š ān spāh (ī) ⟨ud⟩ gund (ī) Ērānagān az ān saxtīh bōxt. Frāsyāp pad ān āhōg Ayrērad ōzad. Ayrērad pad ān pādāšn frazand čiyōn Gōbedšāh [gwkpt'-MLK'] zād.

And from Ayrērad was born Gōbedšāh. When Frāsyāp drove Mānuščihr with the Iranians into the mountain range of Padašx^uārgar, distress and misery were left. Ayrērad besought of the gods a favour, and gained this bliss, that he redeemed the army and troops of the Iranians from this severity. Frāsyāp killed Ayrērad for this fault. To Ayrērad, as a retribution for this, a son was born whose name was Gōbedšāh.

Indeed this variant of the legend shows a remarkable degree of similarity with the apocalypse not only in structure but also in specific content which may be summarized as follows:

Structure:	*Bundahišn:*	*ĴN*
1. Initial situation (power-relation between political leaders).	Frāsyāp keeps Mānuščihr captive in Padašx^uārgar with the army and champions of the Iranians.	The king of Padašx^uārgar is forced to support a king who is "deaf and blind". The King of P. has no troops, army, treasure, or generals.
2. Divine intervention	by the gods (*yazdān*)	by Mihr Yazd
3. Direct intervention by a servant of a god or gods.	by Ayrērad, the Servant of the gods (*yazdān*).	by the Messenger of Mihr Yazd.

Bīrūnī, 220 (text, ed. Sachau 1876, transl. Sachau 1879, 205 f.);

Ṭabarī, I, 435 f. (ed. de Goeje 1879);

Ṭa'ālībī, 107 (ed. Zotenberg 1900); cf. also Šāhnāmah, *passim* (ed. Vullers 1877–79 and Landauer 1884; transl. Mohl 1876–78).

[82] The reading **niyāz* according to Bailey 1932, 951. Bailey *loc. cit.* omits the word *Ērānagān*.

Structure:	Bundahišn:	JN
4. Solution of the conflict.	M. with the army and champions of the Iranians are saved from captivity of F. by A.	The Messenger brings to the King of P. the treasure of Frāsyāp. The King of P. prepares the army and the troops of Zāwul and defeats his enemies.

In the formulas of the Yašts 9:18 and 22, 17:38, 19:77, *Aγraē-raθa* > Aγrērad is mentioned in structural opposition to *Fra(h)rasyan* > Frāsyāp. He is here (and in Yt 13:131) the son of Naru, but in the Bundahišn he is said to be the son of Pašang (BdA 197, 5; 230, 12), and is called Gōbedšāh (BdA 197,5). Later this title of Aγrērad is interpreted as a personal name of his son.

Also in details the apocalypse reflects the legend about Gōbedšāh. In the apocalypse it is stated that it was near the shore of the sea that the servant of Mihr Yazd received the revelations from God. This location is reminiscent of additional information concerning Gōbedšāh in other Pahlavi books:[82a]

Mēnōg ī Xrad 62: 31–33 (Text: K 43 fol. 175v, 15–176r, 3):

> Gōbedšāh [gwpyt′-šh] *pad Ērān-wēz andar kišwar ī Xᵘanirah. ud az pāy ud tā nēm-tan gāw, ud az nēm-tan ī azabar mardōm, ud hamwār pad drayābār* [dlyd'hb'l] *nišīnēd* [YTYBW ⟨N⟩ -yt] *ud ēzišn ī yazdān hamē kunēd.*

Gōbedšāh is in Ērān-wēz in the continent of Xᵘanirah. And from foot and to the middle of the body he is a bull, and from the middle of the body and above he is a man; and he always resides on the seashore and always performs the religious rites to the gods.[83]

Dādestān ī Dēnīg 89 (Text: K 35 fol. 197r, 5–8):

> Gōbedšāh [gwpt-šh] *xᵘadāyīh abar Gōbed būm ham* ⟨*w*⟩*imand ī *ō [or *naz⟨d⟩] Ērān-wēz pad bār ī āb ī Dāityā. abar nigāh dārēd gāw Haδayąs* (Avestan letters) *kē padiš bawēd spurr spurrīh ī hamist mardōm.*

Gōbedšāh's dominion is over the land of Gōbed, whose frontiers are the same as Ērān-wēz on the banks of the River Dāitī. He watches over the bull Haδayąs, through which the perfect perfection of all mankind will come true.[84]

2.5. The author of JN intentionally makes use of similar geographical and historical parallelism as a literary and didactic technique. In 96, for example, the eschatological battle between the King of Padašxᵘārgar and the enemies of Iran will take place in the same geographical location where Wištāsp fought in the beginning of the millenium with the white Xionites, *i.e.* in the White Forest, or, "at that plain". The events in the beginning thus serve as a prototype for those in the end. Stylistically these events are connected by means of spatial contiguity and verbal similarity (*Spēd Xiōnān*

[82a] Benveniste 1932, 369.

[83] Cf. text and transl. Bailey 1932, 952. Pazand text in West 1871, 56; transl. 186.

[84] Cf. text and transl. Bailey 1932, 952; transl. SBE, XVIII, 257.

– *Spēd-Razūr*). The important effect achieved by this technique is not the esthetical alone, but the impression that there exists a real connection or parallelism between the eschatological events and those of the beginning.

The battle is won over the "enemies" (98), including the joined forces of the Arabs, Turks and Romans (Byzantines) mentioned in 95. This is possible through the might of Kayanian Glory and the true faith and the assistance of the gods of Ērān. In particular Mihr, Sroš, Rašn and the holy elements are mentioned. The mythical motif of Mithra assisted by the gods Rašnu and Sraoša[85] (Yašt 10,41) in the battle with the "Mithra-deceivers" is reinterpreted here as a political and eschatological event vaticinated by the sage. A parallel is found in

Bahman Yašt VI, 7–10 (III,8–10) (Text: Anklesaria 1957, 49–50):

7. *ud pad hamkōxšišnīh pad 3 gyāg ardīg* ['ltyh/'lts, DH + K20] *ī wuzurg 3 bār būd bawēd, Spitāmān Zarduxšt.*

8. *ēk pad xʷadāyīh ī Kayōs ka pad ān ī dēwān abāgīh abāg amahraspandān.*

9. *ud dudīgar ka tō Spitāmān Zarduxšt dēn padīrift ud hampursagīh ī tō, Wištaspšāh ud Arjāsp ī xēšm-wišūd pad kārezār ī dēn pad hamkōxšišnīh pad Spēd-Razūr /hād būd kē andar Pārs guft/*

10. *ud sidīgar ka hazārag ī tō sar bawēd, Spitāmān Zarduxšt, ka ān har 3 ō ēd gyāg rasēd, ud Turk ud Tāzīg ud Hrōmīg /hād būd kē dašt⟨ī⟩g ⟨ī⟩ Nišānag guft/ hamāg Ērān dehān ī man Ōhrmazd dād az gāh ī xʷēš, be ō Padašxʷārgar rasēd.*

7. And in internecine combat shall have occurred the great battle, in 3 places, at 3 times, O Spitāmān Zarduxšt.

8. One, in the reign of Kayōs, when the company of the dēws (will struggle) with the Amahraspands.

9. and a second, when you, O Spitāmān Zarduxšt, have received the religion and (had) your consultation, when king Wištāsp and the xēšm-brood Arjāsp (will struggle) in the internecine religious war in the White Forest /some have said in Pārs/.

10. and the third, when your millenium will end, O Spitāmān Zarduxšt, when all those three will arrive to this place, Turks, Arabs, and Romans (Byzantines) /some have said on the Plain of Banners/. (The men of) all the countries of Ērān, which I, Ōhrmazd, have created, will arrive from their own place to Padašxʷārgar.

2.6. The speculative and interpretative activity which we have seen reflected in the ĴN is only one instance of a wide-spread phenomenon, *viz.* that traditional motifs or patterns of thought, and apocalyptic ideas are actualized and reinterpreted in particular historical and social situations. It is noteworthy that such actualizations regularly have occurred in situations of cultural or political conflict or crisis (real or perceived). Old conflict motifs which in the apocalyptic discourse receive a new or additional meaning are thus used as models for the interpretation of the contemporaneous situation. This activity is a prominent characteristic of apocalypticism understood as a social and religious phenomenon. And this phenomenon is in no way restricted to the ancient societies. It is still found

---

[85] On Sraoša as a personification of the Mithra community see Nyberg 1938, 67. For sources and discussion cf. Widengren 1938, 311 ff.

in the apocalyptic or millenarian movements in the Third World, in the Orient and in our own society today.

Abbreviations

AJ   = Ayādgār ī Jāmāspīg
BdA   = Great Bundahišn, ed. *Anklesaria*, s. Bibliography: I. Quoted Pahlavi texts
JN   = Jāmāsp Nāmag
K 20, K 35, K 43 = Fascimile editions of Mss in Codices Avestici et pahlavici Bibliothecae Universitatis Hafniensis

Bibliography

I. Quoted Pahlavi texts

Ayādgār ī Jāmāspīg: *Messina* 1939 = AJ

Bahman Yašt: Zand-ī Vohuman Yasn and Two Pahlavi Fragments, ed. *B. T. Anklesaria*, Bombay 1957.

Dādestān ī Dēnīg: K 35 in *Codices Avestici et pahlavici Bibliothecae Universitatis Hafniensis*, Vol. III, Copenhagen 1934.

Dēnkard: The Complee Text of the Pahlavi Dinkard under the supervision of *D. M. Madan*, Bombay 1911. For Books V and VII cf. *Molé* 1967, 2–121.

Great Bundahišn: The Bûndahishn, ed. by *E. T. D. Anklesaria*, Bombay 1908 = BdA.

Jāmāsp Nāmag: *Modi* 1903, 1–17 (Pahlavi text) = JN; cf. *Bailey* 1930 + 1931; *Benveniste* 1932; *Messina* 1939, 66–74.

Mēnōg ī Xrad: K 43 in *Codices Avestici et pahlavici Bibliothecae Universitatis Hafniensis*, Vol. V, Copenhagen 1936 (Pahlavi text); Pazand text in *West* 1871.

Wizīrkard ī Dēnīg: *Molé* 1967, 122–135.

II. Other texts, translations and studies

Abegg, E. 1928: *Der Messiasglauben in Indien und Iran,* Berlin–Leipzig 1928.

Asmussen, J. P. 1965: X^uāstvānīft. Studies in Manichaeism, Copenhagen 1965.

Avesta: Darmesteter, J. 1892–1893: Le Zend-Avesta. Traduction nouvelle avec commentaire historique et philosophique. I–III, Paris 1892–1893.

Bailey, H. W. 1930: "To the Zamasp-Namak I", in: *BSOS* 6 (1930) 55–85.

– 1931: "To the Zamasp-Namak II", in: *BSOS* 6 (1931) 581–600.

– 1932: "Iranian Studies", in: *BSOS* 6 (1932) 945–955.

Balādurī: Kitab futūḥ al-buldān. Liber expugnationis regionum, ed. de Goeje, Leiden 1866.

Baldensperger, J. P. 1903: *Die messianisch-apokalyptischen Hoffnungen des Judentums* (3rd ed.), Straßburg 1903.

Benveniste, E. 1932: "Une Apocalypse pehlevie: le Žāmāsp-Nāmak", in: *RHR* 106 (1932) 337–380.

– 1932–33: "Le témoignage de Théodore bar Kōnay sur le zoroastrisme", in: *MO* 26–27 (1932–33) 170–215.

Berger, P. L.–Luckmann, T. 1967: *The Social Construction of Reality,* New York 1967.

Betz, H. D. 1966: "Zum Problem des religionsgeschichtlichen Verständnisses der Apokalyptik", in: *ZThK* 63 (1966) 391–409.

Bīrūnī: Albîrûnî, Chronologie orientalischer Völker, ed. Sachau, C. E., Leipzig 1876.
- Albîrûnî, The Chronology of Ancient Nations, transl. Sachau, C. E., London 1879.
Bousset, W. 1903: Die jüdische Apokalyptik, ihre religionsgeschichtliche Herkunft und ihre Bedeutung für das Neue Testament, Berlin 1903.
- 1906: Die Religion des Judentums im Neutestamentlichen Zeitalter. 2nd ed., Berlin 1906.
Bright, J. 1966: Geschichte Israels, Düsseldorf 1966.
Burland, C. A. 1967: The Gods of Mexico, London 1967.
Burridge, K. 1969: New Heaven New Earth, New York 1969.
Christensen, A. 1917: Les types du premier homme et du premier roi. (AEO 14), Stockholm 1917.
- 1932: Les Kayanides (DVSS. PH 19:2), København 1932.
- 1935: Heldedigtning og Fortaellingslitteratur hos Iranerne i Oldtiden, København 1935.
Collins, J. J. 1975: "The Court-Tales in Daniel and the Development of Apocalyptic", in: JBL 94 (1975) 218–234.
- 1979a: "Introduction: Towards the Morphology of a Genre", in: Semeia 14 (1979) 1–20.
- 1979b: "The Jewish Apocalypses", in: Semeia 14 (1979) 21–59.
- 1979c: "Persian Apocalypses", in: Semeia 14 (1979) 207–217.
Czeglédy, K. 1958: "Bahrām Čōbīn and the Persian Apocalyptic Literature", in: AOH 8 (1958) 21–43.
Dexinger, F. 1977: Henochs Zehnwochenapokalypse und offene Probleme der Apokalyptikforschung (StBP 29), Leiden 1977.
Duchesne-Guillemin, J. 1953: Ormazd et Ahriman, Paris 1953.
Eddy, S. K. 1961: The King is Dead, Lincoln, Nebr. 1961.
Eybers, I. H. 1971: "Profetisme in die Ou Testament", in: NGTT 12 (1971) 11–28.
Frey, J. B. 1928: Apocalyptique. In: DBS 1, Paris 1928, 326–354.
Frost, S. B. 1952: Old Testament Apocalyptic. Its Origins and Growth, London 1952.
Ginsberg, H. L. 1948: Studies in Daniel, New York 1948.
Glasson, T. F. 1961: Greek Influence in Jewish Eschatology (BMSPCK), London 1961.
Gray, L. H. 1925: "Ages of the world (Primitive and American)", in: ERE I (1925) 183.
Hamza al-Isfahānī: Hamzae Ispahanensis. Annalium Libri X, ed. Gottwaldt, J. M. E., Lipsiae 1848.
Hanson, P. D. 1971: "Jewish Apocalyptic against its Near Eastern Environment", in: RB 78 (1971) 31–58.
- 1975: The Dawn of Apocalyptic, Philadelphia, Penn. 1975.
- 1976: "Apocalypticism", in: IDBSup (1976) 28–34.
Haran Gawaita: Drower E. S. 1953: The Haran Gawaita and the Baptism of Hibil-Ziwa. The Mandaic text reproduced together with translation, notes and commentary (StT 176), Città del Vaticano 1953.
Hartman, L. 1966: Prophecy Interpreted (CB. NT 1), Uppsala 1966.
Hartman, S. S. 1973: "Iran", in: Theologie und Religionswissenschaft, Darmstadt 1973, 106–123.
- 1976: "Frågan om eventuellt iranskt inflytande på kristendomens och judendomens apokalyptik och djävulsföreställning", in: SvTK 52 (1976) 1–8.
Hengel, M. 1969: Judentum und Hellenismus (WUNT 10), Tübingen 1969.
Hvidtfeldt, A. 1968: "Indianske højkulturers religioner", in: Illustreret Religionshistorie (ed. J. P. Asmussen–J. Laessøe), København 1968.
Instituto Fe y Secularidad 1975: Sociologia de la Religion y Teologia, Madrid 1975.
Isenberg, S. R. 1974: "Millenarism in Greco-Roman Palestine", in: Religion 4 (1974) 26–46.
Kanga, M. F. 1974: "A Critical Study of Epistle I. Ch 6 and 7 of Manuscihr Gōsnjamān", in: Mémorial Jean de Menasce (ed. Ph. Gignoux–A.Tafazzoli), Louvain 1974, 251–262.
Kaufmann, J. 1928: "Apokalyptik", in: EJ(D), Berlin 1928, 2, 1142–1154.
Kippenberg, H. G. 1978: "Die Geschichte der mittelpersischen apokalyptischen Traditionen", in: StIr 7 (1978) 49–80.
Klíma, O. 1968: "Avesta. Ancient Persian Inscriptions. Middle Persian Literature", in: Rypka, J.: History of Iranian Literature, Dortrecht 1968, 1–67.
Koch, K. 1970: Ratlos vor der Apokalyptik, Gütersloh 1970.

– 1972: *The Rediscovery of Apocalyptic* (SBT 2/22), London-Naperville, Ill. 1972.

Kroeber, A. L. 1925: *Handbook of Indians of California*, Smithsonian Institute: Bureau of American Ethnography, Bulletin 78, 868–873, Washington 1925.

Ladd, G. E. 1957: "Why not Prophetic-Apocalyptic?", in: *JBL* 76 (1957) 192–200.

Lebram, J. C. H. 1970: "Apokalyptik und Hellenismus im Buche Daniel", in: *VT* 20 (1970) 503–524.

Lidzbarski, M. 1925: *Ginzā*. Der Schatz oder das Große Buch der Mandäer, übersetzt und erklärt (QRG 13:4), Göttingen 1925.

Lücke, F. 1832: *Versuch einer vollständigen Einleitung in die Offenbarung Johannis und die gesammte apokalyptische Litteratur*, Bonn 1832.

MacKenzie, D. N. 1967: "Notes on the transcription of Pahlavi", in: *BSOAS* 30 (1967) 17–29.

– 1971: *A Concise Pahlavi Dictionary*, London–New York–Toronto 1971.

– 1974: "Finding's keeping", in: *Mémorial Jean de Menasce* (ed. Ph. Gignoux–A. Tafazzoli), Louvain 1974, 273–280.

Markwart, J. 1938: *Wehrot und Arang*, Leiden 1938.

Messina, G. 1939: *Libro Apocalittico Persiano. Ayātkār i Žāmāspīk* (BibOr 9), Roma 1939.

Modi, J. J. 1903: *Jâmâspi, Pahlavi, Pâzend and Persian Texts*, Bombay 1903.

– 1937: *The Religious ceremonies and customs of the Parsees*, 2nd ed., Bombay 1937.

Molé, M. 1963: *Culte, mythe et cosmologie dans l'Iran ancien*, Paris 1963.

–. 1967: *La legende de Zoroastre selon les textes pehlevis*, Paris 1967.

Monchi-Zadeh, D. 1975: *Topografisch-historische Studien zum iranischen Nationalepos*, Wiesbaden 1975.

Moulton, J. H. 1902: "Zoroastrianism", in: *DB(H)*, IV, Edinburgh 1902, 898–944.

Müller, K. 1973: "Die Ansätze der Apokalyptik", in: *Literatur und Religion des Frühjudentums*, Würzburg 1973, 31–42.

Nash, P. 1937: "The Place of Religious Revivalism in the Formation of the Intercultural Community on Klamath Reservation", in: *Social Anthropology of North American Tribes* (ed. F. F. Eggan et al.), Chicago 1937, 377–442.

Nyberg, H. S. 1938: *Die Religionen des alten Iran* (MVAEG 43), Leipzig 1938 [reprint: 1966].

– 1974: *A Manual of Pahlavi II*, Wiesbaden 1974.

von der Osten-Sacken, P. 1969: *Die Apokalyptik in ihrem Verhältnis zu Prophetie und Weisheit* (TEH 157), München 1969.

Otto, R. 1934: *Reich Gottes und Menschensohn*, München 1934.

Plöger, O. 1959: *Theokratie und Eschatologie* (WMANT 2), Neukirchen 1959.

von Rad, G. 1961: *Theologie des Alten Testaments* II, München 1961.

Reitzenstein, R. 1921: *Das iranische Erlösungsmysterium*, Bonn 1921.

Ringgren, H. 1957a: "Apokalyptische Literatur, religionsgeschichtlich", in: *RGG³* I (1957) 463–464.

– 1957b: "Jüdische Apokalyptik", in: *RGG³* I (1957) 464–466.

Rowley, H. H. 1944: *The Relevance of Apocalyptic*, London 1944.

Russell, D. S. 1964: *The Method and Message of Jewish Apocalyptic*, Philadelphia, Penn. 1964.

Šāhnāmah: Firdusii Liber Regum qui inscribitur Schahname, ed. *Vullers, J. A.*, I–II, Lugd. Bat. 1877–79, III, ed. *Landauer, S.*, 1884.

– *Le livre des rois par Abou'l Kasim Firdousi*, transl. *Mohl, J.*, I–VII, Paris 1876–78.

Šahrīhā ī Ērān: Markwart, J., 1931. *A Catalogue of the Provincial Capitals of Ērānshahr*, Roma 1931.

Scheftelowitz, J. 1920: *Die altpersische Religion und das Judentum*, Gießen 1920.

Schmidt, J. M. 1969: *Die jüdische Apokalyptik*, Neukirchen-Vluyn 1969.

Schmithals, W. 1973: *Die Apokalyptik*, Göttingen 1973.

Schreiner, J. 1969a: "Die Symbolsprache der jüdischen Apokalyptik", in: *Bild-Wort-Symbol in der Theologie* (ed. W. Heinen), Würzburg 1969, 55–81.

– 1969b: *Alttestamentlich-Jüdische Apokalyptik* (BiH VI), München 1969.

– 1973: "Die apokalyptische Bewegung", in: *Literatur und Religion des Frühjudentums* (Gütersloh), Würzburg 1973, 214–253.

Semeia 14 (1979): *Apocalypse: The Morphology of a Genre* (Guest Editor: John J. Collins), Missoula, Montana 1979.

Sickenberger, J. 1950: "Apokalyptik", in: *RAC* I (1950) 504–510.

Smith, J. Z. 1975: "Wisdom and Apocalyptic", in: *Religious Syncretism in Antiquity. Essays in Conversation with Geo Widengren.* (Ed. B. A. Pearson), Missoula, Montana, 1975, 131–156.

Steinschneider, M. 1874: "Apocalypsen mit polemischer Tendenz", in: *ZDMG* 28 (1874) 627–659.

Stone, M. E. 1976: "Lists of Revealed Things in the Apocalyptic Literature", in: *Magnalia Dei. The Mighty Acts of God.* (Ed. F. M. Cross–W. E. Lemke–P. D. Miller), Garden City, New York 1976, 414–452.

Stuhlmüller, C. 1968: "Post-Exilic Period: Spirit, Apocalyptic", in: *The Jerome Biblical Commentary.* (Ed. Brown, R. E.–Fitzmyer, J. A.–Murphy, R. E.), London 1968, Vol. 1, 337–343.

Swain, J. W. 1940: „The Theory of the Four Monarchies: Opposition History Under the Roman Empire", in: *CP* 35 (1940) 1–21.

Taʿālibī: *Al-Thaʿālibī, Histoire des rois Perses,* ed. and transl. *Zotenberg, H.,* Paris 1900.

Ṭabarī: *Al-Ṭabarī, Annales,* ed. *de Goeje, J.* et al., Lugd. Batav. 1879 ff.

Tavadia, J. C. 1956: *Die mittelpersische Sprache und Literatur der Zarathustrier* (ITH 2), Leipzig 1956.

Theodor bar Kōnai: in *Pognon, H.* 1898/99. *Inscriptions mandaites des coupes de Khoubair,* Paris 1898/99.

Vawter, B. 1960: "Apocalyptic: Its Relation to Prophecy", in: *CBQ* 22 (1960) 33–46.

Vielhauer, P. 1965: "Apocalypses and Related Subjects: Introduction", in: Hennecke, E.–Schneemelcher, W. (ed.): *New Testament Apocrypha,* Vol. 2, London 1965, 581–607.

Volz, P. 1934: *Die Eschatologie der jüdischen Gemeinde im neutestamentlichen Zeitalter,* Tübingen 1934.

West, E. W. 1871: *The Book of the Mainyo-i Khard.* The Pazand and Sanskrit texts with an English Transl., a Glossary etc., London 1871.

Widengren, G. 1938: *Hochgottglaube im alten Iran* (UUÅ 1938:6), Uppsala 1938.

– 1961: *Iranische Geisteswelt von den Anfängen bis zum Islam,* Baden-Baden 1961.

– 1965: *Die Religionen Irans* (RM 14), Stuttgart 1965.

– 1966: "Iran and Israel in Parthian Times with Special Regard to the Ethiopic Book of Enoch", in: *Temenos* 2 (1966) 139–177.

– 1967: "Zervanitische Texte aus dem 'Avesta' in der Pahlavi-Überlieferung. Eine Untersuchung zu Zātspram und Bundahišn", in: *Festschrift für Wilhelm Eilers,* Wiesbaden 1967, 278–287.

– 1969: *Religionsphänomenologie,* Berlin 1969.

Wikander, S. 1946: *Feuerpriester in Kleinasien und Iran* (ARSHLL 40), Lund 1946.

Wilson, B. 1973: *Magic and the Millenium.* A sociological study of religious movements of protest among tribal and thirdworld peoples, New York 1973.

Winston, D. 1966: "The Iranian Component in the Bible, Apocrypha, and Qumran: a Review of the Evidence", in: *HR* 5 (1966) 183–216.

Worsley, P. 1970: *The Trumpet Shall Sound.* A Study of 'Cargo' Cults in Melanesia, 2nd ed., New York 1970.

Yašts: Lommel, H. 1927. *Die Yäšt's des Avesta,* Göttingen–Leipzig 1927.

Introductory Remarks on Apocalypticism in Egypt

Jan Bergman

1. In Search of Egyptian Apocalypticism

The title and the arrangement of this lecture is due to its early place on the program of the colloquium. Considering the fact that two other lectures, namely those of Jan Assmann and of J. Gwyn Griffiths, will treat particular aspects of apocalyptic in Egypt, I want to start with some general remarks. After that a presentation and discussion of some important ideas in the apocalyptic *Vorstellungswelt* in ancient Egypt will follow. Finally, I will conclude my lecture by giving a few examples of Egypt's contribution to the imagery of Mediterranean apocalypticism.

1.1. It is indeed a challenge to the Egyptologist to try to present ancient Egyptian apocalypticism. Normally one will look in vain in manuals and lexica on Egyptian religion and civilization for an article particularly on "Apocalyptic(ism)". The excellent *Reallexikon der ägyptischen Religionsgeschichte* by H. Bonnet[1] does not offer any article s.v. "Apokalyptik", nor does the great *Reallexikon der Ägyptologie* by Helck – Otto.[2] S. Morenz gives in his *Ägyptische Religion*[3] detailed chapters on "Weltschöpfung und Weltwerden" and "Der Tod und die Toten" but no discussion at all on apocalypticism. This is a rather surprising state of affairs, as Morenz normally tends to profile the structures of Egyptian religion by comparisons with Jewish and Christian materials. Thus one can continue the search, for "apocalypticism" is really an *avis rara* among Egyptologists today. At the same time one may note that articles on "eschatology" are also missing.[4]

1.2. This state of affairs is evidently not only a matter of schooltraditions, etc. In his very profound and stimulating study *Zeit und Ewigkeit im alten Ägypten*, J. Assmann[5] has demonstrated that the dominating concep-

---

[1] Bonnet 1952.   [2] Helck-Otto 1974ff.   [3] Morenz 1960.

[4] G. Lanczkowski is, in this respect, an exception; he is also, as to my knowledge, the only Egyptologist in this generation who has written a monograph on ancient Egyptian prophetism (= Lanczkowski 1960).

[5] Assmann 1975.

tions of time in ancient Egypt exclude "a real eschatological horizon". Even if Assmann does not mention "apocalypticism" in this connection, I know that he could readily have added it. I will return to Assmann's views later on.

1.3. Having reached this point one may reasonably ask: Why then speak of "Egyptian apocalypticism"?

Let me first state that I have not invented the term. In 1925 C. C. McCown published a comprehensive article under the title "Hebrew and Egyptian Apocalyptical Literature".[6] Here we find a presentation of two to three apocalyptic writings from the Middle Kingdom – besides the mention of a series of "indirectly apocalyptical" documents from the same period – and seven specimens from Greek and Roman times (two in Demotic, the others in Greek). Reflections on the relationships between Egypt and Israel, especially as to literature, and on the influence of Egyptian apocalyptic form the setting of this impressive presentation.

Now, all these texts – with one exception – recur in the book *Der Messias* by H. Gressmann,[7] only they are here introduced as "Ägyptische Prophezeiungen". Furthermore, six out of eight texts are individually presented as "Orakel": "Das Orakel von Buto (Mykerinos)", "Das Orakel des Amenophis", "Das Orakel auf Ameni" (= The Prophecies of Neferti), "Das Orakel des Töpfers", "Das Orakel des Lammes" und "Der demotische Orakelkommentar". The others are: "Die wunderbare Geburt der Göttersöhne (Pap Westcar)" und "Die prophetischen Mahn- und Scheltworte des Ipuwêr". McCown also included "The Complaint of the Eloquent Peasant" and " The Dream of Nectanebo". Most of these texts also appeared in the second edition of Gressmann's *Altorientalische Texte*.[8] In sum, 50 years ago many students within the biblical field met with a rather extensive corpus of Egyptian texts presented as parallels to biblical apocalyptic – or prophetic – texts. There was, however, no terminological consensus. And McCown, who seems to have been especially fond of the term "apocalyptic", was well aware of the terminological problem. Already in a footnote to his article we find, as a sort of justification for the title, a reference to an explanation of the sense in which "apocalyptic" is used by him. His definition is as follows:

"a type of thinking and writing which criticizes present evils and promises future improvement, all under the guise of denunciations and predictions that are usually based upon supposedly supernatural visions and revelations."[9]

A. von Gall, who was very critical with regard to calling these texts "prophetisch", writes in this connection:

---

[6] McCown 1925.   [7] Greßmann 1929, edited posthumously.   [8] Greßmann 1926-27.
[9] McCown 1925, 396.

"Wenn sich die ägyptischen Texte mit einer jüdischen Literaturgattung berühren, so sind es die Apokalypsen. Ich erinnere an Dan 2.7.8.10.11, an IV Esra, II. Baruch oder Stücke aus Henoch und vor allem an die jüdischen Sibyllinen, deren Heimat ja gerade in Ägypten liegt. In dieser Literatur wird in der Tat Geschichte in der Form von Weissagen geboten, so daß die Frage berechtigt ist, ob nicht die jüdischen Apokalypsen als *Gattung* viel mehr in Ägypten als in Babylonien, wie man meist annimmt, zu Hause sind."[10]

I have given this long citation to recall that it was in the palmy days of the so-called "religionsgeschichtliche Schule" that "Egyptian apocalypticism" became famous.

1.4. In modern manuals to History of Religions and Biblical Studies, as in the general debate on apocalypticism, these texts seem to play a very modest rôle. That is due to reactions against the "religionsgeschichtliche Schule" and to a much more developed consciousness of the importance of stricter terminology as well. In H. Ringgren's article on "Apokalyptik"[11] we find mentioned "ägyptische Ansätze zur Apokalyptik" with a reference to A. von Gall. G. Lanczkowski does not even mention Egypt in his introductory article to "Apokalyptik" in TRE.[12] Interestingly enough, in the following part on Old Testament apocalyptic J. Lebram[13] has many references to Egypt and its rôle in the early stages of Jewish apocalyptic.

2. Egyptian Apocalyptic Literature?

It is evident that none of the Egyptian documents in question can be designated as a typical apocalypse. Even some criteria in the wide definition of McCown cited above are missing in some of these writings. Nevertheless, it can be useful in our context to make some remarks on this corpus – which is, indeed, a very heterogeneous one – not only to actualize a debate which has been too suppressed, but also to point to some typical Egyptian characteristics.

2.1. As to "the supernatural visions and revelations" these texts have astonishingly little to report. Most interesting in this respect is The Prophecies of Neferti, which preferably should be called the "Visions of Neferti." The following short citations can illustrate this:[14]

"As he deplored what was to happen in the land and evoked the state of the East..., he said: Stir, my heart, bewail this land. ... Tire not while this is before you, rise against what is before you! I shall describe what is before me. I show you the land in turmoil."

The visionary style is also marked by the repeated "I show you...". It is worth noting that this visionary mood and the contents of the vision contrast sharply with the idyllic introduction *(à la Königsnovelle)*: The lector-priest of Bastet does not enter the residence of the king to bring him

---

[10] von Gall 1926, 81. [11] Ringgren 1957. [12] Lanczkowski 1978.
[13] Lebram 1978. [14] Neferti 17 ff.

a message from his goddess. Rather he is summoned by the king who wants entertainment! The concluding formula, "And he who is wise will libate for me, when he sees fulfilled what I have spoken!",[15] indicates a complex tradition history.[16]

2.2. Many of the writings do not manifest a clear change from the present woe to the predicted joy. In some cases the improvement is absent as with "The Oracle of Buto";[17] this, on the other hand, seems to be the only sure case where the goddess of the oracle takes the initiative. Even when the "new age" is effectively marked – as with "the coming of Ameni" in "The Visions of Neferti" – there is surely no "eschatological" event. He comes with a new dynasty, the first in the Middle Kingdom. It could, therefore, be of importance that a priest from Lower Egypt representing one of the holy cities of the Old Kingdom is the one to prophesy of his coming, as he is to come from the south and is to place his residence in Upper Egypt. But what we hear of his deeds is what is expected from every king: "Then Order will return to its seat, while Chaos is driven away."[18]

2.3. The texts are, as should be expected, very king-centred. It is, however, interesting to notice that the king is the receiver, while the sage – or a corresponding person – is the active one. Especially well-known and popular was the pair Amenophis the Sage and Amenophis III – Josephus underlines their name-relationship.[19] (This makes the suicide of the sage even more unexpected. It seems to be a variant of the topic "oracle at the approach of death" or "oracle confirmed by death"; cf. the potter, who dies while prophesying, and the "lamb", whose death is mentioned immediately after the oracle has been delivered. The concluding phrases on the libation to Neferti cited above can possibly be another example of this motif. I have drawn attention to it, as it can also be a "symbolic action" meant to underline the fatality of the message. This, however, would not be applicable in the case of Neferti.)

2.4. The mysterious and hidden character of the apocalyptic message is not at all striking in our texts, with one strong exception, namely, the "Demotic Chronicle" – or better "Patriotic Oracles with Interpretations". Here the obscurity of the original text is highly qualified. That is why interpretations are given in the text, a phenomenon well-known in Egypt ("The Book of the Dead", chapter 17, etc.) and elsewhere (cf. the *pesher*

---

[15] Neferti 70.
[16] That the writing was created originally just to guarantee the cult of the sage Neferti – as von Gall proposes (von Gall 1926, 55) – seems to me very unlikely.
[17] See Herodotus, II 133.
[18] Neferti 69.
[19] Josephus, *Contra Apionem* I, §232.

technique in Qumran). This could be a device to actualize or correct the original oracle, but in this particular case the interpretations seem to be written by the same hand as the basic text.

One concrete example of style should be added. In the "Story of the Birth of the Royal Children" (Pap Westcar) the period for fulfillment of the oracle is stated thus: "first your son, then his son, then one of them".[20] Who does not associate this with a famous apocalyptic saying on "times"? Nevertheless, the contexts are rather different.

2.5. The last example can illustrate that this corpus of texts can be useful as comparative material with regard to apocalyptic literature, whatever definition one may prefer for an "apocalypse". I would not call any of the texts apocalypses. But I can find some apocalyptic motifs and ideas in several of them. A few – especially the "Visions of Neferti" – give me a vague impression of an apocalyptic mode. J. Z. Smith has coined the expression "proto-apocalyptic".[21] I would not oppose using that designation for these remarkable visions.

3. Apocalypticism and the Egyptian World-View

Let us now pass on to the question: Is apocalypticism (in not too vague a sense) on the whole possible according to the ancient Egyptian ideas of time and cosmos? It seems to me very hard to answer this question absolutely in the negative. The multiplicity of approaches is a characteristic Egyptian ideal. And there were many schools of priests with different theologies and philosophies.

3.1. Now, J. Assmann, in the excellent study mentioned above,[22] has treated the fundamental time-structures of the Egyptian world view. With a lot of examples he has illustrated how the two complementary conceptions of "eternity", nḥḥ as a dynamic uninterrupted movement and ḏt as a more static unlimited series of times, together form a total system of *Diesseits* and *Jenseits,* within which creation and death take place and cosmos and chaos change. There are no terminations for this world – when the texts mention "the limits of nḥḥ and of ḏt", these are only, according to Assmann, rhetorical figures. As to the pre-existent world, often alluded to in the texts, Assmann explains it away as a complex process with the double aspect of creation and transformation. He speaks of "a monistic trend", since cosmos and chaos do not combat each other in the beginning. Thus, the world view is monistic, not dualistic, even if there is no radical

---

[20] Pap Westcar 9, 14.
[21] Smith 1975, 147 ff.: "proto-apocalyptic material" and "proto-apocalyptic situations".
[22] Assmann 1975.

monism (as in the Amarna theology). Under these circumstances any eschatology – and any real apocalypticism – is unthinkable.

3.2. Now there are surely a lot of Egyptian texts, especially of magical or funerary nature, which describe a total world catastrophe in very dramatical terms.[23] S. Schott has collected rich material in his article "Altägyptische Vorstellungen vom Weltende".[24] I cite a passage from the Pap Salt 825 (BM 10.051) in his translation:[25]

> "Es wurde nicht Tag... Götter und Göttinnen legten ihre Hände auf ihre Köpfe. Die Erde... Die Sonne ging nicht auf. Der Mond blieb aus... Der Himmel fiel im Finstern... Umgestürzt war die Erde, umgewandt das Wasser. Es zog nicht stromab... Alle Welt klagte und weinte, die Seelen... Götter und Göttinnen, Menschen, Geister und Tote, Vieh und Herden..."

This really smells apocalyptic! But Assmann points to the fact that in the magical context the manipulation of the cosmos is a leading idea, while a determinism rules in eschatology and apocalypticism which excludes every manipulation (as also, one may add, the effects of cult and piety). I, for my part, am not so sure that this logic is very valuable in these matters.

3.3. There is, however, a little group of texts which evidently treats the end of the world. The famous "Dialogue between Atum and Osiris" is the most important testimony.[26] Let me cite only the last section of this very important text:[27]

> "And I – Atum is speaking – will destroy all that I had created, and the earth will return to the primordial water, the Flood, as it was in the beginning. I will remain alone together with Osiris after having changed in other forms, to wit forms of serpents that men do not know and gods do not see."

This really seems to be an excellent proof of the ideal eschatological setting: ἰδοὺ ποιῶ τὰ ἔσχατα ὡς τὰ πρῶτα (Barn 6: 13)[28]. But in the more developed eschatological-apocalyptical thinking something more is needed. This follows from the fact that Gunkel's pattern of "Urzeit und Endzeit" can fit very well even into a cyclical conception of the life of the world. It is quite possible that Atum will restart the whole process. But according to a strict two-eons-doctrine τὰ ἔσχατα must surpass τὰ

---

[23] It may be noted that the corpus of texts discussed above does not contain these "apocalyptical" descriptions! As these are particularly found in "Drohungen an Gott" or magical spells, the persons responsible for gathering the "corpus", being mostly interested in apocalyptical *literature*, passed by these very illustrative formulas! This should be taken as a warning not to monopolize one method!

[24] Schott 1959.   [25] Pap Salt 825, I, 1 ff.

[26] For this complicated tradition see Otto 1962.

[27] This dialogue is found in the 175th chapter of the Book of the Dead, here cited according to Pap Ani III 19.

[28] This passage was written as the motto of the famous book by H. Gunkel, "Schöpfung und Chaos in Urzeit und Endzeit" (= Gunkel 1894).

πρῶτα.[29] It must be admitted that we can find no evidence for such a radical apocalypticism in ancient Egypt.

3.4. But now, back to Assmann's monistic world view. I think that for the ancient Egyptian there was also the alternative of breaking through this monistic system. The powers of chaos, especially the most compact one "The Joined Darkness" (kkw sm3w), seem to me to have a more complicated nature than is generally assumed.[30] I can not argue for this here. But even if I am right, this would not open the way for "new heavens and a new earth" but for *"the second death"*. This expression is, to my mind, a key word for some relations between ancient Egyptian ideas and "The Book of Revelation". As is well-known, ὁ θάνατος ὁ δεύτερος is found three times in Rev (2:11, 20:6, 21:8) but nowhere else in earlier Greek literature. Now, "The Second Death" (mt m whm) is a common term in the Coffin Texts and in the "Book of the Dead", the importance of which is stressed by its frequent appearance in chapter titles.[31] That Christian apocalyptic has got this expression from the Egyptians, masters of *Jenseitslehren*, is undoubtable, even if the exact channels for the transmission can not be determined.

3.5. This conception also is important in the respect that it seems to break the typical cyclical eternity. The question of real apocalypticism in Egypt is dependent on the presence of irreversible processes. To make the quest for eschatology – apocalypticism more successfull, an effort to collect *"telos*-directed processes" in the Egyptian world could be useful. Let me just mention a few: the *bios* as a career, the concept of an ideal age (110 years), the idea that the actual Pharao should not only copy the deeds of the forefathers but surpass them, a lot of interesting reflections in the so-called *Auseinandersetzungs-Literatur*, originating after the fall of the Old Kingdom in the confrontation with new structures in society, etc.

3.6. Here we touch on another topic of interest for a special apocalyptic tradition, namely, traces of a deprivation or degeneration theory.[32] Even if we cannot reconstruct a strict parallel to the "Four-Ages-Doctrine" of Hesiod, there are many striking parallel details (*e.g.,* the succession-myth on the *Naos* of *Haft el Henne*; perhaps the organisation of the divine dynasties by Manetho: Great Ennead, Little Ennead, "The Followers of Horus", 3ḥw or νέκυες, the ordinary dynasties; note here the falling numbers of the years of rule!).

With regard to "The four ages" it is important to underline the fact that many conceptions in Egypt are evidently both spatial and temporal. That will legitimate our consideration of the many examples of the fourfold room: The four cardinal points and their winds, the four main stations on

---

[29] Cf. Rev 21:1 "and the sea vanished".
[30] See the penetrating studies Hornung 1956 and Hornung 1965.
[31] See Zandee 1960, 186 ff.   [32] Cf. Kákosy 1964.

the courses of the two barks of the Sun (identified with Harachte, Re, Atum and Osiris), the four "floors" of the Egyptian cosmos (heaven, sky, earth and netherworld, identified with Re, Shou, Geb and Osiris respectively), the four elements, the four Khnum forms, the four Bas of the Ram of Mendes, etc.etc.

3.7. The series of identifications mentioned above are typical for the multiplicity of approaches of the Egyptian who is thus able to master all the aspects of the fourfold world. A special means for mastering this is represented by the particular type of Egyptian Wisdom called *onomastica*. For developing an apocalyptic world view – and here I think as much in spatial terms as in temporal ones – this onomastica-knowledge was quite important. And the illustrated *Jenseitsführer* are to be reckoned as a qualified type of this genre. These very detailed representations of Hell and Heaven have undoubtedly been a source second to none for the many descriptions of visits in Heaven and in Hell typical of apocalyptic literature; much work remains to be done also here in tracing the paths of the traditions for these very remarkable "mysteries" to be unveiled by the apocalyptists.

The list of important apocalyptic topics, well rooted in the special religious climate of the Nile Valley, could be much longer. But I hope that already the indications given above are enough to give a preliminary idea of what Egypt can offer to those interested in the rich mysteries of apocalypticism.

4. The Role of Egyptian Iconography in Apocalyptic Visions

Before ending these introductory remarks on relations between Egypt and Mediterranean apocalypticism, I feel obliged to point emphatically to the great importance to be attributed to Egyptian iconography in this connection.

Prophecy and apocalyptic are often differentiated roughly as to their preferences for words and images respectively. Thus, auditions normally dominate prophecies, while apocalyptic is characterized by vision. The Word of God comes to the prophet, the vision of God's mysteries is revealed in the apocalypse. To give only one typical example: the strange message to Belshassar according to Daniel 5 is *written* on the wall so that the king can *see* it. It is not addressed to him audibly!

4.1. Now, if any religious culture in the Mediterranean area was an eminently visual one, with a great predilection for concrete and detailed imagery, it was, for sure, the ancient Egyptian civilization. Many collaborating factors can help to prove this statement. The preservation of the pictographic writing of the hieroglyphics as a sacred script for more than

3,000 years is illustrative of this, especially in comparison with the Sumerian and Hittite pictographs which lost their pregnance of visuality.

The early appearance in ancient Egypt of special traditions composed of texts and pictures is a further testimony to the iconographic nature of Egyptian culture. Already in the Coffin Texts we find sections, "the Book of Two Ways" and "The Book of the Field of Hetep", which mark the birth of the picture-book in world history. Here, and in the expanding "*Jenseitsliteratur*" of the New Kingdom[33] one may legitimately speak not only of "books with illustrations" but rather of "pictorial representations" – sometimes even "maps" – with textual explanations and commentaries.

4.2. It is obvious to me that the most impressive Amduat compositions in the Royal Tombs form an excellent point of departure for apocalyptic speculations. Amduat, now the conventional name of a particular book, was for the Egyptians the proper title for this genre of *Jenseitsliteratur*, its meaning being "That which is in Dat" – Dat is the other world located in heaven, or, more frequently, identified with the netherworld. These representations offer a very detailed cosmography, organized in twelve three-storey sections, the inhabitants of which – gods, guardians, demons, men, etc. – are accurately named, sometimes in cryptic writings. In any case, we find here excellent illustrations of the "visits to Hades" and – at least partially – of the "heavenly journeys", which constitute favourite settings for many apocalypses.

Two other factors make these imposing cosmographies even more important for us. First, the organizing principle of the cosmos is the journey of the Sun, with the effect that the twelve sections represent the twelve hours of the night – and, in one case, "The Book of the Day and the Night", of the day, too. Thus, the spatial and the temporal aspects coincide. Evidently, this cosmic time-table could easily form the basis for an apocalyptic one. A certain foundation for a dualistic view can be found in the double representation of the goddess Nut in "The Book of the Day and of the Night": here this Goddess of Heaven is both the "Heaven Above" and the "Heaven Below", or the "Heaven of Day" and the "Heaven of Night". Surely, the Egyptians wanted to stress the unity by giving these complementary representations of Nut, but the hosts of dreadful beings in the Netherworld[34] and all the dangers waiting there could favour a more dualistic-antagonistic interpretation.

The second point to underline is the different forms in which the Sun appears during his journey through the sections of the Dat. Among these changing manifestations the theriomorph sections dominate.[35] It is prob-

---

[33] See Hornung 1972.

[34] Cf. the detailed study Zandee 1960.

[35] The best proof of this is "The Litany of the Sun".

able that we have here one of the causes for the frequent introduction of the protagonists in animal form in the apocalypses. But I am the first to admit that the genesis of the apocalyptic genre seems to be very complex, so that the influence here – as in many other cases[36] – is rather indirect, passing through many unknown links and milieus.

Bibliography

Assmann, Jan 1975: *Zeit und Ewigkeit im alten Ägypten* (AHAW. PH 1975:1), Heidelberg 1975.
Bergman, Jan 1977: "Zum Zwei-Wege-Motiv. Religionsgeschichtliche und exegetische Bemerkungen", in: *SEÅ* 41-42 (1976-77) 27-56.
Bonnet, Hans 1952: *Reallexikon der ägyptischen Religionsgeschichte*, Berlin 1952.
Gall, A. von 1926: *ΒΑΣΙΛΕΙΑ ΤΟΥ ΘΕΟΥ*. Eine religionsgeschichtliche Studie zur vorchristlichen Eschatologie, Heidelberg 1926.
Greßmann, Hugo 1926-27: *Altorientalische Texte und Bilder zum Alten Testament*, 2. Aufl., Berlin 1926-27.
– 1929: *Der Messias*, Göttingen 1929.
Gunkel, Hermann 1894: *Schöpfung und Chaos in Urzeit und Endzeit*. Eine religionsgeschichtliche Untersuchung über Gen. 1 und Ap. Joh. 12, Göttingen 1894.
Helck, W.-Otto, E. 1974ff.: *Lexikon der Ägyptologie*, Wiesbaden 1974ff.
Hornung, Erik 1956: "Chaotische Bereiche in der geordneten Welt", in: *ZÄS* 81 (1956) 28-32.
– 1965: "Licht und Finsternis in der Vorstellungswelt Altägyptens", in: *StGen* 18 (1965) 73-83.
– 1972: *Ägyptische Unterweltsbücher*. Eingeleitet, übersetzt und erläutert von E. H. (BAW.AO) Zürich und München 1972.
Kákosy, László 1964: "Ideas about the fallen state of the world in Egyptian Religion: Decline of the Golden Age", in: *AOH* 17 (1964) 205-216.
Lanczkowski, Günter 1960: *Altägyptischer Prophetismus* (ÄA 4), Wiesbaden 1960.
– 1978: "Apokalyptik/Apokalypsen I. Religionsgeschichtlich", in: *TRE* III (1978) 189-191.
Lebram, Jürgen 1978: "Apokalyptik/Apokalypsen II. Altes Testament", in: *TRE* III (1978) 192-202.
McCown, C. C. 1925: "Hebrew and Egyptian Apocalyptical Literature", in: *HThR* 18 (1925) 357-411.
Morenz, Siegfried 1960: *Ägyptische Religion* (RM 8), Stuttgart 1960.
Otto, Eberhard 1962: "Zwei Paralleltexte zu Totenbuch 175", in: *CEg* 37 (1962) 249-256.
Ringgren, Helmer 1957: "Apokalyptik I. Apokalyptische Literatur, religionsgeschichtlich", in: *RGG*³ I (1957) 463-464.
Schott, Siegfried 1959: "Altägyptische Vorstellungen vom Weltende", in: *AnBib* 12 (1959) 319-330.
Smith, Jonathan Z. 1975: "Wisdom and Apocalyptic", in: *Religious Syncretism in Antiquity*. Essays in Conversation with Geo Widengren, ed. Birger A. Pearson, Missoula, Mont. 1975, 131-156.
Zandee, Jan 1960: *Death as an Enemy according to Ancient Egyptian Conceptions,* Leiden 1960.

---

[36] Cf. Bergman 1977 for the motif of "The Two Ways".

Datierung der jungavestischen Apokalyptik[*]

Sven S. Hartman

1. Einleitung

1.1. Der iranische Einfluß auf Judentum und Christentum wurde von vielen Forschern geltend gemacht[1]. Von schwedischen Forschern, die diese Ansicht vertreten, sei besonders mein Lehrer, Geo Widengren, genannt; das Problem ist allerdings eine Streitfrage. Der vorliegende Artikel will diese Frage aufgreifen und sie mit neuen Argumenten beleuchten, die der wahrscheinlichen Datierung von zwei in diesem Zusammenhang wichtigen Ideekomplexen gelten: 1) die Apokalyptik; 2) die damit verbundene Teufelsvorstellung.

1.2. Was bedeutet das Wort "Apokalyptik"? Man macht sich u. E. oft eine ungenaue Vorstellung davon, wenn man meint, daß es sich ausschließlich um Vorstellungen über den baldigen Untergang der Welt handle. Solche Ideen *können* in den Begriff Apokalyptik mit eingefaßt werden, jedoch handelt es sich in diesem Fall nur um einen Teilaspekt. Die eigentliche Bedeutung des Wortes Apokalyptik ist Weltalterlehre, eine Lehre über den gesamten Weltverlauf, von Beginn bis zum Schluß[2].

1.2.1. Eine Tabelle über einige Weltalterlehren (apokalyptische Systeme) wird unten (Fig. 1) angeführt. Es sei von vornherein festgestellt, daß die verschiedenen Systeme ein und dieselbe Tendenz aufweisen, nämlich eine Degeneration oder stetige Verschlechterung. Im indischen System drückt sich dies auf zwei aus der Tabelle ersichtlichen Arten aus. Teils nimmt die Länge der vier Weltalter ständig ab: 4000 Jahre, 3000 Jahre, 2000 Jahre und 1000 Jahre; teils sind die Farben, die der Gott Viṣṇu während der vier Weltalter (*yugas*) annimmt, die vier Kastenfarben in abnehmender Würde: zuerst die weiße Priesterfarbe, dann die rote Kriegerfarbe, danach die gelbe Farbe des Bauernstandes und schließlich die schwarze Farbe der Dienenden. Dies wiederholt sich in vielen anderen Fällen: die Tugend

---

[*] Dieser Artikel ist größtenteils schon auf Schwedisch veröffentlicht, Sven S. Hartman 1976. Vgl. auch Sven S. Hartman 1975, 170–177 und 1980, 1–9.
[1] Vgl. Sven S. Hartman 1973, 106–123.
[2] Widengren 1969, Kap. 16.

nimmt dauernd ab, ebenso die Lebenslänge der Menschen etc.[3]. – In der Spalte Iran I (Avesta) ist diese schrittweise Verschlechterung nicht so deutlich erkennbar; wir können aber ersehen: aus *Gaya* (= Leben) wird allmählich *Gaya maretan* (= sterbliches Leben). Diese Andeutung eines Verfalls wird von Iran II (die Pahlavi-Schrift Bundahišn) verschärft. Dort wird gesagt, daß die Schöpfung auf folgende Weise entartet: während der ersten 3000-Jahr-Periode ist sie völlig geistig und unsterblich und besteht nur aus Gayōmart (= Gaya maretan) und dem Urstier. Im Verlauf der nächsten 3000 Jahre wird sie zwar materiell, ist aber immer noch unsterblich. Nach 6000 Jahren, zu Beginn der dritten Periode, kommt das Böse in die Welt und Gayōmart und der Urstier werden sterblich. Sie sterben tatsächlich, wonach die übrige Schöpfung entsteht. Wenn das Ende der vierten 3000-Jahr-Periode erreicht ist, geht diese Welt unter und der eschatologische Erlöser erscheint. Es ist der Saošyant, der auf avestisch Astvat.ereta heißt[4]. – In der Spalte Iran III, die auf Material aus der Pahlavi-Schrift Bahman Yašt baut, wird die noch übriggebliebene Weltzeit als ein Baum mit vier Metallzweigen in der fallenden Wertskala Gold, Silber, Kupfer und Eisen geschildert[5]. Dieselbe fallende Wertskala finden wir auch bei Hesiodos – wobei es sich allerdings um den gesamten Weltverlauf dreht – und bei Daniel, Kap. 2, wo es sich, wie auch im Bahman Yašt, nur um die bis zum Weltende noch verbleibende Zeit handelt. Diese Tendenz des Verfalls und der Verschlechterung findet sich also durchgehend bei allen genannten apokalyptischen Systemen, und sie alle weisen auch eine Vierteilung der Zeit auf.

1.2.2. Wie soll man diese Ähnlichkeit erklären? Handelt es sich um etwas Indo-Iranisches, da ja sowohl Indien als auch der Iran diese Vorstellungen umfassen? Ist es gar etwas Indo-Europäisches, zumal auch Griechenland ähnliche Ideen aufweist? Oder berührt es etwas allgemein Menschliches, da ja auch die Semiten durch das Danielbuch vertreten sind? Man pflegt in diesem Zusammenhang vom Einfluß der einen Religion auf die andere – oder umgekehrt – zu sprechen; z. B. vom Iran auf Daniel, oder gerade umgekehrt; oder vom Iran auf Griechenland mit Hesiodos, oder umgekehrt. Wenn man von Einfluß spricht, meint man eigentlich nie *direkten* Einfluß in dem Sinne, daß jemand Bücher ihm fremder Religionen gelesen und dadurch Eindrücke empfangen hätte, oder daß jemand die Literatur anderer Völker vorgelesen und erklärt bekommen hätte. Nein, man denkt dabei hauptsächlich an *indirekten* Einfluß: es gab Zeitströmun-

---

[3] Widengren 1969, 456ff. Vgl. auch Widengren in diesem Band § 4.3.2.1.2., § 5.1.3. und § 6.1.1.

[4] Widengren 1961, 209ff.

[5] Widengren 1961, 183ff. Zur sassanidischen Reinterpretation des Weltzeitschemas vgl. Widengren in diesem Band § 7. Dazu ferner in diesem Band Hultgård § 6.2.1. und Olsson § 2.

Indien	Iran I (Avesta)	Iran II (Bundahišn)	Iran III (Bahman Yašt)	Hesiodos (700 v. Chr.)	Daniel Kap. 2
krta-yuga 400 + 4 000 + 400 weiß	Gaya	3 000 (geistig)	Gold	Gold	Gold
treta-yuga 300 + 3 000 + 300 rot		3 000 (materiell)	Silber	Silber	Silber
dvapara-yuga 200 + 2 000 + 200 gelb	Gaya maretan Zarathustra	3 000 (sterblich)	Kupfer	Kupfer	Kupfer
kali-yuga 100 + 1 000 + 100 schwarz	Astvat.ereta	3 000 (verklärt)	Eisen	Eisen	Eisen
1 000 + 10 000 + 1 000 = 12 000 Jahre		12 000 Jahre			

Fig. 1

gen; die Apokalyptik war damals in Mode, ungefähr wie es heute politische
Strömungen sind. Die meisten jetzigen Menschen haben nicht die Theorien
studiert, die sich hinter ihrer politischen Anschauung verbergen, sind aber
trotzdem davon beeinflußt worden, wenn auch nur indirekt. Im vorliegenden Fall denken wir uns also den Einfluß vor allem als *Ideenströmungen* der
damaligen Zeit.

1.2.3. Wollte man versuchen, die verschiedenen apokalyptischen
Systeme zu datieren und auf diese Art die Urquelle und den Ursprung
freilegen, würde beim Vergleich vielleicht Hesiodos (ungefähr 700 v. Chr.)
'gewinnen', und manche Forscher haben auch den Ursprung der Apokalyptik bei Hesiodos oder in Griechenland sehen wollen. *Das* ist aber eine
vielleicht doch zu einfache Erklärung. Fürs erste ist es nämlich möglich,
Iran I, d. h. die Apokalyptik des Avesta, spätestens auf die Zeit um 600
v. Chr. zu datieren. Außerdem ist es leicht zu zeigen, daß die jüdische – und
später christliche Apokalyptik nicht der griechischen, sondern der iranischen ähnelt. Diese Ähnlichkeit zeigt sich in einer besonderen und entscheidenden Hinsicht: die iranische, wie auch die jüdische und christliche
Apokalyptik ist verknüpft mit der zyklischen Inkarnation eines Urmenschen, eines Propheten und eines eschatologischen Erlösers. Dieser
Umstand ist für die Frage ganz entscheidend, und die iranische Apokalyptik, die mit einer Urmenschengestalt, einer Prophetengestalt und einer
eschatologischen Erlösergestalt verbunden ist, kann also spätestens auf
etwa 600 v. Chr. datiert werden. (Auch im Danielbuch, Kap. 7, im
Henochbuch sowie im Christentum finden wir eine mit derartigen Gestalten verbundene Apokalyptik[6]).

Zuerst wollen wir einen Datierungsversuch vornehmen. Dieser setzt
eine gewisse Erörterung voraus, die etwas Platz beansprucht, aber ich
glaube sagen zu können, daß das Endresultat überzeugend ist. Was wir also
besprechen, ist die Tabellenspalte Iran I (Avesta).

2. Die iranische Apokalyptik mit Erlösergestalten

2.1. Im sogenannten späteren Avesta (d. h. das ganze Avesta mit Aus-
nahme der von Zarathustra herstammenden Gāthā-Hymnen) kommen die
Namen *Gaya* (Leben) und *Gaya maretan* (sterbliches Leben) vor. Die
Namen Gaya und Gaya maretan kommen nur im nicht-gāthischen Teil des
Avesta vor. Diese Namen leiten sich daher wahrscheinlich nicht von
Zarathustra her. Aber die *Wörter* selbst, aus denen die Namen Gaya und
Gaya maretan bestehen, müssen aus den Gāthā-Hymnen herstammen,
näher bezeichnet aus Kap. 30 (Strophe 4 und 6) des Yasna[7] (der ein Teil der

---

[6] Sven S. Hartman 1973, 117.
[7] Text und Übersetzung bei Widengren in diesem Band § 2.2.2.

ersten Gāthā-Hymne ist). Es ist also zu beachten, daß ich zwischen den *Namen* und den *Wörtern*, aus denen der Name besteht, einen scharfen Unterschied mache. In unserem Fall finden sich die Namen nicht in den Gāthās, aber die *Wörter*, aus denen die Namen bestehen, sind dort vorhanden.

2.1.1. Wir wollen *Gaya* und Gaya *maretan* näher untersuchen. Laut einer Exegese der Gāthā-Stelle, an der das Wort *gaya* steht (Yasna 30,4), soll es sich um Gayōmart (der spätere Pahlavi-Name) handeln. (Die Exegese findet sich in der Pahlavi-Schrift Dēnkart[8]). Obwohl die Interpretation falsch sein muß, wird der Name Gayōmart mit "lebend und sprechend" sowie "sterblich" ausgelegt und es wird gesagt, daß Gayōmart dank des guten Gottes Ōhrmazd "lebend und sprechend", aber "sterblich" auf Grund des bösen Ahriman gewesen sei. Da nun Avesta selbst einen Unterschied zwischen Gaya und Gaya maretan macht, indem im späteren Avesta deren *fravašis* unmittelbar nacheinander angerufen werden, und da die Pahlavi-Schriften von einer Schöpfung sprechen, die nicht sterblich ist – nämlich während der ersten sechs Jahrtausende (siehe Iran II, Bundahišn) –, liegt es auf der Hand, daß Gaya allein *dasjenige* geschaffene Wesen bezeichnet, das noch nicht sterblich war, während dagegen Gaya maretan dasselbe erschaffene Wesen bezeichnet, nachdem es sterblich geworden war. (Der Name selbst hat ja diese Bedeutung[9].)

2.1.2. Fortsetzungsweise finden wir, daß Gaya maretan im Avesta zwei spezielle Eigenschaften erhält: 1) er ist der erste gerechte Mensch; 2) er stand in einem sehr nahen Verhältnis zum Urstier[10].

Das Merkwürdige ist nun, daß diese beiden Eigenschaften Zarathustra in den Gāthā-Hymnen zukommen. Also: Gaya maretan erhält im späteren Avesta Eigenschaften, die Zarathustra in den Gāthā-Hymnen zugeschrieben werden.

2.1.2.1. Die *erste* Eigenschaft – daß Gaya maretan der erste gerechte Mensch war – geht aus dem gewöhnlichen Ausdruck "von Gaya maretan zum siegreichen Saošyant" hervor[11], worin man also den gesamten Weltverlauf zusammengefaßt hat, indem man den Anfang und das Ende nennt. Diese Eigenschaft geht aber auch aus dem Ausdruck hervor: "der, der zuerst Ahura Mazdāhs *Gedanken* und *Lehren* zuhörte" (*yō paoiryō ahurāi mazdāi manasča gušta sāsnåsča*), Yašt 13,87; in dieser Ausdrucksweise war man offensichtlich abhängig von einer früheren Gāthā-Stelle über Zarathustra, nämlich Yasna 29,8, wo von *Zarathustra* gesagt wird, er sei derjenige gewesen, "der allein auf unsere Lehren gehört hat" (*yə̄ nə̄ aēvō sāsnå gūšatā*), d. h. auf die Lehren Ahura Mazdāhs.

---

[8] DkM 73,16 ff.
[10] *Ibid.*, 102 ff.
[9] Sven S. Hartman 1965/66, 100.
[11] Z. B. Yasna 26:10; 59:27; Yašt 13:145.

2.1.2.2. Die *zweite* Eigenschaft bei Gaya maretan, nämlich in einem sehr nahen Verhältnis zum Urstier zu stehen, besitzt auch Zarathustra, und dies ganz besonders in dem eben zitierten, berühmten Kapitel Yasna 29. Dort handelt es sich um die Klage und das Gebet des Urstiers, der Stierseele, einen Beschützer zu erhalten, und er erhält als Beschützer dann Zarathustra. Im jüngeren Avesta wird die Stierseele zusammen mit Gaya maretan erwähnt, desgleichen auch in der Pahlavi-Literatur.

2.1.3. Wenn wir auf Grund des Ausgeführten behaupten, daß Gaya marctan im jüngeren Avesta in gewissen Beziehungen ein Äquivalent zu Zarathustra ist, haben wir damit nicht zuviel gesagt. Damit verlassen wir vorerst Gaya maretan und wenden uns dem Saošyant zu, dem eschatologischen Erlöser im jüngeren Avesta und in der Pahlavi-Literatur.

2.2. Auf dieselbe Art, auf die wir Gaya maretan (Gayōmart) als in gewissen Belangen Zarathustra gleichwertig charakterisieren konnten, können wir auch den Saošyant als ein Äquivalent zum selben Zarathustra bezeichnen, allerdings in anderer Hinsicht. Dies wollen wir zu zeigen versuchen[12].

2.2.1. Wir beginnen mit dem Wort *Saošyant*. Es stammt von den Gāthās her und ist dort ein Appellativ (kein Eigenname), der in bezug auf Zarathustra und seine engsten Mithelfer angewendet wird. Im jüngeren Avesta ist das Wort ein Eigenname (wenn es im Singular steht) und wird nur mit Bezug auf den eschatologischen Erlöser, auch Astvat.ereta genannt, gebraucht. In den Gāthās sind also Zarathustra und der Saošyant ein- und dieselbe Person. Im jüngeren Avesta scheinen sie getrennt zu sein. Allerdings ist das Band zwischen ihnen immer stark gewesen, und deshalb wird der kommende eschatologische Erlöser als ein Nachkomme Zarathustras geschildert, ein Abkomme, der in einer Jungfrauengeburt zur Welt kam[13].

2.2.2. Der Saošyant im jüngeren Avesta trägt den Namen Astvat.ereta. Dieser Name besteht aus zwei gāthischen Wörtern, *astvat* und *ašəm,* die zusammen in Yasna 43,16 vorkommen. Der Name des letzten gerechten Menschen, des Saošyant, wurde also auf dieselbe Art gebildet wie der Name des ersten gerechten Menschen, nämlich Gaya maretan: eine Gāthā-Stelle hat das Material, die Wörter, geliefert, nicht aber den Namen als solchen[14].

Wenn man dann eine gewisse Stelle im Yašt 13 (Yašt 13,129) über den Saošyant liest, ist es völlig einleuchtend, daß sowohl der Name Astvat.ereta als auch das, was in der in Rede stehenden Stelle über ihn ausgesagt wird, aus der Gāthā-Stelle Yasna 43,16 herstammt.

---

[12] Sven S. Hartman 1965/66, 106 ff.
[13] Dazu Widengren in diesem Band § 2.2.1.
[14] Sven S. Hartman 1965/66, 106.

2.2.3. Der Saošyant wie auch seine Mithelfer werden *frašō. čaretar* genannt (Yašt 13,17; 19,22; Yasna 24,5) "solche, die etwas *fraša*- machen".

Diese Tätigkeit, "etwas *fraša*- zu machen", hat der Saošyant des jüngeren Avesta (Astvat.ereta) vom vornehmsten Saošyant der Gāthās, d. h. von Zarathustra, übernommen. Dies kann man leicht feststellen, wenn man Yašt 19,89 mit der Gāthā-Stelle Yasna 30,9 vergleicht. Die Yašt-Stelle hat nämlich die Formulierung von der Gāthā-Stelle übernommen. Beide sprechen davon, "das Dasein *fraša*- zu machen". Wiederum stellen wir fest, daß der Saošyant im jüngeren Avesta die Rolle des gāthischen Zarathustra übernommen hat. Eine weitere Analyse zeigt jedoch, daß, wenn Zarathustra etwas *fraša*- macht, bedeutet dies, er macht *gesund in geistlicher* Hinsicht, so daß man sich nicht einem verabscheuungswürdigen Kult mit Tobsucht und Grausamkeit gegenüber dem Vieh, sondern einem guten Kult widmen möge. Wenn der Saošyant im jüngeren Avesta etwas *fraša*- macht, bedeutet dies aber, daß er von Alter, Tod etc. befreit. Das ganze Dasein wird vom kommenden Saošyant zu einem "nicht alternden, nicht sterbenden, nicht welkenden, nicht vermodernden, sondern immer lebenden" (Dasein) gestaltet werden. Dann wird es *fraša*- sein, was wir mit "verklärt" übersetzen können[15].

2.2.4. Wie Gaya maretan und Zarathustra ist auch der Saošyant mit einem Stier verbunden. Dies geht aber erst aus der Pahlavi-Literatur hervor. Man hat diesen eschatologischen Stier als eine Dublette zum kosmischen Stier aufgefaßt, d. h. der Stier des Saošyant wäre bloß eine Dublette zu dem des Gaya maretan. Wahrscheinlich haben sich diese beiden Stiere aus dem Stier entwickelt, der in den Gāthās zusammen mit Zarathustra erwähnt wurde.

Was wir hier über das Verhältnis zwischen dem Saošyant und Zarathustra gefunden haben, wird vom syrischen Schriftsteller Theodor bar Kōnai bezeugt. Laut diesem soll Zarathustra vom eschatologischen Erlöser prophezeit und gesagt haben: "Ich bin er, und er ist ich. Ich bin in ihm, und er ist in mir"[16].

Es gibt viele Forscher, die früher und aus anderen Gründen geltend machen wollten, daß der Saošyant des jüngeren Avesta einen Aspekt Zarathustras repräsentiert. Hier seien besonders Bousset, Reitzenstein, Nyberg und Widengren genannt[17].

2.3. Wir wenden uns jetzt Zarathustra selbst zu.

2.3.1. Wenn wir Zarathustra im jüngeren Avesta betrachten, erhalten wir Belege dafür, daß er dort als ein allumfassender Mensch oder ein

---

[15] *Ibid.,* 107 ff.   [16] Peeters in Bidez/Cumont 1938, II, 128.
[17] Bousset 1907, 205; Reitzenstein 1921, 242 f.; Nyberg 1938, 302; Widengren 1954, 47 f. Vgl. auch Colpe 1969, 256.

vollkommener Mensch aufgefaßt wurde, ein τέλειος ἄνθρωπος (so Kaj Barr[18]), der deshalb den ersten Menschen als *einen* und den letzten Menschen als einen *anderen* Aspekt besitzen konnte. In der Pahlavi-Schrift Dātastān- i dēnīk 2,9; 4,6 und 28,7 wird gesagt, daß Gayōmart, Zarathustra und der Saošyant der Beginn, die Mitte und das Ende der Menschheitsgeschichte vertreten. Dies hat man als eine Aion-Spekulation deuten wollen. Deshalb wollen wir darauf hinweisen, daß gewisse späte Quellen Zarathustra tatsächlich als "den großen Zurvan" bezeichnen, d. h. die Große Zeit, den Großen Aion[19].

2.3.2. Zarathustra ist nicht nur die Totalität, sondern auch die Vollkommenheit[20]. Dies wird augenscheinlich, indem man ihm alle möglichen Superlative verleiht: er ist der Stärkste, der Tapferste, der Schnellste, der Siegreichste, der Wohlwollendste, der am besten Herrschende, der Reichste, der Anbetungswürdigste etc.

2.3.3. Zarathustra wird auch als der Erste in allen möglichen Beziehungen dargestellt: der Erste, der das Gute gedacht, der Erste, der das Gute gesagt, und der erste, der das Gute getan hat. Er ist auch der erste Priester, der erste Krieger, der erste Hirte etc. Deshalb haben manche gemeint, Zarathustra sei als ein Urmensch aufgefaßt worden. Wir wissen aber, daß Zarathustra sowohl als der Erste als auch der Letzte vorgestellt wurde. Diese Aspekte dürfen nicht voneinander isoliert werden, sie gehören zusammen.

2.4. Bisher haben wir die Spalte Iran I der Tabelle über die apokalyptischen Systeme betrachtet. Nun soll dieses System auch datiert werden.

Zuerst müssen wir feststellen, daß es viele andere Namen gibt, die auf dieselbe Weise wie Gaya maretan und Astvat.ereta gebildet worden sind, d. h. sie bestehen aus gāthischen Wörtern, obwohl die Namen an sich nicht in den Gāthās, sondern erst im jüngeren Avesta vorkommen. Es handelt sich dabei um mindestens 35–40 Namen[21]. Der wichtigste aller dieser Namen ist der Name Ahura Mazdāh. Dieser Name verhilft uns sogar dazu, sowohl die iranische Apokalyptik als auch den iranischen Dualismus mit seiner Teufelsvorstellung zu datieren. Die Datierung bezieht sich darauf, wann die Apokalyptik bzw. der Dualismus im Iran *spätestens* aufgekommen sein kann.

3. Datierung apokalyptischer Namen

3.1. Es ist eine Tatsache, daß die höchste Gottheit in den Gāthā-Hymnen *nicht* Ahura Mazdāh heißt[22], was dagegen gewöhnlich der Fall in

---

[18] Barr 1952, 26–36.   [19] Moïn 1948, 111 ff.; Sven S. Hartman 1953, 117.
[20] Sven S. Hartman 1965/66, 113 ff.   [21] Siehe unten § 3.2.3.3. mit Anm. 27.
[22] Bartholomae 1905, 128; Kent 1933, 207 ff.

übrigen avestischen Texten ist. Es scheint mir, daß diesem Umstand nicht die Aufmerksamkeit zuteil wurde, die ihm gebührt. Deshalb möchte ich mich hier ein wenig näher damit beschäftigen.

3.1.1. Die Entwicklung des Namens Ahura Mazdāh[23] veranschaulicht die folgende Tabelle (Fig. 2). Zu beachten ist, daß die Tabelle nur dem Namen an sich gilt, und nicht allen Vorstellungen, die sich mit ihm verbinden. Daß das Wort Ahura (mit vorangestelltem *) tatsächlich in dieser prägathischen iranischen Religion existiert hat, geht aus einigen Stellen im jüngeren Avesta hervor, wo der Name vorkommt. Es sind dies solche Stellen, die zwar mit vedischer, aber nicht mit gāthischer Religion übereinstimmen. Solche Stellen repräsentieren eine Tradition der indo-iranischen oder arischen Religion. An einigen Stellen im Avesta werden Mithra und Ahura als ein Paar und deshalb im Dual genannt. In Yašt 10,113 und 145 haben wir Mithra Ahura, in Yasna 1,11 und 2,11 finden wir die Ordnung Ahura Mithra. Man ist sich darüber einig, daß dieses Paar dem vedischen Paar Mitra-Varuna entspricht, das ebenfalls im Dual geschrieben wird. Das Wort *ahura* kann im Avesta auch als Appellativ gebraucht werden, als Epitheton auf Mithra und Apam Napāt. In diesem Fall entspricht das Wort dem vedischen *asura*.

3.1.2. Anhand des Gesagten erscheint es uns klar, daß sowohl das *ahura* als auch der Name *Ahura* in der prägathischen iranischen Religion existierte. Warum können wir nicht auch annehmen, daß es den Namen Mazdāh, Mazdāh Ahura und Ahura Mazdāh in der prägathischen irani-schen Religion gegeben hat, oder zumindest einen dieser Namen? Ich kann nicht sagen, daß es stichhaltige Argumente dafür gibt. Es erscheint mir natürlich, daß der Mann (Zarathustra), der für eine jede Gottheit neue Namen, und Namen, die meist Tugenden bezeichnen, erfand, zumindest mit dem Wort *mazdāh,* "weise", als Namen der höchsten Gottheit beigetra-gen hat. Im übrigen stellt Avesta die Sache so dar, daß Ahura Mazdāh erst durch Zarathustra einen Kult erhielt. Die anderen Gottheiten werden in den Yašts mit präzarathustrischem Kult dargestellt. Dem ist nicht so bei Ahura Mazdāh. Und laut Vīdēvdāt 2,3 weigerte sich der Urkönig Yima, die Religion Ahura Mazdāhs anzunehmen oder dafür zu propagieren. Es scheint mir, daß das von mir Gesagte stark gegen die Möglichkeit spricht, daß Mazdāh, Mazdāh Ahura und Ahura Mazdāh oder einer von ihnen Gottesnamen in der prägāthischen Religion gewesen seien. Am unglaub-haftesten ist gar die Annahme, daß der Name Ahura Mazdāh schon vor den Gāthās existiert habe. Er erscheint in den Gāthās ja nicht einmal als ein Name, was wir bereits angedeutet haben und worauf wir noch zurück-kommen werden.

---

[23] Für das Folgende siehe Sven S. Hartman 1965/66.

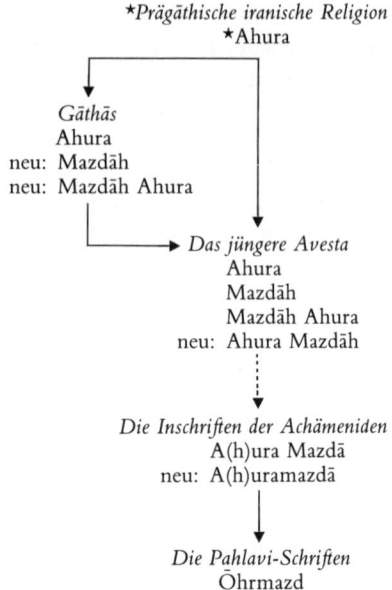

Prägäthische iranische Religion
*Ahura

Gāthās
Ahura
neu: Mazdāh
neu: Mazdāh Ahura

Das jüngere Avesta
Ahura
Mazdāh
Mazdāh Ahura
neu: Ahura Mazdāh

Die Inschriften der Achämeniden
A(h)ura Mazdā
neu: A(h)uramazdā

Die Pahlavi-Schriften
Ōhrmazd

Fig. 2 Vor "Prägäthische iranische Religion" habe ich ein * gesetzt, um anzudeuten, daß wir keine direkten Quellen haben und daß wir deshalb mit Ausgangspunkt von dem, was im Avesta steht, eigene Schlüsse ziehen müssen.

Der Pfeil zwischen dem jüngeren Avesta und den Achämeniden ist strichliert, um anzudeuten, daß es ein Zwischenglied (oder mehrere) zwischen diesen beiden geben kann.

3.2. Bei den Gāthās wird der höchste Gott oft nur Mazdāh genannt (116mal). Manchmal wird er nur Ahura genannt (64mal), manchmal Mazdāh Ahura (28mal). Darüber hinaus gab es noch die Schreibmöglichkeiten Mazdāh + ein oder mehrere Wörter + Ahura (24mal), oder Ahura + ein oder mehrere Wörter + Mazdāh (6mal). An sechs Stellen kommen tatsächlich die Namen Ahura und Mazdāh zusammen und in dieser Ordnung vor. Aber an diesen sechs Stellen ist eine Pause, Zäsur, nach Ahura. (Yasna 28,9a; 29,6a; 33,6c, 11a; 51,15b; 53,1c.)

3.2.1. Wenn nun jemand sagen wollte, daß die Zäsur in der Fragestellung, ob Ahura Mazdāh in den Gāthās als Eigenname vorkommt, keine Rolle spielt, möchte ich folgendes antworten: in diesem Fall diskutieren wir die Sache nicht weiter. Es ist nämlich nicht notwendig, die Frage von der Bedeutung der Zäsur abhängig zu machen. Anstelle dessen möchte ich folgendermaßen argumentieren: der höchste Gott in den Gāthās wird 240mal als etwas anderes als Ahura Mazdāh bezeichnet und 6mal wird er Ahura + Zäsur + Mazdāh genannt. Wenn danach jemand Ahura Mazdāh (ohne Zäsur zwischen den Worten) zum üblichsten Namen des höchsten

Gottes macht, ist dies *nicht* in Übereinstimmung mit dem gāthischen Sprachgebrauch, sondern man hat in diesem Fall etwas Neues dargeboten. Wir können niemals behaupten, daß der höchste Gott der Gāthā-Hymnen Ahura Mazdāh heißt. Dagegen können wir sagen, daß sich dies so beim höchsten Gott des jüngeren Avesta verhält. Ahura Mazdāh ist in den Gāthā-Hymnen kein Eigenname, was allerdings auf das jüngere Avesta zutrifft. Im jüngeren Avesta kommt der Name Ahura Mazdāh äußerst oft, ja viele Hunderte Male, vor. Es ist dieser Name und keiner der gāthischen, der sich weiterpflanzte und zu einem einzigen Wort im A(h)uramazdā der altpersischen Inschriften und zum Pahlavi-Namen Ōhrmazd wurde. Es ist ein Gott namens Ahura Mazdāh, mit dem Zarathustra (hier anachronistisch) im Vīdēvāt und anderen Texten, die dem jüngeren Avesta angehören, gesprochen habe.

3.2.2. Der Zarathustra der Gāthā-Hymnen – und dies ist ja der authentische Zarathustra – kennt jedoch den Namen Ahura Mazdāh nicht. Woher kommt also dann der Name Ahura Mazdāh?

Er kommt und kommt doch wieder nicht von den Gāthās, und damit meine ich folgendes: die beiden Teile des Namens, Ahura und Mazdāh, stammen von den Gāthā-Hymnen her, aber der Name in seiner Ganzheit ist eine Neuschöpfung im nicht-gāthischen Avesta, dem jüngeren Avesta. Diese Annahme erscheint mir notwendig, denn man kann sich ja nicht denken, daß, falls der Name Ahura Mazdāh schon vor Zarathustra existiert hat, dieser den Namen in Mazdāh, Mazdāh Ahura oder nur Ahura verdreht hätte. Dagegen ist es gut denkbar, daß der Name Ahura Mazdāh von einem Redaktor des späteren Avesta geschaffen wurde, der die beidem Wörter den Gāthā-Hymnen entnommen hat.

3.2.3. Diese Lösung ist durchaus möglich, denn es gibt viele andere Beispiele für eine solche Verfahrensweise.

3.2.3.1. Das naheliegendste Beispiel in diesem Zusammenhang ist der Gegenpol Ahura Mazdāhs, Angra Mainyu. Als *Name* des bösen Geistes kommt Angra Mainyu in den Gāthā-Hymnen nicht vor. Aber beide Wörter, aus denen der Name besteht, gibt es dort, wenn auch getrennt (Yasna 45,2). Der Name an sich ist dagegen eine Neuschöpfung im nicht-gāthischen, dem jüngeren Avesta. Und die beiden Wörter wurden dann, später, zu einem einzigen zusammengezogen, nämlich Ahriman ('Αρειμά-νιος[24]), die iranische Teufelsgestalt par préférence.

3.2.3.2. Der erste und der letzte der gerechten Menschen, also Gaya maretan (im Pahlavi Gayōmart) und der Saošyant Astvat.ereta sind zwei weitere Beispiele derselben Verfahrensweise. Was Gaya maretan betrifft,

---

[24] Eudemos von Rhodos bei Damascios (Dub. 125 bis), Aristoteles bei Diogenes Laertius (I 6–9) und Theopompos bei Plutarchos (De Is. et Os. 47): Clemen 1920, 95, 75, 48 ff. Siehe auch Widengren in diesem Band § 5.1.1.

besteht sein Name aus zwei gāthischen Wörtern aus Yasna 30,4 und 6. Diese Wörter sind in den genannten Gāthā-Stellen voneinander getrennt, aber dies scheint keine Rolle gespielt zu haben[25]. Mit diesen beiden gāthischen Wörtern wurde eine Gestalt geschaffen, welche gewisse Eigenschaften erhielt, die in den Gāthās Zarathustra zukommen. Dasselbe ist der Fall mit Astvat.ereta. Die beiden Wörter in seinem Namen kommen in den Gāthās vor (Yasna 43,16), sind dort aber keineswegs ein Eigenname. Auch diese eschatologische Gestalt hat gewisse Eigenschaften des gāthischen Zarathustra erhalten[26].

3.2.3.3. Die beiden letztgenannten Beispiele, der Anfang und das Ende der Reihe von fravašis gerechter Menschen, können natürlich nicht von der Reihe als Ganzheit getrennt werden. Und da finden wir viele Namen, die von gāthischen Namen, Wörtern und Vorstellungen gebildet wurden. In einem anderen Zusammenhang haben wir eine lange Reihe solcher Namen aufgezeigt und wollen sie hier nicht wiederholen[27]. Wir möchten nur darauf hinweisen, daß von vielen Personen, deren Namen auf diese Weise gebildet wurden, gesagt wird, sie seien Nachkommen von Personen, die zur Zeit Zarathustras gelebt haben. Der Brauch, Namen mit gāthischen Wörtern zu bilden, dürfte also gleichzeitig damit begonnen haben, daß Zarathustra Anerkennung und Anhänger gewann.

3.3. Auf Grund des Gesagten erscheint es mir notwendig anzunehmen, daß der Name Ahura Mazdāh in einer nachgāthischen Namengebungsprozedur zustande kam, da auch viele andere Namen auf dieselbe Weise geschaffen wurden, nämlich aus gāthischen Wörtern, die keine richtigen Eigennamen gewesen waren. Ich fasse die wichtigsten Argumente hierfür noch einmal zusammen:

1. Der Name Ahura Mazdāh ist in den Gāthā-Hymnen kein Eigenname.
2. Deshalb ist es schwierig, sich zu denken, daß der Name prägāthisch sein soll.
3. Er dürfte also postgāthisch sein, jedoch aus zwei gāthischen Wörtern gebildet.
4. Am wahrscheinlichsten ist es dann, daß der Name im Zusammenhang mit den übrigen pseudogāthischen Namen geschaffen wurde, wovon wir oben drei Beispiele nannten.

3.4. Das Gesagte bedingt gewisse Konsequenzen für die Datierung der Avesta-Texte. Wenn – wie wir behaupten – der Name Ahura Mazdāh eine Neuschöpfung im jüngeren Avesta ist, müssen große Teile des jüngeren Avesta vor der achämenidischen Zeit datiert werden, denn in den achämenidischen Inschriften kommt ja der Name A(h)uramazdā vor. Dabei ist zu beachten, daß er außerdem noch eine Entwicklung durchgemacht hat, denn seine beiden Bestandteile sind zu einem einzigen Wort zusammengeschmolzen, und eine solche Entwicklung nimmt eine gewisse Zeit in

---

[25] So auch im Hinblick auf den Einwand von Widengren in diesem Band § 2.2.2.
[26] Im übrigen siehe oben § 2.1. und § 2.2.2.   [27] Sven S. Hartman 1975, 176.

Anspruch. Wenn wir deshalb die pseudogāthischen Namenbildungen auf spätestens 600 v. Chr. datieren, ist diese Lösung keineswegs undenkbar.

4. Iranischer Einfluß auf jüdische und christliche Apokalyptik[28]

4.1. Auf Grund der Datierung des Namens Ahura Mazdāh auf spätestens 600 v. Chr. haben wir auch alle avestischen Namen datiert, die auf dieselbe Art gebildet worden sind, nämlich aus gāthischen Wörtern, ohne dabei gāthisch zu sein. Dies bedeutet, daß der Dualismus in Iran zwischen Ahura Mazdāh und Angra Mainyu[29] schon damals vorhanden war. Es bedeutet auch, daß die iranische Apokalyptik mit Gaya maretan, Zarathustra und den eschatologischen Saošyant Astvat.ereta spätestens dann vorhanden gewesen sein muß. Es ist diese Apokalyptik, die mit einem Propheten verknüpft ist, der zugleich Urmensch und eschatologischer Erlöser ist, genau wie es der Fall im Henochbuch und im Christentum ist. In allen drei Fällen haben wir also

1. ein präexistentes Wesen (Gaya – Henoch – Christus);
2. einen Propheten, der mit dem präexistenten Wesen identisch ist;
3. einen eschatologischen Erlöser, der auch mit den beiden vorhergehenden identisch ist[30].

4.2. Es sollen noch einige Worte bezüglich des Dualismus, oder vielleicht richtiger, bezüglich des Teufels, des Satans, des bösen Teils des Dualismus, gesagt werden. Es ist eine Tatsache, daß das Alte Testament keinen richtigen Teufel kennt, wohl aber das Judentum und auch das Christentum. Im Buche Hiob wird Satan erwähnt, aber er ist dort einer der Söhne Gottes, und es sind Gott und Satan (in der Lutherübersetzung "Verkläger" genannt), die gemeinsam prüfen, ob Hiob gerecht ist, auch wenn er Schweres durchmachen muß. Im Buche Hiob gibt es noch keinen richtigen Teufel, aber dieser kommt in spätjüdischen Schriften und im Neuen Testament vor. 'Etwas' ist also geschehen, das ins Judentum und ins Christentum eindrang, und das es früher nicht gab. Dieses 'Etwas' dürfte ein Einfluß des iranischen Ahriman (Angra Mainyu) sein. Und dieser Einfluß ist durchaus nicht unerwartet. Die Juden haben während mehr als zweihundert Jahren unter der persischen Dynastie der Achämeniden gelebt und danach kamen diejenigen, die in Mesopotamien wohnten, unter parthischer Herrschaft. Also: die Teufelsvorstellung kommt aus dem Iran und ist dort seit mindestens 600 v. Chr. nachweisbar.

---

[28] Vgl. nunmehr auch Hultgård 1979.
[29] Zu Angra Mainyu siehe oben § 3.2.3.1. sowie Sven S. Hartman 1975, 175.
[30] Sven S. Hartman 1973, 117.

Bibliographie

1. Quellen

Avesta: Zendavesta I. The Zend Texts, by *N. L. Westergaard,* Kopenhagen 1852–1854.
Avesta, die heiligen Bücher der Parsen I–III, hrsg. von *K. F. Geldner,* Stuttgart 1886–1895.
Le Zend-Avesta, trad. nouv. avec commentaire hist. et philologique I–III, par *J. Darmeste-*
ter, Paris 1892–1893.
Avesta. Die heiligen Bücher der Parsen, übersetzt auf der Grundlage von Chr. Bartholo-
mae's Altiranischem Wörterbuch, von *F. Wolff,* Straßburg 1910, Berlin/Leipzig 1924.
Die Faksimileauflage *"Codices Avestici et Pahlavici Universitatis Hafniensis",* Kopenhagen
1931 ff.
Gāthās: Die Gatha's des Awesta, übers. von *Chr. Bartholomae,* Straßburg 1905.
Zoroastre. Étude critique avec une traduction commentée des Gâthâ, par *J. Duchesne-*
Guillemin, Paris 1948.
Yašts: Die Yäšt's des Awesta, übers. von *H. Lommel,* Göttingen-Leipzig 1927.

Pahlavi-Texte

Bahman Yašt: Zand-î Vohûman Yasn and Two Pahlavi Fragments with Text, Transliteration,
and Translation in English by *B. T. Anklesaria,* Bombay 1957.
Kaikobad Adarbad Nosherwan, The Text of the Pahlavi Zand-i-Vohuman Yasht, Poona
1899.
Die Pahlavi-Kodexe K 20B und K 43 in der Faksimileausgabe *"Codices Avestici et Pahlavici*
Universitatis Hafniensis", Kopenhagen 1931 ff.
Bundahišn: The Bundahishn, being a facsimile of the TD Manuscript No. 2 brought from
Persia by Dastur Tirandaz an now preserved in the late Ervad Tahmuras' Library, ed. by
the late *E. T. D. Anklesaria,* Bombay 1908.
The Bondaheshn, being a facsimile edition of the manuscript TD_1, Iranian Culture
Foundation 88.
The Codex DH, being a facsimile edition of Bondahesh, Zand-e Vohuman Yasht and parts
of Denkard, Iranian Culture Foundation 89.
Die Pahlavi-Kodexe K 20 und K 20B in der Faksimileausgabe *"Codices Avestici et Pahlavi*
Universitatis Hafniensis", Kopenhagen 1931 ff.
Dēnkart: The Complete Text of the Pahlavi Dinkard. Published by "The Society for the
promotion of researches into the Zoroastrian religion" under the supervision of *D. M.*
Madan, Bombay 1911.
Dēnkart, A Pahlavi Text. Facsimile edition of the manuscript B of the K. R. Cama Oriental
Institute Bombay, ed. *M. J. Dresden,* Wiesbaden 1966.
Pahlavi Rivâyat zu *Dātastān i Dēnīk*: The Pahlavi Rivâyat accompanying the Dâdistân î Dînîk,
ed. *E. B. N. Dhabhar,* Bombay 1913.

2. Literatur

Abegg, E. 1928: *Der Messiasglaube in Indien und Iran,* Berlin-Leipzig 1928.
Barr, K. 1952: "Irans Profet som τέλειος ἄνθρωπος", in: *FS. L. L. Hammerich,* Kopenhagen
1952, 26–36.
Bartholomae, Chr. 1904: *Altiranisches Wörterbuch,* Straßburg 1904.
Bidez, J./Cumont, F. 1938: Les Mages Hellénisés, I–II, Paris 1938 [Neudruck 1973].
Bousset, W. 1907: *Hauptprobleme der Gnosis* (FRLANT 10), Göttingen 1907 [Neudruck 1973].
Clemen, C. 1920: *Fontes historiae religionis persicae* (FHR: Fasc. I), Bonn 1920.
Colpe, C. 1969: "Der Begriff 'Menschensohn' und die Methode der Erforschung messiani-
scher Prototypen", in: *Kairos* 11 (1969) 241 ff.
Hartman, S. S. 1953: *Gayōmart.* Étude sur le syncrétisme dans l'ancien Iran, Uppsala 1953.
– 1964: "Aspects de l'histoire religieuse selon la conception de l'Avesta non-gāthique", in:
OrSuec 13 (1964) 88–118.

- 1965/66: "Der große Zarathustra", in: *OrSuec* 14/15 (1965/66) 99–117.
- 1973: "Iran", in: U. Mann (Hrsg.), *Theologie und Religionswissenschaft,* Darmstadt 1973, 106–123.
- 1975: "Der Name Ahura Mazdāh", in: A. Dietrich (Hrsg.), *Synkretismus im syrisch-persischen Kulturgebiet* (AAWG.PH 96), Göttingen 1975, 170–177.
- 1976: "Frågan om eventuellt iranskt inflytande på kristendomens och judendomens apokalyptik och djävulsföreställning", in: *SvTK* 52 (1976) 1–8.
- 1980: *Parsism.* The Religion of Zoroaster (IoR 14,4), Leiden 1980.
Hultgård, A. 1979: "Das Judentum in der hellenistisch-römischen Zeit und die iranische Religion – ein religionsgeschichtliches Problem", in: *ANRW* II.19.1., Berlin-New York 1979, 512–590.
Kent, R. G. 1933: "The Name Ahuramazda", in: Jal Dastur Cursetji Pavry (Hrsg.), *Oriental Studies in Honour of Cursetji Erachji Pavry,* London-Oxford 1933, 207 ff.
Moïn, M. 1948: *L'influence du mazdéisme dans la litterature persane* (*Mazdēsnā wa-ta'tīr-i ān dar 'adabīyāt-i pārsī*) (Publications de l'Université de Teheran 9/1326 [1948], Teheran 1948.
Nyberg, H. S. 1938: *Die Religionen des alten Iran* (MVAEG 43), Leipzig 1938 [Neudruck: Osnabrück 1966].
Reitzenstein, R. 1921: *Das iranische Erlösungsmysterium,* Bonn 1921.
Ringgren, H. 1957: "I. Apokalyptische Literatur, religionsgeschichtlich; II. Jüdische Apokalyptik", in: *RGG*³ I, Tübingen 1957, 463–466.
Widengren, G. 1954: "Stand und Aufgaben der iranischen Religionsgeschichte", in: *Numen* 1 (1954) 16–83.
- 1955: "Stand und Aufgaben der iranischen Religionsgeschichte", in: *Numen* 2 (1955) 47–134.
- 1961: *Iranische Geisteswelt,* Baden-Baden 1961.
- 1965: *Die Religionen Irans* (RM 14), Stuttgart 1965.
- 1969: *Religionsphänomenologie,* Berlin-New York 1969.

Leitende Ideen und Quellen der iranischen Apokalyptik

Geo Widengren

1. Die apokalyptischen Anschauungen in den Gathas

Der originellste Beitrag Zarathustras zur iranischen Religion und zugleich seine für die folgenden Zeiten bedeutsamste Leistung war wohl seine eschatologische Lehre. Denn anstatt der zyklischen Zeitkonzeption der ererbten indo-iranischen Spekulation[1] bietet er eine lineare Zeitauffassung: die Weltentwicklung wiederholt sich nicht *in infinitum,* sondern geht ihrem Ende entgegen[2]. Die eschatologische Perspektive ist aber an sich keine Neuschöpfung Zarathustras[3].

Wenn wir die eschatologischen Motive betrachten, die mit dem Weltende verbunden sind, sehen wir sofort, daß sie in zwei Kategorien zerfallen: einerseits gibt es eine *kriegerische Entscheidung* zwischen den Heeren, den zwei Streitmächten, andererseits finden sich die *naturhaften Elemente* Feuer und geschmolzenes Metall, die sozusagen die Rolle eines kosmischen Schlußordals spielen[4].

1.1. Die kriegerische Entscheidung

1.1.1. Vom kosmischen Endkampf heißt es in den Gathas (Y. 44:15[5]):

hyaṯ hə̄m spādā anaočaŋhā jamaētē,	Wenn die beiden feindlichen Heerscharen sich treffen,
avāiš urvātāiš yā tū mazdā dīdərəžō,	nach jenen Bestimmungen, an denen du, O Mazdā, festhalten willst,
kuϑrā ayā̊ kahmāi vananąm dadā̊?	welcher von den beiden wirst du den Sieg verleihen?

Y.44:13 hat schon von der Vernichtung der Lüge (*drug*) gesprochen; auch Y. 30:8 davon, daß *Xšaϑra,* die Herrschaft, das Reich, denen zugeteilt

---

[1] Wir müssen ja voraussetzen, daß er von dieser Spekulation ausgegangen ist, so wie er in anderen Fällen vom indo-iranischen Erbe ausgegangen ist; vgl. Widengren 1965, 78.

[2] Vgl. Nyberg 1938, 216.

[3] Diese Meinung, Nyberg 1938, 217, ist nicht richtig; vgl. Widengren 1979a, 83. Ich verwende gewisse Formulierungen, die dort zu finden sind.

[4] Vgl. Lommel 1930, 219–222; Nyberg 1938, 228.

[5] Auf diese entscheidende Stelle hat Lommel 1930, 222 hingewiesen.

wird, welche dem *Aša,* der Wahrheit, die Lüge in die Hände liefern. Ja, die Wahrheit selbst wird die Lüge überwinden: Y. 48:1; ferner Y. 30:10 und Y. 48:2[6].

1.1.2. Schon in den Gathas wird vom Kampf zwischen Guten und Bösen gesprochen. In das normale, von der Rechten Ordnung, der Wahrhaftigkeit (*Aša*), geprägte Dasein brechen die bösen Mächte herein: die Lüge (*drug*), die Raserei (*aēšma*) und vor allem *Ahra Mainyu,* der Böse Geist. Diese bösen Mächte vertreten Sünde (*aēnah*) und Tod (*maraka* [*mahrka*])[7].

Am Ende der Welt werden die Bösen für ihre Sünde durch Strafe büßen, Y. 30:8; 32:6−8. Zusammenfassend werden die widergöttlichen Mächte als *daēva*-s bezeichnet, die guten, göttlichen Personen aber als *ahura*-s.

1.1.3. Wie Wikander gezeigt hat, verbergen sich kultisch-soziale Gegensätze hinter diesen Anschauungen. Die Feinde der rechten Ordnung, die Anhänger der *Aēšma,* sind die Männerbündler, für die das Verbum *aēš*-typisch ist, wie in Indien jene die *iṣmin* sind, eben die Gefolgsleute des Gottes Indra sind. Zwei kultisch-soziale Ideologien stoßen hier zusammen[8].

Diese Gegensätze wurden von Zarathustra auf das eschatologische Niveau gehoben. Aber schon in der gegenwärtigen Zeit muß man die bösen Gegner bekämpfen, denn man lebt ja im letzten Zeitalter. Zarathustra hat das Gefühl, die Endzeit zu erleben[9]. Der Endkampf wird hier eingeleitet, wenn Zarathustra seine Anhänger ermahnt, die Feinde mit der Waffe (*snaiϑiš*) zu zerhauen (*aϑā īš sāzdūm snaiϑišā*), Y. 31:18[10].

1.2. Die naturhaften Geschehnisse

1.2.1. Was vom kosmischen Endkampf gesagt ist, gilt auch von den naturhaften Geschehnissen im Kosmos, denen wir uns jetzt zuwenden.

Mit Recht hat Lommel hinter der umgestaltenden Wirkung des Feuers am Ende "einige" alte Mythologien vermutet[11]. Das hatte tatsächlich schon Söderblom gesehen und klar ausgedrückt[12]. Daß Zarathustra die Weltzerstörung durch Feuer aus der traditionellen Religion übernommen hat, kann keinem Zweifel unterliegen. Diese Vorstellung ist nicht nur als indo-iranisch-indisch in Viṣṇu Purāṇa 6,3, sondern sogar als indo-germanisch-nordisch in Völuspa 57 und bei Saxo, Gesta Danorum VIII 4,4 belegt[13].

---

[6] Es ist wiederum Lommel 1930, 223, der auf diese Stelle aufmerksam gemacht hat.
[7] Vgl. Widengren 1961a, 42f.; 1965, 78.
[8] Vgl. Wikander 1938, 59f.   [9] Vgl. Nyberg 1938, 227f.
[10] Für die Bedeutung von *sāzdūm,* √*sā*-, AirWb 1569, vgl. Kellens 1975, 215. Die aus AirWb 1628 in Widengren 1965, 65 entnommene Übersetzung ist also zu korrigieren.
[11] Vgl. Lommel 1930, 222.   [12] Vgl. Söderblom 1901, 194ff., 236f.
[13] Vgl. Ström 1975, 247f.

Das Ende der Welt wird also durch Störungen der gesetzesmäßigen Ordnung herbeigeführt werden, durch Naturkatastrophen und zuletzt durch das Feuer, das sich über die Erde ausgießt. Aber ehe das geschieht, wird die rechte Ordnung auf andere Weise in Unordnung gebracht, und zwar durch Auflösung der normalen Ordnung in der Gesellschaft, wie wir schon oben § 1.1.2. und § 1.1.3. gesehen haben.

1.2.2. Zwischen den beiden streitenden Parteien (*rāna*), den Guten und den Bösen, wird Ahura Mazdā durch ein großes Feuerordal Gerechtigkeit walten lassen und Belohnung und Strafe verteilen. Dieser Gedanke tritt an verschiedenen Stellen in den Gathas hervor und gehört zu den grundlegenden eschatologischen Gedanken Zarathustras, vgl. Y. 51:9; 31:3, 19; 43:12; 47:6.

Durch das rote Feuer (*āϑrā suxrā*) wird Recht im kosmischen Endordal geschaffen[14]. Nicht nur das Feuer allein, sondern auch geschmolzenes Metall (*ayah- xšusta-*) tritt bei dem eschatologischen Ordal in Erscheinung.

1.2.3. Die Gerechten gehen in der Ekstase und nach dem Tode zum himmlischen Dasein, Y. 46:10−11. Als Führer der Rechtschaffenen schreitet Zarathustra über die Brücke der Entscheidung (*Činvatō pərətu*)[15]. So sagt er zu Ahura Mazdā, Y. 46:10:

> Denen, welche ich zum Lobpreis vor Euch geleiten will,
> denen allen voran werde ich die Činvat-Brücke hinüberschreiten.

Als Offenbarer des Gotteswortes und Führer der Gläubigen nach dem Tode nimmt der Stifter tatsächlich die Stellung eines Erlösers ein. Er ist der Saošyant, der seiner Gemeinde "Nutzen" (*savah*) bringt[16]. M. R. sagt Lommel, daß die künftige Wirksamkeit des Saošyant schon durch die futurische Form des Wortes sichergestellt ist. "Daß dieser Begriff mit einer Zukunftserwartung verknüpft ist, geht auch hervor aus Y. 46:3"[17]:

> Wann, O Mazdā, wird die Morgenröte der Tage
> für das Beibehalten des Aša im Dasein herbeikommen,
> (wann) mit gewaltigen Sprüchen die Weisheiten der Saošyanten?
> Welchen wird (Aša) zu Hilfe kommen mit Vohu Manah?
> Mir wähle ich, O Ahura, dich für die Vollendung[18].

---

[14] Vgl. Lommel 1930, 222. Sehr ausführlich darüber Nyberg 1938, 227 ff.
[15] Vgl. Nyberg 1938, 180 f.
[16] Das Wort *saošyant* ist Part. Fut. von √*su-, sav-*; vgl. Nyberg 1938, 230.
[17] Lommel 1930, 227; anders Nyberg 1938, 231.
[18] Für die Übersetzung vgl. Benveniste 1935, 44 und 46. Mit Lommel 1930, 227 nehme ich an, daß Aša Subjekt von *jimat̰*, "wird kommen" ist. Nyberg 1938, 231 sagt: "das Göttliche", aber ein solches Subjekt wird früher nicht erwähnt. Den Terminus *səngha*, Spruch, kann man hier als Richterspruch im eschatologischen Sinn auffassen, vgl. AirWb 1575, 3 mit den dort angeführten Stellen. Nybergs "Ordalentscheidungen" scheint mir an dieser Stelle nicht berechtigt zu sein.

Die Saošyanten werden also mit mächtigen Richtersprüchen kommen mit ihrer Weisheit (*Xratu*) um Aša und Vohu Manah in der Welt Geltung zu schaffen. Die Vollendung (*sạstra*) ist offenbar nahe, denn Zarathustra wählt sich Ahura für diese Vollendung, die sonst in den Gathas *ākərəti*, "Verklärung" heißt[19]. "Die Neugestaltung" der Dinge, die Zarathustra vom kosmischen Ordal erwartet, faßt er am kürzesten in seinem Gebet Y. 30:9 zusammen[20]:

> Mögen wir diejenigen sein, die dies Dasein *fraša* machen!

Die Gottheit ist es zuletzt, die das Handeln der Menschen so gestaltet, daß die Welt *fraša* wird.

Woher die Saošyanten kommen und welche sie – außer Zarathustra – sind, wissen wir nicht. Aber wahrscheinlich sind sie wie Aša und Vohu Manah himmlische Gestalten (so auch Lommel), die in den Endkampf eingreifen.

1.3. Ergebnis der Analyse von den Gathas

Mit diesen Lehren und Hoffnungen tritt uns Zarathustra als *der erste Apokalyptiker* entgegen, was Nyberg mit vollem Recht hervorgehoben hat[21].

Die Kontinuität in der iranischen Eschatologie aller Perioden hat Lommel m. R. stark unterstrichen[22] und diese Kontinuität wird noch deutlicher hervortreten, wenn wir, mit Hilfe der unten § 4.1. dargelegten Methode, welche der damaligen Forschung noch fremd war[23], die auf avestische Texte zurückgehenden Stellen in der apokalyptischen Pahlaviliteratur näher analysieren.

2. Die jungavestische Apokalyptik

In der Zeit nach Zarathustra, als seine Lehre sich im Iran verbreitete, aber zugleich eine Akkomodation an die vor ihm herrschenden Ideen und Praktiken einsetzte, finden wir eine Apokalyptik, in der uns die gathischen Anschauungen in voll entwickelter Form entgegentreten. Dabei ist indessen zu beachten, daß die Gathas keine Lehrtraktate waren; wir können

---

[19] Vgl. Widengren 1965, 88; "Verklärung" ist die konventionelle Übersetzung.

[20] Nyberg 1938, 228.

[21] Vgl. Nyberg 1938, 267.

[22] Vgl. Lommel 1930, 205–236, wo er der Reihe nach die Pahlaviquellen, das jüngere Avesta und die Gathas behandelt.

[23] Lommel war auch kein Kenner der Pahlavisprache. Übrigens weiß ich von keinen anderen Forschern, außer Molé und mir, die versucht haben, die avestischen Vorlagen zu entdecken; vgl. bes. unten § 4.1.

deshalb nicht sicher sein, daß sie *alle* Ideen Zarathustras wiedergeben. Mit diesem Vorbehalt betrachten wir die sog. jungavestische Apokalyptik der Yašts, d. h. die an die göttlichen Wesen gerichteten Opfergesänge, die zusammen mit dem jüngeren Yasna (also Yasna außer den Gathas) den Kernbestand des "jüngeren Avesta" ausmachen.

Dabei richten wir die Aufmerksamkeit auf die neuen Zeichen, die wir in der jungavestischen Apokalyptik finden. Diese sind in zwei Hauptpunkten zusammenzufassen: die *Auferstehung der Toten* und die *Entwicklung der Lehre vom Saošyant*.

2.1. Die Auferstehung der Toten

Die Vorstellung von der Auferstehung der Toten ist den Gathas fremd; sie sprechen nur von der Himmelfahrt der Seele, eine Vorstellung, die sich eben nicht ohne Widerspruch mit dem Gedanken an eine Auferstehung vereinbaren läßt. In den Yašts aber ist die Auferstehung der Toten ein wiederkehrendes Thema. So in Yt. 19:11:

yat̰ irista paiti usəhištąn	*[10]*[24a]	Wenn die Toten auferstehen,
jasāt̰ j̊vayō amərəxtiš	*[8]*	dann wird der Lebendige ohne Verderben kommen[25],
daϑaite frašəm vasna[24] *aŋhuš.*	*[10]*	nach Wunsch wird das Leben *fraša* gemacht werden.

2.2. Die Entwicklung der Lehre vom Saošyant

Sehr bedeutsam für das Verständnis der Lehre vom Saošyant ist die Stelle Yt. 19:89, wo es heißt:

yat̰ upaŋhačat̰ saošyantəm	*[8]*	Wenn (der Glücksglanz) sich zu dem Saošy- ant gesellen wird,
vərəϑrājanəm uta anyā̊scit̰ haxayō,	*[12]*	dem Siegreichen, und zu den anderen Ge- nossen[26],
yat̰ kərənavāt̰ frašəm ahūm,	*[8]*	wenn er das Dasein *fraša* machen wird,
★azarəšəntəm amarəšəntəm	*[8]*	nicht alternd, nicht sterbend,
afriϑyantəm apuyantəm	*[8]*	nicht verwesend, nicht faulend,
yavaējim yavaēsum vasō.xšaϑrəm	*[10]*	ewig lebend, ewig gedeihend, nach Gefallen
usw. wie v. 11.		herrschend
		usw. wie V. 11.

---

[24] Es müßte eigentlich *vasnē* heißen.

[24a] [10], [8] etc. gibt metrische Silbenzählung an.

[25] Mit Bartholomae AirWb 610 und Nyberg 1938, 308 *gegen* Lommel 1927, 177: "für die Lebenden". Für die Form *j̊vayō* statt *j̊ivayō* vgl. Reichelt 1909, § 33,6 und § 131,4.

[26] *Haxi* ist der Gefolgsmann (√hak). Das Wort korrespondiert hier mit der Verbform *upaŋhačat* (√hak-). In Indien sind die Maruten als Gefolgsmänner (*sakhi*) Indras bezeichnet; vgl. Widengren 1969b, 42 (wo ein Verweis auf *haxi* fehlt) und 1965, 15 Anm. 49.

Wir betrachten diese Stelle etwas näher. Hier wird deutlich gesagt, was das Werk des Saošyant ist. Er wird das Dasein der Menschen "ewig lebend", unvergänglich und also *fraša* machen. Das Wort *fraša* umfaßt offenbar alle die Begriffe wie nichtalternd, nichtfaulend usw., die hier aufgezählt wurden. Man kann daher die von Bailey vorgeschlagene Grundbedeutung "stark" akzeptieren[27].

Die Gläubigen sind als die Genossen (*haxayō*; eigtl. Gefolgsmänner) des Saošyant bezeichnet, der selber das Epitheton "siegreich" bekommt. Das deutet auf einen kriegerischen Kampf hin, woraus er und seine Genossen siegreich hervorgehen.

2.2.1. Der Begriff Saošyant wird in dieser Zeit näher fixiert. Eine ganze Mythologie verknüpft ihn mit Zarathustra. Man rechnet mit drei solchen Saošyants: Astvat-Arta, Uxšyat-Arta und Uxšyat-Nəmah; es ist aber unsicher, wie konkret und lebendig man sich die zwei letzteren vorgestellt hat. Sie werden jedenfalls zusammen mit Astvat-Arta in Yt. 13:128 erwähnt[28]. Ihre Namen sind symbolisch: "Die körperhafte Wahrheit" (mit Anknüpfung an Y. 43:16: "Körperhaft möge *Aša* sein" [*Arta*: Nebenform von *Aša*]. Über die Art, wie dieser Name aus zwei Wörtern in dieser Gathastelle gebildet ist, vgl. in diesem Band den Beitrag von S. S. Hartman (§ 2.2.2.); dort wird auch gezeigt, daß Yt. 13:129 von Y. 43:16 ganz abhängig ist); "Der die Wahrheit vermehrt" (Uxšyat-Arta; vgl. Yt. 13:128); "Der die Verehrung vermehrt" (Uxšyat-Nəmah; vgl. *ibid.*).

Sehr früh ist ein Mythos über die wunderbare Geburt dieser drei Saošyants entstanden. Zarathustras Sperma wird in dem See Kansaoya (Yt. 13:62) bewahrt. Dort badet ein unverheiratetes Mädchen, eine Jungfrau, und wird von diesem Sperma befruchtet, Yt. 13:142:

		[Wir verehren die Fravaši]
Kanyā̊ ərədat. fəδryā̊ ašaonyā̊ ...	[8]	des gerechten Mädchens Ardatfedri...,
yaϑā hā təm zīzanāt	[6?]	weil sie den gebären wird,
yō vīspe taurvayāt	[6]	der überwinden wird
daēvāaṱča ṱbaēšā mašyāat	[8]	alle Feindseligkeit[29] der Dämonen und Menschen.

Von dieser Jungfrau wird Saošyant geboren, und in inspirierten Worten besingt der Yašt-Sänger das Hervortreten des Erlösers Astvat-Arta aus dem Kansaoya-See, Yt. 19:92[30]:

---

[27] Vgl. Bailey 1953b, 21–32. In Widengren 1965, 88 Anm. 148 habe ich darauf hingewiesen, aber etwas gezögert, diese Bedeutung zu akzeptieren. Sie scheint mir jetzt die beste zu sein.

[28] Vgl. Nyberg 1938, 306. Seine Skepsis ist indessen wenig begründet, denn die drei Saošyants hängen mit dem Millennien-Schema zusammen; vgl. weiter unten in diesem Paragraphen.

[29] Das Wort *ṱbaēšah*, ein gathischer Begriff, ist nunmehr m. E. (mit AirWb 814f. und Nyberg 1938, 405) besser so als mit "Leid" zu übersetzen.

[30] Mit Geldner, vgl. AirWb 1464, ist *vīspa-taurvairyā̊* (gegen AirWb *ibid.*) zu lesen. Das

yat̰ astvat-ərətō fraxštāite	Wenn Astvat-Arta hervortreten wird
hača apat̰ k̜ansaoyāt̰	aus dem Wasser des Kansaoya-Sees,
aštō mazdā̊ ahurahe	der Gesandte Ahura Mazdās,
vīspa-taurvairyā̊ puϑrō,	Vīspa-taurvairī's Sohn,
vaēδəm vaēǰō yim vārəϑraynəm,	die siegreiche Keule schwingend,
yim barat̰ taxmō ϑraētaonō,	die der starke Thraētaona trug,
yat̰ ažiš dahākō ǰaini.	als Aži Dahāka erschlagen ward.

In der Fortsetzung heißt es, daß *Aēšma,* die Raserei, mit blutiger Keule vor Astvat-Arta und seine Genossen ·fliehen wird; die Wahrheit wird die Lüge besiegen. Dann folgt Yt. 19:96:

⋆vanaite akəmčit̰ manō	[8]	Besiegt wird das Böse Denken (Aka Manah),
vohu manō tat̰ vanaiti	[8]	Vohu Manah (das Gute Denken) besiegt es,
⋆vanaite miϑaoxtō vāxš,	[8]	besiegt wird das falsch gesprochene Wort
ərəžuxδō vāxš təm vanaiti	[8]	das recht gesprochene Wort besiegt es.
vanāt̰ haurvās̆ca amərətās̆ca	[8]	Besiegen werden Heilsein und Unsterblichkeit
uva šuδəmča taršnəmča, ...	[8]	beide, Hunger und Durst, ...
frānāmāiti dužvarštāvarəš	[8]	entfliehen wird der böse Werke Wirkende,
aŋrō mainyuš axšayamnō.	[8]	der Böse Geist, nicht (mehr) herrschend.

Dem Paar Hunger und Durst, das hier als besiegt erwähnt wird, werden wir später in der zervanitischen Apokalypse Zātspr. XXXIV 32 begegnen (§ 5.2.1.). Den Begriff *miϑaoxtō* werden wir auch später in der mitteliranischen Apokalyptik (s. § 6.1.11.) wiederfinden. Und selbstverständlich spielt die Raserei (*Hešm*) dort eine so hervortretende Rolle, daß Stellenverweise hier überflüssig sind.

Dieser Saošyant ist der Erlöser *par excellence.* Die zwei anderen Saošyants haben nur die Funktion, den Übergang von Zarathustra zu dem dritten Sohn zu vermitteln. Ihre Geburt geschieht in analoger Weise und ihre Mütter tragen ähnliche symbolische Namen. Ein verlorengegangenes avestisches Traktat, Spand Nask, erzählte die übernatürliche Geburt der drei Erlöser. Jedesmal am Ende der drei letzten Millennien der Welt tritt einer von diesen Erlösern hervor, während Zarathustra die letzte Dreitausendjahr-Periode einleitete. Das Schema hat folgendes Aussehen[31]:

Bis zum Ende 3000 Jahre – Zarathustra
2000 Jahre – Uxšyat-Arta
1000 Jahre – Uxšyat-Nəmah
0 Jahre – Astvat-Arta

Wort *vaēδa* bezeichnet offenbar nicht ein Wurfgeschoß (so AirWb 1320), sondern, da sie die Waffe des Thraētaonas ist, eben die von ihm getragene Keule, wie Bartholomae selbst bemerkt. "Die stierköpfige Keule" (*gurz i gāvsār*) werden wir in der mir. Apokalyptik wiederfinden (unten § 4.2.2.4.–§ 4.2.2.5.). Für die Prät. Pass. Form *ǰaini* ist "erschlagen" wie ich 1965, 106 übersetzt habe (diese Übersetzung auch bei Nyberg 1938, 312) besser als "getötet" (so Lommel 1927, 185). Für die richtige Auffassung der Verbform vgl. AirWb 490. – Das Metrum ist in diesem Falle nicht leicht zu rekonstruieren.
[31] Vgl. Widengren 1965, 107.

Die Zahl der Saošyanten war als drei fixiert: Sie sind die mythischen Söhne Zarathustras, von drei jungfräulichen Müttern geboren. Die eigtl. konkrete Gestalt ist der letzte, der am Ende der Dreimillennien-Periode, also am Ende der Zeit, hervortritt. Er ist eine sowohl kämpfende wie richtende Gestalt (denn selbstverständlich lebt diese gathische Auffassung fort), aber das kriegerische Wirken dominiert sein Wesen. Darum trägt er auch die typische Waffe, die Keule.

Der Saošyant und seine Helfer werden *frašō. čarətar* genannt (Yt. 13:17; 19:22), denn wie wir oben (§ 1.2.3.) gesehen haben, wird der Saošyant das Dasein *fraša* machen. Eine Erneuerung der Welt findet statt (*frašō.kərəti*; Y. 62:3; Yt. 13:58; Vd. 18:51). Hier finden wir einen deutlichen Zusammenhang mit den Gathas[32].

2.2.2. Auffallend ist, daß Mithra, der sonst in dieser Periode seine alte, neben Ahura Mazdā, dominierende Stellung wieder gewonnen hat und in der mitteliranischen Apokalyptik eine große Rolle spielt, hier in der jungavestischen Apokalyptik nicht einmal erwähnt wird. Wir werden aber später (§ 4.2.1.1. und vgl. § 4.3.2.2.) sehen, daß Mithra tatsächlich *nicht* aus der jungavestischen Apokalyptik verschwunden war. Ferner haben wir, wie Sven Hartman hervorgehoben hat, mit einer anderen Gestalt zu rechnen, von der wir in der folgenden Periode konkretere Angaben bekommen, nämlich Gaya, bzw. Gaya marətan[33]. Der *Name Gaya marətan* hat sich, wie Hartman unterstreicht, aus zwei separaten Wörtern in Y. 30:6 entwickelt. Hier lesen wir nämlich über das Wirken der Dämonen:

at aēšəməm həndvārəntā,	Dann liefen sie zusammen zu Aēšma,
yā bąnayən ahūm marətānō[34].	um durch ihn das Leben der Menschen zu verderben.

Hier finden wir aber das Wort *ahū*, nicht *gaya*, verwendet. Es ist darum zweifelhaft, ob man mit Hartman sagen kann: "die Wörter selbst, aus denen die Namen Gaya und Gaya marətan bestehen, müssen aus den Gāthā-Hymnen herstammen, näher bezeichnet aus Kap. 30 des Yasna"[35]. In der Tat lesen wir Y. 30:4:

atcā hyat tā həm mainyū jasaētəm, paourvīm	Und als diese beiden Geister zusammentra-
dazdē	fen, da setzten sie das Erste Leben
gaēmcā ajyāitīmcā.	und das Nicht-Leben fest.

Man müßte dann annehmen, daß die "jungavestischen" Theologen *pauroyam gayam* (so zu lesen), das Erste Leben, mit *ajyāitīm,* das Nicht-Leben, einerseits mit *ahūm marətānō* kombiniert und andererseits daraus

---

[32] Vgl. Lommel 1930, 225 gegen den Versuch, die Kontinuität zu bestreiten.

[33] *Gaya marətan* > mir. Gayōmart, gelehrtes Lw., sprechechte Form Gēhmurd.

[34] Das Wort *marətānō* ist Gen. Sing. Coll. = das Menschengeschlecht.

[35] Vgl. S. S. Hartman in diesem Band § 2.1.

einen neuen Begriff, *gaya marətan,* geschaffen haben. Prinzipiell meine ich aber, daß Hartman das Richtige gesehen hat. Er hat auch die Aufmerksamkeit auf die Stellen Y. 26:10; 59:27; Yt. 13:145 gelenkt, wo wir den Ausdruck finden:

hača gayāṯ marəϑnāṯ ā saošyantāṯ vərəϑraynaṯ[36].   Von Gaya marətan bis zum siegreichen Saošyant.

Wie Hartman hervorhebt, wird damit der Beginn und das Ende der Weltgeschichte angegeben. Ich will dies dahin qualifizieren, daß wir *vor* Gaya marətan mit Gaya zu rechnen haben, wie Hartman selbst dargelegt hat. Also leitet Gaya marətan die spätere Weltperiode ein, die die eigentliche Geschichte darstellt. Hierbei sei nur bemerkt, daß die Schöpfung des "Sterblichen Lebens", d.h. des kosmischen Urmenschen, die 9000-Jahr-Periode einleitet, der nach der späteren Apokalyptik eine 3000-Jahr-Periode vorangegangen ist.

Für das Verhältnis von Zarathustra, Gaya marətan und Saošyant verweise ich auf Prof. Hartmans Darlegungen[37].

2.3. Zusammenfassung der Paragraphen 1. und 2.

2.3.1. In der Geschichte der iranischen Religion ist Zarathustra der erste Apokalyptiker. Er geht indessen von schon indo-iranischen Voraussetzungen aus. Aber die alte zyklische Zeitauffassung hat er in eine lineare verwandelt. Die Weltentwicklung geht ihrem Ende entgegen. Zwei Kategorien von Motiven sind mit diesem Weltende verbunden: einerseits gibt es eine kriegerische Entscheidung zwischen den guten und den bösen Mächten, andererseits treten uns die naturhaften Elemente Feuer und geschmolzenes Metall entgegen, die sozusagen die Rolle eines kosmischen Schlußordals spielen.

Zwischen den beiden streitenden Parteien wird Gott, Ahura Mazdā, Gerechtigkeit walten lassen und Belohnung und Strafe verteilen. Die sowohl im Kosmos wie in der Gesellschaft in Unordnung gebrachte Ordnung, die Wahrhaftigkeit (*Aša*), wird wieder hergestellt. Die Saošyanten werden mit ihrer Weisheit kommen, die gewaltigen Richtersprüche bringend. Unter ihnen ist Zarathustra, der seiner Gemeinde "Nutzen", d.h. Heil verschafft, aber es gibt auch andere, deren Namen und Herkunft wir nicht kennen. Die Gerechten gehen nach dem Tode über die Brücke der Entscheidung, die Činvat-Brücke, in das himmlische Dasein hinein. Die Bösen Mächte dagegen, Ahra Mainyu und Aēšma (die Raserei) an der Spitze, werden für ihre Sünde durch Strafe büßen.

---

[36] Vgl. S. S. Hartman in diesem Band § 2.1.2.1.; ausführlicher *idem* 1953, 33 und 35.
[37] Vgl. S. S. Hartman in diesem Band § 2.

Der Endkampf wird schon hier eingeleitet. Zarathustra ermahnt seine Anhänger, die Feinde mit der Waffe zu zerhauen. Sie streiten, um die Welt *fraša* zu machen, sie durch Stärkung zu erneuern. Dadurch kommt die Vollendung (*ākərəti*) zustande.

2.3.2. Eine erstaunliche Kontinuität herrscht in der Apokalyptik der Gathas, der Gesänge Zarathustras, und derjenigen des sog. jüngeren Avesta. Zwei neue Motive treten indessen in der jungavestischen Apokalyptik auf, wobei jedoch zu bemerken ist, daß die Gathas keine Lehrtraktate sind, wenn sie auch immer auf die Lehre Zarathustras anspielen. Sie geben also keine zusammenfassende Darstellung seiner Lehre. Mit diesem Vorbehalt haben wir die uns nicht früher bekannten Motive der Apokalyptik betrachtet: die Auferstehung der Toten und die voll entwickelte Lehre von den Saošyanten.

Die Lehre von der Auferstehung ist ein wiederkehrendes Thema in den Yašts, den alten Opfergesängen. Es liegt auf der Hand, daß dieses Thema mit der gathischen Vorstellung von der Himmelfahrt der Seele nur schwer zu vereinbaren ist.

Was den Begriff Saošyant betrifft, wird er jetzt näher fixiert. Eine ganze Mythologie verbindet die Saošyant-Vorstellung mit Zarathustra. Man rechnet mit drei Söhnen Zarathustras, die nacheinander in mythischer Weise durch Jungfrauengeburt geboren werden; Zarathustras Sperma, in dem See Kansaoya bewahrt, befruchtet zu drei verschiedenen Epochen eine badende Jungfrau. Die Namen der Saošyanten, die symbolisch sind, werden aus den Texten herausgelesen. Der dritte Saošyant, der das Weltende einführt, ist der Erlöser *par excellence*. Vor dem Saošyant Astvat-Arta, der die siegreiche Keule schwingt, fliehen Aēšma mit der blutigen Keule und seine Genossen, die Wahrheit wird die Lüge besiegen, das Gute Denken besiegt das Böse Denken, Hunger und Durst werden von Heilsein und Unsterblichkeit besiegt. Die gathischen Heilvollen Unsterblichen, die Ameša Spentas, treten als Mitkämpfer des Saošyant auf. Auch hier endet alle Weltentwicklung mit der doppelten Ausmündung: die Guten Mächte siegen im Endkampf über die Bösen.

Zuletzt soll darauf hingewiesen werden, daß eine feste Chronologie der letzten Zeiten schon herausgearbeitet wird.

3. Das sassanidische Avesta und die Pahlaviliteratur

3.1. Das parthische Schrifttum

In den früheren Kapiteln war von "Avesta" und "avestisch" als von wohlbekannten Begriffen die Rede. Es bedarf aber einer näheren Darlegung, um klarzumachen, was wir unter diesen Begriffen zu verstehen haben, weil offenbar die Vorstellungen, die man sich in der Iranistik fernstehenden Kreisen darüber macht, oft nicht korrekt und jedenfalls höchst unzureichend sind.

Man ist sich nunmehr darüber einig, daß man von einem Avesta *vor* der *sassanidischen Periode* (226−652 n. Chr.) nicht sprechen kann. Es handelt sich hier um den Prozeß einer Kanonbildung, deren einzelne Phasen wir nur unvollständig verfolgen können, deren Resultat uns aber bekannt ist und über deren entscheidende Momente wir gewisse Kenntnisse besitzen.

Wir gehen von den bahnbrechenden Forschungen Nybergs, Baileys und Wikanders aus, deren Resultate wir schon früher zusammenzufassen und weiterzuführen versucht haben[38].

3.1.1. Zuerst haben wir die *parthische* oder *arsakidische Periode* (248 v. Chr. −226 n. Chr.) zu betrachten. Träger der heiligen Überlieferungen im Partherreich waren die medischen Magier, die ihre Stellung als alleinherrschende Priesterschaft aus der *achämenidischen Zeit* (550−331 v. Chr.) geerbt und eher gestärkt hatten[39].

Die alte Art des Tradierens im Iran war eine mündliche Überlieferung[40]. Das bedeutet indessen nicht, daß die Begegnung mit der Schriftkultur im Vorderen Orient und im Mittelmeerraum gar keine schriftliche Überlieferung geschaffen hätte. Im Gegenteil! Wir besitzen Notizen, die zeigen, daß es in parthischer Zeit heilige Bücher unter den Magiern gab.

In der Schilderung, die Pausanias V 27,6 von dem Feuerdienst der in Kleinasien lebenden iranischen Magier gibt, heißt es, daß der amtierende Magier "in barbarischer Sprache" einen Gott anruft und dabei ein Buch benutzt. Diese Angabe aus der Zeit um 150 n. Chr. läßt erkennen, daß eine heilige Schrift, wahrscheinlich vom Charakter der Yašts-Texte[41], im Ritual der Magier verwendet wurde[42].

In noch frühere Zeit würden wir durch die sogenannten "Orakel des Hystaspes" versetzt werden, die auf 100 v. Chr. datiert werden können[43] und auf die wir unten (§ 4.3.2.) ausführlich zurückkommen, wenn wir mit einiger Sicherheit sagen könnten, daß diese Orakel schriftlich fixiert waren, als sie noch in iranischer Sprache kursierten. Leider fehlen uns alle entspre-

---

[38] Vgl. Nyberg 1938, 404–429; Bailey 1943, 149–194; Wikander 1946, 125–191; Widengren 1965, 197–199, 245–259; 1968a, 36–53.

[39] Über die Magier in der medischen und achämenidischen Zeit vgl. die grundlegenden Analysen Nybergs 1938, 335 ff., 374 ff., und über sie in der parthischen Zeit Widengren 1965, 174 ff.; Wikander 1946, 83, 89 ff.

[40] Es ist das große Verdienst Nybergs, diese Tatsache als erster stark unterstrichen zu haben. Bailey 1943, 149 ff. hat dazu viel Material geliefert.

[41] Darüber vgl. Widengren 1965, 197.

[42] Diese offenkundige Tatsache kann man nicht wegdeuten, vgl. Bidez-Cumont 1938, I, 90.

[43] Für eine kurze Diskussion der Datierung vgl. Widengren 1965, 199 Anm. 1 (gegen Windisch 1929 und Bidez-Cumont 1938, I, 217 ff. und II, 362 Anm. 3).

chenden Kriterien. Wir wissen nur, daß sie in griechischer Sprache als Buch gelesen wurden[44], aber ob diese Übersetzung von einer mündlichen oder schriftlichen Quelle herstammt, wissen wir leider nicht[45].

3.1.2. Im Übergang zwischen *parthischer* und *sassanidischer* Zeit gab es Schriften, die angeblich die Lehren Zarathustras, von seinen Schülern aufgezeichnet, wiedergaben. Davon wußte Mani, der diese Angabe mitteilt[46]. Also waren zur Zeit Manis gewisse Religionsurkunden in iranischer Sprache bekannt[47], die unter dem Namen Zarathustras kursierten. In Übereinstimmung damit spricht der manichäische Text M 16 von "einem zoroastrischen Buche" (*zardustagān nibēg*)[48], und Mani gibt ja auch an, daß er die Schriften der früheren Gottesoffenbarer, unter denen nach ihm sich auch Zarathustra befindet, seinen eigenen Offenbarungsurkunden einverleibt habe[49]. Das bekannte sog. Zarathustra-Fragment, M 7,82–118[50] führt Zarathustra selbst als redend ein, legt also die gnostische Botschaft dieses Textes in den Mund des Stifters und könnte *vielleicht* eine der erwähnten zoroastrischen Schriften sein[51].

Auch die Mithrasmysterien kennen in spätparthischer Zeit heilige Schriften. Die Mithrasmagier im Mithräum zu Dura (eine Stadt, die sich mit Intervallen bis 165 n. Chr. in parthischem Besitz befand), die in parthischer Tracht abgebildet sind, hatten in der linken Hand in der Tat eine Buchrolle[52]. Weissagungen über Mithra können also sehr wohl auch schriftlich verbreitet gewesen sein.

Mit dem Zoroastrismus konkurrierte im Partherreich die alte Religion der medischen Magier, nämlich der Zervanismus[53]. Dieser Umstand zeigt, daß der Zervanismus der herrschende Religionstypus unter den Parthern war, als Mani, der von parthischen Eltern geboren war, seine erste Jugend erlebte. Möglich ist, daß die zervanitische apokalyptische Literatur (ebenso

---

[44] Justinus Martyr, Apol. I 44,12.

[45] Meine persönliche Auffassung ist, daß die Quelle eine Schrift war.

[46] Kephalaia, S. 7:27 ff.　　[47] So richtig Cumont 1933, 153 f.　　[48] Müller 1904, 94.

[49] Kephalaia, Kap. 154; T II D 126; vgl. Andreas-Henning 1933, 295 f. [4 f.]. Ausführlicher Schmidt-Polotsky 1933, 41 f. [40 f.], 59 f. [58 f.]. Später Puech 1949, 61 f.

[50] Andreas-Henning 1934, 872 f. [27 f.].

[51] Selbstverständlich könnten ja auch die Manichäer Zarathustra die Offenbarung zugeschrieben haben; vgl. über das Fragment Henning in Andreas-Henning 1934, 872 [27] Anm. 1, der – etwas zu apodiktisch – nur die zweite Möglichkeit zugeben will.

[52] Vgl. die Abbildungen in Rostovtseff et alii 1939, Pl. XVI–XVII.

[53] Für den Zervanismus als die Religion der medischen Magier vgl. Nyberg 1938, 374 ff., 380 ff., 388, wo er dieses Verhältnis klar dargelegt hat. Für den Zervanismus in der parthischen Periode vgl. Widengren 1965, 214 ff. und für den Zervanismus als den iranischen Hintergrund des Manichäismus die einzelnen Bemerkungen in *idem* 1965, 299 ff. und in *idem* 1961, 48–76, systematischer und ausführlicher aber in *idem* 1977, X–XXV sowie in *idem* 1978, 287 f., 302–309 und 312–315. Zwei Jahre später als Nyberg hat Cumont (offenbar von ihm unabhängig) gesehen, daß der Zervanismus die Religion der Magier war, vgl. Bidez-Cumont 1938, I, 72.

wie die Weisheitsliteratur) schriftlich fixiert war und daß die zarathustrischen "Bücher" nichts anderes als zervanitisch gefärbte Traktate oder Übersetzungen avestischer Texte waren. Dieses Problem wird später (§ 3.3.) diskutiert werden.

3.1.3. Die Forschungen Wikanders haben gezeigt, daß die epische Literatur im Iran die mythische voraussetzt[54]. Tatsächlich besitzen wir einen kleinen epischen Text (AZ), in parthischer Sprache geschrieben und ursprünglich poetisch gestaltet[55]. Es war außerdem noch möglich, einen zervanitischen Text in Bdhn als einen ursprünglichen epischen Text aufzuzeigen[56]. Auf den avestischen Hintergrund solcher epischer Texte und ihre literarische und sprachliche Abhängigkeit von Avesta werden wir unten (§ 4.2.1.) ausführlich eingehen. Aber schon hier muß gesagt werden, daß sie von den Yašt-Texten inspiriert worden sind und mit ihnen nahe zusammenhängen. Der Hintergrund ist also das "jüngere" Avesta. Ob sie schon schriftlich fixiert waren, ist schwer zu sagen. Aber weil schon damals heilige Schriften kursierten, ist diese Annahme ansprechend. Das Problem müssen wir aber in einem anderen Kontext näher behandeln (vgl. unten § 3.3.).

3.2. Die zoroastrische Literatursprache

3.2.1. Das sassanidische Avesta war mit einer kommentierenden Übersetzung versehen, die man *zand* nennt. Dieses Wort bedeutet "Wissen" und ist die mir. Form des avest. *zanti*[57]. Der Terminus gehört dem mparth. Dialekt an, denn wir finden dort das entsprechende Verbum *zānādan* (M), und *frazānag* (M), Weiser, ein Wort, das auch in der zoroastrischen Literatur vorkommt. Sonst entspricht dort diesem Stamm *zān-*, aus dem avest. *zan-*[58], der mpers. Stamm *dān-*, aus apers. *dan-*[59], wovon wir *dānak*, Weiser, usw. finden, Formen, die sehr oft im zoroastrischen Schrifttum vorkommen.

Dieses Beispiel ist typisch. Die kommentierte Übersetzung *zand* war in dem, was wir Buchpahlavi nennen, abgefaßt[60].

---

[54] Vgl. Wikander 1950.

[55] Das hat Benveniste 1932 bahnbrechend aufgezeigt, auch wenn man seine Rekonstruktion eines poetischen Originals und seine metrische Analyse nicht gutheißen kann, – vor allem deswegen nicht, weil er sich sassanidischer Dialektformen anstatt parthischer bedient. Vgl. ferner § 4.2.1. mit Anm. 129.

[56] Vgl. Widengren 1967a, bes. 346. Vgl. ferner unten § 4.2.1.1.

[57] AirWb 1660.   [58] AirWb 1659.

[59] AirWb 1659 s. v. *zan-* sondert nicht diese zu zwei verschiedenen Dialekten gehörenden Formen.

[60] Diese Sprache ist eine *Literatursprache,* durch Mischung der zwei Dialekte mparth. (NW)

3.2.2. Dieses Verhältnis, das in unserem Zusammenhang eine wichtige Rolle spielt, können wir durch einige Beispiele, die das Vorkommen des Terminus *zand* komplettieren, näher illustrieren.

In der apokalyptischen Chronologie hat der Begriff "Winter" eine dem Terminus "Jahr" entsprechende Funktion zu erfüllen, wie wir sehen werden (§ 5.1.2.#(5) und vgl. z. B. Bahm. Yt. II 31, 41; III 11). Das mpers. Wort ist *damistān*, aber z. B. in der zervanitischen Apokalypse Zātspr. XXXIV 32 kommt die mparth. Form *zamistān* vor[61]. Ähnlich verhält es sich mit mparth. *zamīk,* Erde, vgl. z. B. Bahm. Yt. II 48, 52f., wo die mpers. Form *damīk* ist[62].

In den Schilderungen der Kämpfe in der Endzeit begegnen gewisse interessante Ausdrücke. Wir werden uns später (§ 4.2.2.2.) mit den sog. "Starkarmigen" bekannt machen, die in DkM 665,18f. *stavr bāzāi* heißen. Hier ist *bāzāi* mparth., wie auch das gewöhnlichere *bāzūk*[63], was der mpers. Form *bādūk* entspricht[64]. Die eschatologischen Feinde sind ferner als *vičārt-vars,* "mit zerteiltem (gcflochtcncm) Haar" charakterisiert, was in Bahm. Yt. sehr gewöhnlich ist[65]. Sowohl *vičārt*, zerteilt, wie *vars*, Haar, sind mparth. Formen, die in mpers. **guzārt* bzw. **gurs* ihre Entsprechungen besitzen[66].

Die Keule, die wir schon in der jungavestischen Apokalyptik (§ 2.2.1.) gefunden haben, spielt, wie wir (§ 4.2.2.4. – § 4.2.2.5.) sehen werden, in den Schilderungen der Pahlaviliteratur eine wichtige Rolle. Der Name *gurz* (*i gāv-sār*), die Keule (mit dem Stierkopf genannt), ist eine mpers. Form;

---

und mpers. (SW) entstanden. Näheres dazu unten § 3.2.3. Schon Tedesco 1921, 249 hat, wenn auch mit ungenügendem Material, festgestellt, daß Buchpahlavi mparth. Elemente enthält. Vgl. Nyberg 1931a, VIII und Bailey 1953, 176, wo als drittes Element auch Sogdisch erwähnt wird, das indessen nur unbedeutende Beiträge zum Wortschatz geliefert hat. Ergänzungen bei Lenz 1926; ferner Einzelbeiträge in der späteren Forschung. Das Buchpahlavi verdient eine dialektologische Spezialuntersuchung. Den Charakter des Buchpahlavi als eine Mischsprache hat Nyberg in seinem Unterricht stark hervorgehoben.

[61] *Zamistān* < avest. *zyam, zəm;* AirWb 1699. Nicht bei MacKenzie 1971, wo sich indessen die kürzere Form *zam* (< *zəm*) findet, S. 97.

[62] Die Form *damīk* ist nicht bei MacKenzie 1971 verzeichnet; man findet sie angeführt bei Nyberg 1974, 57a s. v. *damīk*. Eine deutliche Schreibung findet man an mehreren Stellen in AVN und HN, vgl. West-Haug 1874, 271.

[63] *Bāzūk* < *bāzu-,* AirWb 955. Bei MacKenzie 1971, 18 wird *bāzā* (sic) verzeichnet; zur Form vgl. Geiger-Kuhn 1896, I 2, 172 § 104 A 2), wo viele solche Formen sich finden. Die Form *bāzūk* lebt in *bāzū* fort. Molé 1967, 268a gibt unrichtig die Form *bāzāδ*; vgl. auch unten § 4.2.2.2. mit Anm. 180–181.

[64] Vgl. Andreas-Barr 1933, 123a [35a].   [65] Vgl. unten § 4.2.2.8.

[66] Diese mpers. Formen leben in der npers. Sprache fort, denn laut Geiger-Kuhn 1896, I 2, 64:3a (vgl. auch Steingass) ist *gurs* npers. bewahrt; in der Pahlaviliteratur habe ich sie aber bisher nicht finden können. In der manichäischen Literatur gibt es allerdings *guzār* in der Bedeutung "Entscheidung", vgl. Henning 1933–34, 226 Anm. 27. Zweifelhaft ist die Lesung *gars,* vgl. Geiger-Kuhn 1896, I, 2, 64:3a). Die mparth. Form *vars* (armen. Lw. *vars*) < avest. *varəsa*, AirWb 1374. Nyberg 1974, 204a hätte den mparth. Ursprung unterstreichen sollen.

wir finden aber in der Pahlaviliteratur auch die mparth. Form *vazr*, MX XLIII 9[67].

Ein wichtiges Wort in der Apokalyptik ist *Leben*. Lebendig und Leben können entweder *zīvandak* bzw. *zīvistan* oder *zīndak* bzw. *zīstan* heißen. Jene Formen sind ursprünglich mparth. (*žīvandak*[68] ist ein Präs. Part. von *žīvistar*[69]), während diese mpers. sind. Die mparth. Formen haben jedoch die mpers. Lautentwicklung *ž* > *z* mitgemacht, was den gegenseitigen Einfluß unterstreicht[69a].

3.2.3. Die mparth. Formen entstammen, wie soeben dargelegt wurde, der avestischen Sprache; die aus Ostiran kommenden Parther haben sie von dort mitbringen und den typischen Lautbestand bewahren können. Im Westen haben sie sich in Medien niedergelassen und wohl die medische Sprache im Ganzen übernommen. Medien wurde die Heimat der Parther und medisch ihre Sprache. Hier im NW Iran, wo die medischen Magier der zervanitischen Religion huldigten, entwickelte sich der parthische Dialekt als gesprochene und geschriebene Sprache. Hierbei spielte die alte medische Sprache sicherlich die entscheidende Rolle, aber avestische Einflüsse sind leicht festzustellen. Diese können indessen schon die medischen Magier rezipiert haben[70].

Die mpers. Termini setzen dagegen die apers. Lautentwicklung fort und bewahren als mpers. Sprachstufe den apers. Lautbestand.

Die zoroastrische Literatursprache, die wir Pahlavi nennen, ist also eine durch Mischung von zwei Dialekten, mparth. (NW) und mpers. (SW), entstandene Sprache, wobei aber die Struktur der Sprache vom mpers. Dialekt, d. h. der Sprache der herrschenden sassanidischen Dynastie, geprägt ist, während viele Wörter oder Wortformen dem mpath. Dialekt entstammen. Der *Name* Pahlavi deutet indessen auf parthischen Ursprung hin: *pahlavīk* < *parθavīk*, "parthisch". Schematisch kann die Sprachentwicklung durch ein Falldiagramm veranschaulicht werden (siehe S. 92).

Wie ist dann diese zoroastrische Literatursprache entstanden, die wir, um sie von anderen Typen von Pahlavi zu unterscheiden, als Buch-Pahlavi bezeichnen? Um diese Frage beantworten zu können, müssen wir einiges über die Kanonbildung sagen.

---

[67] Vgl. Widengren 1960, 39, wo der parthische Ursprung des Wortes notiert ist. Noch in Nyberg 1974, 207b vermissen wir eine solche Bemerkung.

[68] *Žīvandak* < avest. *jīva-*, Präs. von *gay-*, AirWb 502.

[69] Vgl. Ghilain 1939, 50.   [69a] Vgl. unten Anm. 221.

[70] Für parthisch als die Sprache des nordwestlichen, "medischen" Irans, vgl. Reichelt 1927, 42. Ich habe dieses Verhältnis in Widengren 1960, 38 hervorgehoben. Wohlbemerkt finden sich medische Sprachelemente schon in der altpersischen Sprache, wie die Forschung schon längst notiert hat. Zur Charakterisierung des Altmedischen vgl. Mayrhofer 1968 und Eilers 1972.

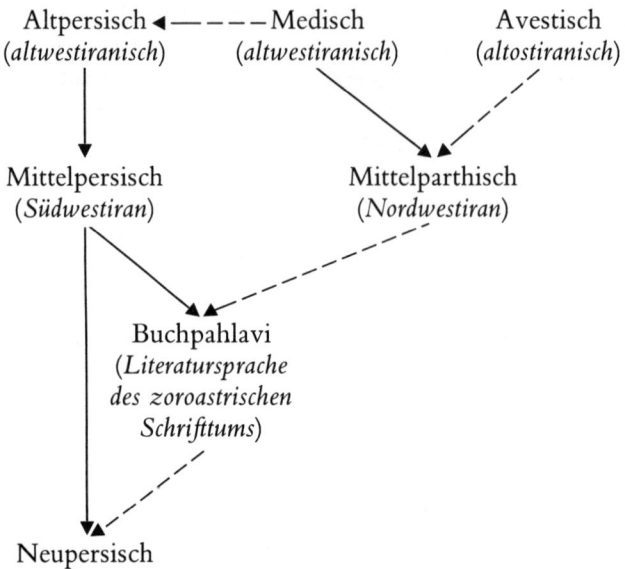

3.3. Die Kanonbildung und die zoroastrische Staatskirche[71]

Die zoroastrische Staatskirche ist durch eine Fusion von zwei mächtigen Priesterschaften zustande gekommen[72]: die medischen Magier, später Mobads genannt[73], mit Šīz (NW) als Kultzentrum schlossen sich mit den persischen Herbads[74], die in Istaxr (SW) ihren kultischen Hauptsitz besaßen, zusammen[75].

Die *schriftliche* Überlieferung der Magier-Mobads (die wir in der Fortsetzung Mobads nennen) wurde dabei mit der *mündlichen* der Herbads vereint. Das ist das unwiderrufliche Ergebnis der bahnbrechenden Forschungen

---

[71] Vgl. die Darlegungen in Widengren 1965, 245–259 und vor allem 1968a, 36–53.

[72] Vgl. Widengren 1965, 260–265.

[73] *Magu-pati*, "Magierherr", *mōgpat*, mit SW-Entwicklung > *mōvpat* > *mōpat*. Vgl. Nyberg 1974, 122b, s. v. *magu* und *magu-pat*, eine klare Darlegung des Unterschieds zwischen den mparth. und den mpers. Lautformen, die beide in den zwei verschiedenen armen. Lw. wiederkehren. MacKenzie 1971, 56 ist nicht nur inkorrekt, sondern auch inkonsequent, denn er gibt einerseits die Form *mowbed,* andererseits aber *mōymard,* trotzdem daß beide Wörter in derselben Weise geschrieben sind: *mgw*! Das von MacKenzie 1967 und 1971 angewandte System der Transkription geht auf das von Henning 1958 entwickelte Prinzip zurück. Warum ausgerechnet die Lautgestalt der mittelpersischen Sprache, so wie sie im 3. Jh. n. Chr. aussah, als normierend gegen die Orthographie der Inschriften, der literarischen Texte und der Lehnwörter im Armenischen zu gelten hat, ist unbegreiflich. Das mitteliranische Stadium der Sprache existierte ja Jahrhunderte früher. Aber solche Fragen können selbstverständlich im Rahmen dieser Monographie nicht diskutiert werden.

[74] *Hērpat* < *ēhrpat* < avest. *aēϑrapati,* AirWb 20.

[75] Für Šīz und Istaxr vgl. Wikander 1946, Register s. v. Istachr und Šīz.

Wikanders. Wir haben ja oben (§ 3.1.2.) festgestellt, daß die medischen Magier in parthischer Zeit *tatsächlich* heilige Schriften besaßen[76].

Wikander hat ferner behauptet, daß diese *schriftliche* Überlieferung eben *zand* genannt wurde[77]. Es ist gut verständlich, daß – wie wir (§ 3.2.1.) sahen – *zand* eine mparth. Form ist, denn die Mobads als die unmittelbaren Nachfolger der medischen Magier, die im Partherreich tätig waren, sprachen und schrieben den mparth. Dialekt (NW), der in Medien herrschend war. Diese schriftliche Überlieferung *zand* war im Kultzentrum zu Šiz in Media Atropatene (Āturpātakān) aufbewahrt[78]. Laut der in Dk überlieferten Geschichtslegende wurde die *mündliche* Überlieferung, später *apastāk*[78a] genannt, in Istaxr in einer Schrift bewahrt. Alexander verbrannte aber dieses Exemplar (*apastāk*) und raubte das andere, in Šiz befindliche (*zand*), weg und sandte es nach Rom: *dēn i mazdēsnān zand stat ō Hrōm frēstāt, apastāk sōxt* (Bdn A 214:12f.). Also stellen *apastāk* und *zand* die zwei Formen der Religion der Mazdayasnier (*dēn i mazdēsnān*) dar; *zand* wird hier – gegen die Gewohnheit – an erster Stelle genannt. Die Verbindung *apastāk* – Istaxr gewinnen wir durch die Brandstiftung Alexanders in Persepolis[79].

Die Schrift in Šiz wird das Original (*bun*) genannt, DkM (III) 405:18[80].

Die religiöse Überlieferung wird unter Artaxšēr I. wieder hergestellt, DkM (III) 406:5 und (IV) 412:11−16. Wichtig zu notieren ist aber, daß Dk IV schon mit einer Sammlung unter dem Arsakidenkönig Valagaš rechnet, DkM 412:5−11. Damit kann nur Valagaš III. (148−191 n. Chr) gemeint sein[81], was tatsächlich mit den angeführten Angaben über heilige Schriften in der Partherzeit gut übereinstimmen würde. Es ist durchaus möglich, daß diese Schriftsammlung in parthischer Zeit den Namen *zand* führte[82].

3.3.1. Die *erste wirkliche Redaktion* von schriftlicher und mündlicher Überlieferung von *zand* und *apastāk* kam aber erst unter Artaxšēr I. (224−240 n. Chr.) und Šāhpuhr I. (240−272 n. Chr.) (DkM (IV) 412:17, 20−21) zustande, denn zu dieser Zeit wirkte Kartēr, der Gründer der zoroastrischen Staatskirche[83].

Eine Schwierigkeit in der Beweisführung Wikanders hat Hartman nach-

---

[76] Diese von Wikander nicht verwerteten Tatsachen bestätigen also seine Resultate.

[77] Wikander 1946, 141.

[78] Vgl. Wikander 1946, 139 ff.

[78a] Für das Wort *apastāk* und dessen Bedeutung vgl. die gründliche Untersuchung von Belardi 1979, wo die zwei früheren Deutungen des Wortes überzeugend kritisiert werden und dazu eine neue Erklärung vorgeschlagen wird.

[79] Meine Bemerkung. Sie erklärt die Legende von der Verbrennung des *apastāk*.

[80] Zum folgenden vgl. die synoptische Zusammenstellung der Angaben in Dk III und IV in Wikander 1946, 134 ff. und in Widengren 1965, 246 f.

[81] Vgl. Nyberg 1938, 408.

[82] Dies ist die natürliche Erklärung der Bezeichnung *zand* für die Šiz-Überlieferung.

[83] Vgl. Widengren 1965, 274 f.

gewiesen[84]. Wikander erwähnt (S. 132f.), daß laut Fārsnāmah (S. 49; tatsächlich 49−50) das Heilige Buch sich in der "Burg des Archivs" (*diz i nifišt* [sic!])[85] befindet. Die Burg aber ist in *Istaxr* belegen. Wikander observierte indes nicht, daß dieses Buch, von Vištāspa empfangen, von Zardušt als *zand* gebracht wurde (S. 50:16−20); ein Buch, in dem die ganze Weisheit auf 12000 Ochsenhäuten mit gold(enen Buchstaben) geschrieben war. Es wird aber in der Fortsetzung gesagt, daß dieses Buch, aus *zand* und *pāzand* bestehend, also nicht nur *zand*, sondern auch *pāzand*, was später den Superkommentar bezeichnet, in Istaxr deponiert wurde (S. 51:2).

Zuerst bemerken wir, daß Zarathustra den *zand* gebracht hat. Hier sollen wir die sozusagen orthodoxe Ausdrucksweise AVN I 7 vergleichen: *ēn dēn čigōn hamāk apastāk u zand*, "diese Religion, nämlich der ganze *apastāk* und *zand*", worauf die Notiz über die mit goldener Tinte beschrifteten 12000 Ochsenhäuten folgt. Die exklusive Erwähnung von *zand* in Fārsnāmah und die damit zusammenhängende Nichterwähnung des *apastāk* führt selbstverständlich auf eine *Šīz*-Tradition hin.

Die Zahl 12000 führt ebenso nach Šīz, denn 12000 ist, wie wir sehen werden, die für den Zervanismus typische Zahl der Dauer der Welt[86].

Dazu kommt die Bezeichnung "Weisheit" für dieses heilige Buch. Hier entspricht das arabische Lw. *ḥikmat* (Fārsnāmah 49:19) dem mir. *xrat*. Und die Magier von Medien haben eben ihre Lehren als "Weisheit" verbreiten wollen. Darum wird auch Zarathustra als *ḥakīm*, Weiser, bezeichnet, d. h. er ist eben ein *frazānak* (mparth.)[87].

Zuletzt soll hervorgehoben werden, daß Vištāspa bei den klassischen Autoren eben als König der Meder betrachtet wird. Das bedeutet, daß die Magier ihn sowohl wie Zarathustra als Medien zugehörig betrachtet haben[88].

Kurz gesagt: Fārsnāmah gibt eine Überlieferung wieder, die eine Šīz-Tradition für Istaxr usurpiert hat. Alles in der Überlieferung außer der Lokalisierung in Istaxr bestätigt die Analyse Wikanders.

Kartēr war ursprünglich ein Hērbad, der seine Verbindung mit Istaxr immer bewahrte, wurde aber später auch ein Mobad, vereint also in seiner Person die Würde der zwei Priesterschaften[89]. Ebenso wurde *zand* mit *apastāk* vereint. Dieser Prozeß der ersten Redaktion begann um die Mitte des 3. Jh. n. Chr. Die Dēnkart-Tradition in Dk III und IV spricht von Artaxšēr I., die in Dk IV auch von Šāhpuhr I., als treibende Kräfte bei der

---

[84] Prof. S. S. Hartman hat mich auf sie aufmerksam gemacht, wofür ich ihm an dieser Stelle danken möchte.

[85] Wikander schreibt *diz i nipišt*.   [86] Vgl. unten § 5.1.2.

[87] Vgl. Widengren 1974, bes. 508–514.

[88] Vgl. Lactantius, Instit. VII 15, 19: *Hystaspes, qui fuit Medorum rex antiquissimus*, … Vgl. Nyberg 1938, 401f. und Widengren 1965, 232–236; 1978, 287f.

[89] Vgl. Widengren 1965, 262, in der Dikussion mit Wikander 1946, der grundlegend bleibt.

Sammlung der Heiligen Schrift. Wikander legte Nachdruck auf die drei Könige, die Bahrām hießen.

Die in DkM (IV) 412:17−22 gegebene Notiz ist für unser Thema sehr wichtig. Sie teilt über die Aktivität Šāhpuhrs I. folgendes mit[90]:

> *nipēkīhā-č i hač dēn bē apar bižiškīh u staryumbišnīh u čandišn u zamān u giyāk u gōhr, dahišn, bavišn, vināsišn, yatak-vihīrīh u gavākīh, apārīk kirrōkīh u afzār andar Hindūkān u Hrōm apārīk-ič zamīkīhā pargandak būt, apāč ō ham āvurt, apāk apastāk apāč handāxt, u har hān druyist paččēn ō hān ganž i Šīzīkān dāt.*

(Šāhpuhr) ließ die Schriften aus der Religion über Heilkunde und Sternkunde und Bewegung und Zeit und Raum und Substanz, Schöpfung, Werden und Vergehen, Qualitätsveränderung und Zunehmen und sonstige Handwerke und Mittel, die in Indien und (Ost-)Rom und in den übrigen Ländern zerstreut waren, wieder zusammenbringen und (sie) wieder mit dem *apastāk* vereinigen und befahl, von allem eine zuverlässige Abschrift in jener Schatzkammer zu Šīz niederzulegen.

Wir notieren hier den von Wikander hervorgehobenen Gegensatz zwischen *nipēk*, Schrift, und *apastāk*, "Avesta", und weiterhin, daß die Schriften (*nipēkīhā*) mit dem *apastāk* vereint wurden, worauf eine zuverlässige Abschrift (*paččēn*) in Šīz deponiert wurde. Diese Textstelle zeigt unwidersprüchlich, daß Wikander recht hat.

Nicht weniger interessant ist die Angabe des Inhalts dieser *nipēkīhā*, ein Thema, mit dem sich Wikander nicht beschäftigt hat, das aber sehr wichtig ist. Die Schriften behandeln Kosmologie, Astronomie und menschliche Aktivitäten. Zu notieren ist, daß *zamān u giyāk*, Zeit und Raum, behandelt werden. Diese Angabe ist mit der Notiz bei Eudemus Rhodius (letzte Hälfte des 4. Jh. v. Chr.) zu vergleichen, wo dieser sagt, daß die Magier das intelligible und vereinigte Ganze teils *Raum*, teils *Zeit* nennen, woraus die Unterscheidung zwischen dem Guten Gott und dem Bösen Dämon oder zwischen Licht und Finsternis entstehe[91]. Hier begegnen wir einer typisch zervanitischen Anschauung[92]. Dieser Vergleich mit Eudemus läßt erkennen, daß die schriftliche Šīz-Tradition, *nipēkīhā* und *zand* genannt, zervanitische Anschauungen vertrat. Dieses Resultat kann uns nicht überraschen, weil ja die medischen Magier den Zervanismus vertraten. Richtig ist auch die Bezeichnung "Weisheit" (*ḥikmah*) in Fārsnāmah, denn die zervanitischen Magier prahlten damit, daß sie Inhaber der Weisheit (σοφία) waren, wie die klassischen Autoren uns mitteilen. Und was ist diese Weisheit (*xrat* in mir. Sprache)? Sie umfaßt nicht nur die Kenntnis der göttlichen Dinge, sondern auch Kunde von dem Ursprung und den Gesetzen der Welt, von den Eigenschaften der Natur und der Beschaffenheit des Menschen[93]. Noch

---

[90] Text nach Nyberg 1964, 109:7 ff. Die Lesung *yumbišnīh* nach *idem* 1974, 227a.

[91] Damascius, Dub. 125 bis. Vgl. unten § 5.1.2. # (4).

[92] Vgl. Widengren 1965, 149 f., wo sich eine ausführliche Diskussion findet. Vgl. schon Bousset (1912–1919), 1979, 215 f. (Hinweis D. Hellholm).

[93] Vgl. Bidez-Cumont 1938, I, 93; II, 17(B6) und Widengren 1974, 511, wo der Zusammenhang mit den Lehren über die Weisheit (*xrat*) im vorausgehenden Abschnitt dargelegt wird.

ein wichtiger Umstand ist schon hier zu notieren: im vorhandenen Avesta fehlen diese Lehren.

3.3.2. Nach der Dēnkartlegende wurde von Šāhpuhr II. (309—379/80 n. Chr.) eine *zweite Redaktion* unternommen. Der mitwirkende Priester war Āturpāt i Mahraspandān, vgl. DkM (IV) 412:2—8: Durch ein Ordal bestätigte dieser die Korrektheit der von ihm vorgetragenen Überlieferung, worauf Šāhpuhr II. die überlieferten *nask*-s neu rechnen ließ und eine Erklärung in Gegenwart auch der Andersgläubigen abgab, daß er nicht mehr einen Menschen von schlechter Religion zulassen wolle[94].

Wir können sicher sein, daß in dieser Redaktion des Avesta die zervanitischen und überhaupt kosmologischen Texte immer noch ihren Platz behielten. Das geht aus der christlichen Polemik hervor, die sich in dieser Zeit und etwa ± 500 n. Chr. gegen zervanitische Anschauungen richtet[95].

Diese Schlußfolgerung, daß nämlich die zervanitischen Lehren noch nach der Avesta-Redaktion unter Šāhpuhr II. in dem Avesta zu lesen waren, läßt sich unzweideutig beweisen durch den Wortlaut gewisser Märtyrerakten, die eben klar aussprechen, daß sie sich in *Abestāg* (spätere Form von *Apastāk*) fanden. Der Obermagier Ādurfrāzgerd führt aus "unserem Abestāg", wie er sagt, eine zervanitische Belohnungslehre an. Der Christ Ādurhormuzd und die Christin Anāhīd greifen in ihrer Polemik gegen den Obermagier eben die zervanitischen Mythen und Anschauungen an[96].

3.3.3. Die *dritte Redaktion*, die letzte sassanidische, fand unter Xosrau Anōšurvān (531—579 n. Chr.) statt. Das königliche Edikt faßt das Resultat in folgenden Worten zusammen:

ōgōn vasīhā apastāk-ēvāčīk pat apēčak gōvišnīh, nipēk-pairāyišnīk hač mātiyān-ayyātkārīh, u pātram-ič aivēnak āvāčīk andar gōvišn-ākāhēnišn dāšt ēstēt, pas-ič hamāk xānīk-dānakīh i dēn mazdēsn[96a].

(DkM (IV) 414:2—6)

Diese Stelle läßt sich folgendermaßen übersetzen[97]:

In solcher Weise ist das zum Avesta-Wort Gehörige in seinem ganzen Umfang in reiner mündlicher Überlieferung *oder* schriftgeschmückt durch die Buch-und-Denkschrift-Verfertigung *oder* in der Sprache des gemeinen Volkes durch mündliche Weitergabe bewahrt, also das ganze quellenmäßige Wissen der Religion der Mazdā-Verehrer.

---

[94] Mit Benutzung der Textgestaltung und Deutung bei Nyberg 1964, 109 und 1974, 227b s. v. *yuvat-srītak* (die Lesung *yuvat* kann ich nicht akzeptieren).

[95] Vgl. Widengren 1965, 283; Nyberg 1931, 70; Christensen 1944, 150ff.

[96] Syrischer Text: *Acta Martyrum et Sanctorum* II, 576ff.; Übersetzung bei Nöldeke 1893, 34ff., oft reproduziert, z. B. bei Bidez-Cumont 1938, II, 108ff. mit Anmerkungen.

[96a] In der Faksimileausgabe Dresden 1966 steht *pāt ram* anstatt *pātram*.

[97] Vgl. Widengren 1965, 254. Transkribierter Text und Übersetzung bei Zaehner 1955, 32 (Text), 9 (Übers.). Ich habe Zaehners Übersetzung als Basis genommen.

Hier begegnen wir drei Arten der Überlieferung:
(1) der mündlichen Überlieferung von *apastāk*;
(2) der schriftlichen Überlieferung davon;
(3) der Überlieferung in mittelpersischer Sprache in mündlicher Form.
Diese dritte Form dürfte wohl bedeuten, daß die Pahlavi-Übersetzung, so wie die komplizierte Schrift mit den aramäischen Ideogrammen mündlich zu lesen war, auch gelehrt wurde, d. h. was wir *Pāzand* nennen, nämlich Buch-Pahlavi in phonetischer Transkription. Wir erinnern hier an die Stelle Bahm. Yt. II 55, wo es heißt, daß Ōhrmazd dem Zartušt sagt:

bē xvǎh u varm bē kun pat zand⟨u⟩pāzand u vičārišn bē čāš ō hērpatān u hāvištān gōv.
Repetiere und lerne auswendig *zand* und *pāzand* und lehre die Erklärung den Herbad-s und den Schülern[98].

Noch an einer anderen wichtigen Stelle wird *zand* erwähnt, nämlich Bahm. Yt. I 7, wo Xosrau Anōšurvān die ihm bei der Avesta-Redaktion behilflichen Priester ermahnt:

u-š patmān hač-aš xvāst ku ēn yasnīhā pat nihān mā dārēt, bē pat patvand i šmāh zānd mā čāšēt. ōišān andar husrav patmān kart.
Und er verlangte von ihnen eine Übereinkunft folgendermaßen: 'Haltet nicht diese yasna-s in Verborgenheit, aber lehret nicht das *zand* außer in eurem Traditionskreis'[99]!

Man kann hier auch z. B. MX XXVI 12 vergleichen:

čigōn hač-ič patvand i ōišān pēšēnīkān i vitartak paitāk.
Wie es eben aus der Überlieferung jener früheren Männer, die hingeschieden sind, offenbar ist.

In Bahm. Yt. hat also *zand* die Stellung eines Kommentars eingenommen: *apastāk* und *zand* haben schon ihren späteren traditionellen Platz als Grundtext in avestischer Sprache und Erklärung in Pahlavisprache bekommen, wozu *pāzand* als eine Art von Superkommentar hinzukommt[100]. Diese Erklärung in Buchpahlavi ist als eine kommentierende Übersetzung zu bezeichnen.
Der Terminus *zand* hat also von einer gewissen Zeit ab seine Bedeutung verändert. Wann ist dies geschehen?

---

[98] Über *varm kartan* vgl. vor allem Bailey 1943, 159f. Das Verbum *xvastan* bedeutet eigtl. treten, aber bekommt die Bedeutung trainieren, vgl. Nyberg 1974, 221b, mit Hinweis auf AirWb 1874f. *xvah-* mit Prät. Part. Pass. *xvarta*. Bartholomae hat den Zusammenhang nicht verstanden. Diese wichtige Bedeutung "repetieren", "trainieren" fehlt bei MacKenzie 1971, 96. Bei Anklesaria IV 67 findet sich die falsche Lesung *xvǎn*.

[99] Vgl. für *patvand* Bailey 1943, 149ff. und Nyberg 1974, 159a. Ich habe früher, West in SBE folgend, mit "Verwandtschaftskreis" übersetzt, finde aber jetzt, daß diese Übersetzung eine zu enge Bedeutung gibt. Die Schüler und Priester, *hāvištān* und *hērpatān*, II 55, sind doch nicht alle verwandt.

[100] Die *Pāzandtexte* sind solche in Pahlavi geschriebenen Schriftstücke, in denen alle Worte in avest. Lettern umschrieben sind, wodurch die Lesung erleichtert wird.

3.4. Die Entwicklung in der Bedeutung von zand

3.4.1. Wann die Bedeutungsveränderung von *zand* eingetreten ist, können wir mit Sicherheit nicht sagen, aber es gibt gewisse Indizien. *Zand* entwickelte sich bedeutungsgemäß aus der Bezeichnung eines zervanitisch gefärbten Schrifttums in altiranischer Sprache der medischen Mobads, das sich zum größten Teil mit Kosmologie, Astrologie, Weltentwicklung einschließlich Apokalyptik, Makrokosmos-Mikrokosmosspekulation und zervanitischen Mythen beschäftigte, zur Bezeichnung einer kommentierenden Übersetzung von Avesta, in der die zervanitischen und kosmologischen usw. Elemente des urspr. *zand* (mit *apastāk* vereint) durch "Zensur" in der Avesta-Redaktion unter Xosrau I. ausgemerzt wurden. Den Zeitpunkt können wir mit Hilfe der christlichen Polemik in den syrischen Märtyrerakten persischer Märtyrer annähernd fixieren, denn in den späteren Mätyrerakten ist die Polemik gegen den Zervanismus verschwunden. Die Polemik richtet sich nunmehr vor allem gegen die Feuer-Verehrung[101].

Die zervanitischen Anschauungen verschwanden aber nicht, sondern wurden in der Pahlavi-Übersetzung (*zand*) beibehalten. Einen typischen Fall finden wir in Y. 30, der berühmten Zwillingsgatha, wo Avesta und Zand in V. 5–6 einen Text bieten, wo wir in der Pahlavi-Übersetzung eine zervanitische Exegese finden[102], die tatsächlich im avestischen Text nicht ohne Basis ist[103]. Nun hat aber Hartman mit Recht darauf hingewiesen, daß die Pahlavi-Übersetzung (*zand*) mit DkM 829:1−5 verglichen werden muß, wo gegen die Anschauung polemisiert wird, daß Ōhrmazd und Ahriman zwei Brüder in einem Mutterleib waren[104]. Wir müssen also damit rechnen, daß sich in der Pahlavi-Übersetzung gewisser avestischer Texte eine zervanitische Überlieferung fände, wenn uns diese Texte noch zugänglich wären.

Aus dem Avesta wurden aber eine Reihe von solchen Elementen ausgesondert. Nur einige Stellen sind zu nennen, die sich in Vd. und in Yašttexten finden. Hier wird nämlich Zervan selbst erwähnt. Zuerst notieren wir die Ausdrücke *darəyəmčiṯ aipi zrvānəm* (Yt. 13:53; 19:26) und *zrvānəm darəyō xvaδātəm* (Vd. 19:13; Y. 72:10). An der letzten Stelle steht dieser *zrvan darəyō. xvaδāta* im Gegensatz zu *zrvan akarana,* die 'Langherrschende Zeit' gegen die 'Unbegrenzte Zeit'.

Hier begegnen wir den zwei in der Pahlavi-Literatur wohlbekannten zervanitischen Begriffen: *Zurvān i dērang xvatāi* (oder *Zurvān i kanārākō-*

---

[101] Vgl. solche Akten wie die des Mār Gīwargīs § 57, wo wir eben eine Polemik gegen die Feuerverehrung antreffen.

[102] Vgl. Schaeder 1930, 288 ff. [90 ff.]; Benveniste 1932−33, 210 ff.

[103] Vgl. Widengren 1965, 75−77; 1961a, 39 f.

[104] Zaehner 1955, 429 hat versäumt, die Beobachtungen Hartmans zur Kenntnis zu nehmen und verstand darum nicht den Zusammenhang; vgl. Hartman 1953, 23−25.

mand) und *Zurvān i akanārak*[105]. Nyāyišn 1:8 spricht demgemäß von den zwei Zurvān-s.

Sehr wichtig ist die Stelle Vd. 19:29 wo es heißt[106]:

paϑ̨m zrvō-dātanąm ǰasaiti yasča drvaite yasča ašaone, činvaṯ-pərətūm mazdaδātąm.

(Die Seele) sowohl des Lügenhaften wie des Wahrhaften kommt hin zu den von Zurvan geschaffenen Pfaden, zu der Cinvat-Brücke[107].

Die unter Xosrau I. unternommene Zensur ist also bis auf die hier oben erwähnten wenigen Stellen vollständig durchgeführt. Die höchste Gottheit Zervan und die mit ihr verbundenen Anschauungen sind aus dem Avesta entfernt – soweit wir den jetzigen Bestand kontrollieren können. Diese *reservatio* ist motiviert, wie wir bald sehen werden.

3.4.2. Ein Rückblick auf die Kanon-Arbeit zeigt, daß jedes entscheidende Moment mit Maßnahmen gegen Andersdenkende vereint war.

Der *erste Kanon* unter Artaxšēr I., Šāhpuhr I. und den Bahrāms steht im Zeichen des Kampfes gegen die religiösen Minoritäten, vor allem die Manichäer (unter den Bahrāms).

Der *zweite Kanon* war mit der Verfolgung der Christen unter Šāhpuhr II. verbunden.

Der *dritte und endgültige Kanon* unter Xosrau I. fand seinen Abschluß während des Kampfes gegen die Mazdakiten.

Von dem Substantiv *zand* entwickelt sich das Wort *zandīk*, das in Pahlavi "Ketzer" bedeutet und eine reguläre adjektivische Bildung ist[108]. Wenn wir dem Wort zuerst begegnen, nämlich in der armenischen Literatur, bezeichnet es aber nicht "Ketzer" im allgemeinen, sondern eben Manichäer[109].

In MX XXX 16 wird indessen *zandīkīh* als eine schwere Sünde erwähnt und die neupers. Übersetzung definiert: *az Ahrēman u dēvān nīkī dānad u bixvāhad*, "(wer) von Ahriman und den Dämonen Gutes denkt und wünscht"[110]. Ein *zandīk* bezeichnet hier eine Person, die Ahriman und die Dämonen auch positiv bewertet. Das ist im Zervanismus der Fall. Schaeder, der sich fragt, wie man sich die semantische Entwicklung zu denken hat[111], sah aber nicht, daß die Stelle in MX XXX 16 zum Zervanismus führt und hat demzufolge nicht verstanden, daß ein genetischer Zusammenhang zwischen Zervanismus, Manichäismus und *zand* besteht[112]. Weil *zand* zer-

---

[105] Vgl. über diese Gestalten Zaehner 1955, 57 und 106.

[106] Wiedergabe der avest. Stellen bei Zaehner 1955, 275.

[107] Man muß den Genitiv als Gen. Part. verstehen; vgl. Reichelt 1909, 258 § 497 mit ähnlichen Konstruktionen, wo der Genitiv eben als Akkusativ des Ziels verwendet wird, ebenfalls mit dem Verbum *gam-* verbunden, was offenbar für Vd. charakteristisch ist. Zaehner 1955, 275: "along". Wie motiviert man diese Übersetzung?

[108] Vgl. Nyberg 1974, 229a; Geiger-Kuhn 1896, I 2, 179 für die Bildung.

[109] Vgl. Hübschmann 1897, 149:225.

[110] Vgl. Schaeder 1930, 285 [87].   [111] *Ibid.*, 285 ff. [87 ff.].

[112] Für den Zervanismus als Grundlage und Ausgangspunkt des manichäischen Systems vgl. Widengren 1977 und 1978. S. auch Anm. 53 und 265.

vanitisch gefärbt und der Zervanismus von der Orthodoxie verworfen war, mußte *zandīk* – als Vertreter des ursprünglichen *zand* – die Bedeutung "Ketzer" annehmen. Demzufolge wurden die zervanitischen Anschauungen – vielleicht doch nicht ganz vollständig – aus dem neuen *zand,* der Pahlavi-Übersetzung, entfernt.

Das sassanidische Avesta in der letzten Redaktion umfaßte 21 Nasks, von denen heute nur ein Nask, der 19., nämlich Vd., bewahrt ist. Dieser Nask ist das Werk der medischen Magier, wie Nyberg gezeigt hat[113]. *Und ausgerechnet hier finden wir die wenigen Spuren der Zervan-Verehrung.* Die kosmologischen Elemente, z. B. die Makro-Mikro-Kosmos-Spekulation, retteten sich indessen von der Zensur und wurden in Dāmdāt-Nask (Nask Nr. 4) behandelt[114]. Dieser Nask ist völlig verlorengegangen, aber der Inhalt ist in verschiedenen Teilen der Pahlavi-Literatur bewahrt, vor allem, wie wir unten (§ 6., bes. § 6.2.2.) sehen werden, im Bundahišn, der in seinen kosmogonischen Kapiteln im wesentlichen nur ein Auszug aus diesem Nask ist[115]. Ähnlich verhält es sich z. T. mit den apokalyptischen Lehren. Diese finden sich heute in vielen Pahlavi-Texten zerstreut. Reste und Andeutungen finden sich aber auch, wie wir (§ 2.) gesehen haben, im jüngeren Avesta.

3.5. Zusammenfassung unserer Resultate

Was zuerst das Priestertum betrifft, findet eine Fusion zwischen Mobads in Šīz und Hērbads in Istaxr statt.

Diese Fusion bringt sodann eine andere Fusion mit sich, nämlich die zwischen dem Schrifttum (*nipēk*), das *zand* heißt und die Überlieferung der Mobads ist, und *apastāk,* der mündlichen Überlieferung der Herbads. Der ganze Kanon bekommt den Namen *apastāk,* während *zand* die Bezeichnung der kommentierenden Pahlavi-Übersetzung (= PÜ) wird.

Die zoroastrische Religion wird eine synkretistische, wo der Zoroastrismus mit dem Zervanismus verquickt wird. Die Spuren des reinen Zervanismus werden aber möglichst vollständig sowohl aus *apastāk* wie aus *zand* entfernt. Im avestischen Text des Vd., eine Schrift, die ein Produkt der Magier ist, bleiben indessen einige unmißverständliche zervanitische Ausdrücke. In *zand* finden sich auch nur schwache Spuren eines *reinen* Zervanismus, dagegen haben sich offenbar in *zand* zervanitische Überlieferungen, *synkretistisch* mit den zoroastrischen verbunden und gemischt, in großem Umfang gerettet. Die kosmologischen, astrologischen, apokalyp-

---

[113] Vgl. Nyberg 1938, 337 ff. Zum Pahlavikompendium Dēnkart vgl. auch Widengren 1968a, 41.
[114] Vgl. Götze 1923, 60 ff.
[115] Vgl. Christensen 1931, 46 mit Verweis auf die Literatur.

tischen usw. Lehren der Mobads behalten ihren bedeutenden Platz auch im sassanidischen Avesta, wo z. B. Sūtkar Nask besonders wichtig ist, wie wir in der Fortsetzung darlegen wollen (vgl. § 4.1.4. und § 7.1.2. bzw. § 7.4.).

Pahlavi als Sprache der Literatur, das sog. Buchpahlavi, wird auch eine Mischsprache wegen der Fusion der Mobads und Herbads. Sie entsteht durch die Mischung des parthischen Dialektes der Mobads (NW) mit dem persischen Dialekt der Herbads (SW), wo der mparth. Einfluß sich hauptsächlich (aber nicht ausschließlich) auf dem lexikalischen Gebiet bemerkbar macht. Wie die Erklärung und Übersetzung *zand* aussah, können wir am besten durch ein Studium des Ritualtextes Nīrangastān verstehen lernen[116].

4. Die mitteliranische Apokalyptik und ihr Hintergrund im "Avesta"

4.1. Das grundlegende Problem

Die mitteliranische Apokalyptik ist uns innerhalb und außerhalb Irans zugänglich. Innerhalb Irans liegt sie in der in Buchpahlavi geschriebenen zoroastrischen Literatur vor[117]. Weil die zoroastrische Literatur, so wie sie uns vorliegt, zum größten Teil nach dem Fall des Sassanidenreiches ±650 n. Chr. niedergeschrieben wurde, werden auch die mitteliranischen apokalyptischen Schriften sehr oft, besonders von Nichtiranisten, die auf diesem Gebiete nicht sachverständig sind, als "spät" oder "nachsassanidisch" bezeichnet. Man ignoriert dabei, hoffentlich in gutem Glauben, die von Iranisten und Religionshistorikern geleistete analytische Arbeit. Um solchen Mißverständnissen vorzubeugen und eine ziemlich allgemein verbreitete Unkenntnis zu beseitigen, ist es notwendig, zuerst das grundlegende Problem etwas ausführlicher zu behandeln.

Wir gehen darum auf die schriftliche Bezeugung und die sprachliche Analyse der Texte ein.

4.1.1. Hier notieren wir zuerst, daß es in Pahlavitexten verschiedene Ausdrücke, *Zitatformeln,* gibt, die darauf hinweisen, daß der unmittelbar folgende Abschnitt aus dem Avesta, der heiligen Schrift der Zoroastrier, geholt und ins Pahlavi übersetzt ist. Solche Zitatformeln werden hier ohne Anspruch auf Vollständigkeit angeführt[118].

| (1) | *pat vēh-dēn ōgōn paitāk ku* | = in der Guten Religion ist es folgendermaßen offenbart . . . |
| (2) | *(ēt) pat dēn ōgōn paitāk ku* | = (dieses) ist in der Religion folgendermaßen offenbart . . . |

---

[116] S. die Exemplifikation in Widengren 1967a, 340ff.; vgl. auch das Beispiel unten § 4.1.3.
[117] Dazu siehe oben § 3.2.
[118] Vgl. Widengren 1967, 279f. und 1968a, 42.

(3) *ōgōn čigōn pat dēn gōvēt ku*	= folgendermaßen, wie man (er) in der Religion sagt . . .
(4) *čigōn gōvēt pat dēn*	= wie man (er) in der Religion sagt . . .
(5) *gōvēt pat dēn ku*	= man (er) sagt in der Religion . . .
(6) *andar dēn ōgōn nimūt ēstēt ku*	= in der Religion ist es folgendermaßen angegeben . . .
(7) *ōgōn paitāk ku*	= folgendermaßen ist es offenbart . . .
(8) *hač dēn paitāk ku*	= aus der Religion ist es offenbart, daß . . .
(9) *ētōn hač dēn mazdēsnān*	= folgendermaßen (geht) aus der Religion der Mazdā-Verehrer (hervor) . . .
(10) *andar apastāk gōvēt ku*	= im Avesta sagt man (er), daß . . .
(11) *hač (pat) apastāk paitāk (gōvēt) ku*	= aus dem (im) Avesta ist es offenbart (sagt man), daß . . .
(12) *paitākīhast pat ākāhīh i hač apastāk*	= aus dem Wissen vom Avesta ist es offenbart[119]. . . .

Auffallend ist, daß die heilige Schrift *Vēh-Dēn*, die Gute Religion, oder *dēn*, die Religion, heißt, während *apastāk* m.W. *nur* in den späteren Schriften Dk und PRDD vorkommt[120]. Die Bezeichnung "Avesta" tritt also erst spät auf, und wann dies der Fall ist, haben wir oben (§ 3.3.2.) schon gesehen.

4.1.2. Ferner gibt es gewisse Ausdrücke, die auf einen *Kommentar* zur heiligen Schrift hinweisen. Ein solcher Kommentar wird nämlich ziemlich oft, auch in den apokalyptischen Pahlavitexten gegeben. Ihr ursprünglicher Standort ist in den Pahlaviübersetzungen der "avestischen Schriften" zu finden. Solche Ausdrücke sind u. a. die folgenden[121]:

(1) *Zand-ākāhīh*	= das Kommentar-Wissen
(2) *hač pōryōtkēš-gōvišn nikēž i vēh-dēn*	= aus den Aussagen der ersten Lehrer, der Auslegung der Religion
(3) *hač nīkēž i vēh-dēn*	= aus der Auslegung der Guten Religion
(4) *pat zand i Vohuman Yasn paitāk ku*	= im Kommentar zu Vohuman Yasn ist es offenbart, daß . . .
(5) *pat zand i Vohuman Yasn, Hōrdat Yasn, Aštāt Yasn paitāk ku*	= im Kommentar zu Vohuman Yasn, Hōrdat Yasn, Aštāt Yasn ist es offenbart, daß . . .
(6) *Māhvindāt guft ku*	= Māhvindāt sagte, daß . . . (auch andere Kommentatoren werden erwähnt).
(7) *hast kē gōvēt (gōvēnd) ku*	= einige sagen, daß . . . .

Solche Ausdrücke in den Pahlavitexten besagen, daß der betr. Satz, Abschnitt oder Wort aus dem Avesta bzw. der kommentierenden Übers. (*zand*) zum Avesta geholt und von den Exegeten näher kommentiert ist, wobei verschiedene Meinungen angeführt werden können, die zeigen, daß man in den verschiedenen Kommentaren verschiedene Ansichten zum

---

[119] Dk VII 1, 44; ungewöhnlicher Ausdruck!

[120] Vgl. auch Wikander 1946, 32 mit Anm. 1.

[121] Vgl. Widengren 1967, 280 und 1968a, 42f.; vgl. auch West 1880, LIII.

Ausdruck gebracht hat. Es gehört aber zu den Ausnahmen, daß die Kommentatoren mit Namen erwähnt werden, wie Māhvindāt und Rōšn in Bahm. Yt. III 3. Zu notieren ist aber, daß manchmal nur das Wort *ku*, "d. h." verwendet wird, worauf eine exegetische Glosse folgt; dies ist z. B. in Bahm. Yt. II 2 der Fall, wo die lange erklärende Glosse nur durch *ku* eingeführt wird.

4.1.3. Sehr wichtig ist auch, daß es gewisse *sprachliche* und *stilistische Kriterien* gibt, die auf einen avest. Hintergrund hindeuten.

In einer gewöhnlichen Prosaerzählung in Pahlavi, wie z. B. KN, das Tatenbuch des Pāpaksohnes Artaxšēr, steht das Verbum am Ende des Satzes – mit einigen wenigen, leicht zu erklärenden Ausnahmen. Das hatte schon West 1880 erkannt, aber diese Einsicht ist seither verlorengegangen[122].

Dieses Kriterium habe ich gründlich analysiert und brauche die Analyse hier nicht zu wiederholen[123]. Ich möchte nur unterstreichen, daß wir zwei ausgezeichnete Beispiele für den Unterschied zwischen der Sprache, die man als "sprachechtes", "authentisches" Pahlavi bezeichnen kann, und der Sprache, die ich als "Übersetzungspahlavi" charakterisieren will, besitzen. Das *erste* Beispiel ist die Schilderung, die in Dk VII 4,84ff. von dem ekstatischen Schauen Vistāšps gegeben wird. Sie geht auf ein verlorenes avestisches Original zurück[124]. Hier steht das Verbum am Anfang des Satzes, und die Syntax ist oft sehr dunkel, weil die Übersetzer der avestischen Texte Wort für Wort übersetzten. Diese Schilderung ist dann zu einer glatten Erzählung verarbeitet, die man jetzt in PRDD 139:13–18 lesen kann. Hier ist das Verbum völlig normal plaziert[125]:

Dk VII 4,84ff.	**PRDD 139:13–18**
u-š ō Nērōsang	*u Ōhrmazd Nērōsang* **frēstīt** *ku*
Yazat **guft** *kē dātār Ōhrmazd ku*	*bē hu-tuxšt* **šav!** *uš ēn* **bē guft** *ku*
bē rav, vāz *Nērōsang . . .*	*mang andar ō mai* **kun!** *frāč ō Vištāsp* **dah!**
stane *tašt i nēvak i apar-nēvaktar*	*hu-tuxš hamgōn* **kart**.
hač hān hutaštakān kart.	*ka-š* **xvart būt**, *pat giyāk* **start būt**.
apar hōm u mang amāh rād **barē**	*u-š ruvān ō Garōdmān* **nīt**.
ō Vištāp.	

Und zum Yazata	Und Ōhrmazd sandte Nērōsang (sagend):
Nērōsang sagte er, der Schöpfer Ōhrmazd:	'Gehe eifrig hin!' Und er sagte dies:
'Gehe hin, steige nieder, O Nērōsang! . . .	'Mische *mang* in den Wein! Gib' zu Vištāsp!'

---

[122] Ich bedaure sehr, früher übersehen zu haben, daß West 1880, LIII und 195 Anm. 4 darauf aufmerksam gemacht hat, daß *sprachliche Kriterien* in einem Pahlavitext auf einen dahinterliegenden avest. Text hindeuten können. Vgl. aber Anm. 124.

[123] S. Widengren 1967, 280ff.; 1967a, 340ff.; 1969a, 183–193.

[124] Vgl. Widengren 1955, 67 [91]; 1979, 347ff. Schon in Widengren 1955 habe ich auf den avest. Hintergrund des Dk-Textes hingewiesen. Dort Anm. 105 sowie 1969, 471 Anm. 51 wurde tatsächlich auf West verwiesen!

[125] Die Übereinstimmungen sind in Fettdruck gedruckt.

Ergreife die schöne Schale, schöner   Eifrig tat er in solcher Weise.
als die anderen gutgearbeiteten Schalen!   Als (Vištāsp) geschluckt hatte, wurde er auf
                                              der Stelle bewußtlos,
Bringe *hōm* und *mang* für unsere Rechnung   und seine Seele wurde zu Garōdmān geführt.
zu Vištāsp!'

Der Unterschied sticht sofort in die Augen. Ein *zweites* Beispiel habe ich anderswo angeführt. Es steht in der PÜ des Avestatraktates Nīrangistān (21:3 usw.) und dem dazu gehörenden Pahlavikommentar, wo wir sehr deutlich den Unterschied in der Plazierung des Verbums beobachten können[126].

4.1.4. Wir nehmen den wichtigsten apokalyptischen Text, Bahm. Yt., als ein Typenbeispiel. Der Text trägt den Namen *Zand i Vohuman Yasn*. Diese Apokalypse ist also die Zand-Fassung des avest. Textes *Vohu Manah Yasna,* was auch aus den schon von uns angeführten Formeln (§ 4.1.2.) hervorgeht; Bahm. Yt. II 1:

> *pat zand i Vohuman Yasn paitāk ku . . .*
> Im *zand* zu Vohuman Yasn ist es offenbart, daß . . .

Aber die jetzige Apokalypse Bahm. Yt. basiert auch auf anderen Zand-Texten, denn wir führten auch eine andere Formel an, I 6:

> *pat zand i Vohuman Yasn u Hōrdat Yasn u Aštāt Yasn paitāk ku . . .*
> Im *zand* zu Vohuman Yasn und Hōrdat Yasn und Aštāt Yasn ist es offenbart, daß . . .

Aus dieser Stelle geht also hervor, daß Bahm. Yt. seinen Inhalt, jedenfalls was das Hauptthema, Zarathustras Vision, betrifft, aus drei Texten geholt hat, nämlich Vohuman Yasn, Hōrdat Yasn und Aštāt Yasn. Diese drei Texte können wir auch innerhalb des Avesta in einem bestimmten Nask lokalisieren, denn schon Bahm. Yt. I 1 heißt es:

> *čigōn hač Stūtkar paitāk ku Zartušt hač Ōhrmazd ahōšīh xvāst.*
> Wie es in Stūtkar offenbart ist, erbat sich Zartušt von Ōhrmazd Unsterblichkeit.

Der Name Stūtkar hat gewöhnlich die Form Sūtkar. Er "hing nur lose mit den Gathas zusammen. Sein Zweck war, nützliche Lehren aus den Gathas zu ziehen und sie durch Legenden zu erläutern" (Dk IX 2−23)[127].

Also sehen wir, daß der Rahmen des Bahm. Yt. aus dem Sūtkar Nask des sassanidischen Avesta stammt. Unsere Aufgabe muß es darum sein, mit Hilfe der schon angegebenen Kriterien zu untersuchen, wieviel vom Inhalt des Textes dem sassanidischen Avesta entstammt.

---

[126] Widengren 1967a, 341; vgl ferner unten § 6.1.2. und § 6.1.3. *et passim.*
[127] Geldner in: Geiger-Kuhn 1904, II, 25 mit Hinweis auf West in SBE XXXVII 173 Anm.

4.2. Analyse von Bahman Yašt Buch III: der eschatologische Endkampf

4.2.1. Die avestischen Bestandteile des Zand-Materials in den epischen Pišyōtan-Fragmenten

In einem durch neue Gesichtspunkte gekennzeichneten Aufsatz hat Benveniste das Vorhandensein einer epischen Dichtung in mparth. Sprache aufgezeigt[128]. Der kleine Text *Abyātkār i Zarērān*, der von dem ersten Glaubenskrieg der Zoroastrier handelt, den Vištāspa, der königliche Gönner Zarathustras, gegen den Xioniterherrscher Arǰataspa führte (vgl. Yt. 5:108f.; 9:30), ist nämlich, wie Benveniste einwandfrei zeigte, als ein kleines Epos in sassanidischer Redaktion enthalten, in dem doch gewisse mparth. Formen noch bewahrt sind. Er hat dabei kurz auf die stilistischen Kriterien hingewiesen, die noch in der Prosabearbeitung des urspr. Epos deutlich zu beobachten sind[129].

Von dieser Erkenntnis ausgehend habe ich einen kurzen zervanitischen Text in Bdhn (Bdhn A 39: 11ff.; Ind. Bdhn 8:6ff.) als ein episches Fragment aufgezeigt[130]. Gegen diesen Hintergrund ist es in diesem Zusammenhang notwendig, einige auffallende Textstücke in Bahm. Yt. III näher zu untersuchen, in denen auch eine avestische "Lokalfarbe", u. a. durch die anormale Stellung des Verbums[130a], sehr deutlich an den Tag tritt. Diese Untersuchung muß freilich einen ausgesprochenen philologischen Charakter haben, was die Lektüre sicherlich nicht so leicht macht, denn nur so ist eine überzeugende Beweisführung möglich.

4.2.1.1. Wir beschäftigen uns zuerst mit Buch III von Bahm. Yt.

I. An erster Stelle kommt eine Strophe der Einführung (= III 26):

u ravēt Nēryōsang-yazat u Srōš-ahlav	Hervor gehen der Yazat Nēryōsang und der Gerechte Srōš
hač vēh Čakāt i Dāitīk	von dem Gipfel des Guten Dāitīk-Flusses
i Kangdiz i Siyāvaxš i bāmīk	zu Kangdiz, gebaut vom glänzenden Siyāvaxš,
u-š vāng kunēnd ku:	und erheben den Ruf folgendermaßen:
'frāč rav, Pišyōtan i bāmīk,	'Geh hervor, glänzender Pišyōtan,
Čitrakmiyān i Vištāspān,	Čitrakmiyān[132], Vištāsp-Sohn,
Kayān xvarrah, i dēn rāst virāstār!	Glücksglanz der Kayanier, richtiger Wiederhersteller der Religion!
frāč rav ō ēn Ērān dēhān i man Ōhrmazd dāt,	Geh hervor zu den von mir, Ōhrmazd, geschaffenen Ländern von Iran,

---

[128] Vgl. Benveniste 1932.

[129] *Ibid.*, 247. Hier möchte ich, mehr als Benveniste es tut, die Wiederholung der stehenden Ausdrücke und Formeln hervorheben. Vgl. oben § 3.1.2. mit Anm. 55.

[130] Vgl. Widengren 1967a, 346 und 351.

[130a] Die anormale Stellung des Verbums im Pahlavitext ist, soweit möglich, in der Übersetzung beibehalten.

[131] Für die Supplierung vgl. die siebente Strophe.

[132] Oder Čibrakmēhān, vgl. Christensen 1931, 56 Anm. 3.

apāč virāy gāh i Dēn　　　　　　　　　stelle wieder her den Thron der Religion
u xvatāyīh ⟨apar druvandān⟩!'[131]　　　und die Herrschaft ⟨über die Lügenhaften⟩!'

Hier werden wir in die iranische Sagengeschichte versetzt. Pišyōtan ist der avest. *Pisi.šyaoϑna*[133], der laut Bahm. Yt. II 1; III 25 auch den Namen Čitrakmiyān (Čihrmiyān [oder *-mēhan*]) führt. Er ist der Sohn des Zarathustrabeschützers Vištāspa (> Vištāsp). Kangdiz ist das wunderbare Schloß, das von Syāvaršan[134], dem berühmten Sagenhelden, gebaut wurde[135]. Dāitīk ist der avestische Fluß *vaŋuhī dāityā*[136]; der *čakāt i dāitīk* ist indessen der Gipfel des Dāitīk, was eigentlich der Gerichtsgipfel ist, wo die Činvat-Brücke sich befindet[137]. Gewiß liegt hier eine Mischung von Dāitīk als Fluß und Čakāt i Dāitīk als Gerichtsgipfel vor[138]. Jedenfalls macht es auch bedenklich, daß *vēh* (< *vaŋuhī*), eigentlich das Epitheton zu Dāitīk, hier zu Čakāt gehört. Es liegt nahe, an eine falsche Übersetzung des avestischen Textes zu denken, weil man Wort für Wort, ohne Rücksicht auf den syntaktischen Zusammenhang übersetzte. Demgemäß habe ich auch übersetzt, denn von einem "guten Gipfel" wissen wir nichts. In Dk VII 3,51 z. B. finden wir eben *Vēh Dāitīk!*

Wo in der mythischen Geographie Dāitīk und Kangdiz ihren Platz haben, ist eine umstrittene Frage[139], auf die wir hier nicht einzugehen brauchen.

II. Die zweite Strophe (= III 27):

frāč ravēt Pišyōtan i bāmīk　　　　　　Hervor geht der glänzende Pišyōtan
apāk ē-sat-u-panǰah mart i ahlav　　　　zusammen mit einhundertfünfzig gerechten
　　　　　　　　　　　　　　　　　Männern,
kē hāvišt i Pišyōtan hēnd,　　　　　　　die die Schüler Pišyōtans sind,
pat siyāh samōr yāmak . . . dārēnd[140]. . .　und die ein Gewand von schwarzem Zo-
　　　　　　　　　　　　　　　　　bel . . . tragen . . .
pas hač hān bē škenēt patiyārak sē-ēvak[141].　Dann zerbricht er ein Drittel jener Feinde[142].

Den eigentümlichen Ausdruck "Schüler" (*hāvišt*) werden wir später (§ 4.2.2.2.) erklären und ebenso die Zahl *150* (§ 4.2.2.3.).

---

[133] AirWb 908.　　　　　　　　　　　[134] AirWb 1631 > *siyāvaxš*.
[135] Vgl. die Verweise bei Markwart 1931, 27.　[136] AirWb 730.
[137] Vgl. Bdhn XXX, 9−10 (A 202:10ff.).
[138] So Markwart 1938, 125f. So übersetzt auch Gnoli 1980, 148. Aber *dāitīk* unterscheidet sich von *dātīk*!
[139] Vgl. Markwart 1938, 122−125, 140; Gnoli 1967, 105 (Kangdiz) und 13f., 38, 97−99 (Dāitīk).
[140] *pat mēnōi vēh* ist offenbar Hinzufügung.
[141] Die Präsensform *škenēt* hat einen kurzen Vokal, wie die Pāzandform *škan* zeigt. MacKenzie 1971, 80 ist also korrekt (gegen Nyberg 1974, 186b).
[142] Hier liegt wiederum eine Wort-für-Wort-Übersetzung vor. Zu konstruieren ist also: *pas hač hān patiyārak sē-ēvak bē škenēt.*

III. Wir gehen zu der dritten Strophe über[143] (= III 30):

frāč ravēt Pišyōtan i Vištāspān	Hervor geht Pišyōtan, der Vištāsp-Sohn,
ō uzdēstačār i vazurg,	zu dem großen Götzentempel,
nišēmak i druvand Gannāk Mēnōi . . .	dem Nest des lügenhaften Bösen Geistes . . .
bē kanēnd hān uzdēstačār,	Sie zerstören jenen Götzentempel
pat ham-kōxšišnīh i Pišyōtan i bāmīk[144].	durch den Kampf des glänzenden Pišyōtan.

Die Worte *uzdēstačār*[145] und *nišēmak i druvand Gannāk Mēnōi* besitzen ihre Entsprechung in den von Frāsiyāp[146], dem Feind des iranischen Volkes, gegründeten *dēvān uzdēstačār* und *nišēmak i bagān*, "Götzentempel der Dämonen" und "Nest der Götter" in ŠE § 7. Wir werden also hier in die Zeit der Kämpfe zwischen dem König der Turier und den iranischen Sagenhelden versetzt.

IV. Dann folgt die vierte, von uns restaurierte Strophe (= III 32):

Mihr i frāxv-gōyōt u Srōš⟨i⟩takīk	Mihr mit den weiten Triften und der wackere Srōš
u Rašn i rāst u Vahrām i amāvand . . .	und der gerade Rašn und der gewaltige Vahrām . . .
⟨rasēnd⟩ ō ayyārīh i Pišyōtan i bāmīk	kommen dem glänzenden Pišyōtan zu Hilfe.
bē zanēnd dēvān i tom-tōhmakān.	Sie schlagen die Dämonen aus dem finsteren Geschlecht.

Mithra, den wir in der jungavestischen Apokalyptik vermißt haben, tritt hier plötzlich und unvermittelt auf[146a]. Er ist von Srōš und Rašn begleitet, die regelmäßig seine Begleiter sind[147].

Das Epitheton Mihrs, *frāxv-gōyōt,* ist die reguläre Pahlavi-Übersetzung des avestischen Ausdrucks *vouru gaoyaoti*, der nur Mithra beigelegt wird[148].

V. Die fünfte Strophe führt den Gegner sprechend ein (= III 33–34):

vāng kunēt Gannāk Mēnōi i druvand	Den Ruf erhebt der lügenhafte Böse Geist
ō Mihr i frāxv-gōyōt ku:	zu Mihr mit den weiten Triften:
'*pat rāstīh ul ēst tō, Mihr i frāxv-gōyōt'!*	'Steh aufrecht in Geradheit, du Mihr mit den weiten Triften'!
pas Mihr i frāxv-gōyōt vāng kunēt:	Dann erhebt den Ruf Mihr mit den weiten Triften:

---

[143] Es folgt in III 29 eine Wiederholung, die hier wiederzugeben nicht notwendig ist.

[144] Zur Umschrift: Nyberg 1974, 80b f. hat seine frühere Etymologie: *gannāk* SW-Entwicklung <*gandāk*, Wechselform von *gandak*, stinkend, aufgegeben, aber zu Unrecht; vgl. Widengren 1965, 322 Anm. 21.

[145] Für die Lesung und Etymologie vgl. Nyberg 1974, 199a f.

[146] Frāsiyāp = avest. *Fraŋrasyan*, AirWb 986.

[146a] Vgl. auch unten § 4.3.2.2.

[147] Über Srōš und Rašn (avest. Sraoša und Rašnu) vgl. Dumézil 1953, 9–18 und kurz zusammenfassend Widengren 1965, 14f. (ohne eigene Forschung).

[148] AirWb 1430.

'ēn nōh hazār sāl pašt-ē i-š kart	'Diesem Vertrag von neuntausend Jahren zufolge, den er[149] geschlossen hat,
tā nūn Dahāk i duš-dēn u Frāsiyāp i Tūr . . .	haben bis jetzt Dahāk mit schlechter Religion und der Turier Frāsiyāp . . .
u ōišān davāl-kustīkān dēvān i vičārt-vars	und jene ledergegürtelten Dämonen mit gescheiteltem Haar,
hazār sālān āvām	während einer Periode von tausend Jahren
vēš hač patmān xvatāyīh kart'.	über das Abkommen hinaus, die Herrschaft ausgeübt'.

Aus den zwei feindlichen Schlachtreihen rufen die Anführer, Mithra und der Böse Geist Ahriman, zu einander[150]. Hier wird auf den im Zervanismus erwähnten Vertrag zwischen dem Guten und dem Bösen Gott hingewiesen, demgemäß Ahriman 9000 Jahre herrschen wird[151]. Wir verweisen auf Zātspr. XXXIV 30, wo sowohl die 9000 Jahre wie *pašt,* Vertrag, erwähnt sind[152]. Das Abkommen heißt auch (wie hier) *patmān* und diesen Terminus finden wir in Bdhn I 13 vor und in I 14 werden die 9000 Jahre erwähnt[153]. Hier aber herrschen die zwei Gegner abwechselnd. Die Vorstellung von 9000 Jahren und die Schlüsselworte *pašt* und *patmān* sowie die Stellung Mithras als Hüter des Vertrages zeigen den klaren zervanitischen Charakter dieses apokalyptischen Motivs[154].

VI. Die sechste Strophe lautet wie folgt (= III 35):

start bavēt hān druvand i Gannāk Mēnōi	Betäubt wird jener lügenhafte Böse Geist,
ka ētōn ašnūt	als er solchermaßen hörte.
Mihr i fräxv-gōyōt bē zanēt	Mihr mit den weiten Triften schlägt
Hēšm i xru-druš, pat stavīh dvārēt	Hēšm mit der blutigen Keule, kraftlos läuft er weg
hān druvand Gannāk Mēnōi apāk višūtakān	jener lügenhafte Böse Geist, zusammen mit den Ausgeburten
u vat-tōhmakān	und denen aus dem schlechten Geschlecht,
apāč ō tār u tom i dōšaxv dvārēt.	zurück zur Finsternis und Dunkelheit der Hölle läuft er hin.

Eine gewöhnliche Ausdrucksweise ist, daß Ahriman *start bavēt,* betäubt wird, wenn er das mächtige Gotteswort vernimmt, z. B. Zātspr. I 4[155], Bdhn A 7:11f.[156]. Einige sprachliche Beobachtungen vervollständigen die

---

[149] Sc. der Böse Geist.
[150] Vgl. Reitzenstein in Reitzenstein-Schaeder 1926, 47f.
[151] Vgl. Widengren 1965, 285f.; Zaehner 1955, 99f. Diese Auffassung ist die radikal pessimistische!
[152] Vgl. Zaehner 1955, 340.   [153] Vgl. *ibid.,* 279f.
[154] Die Wortform *patmān* ist mparth. und auch als mparth. Terminus in der manichäischen Literatur belegt; richtig Nyberg 1974, 158a. MacKenzie 1971, 67 transkribiert fälschlich *paymān,* was die mpers. Form ist, und erwähnt *nicht* die entspr. mparth. Form. S. ferner unten § 5.1.2. # (5).
[155] Vgl. Zaehner 1955, 339.   [156] Vgl. Widengren 1967a, 338, 343.

Lokalisierung im Zervanismus. Sowohl *pašt* wie *patmān* gehören dem mparth. Dialekt an[157]. Aber auch *višūtakān*, die Ausgeburten, ist ein mparth. Wort[158].

Sowohl inhaltlich wie sprachlich führen uns also diese epischen Fragmente zurück zu der zervanitisch-parthischen Überlieferung, dem ursprünglichen *zand*.

VII. Die siebente Strophe (= III 36):

vāng kunēt Mihr i frāxv-gōyōt	Den Ruf erhebt Mihr mit den weiten Triften
ō Pišyōtan i bāmīk ku:	zu dem glänzenden Pišyōtan:
'bē kan, bē zan hān uzdēstačār	'Zerstöre, schlage nieder jenen Götzentempel,
i dēvān nišēmak!	das Nest der Dämonen!
rav ō ēn Ērān dēhān i man Ōhrmazd dāt!	Geh hervor zu den von mir, Ōhrmazd, geschaffenen Ländern von Iran!
apāč virāy gāh i Dēn	Stelle wieder her den Thron der Religion
u xvatāyīh apar druvandān!	und die Herrschaft über die Lügenhaften!
ka tō vēnēnd škanēnd[159]*.'*	Wenn sie dich sehen, brechen sie zusammen.'

VIII. Die achte Strophe (= III 37):

apar rasēt Pišyōtan i bāmīk	Hervor tritt der glänzende Pišyōtan.
bē zanēt hān druž i vas ōž,	Er schlägt jenen Lügenteufel von viel Stärke,
bē kanēt hān uzdēstačār	er zerstört jenen Götzentempel,
ku nišēmak i dēvān[160]*.*	wo das Nest der Dämonen ist.

IX. Die neunte Strophe (= III 38):

frāč rasēt Pišyōtan i bāmīk	Hervor tritt der glänzende Pišyōtan
ō ēn Ērān dēhān i man Ōhrmazd dāt ō Ārang u Vēhrōt[161]*.*	zu den von mir, Ōhrmazd, geschaffenen Ländern von Iran, zu Ārang und Vēhrōt.

---

[157] Für *pašt* wird der mparth. Ursprung von Nyberg 1974, 153b nicht vermerkt. Es kann doch keinem Zweifel unterliegen, daß *pašt*, ein *bindendes* Versprechen, mit mparth. *paštag* (M), gebunden, zusammenhängt. In Zātspr. I 30 finden wir dieses Wort im zervanitischen Kontext. Für *patmān* dagegen vgl. Nyberg 1974, 158a.

[158] Nyberg 1974, 216b registriert nicht das Verbum *višūtan* als mparth. ebensowenig wie *višūtak*, aber schon die Bildung mit *vi-* anstatt mpers. *gu-* zeigt, daß es ein NW-Wort ist. Wir haben die mpers. Entsprechung *gušūdan,* wo indessen die Bedeutung "öffnen" eine abweichende, doch nicht unerklärliche semantische Entwicklung aufzeigt. Aber *gušūdan* könnte sich als eine Wechselform von *gušādan* entwickelt haben und dadurch semantisch beeinflußt sein.

[159] Hier ist die Verbform *škanēnd* offenbar intrans. Wir notieren, daß das neupers. Verbum *šikastan* sowohl intrans. wie trans. ist.

[160] Ich nehme *ku* hier nicht als eine Glosse einführend, sonst gewöhnlich in Bahm. Yt., sondern als relatives Adverb, stammend aus dem NW-Dialekt, vgl. Nyberg 1974, 119b: Kü 2. Das Komplement *nišēmak* wird ja sonst hier immer erwähnt.

[161] Die Lesung in MS DH *Ārang u Vēhrōt* ist sicherlich richtig; vgl. Markwart 1938, 115f., wo man sieht, daß *Ārang* als *Arvand* aufgefaßt wird, die Lesart, die Anklesaria aufgenommen hat. Überhaupt ist Anklesarias Text und Übers. nicht von solcher Qualität, daß man sie als Ausgangspunkt nehmen könnte.

ka druvandān ōi vēnēnd bē škanēnd[162].	Wenn die Lügenhaften ihn sehen, brechen sie zusammen,
ōišān tom-tōhmakān nē aržānīkān . . .	jene Finsternis-Entsprossenen, die Nichts-würdigen . . .
apāč virāyēt ēn Ērān-dēhān.	Wieder stellt er her diese Länder vom Iran.

Auch in diesem Abschnitt gibt es eine klare NW-Form, nämlich *arž-ānīk*[163].

X. Die zehnte Strophe (= III 41):

ētōn gōvēt Pišyōtan i bāmīk ku: '*zat bavāt dēv u zat parīk!*	So spricht der glänzende Pišyōtan: 'Geschlagen sei Dämon und geschlagen Parīk!
zat bavāt dēv, družīh u vattarīh!	Geschlagen seien Dämonen, Lügnerschaft und die Bösen!
zat bavānd tom-tōhmakān dēvān!	Geschlagen seien die Finsternis-Entsprossenen-Dämonen!
xūp *virāst bavāt gāh i dēn u xvatāyīh[164]!'	Gut wiederhergestellt seien der Thron der Religion und die Herrschaft!'

Die Ausdrücke *dēv* und *parīk* führen uns zu den ältesten mythisch-epischen Überlieferungen im Ostiran zurück, wo die *pairīka*-s als mit der *daēva*-Verehrung verbunden erscheinen. Hier hat Wikander ansprechend einen Gegensatz zu den Fruchtbarkeitsriten des Männerbundes vermutet[165]. Die *pairīka* > *parīk* > *parī* hat bekanntlich mit der Zeit ihre negative Bedeutung verloren, ist aber hier in Bahm. Yt. immer noch ein daēvisches Wesen.

XI. Die elfte Strophe (= III 42+52):

frāč rasēt Pišyōtan i bāmīk, *frāč rasēt apāk ē-sat-u-panǰāh mart i hāvišt*	Hervor tritt der glänzende Pišyōtan, hervor tritt er mit einhundertfünfzig Männern, die Schüler sind,
kē siyāh samōr ⟨yāmak⟩ dārēnd *u gīrēnd taxt-gāh i Dēn u xvatāyīh i xvēš.*	die schwarzen Zobel ⟨als Gewand⟩ tragen. Sie ergreifen ihren Thron-Sitz der Religion und ihre eigene Herrschaft.
[. . . ein Fragment] *druž i Āz-čihrak bē zanēt*	[. . . ein Fragment] Die Lügenteufel von der Brut der Lust (Āz) schlägt er,
u Pišyōtan i Vištāspān *ham-gōnak dastvar u rat i gēhān bavēt*[166].	und Pišyōtan, der Vištāsp-Sohn, wird ebenfalls der Dastur und Rat der Welt sein.

---

[162] S. oben Anm. 159.

[163] Vgl. Nyberg 1974, 30b. Er registriert es jedoch nicht als NW-Wort.

[164] Ich habe *virāstar* zu **virāst* emendiert, weil wir erst so einen guten Sinn erhalten und die Konstruktion auf diese Weise mit den drei vorausgehenden Wünschen übereinstimmt: Part. Pass. + Subjunktiv mit optativischer Bedeutung, vgl. Widengren 1967b, 99f.

[165] Vgl. Wikander 1941, 66f.

[166] Die Worte *dastvar* und *rat* bezeichnen Inhaber priesterlich-richterlicher Funktionen. Es ist

Die letzte Strophe stellt fest, daß Pišyōtan den Thron der Religion und die Herrschaft in Besitz nimmt. Das Fragment III 52 erwähnt ihn indessen ein letztes Mal und dürfte also den Rest der Schlußtirade einmal konstituiert haben. Es ist zweifelhaft, ob die erste Zeile hierher gehört oder – wie im jetzigen Text – zum vorhergehenden Stück. Aber Āz, die Lust, ist eine ausgesprochen zervanitische Gestalt[167], und ich nehme darum einen parthischen Ursprung dieser Zeile an.

4.2.1.2. Die Überlieferung über Pišyōtan und seine 150 Schüler begegnet auch in anderen apokalyptischen Texten. So heißt es Dk VII 8,45–46, daß

> die Bösen in ihrem Haß und ihrer Feindschaft fortschreiten werden, bis der Mann mit der siegreichen Keule kommt, der der gerechte Čitrōmiyān ist, mit 150 Männern, die starke, hochgewachsene Schüler sind[168], vorwärts blickende, mit breiten Schultern, stark-armige.

Hier begegnen uns gewisse Ausdrücke, die wir unten (§ 4.2.2.) behandeln werden, nämlich "die siegreiche Keule", die Pišyōtans Waffe ist, ferner "Schüler", ein schon bekanntes Wort, und "stark-armig". Die ganze Stelle ist avestisch, wie die Syntax demonstriert[169].

Eine andere Stelle ist AŽ XVI 51–52, wo Žāmāsp dem Vištāsp u. a. über den eschatologischen Streit prophezeit:

u pas Srōš u Nēryōsang,	Und nachher werden Srōš und Nēryōsang
Pišyōtan, i šmāh pus,	den Pišyōtan, Ihren Sohn,
hač framān i dātār Ōhrmazd,	durch den Befehl des Schöpfers Ōhrmazd
hač Kangdiz i Kayān bē hangēžēnd.	von der (Festung) Kangdiz der Kayanier auf-rütteln[171].
u bē ravēt Pišyōtan, i šmāh pus,	Und hervorgeht Pišyōtan, Ihr Sohn,
apāk ē-sat-u-panǰāh hāvišt,	zusammen mit einhundertfünfzig Schülern,
kē-šān patmōčan ⟨i⟩ *samōr *i siyāh[170].	deren Kleidung *schwarzer *Zobel ist.

Es ist zu notieren, daß XVI 52 von einem avestischen Text übersetzt ist, wie die Stellung des Verbums zeigt. Mit Ausnahme der eigentümlichen Farbenzusammensetzung von weiß und schwarz, die sich in dem nicht-emendierten Text findet, stimmt dieses epische Fragment mit der oben zitierten II. Strophe (Bahm. Yt. III 27) gut überein. Eine dritte Stelle, Bdhn

---

möglich, daß *dastvar* urspr. ein mparth. Wort ist, weil *dast* in der Bedeutung "geschickt" mparth. belegt ist, wie Bailey 1943, 160 als erster bemerkt hat.

[167] Vgl. Zaehner 1955, 166–168. S. auch unten § 5.2.1. und § 5.2.2.

[168] Zu Unrecht betrachtet Molé 1967, 89 (in seiner Übersetzung) *hāvištān* als Glosse.

[169] So auch Molé 1967, 88–89.

[170] Der Text in Messina 1939, 74 ist ohne Zweifel korrupt: *patmōčan spēt u siyāh*, "ein weißes und schwarzes Kleid" gibt keinen Sinn. Trotz der graphischen Schwierigkeit emendiere ich darum in Übereinstimmung mit der konstanten Ausdrucksweise in Bahm. Yt. ܐܘܣܝ zu ܣܘܪ.

[171] Zu "aufrütteln" in der Bedeutung "auferwecken", "auferstehen lassen" s. Widengren 1965, 105 Anm. 11. Die dort angeführte Stelle Bdhn A 223:4f. wird unten § 5.2.3. zitiert.

A 218:2–5, gibt nichts Bemerkenswertes her; diese Stelle ist nicht aus dem Avestischen übersetzt.

4.2.2. *Analyse spezieller Ausdrücke in den epischen Pišyōtan-Fragmenten*

4.2.2.1. Zuerst der Terminus *hāvišt*, Schüler[172]. Gewiß berührt es eigentümlich, daß ein Held wie Pišyōtan von Schülern begleitet ist; und warum sind es 150? Das Wort *hāvišt* stammt aus avest. *hāvišta*[173].

Es ist ein typisch zoroastrisches Wort und findet sich hier und da in der Pahlaviliteratur. Die Lautform mit -*išt* deutet aber auf einen NW-Dialekt hin, also mparth.[174]. Daß Pišyōtan um sich "Schüler" oder Lehrlinge scharte, erklärt sich aus den altiranischen sozialen Zuständen. Seitdem Wikander 1938 das Vorhandensein von Männerbünden im alten Iran aufgewiesen hatte[175], hat sich das Material bedeutend erweitert, und wir überblicken nunmehr die Entwicklung von Männerbund zu Gefolgschaft sowie den Zusammenhang zwischen der Trainierung der Jungen im Männerbund und dem Erziehungswesen in der iranischen feudalen Gesellschaft[176]. Gegen diesen Hintergrund verstehen wir die Einrichtung der *hāvištān*. In der feudalen parthischen Gesellschaft in Armenien entsprechen die *ašakert*-s (armen.) einem mparth. Lw. *ašākirt*[177]. Hier in Armenien besaß ein großer Feudalherr solche "Schüler". Einem solchen entspricht Pišyōtan, der also als ein Meister in einem Männerbund auftritt.

4.2.2.2. Laut Dk VII 8,45f. (M 665: 18f.)[178] sind die *hāvištān* "starkarmig" (*stavr-bāzāi*). Das Wort *bāzāi* ist mparth., denn mpers. heißt es *bādūk*[179]. Daneben finden wir eine andere NW-Form *bāzūk*[180]. Der Ausdruck *stavr-bāzāi* gibt das alte Mithra-Epithet *ugra.bāzu* wieder[181], das wir Yt. 13:136 als Bezeichnung für die Feinde der zoroastrischen Gemeinde

---

[172] In § 4.2.1.1. die II. Strophe [III 27]; XI. Strophe [III 42]; in § 4.2.1.2. Dk VII 8, 45–46; AŽ XVI 51–52.

[173] AirWb 1806. Vgl. Bailey 1953a, 97.

[174] Tedesco 1921, 203 unterschätzt den starken NW-Einfluß in dem SW-Dialekt und auch umgekehrt einen, wenn auch unbedeutenden, SW-Einfluß im NW-Dialekt. Der Fall mparth. *masišt* gegen mpers. *mahist*, Superl. von *mas*, groß, ist doch typisch, aber mit diesen Formen hat Tedesco *ibid.*, 203 Anm. 14 nicht gerechnet. Gegen diesen Abschnitt kann man in vieler Hinsicht Kritik richten. Eigentümlich ist, daß avest. *hāvišta*- in der PÜ *nicht* mit *hāvišt* übersetzt wird. Zu diesem Problem vgl. Wikander 1946, 117ff., wo er eine Feststellung Baileys 1933, 292 weiter ausführt.

[175] "Der arische Männerbund", eine bahnbrechende Untersuchung.

[176] Vgl. vor allem Widengren 1969b, bes. Kap. III.

[177] Vgl. die Literaturnachweise bei Widengren 1969b, 90 Anm. 71.

[178] In § 4.2.1.2. zitiert.   [179] Andreas-Barr 1933, Glossar s. v.

[180] *Bāzūk* < avest. *bāzu*, AirWb 955. Vgl für *bāzūk* und *bādūk* Nyberg 1974, 46a (wo *bāzāi* fehlt). MacKenzie 1971, 18 hat nur *bāzā* (sic) registriert. Vgl. auch oben § 3.2.2. mit Anm. 63 und 64.

[181] Vgl. darüber Widengren 1938, 315f.

antreffen. Mithra, selbst starkarmig, ist also als Herr der Starkarmigen aufzufassen. In Indien ist seine Entsprechung als Gott der Kriegerfunktion, Indra, auch starkarmig (*ugrabāhu*)[182].

4.2.2.3. Die Zahl 150 [183] erklärt sich aus der militärischen Organisation, denn die grundlegende Abteilung war die Fünfzigschaft[184]. Also hatte Pišyōtan zu seiner Verfügung drei Fünfzigschaften.

4.2.2.4. Pišyōtan führt als Waffe laut Dk VII 8,45 *vazr i pērōžkar*, die siegreiche Keule[185], wiederum eine mparth. Form, denn *vazr*[186] entspricht der mpers. Form **gurz* (npers. bewahrt).

4.2.2.5. Die Schüler Pišyōtans tragen ein Gewand von schwarzem Zobel (*samōr*)[187]. Die schwarze Farbe ist auffallend, denn es ist eigentümlich, daß Pišyōtan und seine Gefolgsleute, die hier als Vorkämpfer der Guten Religion auftreten, d. h. zoroastrisiert sind, dennoch eine *schwarze* Tracht tragen.

Auch der Glaubensheld Frētōn[188], den wir als Besieger des bösen Tyrannen Dahāk kennenlernen werden, trägt in Fārsnāmah 36:8 "die stierköpfige Keule" (*gurz i gāv-sār*), die von *schwarzer* Farbe ist (*siyāh rang*).

Dieses Verhältnis ist in der Tat eigentümlich, denn die schwarze Farbe ist das Kennzeichen der bündlerischen Organisation, die die Feinde Zarathustras und seiner ersten Gemeinde gewesen sind, wie eben Wikander demonstriert hat. Was die schwarze Farbe anbetrifft, habe ich dieses Detail zu den Kennzeichen der Männerbündler hinzufügen können[189]. M. R. hat Wikander auch Frētōn als den großen Heros der parthischen Männerbünde erkannt[190]. Sowohl Frētōn wie Pišyōtan sind also zoroastrisierte Führer der Männerbünde, und daher erklären sich die Übereinstimmungen. Es verhält sich nämlich auch in Bahm. Yt. so, daß die Feinde *schwarze* Waffen tragen, II 25: *siyāv zēn barēnd*[191].

4.2.2.6. Die apokalyptischen Feinde sind *Hēšm-tōhmakān*, "aus dem Geschlecht Hēšms stammend", "Hēšm-geboren" (Bahm. Yt. II 36; III 3,

---

[182] Vgl. Wikander 1941, 109ff., 124 und Dumézil 1957, 129–141.

[183] In § 4.2.1.1. die II. Strophe [III 27]; XI. Strophe [III 42]; in § 4.2.1.2. Dk VII 8, 45–46; AŽ XVI 51–52.

[184] Vgl. Widengren 1956, 161 mit Verweis auf Strabo XV 3,18, laut welcher Stelle die Jungen παῖδες genannt werden, der Meister aber διδάσκαλος, Lehrer; vgl. ferner *idem* 1969b, 83 f.

[185] S. § 4.2.1.2.

[186] *Vazr* < avest. *vazra*, AirWb 1392.

[187] In § 4.2.1.1. die II. Strophe [III 27]; XI. Strophe [III 42]; in § 4.2.1.2. AŽ XVI 52.

[188] Frētōn > npers. Farīdūn.

[189] Vgl. Widengren 1938, 342f., 349; 1969b, 35. Als Supplement vgl. Garšāspnāmah V. 1072, wo Garšāsp ein Banner mit einem schwarzen Drachen bekommt.

[190] Vgl. Wikander 1938, Kap. V.

[191] Die mparth. Form *siyāv* hat nur ein MS, die anderen MSS geben mpers. *siyāh*, aber K20 hat *siyāv*!

6, 10, 21, 24)[191a]. Es fällt auf, daß dieser Ausdruck in den epischen Fragmenten nicht verwendet wird. Hier werden die Feinde dagegen *tom-tōhmakān*, "der Finsternis entstammend", genannt[192], obwohl Hešm, wie wir sahen, zusammen mit Ahriman der große Gegner des Guten ist. Hešm hat *xru-druš*, die blutige Waffe (Keule), III 24, 30, 35[193]. Das Epithet ist nur eine Transkription des avest. *xrvī.dru*[194], das Aēšma (> Hēšm) bes. in der Yašt-Literatur bekommt. Die Pišyōtan-Fragmente geben also die avest. Überlieferung von Aēšma wieder, so wie sie in den Yašts zu finden ist.

Das Beiwort *tom-tōhmakān* gibt avest. *təmas-čiϑra* wieder, das wir in Vd., aber auch Yt. 6:4 finden, wo die *daēva*-s so genannt werden[195].

4.2.2.7. Die Feinde tragen einen Ledergurt, sie sind *davāl-kustīkān*, ledergegürtelt, III 34[196] aber auch II 50; III 8, 21 außerhalb der epischen Pišyōtan-Fragmente. Das Wort *kustīk* bedeutet hier "Gurt" und nicht wie gewöhnlich die Gebetsschnur der Zoroastrier[197]. Noch immer kann neupers. *kustī* den Gürtel des xorasanischen Ringkämpfers bezeichnen[198]. In ŠN wird geschildert, wie man beim Ringkampf einander am Gürtel aus Leder faßt, (*davāl i kamar*)[199]. Der Gürtel symbolisiert, daß der Männerbündler an seinen Führer, später der Gefolgsmann an seinen Feudalherrn "gebunden" ist[200]. Der Ledergurt ist auch ein Waffengürtel und hebt den kriegerischen Charakter dieser Männerbünde hervor.

4.2.2.8. Die Gegner werden auch als *vičārt-vars*, "mit zerteiltem Haar", geschildert[201]. Ein vollerer Ausdruck findet sich II 25, wo sie als *vars ⟨i⟩ vičārt ō pušt*, "mit bis auf den Rücken zerteiltem Haar" (d. h. Zöpfe tragend), bezeichnet werden[202].

4.2.2.8.1. In einer wichtigen, aber schwierigen Stelle DkM 220:8–14

[191a] S. unten § 4.2.2.8.4., wo III 21 zitiert wird.

[192] In § 4.2.1.1. die IV. Strophe [III 32]; IX. Strophe [III 38]; X. Strophe [III 41].

[193] K20 hat die schlechtere Lesart *xru-draš*, "mit blutigem Banner". Aus der PÜ des avest. Ausdrucks *xrvī.dru* (AirWb 540), die nur eine Umschreibung ist: *xrudruš*, חרדרוש, hat man *xrudrawš* ~ -*draš* gemacht. Man sollte das armen. Lw. *drauš*, Banner, Fahne (mit Hübschmann 1897, 146:211) vergleichen. Aēšma trägt in den avest. Texten "die blutige Keule", aber nicht "das blutige Banner", das Feldzeichen des feindlichen Heeres, *haēnā* (vgl. AirWb 1729 + 539: *xrūra-, drafša-*). Vgl. auch Wikander 1941, 108.

[194] S. vorhergehende Anm.

[195] Vgl. AirWb 648 s. v. *təmas-čiϑra*.

[196] In § 4.2.1.1. die V. Strophe. Die Stelle III 21 außerhalb der Pišyōtan-Fragmente wird unten § 4.2.2.8.4. zitiert.

[197] Die einzige Bedeutung bei MacKenzie 1971, 52, was ein Mangel ist.

[198] Nach Steingass 1947, s. v. *kustī* 1029a.

[199] Vgl. Widengren 1969b, 155f., Anhang 3.

[200] Vgl. Widengren 1969b, Kap. I.

[201] In § 4.2.1.1. die V. Strophe [III 34]; so auch II 35 und III 6 außerhalb der epischen Pišyōtan-Fragmente.

[202] Vgl. Widengren 1969b, 19; s. auch oben § 3.2.2., vor allem aber unten § 4.2.2.8.5. (Text und Übers.).

werden die dämonischen Feinde als *gurgīk brahnak vičārt-vars dēv* bezeichnet, also als "wolfsmäßige, nackte Dämonen mit zerteiltem Haar".

Es ist ein Zeichen nicht nur des iranischen, sondern überhaupt des indogermanischen Kriegertums, daß die Elitekrieger "nackt", d. h. mit nacktem Oberkörper oder wenigstens ohne Brustharnisch, kämpften[203]. Das Flechtetragen der Krieger hat übrigens auch seine indo-germanischen Entsprechungen[204].

Was *gurgīk* betrifft, hat Wikander gezeigt, daß das Mitglied des Männerbundes als "Wolf"[205] bezeichnet wurde. Besonders wichtig ist, daß der avestische Ausdruck *vəhrko bizangrō*, der zweifüßige Wolf, in der PÜ von Vd. 7:52 bewahrt ist[206].

4.2.2.8.2. Diese zweifüßigen Wölfe werden in DkM 729:13 erwähnt, wo gesagt wird, daß die zweifüßigen Wölfe mehr als die vierfüßigen den Tod verdienen, *andar gurgān zanišntarīh ⟨i⟩ hān i 2 zang hač hān i 4 zang*. Der Pahlaviausdruck *gurg i dō zang* ist eine genaue PÜ des avest. *vəhrkō bizangrō*.

4.2.2.8.3. An der Stelle DkM 730:13 heißt es über die von Nicht-Iraniern unternommenen Plünderungen, daß diese Feinde sowohl Wölfe wie Helfer sind. Helfer (*ayār*) ist aber eine Bezeichnung des Gefolgsmannes, des Mitgliedes des sich aus dem Männerbund entwickelnden Gefolges[207].

Der schlechte Wolf (*hān i vattar gurg*) ist voller Heranstürmen (*voiγən*)[208].

4.2.2.8.4. Wir führen in diesem Zusammenhang Bahm. Yt. III 21 an:

ōišān Hēšm-tōhmakān i Šētāspīk, hēn i frāxvānīk,
u sahm i gurg i dō-zang u dēv i davāl-kustīkān.
(Sie schlagen) jene aus dem Geschlecht Hēšms stammenden, die Šētāsp angehören, die Heerschar mit breiter Front,
und den Schrecken der zweifüßigen Wölfe und Dämonen mit Ledergurt.

Hier begegnet uns eine Konzentration der Ausdrücke, die die Feinde bezeichnen. Wir behandeln hier zuerst den Ausdruck *hēn i frāxvānīk*. Die Bezeichnung der feindlichen Scharen ist in mir. zoroastrischen Texten *immer hēn*[209]. So auch das armen. Lw. *hen*[210].

---

[203] Vgl. Widengren 1969b, 19f. und 33.
[204] Vgl. Wikander 1941, 76 Anm. I; Widengren 1969b, 19.
[205] Vgl. Wikander 1938, 64ff.; *gurgīk, -īk*-Ableitung aus mpers. *gurg* < avest. *vəhrka*, AirWb 1418f.
[206] Vgl. Widengren 1938, 328 mit Korrigierung der Übers.
[207] Vgl. Widengren 1969b, 39.
[208] Vgl. Widengren 1938, 329. Die Bedeutung des avest. Wortes *voiγən* ist von Benveniste und Wikander diskutiert worden, vgl. Wikander 1941, 140ff. Ich finde immer noch, daß der Kontext die Übers. "Heranstürmen" befürwortet.
[209] *Hēn* < avest. *haēnā*, AirWb 1729. Vgl. Nyberg 1974, 99b.
[210] Vgl. Widengren 1969b, 44 Anm. 146. Das armen. Wort bedeutet ein feindliches Heer.

Dieses Wort hat in der parth. Sprache wie in den ostiranischen Dialekten indessen eine *positive* Bedeutung gehabt, wie auch das entsprechende indische *sena*. Das deutet wiederum auf die von Wikander im alten Iran aufgezeigten kultisch-sozialen Gegensätze: Zoroastrismus *versus* altiranische Religion. Der Terminus *haēnā* kann zusammen mit *vōiγnā* in Yt. 8:56,61 erwähnt werden.

Der Ausdruck *hēn i frāxvānīk* gibt die PÜ des avest. Ausdruckes *haēnayā̊ pərəθu. ainikayā̊*, Yt. 1:11; 4:3; 5:131; Y. 9:18 wieder. Hier sehen wir wiederum, wie die Pahlavi-Termini in den Schilderungen der apokalyptischen Feinde aus der PÜ des jüngeren Avesta, zumal der Yašt-Texte, stammen; ein unzweideutiger Beleg dafür, daß der Hauptinhalt des Bahm. Yt. aus der PÜ des Avesta-Textes herrührt.

Ein rätselvolles Wort ist Šētāsp(īh), Šētāsp (und dem Šētāsp angehörig). Außer in Dk VII 8,47 finden wir die folgenden Stellen in Bahm. Yt. III 3, 5, 8, 21. Der Name Šētāsp ist aus der späteren nationalen Überlieferung bekannt, wo er mit einer Abstammung von Tūr eingeführt wird[211]. Die abstrakt-kollektive Form Šētāspīh bedeutet wörtlich "die Šētāspschaft", "die zum Šētāsp gehörenden". Der Name ist unbedingt avestisch, höchstwahrscheinlich *Xšaētāspa, "glänzende Rosse habend"[212]. Eigentümlich ist, daß die nationale Überlieferung über Šētāsp ganz positiv ist. Mit Šētāspīh wird das Koll. *kirsyakīh* verbunden. Wie Wikander (gegen eine abwegige ältere Forschung[213]) gezeigt hat, ist das Wort "eine unmittelbare mittelpersische Fortsetzung von air. *kərəsyāka* mit der gewöhnlichen Abstrakt- oder Kollektivendung"[214]. Und avest. *kərəsa* und *kərəsāni* werden beide in der PÜ mit *kirsyakīh* oder *kirsyak* übersetzt[215]. Wikander hat ferner überzeugend nachgewiesen, daß das Wort *kərəsa* das Mitglied des Männerbundes (als Synonym von *gaδa* und *mairya*) ist, das als *aēšma* > *hēšm* gekennzeichnet wird[216]. Die konkrete Bedeutung können wir nicht angeben. Falls wir überall *Šētāspīh u Kirsyakīh* zu lesen haben, könnten wir zur Not mit "Šētāspanhänger" und "Kirsyakanhänger" übersetzen und darunter die Mitglieder des Männerbundes verstehen. Jedenfalls werden wir auch in diesem Fall zu avestischen Verhältnissen zurückversetzt.

4.2.2.8.5. An der von uns schon kurz erwähnten Stelle Bahm. Yt. II 25 wird von den Feinden gesagt[217]:

---

[211] Vgl. Christensen 1917–34, I, 201, 203, 205; 1931, 133; Justi 1895, 294.

[212] Vgl. Justi 1895, 294a. Unter *šētāspīh* finden wir ganz fantastische Angaben: die Kreuzesritter seien damit gemeint!

[213] Sie sah hier eine Bezeichnung für Christen. Dieser Fehler spukt noch bei Molé 1967, 89.

[214] Vgl. Wikander 1941, 137.   [215] AirWb 469, 470.   [216] Vgl. Wikander 1941, 135.

[217] Zu Text und Übers.: mit K20 ist, wie schon (Anm. 191) gesagt, *siyāv*, die mparth. Form zu lesen. Die meisten MSS haben *nērōk–kartār*. Die exakte Bedeutung ist unsicher. Eigentümlich ist, daß dieses Stück von 5 Zeilen 4 Zeilen mit Reim hat. Diese Stelle gründet sich *nicht* auf eine PÜ eines avest. Textes, wie die Syntax zeigt.

ul-grift drafš hēnd	Hochgetragene Banner haben sie,
siyāv zēn barēnd	schwarze Waffen tragen sie,
u vars vičārt ō pušt dārēnd	und das Haar bis auf den Rücken zerteilt haben sie,
u xortak u nitom bandak	und kleine und niedrigste Dienstmänner,
nērōk-kartār zanišn-pēškār vēš hēnd.	Macher der Gewalt, des Mordens Diener sind sie mehr.

Der Ausdruck *ul-grift drafš*, "ein hochgetragenes Banner habend", kehrt in anderen Beschreibungen der feindlichen Scharen wieder, vgl. III (7), 22. Auch dieser Ausdruck besitzt einen avest. Hintergrund, nämlich *uzgərəptō. drafša*[218].

Ein anderer interessanter Ausdruck ist *afrāstak drafš* (III 22), ein Ausdruck, der avest. *ərəδwō. drafša* in der PÜ wiedergibt[219]. Beide Ausdrücke kommen in Verbindung mit *haēnā* (Yt. 1:11) vor. Die Bedeutung ist "ein hochgehobenes Banner habend". Auch einen dritten Ausdruck finden wir, nämlich *xrū-drafš*, das blutige Banner (Bahm. Yt. II 36). Das würde die PÜ des avest. **xrvī. drafša* sein, das aber im jetzigen Avesta nicht belegt ist. Mit Hinweis auf Bahm. Yt. III 24, 30, 35 erscheint *xrū-drafš* als eine Korruptel für *xrū-druš* (vgl. § 4.2.2.6.).

Wie Wikander gezeigt hat, ist "das Heer mit breiter Front" und hochgerichtetem Banner der altiranische Männerbund, wogegen Zarathustra und seine Gemeinde sich mit Entrüstung wenden[220].

4.2.3. Weitere Schilderungen des eschatologischen Endkampfes in Bahm. Yt. Buch III außerhalb der epischen Pišyōtan-Fragmente

4.2.3.1. Der eschatologische Endkampf trägt den Namen *artīk i vazurg*, den Großen Krieg (Bahm. Yt. III 8). Das ist eine Terminologie, der wir später (§ 5.2., bes. § 5.2.5.) in der zervanitischen Apokalyptik begegnen werden.

Ahriman, der betäubt war (III 41), steht aus Rachgier auf und ermahnt den im Berge Demavand gefesselten Tyrannen Aži Dahāk (vgl. AŽ IV 28–29), den Drachen, sich von seinen Fesseln zu lösen und in die Welt hinauszustürmen (III 55). Wasser, Feuer und Pflanzen bitten Ōhrmazd, daß er Frētōn wieder lebendig mache, so daß er Aži Dahāk erschlage: *Frētōn zīvandak apāč kun bē Aži Dahāk zanēt* (III 58)[221].

Wegen einer schlechten Redaktion der verschiedenen Quellen wird aber

---

[218] AirWb 411. PÜ hat *ul-grift drafš*; AirWb gibt die falsche Lesung *us* für *ul*!

[219] AirWb 351.

[220] Vgl. Wikander 1938, 60ff.; 1941, 107ff.

[221] Die Lesung *zīvandak*, mparth. Form (mit Angleichung im Anlaut an mpers.), ist ganz deutlich. Die Lesung *zīndak* bei Anklesaria ist völlig falsch. Bei MacKenzie 1971 fehlt *zīvandak* (der trotz der klaren Schreibung *zywndk* eine Vermischung mit *zīndak*, geschrieben *zyndk*!, zustande bringt), aber nicht bei Nyberg 1974, 231b. S. auch oben § 3.2.1. zu Anm. 69a.

schon III 56 erzählt, daß Frētōn aufsteht. In III 57 wird geschildert, wie Aži Dahāk, der Drache, loskommt und in der Welt grausam wütet und ein Drittel verschlingt. Was tut dann der auferstandene Frētōn? Darüber erfahren wir hier in Bahm. Yt. nichts.

Anstatt Frētōn tritt jetzt Kersāsp auf und schlägt Aži Dahāk mit seiner Keule tot (III 59–61). "Die siegreiche Keule" heißt aber hier *gaδ i pērōzkar*, also eine andere Bezeichnung, die auf eine von der Pišyōtan-Erzählung verschiedenartige Überlieferung hindeutet. Ausführlicher wird das Töten Aži Dahāks AŽ XVII 6–8 geschildert, wo indessen Kersāsp den Namen Sām i Narīmān führt[222].

Auffallend kurz wird endlich das Ende mit der Ankunft des Sōšyans geschildert. In diesen Schilderungen der Kämpfe bewegen wir uns entschieden im Ostiran zur Zeit der avestischen Verhältnisse. Zugrunde liegen Helden und Traditionen aus der Ýašt-Literatur. Das gilt sicherlich auch von der Rolle, die die Zerstörung des Götzentempels (*uzdēstačār*) und der Götterwohnung (*nišēmak*) spielt, denn wir wissen, daß es solche von Frāsiyāp gegründete im Ostiran gab (ŠE § 7).

4.2.3.2. Die Schilderungen der alten ostiranischen Feinde, die den Männerbünden angehörten, sind indessen an einigen Stellen neueren, rein geschichtlichen west- sowohl wie ostiranischen Verhältnissen angepaßt. Diese zeitgeschichtlichen Zusätze sind leicht zu entdecken, z. B. III 3, wo eine exegetische Glosse, von Māhvindat stammend, sagt, daß die Feinde Rhomäer sind; oder III 7: Türken und Rote ⟨Chioniten⟩ (Karmīr ⟨Xiōn⟩)[223]; III 8: Türken und Rhomäer; III 9: Türken, Tāčīken und Rhomäer; III 34: Alexander, der Rhomäer. Ferner findet sich eine Menge exegetischer Glossen der Art, wie oben (§ 4.1.2.) angegeben.

Dadurch versucht man, den Text sowohl geschichtlich wie topographisch zu aktualisieren[224]. An gewissen, schwer zu deutenden Stellen ist der Text von erklärenden Glossen überfüllt, die jede ihre eigene Erklärung geben, vgl. III 9–10, 19, 21.

4.2.3.3. Ein Vergleich mit Buch II von Bahm. Yt. ist lehrreich, denn dort finden wir kaum eine einzige exegetische Glosse. Das ist ein neues Indiz dafür, daß Buch III hauptsächlich auf der PÜ eines avestischen Textes basiert ist. Aber der Redaktor hat sich bemüht, die legendären, anfangs ganz unzoroastrischen Heroen durch Anknüpfung an zoroastrische rituelle Handlungen zu "zoroastrisieren". Er setzt dadurch eine schon jungavestische Tendenz fort[225].

---

[222] *Sām i Narīmān* = avest. *naire-manah* (AirWb 1053), aus der Familie Sāma (AirWb 1571).
[223] Vgl. Bahm. Yt. II 49 und Bailey 1930–32, 946.
[224] S. ferner unten § 4.3.3. und § 7.3. mit anm. 371. Zu einer solchen Aktualisierung s. in diesem Band den Beitrag von T. Olsson § 2.
[225] Vgl. über die Zoroastrisierung von Zamyād Yt., Yt 19, Lommel 1927, 175; Nyberg 1938, 304f.; Christensen 1925–26, 81ff. (seine Datierung ist sicherlich zu niedrig).

4.2.4. *Zusammenfassung der Analyse von Bahm. Yt. Buch III*

In diesem Abschnitt wurde demonstriert, daß Buch III von Bahm. Yt. ein ziemlich umfassendes episches Fragment als Kernstück bewahrt hat. Dieses Epos, im Stil der alten Yašttexte abgefaßt, lag urspr. in avestischer Sprache vor und schildert Verhältnisse und mythisch-legendäre Gestalten, die der damaligen Epoche angehörten. Der Held ist Pišyōtan, der handelnde Gott ist Mithra, der als Überwacher des Vertrages mit Ahriman auftritt – ein zervanitischer Zug. Pišyōtan ist von 150 "Schülern", die seine Gefolgsmänner sind, umgeben. Ihre Tracht mit der *schwarzen* Farbe deutet auf soziale Verhältnisse hin, die dem alten Zoroastrismus unsympathisch, ja widerwärtig waren. Aber der Text ist gewissermaßen zoroastrisiert worden, so daß Pišyōtan als ein Glaubensheld, der die Dämonen bekämpft und den Götzentempel niederreißt, auftritt.

Es wurden ferner andere Stellen in Bahm. Yt. und anderen Texten untersucht, wo Schilderungen der Feinde des Irans vorkommen, und es wurde aufgezeigt, daß sie avest. Epitheta und avest. Charakterisierungen der Feinde beinhalten, die auf die Männerbünde hindeuten. Wichtig dabei ist, daß sie gescheiteltes Haar haben, *schwarze* Waffen tragen und nackt sind. So werden wir auch hier auf ältere Zustände zurückgeführt. Diese inhaltlichen Kriterien stimmen mit den formalen, sprachlichen, was das Pišyōtan-Epos betrifft, vollständig überein, eine Tatsache, die bes. unterstrichen werden sollte.

4.3. *Analyse von Bahman Yašt Buch II im Vergleich mit den Orakeln des Hystaspes*

4.3.1. *Bahman Yašt Buch II*

Die Verhältnisse in Bahm. Yt. Buch II liegen anders als in Buch III. *Erstens* rein formalphilologisch, denn es ist deutlich, daß der Inhalt nicht in demselben Maße aus der PÜ eines avestischen Textes stammt, wie unsere Analyse demonstrieren wird. *Zweitens* inhaltlich, denn die Unordnung in der Welt und in der Gesellschaft spielen hier eine noch größere Rolle als das Heranstürmen der Feinde.

4.3.1.1. Direkt aus einer PÜ stammen der Zitatformel bzw. Stellung des Verbums im Satze oder der anderen Kriterien wegen in erster Linie folgende Stellen:

II 1, wo es heißt: *pat zand i Vohuman Yasn paitāk ku;*

II 2, wo eine Glosse, mit *ku* eingeführt, folgt;

II 4: *čē mēnīt Spitāmān Zartušt i ahlav*; mit unregelmäßiger Stellung des Verbums;

II 7–8: an beiden Stellen heißt es: *u-š bē dīt Zartušt*; ebenso wie II 4;

II 11–12: *guft-aš Ōhrmazd* bzw. *Zartušt* mit unregelmäßiger Stellung des Verbums anstatt *Ōhrmazd* bzw. *Zartušt guft*;

II 15, mit der unregelmäßigen Stellung des Verbums, ist wegen der inhaltlichen Feststellung *besonders* wichtig: *draxt-ē bun i tō dīt hān gētīh hast i man Ōhrmazd dāt*, "der Stamm des Baumes, den du gesehen hast, ist jene Welt, die ich, Ōhrmazd, schuf". Hier wird also im avestischen Text festgestellt, daß der von Zarathustra geschaute Baum ein Symbol der Welt ist – er ist der Weltbaum.

II 17 zeigt der Satz *bē pālāyēt hamāk gēhān* mit der anormalen Stellung des Verbums, daß auch diese Stelle aus der PÜ eines avestischen Textes herrührt[225a];

II 23 mit der Frage Zarathustras hat wieder die anormale Ausdrucksweise *guft-aš Zartušt* und ist also avestisch;

II 24 mit der Antwort des Ōhrmazd verhält es sich ähnlich; dazu kommt noch der Ausdruck: *rōšn kunam daxšak i hazārak i tō sar bavēt*, "ich will das Zeichen klarmachen, das das Ende deines Millenniums bedeutet"[226];

II 25–26 enthalten avestisches Material, wie wir schon aufgezeigt haben[227].

Hier ist in II 26 ein Satz besonders klar, nämlich *ul dvārēnd ō ēn Ērāndēhān*, "sie laufen Sturm gegen diese Länder vom Iran". Die Stellung des Verbums ist unregelmäßig und der Buchpahlavi-Ausdruck entspricht wahrscheinlich avest. *⋆usdvarənti*[228].

II 29 begegnen wir wieder sicherem avest. Material, denn die Wortstellung *bē kanēnd ēn Ērān-dēhān*, "sie zerstören die Länder vom Iran", ist unregelmäßig;

Zu *II 48* notiert man als avest. den Ausdruck *spandarmat zamīk*, "die Spandarmat-Erde", denn Vd. 2:10 wird die Erde als Spenta Ārmaiti angeredet; derselbe Ausdruck findet sich auch *II 53*;

Zu *II 54* ist die Konstruktion *guft-aš Ōhrmazd* schon mehrmals notiert;

II 55: *ētōn-aš guft Ōhrmazd ō Spitāmān Zartušt*, "in dieser Weise sprach Ōhrmazd zu Spitāmān Zartušt" ist ebenso eine avest. Konstruktion;

In *II 57* ist *pursīt Zartušt hač Ōhrmazd*, "Zarathustra fragte Ōhrmazd" ebenso eine avest. Konstruktion;

II 58 finden wir wiederum *guft-aš Ōhrmazd ō Spitāmān Zartušt*, und in *II 62* kommt wieder *guft-aš Ōhrmazd* vor.

[225a] S. auch unten § 7.2.2.

[226] So scheint es mir notwendig zu übersetzen, wenn wir nicht eine falsche Wiedergabe des avest. Relativpronom. annehmen müssen; vgl. hier Vd. 4:51: *daxšta daxštavanta yā . . .*, "mit dem Zeichen gezeichnet, mit dem . . ." Dann wäre zu übersetzen: "das Zeichen, mit dem das Ende deines Millenniums da ist". Sachlich gibt es keinen Unterschied.

[227] S. § 4.2.2.8.5.

[228] Vgl. AirWb 765, allerdings nicht mit *us* belegt.

4.3.1.2. Diese Übersicht zeigt, daß der Umfang des Materials in Buch II, das sich aufgrund formal-philologischer Kriterien als aus dem sassanidischen Avesta stammend erwiesen hat, bedeutend geringer ist als in Buch III. Hier sind aber zwei Bemerkungen notwendig: *erstens* fordert selbstverständlich der Zusammenhang, daß an vielen Stellen das zwischen zwei "avestischen" Prophezeiungen befindliche Material auch *ursprünglich* aus dem Avesta stammt, z. B. wenn es sich um die Äste des Baumes, die die älteren Perioden der Geschichte Irans symbolisieren, handelt; *zweitens* wenn es um kosmische Motive, die altiranisch oder altindisch sind, geht. Wir geben einige Beispiele:

In II 5—6 wird *Ōhrmazd* als *dātār i gēhān astōmandān ahlav* angeredet. Es ist aber bemerkenswert, daß *gēhān* hier im Plural steht, weil *astōmandān* auch Plural ist. Der Ausdruck bedeutet also "gerechter Schöpfer der körperlichen Wesen", so daß *gēhān* nicht wie gewöhnlich "Welt" bedeutet[229], sondern daß die ganze Anrede die wörtliche Übersetzung von der avest. Anrede in Yt. 1:1 ist: *ahura mazdā . . . dātarə gaēϑanąm astvaitinąm ašāum*. Es kann also keinem Zweifel unterliegen, daß die zwei zusammengehörenden Paragraphen II 5—6 avest. Vorlagen besitzen[230].

Für die Rahmenerzählung verweisen wir auf den Beitrag von Hultgård in diesem Band und stellen hier nur fest, daß der Zusammenhang auch in der avest. Vorlage eine fortlaufende Erzählung erforderlich macht. Darum muß selbstverständlich II 14, wie die damit korrespondierende Stelle II 17, eine avest. Vorlage haben.

Einen ganzen Komplex umfassen die Paragraphen II 23—29, wo II 28 das Treiben der dämonischen Feinde beschreibt, wo wir aber keine avest. Vorlage nachweisen können. Auf II 27 kommen wir später (§ 4.3.2.1.2.) zurück, ebenso auf II 29—32 (*ibid.* und § 4.3.2.1.1.). Es folgen dann mehrere Paragraphen, bei denen man einen sassanidischen Hintergrund vermuten kann, weil teils auf rituelle Verhältnisse, teils auf Folgen der durch Mazdak verursachten sozialen Unruhen (II 38—39) angespielt wird. Erst mit II 41—44 kommt ein avest. Komplex, den wir unten (§ 4.3.2.1.2.) besprechen werden; dies ist auch der Fall mit II 47—48. Mit II 54—55 folgt ein neuer avest. Komplex; so auch II 57—58.

4.3.2. Die Orakel des Hystaspes

In den Orakeln des Hystaspes werden verschiedene Motive angetroffen, die auch in Bahm. Yt. vorkommen und dort eine große Rolle spielen. Daneben werden wir als Vergleich AŽ anführen[231].

---

[229] Nyberg 1974, 82a hat notiert, daß *gēhān* < *gaēϑānām*, aber er gibt den Ausdruck *astōmandān gēhān* an, ohne Yt. 1:1 zu beachten. Auch in der PÜ bleibt *gēhān* also ein Plural, wie die Verwendung der Pluralform *astōmandān gēhān* zeigt.

[230] Die Konstruktion *čē mēnīt Spitāmān Zartušt* deutet ja auf eine avest. Vorlage hin.

[231] Für das Folgende vgl. Widengren 1965, 199 ff., wo auf die ausgezeichneten Untersu-

Wir folgen dem Gang der Ereignisse, so wie sie von Lactantius geschildert werden[232]:

Dies soll eine Zeit sein, in der die Gerechtigkeit preisgegeben und die Unschuld verhaßt sein wird, in der die Bösen in feindlicher Weise die Guten ausplündern werden. Weder Gesetz noch Ordnung noch Zucht im Kriegsdienst wird beobachtet werden, niemand wird den Hunden Achtung erweisen noch die Pflicht der Frömmigkeit anerkennen, weder mit dem andern Geschlecht noch mit Kindern Mitleid kennen: alles wird verworren und gegen (göttliches) Recht, gegen die Rechtsbestimmungen der Natur vermischt sein. Die ganze Erde wird auf diese Weise gleichwie durch eine allgemeine Räuberei verwüstet.

Wenn dies geschehen ist, dann werden die Gerechten und die Anhänger der Wahrheit sich von den Bösen absondern und in die Einöde fliehen. Nachdem er dieses gehört hat, wird der Gottlose, in Zorn entbrannt, mit einem großen Heere kommen, und nachdem er alle Truppen versammelt hat, wird er den Berg, auf dem sich die Gerechten aufhalten werden, umzingeln, um sie zu ergreifen.

Wenn aber diese sich auf allen Seiten umgeben und belagert sehen werden, werden sie mit lauter Stimme zu Gott rufen und die himmlische Hilfe erflehen. Und Gott wird sie erhören und vom Himmel aus 'den Großen König' senden, um sie zu retten und zu befreien und alle Gottlosen mit Feuer und Schwert zugrundezurichten.

4.3.2.1. Zuerst schildern die Orakel *die schlimmen Zustände*, die in der Endzeit über die Welt und im Kosmos kommen werden.

4.3.2.1.1. Hier treten uns eine Reihe von aus der iranischen Apokalyptik wohlbekannten Themen entgegen. Wir finden z. B. das Thema der Gewaltherrschaft, der Gesetzlosigkeit und der allgemeinen *Auflösung in der Gesellschaft*. Hierzu bietet Bahm. Yt. II 29—30 einen Paralleltext:

Und ihr Versprechen und Vertrag haben keine Wahrheit und keine Form, und sie halten nicht die Sicherheit und stehen nicht zu dem Versprechen, das sie machen. Mit Betrug und Gier und übler Herrschaft zerstören sie diese . . . Länder vom Iran.

In jenem Zeitalter . . . werden alle Menschen Betrüger sein, und Ehrung und Wohlgefallen und Seelenfreundschaft werden aus der Welt verschwinden, die Freundschaft des Vaters mit dem Sohne und des Bruders mit dem Bruder werden verschwinden, der Schwiegersohn wird vom Schwiegervater geschieden sein und die Mutter von ihrer Tochter getrennt und anderen Willens als sie sein.

Das Thema der allgemeinen Auflösung der Familienfreundschaft und Liebe wird auch AŽ XVI 8 angeschlagen. Die Mutter verkauft ihre Tochter, der Sohn vertreibt während ihres Lebens Vater und Mutter von ihrer Hausgewalt, ja tötet sie.

Die Orakel des Hystaspes schildern im angegebenen Passus die Flucht der Gerechten in die Einöde. Dieses Thema korrespondiert mit Bahm. Yt. III 10, wo gesagt wird, daß alle Länder vom Iran aus ihrem eigenen Ort

---

chungen von Benveniste 1932a und Cumont 1931 Rücksicht genommen ist. Cumont war hier bahnbrechend. Wir sollten aber auch nicht vergessen, daß es Windisch 1929 war, der die Aufmerksamkeit auf die Orakel des Hystaspes richtete.

[232] Lactantius, Inst. divinae VII 17,9—11; Text bei Bidez–Cumont 1938, II, 370.

[233] III 10 bietet am Ende einen schwierigen, wahrscheinlich korrupten Text, aber die Flucht nach Patašxvārgar ist davon nicht abhängig.

nach Patašxvārgar gelangen. Die Exegeten glossieren hier auch mit anderen Orten. Das Wichtige ist, daß es sich um eine Flucht handelt[233]. Um sein Leben zu retten, verläßt man Frau und Kind und Eigentum (III 11). Das bedeutet, daß man in die Einöde flieht, um sein Leben zu retten[234]. So heißt es auch AŽ XVI 11, daß man in die Ferne geht, *vas martōm ō uzdēhīkīh, bēkānīh u saxtīh rasēt*, "viele Menschen gelangen in Landsflucht, Exil und Plage". Das sind Leute, in deren Augen ihre Kinder unter diesen Umständen von geringem Wert (*xvār*) sind.

4.3.2.1.2. In der Schilderung der bösen Zustände der Endzeit finden sich eine Reihe charakteristischer Züge, die aus den Pahlavi-Apokalypsen wohlbekannt sind. Sie setzen die schon früher in der iranischen Apokalyptik (§ 1.2.) belegten Schilderungen der *kosmischen Störungen* fort. Die Orakel geben an, daß die Länder auch durch beständige Erderschütterungen untergehen werden, Instit. VII 16:4:

> *Eruentur funditus civitates atque interibunt, non modo ferro atque igni, verum etiam terrae motibus adsiduis . . .*

Dies stimmt mit Bahm. Yt. II 48 überein: *Spandarmat zamīk dahān apāč višāyēt*, "die Erde Spandarmat wird ihren Mund auftun". Vor allem aber soll AŽ XVI 13 zum Vergleich herangezogen werden: "Die Erdbeben (*būm-čandak*) werden zahlreich sein und viel Schaden anrichten."

Die Quellen und Flüsse werden austrocknen, Instit. VII 14,4 [7]. Der Mangel an Wasser wird auch AŽ XVI 13 erwähnt, vor allem aber Bahm. Yt. II 42 ausführlich geschildert[235]:

> Der Regen regnet nicht zu seiner Zeit, und wenn es regnet, regnet es mehr Ungeziefer als Wasser, und das Wasser der Flüsse und Quellen wird vermindert, eine Vermehrung findet nicht mehr statt.

Am Himmel ereignen sich furchtbare Zeichen: Kometen, Sonnenfinsternis, Veränderungen der Mondfarbe und Sturz der Sterne (Instit. VII 16,4 [7]).

Diese uranischen Erscheinungen werden ebenfalls in Bahm. Yt. II 31 und 42 geschildert:

> Die Sonne wird unsichtbarer und kleiner werden . . . und den ganzen Himmel wird eine Nebelwolke nachtfinster machen[236].

Dann wird laut der Orakel des Hystaspes das Jahr verkürzt, der Monat verkleinert und der Tag zusammengepreßt (Instit. VII 16,4 [10]).

Bahm. Yt. II 31 behandelt dasselbe Thema:

> Das Jahr und der Monat und der Tag werden kürzer[237].

---

[234] Vgl. Cumont 1931, 83.   [235] Vgl. auch II 41.
[236] Das Wort *nēzm*, Nebelwolke, mparth. belegt, fehlt in MacKenzie 1971.
[237] Man sollte beachten, daß sowohl bei Lactantius wie in Bahm. Yt. von Jahr, Monat und Tag, aber nicht von *Woche* gesprochen wird.

Auch die höchsten Berge werden einstürzen und den Ebenen gleichge-
macht werden. (Instit. VII 16,4 [11]).

Es ist dies eines der bekanntesten Motive der iranischen Apokalyptik,
schon aus spätachemenidischer Zeit bekannt, wie wir unten (§ 5.1.3. und
§ 6.1.13.) sehen werden. In Bdhn XXXIV, A 228:3f. heißt es mit einem
Zitat aus dem Avesta[238]:

Auch dieses sagt man: 'Diese Erde wird ohne Täler und ohne Hügel eine Ebene sein',
ēn zamīk anapēšar u anišēp u hāmōn bē bavēt.

Wegen aller dieser Übel wünscht man sich den Tod (Instit. VII 16,4
[12]). Das wird in Bahm. Yt. II 44 ziemlich breit ausgeführt:

i-šān zīvandakīh andar nē apāyēt u margīh pat āyaft xvāhēnd.
Unter welchen das Leben nicht wünschenswert ist, und sie wünschen den Tod als Gabe.

Tatsächlich kommt der Tod in einem solchen Ausmaß vor, daß vom
Menschengeschlecht kaum ein Zehntel übrigbleibt, von Tausenden kaum
hundert (Instit. VII 16,4 [12]).

Dieses charakteristische Detail kennen wir auch aus Bahm Yt. II 47, wo
wir lesen:

pat ōišān ēn martōm pat 10, 9 pat kust i apāxtar bē apasīhēnd.
Wegen jener Leute (sc. der Niedrigen und Schlechten) verschwinden im nördlichen Bereich
neun von zehn Menschen (von den Adeligen und Großen)[239].

Zu vergleichen ist auch II 27, wo eine graduelle Verminderung des
Staates und der Gesellschaft erwähnt wird, die von einem Gau (*rōstak*) bis
zu einer Schwelle des Hauses (*astānak*) geht.

Es wären auch andere Stellen zu notieren, aber wir erwähnen hier nur
noch ein charakteristisches und sehr wichtiges Thema: In Bahm. Yt. II 32
heißt es:

u martōm kōtaktar zāyēt, "und die Menschen werden kleiner geboren werden".

Hand in Hand mit der physischen Schwäche geht eine Schwächung der
moralischen Kraft, wie gesagt wird:

u-šān hunar u nērōk kam u frēftārtar u vattardāttar bavēnd, spās u āžarm i nān u namak nē dārēnd u-
šān dōšāram pat sayōk nē dārēnd[240].
Und ihre Tugend und Kraft ist geringer, und sie werden trügerischer und schlechter
veranlagt. Sie haben keine Dankbarkeit und keinen Respekt vor Brot und Salz, und auf
Waisen nehmen sie keine Rücksicht.

---

[238] Das Avestazitat bestätigt das Alter dieser Vorstellung; vgl. auch unten § 5.1.3.
[239] Widengren 1965, 206 ist zu korrigieren, denn neun von zehn verfallen nicht nur der
Armut, sondern verschwinden geradezu!
[240] Das Wort *sayōk* (die Lautform ist hypothetisch) ist mparth.; vgl. Andreas-Henning 1934,
906 f. [61 f.]; *sywg,* avest. *saē,* AirWb 1547. Nicht in MacKenzie 1971.

Dieses Motiv kennen wir aus der indischen Weltalterlehre. In der letzten Periode (*kaliyuga*)[241] werden die Menschen kleiner geboren und schwächer. Sie leben nur allerhöchst 20 Jahre. Und diese Menschen sind dem Unglauben, der Ungerechtigkeit und sittlichem Verderben anheim gefallen[242]. Warum diese allgemeine Schwächung in der Welt und in der Menschheit eintritt, werden wir unten (§ 5.1.2. und vgl. auch § 6.1.) erklären.

4.3.2.2. Die *Entscheidungsschlacht* zwischen den dämonischen Feinden Irans und den gerechten Iraniern wird ja auch in Bahm. Yt. Buch II erwähnt, aber der Bericht über den siegreichen Kampf der Iranier findet sich erst in Buch III, ein Kampf, der ja oft in den apokalyptischen Texten erwähnt wird.

Die Orakel schildern in lebhaften Farben, wie die auf dem Berg vom Teufel und seinen Truppen umzingelten Gerechten zu Gott flehen und dieser als ihren Retter den Großen König sendet, Instit. VII 19,5: Er steigt vom Himmel herab als der Anführer des "heiligen Kriegsdienstes" (*dux sanctae militiae*). Ein unauslöschliches Feuer wird ihm vorangehen. Es wird mit der Menge gekämpft, die den Berg umzingelt hat, und das Blut wird wie ein Wildbach fließen. Der gottlose Feind wird, nachdem seine Truppen vertilgt sind, allein fliehen.

Der *dux sanctae militiae* ist Mithra, denn in den Mithramysterien geben die Mysten durch Fahneneid (*sacramentum*) ihren Namen für den heiligen Kriegsdienst. Sie sind die *milites dei*, und er ist ihr *dux*[243]. Mithra tritt ja in Bahm. Yt. III 32–36 als der große Führer im Kampf gegen Ahriman auf[244]. Die Angaben stützen sich wie immer gegenseitig.

Das Feuer, das laut Lactantius dem himmlischen Führer vorangeht, ist eine bekannte Erscheinung in der iranischen Apokalyptik, vgl. Bdhn XXXIV, A 225:6[245] und AZ XVII 15, wo gesagt wird, daß Šahrēvar[246] alle Berge in der Welt anzündet (*tāpēt*).

Zum Motiv der göttlichen Hilfe sollte man auch Bahm. Yt. III 31 vergleichen, wo Ōhrmazd zum Berge Hukairyāt kommt und den Amahraspandān[247] den Befehl erteilt, die himmlischen Scharen, die Yazatas, dem Führer der Gerechten im Kampf gegen die Bösen, Pišyōtan, zu Hilfe zu senden[248].

---

[241] Dazu vgl. § 1.2.1. mit Fig. 1 bei S. S. Hartman in diesem Band.

[242] Vgl. Widengren 1969, 458, 462, wo Indien und Iran miteinander verglichen werden.

[243] Vgl. Reitzenstein 1927, 192. Der Begriff *sancta militia* ist in den Isismysterien aufgenommen, wo er eigtl. unmotiviert vorkommt. Die Mysten Mithras sind *milites sui*, Tertull., De *praescr. haereticorum* 40. Für Mithra als den Anführer im Kriege gegen die bösen Mächte am Ende der Zeiten, den *rex magnus*, vgl. Bidez-Cumont 1938, II, 372.

[244] S. oben § 4.2.1.1.   [245] Vgl. Cumont 1931, 42 ff.

[246] Šahrēvar < avest. *Xšaϑra vairya*.

[247] Amahraspandān < avest. *aməša Spənta*.

[248] Von Bidez-Cumont 1938, II, 372 Anm. 4 richtig angeführt.

Nachdem der gottlose Führer oft besiegt und geflohen war, doch wiederholt den Krieg erneut angefangen hat, wird er endgültig zusammen mit allen Gottlosen überwunden und, nachdem seine Anhänger umgebracht worden sind, gefangen und gefesselt. Endlich muß er die Strafe für seine Freveltaten leiden, Instit. VII 19,6. Aber auch die übrigen frevelhaften Gewaltherrscher, die die Erdscheibe "zerrieben haben", werden zusammen mit ihm gefesselt und zum König geführt. Er wird sie überführen und verurteilen und wohlverdienten Martern überliefern.

Die Götzentempel und Götzenbilder werden niedergeworfen und verbrannt werden, Instit. VII 19,7. Auch Bahm. Yt. III erzählt am Ende von der Tötung des Gewaltherrschers Aži Dahāk und von der Zerstörung der Götzentempel (III 36, 37, 41, 42). Auch Bdhn XXXIII, A 218:2−4, endet damit, daß Pišyōtan mit seinen 150 "Schülern" den Götzentempel zerstört.

Den Namen der großen eschatologischen Schlacht, der Große Krieg (*artīk i vazurg*) haben wir in Bahm. Yt. III 8 vorgefunden, wo gesagt wird, daß die ledergegürtelten Feinde hervorstürmen und daß an drei Orten der Große Krieg dreimal ausgefochten wird. Hier haben wir die Entsprechung der wiederholten Schlachten in den Orakeln des Hystaspes[249]. Eine abweichende Terminologie finden wir AŽ XVI 35, *hān i vazurg kārēčār*[250].

4.3.3. Zusammenfassung

Durch Vergleich mit den Orakeln des Hystaspes, die mindestens um 100 v. Chr. entstanden sind[251], hat sich herausgestellt, daß viel Stoff in Bahm. Yt. II, der aufgrund formal-philologischer Gründe nicht als avestisch zu erweisen ist, schon in der Zeit der Orakel in Form von iranischen apokalyptischen Themata kursierte.

Wenn wir diesen Stoff zu dem vorhandenen avestischen addieren, sehen wir sofort, daß auch der größere Teil von Buch II einen avest. Ursprung besitzt. Sassanidisch ist die Adaption des alten Stoffes an die sassanidischen Verhältnisse, bes. was die letzte Zeit des Reiches betrifft, als die Kriege mit den Byzantinern, Türken und vor allem Arabern den Sturz des Sassanidenreiches herbeiführten[252].

Dazu kommen die Anspielungen auf die Mazdakitenunruhen und die religiöse Zersplitterung, die man als einen Abfall vom rechten Glauben empfunden hat. Typisch ist hier auch das Interesse für Rituale und Feuerdienst. Aber diese Zusätze oder Umformulierungen, die mit der zeitge-

---

[249] Die zoroastrische Überlieferung verteilt indessen diese 3 Kriege auf 3 verschiedene Perioden, Bahm. Yt. III 9; AŽ Appendix I 7. Die Überlieferung ist hier sehr fest. S. auch oben § 4.2.3.1. und unten § 5.2.5.

[250] Die Manichäer haben diese Terminologie vom Zervanismus übernommen, vgl. Widengren 1961, 70.

[251] Vgl. Widengren 1965, 199 Anm. 1.   [252] Vgl. oben § 4.2.3.2. sowie unten §. 7.3.

schichtlichen Deutung zusammenhängen, lassen sich durch kritische Analyse leicht ausscheiden. Eine ins Detail gehende literarkritische Arbeit bleibt ein dringendes Desiderat[253].

5. Die zervanitische Apokalyptik

Wie wir oben (§ 3.1.2.) hervorgehoben haben, war der Zervanismus die Religion der medischen Magier, die ihre Stellung im Partherreich bewahrten und bes. im NW-Iran, Armenien und Kleinasien stark waren[254].

5.1. Analyse von Plutarch De Iside et Osiride 46–47 im Vergleich mit iranischen Texten

Das älteste Zeugnis der zervanitischen Apokalyptik findet man bei Plutarch, wo eine Übersicht über die Weltentwicklung geboten wird[255]:

(46.) Einige meinen, daß es zwei Götter gibt, gleich wie Kunstnebenbuhler, der eine der Schöpfer der guten, der andere der schlechten Dinge. Einige nennen den besseren 'Gott', den andern aber 'Dämon', so wie es eben Zoroaster, der Magier, tat, der 5000 Jahre vor dem trojanischen Krieg gelebt haben soll. Jener nannte den einen Oromazes, den andern Areimanios, und er meinte, daß der eine dem Licht mehr als allen anderen wahrnehmbaren Dingen gleich sei, der andere aber im Gegenteil der Finsternis und Unkenntnis gleiche, daß indessen zwischen den beiden sich Mithras befinde; darum benennen auch die Perser Mithras mit dem Namen 'Mittler'. Er lehrte sie auch, dem einen Gelübde und Dankopfer, dem anderen apotropäische und finstere Opfer darzubringen. Sie zerstoßen nämlich ein Kraut, Omomi genannt, in einem Mörser und rufen dabei Hades und die Finsternis an. Dann mischen sie es mit dem Blut eines geschlachteten Wolfes, bringen es an einen sonnenlosen Ort und werfen es dort weg. Auch von den Pflanzen meinen sie nämlich, daß manche dem Guten Gott, andere dem Bösen Dämon angehören; und von den Tieren die Hunde, Vögel und Igel dem Guten, dem Bösen aber die Wasserratten. Deswegen preisen sie denjenigen glücklich, der die meisten [der letzteren] getötet hat.

(47.) Indessen erzählen auch sie viele mythische Fabeln von den Göttern, unter anderem auch das Folgende: Der eine, Oromazes, aus dem reinsten Licht, der andere, Areimanios, aus dem Dunkel geboren, führen gegeneinander Krieg.

[. . . Hier folgt ein Bericht darüber, wie vom Guten Gott eine Götterreihe in Form abstrakter Begriffe geschaffen wurde . . .[256]]

Ferner versetzte er vierundzwanzig andere Götter in ein Ei. Aber die von Areimanios geschaffenen Götter, die ebensoviele waren, durchbohrten das Ei, ⟨weil sie nach dem Glanz

---

[253] Vgl. den Beitrag von A. Hultgård in diesem Band.

[254] Vgl. Widengren 1965, 174 ff. und 214 ff. mit Hinweis auf die Arbeiten von Bidez-Cumont 1938 und Wikander 1946, z. B. 1–17 und 83 ff., die beide viel Material und eine Fülle von Gesichtspunkten bieten, die aber in Einzelheiten zu korrigieren und ergänzen sind. Nyberg 1938, wo ja der Zervanismus als Religion der medischen Magier zuerst aufgezeigt wurde, behandelt nicht die parthische Periode, geht aber auf S. 392–395 auf den Text von De Iside et Osiride ein.

[255] Text bei Bidez-Cumont 1938, II, 70–72; Text und Übers. bei Griffiths 1970, 190–195; Kommentar *ibid.*, 470–482.

[256] Dazu Näheres unten § 5.1.1.

des Himmels lüstern waren[257]〉, wodurch das Böse mit dem Guten vermischt wurde (ὅϑεν ἀναμέμικται τὰ κακὰ τοῖς ἀγαϑοῖς).

Aber die schicksalsbestimmte Zeit (χρόνος εἱμαρμένος) wird kommen, wenn Areimanios, der Bringer von Seuche und Not, durch diese notwendigerweise völlig vernichtet sein und verschwinden wird (ἀνάγκη φϑαρῆναι παντάπασι καὶ ἀφανισϑῆναι), wenn die Erde flach und eben sein und eine einzige Lebensweise, ein einziger Staat und eine einzige Sprache alle glückseligen Menschen umfassen wird.

Theopompus sagt, daß laut den Magiern[258] abwechselnd nacheinander der eine der Götter 3000 Jahre herrschen und der andere beherrscht wird[259], aber daß während anderer 3000 Jahre sie einander bekämpfen und bekriegen und der eine die Herrschaft des anderen auflöst. Aber zuletzt wird Hades[260] unterliegen und die Menschen werden glücklich sein, indem sie weder Nahrung mehr bedürfen noch einen Schatten werfen. Der Gott, der dieses zustande bringt, wird eine Zeit ruhig sein und ausruhen, die übrigens für einen Gott nicht besonders lang, für einen schlafenden Menschen aber hinreichend ist[261].

5.1.1. Der Gewährsmann wenigstens des Schlußberichtes ist der Historiker Theopompus von Chios (* ca. 378 v. Chr.)[262], der also Anschauungen wiedergibt, die in spätachämenidischer und frühparthischer Zeit maßgebend waren. Man muß Nyberg darin recht geben, daß Theopompus der alleinige Gewährsmann ist[263]. Diese seine Ansicht läßt sich leicht beweisen: der Text gibt nämlich, ganz wie die Berichte in Bdh., Zātspr. und (teilweise) Bahm. Yt. eine Übersicht über die Weltentwicklung vom Kampf am Urbeginn zwischen Ōhrmazd und Ahriman bis zum Schluß der Welt mit dem Verschwinden Ahrimans und dem Glückszustand der Welt. Eigentümlicherweise kann man diese Übereinstimmung nirgends notiert finden[264].

Wir sehen also, wie zwei Götter, Oromazes und Areimanios, gegeneinanderstehen. Eigentlich ist nur der eine, der Gute, ein "Gott", während der

---

[257] Vgl. Zātspr. I 3: "Und er (sc. Ahriman) sah einen Strahl vom Licht, und wegen der Verschiedenheit von seiner eigenen Natur strebte er es zu erreichen, und sein Verlangen nach ihm wuchs ebenso wie nach der Finsternis" (Übers. nach Widengren 1967, 286). Der griechische Text ist an dieser Stelle korrupt, s. Griffiths 1970, 192, 478; Bidez-Cumont 1938, II, 71, 76f. Anm. 17.

[258] Sie werden also ausdrücklich als Gewährsmänner bezeichnet.

[259] An diesem Punkte bietet die deutsche Fassung bei Nyberg 1938, 393 eine falsche Übersetzung.

[260] Für die durchgehende Gleichstellung Ahrimans mit Hades vgl. Bidez-Cumont 1938, I, 59 Anm. 3. Doch ist es bemerkenswert, daß hier *nicht* der Name Areimanios verwendet wird. Dieser Umstand könnte auf zwei Quellen hindeuten.

[261] Für den Ausdruck vgl. Bidez-Cumont 1938, II, 78 Anm. 26.

[262] S. Griffiths 1970, 480 und dort angegebene Lit., vgl. auch Widengren 1965, 216 Anm. 3; 1969, 472 mit Anm. 52.

[263] Man nimmt gewöhnlich an, der Text stamme nicht aus einer Quelle, aber die Datierung ist davon unabhängig, weil die zwei anderen supponierten Gewährsmänner (Eudemus von Rhodos und Eudoxus von Knidos) auch während der Achämenidenzeit lebten; vgl. Bidez-Cumont 1938, II, 72 Anm. 1; Widengren 1965, 216 Anm. 3 und Griffiths 1970, 471.

[264] Auch nicht bei Nyberg 1938, 392ff., der anscheinend die aus zervanitischem Blickpunkt übergreifende Weltbetrachtung des Textes nicht gesehen hat. Seine Analyse ist sonst lehrreich und sollte neben denen von Benveniste und Cumont beachtet werden.

andere, der Böse, ein "Dämon" genannt wird[265]. Tatsächlich sind sie aber ebenbürtige Nebenbuhler, die jeder ihre Schöpfung schaffen. Der Gute Gott schuf zuerst himmlische Wesen, die deutlich die Ameša Spentas sind und abstrakte Namen tragen, danach 24 andere Götter, die er in ein Ei verschloß. Zusammen mit den sechs Ameša Spentas sind sie offenbar die 30 Götter der Tage des Monats[266]. Aber die von Areimanios geschaffenen Götter, die ebensoviele waren, durchbohrten das Ei, wodurch das Böse mit dem Guten vermischt wurde. Diesen Angriff von unten gegen die himmlische Welt kennen wir sowohl aus Bdhn I als auch aus Zātspr. I[267], und die Eigestalt des Universums finden wir in MX XLIV 8:

Asmān u Zamīk u āp u apārīk har čē andarōn xāyak-dēs
Der Himmel und die Erde und das Wasser und alles übrige, was sich im eiförmigen Gebäude befindet.

Die durch diesen Angriff entstandene "Mischung" (*gumēčišn*) ist ja ein Hauptdogma der zervanitischen Religion[268], die ebenfalls in De Iside et Osiride als Resultat des Angriffes klar zum Ausdruck kommt: ὅϑεν ἀναμέμικται τὰ κακὰ τοῖς ἀγαϑοῖς (§ 47 [370 B]).

5.1.2. Der zervanitische Charakter wurde zuerst von Benveniste in einer bahnbrechenden Untersuchung demonstriert[269] und von Nyberg stark unterstrichen[270]. Man hat zwar den zervanitischen Charakter bestreiten wollen[271]; aber ein solches Unternehmen ist aussichtslos. Die Argumente für den zervanitischen Typus der geschilderten Religion der Magier sind zu stark und lassen sich außer durch das schon (§ 5.1.1.) erwähnte Motiv der "Mischung" *hauptsächlich* folgendermaßen zusammenfassen:

(1) Oromazes und Areimanios sind zwei *gleichberechtigte Gegner,* was völlig gegen den Zoroastrismus streitet, aber mit dem Zervanismus übereinstimmt; vgl. alle Mythen über die Zwillinge Ōhrmazd und Ahriman, die wohlbekannt sind.

---

[265] Vgl. Eudemus Rhodius (Damascius, Dub. 125 bis) und dazu Widengren 1965, 149 f., 220; 1969, 134 ff. S. aber auch schon Bousset (1912–1919) 1979, 215 f. (Hinweis D. Hellholm). Noch in dem vom zervanitischen System abhängigen Manichäismus ist nur das Gute Wesen ein Gott, während das Böse Wesen ein Dämon ist, vgl. Widengren 1977, XII f. und 1978, *passim.* Man sollte hier auf Augustin, Contra Faustum XXI 1 verweisen.

[266] Über das Verhältnis der Tagesnamen zu den Yašt-Gottheiten vgl. Wikander 1946, 229 ff.

[267] Bdhn I 2 f. bzw. Zaehner 1937–39, 573–585 *(idem* 1955, 339 ff.). Eine sprachliche und stilistische Analyse der avest. Partien mit Übers. findet sich in Widengren 1967, 281–287. S. auch unten § 6.1.11.

[268] Vgl. Nyberg 1931, 29 f.; Widengren 1969, 460. Für die "Mischung" als "ein Hauptbegriff im manichäischen System" vgl. Widengren 1978, 307 ff. und 313 f., wo auf frühere Darstellungen hingewiesen wird.

[269] Benveniste 1929, 69–117.

[270] Nyberg 1938, 393–395.

[271] Vgl. Zaehner 1955, 13 ff., wo die Argumentation erstaunlich oberflächlich ist und die entscheidenden Argumente nicht einmal erwähnt werden. Auch Cumont in Bidez-Cumont 1938, II, 72 ff. mangelte es offenbar in diesem Fall an nötigen Kenntnissen.

(2) Eben darum wird auch *dem Areimanios geopfert,* was im Zoroastrismus undenkbar ist[272].

(3) Zwischen dem Guten und dem Bösen ist laut diesem Bericht *Mithra* eingesetzt, den die Perser *"Mittler"* (μεσίτης) nennen. Dieser Zug stimmt völlig mit dem zervanitischen Mythus bei Eznik von Kolb überein, der angibt, daß die Sonne als Schiedsrichter (*datavor*) zwischen Ormizd und Ahriman eingesetzt wurde[273].

Im armenischen Text heißt hier die Sonne *aregakn,* aber in der mir. Sprache ist die Sonne auch Mihr (< Miϑra) und Mithra wird eben auch als Sonne aufgefaßt[274]. Mit Recht hat also Benveniste auf diesen Mythus hingewiesen[275]. Mithra ist ja der Gott der Verträge, und in Bahm. Yt. III sind wir ihm als Wächter des Vertrages zwischen Ōhrmazd und Ahriman schon begegnet.

(4) Die schicksalsbestimmte Zeit (χρόνος εἱμαρμένος) ist ja ein deutlicher zervanitischer Begriff, der in MX XXVII 5 den Begriffen *zamān(ak)* und *brēh*[276] entspricht und also in Pahlavi *zamān i brēh* lauten würde. Noch am Ende des Berichtes erscheint der Begriff χρόνος im Zusammenhang mit dem Ausruhen des Gottes nach Vollendung des Weltverlaufes.

(5) Das chronologische Schema von 9000 Jahren, währenddessen Oromazes und Areimanos zuerst je 3000 regieren, sich danach aber 3000 Jahre bekämpfen. Nyberg wollte nur 12000, nicht 9000 Jahre als die authentische zervanitische Weltdauer anerkennen[277]. Benveniste dagegen verteidigte die Zahl 9000, indem er auf MX VIII 11 verwies[278]:

> Ahriman . . . *9000 zamistān pat zamān i akanārak apāk Ōhrmazd patmān kart.*
> Ahriman . . . machte mit Ohrmazd durch die unbegrenzte Zeit einen Vertrag von 9000 Jahren (eigtl. 'Wintern').

Und der Mittler Mithra, der über den Vertrag wacht, spricht (Bahm. Yt. III 34) von dem Vertrag von 9000 Jahren wie auch Ahriman (III 55) feststellt, daß 9000 Jahre verflossen sind[279]. In das 3×3000-Schema fügen sich sowohl die Drei-Zeiten-Formel *kē hast, būt u bavēt,* "der ist, war und sein wird", oder *būt u hast u hamē bavēt,* als auch die drei Epitheta *ašōqar, frašōqar, zarōqar,* die die drei Aspekte des Wesens Zervans beschreiben. Um

---

[272] Von Benveniste 1929, 73 mit Kraft betont. Ebenso Nyberg 1938, 393.

[273] De Deo II, IX, 190; Mariès-Mercier 1959, 471 (Text), 610 (Übers.).

[274] Vgl. Widengren 1938, 94, 158 mit Hinweisen.

[275] Vgl. Benveniste 1929, 89f.

[276] Für diese Begriffe vgl. Nyberg 1931, 54. "Time indeed, is not mentioned in Plutarch", sagt Benveniste 1929, 113. Das ist also nicht richtig. S. ferner Widengren 1969a, 183ff.; 1973, 318f. und oben § 3.3.1. mit Anm. 91f. Auf Eudemus Rhodius (Damascius, Dub. 125 bis) und den Zusammenhang mit dem Zervanismus wies schon Bousset (1912—1919) 1979, 215f. hin (Hinweis D. Hellholm).

[277] Vgl. Nyberg 1931, 57.   [278] Vgl. Benveniste 1929, 107f.

[279] In Widengren 1965, 286ff. habe ich versäumt, auf diese zwei Stellen hinzuweisen; vgl. oben § 4.2.1.1. die V. Strophe [III 34].

ihre genaue Bedeutung hat sich vor allem Nyberg bemüht[280]. Wie man auch diese Wörter deutet, ist es sicher, daß "sie sich auf die drei Stadien im Dasein aller Lebewesen beziehen"[281]. Die Drei-Zeiten-Formel ist auch in der indischen Literatur zu belegen[282]. Fügen wir in der gewöhnlichen iranischen Weise die Ganzheit als ein viertes Glied hinzu und teilen diesem vierten Glied wieder 3000 Jahre zu, bekommen wir die Zahl 12000 Jahre auf vier Perioden verteilt. Diese Zahl gibt eine Anknüpfung an die 12 Monate und die 12 Zodiakalzeichen, ist *aber* von diesen zwei Größen, wie wir sehen, völlig unabhängig. Die 4 Perioden hängen statt dessen offenbar mit einer alten indo-iranischen Spekulation über die 4 Weltperioden zusammen, die auch in Indien bewahrt ist[283]. Zu dieser Spekulation gehört der Gedanke von der Schwächung der Welt in der letzten Periode, wie wir (§ 4.3.2.1.2.) sowohl in Bahm. Yt. wie in den Orakeln des Hystaspes festgestellt haben. Dieser Umstand erklärt sich aus der Vorstellung, daß die Welt der Körper des Allgottes ist, die Elemente seine Körperteile[284]. Die Schwächung der Welt in der letzten Periode bedeutet das Altern des Gottes, das zugleich das Altern der Welt bedeutet. Wenn die Welt als ein Baum gesehen wird, vertreten die 4 Metalle seiner Zweige eine sinkende Leiter: Gold, Silber, Kupfer, Eisen, eine alte indo-germanische Spekulation[285].

Sowohl die 9000 wie die 12000 Jahre als Weltdauer können also als zervanitisch betrachtet werden und sind somit aus den zervanitischen Voraussetzungen gut verständlich[285a].

5.1.3. Wir kehren zur Endzeit zurück und greifen die Motive auf, wie sie der Reihe nach erscheinen:

(1) die schicksalsbestimmte Zeit wurde schon (§ 5.1.2.) behandelt;

(2) Ahriman bringt Seuche und Not. Die Formulierung ist griechisch, der Gedanke aber iranisch[286];

(3) Durch die "Zeit" wird er notwendigerweise vernichtet werden. Das

---

[280] Nyberg 1931, 87 ff. und 1938, 382. Zu vergleichen ist auch Benveniste-Renou 1934, 65 und Bailey 1953b, 37 f. Eine Übersicht der verschiedenen Deutungen bei Widengren 1965, 286 f. Ich finde immer noch die Deutungen Nybergs überzeugend, weil sie mit dem Wesen Zervans am besten übereinstimmen.

[281] Nyberg 1938, 382.   [282] Vgl. Widengren 1965, 287 f.

[283] Vgl. Widengren 1969, 456 ff.   [284] Vgl. Widengren 1965, 8–11.

[285] Vgl. Widengren 1969, 461. Ich habe *ibid.* Anm. 16 notiert, daß das mir. Lw. *azg*, Zweig, im Armenischen, "Geschlecht", "Generation" bedeutet. Vgl. auch § 1.2.1. mit Fig. 1 in S. S. Hartmans Beitrag in diesem Band sowie § 7. unten.

[285a] Zur religionsgeschichtlichen Bedeutung der Schemata der Zeitperioden vgl. Widengren 1966, 161 f. Die Probleme, die damit verknüpft sind, erfordern eine eingehende Spezialuntersuchung, die hier nicht geleistet werden kann.

[286] Vgl. Bidez-Cumont 1938, II, 77 Anm. 18 mit Hinweis auf Dk VII 8,19; s. ferner *ibid.*, 370 Anm. 9 mit Verweis auf *pestilentia et fame* in den *Orakeln des Hystaspes* (Lact. Epit. 66 [71] 3); dazu auch Widengren 1965, 218 Anm. 16, sowie Griffiths 1970, 479.

Vorkommen des Wortes *Ananke* im Ausdruck ἀνάγκη φθαρῆναι . . . καὶ ἀφανισθῆναι zeigt die vom Schicksal gesandte Fügung der Ereignisse. Das Verschwinden Ahrimans von der Erde gehört zum eisernen Bestand der iranischen Apokalyptik, vgl. bes. Bdhn XXXIV und Zātspr. XXXIV;

(4) Die Erde wird flach sein. Diesem Motiv sind wir schon bei der Analyse der Orakel des Hystaspes (§ 4.3.2.1.2.) begegnet, wo wir auch auf Bdhn verwiesen haben;

(5) Die Menschen werden in *einem* Staatswesen leben. Eine wirklich gute Parallele findet man nicht so leicht[287]. Man denkt wohl zunächst an das Regiment des Sōšyans, aber es gibt auch andere Möglichkeiten, von denen jedoch keine überzeugend ist;

(6) Die Menschen werden dieselbe Sprache sprechen; das ist ein Thema, das wir aus Bdhn A 225:15f. kennen: "Alle Menschen zusammen werden einer Stimme sein", *martōm hakanēn ham-vāng bavēnd*;

(7) Alle Menschen werden selig (μακάριοι). Das ist ja, wie bekannt, das Hauptthema in der Schilderung Bdhn XXXIV, A 226:12f.: "und jenes Dasein ist so gerecht, daß man sagt: sie werden in das Paradies Ōhrmazds eintreten";

(8) Die Menschen werden keiner Nahrung mehr bedürfen und sie werfen keinen Schatten mehr. Man hat nicht verstanden, daß diese zwei Umstände zusammengehören. Am Anfang haben die zwei ersten Menschen dadurch mehr und mehr gesündigt, daß sie zuerst Milch, dann Fleisch als Nahrung zu sich nahmen, wodurch sie sich auch der Verehrung der Dämonen hingaben (Bdhn A 102:1ff.). Dadurch sind sie selbstverständlich der Mischung von Licht und Finsternis verfallen. Ihr ursprünglich lichtes Wesen bekommt einen Einschlag von Dunkelheit. Am Ende der Zeiten hören sie aber auf, Nahrung zu sich zu nehmen. Mit dem Fleisch anfangend, enden sie damit, daß sie nur Wasser trinken (Bdhn A 221:1ff.)[287a]; ein aus Avesta geholtes Stück. Diese Überlieferung ist zervanitisch, wie Zaehner sehr verdienstvoll aufgezeigt hat[288]. Bei der Auferstehung wird die Hälfte des Lichtes der Sonne dem Urmenschen Gayōmart gegeben, die andere Hälfte den Menschen (Bdhn A 223:9f.)[289]. Dieser Umstand bestätigt, daß sie nunmehr frei von Finsternis sind und also keinen Schatten werfen; sie sind *asāyak,* wenn auch dieser Ausdruck nicht hier begegnet[290].

(9) Was in Plutarchs Bericht noch Schwierigkeiten bereitet, ist die Angabe, daß der Gott, der die eschatologischen Ereignisse bewerkstelligt, eine Zeit ausruht. Eine aus den iranischen Quellen stammende Erklärung

---

[287] Bidez-Cumont 1938, II, 77 Anm. 20 gibt keine gute Parallelstelle.
[287a] Diese Stelle wird unten § 6.1.1. zitiert.
[288] Zaehner 1955, 176ff.   [289] Vgl. Bailey 1943, 98.
[290] Vgl. avest. *a-saya-*, AirWb 208f.

ist hierfür nicht gefunden[291]. Man gewinnt doch den Eindruck, daß dieser Gott – die über Ōhrmazd und Ahriman stehende Gottheit Zervan mag vielleicht gemeint sein, denn der Bericht ist ja ein verkürzendes Referat – sich ausruht, um dann eine neue Weltentwicklung in Gang zu setzen, so wie es der Fall in der indischen Spekulation ist.

5.2. Analyse der zervanitischen Apokalypse Zātspram XXXIV

Eine bedeutsame zervanitische Apokalypse ist von Zaehner ediert, übersetzt und mit Kommentar versehen worden, nämlich Zātspr. XXXIV[292]. Dieser Text ist gewiß auf einer PÜ des Avesta basiert, denn mit Hilfe oben (§ 4.1.) angegebener Kriterien läßt sich nachweisen, daß viele Paragraphen aus dem Avesta stammen. Zaehner hat bei seiner sonst ausgezeichneten Leistung dieses grundlegende Faktum jedoch nicht gesehen und darum den Text an etlichen Stellen nicht korrekt übersetzt[293].

5.2.1. Was in dieser Apokalypse besonders auffallend ist, ist die große Rolle, die Āz, "Gier", "Lust" spielt. Wir haben diese Gestalt schon in Bahm. Yt. angetroffen[294], aber erst Zātspr. XXXIV lernen wir wirklich ihr Wesen kennen. Zaehner hat an mehreren Stellen in seiner Arbeit ihr Wesen gründlich analysiert und dabei gezeigt, daß sie eine exklusive zervanitische Gestalt ist[295]. Wir finden in dieser Schilderung, daß Āz eine sehr hervortretende Rolle neben Ahriman spielt, dessen Unterführer sie ist. Darüber handelt § 32, wo von Ahriman gesagt wird:

u-š pas vičīt spāhpat sardār i xvat hast Āz, u-š 4 spāhpat pat ham-kārīh frāč dāt hēnd, hast Hēšm u Zamistān u Zarmān u S⟨ē⟩ž, homānakīh i xvarāsān u *xvarbarān u nēmrōč u apāxtar spāhpat. apar vičīt Āz dašnak sardār u hōyak sardār, i hast sud[296], tišn, ētōn-ič Zarmān *sēvan mōdak, ētōn-ič S⟨ē⟩ž frēhbūt u *apēbūt.

Und dann erwählte er als Oberbefehlshaber der Heerführer die Āz selbst und zu ihrer Unterstützung wurden von ihm vier Heerführer gegeben: sie sind Hēšm (Raserei) und Zamistān (Winter) und Zarmān (Alter) und Sēž (Kummer), ähnlich den Heerführern von Ost, West, Süd und Nord. Ferner erwählte Āz Befehlshaber des rechten und des linken Flügels, die 'Hunger' und 'Durst' sind; ⟨in dieser Weise erwählte Hēšm . . .⟩ ⟨und in dieser Weise erwählte Zamistan . . .⟩ und in dieser Weise auch Zarmān 'Totenklage' und 'Weinen', und in dieser Weise Sēž 'Übertreibung' und 'Mangel'.

---

[291] Moulton 1913, 406 Anm. 1–2 registriert verschiedene Vorschläge, teils zur Textgestaltung, teils zur Deutung – alles zu hypothetisch.

[292] Zaehner 1940–42, 377–398, mit wenigen Änderungen abgedruckt in *idem* 1955, 343–354.

[293] Vgl. Widengren 1967b, 90–93.

[294] S. oben § 4.2.1.1., wo III 52 zitiert ist; vgl. außerdem II 41 und III 39.

[295] Vgl. Zaehner 1955, 166.

[296] Das Wort *sud* (alternative Form *šud*) < avest. *šud* (AirWb 1710). Die avest. Formel *šuδəm taršnəmčạ* kehrt also hier wieder, vgl. z. B. Yt. 19:96 und Anm. 300a. Wie gewöhnlich verwischt MacKenzie 1971, 81 durch die Transkription *šuy* den mparth. Ursprung des Wortes. Zaehner dagegen ist korrekt!

Es ist klar, daß dieser Paragraph in unvollständiger Gestalt überliefert worden ist. Āz besaß vier *spāhpatān* als Unterbefehlshaber: Hēšm, Zamistān, Zarmān und Sēž. Āz wählte dann Befehlshaber des rechten und linken Flügels, wie es jetzt heißt. Dann wird aber gesagt, daß Zarmān *šēvan* (Totenklage) und *mōdak* (Weinen) in gleicher Weise verordnete und Sēž *frēhbūt* (Übertreibung) und *apēbūt* (Mangel). Was ist aber aus Hēšm und Zamistān geworden? Sie sind offenbar durch Textfehler ausgefallen. Statt dessen heißt es, daß Āz Befehlshaber des rechten (Hunger) und des linken (Durst) Flügels erwählte. Sie selbst aber als Oberbefehlshaber hatte die unmittelbare Führung des Zentrums. Einen solchen Befehl führten indessen offenbar auch die vier *spāhpatān*. Also sind zwei *spāhpatān* weggefallen[297].

Die Ausdrücke *dašnak* bzw. *hōyak sardār* sind sicherlich die parthischen technischen Termini[298]. Auch die Worte *šēvan* und *mōdak* sind wie *sardār* mparth. und *šēvan* kommt als Lw. im Armenischen als ein Überbleibsel der alten iranischen Volksreligion vor[299]. Der Zoroastrismus wendet sich immer scharf gegen 'Totenklage' und 'Weinen', und wenn diese hier als Befehlshaber der Flügel in der Armee des *spāhpat* Zarmān erscheinen, ist es

---

[297] Zaehner hat den rein militärischen Hintergrund nicht verstanden. Die vier *spāhpatān* der vier Teile des Reiches gehörten offenbar der Organisation des Partherreiches an, aber Xosrau I. griff auf sie wieder zurück; vgl. Christensen 1944, 130 und zum Problem vorläufig Widengren 1976, 298 mit Anm. 411–414.

[298] Das Wort *sardār* ist mparth. und entspricht mpers. *sālār, sārār*. Für die lautliche Entwicklung vgl. mparth. *sard* (im Gegensatz zu npers. *sāl!*), als Lw. im Armenischen bewahrt, vgl. Hübschmann 1897, 236:571 "Jahr"; vgl. übrigens auch Nyberg 1974, 173b, wo richtig angegeben ist, daß das Wort mpers. *sālār* und *sārār* heißt (das letztere Wort wahrscheinlich auch urspr. mparth. vgl. ŠKZ Z. 11,27). Unbegreiflich, daß MacKenzie 1971, 73 *sardār* als *sālār* liest. Die Entsprechung mparth. -*rd* ~ mpers. -*l* gehört ja zu den fundamentalen Lautgesetzen in der Dialektologie; vgl. Tedesco 1921, 205,15 (doch jetzt unvollständig). Mit der falschen Transkription wird der dialektale Ursprung des Wortes verwischt.

Daß *sardār* in der mpers. Fassung von ŠKZ Z. 33 vorkommt, kann die urspr. dialektale Zugehörigkeit nicht verändern, denn es handelt sich hier wahrscheinlich um einen parthischen Titel, der entweder *darīkān sardār* oder *sārār* lautete, später aber in sassanidischer Zeit *darīkpat* hieß, vgl. Maricq 1965, 71 Anm. 15.

[299] Vgl. Hübschmann 1897, 214:482 und vor allem Wikander 1946, 100f. (101 mit Anm. 1), wo er eine Reihe von Belegen in der Pahlaviliteratur gesammelt hat. MacKenzie 1971, 56 gibt die falsche Transkribierung *mōyag* vom Schriftbild *mwdk*, anstatt *mōdak* und hat also nicht gesehen, daß wir in *mōdak* eine mparth. Form zu sehen haben. In der parthischen Sprache ist die √*maud*- belegt, im Gegensatz zu mpers. *mwy*- vgl. Ghilain 1939, 96. Das Wort *āmust* "Mönch" kommt von diesem Verbum, Ghilain 1939, 96 (vgl. Nyberg 1974, 133) **ā-mud-ti*. Das Wort ist eine Übersetzung des syrischen *abīlā,* "Mönch", eigtl. "Trauernder". Auch das Wort *šēvan* ist mparth. Paz.*šīn(a)* ist die mpers. Form, nicht < **šēvan(ak)* wie Nyberg 1974, 186a angibt, sondern aus **šēn-ak* entwickelt. Nyberg verweist aber richtig auf *šīnah*, Pfeife, als Musikinstrument (wegen des klagenden Lautes?). Der Ausdruck *šēvan u mōdak* ist also parthisch und gehört der alten Volksreligion an, wie Wikander bemerkt. In ŠN leben die Ausdrücke *šēvan* und *mōyah* fort, vgl. z.B. Mohl (Ed.) IV V. 4004–05. Hier also die Fortsetzung des mpers. *mōyak*.

verlockend, an dieser Stelle ein Zeichen des zoroastrischen Einflusses unter den zervanitischen Magiern zu sehen[300].

Weil die Stellung von *vičīt* ganz anormal ist, stammt der Paragraph aus dem sassanidischen Avesta. Hierauf deutet auch der Ausdruck *sud tišn*. In der glücklichen Regierungszeit Yimas hatten die Menschen tausend Jahre lang keine Plagen wie Hunger und Durst[300a], Kälte und Hitze. Dann brach der Winter herein, und mit ihrer unveränderlichen Jugend war es zu Ende[301]. Das Alter und der Winter wie die übrigen Plagen, die der Glückszeit Yimas ein Ende bereiteten, werden also in dieser zervanitischen Apokalypse der Gier (*Āz*) zugeschrieben. In Vd. 1:8 heißt es, daß Ahra Mainyu als Landplage *sraskəmča driwikāča*, 'Weinen und Stöhnen' geschaffen hat, was nach Bdn *šēvan u mōd* entspricht. Wir finden also eine deutliche Anknüpfung an Vd. 1[302].

Auch in Zātspr. XXXIV 35 ist der Vertrag zwischen der Guten und Bösen Gottheit für 9000 Jahre gültig. Dieser Vertag setzt voraus, daß während dieser Zeit Āz alle Menschen zu Feindschaft gegen Ōhrmazd und zu Liebe gegen sich selbst überreden wird. Das bedeutet tatsächlich, daß der Vermehrer (*apazāyēnītar*) derselbe wie der Zerstörer (*zatār*) ist. Die syntaktische Konstruktion:

hān čē-t pat ⟨bun⟩ bē *patēstāt ku bē hāčēh harvisp axv i astōmandān ō adōstīh i Ōhrmazd, dōstīh i xvēš.

. . . jenes, was du im ⟨Urbeginn⟩ versprochen hast, nämlich daß du alle körperlichen Wesen zu Feindschaft gegen Ōhrmazd, zu Liebe gegen dich selbst, überzeugen wirst.

Die Stellung von *bē hāčēh* ist ganz anormal und der Paragraph stammt also aus dem sassanidischen Avesta.

5.2.2. Wir müssen auch einige Worte über das Schicksal sagen, das Āz und Ahriman trifft. In § 35 wird gesagt, daß Āz nichts mehr zu verzehren hat, denn sie hat am Ende der 9000 Jahre die Schöpfung Ahrimans verschlungen. Sie besaß drei Kräfte (*zōrān*): eine Kraft besteht im Essen, eine zweite in dem Wunsch zu kopulieren, eine dritte ist die Sehnsucht nach jedem guten Ding. Dieser § 35 ist avestisch, wie die Syntax zeigt.

Wenn *fraškart*, die Wiederherstellung, nahe ist, werden diejenigen, die Ašavahišt gehorchen, vom Schlachten und Essen von Kleinvieh sich wegwenden und ein Viertel von der Stärke von Āz wird darum verschwinden. Die Finsternis wird teilweise heimgesucht und die Kenntnisse werden

---

[300] Vgl. auch Widengren 1965, 36, 193, 318, 325, wo aber auf Zātspr. XXXIV nicht eingegangen wurde. Der Synkretismus zwischen dem Zoroastrismus und der zervanitischen Religion der Magier wurde von Nyberg 1938, 375 ff., zusammenfassend 389, herausgearbeitet.

[300a] Vgl. Yt. 19:96 oben § 2.2.1., wo die Korrespondenz mit Zātspr. XXXIV 32 besonders notiert wird.

[301] Vgl. Lommel 1927, 198 mit Stellenangaben.

[302] AirWb 1645, 778 mit Hinweis auf Darmesteter 1892–93, II, 10.

klarer sein. Dieser § 39 kann aus formalen Gründen nicht als avestisch bestimmt werden.

In § 40 heißt es, daß in den Kindern, die geboren werden, Āz noch kraftloser sein wird und ihre Körper weniger stinkend: ihre Natur wird mehr mit den Göttern vereint sein. Sie werden auch das Trinken von Milch aufgeben und die Hälfte der Stärke, die Āz besitzt, verschwindet. Diejenigen, die jetzt geboren werden, werden wohlduftend (*hubōd*) sein, im Gegensatz zu stinkend (*gandak*), wie auch im Zwillingsmythus Ōhrmazd wohlduftend ist, Ahriman aber stinkend. Die Kinder werden nunmehr ganz wenig Finsternis besitzen (*kamtārīk*) mit geistiger Natur (*mēnōi-čihr*) und ohne Nachkommen, weil sie nicht mehr essen, wie es § 41 heißt (auch hier fehlen syntaktische Kriterien). Im Ganzen stimmt diese Schilderung mit Bdhn XXXIV überein (vgl. § 6.1.1. und § 5.1.3. # (8)).

Dann folgt der sehr wichtige § 42, wo wenigstens der Schluß deutlich avestisch ist:

u pas Āz *dēv, nē ayāftan i nērōk hač Ōhrmazd dāmān ⟨rād⟩, bē ō Ahriman, kē-š pat spāhpatān sardār paitākēnīt, ruzdakīhā andar ō dāmān rat patkārt ku-m sēr hanburt kunēt, čē nē ayāpēm hač Ōhrmazd dāmān xvarišn zōrān.

Und dann, weil sie keine Stärke von den Geschöpfen Ōhrmazds bekommt, appelliert die Dämonin Āz an Ahriman, der sie als Oberbefehlshaber der Heerführer offenbart hatte; in Geizigkeit zum Herrn der Geschöpfe (sagt sie):
'Machet mich satt, zufriedengestellt, denn nicht bekomme ich Kräfte vom Essen der Geschöpfe Ōhrmazds'[303].

Für die Notlage der Āz sollte man Bdhn A 185:13 vergleichen[304]. Die Reaktion darauf wird in § 43 erzählt, wo es heißt:

Auf Befehl Ahrimans läßt sie die kleinen Dämonen zerstören. Zuletzt verbleiben jene vier Heerführer und jene zwei, Ahriman und Āz.

Dieser Paragraph kann aus syntaktischen Gründen nicht als avestisch demonstriert werden, aber er stellt den logischen Schluß des vorigen Paragraphen dar und ist für den Zusammenhang unentbehrlich.

Es folgen dann zwei eindeutig avest. Abschnitte, die §§ 44 und 45[305].

frāč ō zamīk āyēnd Ōhrmazd, Ahriman, Srōš, Āz, ō Ōhrmazd Ahriman zanēt, tāi *baxtīk būt Āz apāk Ahriman čār nē ayāpēt . . . bē čigōn Āz apāk ⟨Ahriman⟩ baxtīk ⟨ne⟩ bavēt, Ahriman ēvtāk, u-

---

[303] Die Übers. Zaehners 1955, 352 habe ich leicht modifiziert. Ich bin geneigt, *zāvarān, die mparth. Form, anstatt Zaehners zō(h)rān zu lesen. MacKenzie 1971, 63 gibt die Lesung *pahikārdan*, die mpers. Form, obgleich die mparth. Form *padkārdan*, die wir hier finden, belegt ist, vgl. Ghilain 1939, 73. Die Präteritumform *patkārt* bereitet Schwierigkeiten. Man erwartet eine Präsensform, und demgemäß übersetzt Zaehner.

[304] Diese Stelle ist angeführt von Zaehner 1955, 193 Anm. 13, vgl. auch S. 171.

[305] Die Stellung der Verba āyēnd, būt (im nicht angeführten Stück ferner hast und hēnd). Dazu noch der Ausdruck ō Ōhrmazd, (wo Zaehner ō streicht), der eine avest. Konstruktion *ava Ahurō Mazdā* wiedergibt, vgl. Reichelt 1909, 287 § 548a. Die Übers. Zaehners ist in der Wiedergabe der Tempora nicht korrekt, weshalb ich sie hier und da korrigiert habe.

š hamēmāl 3, 2 i yut-gōhr i hast Ōhrmazd Srōš, u ēvak i ham-gōhr i hast Āz ⟨i⟩ baxtīktar. ka-š ayār bē ō hamēmālīh ★vašt, hambatīk pērōžīhēt[306].

Vorwärts zur Erde kommen Ōhrmazd, Ahriman, Srōš, Āz. Der Ōhrmazd schlägt Ahriman; solange Āz die Schicksalsgenossin Ahrimans war, wird er kein Mittel finden . . . aber weil Āz ⟨nicht mehr⟩ die Schicksalsgenossin ⟨des Ahriman⟩ ist, bleibt Ahriman allein, und seine Gegner sind drei; zwei von verschiedener Substanz, die Ōhrmazd und Srōš sind, und eine von derselben Substanz, die Āz ist, die ganz besonders seine Schicksalsgenossin war. Wenn seine Helferin sich zur Gegnerschaft gewendet hat, wird der Widersacher besiegt.

Was hier wirklich von Bedeutung ist, ist die Feindschaft der Gier (Āz) gegen ihren Herrn und Meister Ahriman. Dazu wird sie ja genötigt, weil ihr sonst nichts in der Schöpfung übrig ist, wogegen sie sich wenden kann – die vier *spāhpatān* ausgenommen, über deren Schicksal wir nach § 43 aber nichts mehr erfahren. Die böse Macht ist also in sich selbst zersplittert und muß darum dem Untergang anheimfallen. Diesen inneren Zwiespalt im Wesen der dämonischen Macht finden wir nur in der zervanitischen Apokalyptik.

5.2.3. Sōšyans, der zoroastrische Erlöser, spielt in Zātspr. XXXIV eine erstaunlich unbedeutende Rolle. Er wird in den Paragraphen 46 und 48 erwähnt. Wir wenden uns hier § 46 zu[307]:

ka 57 sāl ō fraškart-kartārīh apāč ō zāyišn bavēt i Sōšyans, spurrīkgarīh hān i ★bē ō Zartušt bē dahīhēt.

Wenn 57 Jahre bis zur Wiederherstellung zurückbleiben, wird es zur Geburt des Sōšyans kommen; die Vollendung dessen, was zu Zartušt gehörte, wird gegeben.

Dieser Paragraph ist deutlich avestisch, wie die Stellung von *bavēt* zeigt; dazu kommt noch die geschraubte Ausdrucksweise, wobei *spurrīkgarīh hān i ★bē ō Zartušt bē dahīhet* dem Verständnis Schwierigkeiten bereitet, denn das Subst. *spurrīkgarīh* fungiert hier als finite Verbform, sofern wir nicht eine leichte Emendierung vornehmen wollen und *spurrīkgarīh ⟨i⟩ hān i* usw. lesen.

Die 57 Jahre, die Sōšyans auf Erden sein Erlösungswerk ausführt, ist eine fest fixierte Zahl, für die ich keine Erklärung bei Zaehner oder anderswo gefunden habe. Laut Bdhn XXXIV, A 223:4f. heißt es:

57 sāl Sōšyans rist hangēžēnēt, harvisp martōm ul ēstēnd.

Während 57 Jahren wird Sōšyans die Toten aufrütteln, alle Menschen stehen auf.

Das bedeutet, daß der Sōšyans wie schon in der jungavest. Apokalyptik (§ 2.2.) von seiner Geburt an als Erwecker der Toten wirksam ist. Wie erklärt man nun die 57 Jahre? Hier muß man auf griechische Verhältnisse verweisen. Die Zahl 57 zerlegt man in 3 × 19 = 57. Das ist der dreifache

---

[306] Wegen der formelhaften Wendungen scheint mir die Ergänzung *apāk* ⟨*Ahriman*⟩ notwendig.

[307] Zaehner übersetzt *dahīhēt* als auf Zarathustra hinweisend. Aber der Sinn ist selbstverständlich, daß der Sōšyans das Werk Zarathustras vollendet.

Zyklus des Epimenides. Nach 57 Jahren stand Epimenides auf (Diog. Laert. I, 109–115). Hier kann man also mit einem griechischen Kultureinfluß auf die Magier rechnen. Oder liegt evtl. ein indo-germanisches Erbe vor[307a]? Jedenfalls muß hier ein von den medischen Magiern vermittelter zervanitischer Einschlag vorliegen.

5.2.4. In dieser zervanitischen Apokalypse taucht eine göttliche Gestalt auf, die sonst im Kampf der guten und der bösen Mächte eine unbedeutende Rolle spielt, hier aber in die Handlung mehr eingreift. Das ist Airyaman[308]. In § 38 heißt es, daß der *Airyaman frēstak* dem Artvahišt helfen wird, die Āz zu überwinden. Diese Aussage wird mit *paitāk* eingeleitet, und darum ist dieser Paragraph wahrscheinlich avestisch. Es folgt auch ein Zitat aus der Erzählung von den zwei ersten Menschen mit der Mahnung, kein Kleinvieh (*gōspand*) zu schlachten. Diese Mahnung hängt mit der eschatologischen Erwartung zusammen, denn wir haben ja gesehen, daß am Ende der Zeiten die Menschen mit dem Fleischessen aufhören werden[309].

In § 17 verkündet Ōhrmazd diese Aussendung Airyamans:

apar *frēstam Airyaman frēstak kē-š frazām-kārīh andar xvēškārīh.

Ich werde den Apostel Airyaman aussenden, unter dessen eigenen Aufgaben das Zustandebringen der Vollendung ist.

Die Stellung des Verbums am Anfang des Satzes zeigt, daß diese Aussage Ōhrmazds aus dem sassanidischen Avesta stammt. Das Wort *frazām* ist ein synonymer Terminus zu *fraškart*[310].

Airyaman tritt als Gefolgsmann Mithras auf, er gehört unbedingt dem Mithra-Kreis an. Auch § 48 ist für das eschatologische Geschehen wichtig, denn hier heißt es:

ka hān spurrgar frēstak i hast Sōšyans parvānak Airyaman pat zamīk paitāk bavēt pat ham-handāčakīh pat 30 sālak bē ō mēnōyān ham-*pursēt.

Wenn der Vollender, der Apostel Airyaman, der der Gefolgsmann des Sōšyans ist, auf der Erde offenbar wird, wird er in gleicher Weise mit den geistlichen Wesen 30 Jahre Rat halten[311].

Das Wort *parvānak* ist ein feudaler Terminus, der in der parthischen religiösen Sprache verwendet wird[312].

5.2.5. Das Ende der Zeiten kommt mit dem Umsturz der Ordnung in der Natur. Auf der Erde werden Quellen von Feuer hervorsprudeln, denn

---

[307a] Mit Einfluß skytischer Schamanenvorstellungen rechnet Dodds 1970, 78 [Hinweis D. Hellholm]. Vgl. auch in diesem Band Burkert §§ 1.6. und 3.4.

[308] Vgl. über ihn vor allem Dumézil 1977, 140–145. Er ist eine vor-gathische Gottheit.

[309] Oben § 5.1.3., § 5.2.2. und unten § 6.1.1.

[310] Von *fra-gam* kommt *frazām*, vgl. Nyberg 1974, 78b. Das Verbum *fra-gam* gehört der "jungavestischen" Sprache an.

[311] Die von Zaehner 1955, § 48 gegebene Übers. ist nicht korrekt, vgl. Widengren 1967b, 90.

[312] Vgl. Widengren 1968, 146, 150f.; 1969b, 39, 49.

Ōhrmazd wird durch das Feuer das Ende bereiten[313]. Diese §§ 50–51, deren avestischer Ursprung aus formalen Gründen nicht eindeutig ist, werden von § 52 gefolgt, wo die syntaktischen Kriterien deutlich den avestischen Ursprung verraten:

ka 3 māh ō ristāxēz apāč, ō artīk bavēt i vazurg, čigōn pat bun dām u dahišn andar kōxšišnīh ⟨i⟩ druž. 90 rōč-šapān kārēčār būt, artīk i hast 30 rōč u šap *pat vārān i xrafstr-zatār, 30 rōč šap pat tāčisn hač mēy kē-š urvar pat-iš vaxšēt, 30 rōč šap pat vāt kē āp bē rānēnēt, zamīk adar *dārišn, ul dārišn i gōr u *čakāt bē kart.

Wenn drei Monate bis zur Auferstehung zurück(bleiben), wird es zum Großen Krieg kommen, ebenso wie im Uranfang Schöpfung und Grundlegung mit der Lüge im Kampf waren. 90 Tage und Nächte währte der Krieg: ein Krieg der 30 Tage und Nächte durch Regen als den Schläger von Ungeziefer dauerte, 30 Tage und Nächte durch Ströme von Nebelwolken, wodurch die Pflanzen wachsen, 30 Tage und Nächte durch Wind, der das Wasser treibt, welches das Halten der Erde unten und das Halten oben impliziert, und Höhlen und Gipfel herstellte.

Hier ist die Konstruktion am Anfang des Stückes besonders auffallend[314]. Der § 53 unterstreicht, daß der Große Krieg am Uranfang durch Wasser und Wind stattfand, am Ende aber durch Hitze und Verbrennung mittels Feuers. Die eschatologische Rolle des Feuers wird also stärker als gewöhnlich hervorgehoben. Sehr wichtig ist der letzte Abschnitt, § 54, wo es heißt:

čigōn hān i artīk apar 90 rōč-šapān yazdān apāk dēv-ič u jēh būt, hān pat avdom āškārak-paitākīhā vēnīhēt, šapān andar andarvāi ātaxš-karp, mart-dēs, mēnōyān mēnīt, ātaxšīk ⟨pat⟩ *bārak i asp homānāk škift, apēgumān bavēnd.

Wie während 90 Tagen und Nächten die Götter mit den Dämonen und der Hure jenen Krieg hatten, so wird am Ende in evidenter Offenbarung, von den Geistwesen gedacht, nachts[315] in der Atmosphäre eine Feuererscheinung, in Gestalt eines Mannes, ⟨mit⟩ einem Reittier gleich einem Pferd, feurig, furchterregend, gesehen werden. Sie werden frei von Zweifel sein.

5.2.6. *Wir fassen unsere Ergebnisse zusammen*. Die zervanitische Apokalypse Zātspr. XXXIV 1–54, von der wir hier nur die letzten Teile behandelt haben, geht offenbar auf eine PÜ eines Textes aus dem sassanidischen Avesta zurück. Wegen Raummangels ist es nicht möglich gewesen, alle Paragraphen im Hinblick auf ihren Ursprung zu analysieren. Wir müssen uns damit begnügen, ganz kurz festzustellen, wo ein avestischer

---

[313] Die Übers. Zaehners 1955 in § 50 ist inkorrekt, denn die Verbalform *fražāmīhēt* ist ja Passivum und bedeutet also "das Ende wird bereitet" und *čihrān* ist das Subjekt zum Verbum *bavēnd*, also: "die Saatarten (*čihran*) werden ein kraftloser Ackerbau werden". Zaehners Übers. ist syntaktisch unmöglich: der sing. *varz* kann nicht das Subjekt vom Plural *bavēnd* sein.

[314] Warum das durative Perfektum *bē kart* hier verwendet wird, ist schwer zu sagen. Zaehner, *ibid.* übersetzt mit "makes" als ob *kunēt* geschrieben wäre, was ja inkorrekt ist. Möglicherweise stand im avest. Grundtext ein Aorist.

[315] Das Wort *šapān* (ohne Präpos.) bereitet Schwierigkeiten. Möglicherweise liegt einfach eine Übers. vom avest. *xšapanō*, Zeitakkusativ in Yt. 8:13, vor. Man erwartet dann eine Zahlangabe.

Ursprung als gesichert gelten kann: §§ 6, 7, 8, 9, 10, 11, 12, 13, 14, 15, 16, 17, 18, 19, 20, 21, 25, 26, 27, 30, 32, 33, 35, 36, 37, 38, 42, 44, 46, 48, 49, 52.

Das ist das Minimum, aber in den anderen Fällen wäre eine eingehendere Analyse nötig. Nur soviel sei bemerkt, daß der Zusammenhang hier wie in Bahm. Yt. selbstverständlich mit sich bringt, daß noch fehlende Paragraphen sicherlich der urspr. avest. Quelle angehört haben müssen.

Darüber hinaus sollte man in Zātspr. XXXIV auch auf die Einschläge von mparth. Dialekt im Wortschatz achtgeben, die, wie wir sahen, nicht unbedeutend sind und also vom Ursprung im Kreise der medischen Magier ein Zeugnis ablegen. Man verhehlt sich diesen wichtigen Umstand, wenn man die Pahlaviwörter nicht korrekt transkribiert[316].

Wir haben schon gesehen, daß auf der bösen Seite Āz eine wahrhaft dominierende Gestalt ist. Die Rolle, die Jēh, die Hure, bei der Verführung des Urmenschen Gayōmart gespielt hat, wird nur in § 31 angedeutet. Auf der guten Seite notieren wir die unbedeutende Rolle, die Srōš und Sōšyans spielen. Auffallend ist, daß Mihr (Mithra) nicht erwähnt wird. Seine Aufgabe scheint von Srōš übernommen worden zu sein, aber in gedämpften Farben. Daß Airyaman neben Srōš vorkommt, ist eigentümlich, weil Srōš ein zoroastrisches Substitut für Airyaman ist, wie Dumézil gezeigt hat[317].

Deutlich kommt der *zervanitische* Charakter dieser Apokalypse einerseits durch die geringe Rolle, die Sōšyans spielt, und die Abwesenheit der zwei übrigen mythischen Söhne Zarathustras, sowie andererseits durch die große Rolle, die von Āz gespielt wird, die Andeutung der Verführung Gayōmarts durch Jēh und die bedeutende Stellung, die Airyaman einnimmt, zum Ausdruck.

Jedoch ist die Abwesenheit des Schiedsrichters Mihr (Mithra), der von Srōš ersetzt und *vielleicht nur* vom feurigen Reiter auf dem feurigen Pferd symbolisiert wird, und das Vorhandensein nicht nur von Srōš, sondern auch von Ašavahišt ein Zeichen dafür, daß diese Apokalypse *zoroastrisch* bearbeitet ist, oder besser: daß sie eine *Mischung von Zervanismus und Zoroastrismus* darstellt, so wie wir sie in Bundahišn wiederfinden, wo indessen in der Schilderung der letzten Zustände und Kämpfe der zervanitische Einschlag als sehr gedämpft erscheint. Dieses Verhältnis wird klar hervortreten, wenn wir uns dem Kap. XXXIV des großen Bundahišn zuwenden.

---

[316] Wir haben oben *passim* notiert, daß sowohl Nyberg als auch Zaehner dies tun, während MacKenzie in ganz inkorrekter Weise den dialektalen Unterschied verwischt.

[317] Vgl. Dumézil 1958, 70f.

6. Die letzten Dinge nach der zoroastrischen Überlieferung in Bundahišn XXXIV

6.1. Analyse von Bundahišn XXXIV im Vergleich mit Zātspram XXXIV

6.1.1. Die Schilderung der letzten Dinge beginnt mit einem Schriftzitat aus Avesta, das Urzeit und Endzeit miteinander vereinigt und auf das wir schon früher Bezug genommen haben (§ 5.1.3., aber auch § 4.3.2.1.2.). Hier folgt der betr. Text, Bdhn A 221:1−11[318]:

> *gōvēt pat dēn ku hač hān čigōn Mišyē u Mišyānē kē hač zamīk apar rust hēnd nazdist āp u pas urvar, pas šīr u pas gōšt xvart hēnd, martōm-ič ka-šān murtan nazdist gōšt, ⟨pas⟩ šīr u pas hač nān xvartan bē ēstēnd, u an-āz tāi bē murtān āp xvarēnd ētōn-ič pat hazārak i Hušētarmāh nērōk i Āz ētōn bē kāhēt ku martōmān pat ēvak pihō-xvarišnīh 3 šap u rōč pat sērīh ēstēnd. pas hač hān gōšt-*xvarišnīh bē ēstēnd u urvar u pēm i gōspand xvarēnd. pas hač hān pēm-xvarišnīh ēstēnd. pas hač urvar-xvarišnīh-ič ēstēnd u āp-xvarišn bavēnd.pēš, pat 10 sāl, ka Sōšyans āyēt ō axvarišnīh ēstēnd u nē mīrēnd.*

Man sagt in der Religion: Ganz wie Mišyē und Mišyānē[319], die aus der Erde emporgewachsen waren, zuerst Wasser und dann Pflanzen, dann Milch und dann Fleisch verzehrten, und eben die Menschen, wenn sie zu sterben haben, zuerst das Fleisch, ⟨dann⟩ die Milch, und dann das Brot zu verzehren sich enthalten und bis zum Sterben ohne Lust (nur) Wasser trinken, in derselben Weise wird in dem Millennium des Hušētarmāh die Kraft der Āz (Gier, Lust) sich vermindern, so daß die Menschen durch das Essen eines Gerichts drei Tage und Nächte in Sattheit verbleiben. Nachher werden sie sich jenes Fleischessens enthalten und Pflanzen und Milch von Kleinvieh verzehren. Dann enthalten sie sich jenes Milchverzehrens. Dann enthalten sie sich auch des Pflanzenverzehrens und werden Wassertrinker. Während zehn Jahren bevor[320] der Sōšyans kommt, leben sie ohne zu essen, aber sie sterben nicht.

6.1.2. Danach wird erzählt, wie Sōšyans die Toten aufrütteln wird, und als ein Schriftzitat wird sodann eine Frage Zarathustras an Ahura Mazdā sowie die Antwort des Gottes über die Auferstehung angeführt. Die Fragestellung ist dieselbe wie Zātspr. XXXIV: Wie ist es möglich, daß ein schon toter Körper, dessen Bestandteile von Wind und Wasser entführt sind, wieder auferstehen kann? Die Antwort ist wieder dieselbe wie in Zātspr.: Für Ahura Mazdā war die Neuschöpfung schwieriger als die Wiederherstellung sich gestalten wird. Ein Vergleich zwischen Zātspr. XXXIV und Bdhn XXXIV ist in der Tat sehr lehrreich[321]:

Bdhn A 221:14−222:16	Zātspr. XXXIV 20+6	
u-š passaxv kart ku **ka-⟨m⟩**	*u-m ō ham-passāxtan apāč dātan*	
asmān apē-stūn *pat mēnōyē-bavišnīh*	*hugartar 12 dāmān i-m pat bun bē*	
dūrak-ālak, rōšn hač gōhr ⟨i⟩ xvan-	*dāt, fratom* **ka-m asmān** *vinārt* **astūn,**	I.

---

[318] Für Transkription und Übers. der Bdhn-Stellen vgl. Messina 1935. Kleine Abweichungen von ihm sind nicht notiert.

[319] Für die verschiedenen Namensformen der zwei ersten Menschen, vgl. Hartman 1953, 45−64 und Nyberg 1974, 123a−b.

[320] Die Konstruktion *pēš pat 10 sāl ka Sōšyans āyēt* bietet eine unregelmäßige Syntax. Normal sollte es *pat 10 sāl pēš ka Sōšyans āyēt . . . ēstēnd* heißen.

[321] Die Übereinstimmungen sind in Fettdruck gedruckt. Zur Dialogstruktur von Zātspr. XXXIV 1−20 s. Hultgård in diesem Band § 4.2.1.

āsēn[322] ⟨*dāt*⟩ *u ka-č-am* **zamīk**
dāt kē hamāk axv i astōmand
barēt, u-š **apar-dāštārīhē** *i gētē*
nēst, **ka-m xvaršēt** *u* **māh** *u* **stārak**
andar andarvāi rōšn-karpīhā vāzīt
hēnd **ka-m yōrtāk**[323] *dāt ku andar*
zamīk bē parganēnd u apač rust
pat apa-zōn apač bavēt, **ka-č-am**
andar urvar rang dāt gōnak gōnak
ka-č-am ⟨**andar**⟩ **urvarān** *u apārīk*
čiš **ātaxš** *dāt pat asōčišnīh* **ka-m**
andar burtār ⟨**i**⟩ **māt pus dāt,** *srāyēnī-*
tan[324], **yut yut mōd** *u* **pōst** *u* **nāxun** *u*
xōn *u* **pad**[325] ⟨*u*⟩ *čašm u gōš u apārīk*
pēšak bē dāt
ka-č-am ō āp pād[326]**dāt ku**
bē tāčēt, **ka-č-am abr dāt**
mēnōyīk kē hān i gētē āp
barēt ānōd ku-š kāmak
vārēt u ka-č-am vāi dāt
kē-č *nāmčišt*[327] *pat vāt-nērōk*
adar- rōn u apar, čigōn kāmak,
vazēt, pat dast frāč nē šāyēt
griftan, ēvak ēvak hač ōišān
ka dāt pat-iš duškartar būt,
ku ristāxēzišnīh čē-m andar
ristāxēz ayārīh i čigōn ōišān
⟨*i*⟩ *hast* **ka-m** *ōišān* ⟨*i*⟩ *nē*
būt kart bavēt . . .[328]
apar nikēr ku **ka** *hān i*
nē būt *adak-im bē kart*
hān i **būt,** *čim apač nē*
šāyēt kartan?

*an-***apar-dāštār** *kē-š hač hēč kust*
nē hēnd gētīhān bē dāštār,
u ditīkar ka-m **zamīk** *vinārt mi-* | II.
yānak ⟨*i*⟩ *asmān* *ku ō katār-ič-ē*
nēmak nē nazdīktar būt homā-
nakīh i zartak i xāyak miyān
⟨*i*⟩ *xāyak, u sitīkar* **ka-m xvar-** | III.
šēt *brihēnīt,* 4-*om ka-m* **māh** | IV.
brihēnīt, ⟨5-*om ka-m* **star** *brihē-* | V.
nīt⟩, 6-*om* **ka-m andar urvaran** | VI.
vas *gonak rang u* *čāšišn bē dāt,*
7-om **andar urvar ātaxš pat** | VII.
asōčišnīh bē dāt, *8-om* **ka-m** | VIII.
xōšak ō zamīk bē burt *u pat*
hangām i frāč vaxšišn barōmand bavēnd,
ō xvarišn i martōmān u gōspandān rasēnd,
9-*om* **ka-m andar mātakān zahak** | IX.
bē vinārt, *apar nihuft tāi bē*
vitart[329] *u-m* **yut yut** *andar hān*
arōdišn paitākēnīt ast **xō**⟨**n**⟩ **mōd** | X.
u **drēm** *u* **pad** *u srūv; dahom*
ka-m tanōmand murvān pat parr
⟨**andar**⟩ *andarvāi vādēnīt*[330]:*yāzdahom* | XI.
ka-m āp pād *xargōš homānakīh*
frāč raftār **dāt,** *dvāzdahom* ⟨**ka-m** | XII.
abr dāt⟩ *ul apar burtār i āp,*
vārānēnītār i vārān.

(§ 6)
ōišān dāmān, **ka nē būt** *hēnd,*
am brihēnītan tuvān būt, u nūn
ka **būt** *u višuft apač passāxtan*
hugartar.

---

[322] So nach Nyberg 1974, 220a; für *āsēn ibid.*, 32a. MacKenzie 1971, 6, gibt nur *āhen*, was unrichtig ist, denn mparth. *'swn* garantiert -*s*-, also richtig Nyberg. Alternative Formen im mparth. sind also: *'swn* ~ *'syn*.

[323] Vgl. Bartholomae 1916–25, II, 28 Anm. 1.

[324] Die Lesung ist sicher: *srāyēnītan* ist Kaus. von *srāyītan*, "beschützen". Die Konstruktion ist aber unregelmäßig: entweder muß *rād* hinzugefügt werden oder man muß einen dahinterstehenden avest. Infinitiv annehmen.

[325] Lesung in Übereinstimmung mit Zātspr. XXXIV 20.

[326] Lesung in Übereinstimmung mit Zātspr. XXXIV 20. MacKenzie 1971, 66 *pāy* verwischt den mparth. Ursprung der Wortform, vgl. Nyberg 1974, 147a.

[327] Emendiert als ⟨ܐܘܫܝܣ⟩ aus ⟨ܐܘܫܝܣ⟩ , *nāmist*. TD₁: *nāmdīt*(?).

[328] Das Wort *būt* ist Dittographie von *bavēt*.

[329] *tāi bē vitart*, "bis es nach außen passiert ist". Zaehner fügt ⟨*nē*⟩ hinzu, was unnötig ist, weil die Ausdrucksweise eine gute Meinung gibt. Das Verbum *vitartan* ist mparth.; vgl. Boyce 1954, 197b.

[330] Hier kann man auch *vāyēnīt* transkribieren, weil mparth. nur *vādāg* in Boyce 1954 belegt ist. Sonstige Verbalformen aus *vāy-*, vgl. Ghilain 1939, 71, aus √*vad*-.

6.1.2.1. Schon dieser Vergleich zeigt, daß beide Texte auf eine avestische Vorlage zurückgehen. Das geht klar aus den syntaktisch unregelmäßigen Konstruktionen hervor. Aber die Verschiedenheit der Texte ist so auffallend, daß nur eine Schlußfolgerung möglich ist: sie gehen auf eine avestische Vorlage zurück, die jeder Text nur unvollständig wiedergibt. Wollten wir diese Vorlage rekonstruieren, eine Aufgabe, die hier nicht in Angriff genommen werden kann, so müßten wir die beiden Texte addieren. Hier nur eine Bemerkung: Es ist erstaunlich, daß Bdhn, über Zātspr. hinaus, soviel von der urspr. zervanitischen avest. Vorlage bewahrt hat.

Wir geben ein kurzes Referat von dem Inhalt des betr. Stückes dieser Vorlage, die wie gewöhnlich am ausführlichsten in Zātspr. bewahrt ist[331].

Zarathustra fragt Ahura Mazdā, wie es möglich sei, die Toten auferstehen zu lassen, da die Teile des Menschen schon weit zerstreut waren. Ahura Mazdā antwortet mit einem Hinweis auf sein Schöpfungswerk. In 12 Sätzen (I.–XII.) zählt er seine Schöpfungen auf. Alle diese Sätze werden in genau derselben Weise eingeleitet: *fratom ka-m asmān vinārt āstūn*, "zuerst als ich den Himmel einrichtete ohne Pfeiler". Bdhn hat durchgehend die Zahl der Schöpfungswerke gestrichen und gibt die folgende Formulierung: *ka-⟨m⟩ asmān apē-stūn . . . ⟨dāt⟩*. Bdhn verwendet *niemals vinārt*, ein typisches mparth. Wort[332], gibt aber eine Reihe Eigenschaften des Himmels wieder, die sich in Zātspr. nicht finden, wo aber an Stelle andere Qualitäten erwähnt werden. Dieser Umstand ist typisch und eher ein Beleg dafür, daß die Vorlage inhaltsreicher war als Bdhn und Zātspr. als Einzelschriften betrachtet.

6.1.2.2. Die Vorlage war sicherlich wie Zātspr. disponiert, so daß die zwölf Schöpfungen aufgezählt wurden. Diese sind:

Bdhn	*Zātspr.*
1. der Himmel	1. der Himmel
2. die Erde	2. die Erde
3. die Sonne	3. die Sonne
4. der Mond	4. der Mond
5. die Sterne	5. die Sterne
7. die Farben in den Pflanzen	6. die Farben usw. in den Pflanzen
8. das Feuer in den Pflanzen	7. das Feuer in den Pflanzen
6. das Getreide	8. das Getreide auf der Erde
9. der Sohn im Mutterleib	9. das Embryo im Mutterleib
10. – – –	10. die Vögel
11. das Wasser laufen machen	11. das Wasser laufen machen[333]
12. die Wolken	12. die Wolken

---

[331] Vgl. Widengren 1967, 283 mit Anm. 10, wo hervorgehoben wird, daß Schaeder in Reitzenstein-Schaeder 1926, 208 das gegenseitige Verhältnis zwischen Bdhn und Zātspr. falsch beurteilt hat. S. auch Widengren 1973, 317f.

[332] Das Präfix *vi-* tritt mpers. als *gu-* auf, wie wir schon oben Anm. 158 beobachtet haben. Das mparth. Verbum hat, wie oft der Fall ist, Eingang in die mpers. Sprache gewonnen, vgl. Henning 1933–34, 226.

Es fehlt also in Bdhn die zehnte Schöpfung: die Vögel, und die achte Schöpfung: das Getreide, kommt schon an sechster Stelle.

6.1.2.3. Als eine Summierung folgt in Bdhn A 222:12ff. die Aussage Ahura Mazdās:

> Als ich schuf, war jedes einzelne von jenen (Schöpfungen) schwieriger als das Zustande-bringen der Auferstehung der Toten, denn bei der Auferstehung der Toten werde ich die Hilfe von solchen, die existieren, haben, die nicht existierten, als ich sie schuf. Merke, wenn das, was nicht war, damals von mir geschaffen wurde, warum sollte es dann nicht möglich sein, das wieder zu schöpfen, was existierte?

Es ist im Text auffallend, daß Zātspr. XXXIV 20, aber nicht Bdhn das typisch zervanitische Verbum *brihēnītan* verwendet[334]. Dieses Verbum treffen wir in ausgesprochen zervanitischen Texten wie MX und Zātspr. an. Typisch ist die Stelle Zātspr. II 19. Das Verbum bedeutet sowohl "bestimmen" wie "schaffen". Das ist wiederum ein Zeichen dafür, daß die zervanitische Färbung stärker in Zātspr. als in Bdhn hervortritt.

6.1.3. Ahura Mazdā crklärt, wie er die Auferstehung zustandebringen wird[335]:

Bdhn A 222:16−223:2	**Zātspr. XXXIV 8−14**
čē pat hangām **hač** mēnōi i **zamīk**	apar xvānam zamīk, hač-iš
ast, hač āp xōn, hač urvar mōd	xvašt **ast** u gōšt u pad i
u **hač vāt *gyān**[336] čigōn-šān pat	Gayōmart apārīkān . . .
bundahišn patigrift, xvāham.	apar xvān⟨am⟩ āp i ārang[337] . . . ku
	apar rasēn **xōn** i ōi ristak martōm . . .
	apar xvānam urvar hač ōi xvāham
	vars i rist martōm
	apar xvānam vāt, *hač ōi
	xvāham **gyān** i ōi ristak martōm.

Wir sehen sofort, daß die Stelle in Bdhn eine starke Verkürzung des Zātspramtextes bietet und daß sogar die Pflanzen (*urvar*) ausgelassen sind, was aber wahrscheinlich nur ein Textfehler der Kopisten ist. Ferner stellen wir fest, daß Zātspr. wie gewöhnlich direkt auf die avest. Vorlage zurückgeht, wie die Stellung des Verbums *xvānam*, "ich rufe an", zeigt, während *xvāham,* "ich fordere zurück", eine syntaktisch normale Stellung in Bdhn

---

[333] Nur Zātspr. hat das anschauliche Bild vom Laufen wie ein Hase (*xargōš*) bewahrt, was wiederum ein Zeichen dafür ist, daß Zātspr. i.a. ursprünglicher ist als Bdhn.

[334] Vgl. Nyberg 1974, 49b; und für die Zātspramstelle II 19 Widengren 1969a, 183 (die dortige Stellenangabe IV 4−10 ist falsch!), wo Zervān eben *brīnkar* (dieselbe Wurzel), Schicksalsbestimmer, heißt und die Lebensdauer Gayōmarts bestimmt, *brihēnom* ("ich bestimme").

[335] Die Übereinstimmungen sind in Fettdruck gedruckt.

[336] Man muß hier ‎سوی‎ lesen.

[337] Der Fluß Ārang wird mit Diglit identifiziert, also im Westen lokalisiert, was an sich nicht korrekt ist; vgl. Markwart 1938, 114ff., wo hervorgehoben wird, daß sowohl Bdhn wie Zātspr. Ārang in den Westen verlegen. Das gehört zur westlichen Umorientierung der Kosmologie.

im Satz einnimmt, im Gegensatz zu Zātspr. (hier also ursprünglicher). Der Inhalt ist einfach: Ahura Mazdā fordert die Bestandteile des Körpers von den verschiedenen Elementen zurück, die er geschaffen hatte. Es ist interessant zu beobachten, daß man so eingehend die Argumente gegen die Lehre der Auferstehung widerlegt.

6.1.4. Nachdem die Versammlung Isatvāstars[338] stattgefunden hat, werden die Gerechten und die Ungerechten voneinander gesondert. Die Ungerechten müssen drei Tage und Nächte in der Hölle verbringen, wo sie an Körper und Seele Vergeltung leiden, während die Gerechten während derselben Zeit im Paradies (Garōdmān) Glückseligkeit erleben. In dieser Weise tritt eine Zersplitterung in der Familie ein, der Vater wird vom Sohn, der Bruder vom Bruder, der Freund vom Freund getrennt. Der Gerechte weint über den Gottlosen. Diese Angabe wird als ein Schriftzitat angeführt mit der Zitatformel: *čigōn gōvēt ku* (Bdhn A 224:5 ff.).

Die Schurken der alten Geschichte wie Dahāk und Frāsiyāp erleiden eine Strafe, die man "die Strafe der drei Nächte" nennt, *pātifrās i tišrąm xšafnąm xvānēnd*. Die letzten zwei Wörter werden mit avestischen Lettern geschrieben, ein Zitat aus Vd. 7:52 PÜ, was auf eine avestische Vorlage hindeutet. Die Ausdrucksweise verdient hier notiert zu werden, Bdhn A 224:13–225:1:

ōišān kē-šān xvatāy⟨īh⟩ dušma⟨n⟩īh rād kart ēstēt čigōn Dahāk u Frāsiyāp u vǎhmān apārīk[339] hač ēn aivēnak-ič margaržānān pātifrās dahēnak vitārēnd[340].

Diejenigen, durch welche die Herrschaft wegen Feindschaft ausgeübt ist, solche wie Dahāk und Frāsiyāp und die übrigen derartigen Leute, die des Todes würdig sind, erleiden eine Strafe von zehnerlei Art.

Die "drei Nächte" ist ein Ausdruck, der die eschatologische Schilderung mit Vd. und HN verbindet[341].

6.1.5 Die Schlange Gōčihr [342], ein Sterndämon im Himmelsgewölbe als Gegner von Sonne und Mond bekannt, fällt auf die Erde, die einen ähnlichen Schmerz empfindet wie ein Schaf, dem ein Wolf seine Wolle ausreißt (*pašm rōvēt*[343]). Dieses Ereignis (Bdhn A 225:3 ff.) steht hier so unvermittelt, daß wir es als einen Einschub aus einem anderen Kontext

---

[338] Vgl. über Isatvāstar Christensen 1917–34, II, 22, 47 und die bei Molé 1967, Gloss. registrierten Stellen. Er ist ein Sohn Zarathustras, in sassanidischer Zeit als *mōbadān mōbad* betrachtet.

[339] Eigtl. "die übrigen N.N.".

[340] Die Wortform *pātifrās* ist mparth. im Gegensatz zu mpers. *pātifrāh*, vgl. Nyberg 1974, 155a. Der Unterschied ist bei MacKenzie 1971 wie gewöhnlich verwischt: er gibt anstatt der korrekten Form *pātifrās* nur *pātifrāh*, trotz der Schreibung.

[341] Vgl. hierzu auch Söderblom 1901, 265 f.

[342] *Gōčihr* < *gao-čiϑra*, AirWb 480 f.; vgl. Nyberg 1974, 83b.

[343] Nach TD₁. Das Verbum *rōvēt* (< **rōpēt*) ist denominativ und findet sich im Neupersischen, vgl. Geiger-Kuhn 1896, I 2, 131 C a). Bei MacKenzie 1971 fehlt das Verbum.

betrachten müssen. Zwar versucht Lommel diesen Sturz des Sternes mit den folgenden Ereignissen zu verknüpfen[344], aber dafür bietet der Text keinen Rückhalt.

6.1.6. Dann werden das Feuer und der Yazat Ērmēn, d. h. Airyaman[345], das Metall in den Bergen (*kōfān*[346]) schmelzen lassen, so daß es wie ein Strom auf der Erde steht. Sie lassen dann alle Menschen durch das geschmolzene Metall hindurchschreiten um sie rein zu machen.

Und dem, der gerecht ist, kommt es dann so vor, als ob er beständig in lauer Milch ginge; wenn er ungerecht ist, dann kommt es ihm entsprechend vor, als ob er beständig in geschmolzenem Metall ginge (Bdhn A 225:6ff.).

Hier fehlen alle Zeichen einer avest. Vorlage, aber bezüglich der Datierungsfrage verweisen wir auf die Orakel des Hystaspes (§ 4.3.2.). Und AŽ XVII 15 findet sich außerdem teils eine Abweichung, teils ein paar supplierende Einzelheiten; es heißt nämlich:

Šahrēvar zündet jeden Berg in der Welt an, das Metall steht in der ganzen Welt, alle Menschen schreiten durch den Strom des geschmolzenen (Metalls) hindurch, und makellos und licht und rein werden sie genau so wie die Sonne im Lichte.

Es ist auffallend, daß es hier Šahrēvar ist, der Herr der Metalle, der den Strom von Metall ausgießen ließ; nach zoroastrischer Anschauung erscheint dieser geeigneter dazu als Airyaman. Wenn wir annehmen, daß Airyaman der zervanitischen Tradition angehört, würde Šahrēvar die nicht-zervanitische Tradition vertreten. Das malerische Bild von der lauen Milch fehlt ganz in AŽ.

6.1.7. Dann vereinen sich wieder die getrennten Mitglieder der Familie und Freunde und fragen einander (Bdhn A 225:11ff.):

Wo bist du alle diese vielen Jahre hindurch gewesen und wie war der Richterspruch (*dātistān*) über deine Seele? Bist du ein Gerechter oder ein Ungerechter gewesen?

Zuerst sieht die Seele den Körper und begehrt auf seine Frage Antwort, *u-š pursēt pat hān i guft passaxv,* (Bdhn A 225:15). Hier finden wir tatsächlich ein Zeichen der avestischen Vorlage, nämlich die unregelmäßige Stellung des Verbums *pursēt*. Das bedeutet selbstverständlich, daß auch die Frage schon avestisch war.

Alle Menschen zusammen werden einer Stimme sein und bringen Ōhrmazd und den Amahraspanden hohe Lobpreisung (Bdhn A 225:15f.).

---

[344] Vgl. Lommel 1930, 209.

[345] Das ist die Schreibung in TD$_1$. Die Form Ērmēn ist eine zweite Form, vielleicht unter Angleichung an Ahrmēn. Die Schreibung in TD$_1$ ist deutlich Airyaman, d. h. die avest. Form.

[346] Dies ist die mparth. Form, die mpers. ist *kōhān*, wie die pāzand- und npers. Formen zeigen.

Daß die Menschen alle *ham-vāng bavēnd,* kennen wir schon aus De Iside et Osiride und dadurch wird das Alter dieser Vorstellung bestätigt, wie oben § 5.1.3. dargelegt wurde.

6.1.8. Jetzt wird Sōšyans ein bemerkenswertes Opfer verrichten, wie es heißt (Bdhn A 226:3 ff.)[346a]:

yazišn pat rist-virāyīh Sōšyans apāk ayārān kanēt u gāv i Hatāyōš pat hān yazišn kušēnd, hač frapīh i hān gāv ⟨u⟩ Hōm i spēt anōš virāyēnd, ō harvisp martōm dahēnd u harvisp martōm *anōš bavēnd tāi hamē-ravišnīh.

Ein Opfer für die Wiederherstellung der Toten wird Sōšyans mit seinen Helfern vollziehen und bei jenem Opfer werden sie den Stier Hatāyōš[347] schlachten. Vom Fett dieses Stieres und vom weißen Hōm bereiten sie den Unsterblichkeitstrank und geben ihn allen Menschen, und alle werden unsterblich werden bis in alle Ewigkeit.

Hier liegt im Verhältnis zur normalen zoroastrischen Überlieferung eine Unstimmigkeit vor. *Erstens* unternimmt der Sōšyans laut AŽ XVII 14 eine Kulthandlung (*yazišn*), wodurch er die Lebenden unsterblich (*ahōš*) macht[348]. Dazu ist natürlich kein Unsterblichkeitstrank nötig. *Zweitens* ist ein Stieropfer selbstverständlich eine abscheuliche Tat im Zoroastrismus seit den Tagen Zarathustras[349]. Zoroastrisch gesehen war es undenkbar, sich eine derartige Freveltat als eine Heilstat in der Endzeit vorzustellen. Hier wird tatsächlich "Mithras Stieropfer" am Ende der Dinge vom Saošyant wiederholt[350]!

Aber Mithra gehört in allerhöchstem Maße dem Zervanismus an und wir können darum annehmen, daß dieses Stieropfer von der zervanitischen Religion übernommen worden ist. Dieses sakramentale Stieropfer besitzt natürlich einen ganz anderen Charakter als das nicht-sakramentale, vom Zervanismus verpönte Schlachten und Essen von Kleinvieh. Es ist eine heilige Handlung und wird darum als *yazišn,* Verehrung, Opfer, bezeichnet[351].

6.1.9. Es folgt dann wieder ein Schriftzitat (Bdhn A 226:6 ff):

Auch dieses sagt man: 'Denjenigen, die die Reife eines Mannes besessen haben, denen wird man das Alter von 40 Jahren wiedergeben; denjenigen, die klein und nicht ⟨zur Reife eines Mannes⟩ gelangt waren, denen wird man das Alter von 15 Jahren zurückgeben'[352].

[346a] Textgestaltung nach TD₁.

[347] Für Hatāyōš vgl. Geiger-Kuhn 1904, II, 645 mit Literaturhinweisen.

[348] Messina emendiert zu Unrecht den Text und "verschlimmbessert" zu *anōš.* Diese zwei Wörter werden abwechselnd gebraucht, z. B. hat TD₁ 194:14 *ahōš* anstatt *anōš.*

[349] Vgl. Nyberg 1938, 51, 71; Widengren 1965, 66. Söderblom 1901, 266 hat die mangelnde Übereinstimmung notiert.

[350] Güntert 1923, 397.

[351] Den Zusammenhang mit dem Zervanismus habe ich in Widengren 1954, 44 [36] nicht gesehen, aber wohl – wie Söderblom – den Widerspruch in der Überlieferung.

[352] Es ist wahrscheinlich, daß wir den Text ergänzen müssen: *hān i kē xvurtak nē ⟨ō mart-*

Danach heißt es, daß jedem Frau und Kinder gegeben wird. Man lebt wie in einer gewöhnlichen Ehe, aber ohne Kinder zu zeugen.

Alsdann wird Sōšyans nach dem Befehl Ōhrmazds jedem Menschen Lohn und Entgelt geben in Übereinstimmung mit seinen Taten[353].

Das ist ebenso gerecht, daß man sagt: 'Sie treten ein in das Paradies Ōhrmazds; so wie es jedem selbst geziemt, wird er die Gestalt annehmen, bis in alle Ewigkeit wird er unter seinesgleichen gelangen', *pat ham-apākīh āyēt*[354] (Bdhn A 226:11 ff.).

Die Stellung von *šavēnd*, "sie treten ein", am Anfang des Schriftzitates bestätigt den avestischen Ursprung.

6.1.10. Dann folgt ein neues Schriftzitat (Bdhn A 226:15 ff.):

Auch dieses sagt man: 'Wenn[355] (von jemandem) Verehrung (*yašt*) nicht gebracht ist und *Gētīkxrīt*[356] nicht bestellt ist und den Würdigen ein Kleid als fromme Gabe nicht geschenkt ist, ist er dort nackt und bringt dem Ōhrmazd Verehrung (*yašt*) dar, und der Geist der Throne wird ihm das Werk der Kleidung besorgen.'

Der Satz *u-š mēnoī i gāhān kār i vastrak ō kunēt,* kann durch Vd. 19:31−32 erklärt werden, wo Vohu Manah der Seele den Thron verleiht und Aogem. § 17, wo er gebeten wird, ihr ein goldgesticktes Gewand ebenso wie einen goldenen Thron zu geben[357]. Die alternative Möglichkeit, hier den Geist der Gathas zu sehen, scheint nicht sehr einleuchtend, eben weil Vohu Manah eine eschatologische Funktion zu erfüllen hat. Wir unterstreichen die religionsgeschichtliche Bedeutung dieser Vorstellung von der Bekleidung der nackten Seele[358].

6.1.11. Es folgt dann eine Schilderung des Endkampfes, die sich in markanter Weise sowohl von Bahm. Yt. wie von Zātspr. XXXIV unterscheidet (Bdhn A 227:4 ff.):

Ōhrmazd wird den Gannāk Mēnoi (den Bösen Geist),
Vohuman den Akōman,
Urtvahišt[359] den Indar,
Šahrēvar den Sarv,
Spandarmat die Tarōmat, d. i. Nārahaiθ,

---

patmān⟩ rasīt būt hēnd, entspr. *kē mart-patmān būt hēnd.* Die betr. Wörter sind durch Haplographie ausgefallen.

[353] Mit TD₁ ist *kunīšn passačakīhā* zu lesen.

[354] Das Wort *ham-apākīh,* "dieselbe Gesellschaft", kann auch als ein Kollektivum aufgefaßt werden: dieselben Begleiter.

[355] Bdhn A 226:15−227:3 wird mit *ka* eingeleitet. Ich glaube nicht, daß es notwendig ist, dieses Wort zu *kē,* wer, zu emendieren, weil *ka lectio difficilior* ist.

[356] Das Wort *gētīkxrīt* bedeutet eine Handlung, wodurch der Himmel auf Erden gekauft wird, vgl. West 1880, 127 Anm. 1.

[357] Vgl. Wikander 1941, 26−28, der als erster auf diese wichtigen Stellen aufmerksam machte.

[358] Wir können hier auf Y. 51:13 verweisen, wo die Seele anscheinend als nackt dastehend gedacht wird. Dieses Thema ist in Widengren [1980] näher behandelt worden.

[359] Eine Nebenform von Artvahišt: *arəta* > *ərəta* > *urt.*

Hōrdāt und Amurdāt den Tairič und den Zairič,
und 'Wahre Rede' die 'Lügnerische Rede',
der Gerechte Srōš den Hēšm mit dem blutigen Banner angreifen.

Diese Liste von gegensätzlichen Paaren Bdhn A 227:4 ff. findet sich auch
Bdhn A 47:8 ff., wo doch einige kleine Abweichungen zu notieren sind.
Vor allem ist Wahre Rede, *Rāst-gōvišnīh*, durch *Rāstīh-srav* ersetzt, so wie
der Gegner *Drōg-gōvišnīh* durch *Drōg u Mitōxt*, Lüge und Falschheit. Das
zeigt, daß die sozusagen "kanonische" Liste kleine Abweichungen aufweisen konnte.

Die Liste geht auf Vd. 19 zurück, wo wir eben § 46 die Wörter *draogō
miϑaoxtō* lesen. Zweifellos sollten wir hier also *Drōg Mitōxt* lesen[359a]. Die
zwei Dämonennamen Indar und Sarv sind ebenfalls aus Vd. geholt, wo wir
19:43 lesen: *indrō daēvō *sauru . . . *nā̊ŋhaiϑəm*[360].

Der dritte Name ist wohl der korrupte und mißverstandene Name Nārahaiϑ.
Wir stellen fest, daß Vd. offenbar die Quelle dieser Gegensatzpaare war[361].
Aber wir können noch ein Stück weiter kommen. In Bdhn A 15:7 ff. wird
die Gegenschöpfung Ahrimans beschrieben, wie er die Gegenspieler der
Amahraspanden schuf: Akōman, Indar, *Sarv[362], *Naŋhaiϑ, Tarōmat,
Tarič, Zairič. Der siebente ist er selbst.

Dieser Gegenschöpfung sind wir schon in De Iside et Osiride (§ 5.1.1.)
begegnet, wo die Gegenspieler auch dieselbe Zahl wie die Ameša Spentas
besitzen. Dort greifen sie die Schöpfung des Ōhrmazd an, genau wie dies
in Bdhn der Fall ist. Der Text in Bdhn ist stark zervanitisch gefärbt, und es
liegt hier offenbar ein Einfluß der zervanitischen Überlieferung vor, wie er
schon in De Iside et Osiride (§ 5.1.2.) zu belegen war. Der Endkampf ist
also eine Wiederholung des Kampfes am Anfang der Weltentwicklung,
und das ist in dieser Ausgestaltung eine zervanitische Färbung des uralten
eschatologischen Motivs. Nach dem Kampf bleiben nur zwei Lügengeister
übrig: Ahriman und Āz, genau wie in Zātspr. XXXIV.

Ōhrmazd kommt selbst in die Welt, er selbst als *zōt*[363], erster amtierender
Priester, zusammen mit dem Gerechten Srōš als *rāspīk*, zweiter amtierender
Priester. Ōhrmazd hält den heiligen Gürtel (*aivyāhan*[364]) in der Hand. Das
sind deutlich zoroastrische rituelle Züge, solche, die wir auch in Bahm. Yt.
finden. Durch die Formel der Gathas geschlagen, *pat hān i gāhānīk nīrang
zat,* werden die Instrumente des Ahriman und der Āz wirkungslos. Das ist
eine Entsprechung dessen, was in der Urzeit passierte, als Ahriman durch
das Aussprechen der Ahuna-Vairya-Formel machtlos wurde.

[359a] Zu *miϑaoxtō* s. Yt. 19:96 oben § 2.2.1.
[360] Vgl. AirWb 367f., 1568.
[361] Vgl. Nyberg 1938, 339, wo Vd. 19 und die parallele Stelle Vd. 10 behandelt werden.
[362] Korrupte Schreibung: Sāvul, was in Zaehner 1955, 282 § 36 akzeptiert ist.
[363] *Zōt* < avest. *zaotar*.   [364] *Aivyāhan* < *aiwyāŋhana*, AirWb 98.

Durch denselben Übergang in den Himmel, durch den er hineingestürmt war, stürzt man den Bösen Geist zurück in die Finsternis (Bdhn A 227:11 f.)[365].

6.1.12. Die Schlange Gōčihr wird im geschmolzenen Metall verbrannt. Das Metall fließt zur Hölle und aller Gestank und Schmutz der Erde werden in diesem Metall verbrannt werden und die Erde wird rein(Bdhn A 227:12 ff.). In diesen Schilderungen kann man keine sicheren Spuren einer avestischen Überlieferung entdecken, aber ihr avestischer Ursprung wird durch die allgemeine Übereinstimmung mit den Orakeln des Hystaspes verbürgt.

Dann heißt es aber Bdhn A 228:2 f.:

u bavēt fraškart andar axv pat kāmak i gēhān amarg tāi hamē-hamē ravišnīh.
Und die Erneuerung geschieht in der Existenz mit dem Ziel, daß die Welt unsterblich (sei) bis in alle Ewigkeit.

Hier ist die Konstruktion deutlich avestisch, wobei wir auch das für die PÜ so charakteristische Fehlen eines Verbums im zweiten Teil des Satzes notieren.

6.1.13. Die Schilderung endet mit einem schon in anderem Zusammenhang notierten Vorgang, Bdhn A 228:3 f.:

ēn-ič gōvēt ku ēn zamīk anāpēšar u anišēp u hamōn bē bavēt.
Auch dieses sagt man: 'Diese Erde wird eine Ebene sein, ohne Täler und ohne Hügel'[366].

Damit kehrt die Erde zum Urzustand zurück, so wie sie war, als sie von Ahura Mazdā geschaffen wurde, vgl. Bdhn A 19:10:

Der Berg, der Činvat-Gipfel wird weder Erhöhung noch Erniedrigung besitzen.

Mit diesem Satz endet die Beschreibung, ganz wie in den Orakeln des Hystaspes (§ 4.3.2.1.2.) und in De Iside et Osiride (§ 5.1.3.).

6.2. *Zusammenfassung*

6.2.1. Die zwei Hauptmotive der Apokalyptik, die kosmischen Veränderungen und Katastrophen sowie der kriegerische Endkampf im Kosmos kehren in Bdhn XXXIV wieder, aber mit charakteristischen Nuancierungen. So fehlen in großem Umfang die Schilderungen der Veränderungen in den normalen Vorgängen der Natur. In den Kampfschilderungen fehlt der Terminus "der Große Krieg" (*artīk i vazurg*), der sonst das Schlüsselwort ist. Ebenso fehlt das Thema "die Auflösung der Familie und der Gesellschaft". Vor allem aber notiert man das Fehlen der bekannten mythisch-legendenhaften Themata, die in Bahm. Yt. eine so große Rolle spielen.

---

[365] Man muß *vitār⟨ēt⟩*, oder *vitār⟨ēnd⟩* lesen.
[366] Für Lesung und Übers. vgl. Bailey in Zaehner 1955, 308 zu Bdhn A 19:10.

Bdhn gibt also in Kap. XXXIV nur eine Auswahl aus einem viel reicheren Material, das wir schon zum größten Teil behandelt haben.

6.2.2. Geht die Schilderung in Bdhn XXXIV auf einen verlorenen avestischen Text zurück? Das ist jedenfalls die Meinung Christensens, der die Vorlagen Bdhns zu bestimmen versucht hat. Er meint, daß Kap. XXXIV ganz oder teilweise auf Spand Nask, den 13. Nask, zurückgeht[367] und verweist auf die Angaben Dk VIII 14, 12—15. Christensen verfügte aber nicht über die nötigen formalen Kriterien, um das avestische von dem nicht-avestischen Material unterscheiden zu können. Doch ist es selbstverständlich, daß die formalen Kriterien nur eine Minimalinterpretation zulassen. Es ist also möglich, daß der ganze Stoff in Bdhn XXXIV avestisch ist, aber eine Entscheidung dieser Frage erfordert eine eingehendere Analyse. Nur soviel kann gesagt werden, daß der zervanitische Einschlag hier nicht so umfassend ist wie in Zātspr., wenn er auch, wie wir sahen, gar nicht unbedeutend ist.

7. Die vier Zeiten

7.1. In Dk IX 8,1 lesen wir, daß der siebente *fargard tā və urvātā* des Sūtkar Nask (= Y. 31) davon handelt, daß dem Zarathustra die Natur der 4 Perioden in seinem Millennium gezeigt wurde[367a]:

Erstens die goldene, in welcher Ahura Mazdā dem Zarathustra die Religion zeigte;

Zweitens die silberne, in welcher Vištāspa von Zarathustra die Religion empfing;

Drittens die stählerne, die Periode, in welcher der Hersteller der Gerechtigkeit, Āturpāt i Mahraspandān, geboren wurde;

Viertens die Periode mit Eisen gemischt, in welcher die Autorität der Abtrünnigen und anderer Schurken – im Hinblick auf die Zerstörung der Religionsherrschaft, die Schwächung jeder Art von Güte und Tugend und das Verschwinden von Ehre und Weisheit aus den Ländern Irans – viel Verbreitung findet.

7.1.1. Es gibt auch für diese Periode eine Schilderung der vielen Schrecken und Plagen, die über das Leben der Guten kommen, die in Anständigkeit verbleiben. Wir sehen, daß das allgemeine Schema mit jenem viergliedrigen in Bahm. Yt. I übereinstimmt, daß sich aber auch charakteristische Unterschiede in der Beschreibung der vier Perioden finden. Die Perioden 1 und 2 sind in Bahm. Yt. I als erste Periode zusammengefaßt. Die Periode 3 mit dem Auftreten Āturpāts ist in Bahm. Yt. II 18 die dritte Periode von sieben, während Āturpāt in Buch I überhaupt nicht erwähnt wird, sondern

---

[367] Vgl. Christensen 1931, 48.

[367a] Vgl. § 1.2.1. mit Fig. 1 im Beitrag von S. S. Hartman in diesem Band und s. Anm. 285a oben.

alles auf die Regierung Xosrau Anōšurvāns konzentriert ist. Es ist deutlich, daß hier eine allgemeine Verschiebung der zeitlichen Perspektive eingetreten ist und daß wir mit verschiedenen Schichten innerhalb des sassanidischen Avesta zu rechnen haben. Die vierte und letzte Periode aber besitzt selbstverständlich immer denselben Charakter: es ist eine Zeit der Plagen und Verfolgungen seitens der Feinde Irans, eine Zeit der Auflösung, bis endlich der erlösende Sieg kommt.

Das zervanitische Vierzahlschema ist in der zoroastrischen Apokalyptik an das letzte Millennium angepaßt und hat also seinen Charakter verändert; es ist indessen immer ein Schema, das sich vom goldenen Zeitalter zum Zeitalter des gemischten Eisens als Unglücksperiode streckt[367b].

7.1.2. Weil Dk IX 8,1 ja den Inhalt vom avestischen Sūtkar Nask wiedergibt, auf dem laut Bahm. Yt. I 1, die ganze Rahmenerzählung basiert, gibt diese Stelle summarisch auch den Inhalt des Vohuman Yasn im sassanidischen Avesta wieder, d. h. diese Dk-Stelle referiert die "avestische" Entsprechung des Pahlavitextes Bahm. Yt., wobei man sich daran zu erinnern hat, daß laut Bahm. Yt. I 6 und II 1 der jetzige Text des Bahm. Yt. auch den *zand* zu Vohuman Yasn, Hōrdāt Yasn und Aštāt Yasn verwendet. Durch diese Angabe verstehen wir, wie es dazu kommt, daß Bahm. Yt. in seiner jetzigen Gestalt nicht nur Material aus dem in *avestischer* Sprache geschriebenen Avesta enthält, sondern auch sehr viel späteres Material, das z. T. aus der kommentierten PÜ *zand* stammt.

7.2. Gegen diesen Hintergrund wollen wir das Schema der vier Zeiten noch einmal betrachten, um zu versuchen festzustellen, wie im ursprünglichen, sassanidischen Avesta, d. h. dem in avestischer Sprache geschriebenen Kanon, dieses Vier-Zeiten-Schema ausgesehen hat.

7.2.1. Daß die *zwei ersten* Perioden, diejenige Zarathustras: die goldene, und diejenige Vištāspas: die silberne, dem urspr. Avesta angehören, ist selbstverständlich.

7.2.2. Schwieriger ist die *dritte* Periode, die wir als die stählerne bezeichnen müssen, denn Dk IX 8,1 nennt sie mit diesem Namen, und dies ist auch in Bahm. Yt. der Fall.

Gehen wir nun zu Bahm. Yt. II 17 über, so finden wir, daß die Periode, die nach derjenigen Vištāspas (die hier als die silberne bezeichnet ist), folgt, als die Periode bezeichnet wird, die

die Herrschaft des Kai Artaxšēr (ist), den man Vohuman, den Spanddāt-Sohn, nennt. Er ist es, der die Dämonen von den Menschen scheidet, die ganze Welt läutert und die Religion befördert.

Hier ist also der mythisch-legendäre Vohuman, der Sohn des Spanddāt[368], mit dem Gründer der sassanidischen Dynastie, Artaxšēr Pāpakān,

[367b] Vgl. oben § 5.1.2. # (5).

[368] Vgl. über ihn Christensen 1931, 63 mit der Genealogie S. 70.

identifiziert worden[369]. Diese Identifizierung hat, wie Christensen m. R. sagt, ihren Grund in der gefälschten Genealogie, die Artaxšēr mit Vohuman als Abkömmling verknüpft.

Der eigentliche Herrscher in dieser dritten Periode war also der mythisch-legendäre Vohuman, der Sohn Spanddāts, was auch aus seiner mythischen Tätigkeit klar hervorgeht: er scheidet die Dämonen von den Menschen und läutert die ganze Welt. Zoroastrisch ist schon die Anschauung, daß er die Religion befördert.

Oben § 4.3.1.1. haben wir schon vermerkt, daß der Ausdruck *bē pālāyēt hamāk gēhān* wegen der Stellung des Verbums auf einen avestischen Grundtext hindeutet. Das *formale* Kriterium stimmt also mit dem *inhaltlichen* überein.

Weil die Chronologie nie die stärkste Seite der Iranier war, werden in Bahm. Yt. II 18 die Herrschaft Artaxšērs und diejenige Šāhpuhrs II. als *eine* Periode betrachtet. In dieser als einer einzigen betrachteten Periode trat laut Bahm. Yt. II 18 Āturpāt i Mahraspandān auf – tatsächlich aber während der Regierung Šāhpuhrs II.[370] Wir verstehen darum gut, warum in Dk IX 8,1 Āturpāt i Mahraspandān in die dritte Periode, diejenige Artaxšērs, plaziert wurde.

7.2.3. Über die *vierte* Periode kann kein Zweifel herrschen. Diese Zeit, aus Eisen gemischt, ist die schreckenerfüllte Endzeit und gehört dem avestischen Kanon an, wenn auch die Schilderung in vielerlei Hinsicht modifiziert wurde.

7.3. Aus der vorhergehenden Darstellung ergibt sich folgende Zwischenbilanz: Die Inhaltsangabe Dk IX 8,1 vom siebenten Fargard des Sūtkar Nask zeigt, daß diese Angabe *nicht* auf dem avestischen Text des Sūtkar Nask, sondern auf dem *zand,* also der PÜ dieses Textes, basiert, wo eine zeitgeschichtliche Erklärung des Textes schon zu finden ist. Diese zeitgeschichtliche Tendenz ist im vorliegenden Pahlavitext des Bahm. Yt. noch mehr verstärkt, worauf wir indessen hier nicht eingehen können. Hier sind übrigens viele Deutungen recht unsicher[371].

7.4. Zuletzt müssen wir ein paar Worte über die Authentizität des in avestischer Sprache vorliegenden Textes des Sūtkar Nask sagen. Wir haben schon oben § 3.3. konstatiert, daß die mitteliranische Sprachperiode ± 300 v. Chr. einsetzte. Nach diesem Zeitpunkt war Avestisch eine tote Sprache. Bailey hat aber angedeutet, daß Zusätze zum sassanidischen Avesta in

---

[369] Vgl. Christensen 1931, 98 mit Hinweis Anm. 4 auf Bdhn A 232:11.

[370] Vgl. oben § 3.3.2.

[371] Vgl. Czeglédy 1958 und Destrée 1971. Beide beschäftigen sich mit AŽ und Bahm. Yt., aber nur mit gewissen späteren Partien. Man vergleiche auch in diesem Band die Beiträge von T. Olsson § 2. und A. Hultgård § 6.2.1. Die Resultate, zu denen diese Verfasser gelangt sind, können hier nicht diskutiert werden, s. ferner oben § 4.2.3.2. und § 4.3.3.

avestischer Sprache bis 600 n. Chr. möglich waren[372]. Ich betrachte diese Möglichkeit – von kurzen konventionellen Formeln abgesehen – *als eine rein theoretische.* Den Beweis dafür liefert das Vorhandensein einer PÜ. Hätten die Priester ausreichende Kenntnisse in der avestischen Sprache gehabt, wäre selbstverständlich eine PÜ völlig unnötig gewesen. Der Gegensatz zu den Verhältnissen in Indien ist instruktiv. Dort wurde in den Priesterschulen eine lebendige Kenntnis der Sanskritsprache bewahrt, und darum besitzen wir eben keine Übersetzung der heiligen Schriften in einer späteren Sprache.

7.5. Zusammenfassend können wir somit sagen, daß die hier als "avestisch" bezeichneten Partien von Bahm. Yt. wirklich dem in avest. Sprache vorliegenden Avesta angehören, so wie dieser Kanon *vor* der sassanidischen Zeit tradiert wurde. Mit sassanidischen Zusätzen zu dem avest. Text haben wir nicht zu rechnen, wohl aber, wie soeben ausgeführt wurde, mit Zusätzen und Adaptierungen in der PÜ, die als Vorlage für den Pahlavitext des Bahm. Yt. diente.

8. Schlußbetrachtung

Wir haben hier nicht nur die leitenden Ideen, sondern auch die Quellen der iranischen Apokalyptik untersucht. Dabei sind die Grundzüge in makro- sowie in mikrokosmischer Hinsicht immer die gleichen geblieben: *teils (1) Unordnung in (1a) Kosmos und (1b) Gesellschaft, teils (2) Kämpfe (2a) zwischen den guten und bösen Mächten und (2b) zwischen ihnen und ihren Anhängern unter den Menschen.*

Zwei Hauptströmungen sind aber zu unterscheiden: die zoroastrische, bzw. die zervanitische. Diese läßt sich durch die Schrift De Iside et Osiride aus achämenidischer Zeit datieren. Für jene besitzen wir durch einen Vergleich zwischen den Pahlavischriften und den Orakeln des Hystaspes ein ähnliches Hilfsmittel. Dazu kommen aber auch die inneren Kriterien in der zoroastrischen Pahlaviliteratur, die eine Mischung von zervanitischen und zoroastrischen Überlieferungen darstellt. Durch philologische Analyse war es möglich, aufzuzeigen, daß ein großer Teil des apokalyptischen Stoffes aus dem sassanidischen Avesta stammt. Es war daher notwendig, auf die Kanongeschichte einzugehen. Aufzeichnungen der religiösen Überlieferungen existierten schon in der parthischen Periode unter den medischen Magiern, wie wir durch verschiedene Zeugnisse wissen. Diese

---

[372] Bailey 1943, 172 sagt: "During the Period 600 B.C. to 600 A.D. accretions were always possible, dependent upon the extent of the knowledge the priests had of the Avestan language." Ich wäre bereit, eine theoretische Möglichkeit für die Periode bis ± 0 v./n. Chr. zu diskutieren, was kleine "accretions" betrifft, notiere aber, daß Bailey kein einziges Beispiel erwähnt.

Magier waren indessen die Träger der zervanitischen Tradition. Umfangreicher zervanitischer Stoff ging daher in das sassanidische Avesta über. Bei der letzten Redaktion unter Xosrau Anōšurvān wurde aber dieser Stoff ausgemerzt, so daß nur wenige Spuren davon geblieben sind.

Der zervanitische Stoff, der sich besonders mit der Weltentwicklung befaßte, verschwand aber nicht. Schon früh in der Sassanidenzeit wurde das Avesta mit einer PÜ, später *zand* genannt, versehen. Das war notwendig, weil die avestische Sprache spätestens 300 v. Chr. als lebendige Sprache ausgestorben war. Das Wort *zand* gehört dem mparth. Dialekt an, dessen Träger die medischen Magier waren. Die Religion dieser Magier war aber der Zervanismus. Nun treffen wir in der Pahlavi-Literatur sowohl Einschläge vom Zervanismus wie vom mparth. Dialekt. Sonst ist diese Literatur zoroastrisch und in mpers. Dialekt geschrieben. *Sprachlich* gesehen ist also die Pahlavi-Literatur in einer gemischten Sprache verfaßt, *inhaltlich* ist sie eine Mischung von Zervanismus und Zoroastrismus. Die zervanitischen Elemente stammen aus dem *zand,* der urspr. Bezeichnung der mparth. schriftlichen Überlieferung der zervanitischen Magier. Das Wort *apastāk,* später die Bezeichnung des sassanidischen Avesta, war urspr. der Name der mündlichen Überlieferung der persischen Priester, die hauptsächlich ritueller Natur war.

So liegen die Quellenverhältnisse. Dank der Inhaltsangaben des Pahlavikompendiums Dēnkart besitzen wir gewisse Möglichkeiten zu bestimmen, aus welchem der 21 Nasks des sassanidischen Avesta der apokalyptische Stoff der Pahlavi-Literatur entnommen ist. Hier kommen vor allem Dāmdāt, Čihrdāt, Spand und Stūtkar (Sūttkar) Nask in Betracht.

Völlig falsch ist also die so oft auftauchende Behauptung, daß die apokalyptische Pahlavi-Literatur post-sassanidisch und die dort gefundenen Ideen sehr spät seien. Im Gegenteil sind sie sehr alt, denn sie stammen nicht nur aus dem Avesta, sondern es läßt sich zudem eine erstaunliche Kontinuität der Vorstellungswelt aufzeigen, wobei besonders auffallend ist, daß Bahm. Yt. III auf die älteste Periode des Zoroastrismus Bezug nimmt.

Was die leitenden Ideen betrifft, so sei das Schema der vier Weltperioden, das zervanitisch ist, besonders hervorgehoben. Es ist mit dem Altern und der Schwächung des Hochgottes Zervān verbunden, dessen Körper die Welt ist. Darum bedeutet die Erneuerung der Welt (*fraškart*) eine Verjüngung und Verstärkung der Welt. Die Welt zusammen mit der Menschheit wird zum Urzustand zurückkehren, so wie sie war, ehe der böse Geist Ahriman, der große Gegenspieler des guten Gottes Ōhrmazd, und Ahrimans Helferin Āz, Gier, die von Ōhrmazd organisierte Welt, attackierten. Endzeit und Urzeit bedingen sich in logischer Weise, und der Endkampf schließt mit dem Herabstürzen Ahrimans zur Hölle, ebenso wie er in der Urzeit hinabstürzte und machtlos hingestreckt lag. Dann wird alle Bosheit samt der Hölle vernichtet, und alle Menschen – auch die Sünder – werden gerecht erklärt und glückselig. Das ist die Schlußperspektive. Obgleich die jetzige Welt unter der Herrschaft Ahrimans leidet, kommt doch der Endsieg, und damit endet alle Weltbetrachtung in einer optimistischen Hoffnung.

Abkürzungsverzeichnis

Außer den laut TRE und im Abkürzungsverzeichnis zu diesem Band verwendeten Abkürzungen werden folgende Sigla gebraucht:

AirWb	=	Altiranisches Wörterbuch, s. Bibliographie: Literatur unter *Bartholomae* AirWb
Aogem.	=	Aogemadaēčā
AVN	=	Ardāi Virāz Nāmak
AZ	=	Abyātkār i Zarērān
AŽ	=	Ayātkar i Žāmāspīk
Bahm. Yt.	=	Bahman Yašt
Bdhn	=	Bundahišn
Bdhn A	=	Bundahišn, ed *Anklesaria,* s. Bibliographie: Quellen, Pahlavi-Texte
Dk	=	Dēnkart
DkM	=	Dēnkart, ed. *Madan,* s. Bibliographie: Quellen, Pahlavi-Texte
HN	=	Hādoxt Nask
KN	=	Kārnāmak i Artaxšēr i Pāpakān
M	=	Manichaica
MX	=	Mēnōy i Xrat
PRDD	=	The Pahlavi Rivâyat accompanying the Dâdistân î Dînîk, ed. *Dhabar,* s. Bibliographie: Quellen, Pahlavi-Texte
PÜ	=	Pahlaviübersetzung
ŠE	=	Šahrīhā i Ērān
ŠKZ	=	Šāhpuhr-Inschrift am Kaʿba-ye-Zardušt, in: *Maricq,* s. Bibliographie: Quellen, Inschriften
ŠN	=	Šāhnāmah
Vd.	=	Vendidad (Vīdēvdāt)
Y.	=	Yasna
Yt.	=	Yašt
Zātspr.	=	Zātspram

Bibliographie

1. Quellen

Avesta: Zendavesta I. The Zend Texts, by *N. L. Westergaard,* Kopenhagen 1852–1854.
Avesta, die heiligen Bücher der Parsen I–III, hrsg. von *K. F. Geldner,* Stuttgart 1886–1895.
Le Zend-Avesta, trad. nouv. avec commentaire hist. et philologique I–III, par *J. Darmesteter,* Paris 1892–1893.
Eine Reihe avestischer Texte ist in Faksimileauflage als *"Codices Avestici et Pahlavici Universitatis Hafniensis",* Kopenhagen 1931 ff. herausgegeben worden.
Gāthās: Die Gatha's des Awesta, übers. von *Chr. Bartholomae,* Straßburg 1905.
Zoroastre. Étude critique avec une trad. commentée des Gâthâ, par *J. Duchesne-Guillemin,* Paris 1948.
Yašts: Die Yäšt's des Awesta, übers. von *H. Lommel,* Göttingen-Leipzig 1927.

Nīrangastān: Nīrangistān. Der Awestatraktat über die rituellen Vorschriften, hrsg. von *A. Waag*, Leipzig 1941.
Aogemadaēčā: Aogemadaēčā, ein Parsentractat in Pazend, Altbaktrisch und Sanskrit, hrsg., übers. und mit Glossar versehen von *W. Geiger*, Erlangen 1878.
Hadōxt Nask: Beiträge zur Metrik des Awestas und des R̥gvedas, von *J. Hertel*, Leipzig 1927.

Pahlavi-Texte

Abyātkār i Zarērān: *D. Monchi-Zadeh*, Die Geschichte Zarērs (AUU.SIU 4), Uppsala 1981.
Ardāi Virāz Nāmak: The Book of Ardā Virāf. The Pahlavi Text prepared by Destur Hoshangji Jamaspji Asa, revised and collated with further manuscripts, with an English translation by *M. Haug* and *E. W. West*, Bombay-London 1872 [Neudruck: Amsterdam 1971].
Der Pahlavi-Kodex K 20 in der Faksimileausgabe *"Codices Avestici et Pahlavici Universitatis Hafniensis"*, Kopenhagen 1931 ff.
Ayātkār i Žāmāspīk: Libro Apocalittico Persiano Ayātkār i Žāmāspīk, testo pehlevico, parsi e pazend restitutio, tradotto e commentato, ed. *G. Messina*, Rom 1939.
Bahman Yašt: Zand-î Vohûman Yasn and Two Pahlavi Fragments with Text, Transliteration, and Translation in English by *B. T. Anklesaria*, Bombay 1957.
Kaikobad Adarbad Nosherwan, The Text of the Pahlavi Zand-i-Vohuman Yasht, Poona 1899.
Die Pahlavi-Kodexe K 20b und K 43 in der Faksimileausgabe *"Codices Avestici et Pahlavici Universitatis Hafniensis"*, Kopenhagen 1931 ff.
Bundahišn: The Bûndahishn, being a facsimile of the TD Manuscript No. 2 brought from Persia by Dastur Tirandaz and now preserved in the late Ervad Tahmuras' Library, ed. by the late *E. T. D. Anklesaria*, Bombay 1908.
Der Bundehesh, zum ersten Male herausgegeben, transcribiert, übersetzt, und mit Glossar versehen von *F. Justi*, Leipzig 1868.
The Bondaheshn, being a facsimile edition of the manuscript TD₁, Iranian Culture Foundation 88.
The Codex DH, being a facsimile edition of Bondahesh, Zand-e Vohuman Yasht and parts of Denkard, Iranian Culture Foundation 89.
Die Pahlavi-Kodexe K 20 und K 20B in der Faksimileausgabe *"Codices Avestici et Pahlavici Universitatis Hafniensis"*, Kopenhagen 1931 ff.
Text und Übers. bei *Messina* 1935 (s. 2. Lit.).
Dēnkart: The Complete Text of the Pahlavi Dinkard. Published by "The Society for the promotion of researches into the Zoroastrian religion" under The supervision of *D. M. Madan*, Bombay 1911.
Dēnkart, A Pahlavi Text. Facsimile edition of the Manuscript B of the K. R. Cama Oriental Institute Bombay, ed. *M. J. Dresden*, Wiesbaden 1966.
Kārnāmak i Artaxšēr i Pāpakān: Kârnâmak i Artakhšēr Pâpakân, ed. by *E. K. Antiâ*, Bombay 1900.
The Pahlavi Kârnâmê î Artakhshîr i Pâpakân, ed. by *Peshotan Sanjana*, Bombay 1896.
Mēnōy i Xrat: The Book of the Mainyo-i-Khard. The Pazand and Sanskrit Texts with an English Transl., a Glossary etc. ed. by *E. W. West*, London-Stuttgart 1871.
Der Pahlavi-Kodex K 43 in der Faksimileausgabe *"Codices Avestici et Pahlavici Universitatis Hafniensis"*, Kopenhagen 1931.
Pahlavi Rivāyat zu *Dātistān i Dēnīk*: The Pahlavi Rivâyat accompanying the Dâdistân î Dînîk, ed. *E. B. N. Dhabhar*, Bombay 1913.
Šahrīhā i Ērān: *J. Markwart* 1931 (s. 2. Lit.).
Zātspram: Kap. I und XXXIV hrsg., übers. und erklärt von *R. C. Zaehner*, in: BSOS 9 (1937–1939) 573–585; BSOAS 10 (1940–1942) 377–398, 606–631. Wieder abgedruckt in: *Zaehner* 1955 (s. 2. Lit.).

Inschriften

achämenidische: *R. G. Kent*, Old Persian. Grammar, Texts, Lexicon, New Haven 1950.

sassanidische: M. *Sprengling*, Third Century Iran. Sapor and Kartir, Chicago 1953.
    A. *Maricq*, "Res gestae divi Saporis", in: Syria 35 (1958) 295–360; nunmehr auch in: Maricq 1965 (s. 2. Lit.).

Neupersische Texte

Fārsnāmah: The *Fārsnāmah of Ibnu'l Balkhi*, ed. Le *Strange-Nickolson*, London 1921.
Garšāspnāmah: Asadī, Garšāspnāmah, ed. H. *Yaghmāi*, Teheran 1371 (1939).
    Le livre de Gerchâsp, poème persan d'Asadi de Tous, trad. par H. *Massé*, Paris 1951.
Šāhnāmah: Le livre des rois par Abou'l Kasim Firdousi, éd. par J. *Mohl* I–VII, Paris 1838–1878. [Abgedruckt Vol. I–VII, Teheran 1345 a.H. Diese Ausgabe ist benutzt.]
    Le livre des rois par Abou'l Kasim Firdousi, trad. par J. *Mohl* I–VII, Paris 1876–1878.

Armenische Texte

Eznik von Kolb: L. *Mariès* – Ch. *Mercier* (Ed.), Eznik de Kolb, De Deo (PO 28:3–4), Paris 1959.

Manichäische Texte

F. C. *Andreas* – K. *Barr*, "Bruchstücke einer Pahlavi-Übersetzung der Psalmen", in: SPAW.PH 1933:1, Berlin 1933, 91–152 [Sonderausgabe 3–64].
F. C. *Andreas* – W. *Henning*, "Mitteliranische Manichaica aus Chinesisch-Turkistan II", in: SPAW.PH 1933:7, Berlin 1933, 294–363 [Sonderausgabe 3–72].
F. C. *Andreas* – W. *Henning*, "Mitteliranische Manichaica aus Chinesisch-Turkistan III", in: SPAW.PH 1934:27, Berlin 1934, 848–912 [Sonderausgabe 3–67].
M. *Boyce*, The Manichaean Hymn-Cycles in Parthian, Oxford 1954.
F. W. K. *Müller*, "Handschriftenreste in Estrangelo-Schrift aus Turfan, Chinesisch-Turkistan, II. Teil", in: SPAW.PH 1904:38, Berlin 1904, 1–117.
C. *Schmidt* – H. J. *Polotsky*, "Ein Manifund in Ägypten", in: SPAW.PH 1933:1, Berlin 1933, 4–90 [Sonderausgabe 3–89].

Syrische Texte

Acta Martyrum et Sanctorum, II, IV, ed. P. *Bedjan*, Leipzig 1891, 1894.
Ausgewählte Akten persischer Märtyrer, von O. *Braun* (BKV² 22), Kempten o.J.
Auszüge aus syrischen Akten persischer Märtyrer, von G. *Hoffmann*, Leipzig 1880.
Th. *Nöldeke*, "Syrische Polemik gegen die persische Religion", in: Festgruß an R. von Roth, Stuttgart 1893, 34–38.

Griechische Texte

Plutarch, De Iside et Osiride §§ 46–47: J. *Gwyn Griffiths* 1970, 190–195 (s. 2. Lit.).
    J. *Bidez* – F. *Cumont* 1938 II, 70–72 (s. 2. Lit.).

Lateinische Texte

Lactantius Instit. divinae: Hystaspes Orakel: J. *Bidez* – F. *Cumont* 1938 II, 364–376 (s. 2. Lit.).

2. Literatur

Bailey, H. W. 1930–32: "Iranian Studies", in: BSOS 6 (1930–32) 945–955.
– 1933: "Iranian Studies III", in: BSOS 7 (1933) 275–298.
– 1943: *Zoroastrian Problems in the ninth-century Books*, Oxford 1943.
– 1953: "The Persian Language", in: A. J. Arberry (Ed.), *The Legacy of Persia*, Oxford 1953, 174–198.
– 1953a: "Analecta Indoscythica I", in: JRAS (1953) 95–116.

– 1953b: "Indo-Iranian Studies I. Indo-Iranian pṛkṣá-: fraša-", in: *TPS* (1953) 21–42.

Bartholomae, Chr.: AirWb: *Altiranisches Wörterbuch*, Straßburg 1904.

– 1916–25: *Zur Kenntnis der mitteliranischen Mundarten* I–VI (in: *SHAW.PH* 1916:9; 1917:11; 1920:2; 1922:6; 1923:3; 1924–25:6), Heidelberg 1916–1925.

Belardi, W. 1979: "Il nome dell' 'Avesta' alla ricerca di un significato perduto", in: *Accad. Naz. dei Lincei, Rendiconti della classe d. scienze morali storiche e filologiche*, Serie VIII, vol. XXXIV, Rom 1979, 251–274.

Benveniste, E. 1929: *The Persian Religion according to the Chief Greek Texts*, Paris 1929.

– 1932: „Le Mémorial de Zarēr", in: *JA* 220 (1932) 245–293.

– 1932a: "Une apocalypse pehlevie: le Žāmāsp-Nāmak", in: *RHR* 106 (1932) 337–380.

– 1932–33: "Le témoignage de Théodore bar Konay sur le Zoroastrisme", in: *MO* 26–27 (1932–33) 170–215.

– 1935: *Les infinitifs avestiques*, Paris 1935.

– Renou, L. 1934: *Vṛtra et Vṛϑragna*, Paris 1934.

Bidez, J. – Cumont, F. 1938: *Les mages hellénisés*, I–II, Paris 1938 [Neudruck 1973].

Bousset, W. 1979: "Der Gott Aion" (Aus dem unveröffentlichten Nachlaß [ca. 1912–1919]), in: *Religionsgeschichtliche Studien. Aufsätze zur Religionsgeschichte des Hellenistischen Zeitalters*, hrsg. von A. F. Verheule (NT.S 50), Leiden 1979, 192–230.

Christensen, A. 1917–34: *Les types du premier Homme et du premier Roi dans l'histoire légendaire des Iraniens*, I–II (AEO 14; 14:2), Stockholm 1917; Leiden 1934.

– 1925–26: "Quelques notices sur les plus anciennes périodes du Zoroastrianisme", in: *AcOr* 4 (1925–26) 81–115.

– 1931: *Les Kayanides* (DVSS.PH 19:2), Kopenhagen 1931.

– 1944: *L'Iran sous les Sassanides*, 2. Aufl. Kopenhagen 1944.

Cumont, F. 1931: "La fin du monde selon les Mages occidentaux", in: *RHR* 103 (1931) 29–96.

– 1933: "L'iniziatione di Nerone da parte di Tiridate d'Armenia", in: *RFIC* 61 (1933) 145–154.

Czeglédy, K. 1958: "Bahrām Čōbīn and the Persien Apocalyptic Literature", in: *AOH* 8 (1958) 21–43.

Darmesteter, J. 1892–93: *Le Zend-Avesta*, trad nouv. avec commentaire hist. et philologique, I–III, Paris 1892–93.

Destrée, A. 1971: "Quelques réflexions sur le héros des récits apocalyptiques Persans et sur le mythe de la ville de cuivre", in: *La Persia nel Medioevo* (Accad. Naz. dei Lincei 368), Rom 1971, 639–652.

Dodds, E. R. 1970: *Die Griechen und das Irrationale*, Darmstadt 1970 [Engl. Original: Berkeley/Los Angeles 1951].

Dumézil, G. 1953: "Vísṇu et les Marút à travers la réforme zoroastrienne", in: *JA* 241 (1953) 1–25.

– 1957: "Remarques sur 'Augur, Augustus'", in: *REL* 35 (1957) 126–151.

– 1958: *L'idéologie tripartie des Indo-Européens*, Brüssel 1958.

– 1977: *Les dieux souverains des Indo-Européens*, Paris 1977.

Eilers, W. 1972: Rez. Mayrhofer 1968, in: *ZDMG* 122 (1972) 383–385.

Geiger, W. – Kuhn, E. (Hrsg.) 1896/1904: *Grundriß der iranischen Philologie*, I.2–II, Straßburg 1896–1904.

Ghilain, A. 1939: *Essai sur la langue parthe*, Louvain 1939 [Nachdruck 1966].

Gnoli, Gh. 1967: *Ricerche storiche sul Sīstān* (ISMEO), Rom 1967.

– 1980: *Zoroaster's Time and Homeland* (IUO.SMin 7), Neapel 1980.

Götze, A. 1923: "Persische Weisheit in griechischem Gewande", in: *ZII* 2 (1923) 60–98, 167–177.

Griffiths, J. Gwyn 1970: *Plutarch's De Iside et Osiride*. Edited with an Introduction, Translation and Commentary, Swansea 1970.

Güntert, H. 1923: *Der arische Weltkönig und Heiland*, Halle 1923.

Hartman, S. S. 1953: *Gayōmart*, Uppsala 1953.

Henning, W. B. 1933—34: "Das Verbum des Mittelpersischen der Turfanfragmente", in: *ZII* 9 (1933—1934) 158—253.
- 1958: "Mitteliranische Iranistik", in: *HO* IV.1, Leiden 1958, 20—130.
Hübschmann, H. 1897: *Armenische Grammatik*, I: Armenische Etymologie, Leipzig 1897 [Neudruck: Hildesheim-New York 1972].
Justi, F. 1895: *Iranisches Namenbuch*, Marburg 1895.
Kellens, J. 1975: "L'expression avestique de la perpétuité", in: *IIJ* 17 (1975) 211—215.
Lenz, W. 1926: "Die nordiranischen Elemente in der neupersischen Literatursprache bei Firdosi", in: *ZII* 4 (1926) 251—316.
Lommel, H. 1927: *Die Yäšt's des Awesta* (QRG 15), Göttingen 1927.
- 1930: *Die Religion Zarathustras*, Tübingen 1930.
MacKenzie, D. N. 1967: "Notes on the transcription of Pahlavi", in: *BSOAS* 30 (1967) 17—29.
- 1971: *A Concise Pahlavi Dictionary*, London 1971.
Maricq, A. 1965: *Classica et Orientalia*, Paris 1965.
Markwart, J. 1931: *A Catalogue of the Provincial Capitals of Ērānšahr*, Rom 1931.
- 1938: *Wehrot und Arang*, Leiden 1938.
Mayrhofer, M. 1968: *Die Rekonstruktion des Medischen* (AÖAW 1968:1), Wien 1968.
Messina, G. 1935: "Mito, leggenda e storia nella tradizione iranica", in: *Or* 4 (1935) 257—290.
- 1939: *Libro apocalittico Persiano, Ayātkār i Žāmāspīk* (BibOr 9), Rom 1939.
Molé, M. 1967: *La légende de Zoroastre selon des textes pehlevis*, Paris 1967.
Moulton, J. H. 1913: *Early Zoroastrianism*, London 1913.
Nyberg, H. S. 1929: "Questions de cosmogonie et de cosmologie mazdéennes", in: *JA* 214 (1929) 193—310.
- 1931: "Questions de cosmogonie et de cosmologie mazdéennes", in: *JA* 219 (1931) 1—134, 193—244.
- 1931a: *Hilfsbuch des Pehlevi*, II: Glossar, Uppsala 1931.
- 1938: *Die Religionen des alten Iran* (MVAEG 43), Leipzig 1938 [Neudruck: Osnabrück 1966].
- 1964: *A Manual of Pahlavi*, I: texts, alphabets, index, paradigms, notes and an introduction, Wiesbaden 1964.
- 1974: *A Manual of Pahlavi*, II: ideograms, glossary, abbreviations, index, grammatical survey, corrigenda to Part I, Wiesbaden 1974.
Puech, H. Ch. 1949: *Le manichéisme. Son fondateur-sa doctrine*, Paris 1949.
Reichelt, H. 1909: *Awestisches Elementarbuch*, Heidelberg 1909.
- 1927: "Iranisch", in: *Grundriß der indogermanischen Sprach- und Altertumskunde*, II Bd. 4, Hälfte 2, Berlin-Leipzig 1927.
Reitzenstein, R. – Schaeder, H. H. 1926: *Studien zum antiken Synkretismus aus Griechenland und Iran*, Leipzig-Berlin 1926.
Reitzenstein, R. 1927: *Die hellenistischen Mysterienreligionen*, 3. Aufl. Leipzig 1927 [Nachdruck: Darmstadt 1973].
Rostovtseff, M. I. – Brown, P. E. – Wells, C. B. (Ed.) 1939: *The Excavations at Dura-Europos*. Preliminary Report of the Seventh and Eight Seasons of work 1933—1934 and 1934—1935, New Haven, Conn. 1939.
Schaeder, H. H. 1930: Iranische Beiträge I (SKG.G 5 VII—IX), Halle 1930, 199—296 [Sonderausgabe 1—98].
Söderblom, N. 1901: *La vie future d'après le mazdéisme* (AMG 9), Paris 1901.
Steingass, P. 1947: *A Comprehensive Persian-English Dictionary*, 3. Nachdruck, London 1947.
Ström, Å. V. 1975: Germanische Religion, in: Ström, Å. V. – Biezais, H.: *Germanische und baltische Religion* (RM 19.1), Stuttgart 1975, 5—306.
Tedesco, P. 1921: "Dialektologie der westiranischen Turfantexte", in: *MO* 15 (1921) 184—258.
West, E. W. – Haug, M. 1874: *Glossary and Index of the Pahlavi Texts of the Book of Ardā Virāf . . .*, Bombay-London 1874 [Neudruck: Osnabrück 1978].

West, E. W. 1880: *Pahlavi Texts, translated by E. W. West. Part I, The Bundahish, Bahman Yasht, and Shāyast Lā Shāyast* (SBE V), Oxford 1880.

Widengren, G. 1938: *Hochgottglaube im alten Iran* (UUÅ 1938:6), Uppsala 1938.

– 1954: "Stand und Aufgaben der iranischen Religionsgeschichte" in: *Numen* 1 (1954) 16–83 [Sonderausgabe 2–69].

– 1955: "Stand und Aufgaben der iranischen Religionsgeschichte", in: *Numen* 2 (1955) 47–134 [Sonderausgabe 71–134].

– 1956: "Recherches sur le féodalisme iranien", in: *OrSuec* 5 (1956) 79–182.

– 1960: *Iranisch-semitische Kulturbegegnung in parthischer Zeit* (AGFLNW.G 70), Köln-Opladen 1960.

– 1961: *Mani und der Manichäismus* (UB 57), Stuttgart 1961.

– 1961a: "Das Prinzip des Bösen in den östlichen Religionen", in: *Das Böse* (SJI 13), Zürich-Stuttgart 1961, 25–61.

– 1965: *Die Religionen Irans* (RM 14), Stuttgart 1965.

– 1966: "Iran and Israel in Parthian Times with Special Regard to the Ethiopic Book of Enoch", in: *Temenos* 2 (1966) 139–177.

– 1967: "Zervanitische Texte aus dem 'Avesta' in der Pahlavi-Überlieferung. Eine Untersuchung zu Zātspram und Bundahišn", in: G. Wiessner (Hrsg.), *FS. Wilhelm Eilers*, Wiesbaden 1967, 278–287.

– 1967a: "Primordial Man and Prostitute: A Zervanite Motif in the Sassanid Avesta", in: R. J. Z. Werblowsky (Ed.), *Studies in Mysticism and Religion. Presented to G. Scholem*, Jerusalem 1967, 337–352.

– 1967b: "Philological Remarks on some Pahlavi Texts chiefly concerned with Zervanite Religion", in: *Sir J. J. Zarthoshti Madressa Centenary Volume*, Bombay 1967, 84–103.

– 1968: "Le symbolisme de la ceinture", in: *IrAnt* 8 (1968), 133–155 [= *Mélanges Ghirshman* III, Leiden 1968].

– 1968a: "Holy Book and Holy Tradition in Iran. The Problem of the Sassanid Avesta", in: F. F. Bruce – G. E. Rupp (Ed.): *Holy Book and Holy Tradition*, Manchester 1968, 36–53.

– 1969: *Religionsphänomenologie*, Berlin-New York 1969.

– 1969a: "The Death of Gayōmart", in: J. Kitagawa – Ch. H. Long (Ed.): *Myths amd Symbols. Studies in Honor of Mircea Eliade*, Chicago 1969, 179–193.

– 1969b: *Der Feudalismus im alten Iran* (WAAFLNW 40), Köln-Opladen 1969.

– 1973: "Salvation in Iranian Religion", in: E. J. Sharpe – J. R. Hinnels (Ed.): *Man and His Salvation. Studies in Memory of S. G. F. Brandon*, Manchester 1973, 315–326.

– 1974: "La Sagesse dans le Manichéisme", in: *Mélanges d'histoire des religions offerts à H.-Ch. Puech*, Paris 1974, 501–515.

– 1976: "Iran, der große Gegner Roms: Königsgewalt, Feudalismus, Militärwesen", in: *ANRW* II.9.1, Berlin 1976, 219–306.

– 1977: "Einleitung", in: *idem* (Hrsg.): *Der Manichäismus* (WdF 168), Darmstadt 1977, IX–XXXII.

– 1978: "Der Manichäismus. Kurzgefaßte Geschichte der Problemforschung", in: B. Aland (Hrsg.): *Gnosis. FS Hans Jonas*, Göttingen 1978, 278–315.

– 1979: "Révélation et Prédication dans les Gāthās", in: Gh. Gnoli – A. V. Rossi (Ed.): *Iranica* (IUO.SMin 10), Neapel 1979, 339–364.

– 1979a: Rez. B. Schlerath (Hrsg.): Zarathustra (WdF 169), Darmstadt 1970, in: *GGA* 231 (1979) 52–85.

– [1980]: "Aspects de la notion de *'daēnā'*" [Vortrag vor ISMEO, Rom 28. 10. 1980; erscheint demnächst].

Wikander, S. 1938: *Der arische Männerbund*, Lund 1938.

– 1941: *Vayu*. Texte und Untersuchungen zur indo-iranischen Religionsgeschichte I., Lund 1941.

– 1946: *Feuerpriester in Kleinasien und Iran* (ARSHLL 40), Lund 1946.

– 1950: "Sur le fonds commun indo-iranian des épopées de la Perse et de l'Inde", in: *NC* 2 (1950) 310–329.

Windisch, H. 1929: *Die Orakel des Hystaspes* (VNAW NS 28.3), Amsterdam 1929.
Zaehner, R. C. 1937−39: "Zurvanica II", in: *BSOS* 9 (1937−39) 573−585.
− 1940−42: "A Zervanite Apocalypse I", in: *BSOAS* 10 (1940−42) 377−398.
− 1955: *Zurvan*. A Zoroastrian Dilemma, Oxford 1955.

Description du phénomène de l'Apocalyptique dans l'Ancien Testament

Jean Carmignac

1. Definitions de l'Apocalyptique

Notre présence ici prouve que nous sommes tous plus ou moins Ratlos vor der Apokalyptik[1]. Mais en outre je suis Français, et l'un de vous regrette "die französische Zurückhaltung gegenüber der Apokalyptik[2]".

1.1. Mon premier devoir est donc de vous expliquer cette réserve des Français envers l'Apocalyptique[3]. Elle ne provient nullement, comme on l'insinue, d'une influence de la théologie catholique. Le véritable responsable en est Descartes, qui nous a habitués aux notions claires et précises. Si nous hésitons à parler d'Apocalyptique, c'est parce que nous voudrions savoir si elle est un genre littéraire ou bien un pudding théologique.

1.1.1. Et si l'on opte pour la théologie, quelle est la composition de ce pudding? Voici les principaux ingrédients qu'il peut contenir: prophétie réelle, fausse prophétie, prophétie ex eventu, messianisme, promesse de prospérité ou de châtiment, promesse de salut politique ou spirituel, parousie, résurrection partielle ou générale, jugement dernier, fin du monde, rénovation du monde, création d'un nouveau monde, vie éternelle pour l'individu ou pour la collectivité, révélations sur Dieu, les anges, les hommes[4] et, of course, eschatologie (dont il existe environ 200 espèces[5]). Chaque fois qu'on parle d'Apocalyptique, veut-on inclure absolument tous ces ingrédients ou seulement certains d'entre eux?

1.1.2. Mais si l'on n'emploie pas chaque fois ce terme avec exactement les mêmes composantes, et si on lui attribue tantôt les unes tantôt les

---

[1] Klaus Koch 1970: Ratlos vor der Apokalyptik.   [2] K. Koch 1970, 87.

[3] Selon J. M. Schmidt 1969, 98, c'est K. I. Nitzsch qui a forgé ce terme "Apokalyptik" en 1820. Pourtant on trouve déjà dans les Pensées de Pascal: "Il y a des figures claires et démonstratives, mais il y en a d'autres qui semblent un peu tirées par les cheveux. Celles-là sont semblables aux apocalyptiques, mais la différence qu'il y a, est qu'il (sic) n'en ont point d'indubitables" (1934, n° 650, p. 233). Mais sans doute faut-il voir là dans "apocalyptiques" un adjectif (= aux [figures] apocalyptiques) et non pas un substantif (malgré le Dictionnaire alphabétique et analogique de la Langue Française par Paul Robert).

[4] C'est à cause de cet élément que G. von Rad rattache l'Apocalyptique (comprise en un sens pseudo-théologique) au courant sapientiel (1967, II, 263-277).

[5] Voir mon article de 1971, 365-390, et mon ouvrage "Le Mirage de l'Eschatologie" 1979b.

autres, on viole les règles élémentaires de la logique, car alors on raisonne selon le type suivant: "la seconde dizaine contient le chiffre 13, elle contient aussi le chiffre 17, donc 13 = 17". En fait l'utilisation théologique de ce terme est extrêmement dangereuse, car il est à peu près impossible que *tous les auteurs et tous les lecteurs* la chargent *toujours* des mêmes éléments identiques. Et s'ils ne le font pas strictement, ils sortent du plan scientifique. Si l'on considère que la théologie est une science, on n'a pas le droit de la déconsidérer par des méthodes anti-scientifiques.

1.1.3. Mais alors, dira-t-on, n'est-ce pas appauvrir la théologie que de la priver d'une notion aussi commode? – Non. Car on n'appauvrit en rien la théologie quand on lui demande d'employer un vocabulaire précis et une méthode scientifique[6]. Au lieu de recourir à ce terme-pudding, qu'on prenne la peine de préciser chaque fois les éléments exacts que l'on veut mentionner. On évitera ainsi bien des sophismes, soit en théologie soit en histoire des religions. En réalité on rendra service à la véritable science[7].

1.1.4. Voilà pourquoi toute définition de l'Apocalyptique en fonction d'une théologie doit être, semble-t-il, absolument éliminée.

1.2. Bien entendu, il faut distinguer entre "Apocalypse", qui est une

---

[6] Voici, par exemple, la définition proposée par P. D. Hanson au début de son article sur l'Apocalypticisme (1976b, 28): "A system of thought produced by visionary movements; builds upon a specific eschatological perspective in generating a symbolic universe opposed to that of the dominant society. This symbolic universe serves to establish the identity of the visionary community in relation to rival groups and to the deity, and to resolve contradictions between religious hopes and the experience of alienation by according ultimate meaning solely to the cosmic realm, from which imminent deliverance is awaited".

[7] Heureusement, bien des savants ont déjà réclamé cette clarification du concept d'Apocalyptique. Voici quelques couplets de cette litanie de doléances:

"Ce qui paraît certain, c'est que notre concept d'"apocalyptique" a besoin d'être soumis de toute urgence à un examen critique, parce que son emploi sommaire pour désigner aussi bien un phénomène littéraire qu'un phénomène religieux pose bien des problèmes" (G. von Rad 1967, II, 277).

"One obvious difficulty in a study of this kind is the use of the word "apocalyptic" itself, which is notoriously difficult to define, and which is used in modern literature, secular and religious alike, with a whole variety of meaning and frequently simply as a synonym for the word "cataclysmic"" (D. S. Russell 1978, 21).

"Despite the universal usage of the word "apocalyptic" today, there is no consensus among scholars as to its exact meaning or the extent of what can properly be classified as apocalyptic literature" (A. A. Di Lella 1978, 63).

"That extravagant, many-faceted complex of symbolisms generally associated with "apocalyptic" (G. Edwards 1977, 193).

Selon R. Martin-Achard, "J. M. Schmidt (Die jüdische Apokalyptik) fait remarquer en terminant que le concept même d'apocalyptique est imprécis et mérite d'être soigneusement étudié; il invite aussi les spécialistes à vouer toute leur attention à l'examen des formes littéraires utilisées par les apocalypticiens, estimant que '"le problème principal de la recherche apocalyptique reste un problème de méthode' (p. 313ss)" (1970, 315).

"... Incertezza del significato stesso di "apocalittica", per cui si corre il rischio di fare la storia di qualcosa che non è mai esistito, almeno con la configurazione esatta che noi pensiamo" (Paolo Sacchi 1979, I, 48).

oeuvre littéraire, "Apocalyptique", qui est le genre littéraire employé dans une telle oeuvre, et "Apocalyptisme", qui est la systématisation des caractéristiques de ce genre littéraire. Reconnaissons bien volontiers que la systématisation exprimée par le terme "Apocalypticisme" perd une grande partie de son intérêt, s'il s'agit d'un style littéraire et non plus d'une tendance théologique. Mais ne regrettons pas trop qu'un terme aussi vague et aussi nébuleux disparaisse de l'horizon théologique.

1.3. Ces précisions permettent de proposer une définition (claire, espérons-le) de l'Apocalyptique: "Genre littéraire qui décrit des révélations célestes à travers des symboles[8]".

Malheureusement, je ne suis pas chargé de prouver et d'expliquer cette définition. Mon rôle est seulement de rechercher ce genre littéraire dans l'Ancien Testament.

1.3.1. L'Apocalypse de Jean dans le Nouveau Testament et le livre de Daniel dans l'Ancien Testament sont généralement considérés comme les deux principales réalisations de ce genre littéraire. Et en effet Daniel contient six visions qui sont rapportées (et expliquées) assez longuement: songe de la Grande Statue (2,1-49), songe du Grand Arbre (4,3-24), vision des Quatre Bêtes (7,1-28), vision du Bélier et du Bouc (8,1-27), vision des Soixante-Dix Semaines (9,21-27), vision du Fils d'Homme (10,4-12,4). J'ose espérer que tous vous considérez au moins ces passages (plus peut-être la vision de Mené-Teqél-Farsîn en 5,5-28) comme franchement apocalyptiques.

1.3.2. Mais ici se pose une autre question. Quel sens faut-il donner au terme ἀποκάλυψις "révélation"? S'agit-il seulement d'une révélation transmise par des symboles visuels, ou bien aussi d'une révélation auditive, ou bien même d'une révélation purement intellectuelle? En fait les trois hypothèses sont possibles. Mais les symboles ne sont presque jamais nécessaires dans une révélation intellectuelle et ils ne jouent souvent qu'on rôle nul ou secondaire dans les révélations auditives (comme par exemple

---

[8] Le mot "célestes" a été choisi à cause de son sens très large, qui inclut tout ce qui est préter-humain.

Dans la Revue de Qumrân (1979a, 20) je dis la même chose en des termes un peu différents: "Genre littéraire qui présente, à travers des symboles typiques, des révélations soit sur Dieu, soit sur les anges ou les démons, soit sur leurs partisans, soit sur les instruments de leur action". J. J. Collins (1979, 9) propose comme définition: "A genre of revelatory literature with a narrative framework, in which a revelation is mediated by an otherworldly being to a human recipient, disclosing a transcendent reality which is both temporal, insofar as it envisages eschatological salvation, and spatial, insofar as it involves another, supernatural world". Je serais d'accord, si l'on supprimait le "narrative framework", qui n'est pas essentiel, et surtout la finale, à partir de "disclosing", car elle consitute une regrettable concession, qui mélange à nouveau le contenant littéraire et le contenu théologique. En réalité le genre littéraire de l'Apocalyptique peut convenir à diverses théologies et chaque théologie peut s'exprimer aussi en d'autres genres littéraires.

dans le cas du petit Samuel: 1 Sam. 3,4-18). On constate donc que l'Apocalyptique présente surtout des révélations visuelles, mais qu'elle peut aussi inclure des révélations auditives et surtout des révélations mixtes, à la fois visuelles et auditives.

1.4. De savantes discussions se sont élevées pour déterminer les rapports de l'Apocalyptique avec le courant prophétique et avec la littérature sapientielle. Par de telles discussions leurs auteurs laissent au moins supposer qu'ils conçoivent logiquement l'Apocalyptique comme un genre littéraire, sur le même plan que le genre prophétique ou le genre sapientiel, car les Prophètes et les Sages peuvent exprimer tant de théologies différentes qu'aucune comparaison précise n'est plus possible sur le plan théologique entre l'ensemble des textes apocalyptiques, l'ensemble des textes prophétiques et l'ensemble des textes sapientiels.

1.4.1. Bien que les Sages révèlent à leurs auditeurs ou à leurs lecteurs des informations précieuses ou des directives bienfaisantes, le genre littéraire qu'ils emploient n'est pas caractérisé par l'usage de symboles (même s'ils peuvent, comme tout le monde, recourir à des images poétiques) et donc, malgré G. von Rad[9], on maintiendra une nette distinction entre l'Apocalyptique et la littérature sapientielle.

1.4.2. Entre Prophétisme et Apocalyptique les rapports sont plus intimes, car les Prophètes peuvent s'exprimer à travers les mêmes symboles que les Apocalypticiens[10]. Mais les Prophètes, même lorsqu'ils parlent au nom de Dieu, ne se cantonnent pas dans les révélations: souvent ils dénoncent les péchés, encouragent à la fidélité, décrivent des événements historiques, promettent le pardon ou le châtiment. Certes, les Apocalypses sont toujours des Prophéties[11], mais les Prophéties ne sont des Apocalypses que lorsqu'elles transmettent des révélations et lorsqu'elles les transmettent à travers des symboles. Ainsi l'Apocalyptique est une subdivision de la Prophétie.

2. L'Apocalyptique dans chaque livre de l'Ancien Testament

En supposant l'accord sur cette conception de l'Apocalyptique, qui semble la seule vraiment logique, rationnelle et scientifique, parcourons donc l'Ancien Testament.

2.1. Les premiers chapitres de la Genèse, même s'ils contiennent des révélations et s'ils recourent à des symboles, se présentent plutôt comme un

---

[9] G. von Rad 1967, II, 263-277.

[10] Dans l'Apocalypse de Jean combien de symboles ne sont-ils pas empruntés aux Prophètes?

[11] En se rappelant bien que la Prophétie, au sens biblique, n'est pas seulement l'annonce du futur, mais surtout la prédication de la Parole de Dieu.

récit historique (réel ou fictif, mais cela ne concerne pas le genre littéraire)...

Les révélations faites à Abraham, Isaac et Jacob, n'ont pas une allure spécialement symbolique ...

La bénédiction de Jacob à ses fils (Gen. 49,1-27) accumule les images poétiques, mais on n'oserait pas dire qu'elle parvienne jusqu'au niveau du symbole: voilà bien une Prophétie (vraie ou fausse, peu importe pour nous) qui n'est pas une Apocalypse.

2.2. Dans le reste du Pentateuque, Dieu se révèle certes à Moïse (Exode 19,10-25), mais l'objet de cette révélation est le Code de l'Alliance, d'allure plutôt juridique; les oracles de Balaam (Nombres 23,7-10 + 18-24; 24,3-9 + 15-24) sont des prophéties, dont les images poétiques ne sont pas vraiment des symboles; de même pour le Cantique de Moïse (Deutér. 32,1-43) et pour la bénédiction des Douze Tribus (Deutér. 33,2-29).

2.3. Les livres historiques, même quand ils mettent Dieu en scène, se présentent comme des relations historiques (au sens oriental et biblique du terme), où les éléments symboliques ne sont qu'accidentels.

2.4. Isaïe est appelé au ministère prophétique dans une vision (6,1–13), où des Séraphins purifient ses lèvres. Mais, bien que l'ouvrage soit appelé "la Vision d'Isaïe" (1,1), c'est le seul passage qui se présente explicitement comme une vision. Même les chapitres 24 à 27, qu'on appelle souvent "Apocalypse d'Isaïe" ne rapportent pas vraiment des visions. En un style grandiose, tissé d'images hardies, le prophète décrit de terribles châtiments et de merveilleuses délivrances. Sans doute parle-t-il sous l'influence d'intuitions venues de Dieu et ces chapitres pourraient-ils être le fruit de visions. Mais puisqu'ils ne sont pas explicitement présentés comme tels, j'estime sage et prudent de ne pas les rattacher au genre apocalyptique et de les considérer plutôt comme des prophéties sur les futures interventions de Dieu.

2.5. En Jérémie également, la vocation du prophète (1,4-19) est une véritable vision: "Que vois-tu Jérémie? – Je vois un rameau d'amandier...". Mais ensuite rien de semblable n'apparaîtra plus: Dieu parle souvent à son envoyé, en des termes plus ou moins imagés ou symboliques, mais il ne lui accorde plus de véritable vision. D'ailleurs les deux fois où Jérémie emploie le terme חזון "vision", il s'agit des fausses visions des faux prophètes (14,14 et 23,16). Jérémie promulgue les révélations du Seigneur, il ne les décrit pas.

2.6. En Ezéchiel se mêlent plusieurs genres littéraires: enseignements, menaces, allégories, actions symboliques. A plusieurs reprises, on rencontre de véritables éléments apocalyptiques: la vision inaugurale du Char et des Quatre Etres Vivants (1,1–3,14), la vision de l'Homme de Feu et de Vermeil (8,1-9,11), la vision des Chérubins (10,1-22 et 11.22-25), la grande vision du Temple (40,1 à 48,35). Certaines allégories, comme celle du Grand Aigle (17,3-10), dont Ezéchiel donne aussitôt l'interprétation (17,12-18), sont intermédiaires entre le tableau allégorique et la fresque apocalyptique.

2.7. Dans les douze "Petits Prophètes", Osée, Jonas, Sophonie, Aggée, Malachie ne contiennent pas d'authentiques visions. Ni non plus Joël, car ses dramatiques descriptions du "Jour du Seigneur" sont simplement illustrées par de brillantes images poétiques. Ni non plus Abdias et Nahum, bien que le titre de ces prophéties emploie le terme "Vision" (Abd. 1,1 et Nah. 1,1). Ni non plus Michée ou Habacuc, bien que leur messsage soit annoncé comme "Parole du Seigneur... qu'a vue Michée" (1,1) ou "Oracle qu'a vu Habacuc" (1,1). Par contre de véritables visions sont rapportées en Amos 7,1-9; 8,1-3 et 9,1-6 (Visions des Sauterelles, du Feu, de l'Etain, des Fruits, du Chapiteau) et surtout en Zacharie 1,8-6,8 (Visions des Cavaliers, des Cornes, du Cordeau, de Josué, du Chandelier, du Livre, du Boisseau, des Chars).

2.8. Dans le livre de Job, l'entretien entre Dieu et Satan (1,6-12 + 2,1-6) pourrait fort bien être le thème d'une vision, mais il semble plutôt n'être qu'une péripétie poétique indispensable au drame qui va être exposé.

3. Les songes à l'origine de l'Apocalyptique

3.1. Dans le cours de l'Ancien Testament apparaissent de temps en temps des personnages surnaturels qui conversent avec les humains pour leur transmettre divers messages: depuis le Paradis Terrestre jusqu'à Héliodore (2 Macc. 3,25-30 + 33-34), on pourrait citer les cas d'Abraham à Mambré (Gen. 18,1-19,3), de Jacob à Pénouel (Gen. 32,25-32), de Moïse au Buisson Ardent (Exode 24,9-11 + 15-18), de Gédéon (Juges 6,11-24), des parents de Samson (Juges 13,3-21), de Nathan (2 Sam. 7,4-17), de Gad (2 Sam. 24,11-17), d'Elie (1 Rois 19,5-7 + 9-18). Dans tous ces cas, il s'agit d'apparitions, qui communiquent avec des hommes pour leur transmettre des enseignements ou des directives (= "la Parole du Seigneur"), mais pas de véritables révélations symboliques, comme celles dont la description constitue précisément le genre littéraire "Apocalyptique".

3.2. Dans le livre de Daniel, certaines révélations prennent la forme de songes, ainsi le songe de la Statue (2,19 + 31-45) celui du Grand Arbre (4,7-14 | 17-24) celui des Quatre Bêtes (7,1-27). Le récit de ces songes est exactement semblable à celui des révélations reçues à l'état de veille. On n'a donc pas le droit d'exclure les songes de l'Apocalyptique.

3.2.1. Certes, un songe ne recourt pas nécessairement à des symboles et alors il ne rentre plus dans la catégorie de l'Apocalyptique: ainsi le songe de

Salomon à Gabaon (1 Rois 3,5-15) et les songes de Judas Maccabée sur Onias et sur Jérémie (2 Macc. 15,11-16)[12].

3.2.2. Mais d'autres songes sont décrits dans le même genre littéraire que les révélations apocalyptiques. Ainsi le songe de Jacob à Béthel (Gen. 28,12-15), où l'échelle qui relie la terre au Ciel constitue un véritable symbole; ainsi les songes de Joseph (Gen. 37,5-11 + 40,5 à 41,36) et celui de Gédéon (Juges 7,13-14).

3.3. Certes, ces songes sont exprimés en des récits trop courts pour qu'on ose leur décerner le titre "d'Apocalypses". Cependant ils peuvent nous suggérer une hypothèse sur l'origine du genre littéraire "Apocalyptique".

3.3.1. Les songes ont souvent été considérés comme des révélations célestes et leur élément irrationnel pouvait facilement donner prise à des interprétations symboliques. A plus forte raison, quand de tels songes sont vraiment des prémonitions (naturelles ou non, cela ne concerne pas le genre littéraire), ils passent volontiers pour des prophéties symboliques. N'est-ce pas le récit coloré et dramatique de ces songes qui a donné naissance à des développements, volontiers repris par les prophètes?

3.3.2. Dans cette hypothèse, la racine de l'Apocalyptique se perdrait dans la nuit des temps; les récits de songes, plus ou moins prophétiques, auraient frayé la voie aux interventions plus systématiques des prophètes, occasionnels ou professionnels; à l'intérieur de cette littérature "prophétique" se serait développée la tendance aux vastes fresques symboliques, qui constituent proprement le genre littéraire que nous appelons "Apocalyptique". Le souffle poétique d'Isaïe et de Jérémie leur permettait d'exprimer directement la Parole du Seigneur à travers de brillantes métaphores. Avec Amos, Ezéchiel et Zacharie on s'habitue de plus en plus à des panoramas symboliques qui sont attribués directement à Dieu ou à ses messagers. Ainsi se constitue un genre littéraire que propageront Daniel et d'autres auteurs de la période intertestamentaire, en attendant le Jean de l'Apocalypse[13].

4. Conclusion

A nous de dégager le "droit coutumier" implicitement admis dans ces ouvrages, pour parvenir ainsi à une meilleure compréhension.

A d'autres spécialistes de préciser dans quelle mesure le même genre littéraire se retrouve dans d'autres religions et à d'autres époques. Mais, en ce qui concerne l'Ancien Testament, l'étude de ce genre littéraire ne doit

---

[12] De même on ne rangera évidemment pas dans le genre apocalyptique les songes présentés par A. Leo Oppenheim 1956, 179-373.

[13] On évitera donc de prétendre dater un texte par sa seule appartenance au genre "Apocalyptique".

pas nous laisser "Ratlos", et nous devons plutôt l'entreprendre
"Furchtlos"[14].

Bibliographie

Carmignac, Jean 1971: "Les Dangers de l'Eschatologie", dans: *NTS* 17 (1971) 365-390.
– 1979a: "Qu'est-ce que l'Apocalyptique? Son emploi à Qumrân", dans: *RdQ* 10 (1979) 3-33.
– 1979b: *Le Mirage de l'Eschatologie: Royauté, Règne et Royaume de Dieu...sans Eschatologie,*
    Paris 1979.
Collins, John J. 1979: *Apocalypse: The Morphology of a Genre (Semeia* 14), Missoula, Montana
    1979.
Di Lella, Alexander A. 1978: dans: Hartman, Louis E. and Di Lella, Alexander A.: *The Book of*
    Daniel. A new Translation, with Introduction and Commentary (AncB), New York 1978.
Edwards, G. 1977: "The Historical Background of Early Apocalyptic Thought", dans:
    Merril, A. L./Overholt, T. W. (Eds.): *Scripture in History and Theology. Essays in Honor of J.*
    Coert Rylaardsam, Pittsburgh, Penn. 1977, 193–203.
Hanson, Paul D. 1976a: "Apocalypse, Genre", dans: *IDBSup* (1976) 27-28.
– 1976b: "Apocalypticism", dans. *IDBSup* (1976) 28-34.
Koch, Klaus 1970: *Ratlos vor der Apokalyptik.* Eine Streitschrift über ein vernachlässigtes
    Gebiet der Bibelwissenschaft und die schädlichen Auswirkungen auf Theologie und
    Philosophie, Gütersloh 1970.
Martin-Achart, Robert 1970: "L'Apocalyptique d'après trois travaux récents", dans: *RThPh*
    20 (1970) 310-318.
Oppenheim, A. Leo 1956: "The Interpretation of Dreams in the Ancient Near East, with a
    Translation of an Assyrian Dream-Book", dans: *TAPhS* 46 (1956) 179-373.
Pascal, Blaise: *Pensées*, Édition établie...par Léon Brunschvicg, Paris 1934.
von Rad, Gerhard 1967: *Théologie de l'Ancien Testament*, Traduction française par Etienne de
    Peyer, 2 vol., Genève 1967.
Russell, D. S. 1978: *Apocalyptic Ancient and Modern*, London 1978.
Sacchi, Paolo 1979: "Il 'Libro dei Vigilanti' e l'apocalittica", dans: *Henoch*, vol. 1, Marzo 1979,
    42-98.
Schmidt, Johann Michael 1969: *Die jüdische Apokalyptik.* Die Geschichte ihrer Erforschung
    von den Anfängen bis zu den Textfunden von Qumran, Neukirchen 1969.
Une bibliographie plus complète sur l'Apocalyptique se trouve dans mon article de la Revue
    de Qumrân, 1979, signalé plus haut.

---

[14] La liste des ouvrages et des articles utilisés dans ce travail est indiquée dans J. Carmignac
1979a, 3-33, surtout 3-6 et 33.

The Piety of the Jewish Apocalyptists

J. C. H. LEBRAM

0. Introductory Remarks

0.1. Ever since the early sixties there has been an increasing tendency to apply to research into Jewish Apocalyptic certain methods whose instruments have long been considered modern and technically fruitful in the field of Old and New Testament studies. I have in mind above all tradition-history and form criticism.[1] Yet we cannot help being struck by the fact that the application of these modern methods has not produced any definite solution to the fundamental problems underlying the study of Apocalyptic. We might even say that it has hardly brought us any closer to such a solution. Nor has the discovery of new material in Palestine since the middle of this century put an end to the old controversies. Did Apocalyptic develop among special groups? Did it originate from Prophecy or Wisdom? Is it a specifically Jewish phenomenon or can it be understood in connection with a supranational movement? How significant were Iranian, Egyptian, or generally Oriental influences? How significant, for that matter, were Greek, especially Hellenistic, influences? All these questions, which have accompanied research into Apocalyptic over the years, are still being debated today. At the otherwise highly productive Colloquium held at Uppsala in 1979 it was not even possible to agree on a definition. This obviously suggests that the insolubility of these problems is due to the lack of a definition, or even to the fact that each scholar sets out with a definition of his own. One actually has the impression that scholars applying the new methods proceed with a preconceived idea about a certain historical or intellectual background, and that this is why new research has not produced any very different results to the schools of literary criticism or religious history. The framework of the initial premises is often derived from the nineteenth century or the Enlightenment[2] –

---

[1] See the publications by Koch 1966 and 1970, and Lebram 1974. What should we think of the comments of two authors to the title of the 1970 edition of Koch's book: "J'espère que telle ne sera pas notre situation au terme de notre congrès" (M. Delcor 1977, 41) and "Nous ne le pensons pas" (E. Jacob 1977, 44)?

[2] See Schmidt 1969b, 11–34, 87–156, and 1969a; Lebram 1979.

sometimes, indeed, even from humanism or the Rabbinicism of the Middle Ages and Josephus.[3] What this means is that these premises cannot be submitted to the criteria of truth or accuracy of a historiology geared to ever more subtle problems.

0.2. If the scholars at the Colloquium could nevertheless work together, listen to one another and regard their encounter as fruitful, it is because Apocalyptic literature consists of a number of texts which were innocently assembled under the same title in the mid-nineteenth century on account of their similarity. With regard to each one of these writings one can skirt the problems that have just been raised and provide answers to certain questions, answers which avoid too many generalisations and which concern the position of the authors of these texts, their ideas, their situation and the relationship of the writings to one another. All this might lead to insights which could teach us to understand Apocalyptic a little better, and that would be a startingpoint from which to proceed to a critical classification of these writings as literature, as well as of the ideas that come to light in them.

0.3. One question, for example, might be about the piety of the Jewish Apocalyptists. We get closer to understanding it by trying to establish what the author of such an Apocalypse expected from his reader. For we can surely assume that religious literature is meant to provoke a religious reaction, and this reaction could give us an idea of the author's religious motivation. We thereby enter on a path which also appears to hold out prospects to other scholars in the present state of research. U. Luck,[4] for example, believes he can obtain a new view of the Apocalyptist's motives from the world picture of Apocalyptic, *i.e.* from the Apocalyptist's religious experience and background. G. W. E. Nickelsburg is still more precise: he describes the lament in the concluding parenesis of *1 Enoch* as "a window into the world as the author perceives it".[5] Nickelsburg's research has also shown that such questions open up a broader variety of relationships between the various branches of learning, which can lead from the literary and theological to the social and sociological situation of the Apocalyptist.

1. General Observations

1.0. One of the first difficulties of our research consists in a peculiarity of the basic form of the apocalyptic prediction, the "futurische Geschichtser-

---

[3] *E.g.* the dating by Stiassny 1977, 181–183, 186–192 and Scaliger 1658, 134 about the "Hellenists" and the effect on the debate since the 17th century (De Jonge 1975, 74ff., 106 n. 197.).

[4] Luck 1976, 288.   [5] Nickelsburg 1977, 311.

zählung".[6] This is the essential characteristic of the great post-Biblical Apocalypses, decisive both for their structure and literary form.[7] They present themselves as pure transmissions of knowledge and consequently need not state their parenetical objective explicitly. Sometimes, indeed, they deliberately avoid doing so. This is undoubtedly connected with their peculiarity as a *literary* revelation, as a revelation intended to be read and not heard. The reader must become absorbed in the text; thus, by reflection and discernment, he will learn to understand his own time and situation in the pseudo-prophetic historical reports; and thus, by reflecting on his own, he will draw the consequences of his belief and actions, without actually receiving a clearly formulated summons. This, however, does not apply to every apocalyptic writing. Since we are concerned with the parenetic objective of the Apocalypses the lack of parenesis can be misleading.

Because of the occasional absence of a specific parenesis there has been a somewhat short-sighted tendency to deduce the religious function of Apocalyptic from the system of its revelations. Since the intervention of heavenly forces lies at the end of its expectation of history, apocalyptic literature has been regarded as "Trostliteratur"[8] and has even been described as optimistic.[9] This sounds positively cynical if we think that the reader has years, periods of unspecified length, predicted to him, in which he must endure unbearable labours, tortures and persecutions. On the basis of the chronological computations of the Apocalyptists certain scholars have also decided that eschatological "Naherwartung" is the essential characteristic of Apocalyptic.[10] If, however, we wish to calculate the date when the Kingdom of God is expected to begin from the chronological indications in 4 Ezra, for example, we come up with dates which are generations away from the probable time at which the book was com-

---

[6] The term was suggested by Vielhauer 1964, 410f.

[7] On the form of the Apocalypse see Lebram 1978, 192.

[8] *E.g.* according to Ringgren 1957, 465 and L. Hartman 1975, 9.

[9] Rowley 1963, 178f. I know that Rowley felt that I have misunderstood him. I do, however, regard such formulations as somewhat flippant. Schreiner 1969, 195 also speaks of an "unausrottbaren Optimismus".

[10] K. Müller 1978, 211: "Diese sich neu im alten Glauben an Gottes totale Geschichtssouveränität verankernde 'eschatologische' Hoffnung erlaubt es dem apokalyptischen Betrachter, seinen eigenen Standpunkt stets am 'Ende' der ersten von Gott festgelegten Weltzeit unmittelbar vor dem Einbruch der neuen zu erkennen." Müller 1973, 32 obviously also has such a *Naherwartung* in mind when he refers to "jene vehemente Eschatologisierung des Verständnisses der eigenen Geschichte". We should not, however, overlook the fact that also in Dan it is a *change*, rather than an *end*, of the world which is expected, and that the expectation of this change is far more concrete in Deutero-Isaiah, for example, than in Dan. I agree with Müller's statement that it points to a "Diskontinuität der Überlieferungsstränge", or to put it more simply, to a depreciation of the salvation-history of the past (Müller 1973, 33; 1978, 211).

posed.[11] Owing to the fictitious dating of 4 Ezra and *2 Apoc. Bar.* the reader
is also given the impression that the speed with which "the age is hastening
to its end"[12] cannot be so very great, since some 600 of the years leading to
the end of time have already elapsed before his own birth. Despite the
precision of the various calculations, not even in the Book of Daniel can the
time of the end be chronologically computed. The figures refer to the fall
of Antiochus, which is seen as a sign of the approaching end. Consequently
the duration of the "trouble" in 12:1, which is part of the "end", remains
uncertain,[13] as does the end itself.

1.1. In Apocalyptic, therefore, an optimistic assurance of reaching the
Kingdom of God does not prevail. Salvation is described briefly and not
very specifically. The Apocalyptist knows, of course, that the time of
salvation will come, but this is by no means the main motif of his
religiosity. There are, on the other hand, other features common to the
Apocalypses which can serve to provoke religious reactions. One of these
features is the feeling that human existence is strictly limited, not only in
the chronological sense of transience, but also as historical consciousness.
Our earthly life is tied to a definite period which differs from all other
periods, both because of its special circumstances and forces, and because
of its possibilities and perceptions. One expression of this consciousness is
the fact that the revelation of the apocalyptic seer – like Daniel, Ezra or
Baruch – was not previously known but has now been disclosed to the
present generation,[14] and that this generation needs the revelation. Even the
break in the continuity of Israel's salvation history, which becomes colourless and insignificant, displays the awareness of individual historicity.[15]

---

[11] If we combine the dating of the predictions in 3:1 in the thirtieth year after the capture of
Jerusalem by the Babylonians (= 556 B.C.) with 14:48 (Syr. text), where this date is given as
Anno Mundi 5000, and then compare it all with 14:11, according to which 9½ world ages
have elapsed and 2½ are still to come, we could conclude that the world was due to end in c.
750 A.D. This does not correspond to the time at which the Ezra Apocalypse was composed.
L. Hartman 1975 has shown, moreover, that the dates of the end-time which appear to be so
clear in the Book of Daniel were not even regarded as reliable by the earlier interpreters, and
that the chronological data in other similar time-tables are far too generalized to be used as the
basis of precise computations of the end-time. Hartman does indeed speak of a "Naherwartung", not however, in the sense of a true expectation, but as an "aim to comfort and to
encourage". He observes: "Let us remember also, that this *'Naherwartung'* did not prevent the
author from writing and publishing his booklet" (p. 9). We could add that 1 Macc 1 already
uses the eschatological prophecies of Dan as historical reports.

[12] 4 Ezra 4:26.

[13] This also applies to Dan 12:6 (against Hartman 1975, 2; Plöger, *ad loc.*), הפלאות refers to
the נפלאות in 8:24, which Antiochus *"devises"* (see Lebram 1975, 738), and not to the end-
time.

[14] *1 Enoch* 93:10; cf. Hengel 1969, 329.

[15] Not altogether wrongly, K. Müller 1973, 33 speaks of a "schockartige Großmutation...,
deren Ergebnis in der Diskontinuität der Überlieferungsstränge zutage liegt".

Above all, however, this view of the individual situation is expressed in a sense of necessary imperfection.

1.2. A second feature is also connected with limitation: the author regards contemporary history as a time of evil, in which ever worse things are to be expected. It is life in oppressive, hopeless circumstances, a form of vital consciousness which we find in ancient authors from Hesiod[16] to Juvenal.[17] The hardship and insecurity of life is regarded as a permanent natural state. In the Damascus Document the course of the "time of wrath" from the destruction of Jerusalem by the Babylonians to the rise of the Damascus Sect is reckoned to last 390 years.[18] This means that men have lived in the most appalling conditions since time immemorial; and, as a member of his group, the author does indeed have a sense of expectation but no certainty about when the Kingdom of God will come to pass. What happens is that, for the individual, the decisive change of existence does not reside in the future world-change but is already incurred by the hope of salvation in the hereafter. In this particular text it consists in belonging to the group, while in other cases it often only consists in new revealed knowledge transmitted by the apocalyptic seer. The world in its last days continues as a matter of course, even if only provisionally, with all its hardships.

1.3. This brings us to a third essential trait of apocalyptic existence. The dependency and imperfection of life, the impotence, the tragic circumstances, are not a self-evident experience for the pious man. By nature he would regard life in the time of evil as entirely normal and endurable, like the great "majority". For him the apocalyptic representation of the "schwern, betrübten Zeit"[19] is not the reflection of a spontaneous impression, but the result of a supernatural message, a mystery that can only be disclosed by divine revelation. His vital consciousness thus contains that intellectual trait which we observed in the literary character of the apocalyptic prediction. Not even personal sin is an experience of the conscience which can regain peace and inner assurance by an amendment of a moral, cultic or ritual nature. It enters human awareness through the encounter with an invisible and unknown world disclosed by the apocalyptic revelation.[20] The means to arouse piety and to turn it into a living relationship with the deity are therefore of a rhetorical and literary kind. They were often intended to seem exaggerated and incredible to the outside world, as in the case of the angels appearing in Dan, the

---

[16] Hesiod, Op. 174 ff.   [17] Juvenal, Sat. 13:28 ff.

[18] CD 1:5 ff., cf. also Dan 9:24 and Hengel 1969, 328 n. 470.

[19] Evangelisches Kirchengesangbuch. Ausgabe für die Evang. Landeskirche in Württemberg. Song No. 207: "Ach, bleib bei uns, Herr Jesu Christ", Verse 2.

[20] Cf. the shattering effect of the visions, *e.g.,* in Dan 10:7, 9–12; 4 Ezra 10:28–31.

theophanies and ascensions in *1 Enoch*, and the dialogues with a heavenly
partner in 4 Ezra. They gave the pious man of the Apocalypse the
conviction that he was on a different, special path which segregated him
from the sinners of the corruptible world. They gave him a selfawareness
which was altogether independent of the world.

1.4. None of these experiences of a pious soul can be called apocalyptic as
such, but they can appear in the abstract, separately, or in various combinations, or even all together, outside the literature and thought which we call
apocalyptic. What is characteristic of Apocalyptic, however, is the fact that
the awareness of historicity which the pious man has within him is
connected with a particular period of time in every Apocalypse. The period
has a definite function as "end-time" within a comprehensive chronology
of universal history variable in its details, and it is that period of world
affairs in which God, the Lord ruling over all heavenly beings, leaves the
world to run its course without intervening. The world has now become a
place of all-pervading profanity from which there is no escape. In this last
period of universal history holiness is basically impossible, and evil,
wickedness, will inevitably triumph. The changes of power determined by
divine chronology lead to the rule of monstrous empires which condition
the thought and life of the whole of mankind. The measure of the wicked
will be reached, as it is described in *1 Enoch* 89: 50–90: 18, or as Dan 2 and 7
represents the dominion of the fourth kingdom, "different from all the
kingdoms". Although this period is just before the divine intervention, it is
characterised as a time of non-intervention by God. It is a time in which
sins will not be punished and pious services will not be rewarded. Even the
temple has lost its power of atonement,[21] or is not even mentioned because
of its ineffectiveness.[22] In Tob 14: 5a, for example, the only aspect of the
temple which is emphasised is its inferiority.[23] The apocalyptic revelation
serves to bring home all this to the reader.

1.4.1. What is striking is not only, as we saw, that many Apocalypses
make no mention of the religious consequences of this situation, but that,
whenever anything is said about them, they are described in general and
vague terms.[24] If we cast a superficial glance at the pareneses in the
Apocalypses we see that the pious are usually required to follow the path of
God, His will or His commandments, but we are never able to tell in what

---

[21] Dan 9:24; *1 Enoch* 89:73.   [22] Dan 9:25.

[23] See Lebram 1978, 196f., 198, where, by referring to the Wisdom narrative and Egyptian
texts, I have traced back the fleeting period of the collapse of order as an idea central to
Apocalyptic to the Wisdom tradition.

[24] As, *e.g.*, in 4 Ezra 7:81, 89, 127f.; 8:56. This observation led Frost 1952, 125f. to follow
Charles in accepting a basic contrast between "Apocalyptic" and "Pharisaic" conceptions of
the law.

these consist.[25] We can of course assume that the fulfilment of the traditional Jewish Law is intended, threatened as it is by antinomianism of a Hellenistic-syncretistic stamp.[26] Yet, in spite of no small quantity of source material and the immense amount of secondary literature, the effective religious forces of the time of Antiochus IV have remained obscure. This is due to the fact that in modern historiography the judgement of sources has become a central and very tricky problem. Scholars have consequently concluded that it is impossible to understand exactly what religious demands are being made in the parenetic texts in the Apocalypses – whether, for example, they refer to the Pentateuch or to a special collection of Halakhot.[27] One scholar has even thought, surely erroneously, "daß an keiner Stelle (sc. in the Apocalypses) das Gesetz oder ein Gebot seinem Inhalt nach erwähnt ist".[28] At all events we perceive a great uncertainty about what the everyday religious life of the Apocalyptists and their followers was like, and about what the religious foundations of their belief consisted in. Even if we presuppose a Jewish piety in the general sense, we have to admit that we have gradually become acquainted with so many different forms of such a religiosity that we require a more precise concept of the piety of at least one Apocalypse.

1.4.2. We can also come to the other conclusion that the Apocalyptists felt no concrete need for an ethical-religious standpoint since they were concerned with a very different set of problems. D. Rössler wished to demonstrate this comprehensively. He saw the difference between the apocalyptic and the Rabbinic understanding of the Law in the fact that in Apocalyptic

"es gar nicht um die einzelne Sünde, den einzelnen Verstoß gegen ein Gebot oder die einzelne Verfehlung des Gesetzes bei der 'Ungerechtigkeit' geht, und entsprechend nicht um die Erfüllung des Einzelgebotes bei der 'Gerechtigkeit', sondern vielmehr um eine grundsätzliche Stellung zum Gesetz überhaupt".[29]

According to Rössler the Law is a criterion for belonging to God's people and therefore the consequence, not the basis, of the pious man's relationship with God, while the characteristic of the righteous is less the fulfilment of the commandment than endurance. This thesis is certainly not

---

[25] What is striking is that this vague and general way of expressing God's will can also be found in Egyptian temple inscriptions of the Graeco-Roman period. Otto 1964, 43 ff. ("Nirgends spezialisierte Verhaltensweisen oder Gebote...") thinks that the temple inscriptions which only use the term "man" provide insufficient evidence for such a conclusion. "Dagegen unterrichten hierüber in reichem Maße die biographischen Inschriften und die didaktische Literatur dieser Zeit". Rau's belief (note 30) that the generalised understanding of the concept of law is a phenomenon typical of Wisdom literature is not valid as far as Egypt is concerned, despite certain analogies.

[26] *E.g.* Nissen 1967; Hengel 1969, 322; *et al.*

[27] Rau 1974, 94.   [28] Rössler 1962, 78.   [29] *Ibid.,* 78 f.

tenable in such an abstract form. The earliest Jewish martyrologies were usually concerned with the fulfilment of a single commandment which the tyrant tried to make them infringe. Yet we must agree with Rössler that in substantial portions of apocalyptic literature the requirement of obedience to God and the Law lacks concrete substance. Rau also believes that

"vom äthiopischen Henochbuch her die gängige These vom Gesetz als dem zentrierenden Mittelpunkt des nachexilischen Judentums einer Prüfung zu unterziehen sei".

Taking up an idea of Rössler's, he explains the phenomenon with reference to historical tradition: the general sense in which the word "Law" is used in *1 Enoch* and the infrequent appearance of the term is due to the fact that the book is in a Wisdom tradition in which the concept of Torah does not have a specific, but a general, significance.[30] In his less specialised work M. Limbeck, too, points out that in *1 Enoch* there is a striking analogy between the designation of the astronomical cosmic observance of the Law and the moral law of God[31] – something which could once more call in doubt the identification of the concept of "Law" with the Mosaic legal code.

1.4.3. Despite these uncertainties we cannot deny that there is at least a partial parenesis in the apocalyptic writings and that, even where it is lacking, the author presupposes the requirement of a certain religious attitude. This means that the question about the characteristics and the substance of the pious reaction to the apocalyptic message in the individual Apocalypses is fully justified.

2. Piety in the Book of Daniel

2.0. Daniel, the first great Apocalypse, which must be regarded as an adaptation of various self-contained preliminary stages, was composed in its present form in c. 165 B.C. It is the prototype of the Apocalypse without a parenesis. The fact that it was composed so early in the history of Apocalypses suggests that the absence of a parenesis was authentically connected with the literary form of Apocalypses and their objective, and that the vagueness of many parenetical portions – which we have discussed above – must also be seen in this light.[32] Nevertheless, at the end of the Book of Daniel we have a clear representation of the man who has accepted

---

[30] Rau 1974, 95f. This idea would seem to be supported by many references in Israelite-Jewish Wisdom. We should add, however, that the Wisdom doctrines frequently refer to individual ethical conditions and concrete ways of conduct – a fact which alters the value of Rau's observations.

[31] Limbeck 1971, 65ff.

[32] I have dealt extensively with questions of introduction and form in my article "Daniel/Danielbuch und Zusätze", in: *TRE* 1981, 325–349.

the apocalyptic message, as also of the phenomenon which we can call the pious man of the Apocalypse.

2.1. The most important passage in this respect is 12: 10. In the second half of the verse, which describes the predicament of man after the book of revelation has been composed, we read of two opposing groups:

> "The wicked shall do wickedly and none of the wicked shall understand; but those who are wise shall understand...."

Who the wicked are is quite clear: Antiochus IV and his supporters, but also all the imperial rulers who, by acting violently, have not reckoned with the Almighty God of Israel. They refuse to perceive that the book of revelation is showing them the future of the world and also the path to salvation. They will not read it at all or, if they do read it, they will not understand it. What is slightly less clear is the identity of the wise. We might think of the pious in general who understand the Apocalypse and therefore can be numbered among the saved. Yet, in contrast to the detailed characterisation of the wicked, we read nothing here about their religious attitude. Furthermore, in verses 11: 33 and 35, which we will be examining more closely later (§2.2.1.), the designation מַשְׂכִּיל has a more technical meaning. It means "teacher". The figure of the teacher is contrasted with that of the wicked, but this contrast does not have an ethical-religious significance in Dan 12: 10b; it has a functional one. The wicked who oppress the Jews and who are impressive – they win supporters amongst the Jews – know nothing, so one must not allow oneself to be impressed by them. On the other hand the מַשְׂכִּילים have knowledge which they can pass on. I am consequently inclined to see a deliberate play on words in the contrast between the לֹא יָבִינוּ and יָבִינוּ which is based on the different meaning of בין hif.:

> "And none of the wicked will understand (about the history of the future), but the (apocalyptic) teachers will teach (it)."

2.1.1. Before I go any further in explaining this interpretation of Dan 12: 10, I would like to show that the contrast between the wicked and the wise (to use this term for a change) is intended primarily in a religious sense. The wicked man is full of hybris and this will lead to his ruin, as it did in the case of Belshazzar and Alexander.[33] The wise man, on the other hand, is also the truly pious man who relies on God, and he will assuredly be given a glorious place in the Kingdom of God:

> "And the teachers shall shine like the brightness of the firmament; and those who turn many to righteousness, like the stars for ever and ever."[34]

---

[33] Dan 5:30; 11:3f.; 1 Macc 1:1–17.   [34] Dan 12:3.

By teachers – the term is used without further qualification as it still is
nowadays with reference to certain figures within particular groups – the
author obviously means only those who proclaim the apocalyptic message
as we find it in the Book of Daniel. In contrast to the wicked tempters,
these are indeed perfectly righteous. This applies first and foremost to the
seer of the Apocalypse. In the last verse of the book, 12: 13, he is told:

> "But go your way till the end; and you shall rest, and shall stand in your allotted place at the
> end of the days."

Daniel can probably end his earthly life so soon because he is sufficiently
mature to obtain eschatological salvation.[35] The promise of a גורל at his
resurrection could even mean more than this; it could perhaps imply an
eschatological function for Daniel as a witness or judge at the Last
Judgement.[36]

2.1.2. So, for the apocalyptic author and his readers, the wise, and above
all Daniel, are models of perfect righteousness who are sure to reach the
Kingdom of God, and there is no doubt that this example influences the
piety of their followers. In 12: 10b, however, they are primarily mediators
of the truth to the reader. But what is the position of the latter in the
Apocalypse? In order to answer this question we must keep in mind that in
the first half of Dan 12: 10b a third group is mentioned, the "many":

> "Many shall purify themselves, and make themselves white, and be refined".

The word רבים without an article cannot mean the full assembly of the
community, as it does in Qumran.[37] Here, despite the positive implications, the word does not designate a small group of elect for whom
salvation would be certain, nor does it designate a sect. "Many" indicates a
large number of people, either from all nations or – more probably – from
among the Jews. The "Jews" must be regarded as a spontaneous, instinc-
tive limitation of the horizon, rather than as a deliberate restriction, for the
Apocalyptist will have regarded the Jewish people as a human universe,
consisting of heroes as well as of men depraved and undecided. The
"many" are the people whose souls the Book of Daniel is trying to win.
They are not the godless who rule in the world and fall with it; but neither
are they the righteous who, through visions or martyrdom, have already
earned their way to heaven. They cannot guide, or even change, the world,
and they have to rely on the man already perfect, on the righteous teacher,
in order to reach a decision. They stand between the wicked and the wise.

---

[35] Cf. 4 Ezra 14:9–17; Wis 4:10–15. Dan 12:13 is applied to the death of the seer by
Montgomery, Bentzen and others. Other commentators are less certain; see, *e.g.,* Plöger, *ad
loc.* Together with LXX and Theodotion, I would classify "to the end" in Dan 12:13 as
secondary (as in BHS).

[36] Cf. Wis 4:16ff.   [37] Cf. 1QS 6:1 and often.

2.2. The readers of the Apocalypse of Daniel whose lives continue in this world are presented with two possibilities which the Last Judgement can bring to them: life eternal or the shame of eternal rejection. This applies in Dan 12: 2 to the "many" who are already dead, and there is no indication that those who are still alive in the reader's generation have any other alternative. They themselves are not even sure that they will die before the Day of Judgement. They are therefore the undecided ones who must still make up their minds about their final destiny. Yet there is nothing contemptuous in the author's description of them since he assumes that many will choose salvation; these are the men who must prepare themselves for the Last Judgement. According to Dan 12: 10 they will be purified – for this is how we must understand the hitp. of ברר.[37a] Life is a constant test, from beginning to end. Their trial has an active and a passive side: the verbs לבן hitp. and צרף nif. must be interpreted in the light of their meaning in Isa 1:18,25, where both roots appear, albeit in different forms. We must therefore translate the first as "keeping oneself clean from sins", and the second as "purified by suffering". The main characteristic of this piety is that the believers – we can certainly refer to them with this ethically neutral word – do not feel secure before the approaching Judgement which they will have to face, either after the sleep of death or while still alive (a difference which cannot have affected them very much subjectively). They feel they are not up to the Judgement, and that is why life in the last difficult times in which evil celebrates its triumph unrestrainedly is regarded as a test or a trial in which the pious man must segregate himself, cut himself off from, and purify himself of, all evil. He must bear all temptations, hardships and sorrows as a process of cleansing in order to attain eschatological purity. This alone makes access to the time of salvation possible at the moment of Judgement.

2.2.1. The purification and cleansing terminology is obviously part of a fixed semantic field with which the religious process of the path to eschatological purity is expressed. We encounter it in a slightly different order in Dan 11: 35:

"And some of the teachers shall fall, to refine and to cleanse amongst themselves and to make white until the time of the end, for there is still an interval."

Since the cleansing process of the teacher at this point is still in a period which is the past both for the author and for the reader of the Apocalypse, Dan 11: 35 confirms our assumption that at the time in which the book was composed the apocalyptic teachers had attained the status of perfection, *i.e.* of maturity for the eschatological Judgement. They had already been

---

[37a] KBL³ *ad vocem.*

purified in the past. This reference to the process of purification is also important because it gives us some idea about the situation in which the hope for purity was formulated and what it entailed. If we read about some teachers who fall, they obviously belong to a group in which other teachers can be included, teachers mentioned in the preceding verses, Dan 11: 33, 34:

> "And the teachers of the people shall make many understand, though they shall fall by sword and flame, by captivity and plunder, for some days. When they fall, they shall receive little help.[38] And many shall join themselves to them with hypocrisy."

This text has been regarded as a description of the martyrdom of the "Teachers" who announce the apocalyptic message as it is found in the Book of Daniel. They are ill-treated by the soldiers of the Syrian king and thereby purified. The basic difficulty where this interpretation is concerned, however, resides in the fact that the verb כשל nif. "fall" cannot simply mean the death or the suffering of the pious. It can mean physical stumbling and, on occasion, "sinking down". When it is used of destruction it always refers to a sinner. It may already have been used in a metaphorical sense in the time of the Book of Daniel, as in Qumran literature where the root means "to fall from truth, to go astray".[39] In any case the destruction of the teacher described here is not necessarily a "pious" death or suffering. Verse 35 says clearly that the "falling" of a few teachers led to the purification and cleanliness of other members of the group. Finally, Dan 11: 33 does not speak of the "teachers or the wise who understand" in general, but of the "teachers of the people", a group, in other words, which the author furnishes with an epithet, in contrast to the teachers of a particular group of his own who are always introduced without further qualification. The author, then, has the teachers of another, obviously eschatological, group in mind. From these three observations we can reconstruct the process which the author of the Book of Daniel wishes to describe as follows: a group bearing the name of those "who know their God" are instructed by their teachers to resist the soldiers

---

[38] My translation "little help" (עזר מעט) reposes on the linguistic usage in, *e.g.*, Deut 26:5; 28:62; Neh 2:12; Eccl 5:2; Prov 10:20. The usual translation "a little help" – with a restrainedly positive significance – rests on Porphyry's understanding of the verse as an allusion to the rebellion of the Maccabees. Apart from the fact that neither 1 Macc 1 nor 2 Macc 5–6 (see 5:27!) say anything about an intervention by the Maccabees in Jerusalem, Casey 1976 has shown that the allusion to the Maccabees which Porphyry finds in Dan 11–12 goes back to a Jewish-Maccabean interpretation of the Book of Daniel. I conclude from this that there is no reason to assume that the author of the Book of Daniel here had an allusion to the Maccabees in mind. What is meant is that the Jews, who were rebelling on religious grounds, found no true support since, when they attacked the violators of the temple, they were joined by "hypocrites", *i.e.* men fighting for other motives.

[39] 1QS 11:12 qal; CD 2:16 nif.; 1QS 3:24 hif.

of Antiochus IV in the temple of Jerusalem either by riots in the temple precincts or by an armed attack. This is a false path which leads to the destruction of the group after days of bloodshed. At first the relatively prolonged battles find the group fairly helpless. By and by ever larger circles join it. Their members, however, are only interested in plunder and destruction – or so at least the author of the Book of Daniel believes. Yet this catastrophe leads to the conversion of a few of the misguided teachers who purify themselves and allow what has happened to cleanse them. These would appear to be the very teachers who proclaim the true apocalyptic message.

2.2.2. We can say for sure, then, that the principles of the pious man of the Apocalypse consist in the rejection of all violence, particularly of the implementation of the Kingdom of God by force. At this point we see that the apocalyptic movement behind the Book of Daniel is derived from an opposition to an enthusiastic *Naherwartung*. This emerges, too, from the twice repeated remark that yet another period of time must elapse before the end.[40] The reader is warned against being deluded by false hopes, since it is so easy to be mistaken in one's expectation of the end – a theme which may also have determined the selection of historical events in the account of the struggle between Syria and Egypt in Dan 11. It has been acknow-ledged[41] that this is not an "objective" historical survey, but a selection of individual episodes calculated to inspire the reader with a particular under-standing of the course of history. The events listed all take place in the time of the fourth kingdom in which wickedness is reaching its height. They are as follows: the rise and fall of Alexander; the marriage of the daughter of Ptolemy II Philadelphos with Antiochus II of Syria which leads to her and her son's death and then to the campaign of her brother Ptolemy III Euergetes I in the eastern part of the Seleucid kingdom; the conquest of Ptolemaic Coelesyria (Palestine and Phoenicia) by Antiochus III of Syria; and, finally, introduced by the plunder of Palestine by his predecessor Seleucus IV, the conquest of Egypt by Antiochus IV. In the case of each of these events we have the attempt of a prince of one of the two countries to conquer the other. Were he to succeed the victor would have achieved all earthly power and would fall prey to total hybris. Then, however, the "full measure of the transgressor"[42] would be reached and divine intervention could be expected. But that has not come about. All the events listed are merely "quasi-eschatological" and could consequently give rise to mislead-ing expectations. If such was the attitude of the author of our book, he may well have intentionally provided his reader with a list of disappointed eschatological hopes. That this interpretation of Dan 11: 1-30 is perfectly

---

[40] Dan 11:27, 35.   [41] Clifford 1975.   [42] Dan 8:23.

plausible is shown by Dan 11: 14, which refers to the conquest of Coelesyria by the Seleucid Antiochus III in c. 200 B.C.:

> "In those times many shall rise against the king of the south; and the men of violence among your own people shall lift themselves up in order to fulfil the vision; but they shall fall."

Here too we find the root discussed above, כשל in the nif., which designates the destruction of those who are on the wrong moral path. The aversion towards eschatological groups which allow themselves to be provoked into revolutionary action in the hope of a swift fulfilment of prophetic utterances is clearly present. The cleansing and purification thus also consist in a rejection of all inward or outward participation in the events of the terrestrial world and its history. The pious man of the Apocalypse is solely intent on the heavenly world.

2.3. So we see that the piety of the Apocalyptist has ascetic features. The extent to which these appear in the external behaviour of the pious man cannot be deduced unequivocally from the Book of Daniel. Nevertheless the visions of the seer in the later chapters 9 and 10 presuppose ascetic abstentions: in Dan 9 he prepares himself for the reception of heavenly instructions in the following way:

> "I turned my face to the Lord God, seeking Him by prayer and supplications with fasting and sackcloth and ashes."

In Dan 10 the preparations are more elaborate:

> "In those days I, Daniel, was mourning for three weeks. I ate no delicacies, no meat or wine entered my mouth, nor did I anoint myself at all, for the full three weeks."[43]

That, of course, is the preparation of a legendary figure for a particularly important meeting with the heavenly powers; it should not be taken as too direct an indication of the religious customs of the reader. Yet there are certain allusions to a practical asceticism independent of experiences of revelation; in Dan 1 we are told that the seer drank only water and observed a vegetarian diet in order not to sully himself with the wine and bread of the Babylonian king.[44] In the earlier traditions of the book, on the other hand, we read about another type of piety; Daniel's habit of praying three times a day with his face towards Jerusalem is emphasised; he also encourages the king to give money to the poor and thereby avert the pending catastrophe.[45] This savours of a more generally Jewish, even Syro-Aramaic piety,[46] than the above examples taken from the Hebrew portions where the ascetic ideal of purity is strongly accentuated.

2.3.1. The principal purpose of ascesis among the ancients was not so

---

[43] Dan 9:3; 10:2ff.   [44] Dan 1:8–17.   [45] Dan 6:11; 4:24.

[46] Cf. Dan 4:24 with P. Hermoupolis 1:6–7 (Milik 1967, 581) and see Porten/Greenfield 1968, 230.

much the development of man as his preparation for the cultic or ritual act, entry into a sacred place, the observation of a sacred period, or the performance of a cultic service.[47] What is indicative of the piety in the Book of Daniel is the fact that here purity does not seem to have such a goal. Nevertheless, we find it in a kindred sense in Dan 9 and 10, where the seer prepares himself thus for the meeting with the heavenly world. The connection between vision and cult is emphasised moreover in ch. 9 by the angel approaching the seer at the time of the evening sacrifice. In Dan 11: 35 and 12: 10, on the other hand, we would appear to be dealing with a spiritual evolution whose conclusion is the attainment of a certain maturity at the time of the end – this would also account for the extension of the idea of impurity to participation in military actions. Ascesis as a goal in itself, which has been regarded as a phenomenon genuinely alien to the Jews, enters Qumran literature[48] in a more developed form at a slightly later period, when the book and figure of Daniel, together with other apocalyptic works, were well-known. We get the impression, furthermore, that this way of life bears a certain similarity to – or even displays a certain kinship with – the ascetic ideals of Hellenism which lead from Pythagoreanism to Plotinus.[49] Pythagoras was not without significance in some Jewish circles, and the Jewish philosopher Philo of Alexandria certainly constitutes a landmark in the development of ancient ascesis as we know it.[50]

2.3.2. Yet it seems to me that the motivation of the ascesis in the Book of Daniel originated to a large exent from an apocalyptic modification of ascesis as associated with a cult.[51] I have already shown (§ 1.4.) that the time of the last kingdom in which the author lived was regarded as a time of all pervading profanity. That, as I also pointed out earlier (§ 1.4.), was really felt in a cultic sense. The temple was either not mentioned or had lost its powers of atonement. Consequently the profanity of this last period of history consisted not only in the fact that sin remained unpunished and the pious action unrewarded, but also in the fact that there was no cultic possibility of atonement. In Dan 9: 24 the last period is conceived as a period of seventy weeks of years and is described as follows:

---

[47] Strathmann 1950, 753f. Examples in Stricker 1969, 10: preparation of the priest for the cult; entry of the laity into the temple.

[48] See the discussion in Thiering 1974. The author's conclusion is somewhat one-sided.

[49] Hengel 1969, 449 with extensive bibliography.

[50] Strathmann 1950, 752. The greatest influence was that exerted by Philo with his work on the Theraputae, "De vita contemplativa", in which the Jewish features of the ascetic described should be kept in mind (25; 28; 36. Text: Philonis Opera, ed. min. Cohn-Wendland VI, 32–50).

[51] Peterson 1959, 217ff. has traced early Christian asceticism back to the eschatological expectation of the end of the world.

"Seventy weeks of years are decreed concerning your people and your holy city, to finish the transgression, to put an end to sin, and to atone for iniquity, to bring in everlasting righteousness, to seal both vision and prophet, and to anoint a most holy offering".

The seer's mysterious utterance announces that the cultic ceremonies of atonement will only be completed after the seventy weeks of years, *i.e.* with the beginning of the time of salvation. The time of salvation is therefore a time of cultic festivity, a time when the temple will again emanate its powers of atonement, and a time which will bring about final righteousness. The previous period, by contrast, is the time of preparation in which men are still living in the world of profanity, where, however, they cleanse themselves of their stains and are purified by their distress.

2.3.3. Despite the cultic origin of the ascesis we must realise that it cannot be essentially a matter of ritual purification. This is impossible because atonement rites in a time of profanity cannot be regarded as truly effective. A characteristic of purity, moreover, is a refusal to participate in revolutionary riots, together with the passive endurance of the tribulations produced by the time of profanity. These are expressions of a behaviour which submits itself to the social, as well as to the historical, events, and does not propose to interrupt them by force. The ascesis is consequently spiritualised.[52] The ideal to which the pious man aspires through his purification becomes clearer if we consider the antitype of the pious man, the eschatological transgressor. In the dream in Dan 8 the one who attacks the stars and overthrows the truth is the destroyer of the cosmic social order. He is therefore the enemy of Egyptian *ma'at*[53] and his "great words" are stressed. Now, this feature of Antiochus becomes comprehensible if we consider the linguistic nature of *ma'at*. It is in everybody's mouth.[54] It is pronounced as Jewish wisdom coming forth from the mouth of God.[54a] The special characeristic of Antiochus is the lie, deceit, which is presented in the Egyptian inscriptions and biographical-didactic literature as the very opposite of *ma'at*.[55] Above all, however, Antiochus is proud and does not accept the position accorded him in the cosmic whole. We may conclude

---

[52] The spiritualisation of what is really a cultic purity as an expression of community with God can be found in the literature of late Antiquity and in Jewish literature. Cf. Apuleius, Meth. 9:6: "…*cuius (sc. Isidis) beneficio redieris ad homines, ei totum debere, quod vives.*" Porphyry, De abstinentia 1:57; 2:44, 45: ἀνδρὸς θείου ἡ ἔσω καὶ ἡ ἔκτος ἁγνεία. Julian the Apostate, Or. 5:175b. For Judaism cf. Aristeas 140: the ritual law makes the Jews so holy that the Egyptian priests ἀνθρώπους θεοῦ προσονομάζουσιν ἡμᾶς, ὃ τοῖς λοιποῖς οὐ πρόσεσ-τιν, … ἀλλ' εἰσὶν ἄνθρωποι βρωτῶν καὶ ποτῶν καὶ σκέπτης.

[53] Otto 1964, 27. What is striking is that qualities are attributed to kings and even normal people which were originally attributed only to gods, Otto 1964, 81 ff. We should here compare the work of J. W. van Henten, "Antiochus IV Epiphanes als typhonischer Typus", which will appear in the forthcoming volume of my essays on Daniel.

[54] Dan 7:8b,11. Otto 1964, 24.   [54a] Sir 24:3.   [55] Otto 1964, 22 ff.

that the conduct of the pious man in the framework of apocalypticism forms the opposite of Antiochus' behaviour: on the whole the pious man is required to live in accordance with the cosmic order.

2.4. If the observations I have made so far give us some indication of the piety of the Apocalyptist according to the ideas in the Book of Daniel, these ideas must have been based on a complete faith in the cosmically determined periods of time due to lead to the beginning of a new life in a new order, though not necessarily a new world. This may have led, in its turn, to an accompaniment of the cosmic world period expressed in a particular rhythm of hours of prayer.[56] The passive endurance of evil in the world is the purification which brings the pious to perfection. The most dangerous sin is obviously pride which does not know its own limits. The humility which acknowledges its distance from God and its dependence on Him could also have achieved a form in the confession of sins and in doxologies.[57] It is even conceivable that the boastful and grand words of the transgressor are contrasted with a deliberate silence, a silence about the secrets of the future[58] which God has revealed through His favourite, Daniel. Thus this ascesis, like all asceses, could have been attended by the study of secret writings.[59] Yet it must be emphasised that there is nothing to suggest the formation of a sect in which people would feel that they belonged to a circle of elect segregated from their own nation.[60] All the activities connected with the process of purification were only possible in the domain of the temple services, although the sacrifice does not seem to have had any significance. In its structure this piety resembles that of the teachers of wisdom and we cannot exclude the influence of Egyptian Wisdom doctrines.[61]

---

[56] The praise of God as an expression of harmony with the creation is especially emphasised in *1 Enoch*, Limbeck 1971, 70 ff. For the times of prayer cf. besides Dan 6:11; 9:21, also Philo, *VitCont* 27.

[57] Dan 9:4–23. Such forms of prayer are connected with the Deuteronomistic tradition: 1 Kgs 8:46–51. Doxologies are frequently to be found at the beginning of confessions of sins, *e.g.,* Neh 1:5.

[58] Secrecy and the abstention from political disturbance play an important part in the biographical inscriptions of the later Egyptian period, Otto 1954, 66. Cf. also Tob 12:11. In 1QS 4:6 one of the virtues of the sons of light is "silence about the secrets of truth".

[59] Cf. Philo, *VitCont* 25; Stricker 1969, 15.

[60] On this point I differ from many contemporary scholars, *e.g.,* Delcor 1971, 15.

[61] Barta 1976 has collected all the features of the anonymous deity in the Egyptian Wisdom doctrines. From the point of view of Apocalyptic it is important to realise that the deity knows the future (80 f.); his activity is concealed from men; they only become aware of it when it comes about, and even then the godless still fail to recognize it. The deity loves *ma'at* and behaves towards man as a judge, "gleichsam blind und lediglich als ausführendes Organ". Yet in later writings he removes his verdict from a temporal sphere and applies it to the hereafter. Man then only receives his reward and his punishment after death (83 f.). Ever since the middle kingdom God's particular assistance is directed to the poor and the weak.

3. Apocalyptic Ethics in 1 Enoch

3.0. We also find extensive portions of apocalyptic material, *i.e.* historical reports in the future tense,[62] in the Ethiopic Book of Enoch (*1 Enoch*).
The use of ancient Biblical traditions, on the other hand, plays an important part[63] in the historical episodes intended to explain the contemporary
period. As the choice of his pseudonym shows, the author searches for the
foundations of the contemporary situation in historical events far more
remote than those in Daniel: the flood and the fall of the angels, for
example, are of considerable significance.[64] The historical picture is determined far more extensively and directly by supernatural events and circumstances of cosmic dimensions – a feature which· has undoubtedly
contributed to the attribution of the Book to Enoch.[65] The Book of Enoch
has therefore become a compilation of physical, cosmic, astronomical and
other traditions which do not always have their origin in the Jewish –
Biblical tradition.[66] The incorporation of literary material of non-apocalyptic provenance in an Apocalypse is, of course, something we also find in
Daniel – yet here too the material is ultimately placed in the service of
apocalyptic objectives.

3.1. As in the Book of Daniel, so in *1 Enoch* we must take various literary
levels into account and, because of the variety of the themes and material
digested, we must also reckon with more individual interpolations.[67] It
may be this diversity in so extensive a work which has led far more clearly
than in Daniel to the formation of purely parenetic passages. They stand
out as signposts guiding the reader in the motley jumble of doctrines. The
pareneses are at the beginning and the end of the present-day version of the
book. This does not prove that the various portions were composed at the
same time,[68] but it does show their cohesive function: they are supposed to

---

[62] Above all *1 Enoch* 83–90, 91, 93.

[63] In contrast to all "futuristische Geschichtserzählungen" in Dan, the "Animal
Apocalypse" (85–90) in *1 Enoch* starts with Adam and Eve and the "Apocalypse of Weeks"
(93; 91:12–17) with Enoch himself – a feature which is obviously connected with the choice of
the seer's pseudonym. Yet he also became the pseudonymous originator of the Apocalypse
because of his early appearance in world history. I still regard the wide use of Biblical
historical traditions as the indication of a "Judaization" of the apocalyptic picture of history
which is more developed than in Dan, and is consequently later than the predictions in Dan.

[64] *1 Enoch* 6–11.

[65] In Judaeo-Graeco literature of the second century B.C. and in *Jub* 4:17 Enoch is the first
representative of cosmic-astrological wisdom (Milik 1976, 8–10).

[66] See Stone 1978. Cf. the extensive introduction in Milik 1976, as also the discussion in
Greenfield/Stone 1977.

[67] Cf. the research report in Rau 1974, 5–11.

[68] According to Milik 1976, 5, portions of the opening and concluding pareneses are to be
found in the remains of a copy (En^c) of the Aramaic text dating from the last third of the first
century A.D. Cf. also Rau 1974, 130: "Der Prozeß der sukzessiven Aneinanderreihung der
Überlieferungsblöcke ist erst im äthiopischen Sprachbereich zum Abschluß gekommen".

remind the reader what the revelations of Enoch are ultimately about – the reader's admonition and eschatological salvation. Here too the piety stems from the perception of the revelation.[69]

3.1.1. This connection between the content of the revelation and the religious reaction is impressed on the reader repeatedly, especially in the seer's introductory discourse. In chs. 1-5 Enoch recounts a vision in which it has been disclosed to him that God will appear and plunge mankind into terror, His parousia entailing the destruction of the world. After this the Judgement will take place which will assure the righteous of peace and mercy and the godless of destruction. The readers are then called upon to observe the heavenly bodies which keep to their immutable courses, the heavenly luminaries which rise and set at fixed intervals; the natural events on earth also obey unalterable laws. Enoch draws two different conclusions from these observations: in 5: 1b he admonishes men to perceive and acknowledge the creative power of God in these phenomena; in 5: 4 the apostates are reproached for not having "been steadfast, nor (having) done the commandments of the Lord", unlike the forces of nature, but "ye have turned away and spoken proud and hard words with your impure mouths against His greatness". So the sin of the godless consists in the rejection of revealed information. They do not take seriously the imminent Last Judgement which the seer has announced to them, and they have not taken the divine obedience of the natural forces as an example. Consequently the seer now utters a prediction of woe for those who have turned away and a promise of salvation for the pious. E. Rau, to whom we owe a minute tradition-historical analysis of *1 Enoch* 1-5 and 72-82, thinks that "turned away" in this context can mean those who have not observed the calendar postulated by Enoch because they have not recognised the decrees of the Creator. Just as in Dan 7 Antiochus IV sins not only with his great words, but also by hindering the Jewish ecclesiastical calendar, so here too pride and presumption consist in spurning the feast days.[70]

3.1.2. The reference to natural forces does not, however, stem from the requirement of a particular calendar. In the Wisdom tradition we find a comparison between the perfect and constant obedience of the works of creation and man's attitude to God at a place where there is no question whatsoever of the observance of a liturgical calendar. Sir 16: 4-17:24 is a catechetical summary of the substantial points of the salvation-history world picture of Judaism.[71] The creation and structure of the world are

---

[69] For this feature of apocalyptic piety cf. §1.3.

[70] Rau 1974, 92f. The connection between cosmic and ethical observance of the law in *1 Enoch* is also treated by Limbeck 1971, 68. See also Rau 1974, 125–304.

[71] In my articles of 1964 and 1965 I have treated the Jewish systems of instruction. Cf. above all 1964, 237–239 for Sir 16/17. Rau 1974, 81 also refers to Sir 16:24–17:24.

discussed, then the creation of man, the law-giving on Sinai and finally the
Last Judgement. The whole ends in a call to conversion. About "works" –
we can assume from the summary that it is the cosmic creations and not the
purtenances of the earth which are implied – we read in 6:27 f.:

> "they hunger not neither are they weak, and they cease not from their works. (28) Not one
> thrusteth aside his neighbour. They never disobey His word."

Here an ethical character is attributed to the natural courses which
corresponds to that double precept containing the Law in the Jewish and
Christian traditions: obedience to God and respect for one's neighbour.
While a certain degree of automatic fulfilment of the Law is attributed to
the works of creation, man's uncertain obedience to God is described as
follows:

> "(17, 6) He created for them tongue, and eyes, and ears, and He gave them a heart to
> understand. (7) With insight and understanding He filled their heart, and taught them good
> and evil. (8) He set His eye upon their hearts, to show them the majesty of His works, (9) And
> praise His holy name (10) that they might evermore declare His glorious works. (11) He set
> before them knowledge; the law of life He gave them for a heritage... (14) And He said unto
> them, Beware of all unrighteousness; And He gave them commandment, to each man
> concerning his neighbour."

This extensive contrast between the divine obedience of the works of
creation on the one hand, and of man on the other, gives rise to a lament
about those who have "turned away" in *1 Enoch* 5: 4. God asks the same of
man as He does of the works of creation. Yet in order to do what the works
do automatically, man requires a perception on the basis of which he must
take a decision. He has the possibility of making up his own mind freely, of
conversion, and therefore of having the true human relationship with God,
but he is in constant danger of going astray and falling prey to temptation.
The Law has been given to him as a preserver and a warner. Ben Sira here
sees the pious man in a situation similar to the one he was in the Book of
Daniel. The ideas of *1 Enoch* 1-5, therefore, originate from a more general
situation than a mere dispute over a calendar; and, besides, harmony with
the forces of nature as the fulfilment of God's will is an ideal of piety to be
found in later Wisdom.

3.1.3. As in Sir 16/17, so in *1 Enoch* 2-5 an appeal is made to man's
perception. Yet here those who hear the appeal are in a different situation.
Sentence has already been passed and the description of the creation simply
shows those who have turned away that they have departed from God's
will and commandments. They must therefore reckon with their condemnation at the Last Judgment[72] – and this is what the immutability of the law

---

[72] Rau 1974, 106: "5,4a–d spricht aus, daß 2,1–5,3 nicht Aufruf zur Umkehr, sondern
Anklage ist".

of nature demonstrates to them. Rau has rightly observed that the sentence, which in Dan 7 was passed on Antiochus IV, here concerns men who are perhaps Jews, compatriots of the pious and members of God's people.[73] If we then realise that the Enoch Apocalypse, just like the Book of Daniel, was read by a pious group – a group which thought it should centre its beliefs on an ecclesiastical calendar which differed from everybody else's – the difference between the piety of the reader of Enoch and the piety of the Book of Daniel becomes clear. For Daniel, too, there were the wicked and the perfectly righteous. Yet the reader would not have seen this as a personal conflict but as a conflict which took place on a different social level to that of his own; as an individual he simply had to find the way to eschatological salvation. In *1 Enoch*, however, the border between the righteous and the wicked is within the reader's horizon. Either he, or the group he belonged to, was in permanent spiritual conflict with the godless. It amounts to a religious "class formation" and this gives the apocalyptic parenesis yet another function: to teach the pious man about his relationship with the wicked, about how to observe them, and even about how to consort with them, mainly on an inner level, but also occasionally on an outer one.

3.2. If the piety of the Book of Enoch is defined by the conflict with the wicked, it cannot surprise us that the parenesis should be influenced by the Wisdom tradition. For it is the Wisdom doctrine which elaborated the contrast between the pious man and the sinner, confronting not only the behaviour of each one with that of the other, but also the results of their actions and their respective final destinies.[74] The fact that the Book of Enoch should start with an announcement of the eschatological judgement theophany can be traced back to the topics of Wisdom literature. The literary similarity with Deut 33 has been rightly pointed out, but it is precisely in the Wisdom books, sometimes even at the beginning, that there is a reference to the judgement of the godless to encourage the reader.[75] Thus, in Prov 1: 8-19, after the introduction, the reader is warned about the ways of the godless, and their acts and their end are described. In Wis 1: 3-10 the reader is threatened with the "search" which the all-knowing God will undertake into sin:

"(1:8) Therefore no man that uttereth unrighteous things shall be unseen; Neither shall justice when it punisheth, pass him by. (9) For the counsels of the ungodly shall be searched out; and the report of his words shall come unto the Lord as a proof of his lawless deeds."

---

[73] Rau 1974, 93.

[74] Prov 2:21 f.; 10:24,25–30; 11:5,8,18,31; 12:12,21; 13:5 etc.

[75] Rau 1974, 60 shows that both in *As. Mos.* 10 and in *1 Enoch* the description of the theophany serves the announcement of the coming of God at the Last Judgement. While he emphasises the connection with prophetic traditions, I regard the application of Wisdom structural forms as more important than the provenance of the diction.

Even the contrast between the final destiny of the righteous and the godless in *1 Enoch* 5: 5-9 has parallels in Wis 4:66 ff. *1 Enoch* therefore uses the traditions of the later Wisdom sayings to a far greater extent than Dan. Indeed, in *1 Enoch* the merely apparent reflection of the existence of the godless constitutes a definite difference to Daniel and a strong affinity with the dualism characteristic of Wisdom literature. For in Daniel the evolution of the evil one forms the substance of the historical experience. His Power rests on the dominion of wicked kings and is therefore conceived politically. In the Book of Enoch, on the other hand, evil is in the world because wisdom has withdrawn.[76] That is no more than a mythical formula for the fact that the godless exist. They are part of the pious man's life and consequently, in *1 Enoch*, wisdom is no longer an apocalyptic knowledge of the situation of man in his history but also a perception of his dependence on mythological-cosmic event.

3.2.1. In the Book of Enoch, as the introductory parenesis shows, the religious reality of the pious man does exist, both in his life with the godless and in his conflicts with them. This is demonstrated in a manner so concrete as to be almost coarse in comparison to the other extensive parenetic portion of the book, the concluding section, ch. 91-105, to which G. Beer has given the heading "Das paränetische Buch. Die Lehr-, Mahn- und Rügereden Henochs."[77] It is a discourse addressed by (the departing?) Enoch to his son, and consequently a last cry of warning to antediluvian mankind about its destruction, as well as a call to the readers of the book who are on the brink of the final repetition of this catastrophe. Enoch is presented as "an example of repentance", just as he is in Sir 44:16. The urgency of such repentance at the beginning of the final parenesis is based on an apocalyptic historical prediction[78] which makes it clear to the reader in which period of history he is living. We cannot here go into the much vexed chronological and literary problems of this "futurische Geschichtser- zählung" – problems which have got further confused in the Ethiopic text.[79] Far more important from our point of view is the admonition which follows immediately on the prediction, and which may even have been where it is now in the original version. We read in 92:1 that

"Enoch indeed wrote this complete doctrine of wisdom which is praised of all men and a judge of all the earth".

The actual connection is reminiscent of the same series of literary forms in Tob 14.[80] The literary arrangement is consequently in the Wisdom- apocalyptic tradition.

---

[76] Cf. Luck 1976, 297 f.   [77] APAT II, 298.

[78] It is the much discussed Apocalypse of Weeks (*1 Enoch* 93; 91:12–17) which Nickelsburg 1977, 313 ff. simply treats as a portion of the parenesis.

[79] See Milik 1976 and Dexinger 1977, 97–189.   [80] Tob 14:4–11a.

3.2.2. The indirect link with the author's present life, which is typical of predictions, is also maintained within the admonition. In 94:2 we read:

"And to certain men of a generation shall the paths of violence and of death be revealed, and they shall hold themselves afar from them, and shall not follow them."[81]

This must refer to the days of the writer in which the pious are confronted with the overt appearance of the wicked. The pious are warned neither to tread the paths of evil nor the paths of death:

"Draw not nigh to them, lest ye be destroyed. But seek and choose for yourselves righteousness and an elect life, and walk in the paths of peace, and ye shall live and prosper."

The introductory themes remind us of the opening of Proverbs. Yet 94:5b decidedly assumes the form of an apocalyptic prediction:

"For I know that sinners will tempt men to evilly-entreat wisdom."

Herewith the parenesis turns into a fictitious prediction of the dualistic state in which the author and his readers see their lives. In a sharp antithesis recalling the first part of Wis, the godless and the pious are described in constant alternation.[82] They are addressed by turns; and, at the climax, their respective thoughts are repeated in their own words. From this great similarity in the technique of representing the contrast between the pious and the godless in Wis and *1 Enoch*, we can deduce that both representations are connected with a firm and age-old literary tradition.[83]

3.2.3. The predictive character of the final parenesis entitles us to conclude, first of all, that here, as in the introduction to the book, we are not dealing with an admonition in the true sense of the term, but with the announcement of a judgement. Two groups are represented, obviously the pious and the godless; and the seer imparts how they will behave at the end of time, how they will judge each other, and what sort of destiny awaits them in the hereafter. The godless will perpetrate injustice and violence, and deceit will be their foundation. They will build their houses with sin, acquire gold and silver for themselves. They rely on their riches, commit blasphemy and unrighteousness, indulge in hatred and evil. They inflict evil on their neighbour, lie and transgress. They are rich, themselves imagining that their wealth proves them to be righteous, even against their own consciences. They devour the finest of the wheat and crush the humble and the just. They acquire silver and gold in unrighteousness, have large estates, and adorn themselves with all kinds of jewelry, like women.

---

[81] Here and in what follows I have used the translation in Charles APOT II, 163–281.

[82] Wis 1:16–5:16. Nickelsburg 1977, 327 has also referred to the parallel.

[83] An analysis of the literary structure is not necessary here. It has been performed most conscienciously by Nickelsburg 1977. I cannot, however, accept his conclusion about a "prophetic consciousness" of the author. See also the questions of Coughenour 1978.

They have a regal appearance and influence, just as they have a great deal of property. They rejoice over the tribulations of the righteous. They pervert the words of truth, transgress the eternal law, falsify weights and measures, build houses with the toil of others. They reject the heritages of their fathers and are violent. They torture the righteous and make proud and insolent speeches against God's righteousness. They strip men naked, rob them, acquire wealth and wish to live halcyon days.[84] If we enquire about the properties or the way of life of the righteous on the other hand, they appear quite colourless. They are sufferers who call on God and hope in Him. We discover no more about them than that they fear God and should not sin before Him.[85]

3.2.3.1. These colourful villains have, of course, frequently been identified with historically known groups. Their sins are "social in nature"[86] and they bear all the marks of a class of exploiters. Thus, in 1960 Bo Reicke saw them as the Hasmonaeans in their later stages,[87] and K. Müller followed him.[88] Yet the frequency with which conquerors and oppressed appear, or are regarded as such, in Jewish history, makes such an identification particularly hazardous. The recent attempts[89] to deduce social-historical developments on the basis of the scanty and far from unequivocal sources of postexilic Jewish history might perhaps help us to identify certain social movements, even if we base ourselves on a distortion. But in view of the isolation of the text this does not lead much further than to the support of an hypothesis. Nor is the result very different if we regard those represented as the enemies of the group from which Ethiopic Enoch came.[90] We cannot reject out of hand the possibility that the representation of the godless is directed against a definite historical group or a certain social class, but it is hardly possible to decide with good reason in favour of one rather than another of the various possibilities. I may therefore be entitled to expand the spectrum of possibilities by one more. Since the admonition uses reproaches which can be made as much to social opponents as to national or religious ones, I would like to point to one element which could be applied to a definite aspect of the relationship between the pious and the godless. We once read that, while they were being oppressed, the pious

"complained to the rulers (sc. about the oppressors) in their tribulation, and cried out against those who devoured them."[91]

---

[84] *1 Enoch* 94:6,7,8,9; 95:2,5,6; 96:4,5,7; 97:8,9; 98:2,13,25; 99:2,12,13,14,15; 100:7; 101:7; 102:9.

[85] 95:7; 97:8; 102:4; 101:1 (yet it is not sure whether this passage refers to the righteous).

[86] Nickelsburg 1977, 311.   [87] Reicke 1960, 139 ff.   [88] Müller 1978, 221.

[89] Kippenberg 1978; more ideological consistent are the works of H. Kreissig and J. P. Wejnberg, see the synopses: J. P. Wejnberg 1973 and Kreissig 1976.

[90] See §3.1.1. and note 70.   [91] *1 Enoch* 103:14.

We here catch a glimpse of the predicament of the Jews in the diaspora. In the daily difficulties which an ethnic religious minority would experience when consorting with the host-nation which both sets the general style of life and is prejudiced against the guest-nation – the repeated cause of some very far-reaching disputes – the Jews, like other minorities, were induced to appeal for official protection.[92] This, of course, never led to the improvement of relations between the ethnic groups, as we see in Egypt. But it is perfectly conceivable that the image of the godless which we find here was partly due to the behaviour of an established host-nation, like the Egyptians, towards an ethnic minority.

3.2.3.2. Other observations are more important for the understanding of the piety in *1 Enoch*. Nickelsburg has rightly pointed to the fact that the image of the godless is also determined by traditional characteristics which can be traced back to Jewish Prophecy and Wisdom literature.[93] We can add that the godless are in no way photographs of historical villains but are presented as types which simply lack all those features on which the ideal citizen of the world or the state might pride himself. The godless are men who distort the truth, transgress the eternal Law and make themselves into what they used not to be, *i.e.* sinners.[94] Behind the parenesis there now looms an ideal human image which will be shattered in the last days about which the author is speaking. The words of truth, which are distorted, the eternal Law, which will be transgressed, are here again the Egyptian *ma'at*, which the godless of the last generation renounce. Their violence, their desire to oppress others, is *"isft"*, disturbance, rejection of all social order, the most common antithesis to *ma'at*;[95] and oppression of the poor is automatically connected with this. In the ideal biographical inscriptions collected by Otto, the founder of the inscriptions very frequently appears as the helper of the poor and the oppressed. He "ist einer, der sich dem Furchtsamen zuwendet, wenn sein Fall (sc. vor Gericht) an die Reihe kommt und sein Zeuge auftritt". He is " freigebig zu jedermann, der Helfer der Vaterlandslosen". Someone even says, "Ich rettete den Hilfsbedürftigen vor einem, der stärker war als er, ich machte keinen Unterschied zwischen dem Großen und dem Kleinen."[96] Social behavior is now at the heart of piety – a trait which we can also find in the contemporary Jewish canon of virtue. In the above-mentioned catechism of Sirach (§ 3.1.2.) the content of the Law is expressed with the words:

"And He said unto them, Beware of all unrighteousness. And He gave them commandment, to each man concerning his neighbour."[97]

---

[92] In Elephantine: see APFC, 97 ff. No. 27. In Alexandria: see CJP II, 25–107 No. 150–159.
[93] Nickelsburg 1977, 317 f., 326 f.
[94] *1 Enoch* 99:2.   [95] Otto 1964, 24.
[96] Otto 1954, 95.   [97] Sir 17:14.

There is no doubt that what Otto had observed in Egypt[98] applies here to the Jews: it is by no means true that the mythical or cultic element was neglected in late Egyptian religion; it was simply rationalised and ethicised. People recognised the personal obligations which stemmed from myth and cult. But we must add that, precisely because social order, ethics and conscience had become the centre of religious thought, people had to perceive the "endtime" in the reality of life. The reproach of distorting the truth and transgressing the eternal Law consequently introduces the description of final misery, of complete loss of order.[99]

3.3. The representation of the godless by the author of the Book of Enoch could be called the socialisation of the image of Antiochus. Yet we must remember that this was not presented objectively but was formulated as an address, a parenesis. We saw above that the sinners are obviously condemned,[100] and we are therefore inclined to regard the admonition as the basis for the unpardonability of the godless. This, however, would be purely hypothetical since the godless can hardly be numbered amongst the readers of the Book of Enoch. The object of the parenesis, as I have suggested, is to teach the pious how to consort with the godless. For this purpose the future destiny of the godless in the hereafter is shown us: they will suddenly be destroyed and have no peace; they will perish in judgement, be cut off from "all their foundations" and fall by the sword. The Creator will annihilate them completely. They will be judged and delivered up to the righteous. They will be afflicted by various forms of distress. Their deceit will be openly known, their riches will pass away; they will be murdered and cast into burning ovens; they will die childless and have no rest, no graves; they will die a sudden death. Finally, the Day of Judgement is described on which the righteous will be preserved but the sinners will be destroyed, and will burn in blazing flames. The elements will turn to fighting the godless. All[101] these personal curses and predictions which the pious hear uttered against the sinners can only serve to show the pious reader how worthless, how short-lived and hopeless it is to possess, gain or acquire riches with force and cunning in this world. To a certain extent the reader participates in the judgement of the sinners after having been shown their doings on earth.

3.3.1. If we wonder about the function of this participation in the fall of the godless – reminiscent as it is of late Gothic Judgement scenes – we get the impression that the pious are being put on their guard against tempta-

---

[98] Otto 1964, 84f.

[99] *1 Enoch* 99:3ff., beginning with the typical formula for setting the time of the story "in those days".

[100] See above §3.1.3.

[101] *1 Enoch* 92:7,10; 95:3,4; 97:2–7; 98:3,10–15; 100:4,7,9,13.

tion. Ultimately evil is not the peculiarity of a class or group, but obviously a possibility open to everybody. That is why the parenesis also begins with an exhortation to the pious not to be led astray from the right path.[102] The author regards evil as a temptation: in his opinion the wish to be rich and the wish to rule and oppress others are the primitive temptations which fascinate man. Consequently, in the parenesis the author is concerned with the preservation of the pious. For the pious, too, live in this earthly world; they are surrounded by the false images of a reality which is only transient and corruptible. The portion 102:4-104:8, the climax of the book, which has been brilliantly analysed by Nickelsburg,[103] contrasts the deceptive experience of this life with the divine reality which men experience after death, in an artistically interwoven antithesis. First the souls of the righteous, who die like the sinners and have to descend into the underworld, are consoled. We then come to the sinners who see no difference between themselves and the righteous in death. Yet the speaker knows that the righteous are in the Book of Life and their spirits are happy and will rejoice. In a second discourse the dead sinners are first cursed and then their like-minded companions are quoted, who value their enjoyable and rich existence on earth. In the end the speaker proclaims that the sinners will not escape the Final Judgement. There follows a third discourse, telling the living righteous not to lament the unhappy existence of their dead brothers, since, after the afflictions of this life, the portals of heaven will be opened to them. Finally the living sinners are informed that, contrary to what they think, their sins will be written down by the angels so that their deceit and godlessness will be of no avail to them. Even if the antitheses discerned by Nickelsburg are not equally perceptible everywhere, from the basic structure of these discourses emerges clearly how essential it is for the pious man of the Apocalypse not to let himself be deceived by the appearance of this world. We are here no longer concerned with the course of a chronologically determined line of time and the historical evolution which takes place within it, running parallel to a human evolution. Temporal periods and developments have been replaced by the antithesis of circumstances. The deceptive condition of this world, determined by the loss of order and the suppression of truth, is contrasted with the condition with God after death (or however we should call it), determined by the reality of the divine order. We still find portions of the parenesis which speak of eschatological end-time relations within

---

[102] Cf. 1QS III,21 ff., where the fate of the sons of light on this earth is described: "Und durch den Engel der Finsternis kommt Verirrung über alle Söhne der Gerechtigkeit, und alle ihre Sünde, Missetat und Schuld und die Verstöße ihrer Taten stehen unter seiner Herrschaft entsprechend den Geheimnissen Gottes, bis zu seiner Zeit". (Lohse's translation.)

[103] Nickelsburg 1977, 319 ff.

chronological limits,[104] but they no longer constitute a coherent apocalyptic representation of history. The antithesis of circumstances has become so central that it is sometimes not even clear whether the author is thinking of a judgement after the expiry of history or whether he simply views the other condition as post-mortal.[105] Occasionally the mention of the Day of Judgement only appears as an apocalyptic relic which actually describes the post-mortal condition. As in the New Testament, so also here we sometimes have the impression that the Egyptian representation of judgement immediately after death was influential.[106] It is not the preparation for endtime that determines apocalyptic piety, but the expectation of death.

3.3.2. This explains why the pious man must be a sufferer in this world. In the extensive description of the lot of the righteous in 102:9-15, not a single action is mentioned which expresses piety – no ascetic, cultic or ritual act. The condition of suffering is simply presented in an ever more moving and concrete manner. The pious man must accept his suffering because he would otherwise acknowledge the earthly world as the true reality; he would see dominion and victory in a worldly dimension as the ultimate purpose of life, and consequently deprive himself of an eternal future.[107] He would have crossed the borders of godlessness and encouraged the formation and maintenance of a condition in which not God, but man, prevails. The Enoch parenesis is therefore intended to keep him as a sufferer. The piety of suffering is akin to the piety of poverty, which has also coloured the image of the two classes of men.[108] What is decisive about the condition of the pious – the poor and the suffering – is that it corresponds to the salvific will of God. Whoever is poor, miserable, blind and suffering, needs a saviour God,[109] and only when God appears as a

---

[104] *1 Enoch* 99:4ff., 100:1ff.

[105] This obscure approach to chronological and anthropological categories is also reminiscent of Wis 3–5. Contemporary Judaism displays the combination of both categories in the same work elsewhere too. In the Book of Tobit a chronological eschatology is also assumed in chaps. 13 and 14, while the suffering and insulted Tobit prays in 3:6: "Command my spirit to be taken from me, that I may be released from off the earth and become earth. . . . Command that I be released from this distress, let me go to the everlasting place". "To the everlasting place" we can compare John 14:2 and the primitive Christian tradition in which the martyr reaches the "due" place, *1 Clem.* 5:4; Pol. *Phil.* 9:2. On the problems in general cf. the recent work of Fischer 1978.

[106] Erman 1934, 224ff.

[107] The subtlety of the idea that the pious man must renounce all success in this life in order to gain the hereafter is shown in the lines of the Sermon on the Mount in Matt 6:2,16 with their sentence "they have their reward (in this life)".

[108] Nickelsburg 1978 has dealt extensively with these connections. The connection between the piety of the poor and expectation of the hereafter in the Egyptian religion, which is also important for judging the Enoch parenesis, has been studied by H. Brunner 1961. On the piety of the poor in general see the recent articles by Wißmann, Michel, Keck, J. Maier, all 1979, as also Mussner 1964.

[109] For important observations on the saviour god in Egypt see Otto 1971.

saviour does He truly rule in the world, is He truly God. Thus, the two components of piety, suffering and the praise of God, converge in a single whole in the Book of Enoch.

4. Ezra's Despair

4.0. Unlike *1 Enoch* the fourth Book of Ezra, taken as a whole, has a uniform structure, whatever those scholars may say who think they have spotted certain discrepancies.[110] Also unlike *1 Enoch* it does not contain any coherent parenetic portions. Nevertheless, it would be wrong to conclude that 4 Ezra was closer to Dan than to *1 Enoch*. In *1 Enoch* the author is constantly dealing with man as sinful and unjust, as oppressor and persecutor, in his earthly state and in his future hopes. In Dan, on the other hand, although man is always in the background, he must let history pass him by in apparent unconcern. In 4 Ezra man is central, even if the message is presented in the account of the course of history, starting with the creation and ending with the eschaton. The tension, however, does not arise from history; the reader must actually already be acquainted with its course. What is really gripping are the dialogues. They are contained mainly in the first three "visions" and they arise from questions expressed in the description of a problem. Thus, the book begins with a description of the development of the world in which Israel's disobedience to God affects all peoples from Adam onwards. This leads to the Flood. But with the new propagation of mankind sin again increases; and, although Israel, as the heir of Abraham, receives the Law on Sinai, God does not take away from the Israelites their "evil heart". Jerusalem, therefore, is finally delivered to its enemies because of its sins. This leads to the question:

"When was it that the inhabitants of the earth did not sin before thee? Or what nation hath so kept thy precepts?"

The reply ends:

---

[110] The constantly recurring question of a literary-critical split in 4 Ezra (last discussed by Stone 1968) has been raised once more by Harnisch in a stimulating article in this volume. This is hardly the place in which to argue with him. Nevertheless I do think that it is possible to interpret the data on which he bases the literary inconsistency of visions V and VI in a different manner. Beneath these visions there lies an earlier Apocalypse which the author has taken over, and he has adapted the pre-eschatological account of history to the presentation of a problem. It would make no sense, if the original author were first to speak of the coming of a new age and its omens and then not to inform the reader of the end. The division of vision VII – a vision which has an entirely uniform content – into two different visions does not seem to me to be convincing. The choice of the analogy of form and content as a point of departure is correct. Yet, in a highly intellectual work, the thought process must be regarded as the element which determines the form.

"For just as the earth has been assigned to the wood and the place of the sea to bear its waves, even so the dwellers upon earth can understand only what is upon the earth, and they who are above the heavens that which is above the heavenly height."[111]

Other questions are:

"Show this also to thy servant: must every one give back his soul after death, or shall we be kept in rest until those times come?"[112] and "If I have found favour in thy sight, show me, thy servant, this also: whether in the Day of Judgement the righteous shall be able to intercede for the ungodly, or to intreat the Most High in their behalf: fathers for sons, sons for parents, brothers for brothers, kinsfolk for their nearest, friends for their dearest."[113]

The question about rest after death shows that the problem of the moment in time of life in the hereafter which remains unclear in *1 Enoch*, is here deliberately spelled out.

4.1. The literary form corresponds to a convention, developed in Homer criticism, of extracting problems from a text and answering them.[114] Thus Aristotle had already contrasted and collected ζητήματα and λύσεις. Traditionally akin to this procedure are the incorrect questions put by the disciples in the Gospel of St. John to which Jesus gives the correct answer as it is revealed to him. Similarly Ezra, whom the literary fiction situates thirty years after the destruction of Jerusalem in 586 B.C., is now the erring and unknowing one who receives his answers from an angel or a heavenly voice. According to one hypothesis the seer represents a theological position peculiar to certain Jewish circles which the author wishes to correct by means of this system of questions and answers. 4 Ezra would therefore be the document of a theological debate between conflicting groups of Jews. Yet in view of the Greek parallel and the correspondencies in John, it is equally possible that we are dealing with a particular form of argument which is only apparently advanced against an opponent. However we may wish to solve this problem, it is evident that the apocalyptic revelation of history, which has now grown old, is preassumed. It is a thesaurus from which problems of importance to the author and his readers can be answered.[115]

4.1.1. In this way, man with all his uncertainty and his questions steps into the centre of the Apocalypse. He is embodied in the figure of the seer. If, in Daniel, history is clearly described from the point of view of man, in 4 Ezra a man is described in his relation to history.

4.1.2. The seer's questions revolve round the impossibility for a man to obtain eschatological salvation on this earth. The world in which the seer

---

[111] 4 Ezra 3:35; 4:21.
[112] 4 Ezra 7:75. I follow the Syriac text, where I have replaced *'yn* by *'n*.
[113] 4 Ezra 7:102.   [114] Pfeiffer 1970, 95 ff.
[115] Further information is contained in Harnisch's article in this volume. Koch 1978 is also important for my own hypothesis.

lives is "this age" as opposed to the future one. Not only is the unpunished deployment of "evil" completed in this age of time which comprises the history of the world from the beginning – a deployment which consists in the dominion of evil rulers (as in Daniel) or in the withdrawal of wisdom from this world (as in the Book of Enoch), but this age is above all the age in which nobody can be without sin and in which everybody is going towards his destruction. Ezra expresses this in his prayerlike laments before the messenger of God again and again. Owing to wickedness of heart, Israel's history has turned into the history of disaster. As a result the Law can bear no fruit. According to the literary fiction, in the time of the seer, Israel is even subjected to Babylon, which is no better than Israel herself. Yet the heathen nations live in joy and splendour. The angel Uriel first tells Ezra that corruptible man cannot comprehend the ways of the Most High. But the future age, which is about to come about, will entail the great harvest of the righteous. Admittedly this will only happen when the number of the righteous – "of those like yourself" – is fulfilled. The greatest measure of the course of the world has already elapsed; what is still to come is merely fleeting, like the last raindrops or like smoke after a fire. The last time before the end will be full of panic; unrighteousness will prevail; there will be natural disasters, rebellions, a wicked ruler; good sense and wisdom will disappear. The second vision also begins with the lament over the fate of Israel, who has been delivered up as the one for the many. The reply again points to the incomprehensibility of the ways of God, and again the angel reveals the signs of the end, now until the appearance of men

"who have been taken up (sc. to heaven), who have not tasted death from their birth", *i.e.* seers like Enoch, Elijah and Ezra himself – "and the heart of the inhabitants of the world shall be changed, and be converted to a different spirit."[116]

4.2. If, in the first two dialogues, the confrontation between Ezra, grieving about the hopelessness of existence in the present age, and the angelic messenger Uriel, pointing to the future, is somewhat monotonous, the third vision leads to more impulsive arguments between the two. Ezra's laments become more desperate and more urgent; he explains that the coming of the new age in no way helps the men of our age, as all are full of sin.[117] Even if a few – even if he – were saved, the creation would have lost its meaning since so many would be destroyed.[118] He even appeals for the salvation of the ungodly through the intercession of the righteous[119] and

---

[116] 4 Ezra 6:26.   [117] 4 Ezra 7:62–69, 116–126; 8:4–36; 9:14–16.
[118] 4 Ezra 7:17f., 45–48.
[119] 4 Ezra 7:102f. Ezra even numbers himself amongst the lost. According to the angel (8:48f.) this will win honour for him, but he is nevertheless ordered to free himself from any solidarity with the dwellers on this earth and to turn to future glory.

entreats the mercy and forbearance of God. The angel becomes ever more determined and dismissive in his replies: all Ezra's demands will be unfulfilled because of the righteousness of God. An irrevocable sentence will be passed at the Last Judgement, after which only the righteous will be received into the new age.[120] After this rejection of Ezra a new message comes into the angel's discourse: Ezra belongs to the elect and the saved; he must consequently free himself of the worries and cares of this world[121] and turn his thoughts to the future age. To concentrate one's mind on the coming world is the central requirement of the book. In answer to his last desperate call *plures sunt qui pereunt quam qui salvabantur*, Ezra hears the final sentence damning the mass of mankind but saving himself and the nation of the righteous: *pereat ergo multitudo quae sine causa nata est, et servetur acinus meus et plantatio mea, quia cum multo labore perfeci haec.*[122]

With this demonstration of the unbending justice of God, the seer reaches a crisis which will lead him to a new attitude in his next vision, the fourth. Hitherto he has only been concerned with the cares and problems of the terrestrial world, the present age. In their evolution he recognised the senselessness of the Creation, the collapse of salvation history and, finally, the worthlessness of the Law. This has all convinced him that there is no way to the new world for man. Ezra no longer believes in what the Enoch parenesis proclaims as a matter of course – a completely new life for the oppressed and the suffering in the hereafter. On the other hand the angel urges him to think of future salvation. What remains decisive is that Ezra cannot tread the only possible path to the new age: the fulfilment of the Law. Even when Israel received the Law it could not fulfil it. That was why Jerusalem was destroyed and Israel subjected to heathens, or so thought Ezra with regard to the position in which the literary fiction has placed him. This initial situation had already given rise to the lament in the first vision that the Law with its statutes has been destroyed. The seer receives the unsatisfactory reply that he cannot understand the ways of God and that the new age is imminent.[123] It is from the question about the fulfilment of the Law that finally the crisis of the dialogue in the third vision also arises. Ezra still thinks that there will be no true salvation because of the power of sin and he appeals to God's mercy. The angel maintains that the Law is still valid and that the sinner must consequently be destroyed.

4.3. The fourth vision, the last in which the argument between the seer and the angel plays a part, albeit a more limited one, begins, like the three previous ones, with an indictment by Ezra. But this time it is different from the others and provokes a new reaction. Ezra again begins by stating

---

[120] 4 Ezra 7:19–25, 59–61, 81–99, 112–115, 127–131.
[121] 4 Ezra 7:15–16, 38–40, 46–61.   [122] 4 Ezra 9:15; 9:22.   [123] 4 Ezra 4:22–26.

that the Law has not brought forth any fruit. The fathers were allowed to be vessels (parabolically speaking) in which the Law was preserved. If it produces no fruit its receivers will indeed be preserved as its vessels, but the Law must be destroyed. It would be preposterous if it were to be the other way round in the case of Israel:

"We who have received the Law and sinned must perish, together with our heart, which has taken it in: the Law, however, perishes not but abides in its glory."[124]

Instead of the angel answering, there suddenly appears a woman grieving and disconsolate, weeping for the loss of her son. Ezra, however, encourages her to bear her own fate gallantly and to remember how much more terrible is the misfortune of Zion. Thereupon the face of the woman shines, she utters a cry, and Ezra sees in her stead the new Jerusalem built by God – for the woman, as Uriel says, was the grieving and destroyed city of Jerusalem. God, Ezra discovers, has shown him the future glory of Jerusalem because he has mourned for the city from the depths of his heart. The main problem in this vision is why the appearance of the woman follows so abruptly after the seer's lament. I believe that this might have been meant as an answer to Ezra's assumption that Israel will be destroyed as a vessel of the Law. Jerusalem, which was the city of the temple and the people of God, the place of the Law, and which was perhaps again destroyed in the author's own lifetime, nevertheless remains God's vessel. In future ages it will again become God's city. Thus the spiritually unfruitful nation of God will bear fruit simply because it has been a vessel of the Law, albeit no longer in this, but in a future age. The seer is at first perplexed, but, with the help of the angel, the future time of salvation becomes a sure reality for him. He has even encouraged the mourning woman to trust in God and consequently he, who had hitherto always despaired at the hopelessness of the present age, finds that he can also trust in God for the restoration of Zion, against all expectations and all logic of history. This vision makes him ready for the reception of the apocalyptic revelations which will provide him with perfect consolation.

4.4. We could – though it might be a little unsuitable – describe the fourth Book of Ezra as an "Erziehungsroman" in which the hero finds his way from the earthly to the divine. Nevertheless, he has still not attained his goal with the *peripateia* of the fourth vision. In one of his admirable personal seminars Julius Schniewind pointed to the fact that in the fourth Book of Ezra there is a curious hiatus: the hero first falls into despair about

---

[124] 4 Ezra 9:34–37. This passage cannot have been meant as a lament about a certain situation, but as an argument containing a plea which goes something like: "You cannot allow yourself to do such a thing, God". The appearance of the mourning woman would be the answer to this.

his sins and then, as soon as he sees the eschatological fulfilment in all its glory, all sorrow is forgotten and he lives only for the future. I would like to suggest, however, that what we really find in 4 Ezra is the bridging of this hiatus. As we have seen, the question of the fulfilment of the Law winds its way through the dialogue like a red thread. The Law would be the way leading to the future age. Both angel and seer agree about this. But Ezra doubts the possibility of fulfilling the Law. The vision of the New Jerusalem, however, shows him that the receivers of the Law can ultimately indeed be saved. The new age is open to them. He consequently turns to the "future", just as the angel has told him to do; and, after the end of the apocalyptic revelations, he receives the acknowledgement:

"Thou hast forsaken the things of thyself, and hast applied thy diligence unto mine and searched out my law."[125]

The infringed law, which had led to the fall of Jerusalem, is not useless, in spite of everything; concern with it, belief in it, opens up the way to the Kingdom of God. That is why the story of Ezra ends with his proclaiming once more, in a state of inspiration, the destroyed Law, the entire Torah, and with his dictating it to five scribes.[126] But it is no longer a law which guarantees the satisfaction of hopes in this life, the rebuilding of Jerusalem on the earthly site it has known hitherto, the possession of this world and preservation from terrestrial griefs. It should help men, rather to find the path of God and assist those who desire eternal life to acquire it. The new Torah therefore consists of 94 books, the 24 books of the old canon, accessible to both the worthy and the unworthy, and the other 70, which have only been preserved by the "wise among thy people". This means the apocalyptic books which herald the coming of the new world. The Law written down by Ezra consequently gains a new function: it is the object of apocalyptic interpretation and becomes the means for entering the new age. The fourth Book of Ezra reports how the restorer of the Law was conducted from his despair about the dominion of sin in this age to belief in eschatological salvation, and how he transmitted the Law, understood anew, to the pious.

4.4.1. At first sight the most surprising aspect of the Apocalypse of Ezra is the return to the "official" salvation-history of Judaism. The reader of the

---

[125] 4 Ezra 13:54. Cf. Luck's résumé 1976, 302: "Man muß es mit dem Gesetz wagen, auch wenn man es nicht sieht".

[126] 4 Ezra 18–27. We here see that the dialogue between Ezra and the angel is about the law which was annulled with the destruction of Jerusalem. Its restoration depends on the value it can still have for future generations, after previous generations have been destroyed by it. The appearance of the woman has revealed to Ezra that the salvation of the receiver of the Law depends on the restoration of the Law – something about which Ezra had not hitherto been convinced.

Book of Daniel thinks himself on the edge of salvation-history and at the beginning of a new and terrible historical cycle in which he must prove himself. The seer in 1 Enoch recognises in single mythical Biblical events, expanded in the sense of the Midrash, the roots of his own life and the contemporary predicament of the world. 4 Ezra, on the other hand, reduces the past to Biblical history from Adam to the destruction of Jerusalem. The connection of a freer, "typically apocalyptic", picture of history with the ancient Biblical tradition can be observed at an early stage in Dan 9 and Tob 14. But the significant exclusivity of its application and accentuation points to a new atmosphere – the atmosphere in which 4 Ezra was composed. It must have been a time in which Judaism was to be concentrated and reduced to its essential traditions. The Apocalypse belongs pretty clearly to the period of the first century in which that Rabbinic Judaism developed which was primarily concerned with the purity of Judaism and the authenticity of tradition. Quite apart from whether we wish to follow Harnisch in seeing in the dialogues of the Apocalypse the arguments between two parties represented by the angel and the seer, it is certainly true that in 4 Ezra we are dealing with a dispute – a dispute about the salvific value of the Law. This was also the problem of the period of early Rabbinicism, attested both by Paul and the New Testament, and by burgeoning Christianity in general. The men and the groups from among the Jews who finally converged in Christianity have departed, at least to a large extent, from the Law as a means of salvation, but they have also recognised the Bible as a book of revelation. Many of them had surely come into contact with apocalyptic ideas and hopes. The fourth Book of Ezra, however, which later found its way into the western canon, possibly via spiritualistic groups,[127] sees the Law as a means of salvation which opens the path to the new age, to the Kingdom of God. It should lead the apocalyptic believer to a true obedience to the Law in the Rabbinic sense. There is no suggestion that the reception of the Law was meant in any other way. We must imagine the righteousness which the pious reader of the book wished to fulfil as what Paul regarded as the path to salvation before his experience in Damascus.[128]

4.4.2. In earlier Apocalyptic, represented by Daniel and Enoch, it is more or less taken for granted that the pious who hope for, and try to acquire, eschatological salvation, are members of the Jewish people. Their eschatological situation is a part of the very framework of Jewish history, whether at the moment of the violation of the temple by the troops of Antiochus, or in their existence in the diaspora. Yet, in the earlier sources, the qualification of the pious for eschatological salvation is characterised by

---

[127] Bardenhewer III, 1912, 409.   [128] Davies 1948, 10, 11.

religious universality: either they prepare themselves by ascesis for the time
of salvation, or else they are poor and oppressed and are open to the salvific
will of God. In 4 Ezra the qualification is the fulfilment of the Jewish
Mosaic Law, the characteristic of Judaism as it was conceived Rabbinically,
and it is deliberately and clearly the salvation of Israel which is at stake.[129]
Apocalyptic, so frequently regarded as individualistic and universalistic,
has been Judaised in 4 Ezra. This is also demonstrated in the figure of the
seer, chosen as a pseudonym. Instead of the antediluvian Enoch and the
Daniel temporarily introduced into Jewish history but whose earlier history seems to have taken place in the Canaanite milieu, Ezra, like that very
similar seer Baruch, appears closely connected with the preservation and
transmission of the Hebrew legal canon. In the visions of the heavenly
Jerusalem and of the Son of Man in the shape of a Messiah king who will
renew the Creation and collect the ten lost tribes, themes of prophetic
eschatology are treated in a manner we do not find in earlier Apocalyptic. If
we add the realisation, deeply lamented by Ezra, that the non-Jews who
despised the Law are predestined to eternal destruction,[130] we see that the
Judaisation is also confirmed by the general character of the work.

4.4.3. At the same time, moreover, the doctrine of this Apocalypse
contains traits which must have been quite alien to traditional nomistic
Judaism: traits connected with the radical denial of everything in this life.
God loves His creation, but men have transformed it into the domain of
sin. Any solidarity with God's creatures is branded as an offence, and the
fulfilment of the Law is worthless for existence in the present age. To be
concerned with earthly things means guilt, and the entire instruction of
Ezra has the sole object of getting away from all forms of earthly things
and adjusting to the hereafter. This world is hastening towards its end; any
sojourn in it is useless, not to say dangerous, and consequently Ezra is
removed from the world. There is no question of ascetic tests or of a
suffering which will be rewarded in the hereafter by heavenly joy. Besides
the Judaisation, therefore, there is a radicalisation of the apocalyptic
attitude to the world. To this radicalisation also belongs the author's
strangely ambiguous attitude towards sin. Ezra complains about the sin
from which man cannot espace in this age. He numbers everybody –
himself included – amongst the sinners, and he is told that he must not
mingle himself "with them that have scorned, nor... with those that shall
suffer torment". He has a store of good works, but the unavoidability of
sin cannot be denied.[131] Ezra also returns to this later. The solution of the
difficulty could be that the author – most Rabbinically, incidentally –
believes that one must sin, but that one must also have performed so many

---

[129] 4 Ezra 3:30; 4:23; 5:27–30,40; 6:55ff.; 8:15ff.,26,45; 10:39.
[130] 4 Ezra 9:18–20.   [131] 4 Ezra 7:76f.

good works that they prevail. Man, however, does not know whether he has performed enough good works. Yet all these possibilities, which only benefit a few, do not determine the ideological atmosphere in 4 Ezra. What is decisive is the conviction that here on earth each man, even the most pious, must sin. There is no freedom to lead a completely pure life. The age is not only transient and corruptible, it also ensnares every man in sin. That the traditional Law which has accompanied Israel in the earthly Canaan can no longer even show the way out of such a corruptible age is ultimately proved by the fact that the ancient Law of Moses is a mere fragment, only one piece of the revelation which Ezra has transmitted. Seventy more secret books are necessary to show the way to the new age.

4.4.4. The fourth Book of Ezra obviously intends to pave the way between apocalyptic doctrine and tradition on the one side and the restorative Judaism of its time on the other. But it is precisely in this attempt that we see that Apocalyptic and its piety have evolved in a manner that renders such an objective vain. This certainly applies in so far as it represents a radical rejection of life on earth. The fully developed two-age doctrine had led to a complete devaluation of inner worldly existence. Consequently no genuine apocalyptic ethic could evolve any further. The pious man must bank on a swift destruction of the world which would remove his sin. The Law, the old source of revelation of Judaism, could now only act as a part of a great literary corpus which emanated nothing but hope that might console us till the hour of our death. Only then would man be certain of his fate. The idea of a blind, hopeless and empty life in this world led Apocalyptic to the verge of Gnosis. All that separates the two is the hope of a new age. As the contributions of G. MacRae and H. G. Kippenberg in this volume show,[132] Gnosis does not even have this hope anymore. Its only hope is to free man from the creation.[133]

---

[132] G. MacRae in this volume §2.5.: "What is of course most distinctive of the apocalyptic eschatology of Gnosticism is the total absence of any new creation". According to H. G. Kippenberg in this volume §3.2.3., the Gnostic is convinced that to act ethically is "ein Mittel, die Destruktion des Kosmos voranzutreiben".

[133] These final statements do not of course mean that the concepts of late Apocalyptic have never been combined with orthodox Judaism. For such syntheses we need only look at 4 Ezra and *2 Apoc. Bar.*, not to mention the apocalyptic ideas scattered throughout Rabbinicism. Yet the result of such an attempt, as we have it in 4 Ezra, is so far removed from Rabbinical thought that it can no longer be regarded as part of Rabbinical Judaism.

Bibliography

Ansheshonk: B. H. Stricker, "De wijsheid van Ansjesjonq", in: *JEOL* 15 (1957–1958) 11–13.
Bardenhewer, O. 1912: *Geschichte der altkirchlichen Literatur* III, Freiburg 1912.
Barta, W. 1976: "Der anonyme Gott der Lebenslehren", in: *ZÄG* 103 (1976) 79–108.
Bauer, W. 1971: *Griechisch-deutsches Wörterbuch zu den Schriften des Neuen Testaments und der übrigen urchristlichen Literatur*⁵, Berlin 1971.
Brunner, H. 1961: "Die religiöse Wertung der Armut im alten Ägypten", in: *Saec.* 12 (1961) 319–344.
Casey, M. 1976: "Porphyry and the Origin of the Book of Daniel", in: *JThS* NS 17 (1976) 15–33.
Clifford, R. J. 1975: "History and Myth in Daniel 10–12", in: *BASOR* 220 (1975) 23–26.
Coughenour, R. A. 1978: "The Woe-Oracles in the Ethiopic Enoch", in: *JSJ* 9 (1978) 192–197.
Davies, W. D. 1948: *Paul and Rabbinic Judaism*, London 1948.
Delcor, M. 1971: *Le livre de Daniel*, (SBi) Paris 1971.
– 1977: "Bilan des études sur l'apocalyptique", in: Monloubou (Ed.) 1977, 27–42.
Dexinger, F. 1977: *Henochs Zehnwochenapokalypse und offene Probleme der Apokalyptikforschung* (StPB 29), Leiden 1977.
Erman, A. 1934: *Die Religion der Ägypter*, Berlin 1934.
Fischer, U. 1978: *Eschatologie und Jenseitserwartung im hellenistischen Diasporajudentum* (BZNW 44), Berlin/New York 1978.
Frost, S. B. 1952: *Old Testament Apocalyptic. Its Origins and Growth*, London 1952.
Greenfield, J. C./Stone, M. E. 1977: "The Enochic Pentateuch and the Date of Similitudes", in: *HThR* 70 (1977) 52–65.
Hartman, L. 1975: "The Functions of some so-called Apocalyptic Time-tables", in: *NTS* 22 (1975) 1–14.
Hengel, M. 1969: *Judentum und Hellenismus*¹ (WUNT 10), Tübingen 1969.
Jacob, E. 1977: "Aux sources bibliques de l'apocalyptique", in: Monloubou (Ed.) 1977, 43–62.
de Jonge, H. J. 1975: "The Study of the New Testament", in: *Leiden University in the Seventeenth Century. An Exchange of Learning*, ed. Th. H. Lunsigh Scheurleer and G. H. M. Posthumus Meijes, Leiden 1975, 65–109.
Kippenberg, H. G. 1978: *Religion und Klassenbildung im antiken Judäa* (StUNT 14), Göttingen 1978.
Keck, L. 1979: "Armut III; Neues Testament", in: *TRE* IV (1979) 76–80.
Koch, K. 1966: "Die Apokalyptik und ihre Zukunftserwartungen", in: *Kont.* 3 (1966) 51–58.
– 1970: *Ratlos vor der Apokalyptik*, Gütersloh 1970.
– 1978: "Esras erste Vision. Weltzeiten und Weg des Höchsten", in: *BZ* 22 (1978) 46–75.
Kreissig, H. 1976: "Die Ursachen des 'Makkabäer'-Aufstandes", in: *Klio* 58 (1976) 249–253.
Lebram, J. 1964: "Der Aufbau der Areopagrede", in: *ZNW* 55 (1964) 221–243.
– 1965: "Zwei Bemerkungen zu katechetischen Traditionen in der Apostelgeschichte", in: *ZNW* 56 (1965) 202–213.
– 1974: "Perspektiven der gegenwärtigen Danielforschung", in: *JSJ* 5 (1974) 1–33.
– 1975: "König Antiochus im Buch Daniel", in: *VT* 25 (1975) 737–772.
– 1978: "Apokalyptik/Apokalypsen II, Altes Testament", in: *TRE* III (1978) 192–202.
– 1979: Review: Monloubou (Ed.) 1977, in: *BiOr* 36 (1979) 111–114.
– 1981: "Daniel/Danielbuch und Zusätze", in: *TRE* VIII (1981) 325–349.
Limbeck, M. 1971: *Die Ordnung des Heils*. Untersuchungen zum Gesetzesverständnis des Frühjudentums, Düsseldorf 1971.
Lohse, E. (Ed.) 1964: *Die Texte aus Qumran, Hebräisch und deutsch*, Darmstadt 1964.
Luck, U. 1976: "Das Weltverständnis in der jüdischen Apokalyptik, dargestellt am äthiopischen Henoch und am 4. Esra", in: *ZThK* 73 (1976) 283–305.
Maier, J. 1979: "Armut IV, Judentum", in: *TRE* IV (1979) 80–85.

Michel, D. 1979: "Armut II, Altes Testament", in: *TRE* IV (1979) 72–76.

Milik, J. T. 1967: "Les papyrus araméens d'Hermoupolis et les cultes syro-phéniciens en Egypte perse", in: *Bib* 48 (1967) 546–622.

– 1976: *The Books of Enoch*. Aramaic Fragments of Qumran Cave 4, Oxford 1976.

Monloubou, L. (Ed.) 1977: *Apocalypses et théologie de l'espérance*. Association Catholique Française pour l'étude de la bible. Congrès de Toulouse 1975 (LeDiv 95), Paris 1977.

Müller, K. 1973: "Die Ansätze der Apokalyptik", in: *Literatur und Religion des Frühjudentums*, ed by J. Maier und J. Schreiner, Würzburg/Gütersloh 1973, 36–42.

– 1978: "Die jüdische Apokalyptik. Anfänge und Merkmale", in: *TRE* (1978) 202–251.

Mussner, F. 1964: "Die Armenfrömmigkeit des Jakobusbriefes", in: *Der Jakobusbrief* (HThK XIII, 1), Freiburg 1964, 76–84.

Nickelsburg, G. W. 1977: "The Apocalyptic Message of 1 Enoch 92–105", in: *CBQ* 39 (1977) 309–328.

– 1978: "Riches, the Rich and God's Judgement in I Enoch 92–105 and the Gospel according to Luke", in: *NTS* 25 (1978) 324–344.

Nissen, A. 1967: "Tora und Geschichte im Spätjudentum", in: *NT* 9 (1967) 241–277.

Otto, E. 1954: *Die biographischen Inschriften der ägyptischen Spätzeit* (PÄ 2), Leiden 1954.

– 1964: *Gott und Mensch nach den ägyptischen Tempelinschriften der griech.-röm. Zeit* (AHAW.PH), Heidelberg 1964.

– 1971: "Gott als Retter in Ägypten", in: *Tradition und Glaube, Festschrift K. G. Kuhn*, Göttingen 1971, 9–22.

Pfeiffer, R. 1970: *Geschichte der klassischen Philologie von den Anfängen bis zum Ende des Hellenismus*. (Aus d. Engl. v. M. Arnold), Reinbek bei Hamburg 1970.

Porten, B./Greenfield, J. C. 1968: "The Aramaic Papyri from Hermoupolis", in: *ZAW* 80 (1968) 216–231.

Peterson, E. 1959: "Einige Beobachtungen zu den Anfängen der christlichen Askese", in: *Frühkirche, Judentum und Gnosis*, Freiburg 1959, 209–220.

Plöger, O. 1965: *Das Buch Daniel* (KAT 18), Gütersloh 1965.

Rau, E. 1974: *Kosmologie, Eschatologie und Lehrautorität Henochs*. Traditions- und formgeschichtliche Untersuchungen zum äthiopischen Henochbuch und zu verwandten Schriften, Diss. Hamburg 1974.

Reicke, B. 1960: "Official and Pietistic Elements of Jewish Apocalypticism", in: *JBL* 79 (1960) 137–150.

Ringgren, H. 1957: "Jüdische Apokalyptik", in: *RGG*³ I, 464–466.

Rössler, D. 1962: *Gesetz und Geschichte*. Untersuchungen zur Theologie der jüdischen Apokalyptik und der pharisäischen Orthodoxie² (WMANT 3), Neukirchen/Vluyn 1962.

Rowley, H. H. 1963: *The Relevance of Apocalyptic*. New and Revised Edition, London 1963.

Scaliger, J. J. 1658: *Thesaurus Temporum*. Animadversiones in Chronologica Eusebii², Paris 1658. (Nach Scaligers hinterlassenen Aufzeichnungen verbesserte Auflage seines in erster Auflage 1606 in Leiden erschienenen Werks.)

Schmidt, J. M. 1969a: "Forschung zur jüdischen Apokalyptik", in: *VF* 14 (1969) 44–69.

– 1969b: *Die jüdische Apokalyptik*. Die Geschichte ihrer Erforschung von den Anfängen bis zu den Textfunden von Qumran, Neukirchen/Vluyn 1969.

Schreiner, J. 1969: *Alttestamentlich-jüdische Apokalyptik*, München 1969.

Stiassny, J. 1977: "L'occultation de l'apocalyptique dans le rabbinisme", in: Monloubou (Ed.) 1977, 179–203.

Stone, M. E. 1968: "The Conception of the Messiah in IV Ezra", in: J. Neusner, *Religions in Antiquity* (NumenSup 14), Leiden 1968, 295–312.

– 1978: "The Book of Enoch and Judaism in the Third Century B.C.E.", in: *CBQ* 40 (1978) 479–492.

Strathmann, H. 1950: "Askese I (nichtchristlich)", in: *RAC* I (1950) 749–758.

Stricker, B. 1967–1971: "De praehelleense ascese", in: *OMRM* 48 (1967) 44–55; 49 (1968) 18–39; 50 (1969) 8–16; 52 (1971) 54–70.

Thiering, B. 1974: "The Biblical Source of Qumran Asceticism", in: *JBL* 93 (1974) 429–449.

Vejnberg, J. P. 1973: "Probleme der sozialökonomischen Struktur Judäas vom 6. Jh. v. u. Z. bis zum 1. Jh. n. u. Z.", in: *JWG* 1973/I, 237–251.

Vielhauer, P. 1964: "Apokalypsen und Verwandtes. Einleitung", in: *NTApo*³ 2, Tübingen 1964, 407–427.

Wißmann, H. 1973: "Armut I; Religionsgeschichtlich", in: *TRE* IV (1979) 69–72.

L'apocalyptique qoumrânienne

Marc Philonenko

1. Eschatologie et apocalyptique: Essai de définition

L'eschatologie et l'apocalyptique juives ont fait l'objet d'études, tenues aujourd'hui encore pour classiques. On trouvera, par exemple, dans les ouvrages de Bousset[1] et de Volz[2] de remarquables synthèses qui font appel à toutes les sources anciennes et fondent dans un même ensemble écrits intertestamentaires et textes rabbiniques[3]. La méthode, légitime en son temps, soulève de graves objections.

1.1. Ces matériaux, en effet, proviennent de milieux très différents, voire opposés. Le fait qu'ils nous soient parvenus par des filières séparées, juives pour les textes rabbiniques, chrétiennes pour les écrits intertestamentaires, mérite, à cet égard, de retenir l'attention.

Si les écrits intertestamentaires ont été écartés par le judaïsme rabbinique, c'est qu'ils lui étaient étrangers. S'ils ont été, au contraire, retenus par certaines églises chrétiennes, le plus souvent marginales, c'est qu'ils avaient avec elles comme une parenté. Cette situation reflète une situation plus ancienne, qui est celle du judaïsme à l'époque hellénistique et romaine, marquée par l'opposition du pharisaïsme et de l'essénisme.

Nombre des écrits intertestamentaires doivent être rattachés à l'essénisme[4], d'autres sont à situer dans sa mouvance, quelques-uns ont sans nul doute une autre origine. Mais que l'on nous comprenne bien! Quand nous parlons d'essénisme, nous pensons à un mouvement mystique qui a connu une longue histoire et des tendances diverses et qui avait réussi à s'implanter non seulement en Palestine, mais au dehors.

Il faut rappeler, enfin, que les écrits intertestamentaires nous ont été transmis par des copistes chrétiens, le plus souvent en traduction ou en traduction de traduction. On s'explique dès lors que la critique ait trop souvent cru déceler dans cette littérature adaptations, remaniements ou

---

[1] Bousset-Gressmann 1926.   [2] Volz 1934.
[3] Volz 1934, 4: "Neben der rabbinischen Theologie ist die Hauptfundgrube für jüdische Eschatologie die apokalyptische Literatur."
[4] Voir Dupont-Sommer 1950, 115–116.

interpolations. Il suffit ici de mentionner les discussions serrées sur le livre des *Paraboles* ou les *Testaments des Douze Patriarches*.

Avec la bibliothèque de Qoumrân, nous nous trouvons dans des conditions très différentes. L'authenticité des manuscrits découverts dans le désert de Juda est incontestable. Nous avons là des documents qui nous ont été conservés dans leur langue originale, l'hébreu ou l'araméen, et qui doivent être attribués à un même milieu essénien. Ces manuscrits constituent un ensemble d'une remarquable homogénéité, ce qui ne signifie nullement uniformité doctrinale et terminologique. Ils montrent plutôt, dans la diversité de leurs genres littéraires, une grande richesse de doctrines. Cette constatation s'applique parfaitement, on le verra, à l'apocalyptique.

1.2. Pour lever toute équivoque, indiquons que nous entendons par "apocalyptique" une "révélation" qui porte non seulement sur la fin du monde, les signes qui l'annoncent, les catastrophes qui l'accompagnent, mais encore sur les origines de l'homme et du monde. Nous distinguons, dès lors, l'apocalyptique de l'eschatologie qui s'intéresse seulement à la fin de l'homme – pris dans son destin singulier ou collectif – et à la fin du monde[5].

Les deux concepts d'eschatologie et d'apocalyptique se recoupent donc, mais ne se confondent pas. L'apocalyptique reprend des matériaux mis en oeuvre dans l'eschatologie, mais elle ne considère l'homme que dans la mesure où son sort est lié à celui de l'humanité toute entière et du monde. Il n'y a pas d'apocalyptique individuelle.

L'eschatologie, toute entière retenue par la fin de l'homme et du monde, ne revient pas sur le problèmes des origines. Il n'y a pas d'eschatologie des commencements.

C'est dire qu'une eschatologie sans apocalyptique est possible, mais qu'il n' y a pas d'apocalyptique sans eschatologie[6].

1.3. On ne se propose pas ici de faire un tableau complet de l'apocalyptique qoumrânienne, mais d'en montrer des aspects essentiels à partir de trois documents particuliers, l'"Instruction sur les Deux Esprits", le *Règlement de la Guerre des Fils de Lumière*, le texte sur Melchisédék.

2. L'"Instruction sur les Deux Esprits"

Le rouleau de la *Règle* nous a transmis une catéchèse d'une grande densité doctrinale, l'"Instruction sur les Deux Esprits"[7]. Cette catéchèse, qui a du connaître une existence indépendante, a exercé une influence considérable, tant sur la littérature qoumrânienne proprement dite, que sur d'autres écrits

---

[5] Cf. Widengren 1969, 440–441.   [6] Cf. Goguel 1946, 296.

[7] *Règle* (1 QS) 3,13–4,26. Nous citerons les textes de Qoumrân dans les traductions de Dupont-Sommer 1964.

esséniens, tels les *Testaments des Douze Patriarches*, ou chrétiens, comme la *Didachè*, l'*Epître de Barnabas* et le *Pasteur d'Hermas*.

2.1. Le préambule indique d'emblée le caractère "apocalyptique" de l'"Instruction" qui traite de "la nature de tous les fils d'homme" et de la "Visite" (פקודה) qui leur est réservée[8]. L'auteur de l'"Instruction" dit de Dieu qu'

"Il a créé l'homme
pour qu'il eût l'empire sur la terre.
Et Il a disposé pour l'homme deux Esprits
pour qu'il marchât en eux jusqu'au moment de Sa Visite"[9].

Ainsi se trouve définie la nature de l'homme dans le cadre de l'histoire du monde.

2.2. L'"Instruction" articule l'histoire de ces deux Esprits dans l'homme et dans le monde en trois temps.

Le premier temps est celui de la création de l'homme et des deux Esprits, car le point est capital et fermement établi par l'"Instruction": "Oui, c'est Lui qui a créé les (deux) Esprits de lumière et de ténèbres"[10].

2.3. Le moment présent est celui du mélange. Les deux Esprits sont, en effet, également répartis dans le monde[11], mais ils sont mêlés dans le coeur de chaque homme en des proportions variables[12], si bien que tout homme appartient nécessairement au lot des ténèbres ou au lot de la lumière. Ces deux camps s'affrontent en une lutte farouche. L'Ange des ténèbres et les esprits de son lot font trébucher les fils de lumière[13] que Dieu et son Ange de Vérité relèvent sans cesse[14].

2.4. Le troisième temps est celui de la Visite eschatologique (פקודה). Le mélange de l'Esprit du Bien et de l'Esprit du Mal prend fin par l'extermination de la Perversité[15].

Le *Livre des Mystères*, très proche ici de l'"Instruction", évoque en des formules qui paraissent faire écho à la liturgie du Nouvel An ces temps ultimes:

"Alors l'Impiété se retirera devant la Justice,
de même que les [té]nèbres se retirent devant la lumière;
et de même que la fumée s'évanouit et n' e[xiste] plus,
de même l'Impiété s'évanouira pour toujours,
et la Justice se montrera comme le soleil, norme du monde"[16].

---

[8] *Règle* (1 QS) 3,13–15.
[9] *Règle* (1 QS) 3,17–18.
[10] *Règle* (1 QS) 3,25–26.
[11] *Règle* (1 QS) 4,16–17.
[12] Voir le texte d'un horoscope découvert dans la grotte IV et publié par Allegro 1964, 291–294. Cf. Dupont-Sommer 1966, 239–253; rapprocher Philon, *Quaestiones in Exodum*, I, 23.
[13] *Règle* (1 QS) 3,21–24.
[14] *Règle* (1 QS) 3,24–25.
[15] *Règle* (1 QS) 4,18–19.
[16] *Livre des Mystères* (1 Q27) 1,6–7.

C'est bien là le "terme décisif" de l'histoire du monde, celui du "Renouvellement"[17]. Pour reprendre les termes de l'"Apocalypse" de l'Asclepius, c'est "un renouvellement de toutes les choses bonnes" (*cunctarum reformatio rerum bonarum*), "une restauration sainte et toute solennelle de la nature" (*naturae ipsius sanctissima et religiosissima restitutio*)[18].

Le livre des *Hymnes* décrit la fin des temps comme une conflagration générale. Un déluge infernal de flots enflammés extermine tout sur son passage[19]. C'est la doctrine qu'Hippolyte prête aux Esséniens: "Ils déclarent qu'il y aura un jugement et une conflagration de l'Univers (τοῦ παντὸς ἐκπύρωσιν) que les injustes seront châtiés à jamais"[20].

2.5. L'"Instruction sur les Deux Esprits" a intégré dans sa vision de l'histoire du monde des éléments propres à une eschatologie individuelle. Deux textes parallèles envisagent le sort des justes et des méchants dans ce monde et dans l'autre.

Le premier texte[21] énumère d'abord les récompenses terrestres promises aux justes: "guérison"[22], "abondance du bonheur", "longueur de jours"[23], "fécondité"[24], puis les récompenses éternelles: "joie éternelle"[25], "vie perpétuelle"[26], "couronne glorieuse"[27], "vêtement d'honneur"[28] "dans l'éternelle lumière"[29]. On notera l'absence de toute allusion à la résurrection.

Il est vraisemblable que nous avons là les éléments d'une eschatologie individuelle qui envisage la destinée du juste immédiatement après la mort.

Le second texte[30] dit les châtiments éternels réservés aux méchants, sans paraître faire mention de châtiments reçus ici-bas: "coups qu'administrent les anges de destruction"[31] "en la Fosse éternelle"[31a], "effroi perpétuel", "honte sans fin", "extermination par le feu des régions ténébreuses"[32].

Ce sont là les éléments d'une eschatologie qui envisage la destinée du méchant après la mort.

2.6. Cette eschatologie individuelle ne s'intègre pas parfaitement dans le schéma apocalyptique de l'"Instruction", tel que nous l'avons dégagé. Très caractéristique à cet égard, est la double acception que paraît prendre le

---

[17] *Règle* (1 QS) 4,25. Comparer *Jubilés* 1,29; *IV Esras* 7,75; *II Baruch* 32,6; *Liber Antiquitatum Biblicarum* 16,3; *Apocalypse d'Abraham* 17,14.

[18] *Asclepius* 26 (traduction A.-J. Festugière).

[19] *Hymnes* (1 QH) 3,28–36. Comparer *Vie d'Adam et Eve* 49; *Oracles Sibyllins* III, 84–85; IV, 172; *Asclepius* 26.

[20] Hippolyte, *Réfutation*, 9,27.   [21] *Règle* (1 QS) 4,6–8.

[22] Comparer *I Hénoch* 10,7; 96,3; *Jubilés* 1,29; 23,29.   [23] Comparer *I Hénoch* 5,9.

[24] Comparer *I Hénoch* 10,17.   [25] Comparer *I Hénoch* 5,7.

[26] Comparer *Ecrit de Damas* (CD) 3,20; *I Hénoch* 40,9; 58,3; *II Hénoch* 42,3; 65,9; *Psaumes de Salomon* 3,12; *Testament d'Aser* 5,2.

[27] *Testament de Benjamin* 4,1; *Ascension d'Esaïe* 9,24–25.   [28] Comparer *I Hénoch* 62,15–16.

[29] Comparer *I Hénoch* 92,4.   [30] *Règle* (1 QS) 4,11–14.

[31] Comparer *Ecrit de Damas* (CD) 2,6.   [31a] Comparer *IV Esdras* 7,36.

[32] Comparer *I Hénoch* 103,8; *Testament de Zabulon* 10,3; *Oracles Sibyllins* III, 507.

terme technique פקודה, "Visite", qui désigne tantôt la "Visite" eschatologique[33], tantôt la rétribution promise aux justes ou aux injustes[34].

Le thème de la Visite eschatologique appelle l'idée d'une période intermédiaire. Aucune précision n'est explicitement donnée sur cette période dans l'"Instruction". On peut cependant supposer que l'auteur place implicitement les récompenses promises aux justes après la mort dans cette période.

C'est au jour du jugement que les justes seront purifiés "par l'Esprit de sainteté de tous les actes d'impiété" qu'ils ont pu commettre[35]. Ils accéderont alors à la connaissance angélique et auront enfin la connaissance des mystères du Très-Haut[36].

Quant aux méchants, livrés après leur mort à des châtiments "éternels" dans la Fosse infernale, au jour où la période intermédiaire prendra fin, ils seront exterminés avec la Perversité et l'Impiété qui les habitaient[37].

2.7. Ce jour, tant attendu par les justes, redouté par les impies, nul ne sait quand il viendra. L'auteur du *Commentaire d'Habacuc* commente ainsi le texte du prophète: "Si elle tarde, attends-la; car elle viendra certainement et elle ne sera pas en retard"[38], par: "L'explication de ceci concerne les hommes de vérité, ceux qui pratiquent la Loi, dont les mains ne se relâchent pas au service de la Vérité, quand est reculé pour eux le temps ultime; car tous les temps de Dieu arrivent lors de leur terme, conformément à ce qu'Il a décrété à leur sujet dans les Mystères de sa Prudence"[39].

3. Le Règlement de la Guerre des Fils de Lumière

Le *Règlement de la Guerre des Fils de Lumière contre les Fils de Ténèbres* développe dans toute son ampleur un thème qui n'avait pas été abordé de front dans l'"Instruction sur les Deux Esprits", celui de la grande guerre eschatologique.

Aux derniers jours, les fils de lumière, c'est-à-dire les Esséniens eux-mêmes et les anges des cieux, toutes forces confondues, écraseront les fils de ténèbres, impies et païens rassemblés, et tout particulièrement les Kittim.

3.1. Le *Règlement* apporte d'importants renseignements sur le déroulement de la Guerre qui éclatera au jour fixé par Dieu depuis toujours. La guerre durera 40 ans. Ces 40 ans se répartissent comme suit: d'abord 6 années de préparation suivies d'une première année de moratoire; puis 33

---

[33] Cf. *Règle* (1 QS) 3,18; 4,19.   [34] Cf. *Règle* (1 QS) 3,14; 4,6; 4,11.
[35] *Règle* (1 QS), 4,21. Comparer Tite 3,5.   [36] *Règle* (1 QS) 4,22.
[37] Comparer *I Hénoch* 22,4.14; *Liber Antiquitatum Biblicarum* 46,3.
[38] *Habacuc* II,3.   [39] *Commentaire d'Habacuc* (1 QpHab) 7,10–14.

autres années de guerre; ces 33 années comportent nécessairement 4 années de moratoire; il reste donc 29 années effectives de campagne[40].

3.2. La guerre comprendra sept phases[41]. Durant trois lots, les fils de lumière seront les plus forts; durant trois autres lots, l'armée de Bélial aura l'avantage; dans le septième lot, "la grande Main de Dieu" soumettra les fils de ténèbres aux fils de lumière. Puisque la dernière phase est celle du triomphe des fils de lumière, il s'en suit que la première phase des hostilités est également ouverte par les fils de lumière, auxquels revient donc l'initiative de la guerre.

La victoire est remportée par "la grande Main de Dieu"[42], mais d'autres textes qoumrâniens l'attribuent au Prince de la Congrégation[43].

3.3. Le *Règlement* annonce en termes lyriques ces jours de gloire:

"Alors [les fils de just]ice éclaireront toutes les extrémités du monde,
de façon progressive, jusqu'à ce que soient consommés tous les moments des ténèbres.
Puis, au moment de Dieu, Sa sublime grandeur brillera
durant tous les temps [des siècles] pour le bonheur et la bénédiction;
la gloire et la joie et la longueur de jours
(seront données) à tous les fils de lumière"[44].

Les récompenses promises aux fils de lumière victorieux en cette ultime bataille retrouvent ainsi celles que l'"Instruction sur les Deux Esprits" réservaient aux justes. Les Ténèbres s'effacent définitivement devant la Lumière. La paix règne sur toute la terre[45].

4. 11 Q Melchisédék

Un texte de la grotte XI présente sous des traits extraordinaires, Melchisédék, le roi-prêtre de Salem, auquel, selon *Genèse* XIV, Abraham remit la dîme de tous ses biens[46].

En dépit des lacunes du manuscrit, Melchisédék apparaît là comme le Maître de l'an de grâce, le chef des anges qui exercera la vengeance des jugements de Dieu et délivrera les captifs de la main de Bélial.

4.1. On n'a pas remarqué que la version des Septante de *Daniel* 8,11 atteste de façon concise, certes, mais parfaitement explicite de semblables espérances placées en un grand ange qui délivrera les captifs ($\dot{\epsilon}\omega\varsigma$ $\dot{o}$ $\dot{\alpha}\varrho\chi\iota\sigma\tau\varrho\acute{\alpha}\tau\eta\gamma\varsigma$ $\dot{\varrho}\acute{\upsilon}\sigma\epsilon\tau\alpha\iota$ $\tau\grave{\eta}\nu$ $\alpha\dot{\iota}\chi\mu\alpha\lambda\omega\sigma\acute{\iota}\alpha\nu$)[47].

4.2. On dit de même dans le *Testament de Zabulon* 9,8:

---

[40] *Règlement de la Guerre* (1 QM) 2,9–10.
[41] *Règlement de la Guerre* (1 QM) 1,13–14.
[42] *Règlement de la Guerre* (1 QM) 1,14.
[43] *Ecrit de Damas* (CD) 7,20–21; *Livre des Bénédictions* (1 QSb) 5,20–29.
[44] *Règlement de la Guerre* (1 QM) 1,8–9.   [45] *Testament de Lévi* 18,4.
[46] Voir l'édition de Milik 1972, 95–144.
[47] Texte pourtant cité par Bousset-Gressmann 1926, 327 et par Volz 1934, 199.

"Et, après cela, se lèvera pour vous le Seigneur lui-même, lumière de justice,
et la guérison et la compassion seront dans ses ailes.
C'est lui qui délivrera de Béliar toute la captivité des fils des hommes,
et tout esprit d'égarement sera foulé aux pieds"[48].

4.3. Il y a plus. Le texte sur Melchisédék fait, semble-t-il, allusion au
Maître de justice dont il place la prédication au début du dixième et dernier
jubilé, soit une quarantaine d'années avant l'événement final[49]. Il est tentant
de rapprocher cette période d'environ 40 ans de la période de 40 ans fixée
par le *Règlement* pour la durée de la guerre eschatologique.
Or, l'*Ecrit de Damas* précise que

"Depuis le jour où fut enlevé le Maître unique
jusqu'à ce qu'aient été supprimés tous les combattants
qui sont retournés [a]vec l'Homme de mensonge,
(il y aura) environ quarante ans"[50].

4.4. On est ainsi amené à établir un lien entre la grande Guerre et la mort
du Maître de justice. Sans doute faut-il admettre que, dans les esprits
enfiévrés de certains sectaires du désert de Juda, la mort du Maître avait été
le signal des combats eschatologiques.

5. Conclusion

L'étude de l'"Instruction sur les deux Esprits", du *Règlement de la Guerre*
et du texte sur Melchisédék n'épuise pas toute la richesse de l'apocalyptique
qoumrânienne, mais elle en révèle certaines variantes qu'il serait vain de
tenter d'harmoniser. Ces variations s'expliquent sans doute par les orienta-
tions prises par différents docteurs sur un thème où l'imagination pouvait se
donner libre cours. Elles s'expliquent surtout par la volonté d'intégrer, à
une vision apocalyptique de l'histoire du monde, l'histoire de la secte et de
son fondateur, le Maître de justice dont on pleurait la disparition brutale et
dont on attendait l'éventuel retour.

Bibliographie

Allegro, John Marco 1964: "An Astrological Cryptic Document from Qumran", dans: *JSSt* 9 (1964), 291–294.
Bousset, Wilhelm–Gressmann, Hugo 1926: *Die Religion des Judentums*[3] (HNT 26), Tübingen 1926.
Caquot, André 1973: "Résumé des cours de 1972–1973", dans: *Annuaire du Collège de France*, Paris 1973.

---

[48] Voir aussi *Testament de Dan* 5,10–11.
[49] Cf. Caquot 1973, 389.   [50] *Ecrit de Damas* (CD) B 2,13–15.

Dupont-Sommer, André 1950: *Aperçus préliminaires sur les manuscrits de la mer Morte*, Paris 1950.
- 1964: *Les écrits esséniens découverts près de la mer Morte*[3], Paris 1964.
- 1966: "Deux documents horoscopiques esséniens découverts à Qoumrân, près de la mer Morte", dans: *Comptes rendus des séances de l'Académie des Inscriptions et Belles-Lettres* (1966) 239–253.
Goguel, Maurice 1946: *La naissance du christianisme*, Paris 1946.
Milik, J. T. 1972: "Milkî-sedeq et Milkî-resa dans les anciens écrits juifs et chrétiens", dans: *JJS* 23 (1972) 95–144.
Volz, Paul 1934: *Die Eschatologie der jüdischen Gemeinde*, Tübingen 1934.
Widengren, Geo 1969: *Religionsphänomenologie*, Berlin 1969.

Sur quelques aspects des Oracles Sibyllins juifs

Marcel Simon

1. Introduction

Parmi l'ample littérature apocalyptique juive qui fleurit aux approches et au début de l'ère chrétienne, les trois Livres Sibyllins unanimement reconnus pour juifs représentent sans doute ce que la Diaspora de langue grecque a produit de plus profondément hellénisé, dans la forme et dans l'esprit[1]. Les auteurs anonymes de ces écrits se dissimulent sous le masque des voyantes païennes; ils utilisent le prestige durable dont bénéficient les Sibylles dans tout le monde méditerranéen et le mettent au service du Dieu unique qui leur dicte leur message. Ils connaissent la technique et le contenu des Oracles Sibyllins païens et n'hésitent pas à leur emprunter certains éléments. Ils sont familiarisés avec la littérature profane et avec les règles de la versification traditionnelle. Les récits mythologiques côtoient ici les épisodes bibliques, ou plutôt s'amalgament avec eux. En dépit des nombreux travaux suscités par ces curieux documents[2], la lumière est loin d'être faite sur des textes caractérisés par une épithète qui, dans la langue de tous les jours, au moins en français, est synonyme d'obscur et de mystérieux. Je ne prétends faire plus ici que souligner quelques points et proposer quelques réflexions, avec le seul espoir de clarifier un peu le débat.

2. Objet des Oracles Sibyllins

Et tout d'abord, à qui s'adressent ces oracles? Il me paraît difficile de souscrire à l'opinion de Tcherikover, qui y voit les instruments d'une "propagande parmi des Juifs et pour des Juifs tellement influencés par la littérature grecque qu'ils placent l'hellénisme au-dessus de la Torah et des prophètes d'Israël"[3]. C'est là restreindre indûment le champ d'action de ce genre d'écrits. Il est arbitraire – tout aussi bien que pour Philon – de poser la

---

[1] Livres III, IV et V (quelques interpolations chrétiennes). Edition classique de Geffcken 1902; trad. allemande (Blass) dans Kautsch, APAT, II, 1900; trad. anglaise de Charles, APOT, II, 1913.

[2] Entre autres Kurfess 1951; Nikiprowetzky 1970; Collins 1974.

[3] Cité par Avi-Yonah et Baras I, 1977, 8.

question des destinataires sous forme de dilemme: soit les païens, soit les Juifs, et de séparer trop radicalement ces deux publics. En fait, ils sont visés l'un et l'autre. Il s'agit bien, d'une part, de fortifier dans leur foi des coreligionnaires largement ouverts à la culture grecque et séduits par elle; mais l'objectif poursuivi est en même temps de gagner à cette foi des Gentils en mal de vérité. On ne saurait, pour comprendre ces textes, faire abstraction de la préoccupation missionnaire: l'apocalyptique, ici, est également et peut-être surtout littérature prosélytique. L'évocation des catastrophes annonciatrices de la fin est, fondamentalement, un appel à la conversion des peuples. Ce motif revient à satiété dans les trois Livres. En particulier il constitue comme la trame du Troisième, dans sa seconde moitié (543–656; 732–742; 762–795). Si nos Oracles se présentent comme les vaticinations des Sibylles, il est clair que ce subterfuge pseudépigraphique impressionnera en priorité le lecteur païen. Pour un Juif, si marqué soit-il par le milieu culturel ambiant, le témoignage de la Sibylle ne doit normalement que confirmer et renforcer celui de la Bible, en illustrant une convergence providentielle entre deux courants issus l'un et l'autre de la même inspiration divine: "Teste David cum Sibylla" chantait la liturgie latine du catholicisme, évoquant dans le *Dies Irae* les drames ultimes[4].

2.1. La destination en partie et vraisemblablement en priorité païenne des Oracles est soulignée par la mention, tantôt hostile, tantôt et plus souvent apitoyée, dans chacun des trois Livres, de différentes régions ou villes du monde méditerranéen et proche-asiatique. Les réactions de la voyante, de haine ou de sympathie, varient d'un pays ou d'une cité et aussi d'un livre à l'autre, et l'on a parfois essayé de tirer de ces différences des indices touchant le *Sitz im Leben* de chacun d'eux. Il est cependant à peu près certain que les trois Livres sont d'origine alexandrine. Les différences que l'on relève de l'un à l'autre tiennent sans doute d'une part à l'utilisation de sources d'origine géographique différente; mais en tout état de cause, les cités et régions nommées sont probablement celles où existait un noyau assez important de population juive et où le message, du fait de contacts entre Juifs et païens, avait quelque chance d'être entendu. Les trois écrits n'ont en commun que deux réactions vraiment fondamentales: une égale haine pour Rome, un égal amour pour le peuple élu.

Cette constante que représente la haine de Rome permet d'intégrer nos écrits, bien qu'à une place très spéciale, dans le vaste courant de résistance spirituelle qui traverse le monde antique assujetti[5]. En particulier on a fait très justement remarquer le nombre considérable d'oracles anti-romains répandus dans les régions d'Asie Mineure et de Syrie[6]. Et précisément, le

---

[4] Sur les affinités et les différences entre apocalyptique et eschatologie, Rowley 1947, 23, n. 3.

[5] Cf. Fuchs 1938.   [6] Hengel 1973, 339–340.

Troisième Livre et le Quatrième, en décrivant la revanche divine sur l'arrogance de Rome, signalent que celle-ci devra restituer à l'Asie tout ce qu'elle lui a pris, et davantage encore: trois fois autant selon le Troisième, deux fois et plus selon le Quatrième (III, 250; IV, 145 SS.). Il faut certainement entendre par Asie la partie la plus hellénisée de ce continent, essentiellement l'Asie Mineure, avec laquelle nos auteurs se sentent liés par un commun attachement à la culture grecque.

2.2. Unanimes contre les Romains, les sentiments des Sibylles sont cependant complexes vis-à-vis des pays conquis. A coup sûr, les malheurs qui se sont abattus, s'abattent ou s'abattront sur les nations païennes constituent toujours le châtiment mérité de leurs péchés, parmi lesquels l'idolâtrie, avec le cortège de fautes de caractère moral qui en sont le fatal accompagnement, est le plus universel et le plus grave. Mais ces châtiments suscitent, selon le cas, dans nos textes, et sans qu'il soit possible de discerner clairement les raisons de ces différences, soit la pitié, soit une véritable *Schadenfreude*. Au reste, les Juifs aussi ont péché et méritent ainsi cette punition que représente la ruine du Temple: celle du premier Temple pour la Troisième Sibylle, qui vaticine avant 70, celle du second pour les deux autres, mais avec des nuances sensibles de l'une à l'autre. De ce fait, sans que la voyante oublie jamais la distance qui sépare le peuple élu des nations impies, comme le premier a souffert de par la volonté divine, par la main des Romains, qui seront à leur tour et plus durement encore, bien qu'ils aient été l'instrument de la Providence, punis de leurs forfaits, une certaine solidarité se crée dans le malheur entre Israël et le reste du monde asservi. Le Quatrième Livre ne mentionne Jérusalem et les malheurs de la Judée que très brièvement et comme en passant, dans un long couplet, très attendri, sur les principales villes grecques, menacées elles aussi de terribles calamités, entre "la pauvre Corinthe" et "la pauvre Antioche" (IV, 105–140; sur Jérusalem, quatre vers seulement: 115–118). Le Cinquième Livre, tout en pleurant sur "la malheureuse Hellas" et en énumérant les villes de l'Hellespont et de l'Asie Mineure, de l'Archipel et de la Grèce propre, s'intéresse aussi à l'Egypte. Il déplore d'avoir à lui annoncer de terribles malheurs, alors qu'il faudrait vaticiner bien plutôt contre la race stupide des Perses, que les catastrophes à venir n'épargneront pas (V, 111–114). C'est vraiment un écho d'un passé dont notre auteur se sent spirituellement tributaire qui s'exprime dans cette allusion à l'ennemi traditionnel de l'hellénisme. Rome aussi a recueilli sur ce point les inimitiés héréditaires de la Grèce. Il y a, dans la littérature grecque et latine, même relativement tardive, de nombreuses allusions malveillantes et hostiles aux "barbares" perses (Philon, *Leg. ad Gaium*, 116; Firmicus Maternus, *De er. profan. relig.*, 5, 2; Eusèbe, *Hist. Eccl.*, 7, 31; Ammien Marcellin, *Hist.*, 23, 6). Elle contient par surcroît la menace perse, mais au prix, pour les régions ainsi protégées, d'une tyrannie insupportable. La Perse n'est guère qu'un mauvais souvenir, Rome est l'oppresseur toujours présent.

3. Problèmes de datation

Ainsi qu'il est habituel dans ce genre de littérature, les perspectives sont fréquemment brouillées. Comme le rappelle fort justement V. Nikiprowetzky à propos de la Troisième Sibylle, "c'est s'exposer aux mécomptes les plus graves que de refuser de prendre en considération le caractère souvent *inactuel* des oracles qui y sont rassemblés. La prophétesse prend soin de nous avertir elle-même que ses paroles retracent l'histoire véridique et du passé et de l'avenir"[7]. Plus généralement, en considérant l'ensemble des trois Livres, on constate souvent que le passé et l'avenir s'enchevêtrent en un écheveau confus. D'autre part, comme la Sibylle est censée parler aux origines lointaines de l'humanité, le passé peut, avec le futur, être englobé dans ses prévisions. Comme par surcroît l'histoire ne se renouvelle jamais sous des formes totalement différentes mais comporte des récurrences et des répétitions de faits et d'épisodes identiques ou du moins très analogues, le passé sert en quelque sorte de point d'appui et de garant au futur. Si la "prophétie" s'est vérifiée en ce qui concerne les évènements révolus, il y a là une raison de croire qu'il en ira de même pour les choses à venir. L'histoire se découpe en périodes qui, à intervalles plus ou moins longs, présentent de singulières affinités jusqu'à être parfois presque superposables. C'est une des constantes de l'apocalyptique, et en particulier des Oracles Sibyllins juifs, que ce recours à cette succession d'âges de l'humanité et d'Empires organiquement unis par des liens mystérieux: cf. p. ex. III, 158–161; IV, 47–106[8].

3.1. Un exemple particulièrement net de cette vision des choses réside dans l'usage que la Sibylle fait des dynasties souveraines, de leurs divers représentants, et aussi des triades impériales, qu'il s'agisse de princes antagonistes, associés ou successifs. Le procédé apparaît avec une particulière netteté dans le Cinquième Livre, où ces personnages sont identifiés de façon transparente, à partir de César, par la valeur numérique, en grec, de leurs initiales. Une fois brièvement caractérisés les différents Julio-Claudiens, il est dit qu'après celui qui a pour lettre N (cinquante), soit Néron, "trois rois se détruiront réciproquement": il s'agit, bien évidemment, de Galba, Othon et Vitellius (V, 34). Les trois Flaviens sont sommairement stigmatisés, sans être désignés autrement que par le nombre impliqué dans leur nom (V, 35–39). A cette double triade, la première simultanée et autodestructrice, la seconde constituée de trois princes successifs et étroite-

---

[7] Nikiprowetzky 1970, à propos de III, 819 ss.   [8] Rowley 1947, 35 ss.

ment apparentés, l'une et l'autre de mauvais renom aux yeux de la voyante, succède une nouvelle série de deux fois trois princes qui, dans un tableau peint en noir et blanc et conforme à la lutte que se livrent tout au long des siècles les forces du mal et du bien, alternativement victorieuses, ne sauraient être que bons.

Sur la première de ces triades aucune hésitation n'est possible: Nerva, Trajan et Hadrien, toujours sans être nommés, sont qualifiés de façon parfaitement reconnaissable, et élogieuse (V, 41–49). En revanche, pour ce qui est des trois princes suivants, rien ne les caractérise, rien ne permet d'en deviner les noms. Cette seconde triade, bienfaisante selon toute apparence semble faire en quelque sorte pendant à la triade sanglante Galba, Othon, Vitellius, de même que les trois premiers Antonins s'opposent aux trois Flaviens, qu'un Juif peut et doit englober dans une commune réprobation. Si l'on reconnaît assez communément dans la dernière triade, présentée de manière impersonnelle, Antonin, Marc Aurèle et Lucius Verus, c'est, faute de tout point d'appui dans le texte même, en raisonnant à partir de données historiques fournies par toutes nos autres sources, ce qui ne va pas sans poser un délicat problème de datation.

3.2. Si l'on admet que l'ensemble de ce couplet dynastique fait partie intégrante du livre, et donc qu'il est juif, on comprend mal l'éloge d'Hadrien, directement apostrophé comme "très excellent, très noble" (V, 49), à moins de situer la rédaction de l'ouvrage au plus tard vers 130, avant la seconde guerre de Judée et la construction d'Aelia Capitolina. On pourrait supposer aussi que toute cette spéculation dynastique est un élément surajouté. Mais un païen n'avait aucune raison de dénoncer en Vespasien l'exterminateur des Juifs; un Chrétien ne l'aurait sans doute pas fait non plus en termes aussi abrupts.

Il est donc particulièrement difficile de dater notre texte: début du règne d'Hadrien, ou règne d'Antonin. La première datation a l'avantage de placer l'ouvrage à un moment où Hadrien n'a rien fait encore pour s'attirer la haine des Juifs, et peut donc être salué avec enthousiasme par la Sibylle. Si au contraire il faut reculer le texte jusque sous Antonin ou l'un de ses successeurs, on s'étonne qu'il ne dise rien du tout de ces personnages, et maintienne sans retouches le couplet à la gloire d'Hadrien. Nous inclinons assez naturellement à reconnaître dans ces trois anonymes ceux que nous savons avoir exercé le pouvoir après Hadrien. Mais il se peut tout aussi bien que l'auteur, écrivant sous Hadrien avant la guerre juive, ait tout simplement, pour prolonger un peu les perspectives, avancé ce chiffre de trois qui lui était familier, et qui ne lui faisait courir aucun risque de se tromper. Car même dans une perspective eschatologique il y avait de fortes chances que trois princes – au moins – fussent encore appelés à règner, simultanément ou successivement. Si l'auteur s'abstient ici de donner le moindre détail qui fasse indice, à la différence de ce qu'il a fait pour tous les princes précédents, c'est peut-être qu'au moment où il écrit les trois anonymes ne sont pas encore entrés en scène; a fortiori ne dit-il rien, même allusivement, de Commode. En définitive, la plus forte vraisemblance me paraît être en faveur d'une rédaction au début du règne d'Hadrien: les termes élogieux que l'auteur lui prodigue et la façon – exceptionnelle – dont il s'adresse à lui directement conviennent très bien à un prince récemment monté sur le trône et précédé d'un préjugé favorable.

3.3. La prudence laconique de l'auteur nous incite à être nous aussi prudents. On puisera une raison supplémentaire de l'être en enregistrant, cette fois dans le Troisième Livre, une autre triade, tout aussi mystérieuse: "Trois infligeront à Rome une fin lamentable" (III, 52). Aucune des triades fameuses de l'histoire romaine parfois appelées au secours par les exégètes de notre texte ne saurait faire percer l'anonymat de ces trois personnages. A. Kurfess, 1951, 288 y voit une allusion au second Triumvirat, sous prétexte que, quelques vers plus tôt, il est question des hésitations, finalement surmontées, de Rome à régner sur l'Egypte. L'explication est peu convaincante[9]. Si l'on considère les Oracles Sibyllins comme un livre à clefs, on doit bien reconnaître qu'il s'y trouve quelques fausses clefs, qui n'ouvrent aucune porte. Nous sommes sans doute ici en présence d'un cliché, sans plus de support dans la réalité que les trois têtes de l'aigle de IV Esdras, 12, 23[10]. C'est le chiffre fatidique qui est déterminant en même temps que l'idée de ces triades récurrentes qui nécessairement jalonnent l'histoire humaine. La Sibylle ne risquait rien à annoncer en termes d'une précision très relative des évènements à venir. Ceux qu'elle annonçait rétrospectivement et qui s'étaient effectivement produits garantissaient sa véracité touchant ce qui n'était pas arrivé encore.

4. La Sibylle et l'histoire

Nous saisissons ici l'un des traits les plus caractéristiques de nos écrits, savoir leur position en regard de l'histoire. On peut dire, en schématisant, que la Sibylle est hors du temps. Sans doute, elle est censée proférer ses oracles dans un passé lointain. Mais sa mission prophétique subsiste à travers les siècles. La voyante y est périodiquement rappelée, contre son gré, bien qu'elle demande un répit dans cette tâche harassante, par la volonté divine (cf. p. ex. III, 2; 295; 490 etc.). Et ses prédictions ont d'autant plus de portée qu'elles sont séparées du moment où elles se réalisent par un plus grand intervalle. Comme la Troisième Sibylle se

---

[9] Sur les discussions relatives à cette triade, Nikiprowetzky 1970, 150–154.
[10] Nikiprowetzky 1970, 153.

donne pour la bru de Noé (III, 827), elle peut embrasser d'un regard prophétique tout le développement de l'histoire presque depuis ses origines. Mais en tant qu'elle est divinement inspirée, elle participe de ce type de connaissance qui est le propre de Dieu, pour lequel passé, présent et futur interfèrent jusqu'à se confondre. En d'autres termes, la Sibylle peut, dans cette vision globale et indifférenciée, projeter parfois dans le passé des évènements qui ne sont pas arrivés encore mais qui, inclus de toute éternité dans le plan divin, sur lequel elle soulève un pan du voile, ne manqueront pas de survenir au jour fixé. C'est ce que A. Pincherle a fort bien exprimé à propos de la Cinquième Sibylle: "Son intense exaltation entraîne l'auteur au point de lui faire oublier qu'il parle dans le rôle d'une Sibylle qui prédit l'avenir, et assumer au contraire le personnage de l'écrivain visionnaire et apocalyptique qui, conformément à la nature de ce genre littéraire, *voit* les évènements futurs et pour *les voir* doit de surcroît les apercevoir projetés dans le passé: phénomène décrit, de façon aussi paradoxale qu'efficace et profondément vraie, par le poète: *e degli anni ancor non nati Daniel si ricordò*"[11].

4.1. C'est dans cette perspective que s'explique plus d'un détail déconcertant de nos textes. L'ordre chronologique, même en ce qui concerne les événements réels du passé, n'est pas nécessairement respecté. Il y a d'incessants retours en arrière; des faits très anciens sont mentionnés – au futur – après des événements très récents et à côté de prophéties non encore accomplies. Le procédé est abondamment utilisé dans les trois Livres. Il apparaît avec une netteté particulièrement foisonnante en III, 165–294 et 419–431. Les Titans sont évoqués au futur, les grands empires orientaux et celui de Rome au passé. L'Exode ne vient qu'ensuite, dans un bref passage où alternent les verbes au futur et au passé. Après l'annonce de la ruine, définitive semble-t-il, de Rome, un nouveau retour en arrière nous ramène á la guerre de Troie et au vieil homme mensonger qui, ayant eu le premier connaissance des écrits de la Sibylle, les plagiera sans vergogne et donnera – toujours au futur – de cette guerre un récit habile mais entièrement mensonger. Dans la mesure où le lecteur admet la fiction d'une Sibylle vaticinant avant les événements du passé, il sait qu'ils se *produiront* à coup sûr, puisqu'ils se sont effectivement *produits*. Dans la même foulée, la voyante peut annoncer, laconiquement ou avec détails, des faits qui, eux, ne se produiront peut-être jamais, mais que l'on attend avec confiance, puisque d'autres, ayant été prédits – *post eventum* – se sont réalisés. Ce brouillage, souvent délibéré, doit prouver que le plan divin bouscule les divisions chronologiques servant à jalonner l'histoire humaine, et que la Sibylle elle-même est, si l'on peut dire, méta- ou trans-historique.

---

[11] Pincherle 1922, XXXIV.

4.2. Je voudrais m'arrêter un instant sur un exemple, emprunté à la Cinquième Sibylle, v. 394 ss. Après une malédiction contre Rome, mention très claire est faite de l'incendie du temple de Vesta, puis de la seconde destruction du Temple de Jérusalem, dont la Sibylle a été le témoin comme elle l'avait été de la première. Le texte est, sur plusieurs points, mal assuré. Il est clair du moins que l'auteur établit, bien que de façon assez embrouillée, une corrélation entre la destruction du sanctuaire païen et celle du Temple de Yahvé et semble voir dans la première la conséquence providentielle de la seconde et le châtiment de ce sacrilège (V, 397–401). Mais alors, comment imaginer la succession des faits? Le temple de Vesta a brûlé une première fois, pendant l'incendie de Rome sous Néron, en 64, une seconde fois sous Commode en 191. Une allusion à la seconde destruction serait normale, dans une perspective strictement chronologique, si l'on admet que le châtiment suit nécessairement la faute. Elle est cependant peu vraisemblable, car, à moins d'y voir une interpolation, elle obligerait à rabaisser jusqu'à date certainement trop tardive la rédaction de notre écrit; et par surcroît un fait survenu plus d'un siècle plus tard peut difficilement être considéré comme un châtiment direct de la catastrophe palestinienne de 70.

La même objection interdit également, et a fortiori, si l'on pense qu'il s'agit, pour le temple de Vesta, de l'incendie de 64, d'y voir la punition divine pour la ruine, six siècles auparavant, du premier Temple, qu'on ne saurait d'ailleurs imputer aux Romains. En fait, il est clair que l'auteur pense essentiellement au second Temple et à l'incendie romain de 64. Force est donc d'admettre qu'il ne se laisse pas arrêter par la chronologie. Si, comme il y a lieu de le croire, il établit effectivement un lien entre l'incendie du sanctuaire païen et celui de Jérusalem, il fait du premier le châtiment *anticipé* d'un forfait commis six ans plus tard. Ce procédé, surprenant pour notre logique, ne l'est nullement dans la perspective où se place le visionnaire.

4.2.1. Par une démarche analogue, la Cinquième Sibylle encore, un peu plus loin, décrit au passé la restauration de Jérusalem, la construction du Temple eschatologique, la venue du Messie, pour revenir ensuite à l'annonce, au futur, des calamités ultimes (V, 414–433; 447 ss.). Elle lance une malédiction contre Isis et Sérapis, dont le règne s'écroulera. Sur quoi l'un des prêtres, vêtu de blanc, dira: "Allons, édifions pour le vrai Dieu un beau temple, et renonçons à l'horrible usage hérité de nos ancêtres, qui célébraient processions solennelles et hécatombes en l'honneur d'idoles de pierre" (V, 492 ss.). On pense naturellement au temple d'Onias. Mais le prêtre qui prend cette initiative monothéiste paraît bien appartenir au clergé égyptien, puisque son objectif est de détourner le peuple de l'idolâtrie ancestrale. Et par surcroît ce temple est appelé à disparaître non pas, comme ce fut le cas pour celui d'Onias, sur l'ordre de Vespasien, mais sous les coups d'Ethiopiens (V, 504–507).

Comment entendre tout cela? Il ne me paraît pas indispensable de recourir à l'hypothèse de multiples strates rédactionnelles et d'interpolations plus ou moins habiles. Cet enchevêtrement, à nos yeux incohérent, peut fort bien être, pour l'essentiel, le fait d'un seul et même auteur, qui a pu, certes, utiliser – et l'a sans doute fait – des éléments préexistants, empruntés pour une part à des prédictions païennes plus ou moins déformées, mais que l'on peut néanmoins créditer de la paternité de l'ensemble. Cet incessant mélange de passé et de futur, qui amène parfois à imputer à l'un ce qui appartient à l'autre, est bien dans la ligne habituelle de cette apocalyptique.

4.2.2. Les points fixes, dans ces fantaisies chronologiques, c'est la double destruction du Temple, qui permet de placer après 70 la rédaction ou la compilation de l'écrit, et c'est une référence, possible mais probablement indirecte, au temple d'Onias. Il faut, ici encore, être très prudent. Il n'est pas sûr que celui-ci ait déjà disparu au moment où notre Sibylle compose son ouvrage. On comprendrait mal, si c'était le cas, et si c'est vraiment de lui qu'elle veut parler, pourquoi, fort peu tendre envers les Romains, elle impute cet acte sacrilège aux Ethiopiens. Au demeurant, les textes anciens parlent non pas de destruction, mais de fermeture seulement, en 72–73, d'un sanctuaire dont le rayonnement dans la Diaspora, et même dans la seule Egypte, semble avoir été fort modeste. Si c'est lui qui est visé dans notre texte, on pourrait être tenté de situer celui-ci entre 70 et 73, ou encore de penser que l'auteur n'a vu dans la mesure prise par Vespasien que l'annonce d'autres mesures, plus radicales, imputées aux Ethiopiens, et qui, elles, méritent d'être prédites, parce qu'elles seront vraiment annonciatrices de la fin du monde. L'importance attribuée aux Ethiopiens est liée au fait que la contrée de Gog et Magog est située, dans ce texte seulement, "au milieu des fleuves d'Ethiopie", III, 319–320 (cf. Ezéchiel, 38), alors qu'elle est généralement identifiée aux terres septentrionales. La présente localisation pourrait être l'indice d'une origine alexandrine de notre écrit: les Ethiopiens représentent pour lui une menace plus sérieuse que celle des lointains Barbares du Nord.

En tout état de cause, ce temple égyptien ne sera qu'un temple de transition. Les termes dans lesquels la Sibylle le célèbre ne s'accordent qu'assez mal avec ce que nous savons d'un sanctuaire considéré par la majorité de l'opinion juive, même hors de Palestine, comme dissident, voire impie, et dont les dimensions et le prestige étaient fort modestes. En définitive, j'estime très possible qu'il ne soit pas question du tout, dans notre texte, du temple d'Onias. Nous sommes, assez vraisemblablement, en pleine vision "futuriste", sans appui dans la réalité concrète du présent ou du passé. Elle paraît bien avoir pour point de départ Isaïe 19, qui dans sa seconde partie relate la conversion des Egyptiens, et en particulier le verset 19: "Ce jour-là il y aura un autel à Yahvé au milieu du pays d'Egypte et près de sa frontière une stèle à Yahvé"[12]. L'autel est ici devenu un temple, et ce sanctuaire érigé, chez Isaïe comme chez la Sibylle, par les Gentils et à leur initiative, est le symbole de cet universalisme que nos Oracles ont puisé chez les Prophètes. Mais le temple eschatologique appelé à le remplacer ne pourra, bien entendu, s'élever que dans la ville sainte de Jérusalem.

5. La Sibylle et le Temple

Le destin du Temple tient une grande place dans les trois Livres, mais avec des nuances sensibles de l'un à l'autre. Le Troisième, compilé soit au IIème, soit plutôt dans la seconde moitié du Ier siècle av. J.C., est d'une époque où le sanctuaire est debout, et les profanations d'Antiochus Epiphane et de Pompée n'en ont pas durablement ébranlé le prestige. Mais la fiction qui fait parler la Sibylle dans un passé très reculé lui permet d'annoncer la ruine du Temple – la première, la seule qu'elle connaisse – comme devant se produire dans l'avenir (III, 213, 274, 294) et le lecteur peu critique peut penser à un évènement non encore survenu, et qui sera suivi d'une restauration. Au contraire, la Quatrième et la Cinquième Sibylles vaticinent après 70, pensent essentiellement au Second Temple, en déplorent la destruction et attendent des temps meilleurs pour le peuple élu.

5.1. Il est clair que pour la Cinquième Sibylle comme pour la Troisième, on ne saurait concevoir de judaïsme sans Palestine, sans Jérusalem, sans Temple. Le sanctuaire de l'avenir messianique et eschatologique ne pourra être qu'une réplique améliorée des deux Temples du passé: c'est Dieu lui-même qui le construira (V, 433). Il sera comme il était avant, mais plus magnifique et plus grand (III, 294). Il n'existera plus aucun autre sanctuaire, voué aux faux dieux, et de la terre entière on apportera encens et offrandes à la maison du Grand Dieu (III, 772 ss.). Il n'y a rien de plus, ici, que la vision du pèlerinage eschatologique des nations à Jérusalem. Le Temple sera, à la mesure de ces besoins nouveaux, immense, surmonté d'une tour qui touchera les nuées, visible de partout, de façon que tous les fidèles et tous les justes puissent contempler la gloire du Dieu éternel (V, 252, 421 ss.; 424–425). Cette tour construite par Dieu pourrait bien être une réplique de la tour de Babel, entreprise humaine insensée.

5.2. Nous sommes là dans une perspective assez classique, qui veut que le futur eschatologique ressemble, en mieux, aux aspects les plus glorieux

---

[12] Pincherle 1922, XXXV, estime qu'il ne faut pas exclure une allusion au temple d'Onias; mais il s'agirait alors, en tout état de cause, non pas du temple matériel, mais du temple scripturaire d'Isaïe: hypothèse ingénieuse, sinon absolument convaincante.

du passé israélite. Le Quatrième Livre offre à cet égard une réelle originalité. J'ai noté déjà qu'il ne s'appensantit pas sur les malheurs de la Palestine, mentionnés très brièvement entre ceux qui frappent les pays voisins: "Sur Jérusalem aussi viendra d'Italie la tempête mauvaise de la guerre, qui dévastera le grand Temple de Dieu". La faute incombe d'ailleurs non pas aux Romains, mais aux Juifs eux-mêmes, "lorsque, s'abandonnant à la folie, ils rejetteront la piété et accompliront des crimes affreux dans le vestibule du Temple" (IV, 115–118).

Déjà ce souci de répartir les responsabilités et d'en attribuer la plus large part aux Juifs est significatif. La théologie du livre l'est plus encore. Il s'ouvre sur la dénonciation de l'oracle mensonger de Phébus et la proclamation du grand Dieu unique, créateur et maître de l'univers, et qui n'est pas façonné de mains d'homme, à l'image des idoles muettes de pierre. Dieu "n'a pas pour demeure une pierre dressée dans un temple, muette et sourde, honte et malheur pour les hommes" (IV, 6–9): entendons que son sanctuaire ne renferme aucune idole: c'est là ce qui en fait l'originalité et en souligne l'unique légitimité. Le Temple n'est donc pas explicitement condamné.

Il reste que d'une répudiation de l'idolâtrie à celle du culte même rendu à Jérusalem le glissement était facile, dès lors que l'antique refus divin de se voir construire une demeure (II, Samuel, 7) avait trouvé une ratification brutale dans la ruine du sanctuaire unique. Certes, l'éruption du Vésuve de 79 représente le châtiment de ce qui s'est commis en Palestine. Mais lorsque, incitant les Gentils à se détourner des temples et des autels qu'ils ont édifiés, l'auteur parle de la souillure imposée à ces édifices "par le sang des créatures vivantes et les offrandes des quadrupèdes", on a peine à croire qu'il ne pense pas aussi aux liturgies jérusalémites (IV, 27–30): le vrai culte est de nature exclusivement éthique (IV, 31–34). Il serait en tous cas à l'aise pour les englober rétrospectivement dans cette condamnation, puisque Dieu lui-même permit que fût mis un terme à cette forme de dévotion indigne de lui.

5.3. Cette interprétation n'est pas unanimement admise. V. Nikiprowetzky en particulier pense que seuls les temples païens sont visés. Il est bon de noter à ce propos que l'éruption du Vésuve n'est pas mise par la Sibylle directement en rapport avec la destruction du Temple: elle manifeste la colère de Dieu devant le massacre de "la race innocente des hommes pieux" (IV, 135–136), c'est-à-dire, peut-être, ceux des Juifs qui se sont désolidarisés de l'insurrection, puisque les Zélotes sont dûment fustigés par la Sibylle. Les crimes contre le peuple élu, dans la mesure où il suit la voie droite, sont apparemment plus affreux que la ruine du sanctuaire.

Encore que sa pensée soit assez mal assurée, il semble bien que la Sibylle incline vers une forme plus spiritualisée de culte. La mention brève et sèche de la ruine du Temple ne s'accompagne d'aucune lamentation. Elle pourrait bien traduire une adhésion voilée au nouvel état de choses ainsi créé.

L'argumentation très fouillée de Nikiprowetzky ne m'a pas convaincu. Affirmer, même en se réclamant de l'autorité de Schürer, "qu'il y aurait été presque absurde de la part de notre pseudo-Sibylle de polémiquer contre le Temple de Jérusalem dix ans après sa destruction totale et l'interruption définitive du culte sacrificiel" et que une "sortie contre le Temple" eût, en l'an 80 de notre ère, "semblé un sacrilège gratuit" néglige certains aspects des choses[13]. Certes, la Sibylle poursuit "une fin pratique et urgente", la conversion des païens. Mais précisément la disparition du Temple lui fournit un argument de plus. Détournez-vous de vos errements, moraux et religieux, de la pédérastie et de l'idolâtrie. Renoncez aussi aux sacrifices. Ils sont, paraît penser la Sibylle, mauvais en soi, et non pas simplement dans le cadre du culte païen, puisque même le seul vrai Dieu, en permettant la destruction de son Temple, a signifié qu'il les rejetait.

5.4. Il me paraît difficile d'admettre, faute de textes très explicites, qu'une prise de position rétroactive, et d'ailleurs prudente, soit nécessairement apparue à l'opinion juive tout entière, dans la Diaspora comme en Palestine, blasphématoire. Il a pu se trouver, parmi l'intelligentsia juive hellénisée, familiarisée avec la critique de certains philosophes contre les formes traditionnelles du culte païen, quelques esprits disposés à condamner les sacrifices non pas seulement en tant qu'ils s'adressaient à de faux dieux, mais en soi. Certains textes scripturaires y inclinaient. Dans le raccourci d'histoire de la période nomadique tel que le présentent les *Actes des Apôtres* 7, 36 ss. les débuts du culte sacrificiel israélite sont mis en rapport avec le culte du veau d'or et consacrent l'apostasie du peuple, voué à l'adoration de l'armée du ciel: "M'avez-vous offert des sacrifices dans le désert durant quarante ans?". La pensée spiritualiste des philosophes rejoignait un certain courant prophétique qui, à force de relativiser le culte sacrificiel, juif, était comme une invitation à s'en écarter. Il était difficile, sauf dans des conventicules tout à fait marginaux, de franchir le pas aussi longtemps que le Temple était debout. Mais déjà, pour l'immense majorité des Juifs, l'institution synagogale était une réalité infiniment plus présente que le lointain sanctuaire unique. Il s'en est certainement trouvé pour penser qu'après tout, la ruine de ce dernier et des formes de culte qui lui étaient propres représentait un progrès voulu et ratifié par Dieu. Lorsqu'Etienne, au grand scandale de ses auditeurs, applique au Temple le terme de *cheiropoièton*, qui désigne souvent, dans le vocabulaire de la Diaspora et dans la Septante les oeuvres d'idolâtrie et traduit parfois *elil*, idole, il ne fait peut-être que proclamer tout haut, en pleine Jérusalem, et face au Temple

---

[13] Nikiprowetzky 1970, 233 ss.

encore debout, ce que certains dans la Diaspora inclinaient à penser tout bas et professèrent à leur tour ouvertement une fois le sanctuaire détruit (*Actes*, 7, 48–50)[14]. Moins radicale qu'Etienne, la Quatrième Sibylle témoigne tout au moins d'une certaine tiédeur vis-à-vis du Temple. Il est peut-être significatif qu'à la différence des deux autres, elle ne fasse aucune place, dans son tableau de la fin des temps et de la béatitude sur terre des élus, au sanctuaire eschatologique (III, 702 ss.). Le livre V en revanche parle de la construction et de la destruction subséquente du temple égyptien. Comme il voit dans sa disparition une victoire sur le paganisme, nous sommes fondés à supposer, encore que l'auteur ne le dise pas, qu'un temple eschatologique était appelé à lui succéder.

6. L'universalisme de la Sibylle

Il serait intéressant, et facile, d'enregistrer d'un livre Sibyllin à l'autre, par une étude comparative approfondie, des nuances assez sensibles. Le Quatrième est moins conforme aux schémas traditionnels de l'espérance juive, moins nationaliste en un sens, que les deux autres. Au même titre que son attitude vis-à-vis du culte jérusalémite me paraît significative, à cet égard, son eschatologie: sans faire aucune allusion à un royaume messianique, il n'envisage que le règne final de Dieu, ouvert, après le jugement universel, à tous ceux, Juifs et Gentils, qui auront été reconnus justes. Ces traits ont été judicieusement soulignés par A. Pincherle, qui cependant conclut, à tort, de l'appel à la conversion adressé aux païens et de l'attitude favorable au prosélytisme, à une date de rédaction antérieure à la destruction du Temple, ce qui l'oblige à voir dans l'allusion à l'éruption du Vésuve une interpolation[15]. Nous savons aujourd'hui que le prosélytisme juif a largement survécu à 70. Il n'est pas exclu que dans certains milieux, dont précisément la Quatrième Sibylle apporte un écho, la ruine du Temple, en atténuant le lien du judaïsme avec la Palestine et du même coup son caractère national, ait à certains égards facilité et stimulé la diffusion d'un culte spiritualisé[16].

6.1. Mais par delà ces nuances, l'unité d'inspiration fondamentale des trois Livres ne peut guère échapper au lecteur. Elle traduit la fierté juive d'être le peuple élu. Certes, les péchés réitérés d'Israël ne sont pas dissimulés, ni les châtiments divins qu'ils ont provoqués. Mais l'élection subsiste, les Juifs restent le peuple juste, véritable, sage, saint, pieux (III, 573; IV, 136; V, 154, 161, 226, 384–385), "la race divine et céleste des bienheureux Juifs" (V, 249). La Sibylle cependant ne se contente pas de ce

---

[14] Pincherle 1922, Appendice B, *ΧΕΙΡΟΠΟΙΗΤΟΣ*; cf. Simon 1958, 87 ss., 103 ss.
[15] Pincherle 1922, XXXII.   [16] Simon 1964, 52–86.

brevet d'autosatisfaction. L'élection se double d'un devoir impérieux, qui en est vraiment la raison d'être: Israël est pour les nations un modèle et doit les amener à leur tour au culte du seul vrai Dieu (III, 219–247; 573–600).

6.2. Un souffle universaliste anime ces écrits. La Sibylle est, au même titre que les grands prophètes bibliques, le porte-parole de Yahvé. Elle adresse son message aux Gentils plus directement que les prophètes, et en termes plus intelligibles, puisqu'elle emprunte au monde païen et son propre personnage et une partie de ses vaticinations. Son auditoire, c'est le peuple juif, bien sûr, qui a toujours besoin d'être rappelé à l'ordre; mais c'est aussi et sans doute d'abord la Gentilité, ou plus précisément le monde hellénistique. Elle assigne volontiers un rôle providentiel à tel peuple, Ethiopiens par exemple, ou à tel personnage "barbare". Cyrus est donné, à la suite de Isaïe 45, comme l'exécuteur des volontés divines (III, 286–287). Mais l'intérêt de la voyante se fixe essentiellement sur ce monde grec, où la Diaspora juive est implantée, et qu'elle-même, "tel un feu dépêché vers l'Hellade" (III, 810), connaît bien. Elle le met en garde contre ses erreurs, lui prédit des châtiments terribles s'il y persiste, et s'efforce de l'amener à rejoindre le troupeau des élus. Pour se faire mieux entendre, elle se vêt à la païenne: *Jüdische Propaganda unter heidnischer Maske*, ainsi la définit Schürer; et elle réalise à sa façon, en sa personne et dans son message, cette synthèse de la tradition biblique et de la culture grecque à laquelle s'est appliqué un Philon.

6.3. Les visions apocalyptiques, si abondamment développées, ne sont en réalité qu'un moyen de montrer que la Sibylle sait tout et qu'elle tient cette omniscience de Dieu lui-même, à la différence des pseudo-Sibylles mensongères; moyen aussi de faire pression sur ses lecteurs, de les effrayer par le tableau des maux qui les menacent et de les maintenir, s'il s'agit de Juifs, de les amener, s'il s'agit de païens, dans le droit chemin qui mène au salut. Profondément juifs, ces écrits sont en même temps, en un certain sens, syncrétistes[17]. Mais il ne s'agit là que d'un syncrétisme purement littéraire, qui n'implique pas la moindre compromission avec l'idolâtrie et les faux dieux. Le caractère essentiel de cette littérature semble bien être l'universalisme. Son objet fondamental c'est d'aider, à travers des cataclysmes inéluctables, à la réalisation de ce Royaume de Dieu où les païens eux aussi, associés et non pas asservis à la nation juive, sont appelés à goûter aux joies éternelles: "Bienheureux", s'écrie la Troisième Sibylle, "l'homme qui vivra en ce temps" (III, 371). Le Quatrième Livre s'achève sur ce même cri (IV, 192). C'est là, me semble-t-il, que réside la signification profonde des écrits sibyllins juifs qui, parallèlement au prosélytisme par persuasion

---

[17] Sur le syncrétisme des Sibylles, Pincherle 1922, XXXVII et surtout Nikiprowetzky 1970, 112–194.

diffusé à travers toute la Diaspora, pratiquent une sorte de prosélytisme par la peur.

Bibliographie

Avi-Yonah, M./Baras, Z. 1977: *The World History of the Jewish People*, I, Jérusalem 1977.

Charles, R. H. 1913: *The Apocrypha and Pseudepigrapha of the Old Testament*, II, Oxford 1913.

Collins, J. J. 1974: *The Sibylline Oracles of Egyptian Judaism* (SBLDS 13), Missoula, Mont. 1974.

Fuchs, H. 1938: *Der geistige Widerstand gegen Rom in der antiken Welt*, Berlin 1938.

Geffcken, J. 1902: *Oracula Sibyllina* (GCS 8), Leipzig 1902.

Hengel, M. 1973: *Judentum und Hellenismus*[2] (WUNT 10), Tübingen 1973.

Kautsch, E. 1900: *Die Apokryphen und Pseudepigraphen des Alten Testaments*, II, Tübingen 1900.

Kurfess, A. 1951: *Sibyllinische Weissagungen*, Berlin 1951.

Nikiprowetzky, V. 1970: *La Troisième Sibylle*, Paris 1970.

Pincherle, A. 1922: *Gli Oracoli Sibillini Giudaici*, Roma 1922.

Rowley, H. H. 1947: *The Relevance of Apocalyptic*[2], London 1947.

Simon, M. 1964: *Verus Israel*[2], Paris 1964.

– 1958: *St. Stephen and the Hellenists in the Primitive Church*, London 1958.

Apokalyptik im frühen Griechentum: Impulse und Transformationen

WALTER BURKERT

0. Vorbemerkung

Es ist einfach und naheliegend, das klassische Griechentum als Gegenposition zu jeglicher Apokalyptik aufzubauen. Wenn Apokalyptik überweltliche Botschaft an die Menschheit über die Gesamtheit der Welt und insbesondere ihre Zukunft bedeutet, wozu in der Regel das Motiv des auf außerordentliche Weise erwählten Zeugen gehört, so mag man dem die beiläufige Bemerkung eines Herodot entgegenhalten, übers Göttliche wüßten doch "alle Menschen gleichviel", d.h. so gut wie nichts (2,3.2), oder den Hohn des hippokratischen Autors 'Von der Heiligen Krankheit' gegen die Scharlatane, die da vorgeben "ein Mehr an Wissen zu besitzen" (VI 354 L.), wo doch alles gleichermaßen menschlich und göttlich zugleich sei. Die Sicht der Griechen tendiert auf eine geschlossene, nach ihren immanenten Wesensgesetzen, als φύσις erfaßbare Welt; auch die Götter wirken in der φύσις und durch sie. Ein Durchbrechen der Wesensgesetze, ein Aufreißen der geschlossenen Weltsphäre wird als undenkbar wegdisputiert. Apokalyptik wäre demgegenüber das ausgesprochen Nichtgriechische, ob orientalisch, jüdisch oder christlich, in räumlichen und zeitlichen Bereichen wuchernd, in denen sich das 'Hellenische' nicht oder nicht mehr entfalten konnte.

Doch sind solche allgemeinen Feststellungen von allenfalls partieller Gültigkeit. Auch wenn sich das 'Hellenische' in einem einmaligen historisch-geistigen Prozeß herauskristallisiert hat, blieb es vielfältigen historisch-sozialen Bedingungen unterworfen, hatte es sich als These gegen vielerlei Antithesen durchzusetzen. Im folgenden sei zum einen darauf hingewiesen, daß auch die klassische Literatur der Griechen durchaus entfaltete Apokalypsen kennt, zum anderen sei den bezeichnenden Verformungen nachgegangen, denen apokalyptische Motivik im Griechentum unterworfen war. Auch auf die Vorformen der Daniel-Apokalyptik kann von hier aus einiges Licht fallen.

1. Griechische Apokalypsen

1.1. Zunächst sei dem Rahmenmotiv des entrückten Zeugen nachgegangen. Mit einer echten Apokalypse schließt eines der berühmtesten und meistgelesenen Bücher der griechischen Literatur, Platons 'Staat'. Dies ist freilich nur einer unter den vier großen Jenseitsmythen[1] in Platons Oeuvre – daneben stehen die Mythen im 'Gorgias', 'Phaidon', 'Phaidros' –; doch ist der Schlußmythos des 'Staats' nicht nur äußerlich der umfangreichste und inhaltlich der universellste, er allein führt das charakteristische Motiv des auf außerordentliche Weise erwählten Zeugen ein, 'Er, Sohn des Armenios, der Pamphyler', der aus dem Tod ins Leben zurückgesandt wurde; denn, so wurde ihm im Jenseits bedeutet, "er müsse ein Bote des Jenseits für die Menschen werden" (614d vgl. 619b). Seine Botschaft also gilt 'den Menschen' schlechthin, und sie enthält nicht nur die Beschreibung des Systems von Lohn und Strafe, das in der anderen Welt für Menschenseelen gilt, sondern auch den Einblick in den Aufbau des Universums, jene 'Spindel' der ineinander kreisenden Gestirne, die sich im Schoße der Notwendigkeit dreht. Von der Komposition her sind beide Teile, die Beschreibung der Jenseitswege einerseits, die Wallfahrt zum Thron der Ananke andererseits[2], deutlich getrennt, doch beides zusammen macht den universalen Gehalt der Botschaft aus; bezeichnend, wie der aus unerforschlichem Ratschluß erwählte Zeuge von anonymen Mächten Schritt um Schritt geleitet wird, damit er sieht und tut, was nötig ist, ohne dem Jenseits ganz anheimzufallen. Die Farben des Wunderbaren scheinen im übrigen gedämpft; immerhin tauchen in Gestalt der "wilden, feurigen Männer", die den Tyrannen zum Tartaros schleifen, veritable Teufel auf (615e). Die Bezeichnung 'Apokalypse' für die einzigartige Offenbarung mit Totalitätsanspruch scheint gerechtfertigt – mit einer wesentlichen Einschränkung: es ist nicht Infragestellung oder Negierung der Welt, nicht das 'ganz andere', was da offenbar wird, sondern die Bestätigung dessen, worauf die im dialektischen Gespräch geweckte philosophische Einsicht notwendig führt; keine Gegenwelt und keine neue Welt, sondern diese unsere Welt, nur eben aus jenseitiger, nicht aus menschlich beschränkter Perspektive gesehen; nicht unerhört neues Geschehen und schon gar nicht Handeln eines Gottes, sondern der unabänderliche Kreislauf, in dem Gerechtigkeit und Notwendigkeit zusammenfallen.

1.2. Platons Apokalypse hat unmittelbare literarische Wirkung entfaltet. Wir wissen vor allem von Werken seines Schülers Herakleides Pontikos, die bis in die Kaiserzeit gern gelesen wurden. Zwei Titel sind faßbar,

---

[1] Frutiger 1930, 249–265; Thomas (1938); Kerschensteiner 1945, 136–156.
[2] Burkert 1975a, 97–99.

'Empedotimos' und 'Abaris'[3]. Im einen Fall war erzählt, wie einem Jäger, der in der Einsamkeit rastete, die Unterweltsgötter Pluton und Persephone entgegentraten, ihm die Beschränktheit des menschlichen Sehvermögens nahmen und ihn die Räume des Kosmos durchdringen ließen, wobei anscheinend unsere Erde sich als die rechte Unterwelt erwies und die Zukunft der Seele in den Sternensphären sich offenbarte. Im 'Abaris' kam die Entrückung einer Seele vor, während der Körper wie tot dalag; ein 'Daimon' führte den Visionär durchs Jenseits, zeigend und Weisung gebend. Inwieweit im Detail die Phantasie des Herakleides über Platon hinausging, ist angesichts der kümmerlichen Fragmente nicht zu sagen. Bezeichnend aber ist die Beurteilung dieser Schriftstellerei durch Plutarch – der ja auch selbst in der Nachfolge von Platon und Herakleides Apokalypsen gedichtet hat –. Plutarch schreibt im Buch 'De audiendis poetis': "Was philosophische Lehren betrifft, so haben die ganz jungen Leute mehr Spaß an dem, was scheinbar nicht philosophisch und nicht so ganz ernst gesagt ist, und solchen Darstellungen gegenüber zeigen sie sich aufmerksam und zahm; dies liegt auf der Hand. Denn nicht nur beim Lesen von den Äsopischen Fabeln und von poetischen Stoffen, [sondern] auch am Abaris des Herakleides und am Lykon des Ariston – Seelenlehre vermischt mit Fabeleien – haben sie ihren Spaß und begeistern sie sich" (14e). Eine besonders für Kinder eingängige, weil phantastische Darstellungsweise also, Verzuckerung der soliden Seelennahrung, das ist die Apokalyptik eines Herakleides im Urteil Plutarchs. Offenbar bedurfte es eines anderen Publikums, damit der bei Platon doch spürbare apokalyptische Impuls zur genuinen Wirkung kommen konnte.

1.3. Die Quellenfrage von Platons Apokalypse ist literarisch unlösbar. Daß Platon einer Quelle folgt, entnimmt man den ausdrücklichen Hinweisen auf Kürzungen, etwa was das Sonderschicksal der als Kleinkinder Verstorbenen betrifft (615c). Daß es eine literarisch fixierte Schilderung vom Abstieg des Orpheus in die Unterwelt gab, ist anzunehmen, doch existiert kein einziges altes Fragment aus diesem Gedicht; offenbar gab es auch ein Gedicht des 'Orpheus' über die Katabasis des Herakles, in dem Unterweltsstrafen ausgemalt waren[4]; vom Aufenthalt des Pythagoras in der Unterwelt hat man früh erzählt, in Form der Anekdote, hinter der vielleicht Rituelles steckt[5], doch nichts weist auf eine literarische Fassung. Jedenfalls wären die rekonstruierbaren Katabasis-Erzählungen nicht eigentliche Apokalypsen: anstelle des von höheren Mächten souverän gewählten Zeugen steht hier eine schamanenartige Gestalt, die kraft eigener Macht ins Jenseits eindringen kann; der literarische Rahmen ist, ähnlich wie schon im

---

[3] Fr. 73–75 und 90–97 Wehrli 1953; Burkert 1972, 366–368.
[4] Graf 1974, 141–146.   [5] Burkert 1972, 155–161.

11. Buch der Odyssee, die Abenteuererzählung; dementsprechend wird nicht in einem außerordentlichen, einmaligen Akt der Vorhang weggezogen, es wird vielmehr von dem berichtet, was grundsätzlich immer zugänglich ist.

In eine andere Richtung weist die ausdrückliche Nennung von 'Pamphylien' und 'Armenien', und seit langem hat man auf die seltsame Parallele in der armenischen Erzählung von Ara und Semiramis hingewiesen[6]. Freilich liegt dies auch wieder so weit ab, daß sichere Schlüsse nicht möglich sind. Bemerkenswert ist, daß Ktesias in seiner phantasievollen Persergeschichte, die etwa 20 Jahre vor Platons 'Staat' erschienen ist, auch Wundergeschichten von iranischen und anderen östlichen Ekstatikern einflocht. Das rhetorisch aufgeputzte Zeugnis des Arnobius (1,52) gibt leider wenig her: er fordert heidnische Wundermänner auf, sich dem Vergleich mit Christus zu stellen: "Soll doch jener Baktrier kommen, dessen Taten Ktesias im ersten Buch seiner Geschichte schildert, und Armenios, der Enkel des Zostrianos, und der Pamphyler, der Vertraute des Kyros"[7]. Kyros wurde, nach Ktesias, von einem 'vertrauten' Lehrer in der 'Magie' unterrichtet[8]. Vielleicht lagen hier Anregungen, die Platon mit der Wahl seines 'Zeugen' aufgriff. Ob dabei Ktesias eventuell echt iranische Tradition vermittelt hat, bleibt wohl unbestimmbar.

1.4. Dokumente sicher vorplatonischer Jenseitslehre sind die Goldblättchen, die man in Unteritalien, Thessalien und Kreta in Gräbern fand. Seit 1974 steht durch den Fund von Hipponion fest, daß der Archetyp dieser Texte mindestens ins 5. Jh. zurückgeht und daß sie für Eingeweihte in Bakchische Mysterien galten. Sie geben dem Toten Weisungen, was er im Jenseits finden wird, was er zu meiden, zu tun und zu sagen hat, um 'Erinnerung' zu gewinnen und zur Seligkeit zu gelangen[9]. Ein 'Mehr an Wissen' ist hier vorausgesetzt, ein übermenschlicher Wegweiser, von dem solche Kunde kommt; ob dies Orpheus war, ist nicht zweifelsfrei entschieden. Jedenfalls handelt es sich bei diesen Texten wiederum nicht um

---

[6] Gruppe 1924/37, 37; Kerschensteiner 1945, 138–140; der Text bei Müller-Langlois 1883, 26 f.

[7] FGrHist 688 F 1 f. = Arnob. 1,52: ... Bactrianus et ille conveniat, cuius Ctesias res gestas historiarum exponit in primo, Armenius Zostriani nepos et familiaris Pamphylus Cyri, Apollonius Damigero et Dardanus... Eindeutig ist nur der 'Bactrianus' Ktesias zugewiesen, doch weist auch der Name Kyros auf 'Persika'; andererseits taucht der Name Zostrianos in später Apokalyptik auf, NHC VIII, 1 Porph. V. Plot. 16; Colpe 1977, 155–157. Kolotes hat bereits im 3. Jh. v. Chr. den Er-Mythos vielmehr auf Zoroaster zurückgeführt, Prokl. Resp. II 109, danach die Zoroaster-Fälschung Clemens Str. 5,103, Prokl. a.a.O., Kerschensteiner 1945, 140–142.

[8] Plut. Artox. 3,3.

[9] Zuntz 1971, 275–393; Hipponion: Pugliese Carratelli 1974, 108–126, 229–236; West 1975; Zuntz 1976; ein weiteres Exemplar: Breslin 1977; Merkelbach 1977, 276. Vgl. Burkert 1975a, 81–104.

eigentliche Apokalypsen; das Privatinteresse der individuellen Suche nach Heil und Seligkeit wird nicht überstiegen. Als fernes Vorbild hat man seit langem auf das ägyptische Totenbuch hingewiesen.

1.5. Es bleiben zwei fragmentarisch erhaltene Dichtungen des 5. Jh., auf die man die Bezeichnung 'Apokalypse' anwenden kann, die Καϑαρμοί des Empedokles und das Gedicht des Parmenides. Die Verkündigung des Empedokles wirkt fast wie vorweggenommene Gnosis: vom göttlichen Ursprung ist die Rede, von einer Urschuld der 'Daimones' und ihrer Verbannung in gottferne Bereiche, von der Sühne durch aufeinanderfolgende Wiedergeburten und schließlicher Rückkehr zu den Göttern. Eine paradiesische Urzeit wird ausgemalt und zugleich als künftiges Ziel vor Augen gestellt. Dabei ist der Verfasser selbst der Zeuge, der in Ich–Form berichtet, was er sah und erlebte. Auch von Führung und Belehrung durch eine göttliche Gestalt war offenbar die Rede; doch sind die Einzelheiten der Rekonstruktion umstritten[10].

1.6. Voll entfaltet finden wir indessen das Rahmenmotiv der Apokalyptik im älteren, erhaltenen Text, im Proömium des Parmenides[11]: der Zeuge, der Verfasser, berichtet, wie ihn ein Pferdegespann unter dem Geleit von Göttinnen über die Grenzen der Welt hinausträgt, hindurch durchs 'Tor der Wege von Nacht und Tag' bis zur Göttin. Wehe dem, den ein 'böses Geschick' auf diesen Weg sendet; er aber ist durch göttliche Wahl bestimmt: "Du mußt alles erfahren" (B 1,28), die Wahrheit und auch dazu die 'Meinungen der Sterblichen'. Der Totalitätsanspruch dieser Offenbarung ist nicht zu übertreffen: es geht um das Sein überhaupt, vollständig, in sich geschlossen, "einer wohlgerundeten Kugel vergleichbar" (8,43), außer dem nichts zu denken noch zu sagen bleibt. Damit freilich wird der äußeren Form der Apokalypse zum Trotz das parmenideische Gedicht zum äußersten Gegenpol der Apokalyptik: nicht um Zukunft geht es, gibt es doch weder Vergangenheit noch Zukunft angesichts der Dauer des Seins, nicht um ein Geschehen, ist doch das Werden schlechthin "erloschen" (8,21). Es gibt keinen Kampf der Welten, keinen göttlichen Willen und kein Gericht. Die Alltagswelt als 'Meinung' wird durchsichtig auf das Eine, Seiende, das allein in seiner Gegenwärtigkeit denkbar ist. Was als Apokalypse begann, enthüllt sich als Grundlegung der Ontologie und Logik der Griechen.

Woher für Parmenides die Anregung zu dieser paradoxen Verwendung der apokalyptischen Erzählung kam, ist für uns wiederum verschollen. Das Vorbild der Dichterweihe des Hesiod genügt nicht zur Erklärung. Daß der

---

[10] Empedokles B 112–153a, neuer Text und Kommentar bei Zuntz (1971), 179–274 und Gallavotti 1975. Vgl. Burkert 1975b.

[11] Burkert 1969, Pellikaan-Engel 1974; zu Parmenides im allgemeinen vgl. Mourelatos 1970; Hölscher 1969; Heitsch 1974.

Weg des Zeus zum Orakel der Nacht, die ihm die Schicksalsbestimmungen
für die Welt enthüllt[12], in der alten Theogonie des Orpheus vorkam, ist
jetzt durch den Papyrus von Derveni bewiesen; aber hier ist die 'Enthüllung' in den Urzeit-Mythos verbaut, der Charakter der Verkündigung
gebrochen. Im Proömium der Theogonie des Epimenides[13] kam vermutlich vor, was als Sage weiterlebte, der mirakulöse, generationenlange
Schlaf des Sehers in der Ida-Höhle; im Schlaf sah er die Götter, insbesondere Dike und Aletheia (FGrHist 457 T 4f.), und hierauf beruhte offenbar
sein 'Mehr an Wissen'. Allerdings ist die Traumvision wiederum nicht die
eigentliche Form der Apokalypse. Immerhin findet sie sich auch in jenem
akkadischen Text, der am ehesten 'apokalyptisch' heißen kann, in der
'Unterweltsvision eines assyrischen Kronprinzen'[14], und in dem neuen
aramäischen Bileam-Text (s. u.); Beziehungen zum Vorderen Orient liegen
im archaischen Kreta überaus nahe. Für die leibhafte Entrückung des
Zeugen bleiben die Hinweise auf skythischen Schamanismus, denen nach
Hermann Diels besonders Karl Meuli und E. R. Dodds nachgegangen
sind[15], und insbesondere Aristeas und Bakis; auf sie wird zurückzukommen
sein.

2. Das Motiv des Weltuntergangs

2.1. Ein scheinbar besonders 'apokalyptisches' Thema ist der Weltunter-
gang, $\varphi\vartheta o\varrho\grave{\alpha}\ \tau o\tilde{v}\ \varkappa\acute{o}\sigma\mu ov$[16]. Für die Griechen jedoch ist dieser nicht
Gegenstand mythischer Traditionen oder religiöser Verkündigung, son-
dern naturphilosophischer Spekulation und Diskussion, und zwar von
Anfang an. Mit Anaximandros, dem ältesten der eigentlichen 'Vorsokratiker', tritt scheinbar unvermittelt die Frage nach dem Untergang der Welt
auf, in Symmetrie zur Erklärung ihrer Entstehung: "Woraus aber die
seienden Dinge entstehen, in das hinein gehen sie auch zugrunde, nach der
Notwendigkeit; denn sie zahlen einander Buße und Strafe für das Unrecht
nach der Ordnung der Zeit", so das berühmte und vielumstrittene Fragment des Anaximandros[17]. Theophrast, durch den uns dieses Zeugnis
erhalten ist, bezog es eindeutig auf die Welt als Ganzes, nicht nur auf einen
immanent-kontinuierlichen Prozeß, in dem einzelnes entsteht und verschwindet. Daneben ist von Weltveränderung die Rede, die für Menschen

---

[12] Mit Parmenides verglichen bei Burkert 1969, 17. Die Kolumnen VI–IX des Derveni-
Papyrus sind noch unveröffentlicht; vgl. allgemein zu diesem Dokument Kapsomenos 1964;
Merkelbach 1967; Burkert 1968.
[13] Burkert 1972, 150f.; 1969, 16f.
[14] ANET 109f.; Borger 1967/75, I 495f., II 265.
[15] Meuli 1935; Dodds 1951, 135–178; Burkert 1972, 147–165.
[16] Zusammenfassend Schwabl 1978, 840–850; allgemein Olrik 1922.
[17] Vgl. Kahn 1960, 166–196; Guthrie 1967/81, I 100f.

nicht weniger katastrophale Perspektiven bringt: einst sei die Erde ganz
sumpfig gewesen, dann sei sie allmählich ausgetrocknet; so sind nun Meer
und Land getrennt; einst aber werde das Meer verschwunden, die Erde
ganz ausgetrocknet sein[18]. Vielleicht sollte dann dem kosmischen 'Sommer'
der Austrocknung ein kosmischer 'Winter' folgen, als Buße und Ausgleich
'nach der Ordnung der Zeit'. Das Eindrucksvolle und Einzigartige ist bei
alledem der Stil der Sachlichkeit und Wirklichkeitshinnahme, der das
Unerhörte geistig bewältigt.

2.2. Leidenschaftlicher und verwirrender ist von Werden, Wandel und
Vergehen des Kosmos bei Heraklit die Rede: diese Welt, ungeschaffen,
"war, ist und wird sein: Feuer, das ewig lebt, sich entzündend nach Maßen
und erlöschend nach Maßen" (B 30). Inwieweit dabei sukzessive Weltpha-
sen angesetzt sind oder aber ein dauernder, dialektischer Prozeß gemeint ist
– "der Weg hinab und hinauf ist einer und derselbe" (B 60) –, darum gehen
seit langem die Kontroversen der Interpreten[19], und sie haben darob die
Fragmente des 'dunklen' Philosophen nach allen Regeln philologischer
Kunst einem strengen Verhör unterworfen. Mit Recht sucht man hinter die
stoischen und die gnostischen Interpretationen und Adaptationen zurückzukommen. Zuweilen freilich ging die Kritik zu weit und mußte sich
philologische Widerlegung gefallen lassen. Dies gilt insbesondere von dem
eindrücklichen – bei Hippolytos überlieferten – Satz: "Alles wird das Feuer,
wenn es herankommt, richten und überführen" (B 66). Der notwendige
Doppelsinn von καταλήψεται, 'ergreifen' und 'überführen', erweist sich
als altionisch und damit heraklitisch[20]. Dann aber ist, wie immer die tiefere
philosophische Deutung ausfallen mag, zu konstatieren, daß hier der
Weltuntergang in der bezeichnenden Form der apokalyptischen Drohgeste
erscheint: den Gegnern gilt das Feuer, den "Baumeistern und Zeugen der
Lügen" (B 28), auch den dionysischen Ekstatikern und Mysterienpriestern
(B 14). Wahrscheinlich gehören auch die Angaben des Heraklit über ein
'Großes Jahr'[21] mit der Kosmoszerstörung zusammen.

2.3. Wechselndes Werden und Vergehen der Lebewelt lehrt auch Empedokles in seinem Naturgedicht; nach Aristoteles handelt es sich um wech-
selnde Phasen in einem großen Kreislauf, wobei zwei gegenläufige Mächte
sich gegenseitig ablösen, 'Liebe' und 'Haß'; unsere Welt ist vom 'Haß'
beherrscht und geht zunehmender Auflösung entgegen. Die Rekonstruktion des empedokleischen Weltzyklus ist jedoch von neueren Interpreten
grundsätzlich angefochten worden, und eine Einigung ist nicht in Sicht[22].

---

[18] A 27; Kahn 1960, 65–67.
[19] Verwiesen sei auf Marcovich 1967 und 1978; B 30 = Fr. 51 Marcovich.
[20] Marcovich zu Fr. 82 = B 66 gegen Reinhardt 1942; Kirk 1954, 359–361.
[21] van der Waerden 1952.
[22] Die Rekonstruktion des 'Zyklus': O'Brien 1969; Guthrie 1967/81, II 167–185; dagegen

Vielmehr scheint bezeichnend, daß in den drei genannten Fällen, bei Anaximandros, Heraklit und Empedokles, eben das Problem der vergehenden Welten zu den hartnäckigsten Kontroversen in der Vorsokratiker-Forschung Anlaß gab. Zur Lückenhaftigkeit der Überlieferung und zur methodischen Vorsicht, die Späteres, Atomistisch-Epikureisches oder Stoisches, möglichst fernhalten will, kommt doch wohl ein gewisses Vorverständnis vom 'Hellenischen': Weltuntergang ist eine Extravaganz der Spekulation, die bei den Vätern der Naturwissenschaft nicht am Platze scheint; es sei nicht einzusehen, was zu solchen Thesen jenseits der Erfahrung und jenseits der Aufgabe, diese unsere Welt zu analysieren, überhaupt hätte führen sollen. So ruft denn kritisch-minimalistische Interpretation die Vorsokratiker zu ihrer eigentlichen Pflicht zurück.

2.4. Wenig beachtet wurde in diesem Zusammenhang das Zeugnis über einen zweitrangigen Autor, den Pythagoreer Philolaos aus der 2. Hälfte des 5. Jh.: er lehrte "einen doppelten Untergang des Kosmos: bald fließe Feuer vom Himmel, bald Wasser vom Mond, das durch die Umdrehung des Gestirns ausgegossen wird; die Dämpfe, die davon emporsteigen, seien die Nahrung des Kosmos"[23]. Dies ist so merkwürdig und isoliert, daß man es eben darum ernst nehmen sollte. Man gewinnt den Eindruck, hier werde unbefangen und fast plump formuliert, was bei Denkern wie Anaximandros, Heraklit und Empedokles ganz anders durchdrungen und dem System assimiliert ist: Zerstörung bald durch Feuer, bald durch Sintflut, und doch Selbsterneuerung, 'Ernährung' der Welt eben durch den Prozeß partieller Vernichtung. Durch 'physikalische' Überlegungen freilich ist so eine Behauptung nicht hinlänglich zu erklären; hier muß, vor aller Philosophie, Verkündigung aus einem andersartigen 'Wissen' im Hintergrund stehen.

2.5. Man hat über die Möglichkeiten eines iranischen Einflusses auf Anaximandros und Heraklit seit langem hin und her diskutiert. Die Quellenlage ist derart, daß die Zeugnisse nicht unmittelbar ineinandergreifen, ein zwingender Beweis also nicht möglich ist; so bleibt ein bedauerlicher Spielraum für individuelle Vorlieben der Freunde oder Feinde des Orients. Mir scheint bei Anaximandros die seltsam verfehlte Reihenfolge der Gestirne – von der Erde aus Sterne, Mond, Sonne, und das Unendliche

Hölscher 1965; Solmsen 1965; Bollack 1965/69, bes. I 95–124; Long 1974; dagegen D. Babut 1975, 304 f.

[23] A 18 = Aet. 2,5.3, überliefert durch (1) Plut. Plac. 2,5.3, (2) Stob. 1,20,1g, (3) Stob. 1,21.6d, (4) Galen Hist. philos. 48; dabei liest (2) περιστροφῇ τοῦ ἀστέρος, was der variierte Text von (4) bestätigt; (3) hat ἀέρος, die Plutarch-Codices variieren; für ἀστέρος ein Hauptcodex (Marcianus 521). Mit Diels wird allgemein ἀέρος akzeptiert, doch scheint 'Drehung des Mondes' leichter nachvollziehbar, vgl. ἐπιστροφή einer Mondseite Aet. 2,29,2 (Berosos). Vgl. auch Burkert 1972, 234; 315 Anm. 86. Die Lehre von der doppelten Weltzerstörung erscheint dann bei Berosos (FGrHist 680 F 21 = Sen. q. n. 3,29) und wird auch den Druiden zugeschrieben (Strab. 4 p. 197).

–, die sich mit dem Avesta trifft, nach wie vor sehr auffällig[24]; bei Heraklit[25] ist weniger die Rolle des Feuers überhaupt beweisend als die spezifische Prophezeiung des scheidenden und rächenden Feuers; bei Empedokles kommt der Vertrag der positiven und der negativen Weltmacht dazu, "durch Eide gesiegelt" (B 30,3), wonach ihre Herrschaft zu wechseln hat; von dem entsprechenden Wechsel zwischen Ahura Mazda und Angra Mainyu wissen die Griechen jedenfalls 100 Jahre nach Empedokles[26]. In iranischen Texten ist bekanntlich die Ausmalung von Weltende und Weltgericht, insbesondere das Ordal durch Feuer früher als irgend sonst nachzuweisen[27]. Allerdings sind die Differenzen zwischen Iranischem und Griechischem unübersehbar. Insbesondere ist die iranische Sicht unkosmisch, ausgerichtet auf die ethisch-religiöse Parteinahme, die wiederum im Griechischen ganz wegfällt. So werden die Anwälte der innergriechisch-geschlossenen Geistesgeschichte sich kaum geschlagen geben gegenüber der Gegenthese von der Wirkung hellenisierter Magier auf die frühgriechische Philosophie, wie dies besonders Martin L. West[28] vertreten hat.

Doch gerade wenn man hypothetisch akzeptiert, daß die Weltzerstörungsspekulationen der Vorsokratiker einem Impuls iranischer Eschatologie verpflichtet sind, tritt die Eigenwilligkeit der griechischen Geistesentwicklung um so deutlicher hervor. Mehr und mehr wird der Fremdkörper abgebaut. Demokrit[29] zwar und in seinem Gefolge Epikur hielten an der Möglichkeit einer kosmischen Katastrophe, eines Zusammenstoßes von Welten ausdrücklich fest; doch ist ein solches Ereignis im atomistischen System bar jeden Sinns, ein im Grunde banaler Unfall, ohne Bedeutung fürs persönliche Leben und auch fürs Denken kein Problem, allenfalls als polemisches Argument verwendbar. Auf der anderen Seite steht die Naturphilosophie im Gefolge von Platon und Aristoteles[30], die glaubt, die Ewigkeit der Welt beweisen zu können. Nur die Stoa[31] lehrt entschieden das schließliche Aufgehen unserer Welt im Feuer, die Ekpyrosis; indem dieses Feuer jedoch mit Weltgesetz und Weltvernunft, mit Logos und Heimarmene identisch ist, wird eben damit die Immanenzphilosophie am konsequentesten durchgeführt. Mit wechselnden Mitteln haben sich also alle philosophischen Systeme der Griechen abgeschirmt gegenüber dem spontanen Einbruch der Transzendenz, der echten Apokalyptik. Das 'subversive' Element erscheint gebannt.

[24] Burkert 1963; West 1971, 76–99.   [25] West 1971, 165–202.
[26] Theopompos FGrHist 115 F 65 = Plut. Is. 370b. Vgl. Widengren in diesem Band § 5.1.
[27] Widengren 1954/55, 1, 39–42; 1965, 87f. und in diesem Band § 1.2 und § 4.3.2.1.2. *et passim.* – Später sind die iranischen Lehren in Form der 'Orakel' des Hystaspes' bei den Griechen verbreitet, Widengren 1965, 199–207; Cumont 1931; Bidez/Cumont 1938, II, 357–376. Vgl. dazu jetzt Widengren in diesem Band § 4.3.2.
[28] West 1971.   [29] A 37; A 84
[30] Bes. Fr. 18–21; Effe 1970, 7–72.   [31] Hierzu Mansfeld 1979.

3. Der Mythos von den 'Vier Reichen' und seine Metamorphosen

3.1. Doch nun zum ältesten Impuls apokalyptischer Motivik in der griechischen Literatur und zugleich zum ältesten Zeugnis einer apokalyptischen Konzeption überhaupt: Hesiods Weltaltermythos, durch Quellengemeinschaft verbunden mit Daniel 2 bzw. Daniel 2 und 7. Dieses Problem ist seit Reitzenstein[32] immer wieder diskutiert worden, und es ist hier weder möglich noch nötig, alle Einzelheiten aufzurollen. So mögen die iranischen Texte, die 1000 Jahre nach Daniel das Schema auf den Verfall des Sassanidenreiches anwenden[33], ebenso beiseitebleiben wie die indische Yuga-Lehre, deren Abhängigkeit vom Vorderorientalischen sich mit ziemlicher Sicherheit erweisen läßt[34]. Es bleiben als Grundtexte einerseits Daniel[35]: das 'Bild' aus Gold, Silber, Erz und Eisen mit Füßen von Eisen und Ton, das der fallende Stein zerschlägt, der sich zum Gebirge auswächst; gedeutet auf vier einander folgende Königreiche, beginnend mit Nebukadnezar und endend mit Alexander und den Diadochen –, und andererseits Hesiod: vier sukzessive Metallgenerationen ($\gamma \varepsilon \nu \varepsilon \alpha i$), das goldene, silberne, eherne und eiserne Geschlecht. Hier freilich ist bekanntlich gleich Hesiod-Analyse[36] zu betreiben: das in der Zählung des Textes vierte Geschlecht, das der 'Heroen, die auch Halbgötter heißen', muß ein Einschub in die vorgegebene Metallreihe sein; es fällt in doppelter Weise aus dem Rahmen, indem es nicht mit einem Metall gekoppelt ist und indem es die Systematik der Verfallsreihe unterbricht; zudem sind allein in ihm die Bezüge zur griechischen Normaltradition zusammengedrängt, zur Welt des heroischen Epos mit Thebanischem und Trojanischem Krieg. Den Einschub hat wohl Hesiod selbst vorgenommen; verwendet hat er eine Quelle, die mit der Folge der vier Metalle den Verfall von Welt und Menschen beschrieb.

Dabei sind die Übereinstimmungen mit Daniel so speziell, daß unabhängige Entstehung so schwer zu verfechten ist wie eine Abhängigkeit Daniels von Hesiod. Die Abfolge der vier Metalle, die absteigende Wertskala, die Koppelung mit vier Epochen der Weltgeschichte bilden hier wie dort das

---

[32] Reitzenstein 1924/25 und 1926, 45–68; vgl. Heubeck 1955; Gatz 1967, 7–27; West 1978, 172–177; Schwabl 1978, 783–795. Ohne Zuziehung Hesiods wird die Weltreichslehre über Ktesias auf die Perser zurückgeführt durch Noth 1957, 254–259; Metzler 1977, 285 f. – Abhängigkeit des Daniel von Hesiod nimmt Solmsen 1980, 213 f. an.

[33] Bahman Yašt 1,2–5, SBE V, 191–193; Denkart 9,8, SBE XXXVII, 180 f., beide aus Stutkar Nask; Widengren 1961, 182–184; Gatz 1967, 7–9; Kippenberg 1978. Zu Beziehungen zur Sethianischen Gnosis Colpe 1977, 161–170. Vgl. auch Widengren in diesem Band.

[34] Pingree 1963, 238–240; vgl. Gatz 1967, 11–16.

[35] Rowley 1935; Tatford 1953; Delcor 1971, 78–83, 85–87: Datierung des Textes zwischen 323 und 250. Über Daniel als "Ursprung der Apokalyptik" auch Dexinger 1977, 14–16.

[36] Vgl. Heubeck 1955; Gatz 1967, 3 f.; Matthiessen 1977; West 1978, 174; schwankend Schwabl 1978, 788, 790, 795. Auch die fünf Weltalter des Hesiodtexts sind strukturell verbunden, Vernant 1960, doch ergeben die strukturellen Beobachtungen kein Argument gegen die historische Analyse.

Rückgrat der Schilderung. Dazu kommt ein Relikt der Prophetie im Text des Hesiod. Bekanntlich wird fast die gesamte Schilderung des eisernen Zeitalters in Futurformen gegeben (176–210): es wird kein Ende des Unheils sein, Brüder werden Brüdern, Kinder den Eltern feind sein, Gewalt wird vor Recht gehen, Aidos und Nemesis werden fliehen; dem fügt sich der Prodigienstil ein: das Ende auch dieses Geschlechts wird kommen, wenn die Kinder bereits mit grauen Schläfen geboren werden (181)[37].

3.2. Zeit und Charakter von Hesiods Quelle lassen sich verhältnismäßig eng eingrenzen. Die Quellengemeinschaft mit Daniel weist nach Osten. Dabei schließt das wahrscheinliche Datum Hesiods – um 700 v. Chr. – iranischen Einfluß praktisch aus. Es bleibt der Bereich von Anatolien-Syrien-Mesopotamien, wobei auf die Lokalisierung Daniels in Babylon und die aramäische Sprachform der betreffenden Kapitel gleich hinzuweisen ist. Aramäisch wird seit der Assyrerzeit zur Verkehrs- und Literatursprache des Vorderen Orients. Weiterhin gibt die Metallreihe den Hinweis, daß die Quelle kaum bis in die Bronzezeit zurückgehen kann[38]; wohl aber läßt sich vermuten, daß eine Erinnerung an den einstigen Gebrauch von Bronzewaffen und -geräten – wovon Hesiod (150f.) ausdrücklich spricht – und vielleicht auch an den Glanz der Spätbronzezeit noch erhalten war und hierin der Anreiz lag, den Kontrast von guter alter Zeit und arger Gegenwart im 'Metallmythos' auszugestalten. Von Hesiod aus zu schließen müßte eine prophetische Gestalt der Bronzezeit die Eisenzeit vorausgesagt haben, und von der griechischen Überlieferung aus kann man auf die 'Sibylle' raten. Gewiß, das Zeugnis, daß sie "die Zeitalter nach Metallen einteilte", ist spät und vereinzelt[39], doch Heraklit (B 92), unser ältester Zeuge, weiß, daß die Sibylle "mit rasendem Munde" Botschaft "ohne Lachen, ohne Schminke, ohne Salbe" verkündet, und "sie erreicht tausend Jahre"; "jetzt erreicht mich der alte Götterspruch", sagt man, wenn eine Prophezeiung in Erfüllung geht (Od. 9,507; 11,172). Weissagungen ekstatischer Frauen sind in Vorderasien von Mari bis zur Assyrerzeit wohl bezeugt[40]. Ob auf die späten Zeugnisse über eine babylonische Sibylle viel zu geben ist, ist eine andere Frage. Aus alledem ergibt sich die Hypothese:

---

[37] Eine Parallele ist IV Esr 6,21, West 1978, z. d. St.; Gatz 1967, 18–21; grau geboren ist der etruskische Tarchon, Strab. 5 p. 219, = Tages der Stifter der Etruskischen Disziplin, das Kind senili prudentia, das nur einen Tag lebt? Cic. div. 2,50 und Pease 1920/23, z. d. St.; Lydos ost. 2f.; Pfiffig 1975, 38; vgl. die Sibylle v. Erythrai, die gleich bei Geburt spricht und in kurzer Zeit erwachsen ist, Hermias in Phdr. p. 94, 26f. Couvreur 1901.

[38] Immerhin wird Silber, Gold, Eisen, Bronze (in dieser Reihenfolge; daneben edle Steine) im Ritual eines hethitischen Gründungsopfers aufgezählt, ANET 356.

[39] Serv. Ecl. 4,4. – Heraklit B 92; vgl. allgemein Rzach 1923.

[40] Ellermeier 1968, 60f.; ANET 449f. Vgl. auch Ringgren in diesem Band. Zur babylonischen Sibylle Rzach 1923, 2097–2102.

Quelle von Hesiod und Daniel ist ein aramäischer Sibyllen-Text wohl des 8. Jh., der sich als Prophezeiung aus der Bronzezeit gab und die goldene und die silberne Epoche als die noch bessere Vorzeit beschrieb.

3.3. Soweit ließ sich seit langem kommen; da die aramäische Literatur, auf Lederrollen geschrieben, fast restlos untergegangen ist, endet die Rekonstruktion im Unbeweisbaren. Seit 1976 aber ist eine indirekte, in sich sensationelle Bestätigung veröffentlicht: die aramäisch beschriftete Stele aus dem Tempel von Deir ʿAlla in Palästina, datiert um 700 v. Chr., mit den Schreckensprophezeiungen des bronzezeitlichen Sehers Bileam (Baʿlam)[41]. Zwar sind vom Text nur entmutigend geringe Fragmente erhalten. Doch die Hauptlinien der Deutung stehen fest: der Name des Zeugen, sein Weinen ob der ihm zuteil gewordenen Visionen, einige Einzelheiten der Wahrsagungen sind klar zu lesen; vielleicht ist sogar ein Ende der Unheilszeiten durch die Geburt eines Kindes verheißen. Das ganze ist damit erstaunlich analog zu dem, was als Hesiods Quelle zu erschließen war: eine aramäische Prophetie vom Ende des 8. Jh., einem Weisen der Vorzeit in den Mund gelegt und auf eine schreckliche Gegenwart bezogen.

Unsere Vorstellung von der Hesiod-Daniel-Quelle wird hiermit entscheidend konkretisiert. Als ihren Inhalt wird man unbedenklich die den beiden Texten gemeinsamen Züge ansetzen: die Abfolge der vier Zeitalter, ihre Kennzeichnung gemäß dem absteigenden Rang der Metalle; die Eisenzeit war dabei in der Fiktion als Zukunft gegeben. Offen bleibt nur ein entscheidender Punkt der Rekonstruktion, der eben den Charakter als 'Apokalypse' betrifft: Daniels Gesichte laufen aus auf die Zerschmetterung des letzten Reichs durch das ganz andere, auf Gericht und Gottesreich. Ist Analoges bei Hesiod angedeutet, ist dies der Quelle zuzuweisen? Man hat auf den Wunsch des Dichters hingewiesen, "entweder früher oder später" geboren zu sein (175); Besseres also wird auf das eiserne Zeitalter folgen. Doch von einer eigentlichen Zukunftsperspektive kann keine Rede sein. Auch der Text von Deir ʿAlla bleibt zufolge seines fragmentarischen Zustandes in diesem Betracht mehrdeutig.

3.4. Einen Schritt weiter führen indessen die weiteren Reflexe der gleichen apokalyptischen Konzeption in der griechischen Literatur. Um 600 v. Chr., also etwa 100 Jahre nach Hesiod, ist das Epos 'Arimaspeia' des Aristeas anzusetzen, über das wir vor allem durch Herodot und seinen Zeitgenossen Damastes von Sigeion unterrichtet sind[42]. Dem Anschein

---

[41] Hoftijzer, van der Kooij 1976; Caquot, Lemaire 1977; Ringgren 1977; Müller 1978. Aus etwa der gleichen Zeit, der Regierung der Bokchoris, stammt die 'Prophezeiung des Lammes', vgl. dazu Assmann und Griffiths in diesem Band.

[42] Bolton 1962; dazu Burkert 1963. Hauptquellen Hdt. 4,13–16 und Damastes FGrHist 5 F 1 = Steph. Byz. s. v. Hyperboreioi; Datierung durch den Spiegel von Kelermes, Bolton T. 1.

nach freilich handelt es sich bei diesem Epos um einen Reisebericht in den fernen Norden jenseits des Schwarzen Meeres, wobei, wie so oft, echte Kunde und Fabeleien sich wunderlich mischen. So hat offenbar Aristeas die Vorstellung vom riesigen Nordgebirge, den 'Rhipäen', in die griechische Tradition gebracht, das doch auf unserem Globus nicht zu finden ist und sich vielmehr als Umsetzung des mythischen Götterbergs im Norden in Pseudogeographie entpuppt. 'Von Norden' sehen alttestamentliche Propheten die wilden Völkerscharen kommen[43], und eben dies war auch das eigentliche Anliegen des Arimaspen-Epos, zu erklären, was hinter den Einfällen der Kimmerier steht, die im 7. Jh. wiederholt Kleinasien verheert, das Phrygerreich und Urartu vernichtet haben. Die Kimmerier – so Aristeas – werden von den Skythen aus ihren Stammessitzen verdrängt, die Skythen ihrerseits weichen dem Druck der Issedonen; doch auch diese sind die Getriebenen, bedrängt von den einäugigen Arimaspen, die am Rhipäischen Gebirge den Greifen das Gold abjagen. Aristeas behauptete bis zu den Issedonen gelangt zu sein, von deren Sitten er Grausliches zu berichten wußte: Schädelbecher, als Trinkschalen vergoldet[44], Gleichberechtigung der Frauen – die Amazonen sind nicht fern –, kannibalisches Verspeisen der verstorbenen Väter. Stärker noch und unheimlicher, gar keine eigentlichen Menschen mehr sind die einäugigen Arimaspen. Jenseits des Rhipäischen Gebirges aber leben die 'Hyperboreer'[45], ein Volk wahrhaft frommer Menschen, mit denen der Gott Apollon leibhaft verkehrt; sie kennen keinen Krieg, keine Ungerechtigkeit, keine Krankheit, sie verbringen ihr Leben in heiligen Festen. Gewöhnlichen Menschen freilich ist dieses Land unerreichbar.

Die einheitliche Struktur dieser Sammlung bunter Phantastik wird nun gerade im Vergleich mit Hesiod und Daniel evident: die Abfolge der Zeiten ist hier bis ins Detail ins Geographische projiziert. Vier streitbare Völker, vier kämpferische 'Reiche' folgen aufeinander, um Menschen zu schrecken und zu quälen, eines immer stärker und wilder als das andere: präsent ist das Kimmerier-Unglück, hinter ihnen drohen die Skythen, dann die noch barbarischeren Issedonen, schließlich die nicht einmal mehr ganz menschlichen Arimaspen; bis zu den Issedonen reicht die Erfahrung des Zeugen, das weitere ist indirekte Kunde. Hinter den Arimaspen aber, die dem Epos den Titel gaben, kommt die große Zäsur, das unübersteigbare Gebirge – analog zum Felsblock bei Daniel, der zum Gebirge wird –. Jenseits davon liegt das Reich des Gottes Apollon.

---

[43] Jes 14,31; Jer 1,14; Ez 38f.; vgl. Childs 1959. – Die Ikonographie des Greifenkampfes ist phönikischer Herkunft, Helck 1979, 212.

[44] Dies (Hdt. 4,26) ein ethnographisch 'echtes' Detail, Rieth 1971.

[45] Die Hyperboreer erscheinen auch Hes. Fr. 150,21; Alkaios Fr. 307c; vgl. Burkert 1977, 230.

Obendrein gab sich das Arimaspenepos selbst den Rahmen der Apokalypse. Auch dies ergibt sich aus Herodot: der Autor behauptete – doch
wohl im Proömium des Gedichtes –, er sei "von Apollon ergriffen"
worden, φοιβόλαμπτος[46], und so sei er in die nie zuvor erkundeten Fernen
gelangt. 'Von Apollon ergriffen' ist der ekstatische Seher, ist Kassandra
oder die Pythia. Dies schließt reales Umherwandern nicht aus; aber der
Einbruch des Göttlichen ist Voraussetzung. So ranken sich um Aristeas
Legenden von seiner mirakulösen Entrückung[47]. Man hat dies in Beziehung
zum skytischen 'Schamanismus' gesetzt[48], auch auf die Verbindung zum
Proömium des Parmenides wurde hingewiesen[49]. So erfüllt denn das
Arimaspenepos die Definition der Apokalypse fast vollständig: der vom
Gott erwählte, einzigartige Zeuge bringt die keinem anderen erreichbare
Kunde, die die Katastrophe der Gegenwart deutet und noch Ärgeres
erwarten läßt. M. E. ist nicht zu bezweifeln, daß Aristeas mit der mutmaß-
lichen Hesiod-Quelle in irgendeiner Weise in Kontakt gekommen ist. Die
griechische Transformation freilich ist in diesem Fall so gründlich, daß die
Interpreten die apokalyptische Dynamik in der Regel übersahen und nur
nach Ethnographie und Folklore suchten. In der Tat, das Gottesreich bleibt
unerreichbar fern, die Welt der Hyperboreer läßt sich allenfalls – so bei
Pindar – als poetisches Gegenbild einsetzen, während der Alltag zwingt,
auch mit Kimmeriern und Skythen irgendwie ins Reine zu kommen.

3.5. Eine sehr eigentümliche Version der Vier-Reiche-Lehre taucht in
der Orphischen Theogonie auf: Uranos-Kronos-Zeus-Dionysos lösen einander ab; die voraussagende Deutung erfolgt in der dritten Generation
durch das Orakel der Nacht; das vierte Reich wird zur Katastrophe, indem
die Titanen den Kinderkönig vernichten. Doch wird weitere Diskussion
bis zur Publikation des Derveni-Papyrus zu warten haben (vgl. Orph. Fr.
220; o. Anm. 12).

3.6. Eine letzte Transposition des Schemas taucht unerwartet in der
attischen Komödie auf, in den 'Rittern' des Aristophanes aus dem Jahr
424[50]. Das Stück ist eine wütende Attacke auf den damals führenden und
erfolgreichen Politiker Kleon, der als 'Gerber' apostrophiert ist. Die Handlung wird durch ein Orakel des Sehers Bakis ausgelöst, das findige Sklaven
dem 'Gerber' entwenden. Vier Herrscher werden in ihm für Athen geweissagt, und jeder von ihnen ist ein 'Händler' – Politik als Geschäft –: dem
'Werghändler' folgte der 'Schafhändler', diesem der 'Lederhändler' oder
'Gerber', der jetzt das Heft führt; ihm ist der Untergang bestimmt, wenn
ein "noch ekelhafterer" Händler auftaucht (134), der Wursthändler, der

---

[46] Vgl. Burkert 1963a, 238–240.   [47] Bolton 1962, 119–175; Burkert 1972, 147–149.
[48] Meuli 1935; Dodds 1951; o. Anm. 15.
[49] Burkert 1963a, 239.   [50] Trencsényi-Waldapfel 1966, 232–250.

denn auch providentiellerweise alsbald die Bühne betritt und sich an Unflätigkeit dem 'Gerber' überlegen erweist. So kann er sich beim Volk von Athen, dem 'Demos', installieren. Da aber folgt die verblüffende, utopische Wende: Der Wursthändler ist imstande, den Demos in seinem Kessel wieder jung zu kochen, und damit hebt eine neue Epoche an, in der die verjüngte Demokratie von Athen "über die ganze Welt König sein wird" (1087). Die Parallele zum Daniel-Schema ist frappierend und braucht kaum ausgezogen zu werden. Wir haben die Folge der vier Herrschaften, wir haben die absteigende Linie und den jähen Umschlag, als endlich der Tiefpunkt erreicht ist. Daß die Parallele nicht zufällig ist, zeigt der ausdrückliche Hinweis auf die Orakel des Bakis, die solches vorhersagen; daß die Weissagung im Stadium des vorletzten 'Reiches' bekannt wird, stimmt zu den Andeutungen bei Hesiod. Auch Bakis ist ein ekstatischer Prophet, nicht φοιβόληπτος wie Aristeas, wohl aber νυμφόληπτος: den Nymphen verdankt er sein 'Mehr an Wissen'[51]. De facto sind die Orakel des Bakis anscheinend zur Zeit der Perserkriege bei den Griechen in Umlauf gekommen; ihr entschiedenster Anhänger ist Herodot. Aus seinen Zitaten vor allem haben wir auch eine Vorstellung vom Prodigienstil dieser Texte: "Aber wenn..." begannen sie jeweils, mit kühnen und meist schreckerregenden Bildern, dunkel genug um zu mehrfacher Anwendung zu taugen. Nicht nur Arges, auch utopisches Glück war in ihnen verkündet, "wenn der Wolf das Schaf heiraten wird"[52]. Der Name Bakis[53] weist nach Lydien, und es liegt nahe, das Aufkommen dieser Orakel mit dem Zusammenbruch des Lyderreichs unter der persischen Eroberung (547/6) zu verbinden. Daß dabei auch jenes alte apokalyptische Schema von den vier Reichen zu neuer Aktualität gelangte, ist nicht verwunderlich.

3.7. Dreifach also findet sich die apokalyptische Konzeption von den vier Reichen, auf die der Umschlag zur Seligkeit folgen muß, in der griechischen Literatur gespiegelt, je im 7., 6. und 5. Jahrhundert; in je verschiedener Weise ist dabei stets die eigentlich apokalyptische Spitze abgebrochen, die Absage an die Wirklichkeit zugunsten der göttlichen Utopie. Hesiod verharrt im eisernen Zeitalter, Aristeas setzt Geschichte um in Geographie, und nur die Komödie leistet sich die Phantastik im Bewußtsein der eigenen Narrheit. Daß nur die Komödie auch die unteren Schichten des Menschseins ans Licht bringt, mit der Perspektive der kleinen Leute und Sklaven zumindest spielt, im Kontrast zur aristokratischen Verhaltenheit der übrigen literarischen Genera, ist gewiß von Bedeutung. Und doch verpufft hier im komischen Spiel, was unter anderen historisch-ethnischen und sozialen

---

[51] Aristoph. Pax 1071; Paus. 10,12,11.   [52] Aristoph. Pax 1076.
[53] baki – scheint das lydische Äquivalent zu Dionysos zu sein, Gusmani 1964, s. v. Bakilli –, bakivali. Die griechische Tradition allerdings weist Bakis nach Böotien, Attika oder Arkadien, Kern 1896.

Voraussetzungen sich als revolutionäres Potential erweisen und zu ungeheurer und unheimlicher Wirkung kommen konnte, etwa im Umkreis des 'Daniel'.

3.8. Zum Abschluß noch ein Rückblick auf jene Epoche, in der der mutmaßliche Urtext der Vier-Reiche-Prophetie Gestalt gewann, die Assyrerzeit des 8. Jh. Ein vergleichbarer Keilschrifttext scheint bisher nicht aufgetaucht zu sein und ist kaum zu erwarten. Wohl aber gibt es Vorformen der Vier-Weltalter-Lehre in der Keilschriftliteratur: seit 1936 ist der hethitische Text von den vier Königreichen im Himmel bekannt[54], seit 1969 das Atrahasis-Epos, das über 1000 Jahre lang tradiert und gelesen wurde[55]. Dieses behandelt, wie die erste Zeile programmatisch andeutet, das Verhältnis von Göttern und Menschen überhaupt: "Als Götter Menschen waren" – merkwürdig analog ist die rätselhafte Überschrift, mit der Hesiod den Weltaltermythos einleitet: "daß die Götter und die sterblichen Menschen gleicher Abstammung sind"[56] –. Im Atrahasis-Epos schaffen die Götter die Menschen, um selbst von Arbeit entlastet zu sein; doch nach kaum 1200 Jahren werden ihnen die Menschen lästig, und sie wollen sich ihrer wieder entledigen. Drei Versuche der Vernichtung werden nacheinander unternommen: die Pest, die Dürre, die Sintflut. Doch dank Atrahasis, dem "an Klugheit Überragenden", der mit Gott Ea im Bunde steht, werden die übrigen Götter gegeneinander ausgespielt und scheitern mit all ihren Vernichtungsplänen. Hunger, Seuchen, Sintflut sind Standardthemen in späterer Apokalyptik, und die Gliederung der Menschheitsgeschichte in vier Perioden – zu je 1200 Jahren? – ist das früheste Modell der Zeitalterspekulationen. Der apokalyptische Weltaltermythos ist hiervon kaum zu trennen; und doch ist 'Atrahasis' nach Stimmung und Gehalt das gerade Gegenteil einer Apokalypse: es handelt sich um einen Ursprungsmythos des universellen Trickster-Typs[57], und das ganze ist beherrscht von einem eigentümlichen De-facto-Optimismus, um nicht zu sagen Zynismus: mögen Götter wüten oder weinen, diese Menschheit mit all ihrer Plackerei ist nun einmal unverwüstlich, ob mit, ob gegen die Götter.

Solcher Optimismus scheint in der Eisenzeit verflogen zu sein. Lag es an der Expansion der assyrischen Militärmacht, die eine Bahn der Vernichtung durch die Welt des Vorderen Orients zu ziehen begann? Späthethiter, Syrien, Palästina – Stadt um Stadt wurde da vernichtet, Völker wurden verpflanzt, Flüchtlinge ausgetrieben[58], alte Zentren ausgelöscht. Die histo-

---

[54] Güterbock 1946, 6–12; ANET 120f.

[55] Lambert, Millard 1969; von Soden 1978.

[56] Hes. Erga 108, vgl. West 1978, z. d. St. und Schwabl 1978, 784f.

[57] Duchemin 1974 vergleicht Atrahasis/Ea und Prometheus. Zum Trickster-Typ Ricketts 1966.

[58] Zur Auswanderung nordsyrischer Handwerker nach Westen in dieser Epoche Boardman 1961 und 1967, 57ff., 63ff.; van Loon 1974.

rische Katastrophe großen Stils war da, gesteuert von einem Zentrum, dem 'König der Länder'. In diesem destabilisierten Bereich ist jener geistige Umschlag am ehesten anzusetzen, die Wandlung des alten kosmogonischen Mythos, der den De-facto-Zustand begründet, zur apokalyptischen Prophezeiung. Von Atrahasis zur Lehre von den vier Weltreichen: diese unsere, die vierte Menschheitsepoche, kann und darf nicht endgültig sein; wenn erst die Welt durchs Schlimmste hindurchgegangen ist, muß das andere, Neue, Heilige anbrechen. So entstand die Konzeption, deren Metamorphosen zu verfolgen waren.

Die historische Sonderstellung der Griechen ist dabei ganz konkret in der Tatsache begründet, daß diese den alten Kulturzentren des Ostens nahe genug waren, um von deren Vorsprung voll zu profitieren[59] und jeden Fortschritt mitzumachen, und doch gerade so weit entfernt, daß die militärisch-wirtschaftlich so verheerenden Imperialismen des Ostens sie nicht mehr erreichten. Die assyrische Weltmacht kam am Horizont der Griechen zum Stillstand, die persische Expansion brach sich bei Salamis. Soviel auch in der griechischen Welt vom 8. Jh. bis zu Alexander, ja bis zur römischen Eroberung gestritten und gelitten wurde, so sehr sich Reiche und Arme, die 'Wenigen' und der 'Demos' bekämpften, die sozialen, wirtschaftlichen und politischen Strukturen der πόλεις erfuhren keine radikale Umgestaltung, sondern im wesentlichen kontinuierliche Entfaltung; und so konnte die geistige Kultur jene Form erreichen, die als 'klassisch' sich fast ein Jahrtausend lang erhielt. Wenn im Schatten naher Katastrophen apokalyptische Motivik vordrang, zur Zeit der Assyrer, der Kimmerier und der Perser, konnte sie doch die Grundhaltung nicht aus den Angeln heben: die Wirklichkeit ist zu akzeptieren. Das Sein ist. Als dann später die griechische Welt durch Rom militärisch und wirtschaftlich verwüstet wurde, war die geistige Tradition zumindest der Oberklasse zu fest geworden, um unmittelbar zu reagieren; Apokalyptik blieb im Untergrund[60].

Es könnte bedenklich erscheinen, wenn ein geistiges Phänomen wie Apokalyptik hier immer wieder mit Kriegsgeschichte verzahnt, ja von ihr abhängig erscheint. Doch sollte auch modernste soziologische oder strukturale Betrachtungsweise sich hüten, die archaische Realität der Waffen zu unterschätzen. Friede oder Apokalyptik bleibt eine nur allzu reale Alternative.

---

[59] Jeffery 1976, 25–28.   [60] Vgl. Fuchs 1964.

Bibliographie

Babut, D. 1975: Rez. A. P. D. Mourelatos (ed.), *The Pre-Socratics*, Garden City 1974, in: *REG* 88 (1975) 304f.

Bidez, J., Cumont, F. 1938: *Les mages hellénisés. Zoroastre, Ostanes et Hystaspe d'après la tradition grecque*, I–II, Paris 1938.

Boardman, J. 1961: *The Cretan Collection in Oxford*, Oxford 1961.

– 1967: "The Khaniale Tekke Tombs II", in: *ABSA* 62 (1967) 57–75.

Bollack, J. 1965/69: *Empédocle* I–III, Paris 1965–1969.

Bolton, J. D. P. 1962: *Aristeas of Proconnesus*, Oxford 1962.

Borger, R. 1967/75: *Handbuch der Keilschriftliteratur* I–III, Berlin 1967–1975.

Breslin, J. 1977: *A. Greek Prayer*, Pasadena, Calif. 1977.

Burkert, W. 1963: "Iranisches bei Anaximandros", in: *RMP* 106 (1963) 97–134.

– 1963a: Rez. Bolton 1962, in: *Gnomon* 35 (1963) 235–240.

– 1968: "Orpheus und die Vorsokratiker", in: *AuA* 14 (1968) 93–114.

– 1969: "Das Proömium des Parmenides und die Katabasis des Pythagoras", in: *Phronesis* 14 (1969) 1–30.

– 1972: *Lore and Science in Ancient Pythagoreanism*, Cambridge, Mass., 1972.

– 1975a: "Le laminette auree: da Orfeo a Lampone", in: *Orfismo in Magna Grecia, Atti del XIV convegno di studi sulla Magna Grecia*, Napoli 1975, 81–104.

– 1975b: "Plotin, Plutarch und die Platonisierende Interpretation von Heraklit und Empedokles", in: *Kephalaion, Studies C. J. de Vogel*, Assen 1975, 137–146.

– 1977: *Griechische Religion der archaischen und klassischen Epoche* (RM 15), Stuttgart 1977.

Caquot, A., Lemaire, A. 1977: "Les textes araméens de Deir Alla", in: *Syria* 54 (1977) 189–208.

Childs, B. S. 1959: "The Enemy from the North and the Chaos Tradition", in: *JBL* 78 (1959) 187–198.

Colpe, C. 1977: "Heidnische, jüdische und christliche Überlieferung in den Schriften aus Nag Hammadi VI,", in: *JAC* 20 (1977) 149–170.

Couvreur, P. (ed.) 1901: *Hermiae Alexandrini in Platonis Phaedrum Scholia*, Paris 1901.

Cumont, F. 1931: "La fin du monde selon les mages occidentaux", in: *RHR* 103 (1931) 29–96.

Delcor, M. 1971: *Le livre de Daniel*, Paris 1971.

Dexinger, F. 1977: *Henochs Zehnwochenapokalypse und offene Probleme der Apolalyptikforschung* (StPB 29), Leiden 1977.

Dodds, E. R. 1951: *The Greeks and the Irrational*, Berkeley, Calif. 1951.

Duchemin, J. 1974: *Prométhée*, Paris 1974.

Effe, B. 1970: *Studien zur Kosmologie und Theologie der Aristotelischen Schrift 'Über die Philosophie'*, München 1970.

Ellermeier, F. 1968: *Prophetie in Mari und Israel*, Herzfeld 1968.

Frutiger, P. 1930: *Les mythes de Platon*, Paris 1930.

Fuchs, H. 1964: *Der geistige Widerstand gegen Rom*, 2. Aufl. Berlin 1964.

Gallavotti, C. 1975: *Empedocle, Poema Fisico e Lustrale*, Verona 1975.

Gatz, B. 1967: *Weltalter, Goldene Zeit und sinnverwandte Vorstellungen*, Hildesheim 1967.

Graf, F. 1974: *Eleusis und die orphische Dichtung Athens in vorhellenistischer Zeit*, Berlin 1974.

Gruppe, O. 1924/37: Art. 'Unterwelt', in: *ALGM* VI, 35–95.

Gusmani, R. 1964: *Lydisches Wörterbuch*, Heidelberg 1964.

Güterbock, H. G. 1946: *Kumarbi, Mythen vom churritischen Kronos*, Zürich 1946.

Guthrie, W. K. C. 1967/81: *A History of Greek Philosophy* I–VI, Cambridge 1967–1981.

Heitsch, E. 1974: *Parmenides, Die Anfänge der Ontologie*, München 1974.

Helck, W. 1979: *Die Beziehungen Ägyptens und Vorderasiens zur Ägäis bis ins 7. Jahrhundert v. Chr.*, Darmstadt 1979.

Heubeck, A. 1955: "Mythologische Vorstellungen des Alten Orients im archaischen Griechentum", in: *Gymnasium* 62 (1955) 508–525 (= Hesiod ed. E. Heitsch [WdF 44], Darmstadt 1966, 545–570).

Hoftijzer, J., van der Kooij, G. 1976: *Aramaic Texts from Deir ʿAlla*, Leiden 1976.
Hölscher, U. 1965: "Weltzeiten und Lebenszyklus", in: *Hermes* 93 (1965) 7–33.
– 1969: *Parmenides, Vom Wesen des Seienden*, Frankfurt 1969.
Jeffery, L. H. 1976: *Archaic Greece*, London 1976.
Kahn, Ch. H. 1960: *Anaximander and the Origins of Greek Cosmology*, New York 1960.
Kapsomenos, G. S. 1964: "Ὁ Ὀρφικὸς πάπυρος τῆς Θεσσαλονίκης", in: Ἀρχαιολογικὸν Δελτίον 19 (1964) 17–25.
Kern, O. 1896: Art. 'Bakis', in: *PRE* II (1896) 2801 f.
Kerschensteiner, J. 1945: *Platon und der Orient*, Stuttgart 1945.
Kippenberg, H. G. 1978: "Die Geschichte der mittelpersischen apokalyptischen Traditionen", in: *StIr* 7 (1978) 49–80.
Kirk, G. S. 1954: *Heraclitus, The Cosmic Fragments*, Cambridge 1954.
Lambert, W. G., Millard, A. R. 1969: *Atraḫasīs, The Babylonian Story of the Flood*. Oxford 1969.
Long, A. A. 1974: "Empedocles' Cosmic Cycle in the 'Sixties", in: A. P. D. Mourelatos (ed.), *The Pre-Socratics*, New York 1974, 397–425.
Loon, M. N. van 1974: *Oude lering, nieuwe nering*, Amsterdam 1974.
Mansfeld, J. 1979: "Providence and the Destruction of the Universe in early Stoic thought", in: *Studies in Hellenistic Religions*, ed. M. J. Vermaseren, Leiden 1979, 129–188.
Marcovic, M. 1967: *Heraclitus*, Editio maior, Merida 1967.
– 1978: *Eraclito, Frammenti*, Firenze 1978.
Matthiessen, K. 1977: "Das Zeitalter der Heroen bei Hesiod", in: *Philologus* 121 (1977) 176–188.
Merkelbach, R. 1967: "Der orphische Papyrus von Derveni", in: *ZPE* 1 (1967) 21–32.
– 1977: "Ein neues orphisches Goldplättchen", in: *ZPE* 25 (1977) 276.
Metzler, D. 1977: In: H. G. Kippenberg, *Seminar: Die Entstehung der antiken Klassengesellschaft*, Frankfurt 1977, 285 ff.
Meuli, K. 1935: "Scythica", in: *Hermes* 70 (1935) 121–176 (= *Ges. Schriften*, Bd. II, Basel 1975, 817–879).
Mourelatos, A. P. D. 1970: *The Route of Parmenides*, New Haven, Conn. 1970.
Müller, H.-P. 1978: "Einige alttestamentliche Probleme zur aramäischen Inschrift von Der ʿAlla", in: *ZDPV* 94 (1978) 56–67.
Müller, C., Langlois, V. 1883: *Fragmenta Historicorum Graecorum* V 2, Paris 1883.
Noth, M. 1957: "Das Geschichtsverständnis der alttestamentlichen Apokalyptik", in: *Gesammelte Studien zum Alten Testament*, München 1957, 248–273.
O'Brien, D. 1969: *Empedocles' Cosmic Cycle*, Cambridge 1969.
Olrik, A. 1922: *Ragnarök, Die Sagen vom Weltuntergang*, Berlin 1922.
Pease, A. S. 1920/23: *M. Tulli Ciceronis De Divinatione Libri Duo*, Urbana 1920/23 (repr. Darmstadt 1973).
Pellikaan-Engel, M. E. 1974: *Hesiod and Parmenides*, Amsterdam 1974.
Pfiffig, A. 1975: *Religio Etrusca*, Graz 1975.
Pingree, D. 1963: "Astronomy and Astrology in India and Iran", in: *Isis* 54 (1963) 229–246.
Pugliese Carratelli, G. 1974: "Un sepolcro di Hipponion e un nuovo testo orfico", in: *ParPass* 29 (1974) 108–126.
Reinhardt, K. 1942: "Heraklits Lehre vom Feuer", in: *Hermes* 77 (1942) 1–27 (= *Vermächtnis der Antike*, Göttingen 1960, 41–71).
Reitzenstein, R. 1924/25: "Altgriechische Theologie und ihre Quellen", in: *VWB* 4 (1924/25) 1–19 (= *Hesiod* ed. E. Heitsch [WdF 44], Darmstadt 1966, 523–544).
– 1926: *Studien zum antiken Synkretismus aus Iran und Griechenland*, Leipzig 1926.
Ricketts, M. L. 1965: "The North American Indian Trickster", in: *HR* 5 (1965) 327–350.
Ringgren, H. 1977: "Bileam och inskriften från Deir ʿAlla", in: *RoB* 36 (1977) 85–89.
Rieth, A. 1971: "Schädelbecher und Schädelbecherfunde in ur- und frühgeschichtlicher Zeit", in: *AW* 2,2 (1971) 47–51.

Rowley, H. H. 1935: *Darius the Mede and the four world empires in the book of Daniel*, Cardiff 1935 (repr. 1964).

Rzach, R. 1923: Art. Sibyllen – Sibyllinische Orakel, in: *PRE* II A 2 (1923) 2073–2183.

Schwabl, H. 1978: Art. 'Weltalter', in: *PRE* Suppl. XV (1978) 783–850.

Soden, W. v. 1978: "Die erste Tafel des altbabylonischen Atramḫasis-Mythus", in: *ZA* 68 (1978) 50–94.

Solmsen, F. 1965: "Love and Strife in Empedocles' Cosmology", in: *Phronesis* 10 (1965) 109–148.

– 1980: Rez. West 1978, in: *Gnomon* 52 (1980) 209–221.

Tatford, F. A. 1953: *The Climax of the Ages*. Studies in the Prophecy of Daniel, London 1953.

Thomas, H. W. 1938: *ΕΠΕΚΕΙΝΑ, Untersuchungen über das Überlieferungsgut in den Jenseitsmythen Platons*, Diss. München 1938.

Trencsényi-Waldapfel, I. 1966: *Untersuchungen zur Religionsgeschichte*, Amsterdam 1966.

Vernant, J. P. 1960: "Le mythe Hésiodique des races", in: *RHR* 159 (1960) 21–54 (= *Mythe et pensée chez les grecs* I, Paris 1965, 13–41; vgl. *ib*. 42–79).

Van der Waerden, B. L. 1952: "Das große Jahr und die ewige Wiederkehr", in: *Hermes* 80 (1952) 129–155.

West, M. L. 1971: *Early Greek Philosophy and the Orient*, Oxford 1971.

– 1975: "Zum neuen Goldplättchen aus Hipponion", in: *ZPE* 18 (1975) 229–236.

– 1978: *Hesiod Works and Days*, Oxford 1978.

Wehrli, F. 1953: *Herakleides Pontikos. Die Schule des Aristoteles* 7, Basel 1953.

Widengren, G. 1954/55: "Stand und Aufgaben der iranischen Religionsgeschichte", *Numen* 1 (1954) 16–83; 2 (1955) 47–132.

– 1961: *Iranische Geisteswelt*, Baden-Baden 1961.

– 1965: *Die Religionen Irans* (RM 14), Stuttgart 1965.

Zuntz, G. 1971: *Persephone*, Oxford 1971.

– 1976: "Die Goldlamelle von Hipponion", in: *WSt* 89 (1976) 129–151.

Abkürzungen:
Zu den Abkürzungen antiker Autornamen vgl. Der Kleine Pauly I xxi–xxvi.

Aetas, aevum und saeclorum ordo
Zur Struktur zeitlicher Deutungssysteme

BURKHARD GLADIGOW

Den stark differierenden Anwendungsformen des modernen Begriffs von 'Apokalyptik' scheint zumindest die Zuordnung gemeinsam zu sein, daß in den einzelnen Apokalypsen mit Hilfe eines Stadienmodells eine Bewertung der jeweiligen Gegenwart vollzogen und, sofern es das Stadienmodell zuläßt, qualifizierende Prognosen publiziert werden. Der erste Teil der folgenden Überlegungen soll dem im Kontext solcher Stadienmodelle erzeugten Zeitbegriff und der Struktur der auf ihn basierenden Argumentation (Polemik, Legitimation, Unheils-, Heilserwartung) gewidmet sein. In einem zweiten Teil wird ein historisches Beispiel vorgestellt, das jenseits der traditionellen Vorstellung von Apokalyptik die Zahl von Zeitkontingenten mit dem Schicksal eines Volkes verbindet: die etruskisch-römische Lehre von den *saecula*.

1. Die Sozialdimension von Zeit

1.1. Eine Orientierung an Newtons absolutem, linearem Zeitbegriff hat für längere Zeit auch in den historischen Wissenschaften den Blick auf die Sozialdimension von Zeit versperrt. Erst verschiedenartige Ansätze aus ethnologischen, soziologischen und kulturanthropologischen Materialbereichen[1] machten deutlich, wie unmittelbar 'Zeit', das Generalisationsniveau von Zeit, an die sozialen und kulturellen Bedingungen der jeweiligen Situation gebunden ist. Die Frage nach der Sozialdimension von Zeit

---

[1] Schütz 1974, 62–135; Berger, Luckmann 1977, 25 ff., 38 f., 187 ff.; Leach 1978, 45–49, 63–66; Goody 1968, 30–42.

impliziert jene weitere nach dem Zeithorizont, d. h. nach Anfang und Ende des als 'Zeit' thematisierten Ausschnitts aus der soziokulturellen Wirklichkeit.

Für naturvölkische, vorstaatliche Gesellschaftsformen scheint charakteristisch zu sein, daß ein Bedarf an abstrakter Zeit nicht vorliegt[2]. Ereignis und Situation werden zwar als Folge vorhergehender Ereignisse und als auf folgende wirksam erkannt und dargestellt, eine 'Staffelung' der nicht um die aktuelle Gegenwart zentrierten Ereignisse findet jedoch nicht statt[3]. Gegenwart, Vergangenheit und Zukunft sind zwar im allgemeinen als temporale Aspekte, etwa des Verbums, vorhanden, ohne daß zugleich eine kontinuierliche Sequenz jeweiliger Gegenwart, Zukunft, Vergangenheit 'gedacht' würde.

Als Zeithorizont erscheint jeweils nur, was im Rahmen unmittelbarer oder mittelbarer sozialer Interaktion geschieht oder geschehen kann. Nur in diesem Rahmen wird ein 'früher' oder 'später' thematisiert; insoweit setzen schon einfache Formen von Zurechnung bestimmbare Zeithorizonte voraus[4]. Eine rituelle Wiederholung mythischer Exempla zu typisierten Gelegenheiten erzeugt andererseits sicher noch nicht 'Zeit'; Wiederholung in diesem Sinne 'vernichtet' eher, wenn man so will[5], Zeit als lineare Zeit. Hieraus allerdings unmittelbar eine zyklische Zeitvorstellung abzuleiten, scheint illegitim[6]; es ließe sich eher unterstellen, daß sich unter solchen Bedingungen die Alternative von linearer und zyklischer Zeit gar nicht stellt[7].

Differenzierungen von aktuellen Zeithorizonten und 'ferner' Vergangenheit und ferner und dunkler Zukunft sind allgemein üblich – nur stellt sich auch hier die Frage, ob die Differenzierungsbedingungen schon 'Zeit'[8] darstellen. Ein Bedarf an abstrakter Zeit scheint gering zu sein, solange sich das Problem der Synchronisation aktueller und individueller Zeithorizonte mit anderen nicht stellt.

1.2. Ein Bedarf an differenzierten und zugleich vergleichbaren Zeitebenen sowie an einer Ausdehnung der Zeithorizonte – über den Bereich sozialer Präsenz oder prinzipieller Kommunikationsmöglichkeiten hinaus – wird dann erzeugt, wenn sich kulturelle Subsysteme auseinanderzuentwik-

---

[2] Bellah 1973, 275 ff.; Stanner 1958; für die Hopi Whorf 1950, 67–72; allgemeine soziopsychologische Aspekte Fraisse 1968, 25–29; zu intrakulturellen Differenzen von Zeithorizonten Leshan 1952, 589–592 und Gurvitch 1958, 99–142.

[3] Fraisse 1968, 28 ff.

[4] Differenzierende Argumentation Schott 1968, 166–205.

[5] Eliade 1966, 73 ff.

[6] Momigliano 1966, 1 ff.; Vidal-Naquet 1960, 5 ff.

[7] Gunnell 1968, 63 ff.; Vittinghoff 1964, 571; Luhmann 1977, 160 ff.; 1976, 349 f.; zur ägyptologischen Diskussion Assmann 1975, 43 ff.

[8] Luhmann 1976, 347.

keln beginnen[9], vor allem das des politischen und des religiösen Handelns. Diese Entwicklungsphase von Kulturen beginnt spätestens dann, "wenn prominente gesellschaftliche Prozesse zeremonieller oder politischer Art sich als solche herausheben und wenn sie nicht mehr als gleichsam natürlicher Ablauf religiösen Geschehens erlebt werden" (N. Luhmann[10]).

Unter den Anforderungen von Herrschaftslegitimation und mit dem Ziel gelenkter Herrschaftstradition wird diese Differenz in den Instituten von Inthronisation und publizierter Genealogie zugleich konstituiert und überbrückt. Darüber hinaus kann dann das bloße Faktum der Sukzession von Herrschern als Argument der Legitimität, als 'historischer Anspruch', schließlich als moralisch gewerteter Beweis von Rechtmäßigkeit und religiöser Konformität gewertet werden. Das "primäre mythische Phasengefühl" (E. Cassirer[11]), das in einer einfachen genealogischen Abfolge Modell und Bestätigung finden konnte, wird auf diese Weise zu als Geschichte konzipierter Herrschaftstradition differenziert. In der Konsequenz von Herrschafts- und Stammesgeschichten dieses Typs liegt es, die Möglichkeiten von Irrtum und Verschuldung mitzureflektieren und in ein Verhältnis zu göttlichem Eingreifen (oder dessen Gegenteil) zu setzen[12]. In dem Maße, in dem die historische Tiefenschärfe zunimmt, werden die Abbildungsebenen in einem gewissen Maße variabel, werden die entworfenen Zeithorizonte zu einem Instrument der Interpretation.

Eine Zurechnung von Ereignissen zu Akteuren und der Aufbau von Ereignisketten, wie sie einem erweiterten politischen Aktionsrahmen entsprechen, setzen eine relative Chronologie voraus, die üblicherweise von einer Epochengliederung aus ethnozentrischer Perspektive (bezogen also jeweils auf den eigenen Herrscher) ausgeht. Strukturell ist dies die Transformation des sozialen Zeithorizonts in einen politischen. Mit der 'Politisierung' der Zeit ist ein neues Abstraktionsniveau von Zeit erreicht, auf dem die Konzeption von Zcit bzw. Zeiten zu einer Interpretationskategorie[13], zu einem Deutungssystem wird.

1.3. Ein Fall mit neuen Qualitäten liegt vor, wenn eine Abfolge von wechselnden Zentralherrschaften ('Weltreichen') mit der Entwicklungslogik der durch die verschiedenen Reiche verkörperten Ordnungsprinzipien begründet wird. Mit dem letzten Herrscher des eigenen Volks ist dann jeweils die 'Ordnung' wiederhergestellt, die 'Gerechtigkeit', ein erstrebter Endzustand, usw. erreicht. Das möglicherweise älteste historische Beispiel

---

[9] Brandon 1965; Gunnell 1968; Albrektson 1967.
[10] Luhmann 1976, 348.
[11] Cassirer 1964, 2, 136; vgl. auch Nadel 1968 s. v. Periodization.
[12] Albrektson 1967; David 1949; Gunnell 1968, 39ff.; Luhmann 1976, 346ff.
[13] Luhmann 1976, 349ff.; die analogen Probleme moderner 'Stadienmodelle' diskutiert Döbert 1977, 524–560.

einer derartigen Drei-Reiche-Lehre[14] findet sich in historiographischen
Konstruktionen im Umkreis von Kyros dem Großen: Kyros als dritter in
der Reihe von Herrschern über ein Weltreich; nach den Assyrern und
Medern herrschen nun die Perser. Ihre Herrschaft, Kyros' Herrschaft ist
errungen als Vergeltung für die von anderen früheren Generationen zuge-
fügten Übergriffe. Kyros also als legitimer Nachfolger und Kyros als der
Weltherrscher, der zu seiner Zeit die alte Ordnung als die neue Ordnung
wiederherstellt. Eines der Beispiele für die Wiederherstellung der alten
Ordnung ist die Rückführung der deportierten Völker durch Kyros; hierzu
Dieter Metzler[15], der die Drei-Reiche-Lehre als programmatische Darstellung von Kyros' Herrschaft betrachtet: "Eben damit führte Kyros aber
nicht wie Nabonid etwas Neues ein, sondern restituierte nur die alte,
zeitweilig gestörte Ordnung, wie denn auch frühe – und moderne –
Endzeiterwartungen die Zukunft als Wiederkehr des Urzustandes zu
erwarten pflegen."

Das Dreierschema der Weltherrschaft, das eine der Modellvorstellungen
für eschatologische Konzepte abgegeben hat[16], ist in seinem prinzipiellen
Aufbau allerdings schon im hesiodischen Sukzessionsmythos des Königs-
tums im Himmel[17], in der Abfolge Uranos, Kronos, Zeus durchgespielt
worden. Kronos der Usurpator macht sich in der Theogonie einer Reihe
von Übergriffen gegen Uranos, gegen Rheia und die gemeinsamen Kinder
schuldig und wird von dem dritten in der Reihe der Götterkönige, Zeus,
gestürzt. Zeus, der zwar ebenfalls seine Position durch Gewalt gewinnt,
kann seine Herrschaft dennoch auf das Recht stützen und errichtet eben
jene Rechtsordnung, deren soziale Realisierung[18] Hesiods persönliches
Anliegen ist. Zugunsten dieses dominanten Darstellungsrahmens bleiben
bei Hesiod andere traditionelle Motive, wie das der Trennung von Himmel
und Erde, im Hintergrund.

2. Sinn und Zeit

2.1. In der Konsequenz der bisher vorgestellten Prämissen von Zeithorizonten liegt es, daß zugleich mit der Thematisierung von Zeitkontingenten
Sinnbeziehungen[19] aufgestellt werden. Im Rahmen der Zeithorizonte einfacher sozialer Systeme sind es Sinnbeziehungen auf der Basis unmittelbarer
sozialer Aktion, mit der Konstitution längerfristiger kultureller Systeme ist

---

[14] Metzler 1977, 286.   [15] Metzler 1977, 287.
[16] Zum Dreierschema in Heilserwartungen Topitsch 1960, 249 ff.; vgl. ferner Taubes 1947,
35 ff.
[17] Hesod. theog. 154 ff., 453 ff.; zum Verhältnis zu altorientalischen Sukzessionsmythen
Heubeck 1966, 545–570 und Lesky 1966, 571–601.
[18] Philippson 1966, 667 ff.; Fränkel 1962, 124 ff.
[19] Grundsätzlich hierzu Luhmann 1976, 337–387; Luhmann 1977, 97 ff., 159–174.

es vor allem die Zuordnung von Ereignissen und Handlungen auf einen Herrscher[20], die ein Zeitkontingent begründet. Genealogie und Tatenberichte eines Herrschers bieten gemeinsam einen naheliegenden Rahmen für die Kontingentierung eines Zeitverhältnisses. Das Netz lateraler Sozialbeziehungen bzw. von asymmetrischen Herrschaftsbeziehungen hat seinen zeitlichen Rahmen und damit die Referenz von Sinnbeziehungen zunächst jeweils in bezug auf die Lebensdauer der Akteure bzw. des Akteurs. Mit dem Tode eines Herrschers und dem Auftreten eines neuen beginnt jeweils eine neue 'Zeit'[21].

Wie gering die Ansprüche eines zeitgenössischen Interpreten an eine Kohärenz von Zeithorizonten untereinander sein können, zeigt der Weltaltermythos des Hesiod: Die Menschen eines Weltalters sind in keinem Falle mit denen des vorhergehenden verwandt[22]; jede *aetas* stirbt restlos aus, wird hinweggerafft oder tötet sich in gegenseitigem Kampf. Selbst unter den Prämissen einer Degenerationstheorie wird eine lineare Entwicklung[23] auf dieser Ebene nicht konzipiert, 'Entwicklung' ist in einer Sequenz von Kontingenten dargestellt. Die Kontingente ihrerseits sind durch die Sinnbeziehung ihrer Extrempunkte charakterisiert: durch die Bedingungen, unter denen die Menschen eines Weltalters geschaffen wurden, und jene, unter denen sie vernichtet wurden. Der Darstellungsmodus erlaubt es, Sinnbeziehungen aller einem Zeithorizont unterstellten Ereignisse vorauszusetzen, ohne wirklich die Differenzierungsbedingungen[24] zu beschreiben. Die Frage nach dem Sinnzusammenhang der Kontingente untereinander wird durch die Logik ihrer Abfolge beantwortet.

2.2. Zeitkontingente erlauben es, Systematisierungen zu unterstellen[25], die im Rahmen von Punkt-zu-Punkt-Relationen aller Ereignisse nicht herzustellen sind. Zeitlich-numerische Systematisierungen gehören wohl zu den einfachsten Modellen der Darstellung: πρώτιστα; δεύτερον; τρίτον; τέταρτον; πέμπτοισιν[26], numerisch-qualitative Charakterisierungen, durch Himmelskörper oder Metalle, zu den komplizierteren, insbesondere bei einer Ausweitung der Metaphorik. Ein besonderes Problem stellen Konzepte, bei denen nicht eigentlich die Reihenfolge, sondern die Summe der Kontingente die Aussage trägt[27].

---

[20] Luhmann 1976, 359f.; Eder 1973, 295–299; vgl. auch Balandier 1972, 114–136; zur Charakterisierung von Epochen durch 'große Gestalten' Landmann 1956, 1–9.
[21] Widengren 1969, 360–393; eponyme Jahresbeamte stellen eine Fortführung dieses Prinzips dar.
[22] Hesiod. op. 121, 137f., 152ff., 161ff., vgl. 180.
[23] Zu Entwicklung und Argumentation Dodds 1977, 7–35 und Demandt 1972.
[24] Luneau 1964; Luhmann 1977, 159.
[25] Döbert 1977, 524–560; Landmann 1956.
[26] Cf. Hesiod. op. 109, 127, 143, 157, 174 in der Aufzählung des Weltaltermythos, wozu Gatz 1967, 34.
[27] Vgl. unten §4.

2.3. Mit einer Festlegung abgeschlossener Reihen von Zeitkontingenten wird zugleich die Frage nach ihrer Qualität als Zyklen gestellt, samt der möglichen These einer Wiederholung. Das Konzept einer definierten Zahl von Zeitkontingenten legt – werden nicht dezidierte Aussagen über ein absolutes Ende der/dieser Welt gemacht – Modelle einer ἀνακύκλησις nahe, sei es nach biomorphen Modellvorstellungen[28], sei es nach astronomischen[29].

3. Periodisierungen – Argumentationsstruktur

3.1. Das bisher Diskutierte läßt sich in die These zusammenfassen, daß eine Historisierung der Zeit[30] einem Bedarf an religiös-politischer Legitimierung und Qualifikation von Herrschaft entspringt. Das Interesse, Vergangenheit in den Entscheidungen der in ihr Handelnden präsent zu halten[31], läßt sich zunächst auf den Kreis derer beschränken, für die Geschichte Legitimationsbasis[32] sein kann: die Herrscher. Genealogien, Tatengeschichten und Stammesgeschichten sind darüber hinaus auch immer Argument für das Erhalten eines *status quo* oder das Erreichen eines *status quo ante*[33].

Zeitliche Deutungssysteme größerer Reichweite pflegen demgegenüber ihre Argumentation nicht auf die Bruchstelle selbst, die Zäsur zwischen zwei Perioden, abzuheben, sondern auf eine Situation kurz vor und kurz nach dem Wechsel. Aus der jeweiligen politischen Inanspruchnahme ergibt sich der erwünschte Typ von Synchronisation: Das zeitliche Deutungssystem und die zu interpretierende Gegenwart werden dergestalt zur Deckung gebracht, daß eine auf eine bevorstehende Zäsur zulaufende Entwicklung beschrieben wird – und damit ein zu erwartender grundsätzlicher Wechsel in der Qualität aller Relationen. Oder Synchronie wird so hergestellt, daß ein bereits eingetretener Neubeginn (Sukzession, Territoriumswechsel, Herrschaftswechsel usw.) durch 'sein' Zeitkontingent legitimiert und die Fortsetzung aller Veränderungen ins Positive in Aussicht gestellt wird.

Für den zeitgenössischen Interpreten ergibt sich das Problem, das seinen Intentionen entsprechend synchronisierte Deutungssystem mit den aktuellen und historischen 'Eckdaten' abzugleichen. Hier liegt das Potential an 'Plausibilität' und 'Sinngebung': In dem Maße, in dem die hergestellte Synchronie mit dem Lebensgefühl und Selbstverständnis der Adressaten

---

[28] Gatz 1967, 108–113; allgemein Demandt 1978.
[29] van der Waerden 1952, 129 ff.
[30] Zur Herkunft dieser Formulierung Luhmann 1976, 352 (Anm. 47).
[31] Zu den Darstellungsmodi Cancik 1975.
[32] Eder 1973, 288–299.   [33] Demandt 1972.

einer derartigen Geschichtsinterpretation in Einklang steht und zugleich als Folge 'schicksalhaft vorherbestimmter' Zeitkontingente großer Reichweite darstellbar ist, wird sie als 'richtig' und 'bedeutungsvoll' empfunden. Der Zustimmung zu einer solchen Einordnung entsprechend können dann Ereignisse der Gegenwart mit einer veränderten Einstellung wahrgenommen werden: als beschleunigt und auf ein schnelles Ende zulaufend ('Akzeleration der Zeit'[34]) oder im Falle eines unterstellten Neubeginns in euphorischer Wertung.

Zur Erhöhung der formalen Plausibilität zeitlicher Deutungssysteme sind im wesentlichen zwei Wege beschritten worden. Entweder wird eine als Prospektive hingestellte Retrospektive entwickelt, meist in der Form eines *vaticinium ex eventu* ohne volle zeitliche Deckung, die insofern als Prophetie und zugleich für eine gewisse Zeit geheimzuhalten vorgestellt wird (Beispiel: Danielprophetie). Oder es wird ein weitgehend kontextfreies Zeitraster zurückprojiziert, dessen Zäsuren jeweils auf dem Wege der Divination erkannt werden müssen, dessen aktuelle Zäsur jedoch mit den früheren in keiner notwendigen Beziehung steht (Beispiel: etruskische Säkula-Lehre[35]).

3.2. Neben eine kollektivierende, Epochen zusammenfassende Periodisierung tritt unter noch zu bestimmenden kulturellen Bedingungen[36] ein neuer Typ individualisierender Periodisierungen, auf den wegen der analogen Struktur hier hingewiesen werden soll: die Seelenwanderungslehren der archaischen griechischen Zeit[37]. Auch hier wird ein Stadienmodell von Existenzformen und -zuständen entworfen, bei dem jede Wiedergeburt und jede Existenzform in der Konsequenz einer früheren steht und bestimmend für die folgenden ist. Bedingung der konzeptionellen Möglichkeit ist ein präzisierter Seelenbegriff[38], der 'Identität' über viele Stadien und mögliche Kontinuitätsbrüche hinweg sicherzustellen war. Es ist zu bezweifeln, daß die Lösung des Kontinuitätsproblems einfach aus einer Identifizierung von 'Lebensseele' und 'Totengeist' hergeleitet werden kann: Die Interpretationskategorie einer individualisierbaren Zeit ist auf diesem Wege noch nicht erfaßt.

Der nachhomerische ψυχή-Begriff verdankt sein interpretatorisches

---

[34] Als spezifisch christliche Anschauung interpretiert bei Benz 1977; allgemein zu Katastrophenbewußtsein und Antizipation Jäger 1977, 58ff., 118ff.; zu Zeiterleben und Zeitschätzung Fraisse 1963.

[35] Vgl. unten § 4.

[36] Döbert 1973, 336ff.; R. W. Müller 1977; Gladigow 1979, 47ff.

[37] Burkert 1962, 98–142; eine systematische Interpretation der Seelenwanderungslehren als individualisiertes zeitliches Deutungssystem steht noch aus. Zum Verhältnis von 'Weltprozeß' und 'Seelendrama' Topitsch 1960, 245ff.; 1971, 201ff.

[38] Zu den besonderen Schwierigkeiten einer über das Materielle hinausgehenden Identifizierbarkeit Gladigow 1967, 410ff.

Potential[39] einem Stadienmodell von Existenzformen, dessen Realitätsbezug in den Zäsuren von Geburt und Tod liegt. Das Stadienmodell des 'Aufstiegs', auch hier ist ein Dreierschema bezeugt[40], endet am 'Sitz der Reinen' oder als Aufnahme unter die Götter; der Weg des Abstiegs führt durch unbegrenzte Wiedereinkörperungen – bis vielleicht eine Chance zum Wiederaufstieg genutzt wird. Die Probleme der politischen Stadienmodelle und der individualisierten sind an den wesentlichen Punkten (Tradition/ Kontinuität und Sequenz/Stadium) vergleichbar. Vielleicht stehen auch die Lösungen in einer Beziehung zueinander.

Zeit ist auf dem Weg über den Psychebegriff individualisierbar und wird auf diesem Wege zu einer präsumtiven Theodizee, sichert also das Sinnversprechen von Religion gegen mögliche Falsifikationen. Das Leiden des Gerechten ist eine Strafe aus einem früheren Leben, das Wohlergehen des Ungerechten findet seine Vergeltung in einer späteren Existenz.

Ein derartiges Periodisierungssystem leistet nicht nur, ein Weiterleben, aktives Weiterleben, nach dem Tode denkbar zu machen, sondern auch, eine Verrechenbarkeit von Leistung und Ertrag[41], von Versprechungen von Institutionen und ihren Realisierungen gegen eine empirische Realität aufrechterhalten zu können.

4. Die etruskische Lehre von den saecula

4.1. Die etruskische Lehre von den *saecula*[42] scheint zunächst ein einfaches, relativ kontextfreies System von Zeitkontingenten gewesen zu sein, dessen eigentliche 'Aussage' in der Summe der den Etruskern vorherbestimmten *saecula* gelegen zu haben scheint. Die römischen Antiquare haben dieser Lehre eine gewisse Aufmerksamkeit geschenkt, sie jedoch von Fall zu Fall mit römischen oder griechischen Konzepten kontaminiert.

Nach diesen Nachrichten, Varro und Censorin sind die Hauptquellen, seien dem *nomen Etruscum* 10 *saecula* vorherbestimmt; nach Ablauf dieser Zeiten würden die Etrusker untergehen. Das Besondere der Konstruktion scheint zu sein, daß zwar die Gesamtzahl der *saecula* feststeht, nicht aber die Länge der einzelnen *saecula*. Jedes *saeculum*[43] soll durch das Lebensalter desjenigen Menschen bestimmt sein, der als letzter von denen stirbt, die am Ende des vorhergehenden noch am Leben waren. Es wird also eine Relation aufgestellt zwischen der maximalen Lebensdauer je Generation und der Lebensdauer des ganzen Volkes.

Diese Regelung ist freilich so nur in einem Fall und einer Phase prakti-

---

[39] Topitsch 1971, 181–225; Kelsen 1941. [40] Pind. Ol. 2, 68.
[41] Zum soziokulturellen Rahmen R. W. Müller 1977.
[42] Quellen bei Pighi 1965; zum Gesamtrahmen Thulin 1905, 1906, 1909.
[43] Cens. 17,2; 17,5 ist auf die *Rituales Etruscorum libri* als Quelle verwiesen.

zierbar: Bei der Gründung einer Stadt oder eines Staates bestimmt von den an diesem Tag Geborenen der am längsten Lebende das erste *saeculum: quo die urbes atque civitates constituerentur, de his qui eo die nati essent eum qui diutissime vixisset die mortis suae primi saeculi modulum finire...* (Censorin. 17,5).

4.2. Für die nächsten *saecula* scheint diese Regelung kaum brauchbar; eine weitere Bestimmung sicherte jedoch der Säkularlehre die notwendige Flexibilität. Für spätere *saecula* sollten den Menschen die Wechsel von einem *saeculum* zum anderen durch Zeichen der Götter angedeutet werden[44]. Ein Trompetenton aus heiterem Himmel[45] soll das Ende des 8. *saeculum* im Jahre 88 v. Chr. angezeigt haben, das *sidus Iulium* nach Caesars Ermordung das Ende des neunten[46]. Varro hat aus den *Tuscae historiae*[47] als Dauer der ersten vier *saecula* je hundert Jahre angegeben, des fünften 123 Jahre, des sechsten und siebenten je 119; das achte sei zum Zeitpunkt der Niederschrift noch im Ablauf.

Die Rückkopplung an das allgemeine Divinationssystem geschieht also über *prodigia*. Diese Verbindung von *saeculum*-Wechsel und *prodigium* verlagert nicht nur die Legitimation des zeitlichen Deutungssystems vom Gesamtrahmen auf den aktuellen Anlaß, sondern bietet zugleich eine auffallende Umkehrung der üblichen Prodigienprokuration[48].

4.3. Normalerweise birgt das Prodigium als Bruch einer mit Vertrauen besetzten Ordnung ein gewisses Potential an Katastrophen, Umsturz, Rebellion, Krieg[49] – wenn auf dem Wege der Prokuration nicht das Richtige getan wird. Gilt jedoch die Prämisse 'mit Vertrauen besetzte Ordnung' nicht mehr, herrscht ein 'Krisen- oder Niedergangsbewußtsein[50]', verändert sich auch der Referenzrahmen der *prodigia*: Als Bruchstellen in den Strukturen sind die *prodigia* dann nicht nur "Einbruchstellen unbestimmbarer Möglichkeiten", sondern Indikatoren einer grundsätzlichen Änderung aller Systembeziehungen.

Anläßlich jenes durch Trompetenton angekündigten Wechsels vom 8. zum 9. *saeculum* referiert Plutarch[51] als etruskische Lehre, das Verhalten der Menschen, das Verhältnis zu den Göttern, überhaupt alle Dinge würden

---

[44] Cens. 17,5/6.
[45] Plut. Sull. 7; im folgenden dann die Angabe von 8 *saecula* als die den Etruskern vorherbestimmte Dauer. Sie beruht auf dem fehlerhaften Verständnis der Varronotiz ... *in Tuscis historiis, quae octavo eorum saeculo scriptae sunt* (Cens. 17,6).
[46] Serv. auct. ecl. 9, 46.
[47] Cens. 17,6; zur Datierung der saecula Diehl 1934, 260.
[48] Zum sozialpsychologischen Rahmen Gladigow 1979a, 61–77.
[49] Prodigia als Indikatoren einer Krisenstimmung: Günther 1964, 218ff.; Gladigow 1979a, 74ff.
[50] Zum Wechsel des Interpretationsrahmens in Krisen Jäger 1977, 66–74 ('Katastrophe als Sanktion der Natur').
[51] Plut. Sull. 7.

sich von einem *saeculum* zum nächsten ändern: "Wenn diese Periode ihr Ende erreiche und eine andere eintrete, erscheine immer am Himmel oder auf der Erde ein Wunderzeichen. Daher könnten die, die sich um diese Zeichen kümmerten und sich darauf verstünden, gleich erraten, daß Menschen von anderen Lebensarten und Sitten geboren worden seien, für welche die Götter mehr oder weniger als für die vorhergehenden sorgten. Sie (... das sind die 'Erfahrensten unter den Etruskern') sagten ferner, bei solch einem Wechsel der Generationen erlitten alle Dinge große Veränderungen."

4.4. Aus den bisher vorgestellten Nachrichten läßt sich keine in die Säkularlehre aufgenommene Vorstellung über durchlaufende Entwicklungstendenzen oder eine Logik der Abfolge erschließen. Das zuvor zitierte Plutarch-Zeugnis scheint lediglich eine Lehre zu referieren, nach der ein Wechsel der Qualität eines *saeculum* gegenüber dem folgenden das Entscheidende sei. Auffallend in dem genannten Zeugnis ist, wie nachdrücklich betont wird, daß sich alle Beziehungen synchron veränderten; es scheint so, als ob die Unterstellung eines Zeithorizontes unter eine gemeinsame Kategorie von dem Verhältnis der Götter zu den Menschen abhängig gemacht würde.

Die vier ersten *saecula* der etruskischen Lehre sind schon in der Antike mit den vier Metallzeitaltern in Verbindung gebracht worden[52], darüber hinaus zugleich mit astrologischen Konzepten vermischt. So etwa bei Servius zu Ekloge 4,4: *Sibyllini: quae Cumana fuit et saecula per metalla divisit, dixit etiam, quis quo saeculo imperaret et Solis ultimum, id est decimum voluit...*[53]. Beides scheinen jedoch eher römische Versuche zu sein, die Säkularlehre mit anderen Weltalterlehren in Verbindung zu bringen. In den Kontext der etruskischen Lehre scheint dagegen die Nachricht von einer Weissagung der Nymphe Vegoia zu gehören[54], die Grenzsteine würden im achten *saeculum* von den Menschen in böser Absicht verletzt und von ihrem Platz gerückt; wenn es geschieht, mit katastrophalen Folgen: *tum etiam terra a tempestatibus vel turbinibus plerumque labe movebitur. fructus saepe ledentur ... multae dissensiones in populo.*

Nach der Ermordung Cäsars deutete der etruskische Seher Vulcatius das Erscheinen eines Kometen, des *sidus Iulium*[55], als Zeichen für das Ende des neunten und den Beginn des zehnten *saeculum*. Die Legitimation dieser Prophezeiung[56] geschieht gewissermaßen *ad hominem*: Er erklärt vor der Volksversammlung, die ihn offensichtlich als Sachverständigen geladen

---

[52] Nilsson 1920, 1709.
[53] Kurfess 1951; Überblick über die Positionen der Forschung Gatz 1967, 87–103; Kraus 1980, 608–612.
[54] Grom. p. 350 Lachm.   [55] S. oben Anm. 46.
[56] Zu anderen Formen der Legitimation oben §3.1.

hatte, er prophezeie gegen den Willen der Götter (*invitis deis secreta rerum pronuntiare*) und werde daher gleich sterben, *et nondum finita oratione in ipsa contione concidit*.

4.5. Gegen nicht eingetretene Prophezeiungen eines Wechsels der *saecula* oder nicht eingetretene Untergangsprophezeiungen scheint sich die *disciplina Etrusca* mit der These immunisiert zu haben, in hohem Alter verlören die Menschen die Fähigkeit, die Zeichen der Götter zu erkennen, sie würden einem Wettläufer oder Viergespann gleichen, das sich schon in totem Rennen außerhalb der abgesteckten Bahn befinde[57]. Das Bild unterstellt die Möglichkeit, daß ein *saeculum* schon längst abgelaufen ist, die Menschen es aber noch nicht 'gemerkt' haben. Dies liegt in der Konsequenz der Säkula-Lehre als eines zeitlichen Deutungssystems, dessen jeweilige Synchronisation durch Seher erst 'erkannt' und hergestellt werden muß. Welche Folgen die Unkenntnis über einen Säkulumswechsel für die Menschen haben könnte, ist leider nirgends ausgeführt.

5. Die römischen saecula

5.1. In der Grundkonzeption sind von den etruskischen *saecula,* die zumindest durch ihre alternierenden Qualitäten bestimmt sind, die *saecula civilia*[58] zu unterscheiden, die auf dem Wege der Einsetzung von Festen mit einem Wiederholungsgebot konstituiert werden (*pro certo et constituto numero annorum,* Acro. Hor. c. s. 1) und 'alle hundert Jahre' als einen üblichen Wiederholungszeitraum kennen. So berichtet etwa Varro im ersten Buch von De scaenicis originibus für die *Ludi Tarentini* des Jahres 249 v. Chr. die Festsetzung *uti ... centesimo quoque anno fierent.* Spätere haben diesen *Ludi Tarentini*[59], die ein Modell für Augustus *Ludi saeculares* abgaben, zwei Zyklen, Feiern von 438 und 449, vorangestellt[60], obwohl Varros Bericht auf eine aktuelle Anordnung der *libri Sibyllini,* es gab viele *portenta,* Blitzeinschläge auf Mauer und Turm, verweist. Eine Wiederholung der *ludi* im Jahre 149 ist nicht überliefert, eine verspätete im Jahre 146[61] unsicher; 49 v. Chr. hat mit einiger Sicherheit keine Feier mehr stattgefunden.

Den Rekonstruktionen der zeitgenössischen Sakraljuristen und der späteren Historiker liegt das gemeinsame Interesse zugrunde, eine aktuelle Veranstaltung, die jeweilige Feier, in unveränderliche Zeithorizonte großer Erstreckung einzuordnen. Ein Wechsel der Legitimationsstruktur wird

---

[57] Cens. 14,5; Thulin 3 (1909), 62,2.   [58] Cens. 17,7ff., vgl. 17,1.
[59] Für eine deutliche Trennung der *ludi* der Republik und der kaiserzeitlichen Säkularspiele plädiert Weiss 1973, 205–217; zur Theatergeschichte Erkell 1961, 166–174.
[60] Nilsson 1920, 1699–1704 mit tabellarischem Überblick.
[61] Nilsson 1920, 1699f.

deutlich: Nicht das Gebot der Wiederholung, 'alle hundert Jahre', gibt dem
Ereignis seine 'säkulare' Bedeutung, sondern seine Einfügung in eine
übergreifende und insoweit sinngebende Vergangenheit.

So läßt Augustus für seine *ludi saeculares* des Jahres 17 v. Chr.[62] Säkularfeiern von 126, 236, 346 und 456 voraussetzen und in die Kapitolinischen
Fasten aufnehmen. Der Wechsel auf ein Intervall von 110 Jahren, möglicherweise im Rekurs auf entsprechende griechische Zyklen[63], erleichterte
wohl die Manipulation. Claudius und Domitian haben sich mit den Feiern
von 47 n. Chr. und 88 n. Chr. nicht an den von Augustus neubegründeten
Zyklus gehalten[64]; erst Septimius Severus tritt mit den *ludi saeculares* des
Jahres 204 n. Chr. wieder in die augusteische Reihe ein. Mit der Säkularfeier des Claudius von 47 n. Chr. wird eine Verbindung der Säkularfeste zu
Centenarfeiern *ab urbe condita* hergestellt[65], die 147 durch Antoninus Pius
und in der 1000-Jahr-Feier von 248 (mit einjähriger Verspätung) durch
Philippus fortgesetzt wird. Zosimos beklagt II 7, daß die Säkularreihe nach
Septimius Severus nicht mehr weitergeführt wurde und führt das gegenwärtige Unglück Roms auf die unterlassenen Säkularfeiern zurück: τούτου
δὲ μὴ φυλαχθέντος, ἔδει γ᾽ ἄρ᾽ εἰς τὴν νῦν συνέχουσαν ἡμᾶς ἐλθεῖν τὰ
πράγματα δυσκληρίαν.

5.2. Die Intentionen der ältesten römischen *saecula*-Feiern und die ihnen
zugrunde liegende Vorstellungswelt lassen sich nur indirekt erschließen.
Unter den Begründungen für die erste historisch faßbare Feier von 249
v. Chr. erscheint eine Abwehr von Krankheiten[66], ein Motiv, das bis in die
augusteische Feier weitergeführt wird: *pro sedanda et vertenda pestilentia.*

Eine *pestilentia sedanda* wird Livius 7,3,3 auch als Grund für die rituelle
Nageleinschlagung in die Wand des Jupitertempels auf dem Kapitol im
Jahre 363[67] angegeben. Für den Vollzug dieser Nageleinschlagung wurde in
den Jahren 331, 313 und 263 ein besonderer Beamter eingesetzt[68], der
dictator clavi figendi causa. Wenn Livius etwas später mit Blick auf das
Minervaheiligtum die Jahreszählung als Zweck der Nagelung ansetzt, so
scheinen hier auf den ersten Blick unvereinbare Vorstellungen vorzuliegen.
Man hat daher mehrfach[69] die Ansicht vertreten, die Jahreszählung sei eine
sekundäre Erklärung durch römische Antiquare. In der Tat ist es schwer
einzusehen, daß ein *praetor maximus* bzw. ein Diktator mit Sonderkompe-
tenzen nur zum Zwecke der Jahreszählung tätig geworden sein sollte.

---

[62] Pighi 1965, 23–25; die relevanten *tabulae* der Fasti Capitolini aO 40–42.
[63] Brind'Amour 1978.
[64] Überblick bei Nilsson 1920, 1717–1720; Pighi 1965, 73–103.
[65] Tac. ann. XI 11 und Suet. Claud. 21; zur Problematik Nilsson 1920, 1717f.
[66] Nilsson 1920, 1704f.; Pighi 1965, 8–12.
[67] Mommsen 1859, 175–180; Wissowa 1912, 430.
[68] Mommsen 1887, 156.   [69] Latte 1967, 154.

Auffallend ist weiterhin, daß zwei der vier Daten genau 100 Jahre auseinander liegen, 363 und 263 v. Chr. Mommsen hat hier eine eigene Säkularreihe erschlossen[70], mußte dann jedoch die beiden anderen Daten für falsch erklären.

5.3. Auf den verschiedenen Ebenen der Argumentation erscheint mehrfach das Problem, ob Jahreszählung und Abwehr von Unheil etwas miteinander gemeinsam hätten. Die Verbindung von *defixio* als magischer Festnagelung[71] und ein Definieren von Jahresgrenzen ebenfalls mit Hilfe von Nägeln entspricht wohl der Logik symbolischer Zusammenhänge[72]. Das Setzen zeitlicher Grenzen und ein Fixieren von Unheil sind nur dann grundsätzlich verschiedene Akte, wenn man einen absoluten Zeit- oder Raumbegriff voraussetzt. Beide angesprochene Maßnahmen ziehen ihr Potential aus der weitverbreiteten Vorstellung, Bereiche seien dann 'beherrschbar', wenn man ihre Grenzen rituell definiere. Was für räumliche Ordnungssysteme unmittelbar plausibel ist, gilt in der gleichen Logik symbolischer Zusammenhänge auch für ein zeitliches Ordnen: Wer 'Herr' über die Grenze ist, die Grenze setzen kann, kann Unheil zurückdrängen und die Chance eines Neubeginns nutzen.

Die Thematik der Feier von 249 v. Chr. ist unter diesen Aspekten zu sehen: Es herrschen Krieg, Krankheiten, schwerwiegende *prodigia* werden gemeldet[73]. Die sibyllinischen Bücher, die auf Geheiß des Senats eingesehen werden, empfehlen ein Opfer an Dis pater, die Einführung der *ludi Tarentini* und eine Wiederholung des Festrituals alle 100 Jahre. Das Ritual, das wir für 249 erschließen können, besteht in dem Opfer schwarzer Tiere (*hostiae furvae*), dem Vortrag eines *carmen*[74], möglicherweise einem Pferderennen[75] und Theaterspielen[76]. Der auf dem Tarentum befindliche Altar wird nach Beendigung der dreitägigen Feierlichkeiten wieder vergraben[77]. Insgesamt enthält das Ritual Elemente einer 'Totenfeier für das abgelaufene *saeculum*'[78] und Elemente, die für Prodigiensühnungen charakteristisch sind. Neben *lustrum condere,* das wohl ursprünglich 'das *lustrum* begraben' bedeutete, findet sich auch ein *saeculum condere* in dieser Bedeutung[79]. Die

---

[70] Kritik an Mommsens 'Jahrhundertnagel' schon bei v. Premerstein 1900, 2–4; ferner Nilsson, 1920, 1698 f.

[71] Clemen 1928, 241 f.   [72] Leach 1978, 39–44.

[73] Varro, De scaenicis originibus bei Cens. 17,7; Verrius Flaccus bei Festus s. v. *saeculares ludos* und s. v. *Tarentum,* sowie in den Schol. Hor. carm. saec. 8; Zusammenstellung der Nachrichten bei Pighi 1965, 59–66.

[74] Für 249 v. Chr. ist der Vortrag eines *carmen* nicht sicher; Diehl 1934, 271 anders Latte 1967, 247.

[75] Festus 478, 15 L.

[76] Erkell 1961 will die ludi Tarentini insgesamt auf Theateraufführungen beschränken; dagegen Weiss 1973, 206 Anm. 8.

[77] Zosim. 2,4,2.   [78] Wissowa 1904, 202.208.

[79] Verg. Aen. 6, 792; vgl. Nilsson 1920, 1707.

Vorstellung, man müsse (und könne) einen abgelaufenen Zeitabschnitt 'begraben', ist außerordentlich weit verbreitet[80].

6. Die augusteische Säkularfeier

Das Datum der augusteischen Säkularfeier 17 v. Chr. scheint nach politischen Gesichtspunkten frei gewählt worden zu sein; eine Vorverlegung um 1 Jahr gegenüber einem älteren Plan[81], vom Jahr 16 auf das Jahr 17, ist zu vermuten. Das gegenüber den republikanischen Säkularfeiern grundsätzlich veränderte Konzept[82] war bereits durch Vergils 4. Ekloge vorbereitet[83]: *Ultima Cumaei venit iam carminis aetas, magnus ab integro saeclorum nascitur ordo,* verfaßt am Ende des Jahres 41 vor Christus. Mindestens drei verschiedene Raster zeitlicher Deutungssysteme sind bei Vergil vereinigt: die alte etruskisch-römische Vorstellung der *saecula,* die Vorstellung von Weltaltern, Weltzuständen, die sich zyklisch wiederholen, und schließlich jene analoge und in Analogie gesetzte von 'Lebens'altern der Welt.

Wie schon ausgeführt, basiert der säkulare Rahmen der augusteischen Feier auf Intervallen von 110 Jahren, die hier zum ersten Male als *saeculum civile* erscheinen. Ein Grund für die Wahl dieses Intervalls ist wohl in der Nachricht des Varro[84] berührt, nach der *genethliaci* behaupteten, eine παλιγγενεσία würde sich alle 440 Jahre ereignen – bezogen allerdings auf die Wiedervereinigung von Körper und Seele. Eine vergleichbare Vorstellung könnte der augusteischen Säkularchronologie zugrunde liegen, etwa derart, daß sich nach den vorausgesetzten 4×110 Jahren mit dem Jahre 16/ 17 der *magnus saeclorum ordo* erneuert. Die Vierzahl der *saecula,* die sich so auffallend von der mit dem Jahre 43 v. Chr. angesetzten Zehnzahl der etruskischen Zählung[85] unterscheidet, wurde zugleich mit den vier hesiodischen Weltaltern in Verbindung gesetzt[86], erweitert allerdings durch die Hesiod fremde Vorstellung der ἀνακύκλησις.

Um den augusteischen Ansatz in ein weitreichendes, legitimierendes Referenzsystem einbauen zu können, wurde von den Sakraljuristen Roms eine Reihe von 4 vorausgehenden Säkularfeiern im Abstand von 110 Jahren (126, 236, 346, 456 v. Chr.) fingiert und den amtlichen Fasti[87] hinzugefügt.

---

[80] Usener 1913, 117 ff.

[81] Der Übergang von der kapitolinischen auf die varronische Jahreszählung ist sicher nicht Ursache, sondern Mittel; Radke 1964, 78.

[82] Wissowa 1904; die letzte Konsequenz aus der Verschiedenheit zieht Weiss 1973, 215 mit der Feststellung, "daß es Säkularspiele in der Republik nie gegeben hat".

[83] Kurzer Forschungsbericht bei Kraus 1980, 608–612; eine Bibliographie folgt *ANRW* II 31,2.

[84] Aus *De gente populi Romani,* Augustin, civ. Dei 22, 28.

[85] S. oben §4.   [86] Gatz 1967, 87–103.   [87] Pighi 1965, 40–42.

Warum zwischen den Daten der Reihe und dem Festtermin eine Differenz von einem Jahr besteht, bleibt allerdings unklar. Weiterhin wird ein sibyllinisches Orakel für das Jahr 126 v. Chr. 'erfunden'[88], das das neue Ritual der Säkularfeier von 17 v. Chr. enthält; als Interpret des bei Phlegon und Zosimos überlieferten Orakels ist uns der Sakraljurist C. Ateius Capito überliefert[89], der wohl zugleich auch sein Verfasser ist. Die Idee, die 'Einsetzung' der augusteischen Feier mit ihrer grundsätzlich neuen Ausrichtung des Rituals auf ein Sibyllinum des Jahres 126 v. Chr. zu verlagern, ist wohl ebenfalls C. Ateius Capito zuzuschreiben.

In diesem Konzept kulminiert die Publikationstechnik 'säkularer' Ansprüche: Der Neubeginn wird ex ante legitimiert; er entspricht dem vorherbestimmten *ordo saeclorum;* selbst die Enthüllung des notwendigen Rituals ist um ein *saeculum* zurückverlegt. In der Fiktion einer 440 Jahre zurückreichenden Reihe als säkularem Rahmen der augusteischen Politik zeigt sich jene grundsätzliche Intention, die zu interpretierende Gegenwart und den Zeithorizont, der die Legitimation liefert, möglichst weit auseinanderzuziehen. In der Gegenwart, in Augustus' Politik, erfüllen sich Korrelationen eines weitreichenden und fast die gesamte römische Geschichte umfassenden Deutungssystems, die, insofern sie als Teil eines Ganzen präsentiert sind, als sinnvoll unterstellt werden.

Bibliographie

Albrektson, B. 1967: *History and the Gods* (CB.OT 1), Lund 1967.

Assmann, J. 1975: *Zeit und Ewigkeit im alten Ägypten* (AHAW.PH 1975.1), Heidelberg 1975.

Balandier, G. 1972: *Politische Anthropologie*, München 1972.

Benz, E. 1977: *Akzeleration der Zeit als geschichtliches und heilsgeschichtliches Problem* (AAWLM.G 1977.2), Mainz 1977.

Bellah, R. N. 1973: "Religiöse Evolution", in: C. Seyfarth/W. M. Sprondel (Hrsg.), *Seminar: Religion und gesellschaftliche Entwicklung*, Frankfurt 1973, 267–302.

Berger, P. L.,/Luckmann, Th. 1977: *Die gesellschaftliche Konstruktion der Wirklichkeit*, 5. Aufl., Frankfurt 1977.

Brandon, S. G. F. 1965: *History, Time and Deity*, Manchester 1965.

Brind'Amour, P. 1978: "L'origine des jeux séculaires", in: W. Haase (Hrsg.), *ANRW* 16,2, Berlin 1978, 1334–1417.

Burkert, W. 1962: *Weisheit und Wissenschaft*, Nürnberg 1962.

Cancik, H. 1975: *Grundzüge der hethitischen und frühisraelischen Geschichtsschreibung*, Wiesbaden 1975.

Cassirer, E. 1964: *Philosophie der symbolischen Formen* (1924), Darmstadt 1964.

Clemen, C. 1928: "Die etruskische Säkularrechnung", in: *SMSR* 4 (1928) 235–242.

David, M. 1949: *Les dieux et le destin en Babylonie*, Paris 1949.

Demandt, A. 1972: *Geschichte als Argument*, Konstanz 1972.

– 1978: *Metaphern für Geschichte*. Sprachbilder und Gleichnisse im historisch-politischen Denken, München 1978.

---

[88] Diels 1890.   [89] Zosim. 2,4,2.

Diehl, E. 1934: "Das saeculum, seine Riten und Gebete", in: *RMP* 83 (1934) 255–272, 348–372.

Diels, H. 1890: *Sibyllinische Blätter*, Berlin 1890.

Dodds, E. R. 1977: *Der Fortschrittsgedanke in der Antike*, Zürich/München 1977.

Döbert, R. 1973: "Zur Logik des Übergangs von archaischen zu hochkulturellen Religionssystemen", in: K. Eder (Hrsg.), *Seminar: Die Entstehung von Klassengesellschaften*, Frankfurt 1973, 330–363.

– 1977: "Methodologische und forschungsstrategische Implikationen von evolutionstheoretischen Stadienmodellen", in: U. Jaeggi/A. Honneth (Hrsg.), *Theorien des historischen Materialismus*, Frankfurt 1977, 524–560.

Eder, K. 1973: "Die Reorganisation der Legitimationsformen in Klassengesellschaften", in: K. Eder (Hrsg.), *Seminar: Die Entstehung von Klassengesellschaften*, Frankfurt 1973, 288–299.

Eliade, M. 1966: *Kosmos und Geschichte. Der Mythos der ewigen Wiederkehr*, Hamburg 1966.

Erkell, H. 1961: "Ludi saeculares und ludi Latini saeculares", in: *Eranos* 67 (1961) 166–174.

Fränkel, H. 1962: *Dichtung und Philosophie des frühen Griechentums*, München 1962.

Fraisse, P. 1963: *Psychology of Time*, New York 1963.

– 1968: "Time. Psychological Aspects", in: *IESS* 16, New York 1968, 25–30.

Gatz, B. 1967: *Weltalter, goldene Zeit und sinnverwandte Vorstellungen*, Hildesheim 1967.

Gladigow, B. 1967: "Zum Makarismos des Weisen", in: *Hermes* 95 (1967) 404–433.

– 1979: "Der Sinn der Götter. Zum kognitiven Potential der persönlichen Gottesvorstellung", in: P. Eicher (Hrsg.), *Gottesvorstellung und Gesellschaftsentwicklung* (FRW 1), München 1979, 41–62.

– 1979a: "Konkrete Angst und offene Furcht. Am Beispiel des Prodigienwesens in Rom", in: H. v. Stietencron (Hrsg.), *Angst und Gewalt*, Düsseldorf 1979, 61–77.

Goody, J. 1968: "Time. Social Organization", in: *IESS* 16, New York 1968, 30–42.

Günther, R. 1964: "Der politisch-ideologische Kampf in der römischen Religion in den letzten zwei Jahrhunderten v. u. Z.", in: *Klio* 42 (1964) 209–236.

Gunnell, J. G. 1968: *Political Philosophy and Time*, Middletown Conn. 1968.

Gurvitch, G. 1964: *The Spectrum of Social Time*, Dordrecht 1964.

– 1958: "Structures sociales et multiplicité de temps", in: *BSFP* 52 (1958) 99–142.

Heubeck, A. 1966: "Mythologische Vorstellungen des Alten Orients im archaischen Griechentum", in: E. Heitsch (Hrsg.), *Hesiod* (WdF 44), Darmstadt 1966, 545–570.

Jäger, W. 1977: *Katastrophe und Gesellschaft*. Grundlegungen und Kritik von Modellen der Katastrophensoziologie, Darmstadt/Neuwied 1977.

Kelsen, H. 1941: *Vergeltung und Kausalität*, The Hague 1941.

Kraus, W. 1980: "Vergils vierte Ekloge", in: W. Haase (Hrsg.), *ANRW* II 31,1, Berlin 1980, 604–645.

Kurfess, A. 1951: "Ad Oracula Sibyllina", in: *SO* 28 (1951) 95–104.

– 1952: "Ad Oracula Sibyllina", in: *SO* 29 (1952) 54–77.

Landmann, M. 1956: *Das Zeitalter als Schicksal*. Die geistesgeschichtliche Kategorie der Epoche, Basel 1956.

Latte, K. 1967: *Römische Religionsgeschichte* (HAW V. 4), 2. Aufl., München 1967.

Leach, L. 1978: *Kultur und Kommunikation*. Zur Logik symbolischer Zusammenhänge, Frankfurt 1978.

Leshan, L. L. 1952: "Time Orientation and Social Class", in: *JAbSP* 47 (1952) 589–592.

Lesky, A. 1966: "Griechischer Mythos und Vorderer Orient", in: E. Heitsch (Hrsg.), *Hesiod* (WdF 44), Darmstadt 1966, 571–601.

Luhmann, N. 1976: "Weltzeit und Systemgeschichte", in: H. M. Baumgartner (Hrsg.), *Seminar: Geschichte und Theorie*, Frankfurt 1976, 337–387.

– 1977: *Funktion der Religion*, Frankfurt 1977.

Luneau, A. 1964: *L'histoire du salut chez les Pères de l'Eglise. La doctrin des âges du monde*, Paris 1964.

Metzler, D. 1977: "Reichsbildung und Geschichtsbild bei den Achämeniden", in: H. G.

Kippenberg (Hrsg.), *Seminar: Die Entstehung der antiken Klassengesellschaft*, Frankfurt 1977, 279–312.

Momigliano, A. 1966: "Time in Ancient Historiography", in: *History and the Concept of Time* (HTh.S 6), La Haye 1966, 1-23.

Mommsen, Th. 1859: *Römische Chronologie*, 2. Aufl., Berlin 1859.

– 1887: *Römisches Staatsrecht* 2,1, 3. Aufl., Leipzig 1887.

Müller, R. W. 1977: *Geist und Geld*. Zur Entstehungsgeschichte von Identitätsbewußtsein und Rationalität seit der Antike, Frankfurt a. M. 1977.

Nadel, G. H. 1968: "Periodization", in: *IESS* 11, New York 1968, 581–585.

Nilsson, M. P. 1920: "Saeculares ludi", in: *PRE* I A 2 (1920) 1690–1720.

v. Premerstein, A. 1900: "clavus Nr. 1", in: *PRE* 4 (1900) 2–4.

Philippson, P. 1966: "Genealogie als mythische Form", in: E. Heitsch (Hrsg.), *Hesiod* (WdF 44), Darmstadt 1966, 651–687.

Pighi, J. B. 1965: *De ludis saecularibus populi Romani Quiritium*, 2. Aufl., Amsterdam 1965.

Radke, G. 1964: "Fachbericht Augusteische Dichtung", in: *Gymnasium* 71 (1964) 72–108.

Schott, R. 1968: "Das Geschichtsbewußtsein schriftloser Völker", in: *ABG* 12 (1968) 166–205.

Schütz, A. 1974: *Der sinnhafte Aufbau der sozialen Welt*, Frankfurt 1974.

Stanner, W. E. H. 1958: "The Dreaming", in: W. Lessa/E. Z. Vogt, *Reader in Comparative Religion*, Evanston (Ill.) 1958, 269–277.

Taubes, J. 1947: *Abendländische Eschatologie*, Bern 1947.

Thulin, C. O. 1905–1909: *Die etruskische Disziplin 1–3*, Göteborg 1905–1909.

Topitsch, E. 1960: "Über Leerformeln. Zur Pragmatik des Sprachgebrauchs in Philosophie und politischer Theorie", in: *FS Victor Kraft*, hrsg. v. E. Topitsch, Wien 1960, 233–264.

– 1971: "Seelenglaube und Selbstinterpretation", in: *idem, Sozialphilosophie zwischen Ideologie und Wissenschaft*, 3. Aufl., Neuwied 1971, 155–199.

Usener, H. 1913: "Italische Mythen", in: *idem, Kl. Schriften* IV, Berlin 1913, 93–143.

Vidal-Naquet, P. 1960: "Temps des dieux et temps des hommes", in: *RHR* 157 (1960) 55–80.

Vittinghoff, F. 1964: "Zum geschichtlichen Selbstverständnis der Spätantike", in: *HZ* 198 (1964) 529–574.

van der Waerden, B. L. 1952: "Das große Jahr und die ewige Wiederkehr", in: *Hermes* 80 (1952) 129–155.

Weiss, P. 1973: "Die 'Säkularspiele' der Republik, eine annalistische Fiktion?", in: *MDAI.R* 80 (1973) 205–217.

Whorf, B. L. 1950: "An American Indian Model of the Universe", in: *IJAL* 16 (1950) 67–72.

Widengren, G. 1969: *Religionsphänomenologie*, Berlin 1969.

Wissowa, G. 1904: "Die Saecularfeier des Augustus", in: *idem, Gesammelte Abhandlungen zur römischen Religions- und Stadtgeschichte*, München 1904, 192–210 [Nachdruck: New York 1975].

– 1912: *Religion und Kultus der Römer* (HAW V. 4), 2. Aufl., München 1912.

Apocalyptic in the Hellenistic Era

J. Gwyn Griffiths

1. Introductory Remarks

The accepted view of apocalyptic in earlier discussions is that it was a literary phenomenon of Jewish origin which flourished between 200 B.C. and 200 A.D.[1] It is significant that the scholars who have planned this Colloquium have drastically revised this view even before a word has been uttered in the Colloquium itself. They have boldly included Ancient Egypt, Mesopotamia, and Iran in their scheme, and it is quite unlikely that in so doing they were envisaging that in any of these areas they would draw a blank. It remains true that this type of literature flourished in the time-span mentioned, which includes the Hellenistic era or at least a large part of it. However, since the Jewish contribution will be dealt with in other session, I shall naturally omit this from my survey. Yet I shall give the term 'Hellenistic' a mainly temporal sense.[2] Although much of the material has survived in Greek, this does not necessarily indicate a Greek origin; and in some cases a translation from another language is clearly implied.

2. The Deceitful Plan of Nectanebus

2.1. A well-known story which is heavily coloured with apocalyptic is that which concerns the Pharaoh Nectanebus. It is the story which opens the "Alexander-Romance", and thematically it links the closing phase of Egypt's Pharaonic history with the new era inaugurated by the conquest of Alexander the Great.[3] In the opening sentence Nectanebus is described as *the last king of Egypt*, after whom Egypt lost her prestige. He is also

---

[1] Cf. Jülicher 1894, 2835–36; Sickenberger 1950, 504–10; Bertholet 1976, 40; Grundmann 1967, I, 151 ff.

[2] Often it bears the sense of "Greek" as well, as in W. L. Knox 1944. More acceptable is the idea of "this entire epoch of the Hellenistic-oriental world of religion" as stated by Betz 1969, 136.

[3] For the earliest text see Kroll 1926. The best modern study is that by Merkelbach (with Jürgen Trumpf) 1977.

described as superior to all in magical power, so that he was able to defeat his enemies without soldiers or arms – a remark signally unverified by history, for Nectanebus the Second was defeated by the Persians in their final invasion of Egypt. Among the gods whom he would summon to help him was the Libyan god Ammon. When a messenger announced to him that huge armies from the East had come to attack Egypt, he laughingly replied that power depended not on numbers but on courage. But after filling a bowl with water, a feat of lecanomancy revealed to him that the gods of Egypt were now guiding the ships of *the hostile barbarians*, the term *barbaroi* being here applied to non-Egyptians. Nectanebus then resigned himself to Egypt's loss of independence: *he inferred that the King* (var. *kingship*) *of the Egyptians had now been abandoned by the gods*. After suitably changing his appearance he fled to Pella in Macedonia,[4] where he established himself as an *Egyptian prophet and astrologer*. In the meantime the Egyptians, troubled by his disappearance, consulted the god of the Scrapcum, that is, Sarapis in his Memphite seat; though it is said before this that they consulted *Hephaestus, the primal father of the gods,* where the reference is to Ptah, the creator-god of Memphis. Version *Γ* (ed. Ursula von Lauenstein, 3.23, p. 8) simply has *the gods*, but then mentions *the god in the sanctuary of the Serapeum*. Thus too the text of *β* (ed. Leif Bergson, p. 5). In reply the divine oracle evinces the apocalyptic statement which is all-important in the story:

> After fleeing from Egypt the mighty, noble, and elderly King and ruler will return to the land of Egypt after a time as a young man, having thrown off his elderly form and encompassed the world, granting to us the subjection of our enemies.
>
> (*Hist. Alex, Magni* ed. W. Kroll, 3.5)

Other texts refer to the enemies here as Persians.[5] Clearly the reference is to Alexander, and the sequel explains how he is to be regarded as the son of Nectanebus II, the last Pharaoh of Egypt.

2.2. In Macedonia the fame of Nectanebus as a magician reached Queen Olympias at a time when her husband, Philip, was away at war. She summoned Nectanebus to her and he instantly fell in love with her. She told him that Philip, according to rumour, was about to reject her in favour of another woman. Nectanebus confirmed the truth of the rumour, but said that a god would visit her in a dream and have intercourse with her; and from the union would be born a son who would avenge her on Philip. The god, he said, would be the Libyan Ammon, with golden hair and ram's horns. When the divine visit was duly experienced, Olympias

---

[4] In fact he fled to Ethiopia: see Diodorus Sic. 16.51.1, ed. C. L. Sherman (LCL), 1952, p. 380; cf. Ausfeld 1907, 126.

[5] *β* ed. Bergson 1965, p. 5; *Γ* ed. von Lauenstein 1969, p. 10. The version of A' is in the choliambic metre: see A. D. Knox 1929, 332. (Printed in the same volume as Edmonds 1929.)

declared that she wanted the real thing, not a mere dream (ἄλλο ὄνειρος, ἄλλο αὐτοψία). Nectanebus achieved this by impersonating the god. Before Philip returned, a charmed falcon had given him a dream in which the divine origin of his wife's pregnancy was explained. In spite of suspicions he was suitably impressed by supernatural displays which Nectanebus had performed; and one of these indicated that the son born to be king would conquer the world but die an early death. The sequel made Alexander, when he was twelve years old, cause the death of Nectanebus; but the latter was then recognized by him as his father and buried by him and Olympias with every show of honour.

2.3. This legend is replete with Egyptian ideas and practices, especially in the sections that describe the magical prowess of Nectanebus. We are, however, concerned with its apocalyptic prophecy and the way in which it is implemented; and this indeed is the essential core of the story. In the background is a defeated nation, overrun for the second time by the might of Persia, this time under Artaxerxes III. We recall that Jewish apocalyptic is also often related to crisis and gloom.[6] The Egyptian oracle foretells the return of the dishonoured Pharaoh to his country as a young man; and he will return as a conqueror – moreover as one who has conquered the whole world. From this vantage-point he will deliver Egypt from her enemies, who are identified as the Persians. The felicitous return of a hero or god is of course a universal theme. Cronus or Saturn will return with his Golden Age; King Arthur will return to lead the Celts to victory; and Christ will come again to the world in triumph. If there is a Messianic tone to the confident prognosis which concerns Nectanebus and Alexander, the manner of its implementation is distinctively Egyptian. A god is to have physical union with Queen Olympias, thus engendering a son who will be an avenger. The role of the son in Egypt's royal theology is that of Horus, the son of Osiris. He is Harendotes, *Hr nd it.f, Horus who saves his father*. Still more striking is the idea of divine incarnation. In the Egyptian doctrine of the Pharaoh's godhead the King is divine both as Horus and as the son of Rēꜥ. However, in the New Kingdom an elaborate actualization of the theory was developed in relation to the Theban deity Amen-Rēꜥ. This god was envisaged as visiting the Pharaoh's mother and procreating by her the son whose divinity is therefore warranted by a process of incarnation which is paraded in both reliefs and inscriptions. Hellmut Brunner[7] has published these with a detailed commentary and analysis, and it is only surprising that this theological doctrine, which obviously lived on in Ptolemaic Alexandria, has been so neglected by students of the idea of

---

[6] Cf. Morris 1973, 39ff. A feature of this study is a too rigid adherence to what the author calls (p. 32) "the stubborn fact that apocalyptic is a Jewish and Christian phenomenon".

[7] Brunner 1964. See also the sequel, *id.*, 1977.

incarnation, in spite of the considerable attention paid recently to this idea.[8] In his concluding discussion of 'Nachleben' Brunner[9] naturally mentions the legend about Nectanebus; and he shows how a rite presented in temple reliefs of the Late Era is likewise concerned with divine birth. A translation of the legend is provided by Emma Brunner-Traut[10] and she appends an admirable commentary in which the Egyptian motifs are expounded. She correctly describes (p. 292) the presentation of the incarnation-motif here an "ägyptisch-hellenistische Pervertierung des altägyptischen Königs-mythos".[11] Alexander was greeted, according to a well-known tradition, as the son of Ammon when he visited the god's oracle in Siwa. Yet a remarkable twist is given to the tradition in the later legend, for Alexander appears here not as the true son of the god, but as the illegitimate son of the Pharaoh Nectanebus. Admittedly, the earlier tradition itself is not free of a kind of duplicity, since the god's first appearance to the queen is in the form of the Pharaoh and only afterwards are we told that *He (the god) allowed her to see him in his divine form*; cf. my remarks in *JEA* 51 (1965) 218–19. But the ensuing reality is viewed as an act of divine procreation: see Brunner 1964, 52.

2.4. This raises the question of the motivation of the prophecy and of its claimed realization. At first sight, although it is a work written in Greek, it could hardly have pleased the Greeks in Egypt since Alexander's divine origin is conveyed in a much attenuated form – to put the matter mildly. Nectanebus himself, it is true, was theoretically divine, so that Alexander is at least credited with a vestige of divinity; or at the very least a Pharaonic prestige is thus attached to him. At this point it should be noted that there is evidence outside this legend for the belief that Ammon had impregnated Olympias in the form of a serpent: Plutarch, *V. Alex.* 3.2, records it; and a funerary inscription from Alexandria refers to it, calling Alexander *him whom Ammon procreated, taking the form of a serpent*.[12] In the Nectanebus story the Pharaoh, when he approaches Olympias, is preceded by a serpent; he also appears thus later at a banquet where Philip is present. Emma Brunner-Traut[13] explains the serpent as the royal uraeus. This suits Nectanebus as a Pharaoh, but the other tradition which also involves Ammon suggests that we have here the "Urschlange" with which the god was associated.[14] The ram was likewise a prominent animal form of his, and

---

[8] Hengel 1976, 23 n. 47, refers to Brunner's work, but does not discuss it.

[9] Brunner 1964, 214.

[10] Brunner-Traut 1963, No. 30, pp. 157–163. She also records the early material on pp. 76–87.

[11] *Ibid.*, 292–293. Merkelbach 1977, 79f. accepts these interpretations.

[12] See Merkelbach 1977, 108 with refs.

[13] Brunner-Traut 1963, 293.

[14] Otto 1966, 97; Gwyn Griffiths 1970, 374; Kaplony 1971, 252, points out that Amûn

Nectanebus assumes an aspect of this form too in his ram's horns. It is fairly clear that the legend of Ammon as the serpent-father of Alexander is an aetiological tale explaining the fact that in the Oracle of Siwa he was greeted as the son of Ammon by the prophet of the god.[15] The Libyan Ammon was doubtless not in origin identical with the Theban Amûn, but by the Hellenistic era the two deities were not rigidly differentiated.[16] In view of this it becomes clearer what Pseudo-Callisthenes has done. His revelation of the future is essentially political. Basically it proclaims that although Egypt is now dominated by the Macedonians, a dynastic and theological continuity has been achieved in that Alexander was the son of the last Egyptian Pharaoh. What is thereby satisfied is the national pride of Egypt. If so, one may ask, why was the work not written in Egyptian, that is, in Demotic? It is possible that the Greek is an adaptation, if not a translation, of a Demotic original. Bilingualism was undoubtedly a characteristic of cultured Alexandrians. John Barns[17] may be going too far when he says that in Egypt then there existed "a bicultural society more bilingual than modern Wales". Probably the incidence of Greek as a spoken language would have been limited, for the most part, to the Greek communities. If we consider, however, the literate minority, especially in Alexandria, then a fluid linguistic position emerges. Comparable compositions (to the Nectanebus legend) came into being in the early years of Ptolemaic rule, and as P. M. Fraser[18] remarks, "some exist in a Greek version, some in both (*i. e.* in Greek and Demotic),[19] and the Greek versions are probably translated or adapted" (from the Demotic).

2.5. To a Greek reader the Nectanebus story might reveal "a hostile or semi-hostile intent".[20] Of course it had splendid entertainment value, and Otto Weinreich[21] analyzed it as a type of tale of adultery which became widely popular. Yet the propagandist purpose is all too manifest, and a part

---

appears in the form of a serpent in the Late Period: he cites Sethe 1929, 27 on Amûn as the *Kematef*-serpent whom Sethe connects with the Agathodaemon.

[15] Plutarch, *V. Alex.* 27.3: ὁ μὲν προφήτης αὐτὸν ὁ Ἅμμωνος ἀπὸ τοῦ θεοῦ χαίρειν, ὡς ἀπὸ πατρός, προσεῖπεν. He is here following Callisthenes.

[16] Hamilton 1969, 69, quotes W. W. Tarn approvingly – Ammon was 'merely Amon transplanted to Siwah'. That is too simple a formulation. Syncretism is clearly indicated. See Bonnet 1952 s.v. Ammonium; he points out that the oracle was well known to the Greeks long before this. See also Kákosy 1978, 111–114.

[17] Barns 1973, 13.   [18] Fraser 1972, I, 682.

[19] A good instance is the *Tale of Tefnut*, the Greek version of which was published by West 1969, 161–183 from a papyrus of the third century A.D. It seems likely that the work of Eudoxus, *Dialogue of Dogs*, was also a translation from Egyptian: see Gwyn Griffiths 1965, 75–78. Dr. West 1969, 183, points out that "there was in the second and third centuries a demand for this Greco-Egyptian literature", of which she cites several examples.

[20] Fraser, *loc. cit.* (of Greek translations generally).

[21] Weinreich 1911. See Brunner-Traut 1963, 392; Merkelbach 1977, 78. I have not been able to see Weinreich's work myself.

of it relates to the idea of Alexander's divinity. Tarn[22] argued that the theory that a Pharaoh owed his origin to a divine visitation which produced the incarnation of the god in a human king really meant that the Pharaoh was given a double paternity since everyone knew who his true father was. He urges therefore that the Nectanebus story, as applied to Alexander, "was told in order to get rid of the double paternity, while safeguarding his claim to be pharaoh, by making him the son of the last native Pharaoh ..." Elsewhere, however, in the same study Tarn finds a different emphasis. "One would expect the Romance, of all works," he says (II, 364), "to treat him as divine; but the main thread of the narrative does exactly the opposite." It is not the god Ammon, but the fugitive Egyptian king who has fathered Alexander.

2.6. Such studied ridicule would please an Egyptian reader, one might think; it might also please Greek intellectuals who never accepted the idea of deification. Another Egyptian piece of motivation was to transform the conqueror, by this story, into a hero with native antecedents. They had done the same thing earlier with the Persian conqueror Cambyses by claiming him to be a son of their own people – the offspring of a daughter of the Egyptian King Apries.[23] National pride was mollified by such a fabrication, and of course it was a process affecting not only Alexander himself, but also the Ptolemies who claimed to be descended from him. Merkelbach[24] cites comparable instances, such as the idea that the Persian Cyrus, the conqueror of the Medes, was the son of the Median princess Mandane; and it is of interest that it was applied to Alexander in countries other than Egypt.[25]

2.7. A double motivation, relating to both Egyptians and Greeks, is possible, as Merkelbach convincingly argues. A good example presented by him is the idea of Alexander as an avenger of his father: this suits his role as Horus the son of Osiris, as we have already observed; but it also suits the

---

[22] Tarn 1948, I, 354. Derchain 1968, 208, takes a more favourable view of the interpretation intended. He says that "it must be assumed that it is based on a story that was deliberately spread in Egypt by the first Greek sovereigns in order to create a dynastic legitimacy"; it was, he thinks, "a kind of legalisation for his conquest of Egypt".

[23] Herodotus, 3.2 (a claim rejected by him). Cf. Ausfeld 1907, 123; Eddy 1961, 279. Kaplony 1971, 250–274 gives examples, including one which concerns Nectanebus I in *The Demotic Chronicle*, of the use of fiction in declaring a king's descent, with the intent of making it more honourable. Kaplony also compares with the legend about the birth of Alexander a passage in the Instruction of King Achthoes III (Merikareᶜ): *Kingship is a splendid office even when there is no son or brother who preserves his monuments. But one king promotes another. A man works for his predecessor.* See Volten 1945, 63 ff.; cf. Wilson 1955, 417.

[24] Merkelbach 1977, 79, citing Herodotus, I. 107 ff.

[25] Tarn 1948, I, 144, citing Persian, Egyptian, Jewish, and Arabic traditions. In the history of Wales a similar idea is associated with the annexation of Wales by England in A. D. 1536; the Tudor Dynasty, who achieved this, claimed Welsh connections.

actual activity of Alexander in avenging his father Philip on his murderers.[26] Many writers have ignored the climax of the oracle in the light it throws on motivation: the world-conqueror thus revealed is one who *grants us the subjection of our enemies* (that is, the Persians). There is plenty of evidence to confirm this favourable approach to the conquest achieved by Alexander in Egypt: if he too was a foreigner, he was infinitely preferable to the hated Persian oppressor. Here was a factor which, initially at any rate, assuaged the fervour of Egyptian nationalism[27] and it was a factor which worked beneficently on the minds of both Egyptians and Greeks.

3. The Demotic Chronicle

3.1. It will be noted that this legend, which derives from the early Ptolemaic era (although the first text comes from the third century A.D.), stages two dreams: one is arranged by Nectanebus for Olympias, the other for Philip. The dream as a vehicle of divine purpose is often attested in the Hellenistic era. A composition known to us from papyri and dating from the second century B.C. has been entitled *The Dream of Nectanebus*.[28] This presents a picture of the decay of religion during the same king's reign, but has no revelation of the future. *The Demotic Chronicle* is about a century earlier and it contains, though with many lacunae, a number of prophecies relating to the condition of Egypt. In fact *Chronicle* is a quite misleading title, as Revillout, the French scholar who thus christened it, realized later. He suggested a revised title, *Prophéties Patriotiques*. Eduard Meyer called the text "einen sehr dunkel gehaltenen Kommentar zu noch dunkleren Prophezeiungen".[29] Here, at any rate, is a feature which many have dauntingly ascribed to apocalyptic – a pursuit of *obscurum per obscurius*.

3.2. A little less sardonically Eduard Meyer[30] later described *The Demotic Chronicle* – the name has been allowed to stand – as an eschatological prophecy concerning the history of Egypt in the Persian and Greek eras. The prophecies (there are many of them in a series of oracles) are all composed *post eventum* and *ex eventu*, except for the expression of the hope that a native dynasty will arise from Heracleopolis with the aid of its god

---

[26] Merkelbach 1977, 82.

[27] Cf. Gwyn Griffiths 1979, 174–179.

[28] See Lavagnini 1922, 37–42; Wilcken 1927, No. 81; Hermann 1938, 39–42; Fraser 1972, I, 682f.

[29] See Spiegelberg 1914, 5.

[30] Ed. Meyer 1915, 287–311, this on p. 287. Spiegelberg 1914 provides a translation with the text. Other versions are given by Roeder 1927, 238–249 and by Bresciani 1969, 551–560. For further literature see Kaplony 1975, 1056–1060; Kienitz 1953, 136ff.

Harsaphes, to bring an end to rule by foreigners. The prophecies themselves are said to be inscribed on old tablets; and a priest, probably from
Heracleopolis, makes comments on them to King Nectanebus I. An
example of oracle and comment has this sequence:

> The goddess Mehit (the celestial cow-goddess identified with the uraeus) brings the god of
> Heracleopolis in her apron.
>   This means: Mehit, who is the uraeus on the forehead, will bring the god of Heracleopolis
> (Harsaphes) content of heart to the house of the Pharaoh. It is Harsaphes that will give
> orders to the ruler after the foreigners and the Ionians.
> Be joyful, thou prophet of Harsaphes!
>   The prophet of Harsaphes will proceed in joy (in the time) after the Ionians, for a ruler
> shall have arisen in Heracleopolis.
>   (*Demotic Chronicle*, Recto Col. II, 23 – III, 1, Spiegelberg, pp. 10–16.)

In the phrase "the foreigners and the Ionians"[31] the former group must
refer to the Persians, the latter to the Greek rulers, so that the prophet
envisages the replacement of the Ptolemaic domination by a new native
regime. If we ask why Heracleopolis in Middle Egypt is singled out for the
honour of producing the royal restorer of Egyptian independence, it is
likely that during the third century B.C. a noble family in that city exerted
propaganda in its own favour and in favour also of the local cult of
Harsaphes.[32] The god Thoth also plays a role, for it is stated in Col. II, 4
that *what they* (recent Egyptian Pharaohs) *have done has been written down by
Thoth when he examined their affairs in Heracleopolis.* Thoth is doubtless
regarded here as the scribe of the gods; he is pre-eminently associated with
the writings stored in the libraries of Egyptian temples, as E. A. E.
Reymond[33] shows in her edition of Demotic papyrus texts from the
Fayûm. Incidentally, although this document deals with recent history, it
shows some stylistic affinities to more ancient compositions. *It is a King of
the South that will come,* states the *Prophecy of Neferti* (57f.),[34] whose text
derives from the New Kingdom.

    3.3. A feature of the condemnation of certain Pharaohs is its emphasis on
their failure to act in accordance with "the Law". This is stated of Hakoris
after a more complimentary beginning:

---

[31] Eddy 1961, 291 n. 60, argues that variations in the references to foreigners imply "two
recensions", but this is not convincing.

[32] Cf. Kaplony 1975, 1057, who refers to the rival activity of Sebennytus; in 1971, 258, he
shows that the existence of Khababash, whom he regards as the worthy but unsuccessful son
of Nectanebus II, was an obstacle to the Heracleopolitan theory. The exact origin of
Khababash (or Khabbash) is, however, much debated; see Kienitz 1953, 185–89; de
Meulenaere 1963, 90–93; and Spalinger 1978, 142–152, where he is viewed as a native ruler
and enemy of Persia, but unrelated to Nectanebus II.

[33] Reymond 1977. See esp. p. 39. Some of the writings are, however, associated with Ptah
and Neïth.

[34] Ed. W. Helck 1970, 49; Wilson 1955, 445; cf. Kaplony 1975, 1058.

The fifth ruler who came after the Medes was Hakoris, Lord of the Crown, whose time of sovereignty was made full since he was beneficent to the temples. He was overthrown because he abandoned the Law and did not have solicitude for his brothers.

(*Demotic Chronicle*, Recto Col. IV, 9–10.)

A similar statement is then made concerning Nepherites:

The sixth ruler who came after the Medes was Nepherites. 'He has not lived.' That means, the order was not made to allow him to live. It happened that the Law at the time of his father was abandoned... Thus the sacrilege was avenged after him on his son.

(*Demotic Chronicle*, Recto, Col. IV, 11–12.)

It seems that the reference is to the short reign (of four months) enjoyed by Nepherites II;[35] disrespect of the Law is imputed not to him, but to his father, the idea being that the sins of the fathers are visited on the children. On the other hand, it is favourably stated (III, 19) of Amyrtaius that *the Law was restored in his time* and that he was allowed to proceed in the traditional manner (lit. *of yesterday*). Similarly the hope for the future is that the restored Egyptian ruler will be loyal to the Law:

Rejoice over the ruler that will be, for he will not abandon the Law.

(*Ibid.*, Col. III, 16.)

Here the ideal entertained is previously suggested by the statement (III, 11) that *one will place his eldest son on his throne, for the ruler who will be like Horus the son of Isis*; naturally it is added that Isis herself will rejoice over the future ruler. The concept of law as expressed in the word *hep*[36] dates from the Middle Kingdom and its usages are wide, applicable to the laws of the Pharaoh, of the country, of temples, and of the gods, the word being used mostly in the plural.[37] Greek equivalents of the word in priestly decrees include νόμοι, δίκαιον, and δικαιοσύνη.[38] Occurrences in *The Demotic Chronicle* are interpreted by Nims to mean "law, right, or justice". He cites[39] the use of *ir p3 hp n* in the sense of "punish", as in P. Insinger, 34, 19: He (god) punishes sin and he rewards good – a sentiment which is conceptually close to our theme. With the whole concept of law in Egypt is firmly linked the ideas attached to Maʿat, both as a goddess and as an abstraction, where truth and justice accompany order and harmony; but in the practical application of them the terms *hp* and *wḏ nyswt* ("King's command") are basic.[40]

---

[35] Spiegelberg 1914, 18 n. 11.

[36] *Gm hp*: 'law was (re)discovered.' The article is missing here; in the other *loci* it is *p3 hp*, with the article.

[37] *Wb.* II, 488; Erichsen, *Demotisches Glossar*, 274, where the extended sense of "right, justice" is also noted, as in *ir p3 hp*, "to do right (to some one)". Spiegelberg (1914) lists the occurrences in this text on p. 70. In Demotic the word occurs usually in the singular.

[38] See the fine study by Nims 1948, 243–260, this on p. 244.

[39] Nims 1948, 246.

[40] Cf. Otto 1956, 150–159, esp. 151f. He discusses *The Demotic Chronicle* in his 1970, 147,

3.4. In the period of the Demotic writings, which begin in the seventh
century B.C., *hp* is often associated with the god Thoth and sometimes
bears a wider sense relating to the laws of nature: *hp n ntr*, "the law of the
god", probably implies a set of natural laws.[41] In *The Demotic Chronicle*,
however, as applied to the Pharaohs, the main emphasis is moral, and it is
developed not only with regard to the idea of forsaking the traditional
Law, but also in relation to the success or failure of a regime. It was
disloyalty to the Law that accounted for the failures of the past; and the
restoration of the independent national state will be under rulers beloved of
God. It was Eduard Meyer[42] who first noticed the parallelism between this
view of history, with its simple correlation of moral and material values,
and that found in the Hebrew books devoted to early history, especially
Judges and *Kings*. He also notes that the idea of the "Law" was elaborated in
Egypt from the Twenty-sixth Dynasty onwards, and that in the same
period the Law of Deuteronomy was introduced in Judah. Devotion to the
Torah was of course basic in Jewish historical thought; and it is given
prominence in Jewish apocalyptic.[43]

3.5. The possibility emerges here, then, of the interplay of two national
traditions. Yet a total assessment of the impact of *The Demotic Chronicle* is
prevented by the fact that the beginning and end are lost. Probably the end
was optimistic in its view of the future. Whereas the details given about
Dynasties XXVIII–XXX are strikingly confirmed by Manetho and the
monuments,[44] the moralistic estimation of the character of each reign is too
general and uninformative to be of value.[45] The Twenty-eighth Dynasty
was itself one which ended the previous Persian supremacy, and a repetition of this feat is now longed for. Kienitz[46] points out that many monuments are extant relating to priests of Kings Nectanebus I and II, and some
of these continued to function in the early Ptolemaic era. Clearly such

---

and believes that its purpose is to bridge the discrepancy between the divine world-order and
historical reality. On the question of the correlation which the *Chronicle* inculcates between
political success or failure and the moral conduct of the ruler, Otto avers that the idea is quite
contrary to the traditional Egyptian view which saw the behaviour of the King as identical
with the will of God and as necessarily conducive, therefore, to a good end. Whereas the
Pharaoh, especially as the son of Rē[c] and as the upholder of Ma[c]at, was in the main regarded in
this light, there are a few suggestions of the belief that he could sometimes err. The *Instruction
for Merikarē* is an example, for the King there admits his errors, strategic and moral, and
declares that only moral conduct will stand the test of the *Totengericht*; cf. Brunner 1970, 125 f.
See too the complaint of Tut[c]ankhamûn on a stela, referring to the reign of Akhenaten: *The
Land was topsy-turvy and the gods turned their backs on this land*; see Gardiner 1961, 237.

[41] Reymond 1977, 36.   [42] Ed. Meyer 1915, 298 f.
[43] Cf. Morris 1973, 68–70.   [44] Kienitz 1953, 137.
[45] "Wertlos" according to Kienitz, *ibid.*
[46] Kienitz 1953, 138–139. Manetho was himself a priest who wrote under Ptolemy II. Cf.
Spalinger 1978, 143 ff., where Pseudo-Callisthenes is also discussed.

people might well nurture the hope of a new native regime in association with ambitious noble families. Yet the *Chronicle*, as it stands, tends to merge the national emphasis in the moral urge: the new ruler will not abandon the Law (III, 16).

4. The "Big Dog"

In spite of the favourable attitude adopted by both Alexander and the early Ptolemies towards Egyptian religion,[47] a bitter priestly reaction is revealed in the *Chronicle*. After a mention of *the Ionians* who come to Egypt to rule the country there comes a dictum of the oracle:

The dogs live. The Big Dog, he finds something to eat.

(*Ibid.*, VI, 21.)

The reference is again to 'the Ionians' (= the Greeks in a more general sense), and it has not surprisingly been suggested that the 'Big Dog' is Alexander the Great. One recalls the symbolic animals of Jewish apocalyptic – the fallen angels of *1 Enoch* 86. 3–4 who become bulls and engender elephants, camels, and asses; or the Beast, Dragon, and Lion of *Revelation*. The "Big Dog" has been interpreted as a suitable symbol of Alexander because of the likely allusion to his famous Molossian hounds.[48] But the reference to Persians in V, 15 as *herds of wild beasts* confirms the impression that the symbolism is Egyptian. The animals are all connected with Seth, who by this time is firmly linked to the desert, to foreign lands, and to the forces of chaos. The numerous animal forms assumed by Seth and his followers in the Edfu Temple Texts are a valid parallel. As for the "Big Dog", the mythic prototype may well be Seth himself, for the Seth-animal was originally, in all probability, a member of the canine family.[49]

5. From "The Archive of Ḥor"

5.1. Whereas astrological predictions can be classified as prophecy, they have no close affinity to any definition of apocalyptic, especially as they are usually linked to personal horoscopes. Astrology was of course combined

---

[47] For the tradition that Alexander was crowned in Memphis see Bergman 1968, 92–94. The "Satrap Stela", 3–4, refers to the restoration to Egypt by Ptolemy I Soter of divine images taken to Asia. Cf. Kienitz 1953, 148. Swinnen 1973, 117 n. 1, dubs the statement as a "cliché". Certainly a strong traditional element is present (cf. below, "The Prediction of the Lamb"), but at least the claim to have done so is significant. Cf. Roeder 1959, 98; Lorton 1971, 162; Spalinger 1978, 147–148.

[48] Hall 1930, 75.

[49] Gwyn Griffiths 1960, 32; 37–38. te Velde 1967, 25 thinks it was "an imaginary animal related to the griffin".

with astronomy, and the word ἀστρολογία includes both. An inscription from the third century B.C. from Tell Faraoun concerns an astronomer and snake-charmer named Harkhebi. He is described as one *who observes everything observable in heaven and earth* and as one *who announces rising and setting at their times, with the gods who foretell the future.*[50] The text, however, includes no predictions. On the other hand, it is likely that astrology encouraged, especially in the Hellenistic era, the type of more universal prediction which we associate with apocalyptic.

5.2. Dreams were commonly regarded as vehicles of revelation, and a dream recorded on an ostracon belonging to a group which J. D. Ray[51] has recently edited conveys what may be called a "Little Apocalypse". Together these ostraca constitute what Ray entitles an "Archive", although he engagingly admits (p. xiv) that a more correct title might be "the waste-paper basket of a troubled man". The ostracon in question ("Additional Text" 59, pp. 167 ff.) records two dreams. In the first Imhotep son of Ptah is mentioned, and *Year 26, Mekhir* as the date of the experience. Ray has shrewdly noted that in Brugsch, *Thesaurus*, 981, a festival of Imhotep in the Memphite necropolis is located on 11 Mekhir, so that the date of the dream experience can be confidently dated to March 10th, 155 B.C. In the first dream the priests of the sanctuary of Imhotep request the election of a certain priest to be their leader. The second dream begins with the statement:[52]

(7) I dreamt (that) (8) he was (in) a panic. A great destruction (had) occurred. There were two gods with [him].

The first person represents Hor himself. Less certain is the reference of the "he"; but as the scribe Imhotep has just been mentioned, he may well be intended. The words for "great destruction" are *sk ꜥ3*, where *sk* is presumably connected with the earlier *ski*, "destroy" (*Wb.* IV, 312 f.). At any rate what is envisaged here is a mighty cataclysm, for we are then told:

(10) ... Thoth judges: (11) no province shall remain [among them] in any way (on) earth. They shall not stand.

Your great man – doubtless Imhotep the scribe – is then mentioned in a context which suggests an ordeal of fire. Afterwards Hor is commanded: (17) *Choose a town (of) Egypt.* He confidently replies:

(18) 'Piahthoth and Amen-Rē' lord of Sambehdet are in it and [every god (?)]
(19) is in it.' I said to him, 'Will it be another town [but]
(20) Pi(?)-Thoth? Isis rests in [it ...]

---

[50] See Neugebauer and Parker 1969, III, 214 with refs.
[51] Ray 1976. I am indebted to Mr Ray for calling my attention to this.
[52] Ray's translation has been used.

Ray believes that Pi(?)-Thoth was in the northern Delta, near Buto, and that the town of Temenēsi, where Hor had been a pastophorus of Isis, was more or less the same place. If so, Hor's answer is quite touching. In a cataclysm which threatens the whole of Egypt with destruction, if he may choose one place to survive, then it will be his own endeared *Kleinstadt*, which is blessed by gods, and especially by his beloved Isis.

6. The Prediction of the Lamb under Bokkhoris

6.1. That animals sometimes had the faculty of speech and of perceptive prediction was a belief held by several peoples of antiquity. The best known example is Balaam's ass (Num. 22.28ff.) who not only spoke to her master but was able to perceive, unlike him, that the angel of the Lord was before them on the way. According to the *Iliad* (19.404ff.) one of the horses of Achilles, endowed with speech by the goddess Hera, predicted that the day of his death was near.[53] A popular tradition in Egypt maintained that during the reign of Bokkhoris of Saïs (ca. 718–712 B.C.),[54] a Pharaoh of the Twenty-fourth Dynasty, a lamb spoke. Indeed these words – *a lamb spoke* – are all that quotations from Manetho[55] tell us about the event. By a fortunate chance a Demotic papyrus now in Vienna tells us a good deal more, although it is fragmentary, about the predictions made by this lamb. They are at first of a gloomy nature, to the effect that Egypt faces a catastrophic sequence of events during which the shrines of her gods will be taken away to Nineveh – clearly a reference to the Assyrian conquest of Egypt in 671–774 B.C. The curses of the lamb refer to lamentations in the cities of Egypt:[56]

(14) There is much malediction against it (Egypt). Heliopolis weeps in the East, for it is vanquished ..., Bubastis weeps, ...; one makes the streets of Sebennytus into a vineyard.

(19) The lamb finished its curses against all these (places). Pshenhor spoke to him: 'Shall this happen (before we have?) observed it?'

(20) He said to him: 'It shall happen, while I ... upon the head of the King, which shall be after the end of 900 years, (21) while I have power in Egypt, yet ...

(Vienna P. Dem. D. 10.000.)

Here the description of the woes of the cities, which are said to be cursed by the lamb, recalls a pattern which occurs in the Old Testament, the earliest being in Num. 21.29, מוֹאָב לְךָ־אוֹי *Woe to thee, Moab*; cf. Is. 23.1–8, of lamentation in Tyre and Sidon, and Matt. 11.20 with its woes to

---

[53] For this and much other relevant material see Kákosy 1966, 341–58. The Rev. D. R. Griffiths reminds me that the serpent in the Garden is the first example in the O. T.: it is a talking and prophetic creature.

[54] Hornung 1978, 164.   [55] Ed. W. G. Waddell (LCL), 1948, 164.

[56] For the text see Krall 1898, 3–11; and esp. Janssen 1954, 17–29. Here I translate his Dutch version. I owe this valuable ref. to Dr Eve Reymond.

Chorazin, Bethsaida, and Capernaum. But there are plenty of antecedents in Egypt. Texts involving the execration of Asiatic princes by breaking pottery which bears their names mention cities such as Byblos and Jerusalem.[57] In *The Admonitions of Ipu-Wer* a state of confusion and chaos is portrayed and it is said (10.3) that *Lower Egypt weeps.*[58] On the other hand, the figure of nine hundred years raises the possibility of Iranian influence.[59]

6.2. An attack on Egypt by the Assyrians is then mentioned by the lamb:

> (21) ... He turned his face to Egypt while he withdrew (22) from the ... they shall go out ... the injustice shall go to ruin, right and law shall exist in (23) Egypt. And they shall ... the precious shrines of the Egyptian gods before them to Nineveh in the land (24) of Assyria.
> *(Ibid.)*

Retaliation and restoration, however, are said to follow, culminating in a time of great happiness:

> and it shall happen that the Egyptians will go to the land of Syria and will make themselves master of its provinces and will find (III, 1) the shrines of the gods of Egypt. They ... can speak on account of the well-being which shall happen to Egypt (2) ... the infertile shall (3) exult, and she who has borne (children) shall rejoice because of the good events which shall happen; and Egypt and the generation (?) of men that shall be in Egypt (4) shall say: "O now, would that my father and my grandfather were here with me", in the good time (5) that shall come.' The lamb finished ... (10) This is the end of the book, written in the 33rd year, on the 8th of Mesore, (11) of Caesar (= Augustus) ...

We are told that when the lamb had finished, *he made his purification*, that is, died. Pshenhor took the lamb to King Bokkhoris, who ordered that it should be buried *like a god.*[60] If the papyrus was written in A.D. 7, the evidence of Manetho shows that the work goes back to at least the third century B.C. Popular tradition added some fantastic features to the story: thus the prophetic lamb was credited with eight legs, two tails, two heads, and four horns[61] – another characteristic of apocalyptic elsewhere.[62] There is

---

[57] Cf. Wilson 1955, 328 f.

[58] Gardiner 1909, 72. Cf. the end of the "Israel Stela" of Merneptah: there is joy in Egypt, but distress in Ashkelon, Gezer, and Israel; cf. Wilson 1955, 378. In Schott 1929, 13 ff. (*Urk* VI = texts of the Late and Ptolemaic eras) the cities of Horus are said to rejoice whereas those of Seth are in misery.

[59] Nine thousand years (not nine hundred) are mentioned by Plutarch, *De Is. et Os.* 47 as the Zoroastrian cycle leading to the happy end of the world; see my Comm. (1970), *ad. loc.*, pp. 480 f.; cf. now also Widengren in this volume § 5.1.2. #(5).

[60] Cf. the discussion by McCown 1925, 357–411, this text on pp. 394 f. McCown used Krall's translation (1898); Janssen (1954) presents much improved readings with a fuller and more accurate version.

[61] Aelian, *De nat. animal.* 12.3; cf. Kákosy 1966, 345.

[62] Cf. the animals in Ezek 1:6 ff.; Dan 7:3 ff.; and 2 Esdr 12:10 ff. Daniel's fourth beast may represent Alexander the Great and other Greek kingdoms; cf. Russell 1967, 233; Heaton 1956, 177. Ezekiel is one of the O. T. authors in whom the boundaries between apocalyptic and prophecy become fluid; cf. R. Meyer 1965. They are obviously fluid too in the present discussion.

certainly no lack of fabulous creatures in the Egyptian tradition.[63] The main emphasis of the prediction is on political and national defeat and deliverance, although its final picture of future bliss has a more general ambience. Clearly it is comparable to *The Demotic Chronicle*, but unlike that document does not give any detail about the deliverer who is to come.[64]

7. The Oracle of the Potter

7.1. The creator-god Khnum, a ram-headed deity who was said to have fashioned mankind on a potter's wheel, is probably to be seen in the figure of the prophetic lamb,[65] and the same god may well be represented by the Potter whose oracle is recorded in two papyri now in Vienna and in one of the Oxyrhynchus papyri now in Oxford.[66] One of the Vienna papyri (P. Graf) is dated to the second century A.D.; the other (P. Rainer) is dated to the third, and so is the Oxyrhynchus papyrus. They are all unhappily in a much damaged state. Enough remains to show that there are further similarities between this oracle and the "Prediction of the Lamb under Bokkhoris". The latter text, by the way, or at least its content, is known to the Potter,[67] for in line 34 of the Oxyrhynchus version reference is made to *the evils which the lamb announced to Bakharis* (sic). Among the similarities in content are the mention of foreign invaders – there the Assyrians, but here the Persians or Greeks; the account of present woes to be followed by future triumph and bliss; and the pathetic wish that ancestors may return from the grave to share the blessings now granted. In the end, too, there is a point of similarity: the prophet, like the lamb, dies, and his burial is arranged by the king himself.[68]

---

[63] Cf. Khnum with four ram-heads: Bonnet 1952, 138; and the composite forms in Sauneron 1970, frontisp. and Fig. 2 opp. p. 12. Cf. McCown 1925, 395, citing Ed. Meyer. Khnum is depicted with four heads in the temple of Esna, and Amûn, also ram-headed, was previously thus shown: see the several examples cited by Kákosy 1966, 351. For winged animals see Gwyn Griffiths 1975, 311ff.

[64] Cf. Lanczkowski 1960, 5ff.; Hengel 1974, I, 184f.; II, 124f.

[65] Cf. Kákosy 1966, 345.

[66] P. Oxy. 2332, ed. C. H. Roberts 1954. The Vienna papyri (P Graf. G. 29787 and P. Rainer, G. 19813) were first edited by C. Wessely. A revised edition of all three is provided by Koenen 1968, and his edition is used here. See too his further remarks on readings, 1974, 313–319.

[67] In P. Rainer, 54, the work is called The Defence of the Potter ($\dot{\alpha}\pi o\lambda o\gamma\acute{\imath}\alpha$ $\varkappa\varepsilon\varrho\alpha\mu\acute{\varepsilon}\omega\varsigma$). The god Khnum was called *Lord of the Potter's Wheel: nb nhp* (three instances in *Wb*. II, 294, 12). Cf. Kákosy 1966, 346, citing the study of Struve 1925, 274. The Potter, then, will refer to the god himself, but in an oracular situation he will be represented by a priest and will speak through him. I doubt, however, whether such a person should be regarded as an "incarnation" of the god as Koenen 1968, 180, states.

[68] Cf. Kákosy 1966, 346. The king named is Amenophis. There were four kings of this name in the Eighteenth Dynasty, but one of them, Amenophis III, reigned at the time of the

7.2. This time the woes of Egypt include disturbances in the workings of nature:

The Nile will flow not having sufficient water, but only a little, so that the earth is scorched, but contrary to nature. For in the time of the Typhonians they will say: Poor Egypt, thou art abused by the terrible abuses wrought against thee. And the sun will be darkened, not wishing to behold the evils in Egypt. The earth will not respond to the sowings of seed.

(P. Rainer, I, 1–7.)

But other troubles stem from political and military affairs. Hated enemies are referred to sometimes as *girdle-wearers* (ζωνοφόροι), a term explained by some as referring to the Persians.[69] The oracle says that their city will become a desert (P. Rainer, 43 f.), but the reference is probably to the Greeks, the city being Alexandria. The alien oppressors are also called Typhonians in accordance with a long-established tradition. A feature of the fall of Alexandria is said to be the departure of the native gods to Memphis, the old capital of Egypt:

But that will happen at the end of evils, when the foreigners fall away in Egypt as the leaves fall from a tree. And the city of girdle-wearers will be made a desert, in the same way as my kiln (experienced), because of the lawless deeds which they did to Egypt. The divine statues of Egypt, which had been carried away there, come home to Egypt, and the city by the sea will become a place for fishermen to dry their nets because Agathos Daemon and Mephis proceed to Memphis, so that people passing by will say, 'So this was the all-nurturing city in which every race of men settled down.'   (P. Rainer, 30–38; cf. P. Oxy. 2332, 53–62.)

Memphis was the capital of Egypt from the time of the first unified kingdom under Menes (*ca.* 3100 B.C.), and to an Egyptian conscious of his country's past the *city by the sea*[70] was a recent upstart. Similarly, the cosmopolitan character of Alexandria was an affront to Egyptian national-ism and the feeling is well epitomized in the phrase *the all-nurturing city.*[71]

7.3. Yet there is something remarkably vague for the most part, in spite of its well-founded traditional theology, about the vision which concerns the king from whom deliverance will come:

And then shall Egypt be made to flourish, when the king who has reigned beneficently for fifty-five years comes from the Sun-god as a bestower of blessings, established by the greatest

---

famous scribe and architect Amenhotep son of Hapu, who was later deified. See Wildung 1977, 83 ff. Manetho (ed. Waddell [LCL] 1948, pp. 120–122) ascribed wisdom and knowledge of the future to this Amenhotep, whom he calls Amenophis; so there may be a link here. Similarities of ideas between the predictions of the Lamb and the Potter, and also other prophetic texts, are tabulated by Dunand 1979, 41–67.

[69] Thus Struve 1925, 273; cf. Tarn 1929, 11, following Reitzenstein also. Dunand 1979, 44, rejects this explanation together with others of an "Iranizing" nature.

[70] For a plural reading see Koenen 1974, 316. It is at variance with several other allusions in the singular.

[71] Norden 1924, 55 n. 2, quotes a similar phrase, following Reitzenstein, in Plut. *V. Alex.* 26.

goddess Isis, so that those who survive will pray that the people who have previously died will rise (from the dead) in order to share their blessings.

(P. Rainer, 39–43; cf. P. Oxy. 2332, 63–71.)

The Pharaoh in the ancient tradition was consistently regarded as the son of Rēᶜ; a new native ruler must therefore come from the Sun-god Rēᶜ. In texts of the Temple of Edfu,[72] which were inscribed between 237 and 57 B.C., Rēᶜ or Rēᶜ-Harakhty is the presiding god under whose commands Horus of Behdet (Edfu) – and Horus in other forms – wages his war against Seth and his followers. *Established by the greatest goddess Isis* is another feature of the Potter's future king, and this reflects another basic fact of the Egyptian royal theology: the King is always identified with the god Horus.[73] In the texts of Edfu the Ptolemies are regularly embellished with these attributes. We read, for instance:

The son of Rēᶜ, Ptolemy, who lives for ever, beloved of Ptah ... Horus of Behdet is his name. (Chassinat, *Edfou*, VI, 131, 6–7.)

It is Fairman's[74] view that the priests were nevertheless intensely con-scious that none of the Ptolemies was a "true Horus" and that they really belonged to the Sethian enemies. But it is hard to demonstrate this from the texts.[75] In the case of the Potter's Oracle the anti-Greek emphasis is clinched by the naming of the Greeks in line 33 of the Oxyrhynchus text.

7.4. Let us return to the vagueness of the prophecy. In one point it is puzzlingly precise: the royal deliverer will achieve a reign of fifty-five years. It is probably an ideal number, being half of the ideal 110 years desiderated by the Egyptians for a life-time.[76] In other ways the description of the deliverer is uninformative, and contrasts with *The Demotic Chronicle* and the "Prediction of the Lamb" in this respect. Details accompany other sayings, such as the coming of a hated king from Syria (P. Oxy. 30–31), where Koenen[77] finds an allusion to the sixth Syrian war of 170–168 B.C., the only occasion when the Syrian King actually came to Egypt; and he makes a good case for locating the document to the historical situation of 130 B.C. One objection is the allusion (P. Oxy. 2) to the *city which is being*

---

[72] Chassinat 1931. For a brief conspectus of the material see Fairman 1935, 26 ff. with a translation of "The Legend of the Winged Disk"; also *id.* 1974.

[73] Strangely ignored by Koenen in his otherwise sound discussion, 1968, 180.

[74] Fairman 1974, 32–33.

[75] See my Review in *OLZ* 73 (1978) 449 and my analysis in 1979, 174–179.

[76] Thus rightly Koenen 1968, 190. Less convincing is his statement that 55 is the sum of all the numbers from 1–10 and has an ideal significance through this, since it is based on the Decad. Still less convincing is the idea that the reference to the 55 years in P. Oxy. 2332, 31 ff., which is regarded as an interpolation, means in effect one year more than the 54 years of the reign of Ptolemy Euergetes II. What ancient reader would be able to take that point without any explanation?

[77] Koenen 1968, 187.

founded.[78] However, the events alluded to are not in sequence, and a number of varying prophecies may be here assembled.[79] The lack of detail about the Saviour-king has a rather pathetic aspect when compared with earlier prophecies. It is not he who is marked out as the destroyer of Alexandria; we are told that conflict of Greeks among each other will bring that about. This betrays a lack of confidence in Egypt's ability, during the Ptolemaic era, to produce a triumphant national leader. As a result, the picture becomes more Utopian, and the prophecies become more like an eschatological type of apocalyptic.[80]

7.5. The Oracle of the Potter has evoked parallels with other apocalyptic literature, notably with the Third Sibylline Oracle.[81] The most striking of these is seen in lines 652 f.:

> Καὶ τότ' ἀπ' ἠελίοιο Θεὸς πέμψει βασιλῆα
> ὃς πᾶσαν γαῖαν παύσει πολέμοιο κακοῖο.
> And then from the Sun-god[82] will God send a king
> who will keep the whole earth from evil war.

Whereas the first line here seems to follow the Potter, the second introduces two ideas not found in his work: universalism and the condemnation of war. Yet there is clearly a possibility of mutual influence between the Jewish and Egyptian traditions.[83] Common to the apocalyptic ideas of the two traditions is an intense concern with the history and fate of the nation. Egyptian religion had a strong national basis which found expression even in the Hellenistic Isis-cult.[84] Indeed the saddest "apocalypse" to come from Egypt is that in the Hermetic *Asclepius*, which derives from the fourth century A.D. It expresses the feeling of profound anguish that Egypt has now been deserted by its own gods:[85]

---

[78] See Roberts 1954, 93 n. 3. Cf. Fraser 1972, I, 681. Dunand 1979, 45–46, is sympathetic to Koenen's thesis.

[79] Cf. the way in which the Horus-myth of Edfu includes material about the Hyksos and also, possibly, about later invaders. See Gwyn Griffiths 1958, 76–85 and 1977, 54–60.

[80] Cf. Koenen 1968, 180 ff. It is hard to follow him, however, when he maintains (p. 181) that the statement about the statues "coming back" to Egypt (P. Oxy. 57 f.) implies that the new King will not be able to achieve that. The statues, he avers, will come back of their own accord. One must surely assume, in spite of the expression used, that the King's action is involved. In "The Prediction of the Lamb" the Egyptians are said to do this.

[81] Norden 1924, 55 n. 2, points to verbal parallels.

[82] Nikiprowetzky 1970, 323, translates "Et alors, de l'Orient . . .". He dates the work to ca. 42 B.C. and finds its source in the Jewish community of Hellenistic Egypt. Cf. my Review in *ClR* 23 (1973) 97–98.

[83] Hengel 1974, I, 185. He refers also to the anti-Jewish prophecy in PSI 982 = CPJ 520 with its allusion in line 9 to the "wrath of Isis"; cf. Koenen in *Gnomon* 40 (1968) 258. An oracle recorded by Manetho refers to the "Exodus of the Impure" from Egypt: see Hopfner 1925, 69 ff. (= Josephus, C. Ap. I, 26) and cf. McCown 1925, 400 ff.

[84] See Bergman 1972, 7–28, esp. p. 23.

[85] *Asclepius*, 24 ed. Nock 1945, 326 ff. (Vol. II). Cf. Barns 1973, 18, whose version of this

A time will come when it will be seen that in vain have the Egyptians served the deity with piety and assiduous service, and all their holy worship will be found fruitless and to no profit. For the deity will retire from earth to heaven, and Egypt will be forsaken; and the land which was the home of religion will be left desolate, bereft of the presence of its gods.

Professor Martin Krause kindly reminds me that the Latin text here derives from Greek prototypes, and that behind them is an earlier Coptic composition which is now available in the Nag Hammadi codices (CG VI, 8:65,15—78,43)[86] and which includes clear indications of the survival of ancient Egyptian concepts.[87]

Bibliography

Ausfeld, Adolf 1907: *Der griechische Alexanderroman*, Leipzig 1907.

Barns, John W. B. 1973: *Egyptians and Greeks*. Inaugural Lecture, Oxford 1973.

Bergman, Jan 1968: *Ich bin Isis* (AUU.HR 3), Uppsala 1968.

– 1972: "Zum 'Mythos von der Nation' in den sog. hellenistischen Mysterienreligionen", in: *Temenos* 8 (1972) 7–28.

Bergson, Leif 1965: *Der griechische Alexanderroman*, Rezension *β*, Uppsala 1965.

Bertholet, Alfred 1976: *Wörterbuch der Religionen*, 3rd ed. rev. K. Goldammer, Stuttgart 1976.

Betz, Hans Dieter 1969: "On the Problem of the Religio-Historical Understanding of Apocalypticism", in: *JTC* 6 (1969) 134–156.

Bonnet, Hans 1952: *Reallexikon der ägyptischen Religionsgeschichte*, Berlin 1952.

Bresciani, Edda 1969: *Letteratura e Poesia dell' antico Egitto*, Torino 1969.

Brunner, Hellmut 1964: *Die Geburt des Gottkönigs* (ÄA 10), Wiesbaden 1964.

– 1970: "Die Lehren", in: *HO*, ed. B. Spuler, I.1. *Literatur*, 2nd ed. rev., Leiden 1970, 113–139.

– 1977: *Die südlichen Räume des Tempels von Luxor* (Arch. Veröff. DAI.K 18), Mainz 1977.

Brunner-Traut, Emma 1963: *Altägyptische Märchen*, Düsseldorf 1963.

Chassinat, Emile 1931: *Le Temple d'Edfou*, VI, Cairo 1931.

Derchain, Philippe 1968: "The Egyptian World in the Age of the Ptolemies and Caesars", in: *Hellenism and the Rise of Rome*, ed. P. Grimal, London 1968, 207–241.

Dunand, Françoise 1979: "L'Oracle du Potier et la formation de l'apocalyptique en Égypte", in: *L'Apocalyptique* (EHiRel 3), Paris 1979, 41–67.

Eddy, Samuel K. 1961: *The King is Dead,* Lincoln, Nebr. 1961.

Edmonds, J. M. 1929: *The Characters of Theophrastus* (LCL), London 1929.

Fairman, H. W. 1935: "The Myth of Horus at Edfu – I.", in: *JEA* 21 (1935) 26–36.

– 1974: *The Triumph of Horus*, London 1974.

Fraser, P. M. 1972: *Ptolemaic Alexandria*, 3 Vols., Oxford 1972.

Gardiner, A. H. 1909: *The Admonitions of an Egyptian Sage*, Leipzig 1909.

– 1961: *Egypt of the Pharaohs*, Oxford 1961.

Grundmann, Walter 1967: in: *Umwelt des Urchristentums*, 2nd ed., rev. J. Leipoldt and W. Grundmann, Berlin 1967, 151 ff.

Gwyn Griffiths, J. 1958: "The Interpretation of the Horus-myth of Edfu", in: *JEA* 44 (1958) 75–85.

– 1960: *The Conflict of Horus and Seth*, Liverpool 1960.

---

section is used here. Dunand 1979, 57 ff. gives a valuable list of parallels with the Oracle of the Potter.

[86] See Parrott 1979, 396 f.   [87] Krause 1969.

– 1965: "A Translation from the Egyptian by Eudoxus", in: *CQ* 15 (1965) 75–78.
– 1970: *Plutarch's De Iside et Osiride*, Cardiff 1970.
– 1975: *Apuleius of Madauros, The Isis-Book* (EPRO 39), Leiden 1975.
– 1977: "Horusmythe", in: *LÄ* 17, 1977, 54–60.
– 1979: "Egyptian Nationalism in the Edfu Temple Texts", in: *Glimpses of Ancient Egypt* ed. John Ruffle et al. (FS. H. W. Fairman), Warminster 1979, 174–179.
Hall, H. R. 1930: *British Museum Guide*, London 1930.
Hamilton, J. R. 1969: *Plutarch, Alexander: A Commentary*, Oxford 1969.
Heaton, Eric 1956: *Daniel*, London 1956 (repr. 1972).
Helck, Wolfgang 1970: *Die Prophezeiung des Nfr.tj.* (KÄT), Wiesbaden 1970.
Hengel, Martin 1974: *Judaism and Hellenism* (tr. J. Bowden), 2 Vols., London 1974.
– 1976: *The Son of God*, London 1976.
Hermann, Alfred 1938: *Die ägyptische Königsnovelle* (LÄS 10), Glückstadt 1938.
Hopfner, Theodor 1925: *Fontes Historiae Religionis Aegyptiacae*, Bonn 1922–1925.
Hornung, Erik 1978: *Grundzüge der ägyptischen Geschichte*, Darmstadt 1978.
Janssen, Jozef M. A. 1954: "Over Farao Bokchoris", in: *Varia Historica* (FS. A. W. Byvanck), Assen 1954.
Jülicher, Adolf 1894: "Apokalypsen" in: *PRE* I 2 (1894) 2835–2836.
Kákosy, László 1966: "Prophecies of Ram Gods", in: *AOH* 19 (1966) 341–358.
– 1978: "Zeus-Amun", in: *Jubilee Volume of the Oriental Collection 1951–1976*, Budapest 1978, 111–114.
Kaplony, Peter 1971: "Bemerkungen zum ägyptischen Königtum, vor allem in der Spätzeit", in: *CEg* 46 (1971) 250–274.
– 1975: "Demotische Chronik", in: *LÄ* I (1975) 1056–1060.
Kienitz, F. K. 1953: *Die politische Geschichte Ägyptens vom 7. zum 4. Jahrhundert vor der Zeitwende*, Berlin 1953.
Knox, A. D. 1929: *Herodes, Cercidas, and the Greek Choliambic Poets* (LCL), London 1929.
Knox, Wilfred L. 1944: *Some Hellenistic Elements in Primitive Christianity*, London 1944.
Koenen, Ludwig 1968: "Die Prophezeiungen des 'Töpfers'", in: *ZPE* 2 (1968) 178–209.
– 1974: "Bemerkungen zum Text des Töpferorakels und zu dem Akaziensymbol", in: *ZPE* 13 (1974) 313–319.
Krall, J. 1898: "Vom König Bokchoris", in: *Festgaben zu Ehren Max Büdingers*, Innsbruck 1898, 3–11.
Krause, Martin 1969: "Ägyptisches Gedankengut in der Apokalypse des Asclepius", in: *ZDMG* Suppl. 1 (1969) 49–57 (= XVII. Deutscher Orientalistentag).
Kroll, Wilhelm 1926: *Historia Alexandri Magni (Pseudo-Callisthenes)*, Berlin 1926.
Lanczkowski, Günter 1960: *Altägyptischer Prophetismus* (ÄA 4), Wiesbaden 1960.
von Lauenstein, Ursula 1969: *Der griechische Alexanderroman*, Rezension *Γ*, Vol. III (BKP 33), Meisenheim 1969.
Lavagnini, B. 1922: *Eroticorum Fragmenta Papyracea*, Leipzig 1922.
Lorton, David 1971: "The supposed expedition of Ptolemy II to Persia", in: *JEA* 57 (1971) 160–164.
McCown, C. C. 1925: "Hebrew and Egyptian Apocalyptic Literature", in: *HThR* 18 (1925) 357–411.
Merkelbach, Reinhold 1977: *Die Quellen des griechischen Alexanderromans*. With Jürgen Trumpf, 2nd ed. (Zetemata, 9), München 1977.
de Meulenaere, H. 1963: "La famille royale des Nectanébo", in: *ZÄS* 90 (1963) 90–93.
Meyer, Eduard 1915: "Ägyptische Dokumente aus der Perserzeit", in: *ZPAW*, Berlin 1915, 287–311.
Meyer, R. 1965: "Apokalyptik", in: *LAW*, Zürich 1965.
Morris, Leon 1973: *Apocalyptic*, 2nd ed., London 1973.
Neugebauer, O. and Parker, Richard A. 1969: *Egyptian Astronomical Texts. III. Decans, Planets, Constellations, and Zodiacs*, London 1969.
Nikiprowetzky, V. 1970: *La troisième Sibylle*, Paris 1970.

Nims, Charles F. 1948: "The Term *Hp*, 'law, right', in Demotic", in: *JNES* 7 (1948) 243–260.

Nock, A. D. 1945: *Corpus Hermeticum*, 4 Vols. (Coll. Budé), Paris 1945–1954.

Norden, Eduard 1924: *Die Geburt des Kindes*, Leipzig 1924 (repr. Stuttgart 1958).

Otto, Eberhard 1956: "Prolegomena zur Frage der Gesetzgebung und Rechtsprechung in Ägypten", in: *MDAI.K* 14 (FS. H. Kees, 1956) 150–159.

– 1966: *Osiris und Amun*, München 1966.

– 1970: "Weltanschauliche und politische Tendenzschriften", in: *HO*, ed. B. Spuler, I.1. *Literatur*, 2nd rev. ed., Leiden 1970, 113–147.

Parrott, Douglas M. 1979: *Nag Hammadi Codices, V, 2–5 and VI with Papyrus Berolinensis 8502, 1 and 4* (NHS XI), Leiden 1979.

Ray, John D. 1976: *The Archive of Hor* (Texts from Excavations 2), London 1976.

Reymond, E. A. E. 1977: *From Ancient Egyptian Hermetic Writings*. Part II of *From the Contents of the Libraries of the Suchos Temples in the Fayyum*, Wien 1977.

Roberts, C. H. 1954: *The Oxyrhynchus Papyri*, XXII, London 1954.

Roeder, Günther 1927: *Altägyptische Erzählungen und Märchen*, Jena 1927.

– 1959: *Die ägyptische Götterwelt*, Zürich 1959.

Russell, D. S. 1967: *The Jews from Alexander to Herod*, Oxford 1967.

Sauneron, Serge 1970: *Le Papyrus magique illustré de Brooklyn*, Brooklyn, N.Y. 1970.

Schott, Siegfried 1929: *Urkunden mythologischen Inhalts* (Urk. VI), Leipzig 1929.

Sethe, Kurt Heinrich 1929: *Amun und die acht Urgötter von Hermopolis* (APAW 4), Berlin 1929.

Sickenberger, J. 1950: "Apokalyptik", in: *RAC* I (1950) 504–510.

Spalinger, Anthony 1978: "The Reign of King Chabbash: An Interpretation", in: *ZÄS* 105 (1978) 142–154.

Spiegelberg, Wilhelm 1914: *Die sogenannte Demotische Chronik*, Leipzig 1914.

Struve, Vasili V. 1925: "Zum Töpferorakel", in: *Aegyptus Pubblicazioni* 3, Milano 1925, 273–281.

Swinnen, W. 1973: "Sur la politique religieuse de Ptolémée Ier", in: *Les syncrétismes dans les religions grecque et romaine*, ed. M. Simon, Paris 1973, 115–133.

Tarn, William W. 1929: "Ptolemy II and Arabia", in: *JEA* 15 (1929) 9–25.

– 1948: *Alexander the Great*, 2 Vols., Cambridge 1948.

te Velde, Herman 1967: *Seth, God of Confusion*, Leiden 1967.

Volten, Axel 1945: *Zwei altägyptische politische Schriften*, Copenhagen 1945.

Weinreich, Otto 1911: *Der Trug des Nektanebos*, Leipzig 1911.

West, Stephanie 1969: "The Greek Version of the Legend of Tefnut", in: *JEA* 55 (1969) 161–183.

Wilcken, Ulrich 1927: *Urkunden der Ptolemäerzeit*, Vol. I, Berlin-Leipzig 1927.

Wildung, Dietrich 1977: *Egyptian Saints*, New York 1977.

Wilson, John A. 1955: Translations in *Ancient Near Eastern Texts* (ANET), 2nd ed. James B. Pritchard, Princeton, N. J. 1955.

The Phenomenon of Early Christian Apocalyptic. Some Reflections on Method*

Elisabeth Schüssler Fiorenza

1. Introduction

Although the phenomenon of apocalyptic has generated much discussion in the scholarly world, no comprehensive studies of early Christian apocalyptic have been written in the last decades. E. Käsemann published his provocative and controversial thesis on apocalyptic as the "mother" of early Christian theology almost twenty years ago and K. Koch confessed almost ten years ago that scholars are "*ratlos vor der Apokalyptik*" in order to engender scholarly interest in the phenomenon. Nevertheless, the ensuing discussions have not produced a general consensus on the delineation and evaluation of the phenomenon in early Christianity nor have they produced book-length studies on it. True, numerous analyses of individual aspects of problems of early Christian eschatology have appeared that also discussed the apocalyptic character of New Testament texts and authors.

1.1. One could argue that this research situation is not surprising, since from a history of religions point of view no such phenomenon as early Christian apocalyptic exists. All early Christian apocalyptic texts are expressions of Jewish apocalypticism and therefore do not constitute an independent phenomenon – "early Christian apocalyptic". Typical for such an evaluation is Ph. Vielhauer's phenomenological approach. Although he discusses Christian texts and writings his analysis has no room for a specific early Christian type of apocalyptic, since he defines apocalyptic as a special expression of Jewish eschatology which is at the same time a product of the cultural-syncretistic impact of Hellenism, as well as a reaction against it. Central concepts of Jesus' preaching, namely Kingdom of God and Son of "Man", as well as his imminent expectation of the end-time, link Jesus with apocalyptic. Nevertheless, Jesus' authority is not that of an apocalyptist and his preaching has "nothing to do with Apocalyptic", because "surveys and divisions of history, numerical speculation and divination are absent from it".[1]

---

* Research for this paper was supported by a National Endowment for the Humanities summer stipend.
[1] Vielhauer 1965, 609; 1975, 487.

Since this statement is typical for the stance of NT exegesis, the absence of scholarly research on early Christian apocalyptic as a phenomenon *sui generis* seems to be due to the often unreflected conviction that from a methodological and historical-exegetical but not from a theological point of view Jewish and early Christian apocalyptic represent one and the same phenomenon. Although basic notions in the preaching of Jesus or of Paul are "apocalyptic", these are only expressions of remnants of Jewish apocalyptic. Although Rev is in the Christian canon, because of its strange apocalyptic language and fancy eschatological speculations, it is often judged to be Jewish apocalyptic and therefore as not having achieved the heights of Pauline theology. Even studies of apocalyptic have not paid too much attention to the book while contemporary artists are deeply attracted by the evocative power of its language and imagery.[2]

1.2. H. D. Betz has challenged this research consensus by demanding that Jewish, and subsequently Christian apocalypticism as well, should be "seen and presented as peculiar expressions within the entire development of Hellenistic syncretism". "Christian apocalypticism is doubtless something *new* compared with Jewish apocalypticism, and it is the *new* which needs to be determined."[3] Thus, the objective and task of this paper seems to be spelled out succinctly. However two problems have still to be clarified: *first*, how "newness" ought to be conceived and *second*, what kind of approach such a paper should take.

First: The attempt to delineate early Christian apocalyptic as a distinctive type within the overall context of the apocalyptic phenomenon in the Greco-Roman world should not be misunderstood. Such a delineation of early Christian apocalyptic as something "new" affirms its continuity with Jewish apocalyptic while at the same time maintaining its own distinctive perspective. In short, it is necessary to relinquish the either – or position and to specify the distinctive character of early Christian apocalyptic as a religious literary phenomenon without sacrificing its *historical* position within the context of Jewish and Greco-Roman apocalyptic. Distinctiveness does not exclude continuity. Characteristic elements of early Christian apocalyptic are also present in other contemporary Hellenistic apocalyptic types. "New" only means that these characteristic elements have achieved a special constellation or configuration[4] and emphasis within early Christian apocalyptic.

Second: H. D. Betz proposes that a tradition-historical analysis combined with a phenomenological approach will bring best results in apocalyptic research. "The essence of apocalypticism is – like all other religious

---

[2] Schüssler Fiorenza 1973, 576 ff.
[3] Betz 1969, 155 (emphasis mine).   [4] Mannheim 1952, 59 f.

phenomena – approached most appropriately if one detects its underlying questions and sees how on that basis the tradition, which might be of a quite heterogeneous origin, has been interpreted."[5] However, Betz's own concrete example of how the method should be employed indicates how complicated the relationships between traditions, basic questions and religio-historical environment are. Although I fully accept this approach I have found it impossible to employ it in this paper. Since the object of the paper is not to trace one small segment or motif but to give a comprehensive presentation of the elusive phenomenon of early Christian apocalyptic, another approach was necessary. The scope of this paper is, therefore, at the same time more ambitious and more limited. The paper will review basic research-approaches within the study of early Christian apocalypticism and inquire why they have or why they have not come to describe early Christian apocalyptic as a peculiar constellation within the syncretistic phenomenon apocalyptic within the Greco-Roman world. Such an approach might help to examine some presuppositions and questions which hinder the appreciation of the apocalyptic phenomenon within early Christianity. The following research approaches will be discussed here: the phenomenological-formal genre-pattern approach, the phenomenological "essence" approach, the literary-symbolic and the sociology of knowledge approach.

2. Phenomenological Classification of Early Christian Apocalyptic

The term "apocalyptic" is usually employed either to name revelatory writings, the apocalypses, or to designate the thought-world of these texts. Whereas a tradition-historical approach attempts to delineate the historical genesis and development of apocalyptic, the phenomenological approach is concerned to separate out the different structures from the multiplicity of apocalyptic phenomena. These structures determine apocalyptic as a genre independently of the position in time and space of individual writings and of their attachment to a given cultural environment or situation. A phenomenological analysis presupposes a historical-exegetical analysis of the material. Its main interest is, however, the classification of the apocalyptic phenomena and the definition of their essence. The following presents examples of such a phenomenological classification of apocalyptic literature and its thought-world. Since such an analysis depends in scope on the exegetical analysis of sources, its results are relative to these analyses.

---

[5] Betz 1969, 137.

2.1. The Delineation of the Genre Apocalypse

The Apocalypse group of the SBL Genres Project has just published a preliminary account of its research on the apocalypse as a coherent genre. These studies include all the texts classified as apocalypses and dated between 250 BCE and 250 CE. This attempt to define the constitutive elements, the extent, and the different types of the genre apocalypse, has formulated a "master paradigm" that encompasses all writings historically classified as apocalypses and seems to presuppose as the essence of apocalyptic the notion of transcendence. Although there is considerable variation within the framework of the genre, it nevertheless is an internally coherent paradigm that encompasses the Jewish, Christian, Gnostic, Greco-Roman, and Persian apocalypses.

Apocalypse is a genre of revelatory literature with a narrative framework, in which a revelation is mediated by an otherworldly being to a human recipient disclosing a transcendent reality which is both temporal, insofar it envisages eschatological salvation, and spatial, insofar as it involves another, supernatural world.[6]

The variations within the genre can be distinguished in basically two types of apocalypses, those without "otherworldly journeys" (Type I "historical" apocalypses) and those with (Type II).

2.1.1. The section on early Christian apocalypses reviews 36 different texts of which 24 are classified as apocalypses and 12 as "related" works because one or the other element of the master paradigm is not found in them.[7] Of the 24 apocalypses, in my opinion, only 6 (Rev, *Apoc. Pet.,* *Hermas,* the fragmentary *Book of Elchasai, 5 Ezra* 2:42—48; and the *Asc. Isa.*) can be called Christian and dated with reasonable probability into the first two centuries CE. Related texts of this area that have some form of eschatology but lack the mediated character of revelation are Mark 13, *Did* 16 and *Asc. Isa.* 3:13–4:18.

Five of the apocalypses can be classified as belonging to the "historical" type. They espouse public eschatology, while only one belongs to the heavenly journey type II. However, it has to be noted that the systematic review of history so dominant for some of the Jewish apocalypses is completely absent in the 5 Christian works, whereas the paraenesis by the mediator is found almost solely in the Christian apocalypses. Moreover, the book of Rev, strictly speaking does not belong to either the "historical" or the "heavenly journey" type, since the work does not have reviews of history, is not pseudonymous, and has no developed heavenly journey. Finally, the literary frameworks of the "historical" type apocalypses differ considerably from each other. Rev is written in the form of the apostolic

---

[6] Collins 1979, 9. [7] Yarbro Collins 1979, 104f.

letter, although it consists mainly of visions *Apoc. Pet.* is written in the form of a revelatory discourse similar to the gnostic Christian discourses. *Hermas* has the form of an extended vision but contains mostly hortatory materials. Similarly the fragmentary *Book of Elchasai* and *5 Ezra* contain mainly prophetic admonitions and have only a slight visionary frame.

2.1.2. *In conclusion:* According to the generalized typology of the genre apocalypse, the phenomenon of "apocalyptic" literature appears only very late in early Christianity and is not very prominent. In the NT only Rev can be classified as apocalypse. This result corresponds with Vielhauer's literary-phenomenological classification that presupposes also an unbroken continuity between the phenomena of Jewish and early Christian apocalyptic. After having established the apocalyptic style characteristics (pseudonymity, visionary account, symbolic imaginative language, interpretation systematization, surveys of history in future form, descriptions of the beyond, throne visions, and the not strictly apocalyptic forms of paraenesis and prayer), he analyses in a second step the basic structures of the World of Ideas (*Vorstellungswelt*). Structural patterns that return again and again in diverse contexts are the dualism of the two aeons, universalism and individualism, pessimism and hope for the beyond, determinism and imminent expectation. According to these basic phenomenological structures only Rev is a genuine apocalypse, although Vielhauer also counts the *Apoc. Pet.*, *Hermas*, and the *Asc. Isa.* among the early Christian apocalypses.

Such genre-definitions are able to establish cross-cultural characteristics of the literary genre apocalypse. However, they cannot highlight the unique literary character of individual apocalypses and their peculiar apocalyptic perspective within a certain religious-cultural context. Nor are they able to trace historical developments of the genre as a whole or of special aspects of it.

2.2. Apocalyptic Pattern and Motifs

The preceeding analysis has indicated that the genre of apocalypse is found only very late and only once in the New Testament. This analysis of early Christian apocalypses has therefore to be supplemented by an analysis that can provide literary-phenomenological categories for the delineation and classification of smaller early Christian apocalyptic text-units. L. Hartman has provided such a classification pattern by analyzing literary motifs and structural patterns of more than 65 small text-units of Jewish apocalyptic literature which express the expectation of what is to happen in connection with the eschatological end-time events.

Although the expectations and motifs vary depending on the particular eschatological hope held by the author, a basic pattern with five elements or motif-clusters can be observed: after the increase of sinful or corrupt behavior and climactic catastrophes marking the last times (A) a divine intervention either by God or a redeemer figure like the Messiah or the Son of "Man" will occur (B). This divine intervention will result in judgment (C) with punishment for the wicked (D) and salvation for the faithful (E). This pattern is found partly or totally in texts like *Asc. Mos.* 10:1–10; *1 Enoch* 46:1–8; 4 Ezra 6:13–28. The pattern is not peculiar to Jewish writings but can also be found in Babylonian mythologies. Such a pattern based on Scripture is already found for example in Dan 7:23–27 or Isa 59:1–21. Even whole apocalyptic books can be structured after this pattern.[8]

2.2.1. The contents of the pattern are derived from the concrete situation and experience of the author as well as from the use of Scripture. Scripture can be quoted explicitly but more often it is only alluded to. The author writes a new text composing it either through Scriptural allusions and word- or motif-associations (anthological style) or by using a Scriptural text as its framework (structural style).[9] Both style-forms are found, *e.g.*, in Rev. While Rev is full of Scriptural allusions but has no direct quotations, it can be shown that for instance the inaugural vision in 1:12–19 is patterned after Dan 10.[10] Such a use of Scripture must not necessarily be the fruit of conscious "desk-labors". It still occurs today in enthusiastic groups that are steeped in Scripture. In short, both this end-time pattern as well as the "apocalyptic" style of using Scripture are used in New Testament writings. Both can be used as heuristic tools to delineate apocalyptic texts in early Christianity.

Early Christian writings frequently combine the apocalyptic pattern of eschatological events with paraenesis.[11] Either the apocalyptic pattern is introduced and framed by paraenesis or it is interlaced with hortatory statements. An analysis of Mark 13 par. shows how much the pattern is determined by and used in the context of paraenesis. Similarly the apocalyptic visions of Rev are set within the apostolic letter-framework and introduced by paraenetic messages.[12] Equally, *Did* 16; *Herm. Vis.* IV and the *Apoc. Pet.* serve paraenetic purposes.

This emphasis on paraenesis suggests that early Christian apocalyptic is an expression of early Christian prophecy. Not only does the author of Rev understand his work as a prophetic book but also Q, Matthew, and the Didache reflect early Christian prophetic traditions. Paul apparently under-

---

[8] Hartman 1966, 28–49.   [9] Patte 1975, 172ff.

[10] Schüssler Fiorenza 1972, 193–197.

[11] For the focus on the present social-political situation of the community as well as for the importance of ethical demands in apocalyptic as well as gnostic early Christian thought cf. the contributions of L. Schottroff and H. G. Klippenberg in this volume.

[12] Schüssler Fiorenza 1977a, 350–366.

stood himself also in analogy to the OT prophets and characterizes early Christian prophecy in terms of apocalyptic. Early Christian prophecy and early Christian apocalyptic seem to belong to the same religious phenomenon.

2.2.2. This apocalyptic pattern or some of its motif-clusters occurs in those early Christian texts that are on different grounds acknowledged as "apocalyptic" texts in early Christian literature, *e.g.,* 1 Thess 4:13–5:11; 1 Cor 15; 2 Thess 2:1–13; The Q-Apocalypse Matt 24:26–28, 37–41 par.; the so-called Synoptic Apocalypse Mark 13 par.; Rev; *Did* 16; *Herm. Vis.* IV; and the *Apoc. Pet.* Although with the exception of chs. 15–17 the whole structure of the *Apoc. Pet.* follows this apocalyptic pattern of eschatological events, it nevertheless places its main emphasis on only one of the motif-clusters, namely the punishment of the wicked (chs. 7–13). The *Asc. Isa.* does not follow this pattern at all but is an account of a heavenly journey. Only *Asc. Isa.* 3:13–4:18 contains elements of the pattern.

However, motifs and motif-clusters of the pattern are not only found in materials classified as apocalyptic but in most of the NT writings. Christian writers seem to have emphasized the following motifs within the motif-clusters of the apocalyptic pattern. In the first motif-cluster, the last times before the eschatological intervention, (A) the situation of persecution and trial of the community is stressed. Emphasis is also given to the opponent figures of demonic powers, false prophets and antichrists. Significant is the rejection of the apocalyptic sign-seeking. In the second motif-cluster, the divine intervention, (B) the expectation of the parousia and the coming of the Son of "Man" for judgment (C) is stressed. The "day of the Lord" and judgment are intertwined. Most developed within Christian texts is, however, the last motif-cluster, the time of salvation (E). Here the motifs of Kingdom, exaltation, resurrection and eternal life, new creation, and the eschatological banquet are especially developed.

However, it is important to note that these apocalyptic motifs and symbols of salvation are not only applied to the future but are also used in order to characterize the present situation of Christ or of the Christians.[13] Both the present and the future accentuation of these apocalyptic motifs are found very early in the Christian tradition. It is therefore questionable to declare either the one or the other as secondary or "heretical", as it is often done when presential apocalyptic language is labeled as "gnostic" or "gnosticizing" when applied to Christian existence. Both seem to represent distinct eschatological apocalyptic Christian types that should not be levelled in. However, already in the Pauline literature and especially in later NT texts often one aspect is stressed to correct the other.

---

[13] Cf. Aune 1972 and especially the contribution of W. A. Meeks in this volume.

2.2.3. *In conclusion*: The literary-phenomenological analyses of early
Christian apocalyptic texts clearly establish their intrinsic continuity with
Jewish apocalyptic literature. While the genre analysis dates early Christian
apocalyptic late and finds only one apocalypse in the NT, the literary
pattern- or motif-analyses can show that apocalyptic texts and motifs are
found very early and very often in Christian literature. As Jewish apocalyptic, so do early Christian apocalyptic texts rely mainly on the OT as a
source and motif-arsenal for their own apocalyptic statements. The most
influential Jewish text probably was Daniel 7. However, since it is typical
for apocalyptists to interpret and re-interpret texts in the light of their own
situation, references to OT-Jewish texts must not necessarily point to a
"Sitz im Leben" in a Jewish community, since their point of coherence
(*Haftpunkt*) in the tradition is not necessarily local but could be given with
the apocalyptic pattern and its motif-clusters.

Moreover it has to be pointed out that the apocalyptic pattern seems
always to be intertwined with paraenesis in early Christian texts. Although
Jewish apocalypses also often have a hortatory interest, the paraenetical
element is explicit in the early Christian apocalyptic genre. Finally, most
apocalyptic texts and motif-clusters are found within the framework of
other literary forms, *e.g.,* letters or gospels. This feature seems to be
common to early Christian and Greco-Roman apocalyptic that is also
mostly transmitted in other literary genres. The discussion of the struc-
tural-phenomenological approach has underlined that early Christian
apocalyptic not only shares its patterns, traditions, motifs and language
with Jewish and Greco-Roman apocalyptic but also can give a different
emphasis to certain motifs of the traditional cross-cultural apocalyptic
pattern. The most significant difference consists in that it applies elements
and motifs of the traditional apocalyptic pattern not only to expectations of
the future but also to the present and past of Christ or the Christians.[14] We
must therefore ask whether this difference indicates a significant shift in the
apocalyptic perspective.

3. The "Essence" of Early Christian Apocalyptic

The phenomenological-theological approach seeks to define the shift in
the transition from Jewish to Christian apocalyptic by distinguishing the
"essence" of both apocalyptic phenomena. Despite their *historical* intercon-
nectedness and traditional continuity, an essential difference can be
detected in their *substantive* relationship.

---

[14] Rollins 1970, 454–476.

3.1. The "Essence" Analysis

3.1.1. Although Schmithals speaks about the apocalyptic movement, his approach is nevertheless not sociological but phenomenological. Like most scholars he discusses first the "thought world" (*Ideen- und Lebenswelt*) of apocalyptic in its "classical form" whose characteristic elements are: pseudonymity and *vaticinia ex eventu*, surveys of history as a whole, and predestination, understood in analogy with the Greek cosmos, universality and the process of individualization, two ages and dualism, imminent expectation and hope for salvation.

3.1.2. A second step asks for the specific apocalyptic world view, since apocalyptic is a unique religious phenomenon with a specific understanding of the world, of human existence in the world and of history. The essence of the apocalyptic phenomenon is to be defined as pessimism. However, the apocalyptist does not succumb to pessimism but is sustained by a hope as radical as the apocalyptic pessimism. "This combination of unconditionally negative and absolute positive aspects is made possible by the dualistic doctrine of the two ages."[15]

In comparing this apocalyptic type with the gnostic type of piety Schmithals highlights their similarities and differences. Whereas both share a radical pessimism vis-à-vis the world, gnosis thinks in vertical terms and apocalyptic in horizontal ones. Whereas the pneumatic being of the gnostic is *by its very nature* nonhistorical and entombed in this evil world, apocalyptic piety knows that reality and world were created good, but are historically completely corrupted. Shaped by such a negative understanding of historical reality, apocalyptic piety requires an imminent expectation of God's eschatological intervention in history "in order to explain its abandonment of historical responsibility".[16]

3.1.3. Early Christian apocalyptic derived its central notion of the resurrection from Jewish apocalyptic but insists that the resurrection of Christ has been the onset of the last times. Consequently, the Christian community understands itself as an eschatological community of salvation. However, this "now" of salvation must not be understood in a gnostic way, since it is not at the disposal of the community. Christian interpretation of reality therefore does not, like Jewish or Gnostic apocalyptic literature, despair of world and history but understands the present as the time of salvation. Therefore, Schmithals claims that the cosmological, temporal, and mythic aspects of apocalyptic are accidental and can be eliminated. Since early Christian faith is essentially non–apocalyptic, it is not accidental that no genuine apocalypse was accepted either into the OT or the NT canon. Insofar as early Christian apocalyptic does not share the radical

---

[15] Schmithals 1975, 49.   [16] Schmithals 1975, 108.

pessimism of Jewish apocalyptic but stresses that God is acting in and through Jesus Christ in history, it is substantially nearer to the God of the prophets than to the God of the apocalyptists. In short, no specific apocalyptic type piety is found in early Christianity. Consequently, from a formal-structural point of view Christian apocalyptic texts are a part of Jewish apocalyptic but from an essential-theological point of view they differ substantively from Jewish apocalyptic speculation.

3.2. Essence and Apocalyptic Language

This formulation of the "essence" of early Christian apocalyptic reflects two rather prevalent but nevertheless inadequate assumptions in exegetical scholarship: it is questionable *firstly,* whether the distinction between language, form and content is correct from a linguistic point of view, and *secondly,* whether abstract philosophical language is theologically superior to imaginative language.

3.2.1. The distinction between form and content, language and essence has plagued the discussion of early Christian apocalyptic since Weiss's and Schweitzer's studies showed Jesus and his preaching to be apocalyptic. A. Schweitzer had distinguished between apocalyptic language that binds Jesus to his own time and eschatological language that expresses the true meaning of the apocalyptic concepts, symbols and imagery and thus makes the message of Jesus valid and acceptable for all times.

This distinction between eschatology and apocalyptic has become almost normative in the theological discussion, whereby apocalyptic is often negatively identified with Jewish thought. While apocalyptic is often used in a pejorative sense, eschatology is understood with reference to things eternal and the real content of eschatology is strictly differentiated from the crude ideas and images of apocalyptic. The concept of eschatology, thus detemporalized, may be cast in existential terms. Jesus preaches that persons stand *now* under the necessity of decision. The real understanding of apocalyptic eschatology means that every hour is the "last hour". Therefore Bultmann maintains that not apocalyptic but eschatology is "the mother" of early Christian theology.[17]

3.2.2. NT texts speak of the eschatological apocalyptic events as future but also as already in some sense present for Christ and the Christian community. But after acknowledging the tension between the "already and not yet" the scholarly consensus rapidly dissolves. Since the tension between future and present statements can be interpreted in various ways, the term "eschatological" has been qualified with such adjectives as consis-

---

[17] Schüssler Fiorenza 1976, 271–277.

tent, imminent, apocalyptic, thoroughgoing, futuristic, proleptic, realized, in the process of realization, inaugurated or fulfilled. However, one suspects that such a confused usage of the qualifying term "eschatological" is rooted in theological apologetics.

Such apologetics seem necessary because apocalyptic language is often misunderstood as descriptive instead of as imaginative language. Apocalyptic language seems strange and fantastic: stars fall from heaven, the Son of "Man" comes on the clouds of heaven, angels appear and trumpets are sounded, animals speak and heavenly books are eaten. Yet such apocalyptic language is not an oddity in the NT but central to the understanding of Jesus as well as of the early Christians. Eschatological language in the New Testament is apocalyptic language. As such it is cosmological, mythological, universal, political and symbolical. As mytho-poetic language it cannot be reduced to descriptive factual information. K. Stendahl, therefore, stresses correctly that abstract philosophical language is not theologically preferable since we can speak in imaginative but not in factual language about eschatological hope. To give the impression that abstract eschatological language can better convey this hope than apocalyptic language is misleading.

> I have always loved to think about heaven as a city of gold, the city of gold and pearly gates and a lot of angels around. Some people feel that we should rather speak about the existence beyond existence in existing non-existent existence. ... Abstract imagery is only duller than concrete imagery. But both are imageries.[18]

Early Christian apocalyptic should therefore not be delineated by abstracting the theological eschatological essence or the existential eschatological stance towards life from its apocalyptic language and thought-world. Apocalyptic language is not simply the vehicle for theological-eschatological ideas or concepts but as mytho-poetic language evokes imaginative participation. The metaphoric and symbolic character of apocalyptic language resists any attempt at logical reduction and closed one-dimensional interpretation. Its aim is not explanation and information but the expression of visionary wholeness. It elicits understandings, emotions and reactions that cannot fully be conceptualized and expressed in propositional language. Since apocalyptic language appeals to the imagination it has to be analyzed from a literary perspective.

---

[18] Stendahl 1972, 62.

4. Apocalyptic Language and Theological Perspective
of Early Christian Apocalyptic

A literary critical approach tries to study the special qualities of apocalyptic language and structure without attempting to press all works into a pre-established type and framework or to reduce imaginative to propositional language. Since this approach invites us to enter the unique "world" of the author, it cannot tolerate any systematization of partial aspects or elements found in different works into an ideal type "apocalypse" or their reduction to a one dimensional world-view of "apocalyptic". Whereas many historical, theological, and phenomenological studies negatively evaluate apocalyptic language and form as the mere container and vehicle of timeless theological truth, literary criticism points out that the form of a work is not an instrumental, separable wrapping for the eschatological content. Since literary criticism does not understand apocalyptic writings in terms of theological argument but in terms of evocative power, it can be appreciative of apocalyptic language, imagery, and visions.

However, the choice of apocalyptic language by early Christian authors also indicates a fresh perspective through which reality is understood "in a certain way, a unique way, not entirely commensurate with any other way. A genuine perspective must partly create, justify and interpret the language by which it finds expression".[19] In order to situate the peculiar perspective of early Christian apocalyptic within the context of early Christian community and history and to determine its function within such a context, the literary critical analysis has to be complemented by a historical-sociological analysis. A phenomenological approach which attempts to distill the "essence" of early Christian apocalyptic from its historical-sociological conditioned form and language overlooks that a transformation in language and literary form always includes also a transformation in the sphere of religious essence and validity. One cannot grasp the peculiar early Christian perspective expressed in apocalyptic language and form by distilling its supra-temporal validity but only by understanding apocalyptic language and form as the "creative concretization flowing from historically unique constellations".[20]

5. Literary Analyses of Apocalyptic Language and Form

Although scholars (especially American) have studied the parables from a literary perspective, such an approach to early Christian apocalyptic is still in its very beginnings. In the concluding section of the paper I will therefore first discuss the symbol analysis and second the phenomenologi-

---

[19] Wheelwright 1975, 170.   [20] Mannheim 1971, 90.

cal literary analysis and will focus third on the significance of such literary approaches for the interpretation of Rev.

5.1. The Symbol-Analysis

5.1.1. Perrin argues that Kingdom of God has been misunderstood as apocalyptic conception because its symbolic language character has been overlooked.[21] In his understanding of symbol Perrin follows Wheelwright's distinction between steno- and tensive symbol. Whereas a steno-symbol always bears only a one-to-one relationship and is mostly used in scientific discourse, the tensive symbol can evoke a whole range of meanings and can never be exhausted or adequately expressed by any one referent. Five different modes of the tensive symbol can be distinguished: It can be (1) the presiding image of a work, (2) the primary image of a poet, (3) a symbol of "ancestral vitality", (4) a symbol of cultural range and (5) an archtypal symbol that expresses cross-cultural meanings.[22]

Perrin classifies Kingdom of God as a tensive symbol of cultural range without, however, exploring its other possibilities of meaning. Perrin concedes that as a cultural symbol the tensive symbol Kingdom of God has come to express Jewish expectations for God's final intervention on behalf of Israel or of the faithful remnant. However, he consistently treats it as a symbol of "ancestral vitality" but not as a symbol of "cultural range" by stressing that the symbol evokes the myth of God acting as King on behalf of God's people in history and by overlooking that in the first century CE this myth had found apocalyptic expression.

This corresponds to his tendency to identify apocalyptic symbols with steno-symbols although he concedes that this need not always be the case. Perrin's symbol-analysis thus seems to continue the dichotomy between eschatology and apocalyptic. Moreover, since he maintains that not the symbol but the myth mediates the experience of reality, he seems in effect to subordinate the symbol to the myth that it evokes. The tensive symbol Kingdom of God tends to become a steno-symbol and the myth of God's kingly activity in behalf of the people of God seems to become the *content* of Jesus' message. Nevertheless his analysis has opened up rich possibilities for the interpretation of apocalyptic language, as the following symbol analysis of "resurrection" indicates.[23]

5.1.2. In line with Jewish apocalyptic expectation, Rev speaks of resur-

---

[21] Perrin 1974, 10ff.; 1976, 29ff., 196ff.   [22] Wheelwright 1975, 98–110.
[23] The following exemplification presupposes but does not critically evaluate the exegetical analyses and summaries of Becker 1976, since it is not concerned with exegetical reconstruction but with the demonstration of a method.

rection only with reference to the final resurrection of the dead. However, this does not mean that in Rev the symbol resurrection does not also evoke a specific Christian meaning. A motif-*geschichtlich* analysis has shown that earliest Christian theology used the symbol "resurrection of the dead" (Rom 1:4) only with reference to Jesus Christ. Paul took over this christological understanding from the antiochene-syriac missionary kerygma (1 Thess 1:9f.). In 1 Thess 4:13ff. for the first time he himself thematizes the problem of the resurrection of the dead because of concrete problems in the Thessalonian community. Here Paul expands the traditional parousia-motif-cluster with the motif of the raising of the dead. As God has raised Christ so God will also raise the Christians from the dead so that all can be together with the Lord.

For the first time in the history of Christian theology Paul integrates in 1 Cor 15 the motif of the resurrection of Christ into the apocalyptic symbol context of the general resurrection of all the dead. However, by calling Christ "the first fruits of those who have fallen asleep" (15:20), he marks at the same time the temporal distance of Christ's resurrection from that of the Christians. Paul thus clearly expands apocalyptic expectations. This shows that the apocalyptic tensive symbol resurrection can evoke a wide range of meaning: exaltation of the "Son of Man" and his return for the gathering of the elect (1 Thess 1:10), the direct assumption of the martyrs into heaven (Phil 1:23), the raising of the dead by analogy to the raising of Christ (1 Thess 4:15ff.), and finally the resurrection of Christ as the first of the general resurrection. With these Jewish apocalyptic motifs are associated in 1 Cor 15 the hellenistic motifs of immortality, transformation of the perishable nature and the putting on of the imperishable nature as a garment.

5.1.3. The title of Christ "firstborn of the dead" in Rev 1:5 shares in this Pauline tradition of the symbol. It alludes to Ps 89:27 "... and I will make him the first-born, the highest of the kings of the earth" and points to the resurrection of the dead in Rev 20:5f. The closest parallel to it is the title of Christ "firstborn *from (ek)* the dead in the baptismal hymn, Col 1:18b. However, while Col 1:18b separates Christ from the dead as the first one, Rev 1:5 understands the genitive-construction similarly to Rom 15:20: Christ is the first among the dead who are to follow. The motif evokes also the image of Christ in the inauguration vision "who dies and now is alive" and who has the "keys of death and Hades" (1:18; cf. 2:8). It also evokes the image of the Lamb that was slaughtered and has won the victory, and thereby alludes also to the promises for those who will be victorious in the future. Thus the symbol resurrection evokes here a whole range of ancestral and cultural meanings and alludes to other motif-clusters within the book. The richness of the christological title can therefore not be experienced when it is reduced to one single meaning but only when its whole range of meanings and associated motifs are explored.[24]

5.2. The Literary-Phenomenological Analysis

5.2.1. While the use of symbol-analysis can help us to discover the wide range of meaning certain apocalyptic symbols and motifs can have, a literary-phenomenological analysis indicates the impact of early Christian perspective on the structures of the New Testament literature. The New Testament writings, however, must not be misunderstood as self-consciously created literary works, but as religious proclamation that provokes as a religious narrative, audience participation and catharsis. The structural order of the religious narrative functions to establish order and to overcome chaos. Therefore the religious story can have two functions: either to reenact the past or to carry the reader/hearer forward into the future.

5.2.2. However, when the present is so much dominated by oppressive forces that it seems to be void of divine order and presence, then the hope for the future can become the focus of the religious story. The apocalyptic narrative has the function of carrying the readers forward into the future and of confirming the hope for their future vindication by God. This apocalyptic vision has not only determined the form of Rev, but also the form of the Gospel and Luke's writing of history. "The vision of human existence as caught up in a transcendent struggle which will express itself in a real history culminating in a total victory of good is fundamental for all three forms."[25]

Characteristic in all three forms is the tension between the two functions of religious narrative, namely the re-enactment of the past and the carrying forward into the future. This combination of the two narrative functions reflects "the tension between the fulfillment of God's eschatological reign in Jesus and the unfulfilled hope" within the early Christian apocalyptic perspective. The paradox comes to the fore in the resurrection faith. The resurrection of Christ as an event of the past is at the same time an apocalyptic future event. This disclosure of the future does not, however, "transform reality; in one sense the resurrection is the dawning of a new age, and in another sense nothing is changed".[26]

5.3. The Significance of a Literary Approach for the Interpretation of Revelation

5.3.1. Since it is not possible to highlight here how this combination of the two functions of religious narrative finds its concrete expression in the

---

[24] Schüssler Fiorenza 1972, 200ff.; see also the analysis of P. Hoffmann 1979.
[25] Beardslee 1970, 55.   [26] Beardslee 1970, 27.

Christian form of gospel and of history, I will discuss it with reference to
Rev that is written in the form of "apocalypse". It has, however, always
been noted that absence of pseudonymity and prophecies *ex eventu* is a
significant characteristic that distinguishes Rev from other Jewish or later
Christian apocalypses. Therefore scholars have argued that the epistolary
frame is not accidental but an important integral part of the whole
composition of Rev that marks it as a Christian prophetic book.

J. J. Collins, however, has recently again argued that a careful comparison of Rev with Dan indicates that the perspective of Rev is not very
different from that of other Jewish apocalypses. The lack of *ex eventu*
prophecy and pseudonymity as well as the epistolary framework are only
"superficial differences which do not reflect a significant change of perspective".[27] Since in Dan pseudonymity and *ex eventu* prophecy serve to
interpret the present time of persecution in the light of the imminent
eschatological events, these methods are no longer necessary in Rev
because of the Christian faith-conviction that Jesus Christ has already
inaugurated the end-time.

Contrary to its own intention the argument shows that the faith-
perspective of early Christian apocalyptic had a creative impact on the
structure and composition of Rev. It modified its composition with respect
to basic elements of the cross-cultural genre-type of apocalypse. To
maintain a significant and creative modification of the genre apocalypse
does not deny that Rev represents a special form of this genre. The early
Christian apocalyptic perspective of the "already" and the "not yet" of
future salvation has created its own type of apocalypse.

5.3.2. The "unique world of vision" of the Book of Revelation lives
from the tension between the forward-movement to the future and the
impact of eschatological reality on the present of community and world in
the figure of Christ who was dead and is alive again. Elsewhere I have
attempted to show that this tension between present and future is also
expressed in the composition of the book. The basic movement of the
narrative represents the prophetic movement from promise to fulfillment.
This linear movement is partly deflected through the cyclic form of the
three plague septets. Yet these septets are broken cycles insofar as they
represent a forward-movement to greater fulfillment. The forward-movement of the narrative is also interrupted through the interludes that are
hymns or visions of eschatological protection and salvation. Insofar as the
author interrupts the continuous pattern of sequential narrative and cyclic
repetition the composition of the book expresses the tension in Revelation
between the end-oriented forward-movement and the impact of

---

[27] Collins 1977, 342.

eschatological salvation on the present reality of the community and world.[28]

6. The Function of Early Christian Apocalyptic Language

I have argued that the "newness" or the particular perspective of early Christian apocalyptic cannot be formulated by constructing a cross-cultural apocalyptic grid or type. Nor can it be grasped by distilling the eschatological or theological "essence" from its apocalyptic language expression which then can be discarded. The attempt to classify all apocalyptic language and forms as "Jewish but not Christian" seems to have the same apologetic roots.

Further it has been observed that in distinction to Jewish apocalypses early Christian writings use apocalyptic language not only to express their future eschatological hope but also to characterize the past and present of Christ and the Christians as a part of the eschatological events. This tension between the past, present, and future of salvation has determined the New Testament forms of gospel, history, and apocalypse so that in a certain sense all three forms can be classified as Christian apocalyptic forms. However, they emphasize differently the two poles of religious narrative: the re-enactment of the past and the anticipation of the future. The analysis of the apocalyptic genre and language finally has indicated the interest of early Christian apocalyptic in paraenesis. Some have suggested that such a paraenetic interest and function of early Christian apocalyptic has a de-apocalyptizing impact on its perspective and language. Therefore early Christian apocalyptic must be understood as prophetic because it is derived not from Jewish apocalyptic but conceived by analogy to OT classical prophecy. However, it is questionable whether such a distinction influenced by the discussions of Jewish apocalyptic is applicable to early Christian apocalyptic, since Jewish apocalyptic originated centuries before the NT era. Nevertheless, such a peculiar emphasis on paraenesis indicates a shift in ideas and perspective.[29]

6.1. A sociology of knowledge approach points out that any change in theological ideas and literary forms is preceded by a change in social function and perspective. The traditional apocalyptic elements function now in relationship to a new systemic center. They are changing because they belong to a new historical situation and constellation.[30] If the creative center of early Christian faith is the living Lord active in his community then the traditional Jewish apocalyptic elements and language receive a new

---

[28] Schüssler Fiorenza 1977a, 344–366.
[29] See Schüssler Fiorenza 1980 for a delineation of the discussion and the pertinent literature.
[30] Cf. the works of Mannheim 1952; *idem* 1971 and Schutz 1967.

function. Apocalyptic language is not just the expression of this creative center of Christian belief and community but constitutive for its under-standing. Such a historical-sociological approach permits us therefore on the one hand to grasp the continuity and shift between Jewish and early Christian apocalyptic. On the other hand it enables us to conceive of the so-called opponents in the NT as Christian groups related differently to the common life center of early Christian apocalyptic.

Change does not mean discontinuity but a further development of the ideas and forms from a new systematic centre. Early Christian apocalyptic thus stands in continuity with Jewish apocalyptic but represents "so to speak a new angle of refraction".[31] Whereas Jewish apocalyptic hopes for the imminent intervention of God and understands its literature as a "proleptic" revelation of the eschatological events, early Christian apocalyptic lives from the belief that the end-events have already been inaugurated in the person of Jesus Christ who was dead and is alive again. Early Christian literature is thus the "revelation" of this resurrected Lord and his relationship to the Christian community. The same Jesus who spoke in the past and who will return as the eschatological judge in the imminent future is now active within the Christian community by speaking through apostles and prophets to it. Early Christian apocalyptic literature is there-fore not just a visionary anticipation of the end-events but the proclamation of eschatological salvation and judgment in and through Christian prophets. Early Christian apocalyptic literature is therefore prophetic in character.

Since early Christian apocalyptic does not just hope for eschatological salvation in the near future but also knows that the end-time is already inaugurated through the exaltation and resurrection of Jesus Christ, it no longer thinks in terms of two succeeding aeons and worlds but maintains the contemporaneity of this world and the world to come with respect to Jesus Christ and to the Christian community. There is only one time, the end-time. This theological understanding is, for instance, expressed in the composition of Rev that does not progress in historical development but so-to-speak reveals in ever new images and perspectives the time of the Christian community as the end-time. Eschatological vision and paraenesis have in Rev the same function. They provide the vision of an alternative world and kingdom in order to strengthen Christians in their consistent resistance to the oppressive powers and persecutions of the Roman Empire.[32]

6.2. This central faith-conviction and hope of early Christian apocalyptic

---

[31] Mannheim 1971, 59–115, 114.
[32] Cf. also the contribution of L. Schottroff in this volume and Mealand 1979.

can be expressed with respect to the Christian community in a twofold way by stressing either the future eschatological or the present eschatological perspective. Because of their functional relationship to the systemic center of early Christian faith both types of early Christian apocalyptic, futuristic and realized eschatology, are dialectically interdependent. Either early Christian writers emphasize the future aspect of eschatological salvation in order to balance the experience of realized eschatology in baptism. Or they stress the present realization of eschatological salvation over and against a future oriented eschatology. Both, however, share the same Christian apocalyptic faith-perspective that the future judge Jesus Christ has already in the past inaugurated eschatological salvation and resurrection on the one hand and that the Christians already share in this salvation but have not yet achieved it on the other. Therefore both expressions of early Christian apocalyptic faith have the same prophetic function of encouragement and exhortation. Moreover, both Christian apocalyptic emphases – the predominantly futural as well as the predominantly realized perspective – may not be played out against each other as orthodox and heretical, or as apocalyptic and gnostic but should be seen in their orientation to their common christological center and perspective.[33]

6.3. Both types of apocalyptic language and eschatology can function in a twofold way: either they provide an alternative vision of the world and its determinative powers in order to encourage alternative community structures and to interpret the Christians' experience of persecution and oppressive reality undermining their faith-conviction that Christ is the Lord of the world and God the creator of the cosmos. Or both types can appeal to apocalyptic imagery and eschatological projection in their description of the "afterlife" in order to control[34] the behavior of the individual Christian and the Christian community in this life. While earlier apocalyptic Christian texts express an alternative vision and interpretation of the present Christian experience of oppression and persecution, later Christian apocalypses appeal to the afterlife by describing especially the punishments in vivid colors. They do so in order to ensure the virtuous life of the Christians and the Christian community in the present.

This functional shift within early Christian apocalyptic literature indicates a change in the social-political situation of the Christian community. It signals a shift from an alternative vision of the world and political power to the rejection of the world for the sake of the afterlife, from a counter-cultural Christian movement to a church adapted and integrated into its culture and society, from a social-political, religious ethos to an indi-

---

[33] For the commonalities between gnostic and apocalyptic literature and thought cf. the articles by G. W. MacRae and H. G. Kippenberg in this volume.

[34] Cf. also the analysis of W. A. Meeks in this volume and of Theissen 1978.

vidualized and privatized ethics. This shift in function finally engenders a shift in apocalyptic language and form, from evocative-mythopoetic symbols and political language to allegorical descriptions of eternal punishments and moralistic injunctions against the sins of the individual.

Bibliography

Aune, David E. 1972: *The Cultic Setting of Realized Eschatology in Early Christianity* (NT.S 28), Leiden 1972.

Baumgarten, Jörg 1975: *Paulus und die Apokalyptik* (WMANT 44), Neukirchen-Vluyn 1975.

Beardslee, William A. 1970: *Literary Criticism of the New Testament*, Philadelphia, Penn. 1970.

Becker, J. 1970: "Erwägungen zur apokalyptischen Tradition in der Paulinischen Theologie", in: *EvTh* 30 (1970) 593–609.

– 1976: *Auferstehung der Toten im Urchristentum* (SBS 82), Stuttgart 1976.

Betz, Hans Dieter 1969: "On the Problem of the Religio-Historical Understanding of Apocalypticism", in: *JTC* 6 (1969) 134–154.

Breech, Earl 1978: "Kingdom of God in the Parables of Jesus", in: *Semeia* 12 (1978) 15–40.

Burkitt, F. C. 1914: *Jewish and Christian Apocalypses*, Oxford 1914.

Collins, John J. 1977: "Pseudonymity, Historical Reviews and the Genre of the Apocalypse of John", in: *CBQ* 39 (1977) 329–343.

– (ed.) 1979: *Apocalypse: The Morphology of a Genre (Semeia 14)*, Missoula, Mont. 1979.

Detweiler, R. 1978: *Story, Sign and Self. Phenomenology and Structuralism as Literary Critical Methods*, Philadelphia, Penn. 1978.

Dexinger, F. 1977: *Henochs Zehnwochenapokalypse und offene Probleme der Apokalyptikforschung* (StPB 29), Leiden 1977, 1–93.

Doty, William G. 1970: "Identifying Eschatological Language", in: *Continuum* 7 (1970) 546–561.

– 1972: "The Concept of Genre in Literary Analysis", in: *SBL Proceedings* 2 (1972) 413–448.

Grässer, E. 1973: *Die Naherwartung Jesu* (SBS 61), Stuttgart 1973.

Hanson, P. D. 1976: "Apocalypse, Genre, Apocalypticism", in: *IDBSup* 1976, 27–34.

Hartman, Lars 1966: *Prophecy Interpreted. The Formation of Some Jewish Apocalyptic Texts and of the Eschatological Discourse* (CB.NT 1), Lund 1966.

Hennecke, E./Schneemelcher, W. (eds.) 1965: *New Testament Apocrypha. Volume II: Apocalypses and Related Subjects*, Philadelphia, Penn. 1965, 581–803.

Hiers, R. H. 1966: "Eschatology and Methodology", in: *JBL* 85 (1966) 170–184.

Hoffmann, P. 1979: "Auferstehung", in: *TRE* IV (1979) 450–513.

James, M. R. 1924: *The Apocryphal New Testament*, Oxford 1924.

Käsemann, E. 1960: "Die Anfänge christlicher Theologie", in: *ZThK* 57 (1960) 162–185.

– 1962: "Zum Thema der urchristlichen Apokalyptik", in: *ZThK* 59 (1962) 257–284.

Keller, C. A. 1977: "Das Problem des Bösen in der Apokalyptik und Gnostik", in: M. Krause (ed.), *Gnosis und Gnosticism* (NHS VIII), Leiden 1977, 70–90.

Koch, K. 1970: *Ratlos vor der Apokalyptik*, Gütersloh 1970.

Kocis, E. 1971: "Apokalyptik und politisches Interesse im Spätjudentum", in: *Judaica* 27 (1971) 71–89.

Lanczkowski, G./Lebram, J./ Müller, K./Strobel, A./Schwarte, K. H. 1978: "Apokalyptik/Apokalypsen", in: *TRE* III (1978) 189–275.

Lohse, E. 1971: "Apokalyptik und Christologie", in: *ZNW* 62 (1971) 48–67.

Mannheim, K. 1952: *Essays on the Sociology of Knowledge*, London 1952.

– 1971: "The Problem of a Sociology of Knowledge", in: K. H. Wolff (ed.), *From Karl Mannheim*, New York 1971, 54–115.

Maren-Grisebach, M. 1977: *Methoden der Literaturwissenschaft* (UTB 121), 6th ed., München 1977.

Marshall, I. H. 1978: "Slippery Words: Eschatology", in: *ET* 81 (1978) 264–269.
Mealand, D. L. 1979: *Poverty and Expectation in the Gospels*, London 1979.
Moule, C. F. D. 1964: "The Influence of Circumstances on the Use of Eschatological Terms", in: *JThS* NS 15 (1964) 1–15.
Patte, D. 1975: *Early Jewish Hermeneutics in Palestine* (SBLDS 22), Missoula, Mont. 1975.
Perrin, N. 1974: "Eschatology and Hermeneutics", in: *JBL* 93 (1974) 1–15.
– 1976: *Jesus and the Language of the Kingdom*, Philadelphia 1976.
Rogahn, K. W. 1975: *The Function of Future Eschatological Statements in the Pauline Epistles*, Ann Arbor, Mich. 1975.
Rollins, W. G. 1970: "The New Testament and Apocalyptic", in: *NTS* 17 (1970/71) 454–476.
Rudolph, K. 1971: "Religionsgeschichte und Religionsphenomenologie", in: *ThLZ* 96 (1971) 241–250.
Sand, A. 1972: "Zur Frage nach dem 'Sitz im Leben' der apokalyptischen Texte des Neuen Testaments", in: *NTS* 18 (1972/73) 167–177.
Schenk, W. 1972: "Naherwartung und Parusieverzögerung. Die urchristliche Eschatologie als Problem der Forschung", in: *Theologische Versuche* IV (1972) 47–69.
Schmidt, J. M. 1969: "Forschungen zur jüdischen Apokalyptik", in: *VF* 14 (1969) 44–69.
– 1969a: *Jüdische Apokalyptik*, Neukirchen-Vluyn 1969.
Schmithals, W. 1975: *The Apocalyptic Movement*, Nashville, Tenn. 1975.
Schoonheim, P. L. 1977: "Probleme und Impulse der Neutestamentlichen Apokalyptik", in: Baarda, T./Klijn, A. F. J./van Unnik, W. C. (eds.), *Miscellanea Neotestamentica* I (NT.S 47), Leiden 1977, 129–145.
Schottroff, W./Stegemann, W. (eds.) 1977: *Der Gott der kleinen Leute. Sozialgeschichtliche Auslegungen. Neues Testament*, München 1977.
Schüssler Fiorenza, E. 1972: *Priester für Gott. Studien zum Herrschafts- und Priestermotiv in der Apokalypse* (NTA 7), Münster 1972.
– 1973: "Apocalyptic and Gnosis in the Book of Revelation and in Paul", in: *JBL* 92 (1973) 565–581.
– 1976: "Eschatology of the NT", in: *IDBSup*, Nashville, Tenn. 1976, 271–277.
– 1977a: "Composition and Structure of the Revelation of John", in: *CBQ* 39 (1977) 344–366.
– 1977b: "The Quest for the Johannine School", in: *NTS* 23 (1977) 402–427.
– 1980: "Apokalypsis and Propheteia. The Book of Revelation in the Context of Early Christian Prophecy", in: J. Lambrecht (ed.), *L'Apocalypse johannique et l'Apocalyptique dans le Nouveau Testament* (BEThL 53), Gembloux 1980, 105–128.
Schutz, A. 1967: *Phenomenology of the Social World*, Evanston, Ill. 1967.
Staerk, W. 1936: "Der eschatologische Mythos in der altchristlichen Kirche", in: *ZNW* 35 (1936) 83–95.
Stanton, G. N. 1977: "5 Ezra and Matthean Christianity in the Second Century", in: *JThS* NS 28 (1977) 67–83.
Stendahl, K. 1972: "On Earth as It Is in Heaven-Dynamics in Christian Eschatology", in: J. Papin (ed.), *The Eschaton*, Villanova, Penn. 1972, 57–68.
Theissen, G. 1978: *Sociology of Early Palestinian Christianity*, Philadelphia, Penn. 1978.
Thoma, C. 1969: "Jüdische Apokalyptik am Ende des 1. nachchristlichen Jahrhunderts", in: *Kairos* 11 (1969) 134–144.
Vielhauer, P. 1965: "Apocalyptic in Early Christianity. Introduction", in: Hennecke/Schneemelcher (eds.) 1965, 608–642.
– 1975: *Geschichte der urchristlichen Literatur*, Berlin 1975, 485–528.
Walter, N. 1975: "Zur theologischen Relevanz apokalyptischer Aussagen", in: *Theologische Versuche* 6 (1975), 47–72.
Wanke, G. 1970: "Eschatologie. Ein Beispiel theologischer Sprachverwirrung", in: *KuD* 16 (1970) 300–312.
Weinel, H. 1923: "Die spätere christliche Apokalyptik", in: *Eucharisterion. Festschrift H. Gunkel*, 2. Teil (FRLANT NF 19/2), Göttingen 1923, 141–173.
Wheelwright, P. 1975: *Metaphor and Reality*, 6th ed., Bloomington, Ind. 1975.

Widengren, G. 1969: *Religionsphenomenologie*, Berlin 1969 (especially pp. 440–479).
Wilder, A. 1971: "The Rhetoric of Ancient and Modern Apocalyptic", in: *Interpretation* 25 (1971) 436–453.
– 1976: *Theopoetic. Theology and Religious Imagination*, Philadelphia, Penn. 1976.
Yarbro Collins, A. 1979: "The Early Christian Apocalypses", in: *Semeia* 14 (1979) 61–121.

Apocalyptic Eschatology in Gnosticism

George MacRae

1. Apocalyptic Eschatology

There is growing agreement among contemporary scholars that the phenomenon of apocalyptic cannot be understood or defined by the exercise of cataloguing elements or characteristics found in apocalypses or in literature that is widely acknowledged to contain apocalyptic features.[1] What is at issue is not merely a matter of proper definition but, as Hans Dieter Betz makes clear, the fact that most of the "apocalyptic" characteristics usually listed are common features of religious literature in the Hellenistic world.[2] Attempts to circumvent the practice of listing and to define the phenomenon by what is distinctive of it are more difficult. One such attempt looks for "the pattern of these elements in combination,"[3] and as long as this is not the sole criterion for coming to grips with apocalypticism, it may be acknowledged as a useful one. At some point, even when consciously dealing with patterns of elements, most scholars do not totally abandon the practice of compiling descriptive lists of them.[4]

1.1. For a recent example, one might look at the list of "points of contact" between apocalyptic and Gnosticism with which Carl-A. Keller begins his study of the problem of evil:[5]

a. Apocalyptists and Gnostics use the same forms of literature (apocalypses, dialogues, etc.).

b. Both groups of texts are permeated with Old Testament citations and reminiscences.

c. In both there is the communication of a knowledge that is revealed, essentially secret, and necessary for salvation (also with similarities in content).

d. Both literatures teach that there is a split or conflict in the celestial world that is determinative of certain aspects of human life on earth.

e. In both cases knowledge leads into a clearly circumscribed ethic of ascetical stamp.[6]

f. Apocalyptic and Gnostic writings have in common an expressly polemical attitude against those who live in error and are destined to be lost.

---

[1] Hanson 1976, 28; Betz 1969, 136; Smith 1975, 132.
[2] Betz 1969, 136.   [3] Smith 1975, 132.   [4] Hanson 1976, 31.
[5] Keller 1977, 70–72, briefly summarized here.
[6] Keller rightly observes that extant Gnostic literature advocates asceticism; whether "Gnostic libertinism" is excluded or not deserves further discussion. See also Kippenberg in the present volume; for an opposing view see Schmithals 1975, 108.

On the surface, such a list might provide a starting-point for a discussion of apocalyptic and Gnosticism, but one would have to ask precisely whether the points listed are in every case distinctive characteristics of either apocalyptic or Gnosticism. To be sure, Keller's intention is quite different: he uses the list merely to show that there are enough obvious points of contact between the two to justify a more penetrating comparative study of the problem of evil, making use of the categories of the sociology of religion. But there is another problem in the compilation of a list such as this, namely that although it ostensibly concentrates on the characteristics of apocalyptic literature, it does not clearly distinguish among literary, theological, and social dimensions of either apocalyptic or Gnosticism.

1.2. It is useful, therefore, to be guided by the kind of basic distinctions in definition advocated by Paul D. Hanson, who urges clarity in the discussion of three terms.[7] (a) The first is the literary genre of *apocalypse*, which is properly described by a listing of its formal elements and material contents. That there were Gnostic apocalypses is not in doubt, and the nature of them is discussed elsewhere in this volume.[8] It is important to remember that the presence of apocalyptic thought is by no means conterminous with the use of the literary genre of apocalypse. Indeed, it might be observed that the most characteristically apocalyptic passages in the Gnostic literature of Nag Hammadi do not occur in works labeled (in antiquity) apocalypses–but this may be part of the modern scholar's problem: Is "apocalyptic" an ancient or a modern concept?[9] (b) The second of Hanson's categories is that of *apocalyptic eschatology*, the broadest of the three, which is closely identified with the continuation and transformation of the prophetic eschatology of the Old Testament. Surprisingly, apocalyptic eschatology is the most easily verifiable in the literature of Gnosticism. It is surprising because at first sight one would expect Gnostic literature to so emphasize a totally realized eschatology as to exclude the future-oriented apocalyptic perspective. But that is not the case; a certain apocalyptic perspective remains, as we shall see below, and may be fundamental to the Gnostic world-view. (c) Thirdly, Hanson defines *apocalypticism* as "the symbolic universe in which an apocalyptic movement codifies its identity and interpretation of reality." This category implies certain sociological and anthropological criteria which will not be the subject of the present paper but which are essential to an investigation of the relation between apocalyptic and Gnosticism.[10]

---

[7] Hanson 1976, 29–31.
[8] Krause; see also Fallon 1979a, 123–158; Ménard 1973, 300–323.
[9] Vielhauer 1975, 486.
[10] Hanson 1976, 30–34; Keller 1977, 75–90; Kippenberg in the present volume.

1.3. This third category gives rise to a fundamental question with which the Colloquium inevitably is concerned, but to which the present paper alone cannot give a definitive answer. The question is whether the Gnostic movement is properly understood as an apocalyptic movement. Hanson expressly denies that the abandonment of the mundane concepts of space and time, typical of Gnosticism, is properly regarded as a manifestation of the "symbolic universe of apocalypticism".[11] On the other hand, Walter Schmithals, in a very provocative essay, citing with approval the dictum of Rudolf Otto, "Gnosis is of the very spirit of apocalyptic teaching," even asserts that the statement may be made conversely as well.[12] To a limited extent, the present paper will attempt to take a stand upon this issue, not by exploring the nature of Gnostic apocalypticism with the tools of the social sciences, but rather by seeking evidence of apocalyptic eschatology in Gnostic texts.

1.4. There is one perhaps obvious and in any case much-traveled approach to the question which we may set aside at the beginning, important as are its conslusions. That is the question of the role of Jewish apocalyptic in the *origins* of Gnosticism. The fact that Gnosticism arose out of Jewish apocalyptic (and wisdom) tradition, however radical the revolt against the Jewish matrix may have been, is now very broadly acknowledged, especially in view of the prominent Jewish elements in the Nag Hammadi Gnostic texts.[13] One must not too quickly polarize the discussion by trying to distinguish between what is Jewish and what is Hellenistic. These categories overlap in the Greco-Roman period, but the evidence of Jewish traditions in *every* known form of Gnostic thought in that period is too overwhelming to be ignored. But the historical influence of Jewish apocalyptic on the origins of Gnosticism is also not the subject of this paper. Our question is rather, to what extent is Gnosticism itself a manifestation of apocalyptic eschatology?

2. Gnostic Apocalyptic

At first glance and a priori, the question might seem otiose. Gnosticism is after all the supreme example of realized eschatology, and for a rational understanding of it, it must be so. It is knowledge of self in the present that is the saving principle, even if that knowledge can deal with past and future in its content. Once one knows one's (divine) self, one is already liberated

---

[11] Hanson 1976, 31; MacRae 1966, 302–303 (which needs to be modified in light of Gnostic literature now available).

[12] Schmithals 1975, 93.

[13] Grant 1966, 27–38; Rudolph 1977, 294–299; MacRae 1966; Fallon 1978; and many other contemporary works.

and the future is radically relativized. The celebrated definition of Theodotus is evidence of this:

> It is not the bath (washing) alone that makes us free, but also the knowledge: who were we?
> what have we become? where were we? into what place have we been cast? whither are we
> hastening? from what are we delivered? what is birth? what is rebirth?[14]

Yet, while emphasis on the realized eschatological dimension is not
misplaced, the Gnostic texts themselves remind us that future eschatology
is not completely set aside.[15] Perhaps early Christian Gnosticism is not
theoretically consistent – what form of early Christianity, except perhaps
Marcionite, is after all consistent?

2.1. Instead of listing elements of apocalyptic eschatology in Gnostic
texts, we shall cite some examples of passages that are unmistakably
apocalyptic in language as well as in perspective. Such passages are not
numerous in the texts, but they are sufficiently frequent as to comprise a
regular dimension of the Gnostic myth. In the untitled cosmogonic tractate
of Nag Hammadi Codex II, commonly called by modern scholars *On the
Origin of the World*, we find the following description of the end time:

> Before the consummation [of the aeon], the whole place will be shaken by a great thunder.
> Then the rulers will lament, [crying out on account of their] death. The angels will mourn for
> their men, and the demons will weep for their times, and their men will mourn and cry out on
> account of their death. Then the aeon will begin to ‹... and› they will be disturbed. Its kings
> will be drunk from the flaming sword and they will make war against one another, so that the
> earth will be drunk from the blood which is poured out. And the seas will be troubled by that
> war. Then the sun will darken and the moon will lose its light. The stars of the heaven will
> disregard their course and a great thunder will come out of a great power that is above all the
> powers of Chaos, the place where the firmament of woman is situated. When she has created
> the first work, she will take off her wise flame of insight. She will put on a senseless wrath.
> Then she will drive out the gods of Chaos whom she had created together with the First
> Father. She will cast them down to the abyss. They will be wiped out by their (own) injustice.
> For they will become like the mountains which blaze out fire, and they will gnaw at one
> another until they are destroyed by their First Father. When he destroys them, he will turn
> against himself and destroy himself until he ceases (to be). And their heavens will fall upon
> one another and their powers will burn. Their aeons will also be overthrown. And his (the
> First Father's) heaven will fall and it will split in two. Likewise (the place of) his joy,
> [however], will fall down to the earth, [and the earth will not] be able to support them. They
> will fall [down] to the abyss and the [abyss] will be overthrown.
>
> The light will [cover the] darkness, and it will wipe it out. It will become like one which
> had not come into being. And the work which the darkness followed will be dissolved. And
> the deficiency will be plucked out at its root (and thrown) down to the darkness. And the light
> will withdraw up to its root. And the glory of the unbegotten will appear, and it will fill all of
> the aeons, when the prophetic utterance and the report of those who are kings are revealed and
> are fulfilled by those who are called perfect. Those who were not perfected in the unbegotten

---

[14] *Excerpta ex Theodoto* 78.2 (Foerster [ed.] 1972, 230).
[15] Peel 1970, 155–159.

Father will receive their glories in their aeons and in the kingdoms of immortals. But they will not ever enter the kingless realm.[16]

2.2. For the Gnostic the material world, which came into being through the tragic fault of the cosmic drama, is perishable and must perish. It is characteristic of Gnostic eschatological passages such as this to emphasize the totality and the finality of the destruction by pointing out that the agent of the final destruction ultimately destroys itself as well. In the Valentinian description of the eschaton according to Ptolemy, the agent of destruction is fire:

> When this has taken place, then (they assert) the fire that is hidden in the world will blaze forth and burn: when it has consumed all matter it will be consumed with it and pass into non-existence.[17]

2.2.1. In Valentinian eschatology there is no absolute dichotomy between the reintegration of the spiritual elements into the divine and the total destruction of the material cosmos. Influenced by their position within – or on the margin of – Christianity, the Valentinians allow a place of intermediate repose or salvation, often called "the Middle", for the "psychic" class of people who are other, non-Valentinian Christians.[18] This place, which is also the repository of the psychic element of the highest class of people, the "pneumatics", is at the same time beyond the cosmos – and thus not subject to the destruction of the latter – and yet not a part of the divine Pleroma. A similar distinction of eschatological places of rest is made at the end of the passage cited from *On the Origin of the World*: some will enter "the kingdoms of immortals", but the "kingless realm"[19] is reserved for the true Gnostics.

2.2.2. The futurity of the apocalyptic eschatology in *On the Origin of the World* is unmistakable, but there is usually no suggestion of the immediacy of the final events such as is often found in apocalyptic thought, eloquently phrased, for example, in 4 Ezra 14:10: "For the age has lost its youth, and the times begin to grow old" (RSV). We find an indirect reference to such immediacy in the *Trimorphic Protennoia*, where hostile powers, once the revelation has come into the world, are represented as saying:

> As for the future, let us make our entire flight before we are imprisoned perforce and taken down to the bosom of the underworld. For already the slackening of our bondage has approached, and the times are cut short and the days have shortened and our time has been fulfilled, and the weeping of our destruction has approached us so that we may be taken to the place we recognize.[20]

---

[16] CG II,5: 125,32–127,14. All translations of Nag Hammadi texts are from Robinson (ed.) 1977. On this passage see Tardieu 1974, 74–83; Rudolph 1977, 216–217; Böhlig/Labib 1962, 104–109; Haardt 1964, 315–336; van Unnik 1970, 277–288.

[17] Irenaeus, *Adversus haereses* I.7.1 (Foerster [ed.] 1972, 139).

[18] *Ibid.*, I.6.1 and 7.1–5.   [19] Fallon 1979b, 285.   [20] CG XIII,1: 44,12–19.

2.2.3. In this document there is clearly apocalyptic language in the distinction of the present age and the age to come. The revealing Voice states:

> I shall tell them of the coming end of this Aeon and teach them of the beginning of the Aeon to come, the one without change...[21]

But the same Voice also proclaims: "I am the Aeon to [come. I am] the fulfillment of the All."[22] Thus the language of apocalyptic eschatology is sometimes appropriated in the service of an essentially realized eschatology, and this phenomenon is quite common in many Gnostic works.[23]

2.3. *On the Origin of the World* and *Trimorphic Protennoia* are Christian Gnostic works, or, perhaps better, christianized versions of Gnostic myths, but one should observe how little the apocalyptic language of them is influenced by New Testament apocalyptic texts. To have some sense of contrast, one needs only turn to *The Dialogue of the Savior* where, despite the fragmentary character of the work, there are clear examples of Jesus reinterpreting apocalyptic sayings from the Gospel tradition.[24] But the apocalyptic eschatology of Gnostic sources does not originally stem from contact with Christianity. One of the most graphic apocalyptic passages in the Nag Hammadi texts, which also deserves to be quoted at length, is in a totally non-Christian context. It is from *The Paraphrase of Shem*, and the speaker is Shem:

> After I cease to be upon the earth and withdraw up to my rest, a great, evil error will come upon the world, and many evils in accordance with the number of the forms of Nature. Evil times will come. And when the era of Nature is approaching destruction, darkness will come upon the earth. The number will be small. And a demon will come up from the power who has a likeness of fire. He will divide the heaven, (and) he will rest in the depth of the east. For the whole world will quake. And the deceived world will be thrown into confusion. Many places will be flooded because of envy of the winds and the demons who have a name which is senseless: Phorbea, Chloerga. They are the ones who govern the world with their teaching. And they lead astray many hearts because of their disorder and their unchastity. Many places will be sprinkled with blood. And five races by themselves will eat their sons. But the regions of the south will receive the Word of the Light. But they who are from the error of the world and from the east –. A demon will come forth from (the) belly of the serpent. He was in hiding in a desolate place. He will perform many wonders. Many will loathe him. A wind will come forth from his mouth with a female likeness. Her name will be called Abalphe. He will reign over the world from the east to the west.
>
> Then Nature will have a final opportunity. And the stars will cease from the sky. The mouth of error will be opened in order that the evil Darkness may become idle and silent. And in the last day the forms of Nature will be destroyed with the winds and all their demons; they will become a dark lump, just as they were from the beginning. And the sweet waters which were burdened by the demons will perish. For where the power of the Spirit has gone there are my sweet waters. The other works of Nature will not be manifest. They will mix with the infinite waters of darkness. And all her forms will cease from the middle region.[25]

---

[21] *Ibid.*, 42,19–21.   [22] *Ibid.*, 45,8–9.

[23] Rudolph 1977, 214–215.   [24] CG III,*5*: 122,1ff.   [25] CG VII,*1*: 43,28–45,31.

To be sure, there are elements in this vivid apocalyptic description which can be compared with elements in, for example, Mark 13 – earthquakes, darkness, stars falling from heaven, false leaders appearing with miracles to lead the world astray – but these are what one might call standard materials of apocalyptic and no more original in Mark 13 than in *The Paraphrase of Shem*. In their non-Christian context in the latter work they merely illustrate the independence of the Gnostic apocalyptic development from the Christian sources.

2.4. To the extent that apocalyptic eschatology is characterized by a periodization of history leading into the end time, we should expect to find examples of such periodization in the Gnostic texts. And there are many such examples, often built on the Jewish apocalyptic scheme involving the flood and the fire and the end time, for instance in *The Apocalypse of Adam*.[26] There is another example in *The Concept of Our Great Power*, a not entirely coherent Christian Gnostic work which, if it does indeed contain a reference to the Anomoean heresy (at 40,7) may be as late as the mid-fourth century, or if the reference is a gloss or simply to "dissimilar things", may be a much earlier work.[27] Here the scheme of periodization is developed into what the author calls "the aeon of the flesh", "the psychic aeon", and "the aeon of beauty".[28] Here too the flood and the fire and the eschaton are the basis of the scheme, but the development of it is not clear.

2.5. What is of course most distinctive of the apocalyptic eschatology of Gnosticism is the total absence of any new creation. Given its radically dualist perspective, expressed in the concept of creation as error. Gnosticism can see the end time only as the dissolution of the created world. Even though the Gnostics can speak of "the aeon to come", there is strictly speaking no age to follow the destruction, and such language is but another illustration of the well known ambiguity of the Gnostic use of the word "aeon". Ultimate destiny is the reintegration of the divine particles into God, the dissolution of multiplicity in the restored unity. And with that the whole cosmos disappears. The *Endzeit* is indeed the restoration of the *Urzeit*, but the result is as timeless as the unknown God himself.[29] Gnosticism may thus be described as the ultimate radicalizing of apocalyptic eschatology.

3. Conclusion: Present and Future

One of the elements most characteristic of apocalyptic eschatology is the conviction that salvation lies in the future, indeed in a future beyond the

---

[26] CG V,5: 64,1–85,32. See Perkins 1972, 591–599; Perkins 1977, 387–389.

[27] Parrott (ed.) 1979, 292 and 304.

[28] CG VI,4: 26,1–48,15.   [29] Schmithals 1975, 106.

history of the cosmos.[30] Because of its basic doctrine that it is knowledge that saves, Gnosticism at first sight might seem to be in conflict with this futurity. But in reality both apocalyptic and Gnosticism center on the acquisition (by revelation) and the communication of a knowledge that exercises saving power in the present by its future-oriented content.[31] It is true that the vast bulk of Gnostic revelations are much more obviously centered on the origins of humanity and world, but the perspective is future nevertheless: it is in the return to the precosmic that human destiny lies. And the presence of explicit passages of apocalyptic eschatology in Gnostic revelations is further evidence that the categories of apocalyptic and Gnosticism should not be too sharply divided. The latter is one manifestation of the former, albeit in extreme form.

Bibliography

Betz, Hans Dieter 1969: "On the Problem of the Religio-Historical Understanding of Apocalypticism", in: *JTC* 6 (1969) 134–156 (German original: *ZThK* 63 [1966] 391–409).

Böhlig, Alexander/Labib, Pahor 1962: *Die koptisch-gnostische Schrift ohne Titel aus Codex II von Nag Hammadi*, Berlin 1962.

Fallon, Francis T. 1978: *The Enthronement of Sabaoth: Jewish Elements in Gnostic Creation Myths* (NHS X), Leiden 1978.

– 1979a: "The Gnostic Apocalypses", in: John J. Collins (ed.), *Apocalypse: The Morphology of a Genre*, (*Semeia* 14 [1979]) 123–158.

– 1979b: "The Gnostics: the Undominated Race", in: *NT* 21 (1979) 271–288.

Foerster, Werner (ed.) 1972: *Gnosis. A Selection of Gnostic Texts*, Vol. I, Oxford 1972.

Grant, Robert M. 1966: *Gnosticism and Early Christianity*, rev. ed., New York 1966.

Haardt, Robert 1964: "Das universaleschatologische Vorstellungsgut in der Gnosis", in: Kurt Schubert (ed.), *Vom Messias zum Christus*, Vienna 1964, 315–336.

Hanson, Paul D. 1976: "Apocalypticism", in: Keith Crim *et al.* (ed.), *IDBSup*, Nashville, Tenn. 1976, 28–34.

Keller, Carl-A. 1977: "Das Problem des Bösen in Apokalyptik und Gnostik", in: Martin Krause (ed.), *Gnosis and Gnosticism* (NHS VIII), Leiden 1977, 70–90.

MacRae, George 1966: *Some Elements of Jewish Apocalyptic and Mystical Traditions and Their Relation to Gnostic Literature*, diss. Cambridge University 1966.

Ménard, Jacques E. 1973: "Littérature apocalyptique juive et littérature gnostique", in: *RevSR* 47 (1973) 300–323.

Parrott, Douglas M. (ed.) 1979: *Nag Hammadi Codices V, 2–5 and VI with Papyrus Berolinensis 8502, 1 and 4* (NHS XI), Leiden 1979.

Peel, Malcolm L. 1970: "Gnostic Eschatology and the New Testament", in: *NT* 12 (1970) 141–165.

Perkins, Pheme 1972: "Apocalyptic Schematization in the Apocalypse of Adam and the Gospel of the Egyptians", in: Lane C. McGaughy (ed.), *The Society of Biblical Literature: One Hundred Eighth Annual Meeting. Book of Seminar Papers* (1972), Vol. 2, 591–599.

– 1977: "Apocalypse of Adam: The Genre and Function of a Gnostic Apocalypse", in: *CBQ* 39 (1977) 382–395.

Robinson, James M. (ed.) 1977: *The Nag Hammadi Library in English*, San Francisco 1977.

---

[30] Hanson 1976, 30.   [31] Schmithals 1975, 95.

Rudolph, Kurt 1977: *Die Gnosis. Wesen und Geschichte einer spätantiken Religion*, Göttingen 1977.

Schmithals, Walter 1975: *The Apocalyptic Movement. Introduction & Interpretation*, Nashville 1975 (German original: *Die Apokalyptik. Einführung und Deutung*, Göttingen 1973).

Smith, Jonathan Z. 1975: "Wisdom and Apocalyptic", in: Birger A. Pearson (ed.), *Religious Syncretism in Antiquity: Essays in Conversation with Geo Widengren*, Missoula, Mont. 1975, 131–156.

Tardieu, Michel 1974: *Trois mythes gnostiques: Adam, Eros et les animaux d'Egypte dans un écrit de Nag Hammadi (II,5)*, Paris 1974.

van Unnik, W. C. 1970: "The 'Wise Fire' in a Gnostic Eschatological Vision", in: Patrick Granfield/Josef A. Jungmann (ed.), *Kyriakon. Festschrift für Johannes Quasten*, Münster 1970, Vol. I, 277–288.

Vielhauer, Philipp 1975: *Geschichte der urchristlichen Literatur*, Berlin 1975.

The Literary Genre of Apocalypses
Die Literaturgattung Apokalypse
Le genre littéraire des Apocalypses

Survey of the Problem of Apocalyptic Genre

Lars Hartman

1. Introductory Remarks

As I have understood the task laid before me in this communication, I am to point to some *general* problems that we come across when entering a discussion of genre in apocalyptic. The assessment of apocalyptic genre in specific religions and traditions will then be undertaken by other members of this colloquium.

1.1. Usually "apocalyptic" and "apocalypticism" concern things within the phenomenology of religion and the sociology of religion. But I will concentrate on some problems that have to do with the fact that genre is a *literary* phenomenon. Therefore, that which I give in terms of a *Forschungsbericht* is rather selective and, furthermore, is determined by my way of assessing the genre problem.

1.2. That there is a genre problem in apocalyptic is certain. G. von Rad stated: "in literary respect apocalyptic does not represent a specific 'genre'. On the contrary, it is, in terms of form criticism, a *mixtum compositum...*"[1] On the other hand, there are many scholars in the field, who are quite prepared to discuss and present definitions of apocalyptic, not only as a religious phenomenon, but also as something moulded in a specific literary genre.[2]

1.3. Apparently, such a diversity of opinions is possible only because terms such as "apocalyptic" and "genre" are being used in different ways. Therefore, for my purpose, it is necessary that we first reflect on the genre concept. My next step will be to suggest what seems to me a justifiable description of "genre". Then, I will confront this description with some recent discussions of apocalyptic genre, and, lastly, make a few suggestions for future research in the area.

---

[1] von Rad 1975, 331. Cp. Collins 1979a, 3; Brashler 1977, 83.
[2] See, *e.g.*, Collins and Brashler, *loc. cit.*

2. The Concept of Genre

Commenting first on the concept of genre, I must say that I lack both time and competence to enter upon a presentation of how scholars in the fields of literary criticism and linguistics have wrestled with the questions as to whether genres exist, and if so, in which sense, and what one then should mean by the term.[3] Nonetheless, I will not conceal the fact that I have learnt a good deal from what has been going on in these areas.

2.1. I mentioned that there exists a certain confusion in terminology. That is true, not least among Biblical scholars. Thus, German authors in the fields often use *Gattung* when they speak of smaller literary units such as psalms of individual lament, miracle stories or proverbs. But they can also speak of the *Form* of such texts and mean the same thing. On the other hand, they can discuss, *e.g.*, the *Gattung* of the gospel as well as its *Form* and again in this case mean the same thing with the two terms.[4] English-speaking authors tend to use the word "genre" about whole works such as gospels, collections of oracles, or epic works, whereas "form" is used to designate smaller textual units. In addition, however, "form", both in English and in German, can be used concerning both, let us say, "specific form" and "general form". By "specific form" I mean the specific shape of a given text, and by "general form" structure and other characteristics that occur in several similar literary pieces and that manifest themselves in the shape of the texts.[5] In the following I will use the term "genre" in the general English sense just mentioned.

2.2. Before entering upon genre in detail, let us briefly consider a classical piece of European literature that may prove illustrative of the problem before us, *viz., Gulliver's Travels* by Jonathan Swift. On the surface, the book appears as a travel-book, not least by its matter-of-fact style. But this primary impression is soon dissolved by the contents of the story, with the result that the youngest readers take it rather as a children's story. A reader who has come a little more of age recognizes that such a genre classification also does not fit, for he senses how much ironic criticism of mankind's follies is contained in the story. And, as we know,

---

[3] A useful survey is Doty 1972. Cp. also the discussion in Knierim 1973. A thorough investigation of principles and theories brought forward in literary criticism and linguistics is Hempfer 1973. – At this point I should also mention that I have learnt very much for this paper from my discussions with Mr. David Hellholm whose Uppsala dissertation (1980) goes deeply into these matters confronting form criticism, linguistics and philosophy.

[4] It seems that NT scholars and their OT colleagues differ in their usage: see, *e.g.*, Rendtorff 1956 and Conzelmann 1956, two dictionary articles under the same headline – the former uses *Gattung* of, *e.g.*, hymns and proverbs, whereas the latter refers to *die Gattung des "Evangeliums"* in contrast to *die "kleinen Formen" in den Evangelien*.

[5] Cp. Doty 1972, 434.

this is not enough, fot the work also consists of a slightly disguised political polemic in an allegorical form. As a matter of fact, Swift himself said that the book was written "to vex the world rather than divert it".[6]

2.2.1. Regarded in the genre perspective Swift's *Gulliver's Travels* may give occasion to the following reflections. The work displays features of different kinds of literature, so that a precise genre classification of it seems impossible. It is certain, though, that the text is ironic and allegoric, although interpreters may doubt how far the irony and allegory go. Now it seems obvious that to a large extent the irony and its message depend on the fact that different features, typical of different genres, have been used in an irregular manner. One does not usually write a travel-book to scorge man's weaknesses, nor does one as a rule write stories to jeer at politicians. But when such and similar things are done, the effects can be stronger, because the readers recognize the odd usage of the genre features, consciously or unconsciously. Of course, in order that something should be felt as irregular, something regular must exist. If this regularity is dissolved, the possibilities of irony, parody, satire, etc., diminish, as far as they depend on this feeling of irregularity. For when addressees somehow distinguish between different kinds of literature, they also tend to associate them with specific situations, contents and functions. In other words, the recognition of a genre creates a certain "reader's expectation" (*Lesererwartung*)[7] which determines the understanding and the reception of the addressee. Further, there is often a connection between genre and sociolinguistic situation and function. But, in order that both regular and irregular uses of genres may "work" with the reader, he must have learnt them; his "*Lesererwartung*" has to have been trained.

2.2.2. Thus, it seems to me, the example of *Gulliver's Travels* points to some essential aspects of genre and also indicates why one should bother about genre at all, *viz.*, that it serves the understanding of a text. Or, in N. Frye's words on genre criticism: "its purpose is to clarify, not to classify".[8]

2.3. What, then, is a genre? I leave aside how Plato and Aristotle have already differentiated between lyric, epic and drama, and also how one has thought of genres as established-rule-systems, which should be followed by authors.[9] Instead I think of vaguer but yet distinguishable literary conventions which characterize so many works in a given cultural context

---

[6] Quintana 1975, 858. Much has been written on Swift's literary technique: see, *e.g.*, Price 1953, esp. 95 ff.; Bullitt 1953; Quintana 1967; Leavis 1968.

[7] See, *e.g.*, Weinrich 1971, 30 f., 140.

[8] N. Frye as cited with agreement by Todorov 1974, 962. Hempfer 1973, 105 ff., 160 f., stresses the hermeneutic implications of genre studies.

[9] So, *e.g.*, with Cicero and the Neo-classicism; see, *e.g.*, Weisstein 1968, 143 f.; Hempfer 1973, 41 ff., 57 f., etc.

that one can speak of some type of literature.[10] Such a convention is shared by reader and author: the author accepts it, more or less faithfully, and shapes his text in adherence to it; the reader's expectations and attitude when approaching the text are colored by it, and it affects his understanding of the text. This is to say that discussing genre means discussing something that has to do with communication.[11]

2.3.1. The expression "a given cultural context", used in the preceding paragraph, may appear to be rather vague. It becomes a little more precise, when we also take into account that genre is a structure that functions within a communication between author and readers. When or where the cultural context is so different from the original one of a given text that its genre does not function as genre in at least a similar way any more, then one has passed the limit for the cultural context that provides the literary conventions that determine genre, its use and understanding. This means placing oneself on a certain level of abstraction: if one abstracts further, one gets a wider genre concept and also has to reckon with wider cultural contexts for the genre, implying less precise historically given cultural conventions behind text-making *and* text-understanding. One should, then, in my view, allow the communication aspect to determine how far one goes in abstraction.

2.3.2. A genre convention can manifest itself in various characteristics of a text, and one may discuss to what extent it necessarily must expose this or that feature or quality on the literary surface in order to be referred to a certain genre. But also elements that are not directly visible in the text belong to a genre convention, elements that have to do with its place in the life of the community in which it appears and to which it is directed – we Biblical scholars speak of the *Sitz im Leben* of a text.

3. Constitutive Elements of a Genre

After these rather general deliberations I now venture to enter upon a more specific discussion. I will present to you some groups of phenomena, which, I believe, to a greater or lesser extent, combine to constitute a genre. All of these phenomena – or constituents, as I shall call them – are dealt with more or less at length in works by literary critics, but I have systematized them in a way I have not come across elsewhere.[12]

3.1. The first group of constituents concerns the linguistic[13] characteris-

---

[10] Cp. the presentation by Hempfer 1973, §3.3.6.   [11] Hempfer 1973, 89ff., 98ff., etc.

[12] I restrict myself to referring my reader to the works referred to in n. 3 above, and to the vast literature that is discussed in them. The following discussion of some groups of constituents is a slightly elaborated version of a section in an earlier article, Hartman 1978.

[13] "Linguistic" in the meaning of "*sprachlich*", not "*sprachwissenschaftlich*".

tics of a text and regards its style, vocabulary and phraseology, *e.g.*, turns of phrase like "once upon a time", "they lived happily ever-after", etc. of the children's story; or the "we"-style of certain scholarly works; or the meter, the epithets, etc. of the classical epic.

3.2. My second group has to do with the contents of a text, with what may be called its propositional level. Here, on the one hand, we have to consider characteristics of a work as a whole, on the other, characteristics of parts of it. In the work as a whole one has to take into account the structure of the presentation, the plot, the main themes, and the topic. Some examples would include: (1) the characteristic construction of a detective story, from the discovery of the body, *via* the introduction of more or less hidden clues and of false tracks, and on to the finale, in which the hero presents the solution; (2) the plot patterns of folk tales, be they the ones Propp investigated or others; (3) the manner of writing history in Antiquity: the general narrative sequence, the knitting of the episodes to each other, the insertions of descriptions of places and people, of speeches, etc.; (4) the topic of the romances in Antiquity, *viz.* some sort of love story; and, perhaps, (5) the manner of writing apocalypses: the introduction of a divine revelation in one or another way, the revelation itself, consisting of a series of visions or travels and/or dialogues with a revealer, and a conclusion which often stresses the importance of the revelation.

3.2.1. In sections of the text one has to consider characteristics of a similar kind: the structure of smaller episodes or of other smaller units, motifs, ways of organizing and presenting the material in shorter stories or other literary pieces. Examples of these characteristics include: (1) the repetition with slight variations in the tales, where, say, at a certain stage, three brothers have to fulfil a task, and the first two do not succeed, but the third one does; (2) the motif found in ancient Greek romances, where both the hero and the heroine travel widely after being seperated[14]; and (3) for the apocalypses, the appearance of a heavenly messenger, an *angelus interpres*, who interprets, *e.g.*, a vision.

3.2.2. I suggested above that, in terms of the text as a whole, this group of genre constituents takes into account the structure of the presentation. This was not only meant to cover what one may call the sequence of the elements of a text, like the one in a detective story or in a speech by a rhetor. I want to point out, too, that this "structure" should also be regarded as including the functional relations between the elements.[15] In the example of the ancient romance one should, accordingly, not only notice the motif of travelling, but also how it functions in relationship to the story

---

[14] Cp. Söder 1932; Hägg 1971.
[15] See the discussion in Hempfer 1973, 138 ff., 190.

as a whole and to other elements in it. That is, one has to consider how it is caused by the separation that gets the story rolling, how it connects the episodes, and, above all, how it creates a suspense that is not eliminated until the amorous couple is happily reunited.[16] And, as to the apocalypses, one should *e.g.*, not only observe the appearance of the motif of a heavenly journey but also pay heed to its function within the whole: how it becomes a means to join heaven and earth, so that divine secrets can be brought to human beings; further, how it anchors the authority of the message of the revelation in the divine Being Itself.

3.3. The phenomena dealt with so far exist in a text whether it functions in a communication or not. I now come to some constituents that to a greater or lesser extent bring an addressee into the picture.

3.3.1. First, then, I will examine the characteristics of what could be termed the "illocution" of the text,[17] *i.e.*, what its author wants to say with that which he says. We could also speak of this constituent as the message, or the type of message conveyed by the text. Also in this case one should look both at the smaller units of the work and at the work as a whole. To give an example, let us think of a scholarly paper: a typical message of the passages which refute other scholarly opinions is that things must be the way the author argues. Such refutations form parts of the lecture as a whole, and their messages contribute to the message of the whole. This, in its turn, is of the type that sheds light on or solves one or several scholarly problems. If, instead, somebody at a dinner table uses the literary form of a paper to express his thanks to the hostess for a delightful meal, it might be entertaining, but the "paper" has acquired a non-typical message. In the case of apocalypses, a typical message is one of comfort and exhortation to steadfastness.

In this context of illocution it may often prove useful to distinguish between different semantic functions. This holds true for the "message" both of the text as a whole and of its minor units. As the function of individual clauses may be informative, prescriptive, expressive or performative,[18] so texts and parts of texts can have similar semantic functions. Accordingly, also the fact that a text belongs to a certain genre means that it may have a specific semantic function.

3.3.2. As stated above, also this group of genre constituents concerns the text as a communication. I am here thinking of the usage of a text, which corresponds to a certain audience. The audience has a certain expectation which is colored by things belonging to the constituent groups I have

---

[16] Cp. Hägg 1971, 150f., 173f., 214f., 324ff., etc., and the literature discussed 340f.

[17] The term is, of course, inspired by J. L. Austin. Cp. Urmson 1967, 213.

[18] Here I use the word "performative" in a narrow sense. It may also have a wider meaning: see, *e.g.*, Hempfer 1973, 161ff. – Cp. Hartman 1975/76.

brought forward already. To give an example, let us return to the scholarly paper. It belongs to the cultural convention shared by the lecturer and his audience that the paper has a typical sociolinguistic function.[19] If somebody gives the shape of a lecture to an after dinner speech, the situation is wrong, the audience may be non-typical, and certainly this audience has no expectations for an academic paper. But if enough of the motifs and of the theme points to the real topic of the speech and to its real illocution, it might be a success. A presupposition is, however, that the audience recognizes the unusual shape and understands to appreciate the pleasantry. As to the apocalyptic genre, we do not know of how apocalypses were used in Jewish and Early Christian circles, but, at any rate, there are rather clear indications that the Revelation of John was written to be read at the divine service.

Thus, in general one tends to combine a given genre to a typical sociolinguistic function. But already the assumed example of burlesque[20] in the preceding paragraph, and, above all, the quantity of other material should remind us that we have to beware of assuming a one-to-one relationship between genre and sociolinguistic function.[21]

3.4. The groups of genre constituents I have presented in the paragraphs above are not altogether sharply delimited from each other. For example, one should remember that it is next to impossible to draw a clear-cut borderline between form (both "general" and "specific") and contents. Furthermore, even though one may list some genre constituents in this way, one should not expect to find all the characteristics of a given genre in all instances of it. And, reversely, not all the types of characteristics that *can* constitute genres need necessarily be represented in an individual genre. It is, for example, only for some genres that one has to count on a specific style and phraseology.

We may ask whether some of these constituents are more important than others for demarcating a genre. I have a feeling that, if a text displays a certain set up of stylistic and phraseological features that normally characterize a certain genre, they are relatively decisive indicators.[22] But then they must also go together with other constituents. *I.e.*, the text should have a particular content on the propositional level and represent a specific structure of a particular kind of plot, or a distinct set up of motifs in a

---

[19] Already in ancient rhetoric one was aware of the different functions of rhetoric *genera*: see Lausberg 1960, §61.

[20] I use the term as suggested by Abrams 1971, *ad voc.*

[21] See, *e.g.*, Güttgemanns 1971, 140ff.; Doty 1972, 424; Hempfer 1973, 186ff.; Knierim 1973.

[22] See also Hempfer 1973, 148f. The present writer has suggested some consequences of these observations for the assessment of the gospels in Hartman 1978.

definite hierarchy (§3.2.). Furthermore, it is likely to have a particular kind of sociolinguistic function (§3.3.2.). The kind of illocution for some genres should be next to obligatory (§3.3.1.), but then it ought also to go together with certain features such as themes and motifs in a specific structure (§3.2.) and, as a rule, with a specific use, a sociolinguistic function (§3.3.2.).

4. Recent Contributions to the Discussion of Apocalyptic Genre

Against the background of the foregoing deliberations I now proceed to a brief presentation of a few recent contributions to the discussion of the problem of apocalyptic genre. All of these concentrate on the Jewish and Christian material.

4.1. Thus, Ph. Vielhauer dealt with "the literary characteristics" of apocalypses in his *Geschichte der urchristlichen Literatur*.[23] Under this heading he listed the following "*Stilelemente*": pseudonymity, account of vision, pictorial language (*Bildersprache*), interpretation, systematization (especially through numbering), and furthermore, combinations of smaller forms such as surveys of history in future form, descriptions of the other world, visions of the divine Throne, paraenesis, and prayers. Apparently these phenomena can be referred to my first two groups of constituents (§3.1. and §3.2.). In discussing them Vielhauer also makes a few observations on the literary function and interrelation of some of these elements. He also touches upon certain things that I gathered into my latter groups of genre constituents, *viz.* those concerning illocution and sociolinguistic function (§3.3.1. and §3.3.2.). Thus, the surveys of history are said to aim at creating confidence in the reader who is confronted by the eschatological predictions in the text. The visions of the Throne are meant to clarify the *Unnahbarkeit* of God and prove that the competence of the visionary goes back to Him. Furthermore, the descriptions of future and transcendent secrets are meant to determine the present life of the readers by binding them to God and His will. Although these observations of an experienced *Formgeschichtler* are not presented as the results of detailed literary analyses, it seems to me that they represent some essential insights into how different factors co-operate within a genre.

4.2. In the Supplement to the *Interpreter's Dictionary of the Bible* (1976) Paul D. Hanson has made a contribution to the discussion of apocalyptic genre. Taking as his point of departure the Book of Revelation, he presents

---

[23] Vielhauer 1975, 487 ff. He also dealt with the matter in Vielhauer 1964. There he discussed "*die literarischen Merkmale*" at somewhat greater length but with less specification as compared to the later work.

some typical genre features not only of this book, but also of some Jewish texts. The result is not unlike Vielhauer's, though perhaps with somewhat less attention paid to the literary function of the phenomena. The setting of the genre, says Hanson, was a time of tribulation and persecution, and its principal function was to reveal the future, thereby comforting the oppressed and encouraging them to faithfulness.

4.3. To my knowledge the most thorough-going recent attempts to render further precision to the discussion before us are those brought forward within a workgroup on apocalypse within the SBL Genres Project. I am most obliged to professor J. J. Collins for having provided me with a copy of a paper from his hand which seems to sum up the achievements of this group so far.[24]

4.3.1. In his article, J. J. Collins establishes a master-paradigm by listing recurring features in all the works which are either called apocalypses or regarded as such by modern authors. This paradigm is divided into two main sections, dealing with the framework of the revelation and its contents, respectively. The framework concerns the manner of the revelation, and here Collins lists the medium: is it a visionary or auditory revelation, is it an otherworldly journey or something like a heavenly book? Further, the framework confronts us with the otherworldly mediator, as well as with the human recipient, his pseudonymity, his disposition and reaction.

4.3.2. As to the contents Collins first observes a temporal axis: one finds matters dealing with the beginning of history or prehistory, and, further, reviews of history and revelations of eschatological crises like persecutions and/or other upheavals. Here we also encounter statements on the eschatological judgment and salvation. In gnostic apocalypses, salvation through knowledge is a distinct feature. On the spatial axis Collins refers to revelations concerning otherworldly regions or beings. He further notes that paraenesis through the mediator is relatively rare, being prominent only in a few Christian and gnostic apocalypses. Finally, he lists a couple of concluding elements, in which the recipient is told what to do next, and the action of the text is somehow brought to an end.

4.3.3. Prof. Collins comments on this list reminding us that these elements do not necessarily constitute an entire independent work, and, reversely, that apocalypses may include subsidiary literary forms which are independent of the genre, *e.g.*, prayers. Of course all elements do not appear in all apocalypses, and furthermore not all of them are equally important. But some are constant: thus there is always a narrative

---

[24] Collins 1979a. He applies his analytical method on Jewish texts in the same volume: Collins 1979b.

framework including an otherworldly mediator and a human recipient, and the contents always concern both a future eschatological salvation and present otherworldly realities.

4.3.4. Collins then arrives at a definition of the genre: "'Apocalypse' is a genre of revelatory literature with a narrative framework, in which a revelation is mediated by an otherworldly being to a human recipient, disclosing a transcendent, reality which is both temporal, in so far as it envisages eschatological salvation, and spatial, in so far as it involves another, supernatural world."

4.3.5. If I may compare Collins' exposition with my own grouping of genre constituents above, it appears that the elements that he lists in the master-paradigm all belong to my second group, the one which contained the propositional constituents (§3.2.). This also holds true of the phenomena that are covered by his definition of apocalyptic genre. In dealing with this second group of mine I stressed that one should not only consider plot, themes, and motifs, but also take into account the hierarchic structure and literary interrelations of those elements. It seems that Collins is of a similar opinion; for, in his paper, he finishes a short discussion of the inner coherence of the genre by saying: "an adequate discussion of these matters can only be achieved through the detailed analysis of individual apocalypses and the examination of the precise ways in which the various elements of the paradigm function" (p. 12).[25] I am so convinced that he is right in this statement that I am afraid that his following attempts to establish a typology of the genre risk being a classification with too little respect for the literary functions and interrelations of the elements.[26] (The suggested typology involves a distinction between two main types of apocalypses, those which have an otherworldly journey and those which have not. These two are both divided further into those which have, and which do not have a historical review, respectively.)

4.3.6. Finally, as to my latter groups of constituents, *viz.*, those concerning illocution and sociolinguistic function (§3.3.1. and §3.3.2.), we may

---

[25] I suspect that "function" here covers both the literary function within the text and the function with regard to the readers, including the sociolinguistic one.

[26] Hempfer 1973, 190, states: at genre criticism "ist einem taxonomisch-klassifizierenden Vorgehen, das Texte allein aufgrund des Vorhandenseins oder Fehlens bestimmter Eigenschaften (Elemente) einer bestimmten 'Gattung' zuordnet, ein im eigentlichen Sinne 'strukturierendes' vorzuziehen, das spezifische Relationen zwischen diesen Elementen erstellt, die für den jeweiligen Texttyp bezeichnender sind als die einfache Kumulation isolierter Elemente". (See also 138f.) – In several studies E. Gülich and W. Raible (*e.g.* 1975; 1977; cp. also 1977a) have suggested methods for distinguishing *Teiltexte* within narrative texts and for determining their relationships to each other as well as their function within the text as a whole. In Hellholm 1980 the author analyses the Shepherd of Hermas using their methods. The present writer has tried to apply them to the beginning and ending of the Book of Revelation in Hartman 1980.

note that Collins and the SBL workgroup are aware of the fact that one "must eventually address the history and social function of the genre" (p. 4). However, in discussing the inner coherence of the genre, Collins touches briefly on what I have called illocution and sociolinguistic function. He suggests that the emphasis on transcendence in the texts has to do with a sense of alienation in the milieu of the readers.

5. Communication and Genre

As the work of the SBL group, including that of prof. Collins, seems to be the most advanced so far in the area, I refrain from discussing other contributions of this kind.[27] It seems to me, though, that the time has come to deepen the analysis and to take into account as exactly as possible the hierarchic structure and literary function of the propositional elements,[28] the illocution of the texts, and their sociolinguistic functions.

5.1. One example of how one can work with profit in the direction just mentioned is an article by K. Koch on the first vision of 4 Ezra.[29] He works on form-critical and text-linguistic lines and arrives at results in these areas that seem convincing, based as they are on a thorough analysis of the text as it stands. Taking a firm hold of the text as a text[30] he puts himself into a certain opposition to traditional approaches according to which the text becomes something like a box containing specimens of apocalyptic ideas, of apocalyptic phenomenology.

5.2. Others have also stressed the need for distinguishing between apocalypses and apocalyptic as a religious phenomenon.[31] Thus, Vielhauer and the SBL group also keep apocalyptic genre and apocalypticism apart.[32] This justified distinction can prepare us to be aware of some further aspects which are implied by the genre questions. I will touch upon them briefly.

5.2.1. Thus, apocalypticism as a religious phenomenon can be considered synchronically: one exposes its *Vorstellungswelt* and observes motifs and themes belonging to different times, religions, and cultures.[33] We need not now enter upon a discussion on how far apocalypticism as a religious phenomenon can be assessed as something which refers to common human

---

[27] Brashler 1977. He refers also to the unpublished Parrott 1970; Collins 1977; Perkins 1977 Dexinger 1977, esp. 9 ff.

[28] It is only fair to mention that in Collins 1977 Prof. Collins discusses the literary function of some elements in Rev.

[29] Koch 1978. See also Hellholm 1980.

[30] Cp. also the approach in Breech 1973.   [31] *E.g.*, Ringgren 1957.

[32] Also Stone 1976, 439, and Hanson 1976. Both also distinguish between apocalyptic eschatology in terms of religious ideas and apocalypticism as a sociological phenomenon. As to the latter, see also Raphaël 1977.

[33] See, *e.g.*, Ringgren 1957; Widengren 1969, ch. 16. Also Raphaël 1977.

experiences and ways of thinking and feeling,[34] neither need we try to answer the question as to whether the motifs go back to some kind of religious *universale*, common to all mankind. But it is exactly this question of the relationship between the general and the specific that is relevant, I think, to anyone who reflects on apocalyptic genre.

5.2.2. As I have understood genre, it should be discussed especially under the category of communication. The genre belongs to a cultural set up which author and reader have in common. In the terminology of de Saussure, the genre of apocalypse is part of a *langue*, the linguistic competence of a cultural and linguistic milieu. The individual apocalypse is then a *parole*, a manifestation of this general *langue*. With regard to the groups of genre constituents I have adopted, all of them of course apply both to the *langue* and to the *parole*. Thus, one learns to understand an apocalypse as one learns to understand other phenomena in one's culture, not least the language.[35]

5.2.3. As intimated at the beginning of this paper, this way of looking at things means that I understand apocalyptic genre as being something narrower than, say, narrative as genre. Such a narrower concept of genre then corresponds with a narrower scope in terms of a historically given, cultural context, which contains the conventions that include the genre, its use and understanding.[36]

5.2.4. The way of regarding genre I have intimated in the last paragraphs has some consequences. First, an understanding on the side of the readers that is more or, sometimes, less perfect is to be expected.[37] Second, the literary convention of a genre is fluid, it changes and develops, and admits varied and new usages.[38] Third, although there is normally a certain tendency to connect a given genre to a particular illocution and sociolinguistic function, one should not assume that such a connection is obligatory.[39] Fourth, human beings seem to have a common tendency to ask the questions of why, whence and whither and to give some of the answers to these questions the form of an apocalypse. Thereby one often uses mythical language[40] which contains motifs and themes that appear in quite different times, places and cultures. Nevertheless, on the abstraction level I have assumed, the *langue* comprising an apocalyptic literary genre should be regarded as limited to specific contexts that are relatively coherent culturally. That is, one can bring the Nordic Voluspa into the discussion of the

---

[34] Cp. Sickenberger 1950, 505.

[35] Hempfer here brings in aspects from Piaget (1973, 122f. *et passim*).

[36] See my discussion above §2.3.

[37] *E.g.*, Hempfer 1973, 127. Cp. Hartman 1975/76. As my reader may notice, I do not reckon with "ideal readers" in Chomsky's manner.

[38] See Hempfer 1973, 98f., 192–220; Fowler 1970/71.

[39] Cp. above §3.3.2.   [40] Cp. Delcor 1977.

religious phenomenon of apocalypticism, but not, at least not directly, into the deliberations concerning the literary genre of apocalypse in Jewish, Christian and gnostic circles of late Antiquity. Fifth, one must be aware of the possibility that apocalyptic, or perhaps eschatological motifs and themes, are dealt with in other literary genres. This is, in fact, true, when such motifs appear, *e.g.*, in a halachic discussion in the Mishnah (*m. Soṭa* ix), or, I have been told, in Egypt, where apocalypses are rare, if at all existant, but where apocalyptic (in the sense of eschatology) is well represented.[41]

6. Desiderations for Future Investigations

Finally, I venture to finish this survey with some desiderations for the future investigation of the literary genre of apocalypse.

6.1. Thus, I think that we should take serious account of what is going on in the areas of literary criticism and linguistics. Accordingly, we should advance to detailed studies of individual texts. Thereby we need not necessarily work with exactly the groupings of genre constituents I have presented above, but, nevertheless, continue from mainly listing themes and motifs on to analyses of the hierarchic structure of the elements, unfolding in this way their functions on the propositional level. This should be distinguished from the quest for the illocutionary and sociolinguistic functions of the parts and of the whole, even though, of course, such investigations depend heavily on the results of the former ones. Furthermore, one should pay attention to the communication aspects, *i.e.*, consciously connect the literary analysis with the fact that the genre problem is part of the larger one concerning understanding and interpretation of human expressions in social interplay.

6.2. In this way our work may bring us into a deeper understanding of what the authors of apocalypses wanted to say to which kind of readers in what kind of situation. But in the long run it may also turn out to be even more interesting, as we may recognize that their problems are reminiscent of ours.

---

[41] Cp. now the contributions to this volume by J. Assmann, J. Bergman and J. Gwyn Griffiths.

Bibliography

Abrams, M. H. 1971: *A Glossary of Literary Terms*, 3rd ed. New York etc. 1971.

Brashler, J. 1977: *The Coptic Apocalypse of Peter*. A Genre Analysis and Interpretation (PhD diss., Claremont, Calif. 1977).

Breech, E. 1973: "Theses Fragments I have Shored Against my Ruins: The Form and Function of 4 Ezra", in: *JBL* 92 (1973) 267–274.

Bullitt, J. M. 1953: *Jonathan Swift and the Anatomy of Satire*. A Study of Satiric Technique, Cambridge, Mass., 1953.

Collins, J. J. 1977: "Pseudonymity, Historical Reviews and the Genre of the Revelation of John", in: *CBQ* 39 (1977) 329–343.

– (ed.) 1979: *Apocalypse: The Morphology of a Genre (Semeia* 14), Missoula, Mont. 1979.

– 1979a: "Introduction: Towards the Morphology of a Genre", in: Collins (ed.) 1979, 1–20. (Previously published in the SBL Seminar Papers 1977.)

– 1979b: "The Jewish Apocalypses", in: Collins (ed.) 1979, 21–59.

Conzelmann, H. 1956: "Formen und Gattungen II. NT", in: *EKL* 1 (1956) 1310–1315.

Cross, F. M. Jr./Lemke, W. E./Miller, P. D. Jr. (eds.) 1976: *Magnalia Dei. The Mighty Acts of God,* Garden City, N.Y. 1976.

Delcor, M. 1977: "Mythologie et apocalyptique", in: Association catholique française pour l'étude de la Bible: *Apocalypses et théologie de l'espérance* (LeDiv 95), Paris 1977, 143–177.

Dexinger, F. 1977: *Henochs Zehnwochenapokalypse und offene Probleme der Apokalyptikforschung* (StPB 29), Leiden 1977.

van Dijk, T. A./Petöfi, J. S. (eds.) 1977: *Grammars and Descriptions* (Studies in Text Theory and Text Analysis), (RTT 1), Berlin/New York 1977.

Doty, W. G. 1972: "The Concept of Genre in Literary Analysis", in: McGaughy (ed.) 1972, 413–448.

Fowler, A. 1970/71: "The Life and Death of Literary Forms", in: *NLH* 2 (1970/71) 199–216.

Gülich, E./Raible, W. 1975: "Textsorten-Probleme", in: Moser (ed.) 1975, 144–197.

– – 1977: "Überlegungen zu einer makrostrukturellen Textanalyse: J. Thurber, The Lover and His Lass", in: van Dijk/Petöfi (eds.) 1977, 132–175.

– – 1977a: *Linguistische Textmodelle*. Grundlagen und Möglichkeiten (UTB 130), Munich 1977.

Güttgemanns, E. 1971: *Offene Fragen zur Formgeschichte des Evangeliums* (BEvTh 14), 2nd ed., Munich 1971.

Hägg, T. 1971: *Narrative Technique in Ancient Greek Romances*. Studies of Chariton, Xenophon Ephesius, and Achilles Tatius (Skrifter utgivna av Svenska institutet i Athen, 8°, VIII), Stockholm 1971.

Hanson, P. D. 1976: "Apocalypse, Genre", and "Apocalypticism", in: *IDBSup* (1976) 27–34.

Hartman, L. 1975/76: "The Function of Some So-Called Apocalyptic Time-Tables", in: *NTS* 20 (1975/76) 1–14.

– 1978: "Till frågan om evangeliernas litterära genre", in: *AnASU* 21 (1978) 5–22.

– 1980: "Form and Message. A Preliminary Discussion of 'Partial Texts' in Rev 1–3 and 22:6ff.", in: Lambrecht (ed.) 1980, 129–149.

Hellholm, D. 1980: *Das Visionenbuch des Hermas als Apokalypse*. Formgeschichtliche und texttheoretische Studien zu einer literarischen Gattung. I. Methodologische Vorüberlegungen und makrostrukturelle Textanalyse (CB.NT 13:1), Lund 1980.

Hempfer, K. W. 1973: *Gattungstheorie*. Information und Synthese (UTB 133), Munich 1973.

Hennecke, E./Schneemelcher, W. (eds.) 1964: *Neutestamentliche Apokryphen* in deutscher Übersetzung, 3rd. ed., II, Tübingen 1964.

Jeffares, A. N. (ed.) 1968: *Swift*. Modern Judgements, London 1968.

Knierim, R. 1973: "Old Testament Form Criticism Reconsidered", in: *Interpretation* 27 (1973) 435–467.

Koch, K. 1978: "Esras erste Vision. Weltzeiten und Weg des Höchsten", in: *BZ* 22 (1978) 46–75.

Lambrecht, J. (ed.) 1980: *L'Apocalypse johannique et l'Apocalyptique dans le Nouveau Testament* (BEThL 53), Gembloux-Louvain 1980.

Lausberg, H. 1960: *Handbuch der literarischen Rhetorik*. Eine Grundlegung der Literaturwissenschaft I–II, Munich 1960.

Leavis, F. R. 1968: "The Irony of Swift", in: Jeffares (ed.) 1968, 121–134.

McGaughy, L. C. (ed.) 1972: *SBL ... Book of Seminar Papers ... 1972*, Missoula, Mont. 1972.

McHugh, R./Edwards, Ph. (eds.) 1967: *Jonathan Swift 1667–1967*, Dublin 1967.

Moser, H. (ed.) 1975: *Linguistische Probleme der Textanalyse* (Jahrbuch des Instituts für deutsche Sprache 1973. Sprache der Gegenwart. Schriften des Instituts für deutsche Sprache in Mannheim 35), Düsseldorf 1975.

Parrott, D. 1970: *A Missionary Wisdom Gattung*: Identification, Sitz im Leben, History and Connection with the New Testament (PhD diss., Berkeley, Calif. 1970).

Perkins, Ph. 1977: "Apocalypse of Adam: The Genre and Function of a Gnostic Apocalypse", in: *CBQ* 39 (1977) 382–395.

Philonenko, M./Simon, M. (eds.) 1977: *L'Apocalyptique* (EHiRel 3), Paris 1977.

Price, M. 1953: *Swift's Rhetorical Art*. A Study in Structure and Meaning, New Haven, Conn. 1953.

Quintana, R. 1967: "Gulliver's Travels: The Satiric Intent and Execution", in: McHugh et al. (eds.) 1967, 78–93.

– 1975: "Swift, Jonathan", in: *Encyclopaedia Britannica Macropaedia* 17 (1975) 856–859.

von Rad, G. 1975: *Theologie des Alten Testaments* II, 6th ed. Munich 1975.

Raphaël, F. 1977: "Esquisse d'une typologie de l'apocalypse", in: Philonenko/Simon (eds.) 1977, 11–38.

Rendtorff, R. 1956: "Formen und Gattungen I. AT", in: *EKL* 1 (1956) 1303–1310.

Ringgren, H. 1957: "Apokalyptik", in: *RGG*³ 1 (1957) 463–466.

Sickenberger, J. 1950: "Apokalyptik", in: *RAC* 1 (1950) 504–510.

Söder, R. 1932: *Die apokryphen Apostelgeschichten und die romanhafte Literatur der Antike*, Stuttgart 1932.

Stone, M. E. 1976: "Lists of Revealed Things in the Apocalyptic Literature", in: Cross et alii (eds.) 1976, 414–452.

Todorov, T. 1974: "Literary Genres", in: *CTL* 12 (1974) 957–962.

Urmson, J. O. 1967: "Austin, J. L.", in: *EncPh* 1 (1967) 211–215.

Vielhauer, Ph. 1964: "Apokalypsen und Verwandtes. Einleitung", in: Hennecke/Schneemelcher (eds.) 1964, 407–427.

– 1975: *Geschichte der urchristlichen Literatur*. Einleitung in das Neue Testament, die Apokryphen und die Apostolischen Väter, Berlin/New York 1975.

Weinrich, H. 1971: *Literatur für Leser*. Essays und Aufsätze zur Literaturwissenschaft, Stuttgart etc. 1971.

Weisstein, U. 1968: *Einführung in die vergleichende Literaturwissenschaft*, Stuttgart etc. 1968.

Widengren, G. 1969: *Religionsphänomenologie*, Berlin 1969.

Königsdogma und Heilserwartung. Politische und kultische Chaosbeschreibungen in ägyptischen Texten

Jan Assmann

0. Geschichte als Fest – die Negation der Eschatologie

Wenn man unter Apokalyptik die Enthüllung des Fortgangs der Weltgeschichte versteht auf ein nicht mehr fernes Ende hin, kann es dann Apokalyptik geben ohne Eschatologie? Mit dieser Frage ist das Kernproblem der altägyptischen "Apokalyptik" gekennzeichnet. Denn eine Welt, die "Geschichte als Fest" (Hornung 1966) versteht, in der jeder König schon mit seiner Thronbesteigung alle Chaosmächte überwunden und das Land in den Urzustand des Heils zurückgeführt hat, in der sogar jeder Sonnenaufgang den Feind niederwirft und die Schöpfung erneuert, lebt fortwährend im Heilszustand einer realisierten Eschatologie[1]. Jeder König ist kraft Amtes fast ein Messias: bis auf den Umstand, daß er nie Gegenstand der Erwartung ist[2]. Unheil gibt es in dieser Welt nur im Sinne einer dogmatischen Fiktion und kommt nur im Modus der Behobenheit, des Überwundenseins zur Sprache, um der Rolle des Königs als Heilbringer zum Objekt zu dienen. Schlechte Könige, Könige, die ihre Macht mißbrauchen, den Willen der Götter mißachten und das Volk unterdrücken, kann es in dieser Welt nicht geben, denn der König ist selbst Gott auf Erden und seine dogmatische Rolle ist so festgelegt, daß auch persönliche Schwä-

---

[1] Hornung 1966, vgl. auch Otto 1966b. Wenn hier für Ägypten die Existenz einer "Eschatologie" bestritten wird, dann ist damit eine politische Eschatologie gemeint, die sich im Geschichtsbild einer Kultur ausdrückt. Eine Individualeschatologie hat es in Ägypten natürlich gegeben, und zwar in einer ungewöhnlich elaborierten und differenzierten Form. Ich würde aber vorschlagen, mit Bezug auf diese so vollkommen anders gearteten Vorstellungen vom Leben nach dem Tode den Terminus Eschatologie zu vermeiden und dafür von "Jenseitsvorstellungen" zu reden. Enger mit dem Geschichtsbild verbunden ist die kosmische Ebene. Hier läßt sich die Existenz eschatologischer Spekulationen nicht bestreiten, vgl. unten §1.2. Aber die Ansätze zu einer "Kosmotelie" – auch hier empfiehlt es sich, Weltbild und Geschichtsbild auseinanderzuhalten und für die Vorstellungen vom Weltende einen anderen Terminus zu verwenden – finden sich nur im Kontext der Osirisreligion, während die dominierende Sonnenreligion auf der kosmischen Ebene das Gegenstück zur "realisierten Eschatologie" der Königsideologie darstellt: indem ihr jeder Sonnenaufgang als neue Weltschöpfung und Erneuerung der Zeit gilt, ist hier der Begriff einer Kosmotelie im Sinne gerichteter, auf ein Ende hin ablaufender Welt-Zeit, ebenso negiert wie auf der politischen Ebene.

[2] Zandee 1971, der allerdings diese notwendige Einschränkung übersieht.

che oder gar Bosheit nichts anrichten kann; sie funktioniert sogar noch unter spätrömischen Kaisern, die wahrscheinlich wenig gewußt haben von den rituellen Triumphen, die sie im fernen Philae oder Esna über die Chaosmächte feierten[3]. Natürlich ist diese Welt, in der jede Heilserwartung immer schon erfüllt, jede Verheißung immer schon realisiert ist, die Welt der offiziellen Königsinschriften und formuliert ein Begriffssystem von dogmatischen Fiktionen, das weit entfernt sein kann von der Art, wie das Volk seine Geschichte erlitten und verarbeitet hat. Das Königsbild der profanen Literatur ist denn auch von dem der Königsinschriften in vielen Zügen verschieden[4]. Aber selbst hier werden Abweichungen vom Dogma mit auffallender Zurückhaltung behandelt[5].

Bei dieser Sicht der Dinge liegt der Schluß nahe, daß auch die umfangreichen Chaosbeschreibungen, die uns die Literatur des "Mittleren Reichs" (ca. 2000–1700 v. Chr.), und die kürzeren Unheilsschilderungen, die uns gewisse Königsinschriften des Neuen Reichs" (ca. 1550–1100 v. Chr.) überliefert haben, nichts anderes als besonders ausführliche Formulierungen der dogmatischen Fiktion vom vertriebenen Unheil sind, rituelle Beschwörungen einer glücklich gebannten und ausgeschlossenen Gegenwelt, apokalyptische Angstträume eines übersteigerten Ordnungsdenkens ohne jeden Bezug auf reale Ereignisse und genuine Unheilserfahrung[6]. Diese schon von Luria (1929) vorgetragene Deutung wird neuerdings von M. Lichtheim (1973) und F. Junge (1977) vertreten[7]. Wir wollen uns die Texte selbst ein wenig näher ansehen.

---

[3] Wie zurückhaltend sich Inschriften ausdrücken, wenn die Bezugnahme auf "schlechte Könige" unvermeidbar erscheint, zeigt die Restaurationsstele des Tutanchamun, die zwar die Mißstände der Amarnazeit in Form einer Chaosbeschreibung schildert, die verantwortlichen Könige aber nicht mit Namen nennt: "'sie' haben die Schöpfung zerstört" (vgl. §3.1. mit n. 95).

[4] Posener 1960.

[5] So erwähnt etwa eine aus dem 17. Jh. v. Chr. (Pap. Westcar) überlieferte Legende, die erzählt, wie der Sonnengott selbst in die Thronfolge eingriff und die drei ersten Könige der 5. Dynastie zeugte, damit diese den Göttern Tempel bauen und Opfer darbringen sollten, mit keinem Wort, daß die Könige der vorangehenden Dynastie solches offenbar nicht getan haben. Die Gottlosigkeit der Pyramidenerbauer steht nur zwischen den Zeilen, als logische Präsupposition des göttlichen Eingriffs. Ebenso zwischen den Zeilen stehen die herodesartigen Absichten des Cheops in bezug auf diese Sonnenprinzen. Erst der Grieche Herodot scheut sich nicht, derartige Cheops-Legenden in aller Ausführlichkeit wiederzugeben (Posener 1956, 10–13).

[6] Nur wenn man, wie z. B. Hornung 1966, diese Chaosbeschreibungen auf eine Stufe stellt mit emphatischen Heilsbekundungen, wie sie sich gelegentlich in Inschriften finden (Urk VII 27; Israelstele s. u., §3.4; Taharqa-Inschrift Macadam 1949, Text 24,4), kann man sie problemlos im Geschichtsbild der "realisierten Eschatologie" unterbringen. Mir scheinen hier aber doch zwei verschiedene Topoi und entsprechende gedankliche Zusammenhänge vorzuliegen, die man sorgfältig auseinanderhalten sollte.

[7] Luria 1929; Lichtheim 1973, 149 f.; Junge 1977; vgl. von anderer Seite her auch Schenkel 1975, 29–31.

1. Die Klagen des "Mittleren Reichs"

1.1. Die "Admonitions": das Gott zum Vorwurf gemachte Böse

Der längste und komplexeste Text dieser Gruppe, die sog. Admonitions oder Mahnworte des *Jpw-wr*, ist nur auf einem Papyrus der 19. Dynastie (um 1250 v. Chr.) überliefert; die Vorlage ist aber mindestens 400 Jahre älter und stellt die Endredaktion einer noch weitere 400 Jahre zurückreichenden Überlieferung dar[8]. Der Text ist zweigeteilt: auf die Chaosbeschreibung der Klagen, die uns hier besonders zu beschäftigen hat, folgt das Gespräch mit dem Schöpfergott, das leider durch große Lücken weitgehend unklar bleibt[9]. Die Klagen wiederum sind durch das Prinzip gleicher Spruchanfänge in Serien eingeteilt: die *jw-ms*-("es-ist-doch-so:")-Serie mit ca. 60 erhaltenen Sprüchen und die *mtn*-("seht:")-Serie mit ca. 50 Sprüchen bilden die bei weitem umfangreichsten Korpora, dann folgen zwei kürzere Abschnitte, deren Sprüche mit "zerstört ist..." und "zerstört die Feinde der erlauchten Residenz!" beginnen. In den beiden ersten großen Serien dominieren Aussagen des Typs "die Letzten sind die Ersten, die Ersten sind die Letzten geworden":

> Arme sind zu Reichen geworden,
> wer sich keine Sandalen leisten konnte, häuft jetzt Schätze auf.
> Die Edlen klagen, die Armen jubeln,
> jede Stadt sagt: 'Laßt uns die Herren aus unserer Mitte vertreiben!'
>
> Die Roben trugen, gehen in Lumpen,
> die nicht einmal für sich selbst nähten, tragen feines Leinen.
> Köche haben jetzt Butler,
> Boten senden jetzt andere aus[10].

In der Art einer Überschrift faßt der längste dieser Abschnitte diese Thematik zusammen: "Seht die Verwandlungen der Menschen"[11]. Es geht um die verkehrte Welt im Bereich der Gesellschaft, in der Herren und Sklaven die Plätze getauscht und die Güter ihre Besitzer gewechselt haben; und das in einer hochstilisierten Redeform, die gewiß nicht wie der authentische Augenzeugenbericht historischer Ereignisse anmutet. Luria

---

[8] Edition: Gardiner 1909; beste Übersetzung Lichtheim 1973, 149–163. Zur Textgeschichte s. bes. Fecht 1972, dessen Auffassung wir uns anschließen, gegen van Seters 1964.

[9] Nur diesem 2. Teil gilt die umfangreiche Monographie von Fecht 1972; für die "Klagen" ist eine entsprechende Untersuchung dringend erwünscht. Einstweilen bietet die Arbeit von Herrmann 1957, 8–32 noch immer die eingehendste Analyse.

[10] Adm 2,4−5; 7−8; 7,11−12; 8,2−3. Hier und im folgenden verwende ich aus Raumgründen diese Form des freien Zitats, das charakteristische Sätze aus längeren Passagen zusammenstellt, um einen Eindruck von Thema und Tenor zu vermitteln. Der Leser ist hier wie in den anderen Fällen auf die glänzenden Übersetzungen M. Lichtheims verwiesen, um sich einen Überblick über den Zusammenhang zu verschaffen.

[11] Adm 7,9 mit Lichtheim 1973, 156 n. 18.

hat an einer Fülle ethnologischen Vergleichsmaterials von z. T. verblüffender Ähnlichkeit zeigen können, daß derartige Redeformen oft in rituellen, quasi karnevalistischen Begehungen der verkehrten Welt verankert sind, wo für die Zeit des Festes die gewohnten Ordnungen auf den Kopf gestellt und die Normen des Alltagslebens außer Kraft gesetzt sind. Andere Texte wie z. B. das Lied der Annamiter anläßlich der französischen Eroberung Indochinas zeigen, wie aus demselben ausgeprägten Ordnungsdenken heraus eine Störung gleich als totale Verkehrung der Ordnung gesehen wird, die das Obere zuunterst, das Unterste zuoberst kehrt:

> Le ciel est bas, la terre est haute...
> Ceux qui n'avaient pas de culotte ont aujourd'hui des souliers...
> les filles publiques sont devenues des grandes dames...
> les vauriens sont tout puissants... usw.[12].

Genau dieselbe Entsprechung oder besser Entfernung zwischen historischer Erfahrung und stilisierter Ausdrucksform möchte man auch in den entsprechenden Sprüchen der Admonitions vermuten. Was aber die Stilform dieser Sprüche angeht, so ist sie in Ägypten zwar nicht in Liedern zu festlichen Chaosinszenierungen des "karnevalistischen" Typs nachzuweisen[13], wohl aber, wie P. Seibert gezeigt hat, in der Totenklage[14]:

> Der (sonst) zu trinken liebte, ist (jetzt) im Land, das ohne Wasser ist.
> Der sich (sonst) in reiche Stoffe zu kleiden liebte,
> schläft (jetzt) im abgelegten Gewand von gestern.

Auch der Tod erscheint in diesen Klagen als eine Verkehrung der gewohnten Ordnung, als eine "Verwandlung der Menschen". In den Admonitions wird die Totenklage über ganz Ägypten angestimmt. Nicht auf die Einzelaussagen kommt es an, sondern auf die Gesamtstimmung der "Todesbefallenheit" (Seibert), die sie evozieren. "Leben ist den Lebenden

---

[12] Luria 1929, 415. Luria wendet sich übrigens nur gegen die Deutung dieser Topik als historisch getreue Schilderung einer sozialen Revolution, nicht gegen jeden Wirklichkeitsbezug. Das Lied der Annamiter bezieht sich auf die französische Eroberung Indochinas. Er leugnet nicht, daß hinter derartigen Liedern und hinter den Admonitions geschichtliche Ereignisse stehen können. "Die Übertreibung aber und die Zurückführung all dieser Ereignisse auf ein und dieselbe Schablone – "Das Untere oben, das Obere unten" – ist eine literarische Erscheinung, eine Erscheinung des Stils." Darin ist ihm unbedingt recht zu geben: nur daß das Problem für den Literaturwissenschaftler damit nicht erledigt ist, sondern überhaupt erst beginnt.
[13] Wie etwa in Mesopotamien, s. Luria 1929, 420. Damit soll nicht bestritten werden, daß es derartige Feste möglicherweise auch in Ägypten gegeben hat; nur hat sich bisher nichts nachweisen lassen, auch nicht das "inszenierte Chaos" nach dem Tod eines Königs in Form einer befristeten Anarchie, mit dem Koenen 1957, 36 unter Hinweis auf Meuli 1943, 51 n. 8 rechnet. Die Apokalyptikforschung wird sich aber mit den von Luria aufgezeigten Zusammenhängen beschäftigen müssen: als ein möglicher Sitz im Leben "protoapokalyptischer" Formen ist der von ihm herausgearbeitete Begriff des Festes als innerkulturell inszeniertes Chaos von größter Bedeutung.
[14] Seibert 1967, 20 ff.; Junge 1977, 278 f.; Lüddeckens 1943, Nr. 64 u. 65a.

genommen" sagt ein späterer Text[15], "man lebt in der Nekropole" diagnostiziert Neferti[16].

So löst sich auch der eklatante Widerspruch auf, der zwischen diesen Sprüchen von der verkehrten Welt und jenen anderen zu bestehen scheint, die von einer *allgemeinen* Notlage handeln, wo dem Sturz der Reichen kein Aufstieg der Armen korrespondiert, sondern alles am Boden liegt[17]:

> Groß und klein sagt: 'ach wären wir tot',
> Kinder: 'Ach wären wir nie geboren'. (4,2–3)
> Alles Getier weint mit seinem Herzen,
> das Herdenvieh betrauert den Zustand des Landes. (5,5)
>
> Korn fehlt überall, man hat weder Kleider noch Salben,
> jedermann sagt: 'Es gibt nichts';
> die Magazine sind leer, die Wächter erschlagen. (6,3–4)
>
> Die Herzen sind gewalttätig, Pest herrscht im Land,
> Blut ist überall, kein Mangel an Tod. (2,5–6)
> Der Fluß ist voll Blut, man kann nicht von ihm trinken. (2,10)
> Die Toten werden im Fluß begraben,
> der Fluß ist ein Grab, das Grab ein Fluß. (2,6–7)

Aus diesem Widerspruch, daß einmal beklagt wird, daß die Reichen arm und die Armen reich geworden sind, das andere Mal und im selben Atemzug aber, daß alle gleichermaßen Not leiden und niemand mehr etwas zu essen hat, hat Luria auf die Fiktivität der ganzen Darstellung schließen wollen[18]. Gewiß: wörtlich – als einfache Widerspiegelungen historischer Tatbestände – darf man diese Schilderungen nicht nehmen. Wir haben es mit den Stilformen der Klage zu tun, in deren Topoi und Formulierungsmustern die "Todesbefallenheit" der ägyptischen Welt dargestellt wird, und mit der "Chaosbeschreibung" als einer literarischen Form[19]. Mit der "Literarizität" dieser Chaosbeschreibung ist jedoch keineswegs jeder Wirklichkeitsbezug auszuschließen. Fiktion – gewiß, aber nicht als Verkehrung, sondern als Modell der (ideologisch gefilterten) Realität. Es gibt keine "müßigen" Fiktionen. Auch wenn sie nicht Geschichtsschreibung sind, sind sie doch geschichtlich: sie entspringen einer historischen Situation und haben einen Ort und eine Funktion in der Gesellschaft, die sie überliefert.

---

[15] S. u., §4.1.   [16] Helck 1970, 46 §XII.d.

[17] Die eingeklammerten Zahlen geben die genauen Nachweise im pap. Leiden J 344. Zu dem Motiv "der Fluß ist voll Blut, man kann nicht von ihm trinken" hat bereits Luria 1929, 414 auf die Parallelen in der Elias-Apokalypse, der Asclepius-Apokalypse (Lactanz div. inst. VII.16,6) und im AT (Ex 7,21) hingewiesen.

[18] Bes. 417 f.: "es lassen sich demnach ganz sicher zwei selbständige, einander ausschließende Schilderungen sondern".

[19] So auch Junge 1977, bes. 178–180, vgl. auch Junge 1973/74, 271 f. Das muß vor allem gegenüber Barta 1974/75 betont werden, der diese Texte immer noch als einen "Spiegel" historischer Zustände versteht.

Dazwischen gibt es nun zwei in sich geschlossene Abschnitte, die nicht so sehr allgemeine Mißstände, sondern vielmehr einzelne Vorkommnisse beschreiben oder vielmehr anprangern in dem Sinne "Was nie hätte geschehen dürfen, ist passiert"[20]. Der erste handelt davon, daß Ämter geplündert, Gesetze und Urkunden zerstört, Steuer- und Besitzstandslisten vernichtet und geheime Zaubersprüche profaniert wurden, kurz – mit F. Junges treffender Formulierung: Die Mauern um das Wissen sind niedergerissen[21]. Der zweite behandelt Übergriffe gegen das Königtum: der tote König ist von Räubern aus dem Grab gerissen, die Pyramide ist leer, das Land des Königtums beraubt (oder: arm gemacht) durch wenige Unwissende, die Krone des Sonnengottes ist gestohlen, die Schlange aus ihrer Höhle genommen[22]. Ich möchte darin eine Art "historischen Abschnitt" im Ganzen der Klage erblicken. Wir werden noch sehen, daß auch die anderen auf geschichtliche Situationen Bezug nehmenden Chaosbeschreibungen konkrete historische Details, an deren Authentizität zu zweifeln kein Anlaß besteht, einbetten in die Topik allgemeinen Unheils, weil es in einer wohlgeordneten Welt, in der alles miteinander zusammenhängt und in harmonischem Gleichgewicht steht, keine isolierbaren Störungen gibt und jeder Eingriff in die Lebenszentren dieser Welt wie etwa Götterkult und Königtum das allgemeine Chaos heraufführt.

Gerade im Hinblick auf die anderen Chaosbeschreibungen aber fällt eines auf: das Unheil wird hier nicht ins Kosmische ausgeweitet. Es ist keine Rede davon, daß die Sonne sich verdunkelt, der Fluß austrocknet – im Gegenteil heißt es vielmehr: "Hapi fließt über, aber man pflügt nicht für ihn"[23] –, daß die Winde verkehrt wehen und die Erde unfruchtbar wird. Die Katastrophe wird strikt eingegrenzt auf den Bereich der vom Menschen zu verantwortenden Mißstände. Im Zentrum stehen Dinge wie Bosheit, Gewalt, Respektlosigkeit, Habgier, Verbrechen wie Raub, Wegelagerei, Mord und Totschlag selbst unter engsten Familienangehörigen, Mißachtung aller Bindungen des Rechts und Gemeinsinns, Angst und Terror – "Das Gesicht ist bleich, der Schütze bereit; man nimmt sich den Schild zum Pflügen mit"[24] –. Die Einschränkung des Unheils auf das Böse im Menschen ergibt sich aus dem besonderen Darstellungsinteresse dieser Schrift und wird erst verständlich, wenn man den zweiten Teil, den

---

[20] So formuliert Neferti (Helck 1970, 32 nach oCairo 25224): *tmt ḫpr ḫprtj*.

[21] Vgl. Junge 1977, 283. Es handelt sich um Adm 6,5–12.

[22] Adm 7,1–8. In diesem sich durch seine politische Thematik deutlich aus dem Kontext heraushebenden Abschnitt möchte Fecht 1972, 172–186 den mehr oder weniger wörtlichen Nachklang der als "Prophezeiung der Residenz" (Merikare E 71 vgl. E 108–110) bekannten "Lehre" bzw. Rechtfertigungsschrift Achthoes' I., des Gründers der Herakleopolitendynastie, erblicken.

[23] Adm 2,3.

[24] Adm 2,1; vgl. Neferti 39–41; Töpferorakel pOxy. 2332, 21–22, pRainer 9–10.

"Vorwurf an Gott" hinzunimmt. Alles was die Klagen in ihren schier endlosen Spruchreihen auffahren, dient dazu, das menschliche Böse in seinen zahllosen Manifestationen auszubreiten, um es dem Schöpfergott zum Vorwurf zu machen. Warum läßt er das Böse zu? Er hat kein Organ dafür, er kann es gar nicht wahrnehmen, sich nicht dagegen erzürnen; er scheint über gerecht und ungerecht, behandelt alle gleich und läßt den Dingen ihren Lauf, der notwendig zur Unterdrückung der Schwächeren durch die Stärkeren führen muß. Hätte er das Böse erkannt, er hätte seine Schöpfung sofort widerrufen anstatt sie qualvoller Selbstzerfleischung preiszugeben[25]. Leider bleibt uns die Antwort des Schöpfergottes und der Fortgang des Gesprächs verborgen[26]. Lediglich zwei Gedichte, die den Vorwurf an Gott einrahmen, lassen noch erkennen, wo der Sprecher das Heil sieht: nicht in der Zukunft, sondern in der Vergangenheit:

> Erinnert euch des Räucherns mit Weihrauch,
> der Trankspende mit dem Krug zur Dämmerung!
> Erinnert euch der Ro-, Terep- und Set-Gänse
> und der Opferdarbringung für die Götter!
> Erinnert euch des Aufrichtens der Fahnenmasten,
> der Beschriftung von Opferstelen,
> wenn der Priester die Kapellen säubert und den Tempel reinigt mit Milch[27]!
> ...
>
> Es ist aber doch schön, wenn die Schiffe stromauf segeln,
> (...) wenn das Netz eingezogen wird und Vögel aufgebunden werden,
> (...) wenn die Wege zum Gehen da sind, ... wenn die Hände der Menschen Pyramiden bauen, wenn Teiche gegraben und Gärten angelegt werden für die Götter, ... wenn man in feines Leinen gekleidet ist, ... wenn Betten gerichtet und die Kopfstützen der Fürsten wohlverwahrt sind[28].

Zugleich wird deutlich, daß es nicht die Welt schlechthin ist, deren Untergang hier beklagt wird, sondern die ägyptische Kultur des Alten Reichs. Auch das wird durch alle ägyptischen Chaosbeschreibungen bis hin zur Asklepius-Apokalypse immer wieder deutlich werden: daß die Welt, deren Todesbefallenheit gezeigt wird, den Begriff Ägyptens von seiner Kultur umschreibt. Das Chaos, das diese Welt ständig von innen und außen bedroht, entspricht der Auffassung eines Hobbes vom Naturzustand: *homo homini lupus.*

---

[25] Fecht 1972, 54–119.

[26] Was die These von Otto und Fecht angeht, in einem Abschnitt des Sargtexts Spruch 1130 (s. dazu n. 30) die in den Adm selbst nicht erhaltene Antwort des Schöpfergottes zu sehen, möchte ich mich der Kritik von Junge 1973/74, 271 anschließen. In der Tat scheint mir in diesem Text aus der Sicht des Schöpfers gerade das assertiert, was ihm die Adm zum Vorwurf machen: er hat die Menschen alle gleich erschaffen und fühlt sich für das von ihnen gegen seinen Willen angerichtete Unrecht nicht verantwortlich.

[27] Adm 10,13–11,4.   [28] Adm 13,9–14,2.

1.2. Exkurs: die "Kosmotelie" von Totenbuch Kap. 175 und ihr Vorläufer

In äußerster Prägnanz wird dieser Begriff der Welt als kultureller Schöpfung in einem den Admonitions ungefähr zeitgenössischen Text formuliert, worin der Schöpfergott selbst das Weltende voraussagt:

Die Hügel werden zu Städten werden,
die Städte zu Hügeln.
Ein Haus wird das andere auslöschen[29].

Hier ist nicht von Feuer und Wasser, sondern von Ruinenhügeln, Tells die Rede, von dem, was übrig bleibt, wenn eine Kultur untergegangen ist. Außerdem illustriert dieser Text noch einmal die Stilform der Umkehrung. Hügel und Städte tauschen ihre Rollen wie Grab und Strom, Fluß und Ufer, Herren und Diener. Die Sätze, die vielleicht die einzige Spur einer Eschatologie in ägyptischen Texten darstellen, sind hier in den Zusammenhang einer Rede geraten, in der der Schöpfergott seine Schöpfung rechtfertigt (CT 1130); man hat diesen Text seit langem mit dem Vorwurf der Admonitions zusammengebracht und in ihm so etwas wie eine Antwort gesehen[30]. Im Zusammenhang meines Themas muß ich darauf verzichten, näher auf ihn einzugehen und kann dies um so eher, als das uns interessierende eschatologische Fragment hier sicher nicht an seinem ursprünglichen Platz ist. Es geht um den Gott Osiris und die "Millionen Jahre", die der Schöpfer zwischen sich und dem Totengott eingerichtet hat[31]. Mit der Präposition "zwischen" ist die Idee der Trennung gemeint zwischen Himmel und Unterwelt[32] und mit den Millionen Jahren die Frist, die dieser so eingeteilten, differenzierten und geordneten Welt gegeben ist[33]. "Danach" wird diese Trennung zwischen Himmels- und Totengott wieder aufgehoben und die Welt in die Ureinheit zurückgenommen werden: "Dann aber werde ich mit ihm zusammenbleiben an einer Stelle; die Hügel werden zu Städten werden... usw."

---

[29] CT VII (ed. de Buck 1961), 468a–b; Lichtheim 1973, 132 versteht die Stelle anders: "while hills became towns and towns hills, for dwelling destroys dwelling"; eine solche Darstellung der vergehenden Zeit wäre aber, soviel ich sehe, ein Unikum in der ägyptischen Literatur, setzt sie doch ein Denken in Zeithorizonten voraus, die nicht nur das Schwinden alter, sondern auch das Entstehen neuer Städte umgreifen. Demgegenüber fügt sich die Stelle, als Darstellung des Weltendes verstanden, vollkommen in die Tradition ein und entspricht vor allem der späteren Fassung des Topos im Totenbuch 175. Zur Form des "Kehrspruchs" s. Westendorf 1955.

[30] Vgl. n. 26.

[31] Ein typisches Beiwort des Osiris lautet "Der Millionen Jahre verbringt als seine Lebenszeit"; die Vorstellung einer wenn auch unabsehbar groß bemessenen Zeitspanne scheint das Wesen dieses Gottes zu charakterisieren.

[32] Trennung des Ungeschiedenen ist nach ägyptischer Vorstellung der kosmogonische Akt par excellence, vgl. Morenz 1960, 182f.; Hornung 1971, 164–166, 170ff.; Fecht 1972, 73 und 74 m. n. 33 zu Adm 12,11.

[33] Assmann 1975b, 22–26.

Erst im 175. Kapitel des TB im NR erscheint diese Eschatologie wo sie hingehört, nämlich im Rahmen eines Gesprächs zwischen Osiris und Atum über die Seinsform, die Osiris als gestorbener Gott im Jenseits zu erwarten hat. Die Vorstellung vom Weltende wird hier absolut – und nicht als Ende der geschichtlichen Kultur – formuliert, zugleich aber die Frist ins Unabsehbare verlängert:

(Osiris):
'Wie steht es mit der Lebenszeit?'

(Atum):
'Du wirst Millionen von Millionen Jahren verbringen,
eine Lebenszeit von Millionen.
Ich aber werde alles, was ich geschaffen habe, zerstören.
Dieses Land wird wieder in das Urwasser zurückkehren,
in die Flut wie in ... seinem Urzustand.
Nur ich bin es, der übrig bleibt, zusammen mit Osiris,
nachdem ich mich wieder in eine Schlange verwandelt habe,
die die Menschen nicht kennen und die Götter nicht erblicken'[34].

Hier ist zwar vom Weltende die Rede, aber kaum im Sinne einer Apokalypse. Die Idee des Endes hat hier einen rein theoretischen Sinn; es ist in so weite Ferne gerückt, daß es immer gleich weit entfernt scheint: man kann ihm nie spürbar näher kommen[35]. Daher hat es auch für das äg. Geschichtsbewußtsein keine Relevanz; es kann nicht Gegenstand der Erwartung sein. Es geht dem Text um ganz andere Fragen als der einer Sinngebung der Geschichte, von Heil und Unheil ist hier nicht die Rede[36]. Es war nötig, auf diesen Text einzugehen, weil er zu Mißverständnissen hinsichtlich der Bedeutung eschatologischer Vorstellungen im ägyptischen Geschichtsbild verleiten könnte[37]; im Folgenden aber braucht er uns nicht weiter zu beschäftigen.

---

[34] Zu diesem Text und seiner Überlieferungsgeschichte s. Otto 1962, 249–256; Assmann 1975b, 22–26; Hornung 1971, 157f.; Hornung 1978 (im Druck); Luft 1978, 168f.

[35] Eine entsprechende Struktur hat die Vorstellung von einer mythischen Urzeit: es handelt sich um eine "absolute Vergangenheit" (Frankfort), von der man sich nicht weiter entfernen kann, sondern immer gleich weit entfernt ist. Im Hinblick darauf möchte ich das Zeitbewußtsein, wie es sich in diesen Vorstellungen von Urzeit und Endzeit äußert, "mythisch" nennen und es einem "geschichtlichen" Zeitbewußtsein gegenüberstellen, das sich in einem in Erinnerung und Erwartung vergegenwärtigten Zeithorizont selbst in Bewegung denkt, z. B. am Anfang oder Ende eines Zeitalters (vgl. hierfür die Beiträge in diesem Band von H. Cancik und B. Gladigow).

[36] Soviel aber darf man wohl als ein notwendiges, wenn auch noch nicht hinreichendes Merkmal eines als "apokalyptisch" einzustufenden Phänomens fordern.

[37] Selbst Hornung, der diesem Text eine zentrale Bedeutung für das ägyptische *Welt*bild einzuräumen geneigt ist, rechnet mit einem ausgeprägt uneschatologischen *Geschichts*bild (s. bes. Hornung 1966), während ich gerade deshalb diesen Text auch für das Weltbild für eher peripher halte, um nicht eine so scharfe Trennung zwischen Welt- und Geschichtsbild in Kauf nehmen zu müssen.

1.3. Chacheperreseneb: die Chaos-Klage als Ausdruck pessimistischer Weltsicht

Bevor ich mich dem für unser Thema bedeutendsten Text des MR zuwende, den Prophezeiungen des Neferti, möchte ich kurz auf einige Texte eingehen, die Chaos-Beschreibungen in der Stilform der Klage vortragen. Die Klagen des Chacheperreseneb, erhalten auf einer Schreibtafel der frühen 18. Dyn., werden aus der Zeit Sesostris II. stammen, mit dessen Pränomen der Name des "Autors" gebildet ist, also mitten aus einer Epoche wohlgesicherter Ordnung und Ruhe; nicht einmal der Fiktion nach weisen sie auf die 1. Zz. zurück[38]. Die Klage über das Unheil Ägyptens ist inzwischen zur literarischen Gattung geworden, in der sich der Autor versucht; übrigens nicht, ohne sich eingangs zu wünschen, daß ihm neue Worte zur Verfügung stünden

> neue Rede, die nicht schon vorgekommen ist, frei von Wiederholungen
> keine Aussprüche der Vergangenheit, die von den Vorfahren gesagt wurden[39].

Die folgende Unheilsklage gibt sich, wie bei Neferti und natürlich nach dessen Vorbild, als prophetische Vision:

> Ich habe dies gesagt entsprechend dem, was ich geschaut habe,
> von der ersten Generation bis zu denen, die in Zukunft kommen werden[40].

Die Mißstände Ägyptens werden in sehr allgemeinen Formeln beschworen:

> Alles wandelt sich, nichts ist mehr wie im vorigen Jahr,
> ein Jahr lastet schwerer als das andere.
> Das Land ist aufgewühlt, zerstört, verwüstet.
> Maat ist hinausgeworfen,
> Isfet herrscht in der Ratsversammlung;
> die Pläne der Götter werden mißachtet,
> ihre Opferversorgung vernachlässigt.
> Das Land ist in schwerer Krankheit *(znj-mnt)*[41],
> Jammer überall, Städte, Bezirke schreien laut,
> alle sind gleichermaßen mit Unheil beladen.
> Man achtet keine Würde mehr,
> die Herren des Schweigens sind gestört.
> (...)
> Das ganze Land ist in großem Unheil,

---

[38] Der Text ist auf der hölzernen Schreibtafel BM 5645 überliefert, die Gardiner 1909, 95 ff. als Appendix zu seiner Edition des Pap. Leiden J 344 (Adm) veröffentlicht hat, und die wie der Leningrader Pap. des Neferti aus der 1. Hälfte der 18. Dyn. stammt. Einige Zeilen davon finden sich auf einem unveröffentlichten Ostrakon im Museum von Kairo, worauf Gardiner und Posener hinweisen, das aber auch in der Neubearbeitung des Textes durch Kadish 1973 unberücksichtigt geblieben ist. Der Text gehörte demnach, ähnlich wie die Prophezeiungen des Neferti, aber anders als die Admonitions, der "Lebensmüde" (n. 49) und die "Klagen des Bauern" zu den im Schulunterricht des Neuen Reichs verwendeten "Klassikern".

[39] Recto 2–3.   [40] Recto 6–7.   [41] Vgl. n. 69.

keiner ist frei von Verbrechen
Herzen sind gierig; der Befehle empfing, gibt Befehle,
und beide finden sich damit ab[42].

Die Aspekte des Unheils sind hier sehr anders gewichtet als in den Admonitions. Die Darstellung eines sozialen Umschwungs in der Stilform der Totenklage – "die Ersten sind die Letzten geworden und die Letzten die Ersten" – fehlt hier[43]. Vor allem fehlt alles, was sich einem historischen Aspekt der Klage zuordnen ließe. *Dieser* Text macht es wirklich unmöglich, zu sagen was eigentlich – und ob überhaupt etwas – geschehen ist. Aber er beansprucht auch gar keinen besonderen historischen Bezug. "Was ich gesehen habe" bedeutet nicht Augenzeugenschaft konkreter historischer Ereignisse, sondern visionäre Schau allgemeinen menschlichen Schicksals "von der ersten bis in zukünftige Generationen". Die Gattung der politischen Klage ist hier ins allgemeine gewendet und zum Ausdruck einer pessimistischen Weltsicht umfunktioniert worden[44].

Während die Admonitions dem Schöpfergott vorwerfen, angesichts des Unrechts zu schweigen, macht Chacheperreseneb den Menschen, die es tun und erleiden, diesen Vorwurf: "jeder schweigt darüber"[45] heißt es einmal, und weiter unten "beide finden sich damit ab"[46], und zum Schluß ganz deutlich:

Keiner ist weise genug, es zu erkennen,
keiner zornig genug, seine Stimme zu erheben. (...)
Es schmerzt, zu schweigen zu dem, was man hört,
es ist vergeblich, dem Unwissenden zu antworten.
Einer Rede zu entgegnen, schafft Feindschaft,
das Herz nimmt die Wahrheit nicht an;
man kann den Vortrag eines Sachverhalts nicht ertragen,
der Mensch liebt nur seine eigenen Worte.
Jedermann baut auf Heimtücke,
aufrichtige Rede hat man fallen gelassen[47].

Die Klagen des Chacheperreseneb sind auch an sein eigenes Herz gerichtet ("zu dir sprach ich, mein Herz, daß du mir antwortest! Ein angeredetes Herz darf nicht schweigen"[48]) als das Selbstgespräch eines Vereinsamten, der unter seinen Mitmenschen keine Zuhörer findet.

---

[42] Recto 10–12, Verso 2.

[43] Es kommt außerhalb der Adm überhaupt nur bei Neferti vor, der es aber – unter der Überschrift: "ich zeige dir das Unterste zuoberst" – sehr viel knapper und allgemeiner behandelt.

[44] In diesem Verlust an Anschaulichkeit und Verblassen des Themas ins allgemeine darf man wohl ein Kennzeichen dafür sehen, daß der Text ans Ende einer Tradition gehört, ganz im Gegensatz zu den Adm, die das Chaos in einer Fülle konkreter Einzelsymptome darstellen.

[45] Verso 3, Lichtheim 1973, 148.   [46] *Ibid.*

[47] Verso 3–5, Lichtheim 1973, 148.

[48] Verso 5–6 (Ende des auf der Londoner Schreibtafel erhaltenen Textes).

1.4. Das Selbstgespräch des "Lebensmüden": das Verstummen zwischenmenschlicher Verständigung

Dem "Gespräch eines Mannes mit seinem Ba"[49] liegt dieselbe Situation völliger Vereinsamung zugrunde; das zweite Gedicht des Mannes, dessen 16 Strophen alle mit der Frage beginnen "Zu wem kann ich heute reden?" hat diesen Verlust mitmenschlicher Verständigung zum alleinigen Thema[50]:

> Die Brüder sind schlecht,
> die Freunde von heute lieben nicht ...
> Herzen sind gierig,
> jedermann raubt die Habe seines Nächsten ...
> Freundlichkeit ist geschwunden,
> Gewalttätigkeit wendet sich gegen jeden ...
> Man ist mit dem Übel zufrieden,
> das Gute ist überall zu Boden geworfen ...
> Man hilft dem nicht, der geholfen hat ...
> Jeder wendet sein Gesicht ab von seinen Brüdern ...
> Keines Menschen Herz kann man vertrauen ...
> Ich bin mit Kummer beladen,
> weil mir ein Freund fehlt ... usw.

Wo die Sprache aufhört, setzt die Gewalt ein und es gilt: *homo homini lupus:*

> Die Menschen plündern,
> jeder beraubt seinen Nächsten ...
> Das Land ist Verbrechern überlassen ...
> Unheil zieht durchs Land, und ein Ende ist nicht abzusehen[51].

Setzen wir hier, im Vorgriff auf eine nähere Betrachtung des Textes, die Verse ein, in denen Neferti dieses Thema behandelt:

> Dieses Land wird zerstört, aber niemanden kümmert es,
> keiner spricht, keiner vergießt eine Träne: 'Was ist aus dem Land geworden!'[52].
> ...
> Man gibt nur mit Haß, um den Mund, der spricht, zum Schweigen zu bringen,
> um ein Wort zu beantworten, fährt der Arm mit dem Stock heraus,
> man spricht durch Totschlag.
> Rede wirkt auf das Herz wie Feuerbrand,
> man kann das Wort eines Mundes nicht ertragen[53].

Zum Thema des "Zuhörens" könnte man zahllose weitere Texte anführen. Das beliebteste Sprichwort der Ägypter lautet: "Gut ist es für die

---

[49] Pap. Berlin 3024; die neueste Edition des Textes mit Verweisen auf die ältere Lit. stammt von H. Goedicke 1970.
[50] Goedicke 1970, 155–172, l.103–130; Lichtheim 1973, 166–168.   [51] l.105 f., 122 f., 129.
[52] Neferti Pet. 24, Helck 1970, 21; Lichtheim 1973, 141.
[53] Neferti 48–50, Helck 1970, 39–42; Lichtheim 1973, 142. Zu *wḥd* "ertragen" s. Gardiner 1909, 104.

Menschen, zu hören"[54]. Vor allem aber muß man sich bewußt halten, daß
die äg. Grundbegriffe für Ordnung und Chaos, *maat* und *isfet*, eigentlich
Wahrheit und Lüge bzw. Gerechtigkeit und Unrecht heißen und sich auf
Sprache und Handeln als die Grundkategorien sozialen Verhaltens beziehen[55]. Noch einmal wird deutlich, daß es in diesen Klagen zumindest in
erster Linie weder um Naturkatastrophen, noch um politische Macht-
kämpfe geht, sondern um die Gefährdung der Kultur als einer Ordnung
menschlichen Zusammenlebens und die Angst vor dem Rückfall in die
Barbarei des Naturzustands. Noch in der koptischen Asklepius-Apokalypse ist an bedeutsamer Stelle von dem "Fehlen guter Worte"
(ⲦⲘⲚ̄ⲦⲀⲦⲀⲖⲞⲄⲞⲤ Ⲛ̄Ⲛ̄ⲨⲀⲬⲈ ⲈⲦⲚⲀⲚⲞⲨⲞⲨ) die Rede[56].

Es ist aber kennzeichnend für archaische Gesellschaften, daß der Begriff
einer auf der Sprache, d. h. den Ordnungen gegenseitiger Verständigung
beruhenden Gemeinschaft (und das bedeutet "Kultur" in diesem Zusammenhang) nicht bei den Menschen haltmacht, sondern die Götter und das
heißt: den als beseelt gedachten Kosmos umfaßt[57]. Jeden Morgen und
Abend redet der Ägypter mit der Sonne[58]. Der ganze Kult ist ein Diskurs
mit der Natur, der die Welt kraft der Sprache zusammenhält. Wenn der
Mensch die Sprache verlernt, schweigen auch die Götter (*omnis vox divina
... mutescet*) und ziehen sich aus der Welt zurück (*dolenda secessio*)[59].

2. Politische Prophezeiungen

2.1. Neferti

Dies vorausgeschickt, wird man die Prophezeiungen des Neferti recht
verstehen, deren Chaosbeschreibung die Natur einbezieht. Dieser Text[60],
der auf einem Pap. der 18. Dyn. und einer Reihe von ramess. Ostraka
überliefert, also im NR der bekannteste und einflußreichste Text unserer
Gruppe war, stellt die Darstellung der gestörten Naturordnung gleich an
den Anfang seiner Chaosbeschreibung:

---

[54] Schiffbrüchiger, 182; Lebensmüder, 67 f. u. a.

[55] Die Grundbedeutung von Maat würde ich eher im sozialen als im kosmischen Bezug
sehen, als Richtigkeit sozialen Verhaltens in Wort ("Wahrheit") und Tat ("Gerechtigkeit"),
wobei freilich die Korrespondenz zwischen kosmischem und sozialem Bereich (s. dazu n. 57)
zu beachten ist. H. H. Schmid 1968 stellt m. E. den kosmischen Bezug zu stark in den
Mittelpunkt.

[56] Nag Hammadi Codex VI, 8:73, 21–22 ed. Krause-Labib 1971, 199.

[57] Vgl. Frankforts Begriff der "integration of society and nature", s. dazu Assmann 1979, 20
m. n. 48.

[58] Zur Bedeutung des Sonnenkults und Sonnenhymnik in Ägypten s. Assmann 1975a mit
weiterer Lit.

[59] Asclepius XIII, 25 ed. Nock-Festugière 1960, 329. Zur äg. Auffassung des Kults s. u. a.
Derchain 1962a; 1965; Otto 1964.

Die Sonne ist verhüllt und strahlt nicht, daß die Menschen sehen können,
man kann nicht leben, wenn (sie) Wolken verhüllen ...
der Fluß von Ägypten ist ausgetrocknet,
man quert das Wasser zu Fuß.
Die Flut wird zum Ufer,
das Ufer zur Flut.
Der Südwind wird mit dem Nordwind streiten
und der Himmel in einem einzigen (= ununterscheidbaren) Windsturm sein[61].

Die Schilderung folgt der Dreiheit der "lebenspendenden Elemente"
Sonne, Nil und Wind[62]. Was dieser Störung der natürlichen Ordnungen
zugrunde liegt, wird gegen Ende der Chaosbeschreibung am Beispiel der
Sonne aufgezeigt:

Re wird sich von den Menschen trennen:
Es gibt zwar noch die Stunde seines Aufgangs,
aber niemand kann mehr wissen, wann Mittag ist,
denn man kann keinen Schatten mehr unterscheiden.
Kein Gesicht wird mehr geblendet sein, das (ihn) sieht[63].

Wenn die Götter sich von den Menschen zurückziehen, dann geht zwar
alles scheinbar seinen gewohnten Lauf weiter, aber die Kraft, der Segen
und das Gedeihen fehlen. Eingebettet in diese theologisch begründete
Naturklage sind nun längere Abschnitte, die das Chaos im Bereich
menschlicher Ordnungen beschreiben. Der erste Abschnitt, den man als
den historischen Kern ansprechen möchte, handelt von der Infiltration von
Asiaten im Ostdelta und der damit verbundenen Zerstörung der alimentä-
ren Ressourcen:

Dann werden jene schönen Dinge zugrunde gehen,
die Fischteiche voller Fischaufschlitzer,
überquellend von Fischen und Vögeln.
Alles Glück ist dahin,
das Land vom Elend zertreten
dadurch daß die Asiaten sich daran mästen,
die das Land durchziehen[64].

---

[60] Helck 1970; Lichtheim 1973, 139–145 mit weiterer Lit.; bes. Posener 1956. Der Vollständigkeit halber sei auch die sehr eigenwillige Studie von Goedicke 1977 erwähnt.
[61] Neferti 24–25; Helck 1970, 21–25.
[62] S. hierzu Assmann 1979, *passim*.
[63] Neferti 51–53; Helck 1970, 42f. Das im ersten Zitat rein kosmisch dargestellte Symptom
der gestörten Ordnung wird nun theologisch gedeutet: Re hat sich von den Menschen
getrennt. Dabei hat man aber diese Trennung nicht als Ursache der irdischen Mißstände
aufzufassen, wie es der späteren Geschichtstheologie entspräche (§3.4.), sondern vielmehr als
Folge: Der Sonnengott erträgt das Unrecht nicht, das auf Erden geschieht. Dieser Gedanke
liegt auch dem wahrscheinlich aus der gleichen Zeit stammenden Mythos von der Vernichtung des Menschengeschlechts zugrunde (Brunner-Traut ⁴1976, 69–72, 266–268). Die engste
Parallele zu Neferti findet sich aber im griechischen Töpferorakel (s. n. 81).
[64] Neferti 30–32; Helck 1970, 27.

Die folgenden Abschnitte behandeln das bekannte Thema: der Schwund an gemeinschaftlicher Ordnung und Verständigung und das Vorherrschen von Raub und Totschlag:

> Man wird Waffen des Krieges ergreifen
> ... und Brot mit Blut fordern[65].
> (vgl. Adm: "man nimmt sich den Schild zum Pflügen mit")

Selbst die engsten Familienbande sind zerstört:

> Ich zeige dir den Sohn als Gegner, den Bruder als Feind,
> einen Menschen, der seinen Vater tötet[66].

Der Verlust an Gemeinsinn, der allgemeine Egoismus ("Des Menschen Herz ist auf sich selbst gerichtet") äußert sich auch in der Gleichgültigkeit gegenüber dem Tod:

> Man wird über den Tod nicht mehr weinen
> und kein Trauerfasten halten wegen eines Todesfalls.
> Des Menschen Herz ist nur auf sich selbst gerichtet. ...
> Es gibt keine Klage mehr, die Menschen haben sie ganz aufgegeben.
> Ein Mann sitzt still und kehrt den Rücken,
> während einer einen anderen umbringt[67].

Und schließlich stimmt auch Neferti, aber sehr viel kürzer und in allgemeineren Ausdrücken, das Lied von der Verkehrten Welt der sozialen Verhältnisse an:

> Ich zeige dir das Land in schwerer Krankheit *(znj-mnt)*:
> der Schwacharmige ist jetzt stark-armig,
> man grüßt den, der (sonst) grüßte.
> Ich zeige dir das Unterste zuoberst,
> was auf dem Rücken lag, hat jetzt den Bauch unten.
> Man wird auf dem Friedhof leben.
> Der Bettler wird Schätze aufhäufen,
> (...) die Geringen werden Brot essen,
> die Dienstboten werden erhoben sein[68].

---

[65] Neferti 39–40; für die Par. in Adm und Töpferorakel s. n. 24.

[66] Neferti 44–45; Helck 1970, 35; vgl. Adm 2,13–14: "Der seinen Bruder erschlägt, ist überall"; 5,10: "Gewalt dringt ein bei jedermann; ein Mann erschlägt seinen Vollbruder." Der erste Satz des letzten Zitats ist ein Zitat aus dem "Lebensmüden" (Goedicke 1970, 159f.), der das Thema der zerstörten Familien- und Freundschaftsbindungen ausführlich behandelt. Vgl. auch Töpferorakel Pap. Oxy. 24–25, Pap. Rainer, 11: πόλεμος καὶ φόνος ἀσεβής ἐσται τῶν ἀδελφῶν καὶ τῶν γαμετῶν "Ruchloser Kampf und Mord wird herrschen zwischen Geschwistern und Eheleuten".

[67] Neferti 41–44. Vgl. Adm 9,3: "Seht, ein Mann wird erschlagen zu Seiten seines Bruders, und der sagt nur: 'Greif ihn nur an!', um seine eigene Haut zu retten." Mit "Jeder denkt nur an sich selbst" vgl. Töpferorakel Pap. Rainer 23–24, Pap. Oxy. 38–39: [πὰ]ς [κλα]ιήσει τὰ ἑαυτοῦ κακὰ ἥσσονα ὄντα ἐκείνου "Jeder beweint nur sein eigenes Leid, auch wenn es geringer als das der anderen ist".

[68] Neferti 54–56; Helck 1970, 46f.

Die Technik der Chaosbeschreibung, die auch den anderen Texten eigentümlich ist, läßt sich bei Neferti am deutlichsten beobachten. Sie besteht im Wechsel von ganz konkreten und ganz allgemeinen Ausdrükken, die die Funktion von Symptomen und Diagnose haben. Neferti kommt es vor allem auf die Diagnostik an. Die Kategorie der "Todesbefallenheit", die die konkreten Schilderungen der Admonitions durch die Stilform der Totenklage vermittelt, wird hier geradezu als *nomen ipsum* in Wendungen wie "Man lebt auf dem Friedhof" und "Ich zeige dir das Land in *znj-mnt*" so direkt wie möglich zum Ausdruck gebracht. *znj-mnt* muß ein Wort für sehr schweres Leiden oder Krankheit sein, es kommt in Heilungszaubertexten vor, wird aber auch in den Chaosbeschreibungen des Chacheperreseneb und Tutanchamun im Sinne der Diagnose des Unheils gebraucht, das Ägypten befallen hat[69].

Neferti ist darin Vorbild für alle späteren politischen Chaosbeschreibungen geworden bis hin zum Töpferorakel. Auch die Ausweitung ins Kosmische steht nicht im Dienst rhetorischer Hyperbolik, sondern des Bemühens um eine möglichst umfassende Diagnose der vielfältigen Erscheinungsformen des Unheils. Neferti will den Untergang der Kultur, die auf Maat gegründet ist, deutlich machen und folgt diesem Begriff in alle seine semantischen Dimensionen kosmischer, kultischer und sozialer Ordnung[70]. Was "Kultur" in diesem Zusammenhang bedeutet, haben wir bereits gezeigt: es ist die Schöpfung schlechthin, deren Untergang Neferti als die umfassendste Diagnose an den Anfang seiner Chaosbeschreibung stellt:

Was geschaffen war, ist zerstört.
Re kann mit der Schöpfung von vorn anfangen.
Das Land ist ganz zugrunde gegangen ohne einen Rest,
nicht einmal das Schwarze unter dem Fingernagel ist übriggeblieben
von dem, was er (Re) bestimmt hat[71].

Das Unheil, das in konkreten Symptomen dargestellt wird wie Asiateneinfälle, Bürgerkrieg, viele gleichzeitige Herrscher, Hungersnot und überhöhte Steuern läßt sich auf keinen isolierten Problembereich eingrenzen, weil alles mit allem zusammenhängt im empfindlichen Gleichgewicht der Maat, das immer neu hergestellt werden muß.

Der zweite Teil der Prophezeiung schildert die Wiederherstellung der Maat als das Werk eines Heilkönigs

---

[69] Neferti 38 und 54; Chacheperreseneb Recto 11; Urk IV 2027.11 s. §3.1; Socle Behague f 22ff. s. §4.1.
[70] Zum Begriff Maat s. o., n. 55; dazu Bergman 1972. Zu den 3 semantischen "Dimensionen" des Begriffs – Kosmos, Kult, Geschichte/Gesellschaft s. u., §4.3.
[71] Neferti 22–23; Helck 1970, 19. Vgl. *ibid.*, 46–47; Helck 37–38: "Zerstörung ist im Geschaffenen, Ausfall im Gefundenen, was geschaffen war, ist ungeschaffen."

der aus dem Süden kommen wird, Ameni mit Namen,
der Sohn einer Frau aus Ta-Seti, ein Kind von Oberägypten[72].

Er wird die heiligen Kronen des legitimen Königtums tragen, wird die
Rebellen im Lande unterwerfen und die Asiaten und Libyer vertreiben.

Dann wird Maat auf ihren Platz zurückkehren
während Isfet vertrieben ist[73].

Man weiß, daß mit Ameni Amenemhet I. gemeint ist, der Gründer der
12. Dyn.[74] Ameni ist eine geläufige Kurzform des Namens, die hier
gewählt ist, um auf Menes, den ersten Reichsgründer anzuspielen. Der
Text ist demnach eine Propagandaschrift in Form einer *ex eventu* Prophezeiung, die die umstrittene Legitimität dieses Usurpators auf einer höheren
Ebene als derjenigen legaler Erbfolge rechtfertigen soll. Als ein neuer
Menes ist dieser Ameni der langersehnte Heilbringer, der das Schöpfungswerk der Kultur noch einmal zu vollbringen vermag[75]. Die dogmatische
Fiktion von der vertriebenen Isfet und verwirklichten Maat wird in ihm
geschichtliches Ereignis, das vor aller Augen und Ohren geschehen ist.
Nach Jahrzehnten der Unheilserfahrung ist er der König, der die Heilser-
wartungen einlöst: das ist seine Legitimation.

So mündet auch diese apokalyptische Vision in die dogmatische Deutung der Gegenwart als erfüllter Heilszeit und verwirklichter Eschatologie.
Was als Weltuntergang dargestellt wurde, läßt das Erneuerungswerk des
Königs in seiner ganzen umfassenden Bedeutung einer Neuschöpfung
deutlich werden. Das ist gewiß eine sehr tendenziöse Deutung der
Geschichte. Aber es scheint mir verkehrt, zu bestreiten, daß hier überhaupt
geschichtliche Erfahrung im Hintergrund steht[76].

---

[72] Neferti 57–59; Helck 1970, 49.

[73] Neferti 68–69; Helck 1970, 57. Vgl. zu diesem Topos die Belegsammlung bei Hornung
1966, 64f. m. n. 74.

[74] Posener 1956, 23ff. Daß gerade für Amenemhet I. die Kurzform Ameni inschriftlich
nicht belegt ist, ist kein stichhaltiger Einwand, denn es kommt der Prophezeiung ja gerade
darauf an, den König nicht eindeutig beim Namen zu nennen, sondern in einer beziehungs-
vollen Weise auf ihn anzuspielen. Der Name Ameni läßt sich auch als "der Verborgene"
auffassen.

[75] Amenemhet I. bzw. die von ihm angeregte Prophezeiung nimmt damit auf eine Situation
mangelnden Königtums Bezug, in der der König, d.h. ein wirklicher König, tatsächlich
Gegenstand der Erwartung war. "Mangel an Königtum" ist genau der Ausdruck, den die
Adm verwenden, und zwar im Zusammenhang dessen, was ich ihren "historischen
Abschnitt" nennen möchte: "Seht, es kommt soweit, daß das Land arm gemacht wird an
Königtum durch ein paar Leute, die keine Gesetze kennen." Die (nicht erhaltene) "Prophezei-
ung der Residenz" (s. n. 22) muß sich auf diese Situation beziehen (Posener 1956, 28). Das
besondere "messianische" Sendungsbewußtsein Amenemhets I. kommt auch in dem Horus-
und Nebti-Namen des Königs, *whm mswt* "der die Geburt wiederholt" zum Ausdruck
(Posener 1956, 58).

[76] Dabei scheint es sich mehr um eine ideologische als um eine politische Erneuerung zu
handeln, denn die Reichseinigung war bereits der vorangehenden Dynastie gelungen. Wie

2.2. Töpferorakel und demotische Texte

Es ist lehrreich, diesem Text zwei Jahrtausende vorgreifend das Töpferorakel[77] gegenüberzustellen, das nicht aus dem Bewußtsein erfüllter Eschatologie heraus entstanden und überliefert ist, sondern das eine echte
Prophezeiung darstellt. Trotzdem sind die Übereinstimmungen frappant[78].
Der griechische Text, der auf 3 Pap. aus dem 2. und 3. Jh. n. Chr.
überliefert ist und sich als Übersetzung eines ägyptischen Originals ausgibt, scheint aus dem 2. Jh. v. Chr. zu stammen. Die Prophezeiung ist wie
bei Neferti in eine Rahmenerzählung gekleidet, auf die wir hier ebensowenig wie bei Neferti eingehen können. Die Chaosbeschreibung verbindet
wie bei Neferti konkrete historische Anspielungen auf die *zonophoroi*
genannten Griechen, das als *parathalassios polis* umschriebene Alexandria
und bestimmte Ereignisse, die L. Koenen auf das Jahr 130 v. Chr. beziehen
wollte[79], mit traditionellen Elementen der Unheilstopik, unter denen selbst
hier noch – in einem Text, der gewiß nicht der Oberschicht entstammt –
das Motiv des sozialen Umschwungs auftaucht:

> Krieg wird zwischen Geschwistern und Eheleuten herrschen,
> die Menschen werden sich gegenseitig umbringen
> Not macht egoistisch: jeder hält sein Übel für das schlimmste
> Die Bauern haben nichts zu ernten und müssen versteuern, was sie
> nicht gesät haben; die Not treibt sie mit Waffen gegeneinander.
> Die Sklaven werden frei werden und ihre Herren Mangel leiden.
> Der Vater wird der Tochter den Gatten abspenstig machen
> und Söhne die Mutter heiraten[80].

Auch diese Prophezeiung beginnt wie Neferti mit einer Schilderung der
gestörten Naturordnungen:

> Der Nil wird niedrig sein, die Erde unfruchtbar,
> die Sonne wird sich verfinstern, weil sie das Unheil in Ägypten
> nicht sehen will; die Winde werden Schäden auf der Erde anrichten[81].

Gegen Ende der Unheilszeit aber werden die Gürtelträger sich selbst
zerfleischen und wie Herbstlaub vom Baum Ägyptens abfallen[82]. Dann

---

sehr das Königtum jedoch nach dem Alten Reich verweltlicht war, geht besonders deutlich
aus den von Brunner 1955 dargelegten Zusammenhängen hervor. Die ideologischen Zielset-
zungen der XII. Dynastie hat Posener 1956 aufgezeigt; vgl. dazu jetzt auch Blumenthal 1970.
[77] Zum Text s. Koenen 1968 und 1974, zur Deutung Koenen 1970 und Dunand 1979, die
den Text sowohl in der älteren ägyptischen (Neferti) als auch der zeitgenössisch jüdisch-
hellenistischen Tradition verankert. Mme. Dunand hat mir, durch Vermittlung von G.
Posener, ihre Übersetzung des Textes zur Verfügung gestellt; beiden sei herzlich gedankt.
[78] S. a. die Übersicht bei Dunand 1979, 48 f.   [79] Koenen 1968, vgl. dagegen Dunand 1979.
[80] Oxy. 24–25 vgl. Rainer 11; Oxy. 38–39 vgl. Rainer 23–24; Rainer 24–25; Oxy. 20–22
vgl. Rainer 8–9; Oxy. 45–46; Oxy. 46–48.
[81] Oxy. 13–20; vgl. Rainer 1–8. Ich gebe eine Zusammenfassung.
[82] Rainer 31 f. = Oxy. 53 f. Vgl. zur Symbolik der Entblätterung und Begründung Koenen
1974, 317 f.; 1968, 181 m. n. 6.

werden die Götterbilder *(agalmata)* zurückkehren[83]. Ein Herrscher und Heilbringer *(agathon doter)*, der 55 Jahre regiert, wird von der Sonne gesandt und von Isis auf den Thron gesetzt[84]. Dann wird Ägypten gedeihen, der Nil wieder Hochwasser führen, Sommer und Winter in richtigem Zyklus kommen[85], die Winde mild und wohlgeordnet wehen und die Sonne wieder aufstrahlen und die Bestrafung der Bösen und das Elend der Gürtelträger sichtbar machen[86].

Die Topoi der Chaosbeschreibung sind dieselben wie in den 2000 Jahre älteren Klagen, die Störungen der beseelten Natur, die von der Depravation der Kultur in Mitleidenschaft gezogen ist, sind die gleichen wie in der Darstellung des Neferti und das Wirken des Heilkönigs, der die Welt wiederherstellt, entspricht in allen Details dem traditionellen Königsdogma. Dahinter steht weniger literarische Tradition als das gleiche Weltbild, das im Rahmen des Kults und des Königtums über die Jahrtausende tradiert wurde. Jetzt aber ist der Heilskönig nicht mehr mit irgendeinem König der herrschenden Dynastie gleichzusetzen, sondern reiner Gegenstand der Erwartung geworden. Das Dogma der verwirklichten Heilszeit ist umgeschlagen in eschatologische Heilserwartung[87].

Das Töpferorakel steht darin nicht allein. Das Orakel des Lammes, ein demotischer Text etwas früherer Zeit[88], auf den sich das Töpferorakel ausdrücklich beruft, sieht in dem König Bokchoris der 24. Dyn. (718–12) den letzten legitimen König und sieht alles folgende als eine Unheilszeit an, wobei auch hier die Verschleppung der im Töpferorakel erwähnten Götterbilder eine bedeutsame Rolle spielt. 900 Jahre wird das Unheil währen, bis wieder ein legitimer König das Heil zurückbringt. Darin sind nicht nur, dem immer weiter tradierten Dogma zum Trotz, Perser, Makedonen und Römer inbegriffen, sondern auch noch die Intervalle einheimischer Dynastien. Auch die sog. demotische Chronik[89], die den Heilskönig aus Herakleopolis erwartet, formuliert einen an die deuteronomistische Geschichts-

---

[83] Rainer 34–35 = Oxy. 57–58; vgl. das Orakel des Lammes (n. 88) und Asclepius XIII, 27 (Krause 1969, 55 n. 59).

[84] Rainer 38–41 = Oxy. 63–67; vgl. Koenen 1968, 180, Dunand 1979, 54f. mit Verweisen auf Parallelen zum sonnengesandten König im III. Buch der Sibyllinen und in der Elias-Apokalypse.

[85] Rainer 45–46 = Oxy. 75–77. Koenen 1970, 253 denkt hier an eine Anspielung auf die Verschiebung des um ¼ Tag zu kurzen Wandeljahres im Laufe einer Sothis-Periode und deren Neubeginn um 139 n. Chr.; aber diese Verschiebung scheint man in Ägypten nie als ein Chaosphänomen empfunden zu haben, ebensowenig wie sich mit ihrer Aufhebung irgendwelche Heilserwartungen verbunden zu haben scheinen; so möchte ich auch in dem geordneten Wechsel der Jahreszeiten mehr einen bildhaften Topos der Heilszeit im Sinne von Assmann 1975a, Text 239, 15–20, als eine konkrete kalendarische Anspielung vermuten. Die Sothisperiode spielt im pharaonisch-ägyptischen Denken eine denkbar geringe Rolle.

[86] Rainer 46–49; Oxy. 77–79.   [87] Koenen 1970; Dunand 1979.

[88] Krall 1898; Janssen 1954; Bresciani 1969; Zauzich 1979.

[89] Spiegelberg 1914; Meyer 1915; Johnson 1974.

schreibung erinnernden Begriff des schlechten Königs, der nicht auf Gottes Wege wandelt und das "Gesetz" verläßt[90], und wendet ihn auf einige Könige der einheimischen 30. Dyn. an. Das Geschichtsbild des Volkes hat sich vom Dogma der offiziellen Inschriften weit entfernt. Selbst in den Tempelinschriften findet sich eine Spur dieses veränderten Zeitbewußtseins. Die Topik der Heilszeit, in der Maat auf Erden weilt, das Land überschwemmt und die Leiber gefüllt sind, erscheint jetzt nicht nur in der Vergangenheitsform als Beschreibung der Zeit der Urgötter, sondern wird noch um Merkmale einer verkehrten Welt mit paradiesischem Vorzeichen ergänzt, die ihre Unwiederbringlichkeit und Unauffindbarkeit in der Gegenwart außer Zweifel stellen: "die Mauern fielen noch nicht ein, der Dorn stach noch nicht in der Zeit der Urgötter"[91]. Hier manifestiert sich, aus dem Bewußtsein einer depravierten Gegenwart, dasselbe eschatologische Denken sozusagen in der Gegenrichtung, dem auch die politischen Prophezeiungen der Zeit entspringen. Dieser Umschlag in Mythos und Apokalyptik ist im ägyptischen Königsdogma angelegt. Was sich in Zeiten des Unheils, in denen das Dogma außer Kraft gesetzt ist, in Mythen und Prophezeiungen ausdrückt, ist im Dogma der erfüllten Heilszeit vorgeprägt.

3. Königsinschriften des Neuen Reichs

3.1. Tutanchamun und die Amarnazeit

Das muß in älteren Zeiten nicht unbedingt anders gewesen sein. Es muß doch auffallen, daß die erhaltenen Beispiele politischer Chaosbeschreibungen immer auf Krisenzeiten realer Gefährdung Bezug nehmen. Um rein rituelle Beschwörungen des Chaos im Rahmen des Festes "Geschichte" kann es sich nicht handeln. Die politische Literatur der 1. Zz., die "Prophezeiung der Residenz" und die "Lehre Achthoes' I.", des Gründers der Herakleopoliten-Dynastie, die in der "Lehre für Merikare" zitiert werden[92], die ältesten Teile der Admonitions und was es sonst noch gegeben haben mag an Klagen und Prophezeiungen, entspringt genau wie 2000 Jahre später die politische Prophetie der Spätzeit dem außer Kraft gesetzten Dogma eines "messianischen" Königtums, das in Apokalyptik umschlägt. Auch im NR tauchen politische Chaosbeschreibungen immer nur nach Krisenperioden auf. In seinem Restaurationsedikt benutzt Tutanchamun diese Topik, um die vorangegangene Episode von Amarna als Unheilszeit und sich selbst als Wiederhersteller der Ordnung darzustellen, der "die isfet vertrieben hat in Ägypten und Maat eingesetzt hat auf ihren Sitz und der

---

[90] Meyer 1915.   [91] Kákosy 1964; Otto 1969; Otto 1964, 62ff.
[92] S.o., n. 22 und 75; Posener 1956, 28, 48f.; Krause 1969, 53 m. n. 48.

die Lüge zum Abscheu gemacht hat, so daß das Land wieder ist wie am ersten Schöpfungstag"[93]. Die eigentliche Chaosbeschreibung verbindet wieder konkrete Symptome mit verallgemeinernden Formulierungen im Sinne einer Diagnose:

> Die Tempel der Götter und Göttinnen von Elephantine bis zum Delta waren im Begriff, einzustürzen, ihre Kapellen vom Verfall bedroht,
> zu Hügeln geworden, bewachsen mit Unkraut,
> ihre Götterwohnungen, als wären sie nie gewesen,
> ihre Hallen ein öffentlicher Weg[94].

Als Diagnose verwendet Tutanchamun dieselbe Formel wie Neferti und Chacheperrenseneb: Das Land war in *znj-mnt*. Und als Begründung: Die Götter hatten sich von diesem Land abgewendet. Wenn man ein Heer ausschickte nach Palästina, hatte es keinen Erfolg, wenn man einen Gott oder eine Göttin anrief, kam sie nicht. Denn "sie" – damit können nur die Verantwortlichen gemeint sein – "hatten die Schöpfung zerstört". "Zerstörung ist im Geschaffenen", heißt es bei Neferti, "Verfall im Gefundenen"[95].

Die Chaosbeschreibung des Tutanchamun hält sich strikt im Rahmen des Tatsächlichen: weder ist hier von Bürgerkrieg und allgemeinem Blutvergießen, noch von sozialem Umschwung und Gleichgültigkeit gegenüber dem Leiden die Rede. Die Aufkündigung der göttlichen Einwohnung auf Erden ist ein so schweres Unheil, daß es weiterer Ausmalung der isfet nicht bedarf. Unter Echnaton waren nicht nur die Tempel geschlossen und die Opfer gesperrt, sondern die Götter, allen voran Amun, mit ikonoklastischen Zerstörungen verfolgt worden. Die gewaltsame Vertreibung der Götter aus dem Lande muß auf die Rechtgläubigen einen furchtbaren Eindruck gemacht haben. "Mein Herz sehnt sich danach, dich zu schauen", heißt es in einem Klagepsalm dieser Zeit an Amun.

> Du läßt mich eine Finsternis sehen, die du gibst
> leuchte mir, daß ich dich schauen kann[96]!

Die Prophezeiung des Neferti hat sich noch einmal erfüllt: das Licht göttlicher Einwohnung, das den Kosmos beseelt, hat sich verdunkelt, und es herrscht, wie die Formel lautet, "Finsternis am Tage"[97].

3.2. Sethos I. und der Beginn der 19. Dynastie

Die Zustände der Amarnazeit kommen noch einmal in einem Königstext zur Sprache: dem Denkstein Sethos' I. für seinen Vater Ramses I., den

---

[93] Urk. IV = Helck 1958, 2026,17f.   [94] Nach Urk. IV 2027, 1–10 (gekürzt).
[95] Vgl. o., n. 71. *jrjjt* in ähnl. Sinn auch Urk. IV 390,8: vgl. *ḥḏ jmnjjt* in Totenbuch 175. Zu *znj mnt* s. o., n. 69.
[96] Assmann 1975a, Nr. 147.
[97] Zu dieser Deutung der Wendung s. Assmann 1969, 296 n. 58.

Gründer der 19. Dyn., in Abydos[98]. Leider ist die entsprechende Passage äußerst zerstört. Die einzigen klaren Sätze der Chaosbeschreibung lauten:

> Die Nekropole, keiner kümmerte sich um sie,
> wie Wasser, das (gleichgültig) am Ufer vorbeieilt.
> Die Unterwelt und ihre Verfassung war unbekannt geworden
> durch (Vergessen)[99]...

Das ist ein Aspekt der Amarnazeit, der im Heiligtum des Totengottes Osiris von besonderer Bedeutung gewesen sein muß[100]. Er läßt sich ebenfalls in den Amarnatexten belegen, die die traditionellen Jenseitsvorstellungen nicht kennen und das Wort "Unterwelt" vermeiden[101]. Die folgende Passage lautet in der Ergänzung von Schott:

> (Da befahl der Allherr im Rat der Götter,
> meinen Vater zum Herrscher zu bestimmen),
> ihre Stätten (wiederherzustellen).

Schicksal vor ihnen und Erfüllung verfuhren, wie es befohlen war.

> Sie taten wie geheißen.
> Da aber begann mein Vater mit dem Königtum des Re
> und saß auf dem Thron wie dieser[102].

Man wüßte freilich gerne, ob überhaupt und wie genau ein göttliches Eingreifen in die Thronfolge in diesem Text formuliert war[103]. Man erinnert sich, daß bei Neferti davon keine Rede war. "Ein König wird kommen aus dem Süden" heißt es einfach. Auch Tutanchamun erwähnt mit keinem Wort ein Einschreiten der Götter. Das Töpferorakel dagegen läßt den Heilskönig vom Sonnengott gesandt und von Isis inthronisiert sein.

3.3. Pap. Harris I. und der Beginn der 20. Dynastie

Aber auch dieser Zug entspricht älterer ägyptischer Tradition, wie sich spätestens aus jenen Chaosbeschreibungen ergibt, die sich auf die Unruhen

---

[98] Ed. Schott 1964.   [99] Schott 1964, 18.   [100] Vgl. Otto 1966, 45ff.
[101] Die traditionelle Vorstellung eines nächtlichen *descensus* des Sonnengottes in die Unterwelt als das Reich der Toten wird in den Amarnahymnen ersetzt durch die aus Ps 104 vertraute Schilderung der diesseitigen Nacht, s. Assmann 1975a, 59f.
[102] Schott 1964, 19.
[103] Die im Pap. Westcar überlieferte Legende (vgl. o., n. 5) führt den Wechsel von der 4. zur 5. Dynastie auf göttliches Eingreifen zurück (Posener 1956, 10–13), im Unterschied zu Neferti und auch noch Tutanchamun. Aber bereits die Orakel-Interventionen in der umstrittenen Thutmosiden-Sukzession sowie die Anbringung des Zyklus von der göttlichen Zeugung des Königskindes auf Tempelwänden durch Hatschepsut und Amenophis III. zeigen, daß der göttlichen Initiative in der offiziellen Königstheologie und Geschichtsauffassung gegenüber dem Handlungsspielraum des Königs im Neuen Reich größeres Gewicht gegeben wird.

im Zusammenhang des nächsten Dynastie-Wechsels von der 19. zur 20. beziehen. Vgl. im pHarris I:

> Das Land Ägypten war 'hinausgeworfen',
> jedermann lebte nach seinem eigenen Recht;
> und sie hatten viele Jahre keine Führer bis als später
> das Land Ägypten aus Magnaten und Bürgermeistern bestand
> und einer den anderen umbrachte unter Großen und Geringen.
> Dann folgte eine Zeit aus 'leeren Jahren',
> als Ir-su, der Asiat, als Oberhaupt bei ihnen war,
> nachdem er sich das ganze Land unterworfen hatte.
> Jeder plünderte seinen Nachbarn aus
> und die Götter behandelten sie nicht besser als die Menschen,
> so daß niemand Opfer darbrachte in ihren Heiligtümern.
> Aber die Götter wendeten sich wieder in Gnade um,
> um das Land in seinen normalen Zustand zu bringen
> entsprechend seiner eigentlichen Verfassung,
> und sie setzten ihren Sohn ein, der aus ihrem Leibe hervorkam[104],

nämlich Sethnacht, den Gründer der 20. Dyn., der die Aufrührer tötete, den "Großen Thron Ägyptens reinigte" und wieder ein legitimer König auf dem Thron Atums war[105]. Hier wird nicht die Abwendung der Götter – die natürlich impliziert ist –, sondern ihre Wieder-Zuwendung zu Ägypten ausgedrückt, die ähnlich wie die Rückkehr der Götterbilder im Orakel des Lammes und im Töpferorakel die Wende zum Heil markiert.

3.4. Die Israelstele des Merenptah

Das Motiv begegnet bereits in der etwas älteren Israelstele des Merenptah[106], deren Darstellung des Triumphs das Ausmaß der abgewendeten Katastrophe andeutet:

> Licht, der die Wolke vertrieb, die über Ägypten hing
> und Ägypten das Licht der Sonne wieder sehen ließ;
> Der den Berg von Erz entfernte vom Nacken des Volkes,
> um dem gefangenen Volk Luft zu verschaffen ...
> Der die Tore von Memphis öffnete, die verschlossen waren,
> und den Tempeln wieder ihre Nahrung zukommen ließ[107].

---

[104] Pap. Harris I, 75, 2–7 ed. Erichsen 1933, 91; Faulkner 1966, 26f.

[105] Die von Hornung 1966, 27 für reine dogmatische Fiktion angesehene Darstellung des Pap. Harris I. wird jetzt in einigen entscheidenden Zügen bestätigt durch die neugefundene Stele des Sethnacht aus Elephantine, s. Bidoli 1972. Natürlich ist der Pap. Harris I kein Stück objektiver Geschichtsschreibung, sondern eine traditionelle und daher in überlieferten Topoi gehaltene Chaosbeschreibung, die mit der Realität nur indirekt zusammenhängt. Wer aber jeden derartigen Zusammenhang bestreiten will, muß erklären, warum die überaus zahlreich erhaltenen Zeugnisse offizieller Geschichtsdarstellung von dem Mittel der Chaosbeschreibung so selten Gebrauch machen.

[106] Kitchen 1968, 12–19; Lichtheim 1976, 73ff.   [107] Kitchen 1968, 13,10–14,1.

Nach einer Darstellung des erfolgreichen Abwehrkampfs gegen die Libyer wird eine längere Rede des Allherrn zitiert, der dem König den Sieg zuspricht:

> Gebt das Schwert meinem Sohn,
> dem aufrichtigen, gütigen, mildtätigen Merenptah,
> der für Memphis sorgte und Heliopolis rächte,
> der die Dörfer öffnete, die versperrt waren.
> Er hat Viele befreit, die überall eingeschlossen waren,
> er hat den Tempeln Opfer gegeben,
> er hat den Göttern Weihrauch darbringen lassen.
> Er hat die Großen ihre Besitztümer behalten lassen
> und die Armen ihre Städte besuchen lassen[108].

Am Ende folgt eine sehr eindrucksvolle Schilderung der eingetretenen Heilszeit des Friedens, in der

> man schreitet frei aus auf den Wegen,
> weil keine Furcht mehr in den Herzen der Menschen herrscht.
> Festungen sind sich selbst überlassen,
> Brunnen sind offen für die Boten;
> Wälle und Mauern sind friedlich,
> nur das Licht der Sonne weckt ihre Wachmannschaften ...
> Soldaten liegen schlafend ausgestreckt ...
> Da gibt es kein Rufen mehr in der Nacht
> 'Bleib wo du bist' mit der Stimme eines Fremden.
> Man kommt und geht mit Gesang.
> Re hat sich Ägypten wieder zugewendet
> der Sohn ist bestimmt zu ihrem Schützer[109].

Re hat sich Ägypten wieder zugewendet: diese Vorstellung, daß der freie Wille der Götter und speziell des Sonnengottes die Geschicke des Landes bestimmt, scheint eine Neuerung der ramessidischen Geschichtsauffassung zu sein, die sich in der Spätzeit allgemein durchsetzt: Anch-Scheschonqy V, 2–3:

> Wenn Re einem Lande zürnt, wird dessen Herrscher das Gesetz mißachten.
> Wenn Re einem Lande zürnt, wird es das Gesetz darin aufhören lassen[110].

---

[108] Kitchen 1968, 16,10–17,1.   [109] Kitchen 1968, 18,5–19,1.

[110] Pap. BM 10508, V. 2–3 ed. Glanville 1955. Der entscheidende Satz der Israel-Stele kommt, mit Ersetzung des Re durch Amun, auch in einer Hymne auf Ramses VI. vor, s. Condon 1978, 12 l.4,20 oben und 30 z. St.:
Siehe, Amun hat sich Ägypten wieder zugewendet:
die arm *(nmḥw)* waren, sind jetzt angesehen.

4. Chaosbeschreibungen in Magie und Kult der Spätzeit

4.1. Metternichstele: Krankheit und kosmisches Unheil

Der Große pHarris scheint nach dem zufälligen Befund des Erhaltenen das letzte Glied in der Reihe politischer Chaosbeschreibungen zu sein, bis diese dann in den demotischen und griechischen Prophetien der Spätzeit wieder auftauchen. Inzwischen aber kommen Chaosbeschreibungen in religiösen Texten auf, die zur Spätzeit hin ein immer "apokalyptischeres" Gepräge annehmen. Schon in Zaubertexten des NR drohen Zauberer damit, die Sonnenbarke "auflaufen zu lassen auf der Sandbank des Apopis"[111]. Spätere Zaubertexte malen die Folgen in der Form einer Chaosbeschreibung aus:

Die Sonnenbarke steht still und fährt nicht weiter,
die Sonne ist noch an ihrer Stelle von gestern.
Die Nahrung ist schifflos, die Tempel versperrt,
die Krankheit dort *(znj-mnt)* wird die Störung zurückwenden
auf ihre Stelle von gestern.
Der Dämon der Finsternis geht umher, die Zeiten sind nicht geschieden,
die Figuren des Schattens lassen sich nicht mehr beobachten.
Die Quellen sind versperrt, die Pflanzen verdorren,
das Leben ist den Lebenden genommen
bis Horus gesundet für seine Mutter Isis
und bis der Patient ebenso gesundet[112].

Im Sonnenkult werden, um dieses Unheil abzuwenden, "die 77 Schriftrollen rezitiert auf der Schlachtbank des Apopis, Tag für Tag"[113], um "der Sonnenbarke freie Fahrt zu geben"[114] und "den Ansturm des Wildgesichtigen abzuwehren"[115].

Der Sonnenlauf erscheint in diesen Texten vom Stillstand bedroht und kultischer Mitwirkung bedürftig. Jeder Sonnenaufgang wird jubelnd und aufatmend als ein Sieg über die Chaosmächte gefeiert, die ständig gegenwärtig sind und den Weltlauf gefährden[116]. Wir stoßen hier auf dieselbe Struktur einer permanent realisierten Eschatologie wie beim Königsdogma, das sich auch immer explizit auf den Sonnenlauf als sein Urbild bezieht:

---

[111] Assmann 1969, 295–298, bes. 296 n. 56; Borghouts 1978, 55 Nr. 58.
[112] Klasens 1952, 31 f., 57, 96.
[113] Assmann 1975a, Nr. 17, 6–7.
[114] *Ibid.*, Nr. 54, Vers 3.
[115] *Ibid.*, Vers 4 vgl. allg. Assmann 1969, 210 f.; 1970, 68 f. Ein spätes Exemplar solchen kosmischen Abwehrzaubers ist uns im Pap. BM 10188, 22–32 (Pap. Bremner Rhind) erhalten, ed. Faulkner 1933, 42–88.
[116] S. Assmann 1969, 379 s. v. "Behobene Krisis".

Die Erde wird hell, Re erstrahlt über seinem Land,
er hat gesiegt über seine Feinde[117]!

beginnt ein Lied zur Salbung des Königs am Stufenthron. Das Chaos wird
immer neu besiegt, die Schöpfung jeden Morgen wiederholt.

4.2. Pap. Salt 825 u. a. Texte: kultische Unheilsbannung

Hinter dieser Vorstellung, der Heil und Unheil, Ordnung und Chaos
ständig gegenwärtige Möglichkeiten sind, steht ein Zeitbegriff, der das
genaue Gegenstück zu einem eschatologischen Denken darstellt: denn
dieses sieht die Zeit auf eine vorbestimmte Katastrophe und Erneuerung
zutreiben, während für den Ägypter die Zeit sich fortwährend erneuert in
den Zyklen des Tages und des Jahres. Das Unheil lauert an den Übergangs-
zonen, und die Rituale bewirken, daß sich ein Zyklus nahtlos an den
anderen schließt, um die Kontinuität zu gewährleisten[118]. Auf der Ebene des
Königtums ist uns ein solches Kontinuitätsritual in einem Papyrus aus
Brooklyn erhalten[119], während Ph. Derchain ein funktionell entsprechendes
Ritual aus dem Osiriskult im Pap. Salt 825 erschlossen hat[120]. Beide Texte
stammen aus der Spätzeit. Das ist kein Zufall der Überlieferung, denn
zahllose Einzelheiten weisen darauf hin, daß dieses Bewußtsein einer
ständig imminenten Katastrophe zur Spätzeit hin einen immer dominieren-
deren Zug ägyptischen Denkens darstellt[121].

Das Ritual des Pap. Salt 825 ist in unserem Zusammenhang besonders
interessant, weil es mit einer apokalyptischen Chaosbeschreibung anfängt:

Die Erde ist verwüstet,
die Sonne geht nicht auf
der Mond zögert, es gibt ihn nicht mehr,
der Ozean schwankt, das Land kehrt sich um,
der Fluß ist nicht mehr schiffbar
Alle Welt klagt und weint
Götter und Göttinnen, Menschen, Verklärte und Tote,
Klein- und Großvieh weinen laut[122]...

Was geschehen ist, stand im verlorenen Anfang des Textes, aber Seth
muß der Urheber des Eingriffs in die Weltordnung sein, denn er wird im

---

[117] Pap. Brooklyn 47.218.50 II, 10, ed. Goyon 1972, 58.
[118] Derchain 1965; Assmann 1975b, 28–30. Für die Epagomenen, die 5 Tage "zwischen den
Jahren", gibt es besondere Schutzsprüche, s. Stricker 1948.
[119] Pap. Brooklyn 47.218.50 ed. Goyon 1972.
[120] Derchain 1965, bes. I, 24–28 mit einer Fülle weiterer Beispiele.
[121] Derchain 1965, 28 mit Verweis auf Morenz 1960, 215–223.
[122] Pap. Salt 825, I.1–6; Schott 1959 übersetzt den 5. Vers: "Das Wasser fließt nicht mehr
stromab", was sprachlich nicht ausgeschlossen ist. Vgl. aber Neferti 26–28 und Töpferorakel
Rainer 1–2; Oxy. 13–14.

folgenden bestraft[123]. Seth wird zum Inbegriff des Unheilbringers. In den Sprüchen, die man rezitiert, um sein Kommen abzuwehren, wird das Chaos, das er verkörpert, ausgemalt:

> Weiche zurück, damit die Sonne sich nicht verfinstere
> auf der Sandbank des Zweimessersees!
> Damit der Himmel den Mond nicht verschlucke
> am Vollmondtag in Heliopolis.
> Damit die Schildkröte nicht den Nil schlürfe
> und die Gewässer austrocknen
> damit nicht eine Flamme aus dem Ozean hervorkomme
> und Flamme durch Flamme verbrenne
> damit nicht bekannt würde das Nord- und Südwärtsfahren der Sonne,
> der an Wegen reichen beim Befahren des Himmels
> damit sich nicht die beiden Himmel auf einmal drehen
> und der Himmel sich mit der Erde vereine
> damit nicht die Lade in Heliopolis geöffnet werde
> und das, was in ihr ist, gesehen wird
> damit nicht das Gewand in Memphis gelöst werde
> und der Arm des So und So betrachtet wird
> damit nicht die Lampe in der Nacht des Bösen verlösche
> in jener Zeit, die nicht geschehen soll
> damit nicht der Ozean süß werde
> und von seinem Wasser getrunken wird usw. usw.[124].

Die Sprüche betreffen teils kosmische Katastrophen, teils die Enthüllung von Kultgeheimnissen. Beides hängt aufs engste zusammen:

> damit nicht die vier Sprüche in Heliopolis bekannt werden
> und der Himmel herabstürzt, wenn er sie hört[125].

4.3. Kultvollzug und kosmische Sympathie

Die Idee des Zusammenhangs, einer Sympathie aller Elemente des Kosmos, beherrscht vor allem die spätzeitliche Theorie des Opfers und Kultvollzugs. Besonders aufschlußreich ist hierfür ein Abschnitt des Pap. Jumilhac:

> Wenn wenig Opferbrote auf ihren Altären sind,
> dann geschieht das Gleiche im ganzen Land
> und wenig Leben wird für die Lebenden sein.
> Wenn dieser Ort seiner Libationen beraubt wird ...,
> dann wird die Nilüberschwemmung niedrig sein in ihrem Quelloch,
> und der Mund der Schildkröte versiegelt.
> Ein Jahr der Hungersnot herrscht im ganzen Land,
> es gibt weder 'Lebensbaum' noch Gemüse.
> Wenn man die Osiris-Zeremonien vernachlässigt

---

[123] IV.6–9. Der Eingriff besteht jedenfalls in der Ermordung des Osiris, s. Derchain 1965, 31–34, der allerdings zu dem Schluß kommt, daß in diesem Fall Schu der Schuldige ist.
[124] Urk. VI = Schott 1929, 122–125.   [125] *Ibid.*, 127, 3–6.

zu ihrer Zeit an diesem Ort ...,
dann wird das Land seiner Gesetze beraubt sein,
der Pöbel (*ḥwrw*) wird seine Herrschaft im Stich lassen
und es gibt keine Befehle für die Menge...
Wenn man den Feind nicht köpft, den man vor sich hat
aus Wachs, auf Papyrus oder aus Holz nach den Vorschriften des Rituals,
dann werden sich die Fremdländer gegen Ägypten empören
und Bürgerkrieg und Revolution im ganzen Land entstehen.
Man wird auf den König in seinem Palast nicht hören
und das Land wird seiner Schutzwehr beraubt sein[126].

Die Sonne ist von Stillstand bedroht, der Kult von Vergessen und
Habgier und der König von äußeren und inneren Feinden. Die drei
Ordnungen des Kosmos, des Kults und des Staats sind drei Aspekte ein
und derselben Ordnung, die von permanenter Gefährdung bedroht immer
wieder bestärkt, bewahrt und hergestellt werden muß. Im Sieg der Sonne
über den Finsternisdrachen siegt Pharao über seine Feinde, die Fülle der
Opfergaben auf den Altären und die metikulöse Observanz der Rituale
garantieren Fülle, Wohlstand und soziale Ordnung im Lande und die
Gerechtigkeit des Königs sichert den Segen der Natur[127]. Die Kohärenz
dieses von mutueller Sympathie zusammengehaltenen Kosmos läßt sich an
einem triangulären Modell veranschaulichen, dessen Ecken von Kosmos,
Kult und Königtum besetzt sind[128]. Jeder Eingriff an einem der drei Pole:

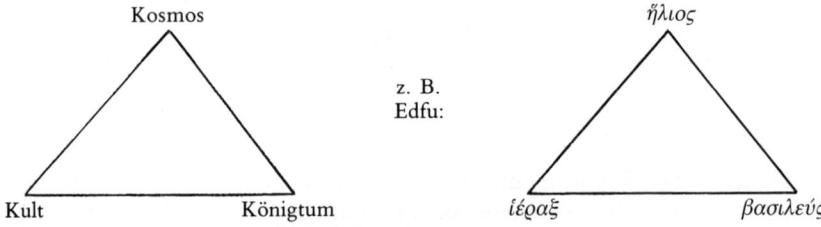

zieht die anderen beiden in Mitleidenschaft. Das Prinzip der Maat-Ver-
wirklichung, das diese Welt im Innersten zusammenhält, verlagert sich

---

[126] Pap. Jumilhac XVII,19–XVIII,11; Vandier 1961, 129 f. (gekürzt).
[127] Zum Zusammenhang der Begriffe "Gerechtigkeit" (Maat) und "Fülle" im ägyptischen
Denken s. Otto 1969 und Assmann 1970, 58–65, vgl. darüber hinaus auch Schmid 1968.
[128] Es handelt sich um dieselbe Dreiheit, die sich, auf die Götterwelt bezogen, als Kult,
Kosmos und Mythos darstellt, vgl. Assmann 1969, 143 n. 22 und 271 f. sowie 1976, 765–771.
Die "mythische" Dimension der Götterwelt entspricht dem mit "Königtum" bezeichneten
Pol, weil sich Mythos auf das geschichtliche Sein der menschlichen Gesellschaft bezieht,
dessen Exponent der König ist. Vgl. ein griechisches Ostrakon aus Edfu, ed. Yoyotte 1969,
das den Gott dieses Tempels als *Helios, Hierax* und *Basileus* anruft. Der Gott, der als "Falke"
im Tempel gegenwärtig und dem kultischen Umgang zugänglich ist, ist zugleich die Sonne
auf der kosmischen und der König auf der politisch-sozialen Ebene der umfassenden Ordnung.

immer mehr von der politischen Ebene des Königtums auf die religiöse Ebene des Kults. Demgegenüber verblaßt das Königsamt immer mehr zu einer priesterlichen Funktion, was sich in den zahlreichen Priestertiteln ausdrückt, mit denen es in den Tempeln umschrieben wird[129]. Oft sind die Kartuschen in diesen Inschriften leer gelassen: "Pharao" wird ein fiktives kirchliches Amt, das die Priester stellvertretend ausüben. Durch diese Fiktion ließ sich der "Weltlauf" auch in den Zeiten der griechisch-römischen Fremdherrschaft noch eine Weile in Gang halten; aber das Bewußtsein des drohenden Endes, der immer dünner werdenden Kulturschicht, muß ständig gewachsen sein.

Dieses Wissen findet seinen Ausdruck in der Asklepios-Apokalypse[130]. In diesem griechischen Text, von dem außer einem Zitat bei Laktanz nur Übersetzungen in koptischer und lateinischer Sprache erhalten sind, laufen die beiden Traditionen der politischen und der rituellen Chaosbeschreibung zusammen. Was hier prophezeit wird, ist der Untergang der ägyptischen Kultur = Religion als der Erkenntnis und zugleich Ins-Werk-Setzung jener Sympathie von Kosmos, Kult und staatlich-moralischer Gemeinschaft, die Ägypten zum "Abbild des Himmels und Tempels der ganzen Welt" machte[131]. Wenn die Götter ihre Einwohnung in diesem Lande aufkündigen (*dolenda secessio*), wird der entgöttlichte Kosmos aufhören, ein Gegenstand der Anbetung und Verehrung zu sein, aber auch Ägypten wird untergehen, denn mit der Gottesfurcht schwinden Gerechtigkeit, Gehorsam und Gemeinsinn.

> Du aber, o Fluß, ein Tag wird kommen, an dem du mehr Blut als Wasser führen wirst, und die Leichen werden höher als die Dämme sein. Und man wird über den Toten nicht so wie über den Lebenden weinen[132]...
> Sie werden die Finsternis dem Licht vorziehen und dem Tod gegenüber dem Leben den Vorzug geben. Den Frommen wird man als Verrückten betrachten und den Gottlosen als Weisen verehren. Den Furchtsamen wird man für stark halten und den Guten bestrafen[133]...
> In jenen Tagen wird die Erde nicht gefestigt sein
> und man wird nicht auf dem Meer segeln,
> und man wird auch nicht die Sterne erkennen, die am Himmel sind.
> Jede heilige Stimme des Wortes Gottes wird über ihn schweigen.
> Die Luft aber wird krank sein.
> Das ist das Greisenalter der Welt: der Zustand der Gottlosigkeit, Rechtlosigkeit und des Fehlens guter Worte[134].

---

[129] Otto 1964, 63–83.
[130] Dem Folgenden liegt die kopt. Fassung in Codex VI (VI, *8* 65,15−78,43) der Bibliothek von Nag Hammadi zugrunde, ed. Krause-Labib 1971, 187−206 (hier 194−200).
[131] Zu dieser für das Verständnis der äg. "Apokalyptik" zentralen Konzeption s. Junge 1978.
[132] 71, 17−23, Krause-Labib 1971, 196; vgl. Asclepius, 24, ed. Nock-Festugière 1960, 328.
[133] 72, 16−25, Krause-Labib 1971, 197; vgl. Asclepius, 25, Nock-Festugière 1960, 329.
[134] 73, 12−22, Krause-Labib 1971, 198−199; vgl. Asclepius, 25−26, Nock-Festugière 1960, 329f.

Die Heilserwartung, die von einem König nichts mehr weiß und auf den Demiurgen selbst hofft, der die vergreiste Welt mit Wasser und Feuer, Krieg und Seuchen zerstören wird um eine neue, heile Welt zu erschaffen: diese Erwartung hat den Boden der ägyptischen Tradition bereits verlassen. Die Unheilserfahrung aber ist ganz in den alten ägyptischen Kategorien von Maat und isfet, göttlicher Einwohnung und Abwendung zum Ausdruck gebracht und macht am Ende dieser jahrtausendelangen Tradition noch einmal in ergreifenden Wendungen deutlich, worum es im Grunde immer ging: um die hauchdünne und von ständigem Untergang bedrohte Schicht der Kultur über dem nie ganz zu bändigenden Treibsand der Barbarei.

Bibliographie

Assmann, Jan 1969: *Liturgische Lieder an den Sonnengott* (MÄSt 19), Berlin 1969.
- 1970: *Der König als Sonnenpriester* (ADAI.Ä VII), Glückstadt-New York 1970.
- 1975a: *Ägyptische Hymnen und Gebete*, Zürich-München 1975.
- 1975b: *Zeit und Ewigkeit im alten Ägypten* (AHAW.PH 1975.1), Heidelberg 1975.
- 1976: "Gott", in: W. Helck, W. Westendorf (Hrsg.), *LÄ* II.5 (Wiesbaden 1976), 756–786.
- 1979: "Primat und Transzendenz. Struktur und Genese der ägyptischen Vorstellung eines 'Höchsten Wesens'", in: W. Westendorf (Hrsg.), *Aspekte der spätägyptischen Religion* (GOF.Ä IV/9), Wiesbaden 1979, 7–42.
Barta, Winfried 1969: *Das Gespräch eines Mannes mit seinem Ba* (MÄSt 18), Berlin 1969.
- 1971: "Zu einigen Textpassagen der Prophezeiung des Neferti", in: *MDAI.K* 27.1 (1971) 35–45.
- 1974/75: "Die erste Zwischenzeit im Spiegel der pessimistischen Literatur", in: *JEOL* 24 (1974/75) 50–61.
Bergman, Jan 1968: *Ich bin Isis*. Studien zum memphitischen Hintergrund der griechischen Isisaretalogien (AUU.HR 3), Uppsala 1968.
- 1972: "Zum 'Mythos vom Staat in Ägypten'", in: H. Biezais (Hrsg.), *The Myth of the State* (SIDA VI), Stockholm 1972, 80–101.
Bidoli, Dino 1972: "Stele des Königs Sethnacht", in: *MDAI.K* 28.2 (1972) 193–200.
Blumenthal, Elke 1970: *Untersuchungen zum Königtum des Mittleren Reichs* I. Die Phraseologie (ASAW.PH 61), Berlin 1970.
Borghouts, J. F. 1978: *Ancient Egyptian Magical Texts* (Nisaba 9), Leiden 1978.
Bresciani, Edda 1969: *Letteratura e poesia dell'antico Egitto*, Torino 1969.
Brunner, Hellmut 1955: "Die Lehre vom Königserbe im frühen Mittleren Reich", in: O. Firchow (Hrsg.), *Ägyptologische Studien* (FS. Hermann Grapow), Berlin 1955, 4–11.
Brunner-Traut, Emma 1976: *Altägyptische Märchen*, Düsseldorf-Köln ⁴1976.
de Buck, Adriaan 1961: *The Egyptian Coffin Texts VII* (OIP LXXXVI), Chicago 1961.
Condon, Virginia 1978: *Seven Royal Hymns of the Ramesside Period* (MÄSt 37), München 1978.
Derchain, Philippe 1962a: *Le rôle du roi d'Egypte dans le maintien de l'ordre cosmique (le pouvoir et le sacré)*, Brüssel 1962, 61–73.
- 1962b: "L'authenticité de l'inspiration égyptienne dans le 'Corpus Herméticum'", in: *RHR* 161 (1962) 175–198.
- 1965: *Le Papyrus Salt 825 (BM 10051), Rituel pour la conservation de la vie en Egypte* (MAB.L 58.1), Brüssel 1965.

Dunand, Francoise 1979: "L'oracle du potier et la formation de l'apocalyptique en Egypte", in: M. Philonenko (Hrsg.), *L'Apocalyptique* (EHiRel 3) Paris 1979, 41–67.

Erichsen, Wolja 1933: *Papyrus Harris I* (BAeg V), Brüssel 1933.

Faulkner, Raymond O. 1933: *The Papyrus Bremner Rhind (BM 10188)* (BAeg III), Brüssel 1933.

– 1964: "Notes on the Admonitions of an Egyptian Sage", in: *JAE* 50 (1964) 24–36.

– 1966: *Cambridge Ancient History XXIII:* Egypt: From the inception of the nineteenth dynasty to the death of Ramesses III, Cambridge 1966.

Fecht, Gerhard 1972: *Der Vorwurf an Gott in den "Mahnworten des Ipuwer"* (AHAW.PH 1972.1), Heidelberg 1972.

Frankfort, Henri 1947: *Kingship and the gods*, Chicago 1947.

Gardiner, Alan H. 1909: *The Admonitions of an Egyptian Sage*, Leipzig 1909.

Glanville, S. R. K. 1955: *The Instructions of 'Onkh-Sheshonqy (BM 10508)*, London 1955.

Goedicke, Hans 1970: *The Report about the Dispute of a Man with his Ba*, Baltimore, Md. 1970.

– 1977: *The Protocol of Neferyt: the Prophecy of Neferti* (The John Hopkins Near Eastern Studies), Baltimore, Md. 1977.

Goyon, Jean Claude 1972: *Confirmation du pouvoir royal au Nouvel An* (BEt LII), Kairo 1972.

Helck, Wolfgang 1958: *Urkunden der 18. Dyn.*, Heft 22, Berlin 1958.

– 1970: *Die Prophezeiung des Nfrtj* (KÄT), Wiesbaden 1970.

Herrmann, Siegfried 1957: *Untersuchungen zur Überlieferungsgestalt mittelägyptischer Literaturwerke*, Berlin 1957.

Hornung, Erik 1966: *Geschichte als Fest.* Zwei Vorträge zum Geschichtsbild der frühen Menschheit, Darmstadt 1966.

– 1971: *Der Eine und die Vielen*, Darmstadt 1971.

– 1978: "Zeitliches Jenseits im alten Ägypten", in: *ErJb* 1978 (im Druck).

– 1979: *Das Totenbuch der Ägypter*, Zürich-München 1979.

Janssen, Jozef M. A. 1954: "Over Farao Bokchoris", in: *Varia Historica* (FS. A. W. Byvanck), Assen 1954, 17–29.

Johnson, Janet F. 1974: "The Demotic Chronicle as an Historical Source", in: *Enchoria* 4 (1974) 1 ff.

Junge, Friedrich 1973/74: Rez. Fecht 1972, in: *WO* 7 (1973/74) 267–273.

– 1977: "Die Welt der Klagen", in: *Fragen an die altägyptische Literatur* (Gedenkschrift E. Otto), Wiesbaden 1977, 275–284.

– 1978: "Wirklichkeit und Abbild", in: G. Wießner (Hrsg.), *Synkretismusforschung*, Theorie und Praxis (GOF), Wiesbaden 1978, 87–108.

Kadish, Gerald E. 1973: "British Museum Writing Board 5645: The Complaints of Kha-kheper-Re^c^-senebu", in: *JEA* 59 (1973) 77–90.

Kákosy, László 1964: "Ideas about the fallen state of the world in Egyptian Religion: Decline of the Golden Age", in: *AOH* 17 (1964) 205–216.

– 1963: "Schöpfung und Weltuntergang in der ägyptischen Religion", in: *AAH* XI.1–2 (1963) 17–30.

– 1966: "Prophecies of Ram-Gods", in: *AOH* XIX.3 (1966) 341–358.

– 1978: "Einige Probleme des ägyptischen Zeitbegriffs", in: *Oikumene* 2 (1978) 95–111.

Kitchen, Kenneth A. 1968: *Ramesside Inscriptions IV*, Oxford 1968.

Klasens, A. 1952: *A Magical Statue Base*, Leiden 1952.

Koenen, Ludwig 1957: *Eine ptolemäische Königsurkunde*, Diss. Köln 1957.

– 1968: "Die Prophezeiungen des Töpfers", in: *ZPE* 2 (1968) 178–209.

– 1970: "The Prophecies of a Potter: A Prophecy of World Renewal becomes an Apocalypse", in: *XIIth intern. Congr. of Papyrology*, Toronto 1970, 249–254.

– 1974: "Bemerkungen zum Text des Töpferorakels und zum Akaziensymbol", in: *ZPE* 13 (1974) 313–319.

Krall, Josef 1898: "Vom König Bokchoris", in: *FS. Büdinger*, Innsbruck 1898, 3–12.

Krause, Martin 1969: "Ägyptisches Gedankengut in der Apokalypse des Asclepius", in: *XVII. Deutscher Orientalistentag, ZDMG Suppl. I*, Wiesbaden 1969, 48–57.

Krause, Martin und Labib, Pahor 1971: *Gnostische und hermetische Schriften aus Nag Hammadi, Codex II und Codex VI* (ADAI.K 2), Glückstadt 1971.

Lanczkowski, Günter 1960a: *Altägyptischer Prophetismus* (ÄA 4), Wiesbaden 1960.

– 1960b: "Eschatology in Ancient Egyptian Religion", in: *Proc. IXth Intern. Congr. for the Hist. of Rel.*, Tokyo 1960, 129–134.

Lichtheim, Miriam 1973: *Ancient Egyptian Literature* I: The Old and Middle Kingdoms, Berkeley-Los Angeles-London 1973.

– 1976: *Id.*, II: The New Kingdom, 1976.

– 1980: *Id.*, III: The Late Period, 1980.

Lüddeckens, E. 1943: *Untersuchungen über religiösen Gehalt, Sprache und Form der ägyptischen Totenklagen* (MDAI.K 11), Berlin 1943.

Luft, Ulrich 1978: *Beiträge zur Historisierung der Götterwelt und der Mythenschreibung* (StAeg IV), Budapest 1978.

Luria, S. 1929: "Die Ersten werden die Letzten sein", in: *Klio* 22 (1929) 405–431.

Macadam, F. Laming 1949: *The Temples of Kawa I*, London 1949.

McCown, C. C. 1925: "Hebrew and Egyptian Apocalyptic Literature", in: *HThR* 18 (1925) 357–411.

Merkelbach, Reinhold 1963: *Isisfeste in griechisch-römischer Zeit*. Daten und Riten, Meisenheim 1963.

Meuli, Karl 1943: *Schweizermasken*, Zürich 1943.

Meyer, Eduard 1915: *Ägyptische Dokumente aus der Perserzeit* (SPAW), Berlin 1915.

Morenz, Siegfried 1960: *Ägyptische Religion* (RM 8), Stuttgart 1960.

Nock, A. D. und Festugière, A. J. 1960: *Corpus Hermeticum* II (Collection Budé), Paris ²1960.

Otto, Eberhard 1962: "Zwei Paralleltexte zu Totenbuch 175", in: *CEg* 37 (1962) 249–256.

– 1963: "Altägyptischer Polytheismus. Eine Beschreibung", in: *Saeculum* 14 (1963) 249–285.

– 1964: *Gott und Mensch nach den Tempelinschriften der griechisch-römischen Zeit* (AHAW), Heidelberg 1964.

– 1966a: *Osiris und Amun*. Kult und Heilige Stätten, München 1966.

– 1966b: "Geschichtsbild und Geschichtsschreibung in Ägypten", in: *WO* 3.3 (1966) 161 ff.

– 1969: "Das 'Goldene Zeitalter' in einem ägyptischen Text", in: *Religions en Egypte hellénistique et romaine* (BCESS), Paris 1969.

Posener, Georges 1956: *Littérature et politique dans l'Egypte de la XII.e dynastie*, Paris 1956.

– 1960: *De la divinité du pharaon* (CSA 15), Paris 1960.

Roberts, C. H. 1954: *The Oxyrhynchus Papyri XXII*, London 1954.

Sander-Hansen, C. E. 1956: *Die Texte der Metternich-Stele* (AAeg VII), Kopenhagen 1956.

Schenkel, Wolfgang 1975: "Repères chronologiques de l'histoire rédactionelle des Coffin Texts", in: W. Westendorf (Hrsg.), *Göttinger Totenbuchstudien*, Beiträge zum 17. Kap. (GOF.Ä IV.3), Wiesbaden 1975, 27–36.

Schmid, Hans Heinrich 1968: *Gerechtigkeit als Weltordnung*. Hintergrund und Geschichte des alttestamentlichen Gerechtigkeitsbegriffs (BHTh 40), Tübingen 1968.

Schott, Siegfried 1929: *Urkunden mythologischen Inhalts* (Urk. VI), Leipzig 1929.

– 1959: "Altägyptische Vorstellungen vom Weltende", in: *AnBib* 12 (1959) 319–330.

– 1964: *Der Denkstein Sethos' I. für die Kapelle Ramses' I. in Abydos* (NAWG), Göttingen 1964.

van Seters, John 1964: "A Date for the Admonitions in the Second Intermediate Period", in: *JEA* 50 (1964) 12–23.

Seibert, Peter 1967: *Die Charakteristik*. Eine ägyptische Sprechsitte und ihre Ausprägungen in Folklore und Literatur (ÄA 20), Wiesbaden 1967.

Spiegel, Joachim 1950: *Soziale und weltanschauliche Reformbewegungen im alten Ägypten*, Heidelberg 1950.

Spiegelberg, Wilhelm 1914: *Die sogenannte Demotische Chronik* (DemSt 7), Leipzig 1914.

Stricker, B. H. 1948: *Spreuken tot beveiling gedurende de schrikkeldagen naar Pap. (Leiden) I. 346* (OMRM 29), Leiden 1948.

Vandier, Jacques 1961: *Le papyrus Jumilhac*, Paris o.J. (1961).

Wessetzky, Vilmos 1942: "Zur Deutung des 'Orakels' in der sog. Demotischen Chronik", in: *WZKM* 49 (1942) 161–171.

Westendorf, Wolfhart 1955: "Der Rezitationsvermerk *ṭz pḥr*", in: O. Firchow (Hrsg.), *Ägyptol. Stud.* (FS. H. Grapow), Berlin 1955, 383–402.

Yoyotte, Jean 1969: "Bakhthis: Religion égyptienne et culture grèque à Edfou", in: *Religions en Egypte hellénistique et romaine* (BCESS), Paris 1969, 127–141.

Zandee, Jan 1971: "Le messie", in: *RHR* 180 (1971) 3–28.

Zauzich, Karl Theodor 1979: "Lamm des Bokchoris", in: W. Helck, W. Westendorf (Hrsg.), *LÄ* III.6, Wiesbaden 1979, 912f.

Akkadian Apocalypses*

Helmer Ringgren

0. Introduction

0.1. There is a certain genre in Akkadian literature which has variously been referred to as "prophecies" or "apocalypses". So far five texts of this genre have been discovered and published, while two others are somewhat different and may not belong to the genre proper. These texts appear as predictions referring to a sequence of kings, whose respective reigns are described in terms of the number of their regnal years and the "good" or "bad" conditions prevailing in the country in their time. The question is whether these texts are real predictions or should be regarded as *vaticinia ex eventu*. At present all probability seems to point to the latter alternative.

0.2. In the following we shall briefly sketch the contents of each of the texts before we discuss their purpose and their possible relevance for the study of apocalyptics.

1. The "Apocalyptic" Texts

We begin by discussing the main group of five texts of which the first three are written in the third person, while the remaining two are in the form of an address in the first person.

1.1. The first text is the one called Text A in the edition of Grayson and Lambert. It seems to have had a mythological introduction; at least Ishtar and Anu are mentioned in the first broken lines. The prophecy itself is built up as a prediction of kings and their regnal years ("A prince will arise and rule for x years"), followed by a description of their respective reigns. It is characteristic of this text that there is an alternation of "good" and "bad" times, as illustrated by the following extract.

A prince will arise and rule for eighteen years.
The land will rest secure, fare well,
(and its) people will enjoy prosperity.

---

* I have utilized the bibliography in the synopsis presented to the Colloquium by Professor Åke W. Sjöberg, Philadelphia, Penn.

The gods will ordain good things for the land,
favourable winds will blow.
The... and the furrow will yield abundant crops.
Sakkan (the god of beasts) and Nisaba (the god of grain) will... in the land.
There will be rain and floods.
The people will enjoy themselves.
But that prince will be put to the sword in a revolution.
A prince will arise and rule for thirteen years.
There will be an Elamite attack on Akkad
and the booty of Akkad will be carried off.
The shrines of the great gods will be destroyed.
Akkad will suffer a defeat.
There will be confusion, disturbance and disorder in the land.
The nobility will lose prestige.
Another man who is unknown will arise,
seize the throne as king and put his grandees to the sword...

The sequence of rulers and the possible historical allusions are shown in the following synopsis.

18 years	good	uprising
13 years	bad	rebellion of Elam, defeat in the gorges of Tupliash
"few days"		He will not be master of the land
3 years	bad	
Lacuna		
? years	good	
8 years	?	
Lacuna		
? years	?	
3 years	bad	hostilities against Akkad; Amorites will put them to the sword
8 years	bad	

As far as we can see, there is no regular alternation of good and bad rulers. This seems to indicate that the author is not following an artificial pattern, but is in some way or other dependent on an existing historical tradition, even if we are not able to identify the events alluded to.[1]

The end of the prophecy is lost so that it is impossible to ascertain the aim of the prophecy.

It might be expected that the sequence of regnal years and the allusions to historical events would make it possible to identify the kings, but so far no convincing result has been reached.

1.2. The second text is the so-called Uruk prophecy, published by Hunger and Kaufman. The preserved part of the text consists of two parts, one (r 3–10) describing a "bad" time, the other (r 11–19) a "good" time. "A

---

[1] See, however, Hallo 1966, 235 ff.

king will arise, but he will not provide justice in the land, he will not give the right decisions for the land". In addition, "he will remove the protective goddess (*lamassu*) of Uruk from Uruk and make her dwell in Babylon" and install the cult of another goddess in Uruk. After him there will be another bad king, about whom no details are given. Then follows a series of five signs of repetition, possibly indicating five more, or a great number of, bad kings, and finally a short reference to another bad king.

But "after him a king will arise in Uruk who will provide justice in the land and will give the right decisions for the land"; he will establish the cult of Anu in Uruk and bring back the protective goddess to the city and rebuild the temples, and there will be a good time. His son will "become master of the world" and "his dynasty will be established forever." So "the kings of Uruk will exercise rulership like the gods".

The text is obviously written from the perspective of Uruk. The problem again is the identification of the kings.[2] We know that Nebuchadnezzar II of Babylon boasts of having returned the *šēdu* of Uruk and the *lamassu* of Eanna to Uruk. It is very probable then that he is the good king referred to in the latter half of the text. As for the king who brought the *lamassu* to Babylon, Hunger and Kaufman opt for Eriba-Marduk. Even if we do not have any exact statement of his having carried off the goddess of Uruk, the general description of the text fits well with what we know about him. The problem is the intermediate period alluded to by the five signs of repetition. In any case it seems probable that the first part of the text is a *vaticinium ex eventu* and that the latter part of the text is meant to exalt Nebuchadnezzar II as the one who restored the cult of Uruk and to predict a glorious future for his dynasty.

1.3. The third text appears as a prophecy uttered by the god Marduk.[3] Text D of Grayson-Lambert forms part of this text.

Here Marduk addresses the great gods and proclaims his intention to reveal his "secrets". After a self-introduction, "I Marduk, the great Lord", etc., he tells his audience that he decided to go to the land of the Hittites and that he stayed there for 24 years. "Who has ever made such a journey?" Then he goes on to report that he went to Elam with all the gods – with dire consequences for his country. No sacrifices were performed, there was chaos in the country, corpses were lying everywhere, brothers and friends fought each other, the rich oppressed the poor.

But when he had completed his years, he desired to go back to Babylon. Here the text changes into the future tense. "A king of Babylon will arise", he will renew the temple, proclaim tax-exemption in Babylon and reinstall Marduk in his dignity. He will renew the processional ship, reassemble the

---

[2] Hunger-Kaufman 1975, 373f.   [3] Borger 1971, 16f.

scattered and make the temples splendid. "He will feed the land the yield of his vegetation." The rivers will yield fish, the fields will be rich in crops, the grass will be abundant, everything will come in order, brothers will have compassion with each other, sons will honour their fathers, and the prince will rule all the lands. For "I, O gods, have a covenant with him". The last part of the text contains a list of sacrifices.

Borger, who published this text, opts for Nebuchadnezzar I (1127–1105) as the king who brought back the statue of Marduk from Elam. It is obviously this event that the text has in view. It is interesting that Marduk tells of his dwelling among the Hittites and in Elam as a deliberate act, while in reality the statue was carried away by force. In any case, the events of the first part are told as a background for the prediction. This text differs from the others in that the first events are not foretold but reported as historical facts.

1.4. The forth text is the Shulgi prophetic speech,[4] part of which is found as Text C in the edition of Grayson-Lambert. It appears as a prediction revealed to the Sumerian king Shulgi by Shamash and Ishtar. First he states in general terms that the countries have been given to the king of Babylon and Nippur and that Elam will be in confusion. Then he reports, much in the style of the royal inscriptions, his deeds and his relationship to Enlil and Ninlil. In the fragmentary columns that follow there is a survey of Babylonian history in the guise of a prophecy. Then we are told that the king of Babylon will have to give his property to Assyria, obviously a reference to Kastiliaš IV who was defeated by Tukulti-Ninurta I (1237–1219). Then there is again a "bad" time, Nippur will be destroyed, a (foreign) prince will triumph, and a king of Babylon will be overthrown. The reference is probably to Kidin-Ḫutrutaš of Elam who destroyed Nippur and overthrew Enlil-nadinšum of Babylon.

Here the *vaticinium ex eventu* ends. The rest is a prophecy of restoration. Though the text is broken it is clear that Bad-tibira, Girshu and Lagash will be rebuilt. Borger concludes that the text aims at one of the late Kassite rulers in the first half of the 12th century, which would mean that this text is somewhat older than the Marduk prophecy.

1.5. Finally, there is the Dynastic prophecy published by Grayson.[5] It seems to have had a brief introductory section which is unfortunately almost totally lost. Of the next section (I 7–25) only the ends of the lines are preserved, but from what is legible it emerges that there is a description of the fall of Assyria and the establishment of the Chaldaean dynasty. The last line contains the formula "For x years he will rule"; the number of the years has been lost.

---

[4] *Ibid.*, 20f.   [5] Grayson 1975, 24ff.

After a lacuna there are broken references to Neriglissar and Labashi-Marduk, followed by a section on Nabonidus.

> A rebel prince will arise...
> The dynasty of Harran [he will establish]
> For seventeen years [he will rule]
> He will oppress the land and the festival of Esagil [he will cancel]
> A fortress in Babylon [he will build]
> He will plot evil against Akkad.

After this a king of Elam is predicted who will remove Nabonidus from his throne and settle him in another land – this is obviously Cyrus. After another lacuna there is a reference to an attack of the army of the Hanaeans, *i.e.* Alexander the Great. "They will plunder and rob him. Afterwards he (the king of Persia) will refit his army and raise his weapon", and aided by the gods of Babylon he will defeat the Hanaeans. This is a problematic statement that runs counter to historical facts, and were it not for the fact that the last fragmentary columns seem to contain allusions to further rulers, *i.e.* the Seleucids, one might suspect that the prophecy was pronounced while there was still hope of defeating Alexander. It seems more probable, however, that the prophecy has ended on a negative note and was composed as criticism of the Seleucids. It ends with a statement that this is secret knowledge that must not be told to the uninitiated.

1.6. From a formal point of view Text A, the Dynastic prophecy and the Uruk prophecy form one group written in the third person, while the Marduk and Shulgi texts are composed in the form of an address in the first person. "Despite this difference the five texts are closely related in form, style and rationale."[6]

2. Other Texts

To this group are often added two more "prophecies" of a somewhat different character, namely Text B of Grayson-Lambert and the very fragmentary text published by Biggs,[7] here referred to as Biggs II.

2.1. Text B, which was re-edited with some additional material by Biggs, differs from the main group through its obvious connections with astrology. "It begins with what seems to be a somewhat mythological report of celestial phenomena and the action taken by the gods Anu-rabu and Enlil in relation to them, reported in the preterite tense, just as the protases of omens are. The rest of the main text consists only of line after line of predictions (*i.e.* omen apodoses)... The predictions include many standard omen apodoses but... there are some unique features. The most interesting of these is a description of a *mīšaru*-act, which is obviously a general alleviation of all sorts of troubles, when the displaced or homeless

---

[6] *Ibid.*, 15.   [7] See below §2.2.

will be gathered back, the poor will become rich... the possessions of the
lowly will be safe",[8] officials will be returned to office, and betrayers will
be executed.

   Some of the predictions do not have precise verbal parallels in the omen
literature, but they are still "completely in the usual omen style". Biggs
concludes that the text "seems to be a collection of omen apodoses gathered
from various sources, just as the standard omen collections probably are".[9]

The king will cause his land to complain, the king of Akkad will not achieve his goal, the king
   of Babylon [will be killed]
The entire land will rebel against the prince who will sit on the throne and he will not conquer
   his enemies, an enemy
will murder the king and his counsellors in the palace. City will turn against city, family will
   turn against family, brother will slay brother, friend will slay friend...

   The temples will be destroyed, citizens of Nippur killed. The gods
consult and restore the king's rule, booty is carried off from Iamut-bal. A
prince who is not considered an heir to the throne seizes the throne and
controls the temples. Then there will be plague and famine, followed by
good times for seven years. Then there is an abrupt reference to the end of
the reign and the death of the king and his family. "The counsel of the land
will change, the entire country will take up arms, and one throne will
overthrow another. Either the great gods will consult one another and the
rule of the king will be short... or there will be an Amorite attack against
the land and there will be destruction of the sanctuaries." Eshnunna will be
reinhabited and Elam will be destroyed. There is no indication of regnal
years, nor any clear allusion to the alternation of "good" and "bad" times.
Allusions to historical events are vague and no identification is possible.
The fact that two alternatives are offered, "Either the gods will consult...
or there will be an Amorite attack", seems to speak against the *vaticinium ex
eventu* interpretation. The description of social disorder seems to be a
standard motif ("brother will slay brother, friend will slay friend"),
similarly, the gathering of the dispersed. The lack of a sequence of rulers
and of identifiable events makes it difficult to date the text, and if it is not a
vaticinium ex eventu the identification of events is not even to be expected.
Biggs suggests the possibility of an Old Babylonian date for the composition.[10]

   2.2. Another very fragmentary text, also published by Biggs (Biggs II)[11]
is similar in so far as it contains astrological elements and has the traditional
omen form with protasis and apodosis. It contains references to the
number of regnal years in three cases.

   The structure of the text will be seen from the following quotation.

---

[8] Biggs 1967, 118.   [9] *Ibid.*   [10] *Ibid.*, 126.   [11] *Ibid.*, 130ff.

[If...] he will die from the sting of a scorpion.
... the ruler will exercise rule for 27 years.
... the elders of the ruler's land will give bad advice and the ruler will bring harm upon his land...
They will kill that ruler in his own town...

It is obvious that much of the phraseology in these two texts is related to that of the omen texts on one hand and to the prophecy texts on the other. From the point of view of style they form a sort of transition from omen text to prophecy. However, it can hardly be proved that this reflects the actual development of the prophecy genre out of omen texts. But the possibility of such a development cannot be ruled out.

3. Function of the Texts

In view of the damaged condition of the texts it is difficult to pass a general judgment on their intention and function. Their form seems to be derived from the omen literature, which is especially visible from the two texts published by Biggs, which we have characterized as a kind of intermediate stage. This makes it hardly probable that they have been intended for public use; rather, they are written with a view to those specialists who generally dealt with *omina*.

3.1. The Uruk prophecy clearly ends with a time of restoration after a period of chaos. Höffken even regards it as an exemple of "Heils-zeitherrschererwartung".[12] The Marduk prophecy also looks forward to a time of restoration, and this seems to be true of the Shulgi prophecy as well. Text A is too broken to warrant a final judgment, while the Dynastic prophecy rather seems to end in a criticism of the Seleucid dynasty – or does it imply an expected restoration after its fall? From this we may venture the tentative conclusion that texts of this genre were published by circles of omen priests who wanted to support a new ruler whom they expected to restore orderly conditions after a period of time which they regarded as an example of bad rule. One presupposition for this is obviously the prevailing royal ideology, according to which the ruler was responsible for almost everything in the country.

3.2. Borger points to the Egyptian prophecy of Neferti[13] – with which Assmann dealt in another paper in this collection[14] – as a parallel, since it was also written as propaganda for a new ruler, emphasizing the chaotic conditions of the previous period. It is interesting to notice that the style of the Neferti text is entirely different from the Akkadian prophecies. This goes to show that similar situations in different countries produced "prophecies" similar in content but different in style, since they adhered to the literary patterns offered by each civilization.

---

[12] Höffken 1977, 57.   [13] Borger 1971, 23.   [14] Assmann §2.1.

3.3. If the interpretation of the Aramaic text about Balaam from Deir 'Allā suggested by Caquot-Lemaire[15] and myself[16] is correct, this text would offer another parallel. Here Balaam receives a vision in which obviously chaotic conditions are described, followed by a prediction of the birth of a "shoot" (*nqr* = Hebr. *neṣær*, Isa 11, 1) and the restoration of happy times. Again, we are tempted to assume that the description of the "bad" time is a *vaticinium ex eventu* and the restoration oracle is intended to support the claims of a new ruler, or the expectations placed on him by certain circles.

4. Conclusion

However, this is not apocalypticism – or should we say, is not yet apocalypticism? The latter expression would imply that we have here a preliminary stage of later apocalypticism proper. From what has been said above it would seem more probable that we have rather to do with parallel phenomena, examples of similar reactions to similar conditions couched in the language and style of the respective milieu.

Thus these texts provide us with valuable comparative material but not necessarily with an earlier stage of what is known as Judaeo-Christian apocalyptics. Our texts provide some of the stones out of which the structure of apocalypticism is built up, and the same can be said of the Iranian and Hellenistic texts examined in this colloquium, but it is only when all the elements come together that the final structure can be called apocalypticism.

Bibliography

Biggs, R. D. 1967: "More Babylonian 'Prophecies'", in: *Iraq* 29 (1967) 117–132.
Borger, R. 1971: "Gott Marduk und Gott-König Šulgi als Propheten. Zwei prophetische Texte", in: *BiOr* 28 (1971) 3–21.
Caquot, A. – Lemaire, A. 1977: "Les textes araméens de Deir 'Alla", in: *Syria* 54 (1977) 189–208.
Grayson, A. K. 1975: *Babylonian Historical-Literary Texts*, Toronto-Buffalo 1975.
Grayson, A. K. – Lambert, W. G. 1964: "Akkadian Prophecies", in: *JCS* 18 (1964) 7–30.
Hallo, W. W. 1966: "Accadian Apocalypses", in: *IEJ* 16 (1966) 231–242.
Heintz, J.-G. 1977: "Note sur les origines de l'apocalyptique judaïque à la lumière des 'prophéties akkadiennes'", in: Philonenko, M. – Simon, M. (eds.): *L'Apocalyptique* (EHiRel 3), Paris 1977, 71–87.
Höffken, P. 1977: "Heilszeitherrschererwartung im babylonischen Raum", in: *WO* 9 (1977) 51–71.
Hunger, H. – Kaufman, S. A. 1975: "A New Akkadian Prophecy Text", in: *JAOS* 95 (1975) 371–375.
Lambert, W. G. 1978: *The Background of Jewish Apocalyptic*. The Ethel M. Wood Lecture delivered before the University of London on 22 February 1977, London 1978.
Ringgren, H. 1977: "Bileam och inskriften från Deir Alla", in: *RoB* 36 (1977) 85–89.
Smith, J. Z. 1975: "Wisdom and Apocalyptic", in: Pearson, B. A. (ed.): *Religious Syncretism in Antiquity*. Essays in conversation with Geo Widengren, Missoula/Montana 1975, 131–156.

---

[15] Caquot-Lemaire 1977, 189 ff.   [16] Ringgren 1977, 88.

Forms and Origins of Iranian Apocalypticism

Anders Hultgård

1. Introduction

1.1. The present study claims to be no more than a preliminary attempt to deal with the forms and the presentation of Iranian apocalypticism and to draw attention to some areas, connected with its origin, where further research should be pursued. Since there may be differences of opinion as to what should be meant by Iranian apocalyptic, it would be fitting to touch briefly upon the question of definition.[1] In this study, I use apocalyptic in its traditional meaning of eschatological teachings which are set in the framework of a cosmic history divided into periods. However, I have also included other non-eschatological materials in so far as they are explicitly found within the apocalyptic scheme. Thus, Iranian apocalypticism concentrates upon the end of the millenium of Zoroaster, on the coming saviours Uxšyatarta and Uxšyatnamah and the signs of their respective periods, and on the final redemption through Ahura Mazda and the last saviour, the Saošyant or Astvatarta.

1.2. Some traditions in the extant Avesta could possibly be termed "apocalyptic", *i.e.* the triple division of world history alluded to in the Avesta, which may be expressed in different ways. It is expressed in one way by the concept of a period of spiritual existence, spoken of as "that which was first" (*paoirya-*, in Avestan). This period is followed by the present, physical existence, also called "the second existence" (Yasna 45:1) and then by the final one with the elimination of the Evil and with the renovation, termed "the last", *apəməm*.[2] In another way it is expressed in the scheme Gaya – Gaya marətan – Astvatarta.[3] The explicit apocalyptic traditions are, however, found only in the Middle Iranian or Pahlavi texts,[4]

---

[1] The general definition of apocalypticism given by Widengren 1969, 440 and 456 includes also the creation and the subsequent course of world history, as far as they are seen in the light of the cosmic scheme. Cf. also S. Hartman in the present volume (§ 1.2.).

[2] For this concept, see Lommel 1930, 144–147.

[3] This concept has been elaborated by S. Hartman 1976 and in his contribution to this volume.

[4] One exception would be Yašt 19:92–96, which describes the appearance of Astvatarta and

and they must therefore be our starting point. These texts present many problems concerning the interpretation, the composition and the age of the materials which they transmit. The main part of the Pahlavi texts seems to have been redacted in the 9th century A.D. For our purpose it is important to notice that most of the Pahlavi books which contain apocalyptic material are compilations of a secondary character. Furthermore, no independent apocalyptic writing like the Book of Revelation in the New Testament and the Jewish apocalypses of Ezra and Baruch survives in the Iranian tradition.

1.2.1. The Bahman Yašt, which is generally held to be an apocalypse, would more accurately be described as a secondary compilation of apocalyptic materials of a diverse origin.[5] Bahman Yašt is the traditional name, but it would be more correct to call it "Zand i Vahuman Yasn". It must be pointed out, however, that the Pahlavi manuscripts transmit this compilation without title, beginning with the usual doxology: *šnāyišn ī dātār Ōhrmazd....* The title "Zand i Vahuman Yasn" is taken by modern commentators from the first words of chap. II and III (I,6 and II): *pat zand ī Vahuman yasn,* "according to the zand of the Vohu Manah yasna".

1.2.2. The text which is termed Jāmāsp Nāmak consists only of some fragments of a more extensive Pahlavi writing.[6] These fragments contain chiefly apocalyptic traditions, but other quite different materials are also found.[7] It is therefore questionable whether the Pahlavi fragments constitute parts of an independent apocalypse. Most of them probably belong to the writing called Ayātkār ī Jāmāspīk,[8] which corresponds in genre more to Bundahišn than to Bahman Yašt. The common setting, *i.e.* questions

---

the renovation of the material world (for the details, cf. Widengren in this vol. §2.2.1.). This passage is, however, not transmitted in the framework of a cosmic history divided into periods.

[5] In the present study I follow the division in chapters and verses found in the edition of Anklesaria 1957. The division of West 1880 is however given in parentheses. For a discussion of the composite nature of Bahman Yašt, see West 1880, l–lvi, Tavadia 1956, 121–124 and Widengren 1961, 181–183; 197–198.

[6] The Pahlavi fragments have been edited by Modi 1903 and West 1904. Transcription and translation are found in Benveniste 1932 and Bailey 1930–32 and Messina 1939. For literary questions and relationship to other texts, see Benveniste 1932, 337–340; Messina 1939, 9–17 and Tavadia 1956, 124–125.

[7] The fragment in ms MU$_4$ also contains exhortations to perform good deeds. The Pahlavi text of ms DP presents three passages with non-apocalyptic materials: (1) Concerning the people in the lakes and the seas; (2) Concerning the question why Ahura Mazda created mankind when he foresaw the evil; (3) Concerning the Mazandarans and the Turks.

[8] This writing has been restored by Messina 1939 from Pahlavi fragments, Pārsi, Pāzand and New Persian versions. Messina 1939, 5 considers it to be a more exact name of the materials termed Jāmāsp Nāmak, whereas Tavadia 1956, 125 regards Ayātkār ī Jāmāspīk as a secondary development of the Jāmāsp Nāmak. On the basis of the manuscript material it is not possible to distinguish between an earlier Jāmāsp Nāmak and the Ayātkār ī Jāmāspīk (as reconstructed by Messina). A literary analysis may perhaps show such a distinction, but this analysis remains to be done.

posed by King Vištāspa and answers given by the wise Jāmāspa (see further §2.1.3.) is distinctive to the materials labelled Jāmāsp Nāmak and Ayātkār ī Jāmāspīk.

1.2.3. Besides Bahman Yašt, the apocalyptic teachings are found within the framework of compositions which as a whole cannot be qualified as apocalyptic writings. In the first place mention should be made of Dēnkart, Bundahišn, the Selections of Zātspram, Ayātkār ī Jāmāspīk and Pahlavi Rivāyat, but other writings such as Dātestān ī Dēnīk, Mēnōi ī Xrat and Pand Nāmak ī Zartušt contain also some apocalyptic traditions.

2. The Setting of the Apocalyptic Materials

2.1. Let us first briefly examine the settings in which the apocalyptic traditions of all these texts are transmitted. The apocalyptic material is usually presented in the same way as the other materials contained in each writing in question. We find, consequentely, different settings according to the general structure of the entire composition.

2.1.1. Bundahišn and Zātspram, for instance, which have a similar general structure, present their materials in sections preceded by a heading which is constructed in the same way throughout the book, *i.e.* by the word *apar*, "concerning", followed by one or two key-terms indicating the chief content of the chapter. Thus, Bundahišn[9] presents the apocalyptic teaching in two sections introduced by the following headings: "Concerning the disasters of each millenium which happened to the land of Iran", *apar vizend ī hazārak hazārak ī ō ērān šahr mat* (XXXIII,1), and "concerning the resurrection and the final body", *apar ristāxēz [ut] tan ī pasēn* (XXXIV,1). Zātspram has no section corresponding to the first one in Bundahišn (XXXIII). The material of chapter XXXIV in Bundahišn is given with a different heading in Zātspram: "Concerning the performance of the renovation", *apar fraškart kartārīh*.

2.1.2. Another type of setting for the apocalyptic traditions is that of "questions and answers" (*pursišn-passaxv*) which is also modelled on the general pattern of the literary work. Thus, the section on the resurrection and the apocalyptic time-table (XXXVII,1–11) in the Dātestān ī Dēnīk begins in the following way: "The thirty-sixth question is that which you ask: 'how will they perform the resurrection...'? The answer is this: ...",

---

[9] The Bundahišn has been transmitted in two versions, a longer one (the "Iranian") represented by the manuscripts DH, TD$_1$ and TD$_2$, and a shorter one (the "Indian") found in the manuscripts M 51b, K 20 and K 20b. The short version lacks chapter XXXIII and the heading of chapter XXXIV has a slightly different wording: *apar čigōnīh ristāxēz ut tan pasēn*. Zātspram chapter XXXV which treats particular aspects of the renovation (*fraškart*) has no equivalent in Bundahišn.

36-om pursišn hān ī pursīt kū ristāxēz čigōn kunēnd ...? Passaxv ē kū ....
Similarly, in the Mēnōi ī Xrat, the opening phrase of each section runs:
"The sage asked the spirit of wisdom the following:", *pursīt dānāk ō mēnōi ī
xrat kū*. Then come the questions functioning as headings of the content of
the section concerned, and the formula "the spirit of wisdom answered
this:", *mēnōi ī xrat passaxv kart kū*, introduces the text properly speaking.
Apocalyptic statements concerning the nine thousand years of the world
and the defeat of Angra Mainyu at the end of this period are found with this
framework in chapters 8 and 28 of the Mēnōi ī Xrat.

2.1.3. As pointed out above, the apocalyptic materials of Ayātkār ī
Jāmāspīk are also transmitted in a setting which belongs to the general
pattern of "questions and answers". Each section opens with a question by
Vištāspa, followed by a more or less extensive answer given by Jāmāspa,
the man next to the king (*bītaxš*). Thus, the apocalyptic chapters XVI and
XVII present the following setting: "King Vištāspa asked: (*pursīt Vištāsp šāh
kū*)... The viceroy Jāmāspa replied: (*guft-aš Jāmāsp ī bītaxš kū*)"....

2.1.4. Dēnkart book VII contains a considerable collection of apocalyptic
traditions. This part of Dēnkart is introduced by the following words:
"The seventh (book); concerning the wonders of the greatest messenger of
the Mazda-religion, Zoroaster the Spitama-son", *Haftom, apar avdīh ī dēn
mazdēst mahist aštak Spitāmān Zartušt*. As the title implies, the book concentrates on Zoroaster, but it is set in a framework of a universal history of the
Mazda-religion. The content is divided into sections (chapters), each one
introduced by the word: "Concerning the miracles..." (*apar avdīh*) followed by an indication of the particular period with which the respective
sections are concerned. The apocalyptic material properly speaking is to be
found in sections 8–11, but already in section 7 we meet with two short
apocalyptic pieces. Their independance is indicated by the headings: "concerning the coming of the destroyers of the realm of the land of Iran"
(7:29–32) and "concerning the breaking down of the Iranian realm"
(7:33–37).

2.1.5. The Pahlavi Rivāyat is a collection of materials which embrace the
whole field of religion. The passages that enter upon a new subject are not
marked by any heading but open either with a short formula variously
worded or with the text itself. The latter is the case with the main
apocalyptic passage (XLVIII) which begins: "After Zoroaster had come to
the consultation with Ahura Mazda...",[10] *pas hač hān ī ka Zartušt bē ō
hampursakīh ī Ōhrmazd mat ....* The most frequent short opening formulas
in the Pahlavi Rivāyat are:

---

[10] Short apocalyptic traditions are also found in chapters XLV, XLIX and LIV.

(a) *ēn-ič paytāk kū* "this also is revealed:"
(b) *dar ī ēn kū* "this subject:"
(c) *ē kū* "this:"

2.1.6. In the Pand Nāmak ī Zartušt[11] we have an example of a Zoroastrian edification literature *(handarz)*. The essential points of the faith are summarized and interwoven with parenetical exhortations like the following: "Of this much you must be fully convinced:", *pat ēn and apēgumān būtan kū*. This sort of exhortation introduces the material where apocalyptic traditions are alluded to.[12]

2.2. The survey of the diverse settings in which the apocalyptic material has been handed down in the Pahlavi writings shows that the setting varies according to the general pattern of the literary work concerned. We have to do with a secondary framework. The independent collections or fragments, the Bahman Yašt and possibly the Jāmāsp Nāmak, are likewise of a secondary nature.

3. The Origin of the Apocalyptic Pahlavi Traditions

The way in which the contents of this framework and of these independent texts are presented makes it clear that we are dealing with summaries, selections or compilations of earlier traditions which have, however, been reworked to fit the time of the post-Sasanian redactors.

3.1. This is seen, firstly, by the explicit reference to an authoritative bulk of traditions, mostly called *dēn* "religion", but the terms *ākāhīh* "knowledge" and *apastāk* "sacred scripture" are also encountered.[13] I give here some examples of the wording of these references taken from the apocalyptic passages of the Pahlavi literature:[14]

pat dēn gōvēt kū "one says[15] in the Religion that"

Bund. XXXIV,1

---

[11] The division of the text into paragraphs follows the edition of Kanga 1960.

[12] The last section of Pand Nāmak ī Zartušt, §54 contains apocalyptic references, but this section seems to be a later addition cf. also Nyberg 1964, XVIIf.

[13] The fact that a bulk of normative traditions underlies the religious Pahlavi writings is rightly emphasized by Widengren 1955, 67 and by Tavadia 1956, 34. Molé 1967, 4 points to the importance of the scriptural basis in Dēnkart book VII as well as in other Pahlavi writings. Widengren 1967, 278–280 has elaborated criteria for discerning Avestan material in the Pahlavi texts. Cf. also note 17 and 26.

[14] A survey of the most current reference-formulas is given by Widengren 1967, 279–280, cf. also Widengren in this vol. §§4.1.1. and 4.1.2. Nyberg 1974, 85 treats the formulas with *guftan*. He distinguishes between "authoritative religious sayings" in which the word *dēn* "religion" occurs and "traditional, extracanonical sayings" which are regularly introduced by the formula *guft ēstēt* "it has been said".

[15] One could also translate: "he (sc. Ahura Mazda) says". This possibility was brought to my attention during the discussion by Prof. S. Hartman.

andar dēn ōgōn nimūt ēstēt kū "it has thus been shown in the Religion that"

Zātsp. XXXIV,1

hač ākāhīh ī im zamānak "according to the Knowledge concerning this period"

Dēnk. VIII,9:1

pat apastāk ōšmurt ēstēt "in the Sacred Scripture it has been mentioned"

Dēnk. VII,8:10

It may be assumed that the abbreviated formulas like *čigōn gōvēt kū* "as one says that" and *paytāk kū* "it is revealed that" also refer to the above mentioned bulk of traditions. No doubt, the corpus of Avestan traditions, collected and authorized in the Sasanian period, is meant by the reference to *dēn, ākāhīh* and *apastāk*. However, the post-Sasanian redactors based the compilations not upon the original Avesta itself but upon its Pahlavi version. This is apparent from some references to different parts of the Avestan collection where the term *zand* is used. For instance, chapter III (II) in the Bahman Yašt is introduced by the words: "according to the zand of Vohu Manah yasna it is revealed that". The genuine title of Bundahišn, which is *zand ākahıh*, also betrays that this compilation has been made from the Pahlavi version.

3.2. Secondly, the basic agreement between the various descriptions of the apocalyptic events in the Pahlavi texts indicates that one draws on a common normative tradition. This fact makes it probable that passages which lack explicit references to tradition are nevertheless based on Avestan texts.[16]

3.3. Thirdly, the linguistic character of many Middle Iranian apocalyptic texts shows their Avestan background.[17] An important criterion is the position of the verb in the sentence. The Avestan language usually puts the verb first. This order is taken over in "translation Pahlavi", whereas in idiomatic Pahlavi the verb generally comes after its subject. Other features which reveal the Avestan base of a Pahlavi text are the peculiar relative constructions and the specific vocabulary proper to "translation Pahlavi".

4. The Forms of the Apocalyptic Traditions

4.1. We must now try to analyse the authorative apocalyptic material in order to find the *forms* in which it was handed down before it was compiled and summarized – or reworked – by the post-Sasanian redactors.

---

[16] Such a passage would be Pahlavi Rivāyat XLVIII.

[17] West 1880, 195 suggests in a short note that some passages in the Bahman Yašt which show a peculiar verbal order are "due probably to the text being originally translated from an Avesta book now lost, or, at any rate, to its author's wish that it might appear to be so translated". Molé 1967 points repeatedly to the characteristic syntax and vocabulary of the "quotation" – passages, which betray their Avestan background. Linguistic and stylistic criteria for discovering Avesta translations are given by Widengren 1967, 280–287 and in this vol. §4.1.3.

4.1.1. A common way of presenting the material is the plain narrative which mostly appears like a dogmatic statement of facts. We find no allusions to earlier forms of apocalypticism. This type of presentation seems to be the result of a free summarizing or reworking of the basic material. Usually such passages are not preceded by references to the normative tradition.[18] Good examples of this narrative, dogmatic "statement"-type are found in Bundahišn XXXIII esp. vv. 1–22, Pahlavi Rivāyat XLVIII and Pand Nāmak ī Zartušt.[19]

4.1.2. Another type in which apocalyptic traditions are recorded in the Pahlavi texts is the *zand*, that is the Pahlavi-translation of Avestan texts with additional explanations given by the translators or the commentators.[20] These explanations are often introduced by special particles, *kū* or *hat*. The passages in which this *zand*-type occurs are regularly preceded by a reference to the authoritative religious tradition, or they are found within a framework that reflects Avestan models. Clear examples of the *zand*-type are Bahman Yašt VI,2–13 and VII,2–14 (III,2–11 and III,12–22) and Dēnkart VII,8:11–19.

4.1.3. In some passages referred to as taken from the normative tradition, we are confronted with material which seems to be neither a typical *zand* nor a narrative-dogmatic summary. Here we may be dealing with direct quotations from the Avesta in its Pahlavi version. Dēnkart VII,11:3 is thus a direct translation of Yašt 19:92–93.[21] Other quotations from lost Avestan passages may be found in Bahman Yašt (*e.g.* IV,1–8 [II,23–27]), and Dēnkart VII (*e.g.* 8:51–54).

4.2. It is in the two latter types of presenting the apocalyptic material, the *zand* and the quotation-passages, that allusions to original forms of the Iranian apocalypticism are likely to appear. The *zand*-passages, however, have often been disengaged from their original context. The same is true of the quotations which seem to be rather short. But clear indications of earlier apocalyptic forms survive.

4.2.1. Some passages, preceded by a reference to the Avesta, begin with a question by Zoroaster addressed to Ahura Mazda who then gives the answer. This pattern may be repeated several times. Although the answers given by Ahura Mazda are generally longer than the questions put forward by the prophet, there is a clear tendency to amplify the passages where

---

[18] Bundahišn XXXIII, 23 has a scriptural reference, *pat dēn gōvēt kū*, but the text continues in the same dogmatic "statement"-style as in vv. 1–22. Moreover, it is not always clear where a presumable quotation ends.

[19] Dēnkart VII, 8:2–10, 9:2–6 and 10:2–3 belong to the same category.

[20] This meaning of *zand* is used in the present study. For a discussion of *zand* and its meanings, see Wikander 1946, 140–141, Tavadia 1956, 24–27, Widengren 1965, 246–259 and Widengren in this vol. §§3.2.1. and 3.4.1.

[21] See Molé 1967, 231.

Ahura Mazda speaks. To give an idea of this form, I reproduce the pattern as it is found in Zātspram XXXIV, 1–20, one of the instances where the form appears to be most complete:

reference to the Avesta:
"It has thus been shown in the Religion that ..."   v. 1

1st question of Zoroaster:
"Zoroaster asked of Ahura Mazda (saying) ..."   v. 1

the prophet asks whether bodily creatures will receive their
bodies back at the *fraškart* (the renovation).

1st answer of Ahura Mazda:
"Ahura Mazda said:"   v. 2

Ahura Mazda replies that they shall receive their bodies back.

2nd question of Zoroaster:
"and Zoroaster asked: ..."   v. 3

the prophet wonders how those who have been torn apart by wild animals
and birds can be healed again.

2nd answer of Ahura Mazda:
"Ahura Mazda said: ..."   v. 4

Ahura Mazda replies with a question to Zoroaster expressed in a
parable about making a wooden casket.

3rd reply of Zoroaster:
"Zoroaster said: ..."   v. 5

the prophet replies as to what should be expected by the point of
the parable.

3rd and final reply of Ahura Mazda:
"Ahura Mazda said: ..."   vv. 6–20

Ahura Mazda answers extensively how he will bring about the resurrection.

4.2.1.1. This pattern of questions and answers, as it appears in Zātspram XXXIV is seldom strictly completed in the Pahlavi texts. In the following apocalyptic passages, however, we find it also clearly preserved: Dēnkart VII,8:23–31, 38–39, 40–43, 51–59 and Bundahišn XXXIV,4–5. In the Bahman Yašt, there is only one introductory question by Zoroaster followed by successive answers of Ahura Mazda in the sections where the pattern has been used: IV,1–66, V,1–10, VI,1–13 and VII,1–39 (II,23–54, II,57–63, III,1–11 and III,12–37). Many passages reveal the original form through allusions and through the circumstance that only part of it has remained. When one suddenly finds in the text that the prophet is addressed with words like "O Zoroaster the Spitama-son" or "O righteous Spitama-son", it may be assumed that Ahura Mazda speaks and that this part of the text draws on an earlier apocalyptic form.[22] Sometimes only the sayings of Ahura Mazda have been retained by the post-Sasanian compilators.[23] Although it clearly appears that Zoroaster is the one who receives the revelations of Ahura Mazda, the questions of the prophet have been suppressed.

4.2.1.2. The presumable origin of this apocalyptic form is the particular encounters of Zoroaster with Ahura Mazda, called *hampursakīh*, during which he received the divine revelations, the *dēn*. *Hampursakīh* may be translated with "consultation, conference" and is also used to denote the encounters of the coming saviours with Ahura Mazda. Whereas Zoroaster has several *hampursakīh*, the saviours have only one.[24] The character of this form, a kind of dialogue between the prophet and God, corresponds also to the literal meaning of *hampursakīh* = *ham* "together" and *pursakīh* from *pursītan* "ask". There is a firm tradition in the Pahlavi texts that Zoroaster had eight encounters (*hampursakīh*) with Ahura Mazda during a period of ten years beginning from the time when the prophet reached the age of thirty years.[25] Although the Middle-Iranian texts refer allusively to the coming of Zoroaster to the *hampursakīh*, there is no clear description of its details. Dēnkart VII,3:51–62 and Zātspram XXI relate the prelude, as it were, to the first *hampursakīh*. They obviously draw upon a common source which they, however, reproduce differently in detail. It is very probable that this source was an authoritative Avestan text.[26]

---

[22] See Bahman Yašt IX, 8 (III, 50), Dēnkart VII, 8:22,45–48 and 9:6. The unexpected introduction of Ahura Mazda speaking in the 1st person is another inconsistency found in some passages, *e.g.* Bahman Yašt IX, 1 (III, 44).

[23] See Dēnkart VII, 8:33–37 and 10:11, Bahman Yašt VIII, 8 (III, 43).

[24] For the encounter of Uxšyatarta and Uxšyatnəmah with Ahura Mazda, see Bahman Yašt IX, 1 (III, 44), Pahlavi Rivāyat XLVIII, 1,22 and 37.

[25] For the *hampursakīh* of Zoroaster, see Dēnkart VII, 3:46,51 and 60, 4:2 and 65, VIII, 13:16 and 14:3, Pahlavi Rivāyat XLVII, 1–5 and Bahman Yašt III, 23 (II, 16).

[26] The Avestan background of Dēnkart VII, 3:60–61 was pointed out by Salemann 1908, 130–131, who reconstructed the Avestan original text, and by Widengren 1955, 67. Cf. also Molé 1967, 40 and Widengren 1945, 60–61. Zātspram as a whole is most probably compiled from earlier, Avestan sources, chiefly Spend Nask and Čihrdāt Nask. Zātspram I, 1 opens with the following statement: *hat pat dēn ōgōn paytāk kū* "now, it is thus revealed in the religion:", a statement which may be interpreted as a reference not only to the content of the first chapter but also to that of the entire compilation. Throughout the book we meet with the phrases *ōgōn paytāk kū* or *ēn-ič paytāk kū* alluding to the scriptural basis of the materials presented. For the Avestan background of chapters IV–XXVI, the "Zardušt-nāmag", see West 1897, xiv–xv and Boyce 1975, 181–182. Zātspram I and XXXIV have been studied by Widengren 1967, 283–287 with respect to an Avestan original; cf. also Widengren in this vol. *passim*.

The account of Dēnkart breaks off curiously just at the point when the prophet, accompanied by Vohu Manah, is leaving to meet Ahura Mazda. I quote here the last part (60–62) where the *hampursakīh* is clearly mentioned (Madan 625:15–22):

u-š ō ōy guft Vahuman kū	And Vohu Manah spoke to him thus:
Zartušt ī Spitāmān bē ēt jāmak	O Zoroaster of the Spitamas
dah kē barē čigōn ōy ō ham pursēm	deposit this vessel[27] which you carry
kē tō dāt hē	so that we may confer with him,
kē man dāt hom	who has created you
kē hač mēnōyān afzōnīktom	who has created me
kē hastān hudāhaktom	who is the most bounteous of the spiritual
kē ōy gōvāk hom kē Vahuman hom	beings,
[kū aštak ī ōy hom]	who is the most beneficent of the corporeal
adak-iš ētōn mēnīt Zartušt kū	beings,
vēh hān kē dātār kē hač ēt aštak vēh	whose spokesman I am;
adak avēšan bē raft hēnd pat apākīh	I, who am Vohu Manah
Vahuman Zartušt-ič	[that is, I am his messenger][28]
Vahuman Zartušt pas.	Thereupon Zoroaster thought thus:
Dēnkart VII,3:60–62	Good is he the creator who is better
	than this messenger. Then they departed
	together, Vohu Manah and Zoroaster,
	Vohu Manah and after him Zoroaster.

The passage that follows only states: "When he (Zoroaster) had returned from the first consultation...", *ka hač hampursakīh ī fratom apāč būt* (VII,4:2). If the Dēnkart text does not offer any details of Zoroaster's encounter with Ahura Mazda and the Aməša Spəntas, the following passage from Zātspram XXI gives a little more information on the circumstances of the *hampursakīh*:

7. *u-š framūt Vahuman bē ō Zartušt kū*	7. And Vohu Manah ordered Zoroaster thus:
apar rav ō hanjaman ī mēnōyan 8.	"Proceed to the gathering of the spiritual
andčand Vahuman pat nō gām bē raft	beings!" 8. As much as Vohu Manah walked
Zartušt pat navad gām ut ka navad	on in nine steps, Zoroaster (did) in
gām šut būt u-š dīt hanjaman ī haft	ninety steps and when he hade gone ninety
Amahraspandān 9. *ka bē ō vist-čahar*	steps, he saw the gathering of the seven
pay i Amahraspandan mat, vazurg	Aməša Spəntas. 9. When he came within
rōšnīh ī Amahraspandān rād adak-iš	twenty four feet of the Aməša Spəntas, he
sāyak ī xveš pat damīk nē dīt 10.	then did not see his own shadow on the
hanjaman gāh būt andar Ēran ut pat	ground owing to the great light of the
kustak i Matān pat bār ī āp ī Dāytī.	Aməša Spəntas. 10. The place of the

---

[27] The word *jāmak* may also mean "garment" and it is so translated by West 1897, 49, Salemann 1908, 130 and Widengren 1945, 61. I prefer, however, with Molé 1967, 175 the meaning "vessel" which better fits the context. Zoroaster fetches water from the river for the *haoma*-ceremony and needs therefore some kind of vessel; for the ritual background of this scene, cf. Boyce 1975, 185. In Dēnkart VII, 3:54 it is said that Zoroaster puts on his garments, the word *varr* or *jāmak* being written with the ideogram *LBWŠY'*. In 3:60 it is, however, written phonetically: *y'mk*.

[28] This is a gloss typical of the *zand*.

11. *Zartušt namāz burt u-š guft kū*	gathering was in Iran and in the region
namāz ō Ōhrmazd	of Matan, on the shore of the waters of
namāz ō Amahraspandān	Daitya.
ut frāč šut pat gāh ī pursišnīkān	11. Zoroaster paid homage and spoke thus:
bē nišast	"Homage to Ahura Mazda!
Zātspram XXI, 7–11	Homage to the Aməša Spəntas!"
	And he went forward and sat down in the
	place of the enquirers.

Then the text continues with a new section "concerning the questions of the enquiring of Zoroaster", *apar frašn pursitārīh ī Zartušt*, where, however, only a summary of the first question and its answer is given (Zātspram XXII, 1–9). Both accounts – Dēnkart VII, 3:51–62 and Zātspram XXI, 1–9 – presuppose a situation where Zoroaster wades into the river Daitya to fetch pure water from the middle of the stream for the *haoma*-ceremony. When coming out of the water, he is met by Vohu Manah who then leads him to Ahura Mazda. Whereas Dēnkart ends its description here, Zātspram gives further details in vv. 8–11 which recall the procedure for consulting an oracle, *i.e.* sitting down in a special place which is qualified as that of the enquirers.[29] Zoroaster's conference with Ahura Mazda and the Aməša Spəntas is furthermore thought to have taken place somewhere by the river Daitya which flowed through the ancient Zoroastrian homeland, the Airyanəm Vaejah. This river has in the Avestan tradition a clear connection with Zoroaster, who according to Yašt 5:104 sacrificed to Anāhitā by "the good Daitya". Zātspram XXI, 1 also records a tradition concerning Daitya that "because of the conference of Zoroaster near by, it is the master of the waters", *čigōn hampursakīh ī Zartušt pat-iš rād rat ast ī āpān*. The tradition underlying Zātspram XXI apparently understood the *hampursakīh* to take place on the earth in a region known for its central role in the first period of the Zoroastrian faith. The account in Dēnkart may also be interpreted in this way, although it stops at the point when Vohu Manah and Zoroaster leave together for the encounter with Ahura Mazda. This poses a problem. Why does the Pahlavi-tradition pass over (Dēnkart) or just touch on (Zātspram) the details of the journey to Ahura Mazda and the nature of the *hampursakīh*-encounter? Was it thought of as an esoteric teching? Or was there a special technique to be used in order to get to Ahura Mazda which, in a later period, was considered unworthy of the prophet? There is another problem. Does the conference of Zoroaster with Ahura Mazda imply a journey to the heavenly world, to the *Garo dəmāna*? If so, did this journey then start from a place near the river Daitya? The question also arises as to

---

[29] Compare the procedure at Delphi in which the enquirer enters the innermost sanctuary for consultation and sits down near the place where the Pythia is seated, cf. Parke 1967, 84. If there is a connection between Zātspram XXI, 11 and the *maga*-concept in Yōišt ī Fryān III, 69, it requires further investigation.

the way the *hampursakīh*-tradition is related to the dream-visions of Zoroaster as recorded in the Bahman Yašt (cf. §4.2.2.).

In any case, the *hampursakīh*-form presupposes an encounter with Ahura Mazda during which Ahura Mazda foretells the eschatological events in their apocalyptic setting.

4.2.1.3. Judging from the Pahlavi-texts, the *hampursakīh*-form was the most important mode of transmitting Avestan apocalyptic traditions. The appearance of a "question – answer" setting in the extant Avesta leads us to the conclusion that the *hampursakīh* was the favourite mode of presenting religious teachings.[30] In fact, the passages dealing with the *hampursakīh*-encounters of Zoroaster understand these to be the occasions when Zoroaster received the whole revelation, the *dēn ī Ōhrmazd*.[31] The extant Avesta has, however, very little to tell of the *hampursakīh* itself. As far as I have been able to ascertain, there are only two passages where the *hampursakīh* is mentioned: Yasna 12:6 and Vidēvdāt 2:1–2. They do not contain any information about the circumstances and the nature of the *hampursakīh*, they just present it as a fact. The first passage, which is found in the ancient Zoroastrian creed, the *Fravarāne* (Yasna 12:1–9), refers to the conferences (*frašna-*) and encounters at which Ahura Mazda and Zoroaster spoke together (*ham+fras-*). Several *hampursakīh*-encounters are here indicated just as in the Pahlavi-tradition. According to the other text, Vidēvdāt 2:1–2, Zoroaster was the first one with whom Ahura Mazda "conferred" (*apərəse*). It may further be deduced from this passage that Zoroaster received the entire revelation (*daēna*) at that time.

4.2.2. The Bahman Yašt contains allusions to another form of Iranian apocalyptic in which the medium of the divine revelation is a vision. In chapters one and three we find two independant versions of the same basic tradition relating how Ahura Mazda reveals the "omniscience" (*harvisp-ākāhīh*) to Zoroaster. In the course of this display, Zoroaster sees in a dream a tree with four branches, originally symbolizing the four ages of the world. The interpretation is then given by Ahura Mazda. This form, a dream-vision, was no doubt also the framework of the Oracles of Hystaspes of which only secondary summaries survive.[32] The Oracles were

---

[30] The pattern presenting Zoroaster asking questions of Ahura Mazda is found in the Gathas (*e.g.* Yasna 31 and 44). In the Yašts one finds the best examples in Yašt 14 dedicated to Vərəthragna and in Yašt 1 (the first part); further Yašt 12:1–6. Hādōxt Nask II and much of the material in Vidēvdāt, *e.g.* II, 1–19 and 39–43, IX, 1–55, appear also to be set in a *hampursakīh*-framework.

[31] Pahlavi Rivāyat XLVII, 2–3 states explicitly that Zoroaster received the *dēn* during his consultations with Ahura Mazda; see also Dēnkart V, 2:6 and VII, 4:47.

[32] The summaries or free renderings are given by Lactantius in the Divine Institutions and in the Epitome of the same work (Lact. Instit. VII, 15–24). The texts pertaining to the Oracles of Hystaspes are found in the collection by Bidez-Cumont 1938, II, 364–376. Cf. Widengren in the present vol. § 4.3.2.

based upon Iranian apocalyptic beliefs and circulated in the Greco-Roman world at least since the first century B.C. In the only extant allusion to the original form of the Oracles, it is said that Hystaspes (the Iranian Vištāspa) transmitted to the memory of posterity a marvellous dream which was expounded by a prophesying youth.[33]

4.3. To sum up this part of the present study, I give below a concise survey of the different ways of presentation and transmission in Iranian apocalypticism from the three viewpoints mentioned.

I. The exterior form or setting:
1. Independant apocalyptic compilations or fragments:
   Bahman Yašt and possibly Jāmāsp Nāmak.
2. The "compendium"-setting.
   a) special apocalyptic sections with headings introduced by *apar*, "concerning":
      Bundahišn XXXIII and XXXIV, Zātspram XXXIV and XXXV, Dēnkart VII,7:29–11:11.
   b) special apocalyptic sections with no heading:
      Pahlavi Rivāyat XLVIII.
3. The "question and answer"-setting:
   Dātestān ī Dēnīk, XXXVI and XXXVII,1–11; Mēnōi ī Xrat VIII,1–16 and XXVIII,1–9.
4. The *handarz*-setting:
   Pand Nāmak ī Zartušt 9–16.

II. Type of presenting the material (the style):
1. The narrative-declarative type.
   Exx.: Bundahišn XXXIII, 1–22; Pahlavi Rivāyat XLVIII; Ayātkār ī Jāmāspīk XVI and XVII.
2. The *zand*-type.
   Exx.: Bahman Yašt VI, 2–12 and VII, 2–14 (III, 2–11 and III, 12–22); Dēnkart VII, 8:11–19.
3. The "translation-Pahlavi"-type (passages translated into Pahlavi from the Avesta and quoted without additional explanations).
   Exx.: Dēnkart VII, 8:51–54 and 11:3, Bahman Yašt IX, 1–8 (III, 44–50).

III. Original "forms":
1. The *hampursakīh*-form.
   Revelations given by Ahura Mazda to Zoroaster during a special consultation (*hampursakīh*) and transmitted in a setting of "questions and answers":

---

[33] The latin text runs: *Hystaspes quoque, qui fuit Medorum rex antiquissimus ... admirabile somnium sub interpretatione vaticinantis pueri ad memoriam posteris tradidit* (Lact. Instit. VII, 15:19).

Bundahišn XXXIV, 4–5; Zātspram XXXIV, 1–20; Dēnkart VIII, 8: 22, 23–31, 32, 33–37, 38–39, 40–43, 51–59, 9:6 and 10:11; Bahman Yašt IV, 1–66, V, 1–10, VI, 1–13, VII, 1–39, VIII, 1–8 and IX, 1b–8 (II, 23–54, II, 57–63, III, 1–11, III, 12–38, III, 39–43 and III, 44b–50).

2. The "dream-vision" form.

A dream or vision received by a person of outstanding importance and expounded by Ahura Mazda or by an inspired human interpreter. Attested receivers: Zoroaster and Vištāspa.

Bahman Yašt I, 1–11 and III, 5–29 (I, 1–5 and II, 1–22); Oracles of Hystaspes.

5. The Apocalyptic Media

5.1. As we have seen, Iranian apocalypticism presents three figures, Zoroaster, Vištāspa and Jāmāspa, through whom divine revelation comes, although in different ways. Zoroaster himself is of course the foremost receiver and transmitter of apocalyptic materials in his capacity of prophet and chief messenger of the Mazda religion.

5.1.1. The priority of Zoroaster as an apocalyptic revealer appears clearly demonstrated when the role of Jāmāspa is made precise. The latter owes his secret knowledge and his ability in foretelling the future to Zoroaster. Ayātkār ī Jāmāspīk expresses this idea by stating that during his lifetime Zoroaster received an order (*framān*) from Ahura Mazda to invest Jāmāspa with an all-embracing knowledge.[34] The same writing records that when king Vištāspa asked whence Jāmāspa had got his secret knowledge, the answer was: "This knowledge has come to me from the religion of Ahura Mazda and Zoroaster".[35] Likewise, in summarizing the content of some apocalyptic Avestan texts, the fifth book of Dēnkart says that Jāmāspa could fortell the signs of different ages, past and future, "from the teaching of Zoroaster", *hač hān ī Zartušt āmōk* (V, 3:4). A kind of apostolic succession is implied in these traditions which is also explicitly confirmed in the statement that Jāmāspa was the second one to be the high priest, *magupatān magupat*, of the Mazda worshippers, Zoroaster being the first one.[36]

5.1.2. The position of Vištāspa as an apocalyptic revealer is more difficult to determine. He is not included in the succession represented by Zoroaster and Jāmāspa. Although the Oracles of Hystaspes show him in the role of an apocalyptic medium, it seems to have been entirely a passive one. What he sees in his dream must be interpreted by someone else. This

---

[34] Ayātkār ī Jāmāspik I, 8–10.
[35] Ayātkār ī Jāmāspīk XIII, 3.
[36] See Zātspram XXV, 7: ... *Jāmāsp ī čigōn pas hač Zartušt magupatān magupat būt.*

interpreter, the *vaticinans puer* in the Oracles, may well have been Jāmāspa in view of the Pahlavi tradition which presents him as a wise seer answering the questions of king Vištāspa. The parallel with the Book of Daniel is striking. King Nebuchadnezzar has a dream-vision which he does not understand but which is interpreted by the wise youth Daniel (Dan 2).[37] The reason why Vištāspa has come to function as an apocalyptic medium is probably due to the impact exercised by the ancient tradition about his heavenly journey (see below §5.4.). The purpose of this journey is to convince Vištāspa that he should accept the religion preached by Zoroaster. It is, however, not stated that Vištāspa receives a revelation or secret knowledge which he in turn should teach and transmit to others. Ayātkār ī Jāmāspīk even draws a clear distinction between the office of the prophetic seer and that of the ruler. Jāmāspa declares, namely, that wisdom and secret science belong to him, whereas Vištāspa has been granted sovereignty and kingship.[38]

5.2. Zoroaster's role as apocalyptic revealer is intimately bound up with the kind of religious type that he represents. The indications given in the Gathas, particularly Yasna 43, suggest that he was a kind of ecstatic visionary who a number of times had an overwhelming experience of the divine, the Mazdā Ahura.[39] It is furthermore noteworthy that already in the Gathas, Vohu Manah plays a prominent part in helping Zoroaster to attain this experience of the supreme god. How was the ecstasy, in which Zoroaster saw and heard Mazdā Ahura, brought about? The Gathas only offer allusions which in addition have given rise to different interpretations. There are, however, good reasons to assume that there were in the early Zoroastrian community several means of attaining the ecstatic vision,[40] *e.g.* chanting,[41] and the use of a specific beverage. The last one is most clearly attested with respect to Vištāspa. Recalling one of the Gathas (Yasna 51) which describes Vištāspa as having received the *čisti* ("insight" in its literal meaning) on the paths of Vohu Manah (v. 16), a subsequent tradition, originally also found in the Avesta, relates how Vištāspa is visited by a divine messenger who urges him to drink a cup of wine or *haoma* mixed with hemp or henbane (*mang*). He then falls into a deep sleep during which his soul is taken to heaven, the *Garō dəmāna*. There he "sees" the happiness and success which will be granted to him if he embraces the religion

---

[37] Bidez-Cumont 1938, II, 367 rightly points out the parallel with the Book of Daniel.

[38] Ayātkār ī Jāmāspīk XIII, 3.

[39] The ecstatic character of this experience has been emphasized by Nyberg 1938, 146–187 and Widengren 1965, 69–74 and 1979a, 56–59.

[40] On the vision, *čisti*, in the Gathas, see Widengren 1979b, 347–353.

[41] For a discussion of chanting and ecstacy in early Zoroastrianism, see Nyberg 1938, 160–163 and Widengren 1965, 72–73.

proclaimed by Zoroaster.[42] The same procedure is used by Artāy Virāz before undertaking his journey to the other world.[43] Now, it appears from a passage in Bahman Yašt, based upon Avestan traditions, that a similar technique was used by Zoroaster,[44] when he had the dream-vision referred to above (§ 4.2.2.). The beverage mentioned in Bahman Yašt consists only of water, but there are grounds to believe that the mention of the *mang* has been suppressed by later tradition.[45] A passage from the Pahlavi Vidēvdāt, hitherto not adduced in this context, supports the view that the original tradition behind the Bahman Yašt knew the narcotic beverage. In IV, 14 mention is made of old women bringing henbane or hemp to be used for abortion and the text adds that this *mang* either was that of Vištāspa or that of Zoroaster (*ayāp hān i Vīštāspān ayāp hān ī Zartuštān*). Considering the data presented above, there is much in favour of the supposition that the *admirabile somnium* of Hystaspes in the Oracles was brought about by drinking the cup of henbane or hemp.

5.3. According to the Bahman Yašt, Zoroaster receives from Ahura Mazda the "wisdom of omniscience" which appears to be closely related to the procedure of drinking the cup of ecstasy:

u-š xrat ī harvisp ākāhīh   And he (sc. Ahura Mazda) put the wisdom
pat āp karp apar dast ī   of omniscience in the form of water in
Zartušt kart u-š guft kū   the hand of Zoroaster and said: "Drink".
frāč xvar ut Zartušt hač-iš   And Zoroaster drank from it and he inter-
frāč xvart u-š xrat ī harvisp   mingled the wisdom of omniscience with
ākāhīh pat Zartušt andar   Zoroaster. Seven days and nights Zoroaster
gumēxt; haft rōč šapān Zar-   was in the wisdom of Ahura Mazda.
tušt andar Ōhrmazd xratīh būt.
          Bahman Yašt III, 6b–8 (II, 5b–6)

It is the conveying of the "wisdom of omniscience", *xrat ī harvisp ākāhīh*, that makes the "seeing" of the visionary possible. Thus, the words immediately following the quoted passage run: "And Zoroaster saw…" *u-š bē dīt Zartušt*. The text then relates the content of the vision. The same is true for Pahlavi Rivāyat XXXVI, 3–14 which draws on the same authoritative tradition as is reflected in Bahman Yašt III, 1–18 (II, 1–13).[46] The text

---

[42] The tradition of Vištāspa's ecstatic journey is found in Dēnkart VII, 4:84–86 and Pahlavi Rivāyat XLVII, 27–32. Its Avestan background and its importance for understanding the type of the visionary in ancient Iran have been pointed out by Widengren 1965, 69–71 and 1979a, 57.

[43] See Artāy Virāz Nāmak II, 21–31.

[44] For the details, see Bahman Yašt III, 5–8 (II, 4–6) and the discussion in Widengren 1965, 69, 72 and 1979a, 58.

[45] Cf. also Widengren 1965, 72 and 1979a, 58.

[46] The relevant section in the Pahlavi Rivāyat is introduced by the words *ēn-ič paytāk kū* "this also is revealed:". A detailed comparison between Bahman Yašt III, 1–18 (II, 1–13) and Pahlavi Rivāyat XXXVI will be made by the present author in a study in preparation.

describes how Zoroaster seeks immortality from Ahura Mazda, which, however, is refused to him. Instead Ahura Mazda grants him a vision.

ut pas Ōhrmazd xrat ī harvisp And then Ahura Mazda transmitted to Zoro-
ākāh [īh] apar ō Zartušt burt. aster the Wisdom of omniscience. Zoroaster
Zartušt har čē būt ētōn bavēt sees everything that came into being, in
ēn gyāk gētāh ut hān-ič ī mēnōi the way it exists, the place of the mate-
hān-ič har kas bē vēnēt u-š dīt rial existence, that of the spiritual
gyāk ī ōy kē amarg būt . . . existence, that of every man. And he saw
               Pahlavi Rivāyat XXXVI, 8–11 the place of him who became deathless . . .

As we have seen from Bahman Yašt III, 6 (II, 5) the "wisdom of omniscience" comes from Ahura Mazda. It is an inherent quality of God. Pahlavi Rivāyat offers a short section illustrating the nature of the omniscience of Ahura Mazda:

dar-ē ēn kū Zartušt hač Ōhrmazd One subject is this: Zoroaster asked Ahura
pursīt kū dānāk harvisp ākāh Mazda thus: "Are you knowing (and) omni-
hē ut Ōhrmazd guft kū dānāk scient?" And Ahura Mazda replied: "I am
harvisp ākāh hom ut Zartušt knowing (and) omniscient." And Zoroaster
guft kū-t dānākīh čigōn ast. said: "Your knowledge, how is it?" Ahura
Ōhrmazd guft kū-m dānākīh ētōn Mazda answered: "My knowledge is like this:
ast ī ka hamāk pēm ī har tis if one should take all the milk of every
andar ō jāmak nād stanēnd ī being (lit. thing) into a vessel of cane,
man ēvak ēvak jutakīhā bē dānam I would be able to tell, one by one, sepa-
guft [an] kū hač pēstān ī kē ut ka rately, where, from whose breast. If one
hamāk āp ī pat gēhān andar ō should allow all the water in the world to
ēt gyāk hilēnd ēvak ēvak jutāk bē enter into this place, I would be able
dānam guftan kū hač katār xānīk to tell, one by one, separately, where, from
ut ka hamāk urvar ī pat hamāk gēhān which source. And if one should compress
xvurt bē afšārēnd ēvak apāč ō all the plants in the whole world into a
gyāk xvēš dānam nihātan. small (bale), I would be able to put them
               Pahlavi Rivāyat XXII back, one by one, in their own place."

The omniscience conveyed to Zoroaster is of the same nature as that of Ahura Mazda. This appears from the description in Bahman Yašt III, 9–10 (II, 7–8):

u-š bē dīt Zartušt pat haft And Zoroaster saw into the seven continents,
kišvar damīk martomān gosp- (he beheld) men (and) cattle, where every
andān kū har ēvak mōd pat pušt fibre of hair (is), how many (they are) on
čand tāk tāk sar ō kū dārēt. the back whereunto each single one has its
U-š bē dīt dar ut draxt kē čē end. And he saw whatever shrubs and trees
čand rēšak ī urvarān pat (there are), what kind, how many; the roots
Spandarmat damīk čigōn rust of the plants in the earth of Spenta Armaiti,
ēstēt ut kū gumēxt ēstēt. how they are grown and where they are
                 mingled.

Jāmāspa also has received this sort of omniscience. According to Ayātkār ī Jāmāspīk I, 10–13 and XIII, 5–7 Jāmāspa himself displays before Vištāspa the kind of knowledge he has.[47] We find in these accounts the same penetrating insight as that which Bahman Yašt ascribes to Zoroaster. The secret science of Ĵāmāspa also comprises a knowledge about apocalyptic matters:

ut patixšāyīh čand ut čigōn	I know the reigns, how many and how (they
ut čē aivēnak ut hān-ič tāi	are) and in what manner and also those until
fraškart ut tan ī pasēn dānam.	the renovation and the final body.

Ayātkār ī Ĵāmāspik XIII, 7

Zoroaster receives the "wisdom of omniscience" in the manner that Ahura Mazda "transmits" it to him.[48] It is a temporary gift as is clearly stated in the Bahman Yašt III, 11 (II, 9):

u-š haftom rōč-šapān xrat ī	And on the seventh day and night he (sc.
harvisp ākāhīh hač Zartušt	Ahura Mazda) took back the wisdom of
apāč stāt.	omniscience from Zoroaster.

Zātspram XXII, 7 also presupposes the occasional character of the omniscient vision:

u-š andar ham rōč sē bār xrat	And he (sc. Ahura Mazda) transmitted (to
ī harvisp ākāh [īh] apar burt.	him) three times on the same day the wis-
	dom of omniscience.

The way in which Ĵāmāspa comes into possession of his omniscience is not explicitly mentioned, except that he has received it by the intermediation of Zoroaster. The texts convey the impression that it is rather an inherent quality. Thus, Ayātkār ī Zarērān makes king Vištāspa honour Ĵāmāspa with the following words:

man dānēm kū tō Ĵāmāsp dānāk	I know that you, Ĵāmāspa, are knowing
ut vēnāk [ut] šnāsāk hē ēn-ič	seeing and wise. You know also this,
dānē kū ka dah rōč vārān āyēt	that when the rain falls for ten days,
čand srišk ō damīk	how many drops fall on the sea and
āyēt ut čand srišk apar drayāp[49] āyēt	how many drops fall on the earth. You
ut ēn-ič dānē kū ka urvarān	know also this, that when the plants
viškōfēt katām hān gul ī rōč	flower, which flowers will blossom
viškōfēt ut katām hān ī šap...	during the day and which will blossom

Ayātkār ī Zarērān § 35–37   during the night...

The text continues with the description of the omniscience which Ĵāmāspa possesses, but there is no allusion to the way in which he has acquired his science. Ayātkar ī Ĵāmāspīk XIII, 8 contains, however, a

---

[47] The term *harvisp-ākāhīh* is not attested with respect to Ĵāmāspa, but we find corresponding expressions: *ākāhīh* "knowledge", *kundākīh* "secret science" (Ayātkār ī Ĵāmāspīk), *dānāk* "knowing" and *vēnāk* "seeing" (Ayātkār ī Zarērān).

[48] The "technical" term for this transmission seems to be *apar burtan*: Zātspram XXII, 7 and Pahlavi Rivāyat XXXVI, 8 or *apar gumēxtan*: Bahman Yašt III, 7 (II, 6).

[49] The transmitted text reads here *srišk* (سىدد) but this seems to be a corruption of *drayāp* (دلسى). I owe this explanation to Prof. D. Monchi-Zadeh, Uppsala; cf. now Monchi-Zadeh 1981, 18.

statement that the soul of Jāmāspa "was in paradise at that time", *man i Jāmāsp pat hān zamān ruvān ī garōdmān*.

5.4. The mention of the soul of Jāmāspa in the paradise leads us to the question whether the giving of omniscient wisdom also includes a heavenly journey undertaken by the visionary. The Iranian tradition knows about the ecstatic journeys to heaven made by Vištāspa and Artāy Vīrāz. These figures are, however, not considered as having "the wisdom of omniscience" which seems to be reserved for the apocalyptic revealers properly speaking, *i.e.* Zoroaster and Jāmāspa. For the latter we have only the allusion quoted above (§ 5.3.) which most probably refers to a heavenly journey. As to Zoroaster, there is a passage in Dātestān ī Dēnīk XXXVII, 43 which appears to link the "conveyance to paradise" (*franāmišn ī ō vahišt*) with the occasion when the "wisdom of omniscience" came upon the prophet from God.[50] The scenes of Zoroaster's visions in Bahman Yašt III (II) and Pahlavi Rivāyat XXXVI are not described; but there is, on the other hand, nothing in the texts that contradicts the supposition that during his "seeing" Zoroaster dwells with Ahura Mazda in heaven.

5.5. To sum up our investigation concerning the apocalyptic media, Zoroaster appears to be the most prominent. He is the only one who figures in the encounters with Ahura Mazda, the *hampursakīh*-consultations. He is granted the divine quality of the "wisdom of omniscience" which makes his "supernatural" seeing possible. As to Zoroaster, the dream-vision form is intimately connected with the theme of omniscient wisdom. There is a certain tension here, because some parts of Zoroaster's vision need an explanation by Ahura Mazda, although one should expect the "wisdom of omniscience" to allow the same perspicacity for future events as for men and nature. The relationship between the *hampursakīh* theme and that of omniscient wisdom remains obscure. Although Zāts-pram XXII, 7 places the giving of the "wisdom of omniscience" in the context of a summary of the *hampursakīh*-questions which Zoroaster addressed to Ahura Mazda, the other texts do not present any connexions at all. Further investigation may, however, yield more in this respect. After Zoroaster, the chief apocalyptic revealer is Jāmāspa, but we know very little about how he attains his secret knowledge and how it was thought of: as inherent quality or as a temporary gift?

6. The Origins of Iranian Apocalypticism

6.1. In the concluding part of the present study, I will touch upon the problems connected with origin in Iranian apocalypticism. To deal with origin involves us in a complex of problems and different approaches.

---

[50] For this passage, see Widengren 1945, 63–64 and 1979a, 59 note 20.

First, there is the question of what is to be meant by "origin" in Iranian apocalypticism. It can imply (1) a study of what is termed "Sitz im Leben" and (2) an analysis of the provenance of the materials of which Iranian apocalypticism is composed from its growth up to the 9th century A.D. when the Pahlavi books were redacted. I believe that both these approaches must be held together in considering the origins of Iranian apocalypticism.

6.2. Then, we are faced with the problem where to begin. As for the "forms", I think that the starting-point for the question of origin must be the Middle-Iranian texts where we find the final exposition of the Iranian apocalyptic system. The time of their redaction, the 9th–10th centuries A.D., provides the first external setting for an interpretation of the origins of the apocalyptic system. The materials handed down up to this time are now being actualized through interpretative additions. They clearly reflect the downfall of the Sasanian empire, the penetration of the Arabs, *tāžīk* in the Pahlavi texts, and the attacks of nomadic Turkish peoples. The expectations of a redemption coming from the east, from India, which appear in the passages concerning Vahrām ī varčāvand (Bahman Yašt VII, 4–5, VIII, 1 [III, 14; III, 39] and Bundahišn XXXIII, 27), may correspond to real attempts to restore the national independance of Iran after its subjugation by the Arabs. Other materials which may be characterized as political oracles, like the one in Jāmāsp Nāmak 88–98, seem also to have been integrated into the final apocalyptic system during the early post-Sasanian period.[51] Thus, one can determine the origin, that is, the provenance, of some of the apocalyptic materials found in the post-Sasanian redaction. These interpretative materials give, at the same time, a new meaning, a new "Sitz im Leben" to the whole apocalyptic system.

6.2.1. Similarly, carrying on the analysis into the Sasanian time, we may assume that this period, so important for the history of Zoroastrianism, has favoured a re-interpretation of some of the basic apocalyptic traditions.[52] Some indications of such a re-interpretation may be mentioned. The two versions of the dream-vision seen by Zoroaster, which are found in the Bahman Yašt, betray a reworking of the original scheme of the ages. In the first version, it is extended to include the period of Xōsrav Anōšurvān (531–579 A.D.). In the second version, the fourfould scheme has been elaborated and mentions still more names from the Sasanian time: the first kings Artašīr and Šāhpur, the priest Aturpāt, the king Bahrām Gōr and the "heretic" Mazdak.[53] Even the summary in Dēnkart IX, 8 of the passage in

---

[51] Cf. Kippenberg 1978, 58–64 and T. Olsson in this vol. § 2.

[52] It is in this period that the final collection and authorization of the Avesta is made and Zoroastrianism is promoted to a kind of "state-religion".

[53] The fact that the legendary son of Vištāspa, called Vahman, is here named Artašīr also bears witness to the Sasanian re-interpretation. For this Vahman see Christensen 1932, 98.

Sutkar Nask – one of the sources of Bahman Yašt – where the four ages of the millenium of Zoroaster were described, has not escaped the re-interpretation since it mentions Aturpāt.[54] Many glosses found in the *zand*-passages have been added in the Sasanian period, as one can see from the names of the commentators incidentally mentioned or from the tendency expressed in the glosses. Thus, the analysis of the apocalyptic system in another crucial period of its transmission enables us to speak of a new and different level of origin.

6.2.2. In this way, as demonstrated by only a few examples, we should follow the development of Iranian apocalypticism, starting from the final exposition in the Pahlavi books, back through time, trying to get behind the Sasanian period into the "dark age", the Parthian period.

6.3. The study of the forms has shown that the basic teachings of the apocalyptic system go back to authoritative Avestan traditions (see §4.2.1.). This means that we will have to date the growth of Iranian apocalypticism to a time considerably antecedent to the birth of Christ. External evidence points to the same conclusion. Plutarch, referring to Theopompus in the 4th century B.C., gives a brief account of Iranian apocalypticism in its zervanite version where the structure of the Middle-Iranian scheme is clearly reflected.[55] Even some details in the account of Plutarch correspond in an astonishing way with what is said in the Pahlavi texts. Plutarch reports that in the end-time the earth will become flat and level, and that men will have one life and one commonwealth and speak one tongue. Furthermore he says that they will need no food in that time. All these details are recorded in the Pahlavi literature, expecially Bundahišn and Ayātkār ī Jāmāspīk.[56]

An important task of further research on Iranian apocalypticism would be to try to reconstruct, on the basis of a formal analysis, the contents and original forms of Iranian apocalypticism in pre-Sasanian times. Having thus got a reliable idea of the apocalyptic teachings of that period, we may then proceed to deal with the question of their origins. The present author prepares a more extensive study along the lines indicated which will take up and develop the observations made in this paper.

6.4. There are two aspects of the origin of Iranian apocalypticism that deserve particular attention.

---

[54] The oracle found in Jāmāsp Nāmak 58–67 appears to have been incorporated into the apocalyptic framework during the late Sasanian period; cf. Czeglédy 1958, 21–43 and Kippenberg 1978, 60. For the Sasanian re-interpretation of the scheme of the four ages, see also Widengren in this vol. §§7.2.2.–7.3.

[55] This account is found in De Iside et Osiride, 46–47: Text and translation in Griffiths 1970, 190–195. For an analysis, see Widengren in this vol. §5.1.

[56] Bundahišn XXXIV, 1–4 and 33; Ayātkār ī Jāmāspīk XVII, 10.

6.4.1. The first one is the relationship between apocalypticism and cult. According to Bundahišn XXXIV, 23 and Zātspram XXXV, 15, in the final stage of the apocalyptic process, the Saošyant with his helpers will perform the rite (*yazišn*) for the restoration of the dead; and he will sacrifice the bull Hatāyōš for that purpose. Such an idea shows the importance of the cult for the priestly circles which transmitted the apocalyptic traditions. But the apocalyptic texts themselves, do they have a ritual "Sitz im Leben"? We indeed find a clear indication of a cultic origin for one apocalyptic text, the Bahman Yašt. The apocalyptic presentation is interrupted in one passage by an Avestan liturgical formula.[57] This formula occurs in the service at the end of each chapter (*hāt*) of the Yasna and the sections (*kardā*) of the Yašts. Sometimes one finds in the Bahman Yašt another formula which betrays an Avestan origin and a ritual context. When Zoroaster addresses himself to Ahura Mazda, he begins with the words: "Ahura Mazda, bounteous spirit, creator of the corporeal beings", *Ōhrmazd, mēnōi apazōnīk dātār ī gēhān astomandān.*[58] This formula is characteristic of the Yašts 1 and 14 (see also Hādōxt Nask I–III and Vidēvdāt II). The references in Bahman Yašt to a *zand* of Vahuman *yasna* supports the theory of a ritual "Sitz im Leben" for the original work. A close examination of further Pahlavi texts will probably yield more in this respect.

6.4.2. The other aspect of the origin of Iranian apocalypticism which will have to be further elucidated is the geographical provenance of the apocalyptic materials. Allusions are often found in this material to rivers, lakes and mountains. A preliminary examination of these allusions reveals that there is a clear eastern Iranian background for some of them. A systematic analysis of the geographical indications found in the apocalyptic materials is needed in order to discern the particular eastern Iranian traditions. There is a tendency, which must have begun to express itself already in the Achaemenian period, to transfer eastern Iranian names to a western context. One example may illustrate this. According to Bahman Yašt, some important apocalyptic events will take place by the river Arang in northeastern Iran. The commentator adds: "someone said that it is the river Euphrat", *hat būt kē Frāt rōt guft.*[59]

6.5. We have in this study emphasized the Pahlavi texts as the basic material for further research on Iranian apocalypticism. In them we find the key which opens up the right understanding of the important and active role which Iranian apocalypticism seems to have played in the ancient Mediterranean and Near Eastern worlds.

---

[57] Bahman Yašt V, 11 (II, 64). Cf. also Tavadia 1956, 122.
[58] Bahman Yašt IV, 1; V, 1; VI, 1; VII, 1 (II, 23; II, 57; III, 1; III, 12).
[59] Bahman Yašt VI, 5 (III, 5).

Bibliography

1. Sources

Avesta: Avesta, die heiligen Bücher der Parsen I–III, hrsg. von *K. F. Geldner,* Stuttgart 1886–1895.

Artāy Virāz Nāmak: The Book of Ardā Virāf, Pahlavi text prepared by Destur Hoshangji Jamaspji Asa, revised and collated with further manuscripts, with an English translation by *M. Haug* and *E. W. West,* Bombay/London 1872 [reprint: Amsterdam 1971].

Ayātkār ī Jāmāspīk: Libro Apocalittico Persiano Ayātkār ī Žāmāspīk, testo pehlevico, parsi e pazend restituito, tradotto e commentato, ed. *G. Messina,* Rome 1939.

Ayātkār ī Zarērān: The Pahlavi Texts contained in the Codex MK copied in 1322 A.C. by the scribe Mehr-Awan Kai-khusru, ed. by *J. M. Jamasp-Asana,* II, Bombay 1913.

Die Geschichte Zarēr's. Ausführlich kommentiert von *Davoud Monchi-Zadeh* (AUU.SIU 4), Uppsala 1981.

Bahman Yašt: The Codex DH, being a facsimile edition of Bondahesh, Zand-e Vohuman Yasht and parts of Denkard, Iranian Culture Foundation 89, fol. 230b–241a.

The Pahlavi Codices K 20 & K 20b, published in facsimile by the University Library of Copenhagen, 1931 (*Codices Avestici et Pahlavici Universitatis Hafniensis* vol. I), fol. 129v–143r.

The Pahlavi Codex K 43, published in facsimile by the University Library of Copenhagen, 1936 (*Codices Avestici et Pahlavici Universitatis Hafniensis* vol. V), fol. 262r–275v.

Zand-î Vohûman Yasn and Two Pahlavi Fragments with Text, Transliteration, and Translation in English by *B. T. Anklesaria,* Bombay 1957.

Bundahišn: The Bundahishn, being a facsimile of the TD Manuscript No. 2 brought from Persia by Dastur Tîrandâz and now preserved in the late Ervald Tahmuras' Library, ed. by the late *E. T. D. Anklesaria,* Bombay 1908.

The Bondahesh, being a facsimile edition of the manuscript TD_1, Iranian Culture Foundation 88.

The Codex DH (see above), fol. 160–230b.

The Pahlavi Codices K 20 & K 20b (see above), fol. 88r–129v.

Codex M 51b, photographs of fol. 205v–251v in the possession of the present author (this codex is described by *Ch. Bartholomae* in "Die Zendhandschriften der K. Hof- und Staatsbibliothek in München", München 1915).

Zand-Ākāsīh, Iranian or Greater Bundahišn, transliteration and translation in English by *B. T. Anklesaria,* Bombay 1956.

Dātestān ī Dēnīk: The Pahlavi Codex K 35, first part, published in facsimile by The University Library of Copenhagen, 1934 (*Codices Avestici et Pahlavici Universitatis Hafniensis* vol. III). Pahlavi Texts, translated by *E. W. West,* Part II, Oxford 1882.

Dēnkart: Dēnkart, A Pahlavi Text. Facsimile edition of the manuscript B of the K. R. Cama Oriental Institute Bombay, ed. by *M. J. Dresden,* Wiesbaden 1966.

The Complete Text of the Pahlavi Dinkard. Published by "The Society for the promotion of researches into the Zoroastrian religion" under the supervision of *D. M. Madan,* Bombay 1911.

Jāmāsp Nāmak: Jâmâspi, Pahlavi, Pazend and Persian Texts by *J. J. Modi,* Bombay 1903.

The Pahlavi Jāmāsp-Nāmak, ed. by *E. W. West* in Avesta, Pahlavi, and Ancient Persian Studies, Strassburg/Leipzig 1904.

Pahlavi Rivāyat: The Pahlavi Rivâyat accompanying The Dâdistân î Dînîk, ed. by *B. N. Dhabhar,* Bombay 1913.

Pahlavi Vidēvdāt: Pahlavi Vendidad, transliteration and translation in English by *B. T. Anklesaria,* Bombay 1949.

Mēnōi ī Xrat: The Pahlavi Codex K 43, published in facsimile by The University Library of Copenhagen, 1936 (see above under Bahman Yašt), fol. 131v–176v.

Pand Nāmak ī Zartušt: Čītak Handarž i Pōryōtkēšān, a Pahlavi text, edited, transcribed and translated into English by *M. F. Kanga,* Bombay 1960.
Yōišt ī Fryān: Appendix I. The tale of Gôsht-i Fryânô; The Pahlevi text, edited by *E. W. West,* in: "The Book of Ardā Virāf"; see above *Artāy Virāz Nāmak.*
Zātspram: Vichitakiha-i Zatsparam with Text and Introduction by *B. T. Anklesaria,* Bombay 1964.

2. Literature

Anklesaria, B. T. 1957: See Bahman Yašt under "Sources".
Bailey, Harold W. 1930–32: "To the Žāmāsp Nāmak" I and II, in *BSOS* 6 (1930–32) 55–85 and 581–600.
Benveniste, Emile 1932: "Une apocalypse pehlevie: le Žāmāsp Nāmak", in: *RHR* 106 (1932) 337–380.
Bidez, Joseph/Cumont, Franz 1938: *Les Mages Hellénisés,* tome II: les textes, Paris 1938 [reprint: 1973].
Boyce, Mary 1975: *A History of Zoroastrianism,* vol. I (HO I, VIII, 1, 2), Leiden/Köln 1975.
Christensen, Arthur 1932: *Les Kayanides* (DVSS.PH 19:2), Copenhagen 1932.
Czeglédy, K. 1958: "Bahrām Čōbīn and the Persian Apocalyptic Literature", in: *AOH* 8 (1958) 21–43.
Griffiths, Gwyn J. 1970: *Plutarch's De Iside et Osiride.* Edited with an Introduction, Translation and Commentary, Swansea 1970.
Hartman, Sven S. 1976: "Frågan om eventuellt iranskt inflytande på kristendomens och judendomens apokalyptik och djävulsföreställning", in: *SvTK* 52 (1976) 1–8.
Kanga, M. F. 1960: See Pand Nāmak ī Zartušt under "Sources".
Kippenberg, Hans G. 1978: "Die Geschichte der mittelpersischen apokalyptischen Traditionen", in: *StIr* 7 (1978) 49–80.
Lommel, Hermann 1930: *Die Religion Zarathustras,* nach dem Awesta dargestellt, Tübingen 1930 [reprint: 1971].
Messina, Giuseppe 1939: See Ayātkār ī Jāmāspīk under "Sources".
Modi, J. J. 1903: See Jāmāsp Nāmak under "Sources".
Molé, Marijan 1967: *La légende de Zoroastre selon les textes pehlevis,* Paris 1967.
Monchi-Zadeh, Davoud 1981: See Ayātkār ī Zarērān under "Sources".
Nyberg, Henrik Samuel 1938: *Die Religionen des alten Irans* (MVAEG 43), Leipzig 1938 [reprint: 1966].
– 1964: *A Manual of Pahlavi,* I: texts, alphabets, index, paradigms, notes and an introduction, Wiesbaden 1964.
– 1974: *A Manual of Pahlavi,* II: ideograms, glossary, abbreviations, index, grammatical survey, corrigenda to Part I, Wiesbaden 1974.
Parke, H. W. 1967: *Greek Oracles,* London 1967.
Salemann, Carl 1908: *Manichaeische Studien,* St. Petersbourg 1908.
Tavadia, Jehangir 1956: *Die mittelpersische Sprache und Literatur der Zarathustrier,* Leipzig 1956.
West, E. W. 1880: *Pahlavi Texts, translated by E. W. West. Part. I: The Bundahish, Bahman Yasht, and Shāyast Lā-Shāyast* (SBE V), Oxford 1880.
– 1897: *Pahlavi Texts, translated by E. W. West. Part V: Marvels of Zoroastrianism* (SBE XLVII), Oxford 1897.
Widengren, Geo 1945: *The Great Vohu Manah and the Apostle of God.* Studies in Iranian and Manichaean religion (UUÅ 1945:5), Uppsala/Leipzig 1945.
– 1954: "Stand und Aufgaben der iranischen Religionsgeschichte", in: *Numen* 1 (1954) 16–83.
– 1955: "Stand und Aufgaben der iranischen Religionsgeschichte", in: *Numen* 2 (1955) 47–134.
– 1961: *Iranische Geisteswelt,* Baden-Baden 1961.
– 1965: *Die Religionen Irans* (RM 14), Stuttgart 1965.
– 1967: "Zervanitische Texte aus dem 'Avesta' in der Pahlavi-Überlieferung. Eine Unter-

suchung zu Zātspram und Bundahišn", in: G. Wiessner (Ed.), *Festschrift für Wilhelm Eilers*, Wiesbaden 1967, 278–287.

– 1969: *Religionsphänomenologie*, Berlin 1969.
– 1979a: Review "Bernfried Schlerath (Hrsg.), Zarathustra (WdF 169)", in: *GGA* 231 (1979) 52–85.
– 1979b: "Révélation et prédication dans les Gāthās", in: Gh. Gnoli/A. V. Rossi (Eds.), *Iranica* (IUO.SMin 10), Napoli 1979, 339–364.
Wikander, Stig 1946: *Feuerpriester in Kleinasien und Iran* (ARSHLL 40), Lund 1946.

Vom profetischen zum apokalyptischen Visionsbericht[*]

Klaus Koch

1. Aufgabenstellung und Methode

1.1. Als das Organisationskomitee des International Colloquiums bei mir wegen eines Vortrages zur Literaturgattung der Apokalypse anfragte, versetzte es mich in Verlegenheit. Denn in "Ratlos vor der Apokalyptik" (1970, 20) hatte ich geschrieben, daß es "formgeschichtliche Untersuchungen zur Apokalyptik noch nicht gibt" und eine literarische Gattung Apokalypse bislang sich höchstens als Arbeitshypothese voraussetzen lasse. In den inzwischen verflossenen zehn Jahren sind zwar einige Beiträge erschienen, die erfolgversprechende Ansätze zeigen, insbesondere das Sonderheft 14 der Zeitschrift Semeia. Jedoch sehe ich mich auch heute noch nicht in der Lage, über eine Literaturgattung der Apokalypse insgesamt eine formgeschichtlich oder textlinguistisch zureichende Darstellung zu bieten. Deshalb beschränkte ich mich auf eine häufig auftauchende, große Partien der Apokalypsen füllende Gliedgattung, nämlich den Visionsbericht. In nahezu allen Büchern, die als Apokalypsen klassifiziert werden, gibt es Partien, in denen der Autor innere Gesichte nach einem strikt aufgebauten Sprachmuster berichtet. Diese Gliedtexte heben sich klar aus dem Kontext heraus und laden zu linguistischer Analyse geradezu ein. Im Buchzusammenhang nehmen sie eine tragende Funktion wahr, man denke nur an die zweite Hälfte des Danielbuches oder an den Hauptteil der Apokalypse Johannes oder die Schlußpartien des IV Esra. Das zugrunde liegende Sprachmuster nenne ich Visionsbericht und setze hinzu, daß er neben dem eigentlichen Gesicht auch dessen Deutung mit umfassen kann.

Erlauben Sie eine mathematische Spielerei. Nehmen wir A für ein apokalyptisches Buch, V für den Visionsbericht, so ergibt sich

$$A = X + V_{1-n}.$$

X steht für andere textliche Bestandteile, die noch nicht klar zu definieren sind, etwa für die Legenden in Dan 1–6 oder die Sendschreiben der

[*] Für Mithilfe danke ich Herrn Till Niewisch und Herrn Günter Baum von der Arbeitsstelle zur Erforschung der profetischen und apokalyptischen Sprache und Literatur an der Universität Hamburg.

Apokalypse Johannes. Das Element V scheint für Apokalypsen insofern konstitutiv zu sein als es da, wo es fehlt, durch eine gleichartige Gattung ersetzt wird wie z. B. den Bericht über die Himmelsreise des Apokalyptikers, der auch visionäre Elemente enthält, aber linguistisch eine abgewandelte Struktur aufweist. Will ich genau sein, hätte ich also zu schreiben:

$$A = X + V/ H,$$

wobei der Schrägstrich alternative Möglichkeiten und H den Bericht über die Himmelsreise bezeichnet.

Ausdrücklich bemerke ich, daß der ins Auge gefaßte Visionsbericht literarisch nie selbständig auftritt, sondern stets als Gliedgattung innerhalb eines größeren Rahmens. Nachdem der Gliedtext analysiert ist, wäre eigentlich nach seiner Funktion im Buchzusammenhang zu fragen. Der Aufgabe nachzugehen, sehe ich mich noch nicht in der Lage. Insofern bleiben meine Ausführungen bewußt unvollständig.

Meine erste These läuft darauf hinaus, daß der apokalyptische Visionsbericht auf ein profetisches Sprachmuster zurückgeht. Allerdings spielen in den profetischen Büchern des Alten Testaments Visionsberichte eine viel geringere Rolle. Doch das Textgefüge ähnelt dem späteren apokalyptischen Typos. Kontinuität wie Diskontinuität zwischen Profetie und Apokalyptik läßt sich hier exemplarisch aufweisen.

Meine zweite These will darlegen, daß sich in dieser sprachlichen Struktur eine bestimmte Weltsicht, ein spezifisches Verständnis über das Verhältnis von Gott und Mensch ausspricht, das ebenfalls Verbindungen zur profetischen Sprache hat, aber weit darüber hinausführt.

1.2. In den Visionsschilderungen eine für die Apokalypsen bezeichnende Sprachform zu sehen, die aus der Profetie herrührt, ist kein neuer Einfall. Schon als Friedrich Lücke 1832 "Apokalyptik" als historischen Sammelbegriff geprägt hat, hat er die Apokalyptik als "symbolischprophetische" Darstellung beschrieben, die lediglich profetische Zukunftsvorstellungen "... auf eine concrete Weise weiter ausbildet ...".

Zugleich sah er im "ungleich größeren Aufwand von Bildern, Symbolen, Allegorien und Personificationen in der Form zusammenhängender Exstasen und Visionen" den bezeichnenden Unterschied zwischen apokalyptischen und profetischen Schriften[1]. Mir will scheinen, daß damit bereits zu Anfang der Apokalyptikforschung erfaßt wurde, wie belangreich die visionären Elemente für unser Thema sind. Seitdem hat die Mehrzahl der Forscher angenommen, daß sich bei den Visionen sowohl Zusammenhang wie Unterschiedenheit gegenüber der Profetie abzeichnen.

Für eine formgeschichtliche Untersuchung verfügen wir heute über bessere Werkzeuge nicht nur als Lücke, sondern auch als die ersten

---

[1] Lücke 1832, 24 f.

Vertreter der Formgeschichte, etwa Gunkel bei seiner Behandlung des IV Esra[2]. Mit Hilfe der Strukturalgrammatik und insbesondere der Textlinguistik hat sich das formgeschichtliche Instrumentarium verfeinert[3]. Für profetische Visionsberichte habe ich anläßlich der Untersuchung des Buches Amos[4] eine entsprechende Analyse vorgelegt. Für Daniel 8 sowie 10–12 hat erstmals Hasslberger 1977 eine Analyse versucht. Erstaunlicherweise sieht er sich nicht imstande, zu entscheiden, ob Daniel 8 eine Gattung vorliege oder nicht[5]. Aber das *hängt* mit seiner m.E. unzureichenden Verwendung der Textlinguistik und dem Verzicht auf makrosyntaktische Fragestellungen zusammen. Im Gegensatz zu seinem Vorgehen eines *working up* – um einen Terminus der amerikanischen Linguistik aufzugreifen – bevorzuge ich eine *working down*-Methode, suche (nach der Abgrenzung der Texteinheit) anhand von Strukturweisern gleichsam von oben nach unten den Aufbau zu erfassen. Induktiv vorgehend, beginne ich

(1.) mit der Analyse eines exemplarischen Danielkapitels (§§2. und 3.). Dem folgt

(2.) der Vergleich mit einem profetischen Visionsbericht und einem Visionsabschnitt aus der alttestamentlichen Apokalypse. Die Ergebnisse werden anhand der Visionsschilderungen in den wichtigsten Apokalypsen insgesamt überprüft und die Kontinuität zur Profetie herausgestellt (§4.). Daran schließen sich

(3.) Erwägungen zur Diskontinuität zwischen Profeten und Apokalyptikern und zum Sitz im Leben an (§5.).

(4.) stelle ich semantische Erwägungen zur metaforisch-symbolischen Chiffrensprache der Texte an (§6.).

1.3. Eine Bemerkung zum *Vorverständnis*. In der öffentlichen Meinung stehen heute Visionen nicht hoch im Kurs, sondern gelten als krankhafte Symptome, Halluzinationen, bestenfalls als Illusionen, denen keinerlei Realitätswert zukommt. Selbst Theologen zollen solch pejorativer Einschätzung Tribut. Nur so erklärt sich wohl, daß die hinter den apokalyptischen Gesichten stehende Weltsicht kaum je erfragt wird. Vielleicht stellen wir einmal unsere Vorurteile zurück und erinnern uns daran, daß es neben diskursiven auch intuitive Erkenntnisse gibt. Intuition aber steht in den Visionen im Vordergrund, wird in ihnen plastisch. Welcher Erkenntniswert ihnen zukommt, werde ich am Ende anzudeuten versuchen.

2. Makrosyntax von Daniel 8

2.1. Rahmung und Aufriß

Die mittelalterliche Kapiteleinteilung hat die danielische Vision von Widder, Ziegenbock und ihren Hörnern als eigenständigen Gliedtext aus-

---

[2] Gunkel in: APAT, 335–350.
[4] Koch 1976, 1, 168f., 291 sowie 2, 86–88.
[3] Koch 1974, 289ff.
[5] Hasslberger 1977, 397.

gegrenzt, als Kapitel für sich genommen. Die Gattungskritik bestätigt diese Aussonderung (s. Übersicht 1), da der Text einen sinnvollen Einsatz und ebenso ein deutliches Ende aufweist. *Anfangs* steht ein *Synchronismus*, eine Zeitformel mit Königsnamen und Selbstvorstellung des Visionärs, wie auch sonst bei alttestamentlichen Neueinsätzen[6].

Der Eingangssynchronismus gehört zu einem erzählenden *Vorspann*, der bis V. 2aα reicht. Die geschichtliche Stunde wird markiert: "Im 3. Jahr des Königtums Belsazzars", der Leser dann auf die Gattung vorbereitet: "Ein חזון wurde sichtbar bei mir" und der verantwortliche Berichter genannt: "Ich, Daniel, sah den חזון ."

Danach wird erst der reale, dann der visionäre Ort genannt (Teil "Vorvision" in der Übersicht).

Zum Abschlußteil gehört wohl schon V. 26b, wo sich der Deuter direkt an den Seher mit der Aufforderung zur Geheimhaltung wendet, mit hervorgehobenem ואתה (Übersicht 1, Teil Abschluß).

Den *Ausgang* bildet V. 27 mit adversativ vorangestelltem ואני , ein Hinweis auf die *Betroffenheit des Visionärs*: "Ich ... war daraufhin tagelang krank" (*erste* und *letzte* Zeile der Übersicht 1, entsprechend 2,46; 7,28; Ez 3,15 u. ö.).

Innerhalb dieses Rahmens hebt der Erzähler *zwei Hauptteile* voneinander ab, indem er zweimal eine stehende Wendung benutzt, nämlich den Szenenweiser der hebräischen Erzählung ויהי + ב + Infinitiv "es geschah, als ..."[7] 8,2aβ.15. Der Szenenweiser wird gattungsspezifisch fortgesetzt: "Es geschah in meinem Sehen ..., daß ich in die Schauung (בחזון) sah" bzw. "daß ich um Einsicht (בינה = Deutung) bat". Beide Hauptteile enden in einer Phrase, die auf das Gesicht von Morgen und Abend hinausläuft V. 14.26 (s. die letzten Kolumnen von Teil 1 und 2 in der Übersicht).

Analysiert man die Ausdrucksebene, zerfällt der Text also deutlich in:

Vorspann 1–2aα
einen 1. Hauptteil 2aβ–14
einen 2. Hauptteil 15–26
Abschluß 26b.27.

Der durch makrosyntaktische Analyse erhobene Aufbau bestätigt sich bei semantischer Vergewisserung des Inhalts. Dann ergibt sich nämlich, daß der *erste Hauptteil* die *Schauung*, der *zweite* die auditive *Deutung* entfaltet.

Allerdings endet schon die Schauung mit einer kurzen Audition V. 13f., die aber nach der Makrosyntax zum ersten Hauptteil gehört und auch durch eine andere Einführung mit Kohortativ ואשמעה sich von der entsprechenden Einführung zur Deutung ואשמע 16 unterscheidet. Zwar

---

[6] Hasslberger 1977, 84f.   [7] Koch 1974, 146, 169.

werden 13 f. oft literarkritisch ausgeschieden, weil a) eine Audition innerhalb der Schauung unpassend und vor V. 15 ff. verfrüht erscheint, b) die
Verse von der Bild- zur Sachebene überwechseln (so zuletzt Hasslberger[8],
der auch V. 11 f. ausscheidet). Doch gleitender Übergang von Vision zu
Audition ist den Apokalyptikern geläufig. Und die Sachebene ist schon
von Anfang an mit der Bildebene vermischt, indem z. B. die Himmelsrichtungen V. 5 ff. wörtlich gemeint sind, andererseits behält "Zertretung" in
V. 14 die Bildsprache von V. 7.10 deutlich bei.

Die aufgewiesenen vier Teile lassen sich Textkonstituenten nennen oder,
fassen wir das Ganze als Erzählung, "Szenen", die sich aus Substanzen
zusammensetzen. Diese ihrerseits bauen sich aus Satzketten mit je einem
beherrschenden Subjekt auf, wie sich gleich zeigen wird.

2.2. Die Schauung V. 2aβ–14

Analysieren wir die beiden Hauptteile nach ihrer Makrosyntax: Wo
finden sich Gliederungssignale, wo wechseln die syntaktischen Subjekte?
Wie werden die "Tempora" gebraucht und verzahnt? Welche Lexeme
werden hervorgehoben?

2.2.1. Die schon bei Profeten gebräuchliche Visions-Eröffnungsnotiz
"die Augen erheben und schauen"[9] erscheint hier ungewöhnlich ausgeweitet V. 2aβ–3aβ. Nicht weniger als viermal im gesamten Abschnitt 8,1–14
wird mit חזון auf die innere Schau verwiesen. Zwei Ortsbestimmungen
werden mit dem visionären Vorgang zusammen erwähnt, sind also für ihn
belangreich.

In den folgenden Sätzen fällt die Wiederholung des Lexems ראה
"Schauen" auf. Mit dem Morfem der 1. Pers. Sing. unterbricht es den Fluß
der Erzählung und blendet dann von den geschauten Subjekten – Tieren,
Hörnern – zum Schauenden und seiner Wahrnehmung zurück. Wozu die
scheinbar überflüssige Wiederholung? Sie unterteilt sichtlich in einzelne
oder Subszenen, bildet also ein Gliederungssignal. Tritt das Präsentativ
הנה hinzu, wirkt der Einschnitt noch stärker V. 3.5 (15). Einem gleichen
Neueinsatz dienen der durch die 1. Pers. Perf. + Partizip herausgehobenen
Satz "ich aber, ich gewann Einsicht" ואני הייתי מבין V. 5 wie auch der mit
dem Lexem שמע (im AT oft mit ראה substituierbar) gebildete Kohortativ
"dann hörte ich" V. 13. Diese Ausdrücke der Wahrnehmung rufen die
(übergeordnete) Kommunikationsebene zwischen Sender und Empfänger
in Erinnerung und dies oberhalb der Ebene Erzählung/Bericht (die Übersicht rahmt die Anfangssignale ein und gliedert danach die Schauung in
parallele Kolumnen von rechts nach links).

---

[8] Hasslberger 1977, 17–19.   [9] Hasslberger 1977, 87 A. 20.

Solche Rückblenden zum schreibenden Subjekt wecken die Frage, ob hier wirkliche Erzählung wiedergegeben werden soll und nicht ein Bericht, bei dem es ebenso auf die Verläßlichkeit des Berichterstatters ankommt wie auf den Geschehensablauf selbst.

2.2.2. Auf die ראה-Einführungsnotiz bzw. ihre Entsprechungen folgen jedesmal eine oder mehrere *Nominalphrase(n)*. Da nominale Sätze im Hebräischen verhältnismäßig selten auftauchen, überrascht die Häufung in Dan 8. Was ist ihre Funktion? Derartige Phrasen lassen vor dem Auge des Sehers eine Hauptgestalt und deren entscheidenden Teile (Hörner) sichtbar werden, und zwar in einem zunächst verweilenden Zustand oder einem Dauergeschehen. Mit dem Ausdruck "Dauergeschehen" umreiße ich den Gehalt partizipialer Nominalsätze: der Widder ist nach drei Seiten hin "am Stoßen" V. 4, der Bock von Westen "im Kommen" V. 5. Ein Ziel solcher Bewegung wird vorerst nicht erkennbar. Anders in der Fortsetzung. Jedesmal erscheint dem Seher zunächst etwas Ruhendes oder sich ständig Vollziehendes. Doch die betreffenden Nominalsätze gehen meist in *Verbalsätze* über, die eine Bewegung der geschauten Gegenstände zu einem Ziel herausstellen. Die Subszenen der Schauung sind also in Momente der Dauer und solcher zielstrebiger Bewegung gespalten. Ein Rhythmus von Dauer und Wechsel, von Zustand und Bewegung herrscht also im ersten Hauptteil vor. – Die meisten Abschnitte enden schließlich mit Aussagen über Erfolg oder Ergebnis; hier werden andersartige, vorwiegend ו-*Perfektsätze* und Lexeme wie גדל, עשה und צלח verwendet: Widder wie Bock wie letztes Horn haben sich großgemacht V. 4.8.11 u.ö.

2.2.3. Eine Abweichung vom gleichmäßigen Aufbau bringt nur die Zeitbestimmung mit Infinitiv in Kol. B₂ V. 8b "während er (der Bock) gewaltig geworden war, war das große Horn schon abgebrochen." Nach einem in V. 8a angezeigten Ergebnis läuft noch einmal eine Geschehenskette an. Aus dem abgebrochenen wachsen vier Hörner und dann ein letztes Horn heraus. Dieses wird so übergroß, daß es zum Himmel reicht und Sterne herunterholt. Die Folgen werden V. 11 f. ausführlich wie nie mit sieben Verbalsätzen vermerkt; der Leser soll hier den entscheidenden Punkt wahrnehmen. Demnach vermute ich, daß die Zeitbestimmung ובעצמו V. 8b einen ähnlichen Einschnitt markiert wie sonst die Rückblenden auf die erste Person des Schauenden, nur daß hier um der dramatischen Zuspitzung willen nicht mehr auf den Wahrnehmungsakt verwiesen wird. Ein Seitenblick auf die Semantik bestätigt die besondere Stellung der Kolumne B₃. Unerhörtes spielt sich ab! Deshalb tauchen bewertende Sememe auf, die bislang vermieden wurden, allesamt nun pejorativ: Empörung (פשע), Zu-Boden-Werfen von Heiligtum und Wahrheit.

2.2.4. Doch die Eröffnung an Daniel ist noch nicht beendet. Eine *Audition* hebt ähnlich der voraufgehenden Vision mit einem Nominalsatz an, schließt daran aber gleich mit ו-Perfekt das Resultat an. Semantisch gesehen, kündet sie kein neues Geschehen, sondern die Befristung des eben Vermeldeten auf 2300 Abend-Morgen. Das läßt den Leser aufatmen: Am Ende wird das Heiligtum (קדשׁ) wieder heilvoll funktionieren! Ohne daß erkennbar wird, wie die heilvolle Wendung sich vollzieht, ist die Schauung plötzlich beendet.

2.3. Deutung V. 15–26

2.3.1. Mit "es geschah in meinem Schauen" wird V. 15, wie oben (§ 2.1.) behauptet, ein neuer Hauptteil eingeleitet. Er widmet sich der Erklärung des ersten. Wie dieser setzt er nicht sofort mit den Gegenständen ein, auf die es ankommt, den Tieren und ihren Hörnern, sondern mit einer umständlichen Vorbereitung. Wie V. 2 wird zunächst die Befindlichkeit des Sehers zum Thema gemacht. Zuerst wird durch Ich-Verweis die Kommunikation mit dem "Empfänger" erneut hervorgerufen. Dann tritt eine zweite Kommunikationsebene oberhalb der Erzählung zutage. Zwischen Daniel und einem neu auftauchenden himmlischen Informationsträger kommt es zu einer *Interaktion*, welche die Deutung als eine zweite, eigenständige Offenbarung von der ersten abheben will (Zwischenteil 4.1 der Übersicht).

2.3.2. Der Anfang der Deutung im engeren Sinn (Lexem ידע) wird durch eine Ankündigung mit Präsentativ herausgehoben V. 19. Die eigentlichen *Identifikationen*, die Aufschlüsselung der bislang geschauten Haupt- und Teilgegenstände, beginnen V. 20, markiert durch abrupt einsetzende nominale Nominalsätze. Wie bei einer mathematischen Gleichung, nur ohne Gleichheitszeichen, wird dem zuerst (vgl. V. 3) geschauten Hauptgegenstand asyndetisch V. 20b eine nominale Erklärung beigegeben. Der Widder mit den auffälligen Hörnern – Könige von Medien und Persien. Der Ziegenbock – König von Jonien. Das große Horn – das ist der erste König. Vier nachwachsende Hörner – vier Königreiche (Kol. A_1 und B_1 unter 4.2. der Übersicht).

2.3.3. Plötzlich wechselt die Satzart. Dem entspricht der Inhalt. Ab V. 23 wird auf Gleichsetzungen verzichtet. Eine Vielzahl von Verbalsätzen gibt nun dem Geschehen dramatischen Charakter, ohne die Notwendigkeit von Gleichsetzung mit früher Geschautem zu berücksichtigen. Durch eine Zeitbestimmung "am Ende ihrer Königreiche" und vielleicht auch durch Übergang zur Poesie (vgl. die Textgestalt in BHS) wird eine Zäsur zum vorangehenden Deutungsschema markiert. Entsprechende Kolumnen aus der Schauung V. 11 f. werden nicht gedeutet, sondern abgewandelt wiederholt: Stark wird seine Kraft, er hat Erfolg und handelt, er macht sich groß und tritt an den Fürsten der Fürsten heran V. 24f. (Übereinstimmun-

gen zwischen Schauung und Deutung sind in der Übersicht unterstrichen).
Aussagen treten nun hinzu, die im ersten Hauptteil noch fehlen: "Er
vernichtet die Starken und das Volk der Heiligen" oder "In Sorglosigkeit
vernichtet er die Vielen" V. 25 (in der Übersicht ausgelassen). Vor allem
überwindet die Deutung den düster klingenden Schluß der Schauung,
indem ohne Anhalt an dieser schließlich ein positives Ende dem Leser
verheißen wird: "Durch eine Nichthand wird es (das letzte Horn) zerbrechen."

2.3.4. Für die in der Schauung angefügte Audition (Kol. C) bedarf es
keiner Deutung. Sie spricht für sich und erhält nur, weil sie mit der
Eingrenzung von Abend-Morgen die Wende des Unheils implizit ankündigt, eine Bekräftigung V. 26a.

2.3.5. Es fällt auf, daß für die Sachhälfte das Lexem מלך "König (sein),
Königtum" mehrfach wiederholt wird und als Deuteschlüssel ab V. 20 die
Kolumnen des zweiten Teiles beherrscht (unterpunktet in der Übersicht).
Würde Dan 8 wie ein Gleichnis Jesu eingeleitet, stünde voran: "Das
menschliche Königtum ist gleich einem Widder und einem Ziegenbock,
die ...". Daß die Sachhälfte durch den Blick auf die Herrscher, auf die
Monarchen im Sinne der Weltherrscher bestimmt wird, ist für den israeliti-
schen Leser nicht so überraschend wie für den modernen. Große Tiere, die
über die Erde jagen, das klingt im alttestamentlichen Umkreis nach
Herrschaft, nach Gewalthabern. Hörner werden auch sonst im Hebräischen auf Könige bezogen (I Sam 2,10; Ps 89,18; 132,17 u. ö.). Dennoch ist
das Gewicht, das wie selbstverständlich der monarchischen Herrschaft bei
der Auflösung der Bilder zukommt, bemerkenswert, weil auch sonst in
den Apokalypsen das Königtum wie von selbst die Sachebene bei Visionen
bedeutet (Dan 2; 7; IVEsr 11f.; syrBar 35–40 u. ö.).

Wenngleich ich mich bei der Strukturanalyse auf wenige Angaben
beschränkt habe, so wird doch, wie ich hoffe, sichtbar, wie überlegt und
kunstvoll Dan 8 aufgebaut ist. Kein einziges Tempus, kein Morfem ist
nachlässig gesetzt, keine Wiederholung ohne Funktion. Ginge es nicht um
den düsteren Ernst apokalyptischer Geschichtsschau, möchte man sich
dem Aufbau geradezu mit ästhetischem Genuß hingeben.

2.3.6. Obwohl die Parallelität des ersten Hauptteils, der Schauung, mit
dem zweiten auf der Hand liegt, ergibt sich doch bei genauerem Hinsehen,
daß überraschenderweise der Deutungsteil nicht so stark durchgeformt ist
wie die Schauung. Das Umgekehrte wäre zu erwarten. Bei der Nacherzäh-
lung eines inneren Gesichtes rechnet man mit der Wiedergabe spontaner
Eindrücke, also mit Brüchen und Sprüngen, während eine Deutung straff
geordnet und logisch vor sich gehen könnte. Warum ist hier das Gegenteil
zu beobachten? Dafür weiß ich nur eine Erklärung anzubieten: für den
zweiten Teil verfügt der Autor offenbar nicht über ein so geprägtes

Sprachmuster wie für den ersten. Spielt hier die Gattungsgeschichte eine Rolle? Ehe das durch Vergleich mit anderen Texten zu prüfen ist, sind einige diachronische Beobachtungen zu Dan 8 selbst angebracht.

3. Überlieferungsgeschichte zu Dan 8 (Diachroner Exkurs)

3.1. Widder und Bock

Ein so genialer Eroberer wie Alexander der Große erscheint hier als bloßer Ziegenbock, ein haariger zudem (שָׂעִיר V. 21)! Ein wenig angemessenes Bild, will uns scheinen; das Symbol eines prächtigen Raubtieres würde uns eher einleuchten. Doch die Gegenüberstellung: König von Griechenland/Syrien = Bock, Könige von Medien-Persien = Widder ist nicht erst durch Daniel aufgebracht worden, sondern greift, wie Cumont[10] aufgewiesen hat, auf die astrale Geografie der Perserzeit zurück, nach der der Zodiakus seine Entsprechungen in zwölf Erdzonen hat, deren Charakter durch das entsprechende Gestirn bestimmt wird. Da die chaldäischen Astrologen ihre Geografie als Hilfsmittel für ihre Zeitdeutung und -voraussage benutzten, nehme ich an, daß sie sich auch mit dem im Altertum berühmten Alexanderzug beschäftigt und ihn als Kampf zwischen dem griechisch-syrischen Ziegenbock und dem iranischen Widder gedeutet haben. Auch die Hörner mögen hier schon eine Rolle gespielt haben; von der Bedeutung dieser Hörner bei späteren iranischen (sassanidischen) Fürsten ist einiges bekannt[11], und die Hörner Alexanders wirken noch im Koran Sure 18 nach, wo der große Grieche als "der Zweigehörnte" erscheint. Was V. 3–8a von Daniel geschaut wird, bestätigt nur ein über Israel hinaus längst verbreitetes Geschichtsbild. Was die einfachen Identifikationen im ersten Teil der Deutung V. 20–22 vermelden, hat nicht nur der Autor, sondern auch der unterrichtete Leser längst durchschaut. Insofern rechnen manche Kommentatoren – zuletzt Hasslberger[12] – zu Recht mit einer älteren Grundlage. Diese könnte außerisraelitisch gewesen sein, da jeder Bezug auf das Bundesvolk fehlt.

3.2. Der Himmelsstürmer

Innerhalb des Bildes wirkt grotesk, daß das nachwachsende Horn eines über die Erde laufenden Bockes plötzlich bis zum Himmel reicht, Sterne herunterholt und zertritt. Dieser Zug ist gewiß hinzugesetzt worden, um den erschütternden Eindruck der Gewaltherrschaft Antiochus' IV. Epipha-

---

[10] Cumont 1909, 263–273.
[11] Lukonin 1967, 207; cf. Amminianus Marcellinus 10,1.
[12] Hasslberger 1977, 401 f.

nes zu verarbeiten und aus geschichtlicher Kontinuität heraus zu begreifen. Das geschieht, indem ein weiteres mythisches Motiv aufgegriffen wird. Nach der profetischen Weissagung Jes 14,12–17 wird sich eines Tages der König von Babel über alle Sterne und den höchsten Gott erheben, jäh abstürzen und dann von den "Böcken" in der Unterwelt willkommen geheißen. Diese Stelle wird vermutlich in der Makkabäerzeit längst eschatologisch interpretiert – das bezeugen andere Jesajaexegesen bei Daniel – und paßt auf Antiochos, der auch König von Babel ist. In die astrale Geografie und Geschichtsdeutung fügt sich ein solcher Hybrismythos ausgezeichnet ein. Auch israelitische Frevelkönig-Himmelsstürmer-Überlieferungen wie die vom Kay Kâûš (= Kambyses?) spielen mit[13]. So legt sich nahe, den Angriff des Seleukiden auf die Verehrung der Götter (Dan 11,36–39 vgl. mit 8,11 f.25) als Angriff auf die Sterne zu versinnbildlichen.

3.3. Himmelsheer und Jerusalemer Kult

Der Frevel erreicht seinen Höhepunkt, als das Horn sich groß macht bis hin zum Fürsten des himmlischen Heeres, was angesichts Jos 5,14 nicht Gott selbst, sondern die höchste Engelsmacht bedeuten wird, also Michael. Dieser ist nicht nur Meister über alle anderen himmlischen Wesen samt den Gestirnen, sondern auch derjenige, der hinter dem Kult auf dem Zion steht und ihn heilsam macht (V. 11 f.). Engel sind die eigentlichen Subjekte des kultischen Handelns am Jerusalemer Tempel, wie besonders die qumranische angelic liturgy klar herausstellt[14]. Diesem Bereich gehört auch Gabriel zu, der für die Deutung verantwortlich ist. Solche Engelgestalten werden hier nicht erstmals bei den Israeliten bekannt und mit dem irdischen geschichtlichen Geschehen in Verbindung gesetzt. Die Angelologie ist wohl keiner zusammenhängenden Überlieferung entnommen, aber sie entspricht bereits gängigen Vorstellungskomplexen und wird vom Autor nicht als neue, überirdische Information aufgenommen.

3.4. Zusammenfassung

Diachrone Untersuchung ergibt also, daß das Kapitel mit überlieferten Stoffen randvoll angefüllt ist. Neu ist nur die Verkoppelung der drei genannten Motivreihen und vor allem die zeitliche Befristung: 2300 Abend-Morgen nur dauert der Spuk. Dazu tritt die Überzeugung von dem bevorstehenden Ende der Zeit (V. 17.19.23). Überkommene astralgeografische Geschichtsdeutung, mythische Scheu vor einem frevelhaften Übermenschen und angelologisch bestimmte Kultauffassung fügen sich zu einer

---

[13] Lewy 1949.   [14] Strugnell 1960, 318 ff.

schlüssigen Deutung des aufregenden gegenwärtigen Weltgeschehens zusammen. Das ist es, was der Autor als überwältigende Offenbarung erlebt, wenn ich einmal den modernen Begriff hier anführen darf.

4. Synchroner Aufweis einer Gliedgattung Visionsbericht in Profetie und Apokalyptik

Um das Anliegen des Verfassers in Dan 8 zu erkennen, ist nötig zu klären, wieweit ein bekanntes Sprachmuster aufgegriffen und wieweit situativ formuliert wird. Wird eine Gattung benutzt, die der Hörer kennt, und die durch Gliederungssignale und stereotype Lexeme eine bestimmte Sinnerwartung bei ihm hervorruft? Dem ist so. Ich weise das zunächst an zwei zeitlich weit auseinanderliegenden Beispielen näher nach, die ich mit dem Aufbau von Dan 8 vergleiche, um dann in einem skizzenhaft gehaltenen zweiten Durchgang die Ergebnisse durch einen Seitenblick auf andere profetische und apokalyptische Texte zu verallgemeinern.

4.1. Heuschreckenvision Am 7,1–3 und Schau des vierten Reiters Apk 6,7f.

4.1.1. Übersicht 2 stellt in Rubrik 1 die Gliederung eines der frühesten profetischen Visionsberichte dar. Wie beim Danielbeispiel heben sich Am 7,1–3 durch Gliederungssignale zwei Hauptteile klar voneinander ab. Als erstes wird eine Schau berichtet, dann folgt das Zwiegespräch des Profeten mit einer unsichtbaren überirdischen Stimme als zweites. Betrachten wir das Gefüge im einzelnen: Ein Vorspann, ein Synchronismus mit Königsjahren, fehlt zwar, doch taucht nachträglich eine Zeitbestimmung auf, die den מלך erwähnt: "Als die Spätsaat aufzugehen begann, es war die Spätsaat nach der Mahd des Königs." Der *Schauungsteil* hebt analog Dan 8 mit einer Eröffnungsnotiz an, gebildet aus dem Lexem ראה (hier hif. statt qal, doch s. Am 9,1). Nach einem Präsentativ wird der Hauptgegenstand im partizipialen Nominalsatz eingeführt, also mit einem Dauergeschehen verbunden: "Einer (war dabei), Heuschrecken zu bilden." Es schließt sich ein Verbalsatz an über eine für des Seher und seine Gemeinschaft fatale Bewegung: "Es geschah, daß sie mit dem Abfressen der Vegetation des Landes fertig waren" (zu Einzelheiten Koch, 1976: 1,200f.268f. und 2,47f.86f.). Der zweite, der *Redeteil* verläuft freilich erheblich anders, im Unterschied zu Daniel bedarf Amos keiner Deutung. Er begreift sofort, was droht; betet nicht um Aufklärung (Dan 8,15), sondern um Verschonung des Volkes. Sie wird denn auch gewährt. Doch das Muster eines himmlisch-irdischen Zwiegesprächs ist hier wie dort das gleiche.

Eine Anmerkung zum Inhalt. Hier hebt zweierlei den amosischen Text von der Danielvision ab. Während der Apokalyptiker die geschauten

Figuren symbolisch meint, versteht der Profet wahrscheinlich alles "real",
was ihm vor das innere Auge tritt. Tauchen Heuschreckenschwärme auf,
sind sie nach seiner und seiner Zeitmeinung tatsächlich von einem geheimnisvoll emsigen Bildner am Ende der Welt geformt worden. Der Wirklichkeitscharakter ist also an beiden Stellen ein verschiedener. Der zweite
Unterschied liegt in der Möglichkeit oder Unmöglichkeit, das Geschaute
abzuwenden. Der Profet rechnet noch damit, der Apokalyptiker nicht
mehr. Trotz solcher Verschiebung auf der Inhaltsebene überrascht, wie fest
die Struktur des Textmusters trotz des Abstandes von 500 Jahren hindurch-
scheint.

4.1.2. Da die Apokalyptik die Religionsgrenzen zwischen Judentum und
Christentum überspringt, greife ich ein weiteres Beispiel aus der Apoka-
lypse Johannes auf, das Gericht vom vierten apokalyptischen Reiter (vgl.
Übersicht 2 Rubrik 3).

Eine Zeitbestimmung steht wie bei Dan voran: "Als das vierte Siegel
geöffnet wurde." Sie ist jedoch insofern von besonderer Art, als sie nicht
auf eine Königsregierung abhebt, sondern auf eine vorangegangene visionäre Wahrnehmung des Sehers, die sich auf einer höheren Ebene vollzogen
hat als die nachfolgende eigentliche *Schau*. Zwischen beiden, dem vorbereiteten Gesicht vom Öffnen der Siegel und dem Hauptgesicht von Pferd und
Reiter, liegt eine Audition: "Ich hörte die Stimme des vierten Tieres:
komm!" Sie tönt gleichsam aus einer Zwischenebene, die unterhalb der
(himmlischen) Ebene des Lammes in der Eröffnung einerseits und oberhalb
des gleich zu berichtenden irdischen Geschehens andererseits liegt. Danach
aber wird der Text nach vertrautem Muster fortgesetzt. Eröffnungsnotiz
und Präsentativ: "Ich schaute und siehe" führen hinüber zu einem
Zustandsbild mit nominalen Phrasen: "Ein fahles Pferd – und der darauf
Sitzende ...." Im Unterschied zu Daniel und Amos wird eine deutende
Identifikation eingeblendet: "Sein Name war der Tod." Dann erscheint ein
zweiter Gegenstand, mit einer begleitenden Bewegung eingeführt: "Der
Hades folgte ihm nach." Die entscheidende *Bewegung* wird durch ein im
passivum divinum berichtetes Ereignis ausgelöst: "Es wurde ihnen Voll-
macht gegeben über ein Viertel der Erde, um zu töten mit dem Schwert
und dem Hunger und dem Tod und durch wilde Tiere."

Bedarf es zusätzlicher Erläuterungen für die strukturelle Übereinstimmung mit Daniel und Amos? Die (Glied-)Gattung des hebräisch-aramäischen Visionsberichts ist also bis in neutestamentliche Zeit und bis in
griechische Texte hinein gebräuchlich geblieben. Kein Wunder, daß einem
Kommentar wie Lohmeyer zu Apk 6 auffällt: "Die Sprache ist stark von
Semitismen durchzogen."[15]

---

[15] Lohmeyer 1953, 59.

Weil der *Deutungsteil* ausfällt, scheint der Text näher bei Amos als bei
Daniel zu stehen. Aber die deutende Zwischenbemerkung über den Reiter
als den Tod läßt erkennen, daß der Wirklichkeitscharakter nicht der von
Am 7, sondern der von Dan 8 ist. Für den Apokalyptiker Johannes existiert
ein fahles Pferd nicht irgendwo real am Rand der Welt, um im eschatologischen Bedarfsfall herbeigeholt zu werden. Vielmehr handelt es sich um ein
Symbol für den schnell dahinfahrenden Tod. Mag auch dessen Personifika-
tion an sich "ernst" gemeint sein wie die des Hades, so gilt das gleiche nicht
für seine Reitergestalt wie denn auch für den Hades ein entsprechendes Bild
fehlt. Die Nähe zu Daniel zeigt sich auch in dem Gesättigtsein mit
spezifischen Überlieferungen. Die vier Plagen, welche die Menschen töten,
sind nach Ez 14,21 eschatologische Wirkungsgrößen. Die vier Pferde, für
die vier Windrichtungen bestimmt, erinnern an Sach 1,8 und 6,1–6. Wie
bei Daniel wird die Verklammerung von umlaufenden Überlieferungen,
insbesondere profetischen Weissagungen, und ihre Einordnung in einen
umgreifenden zeitlichen Entwurf zum Offenbarungserlebnis für den
Autor. Das war bei Amos noch anders. Wenn er einer Heuschreckengefahr
inne wird, dann hat das ein höheres Maß von Spontaneität und hängt nicht
mit vorliegenden Textvorbildern zusammen. Apokalyptisches Erleben
hingegen resultiert aus exegetischer Meditation.

4.2. Verbreitung der Vergleichsebene

Was sich an den ausgewählten Beispielen ergeben hat, läßt sich verallgemeinern. Die Übersicht 3 bietet den Strukturaufriß von 44 Visionsberichten, und zwar aus IReg, Großen und Kleinen Profeten sowie Daniel; dazu
treten deutero- und außerkanonische Belege (Hen, Bar, Test XII, IV Esr)
sowie weitere Abschnitte aus der neutestamentlichen Apokalypse Johannes. Die vorliegende Übersicht ist begreiflicherweise vorläufiger Art, sie
bedarf in jedem Falle näherer Untersuchung (in den Übersichten 1 und 2
werden einzelne Punkte stärker differenziert). Die Darstellung ist so angelegt, daß links die Belege aus der Profetie erscheinen, daran schließen sich
die Spalten Gattungsgliederung und Syntax an; auf der rechten Seite folgen
die Belege für apokalyptische Visionen. Kapitelangabe erfolgt jeweils am
Kopf der Spalte, Zahlen innerhalb der Spalten bezeichnen die Verse.

Verfolgen wir, was sich in diesen Berichten über innere Gesichte zeigt,
so läßt sich ein durch ein ganzes Jahrtausend gleichbleibendes Muster
nachweisen; demnach sind wir berechtigt, von einer Gattung zu reden. Fast
durchweg herrscht Zweiteilung vor. Zuerst wird eine Schauung berichtet,
dann ein Redeteil als Zwiegespräch einer himmlischen Stimme mit dem
Seher. Der zweite Teil fehlt nur, falls wie beim vierten Reiter Apk 6 der
Visionsbericht in eine größere Kette von Texten gleicher Gattung einge-
reiht ist.

4.2.1. *Struktur der Schauung.* Anfangs steht, gewöhnlich nach einer Zeitbestimmung, die bekannte Eröffnungsformel "ich/er schaute" (hebr. ראה , aram. חזה , griech. *ἰδεῖν*). Ein nachfolgendes Präsentativ "und siehe" (והנה / ואלו / וארו / *καὶ ἰδού*) leitet über zu einem zuständlich beschriebenen Hauptgegenstand, der sich an einem belangreichen Ort befindet. Einige seiner Teile werden u. U. zusätzlich beschrieben; evtl. tritt ein zweiter, dritter, vierter Hauptgegenstand hinzu. Danach wird zu Verbalsätzen übergegangen und eine Bewegung signalisiert, auf die der Schaubericht als Klimax zuläuft. Er kann schließlich mit der Feststellung eines Ergebnisses ausklingen. – Ab Ezechiel tritt statt einer bloßen Zeitbestimmung ein ausgestalteter Vorspann (oder eine Vorvision) auf (Rubrik 1), der über die Befindlichkeit des Sehers Auskunft gibt, seinen Ort oder über eine ihn privat betreffende vorbereitende Schau. In einzelnen Apokalypsen weitet sich das zu einer vorbereiteten Aktion des Sehers aus, der mit Fasten oder Beten eine Vision heraufführen will.

4.2.2. *Struktur des himmlisch-irdischen Zwiegesprächs.* Hier variiert das Muster stark. Obligatorisch bleibt, daß entweder Gott selbst oder ein himmlischer Bote das Geschaute kommentiert bzw. aus ihm Folgerungen zieht. Ein Profet wie Amos kann an dieser Stelle mit einer Fürbitte anheben, um das Geschaute abzuwenden; er kann aber auch von der himmlischen Stimme nach dem Geschauten befragt werden und Bescheid geben (Am 7,8; 8,3), um den Gegenstand besonders eindrücklich werden zu lassen. Bei profetischen Texten endet der Teil mit einer göttlichen Schlußrede, die meist die Form einer Profezeiung annimmt und vom Seher öffentlich zu künden ist (Rubrik 5).

Ab Sacharja bahnt sich eine andere Gestaltung des Redeteils an. Der Seher fragt ratlos: "Was sind diese (Bilder)?" und erhält eine Deutung: "Diese bedeuten die und die (metahistorischen Größen)" (Sach 1,9f.; 2,4 u. ö.). Solche *Deutungen* werden stehend bei Dan, syrBar, IV Esr; während äthHen und Apk dabei bleiben, nur Visionsberichte zu bieten, die in sich selbstverständlich sind und nachträglicher Aufschlüsselung nicht bedürfen. (Im Überblick 3 weisen die Rubriken 3 und 4 die verschiedenen Ausgestaltungen des Redeteils aus.)

4.2.3. *Gattungsgeschichte.* Durchmustert man das Gefüge der 44 Visionsberichte – die Zahl ließe sich leicht vermehren –, so bieten sie ein geradezu ideales Material, um die Geschichte einer Gattung zu rekonstruieren. Wo gibt es sonst in der Bibel ein Sprachmuster, das sich so durchgängig bis in das letzte Buch des Neuen Testaments hinein verfolgen läßt und eine wachsende Ausweitung widerspiegelt. Von Amos angefangen, wo wir fünfmal die glatte Zweiteilung von knapper Schauung mit je einem Hauptgegenstand einerseits und einem Redeteil andererseits vorfinden, erweitert sich der Bestand schon bei Jesaja, um bei Ezechiel und Sacharja zusätzliche

Teile aufzunehmen. In der Apokalyptik werden dann alle Teile von Henoch/Daniel bis syr. Baruch/IV Esra/Apokalypse Johannes erheblich ausgeweitet. Dennoch schimmert das Grundmuster weiter durch. Dabei gibt es ältere Muster noch bei jüngeren Autoren; Jeremia z. B. faßt sich nicht weniger knapp als Amos, und Henoch verzichtet auf Deutung, obwohl diese schon bei Sacharja weithin hinzugehört. Doch aufs Ganze gesehen gliedern sich die Apokalypsen zwanglos in die bei den frühen Schriftprofeten anhebende Geschichte der Textsorte ein.

4.2.4. *Verwandte Gattungen.* Im System einer semitischen Sprache wird eine Gattung wie der Visionsbericht nicht isoliert weitergegeben, sondern steht mit anderen in Beziehung, in diesem Fall vor allem mit dem *Traumbericht*, der auch ein Zustandsbild mit Hauptgegenstand bringt, dem schon Gen 40,12.18 eine fachgerechte Deutung (freilich durch Menschen) nachfolgt. Der hebräische Traumbericht entspricht einem mesopotamischen Muster[16], zu dem seit je ein eigener Deutungsteil gehört. Ist es zufällig, daß nach dem Exil bei dem babylonisch beeinflußten Sacharja die Deutung im Visionsbericht neu auftaucht und sie im aramäischen Teil des Daniel-Buches viel schulmäßiger heraustritt (durch das Lexem פשר) als im hebräischen? Auch die hebräische *Späher- und Wächtermeldung* ist zu berücksichtigen, die mit der gleichen Einführungsnotiz und ähnlichen Zustandsbildern ausgestattet wird[17]. Doch die Querverbindungen können hier ebenso weiter verfolgt werden wie parallele apokalyptische Gattungen mit Bericht von einer Himmelsreise oder dem Testament eines Gottesmannes.

4.2.5. *Ergebnis:* Die Entwicklung der Sprachform des Visionsberichtes läßt sich nicht nur durch Jahrhunderte, sondern auch über die Sprachgrenzen hinweg vom Hebräischen zum Aramäischen und Griechischen verfolgen. Das gleiche Grundmuster wird erstaunlich konstant festgehalten. Dennoch bleibt die Verbreitung der Textsorte auf einen verhältnismäßig schmalen, semitisch beeinflußten Raum beschränkt. Obwohl die Apokalyptik als solche einer internationalen Bewegung um die Zeitenwende zuzugehören scheint, wo man sich im gesamten Mittelmeergebiet und Nahen Osten intensiv um "Zukunftserforschung" müht, hat die Gattung dieser Art von Visionsbericht, soweit ich sehen kann, im hellenisierten Teil Israels kaum Fuß gefaßt, tauchte deshalb weder in den Sibyllinen noch den Nag-Hammadi-Schriften auf (hier ist höchstens ein schwacher Nachklang zu bemerken, wenn es in der Paulus-Apokalypse z. B. zweimal heißt: "Ich blickte auf und sah", mit nachfolgender Nominalphrase[18]).

---

[16] Oppenheim 1956; Richter 1963. [17] Reimers 1976, 206.
[18] Robinson (Hrsg.) 1977, 241.

5. Diskontinuität von profetischem und apokalyptischem Visionsbericht. Der veränderte Sitz im Leben

5.1. Stereotype Abweichungen

Trotz des gleichbleibenden Gattungsmusters zeigen sich zwischen profetischen und apokalyptischen Texten im Blick auf die Visionsdarstellungen Unterschiede, deren Hauptpunkte ich kurz umreiße.

(1) Von Gesichten zu erzählen, stellt im Profetenbuch eine Ausnahme dar, in einer Apokalypse wird es zur Regel. Jesaja berichtet von einer einzigen Vision, Jeremia nur von dreien, würden die drei fehlen, würde niemand für das Gesamtbild Jeremias Wesentliches vermissen. Viele Profeten schweigen über diesen Punkt völlig. Unter den Apokalyptikern gibt es dagegen keinen, der auf *Visionsberichte* verzichtet, und wir haben Anlaß, hier ein entscheidendes apokalyptisches Anliegen zu vermuten.

(2) Die *Betroffenheit des Sehers* durch den Visionsvorgang tritt hervor. Ein apokalyptischer Seher spielt bei den Visionen aktiv und passiv mit, während der Profet meist ein bloß Schauender war, der höchstens hinterher wie Amos Fürbitte leistet oder wie Jesaja (6,11) klagt: "Wie lange dies?" Nicht nur, daß Apokalyptiker durch die Schauung zu Boden gerissen werden und der רוח bedürfen, um wieder auf die Beine zu gelangen (Dan 8,27 z. B.), sie treten als Partner den überirdischen Subjekten gegenüber, wagen u. U. wie der IV Esr sogar energische Gegenrede (IVEsr 7,45ff. z. B.).

(3) Eine gegliederte Engelwelt taucht auf. Zwar berichten die Profeten gerade in ihren Visionsberichten von *überirdischen Gestalten*, von denen sie sonst nie sprechen, wie Sarafen (Jes 6), Heuschreckenbildner (Am 7), überirdische Verderber (Ez 9), eine Frau Bosheit (Sach 5,5ff.). Doch bei allem erscheint Jahwe ihnen selbst und bleibt entscheidender Akteur (Ez 1; Sach 3). Die ältesten Berichte stellen sogar Thronratsvisionen dar (IReg 22; Jes 6). In den Apokalypsen jedoch wird Gott für den Visionär in der Regel unsichtbar (Ausnahme Dan 7,9f.). Statt seiner nimmt die Engelhierarchie einen breiten Platz ein und wird zur Offenbarungsquelle bzw. -vermittlung, aber auch zum Antreiber wie Gegenspieler der irdischen Mächte (Dan 8,11f.25).

(4) *Deutung* wird nötig, deren die Profeten nicht bedurften. Schaut Amos Heuschrecken, die vom Ende der Welt aufbrechen und sieht er dort eine geheimnisvolle Gestalt, die sie bildet, dann ist das für ihn Realität. Der Referenzbezug ist durchsichtig. Schaut Jesaja den über dem Jerusalemer Tempel riesenhoch aufragenden Jahwä, so ist auch das für ihn wahrscheinlich blanke Wirklichkeit, nur daß sie das normale Menschenauge nicht wahrzunehmen vermag. Nach profetischem Verständnis eröffnen also Visionen eine Tiefenschau, welche das normale Sehvermögen übertrifft und verlängert, wie heute ein Röntgenschirm den Gesichtskreis des

Betrachters ausweitet, doch taucht keine "Transzendenz" jenseits der Immanenz auf. Selbst Ezechiel hält seine bisweilen skurrilen Gesichte für eine bloße Tiefenschau der alle betreffenden Wirklichkeit; deshalb ist er in der Lage, mitten in der Vision den Namen von Männern zu rufen, die er während der Schauung tätig sieht (11,13). – In apokalyptischen Visionen treten dagegen Symbole hervor, deren Referenzbezug dunkel bleibt und erst ausdrücklich gemacht werden muß. Hinzu kommt, daß ein und derselbe Geschichtsablauf durch mehrere Gesichte und entsprechende Deutungen dargeboten wird. Haupt- und Teilgegenstände der Schauung erscheinen nicht mehr mit der "immanenten" Sache, die sie bedeuten, schlechthin deckungsgleich. Der Apokalyptiker Johannes stellt sich gewiß seinen Christus nicht letztlich in der Gestalt eines Lammes vor, rechnet mit "Konkurrenzgestalten" wie Menschensohn (14,14 nach 14,1 ff.) oder Reitern (19,11 nach 19,7 ff.). Für Daniel sah der historische Alexander gewiß "real" anders aus als ein zottiger Ziegenbock mit Einhorn. Weil nicht mehr der Bereich sichtbarer Wirklichkeit durch die innere Schau einfach vergrößert wird, sondern geschichtliche Kräfte gleichsam mehrdimensional und chiffriert dargestellt werden, wird eine "multiplicity of approaches" möglich, kann eine Größe wie die griechische Herrschaft z. B. durch eisernetönerne Beine eines Standbildes Dan 2 oder durch ein Untier aus dem Meer Dan 7 abgebildet werden. Bezeichnenderweise versteht das Zeitalter der Apokalyptiker die amosische Heuschreckenvision nicht mehr wörtlich, sondern bezieht sie auf den Endfeind Gog, s. LXX zu 7,1. (Auf die apokalyptische Metaforik gehe ich im nächsten Paragrafen noch gesondert ein.)

Was hier als Unterschied zwischen den beiden Arten von Visionsberichten herausgestellt wird, will nicht als starre Grenzziehung begriffen werden. Apokalyptische Gattungsmotive beginnen bisweilen schon bei Ezechiel, ein andermal bei Sacharja; und profetische reichen stellenweise bis hin zum ersten Henoch, im Blick auf das Fehlen eines ausgebauten Deutungsteiles bis hin zur Apokalypse Johannes (s. die leeren Spalten bei Rubrik 4 in Übersicht 3).

5.2. Sitz im Leben – Ähnlichkeit und Differenz

Trotz der genannten vier Unterschiede, die im Laufe der Zeit zunehmen, bleibt der Eindruck einer gleichbleibenden Struktur vorherrschend. Wie ist im hebräisch-aramäischen Sprachgebrauch die Konstanz über ein Jahrtausend zu erklären?

Genügt es, mit bloßen literarischen Nachahmungen zu rechnen? Exegeten der Wellhausenschule haben weitgehend solche Erklärung bevorzugt. Wollen schon Ezechiel oder Sacharja ältere Vorbilder imitieren, wie gele-

gentlich angenommen worden ist? Falls man es für die beiden verneint, hat
man kaum ein Recht, bei den Apokalypsen bloße Nachahmung vorauszusetzen, wo doch jede Schrift eine eigene Ausprägung und Fortschreibung
der Gattung zeigt und von sklavischem Nachäffen nichts zu merken ist.
Unterschiedenheiten bei gleichbleibender Grundstruktur zeigen, daß mit
einer lebendigen Sprachentwicklung zu rechnen ist. Gewiß handelt es sich
dabei nicht um eine Erscheinung der Umgangssprache, sondern um eine
Sondersprache, die in bestimmten Kreisen gepflegt wurde.

Damit stellt sich die Frage nach dem Sitz im Leben. Visionsberichte
wurden offenbar formuliert durch Leute, die sich in visionärer Versenkung
mit Gebet, Fasten und dergleichen übten. Das läßt schon für die Profeten
eine gewisse "Schultradition" voraussetzen[19]. Wenn die Apokalyptiker ein
profetisches Sprachmuster für den Bericht über geheime Erfahrungen
wieder aufgreifen und selbständig umprägen, werden die entsprechenden
psychologischen Praktiken vorauszusetzen sein. Das spräche dafür – der
Frage kann hier im einzelnen nicht nachgegangen werden –, daß sich die
am "Geist" des apokalyptischen Heroen (Daniel, Esra) Interessierten in
eigenen Zirkeln, vielleicht in eigenen Synagogen, trafen und ihre Schrift-
auslegung und Deutungsprobleme einander offenlegten.

6. Textsemantik

6.1. Das Rätsel apokalyptischer Bildersprache

Was die Interpretation apokalyptischer Schriften so schwer macht und
bei manchen Lesern den Eindruck von krauser Phantastik ohne Sinn und
Zweck hervorruft, ist die Eigenart, Dinge und Verhältnisse nicht direkt
anzusprechen, sondern durch eine Masse von "Symbolen" zu chiffrieren,
von Dingen und Bäumen und Himmelswesen statt von Menschen und
historischen Mächten zu reden. Der moderne Exeget findet sich in die
Rolle "derer draußen" versetzt, denen nach der synoptischen Gleichnistheorie Mk 4,10f. das mysterion des Gottesreiches nur ἐν παραβολαῖς und
zum Zweck der Verstockung vorgelegt wird! Hier ist nicht weiter zu
gelangen ohne eine Behandlung des apokalyptischen Metafergebrauchs.

Für die apokalyptische Bildersprache stehen die alttestamentlichen Profeten Pate. Auch sie hatten weithin vermieden, die Dinge beim Namen zu
nennen. Amos z. B. redet nie von den Assyrern, wo er vom Untergang
Israels spricht, und hat sie doch offensichtlich im Auge. Bei ihm wie bei
den übrigen Profeten spielen in Visionsschilderungen (und Symbolhand-
lungen) Metafern und Symbolzeichen eine besonders große Rolle. Insofern
ist eine Analogie zu den Apokalyptikern gegeben. Dennoch empfinden wir

---

[19] Koch 1978.

einen Unterschied, wenn wir von der Profetie zur Apokalyptik übergehen. Die Heuschrecken Am 7 sind wirkliche Tiere, was Widder und Bock in Dan 8 nicht in gleicher Weise sind. Anderswo ist das Ergebnis beim Vergleich vielschichtiger, doch der Unterschied bleibt. So profezeit z. B. Hos 13,4–8 Jahwes Heimsuchung, der sich wie Löwe, Bär und Panther an den Weg Israels legen und es anfallen wird. Hier sind die Raubtiere bildlich genommen, doch das erklärt sich aus dem Kontext, wo vorher von Jahwes Hirtentätigkeit (רעה) geredet wird und damit eine jedermann bekannte "Gebrauchsmetafer" verwendet worden war; um eine Antithese zum bisherigen göttlichen Verhalten herauszustellen, wird im gleichen Bildfeld mit dem Gegensatz zum רעה fortgefahren. Von den drei Raubtieren redet ebenso Dan 7 und bezieht sie auf übermächtige Völker. Doch der Unterschied liegt auf der Hand. Bei Hosea waltet die gewöhnliche Anschauung der zoologischen Spezies vor. Der gemeinsame Charakter der Raubtiere, die Gefährlichkeit für die Herde, wird zur Basis eines einfachen Vergleichs. Bei Daniel hingegen fehlt ein dem Leser geläufiger Bildkontext, die Anschauung wird von vornherein "übertrieben" und aus jeder Alltagserfahrung herausgenommen: ein Löwe mit Adlerflügeln, die nachher ausgerissen werden – das Tier wird sogar zu aufrechtem Gang bewegt und erfährt eine "Herztransplantation". Oder ein Panther mit vier Flügeln und vier Häuptern! Obwohl auch hier Gefährlichkeit für menschliches Leben mitspielt, schwingen doch offenbar auch andere Konnotationen mit und sind von Gewicht.

Verglichen mit dem Profeten fällt weiter das Verschwimmen der Zeitstufen in der Apokalyptik auf. Bei profetischen Visionen liegt entweder die Gegenwärtigkeit des Geschauten auf der Hand (Jes 6) oder seine Zukünftigkeit (so meistens), obschon beides ineinander übergehen kann. Die Heuschrecken, die Amos erschaut, werden in der Ferne schon gebildet, aber werden Palästina erst nach geraumer Zeit erreichen (wenn überhaupt!). Für den Profeten wie für den Leser wird also ein begrenzter, in sich geschlossener Zeitausschnitt offenbar, dessen Relation zur Gegenwart eindeutig ist. Vergangenes bildet keinen Gegenstand für profetische Visionen (Ausnahme Jer 3,6ff.?). Bei den Apokalyptikern, angefangen mit dem Traum von der Völkerstatue Dan 2, werden in die Visionen weite Zeithorizonte abgeschritten, bei denen die Grenzen zwischen Vergangenheit und Gegenwart ebenso zerfließen wie zwischen Gegenwart und Zukunft. Die verschlüsselte Sprache führt dazu, daß der Exeget im dunkeln tappt mit der Frage, ob z. B. Dan 8,25 insgesamt zukünftig gemeint ist oder nur mit seinem letzten Satz. Hat das letzte Horn, das Daniel beim letzten Tier erschaut, die "Vielen" schon vernichtet, als die Apokalypse niedergeschrieben wird, oder wird es das noch tun? Steht sein Auftrumpfen gegen den Fürst der Fürsten noch aus oder nur das Zerbrechen durch die Nicht-Hand?

Von einem abgeschlossenen, überschaubaren Zeitausschnitt kann also nicht mehr die Rede sein.

Wozu all die Verrätselungen und die scheinbar skurrile Darstellungsweise? Schauen wir uns die Sache bei Dan 8 näher an.

6.2. Innere Form der Schauung V. 3–14

Ehe ich die Semantik einzelner Wendungen verfolge, weise ich auf die Erzähltechnik des Verfassers. Sehen wir vom Rahmen ab, läßt sich der *plot* einer einfachen Erzählfolge erkennen, in der zunächst als Aktanten zwei als aggressiv geltende Tiere, Widder und Ziegenbock, hervortreten. Begonnen wird mit dem Widder V. 3, wobei die Aufmerksamkeit sich auf seine Hörner richtet. Nach einem unterbrechenden Rückbezug auf den Sehakt V. 4 läßt die anhebende Erzählung den Widder unmotiviert nach drei Himmelsrichtungen losrasen und alle anderen Tiere überrennen, bis er allein als groß dasteht (הגדיל). Nach einer zweiten Rückblende, mit der der Berichterstatter wieder aus dem Gang der Handlung herausspringt und auf seine Person verweist, wird der zweite Aktant V. 5 eingeführt, wieder mit dem Ton auf dem Horn. Sobald er, der Bock, auftaucht, fliegt er auch schon auf den ersten, den Widder, zu. Ehe es zum Zusammenstoß der beiden kommt, schließt der Berichtende gleichsam die Augen und macht sich nochmals seine Schauung und Reflexion klar, V. 7. Der Sieg des einen über den anderen wird durch fünf Narrative relativ ausführlich gemalt. Dann wird auf längere Verläufe mit ו-perf.-Sätzen umgeschaltet: ein Retter bleibt aus, der Ziegenbock macht sich übergroß (הגדיל). Nach V. 8b erfolgt eine überraschende Wende. Ohne äußere Einwirkung bricht das Horn dem Bock ab, er verliert das Werkzeug seines Sieges. Wird er nun unterliegen? Keineswegs, vier neue Hörner wachsen alsbald nach. Bei dem einen entsteht eine Vergabelung, die sich nach zwei Himmelsrichtungen aggressiv benimmt und dann über alles Frühere hinaus sich auswächst. Riesenhaft lang, ragt seine Größe (הגדיל) bis zum Himmel. Das sich verselbständigende Horn fährt in seinem Angriff fort, reißt Sterne vom Himmel und zertritt sie wie einst der Widder zertreten wurde (רמס wie V. 7).

Mitten im Erzählgang hat der Berichtende eine neue Aktantengruppe eingeführt: Himmelsheer und Sterne. Ergänzt wird sie durch den Fürst des Heeres, sein ständiges Tamidopfer und die Stütze seines Heiligtums. Der Fürst des Himmels läßt sich nicht herabwerfen, wohl aber wird seine irdische Repräsentanz in Opfer und Heiligtum gestürzt. In V. 12 werden noch einmal zwei Narrative gewählt, um die Dramatik zu erhören, bevor eine vorläufige Ergebnisnotiz (ועשתה והצליחה) analog V. 4b die Szene beschließt. Damit bricht die Erzählung ab, an der Stelle, wo die Spannung

beim Leser am höchsten und die Unwahrscheinlichkeit am größten geworden war. Angriff eines Ziegenbocks auf den Himmel und Herabstürzen der Sterne – soll das das letzte Wort sein? Hinzu tritt, daß der Tempel von פשע beherrscht wird. Das heißt, daß das Chaos vorherrscht, die Himmelskräfte sind Garanten der Weltordnung und gewährleisten zusammen mit dem Kult am Tempel den Bestand der Menschheit vor ihrem Schöpfer. Eine "eigentliche" Erzählung müßte also weiterfahren.

Doch Daniel kann es sich leisten, abzubrechen. Er teilt Schauung mit. Die Rubrik חזון, anfangs gleich zweimal herausgestellt V. 2–4, hat darauf vorbereitet, daß das Berichtete u. U. keinen glatten Verlauf nimmt. חזון als Gattungsweiser rechtfertigt auch den Abbruch mitten im Geschehensverlauf. Zwar gibt V. 13 eine Fortsetzung, jedoch auf einer anderen Ebene, derjenigen der Audition. Diese Audition gilt manchen Kommentatoren als höchst ungeschickt angefügt, als "ein weiteres Beispiel für die besagte literarische Unzulänglichkeit, die des Verfassers Stil kennzeichnet"[20]. Ist dem wirklich so oder wird hier vorschnell ein abendländischer Maßstab von sachgemäßer Erzählung unsachgemäß angewendet? Die Audition wechselt von der bislang vorgeführten Tierebene zu einem Bereich von Heiligen über, die über die Zeiten zu befinden haben. Dort war die Uhr des Geschehens für das zertretene Heiligtum angehalten worden. Der Ziegenbock agierte also nicht, so soll der Leser begreifen, derart autark, wie es aufgrund der vorangehenden Schauung erschien. Er war "gesteuert", wie auf der höheren Kommunikationsebene erkennbar wird. Hier wird auch mitgeteilt, daß der traurige Zustand nicht für immer bleibt, sondern nur für 2300 Abend-Morgen. Was dann passiert, bleibt offen. Insofern unterstreicht die Audition nur, daß noch etwas geschehen wird. Die Spannung wird gesteigert, aber noch nicht gelöst.

6.3. Semantik des Visionsteils

Was als Verhalten übermütig gewordener Tiere vorgeführt wird, will nicht amüsante oder schreckliche zoologische Kuriosa schildern. Der Leser wird schnell gewahr, daß die Wörter anderes bedeuten als in der Alltagssemantik, als in ihrem üblichen paradigmatischen Feld.

Zwar fängt es harmlos an. Ein Widder mit einem großen und einem kleinen Horn, am אובל von Susa stehend, und ein Ziegenbock, der vom Westen her auf ihn zurennt, dergleichen kommt vor (wenngleich ich in Unkenntnis altorientalischer Haustiere nicht weiß, ob die Böcke der beiden Tierarten aufeinander loszugehen pflegen und ob im Konfliktfall ein Ziegenbock einen Widder zu Boden werfen kann). Bald mischt sich jedoch

---

[20] Porteous 1962, 105.

Ungereimtes, semantisch Widersprüchliches ein. Bei einem normalen Widder wachsen die Hörner beidseitig gleichmäßig, nicht das eine nach dem andern. Daß kein Tier in West, Nord und Süd sich vor einem Widder retten kann, klingt ebenso unwahrscheinlich wie die Aussage, daß kein (menschlicher oder übermenschlicher) מציל dem Widder entgegentritt. Ein Ziegenbock mit nur einem Horn, das gibt's, aber das befindet sich dann nicht zwischen den Augen. Ein solcher Bock kann nicht über die gesamte Ausdehnung der Erde heranpreschen, ohne den Boden zu berühren! (Manche Ausleger denken hier an ein Märchenmotiv, das aber aus einem Deuterojesaja-Wort [Jes 41,3] stammt.) Bricht einer Ziege das Horn ab, so wächst es nicht nach, jedenfalls nicht vierfach nach und nicht so, daß eine Sprosse bis zum Himmel reichen und Gestirne herunterstoßen kann. Ab V. 10 wechselt die Schau aus der Horizontalen in die Vertikale. Ein Fürst, der hoch droben über den Gestirnen weilte – seine Erscheinung wird bezeichnenderweise nicht beschrieben –, wird mit dem Tamid-Opfer und dem Heiligtum unten (dem Zion, weiß der Leser) eng verbunden. Droben wie drunten greift der Bock an. Die Übersteigerungen des real Möglichen nehmen also zu, bis sie gleichsam an den Rand des Kosmos stoßen. Wiederholt wird von (zwei oder drei) Himmelsrichtungen gesprochen. Die Erde scheint bis an ihren äußersten Horizont hin offengelegt. Die wenigen Aktanten, an sich räumlich begrenzte, angesichts des Universums verhältnismäßig kleine Wesen, bewegen sich in einem gewaltigen homogenen, leer wirkenden Raum ohne jeden Widerstand.

Der hier schreibt, will keine quasinatürlichen Vorgänge wiedergeben, wählt bewußt das Paradox als Ausdrucksmittel und die unübliche semantische Verknüpfung. Das mag der Exeget aus ästhetischem Geschmack heraus beklagen. Zitieren wir etwa Junker, der die Vision als "unvorstellbar" tadelt und fortfährt[21]:

> "Hier ist kein klar und deutlich geschautes Bild mehr. Das Horn erscheint losgelöst von einem Träger als eine selbständige Größe ... es ist eigentlich überhaupt keine Vision mehr, sondern bloße Wirklichkeitsschilderung, wenn das Horn in V. 11 und 12 großtut wider den Fürsten des Himmels, das tägliche Opfer abschafft und die heilige Stätte und die Wahrheit niederwirft."

Kann man jedoch eine Aussage, daß ein König (Antiochos IV.) den Fürsten des himmlischen Heeres angreift, "bloße Wirklichkeitsschilderung" nennen? Daß es dem Seleukiden gelungen sei, Sterne vom Himmel herabzuwerfen, vermelden jedenfalls antike Quellen nicht. Auch läßt sich bezweifeln, ob die vorher angeführten Tiere für den Autor nur ausschmückende Bilder waren, ob er ihnen nicht durchaus einen bestimmten Grad von Wirklichkeit beimißt. Abendländische Ästhetik ist hier fehl am Platze.

---

[21] Junker 1932, 67.

Ehe ich weitere Schlüsse ziehe, gehe ich zum zweiten Teil des Kapitels über und wende mich der Kürze halber sofort der Semantik zu.

6.4. Semantik der Deutung

6.4.1. Wie oben (§2.3.5.) ausgeführt, bringt der erste Teil der Deutung V. 20–22 nichts, was dem Schreiber und seinen gelehrten Lesern unbekannt wäre. Daß das Widdergestirn mit Persien und Medien zusammenhängt und insbesondere mit dessen König, begreift jeder Gebildete, der etwas von astraler Geografie weiß, gleiches gilt für die Identifikation des Bockes (ungewöhnlich höchstens, daß Medien zu Persien geschlagen und Griechenland zu Syrien). Was bezweckt eine solche "Deutung"? "Der Hörnerbesitzer – König von Medien/Persien": heißt das, der Widder stelle eben nichts dar als diese Könige? Falls der astrologische Hintergrund noch in irgendeiner Weise präsent ist, muß das Tier mehr sein als seine irdisch-historische Entsprechung. Dasselbe gilt für den Ziegenbock. In dem einen Fabeltier und dem entsprechenden Himmelszeichen wird das Wesen vieler Herrscher versammelt. Beim zweiten Tier wird übrigens das Plus des tierischen Hintergrunds über die historische Erscheinung hinaus offenkundiger. Denn hier repräsentiert den ersten König nur ein großes Horn, die nachfolgenden Hörner stellen schon für sich genommen Könige dar. Das heißt doch, daß das Tier selbst, das Königtum Jawans, als zusammenhängendes größeres Ganzes im Hintergrund bleibt, und die einzelnen Königreiche – und erst recht Könige – nur als partielle Auskörperung eines umfassenden unsichtbaren metahistorischen Ganzen erscheinen. Statt der Ortsnamen (Susa) und der Himmelsrichtungen in der Schauung werden jetzt Völkernamen angeboten. Nur die Hörner werden bei den Hauptgestalten "gedeutet", sie werden als Waffen benutzt. Demnach soll Gewalttätigkeit die Könige kennzeichnen, und dies gleichsam "von Natur", denn von einer Schuld wird nichts gesagt. Was wird in V. 20–22 eigentlich geklärt? Die Sprache bleibt verschleiert, und was in der Schauung an Einzelzügen geboten war, wird nicht erklärt und bleibt also auch nach dieser "Deutung" als richtig in Geltung.

6.4.2. Der zweite Teil der Deutung V. 23 ff. führt über bereits Gewußtes hinaus und führt Unbekanntes ein. Liefert er Deutung im Sinne einer Auflösung der Rätselsprache? Gibt er mit nüchternen Worten wieder, was die Sache selbst sein soll? Der Anfang ließe sich so fassen: "Am Ende ihres Königtums (der vier Nachfolgereiche) beim Vollenden-Lassen der 'Auflehnung' (LXX) ersteht ein König mit starkem Gesicht." Wie V. 20–22 bildet die Wurzel מלך das tertium comparationis (falls der Begriff erlaubt ist): die Tiere mit ihren Hörnern entsprechen Königreichen und ihren Trägern. Wie dort wird die Ersetzung Volk (עם-קדשים) für Landschaft und Orte

(מקדש) geübt. Die Örtlichkeiten geben bereits in der Schauung die Sache selbst wieder, tragen also schon dort keinen metaforischen Charakter. Durch die zusätzliche Nennung von Völkernamen wird der Schleier kaum gelüftet. Das "starke Gesicht" des Königs V. 23 entspricht dem nach Nord und Süd sich ausbreitenden kleinen Horn V. 9f. Ergibt das aber "die Sache" statt des Bildes, wird nicht eher ein neues Bild eingeführt (mit Wortspiel עַז ≠ עָז ?). "Einsicht in Rätsel" wird ihm zugesprochen, und damit das, was der Seher für sich selbst erfleht (V. 15f.) und nur teilweise empfängt (V. 27). Was hier damit gemeint ist, weiß keiner mehr. Die Vollendung von פשע -Sphären (ἁμαρτίαι) benutzt die gleiche ethische Klassifikation wie V. 13, aber erreicht keine "innerweltliche Realität". Der "freche" König wird mit Namen nicht genannt, also weniger identifiziert als vorher die Könige von Medien-Persien oder Jawan V. 20f. In der Fortsetzung V. 24 erscheint das Ergebnis der Schauszenen V. 12 wieder: "Er hatte Erfolg und vollbrachte es." Das ist einfache Wiederholung und keine Aufklärung. Das Zertrampeln von V. 7.13 wird V. 24 zum Vernichten, für zweimal רמס steht fünfmal שחת . Der frappierendste Zug in der Schauung, der Angriff auf Himmel und Erde wie die Beseitigung des Tamidopfers entfällt. Was aber bietet der zweite Teil als Äquivalent? "Wunderbares vernichten ... Gewaltige vernichten und das Volk der Heiligen ... gegen den Fürst der Fürsten aufstehen." War der Verweis auf die heilige Stätte und den dort geschehenen Frevel im ersten Teil nicht sehr viel konkreter?

6.4.3. *Fazit:* Was wir Deutung nennen und auf den zweiten Teil anwenden, bietet eigentlich keine Deutung, sondern verschiebt bloß die Darstellungsebene. Statt tierischer wie astraler Bilder wird ein menschlich-übermenschlicher Aggressor vorgeführt, dessen Inkognito gewahrt bleibt. Die innere Widersprüchlichkeit im Bild wird eher gegenüber dem ersten Teil noch verstärkt, etwa in dem Satz "gewaltig wurde seine Kraft und nicht durch seine Kraft".

Das Ende dieses Teils V. 25b landet beinahe wieder bei einer Schauung. "Gegen den Fürst der Fürsten ersteht er, und durch eine Nicht-Hand wird er zerschmettert." Der erste rafft knapper als die Vorlage das Geschehen zusammen; sollte man hier nicht eher größere Breite erwarten? Der letzte Satz aber führt die Schauung genau an dem Punkt weiter, wo der Leser oben den Abbruch des Erzählgeschehens bedauerte. Auf den letzten Frevel, bei dem dem Leser gleichsam der Atem stockte, folgt diesmal die notwendige Revanche: der Himmelsstürmer wird gestürzt. Aber wie vollzieht sich sein Zerbrechen? Mit dem Ausdruck "Nicht-Hand" für das entscheidende Subjekt wird ein Widersinn zum Ausdruck gebracht, eine scheinbare Leerformel benutzt, die alle Widersprüche im Vorhergehenden weit hinter sich läßt. Und doch wirkt der Schluß auf den Leser. Im Kontext eines

solchen Visionsberichtes wird selbst eine Nicht-Hand verständlich! Sie
weist auf Transzendenz, und treffender als in dieser *via negationis* könnte
von Gott kaum hier die Rede sein.

6.5. Sprechen in Metafern

6.5.1. Die Besonderheit der apokalyptischen Sprache beachten Exegeten
nur höchst selten. Aus neuerer Zeit kenne ich nur zwei amerikanische
Stimmen, deren Beitrag das Problem aufgreift, aber kaum das letzte Wort
zur Sache bietet. Paul D. Hanson hat in den letzten Jahren mehrfach das
jeweilig andere Verhältnis von "vision" und "reality" zum Kriterium der
Unterscheidung von Profetie und Apokalyptik erhoben[22]. Während jene
eine fruchtbare Spannung zwischen beiden Polen voraussetzt, tut sich bei
dieser eine unübersteigbare Kluft auf: aus der Vision folgt beim Apokalyptiker kein Appell mehr für konkretes politisches Verhalten und Gestalten.
Zweifellos stellt Hanson einen wesentlichen Unterschied der beiden Strömungen israelitischer Religionen zutreffend heraus, aber bewertet ihn
vielleicht doch zu schnell zugunsten der ersteren. Es könnte ja sein, daß die
profetische Ontologie oder Metahistorie naiv war und deshalb von einem
Pol zum andern leichthin überwechseln konnte, während die Apokalyptiker in einer veränderten Zeit sich einer Problemtiefe gegenübersehen, von
denen die Profeten noch nichts ahnten! – Der zweite ist John J. Collins. Er
kennzeichnet die sprachliche Besonderheit apokalyptischer Visionen als
"Allegorie", also als Sprechweise, die etwas anderes meint als sie wörtlich
genommen besagt und sich von anderen Formen metaforischer oder
symbolischer Sprache dadurch unterscheidet, daß sie die zweite Ebene der
Bedeutung ausdrücklich nachträgt. Gegenüber der Danielsprache räumt
Collins jedoch ein, daß "the explicit allusions to a second level of meaning
may be rare and ambiguous on occasion"[23]. In den danielischen Visionen
wird auf "primeval" oder auf "celestial archetypes" zurückgegriffen, um
aufwühlende geschichtliche Erfahrung religiös zu verstehen[24]. Sein Verdienst ist, daß Collins die Bindung apokalyptischer Visionen an überlieferte Stoffe, von denen oben Daniel 8 die Rede war, als konstitutiv
herausstellt.

Dagegen scheint es mir mißlich, daß er den Begriff Allegorie beibehält.
Denn Allegorie meint eine bildliche Rede, für die Substitution vorausgesetzt werden kann; was bildlich gesagt wird, kann in eigentliche unbildli-
che Rede transponiert werden. Dies aber schließt Collins doch wohl aus,
wenn er die Apokalypsen als "disclosing a transcendent reality"[25] begreift.

---

[22] Hanson zuletzt 1978.
[24] Collins 1977, 95 ff.

[23] Collins 1977, 115.
[25] Collins 1979, 9.

6.5.2. Ein Seitenblick auf die moderne Auslegung der Gleichnisse Jesu bei den neutestamentlichen Kollegen hilft ein Stück weiter. Jahrzehntelang hat hier Jülichers Gleichnistheorie gegolten, wonach Jesus seine Gleichnisse formuliert, um allgemeine religiöse Wahrheiten in bildhafte Rede einzukleiden, als "konkrete Vermittlung für Abstraktes". Im Hintergrund stand die antike Theorie, nach der Metafern verkürzte Gleichnisse darstellen und prinzipiell durch eigentliche Aussagen substituierbar sind. Seit Amos N. Wilders Buch über "The Language of the Gospels" (1964) setzt sich jedoch mehr und mehr die Einsicht durch, daß eine echte Metafer und vor allem ein jesuanisches Gleichnis Ausdruck einer eigenen Wirklichkeitssicht ist, also in keiner Weise durch andere Reden ersetzbar erscheint. Es ist hier nicht der Ort, den Verlauf der neutestamentlichen Debatte zu schildern; ich verweise dafür auf Harnischs Literaturbericht[26]; die gleiche Spur wird auch von Philosophen wie Ricoeur (1974) und Linguisten wie Weinrich (1976) verfolgt.

6.5.3. Was ist daraus für apokalyptische Visionen zu lernen? Metafern treten hier viel krasser hervor als in irgendeinem synoptischen Gleichnis. Die Zumutung an die Leser, sich anzustrengen, um einen Sinn zu finden, ist also noch gesteigert gegenüber der neutestamentlichen Parallele. Warum das? Ohne Anspruch auf Vollständigkeit gebe ich drei Mutmaßungen Ausdruck.

(1) Metaforische Rede verweist in diesem Zusammenhang auf eine religiös begründete *Metahistorie*, die den geschichtlichen Weg des Menschen und insbesondere des Gottesvolkes verständlich und sinnvoll werden läßt. Eine tiefe Erfahrung vom Zwang der Verhältnisse, denen gerade die Rechtschaffenen und Frommen sich ausgesetzt sehen, korrespondiert mit der Gewißheit, daß es dennoch "sich lohnt", gut zu handeln und treu zu bleiben, weil letztendlich der Höchste den Grund aller geschichtlichen Wirklichkeit ausmacht. Dabei wird vorausgesetzt, daß politische Figuren auf der Bühne der Geschichte mehr sind als beliebige Individuen und Staaten mehr als die Organisation einer Administration, weiter, daß es Gestirne und Engelsmächte gibt, welche den Geschichtsverlauf maßgeblich beeinflussen, ohne damit menschliche Freiheit auszuschließen. Zwischen Himmel und Erde gibt es mehr Dinge als sich unsere Schulweisheit träumen läßt, von ihnen kann der Visionär metaforisch reden. Wie ich in meiner Darstellung der Profeten[27] darzulegen versucht habe, liegt seit Amos den Profeten an einer solchen Übergeschichte, an Metahistorie. Die Apokalyptiker führen das in ihrer Weise weiter.

(2) Metaforische Rede gestattet, die *Schuldfrage* offen zu lassen. Zwar wird in Dan 8 gegen Ende der Vision vom Empörungsfrevel (פשע) und

---

[26] Harnisch 1979, 53–89.   [27] Koch 1978, 84 ff., 157 ff. und *passim*.

dem Herabwerfen der Wahrheit (אמת) geredet und insofern Schuld als Grund der letzten Geschichtskatastrofe festgehalten. Aber wo und bei wem beginnt die Schuld? Ist das mehrfach betonte Sich-groß-Machen (הגדיל) von persisch-medischem Widder und griechischem Ziegenbock böse oder zeigen sich hier "Naturanlagen", die sich durchsetzen? Soll man einen Schritt weitergehen und schon das Stoßen der Tierfiguren nach den verschiedenen Himmelsrichtungen als sündig und als Eigenwillen brandmarken? Der Apokalyptiker tut es nicht. Er läßt andererseits ebenso offen, wieweit und wo Gott selbst am Werke ist. Zweifellos ist Gott es, der den letzten König fällt V. 25b. Und hinter der befristeten Zeit von 2300 Abend-Morgen steht ebenso göttliche Aktivität. Auch daß ein Widder bei Susa auftaucht und ein Ziegenbock im Westen, mag aus göttlicher Fügung hervorgehen. Doch gesagt wird es nicht. Die metaforische Rede läßt ein Theodizeeproblem gar nicht erst aufkommen. Von apokalyptischem Determinismus zu reden, wie es leider weitgehend in der Bibelwissenschaft üblich geworden ist, ist zumindest im Blick auf Dan 8 unerweisbar.

(3) Metaforische Rede, die nicht in einen Klartext übersetzt wird, reizt zu fortlaufender *Aktualisierung*. Zwar gilt unter historischen Exegeten heute als ausgemacht, daß der Ziegenbock Dan 8 sich auf die Diadochen und der König mit "starkem Gesicht" V. 23 sich auf Antiochus IV. beziehen. In der Tat will der Autor dem Leser solche Bezüge suggerieren. Meint er das jedoch exklusiv und endgültig? Die Leute, die das Danielbuch nach 164 v. Chr. hochgehalten, gelesen und abgeschrieben haben, entnehmen dem Kapitel jedenfalls keine eindeutige Festlegung. Haben sie damit den danielischen Verfasser völlig mißinterpretiert? Sind wir Exegeten heute auf dem richtigen Pfad, wenn wir wähnen, der makkabäische Verfasser habe alle seine Aussagen so punktuell und historisch-kritisch eindeutig gemeint, wie wir es aufgrund unseres wissenschaftlichen Gewissens fordern? Oder stehen konservative Ausleger, die den Ziegenbock Dan 8 auf Rom und den Frevelkönig auf einen noch ausstehenden Antichrist beziehen, dem Anliegen des metaforisch denkenden Autor doch näher als wir gemeinhin wahrhaben wollen?

Lassen Sie mich mit zwei Streiflichtern auf die Geistesgeschichte des Abendlandes schließen. "Ich will keine Bildrede dulden, solange nicht die Sinnwidrigkeit eines wörtlichen Verständnisses nachweisbar ist" schrieb einst Luther gegen Latomus[28]. Die Exegese wäre gegenwärtig nicht das, was sie ist und positiv für Theologie und Kirche leistet, hätte sich dieser Grundsatz nicht durchgesetzt. Und ein zweites: Die Philosophen der Aufklärung haben es Europa eingeimpft, nur jene Sätze für wahr zu halten, die claire et distincte formuliert sind. Moderne Wissenschaft und Technik

---

[28] Zitiert nach Löwith 1959, 53.

gäbe es nicht, hätte diese Losung nicht gesiegt. Und dennoch: hat sich das Abendland mit der Verdammung jeder "symbolischen" Sprache nicht Scheuklappen angelegt? Läßt sich die Wahrheit menschlicher Existenz ohne Metaforik ergründen? Die moderne Lyrik, nicht nur die Surrealisten, hat entschlossen den Weg zurück zur Metafer gewählt. Und ein Naturwissenschaftler wie Heisenberg gesteht heute: "Wir sind gezwungen, in Bildern und Gleichnissen zu sprechen, die nicht genau das treffen, was wir wirklich meinen."[29] Sollte, was für die Naturwissenschaft gilt, nicht auch in der Theologie erwägenswert sein?

Bibliografie

Collins, J. J. 1977: *The Apocalyptic Vision of the Book of Daniel* (HSM 16), Missoula, Mont. 1977.

– (Hrsg.) 1979: *Apocalypse: The Morphology of a Genre* (Semeia 14) Missoula, Mont. 1979.

Cumont, F. 1909: "La plus ancienne géographie astrologique", in: *Klio* 9 (1909) 263–273.

Gunkel, H. 1900: "Das 4. Buch Esra", in: *APAT* Bd. 2, Darmstadt 1962² [= 1900], 331–401.

Hanson, P. D. 1978: *Dynamic Transcendence,* Philadelphia, Penn. 1978.

Harnisch, W. 1979: "Die Metapher als heuristisches Prinzip", in: *VF* 24 (1979) 53–89.

Hasslberger, B. 1977: *Hoffnung in der Bedrängnis.* Eine formkritische Untersuchung zu Dan 8 und 10–12, St. Ottilien 1977.

Heisenberg, W. 1969: *Der Teil und das Ganze,* München 1969.

Junker, H. 1932: *Untersuchungen über exegetische und literarische Probleme des Buches Daniel,* Bonn 1932.

Kautzsch, E. 1900: *APAT* Bd. 2, Darmstadt 1962² [= 1900].

Koch, K. 1974: *Was ist Formgeschichte?,* Neukirchen 1974³.

– 1970: *Ratlos vor der Apokalyptik,* Gütersloh 1970.

Koch, K. u. Mitarb. 1976: *Amos.* Untersucht mit den Methoden einer strukturalen Formgeschichte, Bd. 1–3, Neukirchen 1976.

Koch, K. 1978: *Die Profeten I* (UB 280), Stuttgart 1978.

Lewy, H. 1949: "The Babylonian Background of the Kay Kâûs Legend", in: *ArOr* 17 (1949) 28–109.

Löwith, K. 1959: "Die Sprache als Vermittler von Mensch und Welt", in: W. Schneemelcher (Hrsg.): *Das Problem der Sprache in Theologie und Kirche,* Berlin 1959, 36–54.

Lohmeyer, E. 1953: *Die Offenbarung des Johannes* (HNT 16), Tübingen 1953².

Lücke, F. 1832: *Versuch einer vollständigen Einleitung in die Offenbarung Johannis und in die gesammte apokalyptische Litteratur,* Commentar über die Schriften des Evangelisten Johannes, 4. Theil, 1. Band, Einleitung in die Offenbarung Johannis, Bonn 1832.

Lukonin, W. G. 1967: *Persien 2* (Archaeologia Mundi), München – Genf – Paris 1967.

Oppenheim, A. L. 1956: "The Interpretation of Dreams in the Ancient Near East, with a Translation of an Assyrian Dream-Book", in: *TAPhS* 46 (1956) 179–373.

Porteous, N. 1968: *Das Buch Daniel* (ATD 23), Göttingen 1968².

Reimers, S. 1976: *Formgeschichte der profetischen Visionsberichte,* Diss. Masch., Hamburg 1976.

Richter, W. 1963: "Traum und Traumdeutung im Alten Testament", in: *BZ* 7 (1963) 202–220.

Ricoeur, P./Jüngel, E. 1974: *Metapher – Zur Hermeneutik religiöser Sprache* (Sonderheft EvTh), München 1974.

Robinson, J. M. (Hrsg.) 1977: *The Nag Hammadi Library,* Leiden/San Francisco 1977.

---

[29] Heisenberg 1969, 285.

Strugnell, J. 1960: "The Angelic Liturgy at Qumrân – 4Q Serek Šîrôt ʿOlat Haššabât", in: *Congress Volume Oxford 1959* (VT.S 7), Leiden 1960, 318–345.

Weinrich, H. 1976: *Sprache in Texten*, Stuttgart 1976.

Wilder, A. N. 1964: *Early Christian Rhetoric*. The Language of the Gospel, London 1964.

Einleitung zu den Überblicken 1–3

Die hier angefügten Überblicke 1 bis 3 versuchen, die in der Arbeit entwickelte Sicht der profetischen und apokalyptischen Visionsberichte in formalisierter Weise zusammenzufassen. Dabei wird so vorgegangen, daß zunächst (Überblick 1) eine ausführliche Analyse des apokalyptischen Visionsberichtes Dan 8 vorgelegt wird, die fast den kompletten masoretischen Text in den einzelnen Spalten bietet. Darauf folgt der Vergleich (Überblick 2) dreier Texte, eines alttestamentlich-profetischen, eines alttestamentlich-apokalyptischen und eines neutestamentlich-apokalyptischen, wobei der hebräische bzw. griechische Text in seinen wichtigsten Abschnitten geboten wird. Als drittes schließt sich ein Überblick über 44 Visionsberichte an, die dem Alten Testament, den Apokryfen und dem Neuen Testament entnommen sind (Überblick 3). Auf dieser Ebene wird auf die Aufführung des Wortlautes der einzelnen Texte gänzlich verzichtet, es werden nur noch die für die Gattungsmatrix "Visionsbericht" erheblichen Versangaben geboten.

Die für alle drei Überblicke konstitutive Gattungsmatrix wird am ausführlichsten in Überblick 3 geboten; sie versucht, *alle* Elemente der Gattungsgliederung aufzuführen und ist damit notwendig umfangreicher als die Gattungsgliederungen in den Überblicken 1 und 2. Die Notierung der Gattungselemente geschieht in allen Überblicken übereinstimmend; so ist z. B. das Element 2.1.1 "Eröffnungsnotiz" in allen drei Überblicken gleich notiert.

Überblick 1. *(s. o. nach S. 432)*

Die Analyse von Dan 8 ist von rechts nach links zu lesen. Rechts außen sind die einzelnen Gliederungselemente vermerkt. Nach links schließen sich die jeweiligen Textabschnitte an, wobei diese in den Teilen 2 (Schauung) und 4 (Deutung) in sechs Kolumnen (A$_1$ bis C) unterteilt sind, die sich in beiden Teilen entsprechen.

Innerhalb des Textabdruckes werden drei zusätzliche Markierungen vorgenommen.

– Die *Wiederaufnahme* von Elementen der Schauung im Deutungsteil wird bei den entsprechenden Worten durch Unterpunkten .... kenntlich gemacht,

– *Gattungsweiser* (u. a. חזון) werden eingerahmt,

– Das *Deutungsleitlexem* מלך wird unterstrichen.

(Fortsetzung auf S. 446)

Überblick 2: Vergleich dreier Visionsberichte

Gattungsgliederung/Syntax		Am 7,1-3	Dan 8	Apk 6,7-8
1 VORSPANN				
1.1	Zeitformel/Synchronismus	בתחלת עלות הלקש אחר גזי המלך [ ]	בשנת שלש למלכות	καὶ ὅτε ἤνοιξεν τὴν σφραγῖδα τὴν τετάρ-
1.2	Themaangabe/Selbstvorstellung		חזון נראה אלי אני דניאל..	την
2.0.1	Vorbereitende Wahrnehmung		ויהי בראתי	ἤκουσα φωνὴν τοῦ τετάρτου ζῴου λέγοντος· ἔρχου
2.0.2	Ortsangabe		ואני בשושן...	
2.0.3	Schau über vision. Ort		ואראה בחזן ואני הייתי על..	
2 SCHAUUNG				
2.1.1	Eröffnungsnotiz √ראה √ἰδεῖν	כה הראני אדני יהוה	A וָאשה עני ואראה	καὶ εἶδον
2.1.2	Präsentativ הנה,ἰδού	והנה	והנה	καὶ ἰδού
2.1.3	Begleitgegenstand	יצר		ἵππος χλωρός
2.1.4	Hauptgegenstand A	גבי	איל אחד עמד	καὶ ὁ καθήμενος
2.1.5	Ort von A		לפני האבל	ἐπάνω αὐτοῦ
2.1.6	Teilgegenstände zu A		ולו קרנים	
2.1.7.1	Eröffnungsnotiz		ראיתי	
2.1.7.2	Vorber. Bewegung		האיל מנגח	
2.1.8.	Zwischendeutung			ὄνομα αὐτῷ θάνατος
2.2.1	Eröffnungsnotiz (s.2.1.1)		ואני הייתי מבין	
2.2.2	= 2.1.2		והנה	
2.2.4	Hauptgegenstand B		B₁ צפיר העזים בא	καὶ ὁ ᾅδης ἠκολούθει
2.2.5	Ort Hggst. B		מן המערב	
2.2.6	Teilggst. zu B		קרן חזות	
2.2.7	Vorbereitende Bew. B		ויבא עד האיל...	
2.2.8.1	Eröffnungsnotiz		B₂	
2.2.8.2	(Sprech)Bewegg. (B/A)		....וישכר את שתי קרניו...	καὶ ἐδόθη αὐτοῖς ἐξουσία ἐπὶ τὸ τέταρτον τῆς γῆ- ἀποκτεῖναι ἐν ῥομφαίᾳ καὶ ἐν λιμῷ καὶ ἐν θανά- καὶ ὑπὸ τῶν θηρίων τῆς γῆ
2.2.8.3	Ergebnis	והיה אם־כלה לאכל ...	B₃ ... ולא היה מציל	
2.2.9	(Sprech)Bewegung		...ותעלנה..ארבע..יצא קרן	
2.2.10	Hggst. C (mit 2.1.1 - 2.1.5) und Bewegung		C ...ואשמעה אחד קדוש	

Überblick 2: Vergleich dreier Visionsberichte

Gattungsgliederung/Syntax		Am 7,1-3	Dan 8	Apk 6,7-8
3 REDETEIL	3.1.2 Redeeröffnung des Sehers	וַיֹּאמֶר		
	3.2.1 Anrufung und Bitte	אֲדֹנָי יהוה סְלַח־נָא		
	3.2.3 Klagende Frage	מִי יָקוּם יַעֲקֹב		
	3.2.5 Reaktion יהוה	נִחַם יהוה עַל זֹאת		
4 DEUTUNG	4.1.4 Bitte des Sehers um Deutg.		ויהי בראתי...ואבקשה בינה	
	4.1.3.1 Präsentativ		והנה	
	4.1.3.2 Erscheinung des Deuters		עמד .....כמראה גבר	
	4.1.3.3 Eröffnungsnotiz		ואשמע	
	4.1.3.4 2. Ggstd. und Ort		קול אדם בין אולי	
	4.1.3.6 Sprechbewegung B zu A		....ויאמר גבריאל...	
	4.1.5 (Sprech)Bewegung des Deuters		ויבא./ ויאמר./ ויגע בי..	
	4.1.6 Reaktion des Sehers		ואפלה ./נרדמתי ..	
	4.2.1 Ankündigung der Deutung		ויאמר הנני מודיעך ...	
	4.2.2 Nennung und Deutung A		האיל...מלכי	
	4.2.5 Nennung und Deutung B		והצפר..מלך.	
	4.2.6 Nenng/Deutg Teilgg. B		והקרן..הוא המלך	
	4.2.7 Deutung von Bewegungen		ותעמדנה..ארבע מלכיות	
	4.2.8 Aufnahme/Bekräftigg. C		ומראה...אמת הוא	
5. SCHLUSS - REDE GOTTES	Apod. Weissagg. לֹא + Impf.	לֹא תִהְיֶה		
	und Schlußformel	אָמַר יהוה		
7. ABSCHLUSS	Aufforderung zu Geheimhaltg.		....סתם החזון....	
	und Betroffenheit des Sehers		ואני דניאל נהייתי	

Überblick 3: Versuch ei[...]

1Kg 22	Am 7	Am 7	Am 8	Am 9	Am	Js 6	Jr 1	Jr 1	Ez 1	Ez 2	Ez 8	Ez 37	Sa 1	Sa 2	Sa 2	Sa 4	Sa 5	Sa 5	Sa 6	Sa 3	Gattungsgliederung	Syntax
	(1)					1	1			1		7									1.1 Zeitformel/Synchronismus	בשנת +Zahl + König/ba
																					1.2 (Selbst)Vorst. d. Sehers	Name
									1												2.0.1 Wahrnehmung	VS 1./3. sg
									1	1											2.0.2 Ort des Sehers	ב / ל + Ort
											1										2.0.3 Schau über vision. Ort	√ראה + ל/ב + Ort
																					2.0.4 Reaktion des Sehers	VS 1./3. sg
																					2.0.5 Vorbereitg. d. S.: Fasten	VS 1. sg
																					2.0.6 " : Gebet/Klage	VS 1. sg (+ Anruf)
													1								2.0.7 Schlafnotiz	VS 1./3. sg
						2	1					7									2.0.8 Tagesangabe	יום/לילה + Zahl
19	1	4	7	1	1	1			4	9	2		8	1	5	2	1		1	1	2.1.1 Eröffnungsnotiz √ראה ...	Narr. / Aor.
	1	4	7	1					4	9	2	2	8	1	5	2	1			1	2.1.2 ויראני/ואל/והנה/καὶ ιδου υ	Präsentativ
		4							4	9					5					1	2.1.3 Begleitgegenstand	NS
19	1	4	7	1	1	1			5	9	2	1	8	1	5	2	1		1	1	2.1.4 Hauptgegenstand A	NS
19			7		1	1			5	10		2	8						(1)	1	2.1.5 Ort des Hggstd. A	NS
			7		1				6	10	2		8		3			2			2.1.6 Teilgegenstände von A	NS
		4								10											2.1.7 Vorbereitende Bewegg. A	NSp
												3									2.2.1 Eröffnungsnotiz (= 2.1.1)	Narr / Aor
													7								2.2.2 = 2.1.2	Präsentativ
																					2.2.3 Begleitgegenstand	Nomen/NS
19						2			15				3	7					1		2.2.4 Hauptgegenstand B	NS
						2			15										1		2.2.5 Ort von Hggstd. B	NS
						2			18												2.2.6 Teilgegenstände v. B	NS
						3			19												2.2.7 Vorbereitde. Bewegg. B	NSp ו-Perfekt
20	2	4							3								3		2		2.2.8 (Sprech)Bewegg. (s. Einleitung)	Narr
		4															7		3		2.2.9 " Visionsggste.	Narr
21									26	*			8								2.2.10 Hggst. C (D..) + Bewegung	s. 2.1.1 – 2.1.5
											3										2.2.11 (Sprech)Bew. Visgg.-Seher	Narr
21			8	2	1	11	13	2,1	3,1	9,4	3						5			4	3.1.1 Redeeröffnung Jahwä/Engel	ויאמר X אלי
	2	5			5								9	2		4				4	3.1.2 " Profet	ואמר
	2	5										8	12								3.2 Fürbitte + Reaktion Jahwäs	
			8	2		11	13									2	2	5			3.3 Frage über Geschautes/Antw.	
													9	2		4		6		4	3.4.1 " d. Sehers nach Deutg.	Fragesatz
													9	2		5	3	6	5	4	3.4.2 Redenotiz und Identifik.	ויאמר + NS
													10	2		14			8	6	3.4.3 Nähere Erläuterung	Rel.-Satz/NSp
													10	4				11			3.4.4 Zweck	ל + inf
22						1	9		3	1			4								3.5 Beauftr. mit/ohne Dialog	Imperativ
																					4.1.1 Reaktion d. Sehers auf Vis.	VS 1. sg
																					4.1.2 Umstände d. Deutungsempf.	NS
																					4.1.3 Auftauchen des Deuters	s. 2.1.1ff
																					4.1.4 Bitte des Sehers um Deutg.	VS 1. sg
										11											4.1.5 (Sprech)Bewegg. d. Deuters	VS
																					4.1.6 Reaktion d. Sehers	VS
																					4.2.1 Ankündigg. der Deutg.	VS (הביד)./ NS (פשר)
										11											4.2.2 Nennung und Identif. A	NS
																					4.2.4 evtl. neue Schauung	s. o. 2.1.1ff
																					4.2.5 Nennung und Identif. B	NS
																					4.2.6 " " " Teilg.B	NS
																					4.2.7 Deutung v. Bewegungen	cf 2.2.9
																					4.2.8 Aufnahme (und Bekräftg) C..	NS
																					5 Schlußrede Gottes	
	3	6	8	2	1	11	12	14	10	10	12	13		9			4		(8)	7	6 Mahnung an Empfänger d. Deutg.	
											12										7 Abschluß	

* pml t

kturaufrisses von 44 Visionen

Dan 4	Dan 7	Dan 8	Dan 9	1Hen 14-16	1Hen 83	1Hen 85	2Bar 35-40	2Bar 53-75	4Es 9f	4Es 11f	4Es 13	TJos 19	Apk 1	Apk 4	Apk 5	Apk 8	Apk 10	Apk 13	Apk 13	Apk 14	Apk 14
	1	1	1										1								
1	1	1	2					1				1	9								
2	1	1	2	2	1	1							10								
		2			3			1	26		12,51		9								
		2																			
2	1																				
			3						26	51											
			4					2	27												
					3		36,1			10,60											
									27	11,1	13,1										
7	2	3	8		3	3	1	53,1	38	1	1	8	12	1	1	2	1	1	11	1	14
7	2	3	8		3	2	1	1		2										1	14
		2	9				2	1	2			8			1		1	1	11		14
7	3	3	20		3	3	2	1	38	1	3	8	12	1	1	2	1	1	11	1	14
7	3	3			3	2	1		38	1	3			1	1	2	1	1	(11)	1	14
9	4	3	20					1	38	1		8			1	2	1	1	11	1	14
	4	4		3				2-7	10,25	2	3										
10	7	5		4				8	27	37	5				2						
10	7	5						3	27	37	5				2						
				4	3	3									2		2				
10	7	5			3	3		8	27	37	5	8		2	2	3	3	2		2	15
10		5						8	27	37	5				2		3			2	15
	7	5													3		3				
	8	6		4	3-6					37	5						3				15
11	7					7	4-11	8-10		38	6				2	5		2	12		15
		8				8	37,1	11		12,1				8			3				
	9	13									12	8			6	7					17
				24-16,4					9 39	11,36							4		3		
	15			5			1	12	10,27	12,3	13				4						
		20						55,1-3													
		15f	21					3	29					13							
5	16	15						38	54	34	6	13									
	16	17	21					55,4	30		21			17							
		17									32										
17	16	19	22				39,1	56,1	38	10	25										
7	17	20	24				2	3f	40	11	25		20							4	
8								5-74,4		13	27										
	21																				
20	19/23	21						8		31	30										
	20	21																			
23		22						8-40,3	45	32	32										
		26a									39										
24													10								
		26b				6		4	76	58	37			11	12	13	6				
	28	27							50	35								9	18		

Überblick 2. (s. o. S. 442f.)

Der Überblick 2 ist von links nach rechts zu lesen. Er bietet je einen Visionsbericht aus Amos, Daniel und der Apokalypse Johannes. Die Gliederung ist analog zur Gattungsmatrix aufgebaut, wobei an einigen Stellen noch stärker differenziert wird, z. B. ist das Element 2.1.7 aus Übersicht 1 in 2.1.7.1 "Eröffnungsnotiz" und 2.1.7.2 "Vorbereitende Bewegung" aufgegliedert.

Überblick 3. (s. o. S. 444f.)

Der Überblick 3 bietet den Versuch eines Strukturaufrisses von 44 Visionen. In der Mitte wird die Gattungsmatrix aufgeschlüsselt, die sich in zwei Spalten gliedert. Die linke Spalte führt die Inhalte der Gattungsgliederung auf, die rechte Spalte bietet grammatische und syntaktische Korrelate. Links von der Gattungsmatrix sind alttestamentlich-profetische Visionsberichte aufgeführt, rechts Belege aus Daniel, den Apokryfen und der Apokalypse Johannes.

Jeweils eine Spalte repräsentiert einen Visionsbericht. Das betreffende Kapitel ist am Kopf der Spalte vermerkt. In der Spalte sind die Verse angegeben, in denen das betreffende Gliederungselement aufzufinden ist. Die Versangaben beziehen sich jeweils nur auf den Anfang des betreffenden Unterabschnittes, nicht auf den vollen Umfang.

Gesondert soll hier zu Zeile 2.2.8 aufgeführt werden, daß in dieser Rubrik "Sprechbewegung B – A/ A – B/B – B oder Gott zu A/B" möglich ist.

An Abkürzungen sei aufgeführt:

Hggst – Hauptgegenstand; Bewegg – Bewegung; Visionsggst. – Visionsgegenstand; Beauftr. – Beauftragung; Bewgg. Bewegung; Identif. – Identifizierung.

The Genre of Palestinian Jewish Apocalypses

E. P. Sanders

"When *I* use a word", Humpty Dumpty said in a rather scornful tone, "it means just what I choose it to mean – neither more nor less."

"The question is", said Alice, "whether you *can* make words mean so many different things." ... After a minute Humpty Dumpty began again. "They've a temper, some of them – particularly verbs, they're the proudest – adjectives you can do anything with, but not verbs – however, *I* can manage the whole lot of them!"

1. Traditional Definitions of Apocalypse and Apocalyptic

The topic to be addressed by this paper will amply illustrate that Humpty Dumpty is not the only one who uses words to suit himself. Each of the words in the title of the paper can be and has been used in scholarly discussions to convey at least slightly different realities. I shall leave aside the old question of whether the word "Palestinian" adds any worthwhile limitation to the word "Jewish" when one deals with Judaism in the Greco-Roman era, and restrict the present discussion primarily to the words "genre" and "apocalypse". It is not intended to offer any definitive solutions, and I hope that the paper will not confuse an already confused situation; the intention is to clarify the problems which have arisen and to lay out what is at stake in the current scholarly debate.

1.1. It was once widely – it may be universally – thought that apocalypses are works which include apocalyptic ideas:

By means of the word "Apocalyptic" we designate first of all the literary genre of the Apocalypses, *i.e.* revelatory writings which disclose the secrets of the beyond and especially of the end of time, and then secondly, the realm of ideas from which this literature originates.[1]

The key concept of apocalypticism, and consequently of works called apocalypses, was derived from the principal work from antiquity which has the term ἀποκάλυψις as its lead word, the Apocalypse or Revelation of John. The title was then easily extended to works in which the same theme is at least prominent, Daniel, *1 Enoch*, 4 Ezra and *2 Apocalypse of Baruch*.

1.2. The "realm of ideas" contained in these works can readily be

---

[1] Vielhauer 1965, 582.

expanded beyond the central concept of the revelation of the end, and several scholars have defined apocalypses as works which contain several of a group of ideas and formal elements. The formal elements (visions, for example) are generally connected to the central ideas. It will be useful here to give two influential lists of traits (ideas and formal elements) which have been used to define both apocalypses and apocalypticism:

Vielhauer[2]	Koch[3]
Pseudonymity	Discourse cycles
Account of the vision	Spiritual turmoils
Surveys of history in future-form	Paraenetic discourses
Doctrine of the two ages	Pseudonymity
Pessimism and hope of the beyond	Mythical images rich in symbolism
Universalism and individualism	Composite character
Determinism and imminent expectation	Urgent expectation of the end
Lack of uniformity in expression	Cosmic catastrophy
	World history divided into segments
	Angels and demons
	Promise of salvation (including universalism and individualism)
	The throne of God
	A mediator with royal functions
	The catchword glory

Each of the authors would nuance his list in various ways, but the lists seem to represent fairly how apocalypticism and apocalypses have been most often defined: by a mélange of literary and thematic elements.[4]

1.3. A very important element in the discussion, and one which it is essential to understand in order to grasp the current debate, is the influence of the meaning of the word *Gattung* in form-criticism. A key element in a literary *Gattung* as defined by the originators of form-criticism was a *Sitz im Leben*:

> Besonders unangenehm ist mir das Wort 'formgeschichtlich'...; ich rede vielmehr von 'Literaturgeschichte', die nach 'Gattungen' den Stoff ordnet, 'Gattungen' stelle ich fest a) nach dem gemeinsamen Schatz von Gedanken u[nd] Stimmungen, b) nach dem gleichen Sitz im Leben, c) nach gleichbleibenden Ausdrucksformen.[5]

With this definition of literary investigation in mind, one will readily understand how, when speaking of the literary *Gattung* (translated now into English as "genre") of the apocalypse, scholars such as Koch and Vielhauer, and their predecessors, would look for a mix of formal characteristics (pseudonymity, visions), ideas (imminent end, dualistic world view), and finally a *Sitz im Leben*. Thus Vielhauer proposed that

---

[2] Vielhauer 1965, 583–594.   [3] Koch 1972, 24–33.
[4] Here a glance at the table of contents in Schmidt's (1976) review of scholarship up to 1947 is instructive.
[5] Gunkel to Jülicher 1925, in Rollmann 1981, 283f..

apocalypses were the literature which arose from "those eschatologically-excited circles which were forced more and more by the theocracy into a kind of conventicle existence".[6] One of the problems posed by the study of apocalyptic, in the view of Koch, was that the apocalypse is "a form (*Gattung*) whose *Sitz im Leben* we do not yet know".[7] Raphaël proposed that "apocalyptic discourse is often situated in an intolerable economic, political and social situation".[8] Von Rad urged that such a distinctive literary phenomenon as the late Jewish apocalyptic material must have a *Sitz im Leben*.[9]

2. Criticism of the Traditional Definitions

Criticisms of the way of defining apocalypses which we have been considering have come from several quarters. It has been pointed out that many of the apocalyptic traits which have been used to define apocalypses can be found in works which cannot be considered apocalypses, while many of the works commonly considered apocalypses do not have a majority of the supposed traits of apocalypticism.[10] It would take us too far afield at this point to reiterate all the points which this two-pronged objection can call forward, and one or two examples must suffice.

2.1. With regard to the second point: in defining an apocalypse, Stone argued,

> apocalypticism is not adequate. It makes no sense of at least two of the five independent works bound together under the name I Enoch: parts I and III. Equally large parts of II Enoch, most of III Baruch, sections of II Baruch and of the Apocalypse of Abraham are completely irrelevant if judged by the criterion of 'apocalypticism' or 'apocalyptic eschatology'.[11]

Stone similarly made trenchant observations about the fact that many of the traditional traits occur in works which are not apocalypses.[12] Some of these will be returned to below, as will also the very difficult problem, raised by implication in Stone's remarks, of the possibility of limiting an "apocalypse" to a part of a larger work which is not itself an apocalypse.

2.2. From another angle, Stone brought forward a further criticism of the usual definition of apocalypses: the list of traits given excludes certain important elements of works generally considered apocalypses. The particular elements with which he dealt were the lists of "revealed things", lists which cover such topics as "astronomy and meteorology, uranography and cosmology, the secrets of nature and wisdom...".[13] If Stone's

---

[6] Vielhauer 1965, 598.
[7] Koch 1972, 28; 1970, 34.
[8] Raphaël 1977, 27.
[9] von Rad 1968, 330.
[10] *E.g.* P. D. Hanson 1963, 33; Carmignac 1979, 17.
[11] Stone 1976, 442.
[12] Stone 1976, 440.
[13] Stone 1976, 414, cf. 443.

point about revealed things is taken, it is seen that the whole character of
the discussion about apocalypticism and apocalypses is altered. There is no
necessary connection between cosmological speculation and the prediction
of the coming victory of an oppressed "conventicle". Why should one
more than the other define an apocalypse?[14]

3. Recent Proposals: Preliminary

A way out of this sort of problem was offered by Stone,[15] Hanson[16] and
others: one should distinguish between apocalyptic eschatology, (the
expectation of the end which structures religious perspective), apocalypticism (a "sociological ideology", presumably that of the oppressed), and the
literary genre apocalypse.[17]

3.1. At work in this proposal is an important assumption, an assumption
spelled out by American scholars in particular, not necessarily in connection with the problem of apocalypses: one should distinguish between
genre and *Sitz im Leben*. The form-critical connection of the two, so
important in biblical scholarship since Gunkel, should be severed. This
proposal – in fact, often an assumption – is clear, for example, in many of
the papers prepared for the 1972 meeting of the Task Force on Genre of the
Seminar on the Gospels, a group organized within the Society of Biblical
Literature. Thus, for example, Baird proposed a distinction between
"form" and "genre". A "Form" is "a category for analyzing relatively
small, individual units of literary material". A "genre", which he also calls
"Gattung", is a category "for classifying literary works as a whole".[18] This
definition of *Gattung* (genre), it will be seen, is precisely the opposite of that
of Gunkel and the subsequent form critics. Doty, in an important paper on
genre, makes the very same distinction. "Form" refers to small units,
"genre" to whole works.[19] Once this definition is accepted, the combination of literary forms, motifs, and *Sitz im Leben* to compose a genre, a
combination which we have seen to dominate the definitions proposed by
continental scholars especially, makes little sense.

3.2. On the basis of the growing distinction between "genre" and
"form" one can understand the proposals to distinguish between apocalypticism (the sociological *Sitz im Leben*), apocalyptic eschatology (the dominant theme), and apocalypses (the literary genre), elements which traditional

---

[14] Cf. Carmignac 1979, 16.   [15] Stone 1976, 439.
[16] P. D. Hanson 1976, 29f.   [17] Collins 1979, 3.
[18] Baird 1972, 386. Baird thinks that, after Gunkel, scholars applied the term "form" to
small, individual units. This overlooks the use of *Gattung* for such units by Dibelius,
Bultmann, Grobel, and literally dozens of others who have worked in the form-critical mode.
[19] Doty 1972, 417 and elsewhere.

form criticism would try to hold together. A genre conceived as a whole literary work, as Collins has proposed to me in a helpful letter, can be as broad as a novel: it would be useless to examine a group of novels for a common "Schatz von Gedanken und Stimmungen", a common *Sitz im Leben*, or even tightly related literary forms of expression. All the presuppositions of scholars such as Vielhauer about how "the literary genre apocalypse" should be defined become irrelevant in wide and influential circles, especially in North America.[20]

4. Thoroughgoing Proposals by Collins and Carmignac

From the Apocalypse Group of the Society of Biblical Literature Genres Project has now come a new proposal for the definition of the genre "apocalypse".[21] The proposal is based on the developments just described, and John Collins, the editor of the publication and author of the sections of concern in this paper, accepts the distinction between the genre "apocalypse", the movement "apocalypticism" and the religious view "apocalyptic eschatology".[22] It is the intention of Collins and his collaborators to address only the question of the genre, and to his proposal we now turn.

4.1. The genre is not defined strictly by form, nor by function or *Sitz im Leben*. The only formal element is that there is a narrative framework.[23] The other essential elements of the genre have a coherent and unifying characteristic: to quote Collins, "The key word in the definition is transcendence".[24] The transcendent elements are these: 1) "a revelation is mediated by an otherworldly being to a human recipient"; 2) the revelation discloses "a transcendent reality" which in turn has two characteristics: a) it envisages eschatological salvation and thus has a temporal axis; b) it involves a supernatural world and thus has a spatial axis.[25] These two principal aspects, to repeat, are intrinsically related. Both the revelation and the salvation have to do with the same supernatural or transcendent order.[26]

4.1.1. This general definition permits great flexibility in detail while providing for coherence within the genre. In Collins' view there are two basic types of apocalypse: those "which do not have an otherworldly journey (Type I) and those [which] do (Type II)".[27] Within each principal type there are three sub-types. (a) Some include a review of history, predict an eschatological crisis and involve a cosmic and/or political eschatology. (b) A second sub-type has no historical review but still looks forward to a

---

[20] Not only there: see the paper by L. Hartman in this volume and Carmignac 1979, 19.
[21] Collins 1979.   [22] *Ibid.*, 3.
[23] *Ibid.*, 9. The narrative framework, however, does not appear to be strictly necessary.
[24] *Ibid.*, 10.   [25] *Ibid.*, 9.   [26] *Ibid.*, 11.   [27] *Ibid.*, 13.

resolution of history which has cosmic and/or political dimensions. (c) The third sub-type lacks both the review of history and the public or natural resolution of history and the cosmic order; the eschatology is purely personal.[28] At least one example of each of the sub-types appears under each of the major types; thus one may distinguish six types of apocalypses. This may sound a little vague if it goes entirely unillustrated, and so I shall offer some examples from the two extremes, types Ia and IIc.

4.1.2. Ia is comprised of apocalypses which give a review of history, contain no otherworldly journey, and culminate in a resolution of history which is cosmic and/or political. This type, as Collins notes, "is perhaps the mose widely recognized type". Some of the principal representatives of the type are Daniel 7–12, the Animal Apocalypse from *1 Enoch,* the Apocalypse of Weeks from *1 Enoch, Jubilees* 23, 4 Ezra and *2 Apocalypse of Baruch.*[29]

4.1.3. IIc is comprised of apocalypses which give no review of history and no resolution of the end of history or the cosmic order, but which do contain an otherworldly journey and individual salvation. Here Collins names, for example, *3 Apocalypse of Baruch* and the *Testament of Abraham* chps. 10–15 (in rec. A). He points out that "the majority of the Greco-Roman apocalypses fall in this category: 'the myth of Er' in Plato, Somnium Scipionis in Cicero, the apocalypses in Plutarch and the journey to the underworld in Aeneid VI".[30] This will give some idea of the range of material which can be grouped under the genre apocalypse as Collins defines it.

4.2. Working independently of the Society of Biblical Literature group, Carmignac has arrived more or less simultaneously at a similar definition of the genre "apocalypse".[31]

4.2.1. He insists, first, that to combine genre and theology is to confuse two schemes.[32] He defines the genre thus: An apocalypse is first of all, by definition, a revelation. Yet not every revelation is an apocalypse. Essential to an apocalypse *véritable* is the employment of symbols, though it is also to be noted that the use of symbols in itself does not make an apocalypse. The object of revelation is left open. The only requirement is that there be a "rapport du monde visible avec le monde invisible". The definition is, then, this:

genre littéraire qui présente, à travers des symboles typiques, des révélations soit sur Dieu, soit sur les anges ou les demons, soit sur leurs partisans, soit sur les instruments de leur action.[33]

Excluded as essential are some of the favorite items in most lists: mediating angels, visions, messianism and eschatology.

---

[28] *Ibid.*, 13.   [29] *Ibid.*, 14.   [30] *Ibid.*, 15.   [31] Carmignac 1979.
[32] *Ibid.*, 19.   [33] *Ibid.*, 20.

4.2.2. In a post-script Carmignac relates his definition directly to that of Collins, noting the generally close similarity. He would have stopped the definition after the requirement of a transcendent reality, not regarding as essential to the genre the temporal aspect of salvation.[34] We would add that Collins' definition includes another aspect not regarded as essential by Carmignac, an otherworldly mediator.

5. Positive Results of the Debate

It seems that certain gains have been made which should be registered and consolidated.

5.1. The distinction between "genre", which indicates an entire literary work, and *Gattung* in the sense of the form critics (a small unit with a definite form, representing a certain world of ideas, and having a certain *Sitz im Leben*) should be maintained. It is confusing to identify *Gattung* and genre and then argue that "form" should mean what Gunkel, Dibelius and Bultmann meant by *Gattung*. We should leave form-critical teminology alone: let *Gattung* mean what Gunkel said it meant. If this proposal is accepted, it will mean that translators of German works will have to be cautious in translating *Gattung*, rendering it by "genre" only when it refers to larger works, not to individual units. German scholars may find it useful to adopt the French/English term "genre" to distinguish a larger work from an individual *Gattung*. (In the present volume Koch distinguishes between *Rahmengattung* and *Gliedgattung*, which achieves the purpose in a clear way.)

It will follow from this that the distinction between apocalypticism, end-time (apocalyptic) eschatology, and the genre apocalypse can be confirmed, at least in theory. It is not, again in theory, necessary to define a genre by identifying a *Sitz im Leben* or by seeking its essential world of ideas.

5.2. The enlargement of potential subject matter of apocalypses beyond the end-time events will prove salutary, allowing scholars to give a better account of the material which is actually found in works universally considered "apocalypses".

5.3. Collins' emphasis on transcendence, which seems parallel to Carmignac's citing as the proper object of an apocalypse "le rapport du monde visible avec le monde invisible", is also helpful, pointing as it does to a clearly marked tendency of diverse elements in late antiquity. How marked the tendency is becomes clear in the surveys of works from many different cultural milieux which are included in *Apocalypse: the Morphology of a Genre*.

---

[34] *Ibid.*, 33.

6. Reservations and Criticism

One has, however, some reservations. In many ways the most pressing have to do with a subject which, in this collection of essays, falls more to Professor Hartman than to me: the definition of a genre. I shall briefly mention two points.

6.1. The question of the whole and the parts remains difficult. *1 Enoch* in its present form, while admittedly composite, is usually regarded as an apocalypse. This seems to be implied, for example, in Stone's remark quoted in paragraph 2 above. Collins, however, does not consider *1 Enoch* 91–104 to qualify as an apocalypse, while the other parts of *1 Enoch* are listed as separate apocalypses.[35] Carmignac apparently considers *Jubilees* to be an apocalypse,[36] but Collins lists only chp. 23 as such. Collins considers all of 4 Ezra to be one apocalypse, while Hanson identifies some of its parts as apocalypses.[37] These discrepencies point towards a still outstanding problem in the definition of the word "genre". The notion that a "genre" is a literary category referring to entire literary works (paragraph 3.1.) raises difficulties when applied to works which are compilations. I believe that a strictly literary approach would regard the finished document, as we have it, to be the subject of analysis; but this tends to break down under the inveterate tendency of scholars to pay heed to source-criticism. Collins seems to be reaching, perhaps entirely justifiably, for a definition of genre which is neither *Gattung* nor entire (composite) literary work. In some ways this is not surprising. A novel can contain a lyric poem without the integrity of either being compromised. But if Collins' procedure is to be followed, we shall need *another* title for *1 Enoch* as a whole, or *Jubilees* as a whole, or possibly even for 4 Ezra (if it turns out to be composite, as I continue to think, against the advice of most of my colleagues).[38] If, on the other hand, we follow the lead of Carmignac (and, apparently, Stone), and consider those works which contain elements which they consider essential to apocalypses to be in their entirety apocalypses, then the recent definitions of Collins and Carmignac become subject to the sort of criticism leveled by Hanson, Stone and others against older definitions: a lot of the material is left out of the description. The questions of the whole and the parts and of composite works still leave problems for students of genre.

6.2. There is a potentially more severe problem in the definition of a genre: there is no agreement on what one is.

6.2.1. I find Doty's view helpful, while admitting that it is only one among many:

---

[35] Collins 1979, 45; cf. the list, 28.
[37] P. D. Hanson 1976, 28.
[36] Carmignac 1979, 31.
[38] Sanders 1977, 418.

Generic definitions ought not be restricted to any one particular feature (such as form, content, etc.), but they ought to be widely enough constructed to allow one to conceive of a genre as a congeries of (a limited number of) factors.

He lists for possible inclusion among the cluster of traits which marks a genre the following: "authorial intention, audience expectency, formal units used, structure, use of sources, characterizations, sequential action, primary motifs, institutional setting, rhetorical patterns, and the like".[39] Collins' definition of the genre is this:

'Apocalypse' is a genre of revelatory literature with a narrative framework, in which a revelation is mediated by an otherworldly being to a human recipient, disclosing a transcendent reality which is both temporal, insofar as it envisages eschatological salvation, and spatial insofar as it involves another, supernatural world.[40]

He continues by pointing out that the "key word in the definition is transcendence". When Collins' definition is compared with the "congeries of . . . factors" listed by Doty, it is seen that few of the factors are present.

6.2.2. Let us consider, for example, three of Collins' apocalypses: The *Testament of Abraham* (rec. A, chps. 10–15), *Jub.* 23, and Virgil's *Aeneid*, bk. vi. It is hard to see that among them lies any similarity in authorial intent, audience expectency, formal units, structure, use of sources, characterizations, sequential action, institutional setting, or rhetorical patterns. To prove the negative, that there are no similarities, would require a full study of each of the named works, which is clearly not possible here. I can only fall back on the defence that my study of these works does not reveal any similarities. All three have the revelation of a transcendent reality. With regard to the content of the revelation: *Jub.* 23 reveals something which can be called "eschatological salvation", the *Testament of Abraham* the basis of the judgment of individuals, and Aeneid vi the glory and stability of Rome and of the Augustan regime, as well as a post-mortem judgment. Referring now to Doty's list, we have some agreement in "primary motifs". Is this enough to make a genre? Precisely what has been explained, except the wide-spread desire for revelation? This constitutes something, but is it a literary genre? For my own part, I am dubious. It appears that "genre" has been conceived too loosely (the same could be said of Carmignac's definition), but here I must yield to those who are better equipped to deal with the literary/philosophical questions of what a genre is.

7. Common Characteristics of Jewish Apocalypses

When one turns directly to the Jewish apocalypses (that is, those works always so regarded), there is another feeling of unease. On the one hand I

---

[39] Doty 1972, 439f.   [40] Collins 1979, 9.

must agree that the criticisms leveled at the "old" way of defining apocalypses by Hanson, Stone, Carmignac, Collins and others are right. Often there is little correspondence between numerous of the items in the mixed list of traits which define apocalypses (paragraph 1.2.) and the works generally called apocalypses. It is also true that many of the traditional traits appear in works which are not apocalypses. Yet one cannot help but feel that Vielhauer, Koch and numerous earlier scholars were talking about a definite phenomenon in post-biblical Judaism. There *were* feelings of oppression and hopes of vindication, and these feelings and hopes were expressed in "revelations" which promised either the ultimate restoration of Israel or the vindication of the righteous among Israel. The works usually named as Palestinian Jewish apocalypses (Daniel, *1 Enoch, Jubilees*, 4 Ezra, *2 Apocalypse of Baruch*, the *Apocalypse of Abraham*, and often the *Testament of Levi*), even though they may have been designated "apocalypses" on the basis of an unsophisticated analysis of "genre", can be seen to constitute an identifiable body of literature within Judaism. They are marked off by the combination of revelation with the promise of the vindication or redemption of a group.[41]

7.1. There are other statements to the effect that Israel will be gathered and victorious (Ben Sira 35; Philo, *Praem.* 94–97; 162–172) and there were certainly other revelations (clearly hinted at in Tosefta Hagigah 2.3–4; cf. 2 Cor. 12.1–4). *What is peculiar to the works which have traditionally been considered Palestinian Jewish apocalypses is the combination of revelation with the promise of restoration and reversal.* The presence of the theme of revelation in the works which are to be listed below does not need demonstration, but for the sake of convenience I list here some of the principal passages indicating restoration and reversal in Palestinian Jewish works which have generally been considered apocalypses:

(1) Daniel 7–12: restoration of Israel 12.1–4; for the destruction of the oppressing enemies see, *e.g.,* 11.40–45.

(2) The Animal Apocalypse, *1 Enoch* 83–90: military reversal (presumably based on the Maccabean wars), 90.19; judgment of oppressors, 90.22–26; restoration of the Temple and Jerusalem, 90.28–36.

(3) *1 Enoch* 91–104: the theme of reversal is almost ubiquitous, see for example 94.6–11; restoration of the righteous over the wicked, 96.1; final reversal at the judgment, 98.6–10.

(4) *Jubilees* 23: healing and peace for the righteous, while the adversaries are driven out, 23.29–31.

(5) 4 Ezra: There is no true reversal through chp. 10, even though the eternality of the law is stated and the rebuilding of Zion predicted for the future, see 9.36; 10.27. In subsequent sections the traditional theme of Israel's victory over oppressors appears, see 11.45; 12.31–33; 13.49.

---

[41] It is noteworthy that the apocalypses from the diaspora, such as *3 Apc. Baruch*, have individual salvation, not group redemption.

(6) *2 Apocalypse of Baruch*: reversal and restoration: 51.5; 85.4.

(7) *Apocalypse of Abraham*: reversal and restoration, chp. 31.

(8) *1 Enoch* 1–36: judgment of the wicked and salvation of the righteous (but the wicked are not explicitly said to be former oppressors), 27.2–5; similarly 5.4–9; 10.16f.; the Temple is restored and given to the righteous, chp. 25.

(9) Heavenly Luminaries, *1 Enoch* 72–82: new creation, 72.2; destruction of the wicked, 80.8. The precise themes of reversal and the salvation of the righteous are missing.

(10) The Similitudes, *1 Enoch* 37–71: the themes of reversal and restoration are very frequent, see for example 38.4–6; 46.4; 53.2–7.

(11) Apocalypse of Weeks, *1 Enoch* 93; 91.12–17: reversal and restoration, 91.12f.

(12) *Testament of Levi* 2–5: redemption of Israel, 2.10; intercession for Israel against attackers, 5.6.

7.1.1. Within this list, *1 Enoch* 1–36 does not have the explicit theme of reversal, since the righteous are not precisely said to be oppressed by the wicked. The renewal of the Temple and the giving of it to the righteous, however, seem to imply that "the righteous" are those not otherwise in power. The book of the Heavenly Luminaries perhaps should be excluded. There is destruction and renewal, but the reversal of fortunes of the wicked and the righteous is not a theme of the work. Instead of calling the book of the Heavenly Luminaries an apocalypse, I should rather say that it presupposes the apocalyptic viewpoint but lacks the main theme of apocalypticism.

7.1.2. In Collins' list, these works fall into four different categories. Six are in Ia, one in IIa, four in IIb, and one is considered not an apocalypse. When, however, one makes crucial the question of *restoration*, rather than the *mode* of revelation, different results are achieved. I would exclude the Heavenly Luminaries and put all the rest into one group: Palestinian Jewish apocalypses. They then are seen to be coherent historically, geographically and probably sociologically. By "sociologically" I mean simply this: none of the apocalypses comes from the "mighty". They are either from the oppressed within Israel or from "Israel" conceived of as oppressed. The Maccabean literature is notably without apocalypses.

7.2. One theme does not, of course, make a genre. We have already noted the theme of reversal in Ben Sira and Philo, and to these could be added such items as the prayers in columns 13 and 14 of 1QM, as well as the so-called *Assumption of Moses* (see chp. 10). What do these last mentioned items lack that the apocalypses have? Revelation. I do not dwell on the point because it is obvious and is made with ample clarity by Collins and others, but apocalypses should be, or should intend to be, revelatory; and the form of the revelation should be supernatural. The prayers of 1QM and Ben Sira and the flat predictions of Philo and *The Assumption of Moses* do not qualify. There should be an angel, a vision, an appeal to inspiration by the Spirit, or something of the sort. The last mode of revelation is not

singled out by Collins, and so perhaps I should say something about it.
That is the mode of revelation in *1 Enoch* 91–104, and it seems to be just as
supernatural a mode of revelation as the second-hand angelic revelation and
vision mentioned in the Apocalypse of Weeks (*1 Enoch* 93.2).

7.3. The themes of revelation and the promise of restoration and reversal
appear to me to be *generative* for the works described. Those works contain
much other material, and thus this "definition" is subject to many of the
same criticisms as others.

7.3.1. When one adds the still outstanding problems of how to define
works which are composite and of the very definition of the word "genre",
I shall admit that I have not defined a genre of literature. But it still appears
that there are works which can be called "Palestinian Jewish Apocalypses",
even if they do not constitute one tightly defined literary genre; that these
works are separable from others; and that they point towards historical and
social realities in the history of Israel.

7.3.2. The same things cannot be said of many other proposals. The
revelation of *transcendent reality* (Collins) is as much a concern of the
Hermetic literature, many of the Nag Hammadi works and the Gospel of
John (for example) as of the apocalypses. The feeling that *the world was out
of joint* (cited by Collins as the generative problem of all the apocalypses)[42]
was widespread in the Greco-Roman period. Pseudonymity (as has often
been noted) and angels simply abound in late Judaism. The revelation
which promises reversal and restoration appears to me the most striking
point of the Jewish apocalypses, though they may not constitute a neat
literary genre.

8. Advantages and Disadvantages
of an Essentialist Definition

To summarize: the proposed return to an "essentialist" definition[43] of
Jewish apocalypses suffers from some drawbacks. It does not, for example,
explain a great deal of the material found in the apocalypses. The proposal
does, however, offer some advantages. The themes of revelation and
reversal, when the reversal has to do with a group – either Israel or the
righteous – are in all the works being discussed; and in that combination
they are in no others. They are thus *characteristic* of the Jewish apocalypses.
Further, the revelation of a coming restoration seems *generative* of these
particular works, but again of no others. This seems preferable to the

---

[42] Collins 1979, 27; cf. Betz 1969, 147f.: the feeling of being "helpless in a hostile world".

[43] The old "essentialist" definition was "revelation of the end of time" (*e.g.* Raphaël 1977,
13). "Revelation of restoration and reversal" better represents the point of the material.

appeal to a general *Zeitgeist* (alienation) for the generative problem. If we have correctly identified the generative problem, we have probably identified something about *authorial intent* and *audience expectency*: the authors intended to promise restoration by God from present oppression, and the audience understood the devices being used to make that promise impressive: it was revealed, accompanied by visions, and the like. We probably have not identified a *definite Sitz im Leben* in the sense of the "conventicles" proposed by Vielhauer. At some time or other all Israel may have felt oppressed,[44] and it is impossible to say that the revelation of coming triumph circulated only within small circles in Israel. At any rate, if the Jewish apocalypses as defined here still do not constitute a tight genre, the definition at least meets some of the tests proposed by Doty.

Bibliography

Baird, J. A. 1972: "Genre Analysis as a Method of Historical Criticism", in: *SBL Proceedings* II (ed. Lane C. McGaughy), Missoula, Mont. 1972, 385–411.

Betz, H. D. 1969: "On the Problem of the Religio-Historical Understanding of Apocalypticism", in: *JTC* 6 (1969) 134–156.

Carmignac, J. 1979: "Qu'est-ce que l'apocalyptique? Son emploi à Qumrân", in: *RdQ* 10 (1979) 3–33.

Collins, J. J. (ed.) 1979: *Apocalypse: The Morphology of a Genre*, (*Semeia* 14), Missoula, Mont. 1979.

Doty, W. G. 1972: "The Concept of Genre in Literary Analysis", in: *SBL Proceedings* II (ed. Lane C. McGaughy), Missoula, Mont. 1972, 413–448.

Hanson, P. D. 1963: "Jewish Apocalyptic against Its Near Eastern Environment", in: *RB* 78 (1963) 31–58.

– 1976: "Apocalypse, Genre". "Apocalypticism", in: *IDBSup* (1976) 27–34.

Koch, Klaus 1970: *Ratlos vor der Apokalyptik*, Gütersloh 1970.

– 1972: *The Rediscovery of Apocalyptic* (SBT 2/22), London 1972.

Raphaël, F. 1977: "Esquisse d'une typologie de l'apocalypse", in: *L'Apocalyptique* (eds. Marc Philonenko/Marcel Simon), Paris 1977, 9–38.

Rollmann, Hans: "Zwei Briefe Hermann Gunkels an Adolf Jülicher zur religionsgeschichtlichen und formgeschichtlichen Methode", in: *ZThK* 78 (1981) 276–288.

Sanders, E. P. 1977: *Paul and Palestinian Judaism*, London/Philadelphia, Penn. 1977.

Schmidt, J. M. 1976: *Die jüdische Apokalyptik*[2], Neukirchen 1976.

Stone, M. 1976: "Lists of Revealed Things in the Apocalyptic Literature", in: *Magnalia Dei* (eds. F. M. Cross and others), New York 1976, 414–452.

Vielhauer, P. 1965: "Apocalypses and Related Subjects", in: *New Testament Apocrypha* II (ed. E. Hennecke and W. Schneemelcher, E. t. ed. R. McL. Wilson), Philadelphia, Penn. 1965, 581–607.

von Rad, G. 1968: *Theologie des Alten Testaments II*[5], Munich 1968.

---

[44] All Israel: *e.g.* *T. Levi* 5.6; 4 Ezra 4.23.

Der Prophet als Widerpart und Zeuge der Offenbarung
Erwägungen zur Interdependenz von Form und Sache im IV. Buch Esra

WOLFGANG HARNISCH

1. Tendenzen der neueren Auslegung

Die jüngste Phase der mit dem IV. Buch Esra befaßten Exegese steht im Zeichen einer Wiederentdeckung älterer Auslegungsmuster. Zwar weiß man sich neuen Fragestellungen verpflichtet, doch wird die Lösung der Probleme im Grunde von alten Konzepten erwartet. An drei Beiträgen aus dem Bereich der angloamerikanischen Forschung läßt sich dieser hermeneutische Trend ablesen.

1.1. In einem Aufsatz mit dem Untertitel "The Form and Function of 4 Ezra" versucht E. Breech, den Aufriß von IV Esr als Formular einer prophetischen Tröstung zu würdigen[1]. Nach seinem Dafürhalten übernimmt Esra insofern die Rolle eines Propheten, als er die Not des Volkes Gott übereignet und daraufhin ein göttliches Orakel erwartet. Die ersten drei Gesprächsgänge (3,1–9,22) seien darauf abgezweckt, die religiöse Problematik zu artikulieren, von der sich die Gemeinde Esras betroffen weiß. Demgegenüber bekunde sich in den folgenden drei Visionen und deren Deutung (9,23–13,58) die göttliche Zuwendung. Der Schlußteil (Kp. 14) verstehe sich als eine Art Epilog[2]. Dieser hermeneutische Ansatz, der die Wechselbeziehung von Struktur und Funktion zum Leitmaßstab der Analyse erhebt, wirkt modern. Indessen greift der vorgelegte Entwurf in Wahrheit auf Gesichtspunkte der Interpretation zurück, wie sie vor fast 80 Jahren bereits von H. Gunkel geltend gemacht wurden. Schon Gunkel vertrat nämlich die Auffassung, die drei ersten Visionen seien "der Darstellung der religiösen Probleme", die drei folgenden einer Vollendung der Tröstung des Verfassers gewidmet, und er äußerte bereits die Ansicht, Kp. 14 bilde einen Nachtrag, der dem Ganzen "einen ästhetisch gefälligen Abschluß" verleiht[3].

1.2. Noch stärker macht sich Gunkels Einfluß in den beiden anderen Arbeiten bemerkbar. So wendet sich A. P. Hayman in einem Artikel über "The Problem of Pseudonymity in the Ezra Apocalypse" mit Vehemenz

---

[1] Breech 1973.   [2] Breech 1973, 270 ff., 272 ff., 274.
[3] Gunkel 1900, 335, 347 f. (Einleitung).

gegen die von E. Brandenburger ins Spiel gebrachte und von mir verstärkte These, der Dialog zwischen Esra und dem Engel sei als Ausdruck
einer theologischen Kontroverse zu beurteilen[4]. Für Hayman kommt der
Verfasser von IV Esr keineswegs primär oder gar ausschließlich in den
Offenbarungsweisungen Uriels, sondern auch und gerade in den Klagen,
Fragen und Einwänden des Visionärs zu Wort[5]. Damit ist aber jene
psychologische Sicht der Rollenverteilung restituiert, wie sie Gunkel vertrat. Denn Gunkel war bekanntlich der Meinung, das Zwiegespräch zwischen Esra und dem Engel spiegele die Verfassung eines zwischen Verzweiflung und Hoffnung hin- und herschwankenden Bewußtseins wider.
Die Spannung des Dialogs versteht sich dann als Objektivation eines
seelischen Konflikts. Hayman macht sich diese Deutung zu eigen, und er
distanziert sich von Gunkel nur insofern, als er dessen Schlußfolgerung,
der Apokalyptiker sei "eine zerrissene Natur"[6], zu vermeiden sucht. Für
Hayman übernimmt der ausgesprochene Zweifel vielmehr kathartische
Funktion. Er bildet ein notwendiges Moment im Prozeß der seelischen
Läuterung, und die Einheit der Person bleibt gewahrt, sofern die religiöse
Erfahrung die Kraft besitzt, die Skepsis zu überholen[7].

1.3. Eine fast dogmatische Geltung erfährt diese Auffassung in der
Dissertation von A. L. Thompson über "Responsibility for Evil in the
Theodicy of IV Ezra". Auch dieser Entwurf lebt von der Überzeugung,
daß insbesondere die Äußerungen Esras über den theologischen Ort des
Verfassers Aufschluß geben. Im Ansatz dem religionspsychologischen
Deutungsschema Gunkels und Haymans verpflichtet, orientiert Thompson die Sachinterpretation im übrigen wie Breech an der Frage nach dem
Verhältnis von Form und Inhalt. So meint er, in der Abfolge der Einzelepi-
soden zwei eigenständige Argumentationsstränge voneinander abheben zu
können. Der eine sei heilsgeschichtlich geprägt und auf Israels Geschick
bezogen, der andere trage schöpfungstheologischen Charakter und ziele
auf die Frage nach dem Schicksal der Menschheit. Gelte das erste Argument dem Widerspruch zwischen Israels geschichtlicher Ohnmacht und
dem Wohlergehen der Völker (das Eine – die Vielen), so das zweite dem
Mißverhältnis zwischen dem eschatologischen Verderben vieler und der
eschatologischen Rettung weniger Menschen (viele – wenige). Aus der
unterschiedlichen Verteilung dieser Argumentationsmuster (das heilsge-
schichtliche dominiert in den Episoden I–II und V–VII, das schöpfungs-
theologische dagegen in Episode III, also auf dem Höhepunkt der ersten
drei Gesprächseinheiten) zieht Thompson den Schluß, der Autor der
Schrift suche sich der Enge und dem wirklichkeitsfremden Dogmatismus

---

[4] Hayman 1975, 50 ff.; vgl. Brandenburger 1962, 27 ff.; Harnisch 1969, 60 ff.
[5] Hayman 1975, 49.   [6] Gunkel 1900, 343; vgl. 340, 342.
[7] Vgl. Hayman 1975, 55 f.

einer partikularistisch denkenden jüdischen Orthodoxie zu entwinden, indem er werbend für Perspektiven des theologischen Universalismus eintrete. Freilich erfolge die Kritik am Hergebrachten durchaus auf der Basis und im Rahmen einer Argumentation, die der offiziell wahrgenommenen Sicht des Erwählungsglaubens Raum gibt und am Ende wieder in sie einschwenkt. Sie bleibe eingebettet in eine Problemstellung, die sich in den Bahnen des Überlieferten bewegt[8].

1.4. Sind wir damit einer Lösung des hermeneutischen Problems von IV Esr nähergekommen? Zumindest in zweierlei Hinsicht scheint dies zweifelhaft.

1.4.1. Was an allen drei Arbeiten befremdet, ist zunächst eine auffällige Unterschätzung der Relevanz der Engelaussagen und die damit korrespondierende Verlagerung des Interesses auf die Person und die Äußerungen Esras. Man gibt zwar vor, das, was der Verfasser sagen will, den Worten beider Dialogpartner entnehmen zu wollen. Faktisch dominiert aber eine Orientierung an den Argumenten Esras. Diese Gewichtung der Rollen steht in krassem Widerspruch zur Bewegung des Dialogs selbst. Denn dessen Gefälle läuft offenkundig auf die Engelaussagen zu. Stets ist es Uriel, der das letzte Wort behält. Es mag strittig bleiben, wie die Rolle Esras und das Verhältnis seiner Worte zum Aussagewillen des Ganzen zu beurteilen sind. Keinem Zweifel unterliegt, daß die Antworten des Engels von Anfang an größte Aufmerksamkeit beanspruchen und für die Ermittlung der Intention des Buches von ausschlaggebender Bedeutung sind. In dieser Hinsicht bleiben die genannten Beiträge der angloamerikanischen Forschung somit den kritischen Bedenken ausgesetzt, die gegen Gunkels psychologische Deutung des Dialogs zu erheben waren.

1.4.2. Weil das Gewicht der Offenbarungsworte Uriels verkannt wird, wirken auch die jüngsten Versuche unbefriedigend, Formgesichtspunkte für die Sachinterpretation fruchtbar zu machen. So ist zwar gegenüber Breech einzuräumen, daß die spannungsvolle Bewegung des Gesprächs im Verlauf der Zionvision eine Wendung erfährt. Dies darf jedoch nicht darüber hinwegtäuschen, daß die Fragen, die Esra stellvertretend vorbringt, bereits im ersten Hauptteil der Schrift definitiv beantwortet werden. Die drei ersten Gesprächseinheiten gelten somit nicht nur der Darstellung, sondern zugleich bereits einer Klärung der Verlegenheit, die sich in den Worten Esras ausspricht. Nicht erst in den Traumgesichten des zweiten Hauptteils, sondern schon im Dialog mit dem himmlischen Partner begegnet Esra also einer Instanz, welche die von ihm artikulierte religiöse Problematik löst, allerdings auf eine sehr eigenwillige, dem Seher fremd bleibende Weise. Noch weniger überzeugt, wenn Thompson ähn-

---

[8] Zum Ganzen vgl. bes. Thompson 1977, Kp. IV (157 ff.).

lich wie Gunkel[9] heterogene Argumentationsmuster ausfindig macht und diese dann voneinander isoliert. Dabei ist nämlich völlig außer acht gelassen, daß der Rückgriff auf die Schöpfung in IV Esr "durchweg im Blick auf das unerklärliche Schicksal Israels"[10] erfolgt. Beide Argumentationsstränge sind also aufs engste miteinander verzahnt. Im übrigen erscheint es als ein methodisch fragwürdiges Unterfangen, bestimmte Denkweisen zu formalisieren und deren Textdistribution klären zu wollen, ohne daß zuvor eine Strukturanalyse im Sinne der Formkritik durchgeführt wurde. Weil diese Aufgabe von Thompson nur ansatzweise in Angriff genommen wird, verfängt sich seine Interpretation immer wieder in abenteuerliche Konklusionen[11]. Das Programm einer Erhellung der Form-Inhalt-Relation in IV Esr bleibt Desiderat.

1.5. Fragt man abschließend nach dem positiven Ertrag dieser jüngsten Phase der Diskussion, sind immerhin folgende Gesichtspunkte festzuhalten:

a) Alle drei Untersuchungen verlangen, die Interpretation von IV Esr nicht nur am Dialog zwischen Esra und Uriel in den Episoden I–III, sondern auch und vor allem an den Visionspartien (IV–VI) sowie dem Schlußabschnitt (VII) zu orientieren. Diese Forderung, die zugleich einen Mangel der bisherigen Forschung markiert, besteht zu Recht. Ohne eine Würdigung der Funktion von 9,26–14,48(49f.) im Rahmen der Gesamtdisposition läßt sich das Anliegen von IV Esr in der Tat nicht bestimmen.

b) Stärkste Beachtung verdient das Bemühen von Breech und Thompson, die Frage nach der Interdependenz von Form und Sache zum hermeneutischen Prinzip einer Beschäftigung mit IV Esr zu erheben. Nicht was die Ergebnisse, wohl aber was die leitende Fragehinsicht anbelangt, sind die Arbeiten dieser beiden Exegeten vorbildlich. Zu prüfen, ob und inwiefern sich das Vorverständnis bestätigt, "that the structure and meaning of 4 Ezra are mutually determative"[12], bleibt die hermeneutische Aufgabe einer jeden Interpretation dieser eindrucksvoll komponierten Schrift.

c) In diesem Zusammenhang sind Beobachtungen zur Disposition von Interesse, wie sie als erster Hayman angestellt hat. Anders als Gunkel und Breech ordnet er jeweils die Episoden I–III sowie V–VII zusammen und charakterisiert Visio IV als eine Art Übergangskapitel, das Gelenkfunktion

---

[9] Nach Gunkel (1900, 339) "behandelt der Verfasser zwei verschiedene Probleme; beide Male handelt es sich um eine Theodicee". Zur Skizzierung der beiden Problemkreise vgl. Gunkel 1900, 335 ff., 337 ff.

[10] Harnisch 1969, 60; ähnlich urteilt Reese 1967, 131 und ebd. Anm. 17 (anders allerdings 149, 151).

[11] Vgl. nur Thompson 1977, 217 f., 267 ff.

[12] Breech 1973, 269.

besitzt. Vergleicht man nun den Einleitungs- und Schlußkomplex miteinander, wird der innere Bruch in der Haltung Esras unübersehbar. Dies führt Hayman zu der hermeneutisch grundlegenden Frage: "What can have been the author's purpose in permitting his chief character to undergo such a metamorphosis?"[13] Damit ist zugleich das Hauptproblem angesprochen, mit dem sich die folgenden Erwägungen zu befassen haben.

1.6. In der Erwartung, den Aporien der bisherigen Auslegung beikommen zu können, greifen wir die Frage nach der Wechselbeziehung von Form und Sache in IV Esr erneut auf. Unsere Untersuchung soll dabei einen Weg beschreiten, der von außen nach innen, nämlich von der Makrosyntax des Textes zu den seine Form prägenden kleinsten Einheiten führt, um schließlich zur Frage nach dem Gesamtinteresse der Schrift zurückzukehren.

2. Analyse der Makrostruktur des Werkes

2.1. Aufschlußreichstes Indiz für die kompositorische Eigenart von IV Esr sind die ganz unscheinbar wirkenden Partien, welche den Progreß der Offenbarung anzeigen. Gedacht ist an jene Aussagen, die den Abschluß eines längeren Gesprächsganges und die Eröffnung eines neuen markieren. Achtet man auf diese Stücke, die offenkundig als Dispositionssignale fungieren, präsentiert sich zunächst der Komplex 3,1–10,57 als eine in sich geschlossene Einheit. Sie zerfällt in vier große Offenbarungsepisoden. Die den Aufriß von Visio I–IV tragende kompositorische Absicht wird deutlich, sobald man sich über das Formprinzip der genannten Überleitungswendungen etwas genauer Rechenschaft ablegt. Auf stereotype Weise läuft jede der drei ersten Dialogpartien in einen *Engelauftrag* an Esra aus (5,13; 6,30f.; 9,23–25). Ebenso homogen ist die *Exposition* der jeweils folgenden Episode (II–IV) gestaltet. Sie enthält durchweg einen Vollzugsbericht des Sehers (5,20; 6,35; 9,26) und eine damit unmittelbar verknüpfte Redeeinführung (5,21f.; 6,36f.[14]; 9,27f.), deren Muster z. T. bereits am Auftakt von Visio I sichtbar wird (vgl. 3,1bβ–3).

2.1.1. Die strukturelle Verwandtschaft dieser Stücke ist derart umfassend, daß Anlaß besteht, von einem literarischen Formular (pattern) zu reden. So lassen die *Engelweisungen*, die bei Einhalten bestimmter Auflagen weitergehende Offenbarungen in Aussicht stellen, ein streng gefaßtes Redeschema erkennen, das erst am Schluß (9,23–25) inhaltlich variiert wird:

---

[13] Hayman 1975, 48; zur Charakteristik der Disposition vgl. 47.
[14] Wie in 9,28 ist die Wendung *et dixi* in 3,4; 5,23; 6,38 zum jeweils vorausgehenden Vers zu ziehen.

(1) Rückblick auf die ergangene Offenbarung (eröffnet mit *haec*)
(2) konditionale Offenbarungsankündigung
    (a) Protasis (eingeleitet durch *si*) mit Angabe der Bedingung
        (α) weiteren Bittens (*iterum*)
        (β) siebentägigen Fastens
    (b) futurische Apodosis mit Verheißung weiterer (*iterato, iterum*), und zwar gesteigerter Enthüllung (*horum maiora*).

Mit derselben Konsequenz ist die *Exposition* der sich jeweils anschließenden Episode formuliert, wobei wiederum am Schluß (9,26–28) eine charakteristische Änderung eintritt:

(1) Vollzugsbericht mit Angabe der befolgten Weisung
    (a) siebentägigen Fastens
    (b) (wiederholten) Klagens
    (c) sowie einer ausdrücklichen Bezugnahme auf das Engelmandat
(2) Redeeinführung
    (a) datierte Ereignisformel (*et factum est post dies septem* bzw. *in octava nocte*)
    (b) Doppelaussage über Esras Erregung, bezogen auf die Verfassung
        (α) seines Herzens (*cor meum*)
        (β) seines Geistes bzw. seiner Seele (*spiritus meus, anima mea*)
    (c) Redeeinleitungsfloskel (*et ... coepi [inchoavi] loqui coram Altissimo ... et dixi*).

Wie bereits angedeutet, erfährt die Schematik beim Übergang zur Zionvision eine auffällige Abwandlung. Zwar bleibt die Struktur auch hier erhalten, doch finden sich Züge, die vom Grundmuster abweichen. So fehlt im Engelauftrag der Rückblick auf die Vergangenheit, und die Zukunftsaussage spricht nicht mehr von einer Steigerung des Offenbarungsgeschehens, sondern schlicht vom Wiederkommen und Reden des himmlischen Partners. In den breit entfalteten Konditionalsatz ist eine doppelte *correctio* eingelagert. Diese bringt zum Ausdruck, daß die Bedingung des Fastens nun durch eine siebentägige vegetarische Speise auf offenem Feld abgelöst wird und daß dem Seher für diese Zeit Fleisch- und Weingenuß versagt sind. Die Gebetsforderung steht am Schluß und gewinnt dadurch an Gewicht. Sie ist auch insofern gesteigert, als Esras Bitten *sine intermissione* erfolgen soll. Die Exposition von Visio IV trägt dieser veränderten Lage Rechnung. Der Vollzugsbericht konzentriert sich auf die Kräuternahrung, wobei zu Beginn der erstmalige Ortswechsel (*in campum*) auffällig betont ist (zur Situation von I–III vgl. 3,1a.bα). In der Redeeinführungsformel findet sich vor der eingliedrigen Erregungsaussage (*cor*) ein Satz über Esras lokale Befindlichkeit (*supra foenum*) – ein kompositorisch bedeutsames Detail, wie sich später zeigen wird. Die Redeeinleitungsfloskel ist plerophorisch verbreitert.

2.1.2. Aus diesen Beobachtungen ergibt sich zwingend, daß die Maßregeln des Engels zum Empfang weiterer Offenbarungen auf die besonderen Operationen vor Beginn der Zionvision hinauslaufen. Das an den Naht-

stellen der Visionen sichtbar werdende Formular von Engelauftrag, Vollzugsbericht und Redeeinführung ist bewußt im Sinne einer Klimax gestaltet, so daß beim Leser der Eindruck entsteht, mit der Zionvision habe die
Begegnung zwischen Esra und Uriel ihren Höhepunkt erreicht. Der
Gedanke einer sich steigernden und in der vierten Episode vollendenden
Offenbarungsbewegung wird überdies durch 6,35 nahegelegt. Dort
bezieht Esra das gebotene Fasten auf die ihm auferlegte Erfüllung einer
Dreiwochenfrist. Nimmt man diese Aussage mit dem in 9,24 ausgesprochenen Verbot des Fleisch- und Weingenusses zusammen, wird deutlich,
daß für die Komposition und Reihung der Offenbarungsepisoden I–IV
offensichtlich Dan 10,2 f. Pate gestanden hat:

> Zu jener Zeit übte ich, Daniel, drei Wochen lang Kasteiung: wohlschmeckende Speise aß
> ich nicht, Fleisch und Wein kamen nicht in meinen Mund; ich salbte mich auch niemals, bis
> volle drei Wochen um waren.

Der Verfasser von IV Esr hat das aus Daniel überkommene Dreiwochen-
schema seiner Komposition zugrunde gelegt und durch dessen Aufgliede-
rung in Phasen von jeweils sieben Tagen eine vierteilige Episodenfolge in
Szene gesetzt. Weil das Muster der Gesamtfrist von drei Wochen aber
gewahrt bleibt, gewinnt die vierte Episode Abschlußcharakter[15].

2.2. Wie verhält sich nun die äußerst reflektierte Ökonomie der Darstel-
lung in I–IV zum Aufriß der folgenden Teile des Buches? Auf den ersten
Blick ist ersichtlich, daß die präzis disponierte Anlage der Übergänge, wie
sie in I–IV wahrzunehmen war, bei der Eröffnung von Visio V zerbricht.
Im Engelwort 10,58 f. sind sowohl die konditionale Diktion als auch das
Siebentageschema aufgegeben. Auf einen knapp gefaßten Befehl zum
Bleiben bis zur kommenden Nacht folgt die Ankündigung von Traumgesichten, die der Höchste 'an den Erdbewohnern tun wird in den letzten
Tagen'. Ohne Analogie zu den vergleichbaren Stücken der vorausliegen-
den Teile ist die Nennung des Höchsten, auffällig die Erwähnung von
mehreren Traumgesichten. Insgesamt verrät die Verheißung eine begriff-
lich fixierte Sprache mit systematisierender Tendenz[16]. Die sich anschließende Exposition der Adlervision (10,60; 11,1a) umfaßt einen Vollzugsbericht, der das gebotene Bleiben etwas gezwungen auf den Modus des
Schlafs bezieht, sowie Ereignis- und Traumeröffnungsformel. Auch bei
der Wende zu Visio VI (12,39.51; 13,1) besitzt das Engelwort, das zum
Ausharren anhält und eine weitere Offenbarung des Höchsten ankündigt,

---

[15] Als Hinweis auf die entscheidende vierte Episode lassen sich vielleicht auch die Engeläu-
ßerungen 5,4 und 7,26 interpretieren.
[16] Darauf weisen die geprägte Offenbarungsterminologie (*ostendere, visio somniorum*), der
feststehende Ausdruck *a (in) novissimis diebus*, die undifferenzierte Rede von der eschatologischen Tat Gottes (*facere*) sowie die allgemein gefaßte Objektangabe (*his, qui inhabitant super
terram*).

keine konditionale Form. Im Vollzugsbericht und nur dort wird gänzlich unmotiviert auf das Requisit der Pflanzennahrung zurückgegriffen – eine nach 10,58–60 deplaziert wirkende Imitation des Auftaktes der Zionvision. Überraschend finden an dieser Stelle auch die sieben Tage wieder Verwendung. Doch scheint die chronologische Abfolge von 12,39 und 12,51; 13,1 durch die Zwischenschaltung der Volksszene 12,40b–50 gestört, zumal diese ebenfalls auf die Spanne von sieben Tagen rekurriert (vgl. v.40b).

2.2.1. Diese Ungereimtheiten wirken um so auffälliger, als die für I–IV vorausgesetzte Redesituation keineswegs aufgegeben ist. Immer noch figuriert Uriel, nun freilich ausdrücklich in der Rolle des angelus interpres, als der Partner Esras[17]. Sollte die beschriebene Unausgewogenheit der Visionsübergänge in V–VI etwa als Indiz für eine sekundäre Bearbeitung des Textes zu werten sein? Dann wären Adler- und Menschensohngesicht als spätere Ankristallisationen an die Zionvision zu beurteilen, und der (die) Redaktor(en) hätte(n), um diese Stücke dem Werk einzugliedern, an das Formprinzip der vorgegebenen Visionsübergänge angeknüpft, ohne das Konzept der literarischen Strategie konsequent kopieren zu können. Für den externen Status der Offenbarungsepisoden V und VI ließen sich vielleicht auch Beobachtungen anführen, die aus einem Vergleich dieser Stücke mit der Zionvision erwachsen. Sie betreffen nicht mehr das Problem der Verklammerung, sondern den Charakter dieser Texte selbst. So ist die Partie zwischen Vision und Deuterede, die in der Zionvision einen formtypisch viergliedrigen Dialog[18] mit folgender Deutungsbitte umfaßt, im Adler- und Menschensohngesicht auf eine einzige Äußerung Esras reduziert. Anders als in der Zionvision tragen Deutebitte sowie Einleitungs- und Schlußformel der Deuterede in Visio V und VI das Gepräge einer bereits technisch fixierten Sprache[19]. Eine auffällige Differenz ist auch

---

[17] Es wäre verfehlt, die Ausdrucksweise in 12,34 (vgl. 13,48); 13,32.37.52.54 (Possessivpronomen in der ersten Person Sg.) als Indiz für einen Sprecherwechsel (Uriel – Gott) zu bewerten. Von Gott ist sonst durchweg in der dritten Person (*Altissimus*) die Rede. Die sprachliche Inkonzinnität könnte in einigen Fällen eher den Verdacht einer sekundären Glossierung des Textes nahelegen.

[18] S. u. § 3.1.1.

[19] Dies geht aus einer Gegenüberstellung der Formulierungen von Deutebitte (10,37a; 12,8; 13,15), Einleitungs- (10,40a Syr./Aeth.; 12,8; 13,21a.25a) und Schlußformel der Deuterede (10,49fin.; 12,35; 13,53a) in der Zion-, Adler- und Menschensohnvision hervor. Zu beachten ist auch folgende Differenz: Im Unterschied zum stereotypen Deutemuster (*et quoniam...*) *haec est interpretatio* in der Adler- und Menschensohnvision (12,16.18.20.23.30; 13,22.28) werden Bild und Sache in der Zionvision entweder ohne Deuteformel oder durch die pronominale Wendung *haec est* (*erat*) aufeinander bezogen (10,44.47.48; anders nur 10,43: *haec absolutio est*, ein Ausdruck, dem wohl ein Derivat der Wurzel ptr/pšr entspricht). Nur die Auslegung der Zionvision entspricht somit jenem Typ der Allegorese, der sich traditionsgeschichtlich auf die alttestamentliche Traumdeutung zurückführen läßt und für den gerade "die Verwendung von identifizierenden Pronomina und Kopulae" charakteristisch ist (Klauck 1978, 355; vgl. 67ff.).

insofern bemerkbar, als die Hochschätzung Esras, die vorher dem Orakel des Offenbarers vorbehalten blieb, nun wiederholt in z. T. konditionalen Wendungen vom Betroffenen selbst beansprucht wird (vgl. 10,39.50.57; auch 6,32ff. mit 12,7ff.; 13,14). Andere Indizien für den disparaten Charakter dieser Stücke ergeben sich, sobald man den weiteren Kontext des Buches in Betracht zieht. So wirkt die Anweisung zur Niederschrift des Gesehenen in 12,37a, eine Dublette zu 14,23ff., im vorliegenden Zusammenhang als völlig deplazierter Anachronismus. Insgesamt weist das sprachliche Kolorit des Adler- und Menschensohngesichts nur ganz wenige Berührungspunkte mit den übrigen Teilen des Werkes auf (vgl. z. B. 11,39.44). Rückläufige Korrespondenzen zu den Aussagen der drei ersten Dialogpartien sind allenfalls in den Abschnitten über die Zeichen der Endzeit zu entdecken. Doch ergeben sich daraus nicht unbedingt Anhaltspunkte für die kompositorische Integrität des Ganzen, sind doch in den genannten Texten ganz anders als in Visio V und VI Fragmente einer älteren Zeichentradition dem dialogischen Rahmen eingepaßt, wie eine genauere redaktionskritische Analyse zu zeigen vermag[20].

2.2.2. Auf Grund der genannten Indizien ist ernsthaft mit der Möglichkeit zu rechnen, daß der Komplex der Adler- und Menschensohnvision dem ursprünglichen Entwurf von IV Esr sekundär zugewachsen ist[21]. Auszunehmen sind lediglich die auf 5,16–19 zurückweisende Volksszene 12,40b–50 und vielleicht auch der Schluß des Gesichts vom Menschensohn (13,54f. [56a?]).

---

[20] Als Fragmente einer vorgegebenen Zeichentradition sind in 5,1–12 m. E. die vv.4c–9a.b (mit v.1a als Einleitung?), in 6,18–28 die vv.20b–23 anzusprechen. Beide Stücke wurden redaktionell gerahmt (vgl. 5,1b–4a.b.9c–11; 6,18–20a.26–28) und damit der Dialogsituation wie dem Sachinteresse des Gesamtentwurfs angepaßt. Bei 5,12 und 6,24 handelt es sich wohl um Nachträge (Neueinsatz!). Der Verdacht einer dogmatisch motivierten Glossierung des Textes legt sich für 6,25 nahe. Die Aussage ist einer restaurativen Eschatologie verpflichtet (vgl. PsSal 17,44; 18,6) und dürfte wie 7,27; 9,7f. (beachte die stereotype Form der Stücke) sekundär eingebracht sein.

[21] Für die ursprüngliche Zusammengehörigkeit der Episoden IV und VII läßt sich anführen, daß der in 14,17 verschiedentlich belegte Rückbezug auf den Adler in allen lat. HSS fehlt und daß in der äthiop. Version von 14,8 (vgl. die arab. Übersetzungen und die armen. Version) nur von einem einzigen Traum und seiner Deutung die Rede ist. – Nicht für die Zion-, wohl aber für die Adler- und Menschensohnvision in IVEsr bestätigt sich somit das auf anderem Weg gewonnene Urteil O. H. Stecks, daß es sich bei diesen Stücken um spätere 'Ankristallisationen' handelt, die eine "den Aussagebestand des Werkes umgreifende und ortende Rahmenfunktion nicht haben" (Steck 1967, 191 Anm. 3). Wodurch ist die Erweiterung begründet? Wie U. B. Müller gezeigt hat, geben Visio V und VI einer messianisch geprägten Eschatologie Ausdruck, die national-terrestrisch orientiert bleibt und sich darin mit einer durch PsSal 17f. bestimmten Tradition pharisäischen Denkens berührt (vgl. Müller 1972, 83ff., 107ff.). Sollte der in IVEsr sonst dominierende Dualismus der Zwei-Äonen-Lehre retrospektiv entschärft werden? Mußte sich die dualistische Zeitlehre des IVEsr etwa schon bald eine regressive Überformung durch messianische Vorstellungen gefallen lassen (s. o. Anm. 20 sowie 7,28f.; 13,16–20.22–24; auffällig ist auch 14,9 im Vergleich mit 8,51.62; 4,36)?

2.3. Es ist klar: Die hier vorgeschlagene Hypothese steht im Widerspruch zur gesamten neueren Forschung. Seit Gunkels Verdikt über Versuche einer Quellenscheidung (R. Kabisch) ist die literarische Integrität von IV Esr kaum noch in Zweifel gezogen worden[22]. Weitgehend hält man den Nachweis der Einheitlichkeit des Werkes bereits mit dem ästhetischen Argument einer angenommenen Siebenzahl von Visionen für erbracht. Dabei wird allerdings übersehen, daß sich eine derartige Sicht nur halten läßt, wenn man den auf Visio V und VI folgenden Schlußteil des Buches (VII) als in sich geschlossenen Komplex versteht. Ist diese Prämisse aber zwingend geboten? Wir suchen die Frage zu klären, indem wir uns der Analyse von 13,56b–14,48 zuwenden und dabei wieder auf die Nahtstellen des Textes achten.

2.3.1. Das erste Stück mit überleitender Funktion findet sich 13,56b–14,2a. Die Engelverheißung 13,56b ist weder konditional noch imperativisch gefaßt. Sie begnügt sich mit einer Ankündigung von Rede- und Wundererweis, wobei erstmalig die Spanne von drei Tagen in Erscheinung tritt. Der sich anschließende Vollzugsbericht (13,57f.)[23] umfaßt ein Diktum über die Ortsveränderung (vgl. 9,26), erzähltes Gotteslob statt der üblichen Klageformel sowie eine kurze Angabe über dreitägiges Warten. Die Partie gipfelt in einer Auditionseröffnung (14,1–2a) mit datierter Ereignisformel (*tertio die*), Befindlichkeitsaussage (analog zu 9,27!) und Redeeinführung, die auf Ex 3,4 anspielt und als Sprecher des Folgenden nicht mehr Esra, sondern die geheimnisvoll angedeutete Stimme Gottes vorstellt. In Übereinstimmung mit der üblichen Exegese scheinen die Editoren der Textausgaben durchweg der Auffassung, daß damit die Reihe der gravierenden Dispositionssignale erschöpft ist. Allein, in 14,37f. begegnet eine weitere Wendung, die dem Charakter der sonstigen Expositionen aufs genaueste entspricht (v.37: Bericht Esras über die auf Geheiß eines Dritten vollzogene Mitnahme von fünf Männern, Angabe über Ortswechsel und Bleiben; v.38: Auditionseröffnung mit datierter Ereignisformel [*in crastinum*] und Hinweis auf die ergehende Rede einer göttlichen Stimme). Der Abschnitt bezieht sich auf 14,23–26 zurück, wo wir die entsprechende Auftragserteilung finden: Befehl zur Versammlung und Instruktion des Volkes (dem Esra in der Abschiedsrede 14,28–36 nachkommt) und Anweisungen zum inspirierten Offenbarungsdiktat (mit den

---

[22] Vgl. Kabisch 1889. H. Gunkels Bemerkung (1900, 351), es sei "eine Mißhandlung der schönen Schrift" anzunehmen, daß sie "durch einen ganz elenden Redaktor zusammengeschustert worden sei", hat wie kaum ein anderes Wort in der Exegese des IVEsr Schule gemacht. Verbreitet ist die Meinung, "der kompendienartige Charakter des Buches" verbiete literarkritische Operationen (Plöger 1958, 698).

[23] Von H. Gunkel (1900, 398) fälschlicherweise als Schlußstück der sechsten Episode plaziert.

in 14,37f. wiederholten Bestimmungen über die Auswahl der Schreiber, den gebotenen Ort und die zu wahrende Zeit). Es kann kein Zweifel aufkommen: Zwischen 14,36 und 14,37 muß eine weitere Episodenzäsur angenommen werden. Damit ist aber auch das Dogma der Siebenzahl als ästhetisch motiviertes Fehlurteil erwiesen. Man gelangt entweder zu einer Reihung von acht oder, wie wir vermuten, von sechs Visionen. Das letztere gilt freilich nur, sofern gegen die Zugehörigkeit von Kp. 14 zum Korpus des Ganzen nicht ebenfalls literarische Einwände erhoben werden müssen. Doch läßt der Schlußkomplex sowohl in sprachlicher als auch in sachlicher Hinsicht derart klare Beziehungen zu Visio I–IV erkennen, daß Bedenken dieser Art von vornherein ausscheiden[24].

2.3.2. Im übrigen gewinnt der Verdacht, daß die Episoden VII,1/2 ursprünglich direkt an IV anschlossen, durch unsere Beobachtungen nur an Gewicht. Zu verweisen ist auf die Korrespondenz der Expositionsformulierungen in 9,26 und 13,57 sowie in 9,27 und 14,1. Gerade vor dem Hintergrund der Zionvision erscheint es als überzeugend, daß nun unmittelbar darauf die Klageformel der Exposition durch erzähltes Gotteslob ersetzt wird (13,57f.). Ausgezeichnet fügt sich das neue Zeitsignal der *drei* Tage zum alten der *drei* Wochen. Rhetorisch gesehen geschickt überbietet der Verfasser die zunächst mit Hilfe der drei Wochen angezielte Klimax durch einen zweiten Höhepunkt, der das Offenbarungsgeschehen noch einmal steigert und seiner definitiven Vollendung entgegenführt: Uriels Stimme wird durch die des Höchsten abgelöst, womit das in 10,56 ausgesprochene Versprechen einer (die Doxa-Vision komplettierenden) Audition seine Erfüllung findet. Man kann sogar fragen, ob nicht die letzte Engelweisung ursprünglich in dieser (womöglich durch eine Zeitangabe präzisierten) Verheißung steckte: *et post haec (? – tres dies?) audies, quantum capit auditus aurium tuarum audire.* Im Kontext der vermuteten Episodenfolge erscheint der unbedingte Charakter dieser Ankündigung[25] als sachgerecht: Mit der Zionvision sind alle Konditionen erfüllt. Der Seher hat sich einer unmittelbaren Gottesbegegnung als würdig erwiesen. Sollte diese

---

[24] Folgende Motive aus Kp. 14 finden eine Entsprechung in 3,1–9,25: der Rückbezug auf die Mosetradition (v.3ff.) und das Gesetz (v.22.28ff.), die Beschreibung der Sünde (v.30f.), die Anspielung auf den jesær (haraʿ) (v.34), die Vorstellung vom Endgericht (v.35) sowie die Gegenüberstellung der Gerechten und der Frevler (v.35). Der Gedanke der Entfernung der Wahrheit (v.17) hat ebenso wie der von der endzeitlichen Steigerung des Übels (v.15f.) seine Analogie in 5,1ff. Auch die Vorstellung vom Alterstod dieses Äons (v.16) wurde bereits vorher angesprochen (vgl. 4,26; 5,50ff.). Die Auszeichnung des Mose, der einer Schau des Eschaton gewürdigt wird (v.4f.), korrespondiert der des Abraham in 3,14. Schließlich wahrt die Partie auch insofern den Anschluß an den ersten Hauptteil, als sie einheitlich im Sinne der Äonen-Terminologie geprägt ist, was auf Visio V und VI gerade nicht zutrifft (dort dominiert die Verwendung des Begriffes *terra*).

[25] Vgl. dagegen die konditionalen Offenbarungsankündigungen am Schluß der Episoden I–III.

Erwägung zutreffen, handelte es sich bei 13,56b um ein redaktionell eingebrachtes Stück, dessen Stellung sich der Einschaltung von Visio V und VI verdankt. Diese Vermutung ist um so näherliegend, als Kp. 14 nicht mehr (wie 13,56b suggeriert) den Engel, sondern Gott selbst reden und Wunderbares erweisen läßt. Mit dem Zeitsignal *in crastinum* wird schließlich Visio VII,2 abgesetzt, ein Abschnitt, der nun in der Tat Epilog-charakter trägt, zumal Esra selbst nicht mehr redend auftritt. Anders als bisher angenommen, scheint die Zahl sieben[26] somit in der Offenbarungs-chronologie verankert: Es handelt sich um die Summe der *drei* Wochen (I–IV), der *drei* Tage (VII,1) und *eines* Tages (VII,2).

2.4. *Zusammenfassend ist festzustellen:* Mit großer Wahrscheinlichkeit umfaßt der ursprüngliche Textzusammenhang von IV Esr eine Reihe von sechs[27] Offenbarungsepisoden. Diese ist klimaktisch gestaltet, wie die präzis kalkulierte Abfolge der Dispositionssignale erkennen läßt. Visio IV (+ 13,54f.; 12,40b–50) besitzt überleitende Funktion. Berücksichtigt man diesen Sachverhalt, ergibt sich eine Sequenz nach dem Schema 3/2/1: Lehrgespräch und Kontroverse zwischen Esra und Uriel (I–III), Peripetie der dialogischen Bewegung (IV+VII,1), Epilog mit Besiegelungscharakter (VII,2). Nun gilt es, mit Hilfe einer Analyse der Mikrostruktur des Textes zu klären, inwiefern die proleptisch eingeführten Titel der genannten Komplexe die intendierte Sache treffen.

3. Lehrgespräch und Kontroverse zwischen Esra und Uriel

3.1. Die drei ersten Episoden bilden den weitaus größten Teil des Buches. Die oft sehr knapp gehaltenen Einzelelemente des Zwiegesprächs zwischen Esra und Uriel, nur durch ganz kurze Angaben des Sprecher-wechsels unterbrochen, präsentieren sich in einer stereotyp wirkenden Abfolge von Rede und Gegenrede, die auf den ersten Blick einen inneren Strukturzusammenhang vermissen läßt. Aus der Einförmigkeit der dialo-gischen Bewegung heben sich lediglich die dem Muster der alttestamentli-chen Volksklage nachempfundenen kollektiven Klagelieder Esras 3,4–36; 5,23–30; 6,38–59, die der Exposition im weiteren Sinn angehören, sowie die Engelankündigungen von Zeichen am Schluß der ersten und zweiten Vision ab.

---

[26] Zur Relevanz dieser Zahl in temporaler Hinsicht vgl. die Vorstellung vom siebentägigen Silentium der Endzeit, das die sieben Schöpfungstage der Urzeit rekapituliert (7,30f.), sowie das Motiv von der siebentägigen Schau der Seelen (7,101).

[27] Wie sich später zeigen wird, kann die Zahl sechs als das konstitutive Gliederungsprinzip für den inneren Aufbau der Episoden gelten. Es besteht also eine Korrespondenz zwischen der Makro- und der Mikrostruktur des Textes. In dispositioneller Hinsicht ist die Zahl sieben nur peripher von Bedeutung (vgl. z. B. das Lehrstück 7,76–99).

3.1.1. In einer sehr aufschlußreichen Studie über "Esras erste Vision" hat K. Koch nun den Nachweis erbracht, daß die innere Disposition dieser Partie und, wie er vermutet, wohl auch der beiden folgenden Episoden durch die Abfolge kleinster Gesprächseinheiten vorgegeben ist, die in der Regel einen *viergliedrigen* Wechsel von Esra- und Urielrede enthalten[28]. Die Konsistenz dieser Grundform ergibt sich allerdings weniger aus einer markanten Differenz der Redeeinführungsfloskel[29] als vielmehr aus dem sie tragenden Argumentationsmuster, wie Koch überzeugend dargelegt hat. Charakteristisches Merkmal dieser Einheiten, die geradezu nach dem *Formular eines argumentativen Lehrgesprächs* generiert sind, ist eine Dialogsequenz, in der regelmäßig folgende Elemente einander ablösen: 1. Problemstellung Esras (in der Form von Klagen, Fragen, aber auch Einwänden), 2. bildlich geprägtes Uriel-Argument (in der Form fiktiver Aufgaben oder als Bildwort, Fabel, Gleichnis und Paradigma), oft mit einer imperativischen Wendung eröffnet, 3. kurze Esra-Reaktion (meist bestätigender Art, z. T. auch in der Form einer Rückfrage oder eines Einwurfs) sowie 4. argumentative Schlußfolgerung des Engels, die den Seher offen oder verschwiegen beim Wort nimmt und, indem sie die Bildrede expressis verbis (meist in der Form eines korrekten Vergleichs, gelegentlich auch in der eines Qal Vachomer-Schlusses) auf den zur Debatte stehenden Fall appliziert, überführt[30]. Verstärkt wird die Annahme derartiger Basiseinheiten durch die Art des Redebeginns im ersten Element. Als markante Dispositionssignale können pointiert eingesetzte Anredeformen (*o dominator domine*) fungieren, ein insinuatorisches Wort wie *ecce*, Wendungen der Bitte und (z. T. als Einwand stilisierten) Frage, Niedrigkeitsaussagen und Höflichkeitsfloskeln sowie Selbstreflexionen, die Esras eigenes Reden betreffen. Nimmt man das sich davon abhebende Merkmal äußerster brevitas des dritten Elements hinzu, lassen sich die Zäsuren der viergliedrigen Einheiten problemlos erheben, und zwar auch da, wo der Wechsel von Rede und Gegenrede nicht auf das beschriebene Argumentationsmuster hinausläuft, sondern die Funktion eines Episodenprologs und -epilogs übernimmt.

---

[28] Koch 1978, 49 ff.

[29] So Koch 1978, 52 ff.

[30] Vgl. die Tabellen im Anhang. Nur an einer Stelle (7,45–61) begegnet eine Doppelung von bildlich geprägtem Uriel-Argument und bestätigender Esra-Reaktion, so daß sich eine sechsgliedrige Einheit ergibt. In 5,53 wird der Esra-Kommentar durch die Äußerung einer fiktiven Figur (Gebärende) vertreten, in 4,48 f. ist er durch das Widerfahrnis eines visionären Gleichnisses ersetzt. – Eine sehr enge Formanalogie zu den Lehrgesprächen in IVEsr scheint im Offenbarungsdialog des Poimandres vorzuliegen. Auch dort lassen sich kleinste Gesprächseinheiten (mit unterschiedlicher Gliederzahl) aussondern, und wie in IVEsr behält die Autorität des Offenbarers jeweils das letzte Wort. Im Unterschied zu IVEsr tragen die Dialoge des Poimandres indessen nicht argumentativen, sondern ausschließlich katechetischen Charakter.

3.1.2. Nun findet sich aber (und dieser Beobachtung wird Kochs Arbeit nicht gerecht) in Visio I–III ein zweiter Typ dialogisch geprägter Stücke, der lediglich *zwei Glieder* besitzt. Die eine Variante dieser einfachen Form des Wechselgesprächs begegnet an Stellen, die den Dialog einer Episode eröffnen oder informativ beschließen. Wichtiger ist die andere Variante. Es handelt sich um eine Gesprächseinheit, in der Esra-Diktum (Klage, Vorhaltung, Appell oder Bitte) und gegenläufiges Engel-Votum hart aufeinanderprallen. Wesensmerkmal dieser Stücke ist also, daß sie die Position des Engels nicht auf dem Weg einer überzeugungskräftigen Argumentation schrittweise entfalten, sondern als *Gegenthese* erscheinen lassen, die sich schroff von dem zuvor ausgesprochenen Wort Esras distanziert. Der Vergleich, in den der Widerspruch des Engels auslaufen kann, trägt nun nicht mehr den Charakter einer Konklusion, sondern den einer Illustration der These. Die viergliedrige Einheit scheint kontrahiert und auf die beiden Randaussagen reduziert. Dadurch, daß der Mittelteil ausfällt, entsteht eine qualitativ veränderte Form, die man als *Disputationsstück* bezeichnen kann. Außerordentlich aufschlußreich ist nun die folgende Beobachtung: Während die viergliedrigen Einheiten in Visio I–II das Feld beherrschen, setzen sich in Visio III nach einer kurzen Übergangsphase die Disputationsstücke durch. Das Lehrgespräch geht in eine offene Kontroverse über[31].

3.2. Damit stehen wir vor der Frage nach Aufbau und Sachinteresse der drei ersten Gesprächsblöcke. Auf den ersten Blick ist ersichtlich, daß Visio I und II eine völlig analoge Struktur von jeweils acht Gesprächseinheiten aufweisen (wobei allerdings die Zäsuren in der zweiten Episode anders zu setzen sind als im Dispositionsvorschlag Kochs[32]). Hier wie dort ist eine Dreiteilung erkennbar: Die erste Partie (Gespräch 1–3) gilt dem Nachweis der Unbegreiflichkeit der Wege Gottes, die zweite (4–6) einer Erörterung des Zeitproblems, die dritte (7–8) bezieht sich (mit Ausnahme des Phalthiel-Gesprächs 5,16–19) auf Fragen nach den Modalitäten des Endes. Nur innerhalb der ersten Partie (1.3) sind die gesprächseröffnenden Voten Esras als Klagen, sonst fast ausschließlich als Fragen oder Informationsbitten gefaßt. Bestimmend für den Aussagewillen des Ganzen sind die weisheitlich anmutenden Engel-Konklusionen am Schluß der Gespräche 2–6. Sie beschränken sich entweder darauf, die Klagen Esras mit dem Argument der Unergründlichkeit des göttlichen Verfahrens zurückzuweisen[33], oder sie geben in dialektischer Gegenbewegung zur insinuierten Nähe des Endes zu verstehen, daß die eschatologische Zeit einer allein Gott zugestandenen Voraussicht anheimgestellt bleibt.

---

[31] Vgl. die Tabelle zu Episode III im Anhang.

[32] Vgl. die Übersicht bei Koch 1978, 50f.

[33] In dieser Hinsicht besteht eine bemerkenswerte Sachverwandtschaft mit TestHiob (vgl. 4,5 ff. 13 ff.; 5,36 ff. mit TestHiob 37,6–8; 38,1–6).

3.2.1. Ganz anders verhält es sich mit der dritten Episode. Schon Aufriß und Umfang dieser Partie, die sich in vierzehn Einzelgespräche zerlegen läßt, weisen völlig eigenständige Konturen auf. Wieder scheint eine Drei-teilung anvisiert, die diesmal nach dem Schema 6/6/2 strukturiert ist. Zunächst begegnen wir zwei Sequenzen von je sechs Einheiten (1–6.7–12), deren Finale in beiden Fällen durch einen besonderen Beginn der Worte Esras signalisiert wird (6.12). Die erste Gesprächsrunde (1–6), noch am ehesten mit Episode I–II vergleichbar, gipfelt in der (dispositionell mit den Zeichenreden verwandten) Abhandlung über die sieben Grade der Ver-dammnis und Seligkeit, wobei Esra aufgefordert wird, sich von den Frevlern zu distanzieren (6). Beachtung verdient, daß bereits in diesem Zusammenhang drei Lehrgespräche (2.4.6) durch Disputationsstücke (3.5) unterbrochen sind. Die folgenden sechs Einheiten (7–12), thematisch um das Problem der Fürbitte gruppiert, sind nur noch zweigliedrig. Sie kulminieren in Aussagen, die Esras Appell, Exhomologese und Barmher-zigkeitsbitte schroff zurückweisen. Am Schluß (12) findet sich wiederum die Forderung der Distanznahme gegenüber den Frevlern. Durch eine neue Anredeformel vom rückläufigen Kontext abgesetzt, schließt das ganze mit zwei doppelgliedrigen Stücken (13.14), die sachlich auf den Anfang (1.2) zurückweisen und die Standpunkte der Partner als unversöhnlich kenn-zeichnen. Esra wird letztmalig aufgefordert, sich nicht mehr der Frevler, sondern der Gerechten anzunehmen (13).

3.2.2. Während die Episoden I–II das Anliegen Esras aufs Ganze gesehen nur privativ bedenken und somit eine Art Vorspiel darstellen, das die Praxis der Selbstpreisgabe einübt, erfolgt mit dem Auftakt der dritten Vision insofern eine Wende, als sich der Engel nun zu einer positiven Auskunft grundsätzlichen Charakters bereitfindet. In 7,10bff. 19ff. wird die für das Sachinteresse des Buches maßgebende Orientierung (im Vor-ausgehenden nur durch 4,26ff. präformiert) gedrängt und doch äußerst präzis zur Sprache gebracht. Es handelt sich um *das Postulat einer dualistisch konzipierten Zeitlehre*, in der *die Geschichte dialektisch* verstanden wird. Einerseits erscheint sie als in sich geschlossener Zeitraum der Entfremdung des Menschen von Gott, vom Wohl der Schöpfung durch den adamiti-schen Fall und vom Heil der außergeschichtlichen Zukunft durch die Zäsur des Endgerichts abgetrennt. Andererseits stellt sie sich positiv als befriste-tes Angebot an den Menschen dar, sich dank der Lebensweisung des Gesetzes durch Treue und Gehorsam die Anwartschaft auf den kommen-den Äon zu sichern[34]. Während Esra, immer noch vom Problem der Aporie der Verheißung bewegt, die Möglichkeit des Gesetzesgehorsams anzwei-felt und sich nach weisheitlicher Manier für die Frevler und deren Geschick

---

[34] Zur Sache vgl. Harnisch 1969, 240ff.; 1974, 121ff.

ereifert[35], beharrt der Engel unaufhörlich und in stereotypen Wendungen (Gespräche 3.5.9.12.13) auf dem Gesichtspunkt der Unentschuldbarkeit der Sünder.

3.3. Überblickt man Episode III als Ganzes, gewinnt man den Eindruck einer Auseinandersetzung, die sich mit einem Schlagwort der 'neuen Rhetorik' als 'persuasive Kommunikation' (J. Kopperschmidt) bezeichnen läßt. Es handelt sich um einen Disput, der sich mehr und mehr zuspitzt und von beiden Seiten unerbittlich in der erkennbaren Absicht ausgetragen wird, die Gegenseite für den eigenen Standpunkt einzunehmen. So bedient sich Esra, der kaum noch fragt, sondern anklagt und provoziert, selbst wenn er bittet (vgl. die Vorhaltungen 8,14 und 8,43f.[36] im Kontext der Gespräche 11.12), gelegentlich einer auf Überführung des Partners bedachten Argumentation, wie sie der Engel praktiziert (vgl. 7,106ff.; 8,42ff.). Andererseits mündet der Dialog wiederholt in eine Lage aus, die es nun Uriel erlaubt, gewisse Akzente der oppositionellen Äußerungen Esras gegen diese selbst auszuspielen (vgl. 7,71ff.; 8,37ff. mit 7,62ff.; 8,26ff.). Rede und Gegenrede sind offenbar derselben rhetorischen Strategie verpflichtet[37]. Sosehr nun die Kontroverse den Anschein erweckt, als sei das Plädoyer beider Parteien gleichgewichtig und durch ähnliche Mittel der Sprache bestimmt, sowenig läßt sich übersehen, daß die Bewegung der Auseinandersetzung schriftstellerisch gelenkt ist. *Der Diskurs stellt eine tendenziöse literarische Fiktion dar.* Bewußt ist die Abfolge der einzelnen Gesprächsmomente so angelegt, daß die Voten des Offenbarungsmittlers den Rang des zweiten entscheidenden Wortes einnehmen. Rein von außen gesehen behält der Widerspruch des Engels, meist in die Form einer durch anschließenden Vergleich bekräftigten Feststellung gekleidet, die Oberhand. Wohl begehrt Esra bis zuletzt auf und bleibt trotz z.T. entschärfter Diktion und gewisser Selbstkorrekturen (vgl. z.B. 7,45–48.139) uneinsichtig. Dreimal, und zwar an hervorgehobener Stelle und in gesteigerter Form, bekundet er seine Unnachgiebigkeit (vgl. 7,45.116; 9,14). Dies darf jedoch nicht darüber hinwegtäuschen, daß gemäß dem Stilgesetz vom

---

[35] Zur Bedeutung dieses Motivs in der Weisheit vgl. v. Rad 1970, 262, 272.

[36] Vgl. Hi 10,3.8ff.

[37] Charakteristisch für das argumentative Interesse ist die häufige Verwendung rhetorischer Stilmittel. So finden sich Formen von Hyperbolik (4,30.32), von Paradoxie (8,14.43f.; 9,34f.) und selbst die Figur der Ironie (8,37ff.). Man trifft auf rhetorische Fragen (3,31.32a; 7,15f.), Bildworte und Gleichnisse, oft mit argumentativen Fragen oder Schlußfolgerungen verbunden (passim), auf Vergleiche (5,42; 8,2f.41; 9,15f.), Metaphern (4,30), den Syllogismus (5,45) und Qal Vachomer-Schluß (4,30ff.; vgl. 4,10f. und die gegenläufige Konklusion 4,7–9). Nicht selten begegnen Parallelismus (4,35b; 7,15.21b.26b.46; 9,21) und Chiasmus (6,57f.; 7,103f.), Antithesen (3,30.36; 4,34; 6,55f.57f.; 7,31.65.119ff.), Wiederholungen und Reihungen (passim) sowie der komparativisch geprägte Kettenschluß (7,56), um nur die augenfälligsten Paradigmen zu nennen.

Achtergewicht die eigentliche Autorität den Stellungnahmen des Engels zukommt.

3.3.1. Auf Grund dieser Beobachtungen dürfte nun doch die Vermutung unausweichlich sein, daß sich im Hin und Her von Rede und Gegenrede eine *theologische Kontroverse* widerspiegelt, an welcher der Verfasser selbst beteiligt ist und die er zugunsten der dem Engel in den Mund gelegten Auffassung entschieden wissen will. Mit dem geplanten Ausgang einer Kehre des Geschehens (s. u.) in der Hinterhand kann er es sich leisten, gerade Esra, der zu Großem berufen ist (5,17), zum Sprecher einer religiösen Opposition zu machen, die sich durch die autoritativen Weisungen des Engels anfechten und überholen lassen muß. Freilich ist die Front, die sich in den Worten Esras bekundet, literarisch stilisiert und allem Anschein nach bereits theologisch entschärft. So werden gewisse kritische Bedenken des Sehers, die sich von ihrer Ursprungstendenz her wohl als Ausdruck eines eigenständigen und zugleich aggressiven Seinsverständnisses präsentieren, in der Form der Frage (so Visio I–II) oder Klage vorgestellt und damit abgeschwächt. Möglicherweise sind heterogene Vorstellungselemente in einer Weise miteinander verschlungen, daß der ihnen von Haus aus eignende revolutionäre Sinn nicht mehr erkennbar ist[38]. Gleichwohl erscheint Esra deutlich genug als Widerpart der Offenbarung, und seine Äußerungen tragen sichtlich jene Züge einer Emanzipation vom Hergebrachten, wie sie der Skepsis eigen sind[39].

3.3.2. Zielt das Gefälle des Dialogs dann etwa darauf ab, den Leser zu bewegen, sich von der Identifikationsfigur des klagenden und Gott anklagenden Sehers zu distanzieren? Würde man diesen Schluß ziehen, wäre das

---

[38] Es gibt Anzeichen dafür, daß die Position, der sich IVEsr entgegenwirft, einer radikal dualistischen Strömung entspringt (vgl. 7,62ff.116b Aeth. sowie das Motiv vom jeșær haraᶜ in seiner von Esra beanspruchten Auslegung: 3,20ff.25f.; 4,4; 7,48.62ff. in Verbindung mit 4,30ff.; 8,53). Der Verfasser scheint sich indessen gezwungen zu sehen, latent dualistische Züge schon in dem Part des Dialogs abzubiegen, den er dem Seher überläßt (vgl. die Korrekturen in 3,4f.; ferner 8,7.44 in Verbindung mit 6,6; 9,18fin.). Derartige Wendungen, die jede Problematisierung der Einzigkeit des Schöpfers abwiegeln, sind Indiz für die hintergründige Präsenz eines Dualismus, der sich von dem traditionellen Bekenntnis zu Gott als dem Geber der Thora und dem Herrn der Schöpfung emanzipiert.

[39] Sowohl hinsichtlich der Bundesverheißung als auch im Blick auf die Schöpfungsgedanken wird Esras Kritik an der geltenden Überlieferung im Rahmen eines Beweisverfahrens vorgebracht, das sich wesentlich auf das Argument einer übermächtigen Sündenherrschaft stützt (vgl. nur 3,4ff.; 7,45ff.; 8,35 sowie die Klagen über die Sinnlosigkeit des Lebens 4,12; 5,35; 7,62.116ff.; 8,14 neben 8,15ff.). Als versteckte Anspielung auf die Negation der Skepsis, durch die sich der Verfasser von IVEsr auf den Plan gerufen weiß, lassen sich vielleicht auch der 7,23; 8,58 inkriminierte praktische Atheismus, die 7,22 erwähnten *cogitamenta vanitatis* sowie die Aussagen über den hochmütigen Wandel der Frevler verstehen (vgl. 7,22.79; 8,50.57). Eine ähnliche Beziehung könnte jenen Bemerkungen zugrunde liegen, die Esras Anmaßung verurteilen, weiser zu sein als der Höchste (vgl. 7,19 in Verbindung mit 4,34; 5,33; 8,47). – Zur Sache vgl. auch Perlitt 1972.

Raffinement der literarischen Strategie des Verfassers verkannt. Der Leser ist vielmehr herausgefordert, sich *wie* Esra der Anziehungskraft derjenigen Argumente auszusetzen, die der Offenbarer wahrnimmt. Er soll sich *mit* Esra von der Wahrheit der Offenbarungsreden überzeugen lassen. Nun scheint freilich der Überredungserfolg des Engels am Ende der dritten Episode gescheitert, zumal Visio IV mit einer erneuten Volksklage des Sehers einsetzt. Esra weigert sich ostentativ, den ihm zugemuteten Stellungswechsel zu vollziehen. Damit kompliziert sich aber die Lage des Lesers. Soll er sich auf die Seite des Engels schlagen, obwohl seine Sympathie vielleicht immer noch dem Seher gehört? Eine Lösung des Dilemmas wäre erst dann gegeben, wenn Esra bekundete, daß er der Position des Engels recht geben muß.

4. Die Peripetie der dialogischen Bewegung

4.1. Der wunderbare Rollenwechsel Esras[40]

4.1.1. Ebenso balanciert wie die vorhergehenden Episoden ist die *Zionvision* gegliedert. Verlängert man den Text (wie oben vorgeschlagen) um das Stück der Volksszene 12,40b–50, ergeben sich zwei analog gebaute Dialogfolgen von je drei Einheiten. Zwei doppelgliedrige Gespräche (2.3/5.6), die das Hauptgewicht tragen, werden in beiden Sequenzen durch einen viergliedrigen Prolog (1/4) eröffnet. Als Auftakt des Ganzen fungiert wie in Visio I–III eine kollektive Klagerede Esras (9,29–37). Sie spielt nun allerdings nicht mehr das Unheil der Gegenwart gegen das Heil der Vergangenheit aus. Nach einer deuteronomistisch gefärbten Einleitung, die das Verderben der Väter als selbstverschuldet (!) ausgibt, räsoniert Esra vielmehr mit der Erfahrungsregel von der Beständigkeit eines Gefäßes und der Vergänglichkeit des Inhalts gegen die theologisch zugemutete Erkenntnis, daß das Gesetz bleibt, während Israel, dem doch das Gesetz als Same eingelegt wurde, zugrunde geht – eine spitzfindige Konklusion, die wieder die weisheitliche Argumentation des Engels kopiert. Faktisch übernehmen Esras Worte freilich einen Sinn, dem der Engel ohne weiteres zustimmen könnte. Wichtiger als diese Feststellung ist indessen der Sachverhalt, daß die Klage erstmalig nicht durch eine Engelrede aufgenommen wird. Nach einer narrativen Zwischennotiz, die das Erscheinen einer klagenden Frau

---

[40] Die folgenden Erwägungen berühren sich z. T. mit Gesichtspunkten, wie sie Brandenburger 1977 vorgetragen hat. Besonders seiner anregenden Analyse der Zionvision, die sich mit eigenen Überlegungen trifft, weiß ich mich dankbar verpflichtet. Zu den Ausführungen von diesem Abschnitt vgl. jetzt meinen Beitrag zum Jahreskongreß von SBL 1981 (San Francisco): Harnisch 1981.

zur Rechten (!)[41] Esras festhält (9,38), ergreift der Seher vielmehr erneut selbst das Wort, um von dieser Stelle an bis zum Schluß der *ersten Gesprächsphase* (1–3) den Part der zweiten Redefigur zu spielen, die Antworten gibt und Weisungen erteilt. Liegt darin schon ein bedeutungsvolles Indiz für einen sich anbahnenden Rollenwechsel Esras, so erst recht in der Art, wie er die ihm zugespielte Aufgabe wahrnimmt. Erkundigungsfrage (9,40) und erste Erwiderung (10,6ff.) des Berichts der Frau, die klagend vom Tod ihres einzigen Sohnes beim Betreten des Brautgemachs erzählt, lassen augenfällige Korrespondenzen zu der sonst dem Engel vorbehaltenen Diktion erkennen. So ist der zurechtweisende Teil der Rede (10,6–14), der die Trauer der Frau um den Einen in Relation zum Leiden Zions und der Vielzahl der Verluste der Erde als belanglos hinstellt, in sich als argumentatives Lehrgespräch stilisiert, das alle vier Teile des Formulars (mit Rede und fiktiver Gegenrede) umfaßt[42]. Auf der anderen Seite übernimmt die Frau offensichtlich die Rolle Esras. Beziehungsvoll heißt es von ihr, sie sei aufs Feld geflohen, um ohne Unterlaß zu trauern und zu fasten – eine augenfällige Anspielung auf das Verhaltensmuster des Sehers.

4.1.2. Daß wir es bei dieser Begegnung mit einer Zäsur im Offenbarungsgeschehen zu tun haben, die eine Kehre im Geschick Esras herbeiführt, zeigt sich deutlich an der Art der parallelisierten Redeeinführungen in 9,39 und 10,5. Esra widmete sich der klagenden Frau mit der Bemerkung, er wolle die eigenen Gedanken (*cogitatus*, vgl. 3,1; 5,21) und Reden (*sermones*) zurückstellen (*dereli[n]qui*). Das Peripetiesignal, das mit dieser doppelten Distanznahme von den früheren Erwägungen markiert ist, weist hintergründig auf den Redebeginn 10,20 voraus. Dort beschwört Esra das Weib, ihren Widerspruch aufzugeben und sich statt dessen im Hinblick auf das Unglück Zions und den Schmerz Jerusalems überreden (*persuaderi!*) und trösten (*consolare*) zu lassen (vgl. 10,49). Könnte sachgerechter formuliert werden, worum es dem Engel in seiner Kontroverse mit Esra ging? Veranlaßt durch das Verhalten der Frau, bezieht Esra an dieser Stelle also genau jene Position, die der Engel ihm gegenüber vertrat. Ohne sich dessen bewußt zu sein, nimmt er selbst das Amt des eschatologischen Propheten (vgl. 12,42) wahr, indem er die Frau im Vollzug prophetischen Zorns (*cum iracundia*) tadelt (10,6ff.) und in der Ausübung prophetischer Tröstung in die angemessene, von Vorhaltungen freie und auf Hoffnung gestellte Klage um das Geschick Zions einweist (10,21f.). Beide Reden gipfeln in der Forderung der Selbstpreisgabe, die 10,16 mit der (als konditionale Heilszusage gefaßten) Zumutung verbunden ist, *dem Urteil*

---

[41] Zu 'rechts' als der besseren, Glück verheißenden Seite vgl. nur Ps 45,10; 110,1; Mk 16,5; Mt 25,31ff.

[42] Problemstellung (v.6–8), Argument (v.9–11), fiktive Gegenrede (v.12.13a), zurechtweisende Konklusion in der Form eines Vergleichs (v.13b.14).

Gottes recht zu geben[43]. Unwillkürlich macht Esra in diesem Zusammenhang somit selbst geltend, was der Engel vergeblich von ihm gefordert hatte.

4.1.3. Die *zweite Gesprächsphase*, mit einem Bericht von der wunderbaren Verwandlung der Frau eröffnet (10,25–27a), findet ihren eigentlichen Auftakt in Epiphaniereaktion und Mißverständnis Esras (10,27b–28.32). Der Seher, nun wieder an die Stelle des auf Uriel angewiesenen Dialogpartners versetzt, sieht sich selbst von seinem Begleiter verlassen (*derelinquens dereliquisti*), ja er glaubt sein Anliegen definitiv vereitelt, und das gerade angesichts der vom Leser durchschauten Erscheinung des himmlischen Jerusalem. Doch der *angelus interpres* enthüllt die wahren Beziehungen des Gesichts in einer Deuterede (10,38 ff.), die dispositionell der ersten Antwort Esras an die Frau entspricht. Hauptteil dieser Rede, die mit einem Lehreröffnungsruf (v.38) einsetzt, ist eine von Würdigungen Esras (v.39.50) gerahmte Visionsdeutung (v.40–49). Höhepunkt des Ganzen bilden Erklärungen über Uriels Voraussicht (v.51–54) sowie das Schlußwort v.55–57: eine an das priesterliche Heilsorakel erinnernde Tröstung (mit Invitation zur Schau der Doxa und Verheißung einer Audition) sowie der Makarismus: *Tu autem beatus es prae multis et vocatus es apud Altissimum sicut et pauci*. Als Begründung dieser Auszeichnung Esras, die alle vorausgehenden übertrifft und selbst keiner weiteren Steigerung fähig ist, könnte ursprünglich die Partie 13,54 f. angefügt gewesen sein. Sie gibt zu verstehen, daß Esra deshalb seliggepriesen wird, weil er seine Probleme zurückgestellt (*dereliquisti*), die Sache Gottes (*lex mea*) zu der seinen gemacht, sein Leben in Weisheit geführt und (wie man vielleicht konjizieren darf) Zion (nicht die 'Einsicht')[44] seine Mutter genannt hat (Rückbezug auf 10,7!).

4.1.4. Ausgezeichnet fügt sich in diesen Zusammenhang als Schlußpartie die Volksszene 12,40b–50, die auf 5,16–19 zurückweist[45]. Die Wendung 12,40b, nach der sich die Menge durch das Überschreiten der Frist von sieben Tagen in Bewegung gebracht sieht, bezieht sich offenkundig auf die Weisung Esras in 5,19 zurück[46]. Versetzt man 12,40b–50 an das Ende der Zionvision, ergibt sich eine sehr ausgewogene Disposition der Episodenfolge I–IV, bei der Eingang (I) und Schluß (IV) mit einem besonderen Epilog (Volksszene) versehen und dadurch in ein Korrespondenzverhältnis gebracht sind. In Analogie zum Phalthiel-Spruch 5,17, der Esra als den Hüter Israels in Anspruch nahm, prädiziert das Volk den Seher nun

---

[43] Auf die Zumutung einer derartigen Gerichtsdoxologie läuft auch die Argumentation der Freunde Hiobs hinaus (vgl. v. Rad 1970, 273 f.).

[44] וציון aus וצון* aus יצרד.

[45] Beziehungen zum rückwärtigen Kontext der Episoden I–IV bestehen auch hinsichtlich des Zionmotivs (vgl. 12,44.48 mit 3,28; 5,25; 6,4; 7,26; 8,52; 10,7.20 ff.44; auch 7,6 ff.).

[46] Gegen Müller 1972, 94 f., nach dem sich die Plausibilität der Zeitbestimmung 12,40b durch die Korrespondenz mit 9,23.27 und die Zugabe der beiden Nächte 10,60; 11,1 erklärt.

metaphorisch als 'Leuchte' und 'Hafen', nämlich als den letzten der prophetischen Parakleten[47], der 'wie die Traube von der Lese' übriggeblieben ist (12,41ff.). Die Menge klagt, weil sie sich von diesem Beistand endgültig verlassen glaubt. In hintergründiger Entsprechung zu 10,32 wiederholt sich damit das Mißverständnis Esras (*derelinquere*), wie überhaupt die Klage des Volkes eine der früheren Funktion Esras analoge Rolle spielt (zum Todeswunsch 12,44.45a vgl. 4,12; auch 7,63.69.116). Auf der anderen Seite übernimmt Esra wie zuvor gegenüber der Frau, nun freilich bewußt, den Part des Engels. Seine Trostrede an das Volk (12,46–49), dispositionell in paralleler Stellung zur Deuterede 10,38ff., gibt an die neuen Adressaten weiter, was der Engel ihm zugesprochen hatte (priesterliches Heilsorakel mit entsprechender Begründung).

4.1.5. Im Rückblick erweist sich die Zionvision als eine besonders kunstvoll arrangierte, ja als die am meisten durchdachte Komposition des ganzen Werkes. Mit den Stilmitteln der Hintergründigkeit und Doppelbödigkeit[48], der Paradoxie und des Mißverständnismotivs[49] hat der Verfasser eine Dialogsequenz gestaltet, die auf geheimnisvolle Weise eine Peripetie der Gesprächssituation inszeniert. Esra läßt das Seine und glaubt sich verlassen. Doch ereignet sich damit gerade das Ende seiner Verlassenheit. Er macht das klagende Weib auf die unglückliche Lage Zions aufmerksam, nicht ahnend, daß die Angeredete gerade Zion symbolisiert. Unwissend nimmt er, indem er die Frau zu einer iustificatio Dei veranlaßt, die radikale Forderung der Selbstpreisgabe wahr, die nach den Worten des Engels Gerechtigkeit und Leben erschließt. Der Makarismus des Engels honoriert diesen Rollenwechsel und besiegelt die Kehre: Esra ist in den Kreis derer aufgenommen, die sich als die wahren Adressaten der Verheißung ansprechen lassen dürfen. Damit ist nun endlich eine Lage erreicht, die es dem Leser ermöglicht, sich mit Esra zu identifizieren. Er ist eingeladen, sich in die wunderbar eröffnete Solidarität zwischen Esra und Uriel einbeziehen zu lassen und wie Esra eitlen Gedanken der Skepsis endgültig abzusagen.

4.2. Das Vermächtnis des eschatologischen Propheten

4.2.1. Visio VII,1 macht diesen applikativen Sinn des Ganzen explizit. Der Komplex (13,57–14,36) enthält zwei Gesprächseinheiten (14,1–17.18–36), die jeweils dreigliedrig strukturiert sind, so daß sich die Sprecherfolge der ersten (Gott-Esra-Gott) in der zweiten umkehrt (Esra-

---

[47] Vgl. die treffenden Bemerkungen bei Müller 1974, 54ff.; 1975, 39 z. St.

[48] Zur literarischen Relevanz dieser Stilzüge vgl. Auerbach 1946, 16ff.; Politzer 1966, 330ff.

[49] Vgl. die sehr enge Analogie der Technik des Mißverständnisses im Johannesevangelium (2,30; 3,3f.; 4,10ff.32f.; 6,32ff.; 7,34ff.; 14,4f.7ff.22ff.; 16,17f.); zur Sache vgl. Bultmann 1953, 89 und ebd. Anm. 2 u. ö. (vgl. Register bei Bultmann, 560, s. v.).

Gott-Esra). Der erste Dialog mündet in die Gottesrede 14,3 ff., der zweite
in die Abschiedsrede Esras 14,28 ff. Daß diesem Stück insgesamt die
Aufgabe zufällt, die Konsequenzen der veränderten Lage deutlich zu
machen, zeigt sich bereits an der Exposition. So steht der erzählte Hymnus
(13,57 f.) in wirkungsvollem Kontrast zu den Klageliedern und Klagebe-
richten der vorausgehenden Episoden. Zugleich fungiert er als ein
Bekenntnis der Zuversicht, das dem Makarismus von 10,57 respondiert.
Die unverkennbar auf die Sinaitheophanie anspielende Gesprächseröffnung
des ersten Teils (14,1 ff.) ist darauf angelegt, die nun erfolgende Beauftragung Esras als die eines zweiten Mose[50] erscheinen zu lassen. Dieser
Korrespondenz trägt die Gottesrede ausdrücklich Rechnung, indem sie
zunächst auf die Sendung des Mose zurückblickt (v.3–6), um diese dann als
Typos der Indienstnahme Esras zu beanspruchen (v.7–17). Die dem Seher
geltende Weisung zerfällt in zwei Abschnitte, die jeweils mit einem Hinweis auf das vorgerückte Alter dieses Äons schließen (v.10.15–17; vgl.
schon v.5!). Der erste (v.7–10) fordert zur Geheimhaltung von Vision und
Deutung (Sg. in Aeth., Armen.) auf und kündigt die baldige Entrückung
Esras an. Der zweite (v.[11 f.?]13–17) enthält zehn Imperative, die den
Seher in das prophetische Amt einweisen (v.13a–d) und zur Lösung von
den Belastungen der geschichtlichen Existenz veranlassen (v.13e.14). Wiederum ist der Blick auf die kommende Entrückung gerichtet. Die prophetische Beauftragung Esras erfolgt im Horizont der Abschiedssituation. Als
ein Abschiednehmender soll der Seher sein Haus bestellen, nämlich die
Zurückbleibenden zurechtweisen, trösten und belehren[51]. Mit dieser Charakteristik des prophetischen Amtes sind genau jene Funktionen angesprochen, die Esra bereits in der Begegnung mit der klagenden Frau wahrgenommen hatte. Damit bestätigt sich, daß der Seher schon vor seiner
Berufung unwissend ausgefüllt hat, was ihm nun als Amt ausdrücklich
übertragen wird.

4.2.2. Die zweite Gesprächseinheit (14,18–36) beginnt mit einem Diktum Esras, das pointiert seinen Gehorsam herausstellt (Einwilligung in
Fortgang und Auftrag). Auf das anschließend von Esra angesprochene
Problem einer Unterweisung der späteren Generationen geht die Replik
der Gottesstimme in v.23 ff. ein, indem sie eine auf den Epilog (VII,2)
vorausweisende Reihe von Anordnungen trifft. Den Höhepunkt des
Abschnitts bildet die vordergründig dem Volk, in Wahrheit aber dem
Leser geltende Abschiedsrede Esras v.28–35. Sie beginnt mit einer typischen Anredeformel (v.28) und enthält im übrigen gemäß dem auch sonst

---

[50] Zur Mosetypologie vgl. auch syrBar 84,1–11 und Harnisch 1969, 220 z. St.
[51] Zu dieser dreifachen Aufgabe vgl. Müller 1974, 54.

nachweisbaren Formular des Abschiedssermons[52] drei Teile, nämlich a) einen *Rückblick auf die Vergangenheit* (v.29–32), der die Heilstaten Gottes an Israel mit dem wiederholten Ungehorsam dieses Volkes in Vergangenheit und Gegenwart konfrontiert und das zu Recht ergangene Strafgericht Gottes feststellt; b) eine *konditional gefaßte Heilszusage* (v.33f.) mit Umkehrforderung und der Verheißung postmortal widerfahrender Barmherzigkeit; sowie c) einen *Ausblick auf die Zukunft* des Gerichts (v.35), das über das eschatologische Geschick der Gerechten und der Frevler befindet. Wie O. H. Steck nachgewiesen hat, steht diese Gesetzesparänese Esras (die genausogut vom Engel gesprochen sein könnte!) in der Tradition deuteronomistischer Theologie[53]: Die Lage des Gottesvolkes "ist Gericht und wird auf die Sündengeschichte des Volkes zurückgeführt, zugleich aber ist sie Möglichkeit zum Gehorsam, der über das Bestehen im künftigen Endgericht und somit über das eschatologische Heil oder Unheil entscheidet". Auf diese "exponierte Stelle", an der Esra nun offiziell das Parakletenamt wahrnimmt und mit der Autorität eines von Gott selbst beglaubigten Propheten sein Testament proklamiert, läuft "die ganze Argumentation des 4Esr zu"[54]. Visio VII,1 bildet daher keinen Epilog, sondern die den Höhepunkt der Zionvision überbietende zweite Klimax des Werkes.

4.2.3. Erst die kurze Episode VII,2 (14,37–48), die stärker narrativ geprägt ist und als Redenden nur noch Gott auftreten läßt (v.38.45–47), besitzt den Charakter eines das Ganze besiegelnden Epilogs. Sie schildert Esras Geistbegabung und das bezeichnenderweise vierzig Tage umfassende Diktat von 94 Offenbarungsbüchern. Wie Esra am Ende selbst die Rolle des Engels und damit die Funktion des himmlischen Gesetzeszeugen übernimmt, so läßt er sich nun seinerseits durch die verbriefte Tradition des Gesetzes vertreten, *ut possint homines invenire semitam, et, qui voluerint vivere, in novissimis vivant* (14,22). Freilich soll, wie die abschließende Gottesweisung einschärft, nur der kleinere Teil dieser Schriften der Öffentlichkeit zugänglich sein. Der größere bleibt einer Verwahrung und Würdigung durch den Kreis von Weisen vorbehalten. Ist damit ein Hinweis auf die Trägerkreise und das Traditionsprinzip derjenigen Literatur gegeben, die wir als jüdische Apokalyptik zu kennzeichnen pflegen?

---

[52] Ich verweise auf die soeben erschienene Arbeit von E. von Nordheim (1980), die ich im Manuskript einsehen konnte.

[53] Vgl. Steck 1967, 177ff. G. Reese (1967, 135 Anm. 30) denkt an Dtn 6,20ff. als Textvorlage.

[54] Steck 1967, 178.

5. Offene Fragen

5.1. Mit unserer Analyse sind wir, so steht zu hoffen, bei der Klärung der Korrelation von Form und Sache im IV. Buch Esra sowie im Bemühen um eine Deutung des Gesamtanliegens der Schrift ein Stück weit vorangekommen. Gleichwohl bleibt eine Fülle von Problemen, die noch der Lösung harren. Auf sie soll abschließend wenigstens ansatzweise aufmerksam gemacht werden[54a].

5.2. Was wir bisher außer acht ließen, ist der bemerkenswerte Sachverhalt, daß sich die gesamte Episodenfolge als 'Ich'-Erzählung zu verstehen gibt, in der ein fiktiver Erzähler (Esra) als 'erinnerndes Ich' auf die ihm widerfahrene Vergangenheit im Modus eines 'erinnerten Ich' zurückkommt[55]. Einzig die beiden Schlußsätze 14,49f., die von Entrückung und Titulierung Esras berichten, gehen in 'Er'-Erzählung über. Nun liegt aber, eben weil diese Aussagen die konsequent autobiographische Fiktion des Ganzen sprengen, der Verdacht eines sekundären Nachtrags nahe, und dies um so mehr, als das besagte Stück in der lateinischen Textversion fehlt. Läßt man 14,49f. unberücksichtigt, präsentiert sich der von uns rekonstruierte literarische Zusammenhang als eine durch den Epilog (VII,2) besiegelte *Abschiedsrede Esras mit ausführlicher Einleitung*. Können wir dieser Beobachtung einen hermeneutischen Wink entnehmen, der Anhaltspunkte zur Formbestimmung des Werks in seiner Ganzheit freigibt? Wie gezeigt, ist die Schrift auf die prophetische Berufung Esras und auf den Akt seiner Vermächtnisrede ausgerichtet. Sie will retrospektiv vom Standort dieses Endes her gewürdigt sein. Versteht sich dann etwa der Komplex der Episoden I–III als eine extrem verbreiterte Ausgestaltung des Motivs von der prophetischen Selbstverweigerung, wie es in alttestamentlichen Berufungsberichten begegnet[56]? Fungiert vielleicht der Topos vom Widerspruch des Propheten als Keimzelle der Kontroverse 3,1–9,25 (bzw. 9,37), in welcher sich der zum Zeugen bestimmte Seher ja als Widerpart der Offenbarung erweist? Freilich ist diese Phase des prophetischen Widerstandes nun derart zerdehnt, daß sie ein starkes Eigengewicht erhält. Esra opponiert nicht nur momentan, sondern über einen längeren Zeitraum hinweg gegen das ihn beanspruchende Wort des Offenbarers, und das in der Rolle eines theologischen Kontrahenten. Doch bleibt auch in 4Esr der transitorische Charakter dieser Zeit des Widerstandes der prophetischen Existenz gewahrt. Am Ende erfüllt der Seher gehorsam das ihm übertra-

---

[54a] Zur Diskussion und Kritik meiner Thesen verweise ich auf die Stellungnahmen in Brandenburger 1981 und in Schreiner 1981.

[55] Zur Terminologie vgl. Arnold/Sinemus 1976, 474. Eine sehr enge Formanalogie findet sich im Traktat des Poimandres (s. o. Anm. 30). Auch dort begegnen wir einem Offenbarungsdialog in Ich-Form mit paränetischer Klimax.

[56] Vgl. v. Rad 1965, 64, 66, 74.

gene Parakletenamt, und die vorausliegende Debatte erweist sich nachträglich als 'Episode' im eigentlichen Sinn des Wortes.

5.3. Zur Beobachtung der *prophetischen* Dimension des Ganzen, in die auch manche Berührungspunkte mit Daniel einzubeziehen sind, gesellt sich ein zweiter Gesichtspunkt. Wie aus den Engelvoten von Visio III und schließlich aus Esras Vermächtnisrede ersichtlich, gilt das Sachinteresse der Schrift zweifellos einer *deuteronomistisch* geprägten Gesetzestheologie. Bereits aus der pseudepigraphischen Einkleidung, die Esra in die Zeit nach der ersten Tempelzerstörung (587) ins babylonische Exil versetzt, erhellt die Orientierung an deuteronomistischen Motiven[57]. Offenkundig sieht sich der Verfasser nun aber gezwungen, einer um sich greifenden Diskriminierung dieser Theologie und des sie tragenden Geschichtsbildes zu begegnen. Um das Überkommene vor den Angriffen einer radikalen Skepsis zu sichern, wiederholt er den Anspruch des Gesetzes im neu konzipierten Rahmen einer dualistischen Zeitlehre und behauptet diesen Neuentwurf des Alten "als das Gültige", indem er ihn "mit der Autorität von Offenbarung"[58] versieht. Bildet dieser Konnex einer Problematisierung und einer Neubeglaubigung des Tradierten, die des Aufgebots einer Engelautorität bedarf, ein Wesensmerkmal apokalyptischer Literatur? Ist die mit prophetischer Überlieferung vermittelte Gesetzestheologie deuteronomistischer Provenienz als die Mutter jüdischer Apokalyptik anzusprechen?

5.4. Daß die Dinge so einfach nicht liegen, zeigt der in 4Esr ebenso bemerkbare Einschlag der *Weisheit*. So wird das theologisch Strittige in der Form argumentativer Lehrgespräche entschieden, die wohl auf weisheitliche Muster zurückgehen. Nicht zufällig erscheinen gerade die Weisen als Träger der geheimen Offenbarungsschriften. Nimmt man die Präponderanz weisheitlicher Terminologie hinzu, wird die Nähe zur Weisheitstradition um so augenfälliger. Vor dem Hintergrund dieses Zusammenhangs könnte man fast versucht sein, im Anschluß an G. v. Rad IVEsr als Dokument einer dualistisch bestimmten Weisheitstheologie zu begreifen[59]. Doch steht einer derart einseitigen Traditionsfixierung das genannte prophetisch-deuteronomistische Moment entgegen. Welcher der beiden Dimensionen soll den Ausschlag geben? Oder sind Alternativen dieser Art im Ansatz verfehlt? Müssen wir stärker als bisher mit einer vorgängigen Verflechtung heterogener Überlieferungen und disparater theologischer Tendenzen rechnen[60]? Was besagt diese Korrektur gängiger Klischees dann

---

[57] Vgl. Steck 1967, 177 u. ö.   [58] Steck 1967, 179.

[59] Vgl. v. Rad 1965, 315ff.; 1970, 336ff.; Brandenburger 1968; Luck 1976 sowie die ausgezeichneten Beobachtungen von Reese (1967, 136ff.) zur Rolle der Weisheitstradition in IVEsr.

[60] Zur Sache vgl. die sehr umsichtigen Erwägungen von Steck 1967, 184ff., 205ff., 209ff.;

aber für die Bestimmung von Produzenten und Tradenten einer Literatur, wie sie sich mit dem IV. Buch Esra zur Darstellung bringt?

5.5. Und schließlich: Wie steht es mit der Frage der Abfassungszeit der Schrift, wenn die Adlerallegorie als Fixpunkt einer Datierung entfällt und der bislang angenommene *terminus a quo* fragwürdig werden sollte? Ist es absolut unsinnig zu erwägen, ob der Primärentwurf von IVEsr nicht bereits der Zeit vor 70 n. Chr. oder sogar dem ersten vorchristlichen Jahrhundert entstammen könnte?

Bibliographie

Arnold, H. L./Sinemus, V. 1976: *Grundzüge der Literatur- und Sprachwissenschaft*. Bd. 1: Literaturwissenschaft (dtv WR 4226), 4. Aufl. München 1976.

Auerbach, E. 1946: *Mimesis*. Dargestellte Wirklichkeit in der abendländischen Literatur, Bern 1946.

Brandenburger, E. 1962: *Adam und Christus*. Exegetisch-religionsgeschichtliche Untersuchung zu Röm. 5,12–21 (1.Kor. 15) (WMANT 7), Neukirchen 1962.

– 1968: *Fleisch und Geist*. Paulus und die dualistische Weisheit (WMANT 29), Neukirchen 1968.

– 1977: *Das literarische und theologische Problem des 4. Esrabuches*. Vortrag auf einer Tagung der Projektgruppe Apokalyptik der Wiss. Gesellschaft für Theologie (Bethel 1977).

– 1981: *Die Verborgenheit Gottes im Weltgeschehen*. Das literarische und theologische Problem des 4. Esrabuches (AThANT 68), Zürich 1981.

Breech, E. 1973: "These Fragments I Have Shored Against My Ruins. The Form and Function of 4 Ezra", in: *JBL* 92 (1973) 267 ff.

Bultmann, R. 1953: *Das Evangelium des Johannes* (KEK II), 13. Aufl. Göttingen 1953.

Gunkel, H. 1900: "Das vierte Buch Esra", in: *APAT* II, 331 ff.

Harnisch, W. 1969: *Verhängnis und Verheißung der Geschichte*. Untersuchungen zum Zeit- und Geschichtsverständnis im 4. Buch Esra und in der syr. Baruchapokalypse (FRLANT 97), Göttingen 1969.

– 1974: "Das Geschichtsverständnis der Apokalyptik", in: *BiKi* 1974, 121 ff.

– 1981: "Die Ironie der Offenbarung. Exegetische Erwägungen zur Zionvision im 4. Buch Esra", in: *SBL 1981 Seminar Papers* (hg. von K. H. Richards), Chico, Calif. 1981, 79 ff. (Kurzfassung erscheint demnächst in *ZAW*; engl. Fassung vorgesehen für *SCSt* 1983.)

Hayman, A. P. 1975: "The Problem of Pseudonymity in the Ezra Apocalypse", in: *JSJ* 6 (1975) 47 ff.

Kabisch, R. 1889: *Das vierte Buch Esra auf seine Quellen untersucht*, Göttingen 1889.

Klauck, H.-J. 1978: *Allegorie und Allegorese in synoptischen Gleichnistexten* (NTA N.F. 13), Münster 1978.

Koch, K. 1978: "Esras erste Vision. Weltzeiten und Weg des Höchsten", in: *BZ* N.F. 22 (1978) 46 ff.

Luck, U. 1976: "Das Weltverständnis in der jüdischen Apokalyptik, dargestellt am äthiopischen Henoch und am 4.Esra", in: *ZThK* 73 (1976) 283 ff.

Müller, U. B. 1972: *Messias und Menschensohn in jüdischen Apokalypsen und in der Offenbarung des Johannes* (StNT 6), Gütersloh 1972.

– 1974: "Die Parakletenvorstellung im Johannesevangelium", in: *ZThK* 71 (1974) 31 ff.

– 1975: *Prophetie und Predigt im Neuen Testament*. Formgeschichtliche Untersuchungen zur urchristlichen Prophetie (StNT 10), Gütersloh 1975.

1968, 445 ff. Könnte in dieser Hinsicht nicht auch der paulinischen Charakteristik IKor 1,20 historische Relevanz zukommen?

von Nordheim, E. 1980: *Die Lehre der Alten. I. Das Testament als Literaturgattung im Judentum der hellenistisch-römischen Zeit* (ALGHL 13), Leiden 1980.

Perlitt, L. 1972: "Anklage und Freispruch Gottes. Theologische Motive in der Zeit des Exils", in: *ZThK* 69 (1972) 290 ff.

Plöger, O. 1958: "Esrabücher, III. Das 4. Esrabuch", in: *RGG*³ Bd. II (1958) Sp. 697 ff.

Politzer, H. 1966: "Eine Parabel Franz Kafkas. Versuch einer Interpretation", in: *Deutsche Erzählungen von Wieland bis Kafka* (Interpretationen IV – Fischer Bücherei BdW 721), Frankfurt a. M./Hamburg 1966, 319 ff.

von Rad, G. 1965: *Theologie des Alten Testaments*, Bd. II: Die Theologie der prophetischen Überlieferungen Israels, 4. Aufl. München 1965.

– 1970: *Weisheit in Israel*, Neukirchen 1970.

Reese, G. 1967: *Die Geschichte Israels in der Auffassung des frühen Judentums*, Diss. theol. Heidelberg 1967 (Typoskript).

Schreiner, J. 1981: "Das 4. Buch Esra" in: *JSHRZ*, Band V: Apokalypsen, Gütersloh 1981, 289–412.

Steck, O. H. 1967: *Israel und das gewaltsame Geschick der Propheten*. Untersuchungen zur Überlieferung des deuteronomistischen Geschichtsbildes im Alten Testament, Spätjudentum und Urchristentum (WMANT 23), Neukirchen 1967.

– 1968: "Das Problem theologischer Strömungen in nachexilischer Zeit", in: *EvTh* 28 (1968) 445 ff.

Thompson, A. L. 1977: *Responsibility for Evil in the Theodicy of IV Ezra*. A Study Illustrating the Significance of Form and Structure for the Meaning of the Book (SBLDS 29), Missoula/Montana 1977.

Anhang

Episode I

	Klage u. Aufn.	Gespräch 2	Gespräch 3
E	(3,1a.bα) 3,1bβ–36 *V-Klage* via: 3,31	4,5a *Lehranforderung* rede, Herr	4,11fin.–12 als ich das hörte, fiel ich auf mein Antlitz *Klage* besser, nicht zu sein, als grundlos zu leiden
U	4,1f. *Vergewisserung* erregt sich dein Herz? einsehen willst du den Weg des Höchsten?	4,5b *fiktive Aufgaben* (Imp.) Feuer, Wind, gestern	4,13–18 *Fabel mit argument.* *Schlußfrage* Bäume, Meer
E	4,3a *Bestätigung*	4,6 *rhet. Frage zur Bestätigung der Unlösbarkeit* wer der Geborenen könnte das?	4,19 *Bestätigung* beide eitle Gedanken
U	4,3b–4 *Lehreröffnungsformel* drei Wege/Gleichnisse, bei Lösung Aufschluß über via; quare cor malignum	4,7–11 *Qal Vachomer-Konklusion in Frageform* Unbegreiflichkeit d. Wege Gottes	4,20f. *Konklusion in der Form eines Vergleichs* Irdische erkennen Irdisches, Himmlische Himmlisches

	Gespräch 4	Gespräch 5	Gespräch 6
E	4,22–25 *V-Klage* Israel! was wird er tun für sei- nen Namen?	4,38f. *Einwand in Frageform* hält d. Sünde d. Ernte auf? (prohiberi)	4,44–46 *Informationsfrage* Quantum d. ausstehen- den Zeit
U	4,26–32 *Feststellung* bald (festinare) noch nicht (necdum)	4,40 *Bildwort* (Imp.) Schwangere d. Unaufhaltsame d. Ge- burt (retinere)	4,47 *Ankündigung* (d. Deu- tung eines Gleichnisses)
E	4,33 *Informationsfrage* wie lange?	4,41a *Bestätigung*	[4,48f.] *visionäres Gleichnis* Rauch-Ofen, Regen- Wolke
U	4,34–37 *Lehrauskunft* non festinas mensura temporum	4,41b–43 *Konklusion in der Form* *eines Vergleichs* Eile d. Kammern (festi- nare)	4,50 *Konklusion in der Form* *eines Vergleichs* Maß d. Vergangenheit größer

	Gespräch 7		Gespräch 8
E	4,51 *Informationsfrage* erlebe ich jene Tage?	Ph	5,16–18 *Vorhaltung* non derelinquas nos
U	4,52–5,13 *Weissagung* Zeichen d. Endzeit (5,14f.)	E	5,19 *Weisung* vade a me (5,19fin.)

Episode II

	Klage u. Aufn.	Gespräch 2	Gespräch 3
E	(5,20) 5,21–30 *V-Klage* (5,31)	5,33a *Lehranforderung* rede, mein Herr	5,35b *Klage* warum geboren?
U	5,32 *Lehreröffnungsruf*	5,33b *Rückfrage* liebst du Israel mehr als sein Schöpfer?	5,36f. *fiktive Aufgaben* (Imp.) numera, qui necdum venerunt . . .
E		5,34 *Erklärung* Begreifen von Weg (se- mita) u. Urteil des Höchsten	5,38f. *rhet. Frage zur Bestäti- gung d. Unlösbarkeit* wer könnte dies wissen?
U		5,35a *Ablehnung* das kannst du nicht	5,40 *Konklusion in der Form eines Vergleichs* Unbegreiflichkeit d. Urteils u. d. Liebe Gottes

	Gespräch 4	Gespräch 5	Gespräch 6
E	5,41 *Einwand in Frageform* promissio nur für End- generation?	5,45 *Einwand* Syllogismus	5,50 *Informationsfrage* Mutter jung oder nahe Greisenalter?
U	5,42 *Vergleich* Gericht – Kranz	5,46 *Bildwort* (Imp.) Mutterschoß (per tempus, decem in unum)	5,51f. *Bildwort* (Imp.) Gebärende (Unterschied der früh u. spät Gebo- renen)
E	5,43 *Gegenfrage* in unum facere ut cele- rius iudicium tuum ostendas?	5,47 *Bestätigung* secundum tempus	G [5,53] *Bestätigung* der Differenz
U	5,44 *Lehrsentenz* non potest festinare . . . sustinere	5,48f. *Konklusion* Applikation des Bild- wortes u. Vergleich (per tempus)	5,54f. *Konklusion* abfallende Größe

	Gespräch 7	Gespräch 8
E	5,56 *Informationsfrage* durch wen wird Schöp- fung heimgesucht?	6,11f. *Informationsbitte* um Ende der Zeichen- weissagung
U	6,1–6 *Lehrauskunft* Anfang u. Ende durch Schöpfer allein	6,13–16 (17)18–28(29) 30–34 *Weissagung* Zeichen d. Endzeit
E	6,7 *Informationsfrage* nach Zeitenwende	
U	6,8–10 *Lehrauskunft in allegori-* *scher Form* gehaltene Ferse Esaus	

Episode III

	Klage u. Aufn.	Gespräch 2	Gespräch 3
E	(6,35) 6,36–59 *V-Klage*	7,3a *Lehranforderung* rede, Herr	7,17f. *Einwand* Geschick d. Frevler
U	7,1f. *Lehreröffnungsruf*	7,3b–9 *Gleichnis* v. Meer u. Stadt	
E		7,10a *Bestätigung*	
U		7,10b–16 *Konklusion:* Gleichn.-Applikation, argumentat. Schlußfra- gen (Zwei-Äonen- Lehre)	7,19–44 *Zurechtweisung* Unentschuldbarkeit d. Frevler *Lehrauskunft* Zeichen d. Endes, Gericht

	Gespräch 4	Gespräch 5	Gespräch 6
E	7,45−48 tunc et dixi, dom., et nunc dico *V-Klage* cor malum	7,62−69 *V-Klage* Universalität d. Sünde (sensus)	7,75 *Informationsfrage* Geschick nach d. Tod
U	7,49−52 *Exemplum* Edelsteine, Blei, Ton E 7,53 *Bestätigung* U 7,54−57 *Bildwort* (Imp.) Gold, Silber, Kupfer etc.		7,76−99 *Lehrstück* Sieben Grade d. Ver- dammnis u. Seligk. (Forderung d. Distanz gegenüber Frevlern)
E	7,58 *Bestätigung*		7,100 *Informationsfrage* tempus . . . ut videant?
U	7,59−61 *Konklusion* Wert d. wenigen Ge- rechten	7,70−74 *Abweisung* Unentschuldbarkeit d. Frevler	7,101 *Lehrauskunft* siebentägige Schau

	Gespräch 7	Gespräch 8	Gespräch 9
E	7,102f. *Frage* nach d. Möglichk. d. Fürbitte	7,106−111 *Einwand* Fürbitte in Geschichte Israels	7,116−126 hic sermo meus primus et novissimus *V-Klage* Tat Adams, Universali- tät d. Sünde
U			
E			
U	7,104f. *Feststellung* betr. Gerichtstag *Vergleich* Unvertretbarkeit	7,112−115 *Abweisung* Vorläufigk. dieses Äons, Endgültigk. des Gerichts	7,127−131 *Abweisung* Unentschuldbarkeit d. Frevler

	Gespräch 10	Gespräch 11	Gespräch 12
E	7,132—139 *Appell an Barmherzigkeit* Midrasch zu Ex 34	8,4—36 *Einwand* *Oratio Esrae*	8,42—45 *Einwand* Verweis auf Regen, Mensch = Saat?
U E			
U	8,1—3 *Feststellung* zwei Äonen *Vergleich* Ton-Gold d. Erde (multi-pauci)	8,37—41 *Feststellung* iron. Bestätigung d. Gebets *Vergleich* mit Saat u. Pflanzen (non omnes salvabuntur)	8,46—62a *Zurechtweisung* Unentschuldbarkeit d. Frevler (Forderung d. Distanz gegenüber Frevlern)

	Gespräch 13	Gespräch 14
E	8,62b—63 *Informationsfrage* betr. Zeichen	9,14—16 olim locutus sum et nunc dico et postea dicam *Vorhaltung* Überzahl d. Verworfenen
U E		
U	9,1—13 *Lehrauskunft* Ende Unentschuldbarkeit d. Frevler (Forderung d. Distanz gegenüber Frevlern)	9,17—25 *Abweisung* Tun-Ergehen-Zus.hang heiliger Rest

Episode IV

	Klage/Gespräch 1	Gespräch 2	Gespräch 3
E	(9,26) 9,27—37 *V-Klage* (9,38)	F 9,42b—10,4 *Bericht*	10,17b—18 *Weigerung*
E	9,39f. *Erkundigungsfrage* warum weinst du?		
F	9,41 *Antwort* laß mich weinen		
E	9,42a *Aufforderung* zu erzählen	10,5—17a *Zurechtweisung*	10,19—24 *Zurechtweisung*

	Gespräch 4	Gespräch 5	Gespräch 6
E	(10,25−27a) 10,27b−28 *Frage* *nach Uriel* (10,29f.)	10,34−37 *Lehranforderung* *rede, Herr*	V 12,40b−45a *V-Klage*
U	10,31 *Erkundigungsfrage*		
E	10,32 *Auskunft*		
U	10,33 *Lehreröffnungsformel*	10,38−57+13,54f. (?) *Lehrvortrag*	E 12,45b−49 *Trostrede* (12,50)

Episode VII,1   **Episode VII,2**

Gespräch 1	Gespräch 2	
(13,57f.) G 14,1.2a *Anruf*	E 14,18−22 *Informationsfrage* *Geschick d. Späteren* *Bitte* *um Geistbegabung*	(14,37) G 14,38 *Anruf u. Weissagung* (14,39−44)
E 14,2b *Antwort*	G 14,23−26 *Anweisung*	G 14,45−47 *Anweisung* betr. Veröffentlichung u. Geheimhaltung d. Schriften
G 14,2c−17 *Gottesrede* Beauftragung Esras	E 14,27−36 *Abschiedsrede Esras*	(14,48)

Die Bedeutung der Qumranfunde für die Erforschung der Apokalyptik

Hartmut Stegemann

0. Vorbemerkung

In den 50er Jahren unseres Jahrhunderts galten die Qumranfunde als eine Art Wundermedizin, von der man die Heilung zahlreicher Gebrechen erhoffte, an denen bis dahin die Erforschung des Alten und des Neuen Testaments, des antiken Judentums und der Geschichte der semitischen Sprachen gelitten hatten; und auch der Religionsgeschichte schienen sich durch diese Textfunde ungeahnte neue Möglichkeiten zu eröffnen.

Mittlerweile ist weitgehend Ernüchterung eingetreten, und es gibt heute nur noch wenige Spezialisten, die sich ernsthaft mit der Erforschung der Qumranfunde befassen und deren Ertrag für andere Fachgebiete nutzbar machen.

Was speziell die Erforschung der Apokalyptik anbetrifft, so besteht gegenwärtig eine erhebliche Diskrepanz zwischen der Erwartung, die Qumranfunde könnten wenigstens für diesen Forschungsgegenstand immer noch eine Art Wundermedizin sein, und der Tatsache, daß die bisherigen Ansätze zur Einbeziehung der Qumranfunde in die Apokalyptik-Diskussion so gut wie gar keine allgemein anerkannten oder auch nur weiterführenden Ergebnisse erbracht haben.

Was ist die Ursache dieser seltsamen Diskrepanz? Sind die Qumranfunde selbst zu vieldeutig oder noch unzureichend erschlossen? Oder ist die Apokalyptikforschung sich vielleicht noch gar nicht einig darüber, was denn eigentlich ihr Forschungsgegenstand sei und wie die Texte aus den Qumranfunden sich dazu verhalten?

Meiner Auffassung nach haben die Qumranfunde eine ganz erhebliche Bedeutung für die Erforschung der Apokalyptik, gutenteils freilich in ganz anderer Art, als man dies bislang vermutet hat.

Von der gegebenen Sachlage her halte ich es hier für erforderlich, zunächst einleitend (§ 1.) einige allgemeine Bemerkungen zu den Qumranfunden zu machen, sodann (§ 2.) mein Verständnis der Begriffe "Apokalyptik" und "Eschatologie" darzulegen und anschließend (§ 3.) die Bedeutung der Qumranfunde für die Apokalyptik-Forschung im einzelnen zu erläutern. Schließlich soll (§ 4.) eine knappe Zusammenfassung die wichtigsten Ergebnisse herausstellen und (§5.) ein Nachwort das Problem der Definition von "Apokalyptik" nochmals aufgreifen.

1. Allgemeine Bemerkungen zu den Qumranfunden

In den Jahren 1947 bis 1956 wurden in letztlich 11 Höhlen bei Chirbet Qumran am Toten Meer mehr oder weniger umfangreiche Teile von insgesamt knapp 750 verschiedenen Handschriften in hebräischer, aramäischer und griechischer Sprache gefunden, deren paläographische Daten sie dem Zeitraum vom 3. Jh. v. Chr. bis zum Jahre 68 n. Chr. zuweisen. Bei etwa einem Drittel dieser Handschriften handelt es sich um solche biblischer Bücher. Etwa 500 Handschriften sind nichtbiblischen Werken zuzuweisen, wobei gegenwärtig erst ganz grob abgeschätzt werden kann, in welchen Fällen es sich um Mehrfachkopien des gleichen Werkes handelt. Letztlich dürfte die Anzahl inhaltlich bestimmbarer nichtbiblischer Werke aus den uns erhaltenen Beständen der Qumranbibliothek sich wohl auf höchstens etwa 100 reduzieren lassen, wenn man die Mehrfachkopien solcher Schriften wie einzelner Henoch-Bücher, der "Tempelrolle", der "Hodajot" oder der "Gemeinschaftsregel" je für 1 Werk zusammenfaßt[1].

1.1. Ein abschließendes Urteil zu diesem Punkt ist noch nicht möglich, da bislang nicht einmal die Hälfte aller Qumrantexte ediert worden ist und die Zuweisung oft ganz fragmentarisch erhaltener Handschriften zu Werken, die durch die Qumranfunde erstmalig bekanntgeworden sind, ein besonders schwieriges Geschäft bleibt. Auch befindet sich unter den noch unedierten Qumrantexten eine ganze Reihe von Handschriften, die von Werken stammen, die weder aus der älteren Überlieferung noch aus den bislang edierten Qumranfunden bekannt sind oder deren wahrer Charakter sich anhand der bereits zugänglichen Fragmente noch gar nicht erahnen läßt.

Beispiele für den letztgenannten Aspekt bieten Yigael Yadins Edition der "Tempelrolle" im Jahre 1977[2] oder J. T. Miliks Publikation von Teilen des "Giganten-Buches" aus der Henoch-Literatur im Jahre 1976[3], mit denen jeweils die Zuweisung bereits publizierter, ihrer Bedeutung nach aber bis dahin unbestimmbarer Handschriftenfragmente zu Parallelkopien dieser Werke verbunden war. Voraussichtlich wird es erst in einigen Jahrzehnten möglich sein, unter inhaltlichen Gesichtspunkten einen Gesamtüberblick über alle Texte aus den Qumranfunden zu gewinnen.

---

[1] Neuester Überblick über diese Handschriftenfunde und deren Publikationsstand: Fitzmyer 1975, 11–39.

[2] Yadin 1977, z. B. Vol. III (A): Supplementary Plates, Pl. 35*–40*. Siehe auch van der Ploeg 1978, bes. 112f.

[3] Milik 1976, z. B. 300–304, 309, 334f.

Deshalb steht auch jede Äußerung zur Bedeutung der Qumranfunde für die Erforschung der Apokalyptik unter dem Vorbehalt, daß sie nur vorläufiger Art sein kann und gegebenenfalls aufgrund neuer Textpublikationen revidiert werden muß. Diese für den gegenwärtigen Forschungsstand sehr mißliche Feststellung ist sogar für solche Werke relevant, deren Textbestand uns durch entsprechende Handschriften aus Höhle 1Q seit Jahrzehnten weitgehend oder so gut wie vollständig bekannt ist, wie z. B. die "Kriegsregel" (1Q M) oder die "Gemeinschaftsregel" (1Q S): Erst wenn die noch unedierten Fragmente von Parallelhandschriften aus Höhle 4Q vorliegen[4], ist ein fundiertes Urteil über die literarische Genese dieser Werke, über die relative Eigenständigkeit einzelner ihrer Bestandteile und über die historisch-theologische Wertung bestimmter Textbefunde möglich. Deshalb wird man auch bei derart wohlbekannten Texten sich zunächst auf solche Urteile beschränken müssen, die in jedem Falle möglich sind, gleichgültig, welche weiteren Erkenntnisse die noch unpublizierten Parallelfassungen einst bringen werden.

1.2. Auf der anderen Seite wird man sagen dürfen, daß für ein *vorläufiges* Urteil über die Bedeutung der Qumranfunde für die Erforschung der Apokalyptik bereits eine recht brauchbare Materialbasis gegeben ist. Denn die Handschriften aus 9 der insgesamt 11 Fundhöhlen von Chirbet Qumran sind mittlerweile vollständig ediert, aus Höhle 11Q die allermeisten, aus Höhle 4Q immerhin einige der wichtigsten[5]. Da in solchen Höhlen wie 1–6Q und 11Q offensichtlich nicht eine tendenziöse Auswahl bestimmter Werke vorhanden war wie im Falle der Höhle 7Q, die ausschließlich griechischsprachige Handschriften enthielt, wird man im allgemeinen davon ausgehen dürfen, daß das bereits zugängliche Material einen repräsentativen Querschnitt bietet für die literarischen Gattungen, für die Bevorzugung bestimmter Werke und Lehrgegenstände wie auch für die Mentalität der einstigen Besitzer der Gesamtbibliothek, so daß die weiteren Texteditionen das bereits jetzt feststellbare Bild mehr quantitativ als qualitativ verändern werden, eher weitergehende Erkenntnismöglichkeiten erschließen als jetzt bereits Erkennbares wieder in Frage stellen werden.

Deshalb will ich es trotz der deutlich hervorgehobenen Risiken wagen, mich bereits jetzt schon in relativ grundsätzlicher Weise zur Bedeutung der Qumranfunde für die Erforschung der Apokalyptik zu äußern, zumal dies vor Experten in Sachen "Apokalyptik" geschieht, denen im Einzelfall nicht nur die Bedeutung, sondern auch die Grenzen und die unterschiedliche Tragfähigkeit von mir zu treffender Urteile ohnehin bewußt sind.

---

[4] Fitzmyer 1975, 29f. und 32. Für 1Q M vgl. Hunzinger 1957 und Baillet 1972, für 1Q S Milik 1960, 412–416.

[5] Vgl. oben Anm. 1.

2. Die Begriffe "Apokalyptik" und "Eschatologie"

Ein Hauptproblem bleibt in diesem Zusammenhang freilich noch die Frage, was denn überhaupt gemeint sei, wenn hier von "Apokalyptik" gesprochen wird. Denn je nachdem, wie man diesen Begriff auffaßt, wird man dazu neigen, die nichtbiblischen Qumrantexte entweder als durch und durch "apokalyptisch" zu betrachten oder als Produkte einer Mentalität, der "Apokalyptik" im Grunde fremd bleiben mußte.

2.1. Gänzlich außer Betracht bleiben sollte bei dieser Frage jegliche *tendenziöse* Wertung von "Apokalyptik". Ob man die jüdische Apokalyptik als Fortführung der Prophetie mit anderen Mitteln oder als Gipfel der Möglichkeiten weisheitlicher Lehre auffaßt und gegebenenfalls entsprechend positiv wertet; ob man darin eine "Absage an diese Welt" und deren Realitäten sieht und dann womöglich zu einem negativen Werturteil kommen mag; wie sich "Apokalyptik" zu dem verhält, was man in jüdischer oder christlicher Tradition stehend heute lehrmäßig als essentiell betrachten mag: Derartige Problemstellungen[6] sollen uns hier nicht beschäftigen und auch nicht indirekt beeinflussen. In den Blick genommen werden soll allein das Phänomen der jüdischen und der frühchristlichen "Apokalyptik" an sich, wobei freilich noch immer offen ist, was denn darunter zu verstehen sei.

2.2. Da eine Einigung über einen einheitlichen Sprachgebrauch für den Begriff "Apokalyptik" in absehbarer Zeit kaum erreichbar sein dürfte, bleibt nichts anderes übrig, als daß ein jeder, der diesen Begriff verwenden will, zuvor mitteilt, wie er ihn versteht[7]. In diesem Sinne also meine Position[8]:

Mit "Apokalyptik" bezeichne ich ausschließlich ein *literarisches* Phänomen, nämlich die Anfertigung von "Offenbarungsschriften", die Sachverhalte "enthüllen", die sich nicht aus innerweltlichen Gegebenheiten, beispielsweise aus dem vorgegebenen "Erfahrungswissen" ableiten lassen, sondern die sich dem Autor und dem Leser nur erschließen durch den Rückgriff auf "himmlisches Offenbarungswissen".

Nicht jede Mitteilung "himmlischer Geheimnisse" freilich ist damit zugleich auch bereits "Apokalyptik", ebensowenig jede einzelne "Enthüllung" von Aspekten, deren rechtes Verständnis anderen Menschen verbor-

---

[6] Siehe dazu Schmidt 1969.

[7] Wieviel von dieser Begriffsbestimmung abhängt, wird exemplarisch daran deutlich, daß Herr Kollege Marc Philonenko in seinem Beitrag zu den Qumranfunden im Rahmen unseres Kolloquiums (oben in diesem Band) keinen einzigen jener vier Texte auch nur erwähnt hat, die meiner Auffassung nach möglicherweise in der Qumrangemeinde entstandene "Apokalypsen" sind (siehe unten §3.3.), während umgekehrt seine eigene Textbasis bei mir aus der Diskussion um "Apokalyptik" gänzlich ausscheidet (vgl. unten §3.2.2.).

[8] Im folgenden werden nur einige Grundgedanken ausgeführt. Vgl. weiterhin unten §3.1.1.4. sowie mein "Nachwort" unten §5.

gen ist. Sondern bei "apokalyptischer Literatur" muß es sich schon um ein regelrechtes Buch handeln, das speziell zu dem Zweck abgefaßt worden ist, "himmlisches Geheimwissen" bewußt als solches zu traktieren und es dennoch einem bestimmten Leserkreis zu "offenbaren".

In solcher Absicht sind Teile der Henoch-Literatur abgefaßt worden, die Daniel- und die Johannes-Apokalypse, die syrische Baruch-Apokalypse, das IV Esra-Buch und manch andere jüdische und christliche Schrift. Auch besteht weitgehend Einigkeit in der Forschung, wenigstens die genannten Schriften als "Apokalypsen" zu bezeichnen und sie zumindest als den Kernbestand dessen zu betrachten, was man "Apokalyptik" nennt.

Zum Streit der Gelehrten kommt es erst, wenn man nach dem Inhalt dieser Schriften fragt und damit beginnt, einzelne der darin behandelten Gegenstände wie z. B. Engellisten oder die Gestalt eines "Menschensohnes", die Art der Bildersprache, gedankliche Konzepte wie Dualismus und Zwei-Äonen-Lehre oder eine in diesen Schriften feststellbare Daseinshaltung und Geschichtsbetrachtung als für die "Apokalyptik" charakteristisch zu klassifizieren und alles Vergleichbare in anderweitiger Literatur nun ebenfalls "apokalyptisch" zu nennen.

Meiner Auffassung nach ist ein solches Vorgehen grundsätzlich falsch und vom wissenschaftlichen Standpunkt her illegitim. Nur und erst das Aufgreifen beispielsweise des Zwei-Äonen-Konzepts durch den Autor einer solchen "Offenbarungsschrift" macht dieses Konzept zu einem "apokalyptischen", und es verdient diese Bezeichnung nur im Zusammenhang einer solchen Apokalypse selbst. Jede Umkehr des Verhältnisses schafft lediglich Verwirrung und dient letztlich niemandem. Dies läßt sich leicht deutlich machen, wenn man ein banaleres Beispiel wählt: Der Autor einer Apokalypse kann sich des Briefformulars bedienen, z. B. als formales Konzept für sein Gesamtwerk, für die Gestaltung eines "Himmelsbriefes" oder eines "Sendschreibens" oder für beliebige andere Zwecke. Der Nachweis, daß sich tatsächlich in Apokalypsen "Briefe" finden, wird aber niemanden dazu bringen, aufgrund dieses Nachweises nun auch anderweitige Briefe, beispielsweise die Dienstpost eines Statthalters, als "apokalyptisch" zu bezeichnen. Was bei diesem Beispiel ohne weiteres einleuchtet, muß aber ganz allgemein gelten. "Apokalyptisch" sind Gattungen, Denkweisen, Stoffe und Motive nur im Rahmen von Apokalypsen, nicht darüber hinaus.

Im übrigen ist festzustellen, daß es nicht nur keine eigenständige literarische Gattung "Apokalypse" gibt, sondern auch keine inhaltlichen Kriterien, die nicht nur allen Apokalypsen gemeinsam, sondern in ihrem Vorkommen auch auf diese beschränkt und somit für "Apokalyptik" spezifisch wären. Von daher verbietet sich meines Erachtens jede Ausdehnung des Begriffes "apokalyptisch" über die Apokalypsen hinaus.

Als einzige Ausnahme könnte der Fall gelten, daß jemand eine literarisch vorgegebene Apokalypse bewußt und deren Selbstverständnis entsprechend aufnimmt: Dann, und nur dann ist auch ein solcher Epigone "Apokalyptiker", freilich nur für diesen streng begrenzten Teil seines Gesamtwerkes.

2.3. Ein besonderes Problem schafft in diesem Zusammenhang die Tatsache, daß viele der uns bekannten Apokalypsen auf "Eschatologie" zurückgreifen und diese ihren Zwecken dienstbar machen. Von daher sieht sich mancher Forscher dazu berechtigt, die Grenzen zwischen "Eschatologie" und "Apokalyptik" überhaupt zu verwischen und "eschatologische" Vorstellungen auch dann, wenn sie außerhalb von Apokalypsen begegnen, als "apokalyptisch" zu kennzeichnen.

Tatsächlich aber ist die "Eschatologie" ein gegenüber der "Apokalyptik" völlig eigenständiges, traditionsgeschichtlich auch wesentlich älteres Phänomen[9], dessen Zustandekommen und Ausprägung ganz unabhängig sind davon, ob jemals irgendeine Apokalypse angefertigt und gelesen worden ist oder nicht.

Mit "Eschatologie" bezeichne ich eine spezifische Ausprägung "heilsgeschichtlicher" Orientierung, die von der Zukunft eine "Wende zum Besseren" erhofft. In der Regel wird diese "Wende" bewirkt durch ein göttliches Eingreifen in den Verlauf der Dinge, das als ein "Gericht" oder als eine Strafaktion gegen die "Bösen" in der Welt vorgestellt wird und in dessen Folge sich die "Frommen" eines unbeeinträchtigten Heilszustandes erfreuen dürfen.

Das "Wissen" um eine solche Weiterentwicklung der gegebenen Verhältnisse resultiert im Falle der "Eschatologie" nicht aus "himmlischen Offenbarungen", sondern aus einem vorgegebenen Geschichtsbild, einem "heilsgeschichtlichen pattern". Dieses gestattet es, Mißhelligkeiten und Leiden der Gegenwart als nur temporäre Implikationen eines Geschichtsablaufs zu begreifen, dessen "Wende zum Besseren" künftig bevorsteht und sich ggf. bereits abzeichnet. Doch ist die "Nähe" einer solchen "Wende" nicht unbedingt erforderlich, sondern es kann auch mit längeren Zeiträumen bis zu deren Eintritt gerechnet werden.

Konstitutiv für "Eschatologie" ist allein, daß man eine solche "Wende zum Besseren" von einem künftigen Eingreifen Gottes erhofft. Ein wichtiger Topos in den derart orientierten Stoffen ist die Rede von der אחרית הימים , vom ἔσχατον τῶν ἡμερῶν bzw. von dem letzten Abschnitt auf einer Zeitskala vor Eintritt der erhofften "Wende". Von daher stammt

---

[9] "Eschatologie" läßt sich im Judentum bereits für vorexilische Schriftpropheten nachweisen, während meiner Auffassung nach entsprechende "Apokalyptik" im Judentum frühestens für das 4. Jh. v. Chr. postuliert werden kann.

die Bezeichnung "Eschatologie", und nur im Sinne dieses heilsgeschichtlichen Konzepts soll die Bezeichnung hier verwendet werden[10].

2.4. Viele der uns bekannten Apokalypsen bedienen sich dieses "eschatologischen" Konzepts der Heilsgeschichte, übernehmen eine Fülle von Gegenständen und Motiven aus der "Eschatologie" und sind mitunter so stark von dieser mitgeprägt, daß man zu der Auffassung neigen mag, ohne den Vorgang der "Eschatologie" wäre die "Apokalyptik" nie zustandegekommen. Doch wäre es selbst bei Zugrundelegung dieser Auffassung falsch, aufgrund eines solchen Abhängigkeitsverhältnisses nunmehr die "Apokalyptik" als eine "Tochter" der "Eschatologie" zu betrachten. Denn der für die "Apokalyptik" zentrale Gedanke, der literarisch die Apokalypsen konstituiert, ist nicht das – nur tatsächlich häufig benutzte – Geschichtskonzept der "Eschatologie", sondern die Mitteilung von "himmlischem Geheimwissen", das durch diese Schriften "offenbart" wird und gegebenenfalls eben auch den künftigen Verlauf der Geschichte klären mag.

Die Eigenständigkeit der "Apokalyptik" gegenüber der "Eschatologie" zeigt sich außerdem darin, daß zwar gerade einige ältere jüdische Apokalypsen, die "heilsgeschichtlich" orientiert sind, den traditionsgeschichtlichen Gegebenheiten entsprechend noch stark dem Geschichtsbild der "Eschatologie" verpflichtet sind, dann aber zunehmend an die Stelle der eschatologischen "Wende zum Besseren" der Gedanke des "Endes dieser Welt" zugunsten einer "neuen Welt" tritt, ein "jenseitiger Heilsort" vorgestellt, ja schließlich auf jede Geschichtsspekulation verzichtet werden kann, wie z. B. die christliche Hermas-Apokalypse zeigt. So verbreitet Geschichtsdenken in der "Apokalyptik" auch immer sein mag, konstitutiv kann es für die "Apokalyptik" nicht gewesen sein. "Eschatologie" aber ist bereits vom Begriff her und überall wo sie begegnet notwendigerweise Geschichtsdenken.

3. Die Bedeutung der Qumranfunde für die Apokalyptik-Forschung

Nach diesen ziemlich allgemeinen, von der gegebenen Sachlage her aber erforderlichen Vorbemerkungen kann ich nun endlich zum eigentlichen Gegenstand meines Beitrages übergehen, zur konkreten Bedeutung der Qumranfunde für die Erforschung der Apokalyptik.

Dabei werde ich so vorgehen, daß ich zunächst (§ 3.1.) diejenigen Schriften behandle, von denen man zwar Kopien in den Beständen der Qumranbibliothek gefunden hat, die aber im wesentlichen *unabhängig von*

---

[10] Zur Illustration vgl. meine Hinweise zur "Eschatologie der Qumrangemeinde" unten § 3.4.

der Qumrangemeinde entstanden sind, nämlich Henoch-Schriften, das Jubiläen-Buch und die Daniel-Apokalypse. Sodann will ich (§3.2.) auf solche
Werke eingehen, die man als *spezifische Produkte der Qumrangemeinde*
betrachten könnte, wobei im Einzelfall freilich immer wieder zu fragen
sein wird, ob es sich nicht ebenfalls um ältere Literatur aus vorqumrani-
scher Tradition handelt. Schließlich will ich dann (§3.4.) in aller Kürze die
"Eschatologie" der Qumrangemeinde charakterisieren und versuchen, deren
Eigenständigkeit gegenüber der "Apokalyptik" deutlich zu machen.

3.1. Apokalyptik vor Entstehung der Qumrangemeinde

3.1.1. Die Henoch-Literatur

Vor Entdeckung der Qumrantexte war die Auffassung verbreitet – und
mitunter wird sie heute noch vertreten –, am Anfang aller jüdischen
Apokalyptik stehe das etwa 165/64 v. Chr. abgefaßte biblische Daniel-
Buch. Ergo habe zumindest die jüdische Apokalyptik ihren Ursprung im
palästinischen Judentum zur Zeit Antiochos' IV., und ihre Hauptinteressen
ließen sich durch eine Analyse der Daniel-Apokalypse ermitteln.

Die Entdeckung von Fragmenten von mindestens 20 verschiedenen
Handschriften in den Qumranfunden, die Teile der Henoch-Literatur
repräsentieren, und deren partielle Edition durch J. T. Milik im Jahre 1976
haben dieses Bild gründlich verändert[11].

3.1.1.1. Zunächst ist die Diskussion um die *"Bilderreden"* des Henoch
(äthHen 37–71) neu in Gang gekommen, da sich kein einziges der zahlreichen Qumranfragmente diesem umfangreichen Teil der Henoch-Überlie-
ferung zuweisen läßt. J. T. Milik betrachtet die "Bilderreden" nunmehr als
ein griechisch-christliches Werk, das erst um 270 n. Chr. entstanden sei[12];
andere Untersuchungen neueren Datums weisen sie dem 1. Jh. n. Chr. zu[13].
Jedenfalls ist aufgrund der Qumranfunde nicht nur die literarische Eigenständigkeit der "Bilderreden" evident, sondern auch ein verhältnismäßig
spätes Entstehungsdatum näherliegend als ihre Frühdatierung. Feststehen
sollte auch, daß man die Abfassung der "Bilderreden" künftig nicht mehr
der Qumrangemeinde oder den "Essenern" zuschreiben darf.

3.1.1.2. Statt dessen erweist sich jetzt das bislang nur als Bestandteil des
manichäischen Kanons bekannte *"Giganten-Buch"* als jüdische Henoch-

---

[11] Alle bislang edierten Henoch-Fragmente aus den Qumranfunden sind wiedergegeben bei
Milik 1976, ein Teil davon – nämlich die schon vor 1976 edierten Fragmente – außerdem bei
Fitzmyer and Harrington 1978, 64–79 (Nr. 10–19).
[12] Milik 1976, 89–98, bes. 95f.
[13] So z.B. Knibb 1979 (Ende 1. Jh. n. Chr.); Mearns 1979 (gegen Mitte 1. Jh. n. Chr.).
Weitere Literatur: Harrington 1980, 152.

Schrift aus vorchristlicher Zeit. Es lassen sich nicht nur 10–12 Kopien davon im Rahmen der Qumranfunde nachweisen[14]. Sondern die älteste Kopie stammt bereits aus der 1. Hälfte des 1. Jh. v. Chr.[15]; und in einer Henoch-Handschrift, die aus dem letzten Drittel des 1. Jh. v. Chr. stammt (4Q Hen[c]), erscheint dieses "Giganten-Buch" als zweiter Teil eines größeren Henoch-Corpus, nach dem "angelologischen Buch" (äthHen 1–36) und vor dem "Geschichts-Buch" und dem "paränetischen Buch", die den Schlußteil des äthHen (83–107) bilden[16].

Abgesehen davon, daß J. T. Milik die beiden nur ganz fragmentarisch erhaltenen Handschriften 1Q **23** und 6Q **8** als Kopien des "Giganten-Buches" bestimmt hat[17], hat er leider von den 8–10 Kopien dieses Werkes aus Höhle 4Q bislang nur einige Fragmente aus 4QHenGiants[b] und[c] sowie die erhaltenen Stücke einer einzigen Handschrift ediert, 4QHenGiants[a] als Bestandteil der Handschrift 4QHen[c][18].

So läßt sich bislang über das Gesamtwerk nur wenig mehr sagen, als aus der anderweitigen Überlieferung, die J. T. Milik mit großer Akribie gesammelt und gesichtet hat[19], bereits deutlich ist. Das "Giganten-Buch" ist offenbar literarisch abhängig von dem "angelologischen Buch" (äthHen 1–36) und befaßt sich nähergehend mit den dort genannten Engeln sowie deren Schicksalen, nennt auch im einzelnen die Namen dieser Engel. Die detaillierte "Offenbarung" von Engelschicksalen, das Darstellungsmittel der "Traumvision" und die in den bereits edierten Fragmenten mehrfach belegte Funktion Henochs als dessen, der alles genau aufgeschrieben hat und einzelne Visionen autoritativ deutet[20], machen es möglich, das "Giganten-Buch" als eine "Apokalypse" zu charakterisieren, wenn auch Rahmen und Struktur dieses Werkes noch nicht hinreichend deutlich sind. Entstanden ist es vermutlich im 2. Jh. v. Chr., wobei zunächst noch offenbleiben muß, ob es ein Werk der Qumrangemeinde ist oder außerhalb von ihr angefertigt worden ist.

3.1.1.3. Sicher älter als die Qumrangemeinde ist das *"angelologische Buch"* der Henoch-Literatur (äthHen 1–36), ein in sich bereits kompliziertes literarisches Gebilde, das nun aber durch die Qumranfunde seiner Bedeutsamkeit nach stark aufgewertet worden ist. Gefunden und von J. T. Milik vollständig ediert wurden Fragmente von 5 Handschriften, die diesen Teil des Henoch-Komplexes repräsentieren[21]. Von diesen stammt die Handschrift 4QHen[a] bereits aus der 1. Hälfte des 2. Jh. v. Chr.[22] und enthält insbesondere auch die Anfangskapitel 1–5. Das "angelologische Buch" ist

---

[14] Milik 1976, 9, 57f., 298–339.   [15] *Ibid.*, 57.   [16] *Ibid.*, 6, 58, 310–317.
[17] *Ibid.*, 300–303.   [18] *Ibid.*, 310–317.   [19] *Ibid.*, 298–339.
[20] 4Q HenGig[a] Fragm. 8,4 (Milik 1976, 315); 4Q HenGig[b] 1,II,21 (*ibid.*, 305); 1,III,6 (*ibid.*, 306).
[21] Übersicht Milik 1976, 6.   [22] *Ibid.*, 140.

sicher das Werk eines judäischen Autors, angefertigt vermutlich um die Mitte des 3. Jh. v. Chr.[23]. Die verwendeten Quellenstoffe könnten teilweise samaritanischer Herkunft sein[24].

3.1.1.4. Wahrscheinlich gänzlich samaritanischen Ursprungs ist das *"astronomische Buch"* der Henoch-Literatur[25], wobei die Qumranfunde zeigen, daß dessen Wiedergabe in äthHen 72–82 eine sekundäre Kurzfassung eines ursprünglich wesentlich umfangreicheren Werkes ist[26]. Gefunden wurden Fragmente von 4 Kopien dieses Werkes, von denen J. T. Milik aber bislang nur wenige Stücke ediert hat, diejenigen nämlich, zu denen es textliche Entsprechungen in äthHen 72–82 gibt[27]. Leider ist darunter kein einziges Fragment von 4QHenAstr[a], der ältesten dieser Handschriften, die nach J. T. Milik paläographisch dem Ausgang des 3. oder dem Anfang des 2. Jh. v. Chr. zuzuweisen und damit die allerälteste Handschrift eines Henoch-Buches ist[28].

Weil die meisten Fragmente dieses "astronomischen Buches" aus den Qumranfunden noch unediert sind, kann man gegenwärtig noch kein abschließendes Urteil über das Gesamtwerk fällen. Einige Daten aber stehen bereits jetzt schon fest und sind wichtig genug, in unserem Zusammenhang gebührend hervorgehoben zu werden.

Das durch die Qumranfragmente repräsentierte "astronomische Buch" besteht größtenteils aus Tabellen, die für jeden einzelnen Tag des Jahres Sonnenstand und Mondphasen angeben, außerdem für Sonne und Mond die "Tore" im Osten und Westen, die sie jeweils für ihren "Aufgang" und "Untergang" benutzen; das Rahmenwerk dieser Tabellen bilden allgemeinere Ausführungen zu Kosmologie und Ethik[29]. Zugrunde gelegt wird ein Sonnenjahr von 364 Tagen[30], ein Kalender also, an dem sich später auch die Qumrangemeinde orientiert hat, dessen praktische Anwendung aber durch dieses Werk bereits für das 3., wenn nicht gar für das 4. Jh. v. Chr. nachweisbar wird. Dabei zeigen inhaltliche Implikationen dieses "astronomischen Buches", daß es wahrscheinlich nicht aus Judäa stammt, sondern aus Samaria[31].

Der Name Henochs ist in den bislang von J. T. Milik edierten Fragmenten dieses Werks nicht belegt. Doch gibt es anderweitige Quellenstoffe, die J. T. Milik herangezogen und ausgewertet hat, die Henoch als Vater der Astronomie werten und die sein Wissen darauf zurückführen, daß Engel es ihm offenbart haben[32]. Wenn die noch unedierten Fragmente diesen

---

[23] *Ibid.*, 25–28, 35f.   [24] *Ibid.*, 23f., 31.   [25] *Ibid.*, 9f., 64–68.

[26] *Ibid.*, 8, 273, 274f.   [27] *Ibid.*, 273–297.   [28] *Ibid.*, 7, 273.

[29] *Ibid.*, 274ff. – Aus den Anfangspartien des Werkes stammen die Fragmente von 4Q HenAstr[a], aus den Abschlußpartien die von 4Q HenAstr[d].

[30] Milik 1976, 274f., bes. 282f.   [31] *Ibid.*, 9f., 64–68.

[32] *Ibid.*, 8–22, 275. Besonders wichtig: Jub 4, 17 (*ibid.*, 11f.).

Konnex verifizieren, dann dürfte folgendes deutlich werden: *Stofflich* ist das "astronomische Buch" der Henoch-Literatur im Kern wahrscheinlich ein *Handbuch* für den täglichen Gebrauch samaritanischer Priester gewesen, dessen *Zweck* die *Sicherung der kultischen Ordnung* war. Zur *Legitimation* dieser neuen Kalenderordnung mit ihrem Sonnenjahr von 364 Tagen, die über die von der Thora her zentrale Orientierung an den Mondphasen dominieren sollte, berief man sich auf entsprechendes *"Himmelswissen"*, das dem Henoch durch Engel "offenbart" worden war. So entstand die erste jüdische *"Apokalypse"*[33], und ihr Kern war priesterliches Kalenderwissen.

In wünschenswerter Deutlichkeit verrät dabei das "astronomische Buch" des Henoch, warum es die Behandlung seines Gegenstandes als "Apokalypse" gestaltet, ja vielleicht darüber hinaus, wo die Wurzel der Entstehung von "Apokalypsen" im Judentum überhaupt zu suchen ist. Es handelt sich dabei um einen "historischen Ort", der in diesem Zusammenhang noch so gut wie unbeachtet geblieben ist, um eine Problemstellung, die man bei der Erforschung der Apokalyptik bislang eher als "Randproblem" und vor allem im Zusammenhang mit der meist pseudonymen Verfasserschaft jüdischer Apokalypsen diskutiert hat, der aber wahrscheinlich fundamentale Bedeutung für das Phänomen "Apokalyptik" zukommt: Das *Autoritätsproblem*.

Die religiöse Zentralautorität des nachexilischen Judentums ist spätestens vom 4. Jh. v. Chr. an der Pentateuch, die Thora. Alles, was im religiösen Bereich Anspruch auf Geltung erhebt, muß in der Thora vorgegeben sein oder sich aus der Thora ableiten lassen. Nichts kann Geltung haben und religiös anerkannt werden, was der Thora grundsätzlich fremd ist oder gar in eklatantem Widerspruch zu ihr steht.

Wer diese Sachlage nicht zu akzeptieren bereit war, schloß sich selbst aus der Gemeinschaft des Judentums aus. Wer nicht auf dem Boden der Thora stand, war kein Jude. Wer "Neuerungen" einführen wollte, mußte den Nachweis erbringen, daß sie "thoragemäß" waren, d. h. mit Geist und Buchstaben der Thora vereinbar und gegebenenfalls aus dieser "ableitbar". Deshalb hat selbst ein Philo Alexandrinus noch seine philosophischen Werke durchweg als "Thoraauslegung" gestaltet. Und nur von dieser Voraussetzung her wird die große Bedeutung und der hohe Rang der "Schriftgelehrten" im Judentum verständlich.

Die Thora galt dabei nicht nur als die *zentrale*, sondern auch als die *ausschließliche* Quelle des "Gotteswillens", den Gott dem Mose auf dem Sinai "geoffenbart" hatte. Sollte etwas Darüberhinausgehendes im religiö-

---

[33] J. T. Milik hat das "astronomische Buch" der Henoch-Literatur noch nicht als "Apokalypse" klassifiziert, hält es aber bereits für "the oldest Jewish document attributed to Enoch" (*ibid.*, 8). Dazu Stone 1978, 483–488; Harrington 1980, 151.

sen Bereich Geltung haben, so bedurfte es dafür einer erneuten, "ergänzenden" Offenbarung Gottes. Allein Gott selbst bzw. "der Himmel" oder als seine Organe "die Engel" besaßen die dafür erforderliche Autorität.

Diese Sachverhalte sind allgemein anerkannt, wenn auch im Zusammenhang der Apokalyptikforschung nicht von zentraler Bedeutung für das allgemeine Bewußtsein[34]. Ich will nun versuchen, ihre Relevanz für das Zustandekommen des "astronomischen Buches" des Henoch als – vielleicht erste jüdische – Apokalypse plausibel zu machen.

Grundlage aller kalendarischen Ordnung des nachexilischen Judentums war der Mondzyklus. Ebenso hatte sich das alte Israel orientiert, und dementsprechend setzt auch die Thora ganz selbstverständlich und in vielfältiger Hinsicht einen solchen "Mondkalender" voraus[35].

Wollte man diese Grundorientierung aufgeben zugunsten einer neuen Orientierung am Sonnenzyklus, den traditionellen "Mondkalender" ersetzen durch einen festen "Sonnenkalender" mit jährlich 52 kompletten Wochen bzw. 364 Tagen pro Jahr, dann konnte dies auch die kühnste Thora-Exegese nicht als mit deren Grundorientierung übereinstimmend erweisen. Kein Jude, auch nicht ein amtierender Hohepriester besaß die Autorität, die für die Einführung eines solchen neuen Kalenders erforderlich war. Nur Gott selbst konnte noch eine solche Neuerung einführen, und ein besonders geeignetes Mittel dafür war eine "Offenbarung".

Wenn Gott sich dabei als "Offenbarungsmittler" nicht einen Zeitgenossen des nachexilischen Judentums, sondern ausgerechnet Henoch erwählte, dann implizierte diese Personenwahl, daß dieser "neue" Kalender von Gott her betrachtet schon "gegeben" war, als er sich dem Mose auf dem Sinai offenbarte, also keine nachträgliche "Änderung" des Gotteswillens darstellen kann, sondern – auf eine dem Mose noch "verborgene" Weise – thorakonform sein muß; denn Henoch lebte lange vor Mose.

Wie man die so entstehenden "Widersprüche" zwischen dem "Sonnenkalender" und der Mondorientierung in der Thora letztlich aufzulösen hat, bleibt dann freilich gutenteils Gottes "Geheimnis". Das aber ist eine theologische Kategorie, mit der das nachexilische Judentum zunehmend zu arbeiten gelernt hat, bedeutet also keine Irritation im Grundsätzlichen. Dabei ist es letztlich unerheblich, ob und wieweit man durch entsprechende "Thora-Exegese" einen "Ausgleich" herbeiführt, wie es auf seine Weise z. B. der Autor des Jubiläen-Buches unternommen hat: Entscheidend ist die Sanktionierung des "neuen Prinzips" durch Gott selbst, die

---

[34] Analog argumentieren jetzt allerdings Gruenwald 1980, besonders 3–5, und Hellholm 1980, 191 mit Hinweis auf Vielhauer 1975, 522 und andere.
[35] Siehe dazu Larsson 1973.

Verstehensmöglichkeit des Menschen hingegen eine durchaus "nachrangige" Angelegenheit[36].

So führen uns die Qumran-Fragmente der ursprünglichen Gestalt des "astronomischen" Henoch-Buches nicht nur zeitlich in die Anfänge der jüdischen Apokalyptik. Sondern sie lassen uns darüber hinaus erkennen, wo die eigentlichen Beweggründe für die Entstehung "apokalyptischer Literatur" im Judentum liegen, unabhängig davon, ob bereits vorhandene außerjüdische "Apokalypsen" dafür ein Modell geliefert haben oder ein genuin jüdischer Vorgang zu konstatieren sein sollte. Die Autorität Gottes selbst, "himmlisches Wissen" und dessen "Offenbarung" in Form eines "Buches" sind hier die Konstituenda von "Apokalyptik", was auch immer Gegenstand und Inhalt der "neuen Offenbarung" sein mag, in unserem Fall ein neuer Kalender mit allen seinen detailliert dargelegten Konsequenzen und Implikationen[37].

Die Frage nach dem "Sitz im Leben" *dieser* Apokalypse stellt dann nicht mehr vor die Alternative "Kult" oder "Weisheit", sondern ist eindeutig zu beantworten mit "kultischer Weisheit" oder "Kultwissenschaft". An spezifische Qumrantexte zu erinnern ist in diesem Zusammenhang nur unter dem Aspekt, daß sie unser Wissen um die Vorstellung von der Gemeinschaft mit Engeln im irdischen Kult, und das heißt schwerpunktmäßig im Tempelkult, in erfreulicher Weise bereichert haben[38]. Andererseits zeigt sich mit aller Deutlichkeit, daß jüdische "Apokalyptik" in ihren Anfängen mit Prophetie, aber auch mit Eschatologie überhaupt nichts zu tun hatte, sondern allein durch die Aspekte "göttliche Autorität" und "Himmelswissen" konstituiert worden ist[39].

---

[36] Zum Ausgleichsversuch zwischen Sonnenkalender und Thora durch den Autor des "astronomischen Buches" der Henoch-Literatur siehe Milik 1976, 282 f.

[37] Eine alternative Darstellungsmöglichkeit hat der – m. E. ebenfalls dem 4. oder 3. Jh. v. Chr. einzuordnende – Autor der "Tempelrolle" aus den Qumranfunden gewählt: Er hat ein "6. Buch der Thora" verfaßt, und da Gottes Offenbarung durch Mose nun einmal abgeschlossen vorlag (1.–5. Buch der Thora), läßt er Gott selbst in direkter Rede zu Wort kommen. Daß man im Falle des "astronomischen Buches" nicht analog vorgegangen ist, kann einerseits in der Scheu begründet sein, solch ein "6. Buch der Thora" anzufertigen, andererseits im Gegenstand dieses Werkes, da die "Astronomie" in spezifischer Weise "Himmelswissen" darstellt und insofern von sich aus die Disposition impliziert, "himmlisch geoffenbart" zu werden.

[38] Vgl. z. B. Nötscher 1957, 305–315; H.-W. Kuhn 1966, 66–72; Klinzing 1971, 125–130; Schäfer 1975, 33–40.

[39] Weder formgeschichtlich noch traditionsgeschichtlich steht das "astronomische Buch" der Henoch-Literatur nach allem, was sich darüber bislang feststellen läßt, in irgendeinem Konnex zur *"Prophetie"*. Die "Prophetie" scheidet deshalb nicht nur als möglicher "Sitz im Leben" für dieses Werk aus, sondern darüber hinaus generell als "Sitz im Leben" für die Anfänge der jüdischen "Apokalyptik".
Das gleiche gilt im Falle der *"Eschatologie"*: Die Einführung des (neuen) "Sonnenkalenders" wird nicht "heilsgeschichtlich" begründet oder als Implikat der "Endzeit" bzw. einer künftigen "Heilszeit" betrachtet, sondern empfiehlt sich aus "wissenschaftlichen" Gründen wegen

3.1.1.5. Was die *Henoch-Literatur* insgesamt anbetrifft, so zeigen die Qumranfunde somit, daß von den 5 Büchern des äthHen 2 Bücher ("astronomisches" und "angelologisches" Buch) sicher älter sind als die Qumrangemeinde, ein 3. Buch, das der "Bilderreden", unabhängig von ihr entstand. Das in der Qumrangemeinde dem Henoch-Komplex integrierte "Giganten-Buch" fehlt im äthHen, der die "Bilderreden" aufgenommen hat. Von dem "astronomischen" Buch, das in den Qumranhandschriften stets als eigenständiges Werk auftritt, bietet äthHen nur eine sekundäre Kurzfassung.

Aus diesen Befunden folgt, daß der "Henoch-Pentateuch" im äthHen sicher keine Komposition der Qumrangemeinde ist, wahrscheinlich überhaupt nur solche Henoch-Schriften in sich vereint hat, die nicht der Qumrangemeinde entstammen. Da das 4. und das 5. Buch des äthHen, das "Geschichtsbuch" (83–90) und das "paränethische" Buch (91–107) mit seiner "Zehn-Wochen-Apokalypse" (93,3–10 + 91,11–17), auch inhaltlich keine sonderliche Affinität zu den spezifischen Qumrantexten zeigen, wird man trotz ihres Vorhandenseins in der Qumranbibliothek annehmen dürfen, daß auch diese Henoch-Bücher außerhalb der Qumrangemeinde entstanden sind. Da nach Auskunft des Flavius-Josephus "Engellehren" ohnehin zum "Arkanum" der "Essener" gehörten[40], wird man von vornherein auch gar nicht erwarten dürfen, im äthHen ein Henoch-Buch vorzufinden, das die Qumrangemeinde selbst geschaffen hätte. Allenfalls das "Giganten-Buch" wird man künftig noch als möglicherweise der Qumrangemeinde entstammend betrachten dürfen[41].

---

der prinzipiellen Vorteile einer Orientierung am Sonnenjahr und wegen der hochgradigen "Stimmigkeit" dieses Kalendersystems im Verhältnis zu den Gegebenheiten der jüdischen Wochenzyklen und Festtermine (vgl. allgemein Milik 1959, 170–173, und Milik 1976, 274f., 278, 282f., bes. *ibid.*, 14 unten).

Wir haben mit dieser "Apokalypse" also ein wissenschaftliches Werk vor uns, das in spezifischer Weise von der *"Weisheit"* des Judentums und des Zwei-Strom-Landes gespeist worden ist (vgl. Milik 1976, 8f., 13–18, bes. 13 oben).

Diese Befunde bestätigen eine Auffassung der Sachverhalte, die in neuerer Zeit vor allem durch von Rad 1960, 314–321, erweitert von Rad 1965, 315–330, herausgearbeitet wurde, aber noch längst nicht hinreichend wirksam geworden ist (vgl. dazu Koch 1970, 40–45).

[40] Flavius Josephus, Bell II, 142 (8,7).

[41] Interessant ist die Beobachtung Miliks, daß es unter den Henoch-Handschriften aus den Qumranfunden nur relativ wenige "in the beautiful 'classical' writing of the Herodian era" bzw. aus den letzten 100 Jahren des Bestehens der Qumrangemeinde gibt, nämlich außer 1 Handschrift des "astronomischen Buches" (4Q HenAstr^b) nur noch "some copies of the Book of Giants" (*ibid.*, 7). Hierin wird eine länger andauernde Beliebtheit dieses Werkes im Vergleich mit den übrigen Teilen der Henoch-Literatur in der Qumrangemeinde erkennbar, die durchaus damit zusammenhängen mag, daß allein das "Giganten-Buch" ein Eigenprodukt dieser Gemeinde gewesen ist. Doch wird man mit einem endgültigen Urteil besser noch zuwarten, bis J. T. Milik alle erhaltenen Fragmente des "Giganten-Buches" aus den Qumranfunden einmal veröffentlicht haben wird.

3.1.2. Das Jubiläen-Buch

Durch mindestens 11 Kopien in den Qumranfunden repräsentiert und in einem aus der Anfangszeit der Qumrangemeinde stammenden Gesetzescorpus der "Damaskusschriften" (fragmentarisch erhalten als CD IX–XVI) als Traditionsautorität zitiert worden[42] ist das "Jubiläen-Buch", ein in der Qumrangemeinde offensichtlich beliebtes Werk. In unseren Zusammenhang gehört es, weil es seine Stoffe unter dem Gesichtspunkt darbietet, sie seien dem Mose durch den "Engel des Angesichts" von Gott "offenbart" worden, weshalb dieses Werk den Apokalypsen zuzurechnen ist.

Die bereits edierten Fragmente von 5 Kopien des "Jubiläen-Buches" aus den Qumranfunden, und zwar aus den Höhlen 1Q, 2Q und 11Q[43], stammen paläographisch sämtlich aus "herodianischer" Zeit. 6 weitere Handschriften aus Höhle 4Q sind – ebenso wie ein Jubiläen-Fragment aus den Masada-Funden – noch immer unediert[44], so daß man nicht weiß, ob eine dieser Handschriften paläographisch älter ist als das Entstehungsdatum des Gesetzescorpus der "Damaskusschriften" (CD IX–XVI), bislang unser ältester Zeuge.

Da das "Jubiläen-Buch" den Sonnenkalender mit 364 Tagen im Jahr voraussetzt und bewußt für dessen Geltung eintrat, haben manche Forscher es nach den Qumranfunden als ein spezifisches Werk der Qumrangemeinde betrachtet. Die neuen Daten zum "astronomischen Buch" der Henoch-Literatur[45] zeigen aber, daß dieser Kalender allein kein hinreichender Grund für die Zuweisung eines Werkes zur Qumrangemeinde sein kann. Da die bislang edierten Jubiläen-Fragmente noch sehr dürftig sind, wird man für weitergehende Urteile die Edition der 4Q-Fragmente abwarten müssen in der Hoffnung, daß sie uns hinreichende Einblicke gewähren in die Textgeschichte dieses Werkes und sich daraus Schlußfolgerungen ziehen lassen hinsichtlich des Abfassungsdatums.

Wichtig ist, daß Jub 4,17–22 mindestens zwei, wenn nicht drei Henoch-Bücher bereits kennt, andere offensichtlich noch nicht, so daß die endgültige Datierung der Entstehung des "Jubiläen-Buches" später einmal aus der präzisen Datierung der einzelnen Henoch-Bücher folgen wird[46]. J. T. Miliks Datierung der "Jubiläen" um 128/125 v. Chr.[47] erscheint mir als reichlich spät, ein Datum in der 1. Hälfte des 2. Jh. v. Chr. als näherliegend.

---

[42] CD XVI, 3f.

[43] Editionen: 1Q **17** und **18** in DJD I (1955), 82–84; 2Q **19** und **20** in DJDJ III (1962), 77–79; 11Q Jub: van der Woude 1971.

[44] Fitzmyer 1975, 30 und 40.

[45] Oben § 3.1.1.4.

[46] Vgl. auch das Fragment von 4Q **227** bei Milik 1976, 12.

[47] Milik 1976, 58 mit Anm. 1.

3.1.3. Die Daniel-Apokalypse

Die etwa 165/64 v. Chr. entstandene Daniel-Apokalypse ist unter den Qumranfunden durch mindestens 8 Handschriften repräsentiert, von denen 5 noch unediert sind[48]. Soweit bislang feststellbar, ist die Textfassung dieser Handschriften mit derjenigen des MT – von ganz geringfügigen Varianten abgesehen – identisch, wobei 1QDan[a][49] auch den Übergang vom Hebräischen zum Aramäischen in Dan 2,4 bietet.

Die spezifischen Qumrantexte kommen zwar der Exegese der Daniel-Apokalypse in mancherlei Hinsicht zugute, lassen aber zugleich deutlich erkennen, daß die Daniel-Apokalypse selbst kein Werk der Qumrangemeinde gewesen ist, sondern zu deren Traditionsliteratur gehörte. Auf einige Qumran-Fragmente, die uns Einblick in die literarische Vorgeschichte dieses Werkes gewähren, werde ich im weiteren Verlauf meines Beitrages noch zu sprechen kommen[50].

3.1.4. Zwischenbilanz

So zeigen mehrere Henoch-Bücher, das Jubiläen-Buch und die Daniel-Apokalypse, daß schon vor Entstehung der Qumrangemeinde[51] die Apokalyptik mit einer breiten und vielgestaltigen Literatur im palästinischen Judentum vorhanden war.

Die Hauptbedeutung der Qumranfunde für diesen Teil ist darin zu sehen, daß sie völlig neue Einblicke in die Entstehung der Henoch-Literatur und damit in die Anfänge der jüdischen Apokalyptik gewähren. In der weiteren Diskussion über die "Apokalyptik" dürfte eine Schlüsselrolle dem "astronomischen Buch" der Henoch-Literatur zukommen, sobald J. T. Milik dessen Qumran-Fragmente endlich vollständig ediert haben wird. Fast ebenso bedeutsam ist nunmehr das "angelologische Buch". Dabei wird es besonders wichtig sein, festzustellen, ob und wie die traditionelle Eschatologie mit ihrem spezifischen Geschichtsdenken bereits in die ursprüngliche Fassung des "astronomischen Buches" Eingang gefunden hat und wie ihre Funktion im "angelologischen Buch" zu bewerten ist.

---

[48] Im einzelnen Fitzmyer 1975, 13 und 21.

[49] Text: DJD I (1955), 150; Abbildung: Trever 1965, Plate V. Paläographische Daten von 1Q Dan[a]: "book-hand", Ende der "herodianischen" Zeit (*ibid.*, 333f.).

[50] Unten § 3.2.3.3.

[51] Die "Qumrangemeinde" ist jedenfalls einerseits nach dem Regierungsantritt Antiochus' IV. Epiphanes (175 v. Chr.) entstanden, andererseits längere Zeit vor dem Ende des 2. Jh. v. Chr. (= paläographisches Datum von 1Q S, einer bereits mehrfach redigierten "Ordnung" dieser Gemeinde), wahrscheinlich um die Mitte des 2. Jh. v. Chr. Ich selbst betrachte den Amtsantritt des Makkabäers Jonathan als Hoherpriester zu Jerusalem im Jahre 153/52 v. Chr. als den Auslösungsfaktor für die Bildung dieser "Gemeinde"; siehe Stegemann 1971, 198–252.

3.2. Die spezifische Qumranliteratur

Zur spezifischen Qumranliteratur rechnet man gern alle Schriften, von denen man Exemplare in den Qumranhöhlen gefunden hat, sofern sie nicht zugleich zum Kanon des Alten Testaments im Umfang der Septuaginta gehören.

Bereits meine Ausführungen zu Henoch und Jubiläen haben gezeigt, daß man diese beliebte Betrachtungsweise erheblich einschränken muß. Als "spezifische Qumrantexte" können zunächst nur solche Werke aus den Qumranfunden gelten, die der Gestalt des "Lehrers der Gerechtigkeit" eine autoritative Funktion beimessen, die die spezifische Ordnung der Qumrangemeinde kennen, auf andere Weise deren Sonderstellung im Rahmen des Judentums reflektieren oder wegen ihres formalen oder terminologischen Konnexes mit solchen Schriften diesen *notwendigerweise* zuzuordnen sind.

Dies gilt vor allem für die "pescharim", für die beiden "Damaskusschriften" CD I–VIII/XIX–XX und CD IX–XVI, für die "Gemeinschaftsregel" 1Q S mit ihren beiden Annexen 1Q Sa und 1 Q Sb, für die "Hodajot", für thematische Midraschim wie 4Q Florilegium und 11Q Melchisedeq sowie für manche weitere Schrift. Im Einzelfall bleibt freilich selbst bei diesen Schriften noch immer die Möglichkeit bestehen, daß einzelne ihrer Bestandteile Rezeption älterer Literatur sind, ohne daß diese uns noch eigenständig greifbar sein müßte.

Auf der anderen Seite stehen zahlreiche Schriften aus den Qumranfunden, die zwar "außerbiblisch" sind, aber nicht notwendigerweise zugleich als Produkte der Qumrangemeinde betrachtet werden müssen. Dazu rechne ich z. B. die nichtkanonischen Hymnen in mehreren Psalmen-Handschriften, die Gebetssammlung 4Q Dibre ham-meʾoroth, das Genesis-Apokryphon aus Höhle 1Q, die "Tempelrolle" und viele jener Schriften, von denen nur noch geringe Fragmente erhalten sind, z. B. Weisheitstexte, Hymnen und manche der sogenannten "Paraphrasen" biblischer Bücher, insbesondere solche des Pentateuch[52].

Dazwischen gibt es eine breite "Grauzone" solcher Schriften, bei denen sich kaum feststellen läßt, ob sie Eigenprodukte der Qumrangemeinde waren oder lediglich in deren Bibliothek standen, meist deshalb, weil die uns erhaltenen Fragmente davon zu gering sind, um eine Entscheidung zuzulassen. In anderen Fällen ist die Sachlage kompliziert, beispielsweise im Falle der "Kriegsregel" 1Q M, die vermutlich bereits vor Entstehung der Qumrangemeinde literarisch konzipiert, dann aber von der Qumrangemeinde überarbeitet und somit auch der Sache nach von ihr adaptiert

---

[52] Auf Einzelbegründungen für diese Urteile muß ich in diesem Zusammenhang leider verzichten, zumal keines dieser Werke ernsthaft als "Apokalypse" zu klassifizieren ist.

wurde[53]: Wieweit darf man auch das, was in diesem Rahmen "übernommen" wurde, als für die Qumrangemeinde charakteristisch gelten lassen?

3.2.1. *Werke der Qumranliteratur, die in der Forschung der "Apokalyptik" zugeordnet werden*

Für die Frage nach der Bedeutung der Qumranfunde für die Apokalyptik-Forschung ist die skizzierte Problematik insofern relevant, als die meisten, wenn nicht alle derjenigen "spezifischen Qumrantexte", die man zu den Apokalypsen rechnen könnte, in die genannte "Grauzone" gehören, so daß man für ihr Verständnis weder davon ausgehen kann, sie seien unter Voraussetzung spezifischer Qumrananschauungen zu interpretieren, noch auch einfach davon, es handele sich um ältere Literatur, die von der Qumrangemeinde lediglich benutzt worden ist.

In einem Beitrag in der "Revue de Qumrân" ist J. Carmignac den Fragen nachgegangen, was denn "Apokalyptik" überhaupt sei und wie es um ihre Verwendung "in Qumran" tatsächlich stehe[54]. Er kommt dabei zu Ergebnissen, die meinen eigenen Auffassungen sehr weitgehend entsprechen, so daß ich es mir hier ersparen kann, von ihm Erarbeitetes zu wiederholen. Statt dessen will ich seine Darlegungen knapp charakterisieren und anschließend versuchen, sie in einzelnen Punkten noch näher zu erläutern.

In dem genannten Beitrag setzt J. Carmignac ein mit einer umfassenden Bibliographie zur "Apokalyptik"[55] und wertet die Literatur dann aus unter dem Aspekt, welche Vorstellungen den einzelnen Autoren jeweils als charakteristisch für die "Apokalyptik" gelten und welche Grundauffassungen von "Apokalyptik" in dieser Literatur vorkommen[56]. In kritischer Auseinandersetzung mit dem Vorgefundenen bringt er sodann eine eigene Definition von "Apokalyptik"[57], wobei sein Hauptkriterium der Befund der beiden biblischen Apokalypsen ist, der des Daniel-Buches und der Johannes-Offenbarung. So kommt er zu einem literarisch orientierten Begriff von "Apokalyptik", der jenem sehr nahekommt, den ich selbst eingangs dargelegt habe.

Anschließend behandelt J. Carmignac sämtliche nichtbiblischen Texte aus den Qumranfunden, die in der von ihm gesichteten Literatur als "apokalyptisch" klassifiziert worden sind, insgesamt 17 Positionen[58]. Dabei handelt es sich teilweise um ganze Gattungen wie "pescharim" oder "Gemeindeordnungen", die er jeweils zu einer Position zusammengefaßt

---

[53] Siehe dazu Hunzinger 1957; von der Osten-Sacken 1969, 28–115.
[54] Carmignac 1979. Dankenswerterweise hat mir der Autor noch vor dem Kolloquium in Uppsala die Druckfahnen seines im September 1979 erschienenen Beitrages zugesandt.
[55] Carmignac 1979, 3–6.
[56] *Ibid.*, 7–19.   [57] *Ibid.*, 20–21.   [58] *Ibid.*, 22–32.

hat, teilweise um Einzelschriften wie die "Hodajot" oder die "Kriegsregel", teilweise um "Sammelwerke" wie die Henoch-Literatur. Sein Hauptkriterium bei der Frage, ob es sich im Einzelfall um eine Apokalypse handelt oder nicht, ist jeweils die Feststellung, ob die behandelte Schrift oder Textgattung in spezifischer Weise "himmlisches Geheimwissen" "offenbaren" will oder nicht. Das Ergebnis seines Durchgangs[59], dem ich fast gänzlich zustimmen kann, ist folgendes:

Aus der Diskussion um "Apokalyptik" ausscheiden müssen sämtliche "pescharim" und "Gemeindeordnungen", die "Segenssprüche" 1Q Sb, die "Testimoniensammlung" 4Q **175**, die "Kriegsregel", das sogenannte "Mysterienbuch" 1Q **27**, der als "Patriarchal Blessings" bezeichnete Midrasch aus 4Q, der "Melchisedeq"-Midrasch aus 11Q und die "Tempelrolle", ebenso im wesentlichen die "Hodajot" und das "Genesis-Apokryphon" aus 1Q, in denen nach J. Carmignac allenfalls einzelne Passagen als "apokalyptische Stoffe" betrachtet werden können.

Als "Apokalypsen" zu betrachten seien außer den bereits behandelten Henoch-Schriften und dem Jubiläen-Buch allenfalls ein Werk über das "Neue Jerusalem", die von J. Strugnell teilweise publizierte "Engelliturgie", das "Nabonid-Gebet" in Verbindung mit Pseudo-Daniel, die "'Amram-Visionen" aus 4Q sowie einzelne Passagen in den "Hodajot" und im "Genesis-Apokryphon".

Dieses Ergebnis muß alle diejenigen ernüchtern, die sich daran gewöhnt haben, die Qumrangemeinde als einen Hort der "Apokalyptik" zu betrachten[60].

3.2.2. Aus der künftigen Diskussion um "Apokalyptik" auszuschließende Werke der Qumranliteratur

Bevor ich mich aber denjenigen Werken aus den Qumranfunden zuwende, bei denen man auch weiterhin erwägen kann, daß es sich um "apokalyptische" Literatur handelt, will ich mich zunächst noch kurz zu jenen Schriften aus diesem Fundkomplex äußern, die aus der weiteren Diskussion um "Apokalyptik" ausscheiden müssen[61].

---

[59] *Ibid.*, 32. – In einem Postskriptum (*ibid.*, 33) verweist Carmignac auf die hohe sachliche Übereinstimmung seiner Position mit den Auffassungen von J. J. Collins 1979 und klassifiziert seinen eigenen Qumran-Beitrag als "en partie comme un complément aux travaux de J. J. Collins et de son équipe" (*ibid.*, 33). Für meinen eigenen Beitrag kann ich mich diesem Urteil weitgehend anschließen, gehe aber insbesondere mit meiner Analyse der Henoch-Befunde und deren Auswertung für die Anfänge der jüdischen Apokalyptik über die Positionen von J. J. Collins und J. Carmignac hinaus.

[60] Im Rahmen dieser Auffassung wird die Qumrangemeinde gelegentlich sogar als "apokalyptische Bewegung" eingestuft, ein Fehlurteil, dem durch die Beiträge von J. Carmignac und von mir endgültig der Nährboden entzogen werden soll.

[61] Für die Publikationsorte und sonstige Textwiedergaben der im folgenden genannten Qumrantexte sei hier pauschal verwiesen auf Fitzmyer 1975, 14–39, und Lohse 1971.

3.2.2.1. Die "pescharim", "Midraschim", "Damaskusschrift", "Kriegsregel" etc.

Die *"pescharim"* sind literarischer Ausdruck eines bestimmten eschatologischen Geschichtsverständnisses, das die Erfüllung der Weissagungen der biblischen Propheten im Zusammenhang mit der Geschichte der Qumrangemeinde eintreten sieht. Entsprechend sind auch die thematisch orientierten *"eschatologischen Midraschim"* wie 4Q Florilegium, 4Q Patriarchal Blessing, 11Q Melchisedeq und einzelne Abschnitte in solchen Werken wie der *"Damaskusschrift"* zu werten. In allen diesen Fällen haben wir es mit "Eschatologie" zu tun, nicht mit "Apokalyptik". Das gilt auch für die *"Kriegsregel"*, die nichts anderes ist als eine "Ordnung" für den bevorstehenden eschatologischen Kampf, für dessen Vorbereitung und Verlauf, wobei alle für die Darstellung wesentlichen Elemente aus einem bestimmten Geschichtsbild und aus der Schriftexegese resultieren: In keiner Weise wird "himmlisches Offenbarungswissen" beansprucht, kein Engel tritt auf als Bote oder Deuter, keine "Vision" erschließt das Kommende[62].

Als Konkretion von "Eschatologie", nicht als Apokalyptik wird man aber auch jenen Passus in *1Q Hodajot III, 24–36*[63] werten müssen, der die Schrecknisse schildert, denen die Welt anheimfällt, wenn Gott sein radikales Vernichtungsgericht an den Frevlern vollzieht: Niemand und nichts bleibt verschont. Aber wie alles verläuft, wird dem Frommen nicht als "Geheimwissen" himmlisch offenbart, sondern von ihm selbst dargestellt als von einem, der Gottes Allmacht kennt und preist und der dessen gewiß ist, daß selbst die Schrecken der Endzeit ihm letztlich nichts werden anhaben können. Die Stoffe und Motive dieser Darstellung stammen aus der biblischen Tradition, nicht aus einer "Vision"[64].

3.2.2.2. Das "Genesis-Apokryphon"

Die Tatsache, daß im "Genesis-Apokryphon" einzelne "Visionen" geschildert werden, macht – wie J. Carmignac zu Recht feststellt – das Gesamtwerk nicht zu einer "Apokalypse"[65]. Doch ist die "Vision" als

---

[62] Die Beliebtheit der Klassifizierung der "Kriegsregel" als "apokalyptisches Werk" resultiert aus der naiven Auffassung, eine Schrift, die ausschließlich "Endzeit-Dinge" behandelt, müsse notwendigerweise "apokalyptisch" sein. Hier werden die Möglichkeiten der "Eschatologie" unterschätzt, nicht nur Motive und Vorstellungskomplexe (z. B. Endgericht, messianische Erwartungen) hervorzubringen, sondern auch literarisch eigenständige Werke wie z. B. die "Kriegsregel".

[63] Lohse 1971, 122 f.

[64] Im Falle dieses Hymnus resultiert seine beliebte Klassifizierung als "apokalyptisch" allein aus der Tatsache, daß hier ein "Weltuntergang" geschildert wird, was nach Auffassung vieler Autoren als ein proprium von "Apokalyptik" zu gelten hat. So verbreitet diese Thematik auch immer in Apokalypsen sein mag, so ist sie doch andererseits nicht auf diese beschränkt und kann deshalb nicht als ein "proprium" der Apokalyptik anerkannt werden.

[65] Carmignac 1979, 29 und 32.

Darstellungsmittel durchaus nicht in spezifischer Weise charakteristisch nur für "Apokalypsen", sondern darüber hinaus in Geschichtsdarstellungen und in prophetischer Literatur durchaus üblich. Deshalb sollte man auch das "Genesis-Apokryphon" aus der weiteren Diskussion um "Apokalyptik" gänzlich heraushalten.

3.2.2.3. Die "Tempelrolle"

Was schließlich die "Tempelrolle" anbetrifft, so wird nach allem, was sich trotz der relativ stark zerstörten Anfangspartien dieser Handschrift noch feststellen läßt, der Neubau des Tempels zu Jerusalem nicht "himmlisch offenbart", nicht durch "visionäre Schau" vermittelt, sondern ganz im Stile der Thora göttlicherseits angeordnet[66]. Nicht einmal die Eschatologie spielt hier eine Rolle. Denn es geht in diesem Werk nicht um einen "endzeitlichen" Tempel[66a], sondern einfach darum, bis ins letzte Detail festzulegen, wie der Jerusalemer Tempel beschaffen sein muß, wenn er in jeder Hinsicht dem Gotteswillen entsprechen soll. Der Autor dieses Werkes legt einen ganz konkreten Bauplan vor, von dem er offenbar erwartet, daß er eines Tages architektonisch realisiert werden muß. Daß seine Vorstellungen vom technisch Machbaren dabei für seine Zeit teilweise reichlich utopisch sind, macht sein Werk noch längst nicht zu einer "Apokalypse": Was dem Willen Gottes entspricht, muß realisierbar sein und kann insofern nicht als "utopisch" gelten. Als "Quellen" für die Feststellung des göttlichen Willens gelten dabei ausschließlich Bestimmungen der Thora, Anweisungen Gottes für den Bau des davidisch-salomonischen Tempels und gelegentlich jene Gottesforderungen, die sich bezüglich des Tempels bei Ezechiel finden: Dies alles zu einem einheitlichen Bild zusammenzufügen und daraus die architektonischen Konsequenzen zu ziehen, das ist die Aufgabe, die sich der Autor der "Tempelrolle" gestellt hatte[67].

---

[66] Vgl. dazu oben §3.1.1.4. mit Anm. 37.

[66a] Ein solcher "endzeitlicher" Tempel wird in der Tempelrolle Kol. XXIX, 9f. ausdrücklich als künftiges Schöpfungswerk Gottes selbst(אברא!)genannt und ganz klar unterschieden von dem ansonsten in dieser Schrift dargestellten, von Menschen erbauten Tempel, der zwar bis zum Eschaton "ewige" Wohnstatt dieses Gottes sein soll (Kol. XXIX, 3–9), selbst aber nicht "eschatologisch" qualifiziert ist.

[67] Was hier am Beispiel des Themas "Tempel" vorgeführt wird, gilt entsprechend auch für die anderen Stoffe der "Tempelrolle", die sich mit dem Tempel selbst nur bis Kol. XIII,7 sowie ab Kol. XXX Ende/XXXI Anfang bis XLVII befaßt, ansonsten mit dem Festzyklus und zugehörigen Opfern (Kol. XIII,8 bis XXX Ende/XXXI Anfang) sowie mit vielerlei weiteren institutionellen und halachischen Angelegenheiten (Kol. XLVIII bis LXVI, wo diese – vielleicht unvollendet gebliebene – Handschrift die Textwiedergabe ihrer – möglicherweise weiterreichenden – Vorlage abgebrochen hat). Textübersetzung mit Anmerkungen und Einführung: Maier 1978.

Nur am Rande sei hier vermerkt, daß die ganze "Tempelrolle" keinerlei Anhaltspunkte dafür bietet, daß es sich um ein Werk der Qumrangemeinde handeln könnte[68]. Deren Kritik am Jerusalemer Tempelkult liegt auf einer völlig anderen Ebene als auf der architektonischen[69]; und sollte die "Tempelrolle" tatsächlich den Sonnenkalender mit 364 Tagen pro Jahr voraussetzen, wie Yigael Yadin meint[70], dann kann sie dennoch wesentlich älter sein als die Qumrangemeinde[71]. Bis zum Beweis des Gegenteils halte ich sie für ein Werk des 4. oder spätestens des 3. Jh. v. Chr., das von der Qumrangemeinde lediglich deshalb geschätzt wurde, weil sich der "Gotteswille" darin in mancher Hinsicht "eindeutig" darstellt, wo die sonstige Tradition diffus oder widersprüchlich erscheint. Aber eine solche Wertschätzung bedeutet noch lange nicht, daß sich die ganze Qumrangemeinde voll auf alle Forderungen der "Tempelrolle" hätte einlassen müssen. Tatsächlich sind im Bereich der Bestimmungen für einzelne Feste und in der Halacha die Diskrepanzen gegenüber den spezifischen Qumrantexten größer als deren Übereinstimmungen mit der "Tempelrolle"[72]. Doch muß ich hier auf alle Einzelheiten verzichten und kann mich übereinstimmend mit J. Carmignac darauf beschränken, festzustellen, daß die "Tempelrolle" mit "Apokalyptik" nicht das mindeste zu tun hat.

---

[68] Dies wird von Yadin 1977 in seiner editio princeps der "Tempelrolle" mit großer Selbstverständlichkeit vorausgesetzt und im einzelnen immer wieder nachzuweisen versucht, entsprechend in der weiteren Literatur weitgehend übernommen. Erste Vorbehalte dagegen bereits bei Maier 1978, 11 f., der ansonsten Yadins Grundposition freilich noch teilt.

[69] Siehe dazu meine Ausführungen zur Eschatologie der Qumrangemeinde unten §3.4.

[70] Tatsächlich finden sich für den "Sonnenkalender" charakteristische Daten gern in Yadins Ergänzungen des fragmentarisch erhaltenen Textes der Tempelrolle, weniger im erhaltenen Textbestand (vgl. z. B. Kol. XIV,9). Mit hoher Wahrscheinlichkeit aus dem "Festzyklus" der Tempelrolle erschließbar ist lediglich, daß sie einen regelmäßigen Jahresbeginn mit dem Monat Nisan im Frühjahr voraussetzt, wofür sich im antiken Judentum aber durchaus auch auf der Basis des traditionellen "Mondkalenders" Analogien finden.

[71] Das beweist jetzt neben dem Jubiläen-Buch hinreichend eindeutig das "astronomische Buch" der Henoch-Literatur. Vgl. oben §3.1.1.4.

[72] Stofflich betrachtet erfüllt die Tempelrolle eine doppelte Funktion im Verhältnis zur Thora: 1. Sie gibt eine umfassende Orientierung für religiös bedeutsame Gegenstände, die im Pentateuch (noch) gar nicht oder nur ansatzweise behandelt worden sind (z. B. Tempelbau, Festzyklus, Königtum), ergänzt also die Thora der Sache nach. 2. Sie formuliert "Kompromisse" für Sachverhalte, zu denen sich divergierende Aussagen innerhalb des Pentateuch finden oder Befunde der weiteren autoritativen Traditionsliteratur ("Frühe Propheten", eventuell auch bereits das "Chronistische Geschichtswerk") in einem Spannungsverhältnis zum Pentateuch stehen (z. B. Rechte der Leviten, vielerlei halachische Bestimmungen). Besonders der zweite Aspekt mußte für alle "Schriftgelehrten" von Interesse sein, für die die gleiche literarische Traditionsbasis autoritative Bedeutung besaß wie für die Tempelrolle, auch wenn sie vielleicht von manchen der für diese selbst besonders wichtigen Dingen (z. B. Tempelbau, einige der ab Kol. XIX aufgeführten Feste, Königsgesetz) gar nichts hielten.

3.2.3. Werke, die vielleicht "Apokalypsen" und möglicherweise in der Qumrangemeinde entstanden sind

Wenden wir uns nunmehr den restlichen 4 Texten aus den Qumranfunden zu, bei denen auch J. Carmignac mit der Möglichkeit rechnet, daß es sich um "Apokalypsen" handelt, so wird auch in diesem Punkt das Ergebnis noch magerer sein als es die relativ geringe Anzahl bereits erwarten läßt. Die beiden Hauptgründe dafür sind die, daß es sich in keinem Fall eindeutig feststellen läßt, daß es sich um Schriften handelt, die spezifische Produkte der Qumrangemeinde sein *müßten*, und weiterhin der leidige Umstand, daß die erhaltenen Fragmente aller dieser 4 Schriften erst teilweise ediert sind und das bislang publizierte Material noch kein eindeutiges Urteil darüber erlaubt, ob wir es tatsächlich mit "Apokalypsen" zu tun haben.

3.2.3.1. Das "Neue Jerusalem"[73]

Mindestens 5 aramäischsprachige Handschriften aus den Qumranfunden stammen von einem bislang unbekannten Werk, dessen Gegenstand eine Beschreibung des "Neuen Jerusalem" ist, nämlich die sehr fragmentarischen Handschriften 1Q 32, 2Q 24 und 5Q 15[74] sowie zwei noch unedierte, z. T. wohl umfangreichere Handschriften aus 4Q und 11Q[75]. Soweit sich dies bislang feststellen läßt, wird in diesem Werk – ähnlich wie in Apk 21,2–22,5 – das von Gott im Himmel für die Endzeit vorbereitete "Neue Jerusalem" beschrieben in literarischer Abhängigkeit von Ez 40–48. Den "Apokalypsen" zuzurechnen wäre dieses Werk allein aufgrund des Umstandes, daß der Autor die "Schau" des "himmlischen Jerusalem" einem "Engel" verdankt, der ihn darin herumführt, so daß er die einzelnen Baulichkeiten und deren Maße kennenzulernen und dem Leser mitzuteilen vermag. Von eigentlichen "Visionen" wie in Ez 43,3 und Apk 21,2 findet sich in den bislang edierten Qumranfragmenten noch keine Spur, was aber an dem dürftigen Erhaltungszustand dieser Handschriften liegen könnte.

Paläographisch sind die 3 bislang edierten Handschriften dieses Werkes sämtlich "herodianisch", d. h. den Jahrzehnten um die Zeitenwende einzuordnen. Vom sprachlichen Befund her ist festzustellen, daß es sich um einen westaramäischen Dialekt handelt, den J. T. Milik als "wesentlich

---

[73] Dazu Carmignac 1979, 27 f.

[74] Ediert in DJD I (1955) 134 f., sowie DJDJ III (1962) 84–89 und 184–193.

[75] Einige Textzeilen der Handschrift aus Höhle 4Q sind bereits in DJDJ III (1962) 85 vorauspubliziert worden; im übrigen siehe zu dieser Handschrift *ibid.*, 184–193. Vorläufige Angaben zu der Handschrift aus Höhle 11Q samt Publikation eines Fragmentes davon: Jongeling 1970. Textwiedergabe aller bislang edierten Fragmente des Werkes vom "Neuen Jerusalem" aus den Qumranfunden: Fitzmyer and Harrington 1978, 46–65 (Nr. 6–9).

jünger" einstuft als den des Daniel-Buches[76]: Da dessen Autor sich aber um ein "antiquiertes" Sprachgewand bemüht hat, wird man diesem sprachgeschichtlichen Argument gegenüber reserviert bleiben müssen. Bezüge zu spezifischen Anschauungen der Qumrangemeinde finden sich in den bislang edierten Fragmenten nirgends. So wird man die weiteren Editionen abwarten müssen, bevor ein Urteil darüber möglich wird, ob es sich bei diesem Werk tatsächlich um eine in der Qumrangemeinde abgefaßte "Apokalypse" handelt.

3.2.3.2. Die "Engelliturgie"[77]

Von diesem Werk, dessen Originaltitel "Serek šîrôt ʿôlat haššabbāt" lautet und das in hebräischer Sprache abgefaßt worden ist, gibt es mindestens 4 Handschriften aus Höhle 4Q und eine Handschrift aus den Masada-Funden. Publiziert sind davon bislang nur 2 Fragmente aus 2 verschiedenen 4Q-Handschriften, 4Q Sl 39 und 4Q Sl 40[78].

Das erste dieser Fragmente, das J. Strugnell seiner Handschrift Nr. 39 entnommen hat, teilt Segenssprüche mit, die 7 Engel 7 Arten von "Frommen" zukommen lassen. Auf welche Weise der Autor von diesen "himmlischen" Benediktionen Kenntnis erlangt hat, läßt das edierte Fragment nicht erkennen. Immerhin wäre es gut vorstellbar, daß ihm eine "Vision" oder ein "Offenbarungsengel" dazu verholfen hätte, und jedenfalls handelt es sich um ein spezifisches "Himmelswissen", das hier mitgeteilt wird.

Das zweite dieser Fragmente aus J. Strugnells Handschrift Nr. 40 entstammt einer freien Neuschöpfung der Merkabah-Vision von Ez 1,1–28. Wenn auch die Rahmenpartien (noch?) fehlen, spricht immerhin nichts gegen die Annahme, daß dieser Teil der "Engelliturgie" ebenso wie sein Vorbild in Ez 1 den Charakter einer "Vision" hatte, insofern also dazu geeignet war, Bestandteil einer "Apokalypse" zu sein.

Wie eines Tages das Gesamtwerk der "Engelliturgie" zu klassifizieren sein wird, bleibt abzuwarten. Entscheidend dürfte sein, was von den Rahmenpartien erhalten ist. Das noch unedierte Masada-Fragment bietet offenbar nicht mehr als die Reste zweier Kolumnen mit dem Schluß des "Gesanges" am 5. Sabbath und dem Anfang dessen am 6. Sabbath[79]. Ob es sich um ein spezifisches Werk der Qumrangemeinde handelt, ist ebenfalls noch ungeklärt. Der Sonnenkalender von 364 Tagen im Jahr wird zwar vorausgesetzt[80]; aber diese Tatsache reicht nicht aus für ein abschließendes

---

[76] DJDJ III (1962) 184.   [77] Dazu Carmignac 1979, 28.

[78] Edition der beiden Fragmente von 4Q Sl 39 und Sl 40 in Strugnell 1960. Zu den beiden weiteren Handschriften aus Höhe 4Q siehe *ibid.*, 318f., zu der Masada-Handschrift siehe Yadin 1965, 81 und 105–108.

[79] Siehe Yadin 1965, 106.   [80] So gemäß Yadin 1965, 106f.

Urteil[81]. Die Bezeichnungen für die "Frommen" in 4Q Sl 39[82] passen zwar terminologisch gut zu entsprechenden Gemeindebezeichnungen in spezifischen Qumrantexten, lassen aber solche Bezeichnungen vermissen, die exklusiv nur in der Qumrangemeinde verwendet worden sind. So bleibt auch für diesen Punkt abzuwarten, was die unedierten Fragmente an weitergehenden Erkenntnissen bringen mögen.

Soweit ich sehe, spricht bislang jedenfalls nichts dagegen, daß es sich im Falle der "Engelliturgie" um ein Werk aus der Zeit vor Entstehung der Qumrangemeinde handeln könnte, das vielleicht wie das "angelologische Buch" der Henoch-Literatur aus dem 3. Jh. v. Chr. stammt[83].

3.2.3.3. Das "Nabonid-Gebet" und "Pseudo-Daniel"[84]

Im Jahre 1956 hatte J. T. Milik in der "Revue Biblique" einige kleinere aramäischsprachige Fragmente aus Höhle 4Q veröffentlicht, die ein "Gebet des Nabonid" und weitere Stoffe enthalten, die mit dem biblischen Daniel-Buch, besonders mit dessen Abschnitt 3,31–4,34 verwandt sind, darüber hinaus terminologische Entsprechungen besonders zu Dan 5 bieten[85].

Lediglich wegen dieser inhaltlichen Verwandtschaft mit Stoffen der Daniel-Apokalypse hat J. Carmignac diese Fragmente der "apokalyptischen" Literatur aus den Qumranfunden subsumiert. Doch ist diese Zuordnung m. E. nicht haltbar. Zuletzt hat A. S. van der Woude nach vielen anderen Forschern in einem 1978 erschienenen Beitrag die Fragmente des "Nabonid-Gebetes" gründlich untersucht mit dem Ergebnis, daß sie aller Wahrscheinlichkeit nach der *literarischen Vorgeschichte* unseres biblischen Daniel-Buches einzuordnen[86], also älter als dieses sind und insbesondere auch noch nicht Bestandteil einer "Apokalypse". Das gleiche dürfte für die Fragmente von "Pseudo-Daniel" gelten[87]. So aufschlußreich diese Fragmente auch für die Vorgeschichte der Daniel-Apokalypse sind, sowenig haben sie selbst mit "Apokalyptik" zu tun oder gar mit der

---

[81] Siehe dazu oben §4.1.1.4.

[82] Strugnell 1960, 322ff.; vgl. auch die Liste von Engelbezeichnungen in den erhaltenen Fragmenten von 4Q Sl 37–40, *ibid.*, 331–334.

[83] Aufgrund von Maier 1964 könnte man den Jerusalemer Tempelkult bzw. dort amtierende Priester als "Herkunftsort" dieser "Engelliturgie" betrachten. Andererseits bleibt es vorerst durchaus möglich, dieses Werk der Qumrangemeinde zuzuschreiben, deren "angelologische" Interessen möglicherweise durch das "Giganten-Buch" der Henoch-Literatur weitergehend profiliert werden; siehe dazu oben §3.1.1.5. mit Anm. 41.

[84] Dazu Carmignac 1979, 29.

[85] Milik 1956. Textwiedergabe: Fitzmyer and Harrington 1978, 2–9 (Nr. 2+3).

[86] van der Woude 1978, 126–129. Ähnlich Collins 1977, 4–5, wie bereits in seiner grundlegenden Untersuchung Meyer 1962.

[87] Anders Collins 1977, 5–7, der "Pseudo-Daniel" als abhängig vom biblischen Daniel-Buch betrachtet.

Qumrangemeinde, deren Bibliotheksbeständen wir ihre Kenntnis verdanken.

3.2.3.4. Die "'Amram-Visionen"[88]

Im Jahre 1972 hat J. T. Milik wiederum in der "Revue Biblique" einige
Zeilen eines aramäischsprachigen Werkes aus den Qumranfunden veröf-
fentlicht, von dem insgesamt 5 Kopien vorhanden sind und das mit den
Worten beginnt: "Abschrift des Buches der Worte der Visionen
'Amrams". Fragment 1, Zeile 10 des von Milik edierten Textes 4Q
'Amram[b] Fragment 1 charakterisiert dieses Werk knapp als "Traumvi-
sion"[89].

Solange nicht mehr von diesem Werk bekannt ist, kann man nur sagen,
daß der Darstellungsstil seiner Visionen dem des Daniel-Buches verwandt
ist und daß es sich möglicherweise ebenfalls um eine Apokalypse handelt.
Über Entstehungszeit und Herkunft dieses Werkes, insbesondere auch
über sein Verhältnis zur Qumrangemeinde, läßt sich gegenwärtig noch gar
nichts sagen.

3.3. Das Ergebnis der Paragraphen 3.1. und 3.2.

Als Fazit dieses Durchganges ist festzuhalten, daß es unter den rund 100
nichtbiblischen Werken aus den Qumranfunden[90] abgesehen von sicher
vorqumranischen Werken wie einigen Henoch-Büchern, Jubiläen-Buch
und Daniel-Apokalypse bestenfalls 4 Werke gibt, bei denen es sich möglicherweise um "Apokalypsen" handelt und gegenwärtig noch nicht ausgeschlossen werden kann, daß sie in der Qumrangemeinde entstanden sind,
nämlich

(1) das "Gigantenbuch" der Henoch-Literatur,
(2) die Schrift vom "Neuen Jerusalem",
(3) die sog. "Engelliturgie" und
(4) die "'Amram-Visionen".

Sollte sich durch die abschließende Edition aller dieser erst zu mehr oder
weniger geringen Teilen veröffentlichten Texte herausstellen, daß sie
tatsächlich in der Qumrangemeinde angefertigte Apokalypsen sind, dann
ist deren Anteil an der Gesamtzahl spezifischer Qumrantexte prozentual
nicht größer als der Anteil von Apokalypsen am Kanon des Alten wie des

---

[88] Dazu Carmignac 1979, 30.
[89] Milik 1972, 77–97, bes. 77 und 79 f. Textwiedergabe aller bislang edierten Fragmente von
4Q 'Amram-Visionen: Fitzmyer and Harrington 1978, 90–96 (Nr. 22–26).
[90] Für diese Zahlenangabe siehe oben § 1.

Neuen Testaments[91]. Als "apokalyptische Bewegung" läßt sich die Qumrangemeinde angesichts dieses Sachverhaltes sicher nicht charakterisieren. Andererseits muß ernsthaft mit der Möglichkeit gerechnet werden, daß auch diese 4 Werke entweder gar keine Apokalypsen oder außerhalb der Qumrangemeinde, sei es vor ihrer Entstehung oder neben ihr, verfaßt worden sind.

Als Ergebnis ist also festzuhalten, daß man gegenwärtig noch von keiner einzigen Apokalypse mit Sicherheit behaupten kann, sie sei ein Produkt der Qumrangemeinde. Sollten dennoch einige Apokalypsen in ihrem Kreis entstanden sein, dann als eine Randerscheinung, der man keine große Bedeutung beimessen darf. Zum gleichen Urteil kommt im übrigen J. Carmignac in seinem Beitrag in der "Revue de Qumran"[92].

3.4. Die Eschatologie der Qumrangemeinde

Nur ganz knapp will ich mich abschließend noch zur Eschatologie der Qumrangemeinde äußern, weil deren Eigenart wenigstens teilweise zu erklären vermag, warum man in dieser Gruppe des nachexilischen Judentums kein sonderliches Interesse an Apokalyptik hatte.

3.4.1. Entstanden ist die Qumrangemeinde[93] aus jenen durchaus konservativen Gruppen von Chasidim der Zeit Antiochus' IV., die im Gegenstoß zum Hellenismus die Religiosität ihrer Väter bewahren und sichern wollten. Bereits diese Chasidim hatten partiell eschatologisch orientierte Anschauungen; im Zentrum ihrer Interessen aber stand die Thora und deren Observanz.

Die Qumrangemeinde unterscheidet sich von diesen Chasidim im wesentlichen dadurch, daß sie die Dominanz des "Laien-Elementes" gebrochen und eine priesterlich-hierarchische Gemeindestruktur eingeführt hat. Verbunden war mit dieser Veränderung ein Boykott des Tempelkultes zu Jerusalem aufgrund der Tatsache, daß seit dem Jahre 153/52 v. Chr. nichtsaddoqidische Mitglieder des Hasmonäer-Hauses das Amt des Hohenpriesters innehatten, damit nach Ansicht der Qumrangemeinde die kultische Spitze illegitim und der gesamte Jerusalemer Kult "unrein" war.

3.4.2. Die zentrale Zukunftserwartung der Qumrangemeinde war, daß sie eine "Wende zum Besseren" erhoffte, die darin bestehen sollte, daß Gott die Hasmonäer beseitigte und wieder ein Saddoqid als Hoherpriester amtieren würde. Dies ist der Kern qumranischer "Eschatologie", um den

---

[91] In allen diesen Fällen läge der statistische Anteil von Apokalypsen am "Gesamtwerk" (AT/spezifische Qumrantexte/NT) numerisch bei etwa 4 Prozent.

[92] Carmignac 1979, 32.

[93] Zum folgenden siehe die Einzelnachweise bei Stegemann 1971.

herum sich mancherlei weitere eschatologische Vorstellungen[94] sammelten und entwickelten.

Wenn in dem um 50 v. Chr. abgefaßten Habakuk-Kommentar der Qumrangemeinde (1QpHab) gesagt wird, Gott habe den "Lehrer der Gerechtigkeit" dazu befähigt, "(in rechter Weise) zu deuten alle Worte seiner Diener, der Propheten; [denn d]urch diese hat Gott alles das mitgeteilt, was (dermaleinst) über sein Volk Is[rael] kommen wird" (II,8–10)[95], dann heißt das nicht mehr und nicht weniger, als daß die Qumrangemeinde die Einbeziehung der Prophetenschriften in ihren biblischen Kanon und das Prinzip ihrer eschatologischen Deutung auf alles, was mit der Qumrangemeinde zeitlich zusammenhängt, als durch den "Lehrer der Gerechtigkeit" inauguriert und sanktioniert betrachtet hat. Wie er selbst dies praktiziert hat, zeigt die Inanspruchnahme der biblischen Propheten in den von ihm verfaßten Teilen der Hodajot, die etwa ein Jahrhundert vor den "pescharim" entstanden sind[96]. Die "pescharim" sind demgegenüber von der Auslegungstechnik her ein Werk der späteren Gemeinde: Dadurch, daß sie Satz für Satz nachweisen konnte, daß sich die "Weissagungen" eines der Schriftpropheten bis zum letzten Wort im Zusammenhang mit der Gemeindegeschichte erfüllt hatten, gab sie der Erwartung Ausdruck, daß die "Wende zum Besseren" nun endlich unmittelbar bevorstehen müsse[97].

Der Habakuk-Kommentar zeigt außerdem, daß die Qumrangemeinde im Zusammenhang mit ihrer Prophetenexegese Berechnungen angestellt haben muß über den spätestmöglichen Zeitpunkt für den Eintritt der erhofften "Wende", und Irritationen zu bewältigen hatte, die daraus resultierten, daß die "Wende" nicht zum errechneten Termin eintrat (1QpHab VII,5–VIII,3)[98]. Gerechtfertigt wird dieser "Irrtum" letztlich damit, daß der

---

[94] Vor allem die Vorstellung vom göttlichen "Endgericht" (als Läuterungs-, Scheidungs- oder Strafprozeß) und diverse "messianische" Erwartungen.

[95] Text: Lohse 1971, der allerdings am Schluß ארצו] ו ergänzt statt der meinerseits bevorzugten Lesung ישראל]ו (dazu Stegemann 1971, 56 mit Anm. 97).

[96] Siehe dazu vor allem G. Jeremias 1963, bes. 168–267.

[97] Vgl. dazu auch Stegemann 1963, 241 f. mit Anm. 20.

[98] Text: Lohse 1971, 234–236. Die Entstehung des "Habakuk-Kommentars" datiere ich um das Jahr 50 v. Chr. (vgl. Stegemann 1971, 115–120: Die Tempelplünderung des Jahres 54 v. Chr. ist für den Autor von 1QpHab ein Ereignis der jüngsten Vergangenheit!). – Das zuvor in der Qumrangemeinde errechnete Datum für die endzeitliche "Wende" könnte 100 Jahre nach Entstehung der "Anfangsgemeinde" gelegen haben, die von der Qumrangemeinde auf den Termin "390 Jahre nach der Auslieferung an Nebukadnezar" (im Jahre 586 v. Chr.) datiert worden ist (CD I,5 f.; siehe dazu G. Jeremias 1963, 153–162), historisch betrachtet aber wahrscheinlich in das Jahr 172 v. Chr. gelegt werden muß (Stegemann 1971, 242). Die Gesamtzeit von 490 Jahren (vgl. Dan 9,24–27) hätte sich dann etwa im Jahre 72 v. Chr. "erfüllen" müssen, knapp eine Generation vor Abfassung des "Habakuk-Kommentars". Möglicherweise hat die Tatsache, daß das Jahr 72 v. Chr. ohne das "errechnete" göttliche Eingreifen verging, in der Folgezeit die Anfertigung der "pescharim" bewirkt. Jedenfalls läßt sich für keinen dieser Texte eine Abfassung vor dem Jahre 72 v. Chr. erweisen, angesichts

Mensch die Geheimnisse Gottes nicht voll zu ergründen vermag. Und auch dafür bietet der biblische Prophetentext einen geeigneten Anhaltspunkt, wenn man ihn eben nur hinreichend gründlich studiert und sachgemäß auslegt[99].

Nicht Visionen, nicht Himmelsreisen, nicht durch Vermittlung von Engeln erschlossenes "Himmelswissen" schaffen hier die Grundlage für die Zukunftsorientierung, sondern die überlieferten biblischen Schriften, nicht Henoch oder Daniel, sondern Mose und die biblischen Propheten. Das ist die Grundorientierung der Qumrangemeinde, wobei die Eschatologie eindeutig sekundäre Relevanz und viel geringere Bedeutung hat als die im Zentrum aller Interessen der Qumrangemeinde stehende Thoraobservanz.

Weder ihrem Zustandekommen nach noch in sekundären Entwicklungsstadien läßt sich die Qumrangemeinde als "eschatologische Bewegung" charakterisieren. "Eschatologie" hatte für sie lediglich eine deutlich limitierte Funktion, im Unterschied zu der "Randerscheinung Apokalyptik" immerhin eine *wichtige* Funktion; denn die Trennung vom Jerusalemer Tempelkult war ein schmerzlicher Zustand, weil die Thora die Teilnahme am dortigen Kult verlangte. Dementsprechend massiv war die Hoffnung auf die "Wende" bzw. die eschatologische Orientierung der Gemeinde, aber eben aus den genannten Gründen und in den gekennzeichneten Grenzen.

3.4.3. In unserem Zusammenhang besonders hervorzuheben bleibt schließlich noch die Tatsache, daß keines jener vier Werke, die möglicherweise als in der Qumrangemeinde selbst entstandene Apokalypsen zu betrachten sind[100], Einflüsse der "Eschatologie" erkennen läßt, wenigstens soweit die bislang edierten Fragmente bereits ein Urteil in dieser Beziehung erlauben[101]. Soweit die Qumrangemeinde also überhaupt Apokalypsen

---

von mindestens 17 Exemplaren dieser Gattung aus den Qumranfunden ein recht auffälliger Sachverhalt. Die Abfassung der "pescharim" dokumentiert wahrscheinlich ein halbes Jahrhundert permanenter "Naherwartung" der endzeitlichen "Wende" in der Qumrangemeinde, ein religionsphänomenologisch sehr interessanter, unter diesem Aspekt noch gar nicht hinreichend gewürdigter Umstand: In der Regel rechnet man damit, daß enttäuschte "Naherwartung" bald erlischt, z. B. im Falle der Parusieerwartung des frühen Christentums; die "pescharim" aus den Qumranfunden zeigen nunmehr, daß man im Falle derartiger "Enttäuschung" gegebenenfalls mit wesentlich längeren Fristen bleibender "Naherwartung" als nur ein bis zwei Jahrzehnten rechnen kann.

[99] 1QpHab VII,7f. in Auslegung von Hab 2,3a. Text: Lohse 1971, 234–236. Dazu Strobel 1961.

[100] Siehe oben §3.3.

[101] Auszunehmen von diesem Urteil ist allenfalls vielleicht das Werk über das "Neue Jerusalem" (siehe oben §3.2.3.1.), falls es sich eindeutig als Apokalypse erweisen lassen sollte und zugleich als Ausdruck "eschatologischer" Hoffnung, nicht einfach als Beschreibung "himmlischer" Gegebenheiten. Doch würde eine solche Ausnahme an dem sonstigen Allgemeinbefund so gut wie nichts ändern können.

hervorgebracht hat, sind auch diese nicht aus dem Nährboden der "Eschatologie" erwachsen, sondern unabhängig davon entstanden.

Umgekehrt war aber die "Eschatologie" der Qumrangemeinde offenbar
auch nicht darauf angewiesen, sich in Gestalt von Apokalypsen darzustellen, sondern konnte sich hinreichend in anderer Weise entfalten, in Gebeten, Hymnen, Benediktionen, weisheitlichen Mahnungen, "Kommentaren" zu prophetischen Schriften, thematisch orientierten Midraschim,
Testimonien-Sammlungen, Gemeindeordnungen, und sogar in literarisch
eigenständigen Endzeitschilderungen[102]. Vielleicht wird man die – leicht
noch zu vermehrende – Fülle von Selbstäußerungsmöglichkeiten einer
funktionskräftigen Gemeinde auch dahingehend interpretieren dürfen, daß
hier kaum ein *Bedarf* für Apokalyptik bestanden hat.

Die Apokalyptik hatte ja ihre Hauptfunktion darin, die "himmlische
Autorität" unmittelbar zu beanspruchen, wenn die ansonsten verfügbaren
Autoritäten "versagten". Die Qumrangemeinde aber hat – ähnlich wie
später das "rabbinische Judentum" – das aus Thora, Propheten und einigen
weiteren Schriften bestehende "Vätererbe" als für ihre Belange hinreichende Autoritätsbasis betrachtet, an die man sich auch prinzipiell gebunden sah. "Apokalyptiker" bleiben hier im Grunde "Fremdkörper", denen
man eher mit einer gewissen Reserve begegnet sein mag und auf die man
bestimmt für keinen zentralen Lebens- oder Funktionsbereich der Gemeinde angewiesen war[103].

---

[102] So z. B. die "Kriegsregel" (1QM); vgl. oben §3.2.2.1.

[103] Vgl. Koch 1970, 32. – Im Ansatz guteteils vergleichbar: Rössler 1960. – Interessant sind
in diesem Zusammenhang einige Beobachtungen und Wertungen J. T. Miliks aufgrund des
Befundes der Henoch-Handschriften aus den Qumranfunden. Ausgehend von den paläogra-
phischen Daten dieser Handschriften, die relativ gleichmäßig vom Ausgang des 3. Jh. bis zum
letzten Drittel des 1. Jh. v. Chr. reichen (wobei einige Handschriften sogar aus der Zeit vor
Entstehung der Qumrangemeinde stammen!), stellt er fest: "It is significant in every respect
that, apart from one manuscript of the Astronomical Book (Enastr[b]) and some copies of the
Book of Giants, no manuscript of 4QEn has been found in the beautiful 'classical' writing of
the Herodian era or from the last period of the Essene occupation of Hirbet Qumrân" (vgl.
Anm. 41). "Qumrân scribes and readers must have gradually lost interest in the literary
compositions attributed to Enoch, just as happened, though more rapidly and more drastically, in Pharisaic circles. We should note likewise that an early scroll, En[a] (= 1. Hälfte des 2.
Jh. v. Chr.), had already been withdrawn from circulation and its detached leaves used for
other purposes – for example, the verso of the first leaf for a schoolboy's exercise. Equally
significant, finally, is the absence of the Books of Enoch from other caves at Qumrân, whose
stores formed private libraries. Our copies of 4QEn were no doubt covered with dust on the
shelves, in the chests, or in the earthenware jars of the main library (= 4Q), and only a small
number of Essene readers consulted and borrowed them, particularly during the first century
A.D. – Enochic literature was to have a full-blown renaissance in the early Christian
communities, but this would come about through the medium of Greek translations" (Milik
1976, 7).

Das relative Desinteresse der Qumrangemeinde selbst an der Henoch-Literatur (zur Ausnahme des "Giganten-Buches" siehe oben §3.1.1.5. mit Anm. 41) erscheint mir als sympto-
matisch für deren Einstellung gegenüber der Apokalyptik überhaupt.

4. Zusammenfassung

Zusammenfassend ist festzustellen, daß die *Qumranfunde* erhebliche Bedeutung für die *Erforschung* der Apokalyptik haben, weniger aufgrund einer Bereicherung des Arsenals von Apokalypsen durch entsprechende Produkte der Qumrangemeinde, sondern vor allem dadurch, daß die uns erhaltenen Teile der einstigen Bibliotheksbestände jenes Teils der Gemeinde, der einst Qumran bewohnte, in erfreulichem Maße Einblick gewähren in die Entstehungsverhältnisse der ersten jüdischen Apokalypsen und in die Interessen, denen die Abfassung dieser Literatur zu verdanken ist.

Die Qumranfunde zeigen, daß die Schlüsselrolle für die Frage nach der *Entstehung* der jüdischen Apokalyptik fortan nicht mehr dem Daniel-Buch zukommt, sondern der *Henoch-Literatur*, deren weitergehende Erforschung nunmehr ein vordringliches Desiderat ist. Im übrigen ist von den noch ausstehenden Publikationen weiterer Qumran-Fragmente zu erwarten, daß uns solche Werke wie das "Giganten-Buch" der Henoch-Literatur, die Schilderung des "Neuen Jerusalem", die "Engelliturgie" oder die "'Amram-Visionen", vielleicht auch der eine oder andere noch gänzlich unedierte Text aus den Qumranfunden stofflich in der Apokalyptik-Forschung weiterbringen, letztlich dann auch solche Werke wie das Jubiläen-Buch oder die Daniel-Apokalypse ein neues Profil erhalten.

Vor allem gestatten nunmehr die spezifischen Schriften der Qumrangemeinde, viel deutlicher als bislang möglich zwischen "Apokalyptik" und "Eschatologie" zu unterscheiden und beide Größen sachgemäßer als bisher zu charakterisieren.

Aufschlußreich ist schließlich, daß die Qumranfunde uns endlich und in größerer Anzahl Handschriften jüdischer Apokalypsen aus der Zeit des Zweiten Tempels zugänglich gemacht haben, die erstmalig und eindeutig zeigen, daß die meisten dieser Apokalypsen offenbar in *aramäischer* Sprache abgefaßt worden sind. Hebräisch sind nur das Jubiläen-Buch, die biblische Daniel-Apokalypse (außer deren aramäischem Teil Dan 2,4b–7,28) und die "Engelliturgie" aus den Qumranfunden, falls es sich hierbei überhaupt um eine Apokalypse handelt. Damit ist die verbreitete Auffassung, jüdische Apokalypsen seien in der Regel in hebräischer Sprache abgefaßt worden, endgültig erledigt; insbesondere auch die am Anfang aller jüdischen Apokalyptik stehenden Henoch-Schriften sind durchweg in aramäischer Sprache geschrieben worden.

Die Qumrangemeinde selbst war nach allem, was sich bislang feststellen läßt, keine "apokalyptische Bewegung", sondern hat der Apokalyptik bestenfalls soviel Interesse entgegengebracht wie unser biblischer Kanon Alten und Neuen Testaments. An diesem generellen Urteil wird man auch künftig festhalten können, wenn sämtliche noch unedierten Texte aus den Qumranfunden endlich der Wissenschaft allgemein zugänglich geworden sein werden.

5. Nachwort

In der Abschlußphase des "International Colloquium on Apocalypticism" in Uppsala entwarfen mehrere Teilnehmer "Definitionen" dessen, was ihrer unterschiedlichen Auffassung nach "Apokalyptik" sei. Eine Einigungsmöglichkeit zeichnete sich im Kreise der Teilnehmer nicht einmal ansatzweise ab.

In diesem Zusammenhang hatte ich in Aufnahme meiner obigen Ausführungen und unter weitergehender Bezugnahme auf Aspekte, die für die "Apokalyptik"-Diskussion relevant sind, ebenfalls eine Skizze vorgelegt, die ich nicht als regelrechte "Definition", sondern nur als *Beschreibung* (descriptio) dessen verstehe, was meiner Auffassung nach für jüdische und christliche Apokalypsen in dem Zeitraum vom (4./)3. Jh. v. Chr. bis etwa zur Mitte des 2. Jh. n. Chr.[104] charakteristisch ist und diese von anderer zeitgenössischer Literatur unterscheidet.

Da ein für mich wesentliches Implikat meines Beitrages über "Die Bedeutung der Qumranfunde für die Erforschung der Apokalyptik" darin liegt, den historischen Ansatz jüdischer Apokalyptik nunmehr eher in einem Werk wie dem "astronomischen Buch" der Henoch-Literatur in seiner ursprünglichen Gestalt zu sehen als in der Daniel-Apokalypse, und diese Umorientierung erhebliche Konsequenzen haben dürfte sowohl für künftige Definitionen von "Apokalyptik" als auch für deren Unterscheidung von "Eschatologie", gestatte ich mir, meine damalige Skizze in leicht modifizierter Fassung auch im Rahmen dieses Sammelbandes vorzulegen.

Meiner Auffassung nach lassen sich die uns erhaltenen jüdischen und christlichen Apokalypsen aus dem genannten Zeitraum wie folgt charakterisieren:

5.1. *Apokalypsen* sind literarische Werke, die inhaltlich dadurch gekennzeichnet sind, daß sie das in ihnen Dargestellte als "himmlisch geoffenbart" ausweisen, wobei das gesamte Werk – insbesondere auch in seinem literarischen Rahmen – auf diesen Aspekt des "himmlischen Geoffenbarten" abgestellt ist.

Im einzelnen gelten dabei folgende Kriterien:

(1) Der zentrale Gegenstand eines solchen Werkes (z. B. ein neuer Kalender, eine besondere Lehrauffassung) wird als "himmlisch geoffenbart" dargestellt oder ein bestimmter Sachverhalt (z. B. eine geschichtliche Situation) unter dem Gesichtspunkt behandelt, daß sich dessen rechtes Verständnis für Autor und Leser nur durch "Offenbarung" von "himmlischem Wissen" erschließt.

(2) Die unmittelbare Beanspruchung des "Himmels" (Gott, Engel, himmlischer Erlöser) in diesen Offenbarungsschriften hat ihren Hauptgrund im Autoritätsproblem: Die jeweils "innerweltlich" bereits vorgegebenen religiösen Autoritäten (im Judentum Thora und Propheten; im Christentum "die Schrift", Jesusüberlieferung, Evangelien, Apostelbriefe etc.) bieten von sich aus keine hinreichende Grundlage für das neu Darzustellende, so daß man im Interesse der Legitimation des "Neuen" den "Himmel" gesondert beanspruchen muß[105].

---

[104] Dieser relativ frühe terminus ad quem ist dadurch bedingt, daß ich die "gnostischen" Apokalypsen hier nicht in meine Urteilsbildung einbeziehen möchte, da man in deren Fall mit weiteren Kriterien rechnen könnte, die für die ältere jüdisch-christliche Apokalyptik noch nicht relevant waren.

[105] Siehe dazu oben §3.1.1.4. mit Anm. 34 und §3.4.3. mit Anm. 103.

(3) Als Autoren dieser Offenbarungsschriften fungieren meistens Autoritäten der religiösen Tradition (Pseudonymität, Aspekte der Legitimation, der sachlichen "Zuständigkeit" etc.)[106].

(4) Der Kontakt zwischen Mensch und "Himmel" wird in diesen Offenbarungsschriften in der Regel als Vision, als Audition und/oder als eine "Himmelsreise" dargestellt.

(5) Das rechte Verständnis des – oft bildhaft – Dargestellten wird gegebenenfalls durch eine göttlich autorisierte Mittlergestalt (angelus interpres) erschlossen.

(6) Mit dem "Himmelswissen" verbunden sind in diesen Offenbarungsschriften oft Aspekte wie dessen "Jenseitigkeit" (Transzendenz, Esoterik), "Verborgenheit" (Motiv der "Versiegelung" dieses Wissens) oder "Geheimnis" (Geheimwissen verschiedener Art) oder Interessen apologetischer Art (z. B. "Himmelswissen" kontra "Erfahrungswissen"; neue Betrachtungsweisen kontra traditionelle religiöse Autorität).

(7) Beliebte Gegenstände dieser Offenbarungsschriften sind neuartige, religiös zentrale Lehrauffassungen (z. B. neues Kalendersystem, Determinismus, dualistisches Weltbild), Geschichtsdeutungen (z. B. Weltzeitalter, Zwei-Äonen-Lehre, Eschatologie), Kosmologie, Jenseitsschilderungen (z. B. Gottesthron, Heilsort, Strafort), Angelologie und Heilslehre (z. B. soteriologisch orientierte Paränesen).

(8) Als Darstellungsmittel dieser Offenbarungsschriften dienen beliebige literarische Gattungen; ihr literarischer Rahmen ist meistens narrativ gestaltet[107].

(9) Diese Offenbarungsschriften sind nicht an ein für sie spezifisches soziologisches Milieu ("Sitz im Leben") gebunden oder an bestimmte Gruppen (z. B. Minderheiten, Randgruppen), sondern eher an eine spezifische Bildungsschicht ("Theologen"), an einen besonderen Frömmigkeitstyp (intellektuell, individualistisch) oder an bestimmte Interessenlagen (ein neuartiges Urteil über bestimmte Sachverhalte etc.). Vermutlich haben einzelne Institutionen (z. B. Tempelkult) oder religiöse Amtsträger (z. B. ranghohe Priester, bedeutende "Lehrer") einen wesentlich höheren Anteil an der Anfertigung dieser Offenbarungsschriften als man gemeinhin anzunehmen geneigt ist[108].

(10) Der historische Ort dieser Offenbarungsschriften ist in der Regel eine religiöse Problemsituation, wobei die "Probleme" ganz unterschiedlicher Art sein können (z. B. als erforderlich betrachtete Neuerungen in Kultus oder Lehre; die Auffassung der Sinnlosigkeit des menschlichen Daseins oder der traditionellen Frömmigkeit; religionspolitische oder

---

[106] Hauptausnahme bleibt hier die neutestamentliche Johannes-Apokalypse, die ihren irdischen Autor nennt und deren Darstellung vom "himmlischen" Christus selbst her legitimiert wird.

[107] Die immer wieder unternommenen Versuche, eine eigenständige "Gattung Apokalyptik" zu profilieren (so z. B. noch Koch 1970, 19–24), sollte man endgültig aufgeben. Sie führen lediglich dazu, für Teilbereiche der Apokalyptik auch "gattungsmäßige" Gemeinsamkeiten zu entdecken, schließen dann aber andere Apokalypsen notwendigerweise aus. Allenfalls kann man von einem literarischen "genre" sprechen, wenn man diesen Begriff nicht im Sinne von "Gattung" versteht, sondern sich ausschließlich an inhaltlichen Kriterien orientiert (so z. B. J. J. Collins 1979).

[108] Wenn man den Begriff "Minderheit" überhaupt in diesem Zusammenhang beanspruchen darf, dann am ehesten in dem Sinne, daß man einige Apokalypsen (z. B. "angelologisches Buch" der Henoch-Literatur, Daniel, IV Esra) als Produkte einer "intellektuellen Minderheit" betrachtet. Andere Apokalypsen aber (z. B. das "astronomische Buch" der Henoch-Literatur, Jubiläen-Buch, Hirt des Hermas) sind eher als Produkte der zentralen religiösen Instanzen oder einer "Mehrheit" in ihrem Entstehungsmilieu zu betrachten, wobei die Wahl des Darstellungsmittels "Apokalypse" ihre Ursache hat in Problemen der "Legitimation" des Darzustellenden, nicht in einer – soziologisch faßbaren oder "geistigen" – Minderheitensituation.
Die bisherige Diskussion zu diesem Punkt kann meines Erachtens am ehesten weitergefördert werden durch Beiträge wie die des Herrn Kollegen J. C. Lebram oben in diesem Band.

soziale Notsituationen einer bestimmten Gruppe; Diskrepanzen zwischen Gottes Schöpfer-
willen und der vorfindlichen Weltlage, verbunden mit der Hoffnung auf eine "neue Welt").

(11) Abfassungszweck dieser Offenbarungsschriften ist stets die Einbringung "göttlicher
Ordnung(en)" in eine ansonsten "chaotische" Welt bzw. die Belehrung darüber, daß von Gott
her betrachtet durchaus "in Ordnung" ist, was dem Menschen von seiner religiösen Disposition, seinem Erfahrungswissen oder seinem Erleben her als "chaotisch" oder mit den
göttlichen Absichten unvereinbar erscheint[109].

(12) Den Autoren dieser Offenbarungsschriften erschien die von ihnen gewählte Darstellungsweise vermutlich als der bestmögliche Weg zur Realisierung ihrer Zielinteressen. Ob
dem einzelnen Autor dafür alternativ auch noch andere literarische oder institutionelle
Möglichkeiten offengestanden hätten, entzieht sich in der Regel unseren Feststellungsmög-
lichkeiten[110]. Im übrigen ist durchaus mit der Möglichkeit zu rechnen, daß im Laufe der Zeit
vorhandene Apokalypsen "Schule gemacht" und bewirkt haben, daß man sich entsprechender
Darstellungsmöglichkeiten bediente, ohne dazu unbedingt (z. B. durch das ad (2) gekenn-
zeichnete "Autoritätsproblem") gezwungen zu sein[111].

5.2. *Apokalyptik* bezeichnet

(1) die Anfertigung von Apokalypsen sowie diese selbst als literaturgeschichtliche Gegebenheiten und

(2) die unmittelbare Wirkungsgeschichte dieser Werke.

5.3. *Apokalyptisch*

sind Stoffe, Vorstellungen, Gattungen, Begriffe, Bilder etc., sofern sie in Apokalypsen
vorkommen, und zwar beschränkt auf diesen Bereich und unmittelbare Entlehnungen
daraus[112].

6. Postscriptum

Inzwischen hat Eckhard von Nordheim 1980, 115–118, die Fragmente der "'Amram-
Visionen" aus Höhle 4Q (oben §3.2.3.4.) untersucht und festgestellt, daß auch dieses Werk
keine Apokalypse ist, sondern der *Testamenten*-Literatur zugeordnet werden muß: Formal ist

---

[109] Die populäre Gleichsetzung von "apokalyptisch" mit "chaotisch" (vgl. Koch 1970, 15
mit Anm. 1) verabsolutiert die Formulierungs*voraussetzungen* mancher Apokalypsen und
verkennt völlig deren eigentliche Intention. Pauschal betrachtet sind die Apokalypsen nicht
"Chaos-Literatur", sondern "Ordnungs-Literatur", deren Interesse auf die Einführung einer
neuen "Ordnung" oder auf die Stabilisierung der überkommenen religiösen "Ordnung"
gerichtet ist. Dieses "Ordnungs"-Denken verbindet die Apokalyptik nicht nur sachlich,
sondern wahrscheinlich auch historisch mit der zeitgenössischen jüdischen – und darüber
hinaus altorientalischen – "Weisheit". Siehe dazu die Hinweise auf G. v. Rad und J. T. Milik
oben Anm. 39.

[110] Vielleicht hängt es mit dem – m. E. relativ frühen – Entstehungsdatum des durch die
"Tempelrolle" aus den Qumranfunden zugänglich gewordenen Werkes im 4. oder 3. Jh.
v. Chr. zusammen, daß dessen Autor (noch) ein "6. Buch der Thora" geschrieben und (noch)
nicht die alternative Möglichkeit der Anfertigung einer Apokalypse gewählt hat (siehe dazu
oben §3.1.1.4. mit Anm. 37). In späterer Zeit hätte ihm das Darstellungsmittel der Anfertigung einer Apokalypse vielleicht eher nahegelegen.

[111] Diese Betrachtungsweise könnte etwa im Falle solcher Apokalypsen wie der "Synoptischen Apokalypse" Mk 13, der syrischen "Baruch-Apokalypse" oder des 6. Buches Esra
angebracht sein, vielleicht auch schon für das (wahrscheinlich in der 2. Hälfte des 2. Jh.
v. Chr. entstandene) "Giganten-Buch" der Henoch-Literatur.

[112] Für das Erfordernis dieser Eingrenzung gegenüber einer weithin üblich gewordenen
Verwendung des Begriffes "apokalyptisch" vgl. oben §2.2.

es den TestXII nah verwandt, insbesondere dem TestLev. Die gleiche Auffassung vertritt nun auch Elias Bickerman 1980 in einem "Postscript" zu seiner älteren Untersuchung "The Date of the Testaments of the Twelve Patriarchs", speziell 23.

Damit reduziert sich die Anzahl von Werken aus den Qumranfunden, bei denen es sich möglicherweise um Apokalypsen handelt und zugleich (noch) nicht ausgeschlossen werden kann, daß sie in der "Qumrangemeinde" selbst entstanden sind (vgl. oben §3.3.), auf höchstens noch drei, nämlich

(1) das "Gigantenbuch" der Henoch-Literatur,
(2) die Schrift vom "Neuen Jerusalem" und
(3) die sogenannte "Engelliturgie".

Entsprechend zu modifizieren sind meine Angaben oben §4. sowie in Anm. 91.

Bibliographie

Baillet, Maurice 1972: "Les manuscrits de la Règle de la Guerre de la grotte 4 de Qumran", in: *RB* 79 (1972) 217–226.

Bickerman, Elias 1980: "The Date of the Testaments of the Twelve Patriarchs" (in: *JBL* 69 [1950] 245–260), überarbeitete und ergänzte Fassung in: ders., *Studies in Jewish and Christian History*, Part II (AGJU 9 II), Leiden 1980, 1–23.

Carmignac, Jean 1979: "Qu'est-ce que l'Apocalyptique? Son emploi à Qumrân", in: *RdQ* 10 (1979/81) 3–33.

Collins, John J. 1977: *The Apocalyptic Vision of the Book of Daniel* (HSM 16), Missoula, Mont. 1977.

– 1979: *Apocalypse*. The Morphology of a Genre (Hrsg.) *Semeia* (an experimental journal for biblical criticism, Scholars Press: Missoula, MT) 14 (1979).

Fitzmyer, Joseph A. 1975: *The Dead Sea Scrolls*. Major Publications and Tools for Study (SBibSt 8), Missoula, Mont. 1975.

Fitzmyer, Joseph A. and Harrington, Daniel J. 1978: *A Manual of Palestinian Aramaic Texts* (BibOr 34), Rom 1978.

Gruenwald, Ithamar 1980: *Apocalyptic and Merkavah Mysticism* (AGJU 14), Leiden/Köln 1980.

Harrington, Daniel J. 1980: "Research on the Jewish Pseudepigrapha during the 1970s", in: *CBQ* 42 (1980) 147–159.

Hellholm, David 1980: *Das Visionenbuch des Hermas als Apokalypse*. Formgeschichtliche und texttheoretische Studien zu einer literarischen Gattung, Bd. I: Methodologische Vorüberlegungen und makrostrukturelle Textanalyse (CB.NT 13:1), Lund 1980.

Hengel, Martin 1973: *Judentum und Hellenismus* (WUNT 10), Tübingen 1969, 2. Aufl. 1973, 330–394 und 443–453.

Hunzinger, Claus-Hunno 1957: "Fragmente einer älteren Fassung des Buches Milḥamâ aus Höhle 4 von Qumrân", in: *ZAW* 69 (1957) 131–151.

Jeremias, Gert 1963: *Der Lehrer der Gerechtigkeit* (StUNT 2), Göttingen 1963.

Jongeling, B. 1970: "Publication provisoire d'un fragment provenant de la grotte 11 de Qumrân (11Q Jér Nouv Ar)", in: *JSJ* 1 (1970) 58–64 und 185–186.

Klinzing, Georg 1971: *Die Umdeutung des Kultus in der Qumrangemeinde und im Neuen Testament* (StUNT 7), Göttingen 1971.

Knibb, M. A. 1979: "The Date of the Parables of Enoch: A Critical Review", in: *NTS* 25 (1979) 345–359.

Koch, Klaus 1970: *Ratlos vor der Apokalyptik*, Gütersloh 1970.

Kuhn, Heinz-Wolfgang 1966: *Enderwartung und gegenwärtiges Heil*. Untersuchungen zu den Gemeindeliedern von Qumran (StUNT 4), Göttingen 1966.

Larsson, Gerhard: *The Secret System*. A Study in the Chronology of the Old Testament, Leiden/Köln 1973.

Lohse, Eduard 1971: *Die Texte aus Qumran*. Hebräisch und Deutsch, 2. Auflage Darmstadt und München 1971.

Maier, Johann 1964: *Vom Kultus zur Gnosis.* Studien zur Vor- und Frühgeschichte der "jüdischen Gnosis" (Kairos [St] 1), Salzburg 1964.
- 1978: *Die Tempelrolle vom Toten Meer* (UTB 829), München 1978.
Mearns, Christopher L. 1979: "Dating the Similitudes of Enoch", in: *NTS* 25 (1979) 360–369.
Meyer, Rudolph 1962: *Das Gebet des Nabonid.* Eine in den Qumran-Handschriften wiederentdeckte Weisheitserzählung, Berlin 1962.
Milik, J. T. 1956: "'Prière de Nabonide' et autres écrits d'un cycle de Daniel. Fragments araméens de Qumrân 4", in: *RB* 63 (1956) 407–415.
- 1959: *Ten Years of Discovery in the Wilderness of Judaea,* London/Naperville, Ill., 1959.
- 1960: Rezension von: P. Wernberg-Møller, The Manual of Discipline (Leiden 1957), in: *RB* 67 (1960) 410–416.
- 1972: "4Q Visions de ʿAmram et une citation d'Origène", in: *RB* 79 (1972) 77–97.
- 1976: *The Books of Enoch.* Aramic Fragments of Qumrân Cave 4, Oxford 1976.
Nötscher, F. 1957: "Geist und Geister in den Texten von Qumran", in: *Mélanges bibliques. Festschrift A. Robert* (TICP 4), Paris 1957, 305–315, = ders., *Vom Alten zum Neuen Testament. Gesammelte Aufsätze* (BBB 17), Bonn 1962, 175–187.
Nordheim, Eckhard von 1980: *Die Lehre der Alten,* Bd. I: Das Testament als Literaturgattung im Judentum der hellenistisch-römischen Zeit (ALGHL 13), Leiden 1980.
Osten-Sacken, Peter von der 1969: *Gott und Belial.* Traditionsgeschichtliche Untersuchungen zum Dualismus in den Texten aus Qumran (StUNT 6), Göttingen 1969.
Ploeg, Jan van der 1978: "Une halakha inédite de Qumrân", in: *Qumrân. Sa piété, sa théologie et son milieu,* par M. Delcor (Hrsg.) (BEThL 46), Paris-Gembloux/Leuven 1978, 107–113.
Rad, Gerhard von 1960/1965: *Theologie des Alten Testaments.* Band II: Die Theologie der prophetischen Überlieferungen Israels, 1. Aufl. München 1960, 2. Aufl. München 1965.
Rössler, Dietrich 1960: *Gesetz und Geschichte.* Untersuchungen zur Theologie der jüdischen Apokalyptik und der pharisäischen Orthodoxie (WMANT 3), Neukirchen-Vluyn 1960.
Schäfer, Peter 1975: *Rivalität zwischen Engeln und Menschen.* Untersuchungen zur rabbinischen Engelvorstellung (SJ 8), Berlin/New York 1975.
Schmidt, Johann-Michael 1969: *Die jüdische Apokalyptik.* Die Geschichte ihrer Erforschung von den Anfängen bis zu den Textfunden von Qumran, Neukirchen-Vluyn, 1. Aufl. 1969, 2. Aufl. 1976.
Stegemann, Hartmut 1963: "Der Pešer Psalm 37 aus Höhle 4 von Qumran", in: *RdQ* 4 (1963/64) 235–270.
- 1971: *Die Entstehung der Qumrangemeinde,* Diss. 1965, Bonn 1971.
Stone, Michael Edward 1978: "The Book of Enoch and Judaism in the Third Century B.C.E.", in: *CBQ* 40 (1978) 479–492.
Strobel, August 1961: *Untersuchungen zum eschatologischen Verzögerungsproblem aufgrund der spätjüdisch-urchristlichen Geschichte von Habakuk 2,2ff.* (NT.S 2), Leiden/Köln 1961.
Strugnell, John 1960: "The Angelic Liturgy at Qumrân – 4Q Serek Šîrôt ʿÔlat Haššabbāt", in: *Congress Volume Oxford 1959* (VT.S 7), Leiden 1960, 318–345.
Trever, John C. 1965: "Completion of the Publication of Some Fragments from Qumran Cave I", in: *RdQ* 5 (1964/66) 323–344.
Vielhauer, Philipp 1975: *Geschichte der urchristlichen Literatur,* Berlin/New York 1975.
Woude, Adam S. van der 1971: "Fragmente des Buches Jubiläen aus Qumran Höhle XI (11Q Jub)", in: *Tradition und Glaube. Festgabe für Karl Georg Kuhn,* Göttingen 1971, 140–146 mit Abbildungen Tafel VIII.
- 1978: "Bemerkungen zum Gebet des Nabonid", in: *Qumrân. Sa piété, sa théologie et son milieu,* par M. Delcor (Hrsg.) (BEThL 46), Paris-Gembloux/Leuven 1978, 121–129.
Yadin, Yigael 1965: "The Excavation of Masada 1963/64, Preliminary Report", in: *IEJ* 15 (1965) 1–120.
- 1977: *Megillat ham-Miqaš. The Temple Scroll* (Hebrew Edition), Vol. I–III + III(A), Jerusalem 1977.

The Genre Apocalypse in Hellenistic Judaism

John J. Collins

1. Introduction

1.1. In his introductory comments on "Apocalypses and Related Subjects" for the Hennecke-Schneemelcher edition of the New Testament Apocrypha, P. Vielhauer wrote: "The Sibyllines represent the Apocalyptic of Hellenistic Diaspora Judaism (from which only one real Apocalypse is known, slav. Enoch, which goes back to a Greek original)."[1] Vielhauer's distinction between "apocalyptic" and "real apocalypses" may serve as a useful point of departure for the present study. While the Sibyllines are "related in various respects to the Apocalypses", it is readily granted that they are not formally apocalypses. Vielhauer argued that "There is, however, a basic difference in the function of the two genres. While the Apocalypses are fundamentally a conventicle-literature designed to strengthen a particular community, the Jewish Sibyllines originated as missionary propaganda writings which were turned from the very beginning towards those outside."[2] We shall question whether all apocalypses were "conventicle-literature" or whether the genre can be defined in terms of function at all. The distinction can be established more readily on formal grounds. Apocalypses are revelations and describe the manner in which the revelation is received by the supposed author. The Sibyllines are oracles which are presented directly as the speech of the sibyl.[3] I have suggested elsewhere that the interests of terminological clarity may best be served if we use the word "apocalyptic" primarily with reference to works which are apocalypses, and extend it to other literature only in so far as it resembles the apocalypses.[4] The Sibyllines surely belong in any discussion of apocalyptic literature in the extended sense, but a study of "the Apocalyptic of Hellenistic Diaspora Judaism" must begin, not with the oracles, but with the apocalypses.

---

[1] Vielhauer 1965, 600.   [2] *Ibid.*, 601.

[3] We may add that *Sib. Or.* 3 and 5, the major oracles of Egyptian Judaism, lack the belief in afterlife which is typical of apocalyptic eschatology. See Collins 1974, 110–111. On the provenance of the various Sibylline books see Collins, forthcoming.

[4] Collins 1979, 1–20.

1.2. The present study is based on the assumption that it is in fact possible to identify a literary genre apocalypse. The data and evidence which warrant this assumption can be found in the collection of essays *Apocalypse: The Morphology of a Genre* published in *Semeia* 14 (1979). It is sufficient here to note the definition and the distinct sub-types within the genre. "Apocalypse" is defined as "a genre of revelatory literature with a narrative framework, in which a revelation is mediated by an otherworldly being to a human recipient, disclosing a transcendent reality which is both temporal, in so far as it envisages eschatological salvation, and spatial, insofar as it involves another, supernatural world." Within the bounds of this definition we may distinguish those apocalypses which involve an otherworldly journey (Type II) from those which do not (Type I). Within each of these sub-types we may further distinguish a) "historical" apocalypses which include a review of history, eschatological crisis and cosmic and/or political eschatology; b) apocalypses which have no historical review but envisage cosmic and/or political eschatology; c) apocalypses which have neither historical review nor cosmic transformation but only personal eschatology.[5]

1.3. It is readily apparent that the Sibylline oracles have their closest affinities with Type Ia. However, those works which are apocalypses by this definition and are usually ascribed to the Hellenistic Diaspora, all involve otherworldly journeys and lack the extended reviews of history. They are: *2 (Slavonic) Enoch* (Type IIb), *3 (Greek) Baruch* and the *Testament of Abraham* (Rec. A, 10–15; Rec. B, 8–12) (Type IIc). *The Apocalypse of Zephaniah*, which is known from a quotation in Clement and probable remnants in two sets of Coptic fragments, may also be classified as a Hellenistic Diaspora apocalypse, but will be left aside here because of its fragmentary and problematic character.[6]

1.4. It will be noted that this definition makes no claims about the function of the genre. We will consider the function of these apocalypses individually and consider what light it throws on our understanding of the genre.

---

[5] *Ibid.*

[6] See Charlesworth 1976, 220–223, for a summary and a statement of the problems. Two other works which are not discussed here require mention. The *Apocalypse of Elijah* is a Christian work which incorporates Egyptian Jewish material. Rosenstiehl 1972, 68–73, has argued that parts of chaps. 2 and 3 derive from the first century BCE. I am not convinced by Rosenstiehl's arguments for an early date, but in any case, the work is formally an oracle, like the Sibyllines. Despite its title, it is not an apocalypse by the definition given above. Another Christian apocalypse which may contain an older Jewish core is the story of *Zosimus*. See Charlesworth 1976, 223–228; McNeil 1978, 68–82. It is not clear, however, whether the Jewish stage of this work was already in the form of an apocalypse.

2. *Slavonic Enoch*

2.1. Slavonic Enoch was designated by Vielhauer as the only "real apocalypse" of the Hellenistic Diaspora. Its character as an apocalypse has not been disputed, but its attribution to Hellenistic Judaism is still debated, most recently by J. T. Milik who regards it as a Christian work of the ninth or tenth century.[7] The majority opinion still clearly favors Jewish authorship and an early date.[8] Two considerations weigh heavily against the theory of Christian authorship. First, there is no clearly Christian element in the shorter recension (B), which has been universally recognized as the older recension since the edition of Vaillant.[9] Second, the peculiar requirement that the four legs of a sacrificial animal be tied together (*2 Enoch* 15 and 21, Vaillant pp. 59, 67), would be difficult to explain in a Christian work.[10] The emphasis on sacrifice throughout the book supports the case for Jewish authorship, since in no case is there any allusion to the sacrifice of Christ.[11] The attribution to Egyptian Judaism is generally conceded on the basis of allusions to Egyptian mythology in its cosmology and affinities

---

[7] Milik 1971, 373; 1976, 107–116. His main argument is that the Slavonic reflects the use of a late Greek word *syrmaiographa*, but a single word in the translation is not an adequate basis for dating the whole work. As to the other arguments, dependence on the Similitudes of Enoch is only a factor if one accepts Milik's late date for that work. The alleged correspondence of the angels Arioch and Marioch to Hârût and Mârût of Muslim legend is indecisive since the origin of these figures has not been established.

[8] So Scholem 1962, 64; Philonenko 1969, 109–116; Pines 1970, 72–87; Greenfield 1973, XVIII–XX; Fischer 1978, 38–41.

[9] Vaillant 1952. The older translations of Charles and Morfill 1896, Charles 1913, vol. 2, pp. 425–469 and Bonwetsch 1922 all presupposed the priority of the long recension. Vaillant (x–xi) still regarded *2 Enoch* as a Judeo-Christian work. His argument was partly based on alleged echoes of the NT, especially the beatitudes in Matt 5. This argument has been widely rejected since the correspondences are not exact and do not refer to any elements that are necessarily Christian. See Rubinstein 1962, 1–21; Fischer 1978, 39. Further Vaillant argued that the legend of the birth of Melchizedek presupposed the reference to Melchizedek in the Letter to the Hebrews and was meant to confirm Melchizedek as a proto-type of Christ by having him born miraculously without a human father. On this point he was supported by Rubinstein. Some scholars consider the Melchizedek legend to be a secondary addition, since it has no necessary connection with the story of Enoch and is omitted in some manuscripts (Charles and Morfill 1896, xiii; Fischer 1978, 40). Others have pointed out that the legend is not necessarily derived from the NT but could "have arisen out of a midrash of Ps 110" (Greenfield 1973, XX, following Flusser 1966, 26–27). The existence of Jewish speculation on Melchizedek is shown by 11Q Melch from Qumran. Recently Charlesworth 1979, 315–323, reports that F. Andersen now questions Vaillant's views on the two recensions.

[10] Pines 1970, 75, has noted that the practice is declared contrary to usage by the Mishna treatise *Tamid* and infers that "it may have been an accepted rite of a sect, which repudiated the sacrificial customs prevailing in Jerusalem." The custom was Egyptian in origin.

[11] So also Fischer 1978, 40.

with Philo and other Hellenistic Jewish writings.[12] The most widely accepted date is in the first century CE.[13]

2.2. *2 Enoch* begins with the circumstances which lead up to the revelation. Enoch is weeping and grieving but we are not told why.[14] Then, when he is asleep, two angelic "men" come to escort him on a heavenly tour. Before he departs, Enoch gives a brief exhortation to his sons, to practise sacrifice and avoid idolatry. Then in chaps. 3–9 Enoch is guided through the seven heavens in turn. In the first he sees the angels who govern the stars and the elements. In the second, the place of punishment of the angels who rebelled against the Lord. In the third, the paradise which is at once the original garden of Genesis and the place prepared for the just. On the north of this heaven he sees the place of torture and punishment prepared for sinners. In the fourth heaven he sees the movements of the light of the sun and the moon and the regulation of time. In the fifth, he encounters the Egrigori or Watchers who are mourning the fall of their fellow angels. Enoch tells them that he has seen their condemned brethren and exhorts them to resume their service of God. In the sixth heaven he sees seven angels who supervise the order of the world. Finally in the seventh heaven he comes into the heavenly court. There he is anointed and given garments of glory and he becomes like one of the glorious angels.

2.2.1. There follow two episodes in which Enoch is given direct instruction. First, the angel Vreveil dictates to him "all the works of heaven and earth" and Enoch writes them down in 360 books. Second, God tells Enoch how he created the world. The account is remote from that of Genesis and involves quasi-mythological creatures, Adoil (from whom the great aeon is born) and Arouchaz (who becomes the foundation of creation).

2.2.2. At this point God commands Enoch to return to earth for thirty days to instruct his children and pass on his writings to them. There follows the instruction of Enoch to his sons. This falls into three parts: a) a lengthy exhortation by Enoch, without introduction (chaps. 13–14), b) a

---

[12] See Charles 1913, vol. 2, p. 426; Philonenko 1969 and Fischer 1978, 40. There is a consensus that the book was written in Greek, despite occasional Hebraisms (Pines 1970, 73). Rubinstein 1962, 11, denies that there are any demonstrable Hebraisms as distinct from biblical phraseology.

[13] So Charles, Philonenko, Fischer. The *terminus ante quem* is supplied by Origen, *De Principiis* 1.3.2, which refers to a book of Enoch à propos of the creation of the world. The reference is most easily applied to *2 Enoch* 11 (Vaillant 1952, 29–35). It is not certain that the references to sacrifice must be dated before the temples of Jerusalem and Leontopolis were destroyed, since the sacrificial prescriptions do not in any case conform to the usual practice. The lack of any resentment towards the gentiles makes a date after the revolt of 115 CE unlikely.

[14] Vaillant suggests that Enoch is lamenting the sins of humanity because he knows the flood is coming (Compare *1 Enoch* 83).

similar address to Methusalem and his brothers which appears directly as Enoch's parting testament and c) finally, again a similar address to a multitude of 2,000 men who were assembled to see him. Then Enoch is taken up to heaven (apparently to the seventh) and Methusalem proceeds to offer sacrifice. This concludes the story of Enoch. The legend of Melchizedek is formally a distinct unit, independent of the apocalypse, whether or not it was originally juxtaposed with it in a single composition.

2.3. Unlike many of the better-known apocalypses the revelation in *2 Enoch* is not a response to a specific need or crisis. Enoch is in distress before the angels come to him, but the reason for his distress is not made explicit. It may be simply the general human condition of sin and suffering. The most obvious clue to the purpose of the work lies in the frequency of the exhortations. The actual content of the exhortation is simple enough. It is mainly concerned with natural justice – clothing the naked and feeding the hungry. There are warnings to serve and fear the Lord and avoid idolatry, but there is a striking insistence that whoever offends "the face of a man" offends the face of God.[15] In all of this there is little emphasis on distinctive Jewish customs. The only element in the exhortations that does not fit readily with the dominant universalism is the repeated insistence on sacrifice, with the peculiar requirement that the four legs be tied.[16] This would seem to presuppose a sectarian practice. Yet there is no attempt in *2 Enoch* to polemicize against other practices or to promote the importance of membership in a distinct group.

2.3.1. The exhortations in *2 Enoch* are given a supporting framework by the heavenly journey. In that journey two kinds of material are emphasized, evidence of the order of creation and evidence of an eschatological judgment. The first of these is found in the first, fourth and sixth heaven. Enoch is shown that the sun and moon follow a regular orderly course. The elements are not at the mercy of chance but each has an angel directing it, and these in turn are supervised from the sixth heaven. The ultimate basis for this entire order is the creation, which God describes to Enoch in chap. 11. The implications of this order for human conduct are quite clear. When God is dispatching Enoch to the earth he tells him:

"explique à tes fils tout ce que je t'ai dit et tout ce que tu as vu depuis le ciel inférieur jusqu'au mon trône: toutes les milices, c'est moi qui les ai faites, il n'y a pas qui s'oppose à moi ou ne se soumette pas, et tous se soumettent à ma monarchie et servent ma seule puissance."[17]

Humanity, evidently, should do likewise.[18] God specifies for Enoch the purpose of his mission: that they may know the creator of all things and know that there is no other apart from him.

---

[15] Vaillant 1952, 47.　　[16] *Ibid.*, 59, 67.
[17] *Ibid.*, 33.　　[18] Compare *1 Enoch* 2–5.

2.3.2. In the course of his exhortations Enoch frequently refers back to the created order of the universe. The basis for human respect is that the Lord made man in his own likeness.[19] Enoch begins his testament to Methusalem and his brothers by reminding them of the relations between man and beast established at creation,[20] and his final exhortation to the assembled multitude begins by recounting how God created everything, including humanity.[21] An understanding of the order of the world is the first underpinning of Enoch's message.

2.3.3. The exhortations of Enoch are not based solely on the order of creation. They also appeal to an eschatological judgment. Eschatology figures prominently in the heavenly journey. The third heaven is occupied by Paradise and the place of punishment. The second heaven is the place of punishment for the fallen angels, who are paradigmatic for humanity. The sojourn in the fifth heaven with the Egrigori recalls the fate of the fallen angels as a warning for others. Finally, the transformation of Enoch into the likeness of the angels in the seventh heaven has clear eschatological implications.[22] These eschatological revelations figure prominently in the exhortations of Enoch. The contrasting places of reward and punishment in the third heaven provide the main context in which virtues and vices are articulated. Enoch repeatedly refers to a final judgment.

2.3.4. It is important to realize that the themes of creation and eschatological judgment are not merely juxtaposed in *2 Enoch*. They are intrinsically related to each other. This fact should be obvious from the way in which they are intertwined. In the heavenly journey, cosmological concerns are dominant in the first, fourth and sixth heavens, but eschatological judgment in the second, third and fifth. More directly significant is the way the themes are intertwined in the exhortations. Enoch's summary of the secrets of nature in chap. 13 culminates in his account of the places of reward and punishment, and his moral exhortations are given in this context.[23] The reminder that God created man in his image[24] is balanced with an appeal to the final judgment. In the exhortation to Methusalem, the relation of man and beasts at creation[25] is linked directly to the judgment when even the souls of the animals will accuse mankind. In the final exhortation to the assembled multitude, the creation, with its division of times, finds its counterpart in the final judgment when time will be dissolved.[26] Finally we should note that the references to eschatological

---

[19] Vaillant 1952, 47.   [20] *Ibid.*, 57.   [21] *Ibid.*, 61.

[22] The idea that the righteous dead enjoy an angelic afterlife is widespread in apocalyptic literature. Compare *1 Enoch* 39:5; 104:2,6; *2 Apoc. Bar.* 51:10; Matt 22:30; Dan 12:2–3 (where the stars should be taken as equivalent to the angels). Note also the idea of fellowship with the angels in the Qumran Hodayot. See Collins 1974a, 34–36.

[23] Vaillant 1952, 43, 45.   [24] *Ibid.*, 47.   [25] *Ibid.*, 57.

[26] *Ibid.*, 63.

judgment are frequently presented as references to the places of judgment which are prepared.[27] In short, the cosmology of the heavens has made provision for the judgment. Human destiny is built into the structure of the universe from creation. The eschatological judgment then is scarcely even a different theme from the order of creation. It is the crowning vindication of that order and the most important dimension of the works of creation viewed by Enoch.

2.3.5. The eschatology of *2 Enoch* is primarily concerned with the fate of individuals after death. There is no question of the future establishment of an earthly utopia. Yet this eschatology will be brought into effect by a general judgment which will have cosmic effects.[28] The eschatology of the individual cannot be understood apart from the eschatology of the cosmos. Consequently we can scarcely say that *2 Enoch* is individualistic. The individual is definitely conceived in a context that is both social and cosmic.

2.3.6. It is well known that all apocalyptic eschatology involves a sharp discontinuity between the present and the future. In many apocalypses (*e.g.* 4 Ezra) this is envisaged in terms of an evil present age followed by a good age to come. *2 Enoch* does not especially characterize the present age as evil, but it surely implies a contrast and suggests that the future age is the more ultimately real, since the present world will pass away. The "other world" envisaged by *2 Enoch* is not wholly future. Since it is primarily envisaged in spatial terms, and can be visited by Enoch now, it is a present world, juxtaposed to this one.[29] The present reality of the "other world" is essential to the logic of Enoch's exhortations. The crucial importance of his ethical message is assured, not only by the prospect of a future judgment, but by Enoch's claim that he has seen the places of reward and punishment which are already in existence. The persuasiveness of the message depends on the acceptance of, or belief in, the reality of this "other world." Faith, in the sense of "insight into the heavenly world"[30] is the underpinning for the future hope (and fear) and the basis for present action.

2.3.7. The function of Slavonic Enoch, then, is hortatory. It advocates an ethic that is remarkably universalistic, despite the peculiar insistence on sacrifice. The distinctive character of the work, however, lies in the way it grounds this message in a view of the structure of creation and eschatological judgment. It demands faith or understanding as the basis for action.

---

[27] *Ibid.*, 51, 57, 59.

[28] Fischer 1978, 52, argues that the individual is judged separately, immediately after death, on the basis of a passage in chap. 13 (p. 51): "before man came to be, a place of judgment was prepared for him." However, the passage does not require the interpretation he gives it.

[29] This has been clearly noted by Fischer 1978, 54–55.

[30] I take the phrase from MacRae 1978, 194, who so defines *pistis* in the Epistle to the Hebrews.

3. 3 Apocalypse of Baruch

3.1. In the case of *3 Apoc. Bar.* there is at least a consensus that the work is Jewish, despite some Christian insertions in chaps. 4 and 11–15.[31] There is also a consensus that it originated in the Hellenistic Diaspora, because of its allusions to Egyptian and Greek mythology, and its affinities with other products of Egyptian Judaism.[32] A date about the beginning of the second century is widely accepted.[33]

3.2. *3 Apoc. Bar.*, in its present form, is a shorter and more simple composition than *2 Enoch*, and consists of the heavenly journey, with a brief introduction and conclusion. The introduction gives the circumstances leading up to the revelation: Baruch was grieving over the destruction of Jerusalem. Then an angel appears to show him "the mysteries of God." In the first heaven he sees men who have "the faces of oxen, and the horns of stags, and the feet of goats and the haunches of lambs" (2:3) and are identified as those "who built the tower of strife against God" (2:7). In the second heaven are men whose appearance was like dogs and their feet like those of stags, and are identified as "they who gave counsel to build the tower" (3:5). The contents of the third heaven are most complex (chaps. 4–9). They include Hades and a dragon which devours the bodies of the wicked.[34] They also include the sun and moon and a Phoenix that shields the earth from the sun. In the course of his tour of this heaven, Baruch inquires about "the tree which led Adam astray" and thereby occasions a digression on the vine and the dangers of wine.[35] In the fourth heaven he sees multitudes of birds which sing the praises of God and is told that this is where the souls of the righteous come. The birds are generally assumed to represent the souls of the righteous.[36] Finally, the fifth heaven is marked by a locked gate which is opened by the Archangel Michael. In this heaven the angels bring the merits of humanity in baskets to Michael, who takes them up to God (presumably in a higher heaven). Humanity is rewarded for its

---

[31] Picard 1967, 75–78; Hage 1974, 17–20; Fischer 1978, 72–75; Hughes 1913, 528–530.

[32] Fischer 1978, 75; Picard 1967, 77–78.

[33] Fischer 1978, 75. The *terminus ante quem* is supplied by Origen, (*De Principiis* 2.3.6) who refers to a book of Baruch which treats of seven heavens. *3 Apoc. Bar.* only mentions five heavens, but most scholars assume that the last two were lost in transmission, or perhaps omitted by the Christian redactor. Since the apocalypse begins with Baruch lamenting the destruction of Jerusalem, a date after 70 CE seems plausible. Picard 1967, 77, denies that the work ever referred to more than five heavens. He also disputes the typological significance of the fall of Jerusalem (Picard 1970, 84–90).

[34] The relation between Hades and the dragon is confused. See Fischer 1978, 80–82.

[35] This passage is interrupted by a Christian interpolation which promises that the fruit of the vine shall become the blood of God and that salvation will come through Christ.

[36] Hughes 1913, 539, cites Sanhedrin 92b: "And the soul may say: the body has sinned; for since I am separated from it, I fly in the air like a bird."

merits and punished for the lack of them. The apocalypse ends when Baruch is returned to his place, gives glory to God and exhorts his listeners to do likewise.

3.3. Unlike Enoch, Baruch does not spell out his message in an explicit exhortation at the end.[37] The work still has a hortatory effect, through the list of vices associated with the fruit of the vine in 4:17 and another list of sins that defile the rays of the sun in 8:5.[38] Much of the revelation focuses on rewards and punishments in the afterlife. So the fate of the animal-like builders of the tower and their advisers in the first two heavens stands in contrast to that of the bird-like righteous in the fourth, and the climax of the revelation is the judgment of the merits of humanity by God. All of this is evidently designed to discourage vice and promote virtue.

3.3.1. Yet *3 Apoc. Bar.* does not rely on direct exhortation. As Picard has noted, the work is essentially a story which starts from Baruch's distress over the ruin of Jerusalem. At the end of the story, Baruch has apparently forgotten his distress and is caught up in glorifying God. Picard calls this transition an "apocalyptic cure," which he compares to the "shamanistic cure" discussed by Lévi-Strauss.[39] This cure attains its effect by having the listener identify with Baruch and share his (fictional) experience. So, Picard argues, the problem of Baruch in the apocalypse is the real problem of the author and his circle: an acute sense of exile. Picard refuses to associate this with any contemporary destruction of Jerusalem, but it would surely be very plausible in the aftermath of national disaster, such as the destruction of Jerusalem or the crushing of the revolt in the Diaspora. Baruch's heavenly journey responds to his problem by showing that the "Babylonians" (builders of the tower and their advisers) were severely punished. More fundamentally, there is an implied condemnation of Jerusalem. In 1:2 Jerusalem is the *vineyard* of the Lord. In chap. 4, the vine is the tree that led Adam astray, but was saved from the flood, and now causes all mankind to sin. The apparent digression on the vine then is a symbolic condemnation of Jerusalem and responds directly to the author's problem. Picard's interpretation, that the vine in chap. 4 still refers to Jerusalem, is not explicit in the text, and so must be regarded as less than certain. However, there is no doubt that the apocalypse diminishes the significance of the fall of Jerusalem. In 1:3 Baruch is told not to worry so much about the salvation of Jerusalem. His transition from grief to glorifying God involves no assurance that Jerusalem will be restored. While the apocalypse begins

---

[37] Picard 1970, 90–91, suggests that *3 Apoc. Bar.* was meant to be accompanied by an oral commentary analogous to Enoch's explanations to his sons in *2 Enoch*.

[38] Lists of vices and virtues are especially common in Hellenistic Jewish literature. See Vögtle 1936, 58–73; Conzelmann 1975, 100–101.

[39] Picard 1970, 86–90.

with an opposition of Jerusalem and the nations, it ends with a contrast between individuals who have merits and those who have not. The fate of Jerusalem is of little consequence for the judgment of individuals. It is of interest to note that even the "builders of the tower" and their advisers are not punished for destroying Jerusalem, but for cruelty (in refusing to release a woman for childbirth) and for attempting to discover the nature of heaven. It is not clear whether a specific group of people is symbolized by the tower builders here, but we cannot assume that they are simply the gentile enemies of Judaism.[40]

3.3.2. *3 Apoc. Bar.*, then, replaces the traditional opposition of Israel and the nations with a system of individual rewards and punishments. Unlike *2 Enoch*, it does not even seem to envisage a public general judgment.[41] Yet the individualized judgment is presented as a solution to the public, social problem posed by the fall of Jerusalem. It is also integrated into a view of the total cosmic world order. *3 Apoc. Bar.* is not individualistic in the sense of considering human individuals in isolation from their social and cosmic context.

3.3.3. While the content of the heavenly visions is heavily oriented to the rewards and punishments of the afterlife, these eschatological concerns are intertwined with cosmological speculations, especially in the third heaven. As Picard has noted, the apocalypse proposes an entire "système du monde," which not only distinguishes righteous and wicked but locates them "dans un univers dont les principaux phénomènes physiques sont expliqué."[42] Picard has not, perhaps, adequately noted the otherworldly character of that "universe." What Baruch sees in his journey are those aspects of the world which are not accessible to human knowledge, such as the movements of sun and moon, and properly supernatural regions, the abodes of the wicked and righteous after death. These regions are not presented merely as a fictional world, or only as one to come in the future. They are present, though hidden, realities. The persuasiveness of the book's message depends on the acceptance of this heavenly world as reality, in short, on *faith*. As in *2 Enoch*, the revelation provides the basis for understanding the structure of the world and the way in which human destiny is integrated in it. This understanding can resolve such problems as the fall of Jerusalem by putting them in perspective, and provide positive guidance as to how life should be lived.

---

[40] Picard 1970, 79, n. 6, proposes that there is an allusion to Greek sophists. Nickelsburg (1981, 302) argues that *3 Apoc. Bar.* 16:2–4 alludes to Deut 32:21 and shows that the author interprets the destruction of Jerusalem as punishment for the people's sin.

[41] Fischer 1978, 76–84. There is a reference in 1:7 to a "day of judgment," but this may refer to the day on which Baruch is judged as an individual.

[42] Picard 1970, 95–96.

4. The Testament of Abraham

4.1. The Testament of Abraham is extant in two recensions and there is no consensus as to which is the earlier. Many scholars reject the idea that one recension depends directly on the other, and suppose that both can ultimately be traced to a common original.[43] Nickelsburg has shown persuasively that "numerous elements, *which are simply present* in Rec B, *with no clearly delineated function, are of the essence* of the structure and plot of Rec A," and that therefore the longer Rec A better preserves the outline of the story.[44] Accordingly we will follow Rec A here. There is wide agreement that *Test Abr* is a Jewish work,[45] written in Greek.[46] Egyptian provenance is suggested by several parallels to Egyptian mythology and to other Egyptian Jewish literature.[47] The date is usually put in the first century CE, on the basis of parallels to other Hellenistic Jewish writings.[48]

4.2. While *2 Enoch* and *3 Apoc. Bar.* are universally categorized as apocalypses, the case of *Test Abr* is more complex. All the defining characteristics of an apocalypse cited at the beginning of this essay are indeed present, but the revelation, Abraham's journey on the chariot, takes up only a small portion of the text, while the narrative framework is extended.[49] The work as a whole is not an apocalypse in its dominant form, but the chariot ride, chaps. 10–15 in Rec A and 8–12 in Rec B, must be so

---

[43] Delcor 1973, 13–14; Janssen 1975, 195.

[44] Nickelsburg 1976a, 92. The priority of B is defended by Schmidt 1971 and 1976. Sanders, forthcoming, concludes that the original book contained approximately the contents of Rec. A but that the original wording may be better preserved in B.

[45] Christian authorship was defended by a number of older scholars – M. R. James, Schürer, Weinel – but has found no recent followers. See Janssen 1975, 199.

[46] Delcor 1973, 34; Janssen 1975, 198–199; Sanders forthcoming. Turner 1953 originally argued for a Hebrew original of B, later modified this view to allow the possibility of "Jewish Greek" (1955) and has now abandoned the Hebrew original entirely (so Sanders, who cites a personal letter). Martin 1976, 95–101, suggests that "the producer of Recension A (and possibly also the producer of Recension B) is editing a Greek text which was earlier translated from a Semitic language" but Martin allows that some "additions" may not go back to a Semitic original.

[47] See especially Delcor 1973, 67–68. Janssen 1975, 199–201, objects that Egyptian influence was possible in Palestine, but fails to adduce positive evidence for a Palestinian origin. Schmidt 1971 argues that Egyptian influence is only evident in A, while both A and B show Iranian influence. He concludes that B was composed in Palestine, but there is no reason why Iranian influence should be more likely in Palestine than in Egypt. See the summary and critique of Schmidt's position by Nickelsburg 1976, 15–16.

[48] Delcor 1973, 51. The relation to the Testament of Job, argued by Delcor, is dubious, and in any case, the date of *T. Job* is uncertain. Sanders, forthcoming, argues that so irenic a work would scarcely have been composed in Egypt after 117 CE, and emphasizes the affinities of *Test Abr* with *2 Enoch* and *3 Apoc. Bar.*

[49] It is generally recognized that *Test Abr* is not a testament and is in fact characterized by Abraham's failure to make a testament. See Kolenkow 1974 and 1976.

classified.[50] The relation of this episode to the rest of the work must be considered.

4.3. Nickelsburg has shown that Rec A is "neatly divided into two parallel and symmetrical parts," 1–15 and 16–20. In the first part *Michael* comes to take Abraham, in the second part, *Death*. In both cases, Abraham refuses to go, and asks for a revelation, as a stalling tactic. In the first part the revelation is a ride on the chariot "over all the inhabited world" (10:1). In the second part it is the revelation of the rottenness of Death and the variety of his forms. In both cases, Abraham persists in his refusal, even after the revelation, and in the end he is taken by deceit. Nickelsburg summarizes the message of the book as "The moment of death, and its inevitable consummation, are in the hands of the sovereign God, and there is none who can resist."[51] Yet, the message of the book is more complex than this. As Nickelsburg himself notes, the work is "a veritable parody on the biblical and traditional Abraham."[52] The parody lies not only in Abraham's refusal to die, but also in the defects in his righteousness that are exposed. In his zeal to punish sinners, Abraham is in danger of destroying "the whole creation" (chap. 10). When he sees the judgment, however, he is moved to pity, and recognizes his own excessive zeal as a sin. He repents and is forgiven. It is worthy of note that this is the only way in which Abraham changes in the entire story (he never abandons his resistance to death). A. B. Kolenkow has rightly shown that one major focus of the work is on the recognition of this "new sin".[53] Not only is it the culmination of the heavenly journey of Abraham. It also underlies the second revelation of the varieties of Death. Abraham's sin was the destruction of

---

[50] The apocalyptic character of the work has been questioned by Janssen 1975, 196, but his arguments are weak. The "Zweiteilung in Vision und anschließende Deutung" is prominent only in a few apocalypses and Abraham is in fact accompanied by an *angelus interpres* here. The "Geschichte der vier Weltreiche" is a specific motif which is found in very few apocalypses. In both these cases Janssen seems to make unwarranted generalizations on the basis of Daniel and a few other works as to what is typically apocalyptic. It is true that Abraham is presented in the third rather than in the first person, but Janssen has not shown that this is so significant as to constitute a different genre. It is also true that *Test Abr* lacks the elaborate accounts of heaven and hell which are typical of some Christian apocalypses. It does, however, describe both the judgment and the otherworldly place of judgment. The difference over against other heavenly journeys only concerns the relative degrees of detail. Kolenkow 1976, 147, has suggested that *Test Abr* is "anti-apocalyptic" since it allows the possibility that some of those who go through the wide gate of the wicked may yet escape punishment. There is no doubt that *Test Abr* differs from other apocalyptic writings in its view of a merciful judgment, but different apocalyptic writings can disagree on specific points within a common apocalyptic framework. The fact that *Test Abr* insists on the reality of the judgment and its crucial importance is more significant than the precise way in which the judgment is portrayed.

[51] Nickelsburg 1976a, 87. Compare Schmidt's conclusion summarized by Nickelsburg 1976, 15: "The point of the story is that no one can escape death but that in the light of heavenly reality this death is, in fact, the transition from death (earthly existence) to life…"

[52] *Ibid.*   [53] Kolenkow 1976, 142.

life. Death boasts that he is the destroyer of the world. In Kolenkow's words: "Death's picture of himself puts on a major scale what might seem a minor sin of the righteous – and shows divine reaction to it."[54] The victory of Death is only apparent, since we have already been told in the judgment scene that God does not wish destruction, and does not "requite in death those whom I destroy living upon the earth" (chap. 14).

4.3.1. The two revelatory passages, then, are not mere stalling devices, but provide a crucially important perspective on death and the judgment. The problem raised by the book is the problem of Abraham – the human reluctance to die. The reader can identify with Abraham all the more easily because Abraham is shown to have his flaws and need forgiveness and because his reluctance to die persists to the end. Yet the work provides an "apocalyptic cure". The terror of death is mitigated by the realization that, while only one of the 72 deaths is just, God does not again destroy those who are struck down on earth. The terror of the judgment is mitigated by the revelation that God does not share the severity of "righteous" humans such as Abraham, and accepts intercession. In short, what Abraham is shown in the judgment scene puts the problem of death in perspective. The human reluctance to die will always persist, but it has been robbed of much of its basis. The second revelatory passage, on the nature of Death, is reassuring rather than terrifying, because it is seen in the perspective provided by the judgment scene. The heavenly journey, then, contains the most basic revelation which determines the effect of the book. It also provides the basis for the book's ethical message by showing that mercy rather than severity is pleasing to God.[55]

4.3.2. By contrast with *2 Enoch* and *3 Apoc. Bar.*, *Test Abr* shows little interest in the heavenly world.[56] Abraham is not taken on a tour of the heavens but rides through the sky to view the earth. He does, however, also visit "the first gate of heaven" and the place of judgment. Faith in the existence of these otherworldly places is still essential to the message of the book. While the otherworldly wisdom is less elaborate than in *2 Enoch*, it is still of the utmost importance.

4.3.3. *Test Abr* is almost exclusively concerned with the fate of the individual. Yet it cannot be called individualistic. Its subject is the most universal of human problems, death. Abraham is depicted in such a way as

---

[54] *Ibid.*, 146.

[55] Delcor's suggestion that chaps. 10–15 may be a *corps étranger* shows a failure to grasp the logic of the book (Delcor 1973, 51). Nickelsburg 1976, 21, rightly criticizes Delcor at this point.

[56] Abraham has a far more extensive tour of the heavens in the *Apocalypse of Abraham*. He is also said to have heavenly revelations in *2 Apoc. Bar.* 4:5 and Ps.-Philo's *Liber Antiquitatum Biblicarum* 18:5. Nickelsburg 1976, 25, surmises that *Test Abr* may presuppose familiarity with these traditions.

to emphasize that he too is part of sinful humanity. What Abraham learns on his journey is precisely his solidarity with the rest of humanity, a solidarity already indicated in the opening lines of the book.

5. Conclusions

Now that we have reviewed the three main apocalypses from the Hellenistic Diaspora, we may endeavor to locate them within the spectrum of Jewish writings of their time.

5.1. The initial question is whether they may be regarded as a coherent group, and in what their coherence lies. In fact, each work has a quite distinct purpose. *2 Enoch* advocates a particular ethical content, with a peculiar insistence on sacrifice. *3 Apoc. Bar.* provides a particular perspective on the fall of Jerusalem, which minimizes its importance in the light of individual eschatology. *Test Abr* provides a perspective on death in the light of God's mercy and also sheds light on the value of certain human attitudes. All, however, have an important parenetic aspect. In each case the message of the book is grounded in a view of the world disclosed in an otherworldly revelation. It involves the disclosure of a transcendent reality which is both spatial and temporal. The details of that transcendent reality can vary from one work to another. The inferences drawn from it can also vary. The coherence of these works does not lie in their precise function, but in their underlying conceptual structure: the belief in another, heavenly, world, already existing and in a definite judgment of every individual after death. This structure constitutes the premises for more specific argument. Two apocalypses may disagree diametrically on a specific issue (*e.g.* the possibility of intercession for the dead) but their disagreement falls within an agreed common structure, and each appeals to a similar kind of "evidence" or revelation.

5.2. A second question concerns the relation of these texts to the apocalypses of Palestinian Judaism. The Palestinian apocalypses are commonly described in terms of a pattern involving a review of history, eschatological crisis and heavenly intervention and are thought to represent a response to persecution or political crisis. This description is based on a small group of "historical" apocalypses – Daniel, 4 Ezra, *2 Apoc. Bar.* and some sections of *1 Enoch*.[57] None of the Hellenistic apocalypses we have discussed shows any interest in an historical sequence of this sort, and only *3 Apoc. Bar.* can at all be related to a political crisis. However, this common description of the Palestinian apocalypses is inadequate in several respects. Major sections of *1 Enoch* are not concerned with an historical sequence.

---

[57] These apocalypses are classified as Type Ia in the typology offered in Collins 1979

Further, as M. Stone has pointed out, even the "historical" apocalypses deal at length with cosmological matters and heavenly secrets.[58] Stone has also pointed out that the canonical book of Daniel is "notable among the apocalypses for its lack of interest in such matters."[59] Yet, even Daniel consists of heavenly revelations, mediated by angels, and includes a vision of the divine throne in chap. 7, while the decisive action of the book is represented as the battle of Michael and Gabriel against the angelic princes of Greece and Persia in chaps. 10–12. In short, the present reality of the heavenly world and the actions of heavenly beings is an essential part of the thought structure of even the most "historical" apocalypses.[60] Further, the "vertical" spatial interest has a dominant role in the earliest stages of *1 Enoch*, which must now be dated no later than the third century BCE and which are not obviously influenced by Greek thought.[61] The spatial emphasis in the Diaspora apocalypses then can not be ascribed solely to Hellenistic influence.[62] This is not to deny that the Hellenistic apocalypses have distinctive features over against the Palestinian, and are extreme in their lack of interest in communal salvation, but they still share a common thought structure and stand in the same tradition[62a].

5.3. A third question concerns the relation of these apocalypses to other documents of Diaspora Judaism. We have noted that they involve a kind of *wisdom*, and this wisdom has many affinities with such works as the Wisdom of Solomon and Philo. The contents of *3 Apoc. Bar.*, like those of the Wisdom of Solomon, are defined as μυστήρια θεοῦ and are heavily concerned with the fate of the individual after death.[63] Interest in an otherworldly eschatology and in cosmological matters[64] are precisely the traits that distinguish the Wisdom of Solomon from the older Hebrew wisdom.[65] While the idiom and imagery of the apocalypses is quite different from Wisdom or Philo, the similarities in thought structure are significant.[66]

---

[58] Stone 1976 and 1978.   [59] Stone 1978, 489.

[60] Collins 1977, especially chaps. 5 and 6.

[61] Stone 1978, *passim*.

[62] Fischer 1978 overlooks the continuity of *2 Enoch* and *3 Apoc. Bar.* with the Palestinian tradition.

[62a] Compare the role of faith in the Similitudes of Enoch (Collins, 1980).

[63] *3Apoc.Bar.* 1:6,8; Wis 2:22.

[64] Wis 7:17: "to know the structure of the universe and the operation of the elements." There is of course also some interest in cosmological matters in the Hebrew wisdom literature.

[65] Collins 1977a.

[66] For fuller discussion of the similarities and differences in thought structure see Collins 1977a. Specific parallels to Hellenistic Jewish literature are noted by Charles 1913, vol. 2, p. 426; Picard 1967, 78 and 1970, 83–84; Delcor 1973, 47–51. On the thought structure of the *Testament of Job,* which is closely related to the apocalypses see Collins 1974b.

It should further be noted that the kind of apocalypse represented by the works we have considered – specifically, heavenly journeys – has precedents not only in Palestinian Judaism but also in the Greek tradition, where journeys to the netherworld are found as early as Homer and ascents to the heavens are known from the classical period.[67] The relation of this material to the Jewish heavenly journeys has not yet been adequately explored.

5.4. Finally, there is the question of the function and setting of these texts. We have noted that their specific purposes vary. On a broader level all of them presuppose that the most profound reality and the ultimate destiny of humanity are not found in this world but in the heavens. In this rather broad sense they may be said to reflect a certain alienation from this world, but not to the extent that this world is considered evil or hostile[67a].

More significantly, they all demand the acceptance of a heavenly revelation, which might well be thought to constitute the belief of some esoteric conventicle. However, each of these apocalypses is also distinctly universalistic in its outlook. Whereas apocalypticism is often thought to involve a dualistic view of the world, and to reinforce the morale of a persecuted elect, these works do not reflect persecution and do not even attach any significance to the distinction between Jew and Gentile.[68] There is, of course, always a distinction between righteous and sinners (although even this is modified in the Testament of Abraham) but there is no suggestion that this distinction coincides with identifiable social groups. Neither is there any attempt to promote membership in any particular group. Contrary to the assumption of Vielhauer,[69] not all apocalypses are conventicle literature. Consequently, there is little reason to attribute any of these writings to a specific "milieu fermé" such as the Therapeutae.[70] We cannot, of course, exclude the possibility that these works were produced in a specific organized group (or groups), which was based on faith in the divine revelation. What is important, however, is that the function of the revelation was not to promote or preserve such a distinct group, but to advocate certain attitudes to humanity in general – as typified by the statement in *2 Enoch* that whoever offends the face of man offends the face

---

[67] Attridge 1979 and the bibliography given there. Heavenly journeys are also found in the Persian tradition. See Colpe 1967.

[67a] I have pursued the setting and function of apocalyptic writings further in Collins 1982.

[68] This point is especially emphasized by Sanders, forthcoming.

[69] Above, n. 2.

[70] Delcor 1973, 73, who ascribes *Test Abr* to the Therapeutae. In fact we know far too little about the Therapeutae, and the correspondences between the apocalypses and Philo's account in *De vita contemplativa* are not specific enough to warrant the attribution. Picard 1970, 83–84, sees *3 Apoc. Bar.* as an initiation text for "a mystic Jewish sect" of which the Therapeutae would be an example. He also suggests similar functions for *2 Enoch* and *Test Abr* (*ibid.*, 90–91).

of God.[71] These apocalypses stand as an eloquent witness to the versatility of the genre and the belief in heavenly reality which it involved: it did not always serve to separate sons of light from sons of darkness, but could also serve to enhance the solidarity of common humanity.

Bibliography

Attridge, Harold W. 1979: "Greek and Latin Apocalypses", in: Collins (ed.) 1979, 159–186.
Bonwetsch, G. N. 1922: *Die Bücher der Geheimnisse Henochs, das sogenannte slawische Henoch-buch* (TU 44), Leipzig 1922.
Charles, R. H. and Morfill, W. R. 1896: *The Book of the Secrets of Enoch*, Oxford 1896.
Charles, R. H. (ed.) 1913: *Apocrypha and Pseudepigrapha of the Old Testament*, Oxford 1913.
Charlesworth, J. H. 1976: *The Pseudepigrapha and Modern Research* (SCSt 7), Missoula, Mont. 1976.
– 1979: "The SNTS Pseudepigrapha Seminars at Tübingen and Paris on the Books of Enoch", in: *NTS* 25 (1979) 315–323.
– (ed.) forthcoming: *Old Testament Apocrypha and Pseudepigrapha*, Garden City, New York, forthcoming.
Collins, John J. 1974: *The Sibylline Oracles of Egyptian Judaism* (SBLDS 13), Missoula, Mont. 1974.
– 1974a: "Apocalyptic Eschatology as the Transcendence of Death", in: *CBQ* 35 (1974) 21–43.
– 1974b: "Structure and Meaning in the Testament of Job", in: George W. MacRae (ed.), *SBL Seminar Papers*, Missoula, Mont. 1974. Vol. 1, 35–52.
– 1977: *The Apocalyptic Vision of the Book of Daniel* (HSM 16), Missoula, Mont. 1977.
– 1977a: "Cosmos and Salvation: Jewish Wisdom and Apocalyptic in the Hellenistic Age", in: *HR* 17 (1977) 121–142.
– (ed.) 1979: *Apocalypse: The Morphology of a Genre* (Semeia 14), Missoula, Mont. 1979.
– 1980: "The Heavenly Representative: The 'Son of Man' in the Similitudes of Enoch," in: Nickelsburg and Collins (eds.) 1980, 111–133.
– 1982: "The Apocalyptic Technique: Setting and Function in the Book of the Watchers," in: *CBQ* 44 (1982) 91–111.
– forthcoming: "The Development of the Sibylline Tradition", in: *ANRW*, Berlin forthcoming.
– forthcoming a: "The Sibylline Oracles", in: Charlesworth (ed.) forthcoming.
Colpe, Carsten 1967: "'Die Himmelsreise der Seele' außerhalb und innerhalb der Gnosis", in: Ugo Bianchi (ed.) *Le Origini dello Gnosticismo* (Numen Sup XII), Leiden 1967, 429–447.
Conzelmann, Hans 1975: *1 Corinthians* (Hermeneia), Philadelphia, Penn. 1975 (German original, Göttingen 1969; 2nd ed. 1981).
Delcor, M. 1973: *Le Testament d'Abraham* (SVPT 2), Leiden 1973.
Fischer, Ulrich 1978: *Eschatologie und Jenseitserwartung im Hellenistischen Diasporajudentum* (BZNW 44), Berlin 1978.
Flusser, David 1966: "Melchizedek and the Son of Man", in: *Christian News from Israel* (April, 1966) 26–27.
Greenfield, Jonas C. 1973: "Prolegomenon", in: H. Odeberg, *3 Enoch or the Hebrew Book of Enoch*, New York 1973.
Hage, W. 1974: "Die griechische Baruch-Apokalypse", in: *JSHRZ* V/1, Gütersloh 1974.
Hughes, H. M. 1913: "3 Baruch or the Greek Apocalypse of Baruch", in: Charles (ed.) 1913. Vol. 2, 527–541.

---

[71] Vaillant 1952, 47.

Janssen, Enno 1975: "Testament Abrahams", in: *JSHRZ* III/2, Gütersloh 1975.

Kolenkow, Anitra B. 1974: "What is the Role of Testament in the Testament of Abraham,", in: *HThR* 67 (1974) 182–184.

– 1976: "The Genre Testament and the Testament of Abraham", in: Nickelsburg (ed.) 1976, 139–152.

MacRae, George W. 1978: "Heavenly Temple and Eschatology in the Letter to the Hebrews", in: *Semeia* 12 (1978) 179–199.

Martin, R. A. 1976: "Syntax Criticism of the Testament of Abraham", in: Nickelsburg (ed.) 1976, 95–120.

McNeil, Brian 1978: "The Narration of Zosimus", in: *JSJ* 9 (1978) 68–82.

Milik, J. T. 1971: "Problèmes de la Littérature Hénochique à la Lumière des Fragments Araméens de Qumrân", in: *HThR* 64 (1971) 107–116.

–1976: *The Books of Enoch*, Oxford 1976.

Nickelsburg, George W. E. and Collins, John J. (eds.) 1980: *Ideal Figures in Ancient Judaism* (SCSt 12), Chico, Calif. 1980.

Nickelsburg, George W. E. (ed.) 1976: *Studies on the Testament of Abraham* (SCSt 6), Missoula, Mont. 1976.

– 1976a: "Structure and Message in the Testament of Abraham", in: Nickelsburg (ed.) 1976, 85–93.

– 1981: *Jewish Literature Between The Bible and The Mishnah*, Philadelphia, Penn. 1981.

Philonenko, Marc 1969: "La cosmologie du 'Livre des secrets d'Hénoch'", in: *Religions en Egypte Hellénistique et Romaine*, Paris 1969, 109–116.

Picard, J. C. 1967: *Apocalypsis Baruchi Graece* (PVTG 2), Leiden 1967.

– 1970: "Observations sur l'Apocalypse grecque de Baruch I: Cadre historique et efficacité symbolique", in: *Semitica* 20 (1970) 77–103.

Pines, S. 1970: "Eschatology and the Concept of Time in the Slavonic Book of Enoch", in: R. J. Z. Werblowski and J. C. Bleeker (eds.) *Types of Redemption* (NumenSup XVIII), Leiden 1970, 72–87.

Rosenstiehl, J. M. 1972: *L'Apocalypse d'Elie*, Paris 1972.

Rubinstein, A. 1962: "Observations on the Slavonic Book of Enoch", in: *JJS* 13 (1962) 1–21.

Sanders, E. P. forthcoming: "The Testaments of the Three Patriarchs", in: Charlesworth (ed.) forthcoming.

Schmidt, Francis 1971: *Le Testament d'Abraham: Introduction, édition de la recension courte, traduction et notes*, Thèse Strasbourg (typescript) 1971.

– 1976: "The Two Recensions of the Testament of Abraham: In Which Way did the Transformation Take Place?", in: Nickelsburg (ed.) 1976, 65–83.

Scholem, Gershom 1962: *Ursprung und Anfänge der Kabbala*, Berlin 1962.

Stone, Michael E. 1976: "Lists of Revealed Things in Jewish Apocalyptic", in: F. M. Cross, W. Lemke and P. D. Miller (eds.) *Magnalia Dei: G. Ernest Wright in Memoriam*, Garden City, New York 1976, 414–452.

– 1978: "The Book of Enoch and Judaism in the Third Century BCE", in: *CBQ* 40 (1978) 479–492.

Turner, Nigel 1953: *The Testament of Abraham: a study of the original language, place of origin, authorship and relevance*, Diss. London 1953.

–1955: "The Testament of Abraham, Problems in Biblical Greek", in: *NTS* 1 (1955) 219–223.

Vaillant, A. 1952: *Le Livre des Secrets d'Hénoch, texte slave et traduction francaise*, Paris 1952.

Vielhauer, P. 1965: "Apocalypses and Related Subjects", in: Edgar Hennecke/Wilhelm Schneemelcher (eds.) *New Testament Apocrypha*, Philadelphia, Penn. 1965. Vol. 2, pp. 581–607 (German original, Tübingen 1964).

Vögtle, Anton 1936: *Die Tugend- und Lasterkataloge im Neuen Testament*, (NTA 16,4–5), Münster 1936.

Libri fatales
Römische Offenbarungsliteratur und Geschichtstheologie

HUBERT CANCIK

1. Offenbarung und Geschichte

1.1. imperium sine fine

1.1.1. Der Klassiker der römischen Offenbarungsliteratur ist Publius Vergilius. Vergil führt den etruskischen Beinamen 'Maro'; er stammt aus Mantua, einer etruskischen Stadt, benannt nach der *fatidica Mantus,* der Mutter des Stadtgründers Ocnus. Er schöpft aus römischer Pontifikal- und Auguralliteratur, etruskischer Disziplin ("Lehre"), aus Pythagoreismus und chaldäischer Astrologie. Schon der Antike galt die Aeneis als "heiliges Buch", als "Tempel" und Vergil als *pontifex maximus*[1].

Fast alle antiken Divinationsarten sind in der Aeneis zu finden: Inkubation und Katabasis, Extispicin und Blitzschau, der ekstatische Wahnsinn der gottbesessenen Sibylle und die Lehre des Anchises. Der Vater im Lethe-Hain offenbart (*pandit*) dem Sohne die Zukunft des einzelnen Menschen, des Kosmos und des römischen Volkes (individuelle, kosmologische und kollektive Eschatologie); er belehrt (*docet*), bestärkt ihn (Paraenese), erinnert ihn mit deutlich sibyllinischem Tonfall an seine und des römischen Volkes Aufgabe (Sendung, Bestimmung)[2]:

tu regere imperio populos, Romane, memento.

Vergils Dichtung enthält, worauf schon oft hingewiesen wurde[3], eine römische Geschichtstheologie. Zeichen (*signa*) künden den 'Willen' (*numen*)

---

[1] Maro bezeichnet wohl ein Verwaltungsamt (*aedilis*)? Mantua: Schol. Veron. Vergil, Aen. 10,200 = FGrHist 706, Anhang §4. Quellen Vergils: vgl. z. B. Macrobius 1,24,16 (V. *noster pontifex maximus*). 17 (*scientia iuris auguralis*). 18 (*astrologia totaque philosophia*); 3,2,2f.; 3,9,16; "hl. Buch": Macr. 1,24,13. Astrologie: Serv. Verg. ecl. 4,4: (*Sibylla*) *saecula per metalla divisit.*

[2] Aen. 6,723.759 (vgl. 891).806f.847ff.

[3] Altheim II 1953, 263ff. (Horaz); 276ff. (Livius); 284ff. (Lucan); 294ff. (Vergil und Tacitus); bes. S. 269 (gegen K. Löwith). Altheims Ansätze reichen tief in die 30er Jahre zurück, "Altitalische und altrömische Gottesvorstellung", in: *Klio* 30 (1937) 51ff.; Koch 1935/37 = 1968, 128ff. (Geschichtlichkeit der römischen Götter; Entmythisierung); Kleinknecht 1944 = 1963, 467f.; 472f. (Entmythisierung, Historisierung durch Vergil); 485 ("Geist des historischen Epos der Römer"); Klingner 1965, 310 ("Dieses fast [!] prophetische und

der Götter. Sie "führen" die Flüchtlinge von Troja in die neue Heimat, zur "alten Mutter": Italien – die Flucht als Rückkehr[4]. Damit wird ein 'Plan' (*fata*) in der Geschichte verwirklicht. In die Gründungsgeschichte Roms ist die Bestimmung und Zukunft des Reiches immer wieder eingespiegelt.

Divination ist wichtiger Gegenstand und Gestaltungsmittel dieser Theologie. Es wird genügen, ein Beispiel aus der Aeneis in Erinnerung zu rufen.

1.1.2. Kurz vor dem Ziel zerschlägt ein furchtbares Unwetter die Flotte der Aeneaden; sie werden nach Afrika abgetrieben. In dieser Katastrophe 'offenbart' Iuppiter seinem Kinde Venus, die als Mutter des Aeneas beim Vater für ihre Aeneaden eintritt, die Grundzüge der römischen Geschichte.

"Laß die Furcht", spricht Iuppiter, "der die Sachen der Menschen und Götter mit ewig gültigen Befehlen regiert" (1,229f.); die 'Sendung' (*fata*) und 'Verheißung' (*promissa*) bleiben dir bestehen[5].

> Künden will ich es . . . und weiter (ent)rollen die Geheimnisse der Verkündigungen.

Vergil erinnert durch die figura etymologica an den Zusammenhang von 'Sprechen' und 'Schicksalspruch' (*fari – fatum*).

> fabor enim . . ./ longius et volvens fatorum arcana movebo.

Dem vielschichtigen Ausdruck liegt die Vorstellung von einem Buche zugrunde, in dem das Schicksal von Menschen und Völkern verzeichnet ist. Iuppiter rezitiert sozusagen aus einem *liber fatalis*[6].

---

eschatologische Geschichtsbewußtsein...", sc. bei Vergil: vgl. u. §3.1.). Dieser Forschungsansatz reicht in das 19. Jahrhundert; neben Hegel und Nietzsche ist z. B. Bachofen nicht zu vergessen, vgl. J. J. Bachofen, *Die Sage von Tanaquil* (1870), in: *Gesammelte Werke VI* (1951), 188; 302ff.: "Historisierung des kultischen Gedankens". – Zur neueren Diskussion s. Bailey 1935; Binder 1971; Cancik 1980; Wlosok 1973.

[4] Aen. 3,96ff. (Verheißung Apollo's): ... *antiquam exquirite matrem./ hic domus Aeneae cunctis dominabitur oris/ et nati natorum et qui nascentur ab illis./* – Diese Verheißung entspricht der Iuppiters: das Haus des Aeneas (vgl. *domus divina*) wird überall (*nec metas*), und immer (*sine fine*) herrschen, s. §1.1.2. – Auch der Exodus der Hebräer aus Ägypten (Ex) ist eine Rückkehr.

[5] Aen. 1,257ff.: *manent inmota tuorum/ fata tibi.* Die Paraphrase benutzt mit Bedacht 'moderne' Begriffe.

[6] a) Der Bezug auf *libri* ist bei Vergil nicht eindeutig. Die antiken Kommentare sagen nichts, vgl. Serv. Aen. 1,22 (*sic volvere Parcas: aut a filo traxit volvere aut a libro; una enim loquitur, altera scribit, alia fila deducit*); die neueren schwanken: *volvere – mente agitare* (Ladewig – Schaper) oder "probably a metaphor from a book unrolled" (Conington-Nettleship, [4]1884), ähnlich Marmorale (1952) und Austin (1971). Ein fester Bezug zu den römischen *libri fatales* wurde, soweit ich sehe, bisher nicht angenommen. – Die Übersetzungen schwanken. J. Götte arbeitet die Buchmetapher deutlich heraus: "jetzt will ich künden, ..., will nun weiter entrollen das Buch geheimer Verheißung." R. A. Schröder hält sich offener: "ich künde dir's nun, ... und entfalte dir heut (?) der Verhängnisse tiefstes Geheimnis."
b) Zum Ausdruck *fatorum arcana* vgl. Verg. Aen. 7,123: (*Anchises*) *fatorum arcana reliquit;* die antiken Erklärer dachten hier an Bücher (Schol. a.l.): s. u. §3.2. zu Naevius BP frg. 9* Str. – *movebo* impliziert vielleicht das Ingangsetzen, das durch das Aussprechen selbst schon geschieht.

In der flavischen Epoche hat Silius Italicus in seinem historischen Epos *Punica* die vergilische Geschichtstheologie fortgesetzt und aktualisiert: Domitian tritt an die Stelle des Augustus. In einer kritischen Situation schiebt Silius nach dem Muster des Vergil ein Gespräch zwischen Iuppiter und Venus ein (B. III). Hannibal übersteigt die Alpen; Venus befürchtet das "Ende des Reiches" (*finem imperii* 3,563). Als Mutter und Patronin der Aeneaden (*sanguis tuus*) erinnert sie den Vater an frühere Verheißungen (*concessa urbs*). Iuppiter antwortet mit einer langen Rede über die Zukunft Roms, auch über die Unterwerfung der Juden (571–629). Silius gibt ihr den Titel:

pandit seriem venturi Iuppiter aevi (630).

Er offenbart die Abfolge der kommenden Zeit. Dabei entwickelt Silius das geschichtstheologische Thema, wie das römische Volk von den Göttern geprüft und erzogen werde.

Was literargeschichtlich als bloße Imitatio eines Vergil-Epigonen bewertet wird, ist religionsgeschichtlich die Fortsetzung eines besonderen Zweiges römischer Offenbarungsliteratur und Geschichtstheologie. Diese Geschichtstheologie hat vom Beginn der römischen Literatur bis in die Spätantike – und darüber hinaus – geblüht. Der erste Beleg ist das *bellum Poenicum* des Naevius, ein später die historischen Epen des Claudian, aus der Zeit des hl. Augustinus[7].

1.1.3. Die Offenbarung des vergilischen Iuppiter gibt einen schematischen Abriß der Geschichte der Aeneaden als der Geschichte Roms (263–296): 3 Jahre noch für Aeneas, nach 30 Jahren die *translatio imperii* von Lavinium nach Alba Longa, 300 Jahre bis zur Gründung Roms. Derartige Zahlenreihen sind in spekulativer Geschichtsschau nicht selten (s. § 2.1.). Die Pointe dieser Reihe ist ihre Aufhebung in der Geschichte Roms; die Reihe wird nicht in die Tausender fortgesetzt:

his (Romanis) ego nec metas rerum nec tempora pono:
imperium sine fine dedi (278f.).
Diesen setze ich Ziele weder in Raum noch in Zeit:
ein Reich ohne Ende gab ich ihnen[8].

---

c) Zur Buchmetapher s. Curtius 1961, 306ff.; Leipoldt-Morenz 1953; Lanczkowski 1956. Schicksalsbuch: Phaedrus IV 11: *olim cum adscriptus venerit poenae dies* (vgl. Herm vis 1,2,1: εἰ αὕτη μοι ἡ ἁμαρτία ἀναγράφεται). Seneca, dial. I 5,8: *ille ipse omnium conditor et rector scripsit quidem fata, sed sequitur; semper paret, semel iussit.* Fata Scribunda: Pötscher 1977, 21 (mit Literatur).

[7] Vgl. §3.2. Claudian imitiert Vergil und die unvergilische Tradition Lucans.

[8] Serv. a.l.: *metas ad terras rettulit, tempora ad annos; Lavinio enim et Albae finem statuit, Romanis tribuit aeternitatem.* – Vgl. Cic. Cat. 3,11,26; 4,6,11; 4,10,21. – Für die Folgezeit besonders wichtig wird die Verbindung von 'Weltreich' mit 'Sonne' (Sol-Apollo), vgl. Aen. 7,99–101 (Orakel des Faunus): *quorumque a stirpe nepotes/ omnia* (!) *sub pedibus* (!), *qua Sol utrumque recurrens/ aspicit Oceanum, vertique regique videbunt;* s. Faber 1975, 13ff.; vgl. Dan 2,44.

Ein früheres (?) sibyllinisches Orakel gab eine ähnlich weitreichende Verheißung:

καί σοι πᾶσα χϑὼν Ἰταλὴ καὶ πᾶσα Λατίνων
αἰὲν ὑπὸ σκήπτροισιν ἐπαυχένιον ζυγὸν ἕξει⁹.

Der triumphale Ton eines universalen 'Imperialismus' befremdet den heutigen Hörer. Unter den also Befriedeten – "unter den Füßen des Römervolkes" (Verg. Aen. 7,99 ff.) – waren ja nicht nur Germanen und Perser, sondern auch Juden. Die Befremdung ist berechtigt, darf aber nicht vergessen machen, daß die Verheißung eines *imperium sine fine* (a) in einer katastrophalen Situation – Flüchtling im Schiffbruch – gegeben wird und (b) ausdrücklich das Ende reflektiert. "Ende", "Fall" und "Untergang" sind geschichtliche und geschichtstheologische Erfahrungen, die dem P. Vergilius Maro als Römer und als *vates Etruscus* gut bekannt waren.

Das Ende ist freilich schon vorbei, so glaubte Vergil in den zwanziger Jahren. Der letzte Kampf hat schon stattgefunden – bei Actium, im Jahre 31. Vergil stilisiert die offizielle augusteische Propaganda: Actium – eine Schlacht zwischen Orient und Occident¹⁰, ein Völkerkampf, ein Götterkampf, der an den Titanenkampf erinnert. Jetzt aber thront der Erhabene auf der Schwelle seines Apoll-Tempels. Die Völker aus aller Welt ziehen an ihm vorüber und bringen Tribut: Völkerwallfahrt zum Capitol und Palatin (8,714 ff.), entwickelt aus der religiösen Idee von Victoria, Triumph, Pax.

Actium war die Weltenwende, so Vergil im Siegesrausch und Friedenstraum der zwanziger Jahre. Er war nicht der letzte, der sich so täuschte.

Die Kriegsfurie ist in Eisen geschlagen und fest verschlossen (1,291 ff.): sie bedroht des Augustus Reich ohne Ende nicht mehr. Als Göttermythos formuliert: Die Titanen im Tartarus werden nie wieder Gelegenheit haben, gegen Iuppiter zu rebellieren; seine Herrschaft ist ungestört, die Strafen des "alten Geschlechtes der Erde" sind ewig. Der Tartarus ist doppelt so tief unter der Erde wie der Himmel über ihr; seine Tore können nicht gebrochen werden (*vis ut nulla virum, non ipsi exscindere bello/ caelicolae valeant*); selbst ein Gott, wollte er sich mit den Mächten des Tartarus gegen Iuppiter verbünden, er könnte seine Bundesgenossen nicht aus dem Tartarus holen,

---

⁹ Orakel bei Phlegon, Makrobioi 4 (FGrHist 257 F. 37 V v. 37 f.). Die Datierung (88 v. Chr.?) ist unsicher, spätere Überarbeitungen sind möglich. Die Kategorie des *sine fine* wird in der Aion-Inschrift der Pompei aus Eleusis (74/3 v. Chr. [?], Dittenberger-Hiller, *Sylloge* III³ 1125) deutlich.

¹⁰ Aen. 8,678 ff.: *vires Orientis; Itali – ops barbarica;* Aen. 10,91: der Trojanische Krieg als Krieg zwischen Asien und Europa; vgl. 2,192 ff. (Sinon berichtet ein Orakel über den künftigen Sieg Asiens). Bei der Untersuchung der ersten Stelle tendiert Binder 1971, 214 f. zu dualistischen Formulierungen, die vom Text nicht gedeckt sind, z. B. S. 240 f.: Vergil sehe in der Schlacht von Actium einen Kampf zwischen dem Guten und dem Bösen, zwischen Licht und Finsternis.

selbst nicht mit Kriegsmaschinen[11]. Das ist die mythische Vernichtung der aufrührerischen Potenz.

Augusti Reich, das die Sonne im Aufgang und im Untergang erblickt (7,99ff.), ist der Weltherrschaft Iuppiters konform. Eine traditionsreiche Typologie stellt Augustus in ein mytho-theologisches Spiegelkabinett: Iuppiter, Venus und Apoll schützen den Aeneaden, das Sonnenkind[12]. Augustus ist sozusagen ein neuer Aeneas, ein zweiter Hercules[13], Romulus und Numa zugleich[14].

Dieses Weltbild der Aeneis enthält, um es zu wiederholen, eine individuelle und kosmologische Eschatologie. Das Geschichtsbild ist nicht uneschatologisch, sondern posteschatologisch[15]. Die 'apokalyptischen Motive' sind nicht, wie man sagt, umfunktioniert, vielmehr: dies ist erfüllte (kollektive) Eschatologie aus der Sicht des Siegers. Realisierte 'Apokalyptik' dient der Rechtfertigung von Herrschaft. Die durchaus notwendige Kritik an dieser Geschichtstheologie trifft nicht einen *Mißbrauch* von 'Apokalyptik', richtet sich nicht gegen eine 'Umfunktionierung der orientalischen Apokalyptik': sie muß den *Inhalt* dieser Rechtfertigungen selbst – sowohl der Herrschaft wie des Widerstandes – erfassen.

1.2. Abriß der römischen Geschichtstheologie

Vergils Geschichtstheologie ist der klassische Höhepunkt einer langen, auch vor- und außerliterarisch greifbaren Tradition. Sie wird von den römischen Historikern, Philosophen und Gelehrten vertreten. Trotz aller politisch und weltanschaulich bedingten Unterschiede gibt es im 1. Jh. v. Chr. einen relativ einheitlichen Bestand an 'geschichtstheologischen Dogmen'.

– Die Götter wirken in der Geschichte (*res hominum*), sie senden Zeichen[16];
– die "Aeneaden" stehen unter dem besonderen Schutz (*tutela, cura*) ihrer Stammeltern Venus und Mars[17];

---

[11] Die Titanen im Tartarus werden genannt a) in der Katabasis (6,548ff.), b) auf dem Schild des Aeneas (8,667). Eine politische Deutung des Titanensturzes auf den Sieg Roms z. B. bei Aelius Aristides, Auf Rom 26,103.

[12] Sueton, Augustus 94, bes. §6: der kleine Octavius (Augustus) soll einst – nach langem Suchen, auf einem hohen Turme gefunden worden sein, *iacens contra solis exortum*.

[13] Aen. 8,184ff.: Kampf Hercules' gegen Cacus, der wohl als Prototyp von Actium zu denken ist (Binder 1971, 3 u. ö.). Beachte die Mahnung Euanders an Aeneas (8,364f.): *te quoque dignum/ finge deo* (sc. *Hercule*).

[14] Aen. 6,781ff./788ff./806ff.: Augustus zwischen Romulus und Numa in der Unterwelt. Auch die Titulatur "Augustus" deutet auf Romulus.

[15] Faber 1975, 25ff.

[16] Vgl. z. B. Aen. 1,229f.; Cic. har. resp. 9,19: *deorum numine omnia regi gubernarique*.

[17] Vgl. z. B. Lucrez 1,1–49.

– Rom ist eine heilige Stadt; sie ist mit und neben Alba Zentrum eines auch sakralen Bundes; erst später entwickelt sich der Gedanke des *sacrum imperium*[18];
– Periodisierung der Zeit (*saecula;* vgl. §2.1.);
– der Staat ist 'transpersonal'[19].
Volk, Stadt und Staat – später die jeweilige Dynastie – sind Träger besonderer "Versprechungen". Eine 'Ursünde' – der Betrug des Laomedon und/oder der Brudermord des Romulus – begründet eine Kollektivschuld in der mythischen Frühgeschichte[20]. Mannigfaches Unglück kann so als Strafe bzw. Sühne für diese 'Ursünde' gedeutet werden. Die Götter führen, versprechen, sie zeigen, lohnen und strafen, zürnen, helfen. Das Epochen- und Krisenbewußtsein ist alt und tief verwurzelt. Der Gedanke des 'Endes' ist, wie im nächsten Kapitel gezeigt werden soll, gerade im ersten Jahrhundert weit verbreitet.

Die Begriffe dieser Geschichtstheologie sind aus römischer Religion und griechischer Philosophie entwickelt. Nur wenige Stichworte seien genannt:
– *numen, nutus, voluntas, significatio, consilium, fata deorum;*
– *administratio, regere, gubernare, cura, providentia, Iuppiter custos;*
– *origo, condere, saeculum, finis, casus, occasus imperii, metae rerum;*
– *salus urbis et imperii, servare, eripere, auxilium, praesidium, ducere, augere, defendere, arcere.*

1.3. Zur Begriffsbildung

Die römische Geschichtstheologie wird hier mit Begriffen umschrieben, deren Verwendung teilweise unklar ist. Für den begrenzten Zweck dieses Versuches und der Materialvorlage scheinen folgende Abgrenzungen nützlich[21].

---

[18] Vgl. z. B. Cic. pro Marc. 7,22; Tibull 2,5,23; Livius 4,4,4; 6,23,7.

[19] Vgl. z. B. Livius 28,28,11; Tac. ann. 3,6,3: *principes mortales, rem publicam aeternam esse.*

[20] Serv. auct. Aen. 1,2 (*fato profugus*) zitiert aus einem Buch mit dem Titel "*litterae iuris Etruriae*" einen Spruch des Tages über das Schicksal der Nachkommen von Meineidigen: *eum qui genus a periuris duceret, fato extorrem et profugum esse debere.* Nach Servius hat Vergil in diesem Thema-Satz der Aeneis "aus der Disciplin der Etrusker" geschöpft. Vgl. noch Horaz, epod. 7: *sic est acerba fata Romanos agunt/ scelusque fraternae necis;* Cic. off. 3,41; Verg. Georg. 1,501f.; Aen. 1,292 (*Remo cum fratre Quirinus,* d. i. Romulus) bringt die Versöhnung der Brüder; Lucan 1,95.

[21] Eine Auseinandersetzung mit anderen Bestimmungen dieser Begriffe und ihrer Geschichte kann an dieser Stelle nicht erfolgen. Die vorgetragenen Vorschläge zur Sprachregelung haben einen begrenzten, vornehmlich praktischen Zweck. Sie zielen auf eine Formalisierung der Begriffe, um religionsvergleichende Arbeit zu ermöglichen. Die bekannten theologischen und philosophischen Bestimmungen sind meist religionsspezifisch, d. h. sie gehen von (einer bestimmten Vorstellung von) jüdischer oder christlicher Religion aus.

1.3.1. *Divination* ist ein allgemeiner religionswissenschaftlicher Begriff. Er bezeichnet alles, was zur Klärung der nahen oder fernen Zukunft oder zur Lüftung von Geheimnissen aus der Vergangenheit unternommen wird. Er umfaßt die gesamte natürliche und technische Divination von Los und Traum bis zu Orakel und Prophetie. 'Divinationsliteratur' ist die technische Fachschriftstellerei (*ars*) und – in einem weiteren Sinne – diejenige 'schöne' Literatur, die in einem besonders hohen Maße Themen und Motive der Divination als Rahmen oder Gegenstand verwendet.

1.3.2. *Apokalyptik*[22] ist ein literaturwissenschaftlicher Begriff. Er bezeichnet – wie 'apokryph, arkan, esoterisch' – eine besondere Art von Tradition und Publikation. Der Inhalt dieser Geheim/Offenbarungsliteratur und der Verwendungszweck ("geistiger Widerstand", politische Propaganda, Herrschaftslegitimation, Erbauung) sind durch den Ausdruck 'Apokalyptik' nicht festgelegt. Der jeweilige Offenbarungsmittler ist religionsspezifisch (Musen, Götter, Engel, Moses, Hermes, Sibylle).

1.3.3. *Eschatologie*[23] ist eine Kategorie der Naturgeschichte (Physik), Kosmologie und Geschichte. Eschatologie gibt Kunde von letzten Dingen, und zwar des Individuums oder der Völker oder der Welt. Dementsprechend kann eine individuelle, kollektive und kosmologische Eschatologie unterschieden werden. Eschatologie kann mehr oder weniger mythisch, naturwissenschaftlich oder philosophisch oder religiös angelegt sein. Die kosmologische Eschatologie ist das Gegenstück zu den Kosmogonien, deren Motive sie oft aufnimmt (z. B. Chaos).

1.3.4. *Geschichtstheologie* ist eine spekulative, deutende Darstellung geschichtlicher Tatsachen oder Abläufe mit den Mitteln von Religion und/oder Philosophie und Wissenschaften. Geschichtstheologie tendiert zu generellen Aussagen; sie erkennt und setzt 'Sinn, Werte, Ziele'.

Geschichtstheologie ist also nicht identisch mit Eschatologie; Eschatologie kann Teil einer Geschichtstheologie sein. Andererseits sind Vorstellungen von Verheißung, Willen der Götter, *fatum,* Führung durch die Götter, Erfüllung, Sendung (*dux fatalis*), Prüfung, Fortschritt/Verfall/Ziel prinzipiell möglich auch ohne (explizite) Eschatologie. Das Begriffspaar 'linear/zyklisch', 'geschichtlich/mythisch' ist nicht geeignet, den Unterschied zwischen jüdisch-christlicher und griechisch-römischer Geschichtstheologie zu erfassen[24].

---

[22] Die lateinischen Äquivalente sind *aperire, pandere, patere* bzw. *occultum, abditum, secretum, arcanum.*

[23] Zum Gebrauch dieses Ausdruckes in der Literatur zu Vergil vgl. Norden 1957, 3 ff.: "Die Eschatologie". Klingner (1965, 310), Zinn (1965, 3209), Knauer (1965, 345 ff., 353 ff.) u. a. haben den Ausdruck aufgegriffen. Jeanmaire (1929), Carcopino (1930) u. a. sprechen von "Messianismus". Zur Kritik dieser Ansätze vgl. Heussi 1930; W. Nestle 1946; Gaiser 1961; Jäschke 1976.

[24] Cancik 1976, 111; 1 Anm. 8; 3 Anm. 27; Jäschke 1976, 99 ff.

2. *"Ende" und "Aufschub"*

2.1. *ars auguralis, fulguralis, haruspicina*

Vergils triumphales *imperium sine fine* reflektiert, wie gesagt, das Ende. Das Rom Sullas, Ciceros und Cäsars ist voll von Untergangsspekulationen. Wir wollen eine Auswahl referieren; von einer Untersuchung des sozialen und politischen Ortes dieser Spekulationen muß an dieser Stelle abgesehen werden.

M. Terentius Varro überliefert die mündliche Lehre eines vornehmen römischen Augurn, Vettius[25]: "Er habe ihn sagen hören, daß das römische Volk, wenn es wirklich so sei, wie die Historiker überlieferten über das *augurium* des Romulus bei der Stadtgründung und über die 12 Geier, daß das römische Volk dann bis zu 1200 Jahren gelangen würde, weil es ja 120 Jahre unversehrt überstanden hätte."

Wenn wir als Gründungsjahr Roms das Jahr 753 v. Chr. ansetzen, ergibt sich für den Untergang Roms etwa das Jahr 450 n. Chr. In dieser Epoche endet zwar nicht der römische Staat, wohl aber die römische Religion. Die römische Divination wird von den christlichen Kaisern seit 357 explizit verboten[26].

Im Jahre 65 schlug der Blitz ins Capitol und zerstörte gar eine Statue des kleinen Romulus. Aus ganz Etrurien wurden *haruspices* nach Rom geholt: "Sie sagten, daß Blutvergießen und Brände und Aufhören der Gesetze und Bürgerkrieg im Innern und der ganzen Stadt und des Reiches Untergang nahe wären, wenn nicht die unsterblichen Götter, auf jede nur mögliche Weise besänftigt, durch ihren Willen geradezu das Schicksal selbst abbiegen würden"[27].

Durch außerordentliche Maßnahmen gelang es, die Götter zu versöhnen, der Untergang wurde abgewendet – Cicero entdeckte die catilinarische Verschwörung. Er fühlte sich als "Retter", brachte es freilich nicht zu einem 'heilsgeschichtlichen' Titel als "neuer Romulus", wie später Octavian, sondern nur zu dem Spitznamen "Romulus Arpinas".

Eine Weltenwende sah Ciceros Freund Nigidius Figulus, als Cäsar den Rubikon überschritt[28]. Der "Erneuerer der pythagoreischen Disciplin", so

---

[25] Varro bei Cens. nat. 17,15. – Vgl. die christliche Zahlenspekulation: 6 Schöpfungstage – 1 Tag vor Gott = 1000 Jahre (Ps 89,4; II Petr 3,8) – 6000 Jahre Weltzeit + 1000 Jahre Sabbatruhe (Barn 15,4ff.).

[26] Codex Theodos. 9,16,4 (Constantius a. 357). Behinderungen des römischen Opferkultes und damit auch der Divination gibt es seit der Machtergreifung Constantins: vgl. Cod. Theodos. 9,16,1 (a. 319); 9,16,2; 9,16,3 (a. 321 oder 324); 16,10,1 (a. 320/1).

[27] Cic. Cat. 3,8,19: ... *et totius urbis atque imperi occasum appropinquare dixerunt, nisi di immortales omni ratione placati suo numine prope fata ipsa flexissent.* Zur Deutung selbst vgl. den Bescheid der *haruspices* in Cic. har. resp., s. unten §3.1.; zu *fata flectere* s. unten §2.3.

[28] Lucan 1,639ff.

nennt ihn Cicero, kannte Astrologie, Zahlenmystik und Etruskologie genug, um seine Ansicht belegen zu können[29].

Ein anderer Freund Ciceros, L. Tarutius Firmanus, Verfasser einer griechischen Schrift "über die Sterne", hat das Geburtsdatum Roms berechnet, das Horoskop gestellt und die "*fata* Roms gesungen"[30].

Außer Augurallehre, Blitzlehre und Astrologie wurde auch die Lehre von den *saecula* zur Steigerung oder Kanalisierung von Angst eingesetzt. Daß diese Spekulationen auch die breiten Massen erreichen konnten, lehren Nachrichten über Konfiskation und Verbrennung von *libri fatidici*.

Der *haruspex* Volcanius (Volcatius) sah in dem Kometen, der nach Cäsars Ermordung erschien, ein Zeichen für den Ausgang des neunten und den Beginn des zehnten (und letzten?) *saeculum*. Diese Prophezeiung, so sagte er in der römischen Volksversammlung, künde er gegen den Willen der Götter; er werde deshalb sogleich sterben: "und er hatte seine Rede noch nicht beendet, da brach er mitten in der Versammlung zusammen"[31].

Ein letztes Beispiel möge die politischen Hintergründe dieser Epochen- und Untergangsspekulationen wenigstens andeuten. Im Jahre 43 trat ein namenloser *haruspex* im Senat auf. Er prophezeite, das frühere Königtum kehre wieder; alle außer ihm würden Sklaven werden. Dann verhielt er den Atem und starb als freier Mann[32].

Wenige Jahre darauf schrieb Vergil sein "messianisches Gedicht" und Horaz seinen seherischen Aufruf zur Flucht aus Rom nach den Inseln im Westen[33].

2.2. *Tuscae historiae – libri rituales*

Die etruskische Disciplin hatte, wie die Beispiele zeigen, einen großen Einfluß auf das römische Geschichtsbewußtsein im 1. Jh. v. Chr. Eine Reihe von etruskischen und römischen Autoren ist bekannt: L. Tarquitius Priscus, Iulius Aquila, A. Caecina; Nigidius Figulus, der Pythagoreer; Varro, der "über die *saecula*" schrieb, und der 'Etruskologe' Verrius Flaccus. Es gab etruskische Geschichtsschreibung (*Tuscae historiae*), in denen berechnet war, "wie viele *saecula* diesem Volke (der Etrusker) gegeben waren". Ein *saeculum,* so lehren die etruskischen *libri rituales,* beginnt bei der Gründung einer Stadt oder eines Staates, und zwar mit den Menschen, die am Tage der Gründung geboren werden. Das *saeculum* endet, wenn der letzte von diesen 'Erstgeborenen' stirbt. Da die Menschen das Ende eines *saeculum* nicht immer zweifelsfrei feststellen können, schik-

---

[29] Cic. Tim. 1. Vgl. Schol. Georg. 1,43; Plin. n. h. 2,138f.
[30] Cic. div. 2,98f.   [31] Serv. ecl. 9,46.   [32] Appian, bell. civ. 4,4.
[33] Verg. ecl. 4; Horaz, epod. 16: ... *vate me.*

ken die Götter Zeichen. So sind *saeculum*-Lehre und Divination verknüpft[34]. Ein konkretes Beispiel für diese etruskische Geschichtsschreibung hat sich erstaunlicherweise über den Zusammenbruch der etruskischen Kultur gerettet. Im Scholion Veronense ist ein stark verstümmeltes Stück aus einem Werk des A. Caecina erhalten[35]. Der Gattung nach gehört der Text – er ist ohne Titel zitiert – in die κτίσις-Literatur. Beachtlich ist die Aufmerksamkeit für Riten, die bei einer Stadtgründung nötig sind. Die Erzählung von der Feststellung des Ortes, des Namens und die "Konstitution des Jahres" (*annum constituit*) wirken wie die Anwendung eines etruskischen *liber ritualis*. In diesen war, nach Verrius' Zeugnis, auch über Stadtgründung gehandelt.

Dem etruskischen Volke waren, so stand in den *Tuscae historiae,* zehn *saecula* zugeteilt; man stehe jetzt im achten *saeculum;* "das neunte und zehnte seien noch übrig; wenn diese aber vergangen seien, dann sei es zu Ende mit dem etruskischen Namen" (*finem fore nominis Etrusci*).

Dieses Ende war denn auch nicht fern. Die Römer überzogen ihre 'Bundesgenossen' mit einem furchtbaren Krieg (91–89 v. Chr.). Im Jahre 88 vernahm man einen lauten Trompetenschall aus heiterem Himmel[36]. Die etruskischen Weisen erkannten, daß der Beginn eines neuen *saeculum,* und zwar des neunten[37], angezeigt werde. Vielleicht war es dieses neunte *saeculum,* das nach Volcanius im Jahre 44 endete. "Das Ende des etruskischen Namens", wie die *haruspices* es beobachten, fällt mit der Zerstörung der kulturellen Identität der Etrusker zusammen.

2.3. fata differre (flectere, proferre)

Derartige Spekulationen sind auch in Italien Symptome eines allgemeinen Krisenbewußtseins, Mittel im politischen Kampf der Mächtigen untereinander oder "geistiger Widerstand" von Unterworfenen oder Unterschichten.

---

[34] Varro bei Cens. nat. 17,5–6. – Vgl. Thulin 1968, 3,64f.; F. Schachermeyer, *Etruskische Frühgeschichte,* Berlin/Leipzig 1929, 192ff.

[35] Schol. Veron. Verg. Aen. 10,200 (= FGrHist. 706 Anhang 4a) berichtet u. a. von einem Archon (Tarchon): ibi annum constituit. Vgl. Cens. nat. 17,5. Auch die Suda s. v. Τυρρηνία (*Lexicographi Graeci* I, ed. A. Adler, Leipzig 1935) bezeugt einen 'etruskischen' Historiker, der über die Schöpfung (!) spekuliert und die Dauer bis zum Untergang der Welt berechnet haben soll. In diesem Zusammenhang sei erwähnt, daß Varro, der die *Tuscae historiae* überliefert, auch einen Volnius nennt, der *Tuscae tragoediae* geschrieben haben soll (l. L. 5,55). Hierbei handelt es sich wahrscheinlich um Trauerspiele in lateinischer Sprache, aber mit Stoffen aus Mythos und Geschichte der Etrusker.

[36] Plut. Sulla 7. – In dieselbe Epoche fallen die Sprüche der Vegoia: vgl. Heurgon 1959. Das *finem fore nominis Etrusci* klingt, nach der Vermutung von Sordi 1972, 788f., am Schluß von Vergils Aeneis wieder, wo Iuno emphatisch den Untergang des *nomen Troianum* fordert.

[37] So Thulin, a.a.O.

Wieweit Weissagungen über das Ende eines Staates sich zurückverfolgen lassen, ist unsicher. Bei der Belagerung von Veii (399) wird ein etruskischer *haruspex* von den Römern gefangengenommen[38]. Er gibt, so Livius und Cicero, nach älteren Quellen, die "schicksalhafte Zerstörung des Vaterlandes" preis[39]:

"So also sei es in den Schicksalsbüchern, so in der etruskischen Disciplin überliefert: wenn einmal das Wasser des Albaner Sees sehr gestiegen sei, wenn dann der Römer es richtig ableite, werde ihm der Sieg über die Veienter gegeben; bevor dies geschehe, würden die Götter die Mauern der Veienter nicht verlassen." Die Römer leiteten das Wasser "richtig" (*rite*) ab:

Und das Schicksal ergriff Veii (Liv. 5,19,1);

die Römer zerstörten die Stadt und überführten ihre Götter nach Rom.

Die ursprüngliche Bedeutung dieses Spruches und seine Historizität sind umstritten. Ogilvie vermutet, daß ihm eine *saecula*-Lehre zugrunde liegt[40]. Einen Beweis dafür gibt es nicht. Das Ende der Stadt kann auch anders als durch den Ablauf der ihr zugesprochenen *saecula* begründet worden sein.

In der *saeculum*-Lehre verbinden sich widerspruchsvoll zwei Motive geschichtlichen Denkens: die Einsicht in Notwendigkeit und der Wille, dem Zwang zu entgehen[41]. Daraus entsteht die Lehre vom "Aufschub des Schicksals"[42]:

"Aber man muß wissen, daß gemäß den Büchern der Haruspicin und gemäß den *sacra Acheruntia,* die Tages verfaßt haben soll, die *fata* durch eine bestimmte Weise zehn Jahre aufgeschoben werden (*differri*)."

Einzelheiten dieser etruskischen Lehre vom χατέχον[43] können hier nicht erörtert werden. Wichtig ist zu sehen, wieviel 'eschatologische' Spekulation in diesen "Lehren" enthalten ist. Auf dieser Verbindung von Divination (Zeichen) und Kult (Sühne; Gründungsriten etc.) beruht die (etruskisch-)römische Geschichtstheologie der klassischen Zeit. Die Aeneassage

---

[38] Cic. div. 1,100; Livius 5,14–15; Dion. Hal. 12,10–14; Val. Max. 1,6,3; Plut. Cam. 3f. Vgl. Gagé 1955, 134ff.

[39] Livius 5,15,11: *sic igitur libris fatalibus, sic disciplina Etrusca traditum esse: quando aqua Albana abundasset, tum si eam Romanus rite emisisset, victoriam de Veientibus dari; antequam id fiat, deos moenia Veientium deserturos non esse.* – Quelle ist vielleicht der in Divination sehr erfahrene römische Historiker Q. Fabius Pictor, vgl. Peter HRR p. LXXXVIII.

[40] R. M. Ogilvie, *A commentary on Livy 1–5,* Oxford 1970, 662. Livius bezeichnet 5,14,4 die römischen *libri Sibyllini* als *libri fatales.*

[41] R. Bloch 1966, 159–170.

[42] Quellen: Serv. Aen. 8,398; Cens. nat. 14,6 (und O. Jahn, a. l.).

[43] II Thess 2,7. Ohne Kenntnis der italischen Quellen meint C. Schmitt, *Der Nomos der Erde im Völkerrecht des Ius publicum Europaeum,* 1950, 29: "Ich glaube nicht, daß für einen ursprünglich christlichen Glauben ein anderes Geschichtsbild als das des Kat-echon ... möglich ist." Schmitt hat daraus eine eigene "Katechontik" entwickelt und diese mit römisch-deutscher Reichsmystik verflochten.

ist, wie die Ausgrabungen von Lavinium gezeigt haben, bei den Latinern alt und im Kult verwurzelt. Hinzu kommen Vorstellungen wie Bund (Eid), Gründung, Krise und Erneuerung (παλιγγενεσία), sowie pythagoreische und später stoische Philosopheme.

Dieses 'System' aus Divination, Kult, Mythos, Philosophie und Astrologie[44] trägt auch die Geschichtstheologie Vergils. Sie ist nicht ein kurzatmiges Auftragswerk augusteischer Propaganda – obschon sie auch diesem aktuellen Zwecke dienen will und ihm, wie könnte es anders sein, auch parteilich verhaftet ist. Aber hinter Vergil steht nicht nur eine lange literarische Tradition; Vergil hat das religiöse und mythische Erbe von "ganz Italien" – *tota Italia* war ein politisches Schlagwort der Bürgerkriege! – gesammelt und bewahrt. Ein Blick auf die Divinationsliteratur wird die Dichte dieses religiösen Erbes veranschaulichen.

Vergils *imperium sine fine* ist die Negation einer Negation, die Antwort auf die Untergangsängste der späten Republik, der konservativen Partei, des *nomen Etruscum* und auf die Herrschaftsansprüche des Orients.

3. "Zukunft" – "Hoffnung"

3.1. Die römische Divinationsliteratur

Was mit einem modernen Namen 'Geschichtstheologie' heißt, findet sich unter verschiedenen Titeln in vielerlei Gattungen und Formen in der religiösen Literatur der Römer. Einen Teil dieser religiösen Literatur, die Divinationsliteratur, möchte ich in Auswahl vorstellen. Ich möchte damit einen Einblick geben in die Quellen Vergils und den Erwartungshorizont seines Publikums, in die Verbreitung dieser Vorstellungen und in den Aufbau der religiösen Literatur der Römer.

Im Lexikon des Festus ist folgende Notiz überliefert:

> Marspedis, sive sine r littera maspedis, in precatione solitaurilium quid significet, ne Messalla quidem augur in explanatione auguriorum reperire se potuisse ait[45].

Diese Notiz läßt vier verschiedene Schichten (Typen) von religiöser Literatur erkennen:

(I) *precatio* – der Gebetstext;

(II) *explanatio auguriorum* – technische Erläuterungen zu Texten und Riten im Archiv der Auguren;

---

[44] Serv. Verg. ecl. 4,4: *(Sibylla) quae Cumana fuit et saecula per metalla divisit. dixit etiam, quis quo saeculo imperaret et Solem ultimum id est decimum voluit.* – Verg. Aen. 4,519f.: *conscia fati/ sidera.*

[45] Fest. p. 152f. L. Ein anderes Beispiel: Bei Charisius, p. 285 'Barwick, s. v. *sarcte* ist die Schicht II (*augurales libri*) und IV (Verrius – Festus – Porphyrius – Charisius) vertreten.

(III) *Messalla augur, de auspiciis* – Fachschriftstellerei über *quaestiones augurales* durch einen Fachmann, einen *artium scriptor;*

(IV) Verrius und Festus – Antiquare und Grammatiker, die – in unterschiedlicher Absicht – alte Worte deuten.

Vergil, der alle vier Schichten benutzt, wäre als 'erbauliche/theologische Literatur' in Stufe IV, oder in eine V. Stufe einzuordnen.

Eine ähnliche Schichtung läßt sich in Ciceros Rede "Über den Bescheid der *haruspices*" erkennen[46]:

(I) *Etrusci libri* (§ 53);

(II) das *responsum* der *haruspices* auf die Anfrage (*quaestio*) wegen des Zeichens im *ager Latiniensis;* dieses *responsum* wird im Senat "rezitiert" (§ 9);

(III) die *interpretatio* (§ 36; vgl. § 56) Ciceros:

    (1) Zitation von Lemmata des Bescheides;

    (2) Deutung;

    (3) Homilie in mehr oder weniger engem Anschluß an den Text[47].

Ciceros Rede als ganze läßt sich klassifizieren als Predigt mit Exegese, wobei bemerkenswert ausführlich der zugrunde liegende Text der etruskischen Priester zitiert wird.

Der Bescheid der *haruspices* ist ebenfalls ein formenreicher, sorgfältig komponierter, in altertümlicher Sakralsprache einhergehender Text. Er enthält: den Vorgang (*commissa*, § 40), Drohungen, Vorhersagen (*praedictum*, § 29), Mahnsprüche (*monita*, § 10.40.55.56), Forderungen (*postiliones*, § 20). Die etruskischen Priester schließen mit allgemeinen politischen Ratschlägen: *ne rei publicae status commutetur*. Sie greifen damit unmittelbar und engagiert in den politischen Streit ein. Die Revolution der Volkspartei und des Tribunen Clodius soll nicht stattfinden. Typologisch entspricht die Rede Ciceros einem jener vielfach bearbeiteten Prophetenbücher des Alten Testaments – so wie Vergils Aeneis etwa dem Geschichtswerk des sogenannten Jahwisten entspricht[48].

Aus der Schichtenanalyse der religiösen Literatur der Römer folgt, daß bei einem sachgemäßen Vergleich von jüdisch-christlicher und griechisch-

---

[46] Cicero, *de haruspicum responso in P. Clodium in senatu habita,* etwa Mitte 56 v. Chr. – Zum politischen Hintergrund s. I. Gallo, *Orazioni Clodiane,* Turin 1969.

[47] Zur Form des lemmatisierten Kommentars vgl. E. Klostermann: "Formen der exegetischen Arbeiten des Origenes", in: *ThLZ* 72 (1947) 203–207; G. Lohfink: "Kommentar als Gattung", in: *BiLe* 15 (1974) 1–16; H. Cancik: "Der Text als Bild", in: H. Brunner/R. Kannicht/K. Schwager (Hrsg.): *Wort und Bild,* München 1979, bes. § 3.1.2. Die Form von Text/Interpretation war Cicero als Advokat und Augur vertraut. Diese Form ist die Struktur von Cic. leg. II.

[48] Die Problematik derartiger Vergleiche ist evident, zumal wenn man die quellenkritischen Probleme des jahwistischen Geschichtswerkes oder der deuteronomistischen Bearbeitung von Prophetensprüchen oder Sammlungen von Prophetensprüchen berücksichtigt.

römischer Religion die sogenannte "schöne Literatur", die *theologia philosophorum et poetarum,* immer herangezogen werden muß.

Die Klischees einer simplen Religionstypologie von 'Buchreligion/Kultreligion' oder – noch verführerischer – mythischer ('zyklischer') Naturreligion/geschichtlicher ('linearer') (Offenbarungs-)Religion lösen sich auf, wenn dieses Postulat der vergleichenden Religionsgeschichte auch für die Antike beachtet wird[49].

3.2. libri Sibyllini – fatales – futura continentes

Für die Erforschung der römischen Offenbarungsliteratur und Geschichtstheologie sind natürlich die "sibyllinischen Bücher" von besonderer Bedeutung.

Schon seit dem 6. Jh. sollen sie, aus Cumae importiert, in Rom bekannt gewesen sein[50]. Welche Form, welchen Namen und Inhalt sie damals hatten, ist kaum noch zu erahnen. Mit Sicherheit enthielten sie Sühnungen (*procurationes, remedia*), Anweisungen, die zur Einführung neuer Kulte führen konnten; all dies angeschlossen an die Deutung von mannigfachen Zeichen; vielleicht auch schon Teile des Aeneas-Mythos. Erst seit dem 3. Jh. ist, zumal nach den meisterlichen Forschungen von Hermann Diels[51], der Charakter der Sammlung deutlicher. Zur Zeit Vergils nannte man die Sibyllinischen Bücher *libri fatales* und fand darin *fata et remedia Romana*[52]. Damals muß der Glaube geherrscht haben, daß die Sibylle einst die kritischen Punkte der gesamten Geschichte Roms vorhergesagt habe, mit allen Vergehen, Unglücksfällen und den dann jeweils erforderlichen kultischen Sühnungen. Die Priesterschaft der *XVviri s.f.,* die diese Bücher und mit ihnen den gesamten *graecus ritus* verwaltete, war eine Institution für permanente Reform und Neuerung. Der Bezug auf eine uralte, inspirierte, prinzipiell unveränderliche ('kanonisierte') 'heilige Schrift', die *libri Sibyllini,* ist die Eigenart des *graecus ritus* innerhalb der römischen Religion[53]. Der

---

[49] Mensching 1937; ders. 1959, 65 ff. In dem grundlegenden Werk von Leipoldt-Morenz ist das römische Material nur nebenbei erwähnt (1953, 174 u. ö.), bei Lanczkowski 1956, der "in einem einzigen Buche eine literarhistorische Beschreibung aller heiligen Schriften geben will", übergangen. Vgl. Anm. 24.

[50] Die 'Ursprungsaitiologie' u. a. bei Varro (Lact. inst. 1,6,10 f.); Gell. 1,19; Serv. Aen. 6,72; Dion. Hal. Ant. Rom. 4,62. Zu Interpretation vgl. Gagé 1955, 27 ff. (mit Referat divergierender Ansichten, u. a. von R. Bloch); Radke 1963; ders. 1979, 39–50. Zu vergleichen sind legitimierende Berichte über heilige Bücher, bes. die Nachrichten über den Fund der *Numae libri.* Zu Bücherfunden in der jüdisch-christlichen Tradition vgl. Leipoldt-Morenz 1953; Lanczkowski 1956.

[51] Diels 1890; vgl. Merkelbach 1961.　　　　　[52] Serv. Aen. 6,72.

[53] Die römische Religion enthält drei Teilsysteme, die in sich wieder reich differenziert sind: *patrius ritus, Graecus ritus, Etrusca disciplina.* Auffällig an dieser 'synthetischen Religion' ist nicht der starke Synkretismus, sondern die hohe Selbständigkeit der Teil-Religionen.

Ausdruck "die Bücher" (*libri*, βιβλία) – ohne weitere Bestimmung – waren einem Römer als religiöser Ausdruck durchaus verständlich: es waren die *libri Sibyllini* oder *fatales*.

Vergil hat in seinen Dichtungen auf je verschiedene Weise sibyllinische Literatur berücksichtigt. Er stand dabei, wie gesagt, in einer religiösen und literarischen Tradition, die mit Sicherheit mindestens bis in das 3. Jh. v. Chr. zurückzuverfolgen ist. Eine seiner Vorlagen war das *bellum Poenicum* des Cn. Naevius. Dieser erzählte bereits die Begegnung zwischen Aeneas und der Sibylle[54]. Naevius erzählte weiterhin, daß "Venus dem Anchises – ihrem Geliebten, dem Stammvater der Aeneaden – Bücher gegeben habe, die das Zukünftige enthielten"[55].

> Naevius dicit Venerem libros futura continentes Anchisae dedisse.

Schon Naevius dichtete, daß Venus sich wegen des Schiffbruchs der Trojaner bei Iuppiter beklagte und dieser "seine Tochter tröstete mit der Hoffnung auf die Zukunft":

> primo libro belli Punici ... Venus, Troianis tempestate laborantibus, cum Iove queritur, et sequuntur (sc. bei Naevius) verba Iovis filiam consolantis spe futurorum[56].

Diese Szene, die Naevius in der Krise der punischen Kriege dichtete, hat Vergil in der Offenbarungsrede Iuppiters im ersten Buch der Aeneis nachgeahmt und für die Krise der caesarisch-augusteischen Epoche aktualisiert[57].

Vergil übernimmt damit eine Rolle, die man mit einem oft mißbrauch-

---

[54] Naevius, bell. Poen. frg. 12* Str. bei Lact. inst. 1,6,7ff., vermittelt durch Varro, ant. rer. div. IV.

[55] Macr. 6,2,31 = Naevius frg. 14 Str.

[56] Schol. Aen. 7,123 (Cod. Paris. lat. 7930) = frg. 9* Str. Vgl. Ennius, annal. 1, frg. XIV (Vahlen):
doctusque Anchisesque, Venus quem pulchra dearum
Fari (!) donavit, divinum pectus habere.
Belege zu Anchises als *augur* s. Naevius frg. 25 Str., zu Anchises als *vates* bei Vahlen, a.a.O. Wichtig für die Form der antiken Offenbarungsliteratur ist die Vater-Sohn-Beziehung. Für die Geschichte der römischen Apokalyptik interessant ist der vergilische Bezugspunkt für die späten Kommentatoren. Aen. 7,123 lautet: *Anchises fatorum arcana reliquit*. Das ergibt eine feste Tradition vom 3. Jh. v. Chr. bis in die Spätantike. Vgl. auch Fabius Pictor, ann. frg. 3 (Peter): Aeneas träumt seine (auch Roms?) Zukunft; vgl. hier Anm. 39. – Vgl. Donat zu Vergil, Aen. 1,255ff.: *de futuris enim loqui et significare ventura non nisi deorum rex poterat ... addidit etiam ipse Iuppiter fatorum dispositionem et omnem (!) futuri temporis cursum.* Donat hält dies für eine Art Inhaltsverzeichnis der von Vergil geplanten, aber nicht mehr ausgeführten Bücher der Aeneis. Er nennt die Partie eine *promissio futurorum*.

[57] Dazwischen liegt Ennius, ann. 286ᵃ (aus Serv. Aen. 1,20; Einordnung bei Ennius unsicher): *in Ennio inducitur Iuppiter promittens Romanis excidium Carthaginis.* – Vgl. ann. 290.291; s. hier Anm. 56.

ten Begriff als 'vates' bezeichnet. Sein Freund Horaz hat diese Rolle folgendermaßen charakterisiert[58]:

> orientia tempora notis / instruit exemplis, inopem solatur et aegrum (sc. der 'vates').

Der Römer Caecilius, der bei Minucius Felix eines der wenigen wirklichen Religionsgespräche zwischen Römern und Christen führt, beschreibt die Aufgaben dieser *vates* so[59].

> Inde (templis et delubris) adeo pleni et mixti deo vates futura praecerpunt, dant cautelam periculis, morbis medellam, spem adflictis, opem miseris, solacium calamitatibus, laboribus levamentum.

Diese so erstaunliche Aufzählung pastoraler, sozialer und medizinischer Dienste an römischen Heiligtümern beschließt bei Minucius eine traditionelle Darstellung römischer Staatsreligion und Geschichtstheologie (6,2–7,5). Die Beachtung der göttlichen Zeichen, die Sorge für den Kult hätten das Reich "über die Wege der Sonne" hinausgetragen; Religion habe "den Römern gegeben, gemehrt, gegründet das Reich, da sie nicht so sehr durch Kraft als vielmehr durch Religion und Frömmigkeit stark waren" (25,1).

Das ist der übliche Gottesbeweis des Siegers aus der Geschichte; man konnte es bei den Geschichtsschreibern nachlesen: *specta de libris memoriam* (7,2).

Dies war bequem zu widerlegen. Die Rom- und Religionskritik der Orientalen, Hellenen und Römer selbst hatte hinreichend Material gesammelt[60]. Die Christen hatten auch eine eigene Erklärung für die Erfolge der römischen Divination und Politik: Nicht Götter, sondern Geister und Dämonen sind die Ursache der Größe Roms[61]. Das römische Geschichtsbild ließ sich auch unschwer – unter Wahrung mehr oder weniger starker eschatologischer und politischer Vorbehalte gegen den Staat an sich und gegen diesen Staat mit seiner Geschichte im besonderen – mit dem jüdisch-christlichen Geschichtsdenken verbinden[62]. Der Gott, der Assyrer, Babylonier und Perser erweckt und verworfen hatte, hat auch die römische Geschichte gelenkt. Wenn die Römer, so folgert Augustin[63], den wahren Gott verehrten, "würden sie einerseits ihr Reich auf Erden besser haben, andererseits danach ein ewiges Reich empfangen".

Dies ist die römisch-katholische Korrektur, Überbietung und Bestäti-

---

[58] Hor. ep. 2,1,130 f. Kiessling-Heinze vermuten (a. l.): "H. mag hier geradezu an seines Freundes Virgil Aeneis denken".

[59] Minucius Felix, Octavius 7,6.

[60] Fuchs 1938.

[61] Min. Fel., 26–27.

[62] Nur an die Namen Eusebius, Lactantius, Prudentius, Augustin sei hier erinnert.

[63] Augustin, civ. 4,28.

gung jenes Spruches, mit dem Iuppiter seiner Tochter Venus den Sinn der römischen Geschichte eröffnete, um sie über Leiden und Unglück ihres Sohnes Aeneas zu trösten.

4. Materialien zur römischen Offenbarungsliteratur und Geschichtstheologie

In diesem Kapitel sind in möglichst einfacher und übersichtlicher Form Materialien zur römischen Offenbarungsliteratur und Geschichtstheologie zusammengestellt. Es muß ausdrücklich betont werden, daß es sich in allen Rubriken nur um eine *Auswahl* der Daten, Autoren, Texte, Begriffe und Belege handelt. Zumal aus der sog. schönen Literatur konnten (und brauchten) nur einige Beispiele angeführt werden. Weitere Materialien finden sich in den in der Bibliographie angegebenen Werken, wobei besonders auf Regell und Rohde hingewiesen sei.

4.1. Römische Divinationsliteratur, chronologische Übersicht

um 500	*libri Sibyllini* in Rom.
um 400	*libri fatales* von Veii. Daß sie *saeculum*-Spekulation enthielten, ist eher unwahrscheinlich (Liv. 5,15,11).
249	*ludi Tarentini* oder *saeculares*.
nach 220	Naevius († 201) *bellum Poenicum* (Alterswerk). Erster Beleg für Kenntnis der Sibylle in Rom; Sibylle in Verbindung mit der Aeneassage: Sibyllen- und Aeneastradition sind in Rom wahrscheinlich gleich alt.
nach 216	Politische (hannibalische) und religiöse Krise. Liv. 25,1: Synkretismus; Verbot und Verbrennung von *libri vaticini* aufgrund eines Senatsbeschlusses.
213/12	*carmina Marciana*, Liv. 25,12: aufgefunden im Rahmen der o. g. Inquisition, auf Senatsbeschluß akzeptiert.
207	'carmen' des Livius Andronicus für Iuno Regina mit Tanz von 27 Jungfrauen auf Anordnung der Sib. Bücher; Sühnung des Zwitters von Frusino: Liv. 27,37,5.
192–188	1. Syr. Krieg gegen Antiochos III. – 190 – Sieg v. Magnesia. Übertragung der Weltreichsabfolgelehre vom (griech.) Orient nach Rom möglich. Rom wird Erbe der Seleukiden, auch Erbe des Hasses der unterdrückten Völker: *Hystaspes-Orakel* (1. Jh. v./1. Jh. n. Chr.) bei Lactanz. *Bouplagos-Orakel* bei Antisthenes v. Rhodos: Phlegon

	v. Tralles (FGrHist Nr. 508; Nr. 257,36). Diese Propaganda dürfte Rom erreicht haben.

v. Tralles (FGrHist Nr. 508; Nr. 257,36). Diese Propaganda dürfte Rom erreicht haben.

Rom hat darauf u. a. mit der Aeneadensage (vgl. Plut. Flam. 12) und Einführung des Kultes der kleinasiatischen Magna Mater aufgrund eines Sibyllenspruches reagiert.

189   M. Fulvius Nobilior cos.; vielleicht pythagoreischer Einfluß.

186   Bacchanalienkrise; *externae religiones;* Bücherverbrennung: Liv. 39,15ff.

181   Entdeckung des 'Grabes des Numa' und der *libri Numae*; pythagoreische oder pythagorisierende Schriften (?): Liv. 40,29.

179   M. Fulvius Nobilior *censor;* Patron des Ennius (239–169), des 'Pythagoreers'.

149   M'. Manilius cos., Verfasser der *monumenta,* Sammlung und Erklärung der *leges Numae.*

146   *ludi saeculares* nach Cassius Hemina, Piso Censorius, Cn. Gellius bei Censorin, nat. 17,11.

2. H. 2. Jh. v. Chr.   Cassius Hemina und L. Calpurnius Piso Censorius tradieren die Geschichten von pythagoreischen Numa-Büchern. Sie sind Vorläufer des P. Nigidius Figulus († 45) in der Verbindung von römischer Religion mit pythagoreischer Philosophie.

139   Vertreibung von Juden (Sabazios-Anhängern) und Chaldäern durch den *praetor peregrinus* (Val. Max. 1,3,3).

125   Sibyllinisches Orakel zur Sühnung eines Prodigiums; griech. Überlieferung: Phlegon v. Tralles, mirab. 10; Diels, 1890, 1ff.

ca. 90   Vegoia-Sprüche.

88   Plutarch, Sulla 7: Trompeten-Prodigium, von *haruspices* als Zeichen für Ende des *saeculum* und μετακόσμησις gedeutet.

Juli 83   Beim Brand des Capitols verbrennen die Sib. Bücher, *carmina Marciana* und *commentarii* der *Xviri s.f.* Sie werden ersetzt durch eine Sammlung von Abschriften aus Erythrai, italischen Städten und Privatbesitz: Beweis für die Verbreitung von sibyllinischer Literatur.

?	Vettius *augur* berechnet die Dauer Roms (mündl. Tradition bei Varro, *antiquitates* [*hum.?*] B. 28, erhalten bei Censorin, nat. 17).
2. H. 1. Jh. v. Chr.	*Auctores de disciplina Etrusca:* Tarquitius Priscus; Iulius Aquila; A. Caecina; Caesius.
116–27	M. Terentius Varro, *de saeculo;* Epochengliederung in: *de gente populi Romani* l. IV (Peter HRR II S. 10 ff.): Palingenesia; pythagoreische Zahlenspekulation; universalgeschichtlicher Entwurf.
74/73	Aion-Inschrift der Pompei in Eleusis.
65	Blitzschläge auf dem Capitol, von etruskischen *haruspices* auf *imperii occasus* gedeutet: Cic. Cat. 3,8,19.
63	*Cornelier-Orakel:* Sall. Cat. 47; Cic. Cat. 3,4 ff. L. Cincius, *de fastis.*
53	M. Valerius Messalla Rufus, cos.: Ianus = Aion.
49	Cäsars Übergang über den Rubicon als saeculare Wende gedeutet von Nigidius bei Lucan 1,639 ff.
45	† P. Nigidius Figulus, *sphaera graecanica:* "*novus annus*" Schol. Verg. Georg. 1,43 – "Erneuerer der pythagoreischen Disziplin" (Cic. Tim. 1); Verbindung von etruskischer Disciplin mit Astrologie (Plin. n. h. 2,138 f.), *disciplinas Etruscas sequens* (Arnob. 3,40).
43	† M. Tullius Cicero – a. 56: *de haruspicum responso;* a. 44/43: *de natura deorum; de divinatione; de fato – de auguriis.*
46/45	Cäsars Kalenderreform.
44	*haruspex* Volcanius (Volcatius) über das *sidus Iulium.*
43	anonymer *haruspex* im Senat: prophezeit Rückkehr des Königtums, Sklavenschicksal für alle, außer ihm selbst. Er hält den Atem an und stirbt (App. b. c. 4,4).
41/40	Vergil, ecl. IV (*Cumaeum carmen*). Horaz, epode 16 (*Altera iam teritur . . . vate me*).
22–28/12	Bearbeitung der *Sibyll. Bücher.* Konfiskation von umlaufenden 'nicht-authentischen' Orakeln durch Augustus. Deposition der gereinigten Sammlung der *Sibyll. Bücher* im Apoll-Tempel auf dem Palatin (Suet. Aug. 31).
17	*ludi saeculares; carmen composuit* Q. Horatius Flaccus.

4.2. Römische Divinationsliteratur

4.2.1. I Fachschriftsteller (alphabetisch):

Anonyme Literatur: *augurum libri – ius augurum – augurales libri – augurales – libri de auspiciis* von *"augures populi Romani" – nostri* (sc. *augurum) commentarii – explanatio auguriorum.*

1. Jh. n.	*M. Antistius Labeo*: de officio augurum.
22 n.	† *C. Ateius Capito*: de iure pontificio; de iure augurali (nach Bremer II 1,280 ff.).
1. Jh. v.	*A. Caecina*: de disciplina Etrusca – Blitzlehre, benutzt bei Verrius, Seneca, Plinius.
1. Jh. v. (?)	*Caesius*: de disciplina Etrusca (?).
48 v.	† *Ap. Claudius Pulcher*: libri augurales / auguralis disciplina / de auguriis, Cicero gewidmet.
79 v.	*C. Claudius Marcellus*, proc.: über das Auguralwesen.
2./3. Jh. n. (?)	*Cornelius Labeo*: de oraculo Apollinis Clarii; de disciplina Etrusca (?).
?	*Ennius d. J.* (?): de augurandi disciplina.
Ende 1. Jh. v.	*Fonteius*: de disciplina Etrusca (?).
64 v.	*L. Iulius Caesar*, cos.: libri pontificales (2?); (libri) augurales; auspiciorum libri (16); s. Bickel 1957.
august. Zt. (?)	*Iulius Aquila*: de disciplina Etrusca (?).
1. H. 1. Jh. n.	*M. Manilius*, Astronomicon: Astrologie als Offenbarung, s. 4,916 ff.: *ipse deus vultusque suos corpusque recludit … ut bene cognosci possit* ("erschließt", "offenbart").
213/12 v.	*Marcius*, carmina Marciana.
3. Jh. n.	*Martianus Capella*: de nuptiis Mercurii et Philologiae.
45 v.	† *P. Nigidius Figulus*: Brontoskopie, Astrologie, Nekromantik; Extispicin; Gell. 7,6: *in libro primo augurii privati.*
1. Jh. v.	*P. Servilius augur* (Titel unbekannt).
1. Jh. v. (?)	*Tarquitius Priscus*: lat. transcriptio ex ostentario Tusco: Macr. 3,7,2; ostentarium arborarium: Macr. 3,20,3.
1. Jh. v.	*L. Tarutius Firmanus*: Astrologie in griech. Sprache.
116–27	*M. Terentius Varro*: Astrologie; Ausbildung des vates-Begriffs; Zahlenspekulation; Epochengliederung.
106–43	*M. Tullius Cicero*: de auguriis; de divinatione de fato.

1. Jh. n.	*Umbricius Melior*: de disciplina Etrusca (?).
26 v.	† *M. Valerius Messalla Rufus* (cos. 53): de auspiciis.
ca. 90 v. (?)	*Vegoia*: fragm. in: Corp. agrimensorum p. 350; (libri Vegonici: Amm. Marc. 17,10,2).
1. Jh. v.	*Veranius Flaccus*: auspiciorum libri / de auspiciis.
1. Jh. n.	*Vicellius*: Lydus, ost. 54: ἐκ τῶν Τάγητος στίχων; Astrologie und Erdbebenlehre (?).

4.2.2. II Allgemeine 'religiöse' Literatur:

Cato maior: *de auguribus* (Rede).
Cicero: *de haruspicum responso; de divinatione; de fato; de auguriis.*
Claudian: *de bello Getico* (a. 402 n.).
Fabius Pictor: *annales* frg. 3: Aeneas träumt seine Zukunft; als XVvir (?) Urheber der Sibyll. Orakel bei Phlegon, mir. c. 10: so Diels 1890, 104 ff.
Horaz: epode 16 (... *vate me*).
Livius: Religiöse Historiographie; vgl. den Gebrauch, den Iulius Obsequens (4. Jh. n.?) in seinem *prodigiorum liber* von Livius gemacht hat.
Lucan: Pharsalia I. VI.
Manilius: Astronomicon: Astrologie als Offenbarung: 4,866–935.
Cn. Naevius: *bellum Poenicum,* frg. 9: *libri futura continentes.*
Ovid: *Fasti* 1,89 ff.; 4,1 ff.; 4,191 ff.
Properz: Elegien IV 1: Horus; 2: Vertumnus; 6; 9: Hercules, Kultstiftung an der Ara Maxima.
Seneca: Tragödien: Thyest, Ödipus, Troerinnen; Apocolocyntosis; nat. quaest. II.
Statius: Silve IV 3: Cumaeische Sibylle, Aeneas – Augustus – Domitian.
Silius Italicus: *bellum Punicum,* B. III 557–630: *pandit seriem venturi Iuppiter aevi.*
Tibull: Messalinus' Amtseinführung (II 5).
Vergil: ecl. IV (*Cumaeum carmen*); Aen. I: *imperium sine fine dedi;* Aen. VI: Buch der Sibylle; Aen. VIII: Die Vision auf dem Schild.

4.3. Die primären Divinationsbücher (alphabetisch)

Acheruntia sacra: Serv. Aen. 8,398: von Tages verfaßt; handeln u. a. über das Aufschieben (*differre*) der *fata.*
Acherontici libri: Arnob. 2,62.
augurales libri: Cic. div. 1,72.
fatales libri: s. §4.3.1.

fatidici libri: Sueton, Aug. 31: Augustus als pont. max. läßt Bücher dieser
   Art verbrennen.
Etrusci (-orum) libri: Cic. div. 2,50: Geschichte von Tages; Macr. 3,7,1.
   rituales E. libri: Fest. 358 L.
   E. libri fatales: s. §4.3.1.
   chartae Etruscae: Cic. div. 1,20.
exercituales libri: Amm. 23,5,10.
fulgurales (libri): Cic. div. 1,72.
   ars fulguritarum der etruskischen Nymphe Begoe (Vegoia): Serv. Aen.
   6,72: verwahrt "in templo Apollinis" (!)
   Etrusci libri de fulguratura: Serv. Dan. Aen. 1,42.
l. futura continentes: Naevius, bellum Poenicum frg. 9 Str.
libri haruspicini: Cic. div. 1,72.
   l. haruspicinae (artis): Serv. Aen. 8,398.
litterae iuris Etruriae: Serv. auct. Aen. 1,2: scriptum vocibus Tagae.
(carmina) Marciana: Liv. 25,12.
   libri Marciorum: Serv. Aen. 6,72: in templo Apollinis.
Numae libri: Liv. 40,29 (a. 181 verbrannt); cf. Calpurnius Piso frg. 11 P.
   Numae commentarii: Liv. 1,31,5 (Inhalt: Opfer); Piso, ann. frg. 13,
   nennt dieselben Texte libri.
reconditi libri: Serv. Aen. 2,649.
rituales libri: Cic. div. 1,33 (anscheinend nur von etr. Büchern gebraucht).
ostentarium Tuscum: Macr. 3,7,2.
Sibyllae, -ini libri: Cic. div. 1,98.
   libri: Cic. div. 1,97.
   libri fatales: Liv. 5,14,4: s. §4.3.1.
   versus Sibyllae, -ini: Cic. div. 1,4,98.
   λόγιον Σιβύλλειον: Cass. Dio XLVII 18 (ad a. 44).
Tagetica (sacra): zitiert bei Granius, libro de Italia secundo (Macr. 5,19,13).
   libri Tagetinici: Amm. Marc. 17,10,2.
   disciplina Tagetis: Censor. nat. 4,13.
   praecepta Tagetica (?): Longinian, epist. ad Augustin 234.
   Στίχοι Τάγητος: Lydus, ostent. 54.
Tyrrhena carmina: Lucr. 6,381; vgl. CIL 11 3370 (carmina des Tarquitius
   Priscus).
Tuscae historiae: Censorin, nat. 17,6.
Tusci libelli: Iuven. 13,62.
Tuscorum litterae: Plin. n. h. 2,53,138.
vaticini libri: Liv. 25,1 (einschließlich precationes und ars sacrificandi
   konfisziert und verbrannt); Liv. 39,16,8.
Vegonici libri: s. Vegoia; s. ars fulguritarum.

4.3.1. libri fatales

I. Direkte Nennungen

Arnobius 7,47: si ex libris fatalibus vatumque responsis invitari ad urbem deus Aesculapius iussus est, ... (Einführung des Aesculapkultes).

Censorin 14,6: Etruscis quoque libris fatalibus aetatem hominis duodecim hebdomadibus describi Varro commemorat.

Livius 5,14,4: (deos) pestis eius arcendae causa placandos esse in libris fatalibus inventum sit: die Sibyllinischen Bücher Roms; ebenso: 22,9,9; 42,2,6: ob haec prodigia libri fatales inspecti, editumque ab decemviris est ...; 22,10,10; 22,57,6.

Livius 5,15,11: sic igitur libris fatalibus, sic disciplina Etrusca traditum esse: die Bücher von Veii. Cic. div. 1,100 nennt sie: scripta fata.

Serv. auct. Aen. 2,140: unde ludi Taurei dicti qui ex libris fatalibus a rege Tarquinio Superbo instituti sunt.

Sueton, Iulius 79: ... L. Cottam XVvirum ... ut quoniam fatalibus libris contineretur, Parthos nisi a rege non posse vinci, Caesar rex appellaretur.

Granius Licinianus, B. 35 (p. 15 Fl): ... placuit, id quod numquam alias ac pro collegio, quid in libris fatalibus scriptum esset, palam recitare. Constabat notari carmine Cinna...

II. Umschreibungen

Cicero, har. resp. 9,18: (maiores nostri) fatorum veteres praedictiones Apollinis vatum libris, portentorum expiationes Etruscorum disciplina contineri putaverunt.

Livius 10,8,2: Decemviros sacris faciundis, carminum Sibyllae ac fatorum populi Romani interpretes, antistites eosdem Apollinaris sacri ... videmus. – Vgl. 38,45,3.

Lucan 1,599: (XVviri) qui fata deum secretaque carmina servant.

Seneca, prov. 5,8: irrevocabilis humana pariter ac divina cursus vehit. ille ipse omnium conditor et rector scripsit quidem fata, sed sequitur; semper paret, semel iussit.

Servius, Aen. 6,36 (aus Varro): (Sibylla) a qua sunt fata Romana conscripta.

Servius, Aen. 6,72: novem libri, in quibus erant fata et remedia Romana (die Sibyllinischen Bücher).

Sueton, Augustus 31,1: quidquid fatidicorum librorum Graeci Latinique generis nullis vel parum idoneis auctoribus ferebatur, supra duo milia contracta undique cremavit (sc. Augustus) ac solos retinuit Sibyllinos.

4.4. Römische Divinationsliteratur: Formen und Gattungen

acta: offizielle Aufzeichnungen, beispielsweise der Priesterkollegien, z. B. Opferprotokolle.

annales/historiae: Geschichtswerke mit eingelegten Orakeln, Prophetien.

ars: 'ars' bedeutet sowohl 'Technik, Handwerk' als auch 'Darstellung einer Technik, Fachschriftstellerei'; vgl. *disciplina* – 'Lehre' – als Unterweisung und als Inhalt der Unterweisung. Schriften *'de arte'* und *'de disciplina'* können sowohl (primäre) Lehrbücher als auch Abhandlungen (Traktate, Monographien) sein.

carmen: feierlicher Spruch, Orakel; sakrale Poesie/Prosa.

commentarii: Protokolle, Sammlungen von Vorschriften, Regeln, Beispielen (Fällen).

decretum/edictum: Entscheidung, Gutachten: *decretum collegi* (sc. *augurum*).

dialogische Lehrrede Lydus, de ost. 3,10 B: κατά τινα διαλογικὴν ὁμιλίαν ἐρωτᾷ μὲν δῆϑεν ὁ Τάρχων, ἀποκρίνεται δὲ ὁ Τάγης. Aus ähnlich strukturiertem Text wohl das Vegoia-Fragment (corp. Agrimens., p. 350 Lachmann): wiederholte Anrede an den Empfänger der Offenbarung, *praeceptum* am Ende. Parallelen zu Offenbarungsliteratur κατὰ πεῦσιν καὶ ἀπόκρισιν in der Hermetik.

fabula: ('Mythos') – mit eingelegter Lehrrede, Belehrung über Ritual, Paraenese etc.

fasti: Ovid, *fasti* als Rahmen für Epiphanien und Offenbarung (Kultaitiologien).

instituta: Satzungen: *pontificum et haruspicum instituta.*

interpretatio: Auslegung, Exegese mit Applikation auf aktuelle Anlässe.

ius (augurale, pontificium etc.) a) Gesetzessammlungen (Satzungen); b) Monographien über Sakralrecht; vgl. Begriffe wie *'ars', 'disciplina', 'instituta'.*

lex, leges sacrae: Der Stil sakraler Gesetzgebung ist bewußt imitiert von Cicero (de legibus II) in seiner "Constitution der Religion"; Vorbild sind die *leges Numae.*

libri: der allgemeinste Ausdruck für schriftliche Überlieferung von Offenbarungsgut. 1. *libri Numae:* als Offenbarungsschriften charakterisiert u. a. durch den Inhalt: *occulta quaedam sacrificia,* durch Sanktionen gegen Mißbrauch (Liv. 1,31,8); vgl. den Fund von 'Numae libri' in Numas Grab. 2. *libri augurales, augurum* (s. anonyme Div.-Lit.). 3. *libri Sibyllini,* häufig "die Bücher" schlechthin genannt, z. B. in der Formel *ad libros ire* – die sib. Bücher befragen: Cic. div. 1,97.

litterae: Schriften allgemein; vgl. *volumina, chartae.*

monitum: Mahnspruch (Cic., har. resp. passim).

monumenta: i. S. von: "schriftliche Denkmäler": Cic. div. 1,20 (= de consulatu suo): *artis scripta et monumenta...*

oratio: 'Homilie', 'Predigt', z. B. Rede im Senat oder der *contio* zu den *responsa* oder *decreta* der Priesterkollegien.

praeceptum: Vorschrift, Ratschlag, 'Spruch'. Vegoia-Fragment: imperativisch-adhortative Lehrrede, endend mit einer Verhaltensregel. *Cn. Marcii vatis praecepta* (= *carmina Marciana,* so zitiert bei Isidor, orig. 6,8,12, vgl. Morel p. 6), vgl. *monita, monere* der *haruspices.*

precatio, preces: Liv. 25,1.

responsum: 'Bescheid'. 1. Orakel: Serv. Aen. 3,89; Verg. Aen. 3,94–98: ein *responsum* des Apollon. Verg. Aen. 6,82: *vatis responsa;* Serv. Aen. 6,72: *Sibyllina responsa.* 2. *responsum, respondere,* bes. von *haruspices* gebraucht.

sermo: Rede, Spruch Serv. Aen. 3,445 (aus Varro?): sane sciendum omnia responsa Sibyllae plus minusve centum contineri sermonibus; 6,43: ... responsa enim Sibyllae in hoc loco plus minus centum sermonum sunt. Inveniuntur tamen Apollinis logia et viginti quinque et trium sermonum...; 6,74: ... ut Varro dicit, in foliis palmae interdum notis, interdum scribebat sermonibus.

Traktat, Monographie – ungenauer Terminus für wissenschaftliche, historische, antiquarische Abhandlungen. Beispiele: Cicero, *de divinatione;* Varro, *de saeculo;* Ateius Capito, *de iure pontificio;* Veranius, *de auspiciis;* Cornelius Labeo, *de oraculo Apollinis Clarii.*

4.5. Römische Divinationsliteratur: nach Offenbarungsarten ('hohe Literatur')

Epiphanie: Horus bei Prop. 4,1; Ovid, fasti 1,89ff. 4,1ff.; 4,191ff.

Ekstase: Ennius, Alexander (Cassandra); Verg. Aen. 6,77ff. (die rasende Sibylle); Statius, Silv. 4,3.

Entrückung/Himmelsreise: Cic., de republ. (*somnium Scipionis;* Erklärer: Scipio maior).

extispicium: Lucan, Pharsalia 1,609–638; Seneca, Oedipus, 293–392.

Incubation: Verg. Aen. 7,59–106.

Katabasis: Ennius (s. Lucr. 1,112ff.: *Acherusia templa*). Verg. Aen. 6 (Sibylle und Anchises als Führer und Lehrer).

Nekromantik: Lucan, Pharsalia 6; Seneca, Oedipus 530–658; Silius Italicus, *bellum Punicum* 13,435ff. (Vision: *iam cuncta videbis*).

oraculum, praedictio, monitum, voces: Hor. epod. 16 *contio* (Schlußvers: *vate me*); Verg. Aen. 1,257–296 (*volvens fatorum arcana movebo*); 3,94–98: Orakel des Apollon.

prodigia: Lucan, Pharsalia 1,524–583; Seneca, Thyest 775ff. – 789ff. – 1035: Prodigium – Deutung als dramatisches Strukturprinzip; Livius, passim.

somnium: Fabius Pictor frg. 3; Ennius, Epicharm I; ann. 5f.; s. Lucr. 1,112 und Cic. rep. 6: somnium Scipionis; Ps. Vergil, Culex.

Vision: Verg. Aen. 8,626–728: Die Vision auf dem Schild (literargeschichtliche Form: *descriptio/ ἔκφρασις* vgl. Pausanias 10,28: die Malereien in der Lesche).

Bibliographie

I. Allgemeines

1. Jüdische und christliche Geschichtstheologie

Bultmann, Rudolf 1964: *Geschichte und Eschatologie*, Tübingen ²1964.
Cancik, Hubert 1976: *Grundzüge der hethitischen und alttestamentlichen Geschichtsschreibung*, Wiesbaden 1976.
Heussi, K. 1930: *Vom Sinn der Geschichte*. Augustinus und die Moderne, Jena 1930.
Jäschke, Walter 1976: *Die Suche nach den eschatologischen Wurzeln der Geschichtsphilosophie*, München 1976.
Löwith, Karl 1950: *Meaning in History*. The Theological Implications of the Philosophy of History (1949), Chicago ²1950.
Nestle, Wilhelm: s. unten III. Römische Geschichtstheologie.

2. Heilige Schriften – Buchreligion – Buch als Symbol

Curtius, Ernst Robert 1961: *Europäische Literatur und lateinisches Mittelalter*, Bern/München ³1961.
Lanczkowski, Günter 1956: *Heilige Schriften*. Inhalt, Textgestalt und Überlieferung, Stuttgart 1956.
Leipoldt, Johannes/Morenz, Siegfried 1953: *Heilige Schriften*. Betrachtungen zur Religionsgeschichte der antiken Mittelmeerwelt, Leipzig 1953.
Mensching, Gustav 1937: *Das heilige Wort*, Bonn 1937.
– 1959: *Die Religion*, Stuttgart 1959.

II. Römische Religion

1. Divination

Bickel, Ernst 1957: "L. Caesar, cos. 64 in der Origo gentis Romanae. Die traditionelle Urgeschichte der Römer als Bestandteil ihrer Pontifikal- und Auguralliteratur", in: *RMP* 100 (1957) 201–236.
Bloch, Raymond 1966: "Liberté et déterminisme dans la divination étrusque et romaine", in: *La divination* 1966, 159–170.
Bouché-Leclerq, H. 1879: *Histoire de la divination dans l'Antiquité*, Paris 1879–1882.
La Divination en Mésopotamie ancienne et dans les régions voisines, XIVème Rencontre assyriologique internationale, Paris 1966.
Éléments orientaux dans la religion grecque ancienne. Travaux du Centre d'Études supérieures spécialisé d'histoire des religions de Strasbourg, Paris 1960.
Heurgon, J. 1959: "The Date of Vergil's Prophecy", in: *JRS* 49 (1959) 41–45.
Pfiffig, Ambros J. 1961: "Eine etruskische Prophezeiung", in: *Gymnasium* 68 (1961) 55–64.
Regell, Paul 1878: *De augurum publicorum libris*. Diss. Vratisl. 1878.
– 1881: "Über die Schautempla der Augurn", in: *Fleckeisens Jahrbücher* (1881) 593–637.
– 1882: *Fragmenta auguralia*, Programm Hirschberg 1882.

– 1893: *Commentarii in librorum auguralium fragmenta specimen*, Programm Hirschberg 1893.

Rohde, G. 1936: *Die Kultsatzungen der römischen Pontifices* (RVV 25), Berlin 1936.

Thulin, Carl 1968: *Die etruskische Disziplin*, Teil I–III. Göteborg 1905–1909 = 1968.

2. *XVviri sacris faciundis, libri Sibyllini, Apoll*

Diels, Hermann 1890: *Sibyllinische Blätter*, Berlin 1890.

Gagé, Jean 1955: *Apollon Romain*, Paris 1955.

Radke, Gerhard 1963: "Quindecimviri", in: *PRE* XXIV 1 (1963) 1114–1148.

– 1979: *Die Götter Altitaliens* (1965), Münster ²1979, 39–50.

III. Hellenische und römische Geschichtsphilosophie und -theologie

Altheim, Franz 1951/53: *Römische Religionsgeschichte*, Baden-Baden I 1951; II 1953 (erstmalig 1931–33; englisch: 1938).

Brelich, Angelo 1956: *Tre variazioni Romane sul tema delle origini*, Rom 1956.

Fuchs, Harald 1938: *Der geistige Widerstand gegen Rom in der antiken Welt*, Berlin 1938.

Gaiser, Konrad 1961: *Platon und die Geschichte*, Stuttgart 1961.

Gatz, Bodo 1967: *Weltalter, goldene Zeit und sinnverwandte Vorstellungen*, Hildesheim 1967.

Kajanto, Iiro 1967: *God and Fate in Livy* (Turku 1957); Auswahl bei: Burck, Erich (Hrsg.): *Wege zu Livius* (WdF 132), Darmstadt 1967, 475–485.

Kleinknecht, Hermann: s. unten IV. Vergil.

Koch, Carl 1968: *Der römische Iuppiter* (1935–37), Darmstadt 1968.

Kroymann, Jürgen 1961: "Römisches Sendungs- und Niedergangsbewußtsein", in: *Festschrift H. Hommel*, Tübingen 1961, 69–91.

Nestle, Wilhelm 1946: Griechische Geschichtsphilosophie (1934) in: *idem, Griechische Weltanschauung in ihrer Bedeutung für die Gegenwart*, Stuttgart 1946, 334–372.

Sordi, Marta 1972: "L'idea di crisi e di rinuovamento nella concezione romano-etrusca della storia", in: *ANRW* I², Berlin/New York 1972, 781–793.

IV. Vergil

Bailey, Cyrus 1935: *Religion in Vergil*, Oxford 1935.

Binder, Gerhard 1971: *Aeneas und Augustus*. Interpretationen zum 8. Buch der Aeneis, Meisenheim 1971.

Cancik, Hubert 1980: "Der Eingang in die Unterwelt. Ein religionswissenschaftlicher Versuch zu Vergil, Aeneis 6,236–272", in: Barié, Paul (Hrsg.): *Mythos. Der altsprachliche Unterricht* XIII 2 (Stuttgart 1980) 55–69.

Carcopino, Jérôme 1930: *Virgile et le mystère de la IVᵉ églogue*, Paris 1930.

Faber, Richard 1975: *Die Verkündigung Vergils*. Reich – Kirche – Staat. (AWTS 4), Hildesheim 1975.

– 1976: *Politische Idyllik*. Zur sozialen Mythologie Arkadiens, Stuttgart 1976.

Jeanmaire, Henri 1929: *Le messianisme de Virgile*, Paris 1929.

– 1939: *La Sibylle et le retour de l'âge d'or*, Paris 1939.

Kleinknecht, Hermann 1944: "Laokoon", in: *Hermes* 79 (1944) = in: Oppermann, H. (Hrsg.): *Wege zu Vergil* (WdF 19), Darmstadt 1963, 426–488.

Klingner, Friedrich 1965: *Römische Geisteswelt*, München ⁵1965, 293–311 (Virgil und die geschichtliche Welt, 1943); 645–666 (Rom als Idee, 1927).

– 1967: *Virgil*, Zürich/Stuttgart 1967.

Knauer, Georg N. 1965: *Die Aeneis und Homer* (Hypomnemata 7), Göttingen 1965.

Merkelbach, Reinhold 1961: "Aeneas in Cumae", in: *MH* 19 (1961) 83–90.

Nawratil, K. 1939: "Die Geschichtsphilosophie der Aeneis", in: *WSt* 57 (1939) 113–128.

Norden, Eduard 1957: *P. Vergilius Maro, Aeneis Buch VI* (1903), Stuttgart ³1927 = Darmstadt ⁴1957.

Pötscher, Walter 1977: *Vergil und die göttlichen Mächte*. Aspekte seiner Weltanschauung, Hildesheim 1977.

Rieks, Rudolf 1981: "Vergils Dichtung als Zeugnis und Deutung der römischen Geschichte", in: *ANRW* II 31.2, Berlin/New York 1981, 728–868 (mit sehr reicher Bibliographie; bes. 817 ff.: Aitiologie und Eschatologie).

Wlosok, Antonie 1973: "Vergil in der neueren Forschung", in: *Gymnasium* 8 (1973) 129–151.

Zinn, Ernst 1965: "Vergil", in: *LAW* (1965) 3205–3212.

The Problem of Apocalyptic Genre in Greek and Hellenistic Literature: The Case of the Oracle of Trophonius

Hans Dieter Betz

1. Introduction

In Greek and Hellenistic literature the problem of apocalyptic genre is as complicated as it is known to be in Jewish and early Christian literature. The problem is, to state it generally, which literary genre or genres are specifically associated with texts showing affinities to apocalypticism. So far, the question has not been resolved, so that it may be worthwhile to take a look at the Greek literature, where we not only find various kinds of apocalyptic material but also, characteristic of the Greek mind, consideration of the literary forms and genres, and their purposes and functions. In the following, the case of the famous oracle of Trophonius at Lebadeia will be taken as a test case.[1] Fortunately, we possess a number of quite explicit discussions of the oracle. These discussions show developments as having taken place during its history, which can illuminate certain aspects of the genre problem.

2. The Oracle of Trophonius

The fact that we possess relatively good descriptions of the oracle of Trophonius enables us to follow in some detail how in the course of its history this oracle was gradually transformed and how, in that connection, it came to be connected with afterlife mythology.

2.1. The old Boeotian oracle seems to belong to an archaic cult type, of which several other manifestations in the area, elsewhere in Greece, and even in Ionia are known. Comparing them, A. Schachter[2] has come to the conclusion that this cult type came from the north before the end of the 8th century B.C. and that the sanctuaries are found in places where the

---

[1] On the oracle, see Radke 1939, 678–695; Deubner 1899; Nilsson 1967, 115, 169, 214, 626; 1961, 104, 469f.; Burkert 1977, 143, 186, 308.

[2] Schachter 1967, 1–16; besides the Trophonius oracle, Schachter discusses five Boeotian cults of Apollo, the oracles of Dodona and Delphi, and from Ionia the cults of Apollo of Clarus and Didyma. See also Clark 1968, 63–75.

worshippers of that cult type had settled or migrated. The sanctuaries have in common that they were connected with mountains and springs, employed male prophets, and sometimes used an underground chamber for dream-inspirations. In the course of history, the manifestations of the cult type changed and developed their own peculiar characteristics. Thus, the oracle of Trophonius came to be known by its underground crypt, into which the consultant entered in order to become himself the medium and to have a direct encounter with the god Trophonius himself.

2.2. What interests us here is that none of the older consultations report anything about afterlife mythology. To "descend" (καταβαίνειν) originally means simply to climb down into the crypt,[3] according to Pausanias an underground chamber built like a bread-oven.[4]

2.2.1. When Pausanias visited Lebadeia and the oracle,[5] he reports that the area around the city was filled with numerous temples belonging to a variety of gods. Obviously this speaks for the great reputation the place had acquired, but also for syncretistic developments which no doubt affected also the oracle itself. Thus, the older ritual of waterdrinking as a way to get inspired seems to have undergone secondary developments.[6] According to Pausanias there are now two such rituals: before going down into the crypt the consultant "must drink water called the water of Forgetfulness [Λήϑη], that he may forget all that he has been thinking of hitherto;" after the consultation "he drinks of another water, the water of Memory [Μνημοσύνη], which causes him to remember what he sees after his descent."[7] The names of Lethe and Mnemosyne suggest that the oracle has now been connected with the older mythology of the netherworld, to which these names traditionally belong.[8]

2.2.2. According to Pausanias' report, however, these developments do not appear to have gone very far. He simply states that those who have entered into the *adyton* in one way or another "learn the future," sometimes by vision, sometimes by hearing.[9] There is no indication that anything beyond the traditional inquiry took place.

2.2.3. But Pausanias reports other matters of literary significance. When

---

[3] See the references in Herod. I. 46; VIII. 134; Aristoph. *Nub.* 505–508, with the scholia, ed. Koster 1977, 114–116; Eurip. *Ion* 300, 393f., 404.

[4] Pausanias XXXIX. 10.

[5] Paus. XXXIX–XL. For the nature of the report as eyewitness evidence, see Paus. XXXIX. 14.

[6] This is certainly true of the elaborate rituals proceding the incubation. See on this point Pley 1916, 1256–1262; Nilsson 1961, 470; Deubner 1899, 14ff.

[7] Paus. XXXIX. 8.

[8] On Lethe and Mnemosyne, see Dieterich 1969, 90ff.; Nilsson 1961, 238; Zuntz 1971, 378ff.

[9] Paus. XXXIX. 11. See also Maximus Tyr., *Diss.* XIV. 2.

the inquirer has come out from the crypt, he is again under the guidance of the priests who set him down upon the "throne of Mnemosyne" asking him to relate to them all that he has seen or heard.[10] The inquirer is also obliged to dedicate a tablet upon which the revelation is written down as a testimony.[11] This request we know from Jewish apocalyptic texts as a feature where the testimony is often nothing but the apocalyptic book itself.

2.2.4. Another interesting observation can be made: according to Pausanias, when he returns from the crypt the consultant is "possessed with fear and unconscious of himself and his surroundings."[12] This behavior clearly goes beyond what one should expect from the simple oracular inquiry and suggests an experience more like that in Plutarch's myth of Timarchus.[13] This experience of intense fear, however, must have been so firmly associated with the Trophonius oracle that losing the ability to laugh became a proverbial expression for consulting the oracle.[14]

2.3. More information emerges in Philostratus' account of the visit by Apollonius of Tyana. While Apollonius had consulted the oracle before,[15] he returned to it after making his public speech at Olympia in order to reform it.[16] Before turning to the consultation, Philostratus inserts a brief description of the oracle, which apart from all that agrees with Pausanias contains some new information.

2.3.1. From Philostratus it becomes quite clear that the inquirer does not simply climb down into a crypt but that he actually descends into the netherworld. As he descends he has to hold cakes in his hands to appease dangerous underworld snakes attacking him.[17] The descent is now called *kathodos*, the traditional name for descending into the netherworld. At his return, "the earth brings him back to the surface."[18] This return may occur in the vicinity or far away, beyond Locri, beyond Phocis, but we are told most consultants emerge within the borders of Boeotia.

2.3.2. Apollonius' visit is noteworthy for still other reasons. The priests at first react in a hostile way to his visit, apparently because they were opposed to his ideas of cultic reform. This attempt to reform and thus save the older sanctuaries must have been a cause shared by other philosophers, like, *e.g.*, Plutarch and his work at Delphi. When the priests refused to admit Apollonius, he went to the spring of Hercyne and delivered a lecture

---

[10] *Ibid.*, 13.   [11] *Ibid.*, 14.   [12] *Ibid.*, 13.

[13] See below, section 2.4.

[14] Paus. XXXIX. 13. For the proverb see Radke 1939, 691. Esp. interesting is the story about Parmeniscus of Metapontum from the fifth book of Semus' *History of Delos* (Athen. XIV. 614a).

[15] Philostrat., *Vita Apoll.* IV. 24.

[16] *Ibid.*, VIII. 19–20. Similarly Maximus Tyr., *Diss.* XIV. 2.

[17] *Ibid.*, 19. Cf. Burkert 1977, 300.   [18] *Ibid.*

there about the origin and the proper functioning of the oracle, in which he pointed out as its characteristic feature that the consultant is himself the medium.[19]

2.3.3. Then Appollonius and his followers forced their way into the sanctuary by breaking down the entrance gate. He went down into the crypt wearing the philosopher's mantle as if to give a lecture. To the surprise of everyone the god Trophonius not only approved of the visit, but also rebuked the priests by visions for having opposed it and ordered them to go to Aulis where Apollonius would emerge. When he did emerge there, he brought with him a book containing the teachings of Pythagoras.[20]

2.3.4. As far as the literary forms are concerned, some observations can be made at this point: (1) Probably Apollonius' consultation imitated the famous inquiry of the Delphic oracle by Socrates' student Chaerephon,[21] when he asked the question: "Trophonius, which do you regard to be the most complete and purest philosophy?"[22] (2) But instead of a short oracular answer two events occurred: a long dialog between the god and the philosopher that lasted for seven days, the longest period of inquiry ever recorded, and the number seven ominously pointing to Pythagorean philosophy as the subject of the dialog; and the revelation of the book containing Pythagoras' teachings.[23] (3) This book, we are told, was henceforth kept as a kind of holy book by no less a person than the emperor Hadrian in his most beloved villa at Antium.[24] (4) The revelation of the book was taken to render proof that the oracle of Trophonius is in accord with Pythagorean philosophy. (5) The form of oracular dialog, which seems to be an expansive development of the shorter oracular inquiry, is conducted in the hereafter and leads up to the revelation of a book, features otherwise wellknown from Jewish and Christian apocalyptic as well as from gnostic literature.[25] (6) Noteworthy is also that all this takes place in the process of a prophetic reform.[26]

2.4. The longest and most detailed account of a consultation of the Trophonius oracle is contained in Plutarch's dialog *De genio Socratis*, Chapters 21–22, 589F–592E.[27] The dialog discusses the nature of Socrates' *daimonion* in the first 20 chapters in form of a rational argument called *logos*,

---

[19] *Ibid.*   [20] *Ibid.*

[21] Plato, *Apol.* 20e–21a. See Strycker 1975, 39–49.

[22] Philostr., *Vita Apoll.* VIII. 19.

[23] See note 20, above.   [24] *Vita Apoll.* VIII. 20.

[25] See Speyer 1970, 92, 132; also Speyer 1971, 147.

[26] Cf. the discovery of the Book of the Law in connection with the cultic reform under King Josiah (2 Kings 22–23). *Herm. Vis.* I. 1–4; II. 4. See Boll 1914, 7f.; Dieterich 1969, 84ff.

[27] See D. A. Stoike, in: Betz (ed.) 1975, 272ff.; Vernière 1977, 93–95, 105–107, 243, 292.

but then turns in chapter 21 to the story (*mythos*) of Timarchus of Chaironeia and his visit at the oracle.

2.4.1. Again this visit is associated with Socrates: Timarchus wants to find out the nature of Socrates' *daimonion*.[28] The preparatory rituals are mentioned only in passing. More remarkable is the length of time Timarchus spent in the underworld: two nights and one day, after which the family had given up hope that he would ever return and had begun the burial lamentations. But when he suddenly emerged on the third day, his face was, contrary to the proverbial fear and gloom, cheerful; and after he had worshipped the deity, they left the crowd behind and he began to tell what had happened: "many wonders seen and heard."[29]

2.4.2. The report is composed out of four episodes: (1) the experiences of the soul separating from the body and existing without the body;[30] (2) the vision of the celestial world;[31] (3) the vision of the underworld;[32] (4) the dialog between Timarchus and Trophonius.[33]

2.4.3. Noteworthy is the episodic style and, as part of it, the oracular dialog. The dialog begins when an unseen voice, no doubt that of Trophonius himself, asks Timarchus: "Timarchus, what would you have me explain?" The philosopher, not shy to make the most of a good opportunity, answers: "Everything; for what is here that is not marvellous?"[34] This exchange then leads to the long conversation between the philosopher and the god's voice, which is, however, never clearly identified as such. At any rate, the literary genre of such a dialog is known from Jewish and Christian as well as gnostic sources as that of *erotapocrisis*.[35]

2.4.4. At the outset Trophonius must admit that his explanations are limited to the sublunar spheres and exclude the world of the gods. The reason for this limitation is Plutarch's demonology, according to which Trophonius belongs to the *daimones* in charge of the oracles, that is, to a lower form of deities not to be confused with the celestial realm of the higher gods.[36] Yet, we learn, the realm of Persephone does fall within the competence of Trophonius because hers is the lowest of the realms, Hades. In the dialog itself Timarchus takes up various items from the traditional catalog of *nekyia*, in order to receive the explanation. "What is Styx?" – "It is the path to Hades. . . ."[37] etc.

---

[28] Plut., *gen. Socr.* 590A 5–6.

[29] 590B 9–14. Cf. note 13, above.

[30] 590B 14–C24.

[31] 590C 24 – 590F 25.

[32] 590F 1 – 591A 9.

[33] 591A 9 – 592E 14.

[34] 591A 9–11. Cf. *Corp. Herm.* I.3.

[35] On this form of dialog, see Dörrie & Dörries 1966, 342–370; Rudolph 1968, 85–107; Grese 1979, 59 ff.

[36] Plut., *gen. Socr.* 591A 11–15. On Plutarch's demonology, see esp. *Def. orac.* 415A ff.

[37] 591A 15–16.

2.4.5. But the dialog includes more than such exchanges. In its course, Timarchus views other phenomena, like the souls crying out in terror as they are carried away into Hades.[38] When he sees things he does not understand,[39] the god provides brief lectures on what the vision shows. These lectures, however, contain nothing but middle-Platonic doctrines about the nature of the soul. Hearing these lectures in turn sharpens the vision of Timarchus,[40] so that the dialog moves up to a climax. The climax is reached with the vision of those souls "which from their very beginning and birth are docile to the rein and obedient to their daemon" and from which come the diviners and inspired men.[41] As a familiar figure among them the name of Hermodorus of Klazomenae is mentioned who is, contrary to the revelation, better known by scholarship as Hermotimus of Klazomenae.[42] After his story is told, the god's voice adds mysteriously: "Of these matters you will have better knowledge, young man, in the third month from now; for the present, depart."[43]

2.4.6. With the interview ended, Timarchus tries to find out in vain whose voice had spoken to him.[44] Instead of seeing anyone, he experiences the violent return of his soul into the body. When he recovers, he finds himself in the cave of Trophonius at the same place near the entrance where he had first laid down.[45] His sudden death after three months confirms that the mysterious prophecy at the end had in effect predicted his death – a *topos* in this literature.[46]

2.4.7. With regard to literary form, the telling of the story which Plutarch calls *mythos*, together with the first part called *logos*, completes the argument to be made in the work as a whole.[47] The composition is now complex: (1) In the Platonic fashion the whole work is a dialog that consists of two literary components, the *logos* in the first part and the *mythos* at the end, followed only by a paraenetic interpretation of the *mythos*. (2) The *mythos* itself is an eye-witness account by a third party outside of Plutarch's dialog, a *periegesis* testifying to an experience of a journey to the hereafter. (3) In this testimony, cosmic visions are combined with a revelatory dialog (*erotapokrisis*). (4) The account is also very suggestive with regard to mystery-cult initiations: that Timarchus' descent amounts to a death-and-

---

[38] 591C.   [39] 591D 8–9.   [40] 591F 4–5.   [41] 592C 30ff.

[42] 592C. This reference in effect connects the Trimarchus myth with the whole range of stories about journeys to the afterlife. See on this topic Radermacher 1903; Rohde 1961 I, 300ff.; Dieterich 1969, 128ff.; Ganszyniec 1919, 2413ff.; Cumont 1942; Cumont 1959, 70ff. and *passim*; Ziegler 1943, 1370ff.; Betz 1961, 81ff.; Nilsson 1961, 231ff., 490, 543ff., 600f., 680, 692; Eliade 1972, 21ff.; Graf 1974, with the review by Zuntz 1978, 526–531.

[43] 592E 13–15.   [44] 592E 15–17.   [45] 592E 17–21.

[46] 592E 21–23. See also Homer, *Od.* XI. 134–137; Plutarch, *De sera num.* 566D; Lucian, *Ver. hist.* II, 27–28.

[47] 592E 22, F 27.

rebirth experience is shown by the remarkably close parallel in Apuleius' *Metamorphoses* XI.23, where the cult formula is stated: *"accessi confinium mortis et calcato Proserpinae limine per omnia vectus elementa remeavi, nocte media vidi solem candido coruscantem lumine, deos inferos et deos superos accessi coram et adoravi de proxumo."*[48] (5) Finally, the suggestion is made that Timarchus' story should be honored as a ἱερὸς λόγος and should be dedicated to the god in the traditional manner, that is, as an aretalogy.[49]

2.5. Other developments of the *mythos* connected with the Trophonius oracle can be observed in Lucian's *Necyomantia*, a dialog in the Cynic tradition and dependent upon the lost *Necyia* of Menippus of Gadara.[50] Satirical in nature, Lucian's work presents the familiar *topoi*. Indeed, these *topoi* are very similar to Plutarch's myth of Timarchus, without of course depending on it. The conversion story, fully told in Plutarch, is only implied in Lucian.[51]

2.5.1. The dialog begins with the introductory exchange between Menippus and his friend and leads quickly to the request to tell the story.[52] Noteworthy are allusions to death and rebirth,[53] to the secrecy motif,[54] and to the initiation into the Eleusinian mysteries.[55] The reader is also made to understand that the friend knows already what the story will reveal: what the purpose of the *kathodos* was, who the guide was, what he saw and heard.[56] Only because the friend is initiated into the mysteries of Eleusis can Menippus tell him the story without risking prosecution for ἀσέβεια.

2.5.2. The implication of this remark is that the same mythology is now attached to Eleusis and to the Trophonius oracle. Menippus, however, does not enter into Hades in Greece, but he goes to Babylon where he has heard that the magi of Zoroaster are able to serve as guides.[57] This detour to the orient signifies a new phase of syncretism, for which the old Greek oracles themselves seem no longer sufficient. Because of the crisis in the traditional Greek religion and philosophy, reported in *Necyom.* 3–5, Menippus does not seem to have confidence in the priests at the Trophonius oracle, but he entrusts himself to a magus by the name of Mithrobarzanes. In the end the *magus,* however, shows Menippus a shorter return from the netherworld to Greece – through the cave of Trophonius.[58] That this syncretistic situation existed already at the time of Menippus in the 3rd cent. B.C. seems less likely than the time of Lucian in the 2nd cent. A.D.

2.5.3. Also surprising is the fact that Menippus wishes to consult with

---

[48] Griffiths 1975, 98, lines 11–14; cf. the commentary 296 ff.; Bergman 1982.
[49] 593A 9–10.   [50] See Helm 1906, 17 ff.   [51] Cf. *Necyom.* 6: ἕλοιτο.
[52] *Necyom.* 2.   [53] *Necyom.* 1.   [54] *Ibid.*, 2.   [55] *Ibid.*
[56] *Ibid.*   [57] *Ibid.*, 6.   [58] *Ibid.*, 22.

Teiresias,[59] the famous seer from Thebes, whose oracle Plutarch reports has become silent[60] and whose connection with the Trophonius oracle is certainly secondary. What does Menippus want to hear from Teiresias? – It is the old question: τίς ἐστιν ὁ ἄριστος βίος καὶ ὃν ἄν τις ἕλοιτο εὖ φρονῶν (*Necyom.* 6). This question is asked already in Plato's myth of Er,[61] where we find also the theme of the choice, mentioned in Lucian without further comment.

2.5.4. The *periegesis* is basically the same as in the other underworld stories: after extensive preparatory rituals Menippus follows Mithrobarzanes into the underworld in order to encounter the familiar topography, personalities, and episodes.[62] Characteristically, the *mythos* has been reduced and often consists of simply naming the items supposedly known by the readers already.

2.5.5. On the other hand the story has been enriched by typically Cynic elements, often expanding on older themes. Thus, the criticism of the tyrants and the rich is strongly emphasized and even developed into general social criticism.[63] An excursus on the *condicio humana*[64] is Cynic in nature but has a parallel in the pseudo-Platonic *Axiochus*.[65] When Menippus finally meets Teiresias and asks his question, he gets the answer that the life of the common man is the best.[66] This answer was given also before to Odysseus in Plato's myth of Er (*Rep.* X 620 C), but in Lucian it has become the only answer, no doubt because of its compatibility with the Cynic ideal.[67]

2.5.6. Lucian's dialog is interesting also in view of the Trophonius oracle because it shows how the underworld mythology continues to develop: (1) The *topoi* are assumed to be well known,[68] so that oral transmission seems to play a significant role rather than simple literary dependency. (2) The literary genres continue to be the same even in parodies and satires. (3) Lucian's other stories about the netherworld[69] are evidence that a kind of mythological *koine*[70] has emerged which uses the same kind of *topoi*, not excluding some variations. (4) This mythological *koine* appears to be attached at his time to many oracles not only in Greece, but also to the

---

[59] *Ibid.*, 6, 21.
[60] *Def. orac.* 434C.
[61] See Plato, *Rep.* X 617Eff.
[62] *Necyom.* 8ff.
[63] *Ibid.*, 12–14, 16–20.
[64] *Ibid.*, 16.
[65] Axiochus 366D–367B; cf. Epinomis 973D–974A. See also Tarán 1975, 156.
[66] *Necyom.* 21. The whole revelation, although secret and only whispered by Teiresias into Menippus' ear, amounts to nothing more than a summary of the Cynic way of life.
[67] See Helm 1906, 37f. for parallels.
[68] See Betz 1961, 82, n. 1.
[69] See *De luctu* 2–9; *Cataplus; Dialogi mortuorum,* all of which are inspired by the Cynic philosophy of Menippus of Gadara. See Helm 1906, 17ff., 63ff., 175ff. By contrast, the Nekyia in *Philops.* 22ff. has Epicurean tendencies. It may also be a parody of the stories told by Heracleides Ponticus. See Rohde 1961, 82 n. 4; Lévy 1927, 79ff.
[70] See Betz 1961, 81ff.

mysteries of Eleusis.[71] (5) The mythology has been expanded to include oriental contributions as well as those coming from Cynic philosophy.

3. The Concept of Myth

The developments connected with the Trophonius oracle show that the underworld mythology is consistently referred to by the term μῦθος.

3.1. That μῦθος is a literary term designating a specific genre of narrative can hardly be doubted. It should be noted at the outset, however, that this literary type of *mythos* has not been analyzed adequately.[72] Obviously, the *mythos* of the Trophonius oracle is not a fixed entity but in process, so that the very process of myth-making should be made part of the investigation.

3.2. Somehow Plutarch's myth of Timarchus is related to Plato's myth of Er (*Rep.* X. 614A–621D). But the problem is that the nature of this relationship is far from clear. If Plutarch "imitates" Plato, does he imitate the myth or the myth-making? Why does Plutarch not simply retell Plato's myth? Why does he go on to compose a new myth? If scholars agree that both Plato and Plutarch are the authors of their myths, why do they include elements that come from the so-called Orphic-Pythagorean under-world mythology? In fact, going back from Plutarch to Plato means simply to encounter the same set of problems.

3.2.1. It is puzzling that the large number of studies on Plato's concepts of *mythos* and *logos*[73] do not concern themselves with Plato's myth-making as a literary process. Therefore, if I am not mistaken, the situation in research is still where it was in 1925, when W. Willi formulated the problem in his *Versuch einer Grundlegung der platonischen Mythopoiie*:

> "Die äußere Geschichte des platonischen Mythos haben Religionshistoriker und Mythen-forscher untersucht – noch lange nicht zu Ende. Aber schon das Geleistete hat gezeigt, daß dem letzten Sinn des Mythos so nicht beizukommen ist. Auch das Ästhetische des Mythos hat seit Schleiermacher über C. Justi manchen Vertreter gefunden, aber trotz des Winckelmann-biographen war der Erfolg gering. Die Philosophen haben bei schönen Einzelerfolgen sich viel zu sehr von der Form isoliert. So ist durch den Stand des schon Geleisteten ebenso stark wie durch die entbrannte Auseinandersetzung die Forderung einer Grundlegung des Mythos gegeben."[74]

3.2.2. Not that Willi has solved the problem! Yet, he sees the formal aspects of the problem of the literary genre of *mythos* as over against *logos*, the place of *mythos* in Plato's dialogs, his *Schaltungstechnik*, and the stylistic

---

[71] See Betz 1961, 70 n. 4.

[72] See Kirk 1970; Kirk 1974, 276 ff.; Burkert 1979a, 1 ff.

[73] See Dieterich 1969, 112 ff.; Frutiger 1930, 29 ff.; Friedländer 1954, 182 ff.; Leisegang 1929; Bidez 1945; Edelstein 1949, 463–481; Dörrie 1972; Burkert 1977, 301–306, 446 f.; Burkert 1979, 16–39.

[74] Willi 1925, 3.

characteristics of *mythos*. Very helpful, even if preliminary, are Willi's observations about the eschatological myths.[75]

3.2.3. Willi calls them "Endmythos" and sees that they should be regarded as a literary genre. The great eschatological *Endmythen* in Plato's *Phaed.* 107d–115a, *Phaedr.* 246a–257b, *Gorg.* 522E–527E, and *Rep.* X. 614A–621D are placed at the end of the dialogs, followed only by a brief protreptic discourse. These myths cannot be interpreted simply in the terms of the juxtaposition of *logos* versus *mythos*, traditionally associated with the Sophists.[76] On the contrary, as Plato moves away from the Sophistic concepts, he attributes more and more importance to the eschatological myths.

3.2.4. The Myth of Er (*Rep.* 614A–621D) is set in the context of the theodicy argument.[77] According to that context, the conventional belief is that the just man, finally and in spite of all evidence to the contrary, will be vindicated in life and in death, while the unjust man, like an imprudent chariot racer, seems to do well in the beginning but then collapses in the long run. This argument, according to Plato, is credible only if the *mythos* is added to the *logos*,[78] at which point Socrates tells the famous Myth of Er. This myth relates how a man from Pamphylia by the name of Er, son of Armenius, was slain in battle, but when the dead were gathered on the 10th day in order to be burned, his body had not decayed. He revived on the 12th day on the funeral pyre, whereupon he related "what he has seen in the world beyond."[79] What happened is that between his death and rebirth the man's soul had travelled through the afterlife.

3.2.4.1. His story, the *mythos*, is, however, a highly complex composition of four episodes, and intercalated paraenesis: (1) The first episode (614C–615A) contains a summary of the main points: the vision of two χάσματα, the processions of souls, the Elysian Fields, and the punishment of the wicked in Hades. Then, important points are picked up again and are elaborated further. (2) The second episode (615B–616A) deals with the punishment of the wicked souls, especially of the political tyrants with Ardiaeus the Great singled out, the punishing demons, Tartarus, and climaxes in the witnessing of intense fear. (3) The third episode (616B–617A) contains the vision of the "pillar of light," *i.e.,* the "spindle of Ananke," and the planetary spheres. At this point (616D–617A), a paragraph on astronomy, probably Pythagorean in origin, has also become part of the myth.[80] (4) The fourth episode (617C–618B) describes a scene before the Moirai, beginning with the souls coming before the throne of Lachesis.

---

[75] *Idem*, 47 ff.
[76] See, *e.g.*, Plato, *Protag.* 320C–328C. Cf. Guthrie 1971, 65 ff.
[77] *Rep.* X 612B ff.   [78] 614A.   [79] 614B. Cf. 621B.
[80] See P. Shorey, *Plato VI* (LCL), p. 501, note c.

3.2.4.2. Although the scene occurs outside the limits of time in the afterlife, the description is that of a lot oracle as it might have happened in one of the oracular shrines. A prophet appears, goes up to a speaker's platform and reveals a "*logos* of Lachesis, the daughter of Ananke" (617D–E). The oracle reveals the principles of Greek anthropology and religion, culminating in the Orphic *sententia:* αἰτία ἑλομένου· θεὸς ἀναίτιος. The scene then describes how the priest casts the lots, and the souls choose their παραδείγματα βίου.

3.2.4.3. In 618C, the myth suddenly moves from the eternal world to the here and now, and instead of the prophet now Socrates delivers explanations and paraenesis (618C–619A/B). The choice, we hear from Socrates, between a good and a bad life is ὁ πᾶς κίνδυνος ἀνθρώπῳ, and this not only in the hereafter but also in the here and now. The only important subject of study for the philosopher is this choice for life and death, and it takes "an adamantine faith" in the afterlife to withstand the temptations by the material excesses of life and only those who persevere καὶ ἐν τῷδε τῷ βίῳ κατὰ τὸ δυνατὸν καὶ ἐν παντὶ τῷ ἔπειτα οὕτω γὰρ εὐδαιμονέστατος γίγνεται ἄνθρωπος (619B).

3.2.4.4. After this, the myth switches back to the afterlife, where the prophet proclaims another oracle: "Even for him who comes forward last, if he make his choice wisely and live strenuously, there is reserved an acceptable life, no evil one" (619B). Then we see the foolish man choosing the first lot and opting for tyranny, but he quickly regrets his choice – to no avail. Next comes the philosopher, then all the different souls making their choices, and finally Odysseus choosing the life of an ordinary citizen.

3.2.4.5. The myth reaches its end when Clotho ratifies the choices and Atropos makes them irreversible (620E). Then the souls depart to the Plain of Lethe and to the river Forgetfulness, where all take a drink (621A), in order then to ascend to the stars (621B). At this moment Er's soul suddenly returns to the body and wakes up on top of the funerary pyre.

3.2.4.6. No less important than the myth itself is its subsequent interpretation (621C–D), introduced by Socrates' words: "And so, Glaucon, the *mythos* was saved, as the saying is, and was not lost. And it will save us if we believe it, and we shall safely cross the River of Lethe, and keep our soul unspotted from the world" (621C). At this point Socrates takes over as the mystagogue: "But if we are guided by me we shall believe that soul is immortal and capable of enduring all extremes of good and evil, and so we shall hold ever to the upward way and pursue righteousness with wisdom always and ever, that we may be dear to ourselves and to the gods both during our sojourn here and when we receive our reward..." (621C).

3.2.5. With Socrates' interpretative and paraenetical statements the nature and function of *mythos* have become clear: (1) The genre of *mythos* can do what *logos* cannot do: *mythos* can speak in human words about things that go beyond the human world and language. While *logos* must be understood rationally *mythos* is to be believed.[81] (2) Discussing the immortal life of the soul by rational arguments only remains an incomplete enterprise. (3) Comprehending a subject such as this requires a confrontation with the destiny of one's own soul, and to bring this about is the purpose of *mythos*. (4) By its ability to create φόβος,[82] those who hear the *mythos* and thus "see" the suffering of the wicked under punishment and all the other phenomena in the hereafter are confronted with that "greatest danger for men," the choice between a good and a wicked life. (5) Yielding to the temptation by worldly foolishness, the one who chooses wrongly can always declare the *mythos* to be one of those fables told by women to scare the children.[83] But those who choose wisely see in the *mythos* the truth.[84] (6) Convinced by what the myth wishes to convey, they experience fear: "For no man fears the mere act of dying, except he be utterly irrational and unmanly; doing wrong is what one fears: for to arrive in the netherworld having one's soul fraught with a heap of misdeeds is the uttermost of evils" (*Gorg.* 522E). (7) Without experiencing such φόβος, the soul remains uneducated about itself, about life in this world and in the hereafter.[85] (8) No rational argument (λόγος) alone can motivate a person to live a good life. (9) The *mythos*, however, has the power to persuade the soul. How can the *mythos* have such power? (10) As literary genre and by its language it is related to the oracle: it "indicates" (σημαίνειν) and thus "reveals" what is ὁ τρόπος ἄριστος τοῦ βίου.[86] (11) Like a magical charm the *mythos* must be told again and again.[87] It must be heard and read not as straightforward speech but as oracular revelatory speech. Then it will act out its magical powers, and those who hear it will be forced to make the choice again: αἰτία ἑλομένου· θεὸς ἀναίτιος (*Rep.* X 617E).[88] (12) The soul's choice, however, has its counterpart in the statement about the eschatological judgment: δικαία ἡ κρίσις.[89] (13) Between choice and judgement, the soul is motivated to acquire wisdom and lead a good life. "For the prize is fair, and the hope is great."[90]

---

[81] Cf. *Gorg.* 524B and Socrates' conclusion of his telling of the *mythos*.

[82] Cf. especially *Gorg.* 525B.　　　　　　[83] See *Gorg.* 527A.

[84] See *Gorg.* 523A.　　　　　　　　　　　　[85] See *Gorg.* 527E.

[86] See *Gorg.* 527E. Cf. also *Phaedo* 114C.

[87] *Phaedo* 77D/E; 114D.

[88] This interesting saying, probably Orphic in origin, needs further investigation. See Dieterich 1969, 115, n. 1; Usener 1913, 324, lines 19–21; Guthrie 1966, 167 f., 183.

[89] For this topic, see esp. Plato, *Gorg.* 523E–524A and Dieterich 1969, 116 f. See also Rev. 16:7; 19:2; *Apoc. Pet.* 1. 65, ed. Dieterich 1969, 6, and for further discussion Collins 1977, 367–381.

[90] *Phaedo* 114C. This hope is one of the great themes in *Phaedo* (see 64A, 67B–68B).

3.3. In spite of the fragmentary sources available there are clear indications that the type of myth-making observed in Plato continued in the Academy and that Plutarch's myth of Timarchus is a later representative of that process.

3.3.1. The dialogs of Heracleides Ponticus[91] acquired such a reputation that they represented a literary genre by themselves, called *Heraclidea*.[92] Carrying various titles, they seem to have treated similar themes, all related to the destiny of the soul in the afterlife: (1) Later writers mention a work called *Zoroaster*,[93] a name important for the later Plato and the Academy.[94] It would be interesting to know whether the equation of Er with *Zoroaster* made in later sources[95] was already made here, but nothing is known about the content of the *Zoroaster*. (2) Heracleides' dialog Περὶ τῶν ἐν ῞Αϊδου[96] discusses the doctrine of the soul, and (3) so does the *Abaris*,[97] using the famous shaman from the north to report about his soul's adventures in the afterlife. It is hard to resist the temptation to connect the *Abaris* with the Trophonius oracle because of the hostile snakes mentioned in *Frag*. 74,[98] but the evidence is too slim. *Frag*. 75 contains references to a dialog between *Abaris* and a *daimon*,[99] taking place probably in the afterlife. (4) The dialog entitled Περὶ τοῦ ἄπνου[100] is built around an old legend of a woman seemingly dead but then revived whose soul travelled to the afterlife. The miracle of revival is wrought by no less an authority than Empedocles who told the story to his student Pausanias, a participant in the dialog. Other familiar figures may also have been part of Heracleides' dialog, such as Pythagoras and Hermotimus of Klazomenae. (5) Another dialog entitled Περὶ ψυχῆς[101] contained a vision of the universe and πᾶσα ἡ ψυχῶν ἀλήθεια, reported by a certain Epidotimus, one of the dialog partners. The vision of Hades contained in the dialog may have been parodied by Lucian in his *Philopseudes* 22.[102] *Frag*. 93 reports on an epiphany of the gods Pluto

---

[91] See F. Wehrli 1968, 675–686; also Wehrli 1969a.
[92] See Wehrli 1968, 678f. [93] *Ibid*., 679ff.
[94] See Wehrli 1969a, Fragments 68–70 with the commentary p. 83.
[95] See Fauth 1967, 341f.; Kerschensteiner 1945, 140ff.; Hinz 1972, 774–784.
[96] See Wehrli 1969a, *Frag*. 71–72 with the commentary pp. 83f.
[97] *Ibid*., *Frag*. 73–75 and the commentary pp. 84–86.
[98] Cf. Wehrli, *ibid*., p. 85: "So wird man den sonst verlockenden Gedanken an die Trophoniosgrotte in Lebadeia mit ihren Schlangen… als lokal preisgeben müssen, obwohl sie Ausgangspunkt für eine kosmische Seelenfahrt z. B. bei Plutarch ist (*De genio Socratis* 590b)."
[99] Cf. Wehrli 1969a, 85: "Der belehrende Dämon gehört in die gleiche Tradition wie die Göttin bei Parmenides (Vorsokr. 628B 1, cf. dazu Diels, Parmenides [1897] 14ff.; weiteres zu Klearch fr. 5–10)."
[100] Wehrli 1969a, *frag*. 76–89 and the commentary pp. 86ff.
[101] Wehrli 1969a, *frag*. 90–107 and the commentary pp. 90ff. Is there a relationship between Heracleitus' and Plutarch's Περὶ ψυχῆς?
[102] Rohde 1961 II, 82 n. 4; Betz 1961, 56 n. 4; Wehrli 1969a, 91.

and Persephone. The loss of most of this extremely interesting material makes the establishment of the literary tradition between Plato and Plutarch very difficult.

3.3.2. Even the attribution of existing fragments to extant titles is risky because similar material was evidently treated under a variety of titles. But the contours of the literary process are nonetheless visible: philosophers like Heraclides of Pontus, Clearchus,[103] and others imitated Plato's myth-making in writing their own dialogs. Typical seems to be their taking recourse to legendary material of various origins in order to make similar cases to support the Pythagorean-Platonic doctrines of the soul, the cosmos, and the afterlife. Titles also vary, such as $Περὶ$ $ψυχῆς$, $Περὶ$ $ὕπνου$, etc., or they employ the names of famous shamanistic figures like Pythagoras, Abaris, Hermotimus, etc., or famous holy places, among which the Trophonius oracle seems to stand out.

3.3.3. On the other hand, polemic and criticism against this type of philosophy was also on the rise: (1) The valuable scholion to Aristophanes' *Clouds* 508[104] mentions several comedies and a historical work by Charax of Pergamon with the title *Trophonius*. (2) Philosophical opposition was centered in the Peripatos, and Dicaearchus' work entitled $Περὶ$ $τῆς$ $εἰς$ $Τροφωνίου$ $καταβάσεως$,[105] from which some fragments have survived, seems to have been the major one. Cicero[106] still read it and no doubt used it. (3) It may be intentional that a work by Plutarch, unfortunately lost, carried the same title; it may have been a defense of the oracle against Dicaearchus.[107] Plutarch also says that his brother Lamprias would have a story to tell which he heard from strangers at Lebadeia, but the conversation passes up the chance to hear it.[108] (4) The critical line of the tradition was certainly represented by the Cynic Menippus of Gadara, whose satires Lucian of Samosata imitated.[109] Thus, it is not accidental that Menippus ends his *catabasis* in Lucian's *Necyomanteia* by reemerging in the cave of Trophonius.

3.3.4. In general, however, Plutarch's eschatological myths are the only fully extant examples of this type of myth-making since Plato. In view of the fragments of the intermediate history of the genre, the evidence shows that Plato's type of myth-making continued in the Academy, variations notwithstanding. The method apparently was to use varying legendary traditions of a more popular nature attached to famous names of persons or

---

[103] See Wehrli 1969, *Frag.* 5–10 and the commentary pp. 47 ff. Clearchus' dialog $Περὶ$ $ὕπνου$ contained a report about an encounter with a Jewish philosopher (?) or magician (?).

[104] See note 3, above.

[105] See Wehrli 1967, *Frag.* 13–22 and the commentary, pp. 46 ff.

[106] Cic., *Epist. ad Attic.* XIII. 31, 33.   [107] See Radke 1939, 682.

[108] *Def. or.* 431C.   [109] See note 50, above.

places, to combine them with *topoi* from the *catabasis* literature and the Orphic-Pythagorean mythology concerning the netherworld, the souls, the demons, the gods, and the universe. In the course of the history of the Academy, these doctrines were at each stage brought up to date and pointed against the arguments of the opposition. Plutarch's dialogs and his eschatological myths, therefore, represent the state of the genre at his time. Some literary elements such as the form of the dialog, the concept of *mythos* versus *logos*, and the method of myth-making may not have changed substantially since Plato. But the material to be included has changed considerably through the ever increasing influence of the Orphic-Pythagorean netherworld mythology, the growing importance of cosmic visions, the newly developing doctrines of the soul, mantics, demonology, and the gods. Most importantly, new points of emphasis can be observed in Plutarch which may indicate the underlying reasons for these new developments.

3.5. In general, Plutarch's own concept of *mythos*[110] must be interpreted within the framework of his philosophical theology. By the term μῦθος[111] he refers to a certain type of narrative which is related to his doctrine of revelation.

3.5.1. According to Plutarch, the deity, that is Apollo, does not reveal himself to human beings directly, neither face-to-face nor by speaking.[112] Even Thespesius whose soul was granted a trip to the afterlife was not permitted to see Apollo or speak with him.[113] There was the voice of the Sibyl which he heard,[114] and in *De gen. Socr.* a voice speaks to Timarchus, but it was not clear whose voice it was.[115] On earth, not even the Pythia hears the voice of the god directly. Rather, the god sets her soul in motion, whereupon she becomes ecstatic and begins to utter unintelligible sounds, to be heard and then "translated" into human language by the priests and the exegetes.[116] The oracular speech, therefore, conforms to the Delphic doctrine stated in the famous sentence of Heracleitus:[117]

ὁ ἄναξ, οὗ τὸ μαντεῖόν ἐστιν τὸ ἐν Δελφοῖς,
οὔτε λέγει οὔτε κρύπτει, ἀλλὰ σημαίνει.

---

[110] Plutarch's concept of *mythos* has not been adequately investigated. See Vernière 1977.

[111] Plutarch uses the term in a negative (cf., *e.g., Mor.* 355B, 358E, 395C, 398D, 420B, 435D, 557F, 580C, 589F, 940F) as well as in a positive sense (cf., *e.g., Mor.* 557F, 561B, 563B, 592F, 749A, 761E, 763B–C, 764A; *Fragm.* 157).

[112] See esp. Plutarch, *De E* 384F–385C. See Betz 1975, 87 ff. and 368 s.v. *Revelation*.

[113] *De sera num.* 566D.

[114] *De sera num.* 566D–E.

[115] 592E.

[116] *De Pyth. orac.* 397A ff., 404E ff.; *De def. orac.* 414E, 438A.

[117] Cited by Plutarch, *De Pyth. orac.* 404E.

3.5.2. According to Plutarch oracular speech consists of αἰνίγματα,[118] through which the god reveals his concerns by αἰνίττεσθαι.[119] It is important to see that for Plutarch these αἰνίγματα are not only the oracles but that in principle every phenomenon can become an αἴνιγμα. As far as language is concerned, the shortest αἴνιγμα is the Delphic E.[120] The longer μῦθος is a prose narrative which must be read in the same way as an oracle.[121]

3.5.3. Furthermore, μῦθος and λόγος are not opposites but cooperate with each other in that Apollo works through both. Apollo himself is at the same time ὁ λόγος and ὁ μάντις.[122] His epitheta reveal that as Πύθιος he is the one who causes people to begin "inquiring," which is the beginning of philosophy. As Δήλιος and Φαναῖος he is the one who "makes things clear" and who "reveals;" Ἰσμήνιος he is to those who have ἐπιστήμη, and Λεσχηνόριος he is among those who engage in philosophical dialog. In other words, as λόγος Apollo is the driving force behind all philosophical forms of inquiry, causing someone to see a phenomenon as αἴνιγμα, while at the same time he reveals his "truth" through the medium of the αἴνιγμα.

3.5.4. As oracular narrative, the *mythos* engages the human mind, which contains the *logos*, and creates in it θαυμάζειν καὶ ἀπορεῖν, and the desire to explore and explain the meaning of the *mythos*.[123] Thus, the *mythos*, far from standing in contradiction to the *logos*, is the medium by which the logos accomplishes its goal, the establishment of ἐπιστήμη.[124]

3.5.5. Just as any phenomenon can become an αἴνιγμα, μῦθος can also include any suitable narrative. It is at this point that the philosopher becomes involved in the myth-making itself. Old legends[125] prove no less suitable to serve as μῦθοι than items derived from scientific lore, from cosmology, astronomy, astrology, mathematics, and psychology. Such topics are indeed often found already as part of philosophical school traditions, so that it is almost logical that Plutarch, as did others before him, inserts such philosophical school traditions into existing mythical tales. What can be observed already in Plato's Er myth is only enlarged in Plutarch's *mythoi*: they are continuously expanded to include an ever larger

---

[118] Note the close connection of this concept with Pythagoreanism; cf. *Mor.* 12D, 281B, 354E, and furthermore 154A, 205B, 368D, 385C, 389A, 407, 409D, 671E, 673A, 717A, 988A, 1071C, 1125E, etc.

[119] See Betz 1975, 356 s.v.

[120] *De E* 385C.

[121] Cf., *e.g., De Is. et Os.* 368D; *De E* 398A; *De Pyth. orac.* 407A–B, 409C–D.

[122] See *De E* 385Bff., and Betz 1975, 88ff.

[123] *De E* 385C.

[124] Cf. *De Is. et Os.* 351E–F.

[125] Cf. *De def. orac.* 409F where Plutarch rejects this approach to *mythos*.

share of philosophical school tradition. As a result, what Plutarch calls μῦθος in the positive sense of the term is an amalgam, in which old myths have been melted together with philosophical doctrines, most likely coming from the middle-Platonic school traditions.[126] Negatively, μῦθος describes those materials that are not usable for philosophical interpretation.[127]

3.5.6. Moreover, the door cautiously opened by Plato to foreign myths Plutarch now throws wide open to take in large amounts of Egyptian and Iranian[128] myths and call it μῦθος, too. In the case of the *mythos* of Osiris, Plutarch, perhaps relying on a source, also calls it ἱερὸς λόγος.[129] The notion is peculiar because it can refer both to the mythical narrative and to the σῶμα of Osiris.[130] Specifically, what does Plutarch have to say in regard to the purpose and function of underworld myths?

3.5.7. From his discussions of and with Epicureanism it is quite clear that Plutarch himself is not simply "a believer" in the traditional mythology of the afterlife. At his time not only skeptical philosophers but also the general population have long abandoned these myths as fables and fairytales, believed only by a few superstitious simpletons.[131] Why then does Plutarch still hold on to these myths? In answering this difficult question, one should note that Plutarch shares the view that οἱ πολλοί are not capable of understanding the truth about the deity in the terms of philosophy but that for this reason they need religion: festivals, rituals, and myths.[132] In some way, Plutarch emphasizes again and again, the myths touch upon the truth but only indirectly.[133] But it is not only because of the uneducated masses that the myths are needed.

3.5.8. Although Plutarch himself is so deeply affected by skepticism, he does share the doctrine of the immortality of the soul, a doctrine he recognizes as fundamental to Greek philosophy and religion. If, then, the soul is immortal and if it exists beyond the grave, the doctrine of reward and punishment must be accepted, too.[134] But how can one talk about such

---

[126] See Dillon 1977, 96 ff.

[127] See *De Is. et Os.* 355B, 358E, and *passim*; *Amat.* 764A. See Hani 1976.

[128] See the section on Zoroastrianism *De Is. et Os.* 369D ff. and the frequent parallels to apocalypticism. See Betz 1975, 64 ff. and esp. Widengren in this volume § 5.1. ("Das älteste Zeugnis der zervanitischen Apokalyptik").

[129] See *De Is. et. Os.* 351F, 354A, 358A, 375A. For this concept, see Herodotus II. 81; Plato, *Ep.* VII, 335A; Plutarch, *Quaest. conviv.* II. 3.1, p. 636D.

[130] See for literature Betz 1975, 39.

[131] See especially *De superst., passim; De aud. poet.* 17B–C; *Non posse* 1105A–B. For further references, see Betz 1975, 367, s.v. Myth.

[132] See on this point Adam 1974, 52 ff.; Betz 1975, 229 f.

[133] See *De sera num.* 561B; *De genio Socr.* 589F; *De facie in orbe* 940F; *De Is. et Os.* 358F, 359A, 365D; *Amat* 762A. Cf. Adam 1974, 69 n. 16.

[134] *De sera num.* 560B.

matters in an adequate and convincing way once the old myths have lost their power? Plutarch gives the answer in his dialogs.

3.5.9. The literary form of the dialog as a whole, in which *mythos* plays only a part, contains Plutarch's answer, not the *mythos* alone. The *mythos* must remain part of the philosophical dialog, and the language of the *mythos* must be read as oracular language. For this reasons, too, Plutarch is not interested in "allegorical" interpretation of *mythos*.

3.5.10. The allegorical method accepts myths as given and tries to bring out the true meaning underlying the seemingly irrational narrative.[135] In this way, allegory cannot stir up the human soul and fails to guide it to the response appropriate for the deity.

3.5.11. Since *mythos* cooperates with it, the purpose and function of *logos* must also be taken into account. In a difficult argument, such as "about the deity" in *De sera num. vind.*, the *logos* part cuts a path through the intricacies and complexities, so that καθοδηγῶμεν αὐτοὺς μετ᾽ εὐλαβείας ἀτρέμα πρὸς τὸ εἰκὸς καὶ πιθανόν (558D). Because the *logos* can deal only with τὸ εἰκός, in an argument about the deity it alone is insufficient and must be complemented by a *mythos*: ὕστερον δὲ τὸν μῦθον... κινήσωμεν, εἴ γε δὴ μῦθός ἐστιν (561B).

3.5.12. What can the *mythos* accomplish that the *logos* cannot? For an answer we turn to the myth of Thespesius in *De sera num. vind.* 563Bff., where *mythos* is set in the context of a conversion story.[136] The main witness, Aridaeus-Thespesius, undergoes a sudden conversion which is mysteriously connected with a response given by the Amphilochus oracle at Mallos, to be fulfilled, as we learn later, by the *mythos*.[137]

3.5.12.1. The first function of the *mythos* is named in 563E, where the family and friends of Aridaeus-Thespesius want to hear about the reason for his sudden conversion: τὴν αἰτίαν ἀκοῦσαι τῆς διαφορᾶς, οὐκ ἀπὸ τοῦ τυχόντος οἰομένους γεγονέναι διακόσμησιν εἰς ἦθος τοσαύτην. In telling them the *mythos*, he tells them what he has seen and heard during the journey of his soul to the afterlife. This myth provides the αἰτία in a double sense: It relates the experiences that explain the conversion, and it confronts the hearers of the story as well as its narrator with the old dogma cited by Plato, *Rep.* X. 617E: αἰτία ἑλομένου· θεὸς ἀναίτιος. Viewing the great choice to be made in all its eternal dimensions has caused Aridaeus-Thespesius to make that choice in his own life, of which the observable result is his conversion.

3.5.12.2. The second function is that in order to be motivated for a change of his life-style, his soul must be subjected to a shock-like experi-

---

[135] For the terminology see *Mor.* 19E, 362B, 363D, 409D, 996B. On the subject of allegory in Plutarch, see Griffiths 1967, 79–102; Griffiths 1970, 101f.
[136] See Betz 1975, 219ff.   [137] 563D.

ence of fear. This experience becomes most intense when he views his father, whom he had believed to be a man of decency, confessing the hidden horrible sin of murdering some guests of his in order to take their gold. At that point Thespesius is truly shocked: δι' ἔκπληξιν καὶ δέος, ὑποστρέψαι δὲ καὶ φυγεῖν βουλόμενος (567A).

3.5.12.3. Thus, when Thespesius returns from his experience in the afterlife, he is driven frantic with fear.[138] This outcome is by no means accidental but reflects a theory more fully discussed by Plutarch in his *Non posse suaviter vivi secundum Epicurum*.[139] The theory is named in 1104C with these words: φόβος περὶ τῶν ἐν ˝Αιδου παρὰ τὸ μυθῶδες ἢ τῆς ἀϊδιότητος ἐλπίς... According to Epicurus, "fear of punishment is the only motive to which we can properly appeal in deterring from crime."[140] Plutarch argues that, if Epicurus is right, "we should cram them (*i.e.* the wicked) even fuller of superstitious dread and bring to bear on them the joint array of celestial and terrestrial terrors and chasms and alarms and apprehensions if they are to be shocked by all this into a state of greater honesty and restraint. For they are better off avoiding crime for fear of the next world than committing crimes and spending their lives in insecurity and apprehension."[141] This theory was believed widely in antiquity, and it is without doubt one of the primal reasons for the growing importance of the underworld myths.[142]

3.5.12.4. Finally, as *logos* awakens in the soul rational thought, *mythos* generates the right δόξα about the gods and thus πίστις.[143] Together they enable a person to live a life in εὐλάβεια towards the gods;[144] intellectually, they constitute what Plutarch calls θεολογία.[145]

4. Conclusions

In conclusion, some suggestions and further questions can be formulated.

4.1. While matters of genre are not made explicit in Jewish and Christian apocalyptic texts, comparable Greek sources provide considerable information about the literary genre of *mythos* and ways to interpret it.

---

[138] 568A.   [139] 1101Cff. See Adam 1974, 52ff.   [140] 1104B.   [141] *Ibid.*

[142] See esp. *De sup.* 167A, 169F–170D; *Fragm.* 178. See Betz 1975, 365 s.v. Fear; Betz 1978, 579 s.v. Fear; Bernert 1941, 309–318; Dihle, Waszink, Mundle 1972, 661–699.

[143] *Amat.* 761E: πρὸς πίστιν ὄφελος. See H. Martin in: Betz (ed.) 1978, 503f., 510–512; Adam 1974, 67ff., 71ff.

[144] See especially *De genio Socr.* 551C; *Def. orac.* 420F, and for more passages Betz 1975, 359 s.v. εὐλάβεια, εὐλαβής; Betz 1978, 572, s.v. εὐλάβεια.

[145] See for θεολογία especially Plutarch, *Fragm.* 157 and *De Is. et Os.* 354C, 371A; *De def. orac.* 410B; θεολόγος *De Is. et Os.* 360D, 369B; *De E* 388E; *De def. orac.* 417F, 436D.

4.2. The Greek sources also show how the oracular dialog developed out of the shorter oracular inquiry, and how this origin determines the kind of language used in the *mythos*.

4.3. The crisis of the older oracles appears to have been met by an ever expanding eschatological mythology which became attached to the older oracles and the mystery cults.

4.4. As a result, the increasing reliance on fear more and more determines the function of that mythology as a means to achieve the moral conversion of individuals.

4.5. The main question is, whether these phenomena can be transferred from Greek religion to Jewish and Christian apocalypticism. Ultimately, of course, the answer can be given only on the basis of a larger investigation, but even our brief probing has shown that much could be learned about the questions of literary genre from a full discussion of Jewish and Christian apocalyptic texts in the light of Greek and Hellenistic literature.

Bibliography

Adam Hella 1974: *Plutarchs Schrift non posse suaviter vivi secundum Epicurum*, Amsterdam 1974.

Bergman, Jan 1982: "Per omnia vectus elementa remeavi. Réflexions sur l'arrière-plan égyptien du voyage de salut d'un myste isiaque", in: U. Bianchi–M. J. Vermaseren (eds.), *La soteriologia dei culti orientali nell' impero romano*, Leiden 1982, 671–708.

Bernert, E. 1941: "Phobos", in: *PRE* 39. Halbband (1941) 309–318.

Betz, Hans Dieter 1961: *Lukian von Samosata und das Neue Testament* (TU 76), Berlin 1961.

– (ed.)1975: *Plutarch's Theological Writings and Early Christian Literature* (SCHNT III), Leiden 1975.

– (ed.) 1978: *Plutarch's Ethical Writings and Early Christian Literature* (SCHNT IV), Leiden 1978.

Bidez, Joseph 1945: *Eos ou Platon et l'Orient*, Bruxelles 1945.

Boll, Franz 1914: *Aus der Offenbarung Johannis*, Leipzig & Berlin 1914.

Burkert, Walter 1977: *Griechische Religion der archaischen und klassischen Epoche* (RM 15), Stuttgart 1977.

– 1979: "Mythisches Denken. Versuch einer Definition an Hand des griechischen Befundes", in: *Philosophie und Mythos*, ed. H. Poser, Berlin 1979, 16–39.

– 1979a: *Structure and History in Greek Mythology and Ritual* (Sather Lectures 47), Berkeley and Los Angeles/Calif. 1979.

Clark, Raymond J. 1968: "Trophonius: The Manner of His Revelation", in: *TAPA* 99 (1968) 63–75.

Collins, Adela Yarbro 1977: "The History-of-Religions Approach to Apocalypticism and the 'Angel of the Waters' (Rev 16:4–7)", in: *CBQ* 39 (1977) 367–381.

Cumont, Franz 1942: *Recherches sur le symbolisme funéraire des Romains*, Paris 1942.

– 1959: *After Life in Roman Paganism*, New York 1959.

Deubner, Ludwig 1899: *De incubatione capitula duo*, Gissae 1899.

Dieterich, Albrecht 1969: *Nekyia*, 3. Aufl., Darmstadt 1969.

Dihle, Albrecht, J. Waszink, W. Mundle 1972: "Furcht (Gottes)", in: *RAC* 8 (1972) 661–699.

Dillon, John 1977: *The Middle Platonists*, London 1977.

Dörrie, Heinrich – Dörries, Hermann 1966: "Erotapokriseis", in: *RAC* 6 (1966) 342–370.

Dörrie, Heinrich 1972: *Der Mythos und seine Funktion in der antiken Philosophie* (IBKW 2), Innsbruck 1972.

Edelstein, Ludwig 1949: "The Function of the Myth in Plato's Philosophy", in: *JHI* 10 (1949) 463–481.

Eliade, Mircea 1972: *Zalmoxis. The Vanishing God*, Chicago, Ill. 1972.

Fauth, Wolfgang 1967: "Er", in: *KP* 2 (1967) 341 f.

Friedländer, Paul 1954: *Platon*, Band I, 2. Aufl., Berlin 1954.

Frutiger, Perceval 1930: *Les mythes de Platon*, Paris 1930.

Ganszyniec, Richard 1919: "Katabasis", in: *PRE* 20. Halbband (1919) 2359–2449.

Graf, Felix 1974: *Eleusis und die orphische Dichtung Athens in vorhellenistischer Zeit* (RVV 33), Berlin 1974.

Grese, William C. 1979: *Corpus Hermeticum XIII and Early Christian Literature* (SCHNT 5), Leiden 1979.

Griffiths, J. Gwyn 1967: "Allegory in Greece and Egypt", in: *JEA* 53 (1967) 79–102.

– 1970: *Plutarch's De Iside et Osiride*, Cardiff 1970.

– 1975: *Apuleius of Madaurus. The Isis-Book (Metamorphoses Book XI)* (EPRO 39), Leiden 1975.

Guthrie, W. K. C. 1966: *Orpheus and Greek Religion*, New York 1966.

– 1971: *The Sophists*, Cambridge 1971.

Hani, Jean 1976: *La religion égyptienne dans la pensée de Plutarque* (CEM), Paris 1976.

Helm, Rudolf 1906: *Lucian und Menipp*, Leipzig 1906.

Hinz, W. 1972: "Zoroastres", in: *PRE* 2. Reihe, 19. Halbband (1972), 774–784.

Kerschensteiner, Jula 1945: *Platon und der Orient*, Stuttgart 1945.

Kirk, Geoffrey S. 1970: *Myth: Its Meaning and Function in Ancient and Other Cultures*, Cambridge 1970.

– 1974: *The Nature of Greek Myths*, London 1974.

Koster, W. J. W. 1977: *Scholia in Aristophanem*, vol. III/1, Groningen 1977.

Leisegang, Hans 1929: *Die Platondeutung der Gegenwart*, Karlsruhe 1929.

Lévy, Isidore 1927: *La légende de Pythagore de Grèce en Palästine*, Paris 1927.

Nilsson, Martin P. 1967/1961: *Geschichte der griechischen Religion* (HAW V 2.1 and V 2.2), Band I, 3. Aufl., München 1967; Band II, 2. Aufl., München 1961.

Pley, J. 1916: "Incubatio", *PRE* 9 (1916), 1256–1262.

Radermacher, Ludwig 1903: *Das Jenseits im Mythos der Hellenen*, Bonn 1903.

Radke, Gerhard 1939: "Trophonius", in: *PRE* 2. Reihe, 13. Halbband (1939), 678–695.

Rohde, Erwin 1961: *Psyche*, Band I–II, Darmstadt 1961.

Rudolph, Kurt 1968: "Der gnostische 'Dialog' als literarisches Genus", in: *Probleme der koptischen Literatur* (WBMLUHW.K 1968/1), ed. P. Nagel, Halle 1968, 85–107.

Schachter, A. 1967: "A Boeotian Cult Type", in: *BICS* 14 (1967) 1–16.

Speyer, Wolfgang 1970: *Bücherfunde in der Glaubenswerbung der Antike* (Hypomnemata 24), Göttingen 1970.

– 1971: *Die literarische Fälschung im heidnischen und christlichen Altertum* (HAW I 2), München 1971.

Strycker, E. 1975: "The Oracle Given to Chaerephon about Socrates", in: *Kephalaion, Studies in Greek Philosophy ... offered to C. J. de Vogel*, Assen 1975, 39–49.

Tarán, Leonardo 1975: *Academica: Plato, Philip of Opus, and the Pseudo-Platonic Epinomis*, Philadelphia, Penn. 1975.

Usener, Hermann 1913: *Kleine Schriften*, Band IV, Leipzig 1913.

Vernière, Yvonne 1977: *Symboles et mythes dans la pensée de Plutarque*, Paris 1977.

Wehrli, Fritz 1967: *Die Schule des Aristoteles*, Band I, Basel 1967.

– 1968: "Herakleides der Pontiker", in: *PRE Suppl.* 11 (1968) 675–686.

– 1969: *Die Schule des Aristoteles*, Band III, 2. Aufl., Basel 1969.

– 1969a: *Die Schule des Aristoteles*, Band VII, Basel 1969.

Willi, Walter 1925: *Versuch einer Grundlegung der platonischen Mythopoiie*, Zürich 1925.

Ziegler, Konrat 1943: "Orphische Dichtung", in: *PRE* 36. Halbband (1943) 1370 ff.

Zuntz, Günther 1971: *Persephone*, Oxford 1971.

– 1978: Review of Graf 1974, in: *Gnomon* 50 (1978) 526–531.

Literarische und formgeschichtliche Bestimmung der Apokalypse des Johannes als einem Zeugnis frühchristlicher Apokalyptik

Ulrich B. Müller

0. Vorbemerkung

Weithin ist zugestanden, daß formgeschichtliche Untersuchungen zur apokalyptischen Literatur und der in ihr verwendeten Gattungen rar sind[1]. Ja, es gibt Äußerungen, die solche Erwägungen von vornherein für aussichtslos erklären, weil die apokalyptischen Schriften nur "Mischprodukte der verschiedensten Gattungen" darstellen[2]. Solche Schwierigkeiten sind grundsätzlich zu berücksichtigen, da die in der Apokalyptik benutzten Gattungen oftmals eine lange Geschichte hinter sich haben und manche Veränderung der angenommenen Grundform in Rechnung zu stellen ist. Trotz dieser Problematik bleibt es die Aufgabe der Forschung, die sprachliche Gestalt der apokalyptischen Schriften geschichtlich zu betrachten, da nur so ihre besondere Eigentümlichkeit, ihre Funktion und ihr "Sitz im Leben" annähernd zu bestimmen sind.

0.1. In diesem Referat können wir uns nicht der ganzen frühchristlichen Apokalyptik ausführlich zuwenden. Es wäre zwar reizvoll, die wohl älteste christlich-apokalyptische Schrift zu untersuchen, nämlich die literarische Vorlage von Mk 13. Doch ist ihr genauer Textumfang nur sehr hypothetisch mit Hilfe literarkritischer Sonderungen zu erschließen. Immerhin ist vielleicht soviel deutlich: Es handelt sich um eine Art "Flugblatt", das in einer besonders bedrohlichen Situation des Jüdischen Krieges die Christen Judäas zur Flucht in die Berge auffordert und die tröstliche Nähe des wiederkommenden Menschensohnes einschärft[3]. Der Form nach ist diese Schrift als Mahn- und Trostrede Jesu im Weissagungsstil gehalten. Sie ist von akuter Naherwartung geprägt wie später auch die Apk. Demgegenüber sind die christlichen Apokalypsen der 1. Hälfte des 2. Jahrhunderts anders ausgerichtet. Sie gehen von einer langen Dauer bis zum eschatologi-

---

[1] K. Koch 1970, 20; P. Weimar 1973, 124, 162. Vgl. aber J. J. Collins 1979.

[2] A. Nissen 1967, 246; auch G. v. Rad 1965, 330, Anm. 28.

[3] Zur Rekonstruktion der ursprünglich christlichen Apokalypse vgl. F. Hahn 1975, 240ff.; ihm weitgehend folgend R. Pesch 1977, 264ff. Zur Vorlage könnten m. E. gehören: V. 7.8 (ohne 8 Ende). 9 (ohne einleitenden Satz). 11–13. 14–22.24 (ohne "nach jener Drangsal") – 27.28–31.

schen Ende aus. Bedeutsam ist hier die Petrus-Apokalypse, die nach dem formalen Modell von Mk 13 Belehrungen Jesu über das Jenseits, die Hölle und den Himmel enthält. Das Ganze gibt sich (über Mk 13 hinaus) als Bericht eines Augen- und Ohrenzeugen, des Petrus. Darin hätten wir hier vielleicht "das erste Beispiel dafür, daß eine christliche Apokalypse mit einem christlichen Pseudonym versehen wird"[4]. Über das Buch "Der Hirt des Hermas" ist nicht viel zu sagen. Obwohl es der Form nach eine Apokalypse sein will (vgl. die Visionsberichte in Vis. I–IV), enthält es kaum gattungsspezifische Themen, d. h. keine Enthüllungen über die eschatologische Zukunft oder die jenseitige Welt (abgesehen von Vis. IV)[5].

0.2. Der begrenzte Rahmen dieses Referats läßt nur die ausführliche Behandlung einer apokalyptischen Schrift zu, die allerdings durch ihre literarische und religiöse Bedeutung diese Bevorzugung rechtfertigt. Wir meinen die Apokalypse des Johannes, die Teil des neutestamentlichen Kanons geworden ist. Drei Probleme sollen dabei im Vordergrund stehen. Einmal geht es um das Verhältnis von brieflichem Rahmen sowie der Voranstellung von Briefen oder Sendschreiben (Apk 2–3) und dem ganz anders gearteten apokalyptischen Hauptteil des sonstigen Buches (4,1–22,5). Zum anderen ist der visionäre Hauptteil im Blick auf die Form seiner Visionsreihen zu charakterisieren. Schließlich ist der Frage nach dem literarischen Entstehungsprozeß nachzugehen, der hinter dem komplizierten Aufbau innerhalb des apokalyptischen Hauptteils steht.

1. Brieflicher Rahmen und Briefe in der Apk

Wie sind die *brieflichen* Elemente der Apk zu verstehen?

1.1. Jedenfalls hat das ganze Buch eine briefliche Rahmung. Erkenntlich ist diese am Präskript (1,4f.), das den Verfasser und als Adressaten sieben Gemeinden in der Asia nennt. Dazu gehört eine besonders reich gestaltete salutatio. Endlich fehlt nicht der traditionelle Schlußgruß neutestamentlicher Briefe am Ende des Buches (22,21). Was die Rahmung des Werkes angeht, ist die ganze Apokalypse also als Brief an die sieben Gemeinden der Asia gestaltet (vgl. noch 1,11). E. Schüssler Fiorenza betont zu Recht, "that Revelation as a whole has the form of the early Christian apostolic letter and that the apocalyptic visions, symbols and patterns are set in an epistolary-framework". Dazu stimme, daß der Verfasser seine Autorität nicht durch das literarische Mittel der Pseudonymität ausdrückt und Geschichtsdarstellungen in fingierter Vorzeitigkeit vermeidet[6].

---

[4] P. Vielhauer 1975, 511.

[5] *Ibid.*, 518–522: "Man wird den Hirt des Hermas daher als 'Pseudoapokalypse' bezeichnen müssen." (522); ähnlich P. Vielhauer 1964, 448, 451.

[6] E. Schüssler Fiorenza 1977a, 358. J. J. Collins 1977, 330–333, stellt heraus, daß das Fehlen

1.2. Zu den brieflichen Zügen der Apk gehört, daß dem apokalyptischen Hauptteil 4,1–22,5 sieben Schreiben bzw. Briefe an die genannten Gemeinden vorausgehen (Kap. 2f.)[6a]. Ganz stereotyp sind diese durch Schreibbefehl und Botenformel eingeleitet:

"Dem Engel der Gemeinde in ... schreibe. Dieses sagt der ... (es folgt eine umschreibende Nennung Christi als eigentlichem Sprecher)."

Das eigentliche Korpus jedes einzelnen Schreibens nimmt in Mahnung,

---

der Pseudonymität in der Apk nicht ausreiche, "to indicate a new genre" gegenüber der sonst bekannten jüdisch-apokalyptischen Literatur (332). Er begründet dies zunächst mit dem richtigen Hinweis, daß diese Darstellungsform keinesfalls ausschließlich für apokalyptische Schriften gelte, auch nicht zu ihren unabdingbaren Konstitutiva gehören könne. Weil nun darüber hinaus das Aufkommen der Pseudonymität im jüdischen Bereich mit dem Niedergang der Prophetie zusammenhänge, war der Autor der Apk, der eben gerade sein Werk als Prophetie verstand (1,3; 22,7), frei, auf die Darstellungsform der Pseudonymität zu verzichten (331). Im übrigen herrsche in der Apk die Form indirekter Offenbarung vor ("visions mediated by an angel"), nicht die direkte Offenbarung durch Gott bzw. Christus (4,1–22,5). Deshalb zeige die Apk trotz des Fehlens der Pseudonymität "the same form of mediated revelation as the Jewish apocalypses" (332). Im Blick auf die Pseudonymität trifft es sicherlich zu, daß die Apk sich nicht grundsätzlich von der jüdisch-apokalyptischen Literatur unterscheidet, wenn hier auch eine Besonderheit vorliegt. In ihrer Stilisierung als Brief ist der Sachverhalt jedoch noch differenzierter zu sehen.

[6a] Hier ist kurz zu begründen, warum wir in den sieben Gemeindeschreiben nach der Intention des Verfassers Briefe sehen dürfen, obwohl manche Elemente brieflichen Austausches fehlen und etwa die paulinischen Briefe durchaus andere Formstrukturen aufweisen. Der Schreibbefehl "dem Engel der Gemeinde ... schreibe" zu Beginn jeder Einheit in Apk 1–3 steht in sachlichem Zusammenhang mit der eindeutig brieflichen Einleitung des ganzen Werkes Apk 1,4.5a, dem Briefpräskript. Der Verfasser ist zur schriftlichen Kundgabe dessen genötigt, was er eigentlich mündlich den Gemeinden zu verkünden hatte. Wie in den sonstigen frühchristlichen Briefen ist auch hier die Briefform Surrogat mündlicher Predigt (vgl. IKor 5,3; Kol 2,5). Was die besondere Form der Schreiben in Apk 2–3 angeht, so steht sie wohl in jener Tradition, in der Briefe als Mittel prophetischer Verkündigung auftauchen: "Die Briefe der Apk sind daher ... als Exemplare jener nie ganz ausgestorbenen Gattung des prophetischen Briefes, hier freilich in Verbindung mit Erscheinung und Schreibbefehl, aufzufassen." K. Berger 1974, 214. Zu nennen ist der Brief des Propheten Elia an Joram IIChr 21,12–15 und der Brief Jeremias an die Exilierten in Babylon Jer 29,1–23 (LXX 36,1–23). Beide werden wie die Sendschreiben Apk 2–3 durch die Botenformel eingeleitet: IIChr 21,12; Jer 29,4. Der Brief Jeremias an Baruch in Par Jer 6,17–23 enthält ebenfalls der Botenformel entsprechende Wendungen: 6,20.22 ("spricht der Herr"); der Brief wird zunächst von einem Engel diktiert (6,12–14), der seine Worte durch "so spricht der Herr" autorisiert. Nicht bezogen auf Gott, sondern auf den Briefschreiber selbst tritt die Botenformel auch in dem Brief Baruchs an die 9½ Stämme auf: syrBar 78,2 (vgl. die Beziehung zu 84,7: Verweis auf die prophetische Sendung Baruchs durch Gott). Auch wenn die Sendschreiben Apk 2–3 in der literarischen Formtradition des Prophetenbriefes zu stehen scheinen, geht es nicht an, sie nur von daher zu verstehen. Die Botenformel weist gleichzeitig auf mündliche Verwendung in prophetischer Rede des Johannes hin, da auch sonst innerhalb des Korpus der einzelnen Schreiben weitere Formstrukturen sichtbar werden, die nur aufgrund des Einflusses mündlicher Rede erklärbar sind. Im übrigen stellt der Gebrauch der Botenformel beim Prophetenbrief eine Übernahme von Elementen mündlicher Prophetie dar. Zu dieser Einschätzung der Botenformel siehe schon F. Hahn 1971, 363.366.369f.390–394; U. B. Müller 1975, 47ff. gegen K. Berger 1974, 212f.

Tröstung oder Gerichtsansage zur konkreten Lage der jeweiligen Gemeinde Stellung. Jedes ist individuell gestaltet, was die inhaltliche Aussage betrifft, in der Form aber greift der Verfasser auf prophetische Redestrukturen zurück, die in der alttestamentlich-jüdischen Prophetie gebräuchlich waren[7]. Vorherrschend ist eine bestimmte Form der Paraklese oder Mahnrede (bes. Apk 2,1 ff. und 3,1 ff.), wie sie auch in der Bußpredigt Johannes des Täufers (Mt 3,7–10; Lk 3,7–9) und solchen jüdischen Texten greifbar sind, die in der deuteronomistischen Geschichtsschau wurzeln (z. B. äthHen 91,3–7; 91,18 f.)[8]. Dazu kommt die Form des sog. Heilsorakels (Apk 2,10) und der (unbedingten) Heilsankündigung, die auf das Lob der Gemeinde die Heilsansage folgen läßt (Apk 3,8–10). Wahrscheinlich benutzt der Verfasser bei der Gestaltung seiner Briefe die prophetischen Redeformen, die ihm als urchristlichen Propheten judenchristlicher Herkunft geläufig waren. Die literarische Verwendung mündlicher Redeformen ergibt sich für ihn aus dem Zwang, wegen seiner Entfernung von den Gemeinden dasjenige schriftlich sagen zu müssen, was er eigentlich mündlich den Gemeinden zu verkünden hatte.

1.3. Die aufgezeigten brieflichen Elemente der Apk stehen nun in einer gewissen Spannung zu dem andersartigen Charakter des apokalyptischen Hauptteils 4,1–22,5.

1.3.1. In der dem Präskript vorangestellten Einleitung wird der Inhalt des Buches als Visionsbericht gekennzeichnet (1,2):

"... Johannes, der das Wort Gottes und das Zeugnis Jesu Christi bezeugt – alles, was er gesehen hat."

Dementsprechend nennt der Verfasser seine Ausführungen "Worte der Weissagung" (1,3; 22,7.10.18 f.). Zwar beziehen sich diese Bestimmungen sowohl auf die sieben Sendschreiben (Kap. 2–3) wie die folgenden Visionsberichte, insofern die Abfassung beider Einheiten auf den (doppelten) Schreibbefehl innerhalb der Beauftragungsvision zurückgeht (1,11.19). Doch unterscheidet der Verfasser deutlich zwischen den Sendschreiben und dem apokalyptischen Hauptteil[9]. Im Schreibbefehl 1,19 trennt er die einzel-

---

[7] U. B. Müller 1975, 57 ff.

[8] _Ibid._, 57 ff. Die Paraklese als Bußpredigt hat folgende Struktur (in Klammern Versangaben, die das Redeschema am Beispiel von Apk 3,1 ff. und Mt 3,7–10 darstellen):
1. Urteil über die Gemeindesituation (Anklage) (Apk 3,1b.2b vgl. Mt 3,7b)
2. Mahnung
   a) als appellierende Erinnerung an den empfangenen Heilsstand (Apk 3,3a vgl. Mt 3,9)
   b) als Ruf zur Umkehr (Apk 3,2a.3a vgl. Mt 3,8)
3. Bedingte Gerichtsdrohung (Apk 3,3b vgl. Mt 3,10b).

[9] E. Schüssler Fiorenza 1977a, 362, bestreitet wohl zu Unrecht, daß die Wendung "was geschehen soll danach" (1,19) sich auf 4,1–22,5 bezieht. Ihrer Meinung nach denkt der Verfasser dabei gerade an die sieben Schreiben (Kap. 2–3), "which speak about what is now and what will be in the future". Einer ihrer Gründe ist, daß der Verfasser die sieben Schreiben,

nen Einheiten seines Buches. "Was geschehen soll danach" (1,19) kann sich dabei nur auf den Hauptteil 4,1–22,5 beziehen, weil dieser Teil durch eben diese Formel betont neu eingeleitet wird in 4,1 f. Erst aufgrund einer neuen Geisterfahrung und einer weiteren Vision (4,1 f.) kommt es zur Darstellung dessen, "was danach geschehen soll". Dieser Teil enthält die Enthüllung des endzeitlichen Gerichtsratschlusses Gottes, die visionäre Vorwegnahme seiner Durchführung, nicht aber briefliche Korrespondenz.

1.3.2. Schon formal stoßen beide Elemente zu Beginn des Buches hart aufeinander. Enthält Apk 1,4.5a das Briefpräskript, woran sich eine Doxologie anschließt (1,5b.6), so folgt in 1,7 abrupt, d. h. ohne Überleitungsformel, eine Gerichtsankündigung, die im Ich-Stil das Kommen Christi ansagt, sowie eine Selbstvorstellung Gottes (wieder Ich-Stil), bei der sein Kommen im Vordergrund steht (1,8). W. Bousset betonte die sehr lose Zusammengehörigkeit von 1,4–6 und 1,7f., ja er sah in 1,7f. eine störende Unterbrechung des Zusammenhangs und erklärte das Auftauchen von 1,7f. an dieser Stelle mit der Absicht des Verfassers, mit einem kurzen Motto den Inhalt der ganzen Schrift zu charakterisieren[10]. Doch warum taucht dieses Motto gerade hier auf? Eine formgeschichtliche Beobachtung hilft da weiter. Gerichtsankündigungen haben in vergleichbaren Texten ihren Ort am Anfang einer Schrift[11]. Das beste Beispiel ist äthHen 1,3b–9, wo nach der einleitenden Bestimmung des Buches als Weisheitsrede, die durch den Verweis auf eine empfangene Vision autorisiert wird, eine eschatologische Theophanie geschildert wird[12]. Wie in Apk 1,7 das Kommen Christi angekündigt wird, so in äthHen 1,3b–9 das Kommen Gottes. Vgl. besonders 1,9: "Und siehe, er kommt mit seinen unzähligen Heiligen, um Gericht zu halten über alle . . ." Dabei scheint die Gerichtsankündigung in äthHen 1,3ff. insofern bereits in einer Formtradition zu stehen, als am Anfang von Prophetenbüchern Entsprechendes zu finden ist (Mi 1,3f.; Nah 1,2ff.; Zeph 1,2ff.).

Es wurde festgestellt, daß die Gerichtsankündigung Apk 1,7f. auf den ersten Blick im Kontext disparat erscheint und sich nur aufgrund der dahinterstehenden Formtradition erklären läßt. Ähnlich steht es mit dem ohne Überleitung angeschlossenen Bericht über die Beauftragungsvision des Sehers Johannes 1,9ff. Diese ist in Ich-Form erzählt, obwohl in der Überschrift 1,1–3 und dem brieflichen Präskript 1,4.5a vom Seher in der 3. Person die Rede war. Dieser abrupte Wechsel von der 3. zur 1. Person hat seine Formparallelen, die hier nachwirken. E. Rau hat herausgestellt, "daß der Übergang von der dritten Person in der 'Überschrift' zur ersten in der Schilderung Stilgesetzen prophetischer Überlieferung folgt und

---

"on one level with the so-called apocalyptic visions" stelle, "since he makes the letters clearly part of the inaugural vision". Dieses Argument sticht nicht, da zwar beide Einheiten sich dem Schreibbefehl 1,19 verdanken, aber erst aufgrund gesonderter Auditionen (Schreibbefehle zu Beginn jedes einzelnen Schreibens) und der neuen Vision 4,1f. zustande kommen.

[10] W. Bousset 1906, 190f.   [11] K. Berger 1977, 29.
[12] Vgl. E. Rau 1974, 34ff., 42ff.

sich auch bei Visionsbeschreibungen findet"[13]. Als Beispiel kann zunächst wieder äthHen 1,1–3 dienen. Nachdem in der Überschrift 1,1 von Henoch in der dritten Person die Rede ist (vgl. Apk 1,1–3), geht der Verfasser in 1,2f. unvermittelt zum Selbstbericht in der Ich-Form über. Die plötzliche Ich-Form erklärt sich sachlich aus dem Bestreben, nach der Überschrift die folgende Botschaft des Autors durch das literarische Mittel des Eigenberichts über eine Thronvision zu autorisieren. Indem der Verfasser beansprucht, visionären Einblick in die himmlischen Dinge gehabt zu haben und zu ihrer Mitteilung beauftragt zu sein, soll seine Darstellung Autorität gewinnen. Dieser plötzliche Übergang zum Ich-Bericht findet sich u. a. äthHen 12,3; 37,2; 65,3. Dieselbe Funktion hat die in Apk 1,9ff. geschilderte Beauftragungs-vision (nicht Berufungsvision!).

1.4. Lassen sich Apk 1,7f. und 1,9ff. durch Verweis auf alttestamentli-che und besonders jüdisch-apokalyptische Stilgesetze deuten, sowenig ist die in 1,9ff. enthaltene Beauftragung zum Schreiben von Briefen in den bisher genannten Paralleltexten zu finden. Die Frage stellt sich: Wie kam es dazu, daß der Verfasser Johannes seine Apokalypse mit einem brieflichen Rahmen versah und dem apokalyptischen Hauptteil sieben Gemeinde-schreiben voranstellte? Vergleichbare jüdische Apokalypsen kennen diese Verbindung von Briefelementen und apokalyptischer Belehrung selten. Weder das Daniel-Buch noch das vierte Esra-Buch, das etwa gleichzeitig wie die Apk erschien, lassen briefliche Elemente erkennen, um nur zwei herausragende jüdische Apokalypsen zu nennen. Interessant wird in diesem Zusammenhang die syrische Baruchapokalypse. Sie schließt in Kap. 78–87 mit einem Brief Baruchs an die 9½ Stämme Israels, die jenseits des Flusses wohnen. Anscheinend gab es gattungsmäßige Berührungspunkte zwischen Briefen mit Offenbarungsinhalten und Apokalypsen. Unter dem Oberbe-griff "Offenbarungsschriften" sind "die 'Gattungen' Brief, Testament und Apokalypse häufig nicht so streng voneinander zu scheiden, wie man gewöhnlich annimmt ..."[14]

1.4.1. Aber kehren wir zur syrischen Baruchapokalypse zurück. Sie ist das eindrücklichste Beispiel einer jüdischen Apokalypse, bei der Briefele-mente eine entscheidende Rolle spielen. Nach einer Abschiedsrede Baruchs an das Volk (77,2–10) bittet ihn dieses, auch die Brüder in der Diaspora Babylons zu stärken durch "einen Brief der Unterweisung und ein Schrei-ben der Hoffnung" (77,12). Gemeint ist eine Offenbarungsschrift, die das Volk tröstet in einer Zeit, in der die "Hirten Israels" umgekommen und die "Lampen, die uns Licht geben", erloschen sind. Baruch verweist das Volk zunächst an das bestehende Gesetz, an das sich das Volk halten soll (77,15f.). Dennoch will er einen Brief an die Brüder in Babel und einen an die 9½ Stämme senden (77,17). Diese haben, wie das allein mitgeteilte

---

[13] *Ibid.*, 39.
[14] K. Berger 1974, 207. Ein Beleg dafür ist in gewisser Hinsicht noch grHen 100,6, wo im griechischen Text das sog. paränetische Buch äthHen 92–105 als "diese Worte dieses Briefes" bezeichnet wird.

Schreiben an die 9½ Stämme erkennen läßt, eine dreifache Funktion als Offenbarungsschriften:

(1) Sie wahren die Kontinuität der Offenbarungsverkündigung nach dem Erlöschen der Prophetie, dargestellt durch den Weggang Baruchs (77,12–14).

(2) Der Brief an die 9½ Stämme soll an das Gesetz, an den Bund, an Feste und Sabbate erinnern und ihre Geltung sichern (84,5–8).

(3) Er dient als forensisches "Zeugnis" zwischen dem Schreiber Baruch und den Angeredeten, damit dieser als "Gesandter Gottes" vor Gottes Urteil bestehen kann (84,7).

Angesichts dieser Funktionen ist der Offenbarungscharakter speziell des von Baruch verfaßten Briefes an die 9½ Stämme in der Diaspora deutlich genug. Baruch erscheint hier mindestens ebenso stark als Offenbarungsmittler wie in den das übrige Buch beherrschenden Visionen und Visionsdeutungen. Er ist Gottesbote, unmittelbarer Gesandter Gottes (84,7). Ja, der Verfasser der Baruchapokalypse erhebt ihn in den Rang eines "alter Moses"[15]. Wie Mose dereinst (vgl. Dtn 31,25 ff.) Himmel und Erde als Zeugen gegen das Volk anrief, was die Einhaltung des Gesetzes betraf (84,2–5), so tut es Baruch in dem Brief an die 9½ Stämme (84,6):

"Auch ich, ich sage euch, nachdem ihr leiden mußtet: Seid ihr gehorsam dem, was euch gesagt ward, so werdet ihr empfangen alles von dem Mächtigen ... Darum sei zum Zeugnis zwischen mir und euch denn dieser Brief, daß ihr an die Gebote des Allmächtigen denkt ..."

Nach diesen Überlegungen kann es nicht mehr wundernehmen, daß die syrische Baruchapokalypse mit einem Brief schließt. Dieser hat nach dem Willen seines Verfassers in einer Weise Offenbarungscharakter, daß er als krönender Abschluß des ganzen Werkes dienen kann. Ihn wegen seines scheinbaren formalen Nachtragscharakters oder der bestehenden textlichen Sonderüberlieferung in christlich-syrischen Handschriften als nicht zum ursprünglichen Text der Baruchapokalypse gehörig zu betrachten, ist unbegründet. Die Briefform der Kap. 78–87 schließt sich organisch an das übrige Werk an, insofern der Offenbarungscharakter des Briefes mindestens ebenso deutlich ist wie die vorangehenden Visionen und Visionsdeutungen.

1.4.2. Auf einen Gesichtspunkt ist noch gesondert einzugehen. Man hat darauf hingewiesen, daß Züge des Baruchbriefes, die nicht vom apokalyptischen Konzept des Briefschreibers als endzeitlichem Gesandten und Offenbarungsmittlers geprägt sind, dessen Brief zudem durch ein apokalyptisches Tier, den Adler, übermittelt wird (vgl. Apk 8,13; auch 4,7) – daß diese Züge also auf die Gattung des synagogalen Sendschreibens verweisen, das eine jüdische Synagogengemeinde an die andere senden konnte[16].

---

[15] C. Andresen 1965, 239 f.   [16] *Ibid.*, 239–243.

Zu diesen Zügen gehört wohl die Schlußmahnung des Baruchbriefes (86,1 f.):

"Darum – wenn ihr den Brief empfangen werdet, dann lest ihn vor in euren Versammlungen mit Sorgfalt. Und denkt darüber nach, besonders aber in den Tagen eurer Fasten"[17].

Diese Anweisung hat besondere Bedeutung. Anscheinend gilt das Zeugnis vor der Diaspora als stete Aufgabe, und dieses Mahnschreiben wird "in den Rang eines liturgischen Textes mit gottesdienstlicher Verankerung erhoben"[18]. Der wirkliche Verfasser der Baruchapokalypse stellt die Dinge zunächst so dar, daß Baruch die gottesdienstliche Verlesung nur des Briefes beabsichtigt. In Wahrheit beabsichtigt der Verfasser des Buches aber wohl mehr. Er will mit Hilfe der Fiktion des Baruchbriefes und seiner Verbreitungsnotiz die Publikation seiner ganzen Apokalypse sichern. Sie soll in den Rang gottesdienstlicher Verlesung gelangen und so besondere Geltung bekommen.

1.4.3. Welche Bedeutung für die Apk haben nun diese Beobachtungen zur syrischen Baruchapokalypse? Zunächst einmal diese: Daß Briefe von Offenbarungsmittlern oder sog. Prophetenbriefe[19] denselben apokalyptischen Offenbarungscharakter haben können wie in Visionsberichten mitgeteilte endzeitliche Belehrungen. Von daher ist die Verbindung der sieben Sendschreiben mit dem apokalyptischen Hauptteil innerhalb der Apk durchaus sachgemäß. Eine weitere Übereinstimmung zwischen syrBar und Apk tritt hinzu. Der Verfasser der Apk zielt ebenso darauf ab, daß seine Apokalypse innerhalb der gottesdienstlichen Versammlungen vorgelesen wird wie der Autor der syrBar. Schon in der Einleitung seines Buches schreibt er (1,3):

"… Selig, wer vorliest und die hören die Worte der Weissagung und bewahren, was darin geschrieben ist."

Der gottesdienstliche Charakter der Apk wird auch daran deutlich, daß nach begründeter These der Schlußrahmen des Buches (22,6–21) Anklänge an die urchristliche Herrenmahlsfeier erkennen läßt.

Aus der Abendmahlsliturgie hellenistischer Gemeinden stammt das ἔρχου κύριε Ἰησοῦ (V. 20) (Übersetzung von μαράνα θά). An die Abendmahlsliturgie erinnert der Einladungsspruch ὁ διψῶν ἐρχέσθω, ὁ θέλων λαβέτω ὕδωρ ζωῆς δωρεάν (V. 17). Wahrscheinlich hat die Ausschlußformel für die Gottlosen (ἔξω οἱ κύνες usw. V. 15) den gleichen Sitz im Leben

---

[17] Eine ähnliche Aufforderung zum Vorlesen eines Prophetenbriefes vor dem Volk findet sich in Par Jer 7,19. In Par Jer 6,13 wird der prophetische Brief von vornherein mit den Worten "Sprich zu den Kindern Israels!" in Auftrag gegeben.

[18] C. Andresen 1965, 241.

[19] Vgl. noch die Epistula Jeremiae (LXX) mit ihrer Überschrift: "Abschrift eines Briefes, den Jeremia … gesandt hat, um ihnen kundzutun, wie es ihm von Gott aufgetragen war"; und Par Jer 6,17–23 und 7,23–29.

(vgl. IKor 16,22; Did 10,6)[20]. Anscheinend setzt der Verfasser voraus, daß nach Verlesen seines Buches die Gemeinde zum Höhepunkt des Gottesdienstes, der Herrenmahlsfeier, übergeht. Möglicherweise ist hier dieselbe Situation vorausgesetzt wie am Schluß des paulinischen IKor, insofern gerade dort vermutet werden kann, daß sich die Liturgie des Herrenmahles an die Verlesung des Apostelbriefes angeschlossen hat. Die paulinischen Briefe wurden im Gottesdienst vorgelesen (vgl. IThess 5,27). Dies gilt auch für die sonstigen Briefe des Urchristentums, etwa den IClem, dessen literarischer Charakter den Eindruck eines gottesdienstlichen Textes macht (vgl. das allgemeine Kirchengebet IClem 59,2–61,3): Er war "von vornherein auf gottesdienstliche Lektion berechnet"[21].

Aufgrund dieser Sachverhalte wird der briefliche Rahmen der Apk endgültig klar: Eine als Brief stilisierte Apokalypse konnte am ehesten erwarten, im Gottesdienst vorgelesen zu werden[22]. Daß dies das Ziel des Verfassers war, verrät schon der Makarismus 1,3. Daß hier allerdings Probleme bestehen konnten, ist daraus zu sehen, daß für den Bereich der hellenistischen Missionsgemeinden die Apk die bis dahin erste (uns bekannte) christliche Apokalypse darstellt[23]. Man hat damit zu rechnen, daß die Gattung "Apokalypse", die in jüdischer Tradition steht, eine den kleinasiatischen Gemeinden des 1. Jahrhunderts zwar bekannte, doch wenig vertraute Literaturform war, wie ja auch der Verfasser Johannes mit seiner Theologie und seinem Gemeindeverständnis ganz eigenständig den Gemeinden gegenübertrat; als ursprünglicher Wanderprophet wird er dem judenchristlich-palästinensischen Raum entstammen[24]. Wollte er seiner Apokalypse die Bedeutung gottesdienstlicher Verlesung zukommen lassen, so mußte er sie wenigstens der Form nach den vertrauten Gemeindebriefen anpassen.

1.4.4. Mit der brieflichen Ausgestaltung der Apk hängt wohl auch das Fehlen der Pseudonymität zusammen, die ja ein literarisches Kennzeichen jüdischer Apokalyptik darstellt. Sicher kommt dabei zunächst das besondere prophetische Sendungsbewußtsein zum Ausdruck, das Johannes befähigt, unter seinem eigenen Namen zu schreiben. Als "Knecht Christi" (1,1) erhält er eine besondere Offenbarungsvision des Menschensohnes, die ihn

---

[20] G. Bornkamm 1961, 126f. Trotz der kritischen Einwände, die K. Wengst 1972, 51–54 gegen Bornkamms Deutung des Schlusses der Apk erhoben hat, scheinen mir Bornkamms Hinweise noch immer diskutabel zu sein, ähnlich K. P. Jörns 1971, 182; P. Vielhauer 1975, 500.

[21] M. Dibelius 1975, 49.

[22] W. G. Kümmel 1973, 405; P. Vielhauer 1975, 500.

[23] Vom deuteropaulinischen II Thess (oder gar den eschatologischen Ausführungen in den echten Paulinen) ist hier abzusehen, da diese zwar "apokalyptische" Darlegungen enthalten, aber nicht als apokalyptische Schriften stilisiert sind. Auch die über das MkEv eventuell bekannte synoptische "Apokalypse" Mk 13 (samt Parallelen) gehört nicht hierher, da die ursprünglich apokalyptische Vorlage durch ihre Einarbeitung in das Gesamtevangelium nicht mehr als selbständige Apokalypse erkennbar war. Die Vorlage selbst entstand im judäischen Raum.

[24] U. B. Müller 1976, 46–50. Vgl. bes. Anm. 47.

beauftragt, an die sieben Gemeinden der Asia zu schreiben (1,10–20). Doch
steht das Fehlen der Pseudonymität auch im Zusammenhang gerade dieses
inhaltlichen Auftrags, nämlich Briefe an die ihm *bekannten* Gemeinden zu
verfassen. Er selbst ist den Gemeinden bekannt und will wegen seiner
räumlichen Abwesenheit schriftlich das sagen, was er auch mündlich getan
hätte (Kap. 2–3). Von daher besteht überhaupt kein Grund zur Pseudonymität. In dieser Hinsicht ist die Apk ein literarisches Unikum, wenn
man vom "Hirten des Hermas" absieht, der aber nur bedingt als Apokalypse zu bezeichnen ist.

2. Vorgegebene Formstrukturen in den Visionszyklen

Ehe wir uns nun der formgeschichtlichen Charakterisierung der verschiedenen Visionsreihen zuwenden, ist ein Blick auf die theologisch-
redaktionelle Kompositionsarbeit des Verfassers innerhalb des apokalyptischen Hauptteils zu werfen. Wir können an dieser Stelle allerdings keine
Diskussion über die verschiedenen Vorschläge zur Komposition führen[25],
sondern wollen uns mit einigen Hinweisen begnügen, die sich an die
Ausführungen von K.-P. Jörns anschließen[26].

2.1. Kap. 4–5 sind die Einleitung zum folgenden Endgeschehen. Kap. 4
enthält die Gerichtseröffnung durch Gott, die sich in der Übergabe des
Buches an das Lamm fortsetzt (Kap. 5). Das Buch mit den sieben Siegeln
beinhaltet das von Gott beschlossene Gerichtsgeschehen an der Welt, das
das Lamm durch Öffnen der Siegel in Gang setzt (6,1–8,1). Dabei stellt
diese Visionenfolge quasi eine "Ouvertüre" des eigentlichen Endgeschehens dar, eine Bekanntgabe der endzeitlichen Ereignisse, deren Vollzug
unmittelbar folgt, nachdem das siebte Siegel gelöst ist[27]. 8,2–11,19 schildern die erste Teilrealisierung des Endgeschehens. Noch ist das Ende aber
nicht erreicht; denn mit dem Ertönen der siebten Posaune, die gleichzeitig
als das dritte Wehe erscheint, blickt der Verfasser auf den weiteren Fortgang des endzeitlichen Gerichtsdramas. Kap. 12–14 bringen Konkretionen
der endzeitlichen Situation, in der die endzeitlichen Gegenspieler, das
Lamm, der Satan und seine Machtbastion, das Römische Reich, näher
identifiziert werden. Kap. 15–16 schildern weitere Realisierungen des
universalen Gerichts Gottes. Kap. 17–19,10 führen schließlich hin zur
Vernichtung des widergöttlichen Babels und zum Antritt der Königsherrschaft durch Gott. Der Schlußteil 19,11–22,5 baut darauf auf. Er konkretisiert den in 19,1–10 proklamierten Sieg Gottes, wobei die machtvolle

---

[25] Vgl. nur die Kommentare und Einleitungen zum Neuen Testament. Einen beachtens-
werten neuen Versuch zur Frage der Komposition macht E. Schüssler Fiorenza 1977a. Ich
kann hier leider nicht darauf eingehen. Vgl. neuerdings auch Hahn 1979 und Lambrecht 1980.
[26] Jörns 1971, 176f. und *passim*.   [27] *Ibid.*, 88f.

Erscheinung seines Christus, die Vernichtung des Satans, das Weltgericht bei der allgemeinen Totenauferstehung, neuer Himmel und neue Erde gezeigt werden.

2.2. Ein gestaltendes Element innerhalb der Visionsreihen des apokalyptischen Hauptteils ist noch besonders hervorzuheben: die hymnischen Stücke der Apk. Sie sind nicht als bloße Einschübe in das dargestellte Geschehen zu betrachten, sondern "Teile des Endgeschehens selbst, das der Seher hört und schaut"[28]. Ohne diese Hymnen würden die Visionsreihen fast durchgehend Unheilsbotschaft verkünden; die Hymnen stellen demgegenüber das Heilshandeln Gottes heraus, dem das endzeitliche Gerichtsgeschehen letztlich dient[29]. Formal und funktional gesehen, sind die Hymnen "Responsionen auf ein Handeln Gottes bzw. des Christus"[30]. Dabei wird durch sie deutlich, in welchem sachlichen Verhältnis die in den einzelnen Visionsreihen dargestellten Endereignisse zueinander stehen. Die ersten Hymnen, 4,8c; 4,11 und 5,13 etwa, lassen das visionäre Geschehen noch als totale Prolepse erscheinen. Die Hymnen 11,15b/17f. setzen bereits ein zeitlich vorgerücktes Stadium voraus: Die Plagen der sechs Posaunen haben ein Drittel des Kosmos vernichtet. Und je mehr die hymnischen Stücke an den Schlußhymnus 19,6b–8a heranreichen, um so stärker "verändert sich das Verhältnis von Realisierung und Prolepse"[31].

2.3. Dieser Blick auf die Kompositionsarbeit des Gesamtverfassers war nötig, um von vornherein klarzustellen, daß sich der apokalyptische Hauptteil seines Buches seiner bewußten Gestaltung verdankt. So sehr wir im folgenden auf längst vorgegebene Formstrukturen zu achten haben, so sehr der Verfasser möglicherweise literarische Vorlagen verarbeitet, so ist doch vor allem sein Buch als theologische Aussageeinheit zu begreifen. Bei der nun fälligen Behandlung der einzelnen Visionsreihen ist eine gewisse Beschränkung notwendig. Es kann hier nicht um eine detaillierte formgeschichtliche Analyse aller Visionsberichte gehen, vielmehr werden wir uns nur einigen Besonderheiten der drei Reihen von Siebenervisionen zuwenden, der Öffnung des Sieben-Siegel-Buches durch das Lamm (6,1–8,1), den Posaunenvisionen (8,2–11,19) und den Schalenvisionen (16). Neben der Siebenzahl der darin geschilderten Plagen eint diese Reihen, daß die Rolle der Mittlergestalt, von der die jeweilige endzeitliche Plage ausgeht, das Lamm wie die einzelnen Engel, grundsätzlich gleich ist. Das Lösen der Siegel, das Blasen der Posaunen und das Ausgießen der Schalen haben schöpferische Wirkungen, die Unheil für einen bestimmten Teil der Welt bedeuten.

2.3.1. Wir beginnen mit einer auffälligen Besonderheit der zu behandelnden Visionsberichte, die sie von den meisten jüdisch-apokalyptischen

---

[28] *Ibid.*, 170.   [29] *Ibid.*, 168.   [30] *Ibid.*, 167.   [31] *Ibid.*, 169.

Vergleichstexten unterscheidet, sie aber mit prophetischen Visionsberichten des AT verbindet[32]. Gemeint ist das Fehlen eines besonderen Deutungsteils zur mitgeteilten Vision[33]. Zwar fügt etwa Apk 6,8 eine deutende Identifikation in die Schauung ein; vom Reiter auf dem fahlen Pferd heißt es nämlich: "Sein Name war der Tod"[34]. Dieses Element fehlt z. B. noch bei den Visionsberichten im Amosbuch. Doch unterscheidet sich diese Art der Deutung von dem längst üblich gewordenen ganz eigenständigen Deutungsteil, der sich seit Sacharja, besonders aber in der jüdisch-apokalyptischen Literatur an die Vision anschließt, wobei einleitende Bemerkungen wie Fragen des Propheten bzw. Sehers diesen Teil neu eröffnen (z. B. Sach 1,9ff.; 2,2ff., 4,4ff.; Dan 7,15ff.19; 8,15ff.). Zudem ist zu beachten, daß mehrere der einzelnen Posaunen- oder Schalenvisionen ganz ohne jene deutende Interpretation innerhalb der Schauung auskommen, geschweige denn eine Deutung kennen, die der der jüdisch-apokalyptischen Visionsdeutung entspricht. Immerhin ist die apokalyptische Prägung mancher Visionsberichte der Apk an dem wiederholten "wie" erkenntlich: "(etwas) wie ein großer, feurig brennender Berg" 8,8, "und die Gestalten der Heuschrecken waren wie Pferde, gerüstet zum Krieg" 9,7; "und auf ihren Häuptern war es wie golden schimmernde Kränze und ihre Gesichter waren wie Menschengesichter. Und sie hatten Haare wie Weiberhaare und ihre Zähne waren wie die von Löwen" (9,7–8). Trotz dieser Einschränkung ist das vorherrschende Fehlen eines eigenständigen Deutungsteils bei den Visionen der Apk beachtlich genug.

2.3.2. Diese formalen Beobachtungen lassen gewisse Schlüsse auf den Wirklichkeitscharakter der Visionsberichte zu[35]. Amos versteht das Geschaute noch als reale Wirklichkeit: ein Heuschreckenschwarm zur Zeit, als die Spätsaat zu wachsen begann (7,1), ein Feuerregen, der die große Grundflut fraß und damit auch die Äcker (7,4). Demgegenüber ist in Visionsberichten, die eine gesonderte Deutung enthalten, das Geschaute Symbol, das mit der Sache, die es bedeutet, nicht deckungsgleich ist. Zwar haben die apokalyptischen Visionsbilder, die mit einer eigenen Deutung versehen sind, einen bewußten Hinweischarakter; doch sind sie nicht die Sache selbst.

Viele Visionsberichte der Apk, die keiner gesonderten Deutung bedürfen, zeigen nun durchaus noch Verwandtschaft mit dem Wirklichkeitsverständnis prophetischer Visionen des AT. So ist es wohl bei der ersten und zweiten Schalenvision (16,2–3):

---

[32] K. Koch in diesem Band bes. §§ 5 und 6.
[33] Abgesehen von Apk 7,13ff.; 11,4.6; 14,4; 16,14; 17,9–14.15–18.
[34] Ähnlich Apk 8,11; 9,11; 19,11.16.
[35] Vgl. dazu wieder K. Koch in diesem Band bes. §§ 5 und 6.

"Und der erste (Engel) ging hin und goß aus seine Schale über die Erde. Und es wurde ein schlimmes und böses Geschwür für die Menschen ... Und der zweite goß seine Schale über das Meer aus. Und es wurde zu Blut wie von einem Toten, und jedes lebendige Lebewesen, das was im Meer ist, starb."

Die schöpferische Handlung der Mittlergestalt Engel bewirkt als Plage ein wirkliches Geschwür für die Erdenbewohner, und das Meer wird zu Blut, wenn auch bei dieser Plage das real gedachte Blut eine nähere negative Deutung erfährt "wie von einem Toten". Je mehr solche deutenden Interpretationen auftauchen – Benutzung des apokalyptischen "wie" –, um so mehr verliert die geschaute Größe ihre unmittelbar einsichtige Realität, um so mehr weist sie auf eine dahinter stehende Dimension hin, die erst aufgrund der näheren Interpretation erkennbar ist.

2.3.3. Oft genug hat die geschaute Größe nicht bloßen Verweischarakter, der erst in einer besonderen Deutung entschlüsselt wird, wie es beim vierten Tier in Dan 7 der Fall ist, das furchtbar und stark ist und 10 Hörner besitzt, oder beim Adler mit seinen Flügeln und Häuptern in IV Esr 11. Vielmehr meint die geschaute Größe real das, was sie darstellt: Geschwüre, zu Blut verwandeltes Wasser, Menschen, die von Feuersglut getroffen werden (16,8f.), Blitze, Donner und Erdbeben, die die große Stadt Babylon zerstören (16,18f.).

2.4. Dieses Ergebnis läßt sich durch weitere formale Beobachtungen zu den Visionsreihen der Apk bestätigen. H.-P. Müller hat in seiner Untersuchung "Die Plagen der Apokalypse" ein bestimmtes Formschema erarbeitet, das einen großen Teil der Einzelvisionen innerhalb der drei großen Siebenerreihen bestimmt.

2.4.1. Besonders deutlich erkennbar ist dieses Schema bei den Schalenvisionen Apk 16. Fünf Formelemente gehören dazu:

(I) Zunächst erfolgt die Bevollmächtigung der Engel, die die Plagen auslösen. Dieses Element steht den sieben Einzelvisionen voran. Nur hier werden die Einzelereignisse als Visionsgeschehen charakterisiert (15,5ff.): "Und danach schaute ich und der Tempel des Zelts des Zeugnisses im Himmel wurde geöffnet ...". Es folgen die Erscheinung der Engel (15,6) und die Übergabe der Schalen an sie (15,7). 16,1 enthält dann die eigentliche Beauftragung der Engel, die Schalen des Zornes Gottes über die Erde auszugießen.

(II) Hier geschieht die Ausführung des Auftrags: "Und der erste (Engel) ging hin und goß seine Schale aus über die Erde." In verkürzter Form wiederholt sich diese Bemerkung zu Beginn jeder Einzelvision.

(III) Es schließt sich die Auswirkung der Engelhandlung an. Die 1., 2., 3., 5. und 7. Schalenvision drückt diese Wirkung von schöpferischer Kraft stereotyp durch die Formel $\varkappa\alpha\grave{\iota}$ $\grave{\epsilon}\gamma\acute{\epsilon}\nu\epsilon\tau o$ aus, z.B.: "Und es wurde ein schlimmes und böses Geschwür für die Menschen ..." (16,2). Die 4. und 6.

Einzelvision zeigen Variationen des Schemas: ohne καὶ ἐγένετο. Doch geht es auch hier um die Wirkung der Engelhandlung.

(IV) Die meisten Einzelvisionen sprechen dann von der Folge jener Auswirkung, z.B.: "Und jedes lebendige Lebewesen starb ..." (16,3), "und die Menschen wurden von großer Glut verbrannt ..." (16,9). Die 1. und 3. Vision läßt dieses Motiv vermissen; es stellt ja auch nur eine nähere Präzisierung des vorangehenden Formelements dar, der Auswirkung der Engelhandlung, die die Plage mit sich bringt.

(V) Abschließend wird die Reaktion der Menschen auf Auswirkung und Folge der Engelhandlung geschildert, z.B.: "Und sie (die Menschen) lästerten den Namen Gottes ... und nicht kehrten sie um ..." (16,9; ähnlich V. 11 und 21b). Dieses Element findet sich nur in der 4., 5. und 7. Vision.

Von dem aufgezeigten Formschema sind V. 13–16 nicht erfaßt. Die Verse stellen eine Erweiterung innerhalb der 6. Vision dar, die aber das Vorliegen des Grundschemas auch dort nicht in Frage stellt.

2.4.2. Wir haben die Grundstruktur bisher nur anhand der Schalenvisionen aufgewiesen. Sie findet sich in den beiden anderen Siebenerreihen nur teilweise: nämlich in der 6. und 7. Siegelvision (6,12–17 und 8,1: in erweiterter bzw. verkürzter Form), ferner in den ersten vier Posaunenvisionen (8,2.7–12), wenn auch mit einigen Variationen und unter Verzicht auf das 5. Element, das die Reaktion der Menschen enthält. Wichtig ist aber, daß oft genug die Auswirkung der Engelhandlung (bzw. des Lammes) in Element (III) durch die καὶ ἐγένετο-Formel geprägt ist, die den schöpferischen Charakter der jeweiligen Einzelhandlung durch die Mittlergestalt ausdrückt.

2.4.3. H.-P. Müller[36] hat die Herkunft des Formschemas nachzuweisen versucht. Es findet sich wohl bei der Schilderung der ägyptischen Plagen in Ex 7,8–10,29, wie ja auch inhaltlich Posaunen- und Schalenvisionen nach dem Vorbild der ägyptischen Plagen gestaltet sind. Besonders stammt von dort die Formel καὶ ἐγένετο. Sie ist in Apk 8,7.8; 16,2.3.4.10 eindeutig den Exodusberichten nachgebildet. Neu bei der Übernahme des Formschemas ist nun das Folgende: Element (I), das in Ex etwa von der Beauftragung des Mose handelt, seine Hand über den zu schädigenden Bereich auszustrekken[37], wird in der Apk zum Visionsbericht umstilisiert. Dementsprechend sind jetzt Engelwesen bzw. das Lamm die besonderen Mittlergestalten. Es stellt eine grundlegende Veränderung des ehemals vielleicht volkstümlichen Erzählschemas dar, "daß es hier für apokalyptische Visionsberichte verwendet wird, in denen Himmlische im Dienst der endzeitlichen Plagen agieren ..."[38]. Johannes gebraucht es, um die endzeitliche Durchführung

---

[36] H.-P. Müller 1960, 272–278.   [37] Ex 9,22; 10,12.21.
[38] H.-P. Müller 1960, 272.

des göttlichen Gerichtes an der Welt in visionärer Vorwegnahme darzustellen. Dabei zeigt die Benutzung der καὶ-ἐγένετο-Formel, daß hier jeweils Einzelaspekte dieses Gerichtsprozesses als reales, nicht nur symbolisches Geschehen gemeint sind. In den Plagen erfährt die gottlose Welt wirkliche Vernichtung: Es "werden" Hagel und Feuer, gelangen auf die Erde und vernichten den 3. Teil des Landes; der 3. Teil der Gewässer "wird" zu Wermut, und viele Menschen sterben an dem bitter gewordenen Wasser (Apk 8,7–11). In antithetischer Entsprechung zum Schöpferhandeln Gottes in Gen 1 – vgl. nur 1,3: "Und Gott sprach: Es werde Licht. Und es ward Licht." – stellt Johannes in detaillierten Einzelaktionen die endzeitliche Vernichtung der gottlosen Welt dar.

3. Zur Frage literarischer Vorlagen innerhalb der Visionszyklen

Im folgenden wollen wir uns dem weiteren Problemkreis zuwenden, der Frage nämlich, wie der komplizierte Aufbau immer neuer Visionsreihen des apokalyptischen Hauptteils möglicherweise auch literarisch zu erklären ist. Greift der Verfasser etwa auf bereits geformte Vorlagen zurück, wenn er nicht nur im Anschluß an die Visionsreihe der Öffnung der sieben Siegel (6,1–8,1) die sieben Posaunen- und Schalenvisionen anfügt, sondern auch Visionsstücke einbaut, die keine endzeitlichen Plagenreihen enthalten, sondern das Wirken satanischer Mächte in der Gegenwart der Kirche genauer deuten (vgl. 11; besonders 12–13)? Damit sind in sich relativ geschlossene Einheiten genannt, die der Verfasser jedoch kunstvoll und überlegt einander zuordnet. Die Frage drängt sich auf, ob hinter der besonderen Abfolge immer neuer Visionsberichte nur ein theologischer Plan des Gesamtverfassers steht oder ob ihn die Absicht, vorhandenes Traditionsmaterial in seine Komposition einzubauen, zu dieser "barocken" Gesamtform zwingt. Wir wollen uns jetzt nur der zweiten Möglichkeit zuwenden, ohne daß die schriftstellerische Gestaltungsabsicht des Autors gemindert werden soll. Allerdings werden wir keinen Versuch der Quellenscheidung unternehmen, da dieses Referat dazu keinen Raum gibt. Im übrigen gilt immer noch das Urteil R. Bultmanns: "Mir scheint es methodisch geboten zu sein, für die Analyse der Apk mit schriftlichen Quellen zu rechnen, freilich ohne die Zuversicht, daß wir sie sicher rekonstruieren können"[39]. Doch gibt es eine Möglichkeit, den Umgang des Verfassers mit literarischen Vorlagen deutlich zu machen, ohne daß umfängliche literarkritische Operationen nötig sind. Es geht hier um das merkwürdige Zwischenstück Kap. 10, das zusammen mit 11,1–13 die Reihe der sieben Posaunen unterbricht.

---

[39] R. Bultmann 1927, 506.

3.1. Kap. 10 erscheint auf den ersten Blick als Konglomerat unzusammenhängender Elemente, weshalb hier früher literarkritische Scheidungen beliebt waren. Nichtsdestoweniger wird es sich als einheitliche Komposition des Endverfassers erweisen. Zwei inhaltliche Elemente dieses Textes sind hier zu diskutieren. Zunächst erscheint in 10,1–3a ein "anderer gewaltiger Engel", der in seiner Hand ein geöffnetes "Büchlein" hält und mit lauter Stimme wie ein Löwe brüllt. Diese Schilderung wird jedoch jäh unterbrochen durch neue Szenen, ehe denn wieder vom geöffneten "Buch" in der Hand des gewaltigen Engels die Rede ist (10,8–10). Die erste dieser Szenen soll uns besonders interessieren (10,3b–4):

> "Und als er rief, erhoben die sieben Donner ihre Stimmen. Und als die sieben Donner geredet hatten, wollte ich schreiben. Da hörte ich eine Stimme vom Himmel sprechen: Versiegle, was die sieben Donner geredet haben, und schreibe es nicht auf!"

Die sieben Donner werden mit bestimmtem Artikel als eine offenbar bekannte Größe eingeführt, anschließend aber nicht mehr erwähnt. Was mit ihnen gemeint ist, erscheint zunächst rätselhaft. Jedenfalls genügt der bloße Verweis auf Ps 29,3–9 noch nicht, wo die donnernde Stimme Jahwes siebenmal erwähnt wird. Ansonsten ist die Szene klar. Der Seher erhält das Verbot der Niederschrift dessen, was er bei den sieben Donnern gehört hat.

3.1.1. Wahrscheinlich sind diese sieben Donner parallel zu den sieben Posaunen oder den sieben Schalen zu sehen (8,2–11,19 und 16). Wie jene jeweils sieben endzeitliche Plagen enthalten, so wird es auch bei den sieben Donnern der Fall sein. Bestimmte Plagenreihen will und darf der Seher in seinem Buch veröffentlichen, andere wie die sieben Donner offensichtlich nicht. Möglicherweise enthielt diese Donnerreihe eine eschatologische Ausdeutung jener donnernden Stimmen Jahwes aus Ps 29,3–9, aber diese Erklärung wird eine Vermutung bleiben. Immerhin haben diese Beobachtungen ein Verständnis des Textes angebahnt, wie es schon W. Bousset und andere vor ihm vertreten haben. Die Erwähnung der sieben Donner hat danach einen literarischen Grund. Der Apokalyptiker wollte "eine Quelle, welche sieben Donnervisionen enthielt, absichtlich aus dem Rahmen seines apokalyptischen Werkes ausschließen ... Oder es wäre möglich, daß der Apok. mit dem Intermezzo hat ausdrücken wollen, daß er selbst im Begriff gewesen sei, von neuem ein Siebenzeichen einzuschieben, daß er aber vom göttlichen Geist eines Besseren belehrt sei"[40]. Wenn diese Deutung stimmt, erhalten wir einen Einblick in die Werkstatt des Apokalyptikers. Bestimmte Traditionsstücke kann und will er in sein Werk aufnehmen, andere nicht.

---

[40] W. Bousset 1906, 309.

3.1.2. Diese These findet ihre Bestätigung, wenn wir uns der Erwähnung jenes "Büchleins" in der Hand des gewaltigen Engels zuwenden (10,1–3a.8–10). Dieselbe himmlische Stimme, die dem Seher Johannes verbot, die sieben Donnerstimmen aufzuschreiben, erteilt ihm danach den Auftrag, das Buch im Anschluß an Ez 3,1 ff. zu verzehren. Das "Büchlein" schmeckt zwar im Mund süß wie Honig, im Magen aber wirkt es bitter. Damit wird auf den doppelten Charakter seines Inhaltes angespielt. Mit Recht wird dieser in Kap. 11,1–13 gesehen, und gerade hier ist noch heute zugestanden, daß der Verfasser Quellenstücke verwandt hat (11,1–2 und 11,3–13)[41].

In 10,11 schließlich erhält der Seher Johannes einen erneuten Auftrag (πάλιν!)[41a]. Er muß wiederum weissagen, und zwar über Völker, Nationen, Sprachen und viele Könige. Diese Mitteilung weist über den Inhalt des "Büchleins" weit hinaus. Es geht um die Vorausschau auf die folgenden Visionen, die sich gerade auf Völker und viele Könige beziehen (besonders Kap. 13; 17–18). Wie besonders an dem Gegensatz, die "sieben Donner" nicht aufzuschreiben und das "Büchlein" statt dessen zu "essen", deutlich wird, so wird auch bei 10,11 erkennbar, wie der Apokalyptiker darüber Rechenschaft ablegt, was er an Ausführungen aufnimmt, was nicht. Er fällt damit aus seiner Rolle als bloß berichtender Seher heraus. Unter der Fiktion von Visionen und Auditionen gibt er darüber Auskunft, was Teil seines Gesamtwerkes wird oder was er ausläßt[42].

3.2. Angesichts dieses Tatbestandes stellt sich die Frage, welcher Grund ihn zu diesem Verfahren nötigt. Vor welchem Forum will der Verfasser über seine Gestaltung Rechenschaft ablegen? Denn der betonte Hinweis auf die himmlische Aufforderung, dieses nicht aufzuschreiben, jenes aber zu bringen, hat wohl sicher Legitimationsfunktion vor einer Instanz. Zunächst einmal wird man natürlich geneigt sein, allgemein an die Leser in den sieben angeschriebenen Gemeinden der Asia zu denken. Doch befriedigt diese Auskunft bei näherem Zusehen nicht recht.

---

[41] Vgl. besonders J. Wellhausen 1907, 15; heutzutage E. Lohse 1979, 64–67.

[41a] Die Beauftragung in Apk 10,11 ist wohl auch deshalb nicht mit der von 10,8 (Essen des geöffneten Buches) zu identifizieren, da in 10,11 eine Änderung des Auftraggebers vorliegt (V. 8: "die Stimme, die ich aus dem Himmel hörte" – V. 11: "und *sie* sagen zu mir …").

[42] W. Bousset 1906, 309.314 f. Die rein literarische Erklärung von Apk 10,3b–4 durch Bousset u. a. wurde etwa von R. H. Charles 1920, 261 f.; E. Lohmeyer 1953, 85, bestritten. Beide interpretieren das Verbot, die Stimmen der Donner aufzuschreiben, mit Blick auf die angebliche Parallele IIKor 12,4: Paulus "hörte unsagbare Worte, die einem Menschen nicht erlaubt sind auszusprechen". Doch paßt diese Parallele nicht. Johannes spricht in seinem Werk sonst nie von solchen "Mysterien", die nur ihm als Propheten bekannt sein dürfen. Ihm kommt es sonst vielmehr gerade auf die Kundgabe des "Mysteriums Gottes" an, wie schon der unmittelbare Kontext Apk 10,5–7 beweist (vgl. auch 22,10). Das Zurückhalten der sieben Donner durch die Himmelsstimme hat eher theologisch-kompositorische Gründe: Johannes rechtfertigt, warum er diese endzeitliche Visionenreihe aufnimmt, jene nicht.

3.2.1. Ein Blick auf den Schlußrahmen des Buches 22,6–21 kann uns vielleicht einer differenzierteren Lösung näherbringen. Dieser hat als Ganzer die Funktion, die Ausführungen des Verfassers vor den Adressaten zu legitimieren. Das wird schon in V. 6 deutlich (vgl. 1,1):

"Und er (Christus) sprach zu mir: Diese Worte sind zuverlässig und wahr, und der Herr, der Gott der Geister der Propheten hat seinen Engel gesandt, um seinen Knechten zu zeigen, was in Kürze geschehen muß."

Hier sind Propheten erwähnt; daß diese eine besondere Gruppe im Umkreis des Johannes sind, zeigt der Fortgang in V. 9, wo zwischen den "Brüdern" des Johannes, den Propheten, und jenen unterschieden wird, die die "Worte dieses Buches" bewahren. Apk 22,16 dürfte diese Beobachtung bestätigen:

"Ich, Jesus, habe meinen Engel gesandt, um euch dieses über[43] die Gemeinden zu bezeugen."

Betont wird ein erster Adressatenkreis, "ihr", von den Gemeinden unterschieden. Aus dem Gesamtzusammenhang des Schlußrahmens meint diese von den Gemeinden geschiedene Gruppe am ehesten jene Propheten, deren Bruder Johannes ist[44]. Der Schlußrahmen hat die Funktion der Beglaubigung des ganzen Buches als himmlische Offenbarungsschrift (22,6f.8ff.). Dabei wendet sich der Verfasser letztendlich an alle Leser bzw. Hörer seines Buches. Die fragliche Stelle 22,16 jedoch richtet sich nicht direkt an die Gemeinden, sondern an den Kreis, den er in der 2. Person ("euch") gesondert anredet. Hier bietet der Verfasser Jesus selbst als Offenbarungsursprung auf, um seine Schrift vor dem Forum seiner "Brüder", der Propheten, als himmlisch autorisiert zu legitimieren. Wir stoßen damit auf die Existenz eines apokalyptisch-prophetischen Kreises, zu dem Johannes gehört[45]. Wahrscheinlich hat der Verfasser schon in Kap. 10 diesen Prophetenkreis im Auge, vor dem er die Vernachlässigung der sieben Donnerreihen begründet und die literarische Aufnahme des "Büchleins" (Inhalt: Kap. 11) legitimiert. Diese Propheten sind möglicherweise

---

[43] Μαρτυρῆσαι ἐπί ist hier analog 10,11 προφητεῦσαι ἐπί zu verstehen, W. Bousset 1906, 166.

[44] E. Lohmeyer 1953, 180f.; D. Hill 1971/72, 413; E. Schüssler Fiorenza 1977, 425. Abgelehnt wird diese Deutung von A. Satake 1966, 24f.: "Ὑμῖν bezieht sich vielmehr auf die Gemeindeglieder schlechthin, für die der Verfasser dieses Buch schreibt." Es ist aber sehr fraglich, ob diese Interpretation der doch vorhandenen Differenzierung zwischen "euch" und den Gemeinden gerecht wird. Die direkte Anrede "euch" findet sich sonst nur in den Sendschreiben, immer bezogen auf konkrete Gemeindeglieder einer bestimmten Gemeinde bzw. einem Teil derselben (2,13.24), nicht aber auf die Christen überhaupt.

[45] Diese Folgerung gilt auch, wenn 22,16 nicht jene Propheten im Blick haben sollte. Ihre Existenz scheint durch 22,9 (vgl. 19,10) gesichert zu sein, so auch A. Satake 1966, 57–63.73; vgl. E. Schüssler Fiorenza 1977, 424f. Ich modifiziere damit meine Meinung, die ich in U. B. Müller 1976, 31f., vertreten habe.

auch in 10,7 gemeint: Ihnen ist das "Geheimnis Gottes" verkündet, daß nämlich "keine Zeit mehr ist", vielmehr beim Ertönen der siebten Posaune der endzeitliche Geschichtsplan Gottes sich vollenden wird. Diese ganz "neue" Botschaft ist Verkündigung für die Gegenwart des Verfassers, wie wohl auch der Engel in 10,5 f. sie als neue Offenbarung feierlich beschwört. Nicht schon die alttestamentlichen Propheten hat der Verfasser hier im Blick, sondern christliche Propheten wie er, denen die "neue" Botschaft vom nahen Ende aufgetragen ist[46].

3.2.2. Sind nun diese Propheten des nahen Endes in 10,7 gemeint, zu denen Johannes gehört (vgl. 1,3; 3,11; 22,7.10.12.20), so wird er sie auch im unmittelbaren Kontext ansprechen, wenn er mit Verweis auf die Himmelsstimme die sieben Donner nicht aufschreibt, was wir als Auslassung einer Siebenerreihe von Donnervisionen zu deuten versuchten. Die apokalyptisch stilisierte und gewissermaßen verschlüsselte Rechtfertigung seines literarischen Vorgehens in 10,4 bzw. 10,11 paßt im übrigen eher gegenüber von Gleichgesinnten, die wie Johannes im selben apokalyptischen "Traditionsbetrieb" stehen als gegenüber der Öffentlichkeit der Gemeinden, die in manchen Strömungen sich ganz anderer theologischer Herkunft verdankt[47].

3.2.3. Bei der Betrachtung des Schlußrahmens sind wir auf die Existenz eines Prophetenkreises gestoßen, zu dem Johannes zählt und vor dem er

---

[46] Zu berücksichtigen ist hier W. Boussets Deutung: "Es sind jedenfalls nicht alttestamentliche Propheten gemeint, die Berufung auf diese liegt dem Seher ganz fern. Der Seher hat vielmehr christliche, mindestens zeitgenössische Propheten und Prophetinnen vor Augen, er meint sich und seinesgleichen. Es ist überdies interessant, wie er sich selbst bewußt ist, im Namen eines ganzen Kreises, einer Klasse zu sprechen, er verarbeitet ja in seinem Werk eine ganze prophetische Literatur." 1906, 311. Vgl. auch D. Hill 1971/72, 407. Die in 10,7b vorliegende freie Verwendung von Am 3,7 legt noch nicht den Bezug auf alttestamentliche Propheten nahe, da der ursprüngliche Sinn des alttestamentlichen Textes nicht über die Bedeutung hier entscheidet.

Würden in Apk 10,7 altt. Propheten gemeint sein, widerspräche der Text einer verbreiteten Meinung, nach welcher die alttestamentlichen Propheten zwar auf das Ende hin verkündigten, den Zeitpunkt des Endes aber selbst nicht kannten (1QpHab 7,1–5; vgl. Targ. Koh 1,8 [Bill III, 762]; IPetr 1,10–12). Das spricht dafür, daß Apk 10,7 christliche Propheten meint, denen wie dem Lehrer der Gerechtigkeit in der Qumrangemeinde das Geheimnis des Endes offenbart ist.

[47] U. B. Müller, 1976, 21–26.39 f.; vgl. schon vorher E. Schüssler Fiorenza 1973, 567–574. Die Gemeinden der Sendschreiben unterscheiden sich hinsichtlich ihres Gemeinde- bzw. Amtsverständnisses und besonders ihrer Eschatologie von der Position des Sehers Johannes.

Die Gemeinden von Sardes und Laodizea sind von präsentischem Heilsbewußtsein durchdrungen. Dafür spricht etwa Apk 3,1: "Du hast den Namen, daß du *lebst* ..." und 3,17: "... du sagst: Ich bin reich, reich geworden und habe nichts not ..." Die Überzeugung bereits gegenwärtigen Lebens und erlangter Vollendung prägt diese Gemeinden (vgl. IKor 4,8), was Johannes im Gegenzuge scharf geißelt, weil dieses Bewußtsein für ihn mit dem Mangel an Werken gekoppelt ist (3,1 f.15–17). Was Thyatira betrifft, so verbindet sich dort bei den Anhängern der "Isebel" ein besonderer Erkenntnisstand (2,24) mit sittlicher Freizügigkeit (2,20); vgl. IKor 2,10.

über die Abfassung seiner apokalyptischen Schrift Rechenschaft ablegt. Gleichzeitig drängt sich der Schluß auf, daß in diesem Kreis apokalyptische Traditionsstücke überliefert oder auch verfaßt wurden. Die hypothetisch angenommene Reihe von Sieben-Donner-Visionen müßte in diesem Bereich tradiert worden sein, ähnlich wie anderes Überlieferungsmaterial, das der Apokalypse des Johannes zugrunde liegt, ohne daß wir jeweils genauen Aufschluß über den Umfang einer solchen literarischen Vorlage erzielen können.

Bibliographie

Andresen, C. 1965: "Zum Formular frühchristlicher Gemeindebriefe", in: *ZNW* 56 (1965) 233–259.

Berger, K. 1974: "Apostelbrief und apostolische Rede/Zum Formular frühchristlicher Briefe", in: *ZNW* 65 (1974) 190–231.

– 1977: *Exegese des Neuen Testaments* (UTB 658), Heidelberg 1977.

Bornkamm, G. 1961: "Das Anathema in der urchristlichen Abendmahlsliturgie", in: ders., *Das Ende des Gesetzes*, GAufs. I, 3. Aufl., München 1961, 123–132.

Bousset, W. 1906: *Die Offenbarung Johannis* (KEK XVI), 6. Aufl., Göttingen 1906 (Nachdruck 1966).

Bultmann, R. 1927: Rezension von E. Lohmeyer, Die Offenbarung des Johannes (HNT 16), 1926, in: *ThLZ* 52 (1927) 505–512.

Charles, R. H. 1920: *A Critical and Exegetical Commentary on the Revelation of StJohn* (ICC; 2 volumes), Edinburgh 1920.

Collins, J. J. 1977: "Pseudonymity, Historical Reviews and the Genre of the Revelation of John", in: *CBQ* 39 (1977) 329–343.

– (Hrsg.) 1979: *Apocalypse: The Morphology of a Genre* (Semeia 14), Missoula, Mont., 1979.

Dibelius, M. 1975: *Geschichte der urchristlichen Literatur* (TB 58), München 1975 (Neudruck der Ausgabe 1926).

Hahn, F. 1971: "Die Sendschreiben der Johannesapokalypse", in: G. Jeremias/H.-W. Kuhn/ H. Stegemann (Hrsg.), *Tradition und Glaube*, Festgabe K. G. Kuhn, Göttingen 1971, 357–394.

– 1975: "Die Rede von der Parusie des Menschensohnes Markus 13", in: R. Pesch/ R. Schnackenburg/Od. Kaiser (Hrsg.), *Jesus und der Menschensohn*, Festschrift A. Vögtle, Freiburg 1975, 240–266.

– 1979: "Zum Aufbau der Johannesoffenbarung", in: *Kirche und Bibel*, Festgabe E. Schick, Paderborn 1979, 145–154.

Hill, D. 1971/72: "Prophecy and Prophets in the Revelation of StJohn", in: *NTS* 18 (1971/72) 401–418.

Jörns, K.-P. 1971: *Das hymnische Evangelium.* Untersuchungen zu Aufbau, Funktion und Herkunft der hymnischen Stücke in der Johannesoffenbarung (StNT 5), Gütersloh 1971.

Koch, K. 1970: *Ratlos vor der Apokalyptik*, Gütersloh 1970.

– in diesem Band: "Vom prophetischen zum apokalyptischen Visionsbericht".

Kümmel, W. G. 1973: *Einleitung in das Neue Testament*, 17. Aufl., Heidelberg 1973.

Lambrecht, J. 1980: "A Structuration of Revelation 4,1–22,5", in: ders. (Hrsg.), *L'Apocalypse johannique et l'Apocalyptique dans le Nouveau Testament* (BEThL LIII), Paris–Gembloux/ Leuven 1980, 77–104.

Lohmeyer, E. 1953: *Die Offenbarung des Johannes* (HNT 16), 2. Aufl., Tübingen 1953.

Lohse, E. 1979: *Die Offenbarung des Johannes* (NTD 11), 12. Aufl., Göttingen 1979.

Müller, H.-P. 1960: "Die Plagen der Apokalypse", in: *ZNW* 51 (1960) 268–278.

Müller, U. B. 1975: *Prophetie und Predigt im Neuen Testament.* Formgeschichtliche Untersuchungen zur urchristlichen Prophetie (StNT 10), Gütersloh 1975.

– 1976: *Zur frühchristlichen Theologiegeschichte*. Judenchristentum und Paulinismus in Kleinasien an der Wende vom ersten zum zweiten Jahrhundert n. Chr., Gütersloh 1976.

Nissen, A. 1967: "Tora und Geschichte im Spätjudentum", in: *NT* 9 (1967) 241–277.

Pesch, R. 1977: *Das Markusevangelium*. 2. Teil (HThK II), Freiburg/Basel/Wien 1977.

v. Rad, G. 1965: *Die Theologie des Alten Testaments*. Bd. 2, 4. Aufl., München 1965.

Rau, E. 1974: *Kosmologie, Eschatologie und die Lehrautorität Henochs*, Dissertation Hamburg 1974.

Satake, A. 1966: *Die Gemeindeordnung in der Johannesapokalypse* (WMANT 21), Neukirchen-Vluyn 1966.

Schüssler Fiorenza, E. 1973: "Apocalyptic and Gnosis in the Book of Revelation and Paul", in: *JBL* 91 (1973) 565–581.

– 1977: "The Quest for the Johannine School: The Apocalypse and the Fourth Gospel", in: *NTS* 23 (1977) 402–427.

– 1977a: "Composition and Structure of the Book of Revelation", in: *CBQ* 39 (1977) 344–366.

Vielhauer, P. 1964: "Apokalyptik des Urchristentums. Einleitung", in: E. Hennecke-W. Schneemelcher (Hrsg.), *Neutestamentliche Apokryphen* 2. Bd., 3. Aufl., Tübingen 1964, 428–454.

– 1975: *Geschichte der urchristlichen Literatur*, Berlin–New York 1975.

Weimar, P. 1973: "Formen frühjüdischer Literatur", in: Maier, J. und Schreiner, J. (Hrsg.), *Literatur und Religion des Frühjudentums*, Würzburg/Gütersloh 1973, 123–162.

Wellhausen, J. 1907: *Analyse der Offenbarung Johannis* (AGWG.PH NS 9,4), Berlin 1907.

Wengst, K. 1972: *Christologische Formeln und Lieder des Urchristentums* (StNT 7), Gütersloh 1972.

Die literarischen Gattungen der Apokalypsen von Nag Hammadi

Martin Krause

1. Zu den Nag Hammadi Texten und der Definition "Apokalypse"

Bekanntlich wird jeder, der sich mit dem Handschriftenfund von Nag Hammadi[1] befaßt, mit einer ganzen Reihe ungelöster Probleme konfrontiert. Dazu gehören die so heterogen zusammengesetzte Bibliothek, die neben den die Hauptmasse bildenden gnostischen Schriften auch einige hermetische Texte, Weisheitslehren und philosophische Schriften enthält, deren ehemaliger Besitzer außerdem unbekannt ist, und vor allem der Stand der Bearbeitung dieser Bibliothek.

1.1. Durch die 1972 bis 1977 erschienene Faksimile-Ausgabe[2] sind zwar alle 13 Codices allen Interessierten zugänglich geworden, seit Ende 1977 besitzen wir eine Übersetzung des Fundes in englischer Sprache[3]. Vom größeren Teil der Bibliothek, nämlich von 40[4] der rund 53 Traktate, liegen Ausgaben des koptischen Textes, z.T. mehrfach, vor. Dennoch kann bisher keine Ausgabe und Übersetzung als *endgültige* Textausgabe oder -übersetzung bezeichnet werden. Schuld daran sind im wesentlichen *fünf* Schwierigkeiten, die ich in der Festschrift für Hans Jonas[5] aufgeführt habe, und die ich hier kurz nennen will:

(1) Die Texte sind ins Koptische übersetzt worden, und zwar zu einer Zeit, als die Kopten noch wenig Erfahrungen mit Übersetzungen in ihre Sprache besaßen. Außerdem hat die koptische Sprache keine adäquate Ausdrucksweise für diese Texte. Es gibt daher oft mehrere Übersetzungsmöglichkeiten.

(2) Zwischen ihrer Übersetzung und den uns erhaltenen Abschriften aus der Zeit nach der Mitte des 4. Jahrhunderts liegen mehrere Jahrhunderte Überlieferungsgeschichte. Vor allem bei den nur in einer Kopie erhaltenen Traktaten müssen wir mit Schreibfehlern rechnen.

---

[1] Vgl. Krause 1978, 216–243. [2] The Facsimile Edition 1972 bis 1977.
[3] The Nag Hammadi Library in English, 1977.
[4] 35 bei Krause 1978, 227ff.; dazu VIII,2 (Scholer 1978, 4197 und 1980, 4711); IX,2 (Barc-Roberge 1980); IX, 1–3 und X (Pearson-Giversen 1981).
[5] Krause 1978, 230ff.

(3) Die in *scriptio continua* geschriebenen Texte erlauben zuweilen mehrere Worttrennungen und damit verschiedene Übersetzungsmöglichkeiten.

(4) Die in einem frühen Sahidisch mit Einschlag der Nachbardialekte verfaßten Traktate erlauben zuweilen verschiedene Übersetzungen je nach dem Verständnis einer Form als sahidisch oder nichtsahidisch, und

(5) viele Seiten weisen infolge schlechter Erhaltung Textlücken auf, deren Ergänzung mehr oder weniger hypothetisch ist, vor allem bei den nur in einer Abschrift erhaltenen Texten.

Welche dieser 5 Schwierigkeiten noch zutreffen, werde ich bei jeder Schrift, die wir besprechen, ausführen. Da im Vordergrund der bisherigen Arbeit an den Nag-Hammadi-Texten Textausgaben, Übersetzungen und Kommentare standen, traten literarkritische Untersuchungen[6] in den Hintergrund. Die bisherigen Aussagen über die literarischen Gattungen einzelner Schriften sind z. T. widersprüchlich, wie wir noch sehen werden. Der Hauptgrund besteht darin, daß die in ihrem Titel als Evangelien, Briefe u. a. bezeichneten Texte beim Vergleich mit den literarischen Gattungen des Neuen Testaments neben einigen Übereinstimmungen Unterschiede zeigen. Das hat vor allem die Untersuchung der den Titel "Evangelien" tragenden Schriften gezeigt[7]. Wie steht es mit den fünf Nag-Hammadi-Texten, deren Titel sie als "Apokalypsen" bezeichnen? Es handelt sich um die Adam-, Paulus- und die beiden Jakobusapokalypsen in Codex V und um die Petrusapokalypse in Codex VII.

1.2. Im Januar 1962 hatte Philipp Vielhauer[8] – als ihm der Inhalt dieser Texte nur aus den Angaben von Jean Doresse[9] bekannt war – formuliert: "Wieweit die 'Apokalypsen' oder andere Texte von Nag Hammadi nach Form, Stil und Inhalt in der Tradition jüdischer und christlicher Apokalyptik stehen, läßt sich beim heutigen Stand der Edition nicht sagen." In seiner 1975 erschienenen "Geschichte der urchristlichen Literatur" äußerte sich Vielhauer[10] nicht zur Petrus- und Adamapokalypse, rechnet aber die Paulusapokalypse literarisch zur Apokalyptik, nicht aber die beiden Jakobusapokalypsen.

Bevor wir zu den Apokalypsen kommen und auf die Berechtigung dieser Einteilung Vielhauers eingehen, müssen wir noch den Maßstab für unsere Untersuchungen nennen. Was verstehen wir unter der literarischen Gattung der Apokalypsen? Ich übernehme die von Ph. Vielhauer[11] formulierten Stilelemente der Apokalypsen[12]. Vielhauer nennt folgende "formale

---

[6] Krause 1978, 237 f.   [7] Krause 1975, 85.
[8] Vielhauer 1964, 421.   [9] Doresse 1958, 169–280.
[10] Vielhauer 1975, 526 f.
[11] Vielhauer 1964, 408 ff.; Vielhauer 1975, 485 ff.
[12] Vgl. auch Festugière 1944, I 309 ff.

Eigentümlichkeiten, die man als Stilelemente dieser Literaturgattung ansehen muß"[13]:

(1) Pseudonymität. Als Verfasser werden zur Erhöhung der Autorität Große der Vergangenheit genannt. Deshalb muß das Buch oft versiegelt und bis in die Gegenwart geheim gehalten werden.

(2) Visionsbericht. Die Offenbarungen werden meist als Visionen in Ekstase oder Traum, seltener als Auditionen empfangen. Der Seher wird oft in die Himmelwelt entrückt. Wenn die Offenbarung kurz vor dem Tode erfolgt, ist sie in die Form einer Abschiedsrede gekleidet. Das Geschaute sind Bilder (*Bildersprache*) aus der Natur oder Kunst, Allegorien, zu deren Entschlüsselung es eines *Offenbarungsvermittlers (angelus interpres)* bedarf, falls nicht Gott selbst tätig wird. Außerdem ist eine *Systematisierung* der Ereignisse durch Ordnungsschemata, besonders Zahlen, feststellbar.

(3) In den Apokalypsen sind eine *Reihe kleinerer Formen* anzutreffen. Neben der Darstellung der nahe bevorstehenden Schrecknisse der Endzeit und der Herrlichkeit der neuen Welt werden Geschichtsüberblicke in Futurform geboten. Die genannte Zahl der Perioden schwankt. Sie enthalten auch Jenseitsschilderungen und Thronsaalvisionen sowie Paränesen und Gebete.

2. Die Apokalypsen von Nag Hammadi

An diesen Kriterien sollen im folgenden die im Handschriftenfund von Nag Hammadi überlieferten Apokalypsen gemessen werden. Dabei ergeben sich drei Textgruppen von ungleichem Umfang:

I. Schriften, die den Titel Apokalypsen tragen,
II. Schriften, die *nicht* den Titel Apokalypsen tragen, aber Apokalypsen sind, und
III. Apokalypsen, die ein Teil größerer Schriften sind.

2.1. I. Schriften, die den Titel Apokalypsen tragen

Diese Gruppe kann noch unterteilt werden in

A. Schriften, die zu Recht den Titel Apokalypsen tragen, und
B. Schriften, die zu Unrecht den Titel "Apokalypsen" tragen.

2.1.1. Zu der *Untergruppe IA* gehören drei Apokalypsen, die den Titel zu Recht tragen:

a) die Adamapokalypse,
b) die Paulusapokalypse,
c) die Petrusapokalypse.

---

[13] Vielhauer 1975, 487.

2.1.1.1. Beginnen wir mit der *Adamapokalypse*[14].

Diese Apokalypse ist als 5. Schrift in Codex V auf den Seiten 64,1–85,32 erhalten. Der Titel "die Apokalypse des Adam" steht am Anfang (64,1) und Ende des Traktates (85,32), außerdem beginnt die Schrift mit den Worten: "Die Apokalypse, die Adam seinem Sohne Seth im 700. Jahr verkündet hat" (64,2–4). Auch im Kolophon[15] heißt es: "Das sind die Offenbarungen ($\dot{\alpha}\pi o\varkappa\dot{\alpha}\lambda\upsilon\psi\iota\varsigma$), die Adam seinem Sohn Seth offenbart hat, und sein Sohn hat sie seinem Samen erzählt. Das ist die verborgene Erkenntnis Adams, die er dem Seth gegeben hat – das ist die heilige Taufe derer, die die ewige Erkenntnis kennen – durch die Logosgeborenen und die unvergänglichen Erleuchter, die aus dem heiligen Samen hervorgegangen sind, Jesseus, Mazareus, Jessedekeus, das lebendige Wasser" (85,19–31).

Es liegen bisher drei Textausgaben[16] und mehrere Übersetzungen[17] vor. Von den eingangs genannten 5 Schwierigkeiten trifft nur noch die zuletzt genannte, die Ergänzung der Textlücken, zu, und zwar die Ergänzung der letzten 2–4 Zeilen am unteren Zeilenrand fast aller Seiten, von denen manchmal noch einzelne Buchstaben erhalten sind.

Der Text zerfällt in eine Vorgeschichte (64,5–67,14), die eigentliche Apokalypse (67,14–85,18), in die ein Exkurs (77,27–83,4) eingeschoben ist und das Kolophon (85,19–31), das wir schon kennengelernt haben. Ch. Hedrick[18] hat versucht, zwei Quellen zu unterscheiden, die später ein Redakteur harmonisiert habe. Nach F. Morard[19] hat dieser späte Redaktor sogar mehrere Quellen verarbeitet. Die bisher genannten Argumente für eine Unterscheidung mehrerer Quellen überzeugen mich nicht.

Welche Stilelemente der Apokalyptik sind feststellbar?

(1) Die Pseudonymität. Wie am Anfang der Schrift (64,2–4) zu lesen ist, will Adam in seinem 700. Jahr seinem Sohn Seth diese Lehren mitgeteilt haben. Diese Apokalypse kann auch als Abschiedsrede des Adam interpretiert werden. George MacRae[20] weist darauf hin, daß der Traktat die Form eines Testaments annimmt, weil Adam die Offenbarung seinem Sohn Seth

---

[14] Zur Adamapokalypse vgl. Scholer 1971a, 2412 ff. und die Nachträge Scholer 1971b, 2587; Scholer 1972, 2813 f.; Scholer 1973, 2985 ff.; Scholer 1975, 3472; Scholer 1977, 3882; Scholer 1978, 4163 ff.; Scholer 1979, 4394 ff.; Scholer 1981, 4858.

[15] Morard 1977, 35 unterscheidet zwei Kolophone: 85,19–22a und 85,22b–32.

[16] Böhlig und Labib 1963, 96–117 (Text und Übersetzung), 86–95 (Einleitung); Scholer 1971a, 2393; MacRae 1979, 154–195 (Text und Übersetzung), 151–153 (Einleitung); Hedrick 1980, 229–298 (Text, Übersetzung und Noten), 9–226 (Analyse).

[17] Krause 1971, 17–20 (Einführung), 21–31 (Übersetzung); Krause 1974, 13–15 (Introduction), 15–23 (Translation); Kasser 1967, 316–318 (Einführung), 318–333 (Übersetzung); The Nag Hammadi Library 1977, 256–264 (MacRae); vgl. auch A. 16.

[18] Hedrick 1977, zitiert nach Morard 1977, 35 f. A. 3. Seine Dissertation war für mich bisher nicht erreichbar. Siehe jetzt Hedrick 1980; vgl. A. 16.

[19] Morard 1977, 41.   [20] MacRae 1979, 152.

kurz vor seinem Tode erzählt. Hierzu gehört auch die Bezeichnung der Lehren als Geheimtradition (85,22 f.) und ihre Aufbewahrung auf einem hohen Berge (85,10 ff.)[21].

(2) Visions- bzw. Auditionsbericht in Form eines Traumes. Nach 65,24–66,8 und 67,14–20 geht die Apokalypse des Adam auf Offenbarungen von 3 Männern zurück, die ihm im Schlaf erschienen.

(3) Geschichtsüberblick in Futur-Form. Die eigentliche Apokalypse (67,14–85,18) mit Ausnahme des Exkurses ist ein Geschichtsüberblick in Futur-Form. Er behandelt das zukünftige Schicksal der Nachkommen des Seth und Noah in Anlehnung an das Alte Testament[22]. Hierbei werden drei Perioden unterschieden: die 1. reicht bis zur Sintflut, die 2. bis zu einem Feuer, die 3. bis zur Zeit des Autors. Gebete und Paränesen fehlen.

Die Adamapokalypse weist somit alle 3 von Vielhauer genannten Kriterien auf und kann zur Gattung der Apokalypsen gerechnet werden.

2.1.1.2. Die *Paulusapokalypse*[23]. Sie ist als 2. Schrift in Codex V auf den Seiten 17,19–24,9 erhalten. Der Titel "die Apokalypse des Paulus" steht am Anfang (17,19) und am Ende des Traktates (24,9).

Es liegen bisher zwei Textausgaben[24] und mehrere Übersetzungen[25] vor.

Problematisch ist bisher vor allem noch die Ergänzung vieler Textlücken und ganzer Zeilen, vor allem auf den Seiten 17 und 18 (17: 4 Z., 18: 6 Zeilen am unteren Blattrand). Bedauerlich ist vor allem der schlechte Erhaltungszustand des Anfangs der Apokalypse, so daß wir die Rahmenhandlung nur z. T. noch kennen.

Die Schrift kann unterteilt werden in 1. die bis S. 19,18 reichende Rahmenhandlung: Paulus auf dem Wege nach Jerusalem und 2. die anschließend vom 3. bis zum 10. Himmel führende Reise des Paulus. Während der 3. Himmel (19,23 f.) nur kurz erwähnt wird, wird das Geschehen im 4.–7. Himmel breit ausgeführt. Sehr kurz, nur auf 8 Zeilen, werden abschließend der 8. bis 10. Himmel genannt. G. MacRae[26] will von der Himmelsreise "a scene of judgement and punishment" abtrennen.

Diese Apokalypse – von Hans-Martin Schenke[27] als ein "kümmerliches Machwerk, sozusagen das Produkt eines gnostischen Schülers" bezeichnet

---

[21] Vgl. auch MacRae 1979, 152.   [22] Krause 1971, 18 f.
[23] Zur Paulusapokalypse vgl. Scholer 1971a, 2401 ff. und die Nachträge Scholer 1973, 2981 f.; Scholer 1977, 3877; Scholer 1978, 4159.
[24] Böhlig und Labib 1963, 19–26 (Text und Übersetzung), 15–18 (Einleitung); Murdock und MacRae 1979, 50–63 (Text und Übersetzung), 47–49 (Einleitung). Die letztgenannte Textausgabe unterscheidet sich gegenüber der erstgenannten u. a. auch durch andere Zeilenzählung der Seiten 17 und 18.
[25] Kasser 1969, 259–263; Erbetta 1969a, 348–351; The Nag Hammadi Library 1977, 238–241 (G. W. MacRae und W. R. Murdock); vgl. auch A. 24.
[26] Murdock und MacRae 1979, 48.
[27] Schenke 1966, 25 f.; Schenke 1965, 126; Böhlig und Labib 1963, 15 nennen den Traktat eine kleine, nicht allzu bedeutende Schrift.

– ist vielleicht aus zwei Quellen zusammengearbeitet worden. Dafür spricht weniger der von verschiedenen Kollegen als Kriterium genannte Wechsel von der 3. Person (bis 18,14; 19,18–20,3) zur 1. Person (19,10; 20,5 bis Ende)[28] als der verdorbene Text S. 20,5 ff. und der sich bis S. 21,20 anschließende Inhalt: das Geschehen im 4. Himmel, ohne daß dort die 12 Apostel genannt werden wie in allen anderen Himmeln mit Ausnahme des Siebenten.

Nach Vielhauer[29] kann diese Schrift "literarisch zur Apokalyptik gezählt werden, da sie traditionelle Elemente dieser Gattung enthält". Vielhauer dokumentiert seine Aussage nicht durch Belege. Daher müssen wir fragen: Welche Stilelemente der Apokalyptik sind feststellbar?

(1) Die Pseudonymität. Der Verfasser ist eine Größe der Vergangenheit, wenn auch nicht der weit zurückliegenden Vergangenheit wie in der Adamapokalypse und sonst in der Apokalyptik. Er benutzt die Autorität des Paulus, um eine gnostische Interpretation, d. h. Korrekturen, von Bibelstellen vorzunehmen. Es sind vor allem Act 9,26 f.: die Jünger fürchten sich vor dem nach Jerusalem gekommenen Paulus und glauben nicht, daß er ein Jünger ist. Er erzählt, wie er auf dem Wege den Herrn sah und II Kor 12,2–4: die Entrückung in den Himmel. Gegenüber dem Neuen Testament wird Paulus auf einem Berg, wo in den christlich-gnostischen Texten der Auferstandene zumeist seinen Jüngern seine Lehren mitteilt, verheißen, daß die 12 Apostel, zu denen er gehen wird, ihn willkommen heißen werden ($\dot{\alpha}\sigma\pi\dot{\alpha}\zeta\varepsilon\sigma\vartheta\alpha\iota$ 19,15–18). Außerdem führt ihn die Reise bis in den 10. Himmel.

(2) Visionsbericht. Paulus erhebt auf dem Berg von Jericho, einer Etappe des 1. Teiles der Apokalypse (19,11–13), seine Augen und sieht die Jünger, wie sie ihn willkommen heißen (19,18–20). Der 2. Teil (19,20 bis Ende) findet im 3. bis 10. Himmel statt, da Paulus vom Heiligen Geist (19,20 ff.) in den 3. Himmel entrissen wurde. Der in beiden Teilen auftretende Geist oder Heilige Geist ist als *angelus interpres* tätig.

(3) Während im 1. Teil (S. 18 unten und 19 Anfang) wegen der schlechten Texterhaltung nicht klar ist, was es mit den dort genannten $\dot{\alpha}\varrho\chi\alpha\dot{\iota}$, $\dot{\varepsilon}\xi o v\sigma\dot{\iota}\alpha\iota$, Erzengeln, Kräften und Dämonen auf sich hat, besteht der 2. Teil größtenteils aus Jenseitsschilderungen: im 4. Himmel bringen Engel eine Seele aus dem Land der Toten an das Tor des 4. Himmels und peitschen sie aus. Die Seele fragt, welche Sünden sie in der Welt getan habe, verlangt das Erscheinen von Zeugen. Es erscheinen drei, die gegen sie aussagen. Darauf wird die Seele in einen Körper geworfen (20,5–21,22).

---

[28] So: Tröger 1973, 43; Kasser 1965, 76 ff.; Böhlig und Labib 1963, 16. Murdock und MacRae 1979, 48 dagegen schreiben den Wechsel mehr literarischer Sorglosigkeit als mehreren Quellen zu.

[29] Vielhauer 1975, 527.

Im 5. Himmel sieht Paulus außer seinen Mitaposteln einen großen Engel mit einem Eisenschwert und 3 Engel, die die Seelen zum Gericht treiben (22,2–10). Im 6. Himmel erblickt er außer seinen Mitaposteln ein großes Licht (22,14–21). Im 7. Himmel sieht er einen alten Mann und – falls der Text richtig ergänzt ist – eine Thronsaalschilderung, einen Thron, der siebenmal heller als die Sonne leuchtet. Mit dem Mann entspinnt sich ein Gespräch, an dessen Ende dieser bezweifelt, daß Paulus an den ἀρχαί und ἐξουσίαι vorbeigehen kann. Der Geist empfiehlt Paulus, ihm sein Zeichen zu geben, damit er ihm den Zugang zur Ogdoas öffnet (22,25–24,1). Dort sieht Paulus nur die ihn grüßenden 12 Apostel (24,1–3). Im 9. Himmel grüßt Paulus alle dort Befindlichen (24,4–6) und im 10. Himmel seine Mitgeister (24,6–8).

Wie wir sahen, sind Stilelemente aller drei Gruppen vertreten, wenn auch nur in kleiner Anzahl. So fehlen vor allem Geschichtsüberblicke in Futurform.

K. Rudolph[30] will die Paulusapokalypse in die Gattung der gnostischen "Dialoge", auf die wir noch zu sprechen kommen werden, einreihen. Diese Zuweisung ist m. E. nicht gerechtfertigt. Im gnostischen "Dialog" findet das Gespräch nur zwischen dem "Soter" oder "Herrn" genannten erhöhten Christus und seinen Jüngern statt. In der Paulusapokalypse dagegen spricht Christus als Kleinkind (18,6.13f.) bzw. als "Geist" (18,21; 19,10ff.; 21,25f.; 23,23f.) oder "hl. Geist" (19,20f.26f.) mit bzw. nur zu Paulus – es ist oft gar kein Dialog – und Paulus spricht zum Zolleinnehmer (22,21ff.) und unterhält sich mit einem Greis (23,1ff.). Außerdem finden eine Reihe von Dialogen statt, die weder von Christus noch den Jüngern geführt werden: die Seele spricht 20,14–21,14 mit dem Zolleinnehmer (τελώνης) und den drei Zeugen. Das Gespräch findet außerdem im gnostischen Dialog nur an einem, höchstens an zwei Orten[31] statt, während in der Paulusapokalypse der Gesprächsort mehrfach wechselt: auf dem Wege nach Jerusalem, auf dem Berge von Jericho, in den verschiedenen Himmeln. Ich möchte daher die Schrift nicht zu den gnostischen Dialogen, sondern zur Gattung der Apokalypsen zählen.

2.1.1.3. Die *Petrusapokalypse*[32]. Sie ist als 3. Schrift in Codex VII auf den Seiten 70,13–84,14 erhalten. Der Titel "Apokalypse des Petrus" steht am Anfang (70,13) und Ende (84,14) in griechischer Sprache.

Es liegen bisher eine Textausgabe[33] und mehrere Übersetzungen[34] vor. Der Text ist lückenlos erhalten. Trotzdem ist er teilweise schwer zu

---

[30] Rudolph 1968, 99.   [31] Rudolph 1968, 91.

[32] Scholer 1975, 3481ff.; Scholer 1977, 3898f.; Scholer 1978, 4189ff.; Scholer 1979, 4408; Scholer 1980, 4701.

[33] Krause und Girgis 1973, 152–179.

[34] Werner 1974, 578–582; Brown und Griggs 1975, 131–145; The Nag Hammadi Library 1977, 340–345 (R. A. Bullard), Einleitung von J. Brashler 339–340; vgl. auch A. 33.

verstehen. Ursachen dafür sind die oben als Nr. 1 und 2 genannten Schwierigkeiten: die Arbeit des Übersetzers oder Abschreibers des Textes.

Eine Quellenscheidung ist noch nicht versucht worden. Die Apokalypse kann untergliedert[35] werden in 1. eine Rahmenhandlung am Anfang (70,14–73,14) mit Angabe von Ort und Personen: der Tempel von Jerusalem und der Soter und Petrus, die sich unterhalten, dazu Volk, Priester und Schriftgelehrte, 2. das Corpus der Apokalypse (73,14–80,23): eine Ankündigung der Zeit der Irrung und 3. eine abschließende Rahmenhandlung (80,23–84,13), vor allem eine gnostische Interpretation des Geschehens von Golgatha.

Stilisiert ist die Apokalypse als ein Gespräch des Soter mit Petrus, der in der 1. Pers. berichtet, das unterbrochen wird von Handlungen. Diesem Gespräch liegt nicht das Frage- und Antwortschema des gnostischen Dialogs, den wir noch kennenlernen werden, zugrunde. Vielmehr wird Petrus vom Soter aufgefordert, die Vorgänge sich genau anzusehen und anzuhören.

Welche Stilelemente der Apokalyptik sind feststellbar?

(1) Die Pseudonymität. Der Verfasser soll Petrus sein, der Erlebnisse, die – nach Koschorke[36] – etwa Matthäus 21 bis 28 entsprechen, in gnostischer Interpretation schildert und die er geheimhalten soll (73,14ff. und 83,15ff.).

(2) Visions- bzw. Auditionsbericht. Das Geschehen spielt sich nicht in Ekstase oder Traum ab. Das Geschaute sind keine Bilder, sondern ist eine Vorschau kommender Ereignisse, die aber "richtig" gesehen und gehört werden müssen. Daher wird Petrus mehrfach (z. B. 84,24.31) aufgefordert, zu sehen und zu hören (72,30f.; 73,7f. u. ö.). Der Soter ist tätig entsprechend einem *angelus interpres,* indem er Petrus das Geschaute und Gehörte erklärt.

(3) Geschichtsüberblick in Futur-Form. Der hier gebotene Überblick ist nicht so lang wie normalerweise in den Apokalypsen, denn er umfaßt nur den Zeitraum vom Passionsgeschehen bis in die Zeit des Verfassers, die Koschorke[37] an den Anfang bis Mitte des 3. Jh. setzt. Er betrifft die Auseinandersetzung der Gnosis mit der Großkirche. Auch eine Periodisierung ist nicht durchgeführt. Am Anfang der Schrift (70,15–20) liest man nach Schenke[38] eine verschlüsselte dreigliedrige Zeitangabe.

Mit einigen Bedenken[39] möchte ich diese Schrift in die Gattung der Apokalypse einreihen.

---

[35] Koschorke 1978, 11ff. (literarischer Aufbau).   [36] Koschorke 1978, 12.
[37] Koschorke 1978, 17.   [38] Schenke 1975, 131; Koschorke 1978, 19 A. 2.
[39] Nach Wilson 1978, 355 "handelt es sich nicht um eine Apokalypse des üblichen Typus, sondern um die Wiedergabe einer Offenbarung, die Petrus im Tempel zuteil wird, und zwar bemerkenswerterweise vor der Verhaftung Jesu".

2.1.2. Zu der *Untergruppe IB,* d. h. Schriften, die zu Unrecht den Titel "Apokalypsen" tragen, gehören die beiden Jakobusapokalypsen.

2.1.2.1. Die (1.) *Jakobusapokalypse*[40]. Sie ist als 3. Schrift in Codex V auf den Seiten 24,10–44,10 erhalten. Der Titel "die Apokalypse des Jakobus" steht am Anfang (24,10) – vom Schreiber später nachgetragen – und am Ende des Traktates (44,9–10).

Es liegen bisher zwei Textausgaben[41] und mehrere Übersetzungen[42] vor.

Das Textverständnis wird durch ihren schlechten Erhaltungszustand erschwert. Während auf den Seiten 25–34 mehrere Zeilen am unteren Blattrand nicht vollständig erhalten sind, fehlen auf den Seiten 35–44 oft mehrere Zeilen am oberen und unteren Blattrand.

Die Schrift zerfällt in zwei Teile: 1) 24,11–30,13 und 2) 30,13–44,8. Beide weisen je eine Rahmenhandlung an ihrem Anfang und Ende auf (24,11 und 30,11–13 bzw. 30,13–31,5 und 43,21–44,8), die Zeit und Ort der Handlung nennen: der 1. Teil spielt in Jerusalem (25,15) am Dienstag der Karwoche (25,7f.), der 2. Teil auf dem Berg Gaugelan (30,20f.) einige Tage nach Ostern (30,13–18). Während im 2. Teil neben Jesus, der ⲭⲟⲉⲓⲥ "Herr" genannt wird, und Jakobus noch "seine Jünger" (30,21f.) und eine Menge (30,27; 43,7f.) auftreten, werden im 1. Teil nur "der Herr" und Jakobus genannt. Beide Teile sind Dialoge.

R. Kasser[43] unterscheidet mehrere Quellen. Für die Verarbeitung mehrerer Quellen sprechen nicht nur die beiden Teile, in die das Werk unterteilt werden kann, sondern auch die Verwendung eines Hymnus im 1. Teil (28,7–29,3) und einer valentinianischen Quelle im 2. Teil (33,11–35,25), die wir aus Irenäus (adv. haer. I 21,5) kennen. Im 1. Teil wird (24,26f.) eine Frage des Jakobus zitiert und beantwortet, obwohl sie im Text nicht gestellt wird. Hier ist also Text verloren gegangen. Ferner sei darauf hingewiesen, daß auch der Stil von der 3. Person zur 1. Person (24,11; 25,12; 27,18) wechselt.

Welche Stilelemente der Apokalyptik sind feststellbar? Nur das der Pseudonymität. Der Verfasser benutzt die Autorität des Jakobus, des Adoptivbruders des Herrn (24,14f.), der im 1. Teil allein Empfänger einer gnostischen Sonderbelehrung wird, im 2. Teil zusammen mit anderen Jüngern. Nach 36,13ff. sollen diese Lehren geheim gehalten werden und Addai, der Begründer des syrischen Christentums, soll sie im 10. Jahre

---

[40] Scholer 1971a, 2404ff.; Scholer 1971b, 2586; Scholer 1973, 2983; Scholer 1977, 3878; Scholer 1978, 4160f.; Scholer 1980, 4675.

[41] Böhlig und Labib 1963, 34–55 (Text und Übersetzung), 27–33 (Einleitung); Schoedel 1979, 68–102 (Text und Übersetzung), 65–67 (Einleitung).

[42] Kasser 1968, 164–176; Erbetta 1969b, 333–340; The Nag Hammadi Library 1977, 242–248 (W. R. Schoedel); vgl. auch A. 41.

[43] Kasser 1965, 78f.

aufschreiben. Alle anderen Stilelemente der Apokalyptik fehlen. W. R. Schoedel[44] bezeichnet diese Abhandlung als "apocalypse in the sense that it conveys the secret teaching of the Lord to James". Sie gehört literargeschichtlich nicht zu den Apokalypsen. Vielhauer[45] hat sie nicht in die Gattung der Apokalypsen aufgenommen. Er weist sie – darin K. Rudolph[46] folgend – den gnostischen "Dialogen" zu. Rudolph[47] hat diese Literaturgattung 1968 erstmals beschrieben. Merkmale dieser Literaturgattung sind das Lehrer-Schüler-Schema (Christus als Offenbarer – die Apostel als Offenbarungsempfänger), das sich in Fragen und Antworten konkretisiert. Der Dialog ist eine künstliche Stilisierung, es fehlt eine straffe Gedankenführung. Inhalt des Gespräches sind vielfach exegetische Fragen. Rudolph[48] zählt zu ihr außer dieser Schrift von den Nag-Hammadi-Schriften, die ihm damals bekannt waren, das "Apokryphon des Johannes", die "Sophia Jesu Christi" und die "Paulusapokalypse" – letztere Zuweisung, wie ich meine (vgl. § 2.1.1.2.), zu Unrecht –, ferner das "Evangelium der Maria" aus dem Berliner Codex, die "Pistis Sophia" und die beiden Bücher "Jeu". Zu dieser Gruppe gehört vor allem noch das "Thomasbuch" in Codex II,7 und der "Dialog des Soter" in Codex III,5[49].

Der 1. Teil der Jakobusapokalypse besteht aus 7 Reden des Herrn, an die sich 6 Fragen des Jakobus anschließen, und zwar formuliert Jakobus jeweils aus einem Stichwort Jesu eine Frage. Im 2. Teil sind nur ein Teil der Reden des Jakobus Fragen. Außerdem ersetzt oft eine Handlung des Jakobus eine Rede: Jakobus betet (30,27 ff.), weint (32,13–16), wischt seine Tränen ab (30,23–28). Erst ab 38,12 spricht Jakobus und stellt Fragen. Da dieser Teil schlecht erhalten ist, kann leider nicht entschieden werden, ob die Fragen und Antworten so gut wie im 1. Teil aufeinander bezogen sind.

Der Titel "Apokalypse" für diesen Dialog könnte sich aus der mehrfachen Ankündigung des Herrn herleiten, er wolle dem Jakobus Offenbarungen zuteil werden lassen (+ΝΑϬΩΛΠ ΝΑΚ : 25,6; 26,8; 29,12; +ΝΑΟΥΩΝϨ ΝΑΚ ΕΒΟΛ   30,1 u. ö.). Vielhauer[50] widerspricht der von H. Köster[51] formulierten These, wonach die Gespräche des Auferstandenen mit seinen Jüngern aus der Gattung der Apokalypsen abzuleiten seien. Vielhauer[52] weist auf Verwandtes in beiden Gattungen hin ("Offenbarungen zukünftiger und jenseitiger, vorzeitlicher und kosmologischer Geheimnisse"), aber auch auf "wesentliche strukturelle Unterschiede"[53]: Gespräche sind für die Apokalypse nicht wesentlich, obwohl sie auch dort

---

[44] Schoedel 1979, 65.
[46] Rudolph 1968, 99.
[48] Rudolph 1968, 90.
[50] Vielhauer 1975, 690.
[52] Vielhauer 1975, 690 f.

[45] Vielhauer 1975, 527.
[47] Rudolph 1968, 85–107, bes. 89 f.
[49] Krause 1977, 16.
[51] Köster und Robinson 1971, 182 f.
[53] Vielhauer 1975, 690.

vorkommen, andererseits kommen in den gnostischen Dialogen selten Visionsberichte vor und es "fehlt das Deuten des Geschauten"[54].

2.1.2.2. Die (2.) *Jakobusapokalypse*[55]. Sie ist als 4. Schrift in Codex V auf den Seiten 44,11–63,32 erhalten. Der Titel "die Apokalypse des Jakobus" steht nur am Anfang (44,11–12). Es liegen drei Textausgaben[56] und mehrere Übersetzungen[57] vor. Das Textverständnis wird sehr durch die schlechte Texterhaltung erschwert: keine einzige Seite ist vollständig erhalten. Selbst in den 1976 bzw. 1979 erschienenen Textausgaben weichen verschiedentlich Textlesungen, -trennungen und -ergänzungen voneinander ab, obwohl die Herausgeber ihre Manuskripte ausgetauscht hatten. W.-P. Funk schlägt die meisten Textergänzungen vor, die Ch. Hedrick oft nicht übernimmt.

Die Schrift zerfällt in zwei Teile: 1. Die Apokalypse des Jakobus, die er im Tempel gehabt hat, S. 44,13–61,15 und 2. Das Martyrium des Jakobus. Jakobus steht am Eckstein bzw. der Tempelzinne S. 61,15–63,32[58].

Das Incipit nennt Ohrenzeugen und Ort der Handlung. Gleichzeitig liegt ein Widerspruch zum Titel vor: "Das ist die *Rede* (der Titel lautet "Apokalypse"), die Jakobus der Gerechte in Jerusalem gehalten hat, die Marim, einer der Priester, niedergeschrieben hat. Er hat sie dem Theudas, dem Vater dieses Gerechten, erzählt, weil er ein Verwandter von ihm war" (44,13–20). Diese Aussage kennzeichnet den kunstvoll geschachtelten Aufbau der Schrift, den Funk[59] einleuchtend beschrieben hat; denn in seinen Reden zitiert Jakobus wieder Reden Jesu.

Ein großer Teil der Abhandlung ist in Kunstprosa formuliert, worauf schon A. Böhlig[60] hingewiesen hat. Bemerkenswert sind auch eine Reihe Selbstbezeichnungen Jesu, Ich-bin-Worte (49,5–15), ferner Erlöserprädikationen durch Jakobus αὐτός ἐστιν (58,2–20) bzw. σὺ εἶ (55,15–56,13) und das Gebet des Jakobus (62,16–63,29).

Außer der Pseudonymität wie in der 1. Jakobusapokalypse sind keine Stilelemente der Apokalyptik feststellbar. Andererseits kann die Schrift auch nicht in die Gattung der gnostischen "Dialoge" eingeordnet werden. Hedrick[61] meint: "In the sense that James relates a revelation received from the resurrected Jesus, it may be called a revelation discourse." Funk[62]

---

[54] Vielhauer 1975, 691.
[55] Scholer 1971a, 2408 ff.; Scholer 1972, 2812; Scholer 1975, 3471; Scholer 1977, 3879 ff. Scholer 1978, 4162.
[56] Böhlig und Labib 1963, 66–85 (Text und Übersetzung), 56–64 (Einleitung); Funk 1976, 10–49 (Text und Übersetzung); Hedrick 1979, 110–149 (Text und Übersetzung).
[57] Kasser 1968, 177–186; Erbetta 1969c, 341–347; The Nag Hammadi Library 1977, 249–255 (Hedrick); vgl. auch A. 56.
[58] Funk 1976, 193–198: literarkritische Analyse.
[59] Funk 1976, 11.   [60] Böhlig und Labib 1963, 57.
[61] Hedrick 1979, 106.   [62] Funk 1976, 196.

urteilt: "Obwohl sie ihrem äußeren Rahmen nach mehr zur Gattung der Apostelgeschichte neigt, ist sie doch ihrem Zentrum nach eine echte (nur gleichsam doppelt historisch verpackte) Offenbarungsschrift." Vielhauer[63] meint, beide Jakobusapokalypsen tragen ihren Titel, weil "sie soteriologische und christliche Geheimnisse und Gnosis offenbaren, weil sie Offenbarungsreden sind". Der Titel "Apokalypse" könnte sich – wie schon bei der (1.) Jakobusapokalypse – aus der vierfachen Ankündigung herleiten, er wolle dem Jakobus Offenbarungen zuteil werden lassen: ЄΙϹ ϨΗΗΤЄ ϮΝΑϬѠΛП (bzw.) ОΥѠΝϨ ΝΑΚ ЄΒОΛ (56,17 f.20 f.; 57,4 f.8 f.), ohne daß diese Offenbarungen dann genannt werden (vgl. auch ОΥѠΝϨ ЄΒОΛ 49,21 f.; 55,5.21; ϬѠΛП ЄΒОΛ 46,7).

2.2. II. Schriften, die **nicht** den Titel Apokalypsen tragen, aber Apokalypsen sind

2.2.1. In diese Gruppe gehört die 4. Schrift in Codex VI, die die Seiten 36,1–48,15 einnimmt. Sie hat drei verschiedene Titel, zwei am Anfang (36,1–2) und einen nachgestellten (48,14–15), *"der Gedanke unserer großen Kraft"*[64], nach dem die Schrift allgemein zitiert[65] wird.

Es liegen bisher zwei Textausgaben[66] und mehrere Übersetzungen[67] vor.

Der Text ist mit Ausnahme von zwei Stellen am oberen Blattrand von Seite 47/48 gut erhalten. Trotzdem gibt er für das Verständnis große Rätsel[68] auf, die dem Übersetzer[69] und verschiedenen Quellen[70], die in dieser Schrift verarbeitet worden sein sollen, aber noch nicht herausgearbeitet worden sind[71], angelastet werden.

Unbestritten ist die Bezeichnung der Schrift als Apokalypse[72]. Gründe hierfür wurden bisher noch nicht genannt. Daher müssen wir fragen, welche Stilelemente der Apokalyptik sind feststellbar?

(1) Pseudonymität. Ein Verfasser wird nicht genannt. Er ist verschie-

---

[63] Vielhauer 1975, 527.

[64] Scholer 1978, 4178.

[65] Vgl. Krause 1978, 235 und A. 149.

[66] Krause und Labib 1971, 150–165 (Text und Übersetzung); Wisse und Williams 1979, 293–323 (Text und Übersetzung).

[67] Fischer 1973, 170–175; The Nag Hammadi Library 1977, 285–289 (Wisse); vgl. auch A. 66.

[68] Tröger 1973, 50.

[69] Fischer 1973, 169.

[70] Fischer 1973, 169 f.; Wisse und Williams 1979, 291 f.

[71] Wisse und Williams 1979, 292: "complex literary history".

[72] Colpe 1972, 13 f.: "eine richtige Apokalypse"; Tröger 1973, 50: "eine gnostische Apokalypse"; Rudolph 1977, 51: "eine gnostische Apokalypse"; Wisse und Williams 1979, 292: "a Christian gnostic apocalypse or else a Christian apocalypse with gnosticizing features".

den[73] von der ersten und obersten Gottheit, "unserer großen Kraft", die oft als in der 1. Person sprechend zitiert wird[74].

(2) Es liegt weder ein Visionsbericht noch ein Auditionsbericht vor. Die Hörer oder Leser werden zwar zuweilen aufgefordert, zu sehen (37,24), öfter aber wird ihnen verheißen, daß sie "sehen werden" (36,25; 47,31). Es wird an ihre Erkenntnis appelliert (37,6.24). Bereits am Anfang der Schrift lesen wir: "wer unsere große Kraft erkennen wird, wird unsichtbar werden. Und kein Feuer wird ihn verbrennen können. Und er wird rein sein... und erlöst werden" (36,3ff.).

Mehrfach werden Zahlen genannt, deren Bedeutung nur z. T. einsichtig ist: "von 7 Tagen bis 120 Jahren" (36,11f.), 120 Jahre (38,27f. und 43,19), 72 Sprachen (41,6), 1468 Jahre (46,28)[75].

(3) Geschichtsüberblicke. Die Geschichte wird in drei Äonen eingeteilt. Der erste ist der fleischliche Äon Noahs (38,13f.), der durch die Sintflut zerstört wird (bis 39,15; vgl. auch 41,1f.; 43,14ff.). Der zweite Äon ist der seelische Äon (39,16ff.; 40,24f.; 43,13f.). In ihm erscheint der Retter, wohl Jesus. Der dritte Äon ist der "kommende Äon" (40,32f.). Diese Geschichtsüberblicke werden aber nicht durchgehend in Futurform geboten, sondern Futurformen wechseln mit Vergangenheitsformen ab. Während C. Colpe[76] vermutet, daß mehr "Anspielungen – auf Makkabäerkriege vom nichtjüdischen Standpunkt oder auf den jüdischen Krieg gegen die Römer vom Standpunkt eines neuen pneumatischen Israel aus? – angerührt als wirklich geschildert" werden, sehen die Mitglieder des Berliner Arbeitskreises[77] und K. Rudolph[78] Hinweise auf den jüdischen Krieg 66–73 n. Chr. Mehrfach lesen wir auch Paränesen (36,27ff. u. ö., vor allem 40,1ff.). Die Zuweisung in die Literaturgattung der Apokalypsen ist somit wohl gerechtfertigt.

2.2.2. Nicht sicher bin ich, ob hier eine Schrift angeschlossen werden kann, die unserem Verständnis noch größere Schwierigkeiten als die eben besprochene bereitet. Es ist die 1. Abhandlung in Codex VII, die die Seiten 1,1–49,9 einnimmt und den vorangestellten Titel *"die Paraphrase des Sêem"*[79] (1,1) trägt.

Bisher liegen eine Textausgabe[80] und zwei Übersetzungen[81] vor. Der Text ist sehr gut erhalten, gibt uns aber hermeneutische Probleme auf, die

---

[73] Das zeigt z. B. die Rahmenhandlung 36,3ff., wo von der großen Kraft in 3. Person gesprochen wird, vgl. auch 47,11f. und 47,33f., wo die große Kraft angerufen wird.

[74] Wisse und Williams 1979, 259f. Kommentar zu 36,9 vermuten, daß der Sprecher mit der großen Kraft identisch ist.

[75] Vgl. Colpe 1972, 14 und A. 36.   [76] Colpe 1972, 13.

[77] Tröger 1973, 51.   [78] Rudolph 1977, 215.

[79] Scholer 1971b, 2588; Scholer 1977, 3893ff.; Scholer 1978, 4186f.; Scholer 1979, 4407.

[80] Krause 1973, 2–105 (Text und Übersetzung).

[81] The Nag Hammadi Library 1977, 309–328 (F. Wisse); vgl. auch A. 80.

nicht durch den antiken Übersetzer und wohl auch nicht durch Verarbeitung verschiedener Quellen verursacht worden sind.

Die Abhandlung enthält auch Stilelemente der Apokalyptik:

(1) Pseudonymität. Der Offenbarer nennt sich in der Rahmenhandlung Derdekeas, Sohn des vollkommenen Lichtes (1,4). Offenbarungsempfänger ist Sêem, der "Zuerst-Seiende auf Erden" (1,18ff.).

(2) Visions- bzw. Auditionsbericht. Die Offenbarung soll durch eine Entrückung des Denkens des Sêem aus dem Körper in die Höhe der Schöpfung in die Nähe des Lichtes wie im Schlafe (1,6ff.) vermittelt worden sein. Dabei hört Sêem auch eine Stimme (1,17). Zweimal (41,21f. und 47,9f.) wird später gesagt, Sêem habe sich wie von einem tiefen Schlaf erhoben. Das Gehörte und Geschaute sind keine Bilder, sondern verschlüsselte Geschehnisse aus Natur und Bibel, sicher des Alten, wohl auch des Neuen Testaments, die nicht entschlüsselt werden.

(3) Die Paraphrase enthält eine Reihe kleinerer Formen: Paränesen (32,19ff.), Gebete (8,17; 13,25.35) und Makarismen (40,8ff.; 47,16ff.). Manche Ereignisse werden in Futur-Form berichtet (26,8ff.), darunter auch apokalyptische Ereignisse (z. B. 29,33ff. und 43,31–45,31).

2.3. III. *Apokalypsen, die ein Teil größerer Schriften sind*

In diese Gruppe, auf die ich zum Schluß hinweisen möchte, gehört:

2.3.1. Die *Apokalypse des Asklepius*[82], die in Codex VI die Seiten 70,3 bis 74,17 einnimmt und Teil der 8. Abhandlung des Codex ist, die von S. 65,15 bis 78,43 reicht. Inhaltlich entspricht sie dem hermetischen Asclepius 21 Mitte bis 29. Auf diesen Text gehe ich nicht ein[83], weil ich annehme, daß er von Kollegen hier behandelt werden wird[84].

2.3.2. Die Apokalypse in der Schrift ohne Titel in Codex II[85], für die sich die Bezeichnung *"Vom Ursprung der Welt"*[86] eingebürgert hat. Diese Schrift, die früher als Ganzes für eine Apokalypse gehalten wurde, umfaßt die Seiten 97,24 bis 127,17, die Apokalypse bildet den Schluß. Sie reicht von Seite 126,32 bis 127,17. M. Tardieu[87] hat sie unter dem Titel "le temps eschatologique" auf den Seiten 74–83 seiner Abhandlung über drei gnostische Mythen eingehend behandelt und kommentiert.

2.3.3. In der die *"dreigestaltige Protennoia"*[88] betitelten, in Codex XIII Seite 35–50 erhaltenen Schrift wird die Zeit der Vollendung S. 43,4–44,29

---

[82] Scholer 1975, 3479; Scholer 1978, 4184f.

[83] Vgl. Krause 1969, 48–57.

[84] Vgl. in diesem Band Assmann §§1.4. und 4.3., Griffiths §7.5. und Kippenberg §1.1.3.

[85] Scholer 1971a, 2359ff.; Scholer 1971b, 2582; Scholer 1972, 2811; Scholer 1975, 3467f.; Scholer 1977, 3852f.; Scholer 1978, 4135f.; Scholer 1979, 4386; Scholer 1981, 4852f.

[86] Tröger 1973, 35.   [87] Tardieu 1974, 74–83.

[88] Scholer 1975, 3486f.; Scholer 1978, 4211f.; Scholer 1979, 4417; Scholer 1980, 4715.

beschrieben. Sie weist nach J. Turner[89] Parallelen zur synoptischen Apokalypse Markus 13 und Par. und I Kor 15 auf.

Ich hoffe sehr, daß dieses Kolloquium zu allgemein akzeptierten Definitionen der Apokalyptik – auch ihrer Stilelemente[90] – führen wird, wie dies
1966 in Messina in bezug auf die Begriffe Gnosis und Gnostizismus
geschehen ist.

Bibliographie

Attridge, Harold W. 1979: "Greek and Latin Apocalypses", in: *Semeia* 14 (1979) 159–186.

Barc, Bernard und Roberge, Michel 1980: *L'Hypostase des Archontes. Traité gnostique sur
l'origine de l'homme du monde et des archontes (NH II,4) par B. Barc suivi de Noréa (IX,2) par M.
Roberge* (BCdNH.T 5) Louvain/Québec 1980.

Böhlig, Alexander und Labib, Pahor 1963: *Koptisch-gnostische Apokalypsen aus Codex V von
Nag Hammadi im Koptischen Museum zu Alt-Kairo,* Halle-Wittenberg 1963.

Brown, Scott Kent und Griggs, C. Wilfred 1975: "The Apocalypse of Peter. Introduction and
Translation", in: *BYUS* 15 (1975) 131–145.

Collins, John J. 1979: "Towards the Morphology of a Genre", in: *Semeia* 14 (1979) 1–20.

Colpe, Carsten 1972: "Heidnische, jüdische und christliche Überlieferung in den Schriften aus
Nag Hammadi I", in: *JAC* 15 (1972) 5–18.

Doresse, Jean 1958: *Les livres secrets des gnostiques d'Egypte,* Paris 1958.

Erbetta, M. 1969a: L'apocalisse gnostica di Paolo (II sec.), lettere e apocalissi (*Gli apocrifi del
Nuovo Testamento: versione e commento,* Vol. III; Marietti 1969) 348–351.

– 1969b: La I apocalisse di Giacomo (II. sec.), lettere e apocalissi (*Gli apocrifi del Nuova
Testamento: versione e commento,* Vol. III; Marietti 1969) 333–340.

– 1969c: La II apocalisse di Giacomo (II. sec.), lettere e apocalissi (*Gli apocrifi del Nuovo
Testamento: versione e commento,* Vol. III; Marietti 1969) 341–347.

Fallon, Francis T. 1979: "The Gnostic Apocalypses", in: *Semeia* 14 (1979) 123–158.

Festugière, André-Jean 1944: *La révélation d'Hermès Trismégiste* I, Paris 1944.

Fischer, Karl Martin 1973: "Der Gedanke unserer großen Kraft (Noēma). Die vierte Schrift
aus Nag Hammadi Codex VI", in: *ThLZ* 98 (1973) 169–176.

Funk, Wolf-Peter 1976: *Die zweite Apokalypse des Jakobus aus Nag Hammadi Codex V* (TU
119), Berlin 1976.

Hedrick, Charles W. 1972: "The Apocalypse of Adam: a literary and source analysis", in:
SBL-Proceedings 1972, Vol. 2, Los Angeles 1972, 581–590.

– 1979: "The (second) Apocalypse of James", in: D. M. Parrott (ed), *Nag Hammadi Codices
V,2–5 and VI with P. Berolinensis 8502,1 and 4* (NHS XI), Leiden 1979, 105–149.

– 1980: *The Apocalypses of Adam. A Literary and Source Analysis* (SBLDS 46), Chico, Calif.
1980.

Kasser, Rodolphe 1965: "Textes gnostiques. Nouvelles remarques à propos des apocalypses
de Paul, Jacques et Adam", in: *Le Muséon* 78 (1965) 71–98 und 299–312.

– 1967: "Bibliothèque gnostique V: L'apocalypse d'Adam", in: *RThPh* 17 (1967) 316–333.

– 1968: "Bibliothèque gnostique VI: Les deux apocalypses de Jacques", in: *RThPh* 18 (1968)
163–186.

– 1969: "Bibliothèque gnostique VII: L'apocalypse de Paul", in: *RThPh* 19 (1969) 259–263.

---

[89] The Nag Hammadi Library 1977, 461.

[90] Bei Abfassung des Referates waren mir die Aufsätze von Collins 1979, 1–20; Fallon 1979,
123–158; Attridge 1979, 159–186 und das in Uppsala gehaltene Referat von L. Hartman,
Survey of the Problem of Apocalyptic Genre (vgl. L. Hartman in diesem Band) unbekannt.
Auf eine Stellungnahme zu diesen Arbeiten bei der Drucklegung meines Referates mußte aus
Platzgründen verzichtet werden.

Koschorke, Klaus 1978: *Die Polemik der Gnostiker gegen das kirchliche Christentum unter besonderer Berücksichtigung der Nag-Hammadi-Traktate "Apokalypse des Petrus" (NHC VII,3) und "Testimonium Veritatis" (NHC IX,3)* (NHS XII), Leiden 1978.

Köster, Helmut und Robinson, James M. 1971: *Entwicklungslinien durch die Welt des frühen Christentums*, Tübingen 1971.

Krause, Martin 1969: "Ägyptisches Gedankengut in der Apokalypse des Asclepius", in: *ZDMG suppl.* I (1969) 48–57.

– 1971: In: W. Foerster, *Die Gnosis*. Zweiter Band. Koptische und mandäische Quellen, Zürich und Stuttgart 1971, 1–170.

– 1973: "Die Paraphrase des Sêem", in: F. Altheim und R. Stiehl, *Christentum am Roten Meer*, 2. Band, Berlin-New York 1973, 2–105.

– 1974: In: W. Foerster, *Gnosis. A Selection of Gnostic Texts. English Translation* edited by R. McL. Wilson, II. Coptic and Mandean Sources, Oxford 1974, 1–120.

– 1975: "Zur Bedeutung des gnostisch-hermetischen Handschriftenfundes von Nag Hammadi", in: *Essays on the Nag Hammadi Texts in Honour of Pahor Labib* ed. by M. Krause (NHS VI), Leiden 1975, 64–89.

– 1977: "Der Dialog des Soter in Codex III von Nag Hammadi", in: *Gnosis and Gnosticism. Papers read at the Seventh International Conference on Patristic Studies (Oxford, September 8th–13th 1975)* ed. by M. Krause (NHS VIII), Leiden 1977, 13–34.

– 1978: "Die Texte von Nag Hammadi", in: *Gnosis. Festschrift für Hans Jonas.* In Verbindung mit U. Bianchi, M. Krause, J. M. Robinson und G. Widengren hrsg. von B. Aland, Göttingen 1978, 216–243.

Krause, Martin und Girgis, Viktor 1973: "Die Petrusapokalypse", in: F. Altheim und R. Stiehl, *Christentum am Roten Meer*, 2. Band, Berlin-New York 1973, 152–179.

Krause, Martin und Labib, Pahor 1971: *Gnostische und hermetische Schriften aus Codex II und Codex VI* (ADAI.K 2), Glückstadt 1971.

MacRae, George W. 1979: "The Apocalypse of Adam", in: D. M. Parrott (ed.), *Nag Hammadi Codices V,2–5 and VI with P. Berolinensis 8502,1 and 4* (NHS XI), Leiden 1979, 151–195.

Morard, Françoise 1977: "L'apocalypse d'Adam de Nag Hammadi. Un essai d'interprétation", in: *Gnosis and Gnosticism. Papers read at the Seventh International Conference on Patristic Studies (Oxford, September 8th–13th 1975)* ed. by M. Krause (NHS VIII), Leiden 1977, 35–42.

Murdock, William R. und MacRae, George W. 1979: "The Apocalypse of Paul", in: D. M. Parrott (ed.), *Nag Hammadi Codices V,2–5 and VI with P. Berolinensis 8502,1 and 4* (NHS XI), Leiden 1979, 47–63.

Pearson, Birger A. und Giversen, Søren 1981: *Nag Hammadi Codices IX and X* (NHS XV), Leiden 1981.

Rudolph, Kurt 1968: "Der gnostische 'Dialog' als literarisches Genus", in: P. Nagel (ed.), *Probleme der koptischen Literatur* (WBMLUHW.K 1968/1), Halle 1968, 85–107.

– 1977: *Die Gnosis. Wesen und Geschichte einer spätantiken Religion*, Leipzig 1977.

Schenke, Hans-Martin 1965: "Zum gegenwärtigen Stand der Erforschung der Nag-Hammadi-Schriften", in: *Koptologische Studien in der DDR*, Halle-Wittenberg 1965, 124–135.

– 1966: Rez. von Böhlig-Labib 1963, in: *OLZ* 61 (1966) 23–34.

– 1975: "Zur Faksimile-Ausgabe der Nag-Hammadi-Schriften. Die Schriften des Codex VII", in: *ZÄS* 102 (1975) 123–138.

Schoedel, William R. 1979: "The (first) Apocalypse of James", in: D. M. Parrott (ed.), *Nag Hammadi Codices V,2–5 and VI with P. Berolinensis 8502,1 and 4* (NHS XI), Leiden 1979, 65–103.

Scholer, David M. 1971a: *Nag Hammadi Bibliography 1948–1969* (NHS I), Leiden 1971 (zitiert nach Nr.).

Scholer, David M.: Bibliographia gnostica
1971b Supplementum I, in: *NT* 13 (1971) 322–336.
1972 Supplementum II, in: *NT* 14 (1972) 312–331.
1973 Supplementum III, in: *NT* 15 (1973) 327–345.
1974 Supplementum IV, in: *NT* 16 (1974) 316–336.

1975 Supplementum V, in: *NT* 17 (1975) 305–336.
1977 Supplementum VI, in: *NT* 19 (1977, 293–336.
1978 Supplementum VII, in: *NT* 20 (1978) 300–331.
1979 Supplementum VIII, in: *NT* 21 (1979) 357–382.
1980 Supplementum IX, in: *NT* 22 (1980) 352–384.
1981 Supplementum X, in: *NT* 23 (1981) 361–380.
Tardieu, Michel 1974: *Trois mythes gnostiques*, Paris 1974.
The Facsimile Edition of the Nag Hammadi Codices published under the Auspices of the Department of Antiquities of the Arab Republic of Egypt in Conjunction with the United Nations Educational, Scientific and Cultural Organization, Leiden 1972 bis 1977.
The Nag Hammadi Library in English translated by Members of the Coptic Library Project of the Institute for Antiquity and Christianity, James M. Robinson Director, Leiden 1977.
Tröger, Karl-Wolfgang (Hrsg.) 1973: *Gnosis und Neues Testament*. Studien aus Religionswissenschaft und Theologie, Berlin 1973.
Vielhauer, Philipp 1964: "Apokalypsen und Verwandtes", in: *Neutestamentliche Apokryphen* in deutscher Übersetzung, 3. völlig neu bearbeitete Auflage hrsg. von W. Schneemelcher, Bd. 2, Tübingen 1964, 405–427.
– 1975: *Geschichte der urchristlichen Literatur*, Berlin-New York 1975.
Werner, Andreas 1974: "Die Apokalypse des Petrus. Die dritte Schrift aus Nag Hammadi Codex VII", in: *ThLZ* 99 (1974) 575–584.
Wilson, Robert McLachlan 1978: Apokryphen II, in: *TRE* Bd. III, 1978, 316–362.
Wisse, Frederik und Williams, Francis E. 1979: "The Concept of our great Power", in: D. M. Parrott (ed.), *Nag Hammadi Codices V,2–5 and VI with P. Berolinensis 8502,1 and 4* (NHS XI), Leiden 1979, 291–323.

The Sociology of Apocalypticism and
the "Sitz im Leben" of Apocalypses
Die Soziologie der Apokalyptik
und der Sitz im Leben der Apokalypsen
La sociologie de l'Apocalyptique
et le "Sitz im Leben" des Apocalypses

Social Aspects of Palestinian Jewish Apocalypticism

GEORGE W. E. NICKELSBURG

0. Introduction

0.1. As H. C. Kee has noted recently, most studies of apocalypticism have focused on genre and form or on theological content.[1] Largely lacking in the scholarship, but highly desirable for a better understanding of the documents, are an analysis of the social and cultural factors that gave rise to this literature and its world view, and an attempt to delineate the nature of the communities in and for which these documents were created.

0.2. At least three factors have guided the direction of scholarship on apocalypticism. First, apocalyptic writings have often been studied by persons with strong theological interests and agendas. Secondly, the study of genre and thought-world is based largely on the text itself and on parallel texts. On the other hand, when we inquire into social and cultural factors, community, and *Sitz im Leben*, we engage in a more difficult and often less productive task. We employ the text as a window into the author's *world*; and, as we see through a glass darkly, we attempt to correlate the textual material with a mass – or a minuscule – of extrinsic evidence. Thirdly, social analysis and other cross-disciplinary methods are a relatively recent import to biblical studies, and as is often the case, the canonical scriptures have priority on the goods.

0.3. In this paper I shall: 1) survey the work that has been done toward a social analysis of apocalypticism; 2) summarize the state of the discussion; 3) indicate two methodological problems; 4) sketch a possible approach; and 5) apply it to a specific document.

1. Previous Work

1.1. O. Plöger was the first to provide a scenario for the rise of the Ḥasidim into a fixed group which was responsible for the appearance of early apocalyptic literature.[2] According to Plöger, the Ḥasidim, the mighty

---

[1] Kee 1977, 77.
[2] Plöger 1968, 7–9, 17, 23–24. On the Ḥasidim and Daniel, see also Noth 1958, 372, 381,

warriors mentioned in 1 Macc 2:42, were already "a hard and fast group" at the outbreak of the anti-Seleucid rebellion. "Most probably" they were the same group that hid in caves in the Judean wilderness and were slaughtered by Antiochus's soldiers when they refused to defend themselves on the Sabbath. With some reluctance they abandoned their policy of passive resistance and joined the militant ranks led by the Hasmoneans. With the restoration of the Temple cult and the accession of Alcimus, they were relieved to make peace (1 Macc 7:12–13), although some of them may have adhered to Judas's leadership (cf. 2 Macc 14:6). It is to the circles of the _Hasidim_ that the book of Daniel is to be ascribed. However, the book's interest in eschatology reflects the earlier history of the _Ḥasidim_. Representing a viewpoint later to˙ be developed in Pharisaism, they collected and studied the prophetic oracles; and, opposing the viewpoint later to be seen among the Sadducees, they provided impetus to the movement to canonize the prophetic literature as a supplement to the Pentateuch.

1.2. The most wide-sweeping attempt to place Jewish apocalypticism in its social and cultural setting is to be found in M. Hengel's monumental synthesis, _Judaism and Hellenism_.[3] Hengel begins his discussion by elaborating Plöger's hypothesis, mainly on the basis of data from the Qumran Scrolls.[4] Arguing that the name "Essene" is derived from חסיא, the (Eastern) Aramaic equivalent of the Hebrew חסיד, he finds information about the history of the _Ḥasidim_ in the Damascus Document (CD 1), which dates the emergence of "the root of planting" twenty years before the rise of the Teacher of Righteousness, presumably ca. 175–170 B.C.E. Corroborative evidence is found in the Animal Apocalypse (_1 Enoch_ 85–90), which dates from the time of Judas Maccabeus, and the Apocalypse of Weeks (_1 Enoch_ 93; 91:11–17), which may be earlier. The book of Daniel and possibly the earliest parts of _1 Enoch_ were of Hasidic origin, and the _Ḥasidim_ were the common root of the Essenes and the Pharisees. Citing Plöger's sketch of Hasidic origins with approval, he finds literary evidence for the existence of the early _Ḥasidim_ and their conventicles quite possibly in Psalm 149:1 and, more certainly, in the apocryphal psalms of Qumran Cave 11. The assembly of the "pious" into a relatively closed community took the form of a penitential movement (CD 1; _1 Enoch_ 90:6; 93:9), which reflected a wholesale indictment of post-exilic Judaism, including the Temple cult, and was based on a strong disapproval of "the influence of Hellenistic forms of living and thinking".[5]

1.2.1. The major part of Hengel's discussion of apocalypticism is con-

---

389, 394–395, 397; Bright 1959, 408. See also the important treatment by Tcherikover 1959, 125–126, 196–230.

[3] Hengel 1974, 1. 174–247, 250–254.

[4] _Ibid._, 175–180.   [5] _Ibid._, 179–180.

cerned with the structure of apocalyptic *thought*.[6] This analysis is more properly the subject of the first section of this colloquium; however, two observations are appropriate to this paper. First, in Hengel's view, the apocalyptic world view is a response to the experience of living during the acute crises which many Jews perceived as a threat to the existence of Judaism and which, in turn, led them to lay their lives on the line.[7] This crisis was precipitated by the invasion of Jerusalem by the Hellenistic spirit.[8] As evidence for this invasion, Hengel has amassed mountains of data on the economic, political, and cultural *realia* of second century Palestine.[9] Secondly, according to Hengel, the phenomenon of apocalyptic was itself heavily influenced by Hellenistic thought.[10] In making this assertion, he takes cognizance of the influence of socio-cultural factors on this segment of the history of ideas.

1.2.2. The second part of Hengel's discussion of Jewish apocalypticism is devoted to "Early Essenism," as this is attested in the Qumran Scrolls.[11] Here, too, he is especially interested in the shape of this group's theology. Nonetheless, he discusses the concrete historical circumstances that led to their formation, their self-understanding as "*the eschatological* community of salvation" (1.223), and the social consequences of this self-understanding in their retreat into the wilderness and their community structure. Hengel is, of course, no innovator here. Because of the peculiar contents of the Scrolls, their genres, and their discovery near the ruins of the community that generated and used them, social factors have been an essential part of the discussion of the Scrolls from the beginning. As F. M. Cross noted in 1958,

> The Essene literature enables us to discover the concrete Jewish setting in which an apocalyptic understanding of history was living and integral to communal existence.[12]

1.3. S. R. Isenberg has argued that one can

> understand certain phenomena in Palestinian Judaism in the Greco-Roman period by viewing them from the perspective of social anthropology, viewing relationships of various groups in the light of concepts such as "power" and "access to power," "redemption" and "redemptive media".[13]

The model from which Isenberg derived his categories was K. Burridge's study of millenarian movements in the Pacific islands.[14]

1.3.1. Isenberg describes the development of millenarian movements as follows.[15] In a time of social upheaval a group within the larger society feels itself deprived and oppressed and finds it impossible to fulfil what the

---

[6] *Ibid.*, 181–194, 196–224, 228–247.   [7] *Ibid.*, 194–196.
[8] *Ibid.*, 196.   [9] *Ibid.*, 6–106.   [10] *Ibid.*, 252–253.
[11] *Ibid.*, 218–247.   [12] Cross 1958, 151.   [13] Isenberg 1974, 28.
[14] Burridge 1969, cited by Isenberg 1974, 40, n. 6.   [15] *Ibid.*, 35–38.

established powers define as societal obligations to the power that constitutes the society; they are virtually defined out of the redemptive process. In consequence, they project the causes of their deprivation onto the establishment, which has appropriated for itself the power whose source and authority transcends society, and they perceive the establishment as liars, sons of darkness, misguided, etc. What is required is a new set of assumptions about power and new rules for access to that power; and a new social order is projected to effect these. The new assumptions and rules may be seen as a return to pure original traditions that have been perverted by the establishment. In the second phase new assumptions and beliefs are expressed concretely and tested. The testing may involve hostile words and/or deeds directed at the oppressing power. The millenarian activities may then coalesce into a structured movement if someone appears who is able to articulate the dissatisfactions of the group which feels itself oppressed and who is able to point to a solution. The millenarian prophet transforms and rechannels tradition in such ways that new rules and new assumptions about power can be seen to derive directly from the ultimate power sought by the community. That is, he claims to have received a revelation that authorizes the new order. The prophet may also prescribe new rules, rituals, and community order. The third phase involves either consolidation or dissolution. If the group is tolerated by the power structure, it may become institutionalized and survive. Indeed, it may succeed so well that it becomes a major political force and loses its eschatological focus. On the other hand, it may arouse sufficient hostility that it is crushed by the establishment. Alternatively, it may disappear because it fails to speak to its constituents or because its prophecies are unfulfilled.

1.3.2. Isenberg then briefly applies this scenario to the Qumran community.[16] Cut off from Temple and cult, which they considered to be defiled and presided over by an illegitimate high priesthood, and finding themselves in sharp opposition to the "false" Pharisaic interpretations of the Torah, they exiled themselves in the wilderness, where they constituted themselves as the community of the redeemed. Here they studied and observed the Torah according to the revealed interpretation of the Teacher of Righteousness, they hurled their curses at their enemies in Jerusalem, and they awaited the new order.

1.4. The sociological models of Karl Mannheim and Max Weber are employed by P. D. Hanson in his study of Third Isaiah and Deutero-Zechariah, whom he designates as examples of early apocalyptic eschatology.[17]

---

[16] *Ibid.*, 38–39.   [17] Hanson 1975, especially 211–220.

1.4.1. Although we are not here concerned with these early post-exilic writings, it is important to note that Hanson has attempted to reconstruct their social setting and that he sees a polarity between conflicting groups, interests, and ideologies which is analogous to that posited by Plöger, Hengel, and Isenberg.[18]

1.4.2. In an article on "Apocalypticism," Hanson generalizes his approach, employing categories very close to Isenberg's.[19] Ancient apocalyptic movements have a common *social setting* in which a group experiences alienation due to the disintegration of the life-sustaining socio-religious structures and their supporting myths. Institutional structures may be physically destroyed or a community may find itself excluded from the dominant society and its symbolic universe. The results are chaos, a cultural vacuum, and intolerable strain on the community of the disen-franchised. In their *response* to this setting of alienation, members of apocalyptic movements create a new symbolic universe that replaces the one dominant in the social system responsible for the alienation. The response of apocalyptic eschatology allows the community to maintain a sense of identity and a vision of their ultimate vindication in the face of social structures and historical events that deny that identity and the plausibility of that vision. True identity is derived not from the structures and institutions of the society but from God's redemptive acts, which are effected on the cosmic level. Apocalyptic movements may express their opposition in a variety of forms. They may withdraw and form a new society based on a symbolic utopian universe. They may yield to opposition and go underground and express their identity in a symbolic sub-universe. They may respond with violence, become a revolutionary community, and construct a symbolic counter-universe.

1.5. Ideology, community, *Sitz im Leben*, and function are important considerations for J. J. Collins in his monograph on Daniel.[20] He compares the "viewpoints" of 1 and 2 Maccabees, the *Testament of Moses*, *1 Enoch* 85–90, the book of Daniel, and the Ḥasidim as they are described in 1 and 2 Maccabees and in recent scholarly literature.[21] Criticizing the dominant scholarly reconstruction of the history of the Ḥasidim as an oversimplifica-tion, he espouses the view of Tcherikover and characterizes the Ḥasidim as a party of scribes, prepared from the outset to fight for the Torah and ready to lay down arms when the religious abuses of the Hellenizers were eliminated. Second Maccabees and *1 Enoch* 85–90 may be considered compatible with the viewpoint of the Ḥasidim and may reflect shades of

---

[18] *Ibid.*, 220–279, though Hanson cites none of these authors in this connection.
[19] Hanson 1976, 30–31.   [20] Collins 1977, 191–224.
[21] *Ibid.*, 195–210.

opinion within the party. Contrasted with the viewpoint of these works is the passive resistance espoused by the *Testament of Moses* and the book of Daniel, which should not be considered to be Hasidic in origin. Collins makes an interesting and plausible suggestion about the group in which Daniel was composed, and the book's *Sitz im Leben* and function.[22] Although it was a product of an elite group (the *maśkilîm*), it was intended for popular consumption and was composed as a manifesto that would evoke non-violent resistance to Antiochus's decrees and submission to martyrdom if necessary.

1.6. Having noted the necessity for an investigation of the social setting of Jewish apocalyptic (see above, §0.1.), Kee discusses briefly "The Social Dynamics of Prophetic Movements" as these have been discussed by M. Weber and K. Burridge, and he sketches the Jewish sectarian setting of apocalyptic.[23] In this he follows closely the discussion of Hengel and accepts the hypothesis of the Hasidic origins of apocalypticism.

2. The State of the Discussion

Although we have yet to see a full-scale and methodologically self-conscious study of the social setting of Palestinian Jewish apocalypticism, the past two decades have witnessed a growing awareness of the necessity of viewing apocalyptic thought within its concrete political, economic, and cultural settings.[24]

2.1. An important first step toward the writing of a social history of apocalypticism is the collecting of data on the social *realia* of the times.[25] Hengel's work needs to be extended into the later periods.

2.2. Theoretical discussions have imported models from other disciplines that have sometimes been helpful. These discussions have also uniformly stressed the setting of apocalypticism in times of social upheaval and turmoil, and they have underscored the sense of alienation and powerlessness that permeates the literature of these movements.[26] A key term here is "sense." What counts is not a neutral observer's view of whether things are good or bad, but the apocalyptist's *perception* and *experience* that the times are critical.[27] Without that perception and experience, we do not have the apocalyptic response.

2.3. Apocalyptic responses embody a variety of attitudes and result in different forms of behavior and social organization, as theoreticians like G. Theissen and J. Z. Smith would also remind us.[28] These forms include:

---

[22] *Ibid.*, 210–218.   [23] Kee 1977, 77–87.
[24] Cf. also Nickelsburg 1972 for a similar emphasis.
[25] Smith 1975, 19.   [26] See also Hengel 1974, 1. 194–195.
[27] Isenberg 1974, 35.   [28] Theissen 1978, *passim*; Smith 1975, 20.

passive or militant resistance to persecution or withdrawal from society; a group's understanding of themselves as the elect; the constitution of a more or less structured community.

3. Two Methodological Problems

Recent discussions raise a number of important methodological problems. I shall discuss two of these. The first relates to our use of the sources. In reconstructing the social setting of ancient Jewish apocalypticism, we have several kinds of sources at our disposal: data about social *realia* gathered from literary, epigraphic, and archeological remains; apocalypses – the literary products of apocalyptists and apocalyptic movements; Qumran documents that are not generically apocalypses, and their setting; historical references in such writers as Josephus, Philo, and 1 and 2 Maccabees, which speak, *e.g.*, about the Ḥasidim, or the Essenes or certain Essenes. Our picture of the social setting of ancient apocalypticism is influenced by the priorities that we assign to these sources and by the manner in which we integrate the data derived from them.

3.1. As an example, we may look at the case of the Ḥasidim. What can we know about them? Were they, in fact, a well defined party which was responsible for the composition of Daniel? I do not share the optimism of the scholarly consensus. In elaborating, I must confine myself to a few observations and to the problems which they present for the hypothesis of the Hasidic origins of apocalypticism.[29]

3.1.1. Our only explicit references to a party of the Ḥasidim in the Maccabean period are 1 Macc 2:42 and 7:13 and 2 Macc 14:6. According to the first passage they were mighty warriors – a skill they did not likely acquire from brief training as hesitant recruits. The third passage also mentions their military activities under Judas's leadership. Although the second passage says that they sought to make peace, it does not indicate that they did so with relief and in reversion to a previous thoroughgoing pacifism.[30] The theory that they were initially pacifists is based on two unproven assumptions: a) that the people slaughtered in the caves (1 Macc 2:29–38) were Ḥasidim – an identification that the text does not make; and b) that the refusal of these people to defend themselves on the Sabbath indicates that they were *thoroughgoing* pacifists.

3.1.2. Since this evidence presents the Ḥasidim as warriors and never as pacifists, a theory of the Hasidic authorship of Daniel is problematic for two reasons. First, the book does not espouse a militant ideology. Sec-

---

[29] For an extensive critique of "the Hasidic hypothesis," see Davies 1977.
[30] *Pace* Plöger 1968, 8, 17.

ondly, Daniel was written during the time when (according to 1 Maccabees) the *Hasidim* were making common cause with the Hasmoneans; nonetheless, it describes this warfare as "a little help" (11:34).

3.1.3. Although the "company of the *Hasidim*" (1 Macc 2:42) may have been an established group in 167 B.C.E., we cannot be certain that all occurrences of this term in our literature denote this same group or a specific group who were their predecessors. Some occurrences of קהל חסדים may refer to a gathering of persons construed as "pious" rather than to a tightly constituted group. The term may be used in this broader generic sense in Psalm 149 and the apocryphal psalms of Qumran Cave 11. Also fitting into this category may be the first century *Psalms of Solomon* and their usage of συναγωγαὶ ὁσίων (17:16–[18]) and συνέδριον ὁσίων (4:1), which is generally not brought into the discussion.[31] On the other hand, if one cites Psalm 149 as evidence for the early history of the *Hasidim*, one must also note the militant ideology that pervades the psalm.

3.2. A second methodological problem arising from the recent discussion of the social setting of Jewish apocalypticism relates to the use of models. The theories developed by modern sociologists and anthropologists are based on available and often copious data and are attempts to organize and explain these data. These theories may serve as useful models that help us to understand ancient texts, but primary attention must be given to the documents themselves and to their peculiar contours. The model must not become a die that shapes the ancient materials or a filter that highlights or obliterates textual data in a predetermined way. On the other hand, a model that is helpful in one case may not work in another. It is questionable whether *all* ancient apocalyptists projected the causes of their deprivation on the establishment. The authors of *Jubilees* and the *Testament of Moses* blame the troubles of Antiochan times on the nation's sins. Daniel does not speak in this language. Whether all apocalyptic movements require a prophetic figure to *focus* what is at first *a general sense* of deprivation is questionable. What applies to Qumran and Jesus of Nazareth may not work with Daniel.[32]

4. An Open and Full Agenda

4.1. The recent discussion of Jewish apocalypticism has only begun to reckon with sociological questions. Moreover, much of this discussion has been carried on within a general and theoretical framework. With the

---

[31] For other occurrences of ὅσιος, see 2:36(40); 3:8(10); 4:6(7),8(9); 8:23(28),34(40); 9:3(6); 10:6(7); 12:4(5),6(7); 13:10(9),12(11); 14:3(2),10(7); 15:3(5),7(9).

[32] *Pace* Isenberg 1974, 35–36.

exception of the Scrolls, there has been very little detailed analysis of the social aspects of specific Jewish apocalyptic writings. It is with the individual writings, however, that the task must begin. At the same time, as the discussion in the previous section indicates, much that we would *like* to know about these documents and their settings we *cannot* know, given the present state of our sources.

4.1.1. Allowing for these limitations, here are some of the questions that we may address to the documents as we attempt better to understand them and their social settings. Does the author employ vague and stereotyped language, or can we define specifically the kind of political, economic, cultural, and religious circumstances that have created the author's sense of alienation, deprivation, or victimization? Does the author speak of political persecution or economic oppression? Are the culprits Jews or Gentiles? Is the Temple or the priesthood or the calendar or some other specific tenet of the Law an issue? Can we identify these circumstances and factors and issues with known historical events or situations?

4.1.2. How does the author respond to his circumstances? What attitudes and behavior does he espouse? Does he recommend waiting, cursing the enemies, pacifism, retreat, militant participation in the judgment, gathering as a community?

4.1.3. Is the author's group construed simply as the righteous, opposed to the wicked, or is it thought to be an elect, eschatological community, the sole locus of salvation? In the latter case, can we ascertain the rationale and dynamics that have led to their self-understanding as a community or a sect and the peculiar manner in which that community is construed and organized? For example, do they think of themselves as a new temple because they believe that the old temple has been polluted, and how do they function as temple? It is important that we integrate into a whole: the social factors that led to an apocalyptic response; the thought structure of that response; and the manner in which the response was worked out in life. These elements together constitute a world in which the members of an apocalyptic community live and function in a particular way.[33]

4.1.4. In attempting to understand the dynamics and functioning of an apocalyptic community, it may be helpful to seek models in the Qumran Scrolls and their context, which are unusually rich in these data. Furthermore, with the caveats mentioned above (§ 3.2.), a variety of contemporary models may provide useful perspectives on the ancient documents.[34]

4.1.5. Finally, we must turn our attention to the *Sitz im Leben* and

---

[33] See Smith 1975, 21, who speaks of a "social world" and cites Meeks 1972; cf. Hanson 1976, 31, who speaks of symbolic universes.

[34] See, *e.g.*, the typology of sectarian movements developed by Bryan Wilson, Miller 1979, 164–166.

function of individual works. In attempting to answer this plaguing question, we must be open to the possibility of wide variety. Not all apocalypses or testaments need have served the same function.

4.2. When individual documents have been studied in their own right, we can begin to compare them with one another and to seek possible interrelationships. Did the various parts of *1 Enoch* derive from a common milieu? Are there shades of difference that indicate development or even different origins? How do the Enochic books compare with Daniel, *Jubilees*, and the *Testament of Moses*? What are the relationships between these documents and various of the writings that we know only from Qumran? How do the documents and groups of documents in the apocalyptic corpus relate to others that we might classify as non-apocalyptic?[35]

4.3. We have seen the problems and limitations of reconstructing the history of apocalypticism by mixing data from apocalyptic writings with information about the history of the *Hasidim* which other sources (appear to) provide. The procedure that I have outlined does allow us, however, to learn a great deal about the development of apocalypticism and apocalyptic writings. We can then compare this information derived from individual writings and groups of writings with our historical information about known persons and named groups. In so doing, we may find positive and important correlations. On the other hand, we may discover that because we can know relatively little about the *Hasidim* and other named groups, we can make very few sure correlations. But even if this is the case, our study of the apocalyptic writings will constitute an important step toward charting the history of the rise and development of apocalypticism.

5. *1 Enoch 92–105: A Sketch for a Case Study*

In conclusion I shall briefly discuss a single writing in light of these questions, suggesting some possible answers and indicating the ambiguities attendant to the enterprise. The "Epistle of Enoch" (*1 Enoch* 92–105) depicts high tensions and bitter strife between two categories of people. Although the author usually designates them with generic terms (ἁμαρτωλοί, ἄδικοι, δίκαιοι, εὐσεβεῖς), he fleshes out the vague designations for the sinners with detailed descriptions that depict two kinds of evildoing.

5.1. First, the sinners are the rich and powerful, who persecute and oppress the righteous and lowly.[36] They hoard wealth and possessions

---

[35] This comparative task is at the heart of the discussion by Theissen 1978.

[36] Nickelsburg 1979.

which they have obtained unrighteously, they banquet sumptuously and parade about in resplendent clothing (96:5–6; 97:8–98:2). They impress others into their service to construct their lavish houses (99:13; cf. 94:6–7). In court they bear false witness and hand down unjust verdicts (95:6). They are accused of robbing, torturing, and "devouring" the righteous, of treating them like beasts of burden, and of murdering them. They connive with the rulers, who support their oppressive deeds (103:9–15).

5.1.1. These charges are sufficiently explicit and focused to have led a majority of scholars to conclude that this book was written during the Hasmonean period, most likely during the reign of Alexander Janneus.[37]

5.1.2. Tcherikover goes a step further and compares *1 Enoch* 92–105 with the Wisdom of ben Sira, detailing the great strides that class hatred had made in a century.[38] While Tcherikover's observations are pertinent and his interpretation is plausible, it does not take sufficient note of the different *Sitz im Leben* of Sirach and of *1 Enoch* 92–105. Ben Sira speaks mainly to the rich youth of Jerusalem, calling them to a responsible use of their wealth.[39] Pseudo-Enoch, on the other hand, addresses his "Epistle" primarily to the righteous of his own time (92:1) and offers consolation to these victims of oppression.[40] This consolation takes the form of exhortations to faith and hope and steadfastness, which are explicitly addressed to the righteous. It is also implicit in the many Woes against the sinners. Here the champion of the persecuted and harassed poor indicts the evil deeds of their oppressors and announces the judgment that will befall them. Thus what we learn about the rich comes to us in the form of bitter invectives spoken by their enemies. For this reason, we must treat with caution such loaded legal categories as "robbery, injustice, and murder." Surely there were concrete circumstances and incidents that gave rise to these accusations. Nonetheless, the question remains: could *the poor* of ben Sira's time have employed this kind of rhetoric to damn what they *experienced* as, and *considered to be* oppression, robbery, injustice, and murder? Could they have written *1 Enoch* 92–105? Here Isenberg's comment is pertinent (see above, §2.2.). What counts is not the objective facts as a neutral observer would have perceived them, but the apocalyptist's *experience* and *perception* of his circumstances. In short, we must exercise caution if we wish to use this biased document as a source of information that constitutes a building block for historical reconstruction.[41]

5.2. In a second set of passages, the author makes a variety of *religious* charges against the sinners. Some of the sinners are described as pagans or

---

[37] Martin 1906, xcvi; Charles 1912, 221–222; Nickelsburg 1972, 113.
[38] Tcherikover 1959, 259.   [39] See *ibid.*, 149.
[40] Nickelsburg 1977, 322–326.
[41] Tcherikover (1959, 259–261) uses Sirach as such a source.

apostates. They practise idolatry (99:7), consume blood (98:11), and blaspheme (94:9; 96:7). Other sinners are blamed for disregarding and perverting Torah as the righteous understand Torah. They alter the words of truth and transgress the eternal Law and consider themselves to be guiltless (99:2, Gk.). They reject the foundation and eternal heritage of their fathers (99:14). They are fools who do not listen to the wise (98:9, Gk.). They nullify the words of the righteous (98:14). They write lying and deceitful words and lead many astray with their lies (98:15).[42]

5.2.1. Built into these latter passages is a sharp dichotomy between the members of the author's group, who are the protagonists of wisdom, and their opponents, who are false teachers and who can violate Torah while claiming that they are innocent. That we are not dealing with minor halakhic disputes is evident from the Woe form in which these charges are cast. The sinners will be damned for their conduct.[43] Other evidence in the Apocalypse of Weeks helps us better to define the author's group and their socio-religious self-understanding. The Apocalypse (93:1–10 + 91:11–17) traces the history of the "chosen plant" from Abraham to the choosing of the elect, who will be given "sevenfold wisdom and knowledge" and will function as witnesses of righteousness in the end-time, uprooting the foundations of violence and the structure of deceit. They will take up the sword of judgment against the wicked and will receive the blessings of the eschaton (93:9–10 + 91:11–13, 4QEn^g 1 4:12–18). According to this apocalypse, the community is defined in the following way. They are the righteous, as opposed to the wicked. They are the elect, the true members of the Abrahamic covenant and the recipients of the coming salvation. They possess the revealed, eschatological gift of full wisdom and knowledge. They will function as God's agents in the coming judgment. While this apocalypse could be an interpolation into an extant writing or an earlier tradition incorporated into a later writing, most of its major ideas occur elsewhere in the Epistle. Throughout chaps. 94–105 we hear of the righteous/sinner opposition. The wisdom of the former includes both their understanding of the Law (see above) and the revelation of heaven and the end-time.[44] Their participation in the judgment is affirmed several times (see below). Only the title "the elect" is missing in these chapters.

5.2.2. The Epistle tells us little or nothing about the structure or organization of the author's group. As to their behavior, the author counsels them to stand fast and wait for the judgment. At that time, however, they will wield the sword of the Lord in the great judgment (91:12; 95:3; 96:1; 98:12). The wording of 95:3 is, moreover, reminiscent of

---

[42] On the text of 99:2; 98:9; 98:15, see Nickelsburg 1976, 94, n. 23, 93, 107.
[43] Nickelsburg 1977, 310–312.   [44] *Ibid.*, 315–318.

the ancient language of holy warfare (cf. Num 21:34; Deut 3:2; Josh 8:1–2; cf. Esth 9:5).

5.3. What might be the connections between the Epistle of Enoch and the Qumran community, among whose literary remains have been found fragments of two copies of this work?[45] Similarities include, first of all, a cluster of ideas and terms common to the Damascus Document and the Epistle: the rise of a community called a "planting," which is the recipient of revealed knowledge and which stands in opposition to apostates, who are blind (93:9–10; cf. 94:2; CD 1:7–9); the imagery of the two ways (91:4,18–19; 94:1–4; CD 1:11–16); violation of Torah, construed as inheritance (99:14; CD 1:16); persecution of the righteous (94–103 *passim*; CD 1:20); antagonism to riches (94–103 *passim*; CD 4:17). Another important similarity is the militant ideology that the Epistle and the Qumran War Scroll share with reference to the judgment.

5.3.1. In several respects the Epistle of Enoch differs from the Qumran literature, although the argument from silence should not be pressed. Lacking in 93:10 is the conversion language of CD 1:7–12 and the latter's reference to a prophetic figure.[46] The Epistle gives no counsel to retreat from society. Specific Qumranic exegetical traditions appear to be lacking, although this question should be studied in more detail.

5.3.2. More ambiguous is pseudo-Enoch's attitude toward the Temple. The Epistle does not contain the clear polemics against Temple and cult that characterize the Scrolls. Nonetheless, the Apocalypse of Weeks is strangely silent on the Second Temple. The analogy of the Animal Apocalypse (*1 Enoch* 89:73) may indicate that the author of the Apocalypse of Weeks also thought that the Second Temple was polluted since its construction. How this might fit with the Qumranites' rancour toward the Hasmonean high priesthood is a question we cannot consider here. However, the presence of the Enochic writings at Qumran, together with multiple copies of *Jubilees* with its calendar polemics, may indicate that the Qumranites were heirs of, and participants in an anti-Temple "movement" that was much older than the rise of the Hasmonean high priests.[47]

5.4. While it cannot be shown that the Epistle of Enoch is a product of the Qumran community, it appears to have issued from a group with many affinities to the Qumranites and/or their predecessors. Were these the Ḥasidim? The militant ideology may point in this direction. We have no way of knowing for certain whether the Ḥasidim of 1 Maccabees thought that they were waging eschatological warfare in connection with the

[45] Milik 1976, 207–209, 245–272.
[46] See Miller 1979, 164–166; conversion is characteristic of some, but not all sectarian groups. On the supposed centrality of the prophetic figure, see Isenberg 1974, 36–37.
[47] Hengel 1974, 1. 180.

judgment. *1 Enoch* 90:6–27 may indicate that they did. It associates the opening of the lambs' eyes with the rise of Judas Maccabeus as their champion, and it connects his battles with the eschatological war and final judgment.[48] A few occurrences of εὐσεβεῖς and perhaps two occurrences of ὅσιοι might also suggest a Hasidic origin for the Epistle,[49] but the term δίκαιοι is far more frequent in the document. Names aside, however, *1 Enoch* 92–105, the Animal Apocalypse, and the Damascus Document appear to be evidence of a common religious movement, probably complex and proliferated in its sociology. Its varied contours need to be studied more closely.

Bibliography

Bright, John 1959: *A History of Israel*, Philadelphia, Penn. 1959.

Burridge, Kenelm 1969: *New Heaven New Earth*, New York 1969.

Charles, R. H. 1912: *The Book of Enoch*, Oxford 1912.

Collins, John J. 1977: *The Apocalyptic Vision of the Book of Daniel* (HSM 16), Missoula, Mont. 1977.

Cross, Frank Moore Jr. 1958: *The Ancient Library of Qumran*, Garden City, N.Y. 1958.

Davies, Philip 1977: "Hasidim in the Maccabean Period", in: *JJS* 28 (1977) 127–140.

Hanson, Paul D. 1975: *The Dawn of Apocalyptic*, Philadelphia, Penn. 1975.

– 1976: "Apocalypticism", in: *IDBSup*, Nashville, Tenn. 1976, 30–31.

Hengel, Martin 1974: *Judaism and Hellenism*, Philadelphia, Penn. 1974 (German 2nd edition, Tübingen 1973).

Isenberg, Sheldon R. 1974: "Millenarism in Greco-Roman Palestine", in: *Religion* 4 (1974) 26–46.

Kee, Howard C. 1977: *Community of the New Age*, Philadelphia, Penn. 1977.

Martin, Francois 1906: *Le Livre d'Hénoch*, Paris 1906.

Meeks, Wayne A. 1972: "The Man from Heaven in Johannine Sectarianism", in: *JBL* 91 (1972) 44–72.

Milik, J. T. 1976: *The Books of Enoch*, Oxford 1976.

Miller, Donald E. 1979: "Sectarianism and Secularization: The Work of Bryan Wilson", in: *RelStR* 5 (1979) 161–174.

Nickelsburg, George W. E. 1972: *Resurrection, Immortality, and Eternal Life in Intertestamental Judaism* (HThS 26), Cambridge, Mass. 1972.

– 1976: "Enoch 97–104: A Study of the Greek and Ethiopic Texts", in: *Armenian and Biblical Studies*, ed. Michael E. Stone, Sion Supplements 1, Jerusalem 1976, 90–156.

– 1977: "The Apocalyptic Message of 1 Enoch 92–105", in: *CBQ* 39 (1977) 309–328.

– 1979: "Riches, the Rich, and God's Judgment in 1 Enoch 92–105 and the Gospel According to Luke", in: *NTS* 25 (1979) 324–344.

Noth, Martin 1958: *The History of Israel*, New York 1958 (German 2nd ed. Göttingen 1953).

Plöger, Otto 1968: *Theocracy and Eschatology*, Richmond, Va 1968 (German 2nd edition of 1962, which revised German original, Neukirchen 1959).

Smith, Jonathan Z. 1975: "The Social Description of Early Christianity", in: *RelStR* 1 (1975) 19–25.

Tcherikover, Victor 1959: *Hellenistic Civilization and the Jews*, Philadelphia, Penn. 1959 (Hebrew original).

Theissen, Gerd 1978: *Sociology of Early Palestinian Christianity*, Philadelphia, Penn. 1978 (German original, Munich 1977).

---

[48] On the possible Hasidic origin of *1 Enoch* 85–90, see Charles 1912, 206–207.

[49] On the text of 103:9 and 104:12, see Nickelsburg 1976, 126, 134.

Messianische Hoffnung und politischer "Radikalismus" in der "jüdisch-hellenistischen Diaspora"[*]

Zur Frage der Voraussetzungen des jüdischen Aufstandes unter Trajan 115–117 n. Chr.

MARTIN HENGEL

1. Zum Problem

Die mir durch das Programm des Symposiums vorgegebene Thematik: "Soziologie der Apokalyptik" bzw. "der Sitz im Leben der Apokalypsen" des "hellenistischen Judentums" ist so etwas wie eine Gleichung mit zahlreichen Unbekannten. Man sieht die Aufgabe und weiß zugleich, daß sie unlösbar ist, weil wir darüber zu wenig wissen und die einzelnen Größen daher nicht eindeutig zu erfassen sind.

1.1. Da erscheint zunächst der Begriff des *"hellenistischen Judentums"*, doch ist er viel zu allgemein, denn er umfaßt im Grunde das ganze Judentum der hellenistisch-römischen Zeit, einschließlich des Mutterlandes. Aber auch die exakter benannte Größe des *"griechisch-sprechenden Judentums"* ist alles andere als eine religiöse, soziale oder politisch-geographische Einheit, die sich leicht überschauen ließe. Weiter ist auch der Begriff der *"Apokalyptik"* – wie gerade unser Symposium gezeigt hat – gegenüber verwandten religiösen Vorstellungen und Offenbarungsschriften relativ schwer abzugrenzen und enthält in sich eine zum Teil widersprüchliche Vielfalt von Motiven. *"Den* Apokalyptiker" und *"die* Apokalyptik" im strengen Sinn gibt es noch weniger als *"die* Gnosis" oder *"den* Gnostiker"*. Wir kennen bestenfalls "apokalyptische *Schriften*". Schon ihre Autoren sind uns unbekannt, und dasselbe gilt auch weitgehend von ihrem Leserkreis. Noch komplizierter wird der Sachverhalt, wenn wir das unklare Attribut "jüdisch-hellenistisch" hinzufügen. Denn was soll damit gemeint sein? Apokalyptische Schriften, die in der griechischsprechenden Diaspora entstanden sind und deren Originale in griechischer Sprache geschrieben wurden? War aber nicht gerade auch das palästinische Mutterland zutiefst von der "hellenistischen" Zivilisation beeinflußt und das Griechische dort eine geläufige Sprache[1]? Darf man es darum ausschließen?

---

[*] Der Vortrag ist die stark verkürzte Fassung einer umfangreicheren Studie, die ich in anderem Zusammenhang zu veröffentlichen hoffe. Für das sorgfältige Mitlesen der Korrekturen danke ich Frau Anna-Maria Schwemer und Dr. H. Lichtenberger; für das mehrfache Schreiben des Manuskripts Frl. Monika Merkle.

[1] Zu griechischsprechenden Juden in Jerusalem und Palästina s. Hengel 1975, 152 ff.

Darüber hinaus wurden diejenigen Apokalypsen, die in Aramäisch oder
Hebräisch abgefaßt worden waren, in der Regel ins Griechische übersetzt,
sonst wären sie ja gar nicht zu uns gelangt. Bei zahlreichen "apokalyptischen" Schriften ist es darum umstritten, ob ein semitisches oder griechisches Original zugrunde lag. Bei vielen Werken bleibt es weiter ungewiß,
ob sie nicht christlich "zensiert" wurden oder ob es sich nicht überhaupt
um christliche Apokalypsen handelt, die jüdisches Traditionsmaterial verwenden. Erhalten wurde von der apokalyptischen Literatur des Judentums
in der Regel ja nur das, was späteren christlichen Lesern behagte. Das alles
führt dazu, daß Zeit, Herkunftsort und Milieu dieser Schriften sich häufig
kaum mehr eindeutig bestimmen lassen, so daß auch Schlüsse auf den
"soziologischen Hintergrund" oder auf den "Sitz im Leben" recht hypothetisch werden.

1.2. Man könnte sich nun auf wenige Schriften konzentrieren, bei denen
Entstehungsort und -zeit näher bestimmbar sind, etwa auf die *jüdischen
Sibyllen*. Sie wollten aufgrund ihrer Nachahmung der Sprache Homers in
erster Linie die gebildete Oberschicht, ja vielleicht sogar Nichtjuden
ansprechen. Aber auch bei ihnen ergeben sich erhebliche Unterschiede.
Während z. B. die 3., 5. und 11. Sibylle aus Ägypten stammen, freilich mit
einer zeitlichen Differenz von mindestens 250 Jahren, kommt die kurz nach
79 n. Chr. verfaßte 4. Sibylle aus einem völlig anderen Traditionskreis, der
an Ägypten uninteressiert ist, dafür aber mit den jüdischen Taufsekten
Syriens und Palästinas in Verbindung steht. Außerdem sind gerade die
relativ ergiebigen Sibyllen nach Collins[2] nicht Apokalypsen im strengen
Sinn, sondern nur Orakel, da sie auf direkter Inspiration beruhen. Dagegen
sind die als typisch "hellenistisch" geltenden "Apokalypsen" von der Art
der griechischen Baruchapokalypse oder des Testaments Abrahams mit
ihrer Betonung des Motivs der Himmelsreise und der ganz auf das Indivi-
duum bezogenen Eschatologie für die Frage der sozialen Herkunft des
Verfassers, seiner politischen Anschauungen und seines Milieus – zumindest dem äußeren Anschein nach – relativ wenig aussagekräftig. Sie wollen

---

[2] Collins 1979, 46f. Vgl. *idem*, 1974, 17f.: "The place of the oracle collections in Judaism of
the Hellenistic age was filled by the apocalyptic literature" und S. 110: "Yet we must insist
that the sibyllina at any stage are not fully apocalyptic writings". Ich kann freilich dem Verf.
in seiner Meinung nicht folgen, daß die Sibyllinen keine klare Trennung zwischen der
Herrschaft der Weltmächte und der Gottesherrschaft kennen und daß in ihnen jeglicher
Hinweis auf eine den Tod überwindende Hoffnung fehle. Sib 4,178–190 erwartet nach der
Ekpyrosis die Auferstehung und das Gericht, und in Sib 3,705ff. wird das ewige Leben der
Gerechten im Heiligen Land beschrieben. Richtig ist, daß dort nicht das Heil des einzelnen
Individuums, sondern des ganzen Volkes im Mittelpunkt steht, s. Cavallin 1974, 150: "So we
might say that this Alexandrian Jewish work is the extreme opposite of Philo"; vgl. *idem*,
1979, 293ff. Man sollte sich darum sehr hüten, das sogenannte "hellenistische Judentum" in
irgendeiner Weise als wirkliche Einheit zu betrachten. Sein wichtigstes Band war die
gemeinsame griechische Muttersprache. Religiös war es dagegen vielschichtig.

als religiöse Unterhaltungsliteratur den einzelnen Leser erfreuen, erbauen, und dazu vielleicht noch etwas das Gruseln lehren. Inhaltlich stehen sie der mit "apokalyptischen" Passagen ausgeschmückten religiösen Novelle, von der Art des Testamentum Iobi, von Joseph und Asenath oder der Paralipomena Jeremiae gar nicht so ferne. Von höherer griechischer Bildung unberührt, dienten diese Werke dem religiösen Unterhaltungsbedürfnis[3] der breiten lesekundigen Mittelschicht des griechischsprechenden Diasporajudentums im östlichen Mittelmeerraum.

1.3. Diese Vielfalt, Verschiedenartigkeit, ja Widersprüchlichkeit der sogenannten "apokalyptischen" Quellen verführt dabei leicht zu einer einseitigen Auswertung und zu *fragwürdigen Urteilen.* So kommt eine neuere deutsche Dissertation mit dem Titel "Eschatologie und Jenseitserwartung im hellenistischen Diasporajudentum" von Ulrich Fischer zu dem Ergebnis, "daß in jenem Judentum eschatologische Vorstellungen im Sinne einer kosmologisch-apokalyptischen Zukunftsschau eine weitaus geringere Rolle spielen als individuelle Jenseitsvorstellungen", weiter, daß "auch nationaleschatologische Heilserwartungen im Sinne eines politischen Messianismus ... im Judentum der westlichen Diaspora offensichtlich keine bedeutende Rolle gespielt" haben. Dieses Ergebnis wird unterstrichen durch die abschließende Bemerkung, daß "nirgends in den von uns untersuchten Zeugnissen des hellenistischen Diasporajudentums ... auch nur die geringste Spur einer eschatologischen Naherwartung zu finden" war[4]. Das Ergebnis ist freilich durch eine einseitige Quellenauswahl zustande gekommen, da der Verfasser so entscheidende Zeugnisse wie die jüdischen Sibyllinen, die Zwölfertestamente oder die Abrahamsapokalypse einfach beiseite ließ und auch die Wirkung der griechischen Übersetzungen palästinischer Apokalypsen nur ganz am Rande streifte[5]. Auf das Problem der hellenistisch-orientalischen Orakel und "Apokalypsen" politischen Inhalts (Hystaspes, Töpferorakel, Asklepios oder die 4. Ekloge Vergils) ging er überhaupt nicht ein, ebensowenig auf die jüdisch-apokalyptischen Traditionen in der christlichen Literatur. So ist m. E. die Entwicklung des christlichen Chiliasmus von Apk 20 über Papias, Irenäus bis hin zu Laktanz ohne jüdisch-hellenistische Quellen völlig unverständlich. Fischer muß daher am Ende verwundert die Frage stellen, "wie die christliche Mission unter den Juden der westlichen Diaspora die eschatologische Naherwartung der christlichen Urgemeinde hat 'exportieren' können" und wie die Predigt des Paulus "von der nahe bevorstehenden Parusie" von seinen

---

[3] Vgl. Morton Smith 1972, 223: "Edifying literature can also be intended to amuse. Neither religious, nor even moral concern is an insuperable obstacle to the enjoyment of life."

[4] Fischer 1978, 255, 256, 259.

[5] Fischer 1978, 3 Anm. 4, S. 255; vgl. auch S. 7.

Hörern überhaupt verstanden wurde[6]. Die Frage, ob die Einseitigkeit der von ihm behandelten Quellen u. a. auch soziale Gründe haben könnte (s. u. §3.), kommt ihm überhaupt nicht in den Sinn. Diese Ergebnisse sind typisch für die *Enge*, die die neutestamentlich-judaistische Forschung in Deutschland heute bedroht, und zugleich ein warnendes Beispiel. Mit einer einseitigen Quellenauswahl kann man nahezu alles beweisen.

2. Der jüdische Aufstand unter Trajan[7]

Um der Komplexität der Thematik willen wollen wir einen anderen Weg wählen, der von einem politischen Ereignis von elementarer Gewalt und katastrophalen Folgen ausgeht, das zugleich das Zentrum der griechischsprechenden Diaspora, die jüdische Gemeinde in Alexandrien, aber darüber hinaus auch die Judenschaft ganz Ägyptens, der Cyrenaika und Zyperns, weitgehend dezimierte, ja fast völlig zerstörte.

Der jüdische Aufstand in diesen ehemals ptolemäischen Gebieten unter Trajan 115–117 n. Chr. war wohl die schwerste militärische und soziale Erschütterung, die diese Provinzen zwischen Aktium 31 v. Chr. und der Eroberung Ägyptens durch Zenobia 269/270 n. Chr. heimsuchte[8].

2.1. Die von Dio Cassius[9] überlieferten Zahlen der getöteten "Römer und Griechen" sind gewiß übertrieben (240000 in Cypern und 220000 in der Cyrenaika); daß dieser Krieg jedoch auf beiden Seiten als *Ausrottungs-*

---

[6] Fischer 1978, 259. Zur Kritik s. die Rezension von *Ulrich B. Müller* 1980, 239f., der u. a. auch auf das Phänomen des Aufstands unter Trajan verweist.

[7] Unser Wissen hat sich vor allem durch die Arbeiten von *Applebaum* und *Fuks* ganz wesentlich erweitert. Das zeigt ein Vergleich mit älteren Studien, etwa mit dem immer noch lesenswerten Bändchen von Münter, weiland Bischof von Seeland, 1821, mit Schlatter 1897, 86ff., und 1925, 370ff., ja selbst noch mit der im deutschsprachigen Raum vielzitierten Untersuchung von Bietenhard 1948, 66ff. Grundlegend jetzt Fuks, in: *CPJ* II, 1960, 225ff. und Nr. 436–450; vgl. *idem*, 1953, 131ff. und 1961, 98ff.; dazu Tcherikover in: *CPJ* I, 1957, 85–93; weiter Applebaum 1951, 177ff. und in seiner großen Monographie von 1979, 201–344, der z. Zt. wichtigsten, jedoch zu phantasievollen Untersuchung zum Aufstand und seinen Ursachen. Bei der Abfassung der Studie konnte nur die hebräische Vorlage dieser Monographie verwendet werden. Die Einarbeitung der englischen Fassung war mir erst nachträglich möglich. Eine vorzügliche Zusammenfassung gibt Smallwood 1976, 389ff., vgl. auch 1962, 500ff. Zum neuesten Stand der Diskussion s. Kasher 1976, 147ff. Die wesentlichsten antiken Quellen sind bei Schürer/Vermes/Millar I, 1973, 529 aufgeführt. Hilfreich ist jetzt auch der eingehende Kommentar von M. Stern 1980 zu den einzelnen Quellentexten.

[8] Man könnte noch am ehesten den Aufstand der Bukolen, der räuberischen Hirten im nordwestlichen Nildelta, z. Zt. Mark Aurels 172 n. Chr. vergleichen. Unter ihrem tüchtigen Führer Isidoros, einem Priester, bedrohten sie Alexandrien und schlugen zunächst eine römische Streitmacht, auch schlossen sich ihnen Teile der ägyptischen Bevölkerung an. Sie wurden jedoch von dem aus Syrien herbeigeeilten Avidius Cassius aufgespalten und rasch niedergeworfen (Dio Cassius Epitome 71,4; Script. Hist. Aug. M. Ant 21,2 und Avid. Cass. 6,7). Dazu jetzt A. Henrichs 1972, 48ff. Offenbar waren bei ihrem Aufstand auch religiöse Motive im Spiele.

[9] Epitome 68,32,1–3, Text bei M. Stern 1980, 385 Nr. 437.

krieg geführt wurde, ergibt sich daraus, daß die Cyrenaika von Hadrian später über weite Strecken hin neu besiedelt werden mußte[10]. Der Augenzeuge Appian berichtet andererseits, Trajan habe die Juden in Ägypten "ausgerottet"[11] und Euseb überliefert, der von Trajan wohl gegen Ende 116 n. Chr. eingesetzte Flottenbefehlshaber und Feldherr L. Marcius Turbo habe "in zahlreichen Gefechten und in einem langwierigen und mühevollen Krieg Zehntausende von Juden nicht allein aus Kyrene, sondern auch aus Ägypten getötet..."[12]. Nur in Alexandria blieb ein Rest der jüdischen Gemeinde zunächst erhalten, der – vermutlich verstärkt durch jüdische Flüchtlinge aus der Chora – vom Präfekten gegen Übergriffe der Alexandriner geschützt werden mußte[13]. Die jüdische Gemeinde der Stadt verlor jedoch völlig ihre bisherige Bedeutung, möglicherweise ging sie im Zusammenhang mit dem Bar-Kochba-Aufstand völlig unter. Diesen Nachrichten entspricht, daß die papyrologischen und epigraphischen Belege über Juden in Ägypten nach dem Aufstand für die Dauer des 2. Jh. fast ganz abbrechen[14]. Auf Cypern wurde die Judenschaft gänzlich ausgerottet und das Betreten der Insel für Juden bei Todesstrafe verboten. Der jüdische Landbesitz in Ägypten verfiel, wie A. Świderek nachwies, weitgehend, wenn nicht ganz, der staatlichen Konfiskation[15]. Noch im Jahre 199/

---

[10] Orosius 7,12,6: Quae (i. e. Libya, d. h. die Cyrenaika) adeo tunc interfectis cultoribus desolata est, ut, nisi postea Hadrianus imperator collectas illuc aliunde colonias deduxisset, uacua penitus terra abraso habitatore mansisset. Vgl. Eus. Chron. Hadrian V (121 n. Chr.), *GCS* 47 ed. Helm 1955, 198: Hadrianus in Libyam, quae a Iudaeis uastata fuerat colonias deducit. Die Inschrift Türk Tarih Bell. XI (1947) S. 101 ff. Nr. 19 (*SEG* 17,584) berichtet, daß schon Trajan den Befehl gab, in der Cyrenaika 3000 Legionsveteranen anzusiedeln. Vgl. auch *SEG* 17,809 und Fraser 1950, 78 ff., dazu Applebaum 1979, 270 ff., der eine Ansiedlung dieser Veteranen in Teucheira vermutet (287), und Smallwood 1976, 410 ff.

[11] Bell. Civ. 2,90 (M. Stern 1980, 187 f. Nr. 350): Τραϊανὸν ἐξολλύντα τὸ ἐν Αἰγύπτῳ Ἰουδαίων γένος. Vgl. auch die Schilderung seiner Flucht durch das Delta vor den Juden Arab. F 19 (M. Stern 1980, 185 Nr. 348).

[12] Hist. eccl. 4,2,4: ὃ δὲ πολλαῖς μάχαις οὐκ ὀλίγῳ τε χρόνῳ τὸν πρὸς αὐτοὺς διαπονήσας πόλεμον, πολλὰς μυριάδας Ἰουδαίων ... ἀναιρεῖ.

[13] Das ergibt sich aus den Acta Pauli et Antonini, Act. Alex IX = *CPJ* II, 1960, 87 ff. Nr. 158 vgl. Smallwood 1976, 406 ff.: "The Jewish community in Alexandria now sinks into historical oblivion for a century" (409); etwas anders Applebaum 1979, 295,338. Zu ihrer späteren Neuentwicklung s. Smallwood 1976, 516 ff. Der berühmte Brief Hadrians, Script. Hist. Aug. Quadr. Tyr. 8, in dem der jüdische Patriarch erwähnt wird, ist eine antichristliche und antijüdische Fälschung aus dem Jahre 399 n. Chr., oder wenig später, s. W. Schmid 1966, 178 ff.; vgl. jetzt auch M. Stern 1980, 636 ff. Nr. 537.

[14] Tcherikover CPJ I, 1957, 93: "an almost total annihilation of Egyptian Jewry; strictly speaking, with this period the history of the Egyptian Jews in the Hellenistic-Roman age comes to an end". Smallwood 1976, 406 Anm. 66 weist darauf hin, daß in *CPJ* den fast 450 Dokumenten aus der hellenistischen und römischen Zeit bis 117 n. Chr. nur 50 aus der Zeit zwischen 117 und 337 gegenüberstehen. Nach *CPJ* III 1964, Nr. 460 zahlte von den über 1000 männlichen Erwachsenen des Ortes Karanis nur noch ein einziger die Judensteuer (145/46 oder 167/68 n. Chr.).

[15] Dio Cassius 68,32,2f.; dazu Smallwood 1976, 412 ff.; Applebaum 1979, 297 ff.; Świderek 1971, 45 ff.

200 wurde in Oxyrhynchos ein jährliches Fest über die "Waffenbrüder-
schaft" der örtlichen Bevölkerung mit den Römern bei dem rettenden Sieg
über die Juden gefeiert.[15a]. Die Menschenverluste der Juden in diesen
wichtigen Zentren der Diaspora waren so fast noch größer als die der
beiden Aufstände in Palästina. Die Erhebung muß für die Betroffenen eine
Katastrophe von apokalyptischem Ausmaß bedeutet haben. Zusammen
mit dem Aufstand Bar-Kochbas bildete sie das "Holocaust" des antiken
Judentums.

2.2. Die Juden führten den Krieg mit dem Ziel der *Eroberung*, zumindest
aber der *Zerstörung* der überwiegend heidnischen Territorien. Der Auf-
stand scheint dabei an verschiedenen Orten ziemlich gleichzeitig in der 1.
Hälfte des Jahres 115 aufgeflammt zu sein, als Trajan in das parthische
Mesopotamien einmarschiert war. Zwar wurde die Erhebung in Alexandrien relativ rasch niedergeschlagen, dagegen behielten die Juden auf
Cypern, in der Cyrenaika und dann auch in weiten Teilen der ägyptischen
Chōra zunächst die Oberhand. In Ägypten erreichten ihre Erfolge erst im
Verlauf des Jahres 116 ihren eigentlichen Höhepunkt. Die Aufständischen
brachten weite Teile von der Thebais im Süden bis vor Pelusium im
Nordosten und bis vor die Tore Alexandriens unter ihre Kontrolle[16]. Dabei
wurden sie von ihren Glaubensgenossen aus der Cyrenaika tatkräftig
unterstützt. Applebaum vermutet m. E. mit Recht, daß sie nach einem
übergreifenden strategischen Plan handelten und nach ihrem Sieg in der
Cyrenaika versuchten, die ganze ägyptische Chōra und Alexandrien zu
erobern, um am Ende nach dem Heiligen Lande durchzustoßen. Zugleich
bedrohten sie die Getreideversorgung Roms und hatten, wie der erfolgreiche Aufstand in Salamis auf Cypern zeigt, wohl auch das Ziel, auf See aktiv
zu werden. Sie scheiterten bei dem Ziel, Alexandrien in ihre Hand zu

---

[15a] *CPJ* II, 1960, Nr. 450; vgl. dazu Fuks 1953, 153 f.

[16] Die erste Nachricht stammt aus dem Archiv des Strategen Apollonios aus dem Distrikt
von Hermoupolis in Mittelägypten Ende August/Anfang September 115 n. Chr.: Der Zivil-
beamte wurde durch die Unruhen von seiner Familie plötzlich getrennt, d. h. er wurde wohl
zum militärischen Dienst herangezogen. Seine Frau bittet ihn, er solle sich nicht ohne
militärische Bewachung der Gefahr aussetzen, vielmehr wie andere Beamte die gefährlichen
Situationen den Offizieren überlassen: *CPJ* II, 1960, Nr. 436. Ein Erlaß des Präfekten Rutilius
Lupus berichtet wenig später am 13. 10. u. a. von einem geraume Zeit zurückliegenden, für
die Römer siegreichen Kampf in Alexandrien. Die Erhebung der Juden war dort zu diesem
Zeitpunkt offenbar schon niedergeschlagen: *CPJ* II, 1960, Nr. 435. Möglicherweise gab es
jedoch noch jüdische Angriffe von außen bzw. neue Unruhen in der Stadt, vgl. dazu die
späteren Verhandlungen vor Hadrian *CPJ* II, 1960, Nr. 158. Zum Ganzen Smallwood 1976,
395 ff., 406 ff. *CPJ* II, 1960, Nr. 438 berichtet in der 2. Hälfte des Jahres 116 von jüdischen
Siegen im Distrikt von Hermoupolis, bei der die von den Römern eingesetzten ägyptischen
Bauernmilizen schwere Verluste erlitten. Der letzte Beleg für die Zahlung der Judensteuer aus
Edfu in Oberägypten stammt von einem Centurio Aninios vom 18. Mai 116 n. Chr., danach
brechen die Zahlungsbelege ab. Er ist der einzige jüdische Soldat in römischen Diensten, der
uns bekannt ist: *CPJ* II, 1960, Nr. 229.

bringen. Der Verfasser bemerkt anschließend: "It may be doubted whether there ever arose in the early Roman Empire any movement which so imperilled Roman authority as did the Jewish Diaspora revolt in the reign of Trajan. No one of Rome's subject peoples had risen in active rebellion on this scale..."[17]. Der ganze Verlauf des Krieges gibt dieser Vermutung Recht. Erst zu Beginn des Jahres 117 hören wir von einem Sieg römischer Legionstruppen bei Memphis, die Kämpfe bis zur völligen Niederschlagung des Aufstandes haben jedoch weit über den Tod Trajans am 7. 8. hinaus in die Anfänge der Regierungszeit Hadrians angedauert. Noch im August 118 konnte man im Gau von Hermoupolis wegen der völligen Verwüstung nicht auf dem Landwege, sondern nur auf dem Nil reisen[18].

2.3. Die Kämpfe wurden auf beiden Seiten mit erbarmungslosem Haß als "Religionskrieg" geführt. Dio Cassius berichtet von unsagbaren Kriegsgreueln bis hin zum Kannibalismus, ein Vorwurf, der in anderem Zusammenhang ja auch gegen die Christen erhoben wurde und als Mittel der "psychologischen Kriegsführung" die Angst und den Haß gegen den Gegner schüren sollte[19]. Ein Papyrusbrief aus Mittelägypten illustriert die Furcht der Bevölkerung, die der antijüdischen Greuelpropaganda offenbar Glauben schenkte[20]. Die Juden hatten es vor allem, wie eine Fülle von Nachrichten aus Kyrene[21] und z. T. auch aus Alexandrien[22] bezeugen, auf

---

[17] Vgl. Applebaum 1979, 269 ff., 337 ff., 341 (Zit.). Das geographische Ausmaß des Krieges 66–70 und 132–135 war wesentlich geringer und darum politisch weniger bedrohlich, das gilt selbst für den Aufstand des Civilis in Germanien und NW-Gallien 68–70 n. Chr., der sich nur in einem noch halb barbarischen Grenzgebiet und aufgrund des römischen Bürgerkriegs entfalten konnte.

[18] Hadrian wurde am 9. 8. 117 vom syrischen Heer zum Kaiser proklamiert. Zum Regierungswechsel s. jetzt Temporini 1978, 120 ff. Am 28. November 117 erbittet der Stratege Apollonios beim Präfekten Ägyptens um 60 Tage Urlaub, nachdem ein früheres Urlaubsgesuch, vermutlich wegen der noch unsicheren militärischen Lage, abgelehnt worden war. Seine persönlichen Besitzungen im Gebiet von Hermoupolis seien "durch den Angriff der gottlosen Juden" in so ungeordneten Zustand geraten, daß seine persönliche Anwesenheit dringend notwendig sei. Zu diesem Zeitpunkt scheint der Aufstand im wesentlichen militärisch niedergeschlagen zu sein: *CPJ* II, 1960, Nr. 443. Vgl. auch Script. Hist. Aug. Hadrian 5,2.8 und Euseb Chron. Hadrianus I (117 n. Chr.): Hadrianus Iudaeos capit secundo contra Romanos rebellantes. Zur Verwüstung: *CPJ* II, 1960, Nr. 446 vgl. 447.449.

[19] Epitome 68,32,1 f. Ähnliche Greuel wurden später den Bukolen nachgesagt, s. A. Henrichs 1972, 48 ff. Vgl. dazu jetzt M. Stern 1980, 387.

[20] *CPJ* II, 1960, Nr. 437, dazu Fuks S. 236: "the only thing one can safely say is that the war was conducted ruthlessly on both sides."

[21] Smallwood 1976, 397 ff., 409 f.; Applebaum 1951, 177 ff.; 1979, 269 ff.

[22] In Alexandrien wurde das Heiligtum der Nemesis am Ostende der Stadt, in dem das Haupt des Pompeius begraben war, zerstört: Appian, bell. Civ. 2,90 (M. Stern 1980, 187 Nr. 350). Auch das Serapeion trug schwere Beschädigungen davon, s. Smallwood 1976, 399, 409. Vgl. Applebaum 1979, 267, 295 f., 316 f. Dazu die übertreibende Nachricht Eusebs, Chron. Hadrian I (117 n. Chr.): Hadrianus Alexandriam a Romanis (sic; es ist jedoch mit der armenischen Fassung und der syrischen Epitome Iudaeis zu lesen) subversam publicis

die Zerstörung heidnischer Kultstätten abgesehen. Auf ihrer Seite wurde die großartige Basilikasynagoge in Alexandrien – nach der Zerstörung des Tempels das wichtigste religiöse Bauwerk des Judentums – niedergebrannt[23]. Die formelhafte Redeweise von den ἀνόσιοι Ἰουδαῖοι, die uns mehrfach in den "alexandrinischen Märtyrerakten" begegnet, kam jetzt selbst in offiziellen Urkunden in Gebrauch[24]. Diese alexandrinischen, antijüdischen Propagandaschriften betonen ihrerseits die rettende Macht des *Sarapis* gegenüber den Juden und dem angeblich judenfreundlichen Kaiser[25].

2.4. Der Verlauf des Krieges war so in den ersten eineinhalb Jahren, d. h. bis der Kaiser mit Marcius Turbo seine volle Militärmacht einsetzte, für die militärisch wenig geübten und schlecht ausgerüsteten jüdischen Insurgenten – wenn man von dem durch eine römische Legion geschützten Alexandrien absieht – überraschend erfolgreich. Dies mag durch mehrere Ursachen bedingt gewesen sein. Einmal müßte man den Kampfesmut und die Todesverachtung der Aufständischen hervorheben, die Tacitus kurz zuvor im Blick auf den Jüdischen Krieg begründet hatte: animosque proelio aut suppliciis peremptorum aeternos putant: hinc generandi amor et moriendi contemptus[26]. Nicht minder wesentlich war die *vorzügliche militärische Führung.* Euseb spricht von einem "König" Lukuas[27], der die Juden aus Kyrene nach Ägypten führte und dort erfolgreich den Aufstand befehligte. Die nächste Parallele zu diesem jüdischen König Lukuas stellt der nicht minder kriegstüchtige "naśî' Jiśra'el Schim'on Bar Kokhba" dar. Die militärische Leistung der Juden der Cyrenaika und Ägyptens wird man um so höher einschätzen, wenn man bedenkt, daß die strategische Position Bar Kochbas im unwegsamen jüdischen Siedlungsgebiet Judäas sehr viel

---

instaurauit impensis", vgl. Dionysius Telmaharensis (ed. Siegfried/Gelzer 1884) 62: "Hadrianus Alexandriam, quae a Iudaeis perturbata erat, restituit".

[23] T. Sukka 4,6 (Zuckermandel 198); zur Zerstörung jSukka 5,1 55b Z. 7f.; bSukka 51b; vgl. dazu M. Hengel 1966, 167.

[24] *Act. Alex.* VIII = *CPJ* II, 1960, Nr. 157 col. III Z. 42f. der Vorwurf des Hermaiscus gegen den Kaiser: ἀλλὰ λυπούμεθα ὅτι τὸ συνέδριόν σου ἐπλήσθη τῶν ἀνοσίων Ἰουδαίων. Vgl. weiter IX A = Nr. 158 col. VI Z. 14. S. dazu das Gesuch des Strategen Apollonios an den Präfekten *CPJ* II, 1960, Nr. 443 col. II Z. 4 und Fuks 1953, 157f.; 1961, 103f., der darauf hinweist, daß vor dem Aufstand ἀνόσιοι Ἰουδαῖοι noch keine feste Bezeichnung für die Juden war. Vgl. dazu auch Sevenster 1975, 99ff. und die treffende Bemerkung von Wilcken 1909, 786: "In jener Prägung des ἀνόσιοι Ἰουδαῖοι sehe ich einen Beweis dafür, wie tief der religiöse Gegensatz empfunden wurde."

[25] *Act. Alex.* VIII = *CPJ* II, 1960, Nr. 157 col. III Z. 50ff.: Das von den alexandrinischen Gesandten getragene Standbild des Sarapis fängt an zu schwitzen und erfüllt Trajan und ganz Rom mit Entsetzen. Vgl. auch *Act. Alex.* II = *CPJ* II, 1960, Nr. 154 col. II Z. 47ff.

[26] Hist. 5,5,3; dazu M. Stern 1980, 41ff.

[27] Hist. eccl. 4,2,4: Λουκούᾳ τῷ βασιλεῖ αὐτῶν. Dio Cassius nennt die Anführer in Kyrene Andreas und auf Zypern Artemion. Möglicherweise handelte es sich bei dem ersteren um einen Doppelnamen, so jetzt auch M. Stern 1980, 386.

vorteilhafter war. Er konnte einen Guerillakrieg führen; in den beiden Provinzen ohne natürliche Befestigungen, und mit einer ganz überwiegend feindlichen Bevölkerung, die die Römer militärisch unterstützte, war dies fast unmöglich. Die Verluste der Römer müssen sehr groß gewesen sein, bei einzelnen Einheiten fast bis zu 40%. Ob sie freilich, wie Applebaum aufgrund einer dunklen Notiz in Or.Sib 14,326–28 vermutet, eine römische Legion, darunter Teile der an sich nach Parthien abkommandierten legio III Cyrenaica vernichteten, ist mehr als fraglich. Über die – gewiß harten und für die Juden im ersten Jahr recht erfolgreichen – Kämpfe sind wir nur ganz fragmentarisch unterrichtet[28]. Die Tatsache, daß Trajan auf die Wiedereroberung der Adiabene östlich des Tigris Ende 116 verzichtet und Hadrian Mesopotamien wieder ganz aufgab, hängt wohl nicht zuletzt auch mit der Bedrohung durch den Aufstand der Juden zusammen, der zu einer unmittelbaren Gefährdung des Reiches geworden war.

Mit einem gewissen Recht besteht in der Forschung darum eine weitgehende Übereinstimmung darüber, daß der "König Lukuas" wie Bar Kochba und frühere jüdische "Königsprätendenten" am besten als eine *messianische Gestalt* zu verstehen ist und entsprechend der ganze Aufstand eine *Erhebung mit eschatologisch-messianischem Hintergrund* darstellte. Applebaum bemerkt dazu: "The spirit of the movement was messianic, its aim the liquidation of the Roman régime and the setting up of a new Jewish commonwealth, whose task was to inaugurate the messianic era"[29]. Dies würde aber bedeuten, daß die endzeitlich-politische Heilserwartung auch in den ältesten Kernländern der griechischsprechenden Diaspora im Gegensatz zu der von Fischer geäußerten Meinung recht kräftig gewesen sein muß. Es wäre darum lohnend, der Frage nachzugehen, ob in der "apokalyptischen" Literatur der griechischsprechenden Diaspora gerade Ägyptens Hinweise auf Motive zu finden sind, die für jene einzigartige Erhebung typisch waren.

---

[28] S. dazu jetzt Kasher 1976, 156 ff.; vgl. Applebaum 1979, 312 ff.; s. auch Artemidor, Oneirocrit. 4,24 über einen praefectus praetorii, der "in dem jüdischen Krieg in Kyrene" getötet wurde. Zu Sib 14 (nicht wie Applebaum 1979, 313, vgl. 316, meint Sib 17!) s. Rzach 1923, 2162 ff. Es handelt sich um ein sehr spätes Machwerk. Besonders interessant sind die Zahlenangaben über den Empfang der deposita neuer tirones Asiani bei der Cohors I Lusitanorum am 3. 9. 117 in Ägypten. Bei einer Sollstärke von 360–380 pedites, wurden dieser 126 Rekruten zugeführt, in den 6 Centurionen zwischen 17 und 24; s. dazu J. F. Gilliam 1966, 91–97: "In all likelihood, ..., the 126 tirones Asiani were sent to the cohort largely to replace men lost in the revolt" (96). Neuedition des Textes bei Robert O. Fink 1971, 277 ff. Nr. 74.

[29] Applebaum 1979, 260; vgl. Tcherikover, *CPJ* I, 1957, 89 ff.; Fuks 1961, 103, der zusätzlich noch auf die Verspottung eines jüdischen Königs im Mimus vor dem alexandrinischen Pöbel, *Act. Alex.* IX A = *CPJ* II, 1960, 158a col. I Z. 4–7 verweist; Smallwood 1976, 397; "a messianic crusade". Kritisch, ohne nähere Begründung, dagegen Sevenster 1975, 100 Anm. 61. Vgl. auch jetzt M. Stern 1980, 386: "It seems that he attracted Messianic hopes, being called king by Eusebius".

2.5. Zuvor müssen wir jedoch noch einen Blick auf *Palästina* werfen[30]. Nach der raschen Niederschlagung des parthisch-jüdischen Aufstandes in Nordmesopotamien bis gegen Ende 116 ernannte Trajan den im Osten siegreichen Feldherrn und maurischen Fürsten *Lusius Quietus* zum Statthalter Palästinas, der dadurch zugleich senatorischen Rang erhielt. Gleichzeitig wurde wohl auch die Besatzung dort wesentlich verstärkt. Diese Beorderung des tüchtigen und harten Quietus in die kleine Provinz deutet darauf hin, daß Trajan auch dort *die Situation als recht bedrohlich ansah*[31]. Die rabbinischen Nachrichten vom *"Krieg des Qîṭos"* zwischen den Kriegen Vespasians und Bar Kochbas, die rabbinischen Legenden von Pappos und Lulianos[32] sowie Hinweise in Ps. Spartians Vita Hadriani[33], bei Hippolyt und die Weihung einer vexillatio der legio III Cyrenaica an Sarapis in Jerusalem aus dem Jahre 116 oder 117[34] und andere historische und epigraphische Indizien machen es wahrscheinlich, daß Palästina durch den Aufstand in Ägypten nicht nur bedroht war, sondern daß es dort zu Spannungen und einzelnen Unruhen, wenn auch nicht zu einem wirklichen Aufstand, kam. Besonders auffallend ist die Notiz in syrischen Chroniken, daß sich der jüdische König Lukuas von Ägypten aus Judäa zugewandt habe und von

---

[30] Smallwood 1962, 500ff.; 1976, 421ff.; Applebaum 1979, 300ff., 322ff.

[31] Groag 1927, 1879f.; M. Stern 1980, 389. Lusius Quietus wurde bald nach der Thronbesteigung Hadrians abgesetzt und im Jahr 118 hingerichtet. Seine Tätigkeit in Palästina dauerte nur wenige Monate.

[32] M. Sota 9,14; Seder Olam R. c. 30; beide Texte mit Kommentar bei Krauß 1972, 81f. Vermutlich ist von L. Quietus auch im Zusammenhang der Legende von Lulianos und Pappos und ihrer Hinrichtung die Rede, s. Sifra Emor c. 9,5, ed. Finkelstein 1956, 442; Scholion Meg. Taanit, ed. Lichtenstein 1931/32, 272f., 350, dazu Schlatter 1897, 90f., Krauß 1972, 84f. und Stemberger 1979, 358ff. Die Deutung des "Krieges des Qitos" auf die Katastrophe der griechischsprechenden Diaspora bei Rokeah 1972, 79ff. kann dagegen gar nicht überzeugen, er läßt sich auch nicht mit Schürer/Vermes/Millar I, 1973, 533 einfach auf den Aufstand in Mesopotamien beziehen, da dieser keine rein oder auch nur überwiegend jüdische Sache war. Wir hören von ihm allein durch Euseb, der an allen negativen Nachrichten über die Juden interessiert war, während Dio Cassius nur ganz allgemein von einer Erhebung in Nordmesopotamien spricht, ohne eine jüdische Beteiligung zu nennen: 68,29,4–31,4. Dieser Aufstand brach auch erst im Spätsommer 116 los, als Trajan das ganze Gebiet bereits erobert hatte und die jüdische Erhebung in Ägypten bereits auf ihrem Höhepunkt stand. Der Aufstand der Juden in Mesopotamien im Sommer 116 steht so weniger in Zusammenhang mit der Rebellion in der Cyrenaika und Ägypten als mit der allgemeinen Erhebung gegen die Römer in Nordmesopotamien. Vgl. Lepper 1948, 91–96; Applebaum 1979, 319ff.

[33] 5,2: Lybia denique ac Palaestina rebelles animos efferebant; dazu M. Stern 1980, 618 Nr. 509.

[34] Smallwood 1962, 506f.; Applebaum 1979, 301f. Die Inschrift *ILS* 4393 lautet: (I)ovi o.m. Sarapidi pro salute et victoria imp. Nervae Traiani Caesaris optumi Aug. Germanici Dacici Parthici et populi Romani vexill. leg III Cyr. fecit. Die Legion hatte ihren Standort in Alexandrien, war aber zum Partherfeldzug von dort abgezogen worden. Wahrscheinlich waren dann Teile derselben gleichzeitig mit der Ernennung des siegreichen L. Quietus zum Statthalter nach Jerusalem verlegt worden. Die Weihung in Jerusalem wäre dann auch als religiöse antijüdische Demonstration zu verstehen.

"Lysias", d. h. Lusius Quietus, besiegt worden sei[35]. Umgekehrt legt eine Schimeon b. Jochai zugeschriebene Tradition die Vermutung nahe, daß Juden aus Palästina den ägyptischen Insurgenten zu Hilfe eilten. Sie seien in den Tagen Trajans nach Ägypten gezogen und wie schon zur Zeit Sanheribs und Jeremias "zu Fall gekommen"[36]. Es wäre sonderbar, wenn die Juden, die nach Appian bis vor Pelusium vorgedrungen waren, nicht versucht hätten, auch das palästinische Mutterland zu erreichen, und wenn nicht dort selbst, nach der erfolgreichen Erhebung im Westen und den Rückschlägen der Römer im Partherkrieg, das messianische Fieber aufs Äußerste angestiegen wäre.

3. Zu den Gründen und zur Vorgeschichte des Aufstandes

3.1. Eigenartig ist, daß wir nichts Näheres über die *Gründe* dieser so furchtbaren Insurrektion erfahren. Die politische und soziale Lage der Judenschaft in den drei betroffenen Gebieten war an sich nicht schlechter als im übrigen römischen Reich. Offenbar hatte sich jedoch in den 150 Jahren römischer Herrschaft über Ägypten *ein grundlegender Wandel im Verhältnis gegenüber der heidnischen Umwelt und Staatsmacht vollzogen*, dessen Spuren sich auch in der jüdischen Literatur Ägyptens nachweisen lassen. Man vergleiche nur einmal den Aristeasbrief mit dem im 1. Jh. n. Chr. entstandenen 3. Makkabäerbuch und die 3. mit der 5. Sibylle. Ganz am Anfang scheint die Reaktion auf die römische Eroberung sogar kurze Zeit positiv gewesen zu sein. Eine negative Rolle mag bei dieser verhängnisvollen Entwicklung die Kopfsteuer gespielt haben, die Augustus für alle Bewohner Ägyptens, mit Ausnahme der Bürger Alexandriens, einführte[37], außerdem die Verweigerung des Zugangs zum alexandrinischen Bürgerrecht für die Juden der Stadt durch das Edikt des Claudius[38]. Weiter wird

---

[35] Applebaum 1979, 322: "The epigraphical and literary evidence for the situation in Iudaea at the time of the revolt ... point, in sum, to tension and even to bloodshed, although not to a genuine military outbreak." Zu den syrischen Quellen s. Michael Syrus üs. v. Chabot I, 1899, 172: "A la fin du règne de Trajan, les Juifs d'Egypte se révoltèrent. Ils se constituèrent un roi nommé Lucua. Il les dirigea et vint en Judée. Trajan envoya contre eux Lysias qui en détruisit des myriades. C'est pourquoi Lysias fut établi gouverneur de la Judée" vgl. auch *Bar-Hebraeus Chron. Syr.* ed Bruns/Kirsch 1789, 56. Vermutlich gehen sie beide jedoch nicht auf eine unbekannte Quelle zurück, sondern fassen den Bericht der syrischen Übersetzung von Eusebs Kirchengeschichte (E. Nestle 1901, 122) zusammen. Applebaum 1979, 259 Anm. 69 zitiert noch eine spätere Nachricht von Eutychius ibn Batrik, wonach die Juden zur Zeit Trajans ihren König in Jerusalem gekrönt hätten, was völlig unglaubwürdig ist.

[36] Mekh Ex zu 14,13 (Lauterbach I, 1949, 213); jSukka 5,1 55b Z. 8ff.; LamR 1,16 §45. Schlatter 1897, 89f.

[37] Tcherikover, *CPJ* I, 1957, 60ff., vgl. *idem*, 1963, 1ff.; Smallwood 1976, 231f.; anders Kasher 1978, 196ff.

[38] Tcherikover, *CPJ* I, 1957, 71ff.; II, 1960, 36ff. Nr. 153; Smallwood 1976, 248ff.; anders Kasher 1978, 239ff.

sich auch das Verhältnis zur nichtjüdischen Bevölkerung durch die Pogrome der Jahre 38 und 66 verschlechtert haben, auch die Tempelzerstörung und die Erhebung des fiscus Judaicus verbesserten das Verhältnis zur römischen Macht nicht. Aber all das sind noch keine zureichenden Gründe für den Aufstand, die alexandrinischen Märtyrerakten zeigen ja, wie die Kaiser bis hin zu Trajan und Hadrian z. T. in massiver Weise verleumdet wurden, auf jüdischer Seite zu stehen. So beschuldigte der alexandrinische Märtyrer Hermaiskos Trajan, sein aus Senatoren bestehendes Ratskollegium sei voller "gottloser Juden" (ἀλλὰ λυπούμεθα ὅτι τὸ συνέδριόν σου ἐπλήσθη τῶν ἀνοσίων Ἰουδαίων)[38a].

3.2. Man wird daher zusätzlich davon ausgehen müssen, *daß die jüdische Bevölkerung selbst in sich gespalten war.* Während die Oberschicht aus Gründen der Selbsterhaltung die Loyalität gegenüber Rom bewahrte und versuchte, die unvermeidlichen Spannungen mit der nichtjüdischen Bevölkerung, besonders mit der "griechischen" Majorität in den Städten, in Schranken zu halten, und dabei immer wieder – oft mit Erfolg – beim Kaiser Hilfe suchte, *scheinen die einfachen Schichten sich immer mehr messianisch-politischen Hoffnungen hingegeben zu haben.*

Darauf weisen die Vorgänge in *Ägypten* – nach der Niederwerfung Judäas im Jahre 70 – hin. Damals flüchteten jüdische Aufständische – Josephus nennt hier besonders die *"Sikarier"* – in größerer Zahl nach Ägypten, vermutlich weil sie die berechtigte Hoffnung hatten, bei einem Teil ihrer dortigen Volksgenossen Gehör zu finden. Eine Folge der daraus entstehenden Unruhen war die Schließung des Tempels in Leontopolis[39].

Zu ähnlichen Unruhen kam es in der *Cyrenaika*, wo ein dorthin geflüchteter "Sikarier", der Weber Jonathan, als *Mose redivivus* eine größere Menge aus der einfachen Bevölkerung "in die Wüste führte, mit dem Versprechen, er wolle ihnen Zeichen und Erscheinungen zeigen". Der Vorgang erinnert an die Pseudopropheten in Judäa, wie jenen Ägypter und Theudas, von denen Josephus berichtet. Die Vornehmen meldeten den "Exodus" dem Statthalter Catullus, der die Ausgezogenen niedermachen oder gefangennehmen ließ, aber darüber hinaus zugleich einen Pogrom gegen die jüdische Oberschicht entfachte, der bis nach Alexandrien und Rom fortwirkte. Selbst Josephus wurde in diesem Zusammenhang denunziert und angeklagt, jedoch von Vespasian freigesprochen. Diese Vorgänge mußten zu einer fortdauernden Spannung führen, zumal es schon zu Beginn der römischen Herrschaft zu Unruhen gekommen war. In der Cyrenaika war bereits 87/88 v. Chr. ein jüdischer Aufstand gegen die griechischen Städte ausgebrochen, so daß Sulla den Lukullus dorthin entsandte. Später hatte sich unter Augustus die wirtschaftliche und politische Lage in der Provinz

---

[38a] *CPJ* II, 1960, 83f. Nr. 157 Col. III, 42f.   [39] Jos. Bell 7,408ff.

erheblich verbessert. Wahrscheinlich erzeugte dann wieder der seit Claudius erhobene Anspruch des fiscus, das alte ptolemäische Königsland sei als ager publicus zu betrachten, bei den ehemaligen Kleruchen jüdischer Herkunft eine gewisse Unruhe und wirtschaftliche Unsicherheit; die Auseinandersetzungen um diesen Streit zogen sich lange hin, so daß auch er als auslösendes Moment des Aufstandes keinesfalls ausreicht. Er wird nur *ein* Motiv unter anderen gewesen sein[40].

3.3. Die Gründe des Aufstandes 115–117 erscheinen so als *vielschichtig*; auch wird man zwischen primären und sekundären Ursachen unterscheiden müssen. Zu den letzteren gehört die Verschlechterung der Rechtssituation der jüdischen Bevölkerung gegenüber der ptolemäischen Zeit und damit verbunden die Zunahme der Spannungen gegenüber der römischen Macht.

Ein unmittelbarer äußerer Grund für den Ausbruch des Aufstandes mag der *Partherkrieg Trajans* und der Abzug von einer der beiden in Alexandrien stationierten Legionen darstellen. Die Römer scheinen ihre Besatzungstruppen in Ägypten etwa um die Hälfte vermindert zu haben[41]. Die *eigentliche* Ursache für die Explosion des Jahres 115 wird jedoch nicht primär bei rationalen politischen oder sozialen Erwägungen, sondern im *religiösen Bereich* zu suchen sein, in der alten Hoffnung, die schon die Juden Palästinas nach dem übereinstimmenden Urteil des Josephus, Tacitus und Sueton zum Aufstand verführte, daß der durch die Tora verheißene Messias jetzt "die Weltherrschaft erlangen werde"[42]. Man glaubte, "das Reich Gottes sei nahe herbeigekommen". Möglicherweise war diese Hoffnung durch den großen Krieg mit den Parthern bekräftigt worden, da man in dem erwarteten Sieg der östlichen Heere über die Macht Roms den Vorläufer des Messias sah (s. u. Anm. 54). Euseb und Orosius betonen entsprechend die *plötzliche, unerwartete Leidenschaftlichkeit* der Empörung.

---

[40] Jos. Bell 7, 437ff.; Jos.Ant 14,114ff.; Vita 424f. vgl. Plut. Luc. 2; Romanelli 1943, 223ff. und 1954, 668ff.; Applebaum 1979, 65,202ff.,219ff. Auf ein positives Verhältnis zur römischen Verwaltung deutet z. B. die Ehreninschrift für M. Titius 24/25 n. Chr. aus Berenike hin: Roux 1949, 281ff.; Applebaum 1979, 146ff.,216f. Zum ager publicus s. *op. cit.*, 353 Index s. v. und bes. 208ff.

[41] Kasher 1976, 151ff. Applebaum 1979, 310ff. Von den beiden bei Alexandrien stationierten Legionen, der legio XXII Deiotariana und der legio III Cyrenaica, war die letztere vermutlich schon im Jahr 114 zur Teilnahme an dem östlichen Feldzug abberufen worden. Eine Inschrift von Anfang 115 bezeugt eine ihrer Einheiten in Dura Europos, eine zweite Ende 116/Anfang 117 in Jerusalem, s. o. Anm. 34.

[42] Jos. Bell 6,312f.: τὸ δ' ἐπᾶραν αὐτοὺς μάλιστα πρὸς τὸν πόλεμον ἦν χρησμὸς ἀμφίβολος ὁμοίως ἐν τοῖς ἱεροῖς εὑρημένος γράμμασιν, ὡς κατὰ τὸν καιρὸν ἐκεῖνον ἀπὸ τῆς χώρας αὐτῶν τις ἄρξει τῆς οἰκουμένης. Tac. Hist. 5,13: Pluribus persuasio inerat antiquis sacerdotum litteris contineri, eo ipso tempore fore ut valesceret Oriens profectique Iudaea rerum potirentur. Ähnlich Sueton, Vesp. 4,5, dazu Hengel 1976, 243ff.; Fischer 1978, 158ff.; M. Stern 1980, 61f.

Die Juden "in Alexandrien, in dem übrigen Ägypten und außerdem in
Kyrene seien, wie von einem gewaltsamen, revolutionären Geist gepackt,
angetrieben worden, sich gegen ihre griechischen Mitbürger zu erheben...,"[43] bzw. sie "entbrannten gleichzeitig in unglaublicher Leiden-
schaft... wie vom Wahnsinn dahingerissen"[44].

4. Die 5. Sibylle und der jüdische Aufstand

4.1. Wir besitzen nun eine "apokalyptische" Schrift, das sogenannte
5. sibyllinische Buch[45], in der uns eine ganze Reihe von Motiven des Aufstandes begegnet. Den Hauptteil des Buches (ab v. 52) wird man in der Zeit
Domitians oder Trajans ansetzen dürfen, jedoch noch vor dem Aufstand
der Jahre 115–117, da dieser nicht direkt erwähnt wird. Die Endredaktion
erfolgte dann unter Hadrian, doch noch vor dem Bar-Kochba-Aufstand,
da Hadrian in der einleitenden Aufzählung im Gegensatz zu Trajan positiv
beurteilt wird[46]. Das Werk ist ein Zeugnis für die endzeitliche Hoffnung
ägyptischer Juden, die selbst der gebildeten Oberschicht entstammen, da
sie mit der Sprache Homers umzugehen wissen, heidnische Mythologie
kennen und in Geographie und Geschichte nicht unbewandert sind. Weiter
verfügt die 5. Sibylle über das ganze Arsenal apokalyptischer Schreckensvi-
sionen. Das Weltbild der Verfasser ist beherrscht durch den schroffen
Gegensatz zu den gottlosen Völkern, die dem einen, wahren Gott und
Schöpfer Anerkennung und Ehre versagen und Israel unterdrücken[47]. Ihnen
droht jetzt, in der "letzten Zeit"[48], die mit der Zerstörung des Tempels
beginnt, Gottes vernichtender Zorn:

"Denn allen Menschen zumal ist Mord und Schrecken beschieden,
Wegen der mächtigen Stadt und wegen des Volks der Gerechten,
Welches gerettet stets ward, das besonders die Vorsehung schützte."

(225–227 Üs. n. Kurfeß)

---

[43] Euseb, Hist. eccl. 4,2,2: ... ὥσπερ ὑπὸ πνεύματος δεινοῦ τινος καὶ στασιώδους
ἀναρριπισθέντες, ὥρμηντο πρὸς τοὺς συνοίκους Ἕλληνας στασιάζειν.

[44] Orosius, Hist adv. pag. 7,12,6: incredibili deinde motu sub uno tempore Iudaei quasi
rabie efferati per diuersas terrarum partes exarserunt. Vgl. dazu Applebaum 1979, 259.

[45] Zur 5. Sibylle s. Geffcken 1902a, 22 ff.; Rzach 1923, 2134 ff.; Collins 1974, 75–95; vgl.
auch den Beitrag von M. Simon in diesem Band.

[46] Geffcken 1902a, 23 f., 30; Rzach 1923, 2135 f. Die positive Beurteilung Hadrians mag a)
mit dem Schutz der Reste der Judenschaft in Alexandrien, b) mit der Abberufung und
Hinrichtung des brutalen Lusius Quietus, c) mit seiner Räumung Mesopotamiens und d) mit
seiner zunächst "liberalen", friedvollen, auf Ausgleich bedachten Regierung zusammenhängen.

[47] 276 f.284.403–406.497–500.

[48] ὑστατίῳ καιρῷ 74.348.361.432.447.

Werkzeuge des Gotteszorns sind einerseits kosmische Katastrophen, doch noch sehr viel mehr beschäftigt den Verfasser die – fast genüßliche – Schilderung des κοσμομανὴς πόλεμος[49].

4.2. Urheber des weltweiten Vernichtungskrieges ist der letzte gottlose Weltherrscher. Für den Verfasser ist er identisch mit dem *Nero redivivus*[50]. Die vier Passagen vom Endtyrannen bestimmen den – durchdachten – Aufbau des Werkes[51]. Der Dichter hat dieses Motiv aus der heidnischen Nerosage übernommen, damit das kriegerische Vernichtungsgericht an Rom und an den Völkern durch die widergöttliche Tyrannengestalt vollzogen werden kann und nicht mehr Israel und dem Messias allein zugeschrieben werden muß. Der "Antichrist" wird zum Werkzeug Gottes[52]. Dahinter steckt eine tiefe Ironie. Als der römische Herrscher mit dem höchsten, göttlichen Anspruch wird er zum Todfeind und Zerstörer Roms. Er flieht in den parthischen Osten, zu Persern und Medern, um sich mit Hilfe der barbarischen Völker an den Enden der Erde die zivilisierte Welt, d. h. das römische Reich, zu unterwerfen[53]. Möglicherweise geht diese Sage letztlich selbst auf eine romantische Vorliebe Neros für den fernen Orient zurück. Der parthische Prinz Tiridathes hatte ihm wie einem göttlichen Weltherrscher gehuldigt und aus seiner Hand die Krone Armeniens empfangen, darüber hinaus sollen ihm gegen Ende seiner Herrschaft Astrologen den Verlust der römischen Macht und dafür die Herrschaft über den Osten (Orientis dominationem), einige gar das "regnum Hierosolymorum", und andere schließlich – doch wohl vom Osten aus – die Wiederherstellung seiner früheren Macht geweissagt haben[53a]. Ein derartiger Herrscher konnte nur der "Antichrist" sein.

4.3. Seit in der parthischen Invasion 40 v. Chr. der letzte Hasmonäersproß Antigonos zum jüdischen König eingesetzt worden war, *erwarteten viele Juden das Ende der römischen Herrschaft durch den Sturm aus dem Osten*[54].

---

[49] 362.462.

[50] S. dazu jetzt die Beobachtungen von Collins 1974, 74 f., 82 ff.

[51] 52 ff. 143 ff. 218 ff. 361 ff.

[52] 220: τούτῳ γάρ τοι δῶκε θεὸς μένος ἐς τὸ ποιῆσαι οἷά τις οὐ πρότερος τῶν συμπάντων βασιλήων.

[53] Vgl. 93 ff. 189 ff. 194 ff. 206.

[53a] Dio Cassius 63,1–5; Sueton, Nero 13,40,2.

[54] S. die zahlreichen rabbinischen Belege bei Krauß 1972, 50 ff. über die Zerstörung Roms durch Persien vor dem Kommen des Messias. Freilich gab es auch die umgekehrte Meinung, daß erst wenn Rom seine Herrschaft über die ganze Welt ausgedehnt habe, der Messias kommen werde. Daß das Kommen des Messias durch einen Feldzug Roms im Osten eingeleitet werde, konnte man aus Num 24,24 MT, LXX und Targumim herauslesen. Num 24 war zudem die wichtigste messianische Weissagung für das Diasporajudentum (s. u. §6.2.). Bekannt ist der Ausspruch des Römerfeindes Schimeon b. Jochai aus der Mitte des 2. Jh.: "Wenn du siehst ein persisches Roß angebunden an die Gräber des Landes Israel, dann schaue aus nach den Spuren des Messias." Cant R 8,9 §2 Ende; Lam R 1,13 §41 vgl. Sanh 98a/b. Analog Gen R 42,4: R. Abina Anf. 5. Jh.: "Wenn du siehst, daß sich die Weltmächte

Der Partherkrieg Trajans war, seit der Niederlage Mark Antons 36 v. Chr.,
der erste wirklich große und bedrohliche Krieg zwischen Rom und seinem
östlichen Gegner. Trajan hatte ihn seit geraumer Zeit vorbereitet, am 27.
Oktober 113 Rom verlassen und seit Beginn des Jahres 114 von Antiochien
aus seine Truppen zusammengezogen. Diese Vorbereitungen blieben
gerade in Ägypten, wo eine Legion abberufen wurde, nicht verborgen. Im
Frühjahr 114 marschierte er in Armenien ein, ein Jahr später erfolgte der
Angriff auf das parthische Mesopotamien. Der neue Krieg mußte so die
jüdische Enderwartung aufs äußerste steigern, auch ließ seine stufenweise
Entwicklung genug Zeit zur eigenen Vorbereitung. War jetzt nicht der
langersehnte Augenblick gekommen, da sich die große Weltenwende
anbahnte, die Israel mit Gottes Hilfe die Befreiung bringen würde? Mußte
jetzt nicht die eigene Aktion das Ende vollends "herbeidrängen"[55]? Wenn –
was sehr wahrscheinlich ist – die jüdischen Insurgenten des Jahres 115
endzeitlich motiviert waren, dann müssen sie ähnlich gedacht haben.

In der apokalyptischen Spekulation des in seinem Bildungsniveau weit
über dem Durchschnitt des Diasporajudentums stehenden Verfassers der
Sibylle[56] war alles – entsprechend der alten Kluft zwischen Theorie und
Praxis – viel einfacher. Bei ihm mußte sich Gottes Volk seine Hände kaum
im blutigen Geschäft schmutzig machen, vielmehr wurde das "gottlose,
frevelhafte Reich" durch sein ehemaliges Haupt, den Erzfrevler Nero,
vernichtet. Gott bzw. sein Bevollmächtigter mußte nur noch das letzte
Gericht an diesem und seinen Anhängern vollziehen. Was den Dichter der
5. Sibylle und die Aufständischen verband, waren der *abgrundtiefe Haß
gegen Rom (und Ägypten), der gespannte Blick auf das politische Geschehen im
parthischen Osten und die brennende endzeitliche Erwartung.* Es war wohl dieser
abgrundtiefe Haß gegen den langjährigen Unterdrücker im Zusammen-
spiel mit der eschatologischen Fehldeutung der Ereignisse im Osten, die
den Aufständischen den Anstoß zum Aufstand gab. D. h. die Erhebung
wuchs nicht aus zufälligen Straßentumulten hervor, die es in Alexandrien
immer wieder gegeben hat; sie war – wie auch der Aufstand Bar Kochbas –
vorbereitet und geplant. In der Sibylle tritt uns dieser Haß in der ersten
größeren Passage gegen das gottlose Imperium überdeutlich entgegen
(168–178). Rom soll dort – um es mit einem Satz auszudrücken – zur Hölle

gegenseitig bekämpfen, dann schaue aus nach den Spuren des Königs Messias." Daß diese
Tradition wesentlich älter ist, ergibt sich aus einem Vergleich mit syrBar 70,2–10. Zu den
wechselnden politischen Beziehungen zwischen Rom und den Parthern s. K.-H. Ziegler 1964.
   [55] Zur Vorbereitung des Partherkrieges s. F. A. Lepper 1948, 28 ff.; H. Temporini 1978,
116 ff.; M.-L. Chaumont 1976, 131 ff. Zur Verurteilung des Versuchs, mit Gewalt "das Ende
herbeizudrängen" im späteren Rabbinat s. Hengel 1976, 129 ff.
   [56] Zum Milieu, der Absicht und dem Bildungsniveau der jüdischen Sibyllendichter s.
Hengel 1972, 286 ff. Zur ältesten 3. Sibylle s. jetzt das grundlegende Werk von Nikiprowetzky 1970, bes. 227 ff.

fahren[57]. Hinter dieser Vision von der Vernichtung Roms steht wohl Jes 14,4–21:

"Doch zur Hölle wirst du hinabgestürzt ($\varepsilon i\varsigma$ $\overset{\circ}{\alpha}\delta o\upsilon$ $\varkappa\alpha\tau\alpha\beta\acute{\eta}\sigma\eta$) zur tiefsten Grube" (14,15).

Unter den jüdischen Apokalypsen in griechischer Sprache nimmt die 5. Sibylle in der Schärfe der Polemik gegen die gottlose Weltmacht den ersten Platz ein[58]. Ihre Weissagung steht *in denkbar schärfstem Gegensatz zur römischen Reichsideologie*, zur Vorstellung von der Roma aeterna, wie sie etwa Vergil in der Verheißung Iuppiters an Venus zum Ausdruck bringt:

"his (i. e. Romanis) ego nec metas rerum nec tempora pono: imperium sine fine dedi..."[59]

4.4. Der Vernichtung Roms voraus geht *Gottes Strafgericht über ganz Ägypten*, von Alexandrien bis nach Syene im Süden[60]. Die Begründung

---

[57] $\alpha i\alpha\tilde{i}$ $\pi\acute{\alpha}\nu\tau$' $\dot{\alpha}\varkappa\acute{\alpha}\vartheta\alpha\varrho\tau\varepsilon$ $\pi\acute{o}\lambda\iota$ $\Lambda\alpha\tau\iota\nu\acute{\iota}\delta o\varsigma$ $\alpha\H{\iota}\eta\varsigma$
   $\mu\alpha\iota\nu\grave{\alpha}\varsigma$ $\dot{\varepsilon}\chi\iota\delta\nu o\chi\alpha\varrho\acute{\eta}\varsigma$, $\chi\acute{\eta}\varrho\eta$ $\varkappa\alpha\vartheta\varepsilon\delta o\tilde{\iota}o$ $\pi\alpha\varrho$' $\ddot{o}\chi\vartheta\alpha\varsigma$,
   $\varkappa\alpha\grave{\iota}$ $\pi o\tau\alpha\mu\grave{o}\varsigma$ $T\acute{\iota}\beta\varepsilon\varrho\acute{\iota}\varsigma$ $\sigma\varepsilon$ $\varkappa\lambda\alpha\acute{\upsilon}\sigma\varepsilon\tau\alpha\iota$, $\mathring{\eta}\nu$ $\pi\alpha\varrho\acute{\alpha}\varkappa o\iota\tau\iota\nu$,
   $\mathring{\eta}\tau\varepsilon$ $\mu\iota\alpha\iota\varphi\acute{o}\nu o\nu$ $\mathring{\eta}\tau o\varrho$ $\ddot{\varepsilon}\chi\varepsilon\iota\varsigma$ $\dot{\alpha}\sigma\varepsilon\beta\tilde{\eta}$ $\delta\acute{\varepsilon}$ $\tau\varepsilon$ $\vartheta\upsilon\mu\acute{o}\nu$.
   $o\dot{\upsilon}\varkappa$ $\ddot{\varepsilon}\gamma\nu\omega\varsigma$, $\tau\acute{\iota}$ $\vartheta\varepsilon\grave{o}\varsigma$ $\delta\acute{\upsilon}\nu\alpha\tau\alpha\iota$, $\tau\acute{\iota}$ $\delta\grave{\varepsilon}$ $\mu\eta\chi\alpha\nu\acute{\alpha}\alpha\tau\alpha\iota$;
   $\dot{\alpha}\lambda\lambda$' $\ddot{\varepsilon}\lambda\varepsilon\gamma\varepsilon\varsigma$· "$\mu\acute{o}\nu\eta$ $\varepsilon\dot{\iota}\mu\grave{\iota}$ $\varkappa\alpha\grave{\iota}$ $o\dot{\upsilon}\delta\varepsilon\acute{\iota}\varsigma$ μ' $\dot{\varepsilon}\xi\alpha\lambda\alpha\pi\acute{\alpha}\xi\varepsilon\iota$".
   $\nu\tilde{\upsilon}\nu$ $\delta\grave{\varepsilon}$ $\sigma\grave{\varepsilon}$ $\varkappa\alpha\grave{\iota}$ $\sigma o\grave{\upsilon}\varsigma$ $\pi\acute{\alpha}\nu\tau\alpha\varsigma$ $\dot{o}\lambda\varepsilon\tilde{\iota}$ $\vartheta\varepsilon\grave{o}\varsigma$ $\alpha\dot{\iota}\grave{\varepsilon}\nu$ $\dot{\upsilon}\pi\acute{\alpha}\varrho\chi\omega\nu$
   $\varkappa o\dot{\upsilon}\varkappa\acute{\varepsilon}\tau\iota$ $\sigma o\upsilon$ $\sigma\eta\mu\varepsilon\tilde{\iota}o\nu$ $\ddot{\varepsilon}\tau$' $\ddot{\varepsilon}\sigma\sigma\varepsilon\tau\alpha\iota$ $\dot{\varepsilon}\nu$ $\chi\vartheta o\nu\grave{\iota}$ $\varkappa\varepsilon\acute{\iota}\nu\eta$,
   $\dot{\omega}\varsigma$ $\tau\grave{o}$ $\pi\acute{\alpha}\lambda\alpha\iota$, $\ddot{o}\tau\varepsilon$ $\sigma\grave{\alpha}\varsigma$ $\dot{o}$ $\mu\acute{\varepsilon}\gamma\alpha\varsigma$ $\vartheta\varepsilon\grave{o}\varsigma$ $\varepsilon\ddot{\upsilon}\varrho\alpha\tau o$ $\tau\iota\mu\acute{\alpha}\varsigma$.
   $\mu\varepsilon\tilde{\iota}\nu o\nu$, $\ddot{\alpha}\vartheta\varepsilon\sigma\mu\varepsilon$, $\mu\acute{o}\nu\eta$, $\pi\upsilon\varrho\grave{\iota}$ $\delta\grave{\varepsilon}$ $\varphi\lambda\varepsilon\gamma\acute{\varepsilon}\vartheta o\nu\tau\iota$ $\mu\iota\gamma\varepsilon\tilde{\iota}\sigma\alpha$
   $\tau\alpha\varrho\tau\acute{\alpha}\varrho\varepsilon o\nu$ $o\ddot{\iota}\varkappa\eta\sigma o\nu$ $\dot{\varepsilon}\varsigma$ $"A\iota\delta o\upsilon$ $\chi\tilde{\omega}\varrho o\nu$ $\ddot{\alpha}\vartheta\varepsilon\sigma\mu o\nu$.

[58]   Vgl. Collins 1974, 79: "The outburst against Rome ... is unparalleled in bitterness anywhere in the sibyllina". Fuchs 1964, 68: "Seit diesen Schilderungen aus der Zeit nach der Zerstörung Jerusalems hat der Gedanke von der Vernichtung Roms seinen festen Platz in dem Vorstellungsbereiche der jüdischen Sibyllinen". Die nächste Parallele dürfte Apk 17 und 18 darstellen.

[59]   Aeneis I, 277f.; vgl. den Preis der Siege Cäsars im Osten, die den dauernden Frieden heraufführen:
   "hunc tu olim caelo spoliis Orientis onustum
   accipies secura...
   aspera tum positis mitescent saecula bellis" (289–291).
Eine Verbindung von römischer Reichsideologie und "apokalyptischer" Heilsgeschichte findet sich bei Josephus, wenn er Bell 2,360 in der Rede Agrippas II und 5,367 betont, daß "das Schicksal auf die Seite der Römer übergegangen sei" bzw. daß ihre Weltherrschaft nur mit Gottes Hilfe zustande gekommen sei (2,390), Gott selbst habe, nachdem er früher die Herrschaft auf andere Völker gelegt, dieselbe jetzt auf Italien übertragen. Die jüdischen Vorfahren hätten sich nur deshalb den Römern unterworfen, weil sie wußten, daß Gott mit diesen sei (5,367/368). Das "sine fine" hätte Josephus freilich nie teilen können, s. u. Anm. 99. Zum Ganzen Lindner 1972, 42ff. Vgl. andererseits die Voraussage des Untergangs Roms in der 16. Epode von Horaz und das Orakel des Hystaspes bei Laktanz Inst. 7,15,19: Sublatuiri ex orbe imperium nomenque Romanum. Ähnlich Sib 5,175: $\varkappa o\dot{\upsilon}\varkappa\acute{\varepsilon}\tau\iota$ $\sigma o\upsilon$ $\sigma\eta\mu\varepsilon\tilde{\iota}o\nu$ $\ddot{\varepsilon}\tau$' $\ddot{\varepsilon}\sigma\sigma\varepsilon\tau\alpha\iota$ $\dot{\varepsilon}\nu$ $\chi\vartheta o\nu\grave{\iota}$ $\varkappa\varepsilon\acute{\iota}\nu\eta$. Rom soll spurlos vom Erdboden verschwinden. Vgl. auch Tacitus, Hist 4,54,2f. über die Weissagungen der Druiden, daß der Brand des Capitols 68 n. Chr. die Wende der Weltherrschaft bedeute: Fatali nunc igne signum caelestis irae datum et possessionem rerum humanarum Transalpinis gentibus portendi superstitione vana Druidae canebant.

[60]   52ff. Vgl. 88,194. Auch die benachbarten Gebiete wie die Cyrenaika (195ff.), Kreta, Zypern und Phönizien (450ff.) sind davon betroffen.

desselben liegt in der *Verfolgung Israels*, sie wird etwa in der Gottesstimme
ausgesprochen, die gegen Memphis ertönt, die alte Königs- und Haupt-
stadt Ägyptens, die hier das ganze Land vertritt[61]. Vollstrecker des Gerichts
ist der "Perser", der Nero redivivus, der wenig später angekündigt wird
und das ganze Land mit vernichtendem Krieg überzieht[62]. Doch nicht nur
wegen der Verfolgung der Juden straft Gottes Zorn, sondern auch wegen
des ägyptischen Götzendienstes. Mit den Städten des Landes werden
zugleich ihre Heiligtümer und Götter vernichtet. *Isis*, im Töpferorakel die
Retterin des Landes, verfällt als "dreimal unselige Göttin" wie Rom dem
Totenreich und wird vergessen, mit ihr kommt auch *Sarapis* zu Fall. Durch
den Sturz dieses höchsten Gottes der Alexandriner werden alle erkennen,
daß er nur ein "Nichts" darstellt[63]. Es ist eigenartig, daß der Dichter im
Gegensatz zum sonstigen jüdischen Brauch die heidnischen Götter beim
Namen nennt. Isis, Sarapis, Herakles, Hermes, Zeus, Hera und Poseidon
erscheinen in dieser Häufung nur in seinem Werk[64]. Man wird darin ein
Zeichen der Schärfe der Auseinandersetzung mit den heidnischen Kulten
sehen dürfen. Die Gegner werden beim Namen genannt und in ihrer
Nichtigkeit "entlarvt". Es ging hier um einen zugleich religiösen *und*
politischen Kampf, der sich dann am Ende in den beiderseitigen Gewaltak-
ten des Aufstandes unter Trajan entlud. Die Intensität dieses Kampfes wird
beleuchtet durch ein ägyptisches Orakel, nach dem die "gesetzlosen" Juden
"durch den Zorn der Isis" aus Ägypten vertrieben werden[65].

4.5. Es ist eigenartig, daß der Verfasser mehrfach die *Zerstörung des
Heiligtums* in Jerusalem erwähnt, sie jedoch nie – im Anschluß an die
prophetische Tradition des Alten Testaments – als Gottes Gericht über sein
Volk begründet. Die Vernichtung des Tempels bzw. der Heiligen Stadt
erscheint ausschließlich als Untat Roms[66] und dient nur dazu, das Maß von
dessen Bosheit vollzumachen, Gottes Gericht über die gottlose Menschheit

---

[61] 67–73. Alexandrien wird dagegen – gerade umgekehrt wie im Töpferorakel – als
Hauptzentrum der Juden relativ geschont, 88 ff.

[62] Der "Erzieher" bzw. die "Amme" (τροφός Z. 70 zum Text s. Geffcken 1902) bezieht sich
wohl auf den "Perser", der 93–97 das ganze Land verwüstet.

[63] 75–86.279 f.484–491. Vgl. schon 53: Isis wird auf euhemeristische Weise zur Schwester
der Sibylle gemacht.

[64] Herakles und Hermes 5,87; Zeus: 7.87.131.141; Hera: 140; Poseidon: 157; vgl. auch das
Ende des dionysischen Enthusiasmus bei den Griechen: 264 f.

[65] *CPJ* III, 1964, Nr. 520. Manteuffel 1934–37, 123 bringt das Fragment in Zusammenhang
"mit dem Judenaufstand vom Jahre 115". Vgl. jedoch schon den ägyptischen Priester, Stoiker
und Erzieher Neros, Chairemon, der nach Jos. Ap 1,289 von einer Traumerscheinung der Isis
berichtet, die König Amenophis veranlaßte, die aussätzigen Vorfahren der Juden unter
Führung des Mose und Joseph aus Ägypten zu verjagen. Es handelt sich wohl um ein Zeugnis
jenes älteren ägyptischen Antijudaismus, der den Aufstand 115–117 wie auch die Polemik der
5. Sibylle mit provozierte.

[66] Zerstörung durch Nero: 150 f.226; durch Titus: 408, vgl. 398 ff.

zu motivieren und die Endereignisse einzuleiten[67]. Die Geschichte wird völlig *dualistisch* gesehen: Hier die ganz Guten, und dort die ganz Bösen. Darum ist von Israels Sünde und Umkehr nicht die Rede, sondern nur am Ende von der Aufrichtung des Friedensreiches "für das göttliche und himmlische Geschlecht der seligen Juden", "denn sie werden in Ewigkeit Siegeszeichen (τρόπαια) über die Bösen aufstellen"[68]. Gott wird mit Sicherheit seinem Volk im letzten Kampf gegen alle Feinde helfen und ihm den Sieg geben. Auch hier wird man wieder an analoge Aussagen der *Selbstverherrlichung Roms* erinnert, so etwa, wenn am Ende der Aeneis Jupiter gegenüber Juno das kommende Geschlecht der Römer preist: "supra homines, supra ire deos pietate videbis"[69], oder wenn gesagt wird, daß es die "erhabene Roma" den "Verheißungen (auspicia) Jupiters verdanke, wenn ihre Herrschaft über die Welt, ihr Mut aber bis zum Olymp reiche": "imperium terris, animos aequabit Olympo"[70]. Die eigentliche "theologische" Reflexion, z. B. die Frage nach Gottes Gerechtigkeit, wie sie uns etwa in der doch wohl aus Palästina stammenden zeitgenössischen pharisäischen Apokalypse des 4. Esrabuches begegnet, tritt gegenüber den grausigen Unheils- und verklärten Heilsschilderungen fast völlig zurück.

Auffällig ist weiter die Hervorhebung des darniederliegenden Heiligen Landes aus der Feder eines ägyptischen Juden[71]. Hier scheint sich die Haltung gegenüber dem Mutterland im Vergleich zu früheren Zeiten positiv verändert zu haben. Es würde so verständlich, warum die Aufständischen der Jahre 115–117 auf Palästina zustrebten, weiter, daß der spätere Plan Hadrians, in Jerusalem eine römische Kolonie mit einem Jupitertempel zu errichten, die Juden – nicht nur in Judäa – aufs äußerste provozieren mußte.

Es gehen so beim Verfasser weitläufige hellenistische Bildung und naive Freude an teils realistischen, teils mythologischen Zukunftsgemälden ineinander. Die "fremde" Bildung wird dabei ganz in den Dienst der Verherrlichung des eigenen Glaubens an den einen wahren Gott gestellt[72], um das "letzte Gefecht", den religiös-politischen Machtkampf gegen Rom,

---

[67] Der Brand des Vestatempels in Rom 64 n. Chr. als Vorzeichen der Strafe Gottes für die Tempelzerstörung: 395–401.

[68] 255, Text nach Rzach 1923; vgl. 249; Ἰουδαίων μακάρων θεῖον γένος οὐράνιόν τε.

[69] 12,839.

[70] 6,782. Dieser Vers wurde gerne von römischen Historikern zitiert. Vgl. die Epitome des Werkes von Pompeius Trogus, Justinus 43,3,2, über Romulus: finitimisque populis armis subiectis primo Italiae et mox orbis imperium quaesitum.

[71] Das Heil wird als frommes und friedvolles Wohnen im Heiligen Land und in Jerusalem geschildert, das eine Mauer mit dem Hafen Jope verbindet (250f.) und das ein neuer Tempel schmückt, dessen Turm als Gegenstück des Turms zu Babel allen Menschen sichtbar bis zu den Wolken reicht (420ff.).

[72] Dies gilt schon für die ältere "jüdisch-hellenistische" Literatur, Hengel 1972, 244, 253, 305f.

in grellen Farben auszumalen. Aber eben hier ist zu fragen, ob nicht gerade diese rigoros "nationale" Ausgestaltung der eschatologischen Hoffnung im Grunde selbst in die Nähe zur verhaßten hellenistisch-römischen "Reichsideologie" führt. Die für die Antike einzigartige *Verschmelzung von Volkstum, exklusiver Religion und utopischer Hoffnung* und die damit verbundene Radikalität gab der jüdischen Rebellion in der Cyrenaika und Ägypten jenen unerbittlichen Charakter, den die nichtjüdische Umwelt nicht verstehen konnte und den sie mit der haßerfüllten Formel von den ἀνόσιοι Ἰουδαῖοι beantwortete. Es war der ganz andere Weg des intensiven Torastudiums, verbunden mit einer relativen Freiheit gegenüber der hellenistisch-römischen Kultur, gewissermaßen der Weg nach innen, durch den das palästinische Judentum nach der Katastrophe des Bar-Kochba-Aufstandes unter der politischen und geistigen Führung des Bet-Hillel sich eine ganz neue Zukunft eröffnete[72a]. Im Blick auf die zurückliegenden Katastrophen des 2. Jh.s erscheint darum diese vor allem von dem Redaktor der Mischna, Jehuda han-naśî', vertretene Haltung als wegweisend für die weitere Geschichte des antiken Judentums.

5. Der Messias und der messianische Krieg

5.1. Zunächst wäre zu sagen, daß in der 5. Sibylle der messianische Erlöser weniger hervortritt als der dämonische "Endtyrann" in der Gestalt des Nero redivivus. Gott könnte wie in der 4. Sibylle sein Reich auch unmittelbar, ohne Zuhilfenahme einer Mittlergestalt, aufrichten und die gottlose Menschheit auch ohne dessen Eingreifen vernichten. Diese Tendenz entspricht auch den zeitgenössischen rabbinischen Texten. Die "Erlösung" ist wichtiger als der "Erlöser", die Erlösergestalten sind außerdem variabel und leicht austauschbar. Dennoch spielt der endzeitliche Erlöser eine nicht unwesentliche Rolle[73]. Insgesamt erscheint die Person des "Messias"[74] in der 5. Sibylle viermal, doch beruht eine Erwähnung auf einer christlichen Interpolation oder ist zumindest christlich überarbeitet[75], eine weitere ist verschlüsselt[76]. Der erste klare Beleg[77] geht davon aus, daß der

---

[72a] S. dazu Neusner 1979, 123ff. "The disputes of the Houses were now a matter of a legal study, not of political importance" (125).

[73] S. dazu jetzt Collins 1974, 87ff.

[74] Der Begriff "Gesalbter" erscheint nirgendwo; in 5,68 wird die ungewöhnliche Bezeichnung παῖδες θεόχριστοι auf ganz Israel bezogen.

[75] 256f.; s. schon Geffcken 1902a, 29.

[76] 155–160: Ein Stern kommt vom Himmel, der das Meer und Babylon und Italien (= Rom) vernichtet.

[77] 106–110:
ἀλλ᾽ ὅταν ὕψος ἔχῃ κρατερὸν καὶ θάρσος *ἀηδές*
ἥξει καὶ μακάρων ἐθέλων πόλιν ἐξαλαπάξαι.

Antichrist "auf dem Gipfel seiner Macht ... kommt und die Stadt der Seligen zerstören will", d. h. der Verfasser greift hier das traditionelle Bild des Völkersturms von Gog und Magog auf. Darauf erfolgt die wunderbare Wende:

> "und ein König von Gott her gesandt gegen diese
> wird alle großen Könige und tüchtigsten Männer töten.
> Darauf wird so Gericht sein vom Unsterblichen über die Menschen."

Der zweiten Erwähnung[78] geht die Schilderung der Zerstörung Jerusalems und des Tempels voran. Darauf erscheint der Erlöser als eine "übermenschliche" Gestalt:

> "Denn es kam vom Himmelsgewölbe ein seliger Mann
> der hielt ein Szepter in Händen, das Gott selbst ihm verliehen.
> Der brachte alles trefflich in seine Gewalt
> und gab allen Guten den Reichtum zurück, den frühere Männer
> (ihnen) genommen hatten. Jede Stadt eroberte er von Grund aus
> mit viel Feuer, und die Volksgemeinden der Menschen, die zuvor
> Übeltäter gewesen, verbrannte er."

Man wird diese beiden Aussagen nicht auseinanderreißen dürfen. Der von Gott gesandte "König" und der "vom Himmelsgewölbe kommende selige Mann"[79] meinen dieselbe Person, den "Messias-Menschensohn", bei dem sich der irdisch-königliche und der himmlisch-richterliche Aspekt (man könnte auch sagen Num 24,7.17 und Dan 7,13) verbinden.

5.2. Im Gegensatz zum Menschensohn der Bilderreden des äth. Henoch ist jedoch hier mit keinem Wort von einer Präexistenz des Messias die Rede, und noch mehr als in der 3. Sibylle besitzt er die Funktion des *Weltherrschers und Kriegshelden*[80], zumal er deutlich der Gestalt des Antichristen gegenübergestellt wird, dessen Heer er völlig vernichtet. Wurde zuvor vom Antichrist gesagt, daß "er die ganze Erde besiegen und alles beherr-

---

> καί κέν τις θεόθεν βασιλεὺς πεμφθεὶς ἐπὶ τοῦτον
> πάντας ὀλεῖ βασιλεῖς μεγάλους καὶ φῶτας ἀρίστους.
> εἶθ' οὕτως κρίσις ἔσται ὑπ' ἀφθίτου ἀνθρώποισιν.

Zur Sendungsvorstellung in Judentum s. J.-A. Bühner 1977, 270–373. Vgl. auch Act 3,20; IThess 1,10. Zu hellenistisch-römischen Parallelen s. M. Hengel 1977, 58 ff.

[78] 414–421:
> ἦλθε γὰρ οὐρανίων νώτων ἀνὴρ μακαρίτης
> σκῆπτρον ἔχων ἐν χερσίν, ὃ οἱ θεὸς ἐγγυάλιξεν,
> καὶ πάντων ἐκράτησε καλῶς πᾶσίν τ' ἀπέδωκεν
> τοῖς ἀγαθοῖς τὸν πλοῦτον, ὃν οἱ πρότεροι λάβον ἄνδρες
> πᾶσαν δ' ἐκ βάθρων εἷλεν πόλιν ἐν πυρὶ πολλῷ
> καὶ δήμους ἔφλεξε βρωτῶν τῶν πρόσθε κακούργων
> καὶ πόλιν, ἣν ἐπόθησε θεός, ταύτην ἐποίησεν
> φαιδροτέραν ἄστρων τε καὶ ἡλίου ἠδὲ σελήνης.

[79] Vgl. I Kor 15,47: ὁ δεύτερος ἄνθρωπος ἐξ οὐρανοῦ.

[80] Nikiprowetzky 1970 deutet schon Sib 3,652 den König, den Gott von der Sonne her senden wird und der den Krieg auf der Erde beendet als "un prince guerrier" (Sibylle S. 136).

schen wird"[81], so gilt dies jetzt für den Messias[82]. Jede Stadt – man wird hinzufügen müssen: die Widerstand leistet – wird er niederbrennen, dasselbe gilt von allen "Volksgemeinden" (δήμους), die das heilige und gerechte Gottesvolk Israel unterdrückt hatten. Weiter wird der Erlöser eine Umverteilung der Güter vornehmen: Die Guten, d. h. Israel, erhalten jetzt zurück, was ihnen in früherer Zeit geraubt worden war[83]. Beim heilvollen Ende darf die Expropriation der Expropriateure nicht fehlen.

5.3. Gegenüber der älteren Darstellung des Messias in der 3. Sibylle bringt der Dichter des 5. Buches so eine deutliche Steigerung durch die Betonung des *Vernichtungskrieges*. Nicht nur sein Haß gegen Rom ist innerhalb der sibyllinischen Literatur unübertroffen, sondern auch seine Darstellung des Antichristen und als notwendiges Gegengewicht die des messianischen Krieges. Es wäre dabei irreführend, wenn man im zeitgenössischen Judentum einen grundsätzlichen Gegensatz zwischen dem irdischen Messiaskönig als Kriegshelden und dem Menschensohn-Erlöser als himmlischer Gestalt konstruieren wollte; beide Motive haben sich in vielfältiger, immer wieder neuer Weise verbunden. Das apokalyptische Denken eignet sich in seiner scheinbar widersprüchlichen Vielfalt schlecht für die Zettelkästen und Schubfächer des modernen Forschers und seine reinliche analytische Scheidekunst. Man sollte die Vorstellung einer "reinen Transzendenz" ebenso aus den Beurteilungskategorien der "Apokalyptik" verbannen wie das Zerrbild einer "ausschließlich irdischen Hoffnung". Ähnliches gilt von dem immer wieder in falscher Weise betonten Gegensatz zwischen den Begriffspaaren "irdisch-himmlisch" und "gegenwärtig-zukünftig". Die jüdische "Apokalyptik" war in gleicher Weise an der himmlischen Welt wie an der verklärten Zukunft interessiert. Das erwartete "utopische Paradies" war weder völlig transzendent noch wirklich irdisch. Da die militärisch-destruktive Gewalttätigkeit des Antichristen in der 5. Sibylle in so einzigartiger Weise geschildert wird, mußte dieser gerade auch darin im Messias seinen Meister finden[84]. Daß dieser dabei nicht mehr nur mit menschlichen Waffen kämpft, sondern vor allem mit dem göttlichen Gerichtsfeuer[84a], ist die notwendige Konsequenz seiner gottgegebenen Aufgabe und ein altes sibyllinisches Motiv.

Die Gestalt eines *vom Himmel kommenden Erlösers* mußte entsprechend durchaus nicht zur Vorstellung vom realen eschatologisch-messianischen

---

[81] 108 ff. 365: καὶ πάντα κρατήσει.

[82] 416: καὶ πάντων ἐκράτησε καλῶς, vgl. auch 156 (Messias) und 365 (Antichrist): ὃς πᾶσαν γαῖαν καθελεῖ.

[83] Vgl. ApkAbr 31,6-10 und syrBar 72,2–6.

[84] Die nächste Parallele ist dazu Apk 19,11 ff.: ἐν δικαιοσύνῃ κρίνει καὶ πολεμεῖ.

[84a] Das Motiv erscheint u. a. in IV. Esr 13,4–11 als Kombination von Jes 11,4; Ez 39,6 und Dan 7,12. Zum Feuermotiv vgl. Volz 1934, 318 f.; Hultgård 1979, 570 f.

Krieg in Widerspruch stehen. Ich verweise hier en passant nur auf die
vielfältige Erwartung der Essener mit dem vierzigjährigen Krieg der Söhne
des Lichts gegen die Söhne der Finsternis, den beiden Messiassen aus Aaron
und Israel, und der kommenden Erlösung durch den Lichtfürsten Michael[85].

Selbst ein so hochgebildeter christlicher Theologe wie der Erzieher des
Sohnes von Konstantin, *Laktanz*, kann im 7. Buch seiner Institutiones den
messianischen Krieg in erstaunlicher Weise variieren. Nachdem der *dux
sanctae militiae* vom Himmel herabgekommen ist und das Heer des Antichristen zum großen Hinschlachten in die Hand der Gerechten gegeben
wurde[86], geht der Kampf dennoch weiter: Der Antichrist flieht und erneuert den Kampf viermal "donec quarto proelio confectis omnibus impiis
debellatus et captus tandem scelerum suorum luat poenas"[87].

Man möchte von unserer heutigen Erfahrung aus diese zunächst jüdischen und dann auch christlichen Schilderungen des "letzten Gefechts" eine
gewiß verständliche, aber dennoch allzumenschlich-unmenschliche
Variante des bekannten höchst fragwürdigen römischen Selbstlobs
nennen[88]:

"tu regere imperio populos, Romane, memento
(haec tibi erunt artes), pacique imponere morem,
parcere subiectis et *debellare* superbos."

---

[85] Vgl. Dan 12,1 ff.; äthHen 90,14 ff.; 1QM 17,7 f.; 16,8 ff.; 11QMelch s. Milik 1972, 95 ff.;
zu den beiden Messias v. d. Woude 1957; Starcky 1963, 481 ff. und Liver 1979.

[86] Inst. 7,17,10 f.: et exaudiet eos deus et mittet regem magnum de caelo qui eos eripiat ac
liberet omnesque inpios ferro ignique disperdat; 7,19,5: cadet repente gladius e caelo, ut sciant
iusti *ducem sanctae militiae descensurum* ... et antecedet eum flamma inextinguibilis et uirtus
angelorum tradet in manus iustorum multitudinem illam quae montem circumsederit et
concidetur ab hora tertia usque in uesperum et fluet sanguis more torrentis: deletisque
omnibus copiis inpius solus effugiet et peribit ab eo uirtus sua.

[87] Inst 7,19,6. Vgl. auch die Auslegung von Apk 19,11 bei dem Märtyrerbischof Victorinus
von Pettau (*CSEL* 49, 1916 ed. Haußleiter) p. 137: Equum enim album et sedentem super
eum dominum nostrum cum exercitu caelesti ad regnandum ostendit, cuius in aduentu omnes
colligentur gentes et gladio cadent. Caeterae autem, quae fuerint nobiliores, seruabuntur in
seruitutem sanctorum. Zum endzeitlichen Vernichtungskrieg s. noch T.Sim 6,3 f.; T. Jos
19,8; den himmlischen Krieg (πόλεμος) zwischen Michael und der Schlange Apk 12,7;
19,11 ff.; 20,8 f. In der aus dem 3. Jh. stammenden hebräischen Eliasapokalypse erscheint der
Messias mit einem Heer von 30 000 Gerechten und läßt die Heiden "dahinschwinden" (ed.
Buttenwieser 1897, 19 f.). Zum Motiv des endzeitlichen "Heiligen Krieges" s. auch Hengel
1976, 277 ff., zum Messias als Krieger 281 ff.

[88] Aeneis 6,851–853. Die fata, die die Geschicke der Völker leiten, verkörpern den Willen
Jupiters, dessen Ziel die Überwindung des kriegerischen furor und der gesittete Frieden ist.
Auch in den Sibyllinen folgt auf Vernichtungskrieg und Gericht die Utopie des Friedensrei-
ches. Josephus macht sich bis zu einem gewissen Maße die Idee, daß die Tyche bzw. Gott die
Römer selbst begünstige zu eigen und argumentiert von dieser Basis aus gegen seine
aufständischen Volksgenossen, s. o. Anm. 59.

5.4. Wir sehen aus alledem, daß *Kosmologie* und *Politik* zwar für uns als
zwei völlig verschiedene Dinge erscheinen mögen, für das antike mythische und d.h. auch für das jüdisch-apokalyptische Denken sind sie es
nicht[89]. Gottes Schöpfung und die Geschichte der Menschheit lassen sich
nicht auseinanderreißen. Kriege und kosmische Katastrophen bedingen
sich gegenseitig, ebenso Weltfriede und kosmische Ordnung. Um die
gottlose Weltmacht, in der sich alle Feinde des Gottesvolkes und widergöttlichen Kräfte am Ende der Zeit zusammenschließen, zu zerbrechen,
muß Gott mit noch größerer, übermenschlicher, wunderbarer Macht
eingreifen. Eben dies geschieht im endzeitlichen messianischen Krieg. Ein
traditionsgeschichtlicher Vergleich könnte dabei zeigen, daß an diesem
Punkt weite Teile des griechischsprechenden Diasporajudentums nicht
weniger "militärisch-politisch" dachten als die Juden im palästinischen
Mutterland.

*Aus diesem Grund werden auch die eschatologischen Erwartungen der Aufstän-
dischen zur Zeit Trajans* gar nicht so weit von den Vorstellungen des
Dichters der 5. Sibylle entfernt gewesen sein. Die Gewißheit der rettenden
Reaktion Gottes in der Entsendung einer himmlischen Rettergestalt schloß
die eigene – äußerlich verzweifelt erscheinende – politisch-militärische
Aktion nicht aus, sondern konnte sie als Vorbereitung erfordern. Die
Erwartung des messianischen Endkampfes war zudem, je nach Wechsel
der Situation, vielseitig variierbar, wobei unmittelbare prophetische Weisung, schriftgelehrte Deutung und Umformung der Tradition Hand in
Hand gingen. Im Jüdischen Krieg 66. n. Chr., dessen Ausbruch ja durch
die Erwartung der nahen Erfüllung der messianischen Verheißungen
gefördert wurde und in dem verschiedene Führer mit messianischen
Ansprüchen auftraten[90], hat sich die endzeitliche Erwartung auch nach
schwersten Rückschlägen eher noch weiter intensiviert. Die Führer der
Aufständischen im eingeschlossenen Jerusalem waren sich nicht nur gewiß,
daß Tempel und Stadt – entsprechend der alten Weissagung vom Völker-
sturm – von den Römern nicht erobert werden könnten, "denn die Stadt
gehöre Gott", sondern sie verteidigten den Tempel in der Gewißheit, "daß
dieser auf jeden Fall von dem, der darin wohnt, gerettet werde"[91], eine
Überzeugung, die selbst auf römische Soldaten überging, so daß einzelne
zu den Juden überliefen[92]. Noch unmittelbar vor der Eroberung des Heiligtums verkündete ein zelotischer Prophet für den 10. Ab dem verzweifelten

---

[89] Gegen Collins 1974, 91: "... that the saviour does not operate in the sphere of politics,
but in the sphere of cosmology. Deliverance is seen as a cosmological event. This shows how
deeply the Egyptian Jews had become disillusioned with the political realm".

[90] Hengel 1976, 242ff., 246ff., 296ff.

[91] Jos.Bell 6,98; 5,459; Hengel 1976, 227f.

[92] Dio Cassius 66,5,4; M. Stern 1980, 371ff. Nr. 430.

Volk, "Gott habe den Befehl gegeben, zum Heiligtum hinaufzugehen, dort würden sie die Zeichen der Erlösung empfangen". Wahrscheinlich sollten sie dort die Ankunft des Messias-Menschensohn erwarten[93]. Man wird ähnliche prophetische "Weissagungen" und Orakel auch bei den jüdischen Insurgenten in der Cyrenaika und Ägypten voraussetzen dürfen, deren Erhebung nicht weniger, sondern eher noch mehr verzweifelten Mut voraussetzte als bei den Verteidigern Jerusalems.

Die zeitliche Beschränkung des Vortrags und der vorgeschriebene Umfang des Druckmanuskripts erlauben es nur, den letzten Teil in kurzen Grundthesen zu entwickeln, die nicht mehr ausführlich belegt werden können:

6. Zur Vorgeschichte des Motivs vom messianischen Krieg in der Diaspora Ägyptens

6.1. Die jüdische Diaspora Ägyptens und der Cyrenaika besaß ein ausgesprochenes, durch lange Tradition geprägtes militärisches Selbstbewußtsein, das nicht weniger stark war als das der Bevölkerung des Mutterlandes. Es begegnet uns schon bei dem zweiten griechischen Autor, der über die Juden berichtete, Hekataios von Abdera um 300 v. Chr. Danach habe Mose sich sehr um das Kriegswesen gekümmert und die jungen Männer gezwungen, "sich in Tapferkeit, Ausdauer und im Ertragen von jeder Art von Strapazen zu üben"[94]. Dieses militärische Selbstbewußtsein hängt damit zusammen, daß seit den Tagen des ersten Ptolemäers die sozial führende Schicht der jüdischen Diaspora in Ägypten[94a], der Cyrenaika und vermutlich auch auf Zypern aus Militärsiedlern bestand, die vor allem seit dem Ptolemaios VI Philometor in der Mitte des 2. Jh. v. Chr. in Ägypten einen beachtlichen politischen Machtfaktor darstellten, bis sie – wie das gesamte ptolemäische Heer – von Augustus entwaffnet wurden und ihre mit dem Stande des Militärsiedlers verbundenen Vorrechte verloren[95]. Militärische Tüchtigkeit und Waffengebrauch zur rechten Zeit werden darum auch in der Literatur der ägyptischen Diaspora hochgeschätzt.

6.2. Einen Einfluß dieses kriegerischen Selbstbewußtseins wird man schon in der Übersetzung der wichtigsten messianischen Belegstelle im Pentateuch Num 24,7 f. 17 ff. vermuten dürfen, wo – in starker Abweichung von der hebräischen Vorlage – der Messias als erfolgreicher Krieger und Eroberer gezeichnet wird. Eigenartig ist, daß die späteren Targumim

---

[93] Bell 6,285 f.; Hengel 1976, 248 f.

[94] Diod. Sic. 40,4,6 M. Stern 1974, 26 f. und Kommentar S. 32. Auch nach Artapanos und Josephus ist Mose ein großer Heerführer.

[94a] A. Kasher 1979.

[95] S. dazu Tcherikover, *CPJ* I, 1957, 1–47; Kasher 1978, *passim*; Hengel 1976a, 116 ff.

hier durchweg mehr oder weniger der Deutung der Septuaginta folgen.
Num 24 wurde sowohl in der Diaspora wie auch im palästinischen
Mutterland zum exegetisch und politisch wirkungsvollsten messianischen
Text[96], der in seiner traditionsbildenden Kraft nur noch mit Jes 11 verglichen werden kann. Auch in der Auslegungstradition von Jes 11 wurden die
kriegerischen Züge verstärkt, während das Motiv der Geistbegabung und
der Weisheit abgeschwächt wurde[97].

Die Wirkung dieses messianischen Textes aus dem Pentateuch kann gar
nicht überschätzt werden. Sie tritt uns selbst bei dem sonst so uneschatologischen jüdischen Platoniker Philo entgegen, der in Praem Num 24,7
zitiert und mit der Vorstellung des Kriegsmessias verbindet[98]. Josephus, der
sonst die jüdische messianische Hoffnung ganz unterschlägt, läßt sie bei
seiner Darstellung des Bileamorakels wider seine sonstige Gewohnheit
deutlich durchschimmern[99]. Weitere Hinweise finden sich in den Testamenten der XII Patriarchen, der 3. und 5. Sibylle. Darüber hinaus wird
man in Num 24 jenes "zweideutige Orakel" sehen dürfen, das nach dem
Urteil von Josephus, Tacitus und Sueton die Juden zum Krieg verleitete[100],
und schließlich empfing Bar Kochba von dem "Stern aus Jakob" Num
24,17 seinen Namen[101].

6.3. Es lassen sich so in der Entwicklung des palästinischen Judentums
von der makkabäischen Erhebung und der hasmonäischen Expansion bis
hin zu den Katastrophen der Jahre 70 und 132–135 einerseits und der
ägyptischen Diaspora von ihrer politisch-militärischen Blüte ab der Mitte
des 2. Jhdts. v. Chr. bis hin zu der selbstmörderischen Erhebung der Jahre
115–117 andererseits durchaus gewisse Parallelen aufweisen. In beiden
Bereichen ist eine Intensivierung der messianisch-politischen Hoffnung zu
beobachten, die sich schließlich in Vernichtungskriegen entlud und die aufs
ganze gesehen durch die Verschlechterung der politischen Situation unter
römischer Herrschaft, d. h. in Palästina durch den Verlust der Unabhän-
gigkeit und in Ägypten und der Cyrenaika durch die Aufhebung der
Vorrechte der jüdischen Militärsiedler, bedingt war. Auffallend ist dabei,
daß von den Juden in den ehemals nichtptolemäischen Gebieten, etwa in
Syrien, Kleinasien und Griechenland, wo sich ebenfalls eine sehr große
jüdische Minderheit befand, keine vergleichbaren Unruhen überliefert

---

[96] Dieser Text bedürfte dringend einer eingehenden wirkungsgeschichtlichen Untersuchung. Schon das Zustandekommen des abweichenden Septuagintatextes ist ungeklärt. Am
ausführlichsten wird er bei Vermes 1961, 159ff. behandelt.

[97] S. dazu Hengel 1979, 168ff.

[98] §95: ἐξελεύσεται ... ἄνθρωπος ... καὶ στραταρχῶν καὶ πολεμῶν.

[99] Ant 4,112–125, vgl. 10,208–210 zu Dan 2.

[100] S. o. §3.3. Anm. 42.

[101] jTaan 4,7 68d Z. 49f.: R. Schim‘on b. Jochai lehrte: Aqiba, mein Lehrer, lehrte:
"'Aufgegangen ist ein Stern aus Jakob!' Aufgegangen ist Kosiba aus Jakob!"

werden. Hier blieb man gegenüber der fremden Herrschaft loyal, wie man es schon unter den Persern und den Seleukiden gewesen war. Dies mag damit zusammenhängen, daß die Juden in diesen Gebieten – etwa in den Städten der Westküste Kleinasiens und der Ägäis – ihren Status unter römischer Herrschaft eher als Verbesserung gegenüber der Willkür der früheren Magistrate der einzelnen Poleis empfanden[102].

6.4. Freilich muß man gleichzeitig hervorheben, daß dieser militante Messianismus, der in Palästina wie in Ägypten zur Katastrophe führte, durchaus nicht die einzige Verhaltensweise war. Das in Palästina entstehende Urchristentum, der nach 70 bzw. 135 allein überlebende hillelitische Flügel der Pharisäer und die überwiegend sadduzäische Oberschicht lehnten den Weg der eschatologisch motivierten gewaltsamen Erhebung als einen Gottes Willen widersprechenden Selbstbetrug ab. Auch in Ägypten werden starke Gruppen – gerade in Alexandrien – diesen Versuchen Widerstand geleistet haben. So wurden nach 70 die nach Ägypten geflohenen Sikarier auf Veranlassung der Führer der jüdischen Gemeinde den Römern ausgeliefert[103]. Daß die Aufstände dann schließlich dennoch ausbrachen, läßt sich mit rationalem Kalkül allein kaum mehr begründen, sondern ist in erster Linie dem alle Widerstände überwindenden apokalyptischen Enthusiasmus der militanten Gruppen und dem demagogischen Genie ihrer Führer zuzuschreiben, daneben freilich auch römischen Mißgriffen, so dem Schreckensregiment eines Gessius Florus vor 66 n. Chr., und ·später dem Befehl Hadrians zur Gründung von Aelia Capitolina in Verbindung mit dem Beschneidungsverbot. Um so mehr fällt auf, daß wir überhaupt nichts über die Gründe der Erhebung von 115 hören. Sie muß für die Römer ganz überraschend gekommen sein, denn sie waren in keiner Weise militärisch auf diese "Explosion" des jüdischen Zorns vorbereitet. Die 5. Sibylle zeigt freilich, wie sich die messianisch-militante Hoffnung und der Haß gegen Rom schon in den Jahrzehnten vor dem Aufstand aufs äußerste gesteigert hatten und – das ganze Werk wurde ja erst nach dem Tode Trajans unter Hadrian redigiert – auch nach der Katastrophe weiterwirkten. Die Hoffnung auf die Überwindung der "gottlosen Herrschaft" wurde dabei nicht allein aus der alttestamentlich-prophetischen und späteren jüdisch-apokalyptischen Hoffnung gespeist, sondern zusätzlich von der autochthonen *ägyptischen "Apokalyptik"* beeinflußt, wie ein Vergleich mit dem Töpferorakel und anderen politischen Weissagungen des Nillandes aus hellenistisch-römischer Zeit zeigt. Wahrscheinlich haben jene unbekannten Verfasser der sog. 3. Sibylle aus der Mitte des 2. Jh. v. Chr. und

---

[102] Zu den römischen Rechtsgarantien für die jüdischen Gemeinden s. Smallwood 1976, 138 ff.

[103] Jos. Bell 7,413–416, s. o. §3.2.

der Zeit der Kleopatra VII die an sich heidnische, griechische Form der sibyllinischen Weissagung in Auseinandersetzung mit den fremdenfeindlichen ägyptischen "Apokalypsen" gewählt[104].

6.5. Die Literatur der Diaspora Ägyptens weist jedoch – gerade im Bereich der sogenannten "Apokalypsen" – auch noch ganz andere Schriften auf, in denen die nationale politisch-messianische Hoffnung kaum mehr eine Rolle spielt, sondern sich die Zukunftserwartung auf das *Schicksal des Individuums nach dem Tode* konzentriert. Dazu gehören das Testament Abrahams, die griechische Baruchapokalypse, volkstümliche Offenbarungsschriften, die ihre Fortsetzung in den christlichen Testamenten Isaaks und Jakobs finden und stark an ältere hellenistische und ägyptische Vorbilder erinnern[105]. Hier öffnete sich ein ganz anderer, individueller Weg der Antwort auf die Unterdrückung durch die Fremdherrschaft, der in die Innerlichkeit der persönlichen todesüberwindenden Hoffnung und den kleinen Kreis der religiösen Gemeinschaft der Gleichgesinnten führte. Vielleicht darf man mit aller Vorsicht die Vermutung äußern, daß die nationale, militant-messianische Hoffnung in den breiten, nichtliterarischen Schichten des Judentums der Diaspora der ehemals ptolemäischen Gebiete relativ stark verbreitet war, während in den gebildeteren, literarisch interessierten und produktiven Kreisen die – auf griechischem Einfluß beruhende – individuelle Erwartung stärker im Vordergrund stand. Darüber hinaus mußte man mit Mischformen rechnen. Selbst Philo kennt eine rudimentäre national-militante Zukunftshoffnung. Dies würde auch das einseitige Ergebnis der Untersuchung von U. Fischer (s. o. §1.3.) erklären. Die 5. Sibylle wäre dann nur die Spitze eines Eisberges.

Eine dritte Möglichkeit bildete das *gnostische oder auch hermetisch-mystische Konventikel*. Die politischen Katastrophen konnten schließlich gerade bei den philosophisch (Halb-)Gebildeten zur Verzweiflung am Gott der Väter und guten Weltschöpfer führen, der sein Volk der Vernichtung preisgab. Mußte ein solcher Gott am Ende nicht als grausamer, immer nur strafender Demiurg erscheinen[106]? Hier scheint mir eine der wichtigsten Wurzeln der

---

[104] Zur ägyptischen "Apokalyptik" s. o. in diesem Paragraphen. Der Erfolg der jüdischen Autoren in der Übernahme der Form des heidnischen Orakels zeigt sich in der Formulierung des Laktanz Inst 7,19,9: quod etiam Sibylla cum prophetis congruens futurum esse praedixit.
[105] Macurdy 1942, 213ff. weist auf die Beziehungen zwischen dem Test Abr und der Apokalypse des Pamphyliers Er (s. o. §§ 1.2. und 1.3.) im 10. Buch von Platos Staat hin (614bff.), die selbst wieder vom ägyptischen Totengericht beeinflußt wurde, s. Morenz 1951, 123ff. A. Hultgård 1979, 567 weist auf möglichen iranischen Einfluß hin.
[106] Die palästinische IV Esraapokalypse zeigt ein Ringen um die Frage nach Gottes Gerechtigkeit, das bei negativem Ausgang zum radikalen Bruch mit dem Gott der Väter führen konnte. Man sollte stärker als bisher die tiefgreifende Katastrophe der Jahre 66–70, die durch die mit dem jüdischen Aufstand ausgelösten Pogrome ja auch weite Kreise des Judentums in Syrien und Ägypten, nicht zuletzt in den Metropolen Alexandrien und Antiochien, betraf, für die Herausbildung der – von Anfang an stark jüdisch geprägten – Gnosis in Betracht ziehen.

gnostischen Bewegung zu liegen, die ja ganz stark von der jüdischen Apokalyptik und Weisheit beeinflußt ist und die durch die – auch das ägyptische Judentum betreffende – Katastrophe von 70 n. Chr. m. E. offenbar erst richtig ausgelöst wurde.

Bibliographie

Applebaum, Shimon 1951: "The Jewish Revolt in Cyrene in 115–117 and the subsequent recolonization", in: *JJS* 2 (1951) 177–186.
– 1979: *Jews and Greeks in Ancient Cyrene* (SJLA 28), Leiden 1979.
Bietenhard, Hans 1948: "Die Freiheitskriege der Juden unter den Kaisern Trajan und Hadrian und der messianische Tempelbau", in: *Jud.* 4 (1948) 57–77, 81–108, 161–185.
Bruns, Paulus J./Kirsch, Georgius G. 1789: *Gregorii Abulpharagii sive Bar-Hebraei Chronicon Syriacum*, Leipzig 1789.
Bühner, Jan-A. 1977: *Der Gesandte und sein Weg im 4. Evg.* (WUNT 2. R., 2), Tübingen 1977.
Buttenwieser, Moses 1897: *Die hebräische Elias-Apokalypse*, Leipzig 1897.
Cavallin, Hans Clemens Caesarius 1974: *Life after Death*. Paul's argument for the resurrection of the dead in I Cor 15. Part I: An enquiry into the Jewish background (CB.NT 7,1), Lund 1974.
– 1979: "Leben nach dem Tode im Spätjudentum und im frühen Christentum. I. Spätjudentum", in: *ANRW* II 19,1, Berlin/New York 1979, 240–345.
Chabot, Jean-Baptiste 1899: *Chronique de Michel le Syrien* (1166–1199), Ed. et trad. Bd. 1, Paris 1899.
Chaumont, Marie-Louise 1976: "L'Arménie entre Rome et l'Iran I", in: *ANRW* II 9,1, Berlin/ New York 1976, 71–194.
Collins, John J. 1974: *The Sibylline Oracles of Egyptian Judaism* (SBLDS 13), Missoula/Mont. 1974.
– 1979: "Towards the morphology of a genre", in: *Semeia 14: Apocalypse: The morphology of a genre*, Missoula/Mont. 1979, 1–20.
Corpus papyrorum Judaicarum I 1957, ed. Victor A. Tcherikover/Alexander Fuks, Cambridge/ Mass. 1957.
Corpus papyrorum Judaicarum II 1960, ed. Victor A. Tcherikover/Alexander Fuks, Cambridge/ Mass. 1960.
Corpus papyrorum Judaicarum III 1964, ed. Victor A. Tcherikover/Alexander Fuks/Menahem Stern, Cambridge/Mass. 1964.
Fink, Robert O. 1971: *Roman Military Records on Papyrus* (PMAPA 26), Cleveland, Ohio 1971.
Finkelstein, Louis (Ed.) 1956: *Sifra or Torat Kohanim according to Codex Assemani LXVI*, New York 1956.
Fischer, Ulrich 1978: *Eschatologie und Jenseitserwartung im hellenistischen Diasporajudentum* (BZNW 44), Berlin/New York 1978.
Fraser, P. M./(Applebaum, S.) 1950: "Hadrian and Cyrene", in: *JRS* 40 (1950) 77–90.

Auch in den Hermetica ist der jüdische Einfluß bis in die Liturgie hinein mit Händen zu greifen, s. Philonenko 1975, 204ff. und Zuntz 1972, 150ff. Der deus unicus solitarius destitutus der Juden *und* Christen besaß nach dem Urteil des Heiden Caecilius "adeo nulla vis nec potestas ... ut sit Romanis hominibus cum sua sibi natione captivus" (Min. Felix Oct. 10,3f.). Wenn dieser Gott seinem Volk nicht helfen konnte, mußte er da nicht reif sein zur Abdankung? Oder mußte man seine Hilfe jetzt erst recht wider allen äußeren Augenschein und alle politische Vernunft erwarten? Sowohl die Entstehung der jüdisch-christlichen Gnosis wie die verzweifelten Aufstände der Jahre 115–117 und 132–135 könnten sich so zugleich auch als Versuche erweisen, eine akute religiöse Krise zu lösen.

Fuchs, Harald 1964: *Der geistige Widerstand gegen Rom in der antiken Welt*, Nachdruck Berlin 1964.

Fuks, Alexander 1953: "The Jewish Revolt in Egypt (AD 115–117) in the light of the Papyri", in: *Aeg.* 33 (1953) 131–157.

– 1961: "Aspects of the Jewish Revolt in AD 115–117", in: *JRS* 51 (1961) 98–104.

Geffcken, Johannes (Ed.) 1902: *Die Oracula Sibyllina* (GCS 8), Leipzig 1902.

– 1902a: *Komposition und Entstehungszeit der Oracula Sibyllina* (TU NF VIII, 1), Berlin 1902, Nachdruck Leipzig 1967.

Gilliam, J. F. 1966: "An Egyptian Cohort in AD 117", in: *Beiträge zur Historia-Augusta-Forschung*, hrsg. v. A. Alföldi, Bd. 3, Bonn 1966, 91–97.

Groag, Edmund 1927: Art. "Lusius Quietus", in: *PRE* XIII, 2 (1927) 1874–1890.

Helm, Rudolf (Ed.) 1955: *Hippolytus*, Die Chronik (GCS 36), Berlin ²1955.

Hengel, Martin 1966: "Die Synagogeninschrift von Stobi", in: *ZNW* 57 (1966) 145–183.

– 1972: "Anonymität, Pseudepigraphie und 'Literarische Fälschung' in der jüdisch-hellenistischen Literatur", in: *Pseudepigrapha I*, Vandoeuvres-Genève 1972, 229–308 (Diskussion S. 309–329).

– 1975: "Zwischen Jesus und Paulus. Die 'Hellenisten', die 'Sieben' und Stephanus (Apg 6, 1–15; 7,54–8,3)", in: *ZThK* 72 (1975) 151–206.

– 1976: *Die Zeloten*. Untersuchungen zur jüdischen Freiheitsbewegung in der Zeit von Herodes I. bis 70 n. Chr. (AGJU 1), Leiden/Köln ²1976.

– 1976a: *Juden, Griechen und Barbaren*: Aspekte der Hellenisierung des Judentums in vorchristlicher Zeit (SBS 76), Stuttgart 1976.

– 1977: *Der Sohn Gottes*, Tübingen ²1977.

– 1979: "Jesus als messianischer Lehrer der Weisheit und die Anfänge der Christologie", in: *Sagesse et Religion*, Paris 1979, 147–188.

Henrichs, Albert (Ed.) 1972: *Die Phoinikika des Lollianos*. Fragmente eines neuen griechischen Romans (PTA 14), Bonn 1972.

Hultgård, Anders 1979: "Das Judentum in der hellenistisch-römischen Zeit und die iranische Religion – ein religionsgeschichtliches Problem", in: *ANRW* II 19,1, Berlin/New York 1979, 512–590.

Kasher, Aryeh 1976: "Some comments on the Jewish uprising in Egypt in the time of Trajan", in: *JJS* 27 (1976) 147–158.

– 1978: *The Jews in Hellenistic and Roman Egypt* (PDRI 23), Tel Aviv 1978 (Hebr.).

– 1979: "First Jewish Military Units in Ptolemaic Egypt", in: *JSJ* 9 (1979) 57–67.

Krauß, Samuel 1972: *Monumenta Talmudica*, Darmstadt 1972.

Lauterbach, Jacob Z. (Ed.) 1949: *Mekilta de-Rabbi Ishmael*, Bd. 1, Philadelphia, Penn. 1949.

Lepper, F. A. 1948: *Trajan's Parthian War*, Oxford 1948.

Lichtenstein, Hans 1931–32: "Die Fastenrolle. Eine Untersuchung zur jüdisch-hellenistischen Geschichte", in: *HUCA* 8–9 (1931–32) 257–351.

Lindner, Helgo 1972: *Die Geschichtsauffassung des Flavius Josephus im Bellum Judaicum* (AGJU 12), Leiden 1972.

Liver, J. 1979: "The Doctrine of the Messiahs in Sectarian Literature in the Time of the Second Commonwealth", in: L. Landman (Ed.): *Messianism in the Talmudic Era*, New York 1979, 354–390.

Macurdy, G. H. 1942: "Platonic Orphism in the Testament of Abraham", in: *JBL* 61 (1942) 213–226.

von Manteuffel, Georg 1934–37: "Zur Prophetie in P.S.I., VIII. 982", in: *Mélanges Maspero* II Orient grec, romain et byzantin, Kairo 1934–37, 119–124.

Milik, Joséf T. 1972: "Milkî-ṣedeq et Milkî-reša' dans les anciens écrits juifs et chrétiens", in: *JJS* 23 (1972) 95–144.

Morenz, Siegfried 1951: *Die Geschichte von Joseph dem Zimmermann*, übersetzt, erläutert und untersucht (TU 56), Berlin 1951.

Müller, Ulrich B. 1980: "Rez. Ulrich Fischer, Eschatologie … 1978", in: *ThZ* 26 (1980) 238–240.

Münter, Friedrich 1821: *Der Jüdische Krieg unter den Kaisern Trajan und Hadrian*, Altona/Leipzig 1821.

Musurillo, Herbert (Ed.) 1961: *Acta Alexandrinorum* (BiTeu), Leipzig 1961.

Nestle, Eberhard 1901: *Die Kirchengeschichte des Eusebius aus dem Syrischen übersetzt* (TU NF VI, 2), Berlin 1901.

Neusner, Jacob 1979: *From politics to piety*. The emergence of pharisaic Judaism, New York ²1979.

Nikiprowetzky, Valentin 1970: *La Troisième Sibylle*, Paris/Mouton/La Haye 1970.

Philonenko, Marc 1975: "Le Poimandrès et la liturgie juive", in: Françoise Dunand et Pierre Lévêque (Eds.): *Les syncrétismes dans les religions de l'antiquité, colloque de Besonçon*, Leiden 1975, 204–211.

Reinach, Théodore 1963: *Textes d'auteurs grecs et romains relatifs au Judaisme*, Nachdruck Hildesheim 1963.

Rokeah, David 1972: "The War of Kitos: Towards the clarification of a philological-historical problem", in: *ScrHie* 23 (1972) 79–84.

Romanelli, Pietro 1943: *La Cirenaica romana*, 1943, Nachdruck Rom 1971.

– 1954: "Cyrenaika", in: *CAH* Bd. XI, Cambridge ²1954, 667–675.

Roux, Jeanne et Georges 1949: "Un décret du politeuma des Juifs de Bérénikè en Cyrénaique au Musée lapidaire de Carpentras (Planches III et IV)", in: *REG* 62 (1949) 281–296.

Rzach, Alois 1923: Art. "Sibyllinische Orakel", in: *PRE* 2. RII A2 (1923), 2103–2183.

Schlatter, Adolf 1897: *Die Tage Trajans und Hadrians* (BFChTh 1,3), Gütersloh 1897. Nachdruck in: *idem: Synagoge und Kirche bis zum Barkochba-Aufstand*, Stuttgart 1966, 9–97.

– 1925: *Geschichte Israels von Alexander dem Großen bis Hadrian*, Stuttgart ³1925.

Schmid, Wolfgang 1966: "Die Koexistenz von Sarapiskult und Christentum im Hadrianbrief bei Vopiscus", (Bonner Historia-Augusta-Colloquium 1964/65, Antiquitas Reihe 4), in: *Beiträge zur Historia-Augusta-Forschung*, hrsg. v. A. Alföldi, Bd. 3, Bonn 1966, 153–184.

Schürer, Emil/Vermes, Geza/Millar, Fergus 1973: *The history of the Jewish people in the age of Jesus Christ (175 B.C.–A.D. 135)*, Bd. 1, Edinburgh 1973.

Supplementum Epigraphicum Graecum 1960: 17 (1960).

Sevenster, Jan Nicolaas 1975: *The roots of pagan anti-Semitism in the ancient world* (NT.S 41), Leiden 1975.

Siegfried, C./Gelzer, H. 1884: *Eusebii canonum epitome ex Dionysii Telmaharensis chronico petita*. Verterunt notisque illustrarunt Carolus Siegfried et Henricus Gelzer, Lipsiae 1884.

Smallwood, E. Mary 1962: "Palestine c. AD 115–118", in: *Historia* 11 (1962) 500–516.

– 1976: *The Jews under Roman rule*. From Pompey to Diocletian (SJLA 20), Leiden 1976.

Smith, Morton 1972: "Pseudepigraphy in the Israelite literary tradition", in: *Pseudepigrapha I*. Entretiens sur l'Antiquité Classique, Vandoeuvres-Genève 1972, 189–215 (Diskussion S. 216–227).

Starcky, Jean 1963: "Les quatre étapes du messianisme à Qumrân", in: *RB* 70 (1963) 481–505.

Stemberger, Günter 1979: "Die Beurteilung Roms in der rabbinischen Literatur", in: *ANRW* II 19,2, Berlin/New York 1979, 338–396.

Stern, Menahem (Ed.) 1974: *Greek and Latin Authors on Jews and Judaism*, Bd. I, Jerusalem 1974.

– 1980: *Greek and Latin Authors on Jews and Judaism*, Bd. II, Jerusalem 1980.

Świderek, Anna 1971: "ΙΟΥΔΑΙΚΟΣ ΛΟΓΟΣ", in: *JJP* 16/17 (1971) 45–62.

Tcherikover, Victor A. 1963: "The decline of the Jewish diaspora in Egypt in the Roman period", in: *JJS* 14 (1963) 1–32.

Temporini, Hildegard 1978: *Die Frauen am Hofe Trajans*, Berlin/New York 1978.

Vermes, Geza 1961: *Scripture and Tradition in Judaism*. Haggadic studies (StPB 4), Leiden 1961.

Volz, Paul 1934: *Die Eschatologie der jüdischen Gemeinde im neutestamentlichen Zeitalter*, Tübingen 1934. Nachdruck Hildesheim 1966.

Wilcken, Ulrich 1909: *Zum alexandrinischen Antisemitismus* (ASGW.PH 27), Leipzig 1909, 781–839.

van der Woude, Adam Simon 1957: *Die messianischen Vorstellungen der Gemeinde von Qumrân* (SSN 3), Assen 1957.

Ziegler, K.-H. 1964: *Die Beziehungen zwischen Rom und dem Partherreich*, Wiesbaden 1964.

Zuntz, Günther 1972: "On the hymns in Corpus Hermeticum XIII", in: *idem: Opuscula selecta*, Manchester 1972, 150–177.

Social Functions of Apocalyptic Language in Pauline Christianity

Wayne A. Meeks

1. Paul and Apocalyptic: A Functional Approach

1.1 Almost exactly fifty years ago, Albert Schweitzer completed his book, *The Mysticism of Paul the Apostle*.[1] In it he argued that Paul could be rightly understood only within the context of Jewish and primitive-Christian apocalyptic – a proposal which most theologians found startling, even offensive. The connections between Pauline Christianity and apocalyptic have not become less controversial in the succeeding half-century: witness the reaction to Ernst Käsemann's provocative assertion in 1960 that "Die Apokalyptik ist ... die Mutter aller christlichen Theologie gewesen".[2] Neither the history of ideas nor an existentialist theological hermeneutic has been able to resolve the controversy. A more promising approach is that proposed by John Gager: that we should inquire after the specific *function* of each particular use in the Pauline letters of "end-time language".[3] I want to go somewhat further than Gager did in that brief article by attempting the sort of functional analysis that anthropologists have so successfully developed in their study of modern "millenarian" movements.[4]

1.2. It would be most helpful if we could adopt from the social scientists a unified theory of the functions of millenarian beliefs which could then generate a series of predictive hypotheses to be tested by our historical and exegetical research. Unfortunately, however, there is no such consensus, and it would be naive for me to attempt here my own theoretical synthesis. Nevertheless, there is a fairly broad family resemblance among the analytic methods of several leading anthropologists, despite some fundamental

---

[1] Schweitzer 1930.

[2] Käsemann 1960; Ebeling 1961; Fuchs 1961; response by Käsemann 1962; Bultmann 1964; Becker 1970; Baumgarten 1975; more generally Luz 1968; Delling 1970; Schrage 1974; Benoit 1977; Stuhlmacher 1977.

[3] Gager 1970.

[4] For an introduction to this literature, see the critical survey by Talmon 1962. Gager himself has elsewhere argued for the usefulness of such anthropological method in the study of early Christianity: 1975, chap. 2.

differences in theoretical perspective. For our purposes the common ground may be marked out by stating a few general theses. Based in part in empirical observations, these are not systematically derived hypotheses, but they will serve as convenient signposts:

1.2.1. "Millenarian," or as we may prefer to call them, eschatological beliefs, operate within specific social settings. In order to understand them, we must see what functions they serve for the groups that hold them. Similar verbal formulations may be used for quite different purposes on different occasions or by different groups; in that case, they cannot be said to "mean" the same thing.

1.2.2. Usually it is the revelations received by one or more individual prophets that provide the ordering complex of beliefs for the movement.

1.2.3. Characteristically, the eschatological beliefs introduce innovations in a traditional society, making use of the known and accepted traditions in new combinations in the innovative system of beliefs.

1.2.4. Participants in a millenarian movement are frequently persons and groups who have experienced frustration of their access to social power and to the media through which social power is exercised.

1.2.5. The medium for change in the millenarian movement itself is primarily cognitive. "Social change is preeminently symbol or symbolic change".[5] This implies that apocalyptic beliefs do not merely constitute a compensation in phantasy for real want of power, goods, and status, but first of all provide a way of making sense of a world that seems to have gone mad. An "explanation" of apocalyptic beliefs therefore needs to take account of "cognitive dissonance" theory at least as much as "relative deprivation" theory.[6]

1.2.6. Success in creating a new "plausibility structure" (Berger-Luck-mann) or "mazeway" (Wallace) can enable a group to discover or obtain social power. The apocalyptic myths, radical as they may be in "nihilating" the existing world – that is, the "symbolic universe" of the dominant society – may therefore serve a "conservative" and constructive function for the believing group.[7] That is, they may pave the way for new forms of institutionalization. In such a case the "routinization of charisma" may not entail so radical a change as Max Weber believed.[8]

1.2.7. These theses may suffice to indicate a perspective from which to look at specific uses to which apocalyptic language is put in the Pauline letters. I retain the term "apocalyptic language" rather than Gager's more neutral "end-time language", because it is useful to look at some complexes

---

[5] Smith 1970, 471 (= 1978, 143). Cf. Berger-Luckmann 1966; Wallace 1956; Worsley 1957; Burridge 1969; Douglas 1973.

[6] Aberle 1962; Festinger 1962, 1964.

[7] Kovacs 1976.
[8] See below, §6.2.4.

of motifs that are broader than explicit references to the end of the age, but which characteristically occur in apocalyptic literature. The problems involved in defining "apocalyptic" are notorious,[9] but I believe we could agree that the following characteristics would appear in any literature we would call "apocalyptic," though they need not be regarded as definitive:

1.2.7.1. Secrets have been revealed to the author or prophet.

1.2.7.2. These secrets have to do with a cosmic transformation that will happen very soon. Time moves toward that climax, which separates "this age" from "the age to come."

1.2.7.3. Central among the events to happen "at the end of days" is *judgment*: The rectification of the world order, the separation of the good from the wicked, and assigning the appropriate reward or punishment.

1.2.7.4. Consequently the apocalyptic universe is characterized by three corresponding dualities: (a) the cosmic duality heaven/earth, (b) the temporal duality this age/the age to come, and (c) a social duality: the sons of light/the sons of darkness, the righteous/the unrighteous, the elect/the world.

2. Two Ages, Two Societies: 1 Thessalonians

2.1. The most obviously "apocalyptic" document among the Pauline letters is 2 Thess., but I pass over that letter at present because the still unresolved question of its authenticity would unduly complicate our discussion. I may note, however, that if we pay strict attention to the functions that the apocalyptic language most likely serves in this letter, then many of the reasons for doubting Pauline authorship become less persuasive. If it were accepted as authentic, it would give the clearest example we have of the use of eschatological beliefs by the Pauline leaders for *social* control, not only the control of beliefs. The opening thanksgiving leads into a distinct section (vss. 7–10) which, whether a previously formulated tradition or the author's own work, is in the form of a "judgment theophany" and filled with quotations from and allusions to OT verses (Aus, 1971). This theophany has an antithetical structure; its principal theme is the vindication of the oppressed Christians and the punishment of their oppressors. Hence it serves primarily to emphasize the group's distinctiveness, as a persecuted minority, and their ultimate superiority to those who are now opposing them. The natural counterpart of this distinctiveness is internal coherence, reflected in the praise for their "love of each one of all of you for one another" (vs. 3) as well as for "patience and faith" under persecution (vs. 4). Specific rules are lacking or taken for granted; what is desired is "goodness" and "faith" (1:11). The nearest we come to a specific picture of the desired community life is in the admonitions of 3:6–15, which aim at ἡσυχία by emphasis upon the steady

---

[9] See, *e.g.* Collins 1979 and the contributions in this volume by Collins, Hartman, Schüssler Fiorenza, Sanders, Koch, Betz, Krause.

life of artisans. Those who will not work are not to eat (vs. 10). A further sanction is specified by 3:14: If the ἄτακτοι persist even in the face of this apostolic admonition, they are to be separated from the community – though still regarded as "brothers" (vs. 15). In the apocalyptic section of chap. 2, again the effect is the reinforcement of the solidarity of the Christian group, with their special knowledge, including traditions communicated to them by the apostles (vss. 5–6), and their distinction from "all who do not believe the truth but approve wickedness" (vs. 12), who will be judged at the end.

2.2. In his earliest extant letter, to the Christian groups in Thessalonica, Paul reminds them of their conversion: "How you turned to God from the idols, to serve a living and true God, and to await from the heavens his son, whom he raised from the dead, Jesus who saves us from the coming wrath" (1:9f.). This has the ring of formulaic speech, perhaps not coined by Paul himself,[10] but it states motifs that persisted in Paul's missionary preaching and in his subsequent "reminders" to his congregations. Thus his opening greeting to the Galatian Christians, written a few years later, speaks of "Jesus Christ, who gave himself for our sins, that he might rescue us from the present evil age according to the will of our God and Father..." (Gal 1:4). And in what may be the last of his authentic letters, addressed to Philippi, he says, "Our πολίτευμα is in the heavens, whence we are expecting as Savior the Lord Jesus Christ, who will transform the body of our humility to conform with the body of his glory, by exercise of the power he possesses even to subject the universe to him" (Phil 3:21). The apocalyptic elements are rather clear, especially the correlation of the three dualities, heaven/earth, this age/the coming age, the worshippers of the living and true God/the outsiders who worship idols.

2.2.1. The statement in 1 Thessalonians stands within the opening thanksgiving, which is unusually extended.[11] In that context it provides a summary and transition between two sections that have two closely related epistolary uses: (A) philophronetic, establishing the relational context for the paraenesis that is the principal content of the letter as a whole;[12] (B) introducing two major themes: (a) the importance of the εἴσοδος of the Christian missionaries in Thessalonica and the conversion of the addressees and (b) the θλῖψις which the latter share with the apostles and with Christians in other places.

2.2.2. The motif of shared or analogous θλῖψις is further specified in 2:14:

---

[10] Dibelius 1937, 7; Best 1972, 86, finds two 3-line stanzas; see further literature cited there.
[11] Schubert 1939, 16–27.
[12] Malherbe 1980.

For, brothers, you have become imitators of the churches of God that are in Judaea in Christ Jesus, because you have suffered the same things at the hands of your own people as they at the hands of the Judaeans....

It is the new Christians' ἴδιοι συμφυλέται who have shown hostility toward them. The phrase is usually translated "your own countrymen," but it may suggest a rather closer relationship: people who belong to the same φυλή or "tribe".[13] Luther's "Blutsfreunden" is thus preferable to the English versions. The point is that, in whatever subdivision of the *polis* the Christian had formerly felt what we might call "their ethnic identity," now they found hostility. The very groups with whom formerly they shared ties of kinship and racial or local origins were now their enemies. The reasons for this hostility are not too difficult to imagine. Unlike the many little clubs that were so much a part of city life in the Roman empire, unlike even the multitude of cults into which one might be initiated, the Christians were exclusive. If one were baptized into Christ Jesus, he could not also be initiated into the cult of Dionysus or Serapis, nor could he participate in many civic and social ceremonies that were, however innocuous to most, to the Christian as to the Jew idolatrous.[14] Furthermore, Christian initiation was a rite of passage in which the whole hierarchy of identities seemed to be dissolved: here there was no longer Jew nor Greek, slave nor free, even male and female. Here one took off the old and put on a new humanity; all became brothers and sisters to each other and children of God. Old ties of kinship were dissolved, and a new, fictive kinship was established.[15] This all seemed terribly subversive to the basic institutions of society.[16]

2.2.3. A few sentences later, Paul puts the θλῖψις of the Thessalonian Christians into an interesting context:

I sent Timothy ... to strengthen you and to appeal to you, for the sake of your faith, that no one be shaken by these afflictions (θλίψεις). For you yourselves know that we are destined for this. For when we were with you, we told you in advance that we were going to be afflicted (θλίβεσθαι) – just as it happened, and you know. (3:2–4)

Commentators have debated whether Paul here is employing a specific Jewish eschatological notion, that just before the turn of the ages the righteous are destined to suffer.[17] The strong language of destiny in the

---

[13] Latte 1941.   [14] Nock 1933; Walter 1979.

[15] Meeks 1974; 198?, Part VII.1.; 1983.

[16] Balch 1974; Malherbe 1977, 50–53; Pax 1971, 1972.

[17] Dan 12:1; *Jub.* 23:13f., 18f., 22; *2 Apoc. Bar.* 70:2f., 5, 8–10; *4 Ezra* 5:1–12; 13:30f.; 14:16f.; Mark 13:7f.; Rev *passim*; The notion of the "travail of the Messiah" (חבלי של משיח), which occurs in later rabbinic literature that can hardly be regarded as apocalyptic in any sense, is presumably a relic of this belief: *bŠabb* 118a, *Ketub* 111a, *Sanh* 98a; *Mekilta Vayassa* 6 (printed edd.; Lauterbach II:123, 32n), all cited by Dibelius *ad loc.*

passage lends support to that view.[18] The interesting thing here is that Paul is reminding the Christians of something they were *taught* when they were first converted. The expectation of suffering was part of the catechism, so to speak, of the churches in the Pauline mission areas.[19] When that prediction is fulfilled, then, the experience strongly reinforces the boundary between the converts and the larger society, their συμφυλέται, to which they formerly belonged.

2.2.4. This is not quite a case of "theodicy" in the sense that some sociologists, like Peter Berger, use in talking about millenarian sects,[20] at least not in a direct or simple way. The apocalyptic language, if that is what it is, does not provide an *answer* to the problem of the experienced suffering. Rather, the case is almost the reverse. It was the baptismal ritual, the catechetical instruction, and the continuing discipline of the Christian community that separated the converts from their *symphyletai*, and the "cognitive dissonance" produced by that separation was sharply *emphasized*, not relieved, by the promise that they would be persecuted. When they in fact experience hostility, Paul uses that fact as a means for interpreting their identity as Christians. Their separation from their neighbors has had its predicted outcome, so the complex of teaching that accompanied and effected that separation is confirmed. In that sense, then, the experience of hostility itself is employed to reduce dissonance: the experience helps to make sense of the separation and thus to reinforce the boundaries between the group and the larger society.

2.2.5. Moreover, the language of destiny sets the identity of the Thessalonian Christians into a cosmic, theological context. Visibly they are a tiny club gathering cautiously in someone's house in Thessalonica. But Paul is teaching them that "really" their troubles are part of a comprehensive pattern of God's activity in and for the world. Notice how Paul speaks in 1:6 and 2:14: "You became imitators (μιμηταί) of us and of the Lord…"; "You became imitators of the churches of God that are in Judaea in Christ Jesus." This "imitation" has not been an active choice on their

---

[18] Best 1972, *ad loc.*

[19] Hill 1976 has reached a similar conclusion from study of 1 Peter, building on earlier work by E. Selwyn. See Acts 14:22, where Paul and Barnabas, on a return trip through Lystra, Iconia, and Pisidia, exhort their earlier converts ἐμμένειν τῇ πίστει καὶ ὅτι διὰ πολλῶν θλίψεων δεῖ ἡμᾶς εἰσελθεῖν εἰς τὴν βασιλείαν τοῦ θεοῦ. On this verse, quite exceptional to Luke's own view of suffering, see Adams 1979, 119. Walter 1979, 423, suggests that Thessalonica may have been the first place Paul introduced such a forewarning. Note also the importance of the θλῖψις/παράκλησις motif in the opening blessing of 2 Cor 1:3–11, esp. vs. 7: ὡς κοινωνοί ἐστε τῶν παθημάτων οὕτως καὶ τῆς παρακλήσεως. A similar warning becomes part of the ritual for receiving proselytes to the Jewish community in the aftermath of the Bar Kochba war: *bYebam* 47a.

[20] Berger 1967, 50–79.

part. Rather, their experience has set them within a larger pattern of which God is the author. The experience is that of affliction or, more precisely, the fact that their "receiving the word" brought with it both "much affliction" in the hostility of their former *symphyletai* and also "joy" in the intimate new fellowship of the community, an irrational joy which must therefore be the gift of "the Holy Spirit" (1:6). Paul's interpretation of this experience established solidarity with other Christian groups which the Thessalonian Christians have never seen – far away in Judea – but also with the Apostle, who has also suffered throughout his mission (2:2), and finally with "the Lord." That Lord, of course, is Jesus, God's "Son, whom he raised from the dead." That is, the Christians' experience of joy in the midst of suffering, of internal solidarity against external hostility, Paul declares to be an analogue to the eschatological event that is the center of his message, "Christ and him crucified." To put it another way, Paul has thus made of the announcement of the crucified and risen Messiah not just the report of a miraculous event, but a powerful, comprehensive metaphor that works to place many kinds of experiences within a pattern of God's paradoxical action. As a result, where only weakness and affliction appear to be present, through this metaphor one may discover potential power – for one is now part of a world-wide fellowship grounded in God's own action.

2.3. We have not yet looked at the passage that is most vividly apocalyptic in style, 4:13–5:11. Here Paul has put together three separate bits of tradition, each of apocalyptic cast: (A) The "saying of the Lord" 4:15–17, that draws a verbal picture of extraordinary events, "when the Lord himself, with a cry of command, with the voice of an archangel, with the trumpet of God, shall descend from heaven, and the dead in Christ shall arise first..."; (B) The saying about the coming of the Day of the Lord "like a thief in the night" (5:2), which we find also later in the synoptic gospels, in Revelation, and in 2 Peter; (C) The dualistic admonition to "watch," addressed to the "sons of light," who are distinguished from "the sons of darkness" (5:4–8).

All these apocalyptic images are cited by Paul in response to one problem: the death of some members of the congregation. These people who have died prematurely, the Thessalonian Christians fear, have been separated from those who await the coming of God's son from heaven. Here again we see that Paul is not offering any general theodicy, any general "solution" to the problem of death. It is not the problem of death as a universal phenomenon that is addressed here, but just the power of death to shatter the unique bonds of intimate new community. By using the apocalyptic scenario of the return ($\pi\alpha\varrho o\upsilon\sigma i\alpha$) of Jesus, Paul declares that the community of Christians crosses even the boundary of death, "that we, the living, who survive until the Parousia of the Lord, will certainly not precede those who have died" (4:15). "Then we the living, the survivors, *together with them* will be caught up in clouds to meet the Lord ... and thus we shall always be with the Lord" (4:17).

2.4. There is one last question we must deal with before leaving 1 Thessalonians: the function of the apocalyptic sections within the form and function of the whole letter. My colleague Abraham Malherbe has demonstrated that 1 Thessalonians follows the rhetorical pattern of a paraenetic letter, that is, a letter devoted to reminding people of moral standards and examples and urging them to follow them.[21] Now in almost every apocalyptic writing we find prominent elements of paraenesis;[22] here in a paraenetic letter we have discovered a number of elements of apocalyptic. How do they work together? Space does not permit an analysis of the whole literary structure of the letter, but a few observations may suggest the kinds of functional connections that are present.

2.4.1. On a simple level, the threat of a Final Judgment can of course act as a sanction for maintaining acceptable behavior. Paul does not hesitate to use this sanction in his other letters, *e.g.* Rom 14:10: "You, why do you judge your brother? You, why do you despise your brother? For we shall all stand before the judgment seat of God." And he can often quote what was evidently an early Christian catechetical formula, "Those who do x, y, and z will not inherit the Kingdom of God".[23] These threats remain mostly implicit in 1 Thessalonians, but the rules for sexual behavior are backed by the warning, "The Lord is an avenger for all these things" (4:6, cf. vs. 8).

2.4.2. On the whole, though, the connection between apocalyptic expectation and immediate moral admonition in 1 Thessalonians is more subtle. The "endtime language" reinforces the sense of uniqueness and solidarity of the community, as we have seen. And that in turn produces a disposition, if the admonitions are successful, to act in a way appropriate to the community's health. Appropriate behavior would include internal discipline and obedience of leaders (5:13–22). It also would include behavior that will be benign in the eyes of outsiders. The ethos that is recommended is that of quiet, decent artisans: "Be ambitious to live quietly and to mind your own business and to work with your own hands, as we instructed you, that you may behave decently vis à vis the outsiders and may need nothing" (4:11f.).

2.5. I have dealt with 1 Thessalonians at some length because, if we do

---

[21] Malherbe 1980.

[22] Vielhauer 1965, 587; Hartman 1966, 174–177, urges that in the earliest stages of the eschatological "midrash" underlying both 1 and 2 Thess and Mark 13 par, apocalyptic and paraenesis are much more closely joined than is usual in Jewish apocalyptic.

[23] 1 Cor 6:9f.; 15:50; Gal 5:21; Eph 5:5; cf. Dahl 1965, 62f.; Gager 1970, 333f.

undertake to bring to historical study of religion in antiquity some of the perspectives and methods of the social sciences, it is all the more imperative that we respect the integrity of the texts we are trying to understand. Within the assigned limits of this paper, however, I shall be able only to mention a few examples of other ways in which apocalyptic language works in other letters of the Pauline corpus, without being able to analyze the contexts in detail.

3. The End as Warrant for the New: Galatians

3.1. In Gal 1:4 is a clause that sounds very much like the one with which we began in 1 Thess 1:10: "... Jesus Christ, who gave himself for our sins, in order to rescue us from the present evil age." But in 1 Thessalonians the emphasis was on *waiting* for the Jesus "who saves us from the coming wrath". Here Jesus has already done something to pluck us out of "this present evil age". The emphasis throughout Galatians is on present fulfillment of eschatological hopes.

3.2. Now Paul writes to the churches of Galatia to deal with an acute crisis in authority. He speaks of agitators who have come in, introducing "another gospel," which he insists is false – for there can be no other gospel than the one he preached before. But from the point of view of these rival apostles, whoever they may have been, it is Paul who is the innovator. For the followers of Messiah Jesus were obviously a sect of Judaism, and Paul has radically violated the standards of Judaism by permitting Gentiles to join the community without circumcision and without the requirement to keep the sabbath and festivals and the rules of purity. Proselytism of Gentiles, the new apostles probably argued, was a laudable goal, and certain concessions might be made at first to make it easier for them to take the difficult step of conversion. But later this incomplete faith must be completed by learning to observe the commandments.[24]

3.2.1. That is, they probably understood Paul's approach to the Gentiles as a tactical concession, like that made by the Jewish merchant Ananias, who according to Josephus was responsible for the conversion of the royal household of Adiabene to Judaism. When King Izates himself wanted to be circumcised, Ananias became afraid of a hostile reaction from the king's subjects. He urged the king merely to be a god-fearer without taking the ultimate step of circumcision. Then a bit later there came another merchant, Eleazar, who advised the king that he was thus failing to carry out the Law of God (Jos. *Ant.* 20.34–38). Paul's rivals in Galatia must have seen

---

[24] Gal 3:3 may parody an assertion by the opponents that they wish to "complete" (ἐπιτελεῖσθαι) what Paul has "begun"; so Oepke, cited with approval by Schlier 1965, *ad loc.*

in him a cautious Ananias, in themselves, the faithful Eleazar who would complete his work.

3.2.2. Paul saw things quite differently. For the Gentile Christians now to wish to be "under the Law" would be a step not forward but backward, equivalent to a return to paganism (4:8–11). It would not be an act of obedience to God's will, but of disobedience of the new order established by the Messiah's coming.

3.2.3. To back this extraordinary claim, Paul emphasizes that his innovation was not based on mere human authority, but was received δι᾽ ἀποκαλύψεως, "by revelation" (1:12; compare 1:16, ἀποκαλύψαι and 2:2 κατὰ ἀποκάλυψιν). Furthermore, prior to that revelation, Paul himself had been a "zealot" for the traditions of the fathers (1:14). And the revelation itself is warranted by the scripture and tradition of Israel, as he undertakes to show by intricate exegesis in chapters 3 and 4.

3.2.4. The midrash in those chapters is too complex to rehearse here. Nils Dahl has shown that in chap. 3 Paul has constructed his dense argument by weaving together a series of specific texts and allusions and depending upon traditional interpretations of certain messianic proof-texts and on rules of exegesis that we find explicitly formulated in later rabbinic literature.[25] For example, the tradition that the term "seed" in 2 Sam 7:12 and hence also in Gen 17:7 referred to the Messiah is combined with the promise of Gen 49:10, "Until there shall come the one to whom it belongs",[26] as in the comment from Qumran on the latter passage, "Until there comes the legitimate Anointed One, the Shoot of David, for to him and to his seed has been given the covenant of Kingship for eternal generations" (4QPB 3f.). The passage is understood in the sense of a legal phrase that often occurs in Jewish sources, when a certain rule or institution is valid only "until there shall come" an agent from God. For example, the Rule of the Community from Qumran specifies that the sect is to "walk in these first ordinances until there shall come a Prophet and the Anointed of Aaron and of Israel" (1QS 9:11). Paul is more radical. He not only insists that the Messiah has already come, but the fact that Jesus as crucified stands under the curse of the Law (Deut 21:23) also leads him to an unheard-of deduction. The temporary ordinances that were valid only until the Messiah came include not just some particular rules, but "the Law" as such, *i.e.* the whole body of commandments that distinguished Jews from Gentiles.

3.2.5. Comparison with the Qumran sect is suggestive in another way as well. That group had withdrawn from the main institutions of Judaism to

---

[25] Dahl 1971; in more detail, Dahl 1973.

[26] The enigmatic שׁילה of the MT was apparently read as שׁלו; cf. LXX, ἕως ἂν ἔλθῃ τὰ ἀποκείμενα αὐτῷ.

establish a "community of the new covenant" in the wilderness by the Dead Sea. They were led by priests who regarded the credentials of the priests in charge of the Jerusalem temple as false and the temple itself as polluted. They undertook to build a *new* community, composed of "volunteers for the Torah," who would take upon themselves a new, rigorous discipline of separation from all impurity and radical obedience to the laws of Moses as interpreted by the Teacher of Righteousness and his successors, the priestly leaders of the sect. These radical innovations were justified, in their interpretations, by their belief that they were living at the End of Days. In a similar way, the even more radical innovations of the Pauline Christians are supported by the claim that the Messiah has already come. Obviously the content of the innovations is as different as can be: instead of rigorous application of the Law, abrogation of its legal use; instead of separation from all but the pure Israel, insistence on the unity of Jew and Gentile. Yet in both cases eschatological beliefs provide warrant, within a traditional context, for sharply modified practice.

4. Apocalyptic Exegesis of Scripture

4.1. In recent years students of apocalyptic have observed that it is essentially an exegetical literature. For example, Gerhard von Rad can say, "Überhaupt wird man die geistige Leistung der Apokalyptiker ziemlich erschöpfend mit dem Begriff 'Interpretation' umschreiben können".[27] Professor Hartman has demonstrated how fruitful that observation can be made, in his book that has already become something of a classic.[28] Apocalyptic interpretation is characterized by a very peculiar angle of vision. This is nicely illustrated by a well-known passage from the *pesher* on Habakkuk from Qumran Cave 1, a comment on the verse, "Write down the vision and make it plain upon the tablets, that he who reads may read it speedily." The interpretation of this is: "God told Habakkuk to write down the things that were to come upon the last generation, but he did not make known to him the consummation of the time. And the interpretation of the statement, 'That he who reads may read it speedily,' applies to the Teacher of Righteousness, to whom God did make known all the secrets of the words of his servants the prophets" (1QpHab 7:1–5). For the apocalyptic interpreter, the present moment and his own sect are the focus of all revelation. All that is past is prologue to what is about to happen; all that has been written and spoken in the sacred tradition was pointing to this group and this time.

---

[27] von Rad 1961, II:321 (referring specifically to Daniel).
[28] Hartman 1966.

4.2. Now precisely the same hermeneutical monopoly is implicit in the exegesis by Paul that we have already seen in Galatians. And the typically apocalyptic logic of this position is stated candidly by Paul in two places where he cites passages of scripture in order to derive guidelines for Christian behavior. To the Corinthians: "These things happened τυπικῶς (as models or examples) to those people, but they were written down for our admonition, to whom the end of the ages has come" (1 Cor 10:11). And again to the Romans (15:4): "For whatever was written before was written for our instruction...." Here is the warrant for reading the whole scripture in new ways – sometimes radically new – and for the benefit of a particular group.

5. The Future as Restraint on Enthusiasm: 1 Corinthians

5.1. The Corinthian correspondence is rich in eschatological, and even specifically apocalyptic, language. The following list, by no means exhaustive, will give an idea of the range of expression and of epistolary contexts in 1 Corinthians:

... so that you are not lacking in any spiritual gift, as you wait for the revealing [ἀποκάλυψις] of our Lord Jesus Christ; who will sustain you to the end, guiltless in the day of our Lord Jesus Christ. (1:7f., opening thanksgiving)

... a secret and hidden wisdom of God, which God decreed before the ages.... 'What no eye has seen, nor ear heard, nor the heart of man conceived, what God has prepared for those who love him,' God has revealed to us through the Spirit. (2:6–10)

... each man's work will become manifest; for the Day will disclose it, because it will be revealed with fire.... (3:13; cf. vss. 10–15)

If any one destroys God's temple, God will destroy him. (3:17)

... Do not pronounce judgment before the time, before the Lord comes, who will bring to light the things now hidden in darkness and will disclose the purposes of the heart. Then every man will receive his commendation from God. (4:5)

... You are to deliver this man to Satan for the destruction of the flesh, that his spirit may be saved in the day of the Lord. (5:5)

Do you not know that the saints will judge the world?... Do you not know that we are to judge angels? (6:2,3)

Do you not know that the unrighteous will not inherit the kingdom of God? (6:9)

The body is not meant for immorality, but for the Lord, and the Lord for the body. And God raised the Lord and will also raise us up by his power. (6:13f.)

I think that in view of the present distress it is well for a person to remain as he is.... I mean, brethren, the appointed time has grown very short.... For the form of this world is passing away. (7:26–31)

For as often as you eat this bread and drink the cup, you proclaim the Lord's death until he comes. (11:26)

But when we are judged by the Lord, we are chastened, so that we may not be condemned along with the world. (11:32)

Then comes the end, when he delivers the kingdom to God the Father after destroying every rule and every authority and power. (15:24)

Lo! I tell you a mystery. We shall not all sleep, but we shall all be changed, in a moment, in the twinkling of an eye, at the last trumpet. For the trumpet will sound, and the dead will be raised imperishable, and we shall be changed. (15:51 f.)

If any one has no love for the Lord, let him be accursed. Maranatha. (16:22)[29]

5.1.1. The specific epistolary uses of such language range here from the initial establishment of friendly relations (*philophronesis*) by praise of the addressees in the opening thanksgiving, through warrants for general and specific sorts of behavior (*paraenesis*) and for internal discipline, to highly ironic, even sarcastic twists of phrases shared with the addressees, which must be intended to alter some specific attitudes held by an important group within the Corinthian congregations. This last use is most striking, and may even be regarded as characteristic of 1 Corinthians. The best known instance of the ironic usage is 4:8, which has become the key for recent interpretation of this letter:

Already you are filled! Already you have become rich! Without us you have become kings! And would that you did reign, so that we might share the rule with you!

There is a fairly wide consensus among exegetes that this passage, taken in context with the many statements emphasizing the future and temporal sequence throughout the letter, especially in chapter 15, enable us to discern one major issue behind the varied problems addressed by the letter. As it is commonly put, the issue is between the "realized eschatology" of the group called the *pneumatikoi* or the *teleioi* in Corinth and the "futurist eschatology" or "eschatological reservation" of Paul.[30]

5.1.2. To put this same issue in functional terms will enable us to compare it with uses of apocalyptic language we have seen in the other letters. The *pneumatikoi* of Corinth are using eschatological language, especially in forms that have already been adapted in the ritual of baptism, to warrant their claim to transcend some norms of ordinary behavior and to support their conviction that their status is superior to that of persons still concerned with the fleshly world, including "weak" and "psychic" Christians. Against them Paul uses eschatological language with emphasis upon the future tense, in order to emphasize the imperfection of the present status of Christians, including the inconclusiveness of boundaries – especially internal boundaries between different groups within the community, but also external boundaries between the community and the world.[31]

5.2. On the face of it then, Paul's employment of apocalyptic categories here seems to be the reverse of that in Galatians. There he used the present

---

[29] The translation of all these passages is from the RSV.

[30] *E.g.*, Käsemann 1960; 1962; convenient reviews of literature in Wilson 1968 and Boers 1967; see also Koester 1961; Funk 1966, 279–305; Pearson 1973, chap. 4; Dahl 1967; Thiselton 1978; Horsley 1978.

[31] Meeks 1979.

experience of factors traditionally associated with the messianic age to warrant a radical innovation, abandoning the use of the Mosaic law to set boundaries between Jew and Gentile. Here he uses future eschatological language to *restrain* innovation and to counsel stability and order: "In view of the present [or "impending"] distress, it is well for a person to remain as he is." However, it is important to recognize that this "conservative" use of apocalyptic language is in dialectic with an "innovative" use by the *pneumatikoi* that is structurally analogous to the use that Paul himself made in the letter to Galatians. This shows that the warrant-for-innovation function of apocalyptic language was understood and used in the Pauline congregations by those who had learned from him – though not necessarily with the same results.

5.3. If we look at the social consequences intended by Paul's diverse use of apocalyptic in these different situations, however, we see much greater consistency. The central focus in all three letters we have examined has been the solidarity and stability of the congregations. Use of apocalyptic language in support of that solidarity and stability varies with the nature and source of the threat to the community perceived by Paul and his fellow-workers.

6. Conclusions

6.1. Even this partial survey has shown that the apocalyptic beliefs held by leaders of the Pauline groups and referred to in their letters were complex. They lent themselves to a wide variety of epistolary uses and, we are able to surmise by extension, a variety of functions in the lives of the congregations. Some of the specific functions were these:

6.1.1. To emphasize and legitimate boundaries between the Christian groups and the larger society.

6.1.2. To enhance internal cohesion and solidarity.

6.1.3. To provide sanctions for normative behavior.

6.1.4. To warrant innovations over against the Jewish norms and structures from which Christianity emerged.

6.1.5. To resist, on the other hand, deviant behavior that led to disruption of the Christian community.

6.1.6. To legitimate the leadership of Paul and his associates against challenges.

6.1.7. To justify radical interpretation of scripture and tradition.

6.2. The list could be extended and of course each item could be subdivided. However, the list of functions in itself, even if it were exhaustive, could not alone answer the question whether Pauline Christianity was a "millenarian movement" or, more precisely, whether "millenarian movement" is a useful model or pure type to serve as a base-line in describing the Pauline communities. This is a systemic question. In order to answer it we must discover whether the instances of apocalyptic-like language we have looked at are only fragments or whether they function together as parts of a larger complex of symbols. If the latter, then we must inquire whether the whole symbol-complex works in the way that the foundational myths of a millenarian movement work. Note that this is quite different from the old question whether Paul was a systematic theologian.

6.2.1. Among anthropologists studying modern millenarian movements, even those working from a neo-Marxist perspective, there has been a converging recognition in recent years that the belief system of such a group has a constitutive and not just a reflexive function. For such a group to organize and persist, there must be a prophet who provides, by a revelation, a new myth. This myth, which invariably includes many traditional beliefs and images but in novel combinations, must have explanatory power for coping with present distress. That is, it must enable the adherents to reduce their "cognitive dissonance". It must provide a vision of a radically better future order. It must provide an ordering center for the formation of the emergent community and for its identity over against the dominant society. By thus providing a comprehensive cognitive map, an alternative vision of reality, it offers access to social power, if only within that counter-cultural community.

6.2.2. Did Paul and his associates provide to the churches they founded a mythic complex of that sort, and did it function for them in such a way that Paul thus filled at least in part the role of a "millenial prophet"? I believe that the answer is 'Yes,' as we can see rather easily by returning to a motif we first noticed in 1 Thessalonians. The letter focused on the experiences of separation, hostility from without, and suffering, incorporating these experiences into a master complex of metaphors built upon the kerygma of the crucified Messiah, Son of God, and replicated in the reported experiences of both the apostle and of other Christian groups elsewhere. In a way which is quite characteristic of apocalyptic seers, Paul wove into that metaphoric complex traditional images and beliefs, which were often warranted by a sharply perspectival reading of scripture, all skewed and reshaped by the radically new event, the crucifixion and resurrection of Messiah Jesus. In Galatians, that same complex of tradition, event, and metaphor legitimates the innovative practice of the Gentile-Christian congregations and defends Paul's consistency. In the Corinthian correspondence, it serves as a paradigm for testing appropriate modes of relationships of power within the Christian groups.

6.2.3. It is of course not news to any student of Paul that the proclamation of the crucifixion and resurrection of Jesus is the heart of his theology.

But the social context and consequences of this theological complex have not often been recognized. These can be rather sharply focused by juxtaposing an insight of Kenelm Burridge, that access to social power is a key to the birth of a millenarian movement, with some acute observations by John Schütz about the "hermeneutic of power" in the Pauline letters.

6.2.4. Burridge proposes a working definition of religion and religious activity: "The redemptive process indicated by the activities, moral rules, and assumptions about power which, pertinent to the moral order and taken on faith, not only enable a people to perceive the truth of things, but guarantee that they are indeed perceiving the truth of things."[32] Millenarian movements offer a new vision of "the truth about power". This new vision not only serves psychological needs by alleviating the cognitive dissonance experienced by people for whom the "redemptive process" of the dominant society is not working well, it also serves as the organizing center of the new countercultural community, within which the new paradigms of power can actually be expressed and tried out in microcosm. In some instances the new enjoyment of social power within the group can carry over into new forms of relationship to the larger society as well. Thus the "cargo cults" studied by Burridge and others not infrequently serve as bridges to political action by native groups and to eventual participation in the "modernized" society.

6.2.5. Schütz defines authority as "the interpretation of power". The *auctor* is a person who augments power by inspiring and focusing the power of others.[33] And the metaphorical elaboration of the crucifixion/resurrection kerygma into a complex paradigm is the central way in which Paul does that for the communities he has founded. Schütz may exaggerate the consistency with which Paul employs this paradigm, and he perhaps pays too little attention to more mundane modes of power at work between Paul and his associates, rivals, and communities.[34] Nevertheless, he shows very clearly how the apostle's work of metaphor-construction has provided a new and prolific vision of "the truth about power" that makes possible the formation of new communities in which persons enjoy power which they did not possess previously. That seems precisely analogous to the role of the "millenial prophet" described by Burridge. Moreover, Holmberg carries Schütz's revision of Weber further to show that institutionalization is not the antithesis of a charismatic movement but implicit in such a movement from the beginning.[35] It is not so paradoxical as it appears, then, for an apocalyptic movement to develop institutions, as

---

[32] Burridge 1969, 6f.   [33] Schütz 1975, 12f.
[34] See the criticisms by Holmberg 1978, 133f., 205.
[35] Holmberg 1978, chap. 6; cf. Kovacs 1976; Dahl's observations about the Qumran community point in the same direction: Dahl 1964.

the Pauline leaders clearly were doing and as commonly occurs in modern millenial groups.

6.3. Can we say then that Pauline Christianity was an apocalyptic movement? That conclusion would be too hasty, for two reasons: (A) Pauline Christianity was a complex phenomenon; only some aspects of it are illuminated by comparisons with ancient and modern apocalyptic movements. (B) In order to judge the extent to which the movement as a whole could be accurately characterized as "apocalyptic" or "millenarian", we would need to agree on a functional definition of an apocalyptic movement as an ideal type, and second, we would have to construct a total description of Pauline Christianity, including its social forms and relationships and the social functions of its beliefs. If either of these steps is possible, it is certainly not within the scope of the present essay.[36] Nevertheless, I hope that I have demonstrated that inquiry into the social functions of belief structures is a useful and flexible instrument for historical inquiry, that there are important aspects of Pauline Christianity that are best understood by comparison with analogous forms and functions in apocalyptic movements, and that attempts to delineate apocalypticism should in every instance include careful attention to the social functions of the apocalyptic beliefs.

Bibliography

Aberle, David 1962: "A note on Relative Deprivation Theory as Applied to Millenarian and Other Cult Movements", in: Sylvia L. Thrupp (ed.), *Millenial Dreams in Action: Studies in Revolutionary Religious Movements,* Comparative Studies in Society and History, Suppl. II, The Hague 1962, 209–214.

Adams, David R. 1979: *The Suffering of Paul and the Dynamics of Luke-Acts,* unpublished diss., Yale 1979.

Aus, Roger 1971: *Comfort in Judgment. The Use of Day of the Lord and Theophany Traditions in Second Thessalonians I,* unpublished diss., Yale 1971.

Balch, David 1974: *'Let Wives be Submissive...': The Origin, Form, and Apologetic Function of the Household Duty Code (Haustafel) in I Peter,* unpublished diss., Yale 1974.

Baumgarten, Jörg 1975: *Paulus und die Apokalyptik. Die Auslegung apokalyptischer Überlieferungen in den echten Paulusbriefen* (WMANT 44), Neukirchen 1975.

Becker, Jürgen 1970: "Erwägungen zur apokalyptischen Tradition in der paulinischen Theologie", *EvTh* 30 (1970) 593–609.

Benoit, Pierre 1977: "L'évolution du langage apocalyptique dans le Corpus paulinien", in: *Apocalypses et théologie de l'esperance.* Congres de Toulouse (1975) (LeDiv 95), Paris 1977.

Berger, Peter 1967: *The Sacred Canopy.* Garden City, N. Y., 1967.

Berger, Peter and Luckmann, Thomas 1966: *The Social Construction of Reality: A Treatise in the Sociology of Knowledge,* Garden City, N. Y., 1966.

---

[36] I have essayed a programmatic sketch of the second, a sociological description of the Pauline communities, in Meeks 198?. A book on the same topic, entitled *The First Urban Christians,* will appear in 1983.

Best, Ernest 1972: *The First and Second Epistles to the Thessalonians* (BNTC/HNTC), London/ New York 1972.

Boers, Hendrikus W. 1967: "Apocalyptic Eschatology in 1 Corinthians 15", in: *Interpretation* 21 (1967) 50–65.

Bultmann, Rudolf 1964: "Ist die Apokalyptik die Mutter der christlichen Theologie?", in: W. Eltester (ed.), *Apophoreta: Festschr. für E. Haenchen,* Berlin 1964, 64–69. Reprinted in: *Exegetica,* Tübingen 1967, 476–482.

Burridge, Kenelm 1969: *New Heaven, New Earth: A Study of Millenarian Activities,* London and New York 1969.

Collins, John (ed.) 1979: *Apocalypse: The Morphology of a Genre (Semeia,* 14), Missoula, Mont. 1979.

Dahl, Nils A. 1964: "Eschatologie und Geschichte im Lichte der Qumrantexte", in: E. Dinkler (ed.), *Zeit und Geschichte: Dankesgabe an R. Bultmann zum 80. Geburtstag,* Tübingen 1964, 3–18. Eng. trans. in *The Crucified Messiah and Other Essays,* Minneapolis, Minn. 1974, 129–145.

– 1965: *Kurze Auslegung des Epheserbriefes,* Göttingen 1965.

– 1967: "Paul and the Church at Corinth according to 1 Corinthians 1–4", in: W. R. Farmer et al. (edd.), *Christian History and Interpretation: Studies Presented to John Knox,* Cambridge 1967, 313–335. Reprinted in: *Studies in Paul,* Minneapolis, Minn. 1977, 40–61.

– 1971: "Widersprüche in der Bibel, ein altes hermeneutisches Problem", in: *StTh* 25 (1971) 1–19. Norw. orig. in: *SvTK* 45 (1969) 22–36; Eng. trans. in: *Studies in Paul,* Minneapolis, Minn. 1977, 159–177.

– 1973: *Paul's Letter to the Galatians: Epistolary Genre, Content and Structure.* Privately printed for the SBL Paul Seminar 1973.

Delling, Gerhard 1970: "Zur eschatologischen Bestimmtheit der paulinischen Theologie", in: *Zeit und Endzeit: Zwei Vorlesungen zur Theologie des Neuen Testaments* (BSt 58), Neukirchen 1970, 57–101.

Dibelius, Martin 1937: *An die Thessalonicher I II* (HNT 11), Tübingen ³1937.

Douglas, Mary 1973: *Natural Symbols: Explorations in Cosmology,* London ²1973.

Ebeling, Gerhard 1961: "Der Grund christlicher Theologie", in: *ZThK* 58 (1961) 227–244.

Festinger, Leon 1962: *A Theory of Cognitive Dissonance,* Stanford, Calif. ²1962.

–1964: *When Prophecy Fails: A Social and Psychological Study of a Modern Group that Predicted the Destruction of the World,* New York ²1964.

Fuchs, Ernst 1961: "Über die Aufgabe einer christlichen Theologie", in: *ZThK* 58 (1961) 245–267.

Funk, Robert W. 1966: *Language, Hermeneutic, and Word of God,* New York 1966.

Gager, John G. 1970: "Functional Diversity in Paul's Use of End-Time Language", in: *JBL* 89 (1970) 325–337.

– 1975: *Kingdom and Community: The Social World of Early Christianity* (Prentice-Hall Studies in Religion), Englewood Cliffs, N. J.,. 1975.

Hartman, Lars 1966: *Prophecy Interpreted: The Formation of Some Jewish Apocalyptic Texts and of the Eschatological Discourse Mark 13 par.* (CB.NT 1), Lund 1966.

Hill, David 1976: "On Suffering and Baptism in I Peter", in: *NT* 18 (1976) 181–189.

Holmberg, Bengt 1978: *Paul and Power: The Structure of Authority in the Primitive Church as Reflected in the Pauline Epistles* (CB.NT 11), Lund 1978.

Horsley, R. A. 1978: "'How can some of you say that there is no resurrection of the dead?' Spiritual Elitism in Corinth", in: *NT* 20 (1978) 203–231.

Käsemann, Ernst 1960: "Die Anfänge christlicher Theologie", in: *ZThK* 57 (1960) 162–185. Reprinted in: *Exegetische Versuche und Besinnungen,* II, Göttingen ²1965, 82–104. Eng. Trans. in: *New Testament Questions of Today,* London 1969, 82–107.

– 1962: "Zum Thema der urchristlichen Apokalyptik", in: *ZThK* 59 (1962) 257–284. Reprinted in *ExVuB* II, 105–131. Eng. trans. in: *New Testament Questions of Today,* London 1959, 108–138.

Koester, Helmut 1961: Review of U. Wilckens, *Weisheit und Torheit*, in: *Gnomon* 33 (1961) 590–595.

Kovacs, Brian 1976: "Contributions of Sociology to the Study of the Development of Apocalypticism: A Theoretical Survey". Unpublished paper presented at the Society of Biblical Literature, St. Louis, October 1976.

Latte, Kurt 1941: "Phyle", in: *PRE* 39 (1941), 994–1011.

Luz, Ulrich 1968: *Das Geschichtsverständnis des Paulus* (BEvTh 49), München 1968. Esp. chap. 6, "Überblick über die Zukunftsaussagen bei Paulus", 301–317.

Malherbe, Abraham J. 1977: *Social Aspects of Early Christianity*, Baton Rouge, La., 1977.

– 1980: "Hellenistic Moralists and the New Testament", in: *ANRW* II.28. Berlin–New York (forthcoming).

Meeks, Wayne A. 1974: "The Image of the Androgyne: Some Uses of a Symbol in Earliest Christianity", in: *HR* 13 (1974) 165–208.

– 1979: "'Since Then You Would Need to Go Out of the World': Group Boundaries in Pauline Christianity", in: T. Ryan (ed.), *Critical History and Biblical Faith: New Testament Perspectives*, Villanova, Pa., 1979.

– 198?: "The Social World of Pauline Christianity", in: *ANRW* II.27. Berlin–New York (forthcoming).

– 1983: *The First Urban Christians*. The Social World of the Apostle Paul, New Haven, Conn. – London 1983.

Nock, Arthur Darby 1933: *Conversion: The Old and the New in Religion from Alexander the Great to Augustine of Hippo*, Oxford 1933.

Pax, Elpidius 1971: "Beobachtungen zur Konvertitensprache im ersten Thessalonicherbrief", in: *SBFLA* 21 (1971) 220–261.

– 1972: "Konvertitenprobleme im ersten Thess.", in: *BiLe* 13 (1972) 24–37.

Pearson, Birger A. 1973: *The Pneumatikos-Psychikos Terminology in 1 Corinthians* (SBLDS 12), Missoula, Mont., 1973.

von Rad, Gerhard 1961: *Theologie des Alten Testaments*, München 1961.

Schlier, Heinrich 1965: *Der Brief an die Galater* (KEK 7), Göttingen [13]1965.

Schrage, Wolfgang 1974: "Leid, Kreuz und Eschaton. Die Peristasenkataloge als Merkmale paulinischer theologia crucis und Eschatologie", in: *EvTh* 34 (1974) 141–175.

Schubert, Paul 1939: *Form and Function of the Pauline Thanksgiving* (BZNW 20), Berlin 1939.

Schütz, John Howard 1975: *Paul and the Anatomy of Apostolic Authority* (MSSNTS 26), Cambridge 1975.

Schweitzer, Albert 1930: *Die Mystik des Apostels Paulus*, Tübingen 1930. Reprinted with an introduction by W. G. Kümmel as UTB 1091, Tübingen 1981. Eng. trans. by W. Montgomery, London 1931, New York 1968.

Smith, Jonathan Z. 1970: "A Place to Stand", in: *Worship* 44 (1970) 457–474.

– 1978: *Map is not Territory*: Studies in the History of Religions, Leiden 1978.

Stuhlmacher, Peter 1977: "Zur paulinischen Christologie", in: *ZThK* 74 (1977) 449–463.

Talmon, Yonina 1961: "Pursuit of the Millenium: The Relation between Religious and Social Change", in: *AES* 3 (1962) 125–148.

Thiselton, Anthony C. 1978: "Realized Eschatology at Corinth", *NTS* 24 (1977–78) 510–526.

Vielhauer, Philipp 1965: "Introduction" (to Apocalypses and Related Subjects), in: E. Hennecke and W. Schneemelcher (edd.), *New Testament Apocrypha* (Eng. trans. ed. R. McL. Wilson) II, Philadelphia, Penn. 1965, 581–607.

Wallace, Anthony F. C. 1956: "Revitalization Movements", in: *AmA* 58 (1956) 264–281.

Walter, Nikolaus 1979: "Christusglaube und heidnische Religiosität in paulinischen Gemeinden", in: *NTS* 25 (1978–79) 422–442.

Wilson, Jack H. 1968: "The Corinthians Who Say There is No Resurrection of the Dead", in: *ZNW* 59 (1968) 90–107.

Worsley, Peter 1957: *The Trumpet Shall Sound: A Study of 'Cargo' Cults in Melanesia*, London 1957.

Die Gegenwart in der Apokalyptik der synoptischen Evangelien

Luise Schottroff

0. Vorbemerkung

Trotz der geradezu apokalyptischen Ausmaße der Forschungsgeschichte zu Mk 13 möchte ich dieses Kapitel zunächst in den Mittelpunkt stellen. Die Diskussion der markinischen Apokalypse hat nämlich wichtige Ergebnisse erbracht, die für die Frage nach dem "Sitz im Leben" der Gesellschaft nützlich sind. Ich möchte anhand von Mk 13 exemplarisch zeigen, daß das frühe Christentum eine apokalyptische Bewegung ist, deren theologische Inhalte und theologische Eigenart aus dem Zusammenhang der Lebenswirklichkeit der Menschen, die in ihr zu Wort kommen, zu verstehen sind. Ich halte also Mk 13 – oder andere apokalyptische Aussagen in der synoptischen Tradition – für zentrale Aussagen in ihr. Und: Ich halte die sozialgeschichtliche Frage für eine historisch und theologisch zentrale Frage – nicht für ein nebensächliches Problem.

Es soll hier also vor allem um die Gegenwart der markinischen Gemeinde und ihre Deutung in den apokalyptischen Weissagungen von Mk 13 gehen. Da die apokalyptischen Weissagungen durch ihre Verschlüsselung und Unbestimmtheit Probleme aufgeben, möchte ich eindeutige Aussagen über ihren Sinn auf einer bestimmten historischen Ebene erreichen, indem ich konsequent redaktionsgeschichtlich frage. D. h. Einzelaussagen in Mk 13 sollen im Gesamtzusammenhang des Markusevangeliums verstanden werden. Die Frage nach der von Mk benutzten Tradition ist dabei nur von mittelbarer Bedeutung. Selbst ein Satz der Jesustradition, den Markus unverändert übernimmt, gewinnt im Gesamtzusammenhang des Markusevangeliums und seiner historischen Situation einen bestimmten markinischen Sinn[1]. Eben dies gilt für den Umgang des Mk mit der apokalyptischen Gedankentradition. Traditionelle Motive gewinnen im konkreten Zusammenhang einen konkreten Sinn.

In einem zweiten Arbeitsschritt sollen nach der Analyse von Mk 13 auch

---

[1] Obwohl sich die historische Einordnung des Markusevangeliums durch Marxsen nicht bewährt hat, ist die Konsequenz, mit der er die redaktionsgeschichtliche Frage gestellt hat, voll zu bejahen, s. Marxsen 1959, besonders 108–112.

die apokalyptischen Kapitel des Matthäus- und Lukasevangeliums unter
denselben Fragestellungen und methodischen Voraussetzungen untersucht
werden.

1. Die eschatologische Datierung der Gegenwart in Markus 13

1.1. Die Zerstörung des Tempels ist nahe Vergangenheit

Jesus weissagt die vollständige Zerstörung des prächtigen herodianischen Tempels (13,2). Diese Weissagung ist für Markus bereits eingetrof-
fen. Das zeigen innerhalb von Mk 13 vor allem v.20 und 21. Gott hat
wegen der Auserwählten die Tage der Fluchtkatastrophe in Judäa verkürzt,
sonst wäre die Bevölkerung restlos umgekommen. Der Aorist ἐκολόβω-
σεν blickt zurück, v.20 ist ein vaticinium ex eventu, aus der Realität
genommen und nicht aus apokalyptischer Tradition[2]. Der Neueinsatz v.21
καὶ τότε wendet sich einer späteren Zeit (d.h. der Gegenwart z.Zt. des
Evangelisten) zu. Die Ereignisse von v.14–20 sind für Markus Vergangenheit, die angekündigte Aufrichtung des "Greuels der Verwüstung" (13,14)
ist für ihn in der Eroberung Jerusalems durch Titus und vor allem in der
Zerstörung des Tempels Wirklichkeit geworden. Einen ähnlichen Eindruck vermittelt das Markusevangelium auch außerhalb von Kapitel 13,
vor allem in 12,9 (im Kontext mit 12,10f.). Die vormarkinische prophetische Gerichtsankündigung gegen Israel (12,9) ist für Markus bereits durch
die Geschichte bestätigt worden.

Aus 13,2, aber auch aus 13,14–20 spricht unmittelbare Betroffenheit über
die Zerstörung des Tempels; hier wird nicht gedroht, Gericht angekündigt, sondern (wenn auch in Form einer Weissagung) geklagt. Josephus
berichtet im selben Ton von der Schleifung des Tempels und der Stadt
(Bell VII,1–4) und behauptet sogar, daß Titus Erbarmen gefühlt habe, als
er die zerstörte Stadt auf dem Rückweg nach Alexandrien noch einmal
wiedergesehen habe. Er verglich (sagt Josephus) die "trostlose Wüstenei
vor seinen Augen mit dem einstigen Glanze der Stadt" und bewegte "die
erhabene Größe der nun zertrümmerten Bauwerke in seinem Gedächtnis"
(Bell VII,112f.). Mag auch in 13,19 Tradition (Joel 2,2; Dan 12,1) aufgenommen sein, so ist doch der Gedanke in diesem Zusammenhang Aus-

---

[2] Motivparallelen aus apokalyptischen Texten decken den Gedanken von Mk 13,20 nicht,
auch nicht grBar 9,7 (Gott verkürzt die Tage des Mondes *aus Zorn*). Für weitere Information
s. Pesch 1977 z.St.

Es wäre möglich, den Aorist anders zu erklären: Gott hat bereits seinen ursprünglichen
Zukunftsplan für Judäa revidiert – diese Erklärung wirkt jedoch sehr angestrengt. Daß
Markus literarische Fiktion (Jesus weissagt) durchbricht – wie in v.20 – ist auch in v.19 ἕως
τοῦ νῦν zu beobachten, s. Pesch 1968, 152.

druck der Betroffenheit: Das Elend Judäas ist eine Bedrängnis, wie es sie
noch nie gegeben hat und nie mehr geben wird[3]. Die aufgeführten Gründe
ergeben m. E. eine ausreichende Evidenz dafür, daß die Ereignisse des
Jahres 70 für Markus nahe Vergangenheit sind[4]. Die Zerstörung des
Tempels und Eroberung Jerusalems ist nach Meinung des Markus Strafe
Gottes für die Tötung Jesu (12,9). Sie ist ein Ereignis, das aus Gottes Plan
für die Endphase der Geschichte kommt, denn im Sinne des Markus ist
auch 13,2 Weissagung eines Ereignisses, das zu den Wehen der Endzeit
gehört (s. besonders 13,19), ja ihr grauenhafter Höhepunkt ist. Die judäi-
sche Katastrophe weckt die Frage "wann kommt die Vollendung für dieses
alles" (v.4 nach v.2), d. h. wann kommt das Ende der Geschichte und der
Beginn der Königsherrschaft Gottes. D. h. nach der Zerstörung des Tempels hat es auch unter Christen die Hoffnung (und Furcht zugleich)
gegeben, nun sei das Ende nahe. Markus beurteilt die Lage jedoch anders;
zwar gehört die Tempelzerstörung zu den Endereignissen, sie signalisiert
aber nicht das unmittelbare Ende. Auch wird das Leiden seiner Gegenwart
nicht (wie etwa im IVEsr) als Folge des jüdisch-römischen Krieges verstanden. Die markinische Gemeinde ist von Jerusalems Schicksal betroffen,
leidet aber nicht an *diesem* Schicksal, sondern an einer Verfolgung um
Christi willen (13,9–13).

1.2. Eschatologische Datierung der Gegenwart

Zweimal kommt Markus auf die *Pseudomessiasse* zu sprechen – unter
diesem Begriff fasse ich die Gefahren von v.5f. und v.21–23 zusammen.
Sie sagen "ich bin" der Messias[5] und über sie wird gesagt "da ist der
Messias" (v.21). Mit dieser Proklamation wird zugleich eine eschatologische Behauptung aufgestellt, eine eschatologische Datierung vorgenommen: "jetzt ist das Ende nahe". Lukas hat zu Recht die Proklamation
ergänzt "ὁ καιρὸς ἤγγικεν" (Lk 21,8). Es gibt Christen, die geneigt sind,
solchem Messias zu glauben (v.21), die sich verführen lassen könnten (v.6).
Wie wir uns solche Messiasgestalten und die Folgen ihrer eschatologischen
Datierung vorzustellen haben, ist vor allem aus Josephus bekannt. Schon
vor dem Kriege gab es jüdischen Messianismus (s. nur Act 5,34–39) und
die Auseinandersetzung der Nachfolger Jesu mit solchem Messianismus

---

[3] Auch Kümmel, der die Evidenz einer zeitlichen Ansetzung des Markusevangeliums nach
70 bestreitet, sieht, daß Mk 13 "doch wohl zum mindesten die drohende Nähe des jüdischen
Krieges spüren läßt". Kümmel 1973, 70.

[4] Eine ähnliche Datierung wird zunehmend vertreten, s. die entsprechende Auflistung bei
Kümmel 1973. Hinzu kommt z.B. Stegemann 1974.

[5] So ist v.6 mit Mt 24,5 zu ergänzen im Blick auf v.21–23 trotz des ἐπὶ τῷ ὀνόματί μου, das
eben nur bedeuten kann: "in meinem, des Messias, Namen".

gab es auch schon, wie die Logienquelle zeigt (Mt 24,26f. par.). Aus der
Zeit nach 70 berichtet Josephus von verschiedenen messianischen Unruhen
in der Diaspora. Die Aktion des Webers Jonathan in der Kyrenaika
(Josephus, Bell VII,439) darf man wohl als Illustration für Markus benutzen. Der Prophet-Messias kündigt σημεῖα (τῆς σωτηρίας kann man mit
Josephus, Bell VI,285 ergänzen) an. Die verzweifelten Menschen, die
nichts mehr zu verlieren haben (s. VI,286 "über Furcht und Gefängnis
schon hinaus"; VII,438 ἄποροι), verlassen ihre Wohnungen und ziehen in
einem gemeinsamen Zug in den sicheren Tod[6]. Man erwartet das unmittelbare rettende Eingreifen Gottes. Die Römer haben solche Bewegungen,
auch wenn sie wie die oben genannten unbewaffnet waren, als Bedrohung
empfunden und die Menschen umgebracht (VII,440).

Solche apokalyptische Panik hält Markus bei den von ihm angeredeten
Christen für möglich.

Der Ruf nach dem Ende, die zugleich furchtsame und hoffende *Frage*
"*wann* endlich kommt das Ende" ist auch die Frage der Christen und des
Markus (v.4). Sie kommt aus dem Leiden an gegenwärtiger Not; sie drückt
verzweifelte Sehnsucht aus[7]. Sie ist der Hintergrund für solche Panikaktio-
nen. In 13,7 wird solch eine Situation angesprochen. Auf Kriegsnachrichten und Kriegsgerüchte reagieren die Menschen mit Aufregung[8] und
erwarten das Ende. Markus will, daß sie nüchterner reagieren. Er teilt die
Einschätzung, daß die gegenwärtige Not zu den Enddrangsalen gehört,
rechnet aber mit längeren Zeiträumen und weiterer Steigerung der Enddrangsale (v.8). Indem er die Gegenwart eschatologisch datiert als ἀρχὴ
ὠδίνων und οὔπω τὸ τέλος will er die Nüchternheit erreichen, um die er in
13,33 explizit bittet. Die sehnsüchtige Frage nach dem "Wann" nimmt er
ernst, das ganze Kapitel ist eine Antwort auf die Frage v.4. Die richtige
Antwort auf die Frage ist nicht Endpanik, sondern die nüchterne Einordnung der gegenwärtigen Leiden in die Endgeschichte.

Mehrfach werden die Jünger angeredet: βλέπετε (13,5.9.23.33); Mk
drückt in diesen Aufforderungen die richtigen Verhaltensweisen aus, wie
man zu einer nüchternen eschatologischen Datierung der Gegenwart

---

[6] Zum Wüstenzug Josephus, Bell VII,438 s. Hengel 1976, 238f., 255ff. Zum (faktischen)
kollektiven Selbstmord vgl. auch Josephus, Bell VI,282–287 und die Geschichte aus Kreta bei
Socrates, Hist. eccles. VII,38, auf die Meyer 1940, 87f. aufmerksam gemacht hat. Zum
nichtmilitärischen prophetischen Messianismus s. besonders Meyer 1940, 84ff.

[7] Das gilt für Dan 8,13; 12,6 wie für die Fragen nach dem Ende in IV Esr (s.u.).

[8] θροεῖσθαι als Aufregung angesichts des unmittelbaren Endes wie II Thess 2,2.
θροεῖσθαι wird kaum nur Angst meinen, denn das Ende wird ja *erhofft.* Für diese Deutung
spricht sowohl die Differenz zwischen θροεῖσθαι und πτοεῖσθαι, die aus Lk 21,9 als
Parallele zu Mk 13,7 und aus der Textgeschichte von Lk 24,37 spricht, als auch das
Nebeneinander mit σαλευθῆναι ἀπὸ τοῦ νοός in II Thess 2,2. Lk in 21,9 denkt an die Furcht
vor den letzten Drangsalen, s. auch Kelber 1974, 116f.

kommt. Das eigene Schicksal (v.9) gehört zu den Enddrangsalen, man soll wissen, daß sie zu Gottes Plan gehören (v.23 προείρηκα). Aber nüchtern hinsehen muß man (v.5.33). Im Gleichnis vom Feigenbaum wird dann erklärt, wie man das unmittelbare Ende erkennt. ἐγγύς ist das Ende erst, wenn der Menschensohn auf den Wolken kommt. [Im Kontext von 13,24–27 bezieht sich ταῦτα v.29 auf 24–27, jedenfalls nicht auf gegenwärtige Ereignisse.] Obwohl Markus also hektische "Naherwartung" verhindern will, teilt er doch die grundsätzliche Einschätzung, daß das Ende in absehbarer Zeit[9] kommt (v.30), er teilt selbst auch "Naherwartung". Jesu Lebenszeit war bereits der Beginn der Endgeschichte (1,14f.), er war als Messias-Gottessohn da. Die End*geschichte* umfaßt für Markus die Zeit seit der Verkündigung Jesu bis zur Verkündigung des Evangeliums unter allen Völkern (13,10). Für die Vergangenheit Jesu wie die Gegenwart der Gemeinde gilt ἤγγικεν ἡ βασιλεία τοῦ θεοῦ (1,15). Die Wörter "Naherwartung", "Enthusiasmus" und "Parusieverzögerung" sind nicht besonders geeignet, um die Sachverhalte der apokalyptischen Erwartungen in der synoptischen Tradition zu bezeichnen, weil sie zu einseitig den Blick auf die Vorstellung von den Zeitspannen lenken. Entscheidend sind die Verhaltensweisen, die mit den verschiedenen Formen von Naherwartung verbunden sind: Reagiert man auf die Leiden der Gegenwart mit θροεῖσθαι oder mit ἀγρυπνεῖν – das ist entscheidend. Die Endsehnsucht und Aufregung, mit der Markus sich auseinandersetzt, sollte man nicht als Position von "Gegnern" oder als "Irr*lehre*" ansehen, sondern als Lebensäußerung leidender Menschen[10].

1.3. *Die eschatologische Datierung der Gegenwart im IV Esrabuch*

Im IV Esrabuch läßt sich eine vergleichbare theologische Bemühung um die eschatologische Datierung der Gegenwart beobachten. Der Seher ist ungeduldig, "wie lange noch" (4,33; 6,59), werde ich es erleben (4,51), "zu welcher Zeit" (8,63)? Er ist ungeduldig, weil Israels Leiden unerträglich sind (6,59; 4,23f. als Hintergrund von 4,33), denn die Völker haben Israel überwältigt (6,57)[11]. Hätte Gott nicht das Gericht schneller kommen lassen können, indem er alle Geschlechter zugleich geschaffen hätte (5,43)? Göttli-

---

[9] Die naheliegendste Erklärung für ἡ γενεὰ αὕτη ist "diese Generation" im Sinne der Lebenszeit der Lebenden. Diese Erwartung deckt sich durchaus mit 13,7.8. Auch in 13,30 durchbricht Mk wieder die fiktive Situation (Jesus weissagt zu seinen Lebzeiten).

[10] In der Beschreibung der "Naherwartung" des Markus und der "Naherwartung", mit der er sich auseinandersetzt ("apokalyptisches Fieber"), stimme ich mit Pesch 1968 (s. besonders 235–243) überein, ich meine jedoch, man sollte "(die) eschatologische Irrlehre, (den) apokalyptische(n) Schwarm" (104) nicht als eine *Lehr*position, sondern als Ausdruck einer Leidenssituation begreifen, der Markus verständnisvoll und liebevoll begegnen will.

[11] Weitere Angaben zur Leidenssituation Israels, s. auch 10,21ff.

che Offenbarungen oder ein Offenbarungsengel antworten, kritisieren und wollen dem Seher zu einer anderen Haltung verhelfen: Zwölf Teile hat die Weltgeschichte, jetzt ist sie in der Mitte des 10. Teiles (14,11 f.). Die Vergangenheit ist viel länger als die Zukunft der Geschichte (4,45), der Äon eilt mit Macht zu Ende, die Schöpfung ist alt geworden (5,55; 14,10.15). Das persönliche Schicksal des Sehers wird nicht vorhergesagt; auf seine ungeduldigen Fragen wird geantwortet mit der Ausmalung der Zeichen des Endes (4,52ff.; 6,12ff.; 9,3f.; 13,29ff.). Nach diesen Zeichen kommt das Ende (7,26). Die Leiden der Enddrangsale sind furchtbar: Es gibt Kriege, die Natur gerät aus den Fugen. "Da wird die Ungerechtigkeit viel sein, mehr noch als du jetzt selber siehst, und als du von früher gehört hast" (5,2). Das Leiden der Gegenwart wird sich noch weiter steigern, "denn viel schlimmere Leiden, als die du selber erlebt hast, sollen noch geschehen" (14,15). Der Seher wird darauf verwiesen, daß er die gegenwärtigen Leiden einzuschätzen lernen soll. Er *selbst* muß sie in ihrer eschatologischen Qualität einschätzen, sie eschatologisch datieren. Auf die Frage "zu welcher Zeit" (geschehen die Zeichen)? antwortet Gott: "Das ermiß du bei dir selber; und wenn du siehst, daß ein Teil der angekündigten Zeichen vorüber ist, dann wirst du erkennen, daß nun die Zeit gekommen ist ..." (8,63–9,2). In den göttlichen Offenbarungen wird die Ungeduld kritisiert und die "Wann"-Frage *nicht* mit Terminangaben beantwortet. Der Seher wird vielmehr auf Gottes Plan verwiesen und darauf, die Gegenwart in ihrem Verhältnis zu den eschatologischen Drangsalen selbst einzuschätzen. Daß die Geschichte sich mit der Geschichte des Adlers – d. h. des römischen Weltreiches – in ihrem Endstadium befindet, ist auch die Meinung der göttlichen Offenbarungen[12].

Trotz aller Unterschiede der theologischen Gedanken in IV Esr und Mk 13, die hier nebensächlich sind, ist m. E. festzuhalten, daß die Bewältigung der Verzweiflung durch eine nüchterne eschatologische Datierung der Gegenwart beide Texte eng miteinander verbindet. Mk 13,7f. und IV Esr 8,63–9,2 sind sachliche Analogien. (Natürlich geht es hier nicht um literarische Verwandtschaft.) Die Gegenwart soll als Drangsal der Endgeschichte verstanden werden, deren Leiden sich noch steigern werden. Markus und IV Esr bekämpfen Hoffnungslosigkeit, die Panik und Ungeduld hervorbringt, und predigen Hoffnung auf Gottes Plan, der – wenn auch nach schrecklichen Leiden – das Heil bringen wird.

---

[12] Insofern würde ich die Charakterisierung der Offenbarung als "Neutralisierung der Naherwartung" (Harnisch 1969, besonders 268ff.) modifizieren, weniger den Aspekt der Zeitspannen in den Vordergrund stellen. Es geht um Ungeduld, die aus der als verzweifelt empfundenen Lage der Juden im Römischen Reich kommt und die die gegenwärtigen Leiden mit einem göttlichen Paukenschlag beendet sehen möchte und darum, diese Ungeduld aufzugeben und sich Gottes Plan anzuvertrauen. Die Wann-Frage kommt m. E. nicht aus einer durch enttäuschte Erwartung bewirkten Skepsis (Harnisch 318).

1.4. Die Deutung der Gegenwart in Markus 13

Die nahe Vergangenheit und die Gegenwart, die als Katastrophe erlebt werden, werden in Mk 13 gedeutet. Verzweifelten soll Mut gemacht werden. Die Leiden der Gegenwart sind von Jesus geweissagt (s. auch die explizite Feststellung v.23), sie sind von der Schrift geweissagt (s. die explizite Feststellung v.8 und die zahlreichen Schriftbezüge); sie haben *einen Sinn*[13] *und ein Ende*. Wer in seinen Leidenserfahrungen die von Jesus vorhergesagten Enddrangsale wiedererkennt (v.23), verhält sich nüchtern und gelassen (s. o. §1.2.), ist in der Lage durchzuhalten (ὑπομένειν v.13), nicht abtrünnig zu werden, wie es in Mk 4,17 heißt, wo es um denselben Sachverhalt geht. Wer den Plan Gottes erkennt und seine Gegenwart auf ihn beziehen kann, der lebt in der Hoffnung, daß das kleine Senfkorn ein Baum sein wird, unter dem die Vögel des Himmels wohnen werden, daß die βασιλεία τοῦ θεοῦ der ganzen Welt eine andere Gestalt geben wird (4,30–32). Der Menschensohn wird zum Gericht kommen und wird die weit zerstreut in der Welt lebenden Auserwählten einsammeln lassen. Obwohl das apokalyptische Kapitel des Markus so viele Katastrophen- und Leidensweissagungen enthält, ist das Ziel ein positives: es will Mut machen, Hoffnungen geben und Sinn erkennen lassen – darin ist Kapitel 13 eine Kurzfassung der Ziele des gesamten Markusevangeliums (gerade auch in seiner Predigt der Leidensnachfolge). Daß Vergangenheit, Gegenwart und die geschichtliche Zukunft vor dem Ende so negativ dargestellt werden – als die Drangsale, die dem Ende vorangehen –, hat seine Ursache nicht in einem wie immer zu erklärenden Pessimismus, sondern in der realen Situation der Menschen, um die es hier geht.

2. Die Leiden der Gegenwart in Markus 13

2.1. Die Behauptungen des Markus

Markus behauptet, daß Christen vor Behörden verhört werden (v.9.11) und daß sie genötigt sein werden, ihren christlichen Glauben in diesen *Verhören* darzulegen, so daß das Evangelium auch den Verfolgern zu Ohren kommt (εἰς μαρτυρίαν αὐτοῖς v.9c wird man im jetzigen Kontext mit v.10 wohl durchaus positiv auffassen dürfen[14]). Verfolgungssituation und Völkermission gehören für Mk zusammen. An welche Behörden Markus denkt, ist schwer dem Text zu entnehmen. In v.9 benutzt er gerade in der Aufzählung der Behörden Tradition, die vielleicht ursprünglich palästinische Verhältnisse voraussetzte, und die jetzt durch die Plurale

---

[13] S. dazu besonders Robinson 1956, 92f.
[14] S. etwa die Diskussion dazu bei Pesch 1968, 128f.

verallgemeinert ist. Er scheint nicht sagen zu wollen, daß die Schläge in jüdischen Synagogen zu den Verhören vor heidnischen Behörden führen, zählt vielmehr beides nebeneinander auf. Schwerpunkt der Verfolgung sind die heidnischen Verhöre.

Markus behauptet, daß die Christen durch *Denunziation* in diese Verhöre geraten. In v.12 geht es um Denunziation durch Familienmitglieder. Das παραδιδόναι (in v.9 und) v.11 könnte im Zusammenhang mit v.12 einen analogen Vorgang meinen: durch Dritte den Behörden angezeigt bzw. denunziert werden, so wie Jesus durch Judas und das Synedrium denunziert wurde (14,10; 15,1–3).

Markus behauptet, daß die Christen mit *dem Tode bestraft* werden (v.12 vgl. 8,35).

Markus behauptet, daß die Christen von allen *gehaßt* werden (v.13).

Diese Sachverhalte sind es wohl auch, an die Markus denkt, wenn er von διωγμός und θλῖψις in 4,17 spricht (vgl. 10,28–30; 8,34f.).

Zur Charakteristik der gegenwärtigen Leidenssituation der markinischen Gemeinde wird man auch v.7.6.21–23, also Kriegsnachrichten und *Kriegsgerüchte* und die *Anfälligkeit für Pseudomessiasse* rechnen dürfen.

Markus behauptet, die Verfolgung der Christen sei eine "um meinetwillen" (8,34; 13,9), "um des Evangeliums willen" (8,34), "um des Wortes willen" (4,17); der Haß aller geschehe "um meines Namens willen".

Wenn auch deutlich ist, daß Markus in den Aussagen über die Verfolgung an apokalyptische Tradition anknüpft – und an christliche Martyriumstradition –, so muß man doch seine Aussagen ernst nehmen. Das zeigt gerade v.12, der an das bekannte apokalyptische Motiv von der Auflösung der Familien anknüpft (und an die Verwendung dieses Motivs in vormarkinischer christlicher Tradition, wie wir sie aus Q kennen, Mt 10,34ff. par.). Daß Familienmitglieder die Märtyrer dem Tode ausliefern, ist m.W. nicht aus Motivtradition zu erklären[15]. Man sollte die Aussagen des Markus auch nicht in der Weise abschwächen, daß man annimmt, es handele sich in Wirklichkeit um unbedeutende Vorfälle, die als Verfolgung angesehen wurden[16] oder: Markus beziehe sich auf die für ihn bereits in der Vergangenheit liegende Verfolgung von Christen durch Nero in Rom[17]. Die Leidensnachfolge ist ein so zentrales Thema des Markusevangeliums (und des Kapitels 13), daß seine Aussagen ernstgenommen werden müssen und versucht werden muß, die von ihm angesprochene Situation historisch zu verifizieren.

---

[15] S. die Materialsammlung in Pesch 1977, z.St.
[16] Riddle 1934, 284f.
[17] So z.B. Pesch 1977, 288.

2.2. Historische Verifikation

Die Rolle der Zerstörung des Tempels in Markus 13 spricht dafür, das Markusevangelium in der Regierungszeit Vespasians (69–79) anzusetzen[18]. Außerchristliche Quellen für eine "Christenverfolgung" durch Vespasian sind nicht bekannt, christliche Quellen darüber sind spät[19] und für unsere Frage ohne Aussagekraft. Euseb (H. E. III 17 vgl. IV 26 [Melito]) behauptet sogar ausdrücklich, Vespasian habe die Christen nicht verfolgt (s. auch Tertullian, Ap. V,8), allerdings ist diese Behauptung zweckorientiert. Man will die guten Kaiser, die die Christen nicht verfolgt haben, den schlechten Kaisern konfrontieren. Zunächst spricht also diese Quellenlage gegen die hier vorgetragene Annahme, daß Markus z. Zt. Vespasians schreibt und auf eine Christenverfolgung Bezug nimmt. Vespasian hat den jüdischen Messianismus auch nach der Eroberung Jerusalems gefürchtet (Josephus, Bell VII, 420f.: ὁ δὲ τῶν Ἰουδαίων τὴν ἀκατάπαυστον ὑφορώμενος νεωτεροποιίαν καὶ δείσας, μὴ πάλιν εἰς ἓν ἀθρόοι συλλεγῶσι, καὶ τίνας αὐτοῖς συνεπισπάσωνται; vgl. auch Euseb, H. E. III 12) wie andere Kaiser vor ihm und nach ihm[20]. Zwar kann man nicht ohne weiteres annehmen, daß aus der Optik römischer Behörden dieser Zeit Juden und Christen noch nicht unterschieden werden, man kann jedoch diese Möglichkeit erwägen. Vor allem das Hegesippzitat bei Euseb H. E. III 19–20 unterstützt diese Vermutung. Nachkommen aus der leiblichen Verwandtschaft Jesu, die Christen sind, werden Domitian angezeigt als "ἐκ γένους ὄντας Δαυίδ". Domitian fürchtete die παρουσία τοῦ Χριστοῦ (d. h. eines jüdischen Messias, der einen antirömischen Aufstand führen könnte). Bei dem Verhör erklären die Angeklagten die Eigenart ihres Messiasglaubens; die βασιλεία des Χριστός sei οὐ κοσμικὴ μὲν οὐδ' ἐπίγειος. Wegen dieser Erklärung und ihrer Armut werden sie freigelassen. In eine ähnliche Richtung deutet, daß die vornehme Römerin Domitilla, die durch Domitian verbannt wurde, nach Meinung Eusebs wegen ihres christlichen Bekenntnisses bestraft wurde (Euseb, H. E. III 18), nach dem Bericht des Dio Cassius (67,14,1f.) wegen "ἀθεότης, derentwegen auch andere ἐς τὰ τῶν Ἰουδαίων ἤθη ἐξοκέλλοντες" verurteilt wurden. Wieweit also die domitianische Christenverfolgung aus der Optik der Verfolger eine Judenverfolgung war, wird man sich fragen müssen[21].

---

[18] Allerdings sehe ich keine Evidenz für eine Lokalisierung nach Rom.

[19] Giet 1957, 133f. erwähnt Hilarius v. Poitiers, Chrysostomus, Theodoret als Zeugen für eine Christenverfolgung durch Vespasian.

[20] Man könnte z. B. auf den Satz des Claudius in seinem Brief an die Alexandriner verweisen, in dem er die Juden als τῆς οἰκουμένης νόσος bezeichnet, womit ihre politische Unruhe gemeint ist (s. Tcherikover and Fuks 1960, 41 Zeile 100; zur Interpretation von νόσος s. a.a.O. 54), oder auf Domitians Verfolgung von Davididen (Euseb, H. E. III 19f.).

[21] Zur Diskussion über die Domitianische Christenverfolgung s. Moreau 1961, 35ff. und Vogt 1954, 1167ff.

Aufgrund dieser Überlegung kann man die Möglichkeit einer Verfolgung von Christen, die von Juden oder jüdisch Lebenden nicht unterschieden werden, auch durch Vespasian annehmen. Sichere Nachrichten von direkter Evidenz für oder gegen eine Christenverfolgung gibt es nicht.

Sehr viel klarer wird die Situation, wenn man von der inhaltlichen Überlegung ausgeht, was eigentlich "Christenverfolgung" in dieser Zeit heißt, und die Religionspolitik Vespasians in Rechnung stellt. Um die These vorwegzunehmen: Aufgrund solcher historischer Überlegungen wird das Markusevangelium zu einem klaren Dokument einer natürlich lokal begrenzten "Christenverfolgung" auch zur Zeit Vespasians.

"Christenverfolgungen" im 1. Jahrhundert sind Konflikte mit der "Loyalitätsreligion"[22] der Kaiserzeit. Solche Konflikte haben nicht nur Christen, sondern auch Juden und viele andere Menschen. Christenverfolgungen sind also kein isoliertes Phänomen, sondern ein Glied in einer langen Kette von politischen Drucksituationen, die die staatlichen Machtansprüche sichern sollen. Die nichtjüdische alexandrinische Bevölkerung hat sich z. B. dieses Instruments bedient, als sie die Bemühung der jüdischen Bevölkerungsgruppe um weitere Rechte in der Stadt zunichte machen wollte (38 n. Chr.). Sie schrien "wie aus einem Munde, in den Synagogen sollten (Kaiser-)Bilder aufgestellt werden". Sie wußten, daß damit die Juden in den Konflikt zwischen Tora und Loyalität zum römischen Staat geraten und gezwungen sind, sich staatlichen Verfolgungsmaßnahmen auszusetzen (Philo, Flacc 41–54). Die Juden Alexandrias haben sich durch Loyalitätserklärungen gegenüber dem Kaier zu wehren versucht. Diese Loyalitätserklärungen mußten die Forderungen der Tora berücksichtigen (s. etwa a.a.O. 97; LegGai 280, 236). Die Tora verbietet ihnen nicht "Gebete, Stiftung von Weihgeschenken" und tägliche Opfer bzw. Opfer an Festtagen (LegGai 280), wohl aber die Aufstellung eines Kaiserbildes in der Synagoge, durch die der Anspruch Gottes verletzt wird. Die Opfer werden Gott dargebracht, nicht dem Kaiser oder seinem Genius[23], werden aber als Opfer für ($\dot{v}\pi\acute{e}\varrho$) den Kaiser verstanden. Das spricht Gaius (Caligula) selbst empört aus ($\tau\epsilon\vartheta\acute{v}\varkappa\alpha\tau\epsilon,\ \dot{a}\lambda\lambda'\ \dot{\epsilon}\tau\acute{e}\varrho\omega,\ \varkappa\ddot{a}v\ \dot{v}\pi\dot{\epsilon}\varrho\ \dot{\epsilon}\mu\sigma\tilde{v}$ a.a.O. 357). Diese Formulierung zeigt, wie schmal für einen frommen Juden der Grat war zwischen seinem Monotheismus und den religiösen Loyalitätsbezeugungen gegenüber dem römischen Staat. Caligula verlangte, daß ihm – nicht einem anderen Gott – geopfert werden sollte.

Bewußt wähle ich jetzt ein zeitlich weit entferntes zweites Beispiel für einen Loyalitätskonflikt, der zur Verfolgung führt: die Verhöre der Chri-

---

[22] Ich nehme hier den m. E. sehr treffenden Ausdruck von Latte 1967, 314 ff., auf. Er trifft die Sache besser als z. B. der Begriff "Kaiserkult".

[23] S. dazu Smallwood 1961, 240 f.

sten in Scili in Numidien im Jahre 180 n. Chr. (Acta Scilitanorum)[24]. Der römische Prokonsul Saturninus formuliert die behördliche Loyalitätsforderung: "Et nos religiosi sumus, et simplex est religio nostra, et iuramus per genium domni nostri imperatoris, et pro salute eius supplicamus, quod et vos quoque facere debetis" (§ 3). Die Christen geben Loyalitätserklärungen ab "imperatorem nostrum observamus" (§ 2), weisen auf ihre Steuerzahlung hin (§ 6), drücken aber ihren Monotheismus aus "imperium huius seculi non cognosco; sed magis illi Deo servio, quem nemo hominum vidit ... cognosco domnum meum, regem regum et imperatorem omnium gentium" (§ 6). Die Christin Donata benutzt die knappe Formel "Honorem Caesari quasi Caesari; timorem autem Deo". Sie werden zum Tode verurteilt, weil sie es ablehnen, "ad Romanorum morem" zurückzukehren (§ 14). "Mos Romanorum" ist die römische religio, die der Prokonsul § 3 erklärt hat, sie verlangt den Eid bei dem Genius des regierenden Kaisers und supplicia pro salute des Kaisers[25]. Ein direkter Anspruch auf Gottheit des Kaisers wird im übrigen nicht gestellt. Es geht um Eid und Opfer bezogen auf den Genius des Kaisers. Wie der Konflikt der alexandrinischen Juden zeigte, ist der schmale Grat, auf dem Juden und Christen gehen müssen, wenn sie die Grenze zwischen römischer Loyalitätsreligion und christlichem bzw. jüdischem Monotheismus ziehen, derselbe. Die römische Religionspolitik (der staatlichen Loyalitätsreligion) ist im Prinzip seit Augustus durch das ganze erste und zweite Jahrhundert dieselbe geblieben. Das spezielle Problem, ob sich ein Kaiser auch in Rom ϑεός nennen läßt, ist nur die Spitze des Eisbergs. Loyalitätskonflikte entstanden für Juden und Christen auch unabhängig von dieser speziellen Forderung.

Die Gelegenheiten, bei denen es zu solcher verbalen Gratwanderung kommt, sind verschiedenartig. Im 1. Jahrhundert haben Behörden von sich aus diese Feststellungen und Verhöre gegenüber Juden und Christen nicht in Gang gesetzt; nur aufgrund von delatio/Denunziation (s. Trajan, in: Plinius, Ep. X 97) kamen sie in Gang. Trajan schränkt die Praxis ein: anonyme Anzeigen dürfen nicht mehr berücksichtigt werden. Die Rolle dieser Anzeigen oder Denunziationen[26] im Alltag des römischen Reiches scheint beträchtlich zu sein. Selbst Josephus, dem Illoyalität nun wirklich nicht nachgesagt werden kann, ist mit Hilfe dieses mißbrauchbaren Instrumentes in Verdacht geraten (Bell VII, 447–450; Vita 424–425). Er wurde von dem Rebellenführer Jonathan bezichtigt, den Aufstand in der Kyre-

---

[24] Text nach Wlosok 1970. "Die 'Acta Scilitanorum' sind ein authentischer christlicher Märtyrerbericht, der die amtliche Protokollform ... angestrebt hat", Wlosok 42.

[25] Wlosok 1970, 43 interpretiert nach Plinius, Ep. X, 96,4b–9 zu Recht "mit Opferspenden" für das Heil des Kaisers flehen, s. auch 30 A. 73.

[26] S. dazu auch Sherwin-White 1963, 18.

naika mit Waffen und Geld unterstützt zu haben. Vespasian glaubte dieser Anschuldigung in diesem Falle nicht.

Welches Ausmaß die Anschuldigungen wegen Illoyalität unter Domitian angenommen hatten, zeigen Maßnahmen Nervas bei seinem Amtsantritt (Dio Cass. 68,1–3). Sklaven und Freigelassene, die ihre Herren angezeigt hatten, wurden hingerichtet. Auch viele andere Denunzianten, unter ihnen ein Philosoph, wurden zum Tode verurteilt. Solche, die wegen ἀσέβεια, dem Staatsverbrechen, angeklagt waren, wurden amnestiert, Flüchtlinge konnten zurückkehren. Es wurde generell verboten, irgend jemanden wegen ἀσέβεια oder jüdischer Lebensweise anzuzeigen.

Als Christ angezeigt zu werden hieß inhaltlich, der Illoyalität gegenüber dem römischen Staat (bzw. seiner Verkörperung – dem Kaiser) verdächtigt zu werden. Auch Vorwürfe wie "odium humani generis" oder "Atheismus" laufen sachlich auf dasselbe hinaus[27]. Selbst die Anschuldigung, (nichtpolitische) Schandtaten ("flagitia") begangen zu haben, ist von dem politischen Kern dieser Konflikte nicht zu trennen[28]. Die Anschuldigung, die nach Act 16,20f. gegen Paulus und Silas in Philippi erhoben wurde, trifft den Sachverhalt von Christen- (und Juden-)Verfolgungen im ersten Jahrhundert generell: politische Unruhe und abweichende "Sitten" werden – oft in Wahrheit aus ganz anderen Gründen – zur Anzeige gebracht. Diese Konflikte sind nicht nur für Juden und Christen eine dauernde Gefährdung, sondern für einen viel größeren Kreis von Menschen, gerade auch weil dieses Instrument so leicht mißbrauchbar war. Das Ausmaß der staatlichen Unterdrückung potentieller Unruhe in der Bevölkerung wird daran klar, daß auch ganz unpolitische Verbände – wie z. B. ein Feuerwehrverein – verboten wurden, und Trajan ein Verbot für hetaeriae – Vereine – erließ[29].

Die Vorstellung, daß Konflikte mit der Staatsreligion unter den besonders verhaßten Kaisern Caligula, Nero, Domitian eine besondere Rolle spielen, ist zweifellos unzutreffend. Vespasian – um dessen Zeit es hier geht – hat eine sehr konsequente Religionspolitik betrieben, um seine Herrschaft religiös auszudrücken und zu sichern und um eine Familiendynastie in Gang zu setzen. Bereits in den Jahren des Bürgerkrieges hat er z. B. seine Machtergreifung dadurch religiös vorbereitet, daß er in den römischen Provinzen mit lokalen Kulten Verbindungen einging. So ist z. B. die

---

[27] Odium humani generis = "gemeinschaftsfeindliche Gesinnung" (Wlosok 1970, 21) war nach Tacitus (Ann. 15, 44,4a) der eigentliche Grund für die Verurteilung der römischen Christen durch Nero. Atheismus wird z. B. bei Dio Cass. 67,14,1f. in Zusammenhang mit "nach jüdischen Sitten" leben gebracht.

[28] Der Vorwurf der "flagitia" spielt z. B. bei Neros Verfolgung und bei Plinius eine Rolle (Tacitus, Ann. 15, 44,2; Plinius, Ep. X, 96,1f.).

[29] Plinius, Ep. X, 96,7–8; X,33.34. "Writing about persecution, brief mention should be made of the other groups which suffered restrictions in some form, so as to avoid the impression that it was the Christians only who suffered in this way", Cuss 1974, 154.

Heilung eines Blinden und eines Lahmen in Alexandrien einzuschätzen – als Bund mit dem Serapis-Kult –, aber auch die Deutung jüdischer messianischer Erwartungen auf *seine* Machtergreifung[30]. Nach seinem Herrschaftsantritt in Rom hat er den Kult der Pax, der Victoria und vieler anderer römischer Gottheiten, die Roms Machtanspruch religiös ausdrückten, gefördert[31]. Gerade die Religionspolitik und Machtpolitik Vespasians bot ausreichend Möglichkeiten, daß auch Christen in die Mühlen der staatlichen Behörden geraten konnten.

Betrachtet man die Behauptungen des Markusevangeliums über die Christenverfolgung seiner Gegenwart auf diesem Hintergrund, so läßt sich nur konstatieren, daß das Markusevangelium mit hoher Wahrscheinlichkeit eine zuverlässige historische Quelle auch für die reale Situation von Christen irgendwo im Römischen Reich zur Zeit Vespasians ist. In den Verhören, in die sie durch Denunziation geraten, können sie sich um ihr Leben bringen. "Sorgt nicht, was ihr reden sollt" (13,11). Nimmt man die Informationen, die wir über solche Verhöre haben, so wird verständlich, warum diese Menschen auf die Hilfe des Heiligen Geistes hofften. In diesen Verhören werden die markinischen Christen versucht haben, im Sinne von Mk 12,17 eine sehr nuancierte Loyalitätserklärung abzugeben auf dem schmalen Grat, auf dem vor ihnen und nach ihnen viele Juden und Christen versucht haben, dem maßlosen Machtanspruch des Römischen Reiches gegenüber standzuhalten. Vespasian hat zwar nicht unmittelbar verlangt, daß er als Gott verehrt wird, aber die *Unterscheidung* von Mk 12,17 zwischen Zugehörigkeit zu Gott und zum Staat ist trotzdem eine Verweigerung des geforderten Gehorsams. Plinius d. Ä., ein Zeitgenosse, bringt den Anspruch des Staates auf eine eindringliche Formel: "Gott zu sein bedeutet für den Sterblichen, dem Sterblichen zu helfen, und dies ist der Weg zum ewigen Ruhm. Ihn gingen die vornehmsten Römer, auf ihm wandelt jetzt göttlichen Schrittes zusammen mit seinen Kindern der größte Herrscher aller Zeiten, Vespasianus Augustus, der erschlafften Welt zu Hilfe kommend. Dies ist die älteste Sitte, hochverdienten Männern sich dankbar zu erweisen, daß man solche Helfer unter die Götter versetzt" (Nat. Hist. II 18f.). Aus der Optik der Behörden war das Verhör und das mögliche Urteil keine Christenverfolgung ebensowenig wie die Tötung Jesu Christenverfolgung war. Aus der Optik der Christen stand aber

---

[30] Zur Heilung in Alexandria s. Tacitus, Hist. IV, 81 und Sueton, Vespasian 7; zur Interpretation s. Scott 1936, 9ff.38 und Morenz 1975, 551–560; Zur Weissagung für die Herrschaft Vespasians in Judäa s. Josephus, Bell VI 312f.; III, 401f.; IV, 623; Tacitus, Hist V, 13; Sueton, Vespasian 4.

Zur Religionspolitik, die mit den zahlreichen omina und σημεῖα für die zukünftige Herrschaft Vespasians verbunden ist, s. besonders Scott 1936, 1–19.

[31] Zur Religionspolitik in Rom Scott 1936, 20–39.

gegenüber dem Machtanspruch des Staates ihr Glaube und ihr Evangelium
auf dem Spiel. Sie waren keine politischen oder militärischen Aufrührer;
ihr Versuch gemeinsamen Lebens und ihre maßlosen Hoffnungen jedoch
mußten zu Konflikten führen.

3. Zusammenfassung der Deutung von Markus 13

Markus deutet die unmittelbare Vergangenheit und die eigene Gegenwart in Gestalt von Zukunftsweissagungen Jesu. Aus der Vergangenheit
steht vor allem die Zerstörung des Tempels im Mittelpunkt des Interesses.
Die Betroffenheit über das göttliche Strafgericht an Israel soll aber nicht
falsch verstanden werden: als stünde das Ende unmittelbar bevor. Auch
messianische Propheten treten auf und die Christen der Markusgemeinde
sind in ihrer Sehnsucht nach dem Ende potentielle Anhänger einer *solchen*
messianischen Bewegung. Markus lehnt diesen Messianismus (es muß
nicht nur bewaffneter Messianismus sein) ab. Er fürchtet wohl die apokalyptische Panik und den illusionären Charakter solcher Bewegungen. Die
Sehnsucht nach dem Ende, die "Wann"-Frage, nimmt er jedoch ganz ernst
und beantwortet sie mit der Aufforderung, das eigene Schicksal richtig
einzuschätzen (13,9). Die Gegenwart soll verstanden werden als "Anfang
der Wehen" (13,8), die sich aber noch schrecklich steigern werden. Wenn
dann aber der Menschensohn kommen wird – und Markus rechnet damit
in absehbarer Zeit – *dann* wird man genau wissen, daß das Gericht "nahe"
ist (13,29f.) – und die Errettung und Sammlung der Auserwählten (13,27).
Markus setzt sich mit einer Endpanik auseinander. Die Menschen sollen
nicht ϑροεῖσϑαι (13,7), sondern ἀγρυπνεῖν (13,33). Die Geschichte und
die Gegenwart haben einen von Gott geplanten Sinn (13,23) und ein Ende.
Die Weissagungen haben die Absicht, die Menschen in einer Leidenssituation zu stärken. Die Leiden der Gegenwart sind die Bedrückungen und
Gefährdungen einer Verfolgung der Gemeinde. Die Behauptungen, die
Markus über diese Verfolgung macht, decken sich mit den uns bekannten
Informationen über die Situation von Juden und Christen im Römischen
Reich bereits lange vor und noch lange nach Markus. Die Religionspolitik
und Machtdurchsetzung der Kaiser ist ihr Hintergrund. Aus der römischen
Optik werden Unruhestifter verfolgt, aus der christlichen Optik handelt es
sich um "Christenverfolgung". Die christliche Behauptung ist jedoch
insofern zutreffend, als sich aus dem Glauben an den Messias Jesus und den
Gott Israels, aus der vita christiana der *Gemeinde* und ihren Hoffnungen
und Zielen diese Konflikte ergeben mußten. In den Gemeinden wurde
schließlich bewußt versucht, die Machtstrukturen der Gesellschaft aufzu-
heben (Mk 10,42–45) und das Leben miteinander umfassend neu zu gestalten in der Hoffnung auf den Messias Jesus und die Königsherrschaft

Gottes. Der christliche Messianismus verstand sich selbst nicht als politische Bewegung, wurde aber vom Staat – zu Recht – als politische Gefahr eingeschätzt.

Apokalyptische Weissagungen sind hier eine theologische Auseinandersetzung mit einer als drückend empfundenen Gegenwart. Sie sind Ausdruck einer absolut ernstgenommenen *Gegenwart*. Das Ziel dieser Auseinandersetzung mit der Gegenwart ist ein positives. Der Glaube an den schon gekommenen Messias Jesus befähigt die Menschen, "sich aufzurichten und die Häupter zu erheben", wie Lukas einige Zeit später dieselben Gedanken formuliert (Lk 21,28).

4. Die Gegenwart als Anfang des Endes in den apokalyptischen Jesusreden des Matthäus und Lukas

In diesem Abschnitt soll gezeigt werden, daß die eschatologische Deutung der Gegenwart, die in Markus 13 zu beobachten ist, auch für die späteren Evangelien des Matthäus und Lukas im Zentrum der apokalyptischen Weissagungen steht. Auch diese Evangelien müssen von ihrer historischen Gegenwartssituation und ihrer Erwartung der Königsherrschaft Gottes her verstanden werden.

4.1. Matthäus 24

Die für das Matthäusevangelium gewichtige eschatologische Rede Jesu (Mt 24,3–25,46) ist auf Probleme der Gegenwart konzentriert. Das zeigt sich in der Breite, mit der richtiges Verhalten erklärt wird (vor allem ab 24,45), aber auch in der Darstellung der Verfolgungsnot (24,9–14), die gegenüber Mk beträchtliche Änderungen erfahren hat.

Die Zerstörung des Tempels 70 n. Chr. liegt für Mt länger zurück als für Mk. Daß sie das Gericht Gottes über Israel ist, wird noch schärfer betont als bei Mk (s. Mt 23,13–24,2). Für Mt steht dieses Gericht Gottes nicht in einem Zusammenhang mit Ereignissen, die der Parusie Christi unmittelbar vorausgehen. Mit 24,3 fängt für Mt nach der Gerichtsrede gegen die Führer Israels (23,13–24,2) eine neue Rede Jesu über die Zeichen für die Parusie an. In ihr spielt die Zerstörung des Tempels keine Rolle mehr (zu 24,15–22 s. u.).

Daß in der Schilderung der *Verfolgung* (24,9–14) Probleme der *Gegenwart* ausgesprochen werden, ist schon aus dem Inhalt der Verse ersichtlich. Die ϑλῖψις der Jünger umfaßt Todesgefahr (v.9a), allgemeines Verhaßtsein (v.9b), Abfall von Christen – vermutlich unter dem Eindruck des Verhaßtseins (s. καὶ τότε v.10a), Auslieferung von Christen durch (ehemalige?) Christen[32] (v.10 ἀλλήλους παραδώσουσιν), Haß innerhalb der Gemeinde (v.10b), erfolgreiche Verführung von Christen durch Pseudopropheten (v.11 vgl. 7,15.23), so daß die Gesetzlosigkeit um sich greift und der Zusammenhalt der Gemeinde fragwürdig wird: Die Liebe der Vielen ist erkaltet (v.11). Das ist ein anschauliches Bild der Verfolgungsnot und der Zerstörungen, die sie für die Gemeinde mit sich bringt. Die innergemeindlichen Konflikte sind verquickt mit Denunziationen und Todesgefahr. Durch die – wenn auch sehr freizügige – Benutzung apokalyptischer Motivtraditionen deutet Mt diese Situation: daß Christen sich gegenseitig preisgeben und hassen, steht für ihn für die schon immer befürchtete Zerreißung der Familie in den Wehen der Endzeit (s. o. zu Mk 13,12). Daß die Gesetzlosigkeit zum Ende hin zunimmt (v.12) hat z. B. auch IV Esr (5,2) befürchtet. Die gegenwärtige Notsituation gehört also zu den Enderereignissen – oder wie er in v.8 (mit Mk 13,8) sagt – sie ist der *Anfang der Wehen*[33]. Mt nimmt einzelne Sätze und Wörter aus Mk 13,9–13 auf (zu Mt 10,17–22 s. u.) und gestaltet die Darstellung der Not der Gemeinde unverhältnismäßig selbständig. In anderen Partien der Rede hält er sich enger an die Vorlage Mk 13. Mt 24,9–14 ist "von grundlegender Bedeutung für den Evangelisten"[34] und nicht eine blasse Zusammenfassung zum Ersatz für das Stück Mk 13,9–13, das in der Aussendungsrede (10,17–22) schon 'verbraucht' worden ist[35].

Die Mahnung auszuharren (Mt 24,13) besagt als Abschluß von v.9–12 nicht nur, daß die Christen unter dem Druck der Verfolgungssituation zu ihrem Bekenntnis stehen sollen (wie Mk 13,13), sondern auch, daß sie die Liebe in der Gemeinde, die so bedroht ist, durchhalten müssen[36].

Während Mt in 10,17–22 die Verfolgung der Jünger in der Zeit, als sie noch nur in Palästina umherzogen, dezidiert als Verfolgung durch *Juden* versteht, denkt er hier vor allem an eine Verfolgung durch Heiden (ὑπὸ πάντων τῶν ἐθνῶν). Auch wenn πάντα τὰ ἔθνη alle Völker einschließlich des Judenvolkes meint, so ist doch der Blick primär auf die Verfolgung durch Nichtjuden, d. h. durch den Haß der Bevölkerung und die Verfolgung durch römische Behörden gerichtet.

---

[32] Auch in der Neroverfolgung haben Christen Mitchristen preisgegeben (Tacitus, Ann. 15,44), vermutlich durch Folter dazu gezwungen.

[33] Weitere Argumente für die Einordnung der Ereignisse von Mt 24,4b–14 als die Zeit des Anfangs der Wehen s. bei Lambrecht 1972, 319–321.

[34] Luz 1971, 145.

[35] S. z.B. Klostermann 1927, z. St.; Hare 1967, 124: v.9 sei "an editorial résumé". Hare versteht v.9ff. als Zukunft (aus der Optik des Mt) und 10,17–22 als "instructions relevant to the church's mission" (98), als Verfolgung durch Juden, die "Dauersituation" (Marxsen 1959, 138) der Kirche sei (Hare 1967, 100). Zur Deutung von Mt 10,17–22 s. u.

[36] So zu Recht Pesch 1970, 231.

Mt benutzt Mk 13,9–13 zweimal, in Mt 10,17–22 und 24,9–14. Obwohl er in der Aussendungsrede *auch* an die Situation der Kirche seiner Gegenwart denkt (s. besonders 10,24 ff.), ist doch 10,17–22 "historisierend" zu deuten auf die Verfolgung durch Juden (s. besonders die Zufügung αὐτῶν in v.17) *damals in Palästina*, als der Missionsauftrag Jesu die Heiden noch ausschloß (10,5b.6). Mt 10,5b.6 und die unterschiedliche Gestaltung von 10,17–22 und 24,9–14 sind die wichtigsten Argumente dafür, daß Mt in 10,17–22 von einer vergangenen Verfolgung spricht (und daß die Juden an der gegenwärtigen Verfolgung durch Nichtjuden nicht aktiv beteiligt sind). Daß die Verfolgung in Palästina auch zum Zeugnis vor Heiden (10,18) wurde, liegt an der politischen Situation in Palästina (ἡγεμόνες). Auch die historisierenden Aussagen (Mt 10,17–22) sind in gewisser Hinsicht transparent für die Verfolgung der Kirche der Gegenwart, die aber nicht mehr eine Verfolgung durch Juden ist. Wenn Mt diese Unterscheidung vergangener und gegenwärtiger Verfolgung nicht wichtig wäre, gäbe es keinen einleuchtenden Grund für die zweimalige Verwendung von Mk 13,9–13 und die jeweiligen Umgestaltungen dieser Tradition[37].

Die Situation der Verfolgung hat sich Markus gegenüber nicht grundsätzlich gewandelt. Die Sorge des Markus, daß Christen aus Angst abtrünnig werden könnten, hat sich inzwischen bestätigt und die innere Situation einer Gemeinde ist noch schwieriger geworden.

Die Not der Gegenwart ist der *Anfang der Endzeitwehen* (24,8), die sich noch furchtbar steigern werden (v.15–22 ist für Mt Zukunft)[38]. Dann aber, wenn die Wehen durchgestanden sind, wird gleich das Ende kommen (24,29), das Völkergericht und die Sammlung der Erwählten. Diese Hoffnung ist eine wirkliche, ernsthafte Zukunftserwartung, einer heilvollen Zukunft der Welt unter der βασιλεία τῶν οὐρανῶν – in absehbarer Zeit (v.34).

Die starke Ausgestaltung einer eschatologisch begründeten Ethik bei Mt sollte nicht als Ausdruck einer abgeschwächten apokalyptischen Erwartung verstanden werden. Auch "Parusieverzögerung" ist nicht als Problem im Spiel. Der Sklave, der damit rechnet, daß der Herr erst später kommen wird (24,48), nimmt den Herrn und sein Kommen nicht ernst genug. Die törichten Jungfrauen haben das Öl nicht deshalb nicht vorbereitet, weil ihre Erwartung schon einmal enttäuscht wurde, sondern weil sie sich nicht ernsthaft genug vorbereitet haben (25,5). Daß vom χρονίζειν des Herrn geredet wird, besagt nicht Enttäuschung ursprünglicher Hoffnungen, sondern soll mahnen, die Erwartung durchzuhalten, nicht zu schlafen. Wachsamkeit und Geduld ist gefordert[39].

---

[37] Luz 1971 betont zu Recht die Transparenz der Missionsrede für die Gegenwart des Mt und ihre "Mischung" von historisierenden und gegenwartsbezogenen Aussagen, versteht aber 10,17–22 als gegenwartsbezogen (s. besonders seine m. E. nicht tragfähigen Argumente 144 f.). Die ähnliche Deutung Hares wurde in Anm. 35 beschrieben (seine Argumente a.a.O. 97–99). 10,17–22 wird m. E. zutreffend gedeutet als vergangene Verfolgung durch Juden von Hoffmann 1972, 257; ähnlich Walker 1967, 77.

[38] S. die Argumente z. B. bei Strecker 1971, 239; Pesch 1970, 232. Anders Lambrecht 1972, 321 ff.

[39] S. zu der Problematik der sog. "Parusieverzögerung" schon oben zu Mk 13. Für die hier

4.2. Lukas 21

In der Endzeitrede Jesu im Lukasevangelium (21,10–36) liegt die *Zerstörung des Tempels* (21,5–7, 20–24) wie im Matthäusevangelium weiter zurück. Lukas reflektiert auch das Geschick der Juden in der Zeit nach 70 n. Chr. (21,24). Die Eroberung Jerusalems hat für Lk (wie für Mt) nichts mit unmittelbaren Endereignissen zu tun (s. v. 7 diff. Mk; v. 9 diff. Mk; v. 20 ἤγγικεν ἡ ἐρήμωσις αὐτῆς; v. 24; vielleicht fehlt eine Parallele zu Mk 13,15 wegen der in diesem Motiv enthaltenen Vorstellung von der eschatologischen Katastrophe). Auch die Ankündigung der Pseudomessiasse (21,8), die Kriegs- und Unordnungsnachrichten (21,9) werden noch weiter von den Endereignissen abgerückt als in Mk (s. 21,9 πρῶτον) und gehören für Lk vielleicht auch zu den vergangenen Ereignissen im Umkreis der Eroberung Jerusalems[40]. Erst mit v. 10 kommt Jesus auf eigentliche Endereignisse zu sprechen. Lk macht dies deutlich, indem er Jesus noch einmal eine neue Rede beginnen läßt (v. 10 Τότε ἔλεγεν αὐτοῖς).

Die *Gegenwart* ist auch für Lukas die Zeit der Verkündigung des Evangeliums von Christus vor den Heiden (21,24). Jetzt sind die *"Zeiten der Heiden"*, in denen die Völker Israel niedertreten und in denen ihnen das Heil angeboten wird[41]. Sie werden zu Ende gehen mit dem Gericht über Juden und Heiden, die nicht umgekehrt sind (Lk 21,24 ist die lukanische Fassung von Mk 13,10).

Die *eschatologischen Drangsale* (v. 10 f., 25 f.) enthalten geschichtliche und kosmische Ereignisse (wie in Mk 13). Mag man streiten, ob z. B. die Angst der οἰκουμένη vor der Zukunft (v. 26) im Sinne des Lukas Zukunft ist oder Gegenwart, man wird jedoch in jedem Fall sehen müssen, daß hier gegenwärtige Erfahrungen angesprochen werden[42]. Die großen Zeichen an den Gestirnen (v. 11.25) sind ebenfalls für Menschen, die in derselben Welt leben wie etwa Tacitus, Josephus oder Vespasian, durchaus nicht nur als unbedingt zukünftige Ereignisse anzusehen. Lukas und seine Gemeinde müssen sich fragen, ob solche Himmelszeichen nicht schon geschehen sind[43]. Andere Ereignisse im Verlaufe der Enddrangsale sind zweifellos

---

angesprochene verbreitete Deutung von 24,48; 25,5 als Kronzeugen der "Parusieverzögerung" s. nur Grässer 1960, z. St.

[40] Nicht überzeugend ist die Deutung von v. 9 durch Keck auf Spaltungen und Parteiungen innerhalb der christlichen Gemeinde, s. Keck 1976, 97 ff.

[41] S. die zutreffende Interpretation der καιροὶ ἐθνῶν durch Keck 1976, 224–231.

[42] Vgl. z. B. Philo, LegGai 116–119. Auch Röm 8,22 möchte ich in diesen Zusammenhang bringen. Geiger 1973, 223 sieht zu Recht einen Realitätsbezug für 21,26.

[43] Zur apokalyptischen Motivtradition s. Keck 1976, 232. Gestirnzeichen spielen auch für politische Ereignisse im Römischen Reich und bei Nichtjuden eine Rolle. Σημεῖα πονηρά (ein Komet, ungewöhnliche Mondereignisse, zwei Sonnen) wurden von den Menschen im Jahre 69 gesehen (Dio Cass. 64,8,1) und politisch gedeutet. Damit soll hier nur gesagt werden, daß Gestirnzeichen für das Bewußtsein von Juden und Heiden nicht transgeschichtliche Ereignisse sein müssen.

ausschließlich als zukünftig vorgestellt (z. B. der Völkerkampf v. 10). D. h. wir haben hier wie im Markusevangelium eine Darstellung der Endwehen, die bei den Lesern (oder Hörern) die Frage wecken muß (und soll), was davon Gegenwart ist und was Zukunft.

Die Verfolgung der Gemeinde (v. 12–19) beschreibt Lukas so, daß eindeutig die Geschicke des Stephanus und Paulus, wie er sie in der Act beschreibt, in den Blick geraten. Juden liefern die Christen an die Behörden aus (v. 12). Die Auseinandersetzung mit den (jüdischen) Widersachern, die der Botschaft widersprechen (v. 14 f.), nimmt eine zentrale Rolle in dem Verfolgungsgeschehen ein. Sie fehlte übrigens bei Markus. Die Situation, in der der Christ für sein Reden die Hilfe Christi bzw. des Heiligen Geistes braucht, ist bei Markus das Verhör vor römischen Behörden, bei Lukas jedoch die Auseinandersetzung mit Juden u. U. auch vor den Ohren römischer Behörden. Lukas denkt in v. 4 f. sicher an die vollmächtige Rede wie er sie z. B. in Act 28,25–28 beschreibt. Gegenüber dieser Auseinandersetzung wird die Todesbedrohung als zweitrangig empfunden, obwohl auch Tötungen vorgekommen sind (ἐξ ὑμῶν diff. Markus, allerdings wie in der Logienquelle, s. Lk. 11,49 par.). Aus 21,12–19 im Zusammenhang mit der Apostelgeschichte ergibt sich die Frage, ob für Lukas die Verfolgung ein Geschehen vergangener Kirchengeschichte ist, das keine unmittelbare Relevanz für die Gegenwart hat oder ob er Drucksituationen seiner Gegenwart implizit *mit*ausdrückt. Ist für ihn die Verfolgung der Apostel damals transparent für die Konflikte seiner Zeit? In 12,1–12 hält Jesus eine Rede an die Jünger vor dem Volk. Er ermahnt sie, sich öffentlich zu ihm zu bekennen und nicht aus Furcht vor dem Tod zu heucheln und nur "im Dunkeln" (v. 3) und "in der Stube" zu reden, denn die Sache wird in jedem Fall öffentlich werden. Lukas verwendet in dieser Rede zwar ältere Tradition, der Gesamtgedankengang 12,1–12 ergibt aber eine neue Problemstellung: er redet zu Christen, die aus Angst vor den politischen Verfahren der Römer ihr Bekenntnis *vor Juden* verschweigen. M. E. muß man mit der Aktualität der Verfolgung in diesem Sinne für die lukanische Gemeinde rechnen; die lukanischen Besonderheiten vor allem in 12,1–12 und 21,12–19 erlauben diesen Schluß[44]. Lukanische Verfolgungsaussagen (z. B. 8,13–15) sind für seine Gegenwart transparent. Die von ihm geforderte ὑπομονή (in diesem Zusammenhang 21,19) bedeutet das Durchhalten und Aushalten dieser Bedrohung auch bis zum Einsatz des Lebens. Lk 21,19 verheißt wie Mk 13,13 dem Standhaften das ewige Heil.

---

[44] Wichtig ist in diesem Zusammenhang der Versuch Braumanns 1963, 120 f., primär die Verfolgung der Kirche – und nicht die sogenannte Parusieverzögerung – als hermeneutischen Schlüssel für Lukas zu verwenden. Weiteres Material zur Forschungsgeschichte Keck 1976, 200, Anm. 410.

Die eschatologische Datierung der Gegenwart und die Deutung gegenwärtiger Leidenserfahrungen sind auch für Lukas das Ziel der apokalyptischen Rede Jesu. 21,28 drückt das für ihn Entscheidende in einem Satz aus: Wenn diese Geschehnisse anfangen, d. h. *wenn die eschatologischen Drangsale (v.25f.) auftauchen, sollen die Menschen sich aufrichten und ihre Häupter erheben,* "denn eure Erlösung naht sich". Die verbreitete Auslegung von 21,28 auf die Hoffnung, die die Menschen in ferner Zukunft einmal haben sollen[45], wird diesem Satz wie überhaupt dem Lukasevangelium nicht gerecht. Lukas hätte den leidenden Menschen dann wirklich nur einen billigen Trost zu bieten. Aber nicht nur der theologische Aspekt spricht gegen diese verbreitete Deutung, auch exegetisches Material: 1. ἀρχομένων ist in dieser "fern"-eschatologischen Deutung überflüssig. Tatsächlich aber drückt Lk hier dieselbe eschatologische Datierung aus wie Mk 13,8 (ἀρχὴ ὠδίνων). 2. Lk 18,1–8 zeigt, daß Lukas das Heil herbeisehnt und ἐν τάχει erhofft. 3. Die gespannte Erwartungshaltung, z. B. 12,35f.; 21,36 mag Tradition sein, aber eben mit Leben gefüllte Tradition, sonst wären solche Sätze für ihn sinnlos[46].

Lukas will mit 21,28 (und 21,31)[47] auf seine Gegenwart hinweisen. Jetzt sollen die Menschen erkennen, daß die Königsherrschaft Gottes naht; und sie sollen ihre gegenwärtigen Bedrückungen[48] als Beginn der Endzeitwehen verstehen und ihren Sinn und ihr Ende erkennen.

4.3. Zusammenfassung

Zusammenfassend läßt sich zu den Endzeitreden im Matthäus- und Lukasevangelium sagen, daß die entscheidenden Gedanken zur Endzeit, die in Mk 13 begegnen, auch hier anzutreffen sind:

Die Gegenwart ist Anfang der Endzeitwehen (Mk 13,8; Mt 24,8; Lk 21,28). Die Gegenwart ist die Zeit der weltweiten Verkündigung des Evangeliums (Mk 13,10; Mt 24,14; Lk 21,24). Nach der Ausbreitung des Evangeliums unter den Völkern kommt das ersehnte Ende. Die Gegenwart

---

[45] S. vor allem Conzelmann 1964, 219: "Wenn das Ende kommt, ist das Leiden vorbei". 124: "der quantitativen Dehnung der Zeit entspricht die qualitative Bestimmung durch das Leiden, welches das erhoffte Ende in 'unendlicher' Ferne erscheinen läßt".

[46] Entgegen der seit Conzelmanns Lukasdeutung in der Forschung geradezu kanonisch gewordenen Sicht des Lukas, für den das Ende in "metaphysische Ferne" gerückt (Conzelmann 1964, 104) sei, haben besonders Bartsch 1963 *passim* und Geiger 1973, 258 die Bedeutung einer "Parusieverzögerung" für Lukas zu Recht bestritten.

[47] Markus bezieht diese Aussage (s. o.) darauf, daß erst, wenn der Menschensohn auf den Wolken kommt, das Ende ἐπὶ θύραις sei – er versucht Endpanik zu verhindern. Lk sagt statt dessen ἐγγίζει ἡ βασιλεία τοῦ θεοῦ. Trotz solcher Veränderungen ist ihre Zukunftsvorstellung nicht unterschiedlich.

[48] V.12 πρὸ δὲ τούτων πάντων bezieht sich auf die Geschehnisse von v.10f., die für ihn i. w. (s. o.) noch Zukunft sind, zukünftige Steigerung der eschatologischen Drangsale.

ist eine Leidenszeit. Die Leiden der Gegenwart werden in gesellschaftlichen und politischen Dimensionen erlebt (Verfolgung der Gemeinde) – wie übrigens auch die noch befürchteten Steigerungen der Enddrangsale (Völkerkampf usw.). Die theologische Absicht ist es in allen drei Endzeitreden, die Gegenwart zu deuten, ihr einen Sinn zu geben und Mut zu machen zum öffentlichen Bekenntnis (Mk 13,13; Mt 24,13; Lk 21,19). Gemeinsam ist allen drei Evangelien die Erwartung der Herrschaft Gottes, die die Erfahrungen und Hoffnungen der Gegenwart prägt. – Und darin sind diese Evangelien in der Sache eng verbunden mit den in ihnen verarbeiteten älteren Traditionen über Jesus von Nazareth, die auf allen historischen Ebenen von eben dieser Erwartung geprägt sind.

Alle drei Evangelien sind historische Quellen für die Situation von Christengemeinden im Römischen Reich nach 70 n. Chr., die sich im Laufe der Jahre, die zwischen Markus und Lukas liegen, offensichtlich nicht grundlegend gewandelt hat.

Bibliographie

Bartsch, Hans-Werner 1963: *Wachet aber zu jeder Zeit! Entwurf einer Auslegung des Lukasevangeliums,* Hamburg 1963.

Braumann, Georg 1963: "Das Mittel der Zeit. Erwägungen zur Theologie des Lukasevangeliums", in: *ZNW* 54 (1963) 177–145.

Conzelmann, Hans 1964: *Die Mitte der Zeit* (BHTh 17), 5. Aufl., Tübingen 1964.

Cuss, Dominique 1974: *Imperial Cult and Honorary Terms in the New Testament,* Fribourg 1974.

Geiger, Ruthild 1973: *Die lukanischen Endzeitreden.* Studien zur Eschatologie des Lukasevangeliums (Dissertation Würzburg 1971), Frankfurt a. M. 1973.

Giet, Stanislas 1957: *L'Apocalypse et l'histoire,* Paris 1957.

Grässer, Erich 1960: *Das Problem der Parusieverzögerung in den synoptischen Evangelien und in der Apostelgeschichte* (BZNW 22), 2. Aufl., Berlin 1960.

Hare, Douglas R. A. 1967: *The Theme of Jewish Persecution of Christians in the Gospel according to St. Matthew* (MSSNTS 6), Cambridge 1967.

Harnisch, Wolfgang 1969: *Verhängnis und Verheißung der Geschichte* (FRLANT 97), Göttingen 1969.

Hengel, Martin 1976: *Die Zeloten* (AGJU 1), 2. Aufl., Leiden 1976.

Hoffmann, Paul 1972: *Studien zur Theologie der Logienquelle* (NA 8), München 1972.

Keck, Fridolin 1976: *Die öffentliche Abschiedsrede Jesu in Lk 20,45–21,36,* Stuttgart 1976.

Kelber, Werner H. 1974: *The Kingdom in Mark,* Philadelphia, Penn. 1974.

Klostermann, Erich 1927: *Das Matthäusevangelium* (HNT 4), 2. Aufl., Tübingen 1927.

Kümmel, Werner Georg 1973: *Einleitung in das Neue Testament,* 17. Aufl., Heidelberg 1973.

Lambrecht, J. 1972: "The Parusia Discourse", in: M. Didier (Hrsg.), *L'Évangile selon Matthieu,* Gembloux 1972, 309–342.

Latte, Kurt 1967: *Römische Religionsgeschichte* (HAW 5,4), 2. Aufl., München 1967.

Luz, Ulrich 1971: Die Jünger im Matthäusevangelium, in: *ZNW* 62 (1971) 141–171.

Marxsen, Willi 1959: *Der Evangelist Markus* (FRLANT 69), 2. Aufl., Göttingen 1959.

Meyer, Rudolf 1940: *Der Prophet aus Galiläa,* Leipzig 1940.

Moreau, Jaques 1961: *Die Christenverfolgung im Römischen Reich,* Berlin 1961.

Morenz, Siegfried 1975: "Vespasian, Heiland der Kranken", in: ders., *Religion und Geschichte des alten Ägypten,* Köln 1975, 551–560.

Pesch, Rudolf 1968: *Naherwartungen*, Düsseldorf 1968.
– 1970: Eschatologie und Ethik, Auslegung von Mt 24,1–36, in: *BiLe* 11 (1970) 223–238.
– 1977: *Das Markusevangelium* (HThK II 2), Freiburg 1977.
Riddle, Donald W. 1934: Die Verfolgungslogien in formgeschichtlicher und soziologischer Beleuchtung, in: *ZNW* 33 (1934) 271–289.
Robinson, James M. 1956: *Das Geschichtsverständnis des Markusevangeliums* (AThANT 30), Zürich 1956.
Scott, Kenneth 1936: *The Imperial Cult under the Flavians*, Stuttgart 1936.
Sherwin-White, Adrian-Nicholas 1963: *Roman Society and Roman Law in the New Testament*, Oxford 1963.
Smallwood, Mary E. 1961: *Philonis Alexandrini Legatio ad Gaium*, Leiden 1961.
Stegemann, Ekkehard 1974: *Das Markusevangelium als Ruf in die Nachfolge*, Diss. (ungedruckt), Heidelberg 1974.
Strecker, Georg 1971: *Der Weg der Gerechtigkeit* (FRLANT 82), 3. Aufl., Göttingen 1971.
Tcherikover, V. A. and Fuks, A. (Hrsg.) 1960: *Corpus Papyrorum Judaicarum*, Vol. II, Cambridge/Mass. 1960.
Vogt, Joseph 1954: "Christenverfolgung I", in: *RAC* II (1954) 1159–1228.
Walker, Rolf 1967: *Die Heilsgeschichte im ersten Evangelium* (FRLANT 91), Göttingen 1967.
Wlosok, Antonie 1970: *Rom und die Christen*, Stuttgart 1970.

Persecution and Vengeance in the Book of Revelation

Adela Yarbro Collins

1. Introduction

1.1. Since consensus has not yet been reached on the definition of the literary genre apocalypse or the phenomenon of apocalypticism, generalizations about the function of apocalypticism would be premature at this stage of the discussion. The most appropriate approach for the present seems to be the investigation of the function of particular apocalyptic writings in their historical settings. This article presents such an investigation of the book of Revelation. In the course of this study, a common generalization about apocalypticism will be tested, namely, that it arises in social settings of crisis or alienation. It will be shown that this theory does hold for Revelation, but that the crisis is much more a matter of perspective than of an objective reality about which various observers would agree. The conclusions reached in this article imply that a major function of apocalyptic language is to resolve a social crisis on the level of the imagination, a resolution which, of course, has implications for action. A further issue addressed by this study is the question of the moral evaluation and theological significance of the way in which the book of Revelation resolves its social crisis.

1.2. The majority of commentators agree that, at least on one level, the book of Revelation portrays the Roman empire in a highly unflattering light and predicts the destruction of the city of Rome and the political and economic system associated with it.[1] This interpretation raises a number of historical and theological questions, which may be summarized by two basic queries. What motivated such a thorough-going and violent attack on Rome? How is that motivation to be evaluated?

1.3. A number of commentators respond to such questions indirectly by making assertions about the attitudes of the author and readers and about

---

[1] Kümmel 1966, 322, 327–329; commentators who take this view are, for example, Bousset, Charles, Beckwith, Allo, Kiddle-Ross, Lilje, Barclay, Glasson, Caird, and Kraft (for ch. 17).

the relation of the text to reality. For example, in commenting on 18:20, Bishop Lilje wrote:

> Because God executes judgment, the call for repayment must not be understood in the petty sense of human revenge. "*Sancti sancto modo reddent*" – "the saints 'repay' in a holy manner" – means that they are not animated by joy over destruction, but by certainty that God achieves his purpose, in spite of the arrogance of this secular power.[2]

Among the commentators it is perhaps William Barclay who has made the most thorough attempt to answer the kinds of questions raised above. He emphasizes, for example, that 18:6–8 does not call for the execution of vengeance by human beings; vengeance belongs to God. Further, he argues that the passage "is not a case of grim, savage, harsh, vengeful law and justice; it is simply the expression of the great truth that every man is working out his own judgment".[3] In these and similar comments, Barclay resembles most of the other commentators. On the other hand, after designating 18:1–3 a doom song and pointing out parallels in the Old Testament prophets, he admits, "It may be that we are far from the Christian doctrine of forgiveness; but we are very close to the beating of the human heart".[4] Further he argues that John's indictment of Rome was justified. Evidence is presented of extremes of luxury, ostentation, gluttony and waste. It is pointed out that even Roman writers attacked this extravagant life-style.[5] Nevertheless, in commenting on 18:20, Barclay frankly states that it "is not the more excellent way which Jesus taught." Perhaps by way of excuse, he reminds his readers that the call for rejoicing was written out of terrible suffering. In spite of the element of vengeance, it is the voice of faith, of utter confidence that "no man on God's side could ultimately be on the losing side, ..."[6]

1.4. Biblical scholars and theologians have been most concerned about the impression Revelation gives of a desire for revenge and the theological problems thereby raised. A somewhat different reading of the book was suggested by D. H. Lawrence, one which is, if anything, even more disturbing and challenging for the Christian who accepts Revelation as Scripture. He argued that the book, especially chapters 12–22, is an expression of the anger, hatred and envy of the weak against the strong, even against civilization and nature itself.[7] Lawrence found the latter half of Revelation to be a rather boring historical allegory.

> Only the great whore of Babylon rises rather splendid, sitting in her purple and scarlet upon her scarlet beast. She is the Magna Mater in malefic aspect, clothed in the colours of the angry sun, and throned upon the great red dragon of the angry cosmic power. Splendid she sits, and

---

[2] Lilje 1957, 234.
[3] Barclay 1960, 2. 198–199. See also Klassen 1966, 300–311; Wright and Fuller 1957, 337.
[4] Barclay 1960, 2. 195.   [5] *Ibid.*, 200–211.
[6] *Ibid.*, 213–214.   [7] Lawrence 1976, 11–12.

splendid is her Babylon. How the late apocalyptists love mouthing out all about the gold and silver and cinnamon of evil Babylon! How they *want* them all! How they *envy* Babylon her splendour, envy, envy! How they love destroying it all! The harlot sits magnificent with her golden cup of wine of sensual pleasure in her hand. How the apocalyptists would have loved to drink out of her cup! And since they couldn't: how they loved smashing it![8]

1.5. In this article the contentions that the book of Revelation expresses vengefulness and envy will be assessed as a way of determining the function of the work. The methods used will be literary and historical analysis. After introductory remarks about the structure and composition of Revelation, the function of persecution in the book as a whole will be treated. It will be shown that the eschatological woes and the destruction of the earth are portrayed as divine retribution for the persecution of the saints. Next, the attitude toward the persecutors expressed in Revelation 18 and the probable motivation of the author for taking such a stance will be examined. In the conclusion, we will return to the question of how that motivation ought to be evaluated.

1.6. The writer of this article has argued elsewhere that the book of Revelation is organized into two great cycles of visions, 1:9–11:19 and 12:1–22:5.[9] Each of these cycles is composed of three series of seven: I. messages, seals and trumpets; II. seven unnumbered visions, seven bowls, and another series of seven unnumbered visions. The structure of the book may be summarized as follows:

I. Prologue	1:1–8
Preface	1:1–3
Prescript and sayings	1:4–8
The seven messages	1:9–3:22
The seven seals	4:1–8:5
The seven trumpets	8:2–11:19
II. Seven unnumbered visions	12:1–15:4
The seven bowls	15:1–16:20
Babylon appendix	17:1–19:10
Seven unnumbered visions	19:11–21:8
Jerusalem appendix	21:9–22:5
Epilogue	22:6–21
Sayings	22:6–20
Benediction	22:21

Beginning with the seven seals, each series expresses the whole message of the book in its own particular way. The constant elements of the message are a. persecution, b. punishment of the persecutors and c. salvation.[10]

1.7. The first great cycle of visions introduces these elements in an apparently purposefully veiled and fragmentary way. The second cycle

---

[8] *Ibid.*, 87–88; see also 114–115.
[10] *Ibid.*, 32–44.

[9] Yarbro Collins 1976, 19–32.

maintains the mythic and symbolic language of the first, but presents the
message of the book in a gradually fuller and more coherent manner. In
particular, the second cycle is more explicit about the historical context of
the visions. The first cycle makes clear that persecution is of major
importance, but it is only in the second cycle that the identity of the
persecutors is made explicit, the Roman authorities.

2. *The Function of Persecution in Revelation*

2.1. *The First Cycle of Visions*

2.1.1. The opening vision with its seven messages mentions two incidents of actual persecution and expresses the expectation of many more. In
1:9, John refers to himself as your συγκοινωνὸς ἐν τῇ θλίψει ... καὶ
ὑπομονῇ ἐν Ἰησοῦ. In themselves, θλῖψις and ὑπομονή are rather
general terms. The context suggests that they refer to the great eschatological crisis which involves persecution. Immediately following the remark
cited above is the comment that he was on the island of Patmos on account
of the word of God and the testimony of Jesus. Three interpretations of this
remark have been proposed: that John went to Patmos a. to preach the
gospel, b. to await revelatory visions, or c. because he was sent there by
some agent of Rome.[11] It is unlikely that John went to Patmos to preach or
teach because of the small size of the island.[12] The second theory, that John
went to Patmos to receive revelatory visions, was rejected by Bousset and
Charles, but revived recently by Kraft.[13] Kraft cites a number of passages as
parallels to Rev 1:9 and concludes that early Christian prophets withdrew
to isolated places to receive revelations and to meditate. The likelihood of
this interpretation is called into question by the fact that διά with the
accusative in every other passage in Revelation where it occurs gives the
grounds and not the purpose.[14] It is not an impossible theory, but the third
has more in its favor. In two other passages, "the word of God and the
testimony of Jesus" are associated with persecution (6:9, 20:4). It is likely
that Patmos was used by the Romans as a place of political banishment.[15]

---

[11] Bousset 1896, 223; Charles 1920, 1. 21–22; Kraft 1974, 40–41.

[12] According to Pliny the Elder (*NH* 4. 69–70), Patmos was only about thirty miles in
circumference.

[13] The references are given in note 11.

[14] Charles 1920, 1. 22.

[15] Three of the islands mentioned by Pliny as part of the same group as Patmos (*NH* 4.
69–70) are mentioned elsewhere as places of political banishment: Gyara (or Gyarus, Gioura;
Tac. *Ann.* 3. 68, 4. 30, Juvenal, *Sat.* 1. 73–74), Donusa (Tac. *Ann.* 4. 30) and Amorgus
(Hypere, Patage, or Platage; Tac. *Ann.* 4. 30).

Early Christian tradition says that John was banished to Patmos.[16] The evidence thus supports the theory that John's presence on Patmos was due to Roman hostility. Near the very beginning of the book, therefore, we find the theme of persecution and the Roman empire linked implicitly.

2.1.2. The second clear case of persecution involves Antipas (2:13), whose death is mentioned in the message to Pergamum. The Christians in Pergamum are praised for holding Christ's name and not denying his faith, even in the days of Antipas, "my witness, my faithful one, who was killed among you. ..." The wording implies that Antipas died because of his faith in Christ. The circumstances of his death are not given, but it is hinted that the Romans were involved. Framing the mention of Antipas' death are the remarks, "I know where you dwell, where the throne of Satan is" and "where Satan dwells". These cryptic remarks have been interpreted in various ways. In part, the difference of opinion is due to a scarcity of evidence regarding the Roman administration of Asia, that is, about which city was the capital, where the governor resided and so forth.[17] The book of Revelation as a whole clearly implies that "Satan's throne" is linked in some way with Rome. In chapters 12–13, Satan is portrayed as the one who calls forth the beast and gives it his own power and throne and great authority (13:2). There are indications in chapters 13 and 17 that, on one level of meaning, the beast symbolizes the Roman empire.[18] One of its activities is the persecution of the saints (13:7, 10). The imperial cult is also reflected there (13:8, 12, 15). The interpretation of "Satan's throne" as the residence of the Roman governor or the place where he made judicial decisions illuminates the message to Pergamum as a whole. The sharp two-edged sword of Christ mentioned in the greeting (2:12) and in the threat (2:16) is then contrasted implicitly with the "sword" of the Roman governor.[19] Antipas' epithet ὁ μάρτυς is more clearly shown to have a basically forensic meaning.[20] It is possible, however, that by John's time Ephesus had become the seat of the governor of Asia. In that case, "Satan's throne" is best understood as a reference to Pergamum as the oldest and

---

[16] Bousset 1896, 223, 147; Charles 1920, 1. 22; Caird 1966, 22; Sanders 1963, 75–85; Robinson 1976, 222–224; Johanna Schmidt, "Patmos", in: *PRE* XVIII 4 (1949) 2183–2184.

[17] Bousset 1896, 245–246; Beckwith 1919, 457–458. Ramsay argued that Pergamum was the capital of the province of Asia in John's time (1905, 289–290). Pellett says that Pergamum was the capital originally, but that by the time of Augustus, Ephesus had been made capital and the place where the governor had to land and take office (1962, 258). According to Jones, the governor held his courts in several cities in the western coastal district (1971, 61) including Pergamum.

[18] Yarbro Collins 1976, 172–183.

[19] Caird 1966, 37–38; Farrer 1949, 190–191; Sherwin-White 1963, 4–5, 8–11.

[20] Trites argues for such a meaning of μάρτυς in Rev 2:13 (1977, 159–161, 167, 173).

probably the most prominent center of the imperial cult in the province.[21] The implication would be that Antipas' death was associated with his refusal to participate in the imperial cult.

2.1.3. John's banishment and Antipas' death are clear examples of persecution, but they are spoken of in an indirect way. The general tone of the messages implies that further persecution is expected. The virtue of endurance or steadfastness (ὑπομονή) is emphasized (2:2–3, 19; 3:10). The eschatological character of this endurance is indicated by its association with tribulation (θλῖψις) in 1:9 and with the hour of testing which is about to come upon the inhabited world (3:10). The expectation of further persecution is explicit in the message to Smyrna (2:10). Members of the community there are apparently threatened by imprisonment and death. The impending persecution is described as tribulation and testing. The juxtaposition of this prediction with an attack on the local Jews would not, of course, exclude the agency of the Roman governor, who was responsible for keeping order.[22]

2.1.4. In the next series of seven, the seals, it is even more clear that persecution is depicted in Revelation as a major eschatological event.[23] In the vision of the fifth seal, the souls slain for the witness they had borne cry out for vengeance on their persecutors (6:9–11). The reader is not given any information, however, about the circumstances of their deaths or the identity of the persecutors. The vision which provides a transition from the seals to the trumpets alludes to persecution indirectly by mentioning the prayers of the saints and the altar (8:3). These two elements recall the vision of the fifth seal with the souls under the altar praying to God for vengeance. In the transitional vision, an angel offers the prayers of the saints in a heavenly ritual. The symbolism of this ritual implies that the destruction which follows the trumpets is the divine answer to the saints' prayer. Once again, no details are given about the opponents of the saints and the destruction affects the whole earth. There is only a hint that the trumpets are directed against a particular group. The fifth trumpet is directed against people who lack the seal of God on their foreheads. Other passages in Revelation imply that these are the followers of the beast; on one level of meaning, then, they are supporters of the Roman order (13:3–4, 8, 12–17; 17:8).[24] In the first great cycle of visions, persecution is clearly an important element in the eschatological message of Revelation. There are hints about the nature of this persecution in the first cycle, but it

---

[21] Bousset 1896, 246; Charles 1920, 1. 60–61; Kraft 1974, 64; Beckwith 1919, 458; Caird 1966, 37. On Pergamum's role as a center for the imperial cult, see Magie 1950, 1. 447–449.
[22] Bousset 1896, 242–243; Charles 1920, 1. 56–58; Caird 1966, 35; Sherwin-White 1963, 2.
[23] Yarbro Collins 1977a, 249.   [24] Yarbro Collins 1976, 158–161.

is only in the second great cycle of visions that the Roman empire is revealed as the proximate enemy of Christians.

2.2. The Second Cycle of Visions

2.2.1. In the first series of unnumbered visions (12:1–15:4), the persecuting beast and his cohort arise bearing unmistakable traits of Rome (13:1–18).[25] In the fifth vision of the series (14:6–13), three angels appear, each with a message. The second angel announces, "Fallen, fallen, is Babylon the great, who gave all the nations to drink of the wine of the wrath [or passion] of her harlotry" (14:8). Commentators agree that "Babylon" is a symbolic name here. Most hold the opinion that the city of Rome is being characterized as the new Babylon.[26] The reasons generally given are a. that Babylon was a synonym for Rome in Jewish and Christian literature of the first century C. E.,[27] b. both Babylon and Rome were associated with moral corruption, as well as with power,[28] c. both Babylon and Rome were capitals of a world empire which was the foe of God's people.[29] In the Targums and the rabbinical literature, Rome is called by the name of another traditional enemy of the Jews, Edom.[30] The selection of the name "Babylon" for Rome in Revelation, and probably in the other relevant texts, is best explained by a quite specific shared trait. Babylon was the first and Rome the second city to be associated with the destruction of the temple in Jerusalem. This parallel is not explicitly drawn in Revelation, but is clear in the Jewish texts which use "Babylon" as a name for Rome. The parallel is obvious in the literary fictions of 4 Ezra and 2 Apoc. Bar. Further, when "Babylon" is referred to in these works, the desolation of Zion or the equivalent is always mentioned.[31] The reason for calling Rome "Babylon" in book five of the *Sibylline Oracles* is equally clear.[32] The Nero legend is reflected in an oracle which speaks of a king fleeing "Babylon" and going to the Medes and the Persians.[33] In the same oracle, it is said that this king seized the temple of God and that eventually

---

[25] See note 18 above.

[26] Bousset 1896, 443; Charles 1920, 2. 14; Beckwith 1919, 656; Allo 1933, 239; Lilje 1957, 203; Barclay 1960, 2. 145–146; Glasson 1965, 86.

[27] Bousset 1896, 443; Charles 1920, 2. 14, 62; Allo 1933, 239. The relevant texts are *2 Apoc. Bar.* 11:1; 67:7; 4 Ezra 3:28–31; *Sib. Or.* 5:143, 159; 1 Pet 5:13.

[28] Kiddle-Ross 1940, 333; Barclay 1960, 2. 145–146.

[29] Beckwith 1919, 158–159, 656; Lilje 1957, 203; Glasson 1965, 101.

[30] Bousset 1926, 218. Bill. 4. 1257; Hadas 1929, 369–387.

[31] In addition to the texts cited in note 27, see *2 Apoc. Bar.* 10:1–3, 4 Ezra 3:1–2. On the parallel between Revelation and these two Jewish apocalypses, see Bogaert (1977).

[32] *Sib. Or.* 5 is a Jewish composition, dating to about 100 C.E.; Collins 1972, 73–75.

[33] *Sib. Or.* 5: 137–154; on the Nero legend, see Yarbro Collins 1976, 176–183.

others in power destroyed a great city and righteous people. In the
following oracle, the destruction of "Babylon" and the land of Italy is
foretold. The reason for the destruction is that many holy, faithful Hebrews and a true people have perished.[34]

2.2.2. The brief announcement of Babylon's fall in 14:8 is the only
appearance of Babylon in the first series of visions in the second great cycle
(12:1–15:4). Besides chapter 13, the beast is mentioned in the announcement of the third angel (14:9–11) and in the climactic vision of salvation
which closes the series (15:2–4).

2.2.3. The concluding vision of salvation in 15:2–4 is interlocked with
the opening vision of the next series, the seven bowls.[35] Like the seals and
trumpets, the bowls are universal and cosmic in their effects.[36] The
trumpets, as noted above, contain a slight hint that they are directed against
a particular group (9:4). It was also noted that the trumpets are presented as
the answer to the prayer of the saints for vengeance (6:9–11 and 8:3–5).
These two elements are also present in the bowls. The third bowl has a
distinctive commentary which designates that particular plague as a punishment on those who have shed the blood of the saints (16:5–7).[37] The
persecutors are not explicitly identified in the third bowl, but the context
suggests who they are. The first and fifth bowls are directed against the
beast and its followers. As we have seen, on one level, the beast represents
Rome. The bowls are introduced as the result of God's wrath (15:1). One
of the effects of the seventh bowl is the fall of Babylon, which is
characterized as the result of the wrath of God (16:19). This characterization recalls the opening remark and shows that the fall of Babylon is the
climax of the seven bowls. The implication is that the plagues of the seven
bowls are God's judgment on the whole earth for its complicity in Rome's
persecution of the people of God. The allusion in 9:4 to those who lack
God's seal is clarified by reference to the followers of the beast and to
Babylon in the bowls. The symbolic act of the angel in 8:3–5 is clarified by
the commentary on the third bowl. The two series suggest that the
eschatological judgment, and perhaps even the destruction of the world, is
divine vengeance for the blood of the saints.

---

[34] *Sib. Or.* 5: 155–161.

[35] Yarbro Collins 1976, 16–19.

[36] On the relation of the seven bowls to the traditional plagues against Egypt, see Müller
1960, 268.

[37] On the interpretation of the third bowl and on the history-of-religions approach to
apocalypticism in general, see Betz 1969, 134–156; Yarbro Collins 1977, 367–381.

3. Attitude Toward the Persecutors

3.1. Revelation 18

3.1.1. Chapters 17 and 18 elaborate the judgment of Babylon announced in 16:19 and 19:1–10 presents heavenly rejoicing over the fulfillment of that judgment. Revelation 18 is perhaps the passage that has most deeply offended the moral sensibilities of readers, Christian and non-Christian alike. James L. Price claims that in the brighter scenes of the book "all darkness is not dispelled, nor do the songs of the saved drown the woeful dirges". He refers to chapter 18 as "taunt songs" and "impassioned songs of hatred against Rome".[38] These remarks imply certain conclusions about the form of Revelation 18 and how it functions in the book as a whole.

3.1.2. Let us begin with the question of form. Revelation 18 consists of three units: a report of a vision (vss. 1–3), a report of an audition (vss. 4–20) and a narrative account of a symbolic action performed by an angel (vss. 21–24).[39] Each of these units contains smaller forms, most of which are sayings. The angel who appears in the opening vision speaks a dirge over Babylon.[40] Since this dirge is spoken over an enemy of "Israel", rather than over "Israel" itself, it functions primarily as an announcement of judgment. Vs. 2b is the announcement itself and vs. 3 gives the reason or grounds for the judgment.[41] This shift in the traditional function of the dirge was already present, however, in at least some of the prophetic dirges spoken over Israel (for example, Amos 5:1–2).[42] In some cases, the dirge became an ironic taunt-song; Isaiah 14 is an example. But the element of irony or scorn is not always present.[43] The irony in Rev 18:1–3 results more from the image of the harlot than from the use of the dirge.

3.1.3. The speech of the heavenly voice reported in 18:4–20 contains sayings of several different forms. Five of them are dirges. Three of these dirges begin with "woe, woe!"[44] Within the immediate literary context, all

---

[38] Price 1961, 563–564.

[39] So also Lohmeyer 1953, 147. For a more detailed study of the form and function of Revelation 18, see Yarbro Collins 1980.

[40] The form of Rev 18:2b–3 is similar to that of Isa 21:9 and Amos 5:1–2; on the dirge in the prophets see Tucker 1971, 67–68; Westermann uses the terms "lament" and "death-lament" (1967, 202–3). For a study of the history and function of the dirge, see Jahnow (1923).

[41] The same is true of Isa 21:9. On the announcement of judgment as a prophetic form, see Tucker 1971, 61–65; Westermann 1967, 129–190. March follows K. Koch in using the term "prophecy of disaster" (1974, 159–160).

[42] Stählin 1938, 838–840.

[43] Stählin emphasizes this aspect *(ibid.)*, while Westermann indicates the range of attitudes and emotions (1967, 202–203).

[44] Some of the sayings classified by Westermann as laments begin with "Woe!" (הוֹי ; οὐαί; for example, Jer 10:19–20 and Isa 1:4 (1967, 202–203). Although they also begin with

these are presented as genuine expressions of sorrow. One is addressed to Babylon by an unidentified voice (vs. 14) and the others are uttered by her friends. There are literary indications, however, that the reader is not intended to sympathize with Babylon's friends in their mourning. The first of these appears within the introduction to the dirge of the kings of the earth. They are not presented neutrally; rather the reader is invited to judge against them for having prostituted themselves and lived wantonly with Babylon (18:9). In the context of the book as a whole the dirge of the kings functions as an announcement of judgment. This function is made clear by the ending of the dirge, "in one hour your *judgment* came" (vs. 10; emphasis added).

3.1.4. None of the other dirges expresses its intended function as clearly. If read in isolation, they could evoke a certain pathos and sympathy. The themes of wealth and luxury are emphasized; to determine the response these passages were intended to evoke we must consider how the theme of wealth is treated elsewhere in the book. We shall return to that question. The last dirge is followed abruptly by the call for rejoicing in vs. 20, addressed to the saints, the apostles and the prophets. Obviously, the reader is intended to identify with these groups and thus to rejoice rather than to join in the laments of Babylon's friends. The reason for rejoicing is clear enough in general: God has passed judgment on her. The reason is phrased, however, in a very terse and ambiguous way.[45] However it should be translated, the wording implies that Rome and the Christians are engaged in a legal battle. On one level of meaning, the heavenly court with God as judge is meant. It is probable that the earthly level is involved as well, and that actual Roman trials are alluded to here in which judgment was passed or expected to be passed against Christians.[46] The underlying message then is that the present situation will be reversed: she will be judged as she now judges you. The position of this verse is climactic. It suddenly cuts off the rhythmic and powerful dirges and foreshadows the rejoicing of 19:1–10. Its role in the chapter implies that its underlying message expressed the primary motivation for the composition of at least this particular chapter. The hope articulated here involves a reversal of roles of the persecutor and persecuted. It would be less than honest to deny that, read in its historical context, this hope is tainted by vengefulness.

הוי , the woe oracles are quite different in form from Rev 18:10b, 16, and 19b; on the woe oracles see Tucker 1971, 66; Westermann 1967, 190–194; March 1974, 164–165.

[45] Bousset 1896, 486–487; Charles 1920, 2. 111–112; Caird 1966, 229–230.

[46] The same two levels of meaning seem to be operative in Rev 12:10–12; see Yarbro Collins 1976, 138–142.

3.2. The Author As Jew

3.2.1. In order to clarify and evaluate the motivation behind this apparent vengefulness, we must inquire further into the historical context of the book of Revelation. The writer of this essay agrees with the majority of commentators and New Testament scholars of this century in dating the composition of Revelation to about 95 C. E., in accordance with Irenaeus' testimony.[47] As noted at the beginning of this article, a number of commentators explain the stance of Revelation toward Rome as the result of terrible suffering. John A. T. Robinson has remarked recently,

> One thing of which we may be certain is that the Apocalypse, unless the product of a perfervid and psychotic imagination, was written out of an intense experience of the Christian suffering at the hands of the imperial authorities, represented by the 'beast' of Babylon.[48]

Robinson and others have pointed out how little evidence there is for a persecution of Christians under Domitian.[49] The axiom quoted above combined with the paucity of evidence for a Domitianic persecution contribute to Robinson's conclusion that Revelation was written between 68 and early 70 C. E. (*before* the destruction of Jerusalem).[50] The intense suffering he mentions is Nero's repression of Christians in 64, and he finds Revelation intelligible only if its author experienced that persecution, personally and directly in Rome itself.[51] In this particular aspect of Robinson's argument, it is clear that he is influenced by *a priori* value judgments about what is an acceptable relationship between John's imagination and reality. If the scholarly consensus about the date of Revelation is correct, how is the argument concerning suffering to be assessed?

3.2.2. A discussion of this question must include the self-understanding of the author of Revelation *vis-à-vis* Judaism. His stance is certainly complex and ambiguous. In the message to Smyrna, he refers to the blasphemy of those who say that they are Jews and are not, but are a synagogue of Satan (2:9). A similar attack is made on the Jews of Philadelphia (3:9). There is no good reason to think here of Judaizers rather than actual Jews of the local synagogues. Jewish hostility to the early Christian missionary effort is well attested for both the first and second centuries.[52] The wording of these attacks implies that, in those two cities at least and

---

[47] Kümmel 1966, 327–329; Feuillet 1963, 75; Böcher 1975, 41. The writer has recently reexamined the evidence for the date of Revelation in light of recent research; see Yarbro Collins 1981. A briefer form of that article has also been published (Yarbro Collins 1981a).

[48] Robinson 1976, 230–231.

[49] *Ibid.*, 231–233 and the literature cited there, especially on 233, note 64.

[50] *Ibid.*, 248–253.

[51] *Ibid.*, 231, 252.

[52] Bousset 1896, 242–243; Charles 1920, 1. 56–58; Robinson 1976, 273–274. In support of the theory that the group referred to are local Jews, see Schüssler Fiorenza 1973, 572.

probably throughout Asia Minor, the followers of Jesus were not welcome in the synagogues. At the same time, the remarks imply that John was not content to find a new name to express his own self-understanding and that of his community of faith, but that he claimed the name Ἰουδαῖοι.

3.2.3. John's attitude toward Jerusalem seems to have been equally ambiguous. The designation of Jerusalem as "Sodom" and "Egypt" in 11:8 implies a significant degree of alienation from the historical city and probably from some Jewish leaders. On one level, John would surely have viewed the destruction of Jerusalem as God's punishment on the city for the rejection of the Messiah (the crucifixion of Jesus is explicitly mentioned in 11:8). On the other hand, the two witnesses of chapter 11 are to appear in Jerusalem. Even though they will be rejected as Jesus was, their ministry eventually results in repentance (11:13). Such repentance is portrayed nowhere else in Revelation and perhaps reflects the author's concern for the eventual conversion of the Jews. Also, Jerusalem is a major symbol of salvation in the book (3:12; 21:2, 10).

3.2.4. John's attacks on the Nicolaitans and the followers of "Jezebel" provide evidence for his stance over against both Judaism and the surrounding Greco-Roman culture. The Nicolaitans are mentioned in the messages to Ephesus (2:6) and Pergamum (2:15). Their teaching was identical to that of the followers of "Balaam" (2:14) and "Jezebel" (a leader of the community at Thyatira; 2:20). They all probably constituted a single tendency in various Christian communities of Asia Minor.[53] John's criticisms focus on their allowing their followers to eat meat sacrificed to idols and πορνεῦσαι, to engage in prostitution or some other form of sexual immorality.[54] It is probable, at least for the issue of eating meat, that the literal meanings of the words are intended. It is just as likely, however, that the dispute is not a narrow one over practical problems.[55] Rather, two different perspectives on the relation between faith and culture are at odds. Πορνεύω had come in Jewish tradition to represent idolatry. John uses the word in a metaphorical sense elsewhere in relation to "Babylon."[56] At stake here was the question of assimilation: what pagan customs could Christians adopt for the sake of economic survival, commercial gain, or simple

---

[53] Bousset 1896, 248–249, 254; Charles 1920, 1. 64, 69–70. Schüssler Fiorenza points out some differences between the followers of Jezebel and the Nicolaitans, but ultimately sees them both as part of the same general movement (1973, 568–570).

[54] Bauer-Arndt-Gingrich, s.v. πορνεύω.

[55] Against Bousset (1896, 278–279) and Charles (1920, 1. 63, 69–70) who see the basic issue, but in too simple and narrow a perspective; in agreement with Lohmeyer (1953, 31), Caird (1966, 38–41, 44), and Kraft (1974, 65, 71).

[56] Rev 17:2; 18:3,9; πορνεία is used metaphorically in all but one of its occurrences outside the messages (14:8; 17:2, 4; 18:3; 19:2). In the one case in which it is probably used literally, πορνεία is associated with idolatry (9:20–21).

sociability? As many commentators have noted, the social and economic associations of Asia Minor, including the ones organized for basic kinds of assistance to members, had a religious aspect. Such was true of the trade guilds; membership in such guilds has been posited especially for the Christians of Thyatira.[57] Beckwith rejects Ramsay's suggestion that these Christians were being asked by John to withdraw from the trade guilds.[58] Beckwith implies that they were simply being asked to avoid compromising their faith while remaining members. Unlike Paul, John does not allow for any exceptions to the rule that meat sacrificed to idols must be avoided.[59] It is not obvious that John's strict position on that issue was compatible with continued membership in a guild. Further, there are indications elsewhere in Revelation that the author was calling for actual, social, political and economic withdrawal from the life of the cities of western Asia Minor. In 13:16–17 it is said that the beast from the land creates a situation in which no one can buy or sell unless one has the mark, the name of the beast, or the number of its name. The writer of this article has argued elsewhere that "the mark etc." refers here to Roman coins and that the author is calling for separatism and economic boycott.[60] In view of that indirect exhortation, the call to "come out of her, my people" (18:4) takes on the concrete meaning of social separation.

3.2.5. Given this hostility to the surrounding culture, the breach with the synagogue and the destruction of the temple must have been extremely unsettling and threatening events. Culturally speaking, John found himself on the boundary, neither fish nor fowl. In this state, he seems to have identified with the Jews, in spite of the apparent split. He used the Hebrew text of the Bible and wrote a Semitizing Greek.[61] He adopted the attitude of hostility to Rome which was dominant among Jews after the destruction of the temple and whose roots were in the insults of Pompey, Varus, Pilate, Caligula, Gessius Florus, and Nero.[62] Besides *2 Apoc. Bar.* and 4 Ezra, the book of Revelation has affinities with the fifth book of the *Sibylline Oracles*; in spite of its clear rejection of violent resistance, Revelation has similarities also with the theology of the Zealots.[63] This general hostility to Rome on religious and political grounds was greatly intensified by knowledge of Nero's atrocities against Christians in 64.[64] That event, in addition

---

[57] Allo 1933, 46–47; Charles 1920, 1. 69; Beckwith 1919, 463–464; Ramsay 1905, 316–353.
[58] Beckwith 1919, 464–465.
[59] On Paul's position, see Schüssler Fiorenza 1973, 572–573.
[60] Yarbro Collins 1977a, 252–254.
[61] Charles 1920, 1. lxvi–lxxvii, cxvii–clix; Vanhoye 1962, 436–476.
[62] Smallwood 1976; Grant 1973, esp. 205, 231, 236, 248–249; Collins 1972, 78–79.
[63] Collins 1972, 79; Yarbro Collins 1977a, 252–254, 256.
[64] Frend 1965, 161–165; Dibelius 1956, 2. 204–209.

to Nero's involvement in the Jewish War, explains Nero's role as an Antichrist-like, eschatological adversary in Revelation.[65]

3.3. The Author As Christian

3.3.1. Nero's treatment of the Christians in Rome should probably be seen in the context of the traditional Roman hostility to foreign cults and religious practices thought to have a socially and politically dangerous character.[66] It is likely that his decision was influenced by popular animosity toward Christians.[67] It is improbable that Nero issued a general law prohibiting Christianity or that the Senate produced a *senatus consultum* against Christians. It is more likely that Nero acted on the basis of his police power and that the affair was specific and local.[68] Nevertheless, it seems to have had wider implications and effects. First of all, the hatred of the populace of Rome for the Christians was probably typical of the attitudes of the citizens of many provincial cities as well. Such hatred would certainly have a social impact and perhaps a political one as well. Secondly, Nero's conclusions about his rights and duties in dealing with Christians in terms of Roman law could have been drawn independently by other authorities. For example, provincial governors had police power and were expected to keep order. Further, Nero's action was probably well-known and would have set a precedent.[69] By the time Pliny the Younger encountered Christians in Bithynia (about 112), a provincial governor could conclude that it was his duty to execute any unrepentant, adult, male Christian who was properly accused.[70] It was probably on some such basis that Antipas was executed in Pergamum (2:13).[71]

3.3.2. John's own experience was rather different. As noted above, he does seem to have been affected by some sort of Roman repression. Tertullian and Jerome testify that John's was a case of *relegatio in insulam*.[72] In the imperial period, *relegatio* was normally banishment for life to a particular island for specific offenses or because the person involved

---

[65] Frend 1965, 169–170; Josephus, *Bell* 1. 21, 3. 1; Yarbro Collins 1976, 174–190.

[66] Frend 1965, 104–120, 163.

[67] *Ibid.*, 162–163; Dibelius 1956, 208–211.

[68] Frend 1965, 165–166.

[69] *Ibid.*, 167–169.

[70] Pliny *Letters* 10. 96–97. Even though Pliny raises the question whether it is the *nomen ipsum* or only the *flagitia* associated with it which are punishable, his decisions on particular cases, which are confirmed by Trajan, show that adherence to the cult is the decisive issue.

[71] The fact that Antipas is called ὁ μάρτυς μου ὁ πιστός μου supports the theory that he was tried and executed by the provincial governor, rather than killed by a local mob as Schüssler Fiorenza suggests (1973, 570, note 29); see the discussion relating to notes 19 and 20 above.

[72] Tert *de praescr.* 36; Jerome *de vir. ill.* 9.

threatened the public interest. Among the offenses so punished were *ars magica* or *ars mathematica*.[73] Jewish and Christian prophecy was probably viewed by Romans as such.[74] A provincial governor could pass a sentence of *relegatio*.[75]

3.3.3. Another possibility is that John's sentence was *deportatio in insulam*. *Deportatio* was more severe than *relegatio* and differed from it primarily in the forcible removal of the condemned to the place of exile. *Deportatio* was imposed for a variety of offenses, but was originally applied to political offenders and most often used as a political measure. The provincial governor could not impose a sentence of *deportatio* himself, but could only recommend it in specific cases to the emperor.[76]

3.3.4. Given Nero's precedent and the death of Antipas, it is somewhat puzzling that John was banished rather than executed. William Ramsay conjectured that John's sentence could not have been *deportatio*, but that he was sentenced to hard labor in the quarries of Patmos. His reasons were that *deportatio* was reserved for persons of standing and wealth and that it was too lenient a punishment for a Christian at that time.[77] J. N. Sanders argued that John's was a case of *relegatio*, that such a sentence was reserved for the aristocracy, Roman or provincial, and that persons were usually relegated to islands far distant from their residences. He concluded that a. John could not have been expelled from Ephesus; the city in question may have been Jerusalem, Alexandria or Rome, b. John must have been a member of the Jewish aristocracy, probably a Sadducee and c. he must have been banished before there was precedent for capital punishment of Christians, that is, before 64 C. E.[78]

3.3.5. There is little supporting evidence for Ramsay's theory of hard labor.[79] The fact that *deportatio* and *relegatio* were normally reserved for the upper class is problematic. There may have been exceptions, however, and not much is known about John's origins and social standing. Sanders' argument that John could not have been relegated from Ephesus to Patmos is not compelling. He gives three examples of people being removed to places far distant from the place of expulsion.[80] One of those is Eusebius' reference to Flavia Domitilla's removal from Rome to Pontia, an island

---

[73] Kleinfeller, G., "Relegatio", in: *PRE* IA1 (1914) 564–565; see Juvenal *Sat.* 6. 553–564.

[74] MacMullen 1966, 128–162, esp. 142–162.

[75] Pliny *Letters* 10. 56–57; Sherwin-White 1963, 77.

[76] Kleinfeller, G., "Deportatio in insulam", in: *PRE* V2 (1905) 231–233.

[77] Cited by Caird 1966, 21.

[78] Sanders 1963, 76–77. According to Polycrates, John, who reclined on the breast of the Lord and who sleeps at Ephesus, was a priest wearing the plate (πέταλον) (cited by Eusebius, *HE* 5.24.3). I am indebted to M. Hengel for this reference.

[79] Victorinus says that John was *in metallo damnatus* (*In Apoc.* 10. 11).

[80] Sanders 1963, 76.

opposite Campania. Relative to the other two examples, that removal was
of no great distance. It was common practice for the emperors to exile
someone from Rome to another mainland city or to an island off the coast
of Italy.[81] So, while removal from almost any city of Asia Minor to Patmos
would have been a relatively short one, it would by no means have been as
unusual as Sanders implies. The relative leniency of the punishment does
not necessarily imply that he was sentenced prior to Nero's execution of
Christians in Rome. If there was no general law, the precedent would not
have been absolutely binding. There is another possibility. As we have
noted, Rev 2:9 and 3:9 imply that John regarded himself as a true or real
Jew. The governor would have been likely to accept that self-definition if
John was a native Palestinian. The fact that he apparently knew Hebrew
makes it somewhat more probable that he was born in Palestine rather than
in the Diaspora.

3.4. The Author As Resident of Asia

3.4.1. Besides the author's perspective as a Jew and a Christian in conflict
with Rome, his experience as a resident of the Roman province of Asia is
significant for an understanding of the book of Revelation. In his epilogue
to a chapter on Roman domination in the eastern Mediterranean from
Mithridates to the civil wars, M. Rostovtzeff emphasizes two aspects of the
social and economic situation. First, he argues that the period was one of
brilliant economic progress for Asia Minor, due to the closer economic ties
between East and West and the new opportunities for the economic
growth of the East presented by the establishment of the Roman world
state.[82] On the other hand, Rome's promise to provide security was empty
and the great burden of taxation to pay for the civil wars fell most heavily
on Greece and Asia Minor.[83] The burden of taxation was borne especially
by the working and middle classes, while the provincial elite and the Italian
immigrants, the *negotiatores* (including merchants and shipowners) amassed
fortunes and enjoyed a privileged status.[84] Under the early Roman empire,
Asia Minor thrived in agriculture and commerce.[85] By the time of Vespasian, and on into Hadrian's rule, two social factors were characteristic of
the eastern provinces: a continuous conflict between the rich and the poor
and universal opposition to the administrative methods of the Roman
governors.[86] Under Vespasian and his sons, there was widespread criticism

---

[81] Suet *Aug.* 45 (implied), 65 (Postumus to Surrentum), *Tib.* 50 (Julia to Rhegium).
[82] Rostovtzeff 1941, 2. 1015, 1019.
[83] *Ibid.*, 1016.   [84] *Ibid.*, 1018.
[85] Rostovtzeff 1926, 65, 90.   [86] *Ibid.*, 111.

of the empire based on the philosopical distinction between the tyrant and the king.[87]

3.4.2. In discussing the empire under the Flavians and the Antonines, Rostovtzeff is warmly eloquent about the quality of city life. He suggests that the cities of this period were not inferior to many modern European and American cities in comfort, beauty and hygiene.[88] Nevertheless, he points out that none was self-sufficient. All were dependent on the regular or emergency import of food, a very precarious business.[89] Rostovtzeff closes the chapter with some telling observations:

> Such were the cities of the Roman empire. The picture of their social conditions is not so attractive as the picture of their external appearance. The impression conveyed by our sources is that the splendour of the cities was created by, and existed for, a rather small minority of their population; that the welfare even of this small minority was based on comparatively weak foundations; that the large masses of the city population had either a very moderate income or lived in extreme poverty. In a word, we must not exaggerate the wealth of the cities; their external aspect is misleading.[90]

3.4.3. Rostovtzeff's assessment of economic conditions in the province of Asia under the Flavians is the background against which the theme of wealth in Revelation must be understood. In Revelation 18, it is implied that among the reasons for Rome's predicted destruction are her wealth (17:4, 18:16) and her role as a source of wealth for merchants (18:3, 15) and shipowners (18:19). The first reason given by the angel with the great stone for Babylon's demise is that her merchants were οἱ μεγιστᾶνες τῆς γῆς (18:23). As was noted above, the messages to Pergamum and Thyatira oppose assimilation to the surrounding Greco-Roman culture. It is not improbable that the Christian faith and life-style as John understood them were incompatible with ordinary participation in the economic and social life of the cities of Asia Minor. Such a conclusion is supported by the fact that the Christians in Smyrna are portrayed as economically poor and threatened by persecution (2:8–11), but those of Laodicea as wealthy and apparently avoiding persecution (3:14–22).

3.4.4. It was noted above that the motif of the reversal of roles appears in Revelation 18 in connection with the theme of persecution. That motif is related to the traditional element of the reversal of fortunes, which seems to play a role throughout Revelation.[91] Those who have power and wealth in the present are portrayed as idolatrous and murderous while the truly faithful are expected to be poor. The judgment as described in 6:12–17 affects everyone, but the kings of the earth, οἱ μεγιστᾶνες, the generals

---

[87] *Ibid.*, 109–115.
[88] *Ibid.*, 127–135.
[89] *Ibid.*, 137.
[90] *Ibid.*, 179.
[91] It is found also in Luke 1:51–53, 6:20–26; see Beardslee 1970, 66–68. On the use of this motif in Egyptian texts, see the article by Jan Assmann in this volume (paragraph 1.1.).

and the rich are singled out. In 5:12 it is proclaimed that the Lamb is worthy to receive power and wealth among other things. A contrast is presumably implied with those who actually have wealth and power, and the Lamb's reception of them involves his followers too (5:10; 20:4–6; 21:24–26; 22:5). Such motifs of reversal can be read symbolically on a number of levels of meaning. There are sufficient indications, as we have seen, that the themes of persecution and of wealth were meant to be read, in part at least, on the literal, historical level. Some persecution had been experienced, more was expected; a disparity of wealth existed and economic survival was a problem.

4. Conclusion

4.1. We began by asking what motivated the thorough-going and violent attack on Rome found in the book of Revelation. It is natural to assume that such an attack is based, in significant part, on personal experience of conflict. A plausible reconstruction of such conflict was proposed on the basis of the traditional date, about 95 C.E. The antagonism was precipitated by the destruction of Jerusalem in 70 C.E. and Nero's slaughter of Christians in Rome in 64 C.E. Other incidents probably also played a role, notably the death of Antipas and John's banishment, but there is no need to posit a widespread or recent outbreak of persecution by Roman authorities against Christians. The other major root of the conflict seems to be the disparity of wealth and privilege between the provincial elite and the ordinary people of Asia Minor. Resentment at the disparity was probably aggravated by the fact that opportunities for advancement were tied to acceptance of pagan religious rites, unless one were accepted as a member of a powerful, local Jewish community.

4.2. Our second question was how that motivation ought to be evaluated. The idea that God executes judgment does not exclude the human feeling of envy or desire for revenge.[92] It is easy to deceive ourselves that our not very noble purpose is in reality God's purpose. In relying on "the great truth that every man is working out his own judgment", Barclay overlooks the real tension between that image and those of Revelation.[93] There is no immanent law of justice portrayed there, but creatures who pray and a Creator who acts. Even if a case could be made that the evil in the Roman order outweighed the good, one must ask whether prayers (and their equivalent) for the destruction or impoverishment of one's enemies

---

[92] Against Lilje; see the discussion related to note 2 above.
[93] See note 3 above.

should ever be encouraged. Justice may seem to call for them at times, but there is also the very real danger of becoming like the oppressor in one's opposition.

4.3. One option open to the theologian is to apply the imagery of Revelation only to collective human realities, to institutions, such as cities, corporations, nations, governments and even the Church. Such an approach has been taken by Jacques Ellul and, with less distortion of the historical meaning of the book, by William Stringfellow.[94] For the sake of integrity, this approach must explicitly prescind from the most probable historical meaning of Revelation, that is, the meaning intended by the author. Historically speaking, the book certainly applied to such collective realities, but also to individual human beings. An advantage of this approach is that it maintains a valid and powerful aspect of the meaning of Revelation, while avoiding the most obvious theological problems which it raises. A disadvantage of this approach, at least as Ellul and Stringfellow apply it, is that the imagery loses much of its specificity and thus a good deal of its power. The point is no longer that a *particular* city or nation is the harlot, but that all are. The message of Revelation seems rather to be that the primordial forces of destructive power and death are, from time to time, embodied in *particular* institutions.

4.4. Revelation's call for vengeance and the possibility of the book's function as an outlet for envy give the book a tremendous potential for real psychological and social evil. Its dangerous power must be recognized and dealt with. At the same time, these elements have a relative and limited validity. It may not always be psychologically possible to love one's enemies or rejoice in their good fortune. At least Revelation limits vengence and envy to the imagination and clearly rules out violent deeds. Revelation's portrayal of the Roman empire is one-sided and thus distorted. Nevertheless, it reminds us that creation and human life are not unalloyed goodness and light. The splendour of Rome was achieved through the unwilling sacrifice of many. The book of Revelation may serve as a reminder to the privileged that the system which benefits them may be causing real hardship to others.

Bibliography

Allo, E.-B. 1933: *Saint Jean*. L'Apocalypse (EtB), 4th edition, Paris 1933.
Barclay, William 1960: *The Revelation of John*. Volume 2 (Chapters 6–22), Philadelphia. Penn. 1960.
Beardslee, William 1970: "Uses of the Proverb in the Synoptic Gospels", in: *Interpretation* 24 (1970) 61–73.

---

[94] Ellul 1977; Stringfellow 1973.

Beckwith, Isbon T. 1919: *The Apocalypse of John*. Studies in Introduction with a Critical and Exegetical Commentary, New York 1919.

Betz, Hans Dieter 1969: "On the Problem of the Religio-Historical Understanding of Apocalypticism", in: Robert W. Funk (ed.), *Apocalypticism. JTC* 6 (1969) 134–156. (German original in: *ZThK* 63 [1966] 391–409.)

Böcher, Otto 1975: *Die Johannesapokalypse*, (EdF 41), Darmstadt 1975.

Bogaert, P. M. 1977: "La ruine de Jérusalem et les apocalypses juives après 70", in: *Apocalypses et théologie de l'espérance* (LeDiv 95), Paris 1977, 123–141.

Bousset, Wilhelm 1896: *Die Offenbarung Johannis* (KEK 16), 5th edition, Göttingen 1896.

– 1926: *Die Religion des Judentums im späthellenistischen Zeitalter*, H. Gressmann (ed.), (HNT 21), 3rd edition, Tübingen 1926.

Caird, G. B. 1966: *A Commentary on the Revelation of St. John the Divine* (HNTC), New York 1966.

Charles, R. H. 1920: *A Critical and Exegetical Commentary on the Revelation of St. John* (ICC), New York 1920.

Collins, Adela Yarbro 1976: *The Combat Myth in the Book of Revelation* (HDR 9), Missoula, Mont. 1976.

– 1977: "The History-of-Religions Approach to Apocalypticism and the 'Angel of the Waters' (Rev 16:4–7)", in: *CBQ* 39 (1977) 367–381.

– 1977a: "The Political Perspective of the Revelation to John", in: *JBL* 96 (1977) 241–256.

– 1980: "Revelation 18: Taunt-Song or Dirge?" in: Jan Lambrecht (ed.), *L'Apocalypse johannique et l'Apocalyptique dans le Nouveau Testament* (BEThL 53), Gembloux/Leuven 1980, 185–204.

– 1981: "Myth and History in The Book of Revelation: The Problem of Its Date", in: Baruch Halpern and Jon D. Levenson (eds.), *Traditions in Transformation*. Turning Points in Biblical Faith, Festschrift for Frank Moore Cross, Winona Lake, Indiana 1981, 377–403.

– 1981a: "Dating the Apocalypse of John", in: *BR* 26 (1981) 33–45.

Collins, John J. 1972: *The Sibylline Oracles of Egyptian Judaism* (SBLDS 13), Missoula, Mont. 1972.

Dibelius, Martin 1956: "Rom und die Christen im ersten Jahrhundert", in: *SHAW.PH* 1941–42:2. Reprinted in: *idem, Botschaft und Geschichte: Gesammelte Aufsätze, zweiter Band. Zum Urchristentum und zur hellenistischen Religionsgeschichte*, Tübingen 1956, 177–228.

Ellul, Jacques 1977: *Apocalypse*. The Book of Revelation, New York 1977.

Farrer, Austin 1949: *A Rebirth of Images*. The Making of St. John's Apocalypse, Westminster 1949.

Feuillet, André 1963: *L'Apocalypse*. État de la question (SN.S 3), Paris 1963.

Frend, W. H. C. 1965: *Martyrdom and Persecution in the Early Church*. A Study of a Conflict from the Maccabees to Donatus, Oxford 1965.

Glasson, T. F. 1965: *The Revelation of John* (CBC), Cambridge 1965.

Grant, Michael 1973: *The Jews in the Roman World*, New York 1973.

Hadas, Moses 1929: "Roman Allusions in Rabbinic Literature", in: *PQ* 8 (1929) 369–387.

Jahnow, Hedwig 1923: *Das hebräische Leichenlied im Rahmen der Völkerdichtung* (BZAW 36), Gießen 1923.

Jones, A. H. M. 1971: *The Cities of the Eastern Roman Provinces*, 2nd edition, Oxford 1971.

Kiddle, Martin 1940: *The Revelation of St. John*, assisted by M. K. Ross, (MNTC), London 1940.

Klassen, William 1966: "Vengeance in the Apocalypse of John", in: *CBQ* 28 (1966) 300–311.

Kraft, Heinrich 1974: *Die Offenbarung des Johannes* (HNT 16a), Tübingen 1974.

Kümmel, Werner, G. 1966: *Introduction to the New Testament*, founded by Paul Feine and Johannes Behm, 14th rev. edition, Nashville, Tenn. 1966.

Lawrence, D. H. 1976: *Apocalypse*, New York 1976 (1st edition 1931).

Lilje, Hanns 1957: *The Last Book of the Bible*. The Meaning of the Revelation of St. John, Philadelphia, Penn. 1957.

Lohmeyer, Ernst 1953: *Die Offenbarung des Johannes* (HNT 16), 2nd edition, Tübingen 1953.

MacMullen, Ramsay 1966: *Enemies of the Roman Order*. Treason, Unrest and Alienation in the Empire, Cambridge, Mass., 1966.

Magie, David 1950: *Roman Rule in Asia Minor*, Princeton, N. J. 1950.

March, W. E. 1974: "Prophecy", in John H. Hayes (ed.), *Old Testament Form Criticism*, San Antonio, Tex. 1974, 141–177.

Müller, Hans-Peter 1960: "Die Plagen der Apokalypse: Eine formgeschichtliche Untersuchung", in: *ZNW* 51 (1960) 268–278.

Pellett, David C. 1962: "Asia" in George A. Buttrick (ed.), *IDB* Volume 1, A–D, Nashville, Tenn. 1962, 257–259.

Price, James L. 1961: *Interpreting the New Testament*, 2nd edition New York 1961.

Ramsay, William 1905: *The Letters to the Seven Churches of Asia*, New York 1905.

Robinson, John A. T. 1976: *Redating the New Testament*, Philadelphia, Penn. 1976.

Rostovtzeff, Michael 1926: *The Social and Economic History of the Roman Empire*, Oxford 1926.

– 1941: *The Social and Economic History of the Hellenistic World*, Oxford 1941.

Sanders, J. N. 1963: "St. John on Patmos", in: *NTS* 9 (1963) 75–85.

Schüssler Fiorenza, Elisabeth 1973: "Apocalyptic and Gnosis in the Book of Revelation and Paul", in: *JBL* 92 (1973) 565–581.

Sherwin-White, A. N. 1963: *Roman Society and Roman Law in the New Testament*, Oxford 1963.

Smallwood, E. Mary 1976: *The Jews Under Roman Rule* (SJLA 20), Leiden 1976.

Stählin, Gustav 1938: "II. Die Totenklage der Propheten", in: *ThWNT* III (1938) 838–840.

Stringfellow, William 1973: *An Ethic for Christians and Other Aliens in a Strange Land*, Waco, Tex. 1973.

Trites, Alison A. 1977: *The New Testament Concept of Witness*, Cambridge 1977.

Tucker, Gene M. 1971: *Form Criticism of the Old Testament*, Philadelphia, Penn. 1971.

Vanhoye, Albert 1962: "L'Utilisation du livre d'Ezechiel dans l'Apocalypse", *Biblica* 43 (1962) 436–476.

Westermann, Claus 1967: *Basic Forms of Prophetic Speech*, Philadelphia, Penn. 1967.

Wright, G. Ernest – Fuller, R. H. 1957: *The Book of the Acts of God*. Christian Scholarship Interprets the Bible, Garden City, N.Y. 1957.

Ein Vergleich jüdischer, christlicher und gnostischer Apokalyptik

Hans G. Kippenberg

1. Apokalyptik in gnostischen Texten

1.1. Seit dem Bekanntwerden der Nag-Hammadi-Bibliothek steht das Verhältnis von Gnosis und Apokalyptik wieder zur Debatte. Wir haben bereits gehört, daß Apokalyptisches dem Inhalt und der Form nach auch in der Nag-Hammadi-Bibliothek begegnet[1]. Ergänzend hierzu soll an dieser Stelle von dem inhaltlichen Verhältnis zwischen jüdischer, christlicher und gnostischer Apokalyptik die Rede sein. Denn gerade die Nag-Hammadi-Schriften machen uns deutlich, daß die glatte Unterscheidung zwischen der apokalyptischen Erwartung eines zukünftigen Endes der Welt und der gnostischen Entweltlichung in der Gegenwart in vielen Fällen nicht aufgeht. Zahlreiche gnostische Texte sprechen die Erwartung eines zukünftigen Endes der Welt aus[2], ohne daß hier eine mit dem Anfangszustand identische Wiederherstellung gemeint ist. In diesem Falle wäre die dazwischenliegende Geschichte bedeutungslos. Jedoch findet sich in den Schriften die Idee, daß geschichtliche Ereignisse den Prozeß der Befreiung des gefallenen Lichtes aus den Fesseln der Materie anzeigen. Ich darf als Beispiel drei Texte heranziehen.

1.1.1. In der Schrift 'Über den Ursprung der Welt' (NHC II 5) heißt es (NHC II 125,32–126,11)[3]:

"Vor dem Ende (des Aion) wird der ganze Ort wanken infolge eines großen Erdbebens. Dann werden die Archonten trauern (und schreien über ihren) Tod, die Engel werden ihre Menschen betrauern und die Dämonen werden ihre Zeiten beweinen, und ihre Menschen werden klagen und schreien über ihren Tod. Dann wird der Aion anfangen zu zittern, seine Könige werden sich berauschen am Flammenschwert und gegeneinander Krieg führen, so daß

---

[1] Siehe die Kongreßbeiträge von G. MacRae und M. Krause in diesem Band sowie F. T. Fallon 1979.

[2] Eine Zusammenstellung und Klassifikation diesbezüglicher Textstellen hat M. L. Peel 1970 vorgelegt.

[3] Für die Übersetzung des Koptischen bin ich selber verantwortlich, wenn ich auch jedesmal die vorhandenen Übersetzungen zu Hilfe gezogen habe. Die Abkürzung der Schriften sowie deren Seitenzählung folgt J. Robinson (Hg.) 1977. Text und dt. Übersetzung von "Über den Ursprung der Welt": A. Böhlig – P. Labib 1962, 104–108 (nach der dortigen Zählung 173,32–174,11).

die Erde trunken wird vom vergossenen Blut und die Meere aufgewühlt werden durch jene Kriege. Dann wird die Sonne sich verfinstern und der Mond wird sein Licht verlieren."

Alsdann – ich fasse den Fortgang mit meinen Worten zusammen – verändern die Sterne ihren Lauf, legt die Pistis Sophia den Zorn an, um das Böse zu vernichten, kehrt das Licht zu seiner Wurzel zurück und wird die Herrlichkeit des Ungezeugten offenbar (NHC II 127,4–6). So kündigt sich in den mörderischen Kriegen der Könige die endzeitliche Befreiung des Lichtes an.

1.1.2. Noch sehr viel direkter knüpft die Schrift 'Der Gedanke unserer großen Kraft' aus Kodex VI an zeitgeschichtliche Ereignisse des ersten Jahrhunderts n. Chr. an. Der endzeitliche Weltenbrand wird durch Ereignisse in Judäa angekündigt. Es heißt NHC VI,4 43,34–44,10[4]:

"Der Archont kam herab mit den Archonten des Westens nach dem Osten; denn an jenem Ort hat der Logos sich zuerst gezeigt. Dann bebte die Erde und die Städte wurden zerstört. Dann fraßen die Vögel und sättigten sich von den Toten. Die Erde klagte mit der bewohnten Erde und sie wurden verwüstet."

Der jüdische Krieg 66–70 n. Chr. wird als Krieg der Archonten gegen den im Osten erschienenen Logos dramatisiert. Die endzeitliche Erlösung bereitet sich in historischen Ereignissen vor.

1.1.3. Prinzipiell nicht anders denkt der 'Asclepius'-Traktat, der schon früher in einer lateinischen Übersetzung bekannt war und der jetzt in einer älteren koptischen Version in der Nag-Hammadi-Bibliothek gefunden wurde (NHC VI,8 65,8–78,43)[5]. In diesem Traktat hermetischer und gnostischer Tendenz ist eine kleine Apokalypse eingepaßt (70,2–74,17). In der Art anderer ägyptischer Prophezeiungen weissagt sie eine Zeit schrecklicher Fremdherrschaft über Ägypten, auf die das Ende der Welt und eine Apokatastasis folgen werden. Die Unterwerfung Ägyptens unter griechische und römische Fremdherrschaft ist Auftakt eines Endgeschehens – und zwar nicht nur für den Autor des eingelegten Textes, sondern auch für den Verfasser des Gesamttraktates.

1.2. Es ist deutlich, daß dieser Umstand uns zu einer Überprüfung des Verhältnisses von gnostischem und apokalyptischem Denken veranlassen sollte. Selbstverständlich kann man nicht ausschließen, daß apokalyptische Formen mit gnostischen Inhalten aufgefüllt worden sind und Pseudomorphosen bilden. Doch sprechen schon die drei genannten Texte nicht unbedingt hierfür.

Nun ist in einer der in der Nag-Hammadi-Bibliothek gefundenen Schriften – nämlich in der zweiten Apokalypse des Jakobus – ein Ereignis des

---

[4] Text und dt. Übersetzung: M. Krause – P. Labib 1971, 159f.
[5] Engl. Übersetzung bei J. Robinson (Hg.) 1977, 300–307. Kurze Kommentierung mit Verweis auf weitere Literatur bei K.-W. Tröger (Hg.) 1973, 55–57.

ersten Jahrhunderts interpretiert, das auch in jüdischer und frühchristlicher Apokalyptik eine zentrale Rolle einnimmt: die Zerstörung von Stadt und Tempel Jerusalems durch Titus 70 n. Chr. Dieses Ereignis war in jeder Hinsicht von überragender Bedeutung. Es vernichtete Institutionen, in denen sich ethnische Autonomie partiell erhalten hatte, es machte die Bauern endgültig von fremden Grundeigentümern abhängig und es führte zur Beendigung des Tempelkultes. Die Erbitterung im Kampf machte den Zeitgenossen bewußt, daß hier Prinzipielles entschieden wurde[6]. An den Deutungen, die dieses Ereignis in den drei Traditionen gefunden hat, läßt sich gut die unterschiedliche Einbringung des Zeitgeschichtlichen in das Erlösungsdenken studieren. Zugleich können wir die interessante These von R. M. Grant, nach welcher der Impetus gnostischen Denkens aus dem Scheitern apokalyptischer Hoffnungen gekommen sei[7], in unsere Überlegungen mit einbeziehen.

2. Drei Deutungen des Falles von Jerusalem

2.1. Der Fall Jerusalems ist außer in der erwähnten zweiten Apokalypse des Jakobus in der kleinen Apokalypse des Markusevangeliums, in der Johannesapokalypse, in der syrischen Baruch-Apokalypse und im IV. Esrabuch verarbeitet worden[8].

2.1.1. Der älteste Text ist die kleine Apokalypse in Mk 13. In ihr ist eine literarische Vorlage (ein Flugblatt) aufgenommen, das auf die Jahre 38–40 n. Chr. zurückgeht. Damals fürchteten Bewohner Judäas, daß der römische Kaiser Caligula den Jerusalemer Tempel durch Aufstellung einer Statue von sich schänden werde. Erinnerungen an Antiochus IV Epiphanes wurden wach, der 167 v. Chr. den Jerusalemer Kult dem westsemitischen Gott Ba'alšamēm geweiht hatte. Vor allem das Danielbuch und seine Klage über den 'Greuel der Verwüstung' (12,11) hatte die Erinnerung an dieses Ereignis wach gehalten. Und aus diesem Buch stammte auch die Hoffnung, daß nach der Schändung des Tempels und großer Drangsal der Menschensohn mit den Wolken des Himmels kommen werde. Ich zitiere die Verse, die zu dem apokalyptischen Flugblatt gehört haben werden (in der Rekonstruktion von R. Pesch)[9], im Zusammenhang:

Mk 13, 14–17.19f.24–27:

"Wenn ihr aber den 'Greuel der Verwüstung' stehen seht, wo er nicht sollte – wer es liest, merke drauf –, dann sollen die in Judäa ins Gebirge fliehen; wer auf dem Dach ist, soll nicht

---

[6] A. Schlatter 1923; P. Prigent 1969.   [7] R. M. Grant 1966, 34.

[8] Einen Vergleich zwischen jüdischen und christlichen Apokalypsen hinsichtlich des Falles von Jerusalem hat bereits P. M. Bogaert 1977 durchgeführt.

[9] Bei der quellenkritischen Rekonstruktion bin ich insgesamt R. Pesch 1968 gefolgt; das Resultat seiner Rekonstruktion auf S. 209.

herabsteigen, um etwas aus seinem Hause zu holen, und wer auf dem Feld ist, soll nicht zurückkehren, um seinen Mantel zu holen. Wehe aber den Schwangeren und den Stillenden in jenen Tagen... Denn jene Tage werden eine Drangsal sein, wie es sie von Anfang der Schöpfung an nicht gegeben hat. Und wenn der Herr die Tage nicht verkürzt hätte, würde kein Fleisch gerettet werden... Aber in jenen Tagen 'wird die Sonne sich verfinstern und der Mond wird seinen Schein nicht geben', und 'die Sterne werden vom Himmel fallen und die Kräfte in den Himmeln werden erschüttert werden'. Und dann wird man 'den Sohn des Menschen auf den Wolken kommen' sehen mit großer Macht und Herrlichkeit. Und dann wird er die Engel aussenden und die Auserwählten sammeln von den vier Winden her, vom Ende der Erde bis zum Ende des Himmels."

Es ist schwer zu entscheiden, ob dieses Flugblatt jüdischer oder christlicher Provenienz ist[10]. Es ist deshalb so schwer, weil uns aus diesem Zeitraum keine anderen Texte dieser Art erhalten sind und weil auf der anderen Seite zu den späteren jüdischen und christlichen Apokalypsen doch inhaltliche Unterschiede bestehen. So ist die Kürzung der Tage in späteren jüdischen Apokalypsen eine Drohung im Hinblick auf das bevorstehende Gericht (syrBar 20,1 f.; 83,1 f.; äthHen 80,2), während sie hier ausdrücklich begrüßt wird. Auf der anderen Seite fügt sich die Vorstellung, die Parusie des Auferstandenen sei Schlußpunkt einer Serie beobachtbarer Vorgänge, nicht zur dominanten Idee des frühen Christentums: "Niemand kennt Tag und Stunde" (V.32). So bleibt die religionsgeschichtliche Zuordnung des Flugblattes in der Schwebe.

Die Christen der Zeit nach 70 n. Chr. haben in diesem Flugblatt eine Ankündigung der Zerstörung des Tempels erblickt. Sie haben damit das schreckliche Geschehen zu einer Etappe hin zur Parusie gemacht. Kein Gedanke wird auf eine mögliche Wiederherstellung des Tempels verschwendet. Die Zerstörung noch des Heiligsten ist ein Fortschritt zur Erlösung. Ganz ähnlich verbindet auch die Johannesapokalypse mit der Zerstörung Jerusalems die größten Hoffnungen[11]. Im Zusammenhang dieser Deutung erhält das Motiv der Flucht einen anderen Sinn. Anfänglich als die reale Flucht aus der dem Gericht ausgelieferten Stadt gemeint, wird es nun – nach den Ereignissen – zur Aufforderung, sich vom Judentum zu lösen[12]. Die objektive Vernichtung muß durch die subjektive Aufkündigung der tradierten Loyalitäten vollendet werden.

2.1.2. Ich darf hiermit die Aussage der syrischen Baruch-Apokalypse konfrontieren, die am Anfang des 2. Jh. n. Chr. von einem Juden in Palästina verfaßt wurde[13]. Hier wird die Tempelzerstörung mit der babylonischen Eroberung des Jahres 587 v. Chr. identifiziert – eine Idee, aus der die Wiederherstellung des Tempels wie von selbst folgt. Die Zerstörung war nicht total, und sie war vor allem nicht das Werk der Feinde.

---

[10] R. Pesch 1968, 216 f. [11] P. M. Bogaert 1977, 135–141.
[12] R. Pesch 1968, 145–149.
[13] So die Annahmen von A. F. J. Klijn 1976, 107.

syrBar 80,1–3[14]:

"Die Feinde hatten (schon) die Stadt eingeschlossen, da wurden von dem Höchsten Engel ausgesandt. Sie brachen die Befestigung der starken Mauer ab und rissen ihre festen Eisenekken nieder, die sonst nicht hätten eingerissen werden können. Dagegen versteckten sie die heiligen Geräte, damit der Feind sie nicht besudeln könnte. Und als sie das getan, überließen sie dem Feind die abgebrochene Mauer, das ausgeraubte Haus und den verbrannten Tempel und auch das überwundene Volk; denn es war preisgegeben worden, damit die Feinde sich nicht rühmen sollten und sagen: 'Wir haben es so überwunden, daß wir sogar das Haus des Höchsten im Krieg verwüstet haben.'"

So interpretiert deuten die Ereignisse auf eine fällige Revidierung hin. Strikt gesprochen ist das Heiligtum gar nicht zerstört, sondern sind es allein die Mauern. Die Äußerlichkeit verweist auf die Chance endzeitlicher Erneuerung (32,4). Der Verfasser denkt nicht an eine radikale Neuordnung, sondern an eine endzeitliche Reform. Darum finde ich auch den Begriff 'revolutionär', den C. A. Keller auf dieses Verhalten zur Welt appliziert, nicht passend[15]. Die Zerstörung bleibt etwas Äußerliches und wird durch eine verborgene Kontinuität gehörig relativiert. Der Verfasser läßt keinen Zweifel daran, daß gerade in dieser Zeit den tradierten Loyalitäten die Treue gehalten werden muß. Das Volk Israel – der ethnische Verband – besteht trotz allem weiter.

syrBar 85,3[16]:

"(Bei ihren Vätern) sind versammelt jetzt aber die Gerechten, und die Propheten sind entschlafen. Auch wir verließen unser Land, und Zion ist uns weggenommen. Nichts haben wir jetzt mehr, nur den (All)mächtigen noch und sein Gesetz."

Es besteht ein logischer Zusammenhang zwischen der Darstellung der Zerstörung und den praktischen Konsequenzen für die Betroffenen: das Eigentliche, die Tradition konnte nicht vernichtet werden. Allerdings ist mit dieser Idee dem Wunsch nach einer Beschleunigung der Tage die Bremse angelegt. Denn die jetzige Generation muß sich mittels der Gesetzestreue die Hoffnung erst noch verdienen (85,9). Ein leiser Zweifel, daß dies möglich ist, liegt über unserer Schrift[17]. So sehr die Wiederherstellung ersehnt wird, so sehr ist sie doch zugleich auch ein Gerichtstag, der die letzte Gelegenheit zu Reue und Gebeten nimmt (85,12). Die Konstruktion des IVEsr folgt im großen und ganzen einer ähnlichen Logik[18].

---

[14] Dt. Übersetzung aus A. F. J. Klijn 1976, 176 f.

[15] C. A. Keller 1977, 84.

[16] Dt. Übersetzung aus A. F. J. Klijn 1976, 182.

[17] So auch die Beobachtung von J.-É. Ménard 1973, 147.

[18] Auch IV Esr bezieht sich auf die Zerstörung Jerusalems (10,48) und erwartet die Wiederkehr der unsichtbaren Stadt und des verborgenen Landes (7,26). Eine interessante Nuance ist die Idee, daß auch das Gesetz der Väter vernichtet ist (4,23; 14,21). Doch werden daraus keine praktischen Folgen gezogen (siehe 9,37).

2.1.3. Vergleichen wir hiermit einen gnostischen Text: die zweite Apokalypse des Jakobus aus der Nag-Hammadi-Bibliothek. W.-P. Funk, der den Text herausgegeben und kommentiert hat, datiert die Schrift mit Vorbehalten in die erste Hälfte des zweiten Jahrhunderts und denkt an eine Abfassung im judäischen Gebiet[19]. Die Schrift überliefert eine Rede, die Jakobus, der Verwandte von Jesus, in Jerusalem gehalten hat und in der er Jesu Offenbarung an ihn mitteilt. Jakobus gilt in der Schrift als Vermittler der Offenbarung. In einer Rede an seine Richter kündigt er deren Verurteilung an. Das Urteil steht noch aus, aber es wird demnächst vollstreckt werden. So werden die Ereignisse der Steinigung des Jakobus und der Tempelzerstörung miteinander verbunden. Eine solche Verbindung kennt nebenbei auch Euseb, der sie als ein – ansonsten unbekanntes – Zitat aus Josephus überliefert: "Das (sc. die Zerstörung Jerusalems) widerfuhr den Juden als Rache für Jakobus den Gerechten"[20]. Doch ist die Verbindung in unserer Schrift mit einer gnostischen Variante versehen. Der Text lautet folgendermaßen:

NHC V,4 60,1–23[21]:

"und er läßt mich hören das Verstummen eurer Trompeten, eurer Wasserrohrflöten und eurer Harfen für dieses Haus. Der Herr (gemeint ist der Demiurg – HGK), der euch gefangengenommen hat[22], verschließt eure Ohren, damit sie nicht den Klang meiner Rede hören und ihr in euren Herzen aufmerken könntet auf mich, den ihr 'den Gerechten' nennen werdet. Deshalb sage ich euch (vom Herrn): 'Seht, ich habe euch euer Haus gegeben, von dem ihr sagt, Gott habe es geschaffen, und in (dem) der, der darin wohnt, verheißen hat, euch in ihm ein Erbteil (KLHPONOMIA) zu geben. Dieses werde ich niederreißen zu Untergang und Verspottung derer, die in Unwissenheit sind'".

Das Verstummen des Tempelkultes ist nicht Rache für die Hinrichtung des Jakobus durch den jüdischen Hohenpriester Ananus 62 n. Chr. (Josephus Ant XX 197–203), sondern sie ist Folge der in dieser Verurteilung sich aussprechenden Unwissenheit. Die Botschaft des Jakobus war, daß die Verheißungen des Demiurgen schlechte Ratschläge sind (53,14f.), 'tote Hoffnung' (62,18). Ist diesem Demiurgen doch nur eine zeitlich begrenzte Herrschaft zugemessen worden (53,20f.). Das Verstummen des Tempelkultes kündigt an, daß die Frist des Weltenherrschers abläuft. Seine Verheißungen, womit die alttestamentlichen innerweltlichen Hoffnungen gemeint sind[23], erweisen sich als unwirksam.

Der Verfasser unserer Schrift sieht in dem Ereignis die Vernichtung von leeren Verheißungen. Und damit sind zugleich neue Rechtsverhältnisse

---

[19] W.-P. Funk 1976, 209.
[20] Hist. Eccl. II 23,20ff. – siehe W.-P. Funk 1976, 170.
[21] Text und dt. Übersetzung: W.-P. Funk 1976, 42f.
[22] Ich folge der Konjektur von Funk, das überflüssige ⲈⲂⲞⲖ ⲘⲡⲬⲞⲈⲒⲤ von Zeile 7 nach Z. 14 zu versetzen (1976, 169).
[23] So Funk 1976, 132.

gesetzt. Der Verfasser erläutert dies an dem Verwandtschaftsverhältnis von Jakobus und Jesus, das in der Schrift paradigmatisch benutzt wird. Beide gelten als Vettern, die von derselben Mutter großgezogen worden sind (50,16–23)[24]. Die Regeln dieser durch Verwandtschaft gebildeten Beziehung aber werden durch die Offenbarung Jesu an Jakobus außer Kraft gesetzt.

NHC V,4 51,19–22[25]:

"Dein Vater ist nicht mein Vater. Aber mein Vater ist dir zum Vater geworden".

Im Hintergrund steht hier die Antithese von Demiurg und höchstem Gott. Das Erbe des Demiurgen wird auf den Wegen der Verwandtschaft weitergegeben, das des höchsten Gottes erfordert nichts denn Wissen. Auch der Gnostiker – wie schon der frühchristliche Apokalyptiker – fügt der äußeren Zerstörung des Tempelkultes die individuelle Leistung der Verneinung tradierter Gegenseitigkeiten hinzu.

NHC V,4 53,8–19[26]:

"Und sein Erbe (das des Demiurgen – HGK) wird sich als klein herausstellen – (eben) das, dessen er sich gerühmt hat, daß es groß sei. Auch sind seine Gaben keine Wohltaten. Seine Verheißungen sind schlechte Ratschläge. Denn du gehörst nicht zu (den Kindern) seines Erbarmens, sondern er übt Gewalt an (?) dir. Er will uns Unrecht tun. Und er wird herrschen für eine Zeit, die ihm zugemessen wurde".

Auflehnung und Protest spricht aus diesen Worten, wie sie Hans Jonas auch für andere gnostische Motive nachgewiesen hat[27]. Diese Bezeichnung trifft den Sachverhalt sicher genauer als die von C. A. Keller vorgeschlagene der 'introversionistischen' Antwort des Gnostizismus auf die Welt. Überhaupt ist die Übernahme und Anwendung der Kategorien von Bryan Wilson für unsere Thematik nicht unproblematisch[28]. Er hatte sie nämlich aus einem Vergleich christlicher Sekten entwickelt[29]. Hier mögen sie angemessen sein, da christliche Sekten keine anderen expliziten Bedingungen der Mitgliedschaft kennen als die Zustimmung zu Glaubensanschauungen. Aber dies gilt doch nicht für das Verhältnis von apokalyptischen und gnostischen Gruppierungen im ersten Jahrhundert nach Christus. Deren

---

[24] Ich habe den Befund vereinfacht. Das Problem ist durch Funk 1976, 120–122 ausführlich behandelt.

[25] Text und dt. Übersetzung: Funk 1976, 24f.

[26] Text und dt. Übersetzung: Funk 1976, 28f.

[27] H. Jonas 1964, 214–251.

[28] B. Wilson 1975.

[29] B. Wilson 1975, 4 und 18. Genauer gesagt hat er sie aus einem Vergleich religiöser Bewegungen bei unterentwickelten Völkern und christlichen Bewegungen seit der Reformation entwickelt. Nebenbei muß beachtet werden, daß B. Wilson in dem von ihm herausgegebenen Band *"Patterns of Sectarianism"*, London 1967, die gnostische Sekte als einen eigenen Typ neben der "introversionistischen" geführt hat (S. 28f.). Keller kann sich also auf Wilson überhaupt nicht berufen.

Differenzen gehen eben nicht vorrangig entlang inhaltlicher Antworten auf die Welt – wobei diese Unterschiede sicher auch eine Rolle gespielt haben –, sondern sie verlaufen in der Stellungnahme zu den tradierten Loyalitäten. Aus diesem Blickwinkel betrachtet aber ist nicht die Apokalyptik revolutionär zu nennen, wie C. A. Keller es tut, sondern der Gnostizismus.

2.2. R. M. Grant hatte die Ansicht geäußert, daß der Impetus gnostischen Denkens aus dem Scheitern apokalyptischer Hoffnungen gekommen sei. Legen wir die drei besprochenen Versionen des Falles von Jerusalem nebeneinander, dann bestätigen sie ein gutes Stück dieser These. Um es negativ zu formulieren: das Verhältnis dieser Texte kann nicht ausschließlich ideengeschichtlich bestimmt werden. Der Deutungsrahmen partizipiert am Gang der Ereignisse und ist kein feststehendes Schema. Alle drei Texte erheben die Kultvernichtung zum Symptom einer Krise, die die Gesamtheit der überlieferten Sinngebungen und alltäglichen Handlungsnormen erfaßt hatte. Und tatsächlich hatte ja die gesellschaftliche Entwicklung dazu geführt, daß Institutionen segmentärer Solidarität längst desavouiert waren. Die traditionellen Institute der Abarbeitung von Schulden, des agnatischen Erbrechtes, des Loskaufs sind in diesen Jahren längst nicht mehr in Kraft, wiewohl sie doch aufs engste mit den religiösen Normen verbunden waren[30]. Zu den traditionellen Mitteln des Heilserwerbs gehörte neben der Loyalität gegenüber den Vätern und Stammesgenossen sowie der Treue zur Tradition aber auch das Opfer im Tempel. Die Vernichtung des Tempels verstärkte den Zweifel an den tradierten Mitteln des Heilserwerbes insgesamt. Alle drei Versionen reagieren auf eine *Krise der tradierten Mittel*. Gerade auch die Baruch-Apokalypse, die ja diese Krise zu verkleinern beabsichtigt, weist durch dieses Bemühen – durch die sublime Leugnung von Vernichtung und die Beschwörung von Gesetzestreue – auf das gemeinsame Problem dieser Jahre hin. Sicherlich sind zwischen den drei Versionen die neuen Konditionen des Heilserwerbs strittig. Das Problem aber, die Krise der tradierten Mittel, haben sie nicht selbst geschaffen, sondern als ein gesellschaftliches vorgefunden. In diesem Sinne hat die These von Grant gute Gründe auf ihrer Seite. Einschränkend aber muß sofort hinzugefügt werden, daß es keine Krise an sich gibt, es sei denn im Medium ihrer Diagnose. Schon vor dem Fall Jerusalems und unabhängig von diesem haben wir gnostische Zeugnisse für die Kritik tradierter Mittel religiösen Handelns und tradierter Rationalisierungen des Sinnlosen[31]. Als solche Feststellung von Krisen ist die gnostische Kritik von spezifischen historischen Situationen zugleich auch wieder unabhängig.

---

[30] Dies habe ich ausgeführt in H. G. Kippenberg 1978.

[31] Dies ist Thema eines Aufsatzes von mir "Die gesellschaftlichen Bedingungen des Gnostizismus in Vorderasien", der irgendwann in *ANRW* erscheinen soll.

3. Die Umformung frühchristlicher Apokalyptik

3.1. Diese Feststellung bewahrheitet sich gerade auch in dem Verhältnis zur frühchristlichen Apokalyptik, zu dem uns die Nag-Hammadi-Schriften ebenfalls neue Einsichten vermitteln. Vorwegschicken möchte ich eine grobe Kennzeichnung dessen, was frühchristliche Apokalyptik heißen soll. Trotz der neueren Literatur zum Thema scheint mir die Formulierung von Ernst Käsemann immer noch sehr zutreffend: "Die Wiederkunft Jesu als des himmlischen Menschensohnes ist ja die zentrale Hoffnung, welche die ältesten Jünger direkt aus der Ostererfahrung ableiteten, und als solche ihr eigentlicher Osterglaube. So wird das Ostergeschehen auch erst relativ spät auf Jesus selber beschränkt, ursprünglich jedoch als Anbruch der allgemeinen Totenauferweckung verstanden, also *apokalyptisch*, nicht als isolierbares Mirakel gedeutet"[32]. Ich halte diese Kennzeichnung deshalb für treffend, weil sie besser als der häufig gebrauchte Begriff der Naherwartung die Grenzen zur jüdischen Apokalyptik markiert. Denn Naherwartung – darauf hat K. Schubert zu Recht hingewiesen[33] – gibt es auch im Frühjudentum. Der Unterschied liegt in der Idee, daß Jesu Auferstehung einen Prozeß eingeleitet hat, der unweigerlich mit seiner bevorstehenden Ankunft in messianischer Herrlichkeit (der παρουσία im Neuen Testament) enden wird (I Kor 15,20–28)[34]. Idee ist allerdings ein schwacher Begriff für diesen Sachverhalt, denn diese Glaubensanschauung zieht einen hochgradigen Aktivismus nach sich: das innerweltliche Handeln wird mit radikalen Anforderungen der Endzeit konfrontiert.

3.2. Es war Hans Blumenberg, der in einem 1958 erschienenen Aufsatz 'Epochenschwelle und Rezeption'[35] die These entwickelt hat, daß der antike Gnostizismus seine Entstehung der Krise dieses apokalyptischen Aktivismus – von ihm mit Naherwartung bezeichnet – verdanke. Die Apokalyptik habe als Naherwartung nicht einfach ihren zeitlichen Vorbehalt verkürzt, sondern vom Mythos abgelassen "und sich absoluten Forderungen unterstellt, die überhaupt nur unter der Prämisse der äußersten Kurzfristigkeit durchgehalten werden können. Die Enttäuschung führt dann in eine Krise, die entweder in die allegorisierende *Spiritualisierung* der Eschatologie oder in den das Ende verbürgend vorwegnehmenden *Sakramentalismus* ausmündet"[36] – in Gnostizismus also und kirchlichen Sakramentalismus. Wir werden diese Hypothese in unsere Überlegungen mit einbeziehen, wenn wir den Weg der frühchristlichen Apokalyptik in den Schriften von Nag-Hammadi verfolgen.

---

[32] E. Käsemann 1964, 110 (Hervorhebung von mir).
[33] K. Schubert 1964, 1–54.
[34] Zu diesem Begriffsverständnis Oepke 1954, 863.
[35] Blumenberg 1958, 94–120.   [36] *Ibid.*, 112f.

3.2.1. Auch in bezug auf die frühchristliche Apokalyptik gilt, was wir eingangs allgemein festgestellt hatten: daß die glatte Unterscheidung zwischen der apokalyptischen Erwartung eines nahenden Endes der Welt und der gnostischen Entweltlichung in der Gegenwart nicht aufgehen will. Ich darf dies am Philippusevangelium zeigen, das laut M. Krause in der 2. Hälfte des 2. Jh. n. Chr. irgendwo im griechisch-syrischen Sprachgebiet entstanden sein dürfte und der valentinianischen Gnosis nahesteht[37]. In ihm wird die Auferstehung aus einem Vorgang nach dem Tode zu einem Geschehen vor dem Tode.

NHC II,3 73,1–5[38]:

"Welche sagen, daß man zuerst sterben wird und (erst danach) auferstehen wird, irren sich. Wenn man nicht zuerst die Auferstehung empfängt, (noch) während man lebt, und wenn man (dann) stirbt[39], wird man nichts empfangen".

Damit ist aber keinesfalls der Erwartung eines zukünftigen Weltendes abgeschworen. Das zeigt eine Auseinandersetzung des Verfassers mit Auferstehungsleugnern.

NHC II,3 57,11–19[40]:

"Du sagst: 'Das Fleisch wird nicht auferstehen'. Aber sage mir: 'Was wird auferstehen, damit wir dich ehren?'. Du sagst: 'Der Geist ($\pi\nu\epsilon\tilde{\nu}\mu\alpha$) ist im Fleisch und auch dieses Licht ist im Fleisch'. Auch dieses ist ein logos (Wort?), das im Fleisch ist. Denn was immer du sagen wirst, du sagst nichts außerhalb des Fleisches. Es ist nötig, im Fleisch aufzuerstehen, da alles in ihm ist".

Der Verfasser des Philippusevangeliums besteht auf Elementen unrealisierter Eschatologie. Er steht damit innerhalb der Nag-Hammadi-Bibliothek keineswegs allein. So lesen wir im Evangelium der Wahrheit

NHC I,3 37,34–38,4[41]:

"Der Vater nämlich kennt ihrer aller Anfang und Ende. An ihrem Ende nämlich wird er sie fragen, was sie getan haben. Das Ende aber ist das Erkenntnis-Empfangen über das, was verborgen ist. Das aber ist der Vater, von dem der Anfang ausgegangen ist, der, zu dem alle, die von ihm ausgegangen sind, zurückkehren werden".

Es sind tatsächlich nur Beispiele, die ich hier nenne. M. Peel hat das gnostische Schrifttum insgesamt auf eschatologische Vorstellungen hin gemustert und die Endzeit Spekulation sowie die Auferstehungsidee in

---

[37] So M. Krause in W. Foerster (Hg.) Band 2 1971, 93 f.

[38] Text: J.-É. Ménard 1967, 90 (nach seiner Zählung 75,1–5). Dt. Übersetzung: M. Krause in W. Foerster (Hg.) 1971, 113. Eine Besprechung des gnostischen Begriffs der Auferstehung ist durch J.-É. Ménard 1975 erfolgt.

[39] Zur Konstruktion als Eventualis siehe W. Till 1961, §334.

[40] Text: J.-É. Ménard 1967, 58 (nach seiner Zählung 59,11–19). Dt. Übersetzung: M. Krause in W. Foerster (Hg.) Band 2 1971, 99 f.

[41] Text: M. Malinine, H.-Ch. Puech, G. Quispel 1956. Dt. Übersetzung: M. Krause in W. Foerster (Hg.) Band 2 1971, 80.

zahlreichen Texten angetroffen[42]. Die Verwandlung der Auferstehung zu einem gegenwärtigen Vorgang kann deshalb nicht einem systematischen Interesse an Vergegenwärtigung der Eschatologie entsprungen sein. Der Grund muß in etwas anderem liegen.

3.2.2. Er liegt meines Erachtens in der gnostischen Konzeption der Ethik beschlossen. Eines der wichtigsten Resultate des Fundes von Nag-Hammadi ist die Erkenntnis, daß nicht etwa der Libertinismus, sondern die Askese als die älteste und wohl auch vorherrschende gnostische Ethik zu gelten hat. So wenigstens beurteilt K. Rudolph den Befund[43]. Eine asketische Weltentsagung steht jedoch in anderen Zweckrelationen als der Libertinismus. Sehr schön hat H. Jonas den Zusammenhang des letzteren beschrieben: der Immoralismus geht davon aus, daß der Pneumatiker kraft seiner 'Natur' erlöst ist und diese Natur die Unveränderlichkeit einer echten Substanz hat[44]. Dagegen belastet eine Ethik der asketischen Weltentsagung das individuelle Handeln mit der Verantwortung für den Gesamtprozeß der Welt, steuert auf eine Konvergenz von individueller Abschleifung des Daseins und universaler Beendigung der Demiurgenherrschaft zu. Ich darf diese Hypothese an einer Stelle aus der 'Exegese über die Seele' – einer Schrift, über deren Entstehungszeit leider keine Einmütigkeit erzielt wurde[45] – erläutern.

NHC II,6 134,6–15[46]:

"Es ziemt sich aber, daß sich die Seele selbst (wieder) gebiert und wieder wird, wie sie früher war. Die Seele bewegt sich nun selbst. Und sie empfing das göttliche Wesen vom Vater, so daß sie neu wurde, damit man sie wieder an den Ort nimmt, an dem sie zuerst war. Das ist die Auferstehung, welche es gibt von den Toten. Das ist der Loskauf aus der Gefangenschaft. Das ist das Hinaufsteigen zum Himmel. Das ist der Weg hinauf zum Vater".

Im Handeln des Gnostikers wird ein Stück Ende der Demiurgenherrschaft vorweggenommen. Die Hinwendung zu Wissen und Askese ist Teil der Geschichte der Endzeit.

3.2.3. Daß die Auferstehung zu einem gegenwärtigen Phänomen wird, das hat seinen Grund in der gnostischen Konzeption ethischen Handelns. Es ist der Modus individueller Beteiligung am Gesamtprozeß der Erlösung. So schreibt der Verfasser des Rheginusbriefes, der valentinianischen Kreisen entstammen dürfte[47],

---

[42] Siehe auch neben dem Aufsatz M. L. Peel 1970 sein Buch 1974.

[43] K. Rudolph 1977a, 258–264.

[44] H. Jonas 1964, 234 f.

[45] M. Krause denkt an das Ende des 2. Jh. und an valentinianische Herkunft (in Foerster (Hg.) Band 2 1971, 126); der Berliner Arbeitskreis für koptisch-gnostische Schriften entdeckt in der Schrift eine der ältesten Formen des gnostischen Mythos (K. W. Tröger [Hg.] 1973, 36).

[46] Text und dt. Übersetzung: M. Krause – P. Labib 1971, 80 f.

[47] So M. L. Peel 1974, 9.

NHC I,4 49,25–35[48]:

"Wenn du die Auferstehung hast und dennoch weiterlebst, als ob du sterben würdest...,
warum verwerfe ich dann deine Ungeübtheit? Es ziemt sich für einen jeden, sich auf
vielfältige Weise zu üben, und er soll erlöst werden von diesem Element, damit er nicht
irregeführt werde, sondern sich selbst wieder empfange als den, der er zuerst war".

Die Umgestaltung frühchristlicher Apokalyptik in gnostischen Schriften
ist durch den Begriff von Vergegenwärtigung der Eschatologie nicht
zureichend erfaßt. Auch in diesen Texten wird ein kosmischer Gesamtprozeß vorausgesetzt. Das treibende Motiv liegt eher in der Idee, das Handeln
sei Mittel, die Destruktion des Kosmos voranzutreiben. Dagegen hat ja das
frühe Christentum die Vorstellung ausgeprägt, man müsse in den weltlichen Ordnungen leben als lebe man nicht in ihnen, da den Anforderungen
der Endzeit allein durch Wachsamkeit Rechnung getragen werden kann.
So lasten die weltlichen Ordnungen als höchst reale auf dem Christen,
während sie dem Gnostiker zur Illusion geworden sind. Eher ist die Welt
eine Illusion als die Auferstehung, heißt es im Brief an Rheginus (NHC I,4
48,15f.). Und daran schließt sich eine Ausführung an, die die gnostische
Desillusionierung der Welt zeitgeschichtlich demonstriert.

NHC I,4 48,21–28[49]:

"Diejenigen, die leben, werden sterben. Wieso leben sie in einer Illusion? Die Reichen sind
arm geworden, und die Könige wurden gestürzt, alles pflegt sich zu wandeln. Die Welt ist
eine Illusion".

Eine solche Haltung ist – wie gesagt – von spezifischen Situationen
unabhängig. Sie taugt für verschiedene historische Lagen und sie kann auch
in Kritik an gegenteilige Rationalisierungen übergehen. Die Umgestaltung
der frühchristlichen Apokalyptik gehört in diesen Zusammenhang gnostischer Kritik. Diese hätte sich schwerlich so nachhaltig Gehör verschaffen
können, wenn nicht im Frühchristentum eklatante Aporien entstanden
wären. Es scheint mir nicht möglich, die Entstehung antiken gnostischen
Denkens insgesamt aus dem Problem der Parusieverzögerung abzuleiten.
Andererseits aber ist schwerlich von der Hand zu weisen, daß die frühchristliche Ethik des Aufbruchs aus den traditionellen Verhältnissen sich im
Laufe der Jahre in Widersprüche ohnegleichen verwickelt hat. Haustafeln
ermahnten die Christen dazu, der Obrigkeit untertan zu sein sowie die
Unterordnung als Sklaven und Frauen willig zu akzeptieren – dies alles im
Vertrauen auf die Vorläufigkeit der Verhältnisse[50]. Da galt denn das
Sprichwort: Nichts ist so dauerhaft wie das Provisorium. Daß hiergegen

---

[48] Text und dt. Übersetzung: M. L. Peel 1974, 203 und 44.
[49] Text und dt. Übersetzung: M. L. Peel 1974, 202 und 43.
[50] Die neutestamentlichen Aufforderungen zur Unterordnung hat Delling 1969, 43–46
zusammengestellt.

polemisiert wurde, ist selbstverständlich. Daß Gnostiker eine ansprechende Lösung dieses Dilemmas anboten, darin wird man H. Blumenberg ganz sicher folgen können. Sie gaben dem weltlichen Handeln den Zweck der Unterbrechung der kosmischen Reproduktion, den Zweck des Auszugs aus der Welt[50a].

4. Soziologische Verortung

4.1. Unser Einblick in die sozialen Zusammenhänge des antiken Gnostizismus ist noch immer recht unbefriedigend. Sicher ist positiv zu verzeichnen, daß der 1966 auf dem Messina-Kongreß geäußerte Wunsch nach einer Vertiefung der Kenntnisse der soziologischen Aspekte des Gnostizismus zum Teil in Erfüllung gegangen ist. Wir wissen heutzutage mehr über die soziale Zusammensetzung der gnostischen Gemeinden (Angehörige der mittleren und unteren Schichten), über gesellschaftskritische Intentionen in gnostischen Texten und über den Ursprung gnostischen Denkens im Laienintellektualismus hellenistischer Städte. Und doch ist die bislang erworbene Kenntnis, die K. Rudolph vor kurzem noch einmal gut zusammengestellt hat[51], noch unbefriedigend. Sie ist es deshalb, weil keines der genannten Merkmale dem Gnostizismus allein eignet, sondern auch den konkurrierenden Bewegungen der jüdischen Apokalyptik und dem Frühchristentum. J. J. Collins verortete die jüdische Apokalyptik unter den maśkîlîm, den Weisen von Dan 11,33.35 – herrschaftskritischen Intellektuellen jüdischer Herkunft, die ihre Anhänger bei Mittel- und Unterschichten fanden[52]. Und die Ansätze zu einer Soziologie des Frühchristentums, die wir vor allem G. Theißen zu danken haben, laufen auf nichts prinzipiell anderes hinaus: eine städtische Bewegung, deren Wortführer gebildeter, deren Anhänger einfacher Herkunft waren und die ebenfalls Distanz zur politischen Ordnung hielt[53]. Man muß schon die Themen einer Soziologie des Gnostizismus beträchtlich erweitern, wie es H. A. Green sehr richtig vorschlägt, um die Unterschiede auch zu den konkurrierenden Bewegungen in die soziologische Analyse einzubeziehen[54]. Die Prozesse von Institutionalisierung und interner Stratifikation sind in dieser Hinsicht erfolgversprechend[55].

[50a] Das kritische Verhältnis der Gnostiker zur entstehenden Orthodoxie hat E. Pagels 1979 zum Angelpunkt der Interpretation der Nag-Hammadi-Schriften gemacht.

[51] K. Rudolph 1977b.

[52] J. J. Collins 1975 und 1977, 212f.

[53] G. Theissen 1973, insbesondere S. 266f. Ob die Jesusbewegung dagegen nicht vielleicht eindeutig in untersten gesellschaftlichen Gruppen von Armen und Hungernden anzusiedeln ist, fragt zu Recht W. Stegemann 1979. Dem von W. A. Meeks (Hg.) 1979 herausgegebenen Band verdanken wir eine wesentliche Erweiterung der für eine Soziologie des Urchristentums relevanten Themen.

[54] H. A. Green 1977.   [55] *Ibid.*, 171 und 176.

4.1.1. Dennoch darf man meines Erachtens bei einer Erweiterung der soziologischen Themen nicht stehenbleiben. Die Art und Weise, wie die soziologische Fragestellung seit dem Messina-Kongreß angegangen wurde, ist von einem auffälligen Widerspruch gekennzeichnet. Man adoptierte nämlich einen Gesellschaftsbegriff und eine Methode, die von vorneherein eine Soziologie von Symbolsystemen erschwerte. Das mag ein Zitat aus einem Aufsatz von G. Theißen belegen. Dort heißt es von mythischen Symbolen: "Anders als poetische Bilder stellen sie *keine soziale Realität* dar, die dann als Ganzes für etwas anderes transparent werden soll, sie thematisieren sehr viel direkter dies 'andere': das Handeln von Göttern, Engeln und Dämonen. Sie benutzen dazu freilich Bilder aus dem vertrauten sozialen Leben: Gott wird als König vorgestellt, der Engel als sein Hofstaat"[56]. Hält man – wie es Theißen hier tut – an einem universalen Kriterium von sozialer Realität fest und definiert diese Realität als beobachtbare empirische Beziehungen von Menschen untereinander, dann wandert alles das, was dem Beobachter nicht real erscheint, ab ins Reich der Symbole. Je mehr der Historiker Gesellschaft auf das zu Beobachtende und Prüfende beschränkt, um so mächtiger und chaotischer wird dieses himmlische Reich.

4.1.2. Auffällig nenne ich diese Adoption des soziologischen "Positivismus" deshalb, weil sie in hohem Grade einseitig war. Aus der ausgebreiteten ethnologisch-philosophischen Literatur über die symbolische Vermittlung von sozialen Beziehungen und kollektiven Erfahrungen hätte man ganz andere Ansätze in die Untersuchung einbringen können. So ist ein produktives Experimentieren auf diesem Gebiet leider ausgeblieben. Ich möchte mir die Gelegenheit hierzu nicht entgehen lassen und versuchen, die Differenzen zwischen gnostischer, jüdischer und frühchristlicher Apokalyptik zu soziologisieren.

4.2. Ich nehme meinen Ausgang bei A. MacIntyre. Er hat dargelegt, daß jede gesellschaftliche Handlung einer Beschreibung durch die Handelnden bedarf, anders wäre sie lediglich eine physische Bewegung. Glaubensanschauungen und Handlungen stehen nicht in einer irgendwie gearteten Kausalitätsbeziehung, da diese äußerlich wäre, sondern sie sind innerlich miteinander verbunden. Sie können nicht als separate 'Dinge' angesehen werden, sondern stehen in einem Verhältnis der Logik zueinander. "Weil Handlungen Glaubensanschauungen ausdrücken, weil Handlungen ein Vehikel unserer Glaubensanschauungen sind, können sie als konsistent oder inkonsistent mit Glaubensanschauungen, zu denen man sich bekennt, beschrieben werden... Das Verhältnis von belief zu action ist nicht äußer-

---

[56] G. Theissen 1975, Zitat S. 294 (Hervorhebung von mir).

lich und kontingent, sondern innerlich und konzeptionell"[57]. Unter solcher Voraussetzung verändert sich die Aufgabe einer soziologischen Erklärung. Eine kausale Erklärung aus Antezedentien würde den Gegenstand aus der Klasse der Handlungen in die Klasse der physischen Bewegungen überführen[58]. Daher schlägt MacIntyre eine andere Strategie vor. "Aus einer Reihe verschiedener Argumentationsstränge ist daher hervorgegangen, daß die Suche nach Antezedentien einer Handlung nicht die Suche nach einer invarianten kausalen Verbindung ist, sondern die Suche nach vorhandenen Alternativen und die Frage, warum der Handelnde eher die eine als die andere aktualisiert hat... Die Erklärung einer Wahl zwischen Alternativen erfordert eine Klarlegung, was das Kriterium des Handelnden war und warum er eher von dem einen als dem anderen Kriterium Gebrauch machte und eine Erklärung, warum der Gebrauch dieses Kriteriums denen rational erschien, die es in Anspruch genommen haben"[59].

4.2.1. Man wird den von mir behandelten Gegenstand der gnostischen Apokalyptik nicht als besonders zentral oder spezifisch für den antiken Gnostizismus insgesamt betrachten können. Das aber hat zugleich den Vorteil, daß die Traditionsformationen auch nicht so überaus kunstvoll getrennt worden sind, wie dies etwa bei den Gottesvorstellungen geschehen ist. So lassen sich die prägenden Gewalten, die auf sie eingewirkt haben, umstandsloser an den Oberflächen ablesen.

4.2.2. Die Frageweise von MacIntyre ist den Eigenschaften unseres Gegenstandes in besonderer Weise zugetan. Es ist schon erstaunlich, wie in einer vollkommen unbedeutenden Randprovinz des römischen Reiches innerhalb kurzer Zeit radikal neue Grundtypen menschlichen Handelns in ihrer Logik ausbuchstabiert worden sind. Die Konsistenz, die wir hier beobachten, war sicher von der Konkurrenzsituation diktiert, in der die drei Entwürfe gestanden haben. Zugleich treffen wir in dieser Konsistenz aber auch auf Interessen an Alternativen, die ihrerseits auf unterschiedliche Entscheidungskriterien der damals Lebenden zurückweisen. Zur Alternative standen:

Endzeitvorstellung		*ethische Forderung*
die Erwartung des Anbruchs eines neuen Äons, der die Fremdherrschaft von Israel nimmt	&	die unbeirrbare Treue zum Gesetz des Mose
die Erwartung, daß die Auferstehung Jesu Christi das Kommen des Gottesreiches eingeleitet hat	&	eine innerweltliche Askese (man verbleibt in den innerweltlichen Institutionen und trägt dem Liebespostulat des Gottesreiches Rechnung)
die Erwartung der Vernichtung des Weltherrschers und seiner Schöpfung	&	eine weltflüchtige Askese.

---

[57] A. MacIntyre 1967, Zitat auf S. 52 (Übersetzung von mir).
[58] *Ibid.*, 57.   [59] *Ibid.*, 61 (Übersetzung von mir).

Als vierten im Bunde muß man selbstverständlich die politischen Positionen, wie sie von Sikariern und Zeloten vertreten wurden, hinzudenken. Sie sahen im militärisch-politischen Handeln ein Mittel, dem Willen Gottes in direkter Aktion Geltung zu verschaffen. Demgegenüber gehen die religiösen Entwürfe davon aus, daß die tradierten Mittel des Handelns wie Opfer, brüderliche Solidarität der Israeliten, Anerkennung des Eigentums Jahwes am Land durch kein politisches Handeln mehr gerettet werden können. Daher die allen drei gemeinsame Irrationalisierung der vorgefundenen Verhältnisse. Der Alltag hat sich von den bewährten Mitteln der Erlangung göttlichen Wohlgefallens frei gemacht, Normen der dämonischen Gegenwelt beherrschen ihn.

4.3. Wenn wir unseren Vergleich ausdehnen auf die drei Stellungnahmen zum Fall Jerusalems, dann entpuppt sich das scheinbar rein Theologische als die *Diagnose einer Krise*, in die das jüdische Religionsvolk durch die hellenistische und römische Fremdherrschaft geraten war. Das Ereignis wird verstanden als

– eine zeitweilige Unterbrechung des Kultes und befristete Zerstörung der Stadt;
– das Zeichen der nahenden Vernichtung der weltlichen Ordnungen;
– das Zeichen einer falschen Hoffnung.

Die Konsistenz dieser Stellungnahmen ist sicher auch durch das rationalistische Bedürfnis des Intellektualismus geprägt, das die Konzeption der 'Welt' als eines 'Sinn'-Problems vollzieht[60]. Entscheidender aber ist, daß in die Diagnosen entgegengesetzte gesellschaftliche Optionen eingegangen sind. Die Wahl der einen oder anderen Version ist nämlich zugleich auch eine *Entscheidung* in den gesellschaftlichen Beziehungen:

– zur unbeirrten Loyalität zu den Traditionen der Väter;
– zum Bruch mit diesen Loyalitäten;
– zur Verneinung welterhaltender Institutionen.

Die Frageweise von MacIntyre bringt so recht gut ans Licht, welche gesellschaftlichen Entscheidungen mit den symbolischen Differenzen integral verbunden waren. Sie haben die prägenden Gewalten gebildet, die wir an den Umformungen der Apokalyptik abgelesen haben.

4.4. Ich möchte zum Schluß noch feststellen, daß das soziologisch Beachtliche keineswegs allein in der Rückkoppelung dieser apokalyptischen Entwürfe auf gesellschaftliche Entscheidungen liegt. Nicht minder bedeutsam ist, daß von Beginn an die Diagnosen sich von der historischen Situation gelöst haben – aus einem Mittel zum Zweck an sich wurden. Damit wurde ihnen der Status einer eigenständigen Lebensform vermittelt.

---

[60] M. Weber 1972, 307 f. Die wachsende Bedeutung Webers für eine Religionssoziologie des antiken Judentums zeigt sich in dem von W. Schluchter (Hg.) 1981 herausgegebenen Band sowie in einer 1979 erschienenen Studie von C. Colpe.

Ethische Religiosität unterstellte alles menschliche Handeln, nicht allein das einer spezifischen Situation, transzendenten Zwecken.

Bibliographie

Blumenberg, H. 1958: "Epochenschwelle und Rezeption", in: *PhR* 6 (1958) 94–120.

Bogaert, P. M. 1977: "La ruine de Jerusalem et les apocalypses juives après 70", in: L. Monloubou (Hg.) 1977, 123–141.

Böhlig, A. – Labib, P. 1962: *Die koptisch-gnostische Schrift ohne Titel aus Codex II von Nag Hammadi im Koptischen Museum zu Alt-Kairo*, Berlin 1962.

Collins, J. J. 1975: "Jewish Apocalyptic against its Hellenistic Near Eastern Environment", in: *BASOR* 220 (1975) 27–36.

– 1977: *The Apocalyptic Vision of the Book of Daniel*, Missoula, Mont. 1977.

– (Hg.) 1979: *Apocalypse: The Morphology of a Genre (Semeia* 14), Missoula, Mont. 1979.

Colpe, C. 1979: "Die gnostische Anthropologie zwischen Intellektualismus und Volkstümlichkeit", in: P. Nagel (Hg.), *Studien zum Menschenbild in Gnosis und Manichäismus*, Halle 1979, 31–43.

Delling, G. 1969: Artikel ὑποτάσσω in: *ThWNT* 8 (1969) 40–47.

Fallon, F. T. 1979: "The Gnostic Apocalypses", in: J. J. Collins (Hg.) 1979, 123–158.

Foerster, W. (Hg.) 1971: *Die Gnosis*. Band 2. Koptische und Mandäische Quellen, Zürich (BAW.AC) 1971.

Funk, W.-P. 1976: *Die zweite Apokalypse des Jakobus aus Nag-Hammadi-Codex V* (TU 119), Berlin 1976.

Grant, R. M. 1966: *Gnosticism and Early Christianity*, 2. ed. New York 1966.

Green, H. A. 1977: "Suggested Sociological Themes in the Study of Gnosticism", in: *VigChr* 31 (1977) 169–180.

Jonas, H. 1964: *Gnosis und spätantiker Geist*. 1. Teil. Die mythologische Gnosis, 3. Aufl. Göttingen 1964.

Käsemann, E. 1964: "Zum Thema der urchristlichen Apokalyptik", in: ders., *Exegetische Versuche und Besinnungen*, Göttingen 1964, 105–131.

Keller, C. A. 1977: "Das Problem des Bösen in Apokalyptik und Gnostik", in: M. Krause (Hg.) 1977, 70–90.

Kippenberg, H. G. 1978: *Religion und Klassenbildung im antiken Judäa* (StUNT 14), Göttingen 1978.

– im Erscheinen: "Die gesellschaftlichen Bedingungen des Gnostizismus in Vorderasien", in: *ANRW*, im Erscheinen.

Klijn, A. J. F. 1976: "Die syrische Baruch-Apokalypse", in: *JSHRZ* Band V, Gütersloh 1976, 103–191.

Krause, M. 1971: Koptische Quellen aus Nag Hammadi. Eingeleitet, übersetzt und erläutert von M. Krause, in: W. Foerster (Hg.) 1971, 7–170.

– (Hg.) 1975: *Essays on the Nag-Hammadi-Texts* (NHS III), Leiden 1975.

– (Hg.) 1977: *Gnosis and Gnosticism* (NHS VIII), Leiden 1977.

Krause, M. – Labib, P. 1971: *Gnostische und hermetische Schriften aus Codex II und Codex VI*, Glückstadt 1971.

MacIntyre, A. 1967: "A Mistake about Causality in Social Science", in: P. Laslett and W. Runciman (Hg.), *Philosophy, Politics and Society* 2, Oxford 1967, 48–70.

Malinine, M., Puech, H.-Ch., Quispel, G. (Hg.) 1956: *Evangelium Veritatis. Codex Jung*, Zürich 1956.

Meeks, W. (Hg.) 1979: *Zur Soziologie des Urchristentums*, München 1979.

Ménard, J.-É. 1967: *L'Évangile selon Philippe*, Strasbourg 1967.

– 1973: "Littérature apocalyptique juive et littérature gnostique", in: ders. (Hg.), *Exégèse biblique et judaisme*, Strasbourg 1973, 146–169.

– 1975: "La notion de 'résurrection' dans l'épître à Rhèginos", in: M. Krause (Hg.) 1975, 110–124.

Monloubou, L. (Hg.) 1977: *Apocalypses et Théologie de l'Espérance* (LeDiv 95), Paris 1977.

Oepke, A. 1954: Artikel παρουσία in: *ThWNT* 5 (1954) 856–869.

Pagels, E. 1979: *The Gnostic Gospels,* New York 1979.

Pesch, R. 1968: *Naherwartungen.* Tradition und Redaktion in Mk 13, Düsseldorf 1968.

Peel, M. L. 1970: "Gnostic Eschatology and the New Testament", in: *NT* 12 (1970) 141–165.

– 1974: *Gnosis und Auferstehung.* Der Brief an Rheginus von Nag Hammadi, Neukirchen 1974 (zuerst im Englischen erschienen, London 1969).

Prigent, P. 1969: *La fin de Jérusalem,* Neuchâtel 1969.

Robinson, J. (Hg.) 1977: *The Nag Hammadi Library in English,* Leiden 1977.

Rudolph, K. 1977a: *Die Gnosis.* Wesen und Geschichte einer spätantiken Religion, Göttingen 1977.

– 1977b: "Das Problem einer Soziologie und 'sozialen Verortung' der Gnosis", in: *Kairos* 19 (1977) 35–44.

Schlatter, A. 1923: *Der Bericht über das Ende Jerusalems* (BFChTh 28:1), Gütersloh 1923.

Schluchter, W. (Hg.) 1981: *Max Webers Studie über das antike Judentum,* Frankfurt 1981.

Schubert, K. 1964: "Die Entwicklung der eschatologischen Naherwartung im Judentum", in: ders. (Hg.), *Vom Messias zum Christus,* Wien 1964, 1–54.

Stegemann, W. 1979: "Wanderradikalismus im Urchristentum?", in: W. Schottroff/W.Stegemann (Hg.), *Der Gott der kleinen Leute,* Band 2, München 1979, 94–120.

Theissen, G. 1973: "Wanderradikalismus. Literatursoziologische Aspekte der Überlieferung von Worten Jesu im Urchristentum", in: *ZThK* 70 (1973) 245–271; jetzt auch in Theissen 1979, 79–105.

– 1975: "Die soziologische Auswertung religiöser Überlieferungen", in: *Kairos* 17 (1975) 284–299; jetzt auch in Theissen 1979, 35–54.

– 1979: *Studien zur Soziologie des Urchristentums* (WUNT 19), Tübingen 1979.

Till, W. 1961: *Koptische Dialektgrammatik,* München 1961.

Tröger, K. W. (Hg.) 1973: *Gnosis und Neues Testament,* Berlin 1973.

Weber, M. 1972: *Wirtschaft und Gesellschaft,* 5. Aufl. Tübingen 1972.

Wilson, B. R. 1975: *Magic and Millennium,* Herts 1975.

Conclusion and Evaluation
Zusammenfassung und Auswertung
Bilan et perspectives

"Apokalyptik in der Diskussion"
Kurt Rudolph

1. Sinn und Zweck internationaler Colloquia

Sinn und Zweck internationaler Colloquia über gewichtige Forschungs-
themen bestehen grundsätzlich in dem, was man als "Standortbestim-
mung" bezeichnen kann, in die die vergangenen und gegenwärtigen
Trends einfließen und aus der die zukünftigen Aufgaben sichtbar gemacht
werden sollen. Bloßes schriftliches Publizieren kann auf die Dauer zum
"Aneinander-vorbei-schreiben" führen, mündliche Diskussionen in lebendiger Rede und Gegenrede dienen dagegen nicht nur dem persönlichen
Austausch (mit dem nicht zu unterschätzenden gegenseitigen Kennenlernen in der internationalen Republik der Gelehrten), sondern der Erarbei-
tung gemeinsamer Positionen und damit ohne Zweifel der Anregung für
die weitere Forschung[1].

Das was man gemeinhin als Apokalyptik (Apk) bezeichnet, hat in den
letzten Jahrzehnten einen ähnlichen Stellenwert erhalten wie Gnosis und
Gnostizismus. (Die Sachlage ist tatsächlich ähnlich, und historische und
literarische Verbindungen nicht zu bestreiten.) Publikationen und Konfe-
renzen versuchen einen Querschnitt durch die Forschungslage zu gewinnen
und die Trends entweder zu beschreiben oder – bewußt oder unbewußt –
aktiv zu bestimmen. So ist das Ziel unseres Kolloquiums über Apk in
dreifacher Weise angegeben worden: Untersuchung der gegenwärtigen
Forschungslage, Herausstellung neuer Gedanken und Methoden, Stimulie-
rung der weiteren Arbeit (Programmheft S. 5). Durch eine einsichtige und

---

[1] Bedauerlicherweise war der Verfasser selbst nicht in der Lage, der ehrenvollen Einladung
des Organisationskomitees und der Königlich-Schwedischen Akademie der Literatur,
Geschichte und Altertumskunde zu folgen und die Schlußdiskussion persönlich zu leiten, so
daß er nur die schriftlichen Vorträge zur Verfügung hatte, nicht die Diskussionen und
Aussprachen. Gegenüber den auf dem Kongreß gehaltenen Referaten, die mir als Papers
vorlagen, haben eine Reihe Autoren die Druckfassungen erheblich erweitert oder verändert;
ich habe versucht, auch diesem Prozeß der Weiterarbeit gerecht zu werden, ohne auf
Vollständigkeit Wert zu legen.
Abgekürzt werden: Apk = Apokalyptik; apk = apokalyptisch; Apkse = Apokalypse (außer
bei Buchtiteln, wo dafür Apk verwendet wird).

übersichtliche Gliederung wurden vom Organisationskomitee bereits die
Weichen für die möglichst effektive Erreichung der gesteckten Ziele
gestellt: die Vorstellungswelt der Apk, die Literaturgattung, Soziologie
und "Sitz im Leben", Funktion und historischer Kontext. Die Einschränkung auf die antike Mittelmeerwelt und den vorislamischen Nahen Osten
war sicherlich mehr einem pragmatischen Bedürfnis nach Begrenzung
entsprungen als einer grundsätzlichen Abgrenzung oder Ausklammerung
gleichberechtigter, gleichgewichtiger apk Sachverhalte in den übrigen
geographisch-kulturellen Provinzen der Religionsgeschichte bis in die
Gegenwart (der Islam etwa wäre als Fortbildung biblischer Tradition
ebenso einzubeziehen gewesen wie die indisch-fernöstlichen Räume). Das
Material, soweit es als apk im einen oder anderen Falle zu thematisieren ist,
wurde in den 33 vorliegenden Referaten zwar recht ungleich vorgeführt
und interpretiert, aber durchaus entsprechend dem Gewicht der Bedeutung
in der Forschungs- und Traditionsgeschichte (hier im Sinne der die vorder-
orientalisch-europäische bzw. jüdisch-christliche Religionsgeschichte bis
heute prägenden Überlieferungs- und Ideenkomplexe). Der at-lich-jüdi-
schen Apk galten allein 11 Beiträge, der frühchristlichen und gnostischen
Apk 7, den griechisch-römischen und hellenistischen relevanten Quellen 6,
den altägyptischen 2 (bzw. 3), den iranischen 4 und für Mesopotamien nur
einer. Ein Fazit aus dem Reichtum des Vorgetragenen zu ziehen, noch dazu
wenn man nach der Erfüllung der angeführten Zielstellung fragt, ist
natürlich nicht leicht und nicht frei von subjektiven Interessen und Ein-
schätzungen. Versuchen wir es trotzdem!

2. Der Stand der Forschung

Zum Stand der Forschung, wie er sich in den Beiträgen widerspiegelt,
lassen sich, neben den auf das Spezifikum konzentrierten Ausführungen,
einige übergreifende Sachkomplexe feststellen, die von generellem Interesse sind. Dazu gehört in erster Linie die leidige, aber unumgehbare
Definitionsfrage. Kaum einer der Beiträger hat sich darum gedrückt, dem
bloßen Vorverständnis von Apk zu folgen, sondern sich Gedanken über
einen mehr oder weniger festen Rahmen, unter dem man Apk, apk oder
Apkse verstehen kann, gemacht, indem verschiedene "Merkmale" zu
einem heuristischen Beschreibungsmuster verbunden wurden. Wir möchten darauf zuerst eingehen, weil von dieser Fragestellung ohne Zweifel
entscheidende Wege für die Erfassung von Apk und apk Sachverhalten
gebahnt werden. Die am Schluß unternommenen Definitionsversuche
(offenbar im Anklang an die auf dem Gnosiskongreß 1966 in Messina
vorgelegte Beschreibung von Gnosis und Gnostizismus) sind im vorliegenden Band nicht mit aufgenommen worden, müssen also beiseite bleiben.

2.1. Aus T. Olssons Ausführungen ist zu lernen, daß am Beginn der neueren Apk-Forschung der Schleiermacher-Schüler und Erweckungstheologe Friedrich Lücke (1787–1855) steht, der in seiner Einleitung in die Offenbarung Johannes und in die gesamte apk Literatur (1832) die Apk als "Endzeitprophetie" bestimmte, ein Wesenszug, der bis heute als herausragendster immer wieder genannt wird. Er ist wie die meisten weiteren Kennzeichnungen am Inhalt der apk Texte orientiert. Wir finden so: visionäre "Geschichtsschau" der Endzeit (Widengren), Enthüllung über den Fortgang der Weltgeschichte auf ein nicht mehr fernes Ende hin (J. Assmann), überweltliche Botschaft über die Gesamtheit der Welt, bes. ihre Zukunft (W. Burkert), Zukunftserforschung (K. Koch). Hervorgehoben wird ferner der esoterische und visionäre Charakter des Verkündeten, die Rolle von Weltalterlehren (bes. von S. Hartman) und eschatologische Themen. Das Verhältnis zur Eschatologie ("Endzeitlehre") ist dabei strittig, eine strenge Trennung wird verschiedentlich gefordert (J. Carmignac, H. Stegemann, H. Cancik), obwohl praktisch (textlich!) schwer durchführbar, so daß man M. Philonenko zustimmen muß, wenn er sagt, daß eine Eschatologie ohne Apk möglich ist, aber nicht umgekehrt. Apk ist eine bes. Art eschatologischen Denkens.

Recht kritisch äußert sich T. Olsson zur terminologischen Fragestellung, da die Bezeichnung Apk ein, mit Wittgenstein zu sprechen, typischer "umbrella term" für ein *mixtum compositum* sei, von dem sich die Forschung bisher durch Trugschlüsse habe blenden lassen[2]. Strenggenommen sei "Apk" kein eigenständiges Gebiet von Religion, sondern Teil verschiedener Überlieferungen (welcher ist das nicht?). Daher sei es besser zu unterscheiden: Apk ("apocalypticism") als relativ geschlossenes Gesamtsystem von "apk Ideen", die auch außerhalb von Apk anzutreffen sind, und "Apksen" als literarischer Typ und Ausdruck von Apk. Auf diese Weise würde man dem universalen, aber immer kontextabhängigem Phänomen von Apk mehr gerecht (O. zieht daher auch aztekische Beispiele heran). Charakteristisch sei ihre Beziehung zu einer "offenbarten Weltschau" (revelatory worldview), die auf dem Glauben an eine Verbindung von Mensch und Überwelt basiert und göttliche Geheimnisse oder Pläne für Vergangenheit, Gegenwart und Zukunft dieser Welt vermittelt. Ihre Aktualisierung in Krisenzeiten macht es möglich, sie vielfältig (auch außerhalb von Apk als "apk Ideen") anzutreffen, aber immer bezogen auf einen

---

[2] Zur Forschungslage vgl. auch den Bericht von J. Barr 1975, der u. a. auch den Unterschied zwischen englischer und deutscher Apk-Forschung herausstellt (31 ff.): ist erstere ohne rechtes theoretisches Programm mehr an der Rekonstruktion, Emendation und den Lehren orientiert mit recht rationalistischen, aber auch apologetischen Zügen, so die letztere mit leitenden Gesichtspunkten (G. von Rad, K. Koch), aber auch mit theologischen Implikationen, die zu "obskuren und abstrusen Behauptungen" (W. Pannenberg, J. Moltmann) führten.

festen Kontext oder Inhalt, der eine generelle Bestimmung eben ausschließe. Bei aller Berechtigung dieser Argumente bleibt es doch die Aufgabe, einen *terminus technicus* mit gültigem Anwendungsbereich zu schaffen, der es erlaubt, die Kontinuität der Forschung zu wahren ohne sie einzuengen und konturenlos zu machen. Praktisch verwendet O. auch den Begriff so: er ist das Band, der die drei von ihm unterschiedenen Formen trotz Differenzen zusammenhält (eben als "Schirmbegriff"). Auch hier gilt, wie in bezug auf die Eschatologie: Apk ist eine spezielle Art "offenbarter Weltanschauung" und diese Spezialität gilt es herauszuarbeiten.

Nun ist es stets sinnvoll, sich die Wortgeschichte selbst vor Augen zu führen, wie es M. Smith recht gründlich wenigstens für die jüdischchristliche Gräzität getan hat. Danach ist der Titel "Apk" nicht vor der 2. Hälfte des 1. Jh. greifbar und in den sog. Apksen selbst nur selten anzutreffen (in der Apk Joh nur im Präskript). Für Paulus und seine Schule ist der Begriff im herkömmlichen Sinn "Offenbarung, Vision, Enthüllung" ohne Beziehung auf literarische Zeugnisse. Erst im 2. Jh. (dem Zeitalter gesteigerter Produktion solcher Werke) erfolgt die spezielle Anwendung auf "Offenbarungstexte", was sich in der handschriftlichen Überlieferung fortsetzt und zu den Eintragungen in die ältere Überlieferung führt; in dieser Tradition steht letztlich auch die neuzeitliche Forschung, die in zunehmendem Maße der Literaturgattung selbst ihre Aufmerksamkeit zuwandte.

2.2. Diese der äußeren Form, dem literarischen Genre, gewidmeten Untersuchungen machen sich auch in unserem Symposion sehr stark geltend. Radikale Stimmen möchten vom Inhalt überhaupt weg und Apk nur vom literarischen Gesichtspunkt (von der "reinen" Literaturbetrachtung) her angehen bis zur Abblendung vom historisch-politischen und sozialen Hintergrund. So stellt L. Hartman die Genre-Frage ins Zentrum seines Forschungsüberblicks. J. J. Collins versucht vier literarische Typen frühjüdischer Apken aufzustellen, die allgemein menschliche Probleme zum Ausdruck bringen und keinen speziell historisch-sozialen Kontext verraten sollen, d. h. keine wie auch immer geartete "Konventikelliteratur" (Vielhauer) sind. Für ihn sind Apksen ein Genre der Offenbarungsliteratur mit einer Rahmenerzählung, in der von einer Offenbarungsmitteilung berichtet wird, die ein außerweltliches Wesen an ein menschliches ergehen ließ; enthüllt wird eine transzendente Wirklichkeit in ihrem zeitlichen und räumlichen Aspekt. In ähnlicher Weise haben J. Carmignac und H. Stegemann Apk zunächst als literarisches Phänomen verstanden. Für letzteren ist sie "Anfertigung von 'Offenbarungsschriften', die Sachverhalte 'enthüllen', die sich nicht aus innerweltlichen Gegebenheiten ... ableiten lassen, sondern die sich dem Autor und dem Leser nur erschließen durch den Rückgriff auf 'himmlisches Offenbarungswissen'". Das setzt grundsätzlich ein Buch als Mittler des esoterischen Wissens voraus. Als entscheidend gilt demnach der Rahmen, nicht der Inhalt, der strittig ist; aber es gibt auch keine eigenständige literarische Gattung "Apk"; jede Apkse kann verschiedene Motive und Stilformen umfassen, die als solche nicht entscheidend sind. Stegemann zieht sich daher auf den Topos "Geheimwissen" als Kriterium für Apk (gegenüber der Eschatologie) zurück und sieht ihren Ursprung im priesterlichen Kalender- oder Kultwissen, nicht in der Prophetie. Damit wird deutlich, in welcher Weise die literarische Beurteilung auch zu einer neuartigen Ursprungsbestimmung führen kann (s. u.). Doch kommen andere Betrachtungen dieser Art zu wesentlich anderen Folgerungen: K. Koch, der das Wesen apk Literatur in den Redezyklen über Weltverlauf und Eschaton als ein Zwiegespräch zwischen einer himmlischen Stimme und einem Seher sieht, verankert die Apk im prophetischen Visionsbericht, der ein altes Gattungsmuster des AT ist. M. Krause schließt sich P. Vielhauer an, indem er drei literarische Gattungsmerkmale für Apksen als wesentlich betrachtet: Pseudonymität, Visionsbericht, historisch-futuristische Aussagen (in Gestalt von kleinen Formen). Letzteres ist jedoch ein Rückgriff auf einen wesentlich inhaltlichen Zug. Verwiesen sei noch auf H. D. Betz, der als Testfall für das literarische Genre apk Stoffe im Griechischen das Trophonius-Orakel, wie es Plutarch gestaltet hat, untersucht und dabei feststellt, wie die literarische Dialogform (*Erotapokriseis*) der Orakelüberlieferungen eine neue Funktion im platonisch bestimmten (vergeistigten) Mythosverständnis erhält. Auf den Vorgang von Revitalisierungen und Aktualisierungen älterer Texte und Vorstellungen ("Konfliktmotive") in Apken hat vor allem T. Olsson Wert gelegt und an einem mittelpersischen Text demonstriert (s. u. §3.4.). Daß es dabei zu Verschiebungen, Neubewertungen, Umdeutungen usw. kommt, ist vielfach gerade das Charakteristische für apk Traditionsgeschichten (für das AT vgl. K. Koch).

Nun ist eine rein literarische Betrachtung nicht fehl am Platze, doch scheint sie zuwenig zu beachten, daß sich Inhalt und Form nicht so leicht trennen lassen, ja ihre Auseinanderreißung dem Tatbestand nicht Rechnung trägt. Die Form-Inhalt-Relation ist daher mehr in einem dialektischen Aufeinanderbezogensein zu sehen (wie es etwa W. Harnisch am Beispiel des IV Esra deutlich gemacht hat). So ist auch die von E. P. Sanders geübte Kritik an der ahistorischen Betrachtung von J. J. Collins sicher berechtigt; es geht um den Zusammenhang von sozialen und historischen Gegebenheiten, wie sie sich in den Apksen Ausdruck verschaffen, auf der einen, und dem davon und der Tradition bestimmten literarischen Genre auf der anderen Seite. Die soziologische Analyse ist hierfür ein neues heuristisches Erkenntnismittel, wie wir noch sehen werden (s. u. §2.5.).

In welcher Weise die Terminologie das Grundproblem für die Erfassung oder Beschreibung von Apk bzw. apk Stoffen sein kann, zeigen die ägyptologischen Beiträge, indem hier (bes. bei J. Bergman sichtbar) keine Klarheit zwischen Apk, Orakel und Prophezeiung herrscht. Daher muß J. Assmann trotz seiner eingangs gegebenen "Definition" von Apk (s. o. §2.1.) feststellen, daß in Ägypten jeder historische Bezug in den Weltendeschilderungen (die den mythischen Chaosbeschreibungen entstammen und durchaus in Krisenzeiten beschworen werden) fehlt und hier Apk ohne "politische" Eschatologie antreffbar sei, was m. E. dem Begriff selbst widerspricht und ihn unbrauchbar macht (denn "private", "individuelle Eschatologie" i. S. von Jenseitslehren und eschatologische Spekulationen im Zusammenhang von Kosmoslehren, wie im Osiriskult in Ansätzen greifbar, genügen dazu nicht). In ähnlicher, ja gleicher Weise steht dieses Problem für den griechischen und römischen Bereich an, wie die Beiträge von Burkert, Cancik und Gladigow zeigen. Es ist das leidige Problem der Übertragbarkeit historisch verankerter Termini, das der Religionswissenschaft von jeher zu schaffen gemacht hat und worauf wir noch zurückkommen werden.

2.3. Die berechtigte Forderung J. Assmanns *"Contra definitionem pro descriptione"* enthebt natürlich nicht, Merkmale apk Sachverhalte und Literaturformen in präziser Weise zu einer Rahmendefinition zusammenzufassen, zu einer charakterisierenden, nicht typologisierenden, doch bleibt dies noch eine zukünftige Aufgabe. Apk und Apkse sind aufeinander bezogen anzusehen: letztere ist literarische Manifestation eines apk Sachverhalts, der wiederum nur in Gestalt dieser Manifestation greifbar ist. Unter Verwendung und kritischer Weiterführung der (von H. D. Betz, S. Hartman, M. Krause, H. Stegemann) vorgeschlagenen "Definitionen" gehören zur Apk wesentlich folgende Kennzeichen: linearer, mehr oder weniger periodisierter Geschichtsverlauf, "Endzeitprophetie" (eschatologisches Element), pessimistische Weltbetrachtung, Jenseitslehren, Polarisierungen (duale oder dualistische Züge), Unheils- und Heilszeitvorstellungen, esoterisches Wissen um diese Vorgänge in Korrespondenz zu Offenbarungen und Visionen besonderer Art, niedergelegt in schriftlichen Dokumenten; vorausgesetzt wird eine sozialreligiöse Unheilssituation, deren Bewältigung Wurzel der Apk ist. Sie ist wohl durchweg eine Spätzeiterscheinung, Produkt einer Krisenstimmung. Apksen sind Offenbarungsschriften (ἀποκαλύπτειν!), in denen sich obengenannte Merkmale wiederfinden. Ihre Form erhalten sie durch eine Rahmenerzählung, Auditions- oder Visionsberichte, Himmelsreisen, Dialoge (*Erotapokriseis*) und Paränesen. Die häufige Verwendung von Bildern, Metaphern und Symbolen erfordert jeweils entsprechende "Deutungen". Der Verfasser, unter dem Deckmantel der Pseudonymität einer religiösen oder göttlichen Person legitimiert bzw. autorisiert, steht entweder in Beziehung zu einem

Offenbarungs- oder Visionsempfänger oder ist mit ihm identisch. Offenbarungssender ist eine transzendente, "metahistorische" Wirklichkeit, die unterschiedlich figuriert erscheint (bis zur *theologia negationis*). Diese phänomenologische Beschreibung, die den generellen Gebrauch der Begriffe Apk und Apkse rechtfertigt, muß durch Feststellung des *proprium* des jeweiligen Überlieferungsbereichs oder religiösen "Referenzrahmens" ergänzt werden, die es erlaubt eben von jüdischer, christlicher, iranischer u. a. Apk bzw. Apkse zu sprechen. T. Olsson hat dies mit seiner Forderung nach der Berücksichtigung des Kontextes und des jeweiligen "Wertsystems" unterstrichen, die generelle Aussagen eben sehr erschweren und die Eigenständigkeit apk oder ihr verwandter Überlieferungen trotz formaler Übereinstimmungen in den Mittelpunkt der Betrachtung rücken.

2.4. Diese der Eigenart dienenden Untersuchungen, die ich für einen neuen methodischen Zugang betrachte, sind vor allem von Frau E. Schüssler-Fiorenza unternommen worden. Das Ungenügen der bloßen phänomenologischen, auf Essenz zielenden, der formal-literarischen, das Genre-Pattern erfassenden, und der soziologischen, den Hinter- und Untergrund der Träger und Verfasser aufhellenden Arbeiten, ist dazu angetan, die Besonderheit etwa der christlichen gegenüber der jüdischen Apk herauszustellen. Dazu gehört neben der Paränese vor allem die Gestalt Christi selbst, der durch seine Auferstehung den apk Prozeß eingeleitet hat und so die typische dialektisch verschränkte Spannung christlicher Erwartung zwischen Erfüllung (realisierter Eschatologie) und Nichterfüllung ("futuristische" Eschatologie) hervorruft. Zur Illustration dient in erster Linie die Apk. Joh., worüber A. Y. Collins und U. B. Müller im einzelnen gehandelt haben (s. u.). Auch bei H. G. Kippenberg, der die frühchristliche Apk im Anschluß an E. Käsemann charakterisiert, ist der Impetus wirksam, das Schiboleth der gnostischen Apk zu ergründen, nämlich in der Verneinung jeder traditionellen Hoffnung und in der Verfolgung der Destruktion des Kosmos im praktischen Verhalten. Natürlich gehören in diese Proprium-Suche überhaupt alle Beiträge, die sich den Spezialgebieten und -texten gewidmet haben, wobei es sich immer wieder herausgestellt hat, daß einerseits mit einem bestimmten Apk- bzw. Apkse-Begriff produktiv zu arbeiten ist, andererseits Sachverhalte zur Sprache kommen, die sich herkömmlicherweise schwer darunter subsummieren lassen. Dazu gehören die Ausführungen von H. D. Betz, W. Burkert, B. Gladigow und H. Cancik über das griechisch-römische Material ebenso wie die von J. Assmann, J. Bergman und J. G. Griffiths über Ägypten oder die von H. Ringgren über Mesopotamien. In allen diesen Beiträgen sind eben nicht die sonst die Apk-Debatte beherrschenden jüdisch-christlichen Apksen Gegenstand der Betrachtung, sondern davon recht abweichende Formen und Sachverhalte, die es aber trotzdem ermöglichen sollen, sie in den apk

Rahmen einzubeziehen, obwohl sie ohne Schwierigkeiten auch unter
andere Kategorien subsumiert werden können (wie Orakel, Weltalterspe-
kulationen, Unterwelts- und Chaosbeschreibungen, Heilszeitverhei-
ßungen).

Für das frühe Griechentum führt Burkert den *Er*-Mythos aus Platons
"Staat" als eine echte Apkse an (obwohl ohne Aufbau einer Gegenwelt und
Negierung der bestehenden), ferner besitzen die orphischen Totenpässe
formale Ähnlichkeiten mit Apksen, wie auch die *Katharmoi* des Empedokles und das Proömium des Parmenides. In den apk Zügen der philosophisch geprägten Weltuntergangsvorstellungen sind iranisch-apk Einflüsse
möglich, aber nicht sicher. Alle philosophischen Systeme der Griechen
haben sich gegen die Apk abgeschirmt, ebenso wie in der sonstigen
Literatur, die heranziehbar ist, wie das *Arimaspeia*-Epos des Aristeas oder
die Vision der 4 Reiche in der orphischen Theogonie und in Aristophanes'
"Rittern", die apk Spitze abgebrochen wurde. Es gibt Parallelen bzw. erst
jüngst entdeckte gemeinsame orientalische Wurzeln in der absteigenden
Skala der Weltreichelehre bei Hesiod und Daniel – dies ist aber schon alles.
In Griechenland gab es vom politisch-historischen Hintergrund keinen
Boden für die Apk (s. u.). In gleicher Weise sind die römischen *libri fatales*
oder *Sibyllini*, wie sie H. Cancik vor uns ausbreitet, bemerkenswerte
Beispiele   einer   buchreligiösen   Offenbarungsliteratur   (Sibyllinische
Bücher!), die die röm. Geschichtstheologie bestimmt hat. Ihre Ähnlichkeit
mit den at-lichen Prophetenbüchern, kann nicht über ihren anderen
Ursprung, die etruskische Disziplin der Divination, hinwegtäuschen und
darüber, daß in Rom eine "post-eschatologische Apk" bestand, eine auf
den Herrscherkult bezogene Realisierung (nicht Umfunktionierung) apk
Vorstellungen erfolgte (wofür Vergils Äneide der beste Beweis ist). Untergangsspekulationen sind z. Zt. Cäsars anzutreffen als Widerstandsäußerun-
gen unterdrückter Schichten; auch sie zehren vom Divinationskult und der
Säkularlehre. Letztere, mit der sich auch Gladigow näher beschäftigte, ist
von Haus aus ein kontextfreies System von Zeitkontingenten, von 10
Saecula ohne inhaltliche Differenzierung, das der Kalenderrechnung bzw.
dem Festkalender (*Defixio*) entstammt und für apk Vorstellungen Ansätze
hat, aber i. S. der fiktiven Realisierung der Herrschaftslegitimation. So ist
zwar nur in abgewandelter Weise von römischer Apk die Rede, doch
erlaubt das Material in gattungsmäßiger Hinsicht und auch in den Offen-
barungsarten (Entrückung, Ekstase) Vergleiche mit dem jüdisch-christlichen Bereich. Die sibyllinischen Bücher sind ein sprechender Beweis für
den Nährboden, auf dem die jüdisch-christliche Sibylle gedeihen konnte.
Nach M. Simon haben wir es dabei mit der Adaption der biblischen
Botschaft an die hellenistische Kultur zu tun.

Sowohl in Mesopotamien als auch in Ägypten sind Heilszeiterwartungen, die sich um den König gebildet haben, Hauptreservoir dessen, was als apk Literatur herangezogen werden kann. Im eigentlichen Sinne apk Sachverhalte sind für beide Bereiche nur in abgewandelter Weise nachweisbar, eben als *proprium* dessen, was man als babylonische oder ägyptische Apk bzw. Apksen bezeichnen könnte. J. Bergman hat m. R. auf das Fehlen eines eschatologischen Zeitbegriffs als Haupthindernis für die Entstehung von Apk i. S. des Judentums in Ägypten hingewiesen (ebenso J. Assmann). Es gibt daher keine "typische" apk Literatur hier, höchstens Züge oder Motive (die aber nicht die alte Ansicht A. von Galls rechtfertigen können, daß sie Vorläufer der biblischen Apk gewesen sind). Es sind das Chaos-Ordnung-Schema, die Vorstellung vom 2. Tod, Jenseitslehren, Degenerationstheorie, Zeitraumvorstellungen. Konkreter hat J. Assmann sich des Themas angenommen und den Topos von "Königsdogma und Heilserwartung" zum Leitfaden genommen. Es ist realisierte Apk (wie in Rom), die uns hier entgegentritt, gebunden an die Herrschaftslegitimation, gespeist aber aus dem altägyptischen Bewußtsein um die Empfindlichkeit der Kultur für Barbarei und Chaos. Die Chaosbeschreibungen sind daher Quell apk Sachverhalte, abgesetzt gegen die um den König als Repräsentant der Kultur zentrierte Heilszeit[3]. Merkwürdigerweise nimmt im Laufe der ägyptischen Geschichte das Wissen um das Ende zu, die Furcht vor dem Chaos, geboren aus politischen Krisenzeiten, bis schließlich in nachchristlicher Zeit eine echte eschatologische Heilserwartung auch in Ägypten heimisch wird (Töpferorakel, Asklepius). Herangezogen werden von den Ägyptologen für diesen Tatbestand: die "Mahnworte ('Admonitions') des Ipuwer" ("eines Weisen", nicht Propheten!) das "Gespräch zwischen Atum und Osiris" (Totenbuch, Spruch 175), diverse Chaosschilderungen, die "Prophezeiung des Neferti", die "Demotische Chronik", das "Orakel eines Lammes unter König Bokchoris" und das "Töpferorakel". Griffiths stellt dazu noch die hellenistische Legende vom Traum des Pharao Nectanebus (als Teil des Alexanderromans), die, geboren aus der Krise der persischen Fremdherrschaft in Ägypten, eine Befreiungsideologie enthält.

Für die Keilschriftliteratur hat H. Ringgren 7 fragmentarische Texte des 1. Jh. v. Chr. besprochen, die man in diesen Zusammenhang am ehesten heranziehen kann und die schon Å. Sjöberg in seiner kurzen Information für den Kongreß im Auge hatte. Es handelt sich auch hier um "Heilszeiterwartungen", die sich aus der Königsideologie gebildet haben und die um das Thema von "Unordnung" (Chaos) und "Ordnung" bzw. schlechte und gute Regierung (Herrscher) kreisen (letzteres wird jeweils erwartet). Stilistisch gehören sie in den Bereich der Omenliteratur, die esoterischen

---

[3] Assmann knüpft dafür an die These von S. Luria 1929 an, daß möglicherweise "proto-apk Formen" ihren Sitz im Leben des Festes als "innerkulturell inszeniertes Chaos" haben.

Charakter hat. R. vermutet daher hier ihren Ursprung. Es lassen sich Parallelen zum ägyptischen Neferti-Orakel aufzeigen, noch bessere zu dem neugefundenen aramäischen Balaam-Orakel von Deir ʿAllā. Mit Apk hat dies aber ebensowenig zu tun, wie R. richtig feststellt, so daß wir hier kein Vorstadium der jüdisch-christlichen Apk vor uns haben, höchstens Bruchstücke für deren Bau (z. B. die futuristischen Aussagen oder "Prophetien", Herrscherabfolgen, astrologische Berechnungen, seltsame Erscheinungen). Beachtenswert bleibt, daß das alte Mesopotamien gleiche Reaktionen auf ähnliche (politische, gesellschaftliche, ökonomische) Bedingungen (Krisenzeiten) aufweist, die der religiös-politischen Artikulation von Heilserwartungen (z. T. *vaticina ex eventu*) dienten und um den Bestand der altorientalischen Gesellschaft, ihre Identität und Stabilität, in der Spätzeit kreisten (unter Aufnahme älterer Traditionen natürlich). Die einzige echte Apk neben der jüdisch-christlichen bietet im alten Orient der Iran in Gestalt der zoroastrischen Endzeiterwartungen (s. dazu §3.4.).

2.5. Neben den literaturwissenschaftlichen Bemühungen (s. §2.2.) sind es vor allem die soziologischen, die man als "neue Methode" ansprechen kann (auch wenn sie oft nicht so "neu" sind als sie erscheinen). Dieser Betrachtungsweise verdanken wir eine Reihe bemerkenswerter Einsichten, insbesondere natürlich in den Träger- und Verfasserkreis, d. h. in die Genese apk Sachverhalte und Literatur. Verständlicherweise sind auch sie vielfach hypothetischer Natur und beruhen oft auf einem hermeneutischen Zirkelschluß, aber die Fruchtbarkeit dieses methodischen Zugangs steht außer Frage. Im Vordergrund steht dabei die jüdisch-christliche Apk, da von ihr die größte literarische Hinterlassenschaft vorhanden ist (daher auch patternbildend!) und der "Sitz im Leben" durch historische und sozialökonomische Untersuchungen untermauert werden kann. Daher hat sie auch in dieser Hinsicht Musterwirkung gezeitigt. Zunächst sei auf J. C. H. Lebrams Beitrag dazu hingewiesen, der zwar keine soziologische Analyse vorlegt, aber durch eine neue Fragestellung, nämlich die nach der Frömmigkeit apk Literatur und ihrer Leser (dem Erwartungshorizont), ohne Zweifel wichtige Einsichten in die Trägerschicht vermittelt. Die Befragung repräsentativer Zeugnisse (Daniel, Henoch, IV Esra) führt zu dem Ergebnis, daß wir mit intellektuellen, der "Weisheit" verpflichteten Schichten zu tun haben, die eine Verinnerlichung und Spiritualisierung herkömmlicher Religionspraktiken das Wort reden, ja eine individuelle, pietistische Religiosität pflegen, die ihr Vertrauen zwar auf Gott und Gesetz richten, aber noch mehr von dem ehernen Ablauf der kosmischen und historischen Entwicklung bis zum schlimmen Ende überzeugt sind. Die paränetischen Forderungen zielen mehr auf Askese, Ausharren, Leiden als auf Auflehnung, Revolution. Rituelle Gesetzesfrömmigkeit ist nicht gefragt; die apk Frömmigkeit ist ein neuer Abschnitt in der jüdischen

Religionsgeschichte, die das Vertrauen in die herkömmlichen Strukturen und Heilsmittel verloren hat, vor allem aber einen Weltpessimismus an den Tag legt und das esoterische Wissen um den Weltlauf und das vom Gesetz verlangte endliche Heil für die Frommen als einziges Heilsmittel akzeptiert (womit, wie Lebram m. R. feststellt, schon der Boden für die Gnosis bereitet ist)[4].

Auch von anderer Seite, aber mit betont soziologischer Fragestellung, ist der Frage nach der Trägerschicht nachgegangen worden. M. Hengel, der den historischen Hintergrund des jüdischen Aufstandes unter Trajan (115–17) auslotet und die Zerstörung der jüdisch-ägyptischen Gemeinden als Holokaust dieser Zeit versteht, sieht in den kriegerischen Zügen des apk Messias-Menschensohnes und dem Romhaß (5. Sib. 168–178.414–19) eine Widerspiegelung der realen Vorgänge, ohne sich auf eine bekannte Träger-gruppe festzulegen. Ob dafür die häufig ins Spiel gebrachten Ḥasidīm, über deren eschatologische Auffassungen wir nichts wissen, in Frage kommen, bleibt nach G. W. E. Nickelsburg nach wie vor offen. Daß die Qumrange-meinde ausscheidet, ist jetzt so gut wie sicher (vgl. Carmignac und Stegemann; unten §3.1.). Daher lassen sich nur allgemeine Feststellungen treffen, wie von W. Meeks, der an eine charismatische Gruppe denkt, die von vornherein eben durch ihre Lehren zur Institutionalisierung überging, oder von K. Koch, der eigene Zirkel von visionären Schriftauslegern bzw. -deutern "vielleicht in eigenen Synagogen" (!) vermutet. Apk Erwartung stärkt die soziale Bindung, führt zur Gemeindebildung und zur Schaffung neuer (unter Verwendung alter) "Plausibilitätsstrukturen" in einer Krisen-zeit[5]. Daß wir mit einer unterdrückten Minderheit zu tun haben, die eine Befreiung i. S. einer Restauration alter, vom Gesetz geforderter Zustände erhofft, und zwar in Verbindung mit einer Bestrafung der Feinde und Ungläubigen, ist von E. P. Sanders betont worden, für den keiner der apk Texte aus den Kreisen der "Mächtigen" stammt (also nicht aus der mit Rom kollaborierenden jüdischen Oberschicht), aber auch nicht aus bestimmbaren Konventikeln oder einem ausgemachten "Sitz im Leben", da sich ja ganz Israel (?) unterdrückt fühlte; der allgemeine Zeitgeist sei der sichere Referenzrahmen, der Verfasser, Hörer und Leser verband.

---

[4] Vgl. Rudolph 1967, 117 f., 118 ff.; 1975, 788 f., 792 ff.; 1980a, 232 ff.

[5] Von da aus kommt P. Eicher 1979, 119 zu einer ganz anderen Einschätzung der jüdischen Apk, nämlich als ein "reaktionärer Krisenkult gegenüber der hellenistischen Skepsis und Aufklärung"; der Einsatz von Divination und Offenbarungen dient der Abwehr von Auflö-sungserscheinungen; außerjüdisches Wissen wird durch Resakralisierung legitimiert (120). Dazu auch B. Lang ebd. (1979), 127 ff., der die Apk als einen Prozeß der Segmentierung der Religion aus der Gesellschaft versteht, die eine Legitimierung durch "Offenbarungen" benötigt. Vielleicht ist hier ein Grund zu suchen für die Tatsache, daß die Apksen im rabbinischen Judentum keine Heimstatt fanden.

Daß kriegerische Verwicklungen besonderer Art, die zur Unterdrük-
kung eines Volkes oder Volksteils führen, Nährboden für apk Erwartungen sind, wird auch aus anderen Bereichen deutlich, ebenso da, wo ein
Land, wie Griechenland, kontrastdiagnostisch eben von derartigen militärischen Katastrophen des Orients verschont blieb und daher keine Apk
entstand (so W. Burkert). Die römische Offenbarungsliteratur ist, wie H.
Cancik bemerkt, offen für Widerstandsauslegungen und Katastrophen-
schilderungen. Das gleiche für Ägypten und Mesopotamien mit den aus
Krisenzeiten geborenen "Prophezeiungen", "Orakeln" und "Omina" (s.
§2.4.). Auch die Apk. Joh. atmet derartige Luft: antirömischer Haß und
soziale Spannungen in den kleinasiatischen Gemeinden (A. Y. Collins).
"Gesellschaftliche Entscheidungen" sieht H. G. Kippenberg hinter den apk
Deutungen des Falles Jerusalems wirksam (analysiert bei Mk 13, syrBar
und IV Esra, NHC-ApcJac I). Allgemein wird daher von einer "Krisen-",
"Unheils-" oder "Problemsituation" (Stegemann) als Wurzel apk Schriften
gesprochen. Im Hinblick auf die iranisch-zoroastrische Apk ist dies nur von
T. Olsson für das mpers. Jāmāsp Nāmag näher behandelt worden, das
Ausdruck des Verlustes von Kommunikation und Integration in der spät-
und nachsassanidischen Gemeinde ist. Der Ursprung ist auch hier in der
von Zarathustra gedeuteten, wenn nicht mit eingeleiteten Umbruchslage
im alten Ostiran zu suchen, fortgeführt in den großen Veränderungen
unter Achämeniden, Arsakiden und Sassaniden, bis der Islam eine für die
Zoroastrier katastrophale Situation schuf, die fast das Ende bedeutete: in
dieser Zeit wurde die Endgestalt der apk Tradition ausgeführt (s. u. §3.4.).

3. Einige Hauptproblemkreise der Apokalyptikforschung

Unter den Beiträgen schälen sich einige Hauptproblemkreise heraus, die
schon länger die Apk-Forschung beschäftigt haben.

3.1. Dazu gehört in erster Linie der "klassische" und schon mehrfach
gestreifte Bereich der jüdisch-christlichen Apk, der sich der biblischen
Überlieferung verpflichtet weiß, denn Elemente der apk Literatur
(Träume, Visionen, Prophezeiungen u. a.) finden sich schon vor Daniel im
AT. Trotzdem ist bis heute das Problem sehr umstritten, an welcher
spezifischen Traditionskette des AT die apk Literatur eigentlich hängt. J.
Carmignac spricht sich entschieden für die prophetische aus. Auf sehr
exaktem, textlinguistischem Wege hat K. Koch diese Frage einer Lösung
näher geführt, indem er die Gattung des "Visionsberichtes" als Klammer
zwischen Prophetie und Apk betrachtet. Der Schulzusammenhang läßt
sich bei der späteren Prophetie (Sach, Ez) festmachen, wobei die Zunahme
an Realitätsverlust, Verschwommenheit, Übertreibung bzw. Übersteige-
rung in der metaphorischen und symbolischen Redeweise als typisch für

die Apk zu gelten hat. Auch mit einem Einschlag der Sapientia-Literatur (bzw. Tradition) muß gerechnet werden, wie schon vielfach festgestellt wurde (vgl. oben Lebram). Auf einen weiteren Faktor hat W. Harnisch in seiner Fallstudie zum IV Esra hingewiesen: die deuteronomistische Gesetzeslehre. In diese Richtung zielen auch die Bemerkungen von H. Stegemann, allerdings in einer die prophetische Herkunft ablehnenden These: danach sei das priesterliche Kalender- und Kultwissen, das durch Offenbarung vermittelt und daher esoterisch ist, Wurzel der Apk. Die Problemstellung bleibt also bestehen: die alttestamentliche Tradition ist offenbar in vielfältiger Weise Erblasser für die Apk gewesen, was zu ihrem Charakter als Spätzeitprodukt passen würde[6].

Eine große Bedeutung in der Apk-Forschung kam seit ihrer Entdeckung den Qumranfunden zu. Man glaubte eine Zeitlang, daß wir hier eine der Trägergruppen greifen könnten. Nun haben sowohl J. Carmignac[7] als vor allem H. Stegemann nachweisen können, daß dieser "Wunderschlüssel" nicht paßt. Trotzdem führten diese Funde zu neuen Einsichten. Dazu gehört in erster Linie, daß jetzt die älteste apk Schrift nicht mehr Daniel ist, sondern Teile des Henochbuches (I, 1–36; 72–82), die in Qumran gefunden, aber nicht dort entstanden sind. Damit erweitert sich der Zeitraum der Apk bis in das 3. Jh. v. Chr. (nach Stegemann ist sogar aufgrund des in Hen. erhaltenen Kalenders mit dem 4. Jh. zu rechnen; als Ort kommt Samarien in Frage). Qumran war kein Hort der Apk, höchstens ein Überlieferungsort (neben Jub fanden sich 8 Dan-Handschriften). Als spezifisch apk Literatur aus der Qumrangemeinde haben bis jetzt nur zu gelten: das "Gigantenbuch" (Henochliteratur), das "Neue Jerusalem" (fragmentarisch, herodian. Zeit) und die sog. "Engelliturgie" (3. Jh. v. Chr.?); das "Nabonid-Gebet" und "Ps.-Daniel" gehören in die Vorgeschichte apk Literatur, d. h. des Danielbuches. Immerhin hatte die Qumrangemeinde ein erhöhtes Interesse an apk Schriften; sie als völlig uneschatologisch hinzustellen, halte ich für eine (zwar verständliche) Überreaktion auf die bisherige Auffassung.

3.2. Im Erbe der frühjüdischen Apk steht literarisch und historisch (auch existentiell!) die ur- und frühchristliche Apk. Dabei stellt sich allerdings schon bei Jesus von Nazareth und seiner Gemeinde die Frage nach dem Gewicht der apk Vorstellungswelt. L. Schottroff hat an dem als "Flugblatt" (R. Pesch, aufgenommen auch von U. B. Müller und H. G.

---

[6] I. Gruenwald 1979a bezeichnet die Apk als "Para-Prophetie" (93) und verankert sie mehr in der prophetischen Tradition; charakteristisch sei für sie das Vorhandensein von Engelwesen und Himmelsreisen. Zum Thema der Himmelsreisen s. zuletzt A. Segal 1979, 1333–1394. Keine Rolle spielte auf dem Kongreß das Thema Apk und Merkabah-Spekulation (gewöhnlich "Mystik" genannt); dazu ausführlich jetzt Gruenwald 1979b.

[7] Vgl. Carmignac 1979, 22–32.

Kippenberg) bezeichneten apk Stück Mk 13 gezeigt, daß die Jesusbewegung ohne Zweifel eine apk Bewegung gewesen ist, auch wenn diese Apkse erst aus der Zeit Vespasians (69–79) stammt und eine Reaktion auf Christenverfolgungen und die Zerstörung Jerusalems i. J. 70 n. Chr. ist (auch die Parallelen Mt 24 und Lk 21 drücken keinen grundsätzlichen Wandel in der Verfolgungssituation aus). Daß auch Paulus ein "millenial prophet" gewesen ist, nimmt W. Meeks aufgrund einer Analyse seiner Sprache in den Briefen (I, II Thess, Gal, I Kor) an; es handele sich hier um eine "End-Zeit-Sprache". Die paulinische Schule kann man dagegen nicht als apk Bewegung bezeichnen; für sie hatte die Apk nur eine dienende Funktion im Gemeindeaufbau. Die apk Unterströmung des Urchristentums verschafft sich dann noch einmal vehementen Ausdruck in der "Apk. Joh.". Bekanntlich hat sie F. Engels 1883 in einem feuilletonistischen Artikel als älteste und wichtigste Schrift des NT bezeichnet, da sie den für ihn revolutionären, antirömischen Charakter des Urchristentums am klarsten zum Ausdruck brächte[8]. Nun, chronologisch gehört sie an das Ende des 1. Jh., wie A. Y. Collins erneut zeigt, und ist ebenfalls eine Reaktion auf Christenverfolgungen und die Zerstörung Jerusalems, aber auch auf soziale Spannungen (s. o.). Ihre "evokative Sprache" ist ein Kennzeichen frühchristlicher Hoffnung, die von Erfüllung (in Christus) und Nichterfüllung (Wiederkehr Christi) lebt; in ihr drückt sich aber auch eine einschneidende Veränderung in der Weltsicht und Ethik aus: eine antikosmische, jenseitsgerichtete und individualistische und innergemeindliche Einstellung ohne sozialpolitisches religiöses Engagement (so E. Schüssler Fiorenza). Als Literaturdokument ist der Briefcharakter der Apk. Joh. (der sonst nur noch im syrBar anzutreffen ist) offenbar ein Mittel gewesen, sie liturgisch im Wortgottesdienst vorzutragen und als himmlische Offenbarungsschrift vor einem Kreis von Propheten zu rechtfertigen (so U. B. Müller). Kultisch-liturgische Verwendung apk Schriften diente ihrer Erhaltung über Generationen hinweg, hielt ihr Gedankengut lebendig bei gleichzeitiger Entschärfung bzw. Entaktualisierung.

3.3. Neben den o. g. Qumrantexten hat der Nag-Hammadi-Fund die einzigen neuen Quellen auch zur Apk-Forschung ans Tageslicht gebracht, damit nicht nur den Bestand der frühchristlichen Apksen bereichert, sondern auch der alten Frage nach dem Verhältnis von Apk und Gnosis neuen Auftrieb gegeben. M. Krause hat als vorzüglicher Kenner den tatsächlichen Bestand an NHC-Apksen vorgeführt: es sind die PlsApk (NHC V 2), AdApk (V 5), PetrApk (VII 3), Noēma (VI 4); unsicher bleibt

---

[8] Marx/Engels 1958, 165–170, 262–279; 1976, 127–132, 138–152. Der erste Aufsatz erschien 1883 in der englischen Zeitschrift "Progress", Vol. 2, 112–116, der zweite in der "Neuen Zeit" Jg. 13, 1894/95, Band 1, Heft 1, 4–13; Heft 2, 36–43.

ParSem (VII 1; in ihr dominiert zwar die Urzeit, vgl. aber den apk Abschnitt 43,28–45,31). Zu Unrecht tragen die JakApksen (V 3.4) diesen Titel. In einer ganzen Reihe von Texten sind apk Einsprengsel enthalten, wie in SOT (II 5,126,37–127,17), 3 Protenn (XIII 43,4–44,29) und AscApk (VI 8). G. MacRae fügt noch DialSot (III 5) hinzu, da hier apk Traditionen ausgelegt werden. Obwohl Gnosis im Kern "realisierte Eschatologie" ist, sind apk Sachverhalte in erheblichem Maße beibehalten worden, die das Weltende allerdings nicht als Übergang zu einer "neuen Schöpfung" verstehen, sondern als Reintegration der göttlichen Lichtwelt und gleichzeitiger Vernichtung des Kosmos, so daß die Endzeit die Urzeit wiederherstellt. Man kann dies mit MacRae als eine Radikalisierung der apk Eschatologie überhaupt bezeichnen. Sicherlich lebt die Gnosis auch von der christlichen Tradition, aber ihr apk Grundzug ist unabhängig davon direktes Erbe der jüdischen Apk: für beide ist das esoterische Wissen ein Heilsmittel und die dualistische Weltsicht bestimmend[9]. Das *proprium* gnostischer Apk hat, wie schon angeführt, auch H. G. Kippenberg zu erfassen gesucht, dabei allerdings die erste Jakobus-Apkse benutzt, die nicht als Apkse im engeren Sinne gelten kann. Davon unberührt ist allerdings die treffende Beobachtung vom Zusammenhang gnostischer Apk mit der praktisch-ethischen Forderung der Kosmosdestruktion. Leider ist auf dem Symposion niemand der reichen manichäischen Eschatologie mit ihren apk Bestandteilen nachgegangen, die gerade für die eben skizzierten Probleme erhebliche Aussagekraft besitzen.

3.4. Für die biblische Apk war und ist bis heute die Beeinflussung durch die iranisch-zoroastrische Tradition dieses Genres immer ein ernsthaftes Problem gewesen[10]. Es ist daher sehr begrüßenswert, wenn die Iranisten ohne Rücksicht auf diese Fragestellung erst einmal den Quellenbestand und sein Alter zur Darstellung gebracht haben[11]. In umfassender Weise hat Geo Widengren die leitenden Ideen iranischer Apk vorgeführt, zu denen vor allem die vom Kampf zwischen den guten und bösen Mächten gehört, von denen die ersteren bei der großen Entscheidung am Weltende siegen werden. Angefangen von den Gāthās bis zu den spät- und nachsassanidischen Texten läßt sich eine gewisse Kontinuität in diesem Bereich nachweisen. In Aufnahme einer bekannten Charakterisierung Zarathustras als ersten Apokalyptikers des Orients durch H. S. Nyberg, sieht W. die Geburt

---

[9] Vgl. Rudolph 1980b, 297 ff.

[10] Letzte Übersicht bietet in abgewogener Beurteilung A. Hultgård 1979, 512⁻590. Unklar bleibt bis heute, auf welchen Kanälen diese unleugbaren Einflüsse in das Judentum gelangt sind. Sie erfolgten im Zuge des babylonischen Exils (vgl. Dt-Jes.; aram. Teile von Esra und Neh) und dem Kulturkontakt nach den Alexanderzügen. Sprechendes Beispiel ist auch das Qumranschrifttum (dualistische Züge).

[11] Eine zusammenfassende Darstellung dazu bietet Kippenberg 1978, 49 ff.

der iranischen Eschatologie und Apk durch Verwandlung der indoirani-
schen zyklischen Zeitauffassung in eine lineare in dieser frühen (den großen
biblischen Propheten nahestehenden) Zeit (10.–6. Jh. v. Chr.?). Es läßt sich
nicht bestreiten, daß der Iran tatsächlich für diesen Themenbereich die
ältesten Zeugnisse besitzt, auch wenn in den einzelnen Bestandteilen noch
manche nicht nur chronologische Unsicherheit steckt. Durch ein literarisches und sprachliches Rückschlußverfahren lassen sich mit Heranziehung
der wenigen nichtiranischen (griechisch-lateinischen) Belege (Plutarch,
Hystaspes-Orakel) in ideengeschichtlicher Manier wesentliche Lehrgehalte
und Formelemente aus den relevanten Pehlevitexten bis in den sonst nicht
erhaltenen sassanidischen Avestakanon verfolgen, wobei W. bekanntlich
mit zwei Hauptströmungen rechnet, der zoroastrischen und zervanitischen, die beide ihr Teil zur Ausgestaltung apk Ideenwelt beigetragen
haben (so ist z. B. die Vier-Weltperioden-Lehre zervanitisch). Aber auch
aus dem erhaltenen Avesta (in Frage kommen die Gāthās, der jüngere
Yasna und die Yäšts) ergibt sich das hohe Alter dieses Glaubensgutes
(Weltende mit kriegerischer Entscheidung, Feuer- und Metallordal, End-
zeitheiland, Auferstehung, Neumachung der Erde). Konzentriert auf die
literarische Form und damit Pionierland betretend hat sich A. Hultgård der
eben nur mitteliranisch erhaltenen apk Literatur gewidmet. Diese m. E.
erstmalige Formanalyse führt zu der Feststellung, daß die apk Traditionen
entweder im Dialogstil (*Erotapokriseis*) oder Visionsbericht gestaltet sind
und ihr Ursprung in der avestischen Überlieferung gesucht werden muß,
auch wenn die redaktionelle Endgestalt bekanntlich in das 9./10. Jh.
gehört. Weitere Zeugnisse dafür sind die griechischen Berichte (Theopomp
und Plutarch), der vermutlich rituelle Ursprung des Bahman Yašt (als apk
Haupttext) und der geographische Horizont, der nach Ostiran verweist,
während die Pehlevi-Auslegung westiranische und mesopotamische Verhältnisse voraussetzt. Auch S. Hartman tritt für ein altavestisches, vor-
achämenidisches Alter der jungavestischen Apk ein (spätestens um 600
v. Chr.). Er bedient sich dabei der bisher wenig ausgewerteten Tatsache,
daß eine ganze Reihe zoroastrischer *termini technici (Gaya marĕtan, Astvatĕ-
rĕta, Ahura Mazdā)* zwar aus der nachgathischen Periode stammen, ihr
"Wortmaterial" aber bereits in den Gāthās vorhanden ist. Sicherlich haben
wir damit kein unanfechtbares heuristisches Mittel der Datierung, aber es
eröffnet einen neuen Zugang zu dieser spröden Materie, der nun einmal
nur mit allerlei Kniffen wissenschaftlicher Praxis beizukommen ist. Spielen
in den genannten iranistischen Untersuchungen ideen- und literargeschichtliche Gesichtspunkte die Hauptrolle, so fragt T. Olsson zusätzlich
nach den treibenden Faktoren für diese "apk Aktivität" in Iran. Anhand des
nur fragmentarischen und uneinheitlich überlieferten mittelpersischen
Jāmāsp-Nāmag wird die Aktualisierung der alten apk Tradition des Zoro-

astrismus aufgezeigt: ihr Legendenschatz gibt die Modelle für neue literarische Schöpfungen, die aus politisch-religiösen Krisenzeiten (Römer, Araber, Türken) geboren sind. Die Wiederbelebung alter "Konfliktmotive" dient immer wieder der Auseinandersetzung zwischen iranischer und nichtiranischer Welt, sei es in politischer, religiöser oder ethischer Hinsicht. Die kulturelle Identität des zoroastrischen Irans (auch nach dem Sieg des Islams!) wird verteidigt durch die Hoffnung auf die Zukunft, die der Retterkönig (Pēšyōtan) bringt durch die Wiederherstellung der alten Pracht. Auf diese Weise wird auch von dieser Seite bestätigt, daß die Apk von der Aktualität politisch-gesellschaftlicher Ereignisse lebt und getragen wird. Diesen Gesichtspunkt sollte man noch stärker bei diesen Untersuchungen berücksichtigen.

Ein bemerkenswertes Zeugnis irano-hellenistischer Apk aus dem 1. Jh. v. Chr., das diesen gleichen Geist politisch-religiöser Konfliktsituation atmet, das sog. Hystaspes-Orakel, hat wenigstens nachträglich bei Olsson und Widengren doch noch eine gebührende Beachtung gefunden[12]. Nicht berücksichtigt wurden die altindischen und indogermanischen Quellen.

4. Die Anregung der weiteren Forschung

Die vielfältigen Beiträge, die wir versuchten unter einigen Gesichtspunkten zu betrachten und zusammenzufassen, werden ohne Zweifel die weitere Forschung stimulieren. Nicht nur die notwendige Arbeit an den Quellen muß mit Hilfe neuer Methoden, wozu die literaturwissenschaftliche und soziologische in erster Linie gehören, fortgesetzt werden, sondern es bedarf neben der Eruierung der Vorgeschichte apk Sachverhalte auch einer intensiven Bearbeitung ihrer Nachgeschichte bis in die heutige Zeit. Apk ist ein lebendiger Quell der Krisenbewältigung und Hoffnungssuche der Menschheit durch die Jahrtausende gewesen und ist es auch bis heute, mitunter in verwandelter "profaner" Art und Weise. Wenn Religionswissenschaft in einer Art dialektischer Verschränkung von religionsgeschichtlicher Einzelforschung und religionssystematischer bzw. -vergleichender Betrachtung besteht, also lokale Spezialanalyse und universale Sicht in sich vereinigt, um damit ihr *proprium* zu demonstrieren[13], so ist auch bei der Behandlung der Thematik Apk davon auszugehen. Anders lassen sich z. B. die Fragen der "Definition" nicht bewältigen, ebenso nicht die Probleme der "Symbolsprache" apk Texte, die nur am Rande aufklangen, und die der historisch-politischen und religiösen Kräfte, die sich in den Apksen zu Wort melden. Kann man, wie es offenbar die Themastellung beabsichtigte,

---

[12] Vgl. dazu auch Kippenberg 1978, 70 ff.
[13] Vgl. zu dieser religionswissenschaftlichen Problematik Rudolph 1973, 116 ff.; 1981, 99 ff.

von einem Zusammenhang der verschiedenen Ausprägungen von Apk in der alten Mittelmeerwelt und dem Vorderen Orient sprechen, also von einer "internationalen apk Bewegung" von Iran bis Rom? Die Frage so zu stellen, heißt m. E. sie zu verneinen. Die Eigenschaften jeweiliger Apk, wie wir sie in §2.4. zusammengestellt haben, lassen es trotz gewisser Gemeinsamkeiten im Genre und in der Motivierung nicht zu. Wir können nur einige Kreise feststellen, die zugleich in einem inneren Traditionszusammenhang, ja -geschichte, stehen. Dazu gehört in erster Linie der jüdisch-christliche, der, wie wir jetzt wissen, vom 3. Jh. v. Chr. bis ca. 3. Jh. n. Chr. umfaßt, und der sich tatsächlich unter dem biblischen Vorzeichen bis in die westliche Mittelmeerwelt ausgebreitet hat, wobei er sich lokalen apk Traditionen angepaßt oder sie in sich aufgenommen hat (betr. Ägypten und Rom). In die Vorgeschichte der jüdisch-christlichen Apk gehört auf alle Fälle die iranische, die am stärksten eingewirkt haben muß, da weder die hier sichtbaren Vorstellungen von Weltgericht noch die von Auferstehung und Erlöser in der älteren biblischen Überlieferung vorhanden sind. Heilszeit- und Unheilszeitorakel mesopotamischer und ägyptischer Provenienz sind ohne Zweifel auch in diese apk Bewegung eingegangen, waren sie doch schon teilweise für das israelitische Königtum rezipiert worden (Davidideologie). So finden wir unter dieser Betrachtung doch so etwas wie eine "internationale" Strömung wieder, allerdings als ein traditionsgeschichtlicher Komplex, der unter jüdisch-christlichen Vorzeichen die damalige Welt erobert hat, mit seiner differenzierten Vorgeschichte und, wie schon angedeutet, auch seiner, nun wirklich universell-ökumenisch werdenden Nachgeschichte, deren Zeuge und Beteiligte wir noch heute sind. Die messianisch-apokalyptischen Bewegungen in Asien, Afrika und Amerika, wie sie sich mit Beginn der Christianisierung und Kolonialisierung überall plötzlich bildeten, sind ein Produkt dieser Geschichte: aktualisierte, neuformulierte Apk, geboren aus ähnlichen Gründen wie vor über 2000 Jahren, eingelassen in die Geschichte menschlicher Glaubenshoffnung. Das Thema Apk sprengt die Grenzen bloßer wissenschaftlicher Beschäftigung und stellt existentielle, aktuelle Fragen.

Bibliographie

Barr, James 1975: "Jewish Apocalyptic in Recent Scholarly Study", in: *BJRL* 58 (1975) 9–35.

Carmignac, Jean 1979: "Qu'est-ce que l'Apocalyptique? Son emploi à Qumrân", in: *RdQ* 10 (1979) 3–33.

Eicher, Peter 1979: "Offenbarungsreligion" in: P. Eicher (Hrsg.), *Gottesvorstellung und Gesellschaftsentwicklung* (FRW 1), München 1979, 109–126.

Gruenwald, Ithamar 1979a: "Jewish Apocalyptic Literature", in: H. Temporini/W. Haase (Hrsg.), *ANRW* II 19, 1, Berlin/New York 1979, 89–118.

– 1979b: *Apocalyptic and Merkavah Mysticism* (AGJU 14), Leiden 1979.

Hultgård, Anders 1979: "Das Judentum in der hellenistisch-römischen Zeit und die iranische Religion – ein religionsgeschichtliches Problem", in: H. Temporini/W. Haase (Hrsg.), *ANRW* II 19,1, Berlin/New York 1979, 512–590.

Kippenberg, Hans Gerhard 1978: "Die Geschichte der mittelpersischen apokalyptischen Traditionen", in: *StIr* 7 (1978) 49–80.

Lang, Bernhard 1979: "Die höheren Offenbarungen: Zur kulturellen Strategie der jüdischen Apokalyptik", in: P. Eicher (Hrsg.) 1979, 127–129.

Luria, S. 1929: "Die Ersten werden die Letzten sein", in: *Klio* 22 (1929) 405–431.

Marx, Karl/Engels, Friedrich 1958/1976: *Über Religion*, Berlin 1958 (1. Aufl.), 1976 (veränderte 2. Aufl.).

Rudolph, Kurt 1967: "Randerscheinungen des Judentums und das Problem der Entstehung des Gnostizismus", in: *Kairos* 9 (1967) 105–122; abgedruckt in: Rudolph (Hrsg.) 1975, 768–797.

– 1973: "Das Problem der Autonomie und Integration der Religionswissenschaft", in: *NedThT* 27 (1973) 105–131.

– (Hrsg.) 1975: *Gnosis und Gnostizismus* (WdF 262), Darmstadt 1975.

– 1980a: "Sophia und Gnosis. Bemerkungen zum Problem 'Gnosis und Frühjudentum'", in: K.-W. Tröger (Hrsg.), *Altes Testament – Frühjudentum – Gnosis*, Berlin 1980, 220–237.

– 1980b: *Die Gnosis*. Wesen und Geschichte einer spätantiken Religion, 2. Aufl., Leipzig 1980.

– 1981: "Basic Positions of Religionswissenschaft", in: *Religion* 11 (1981) 97–107.

Segal, Alan F. 1980: "Heavenly Ascent in Hellenistic Judaism, Early Christianity and their Environment", in: H. Temporini/W. Haase (Hrsg.), *ANRW* II 23, 2, Berlin/New York 1980, 1333–94.

Abbreviations

(1) For the abbreviations of names for Biblical Books with the Apocrypha and of the names of Pseudepigraphical and Early Patristic Books the following two systems have been utilized:
(a) The system of the *Journal of Biblical Literature (JBL): Instructions for Contributors*, in: *JBL* 95 (1976) 331–346 (here: 335–338) has been adopted for the ESSAYS IN ENGLISH;
(b) The system of the *Theologische Realenzyklopädie (TRE): Abkürzungsverzeichnis*, ed. S. Schwertner, Berlin–New York 1976 (here XIV–XVIII) has been used for the ESSAYS IN GERMAN.

(2) For the abbreviations of Periodicals, Reference Works, Serials *et cetera* the system of the *TRE* has been adopted for ALL ESSAYS.

Abbreviations which either are not represented in or diverge from the *TRE* are found in the following list of abbreviations.

(3) Separate lists of additional abbreviations are found in a number of articles relating especially to these essays.

LIST OF ABBREVIATIONS

AEO	Archives d'études orientales. Uppsala/Stockholm 1, 1910–20, 1934.
AGFLNW.G	Arbeitsgemeinschaft für Forschung des Landes Nordrhein-Westfalen. Köln-Opladen 1, 1953 ff.
ARSHLL	Acta Regiae Societatis Humaniorum Litterarum Lundensis. Lund 1, 1920 ff.
AUU.HR	Acta Universitatis Upsaliensis. Historia Religionum. Uppsala 1, 1961 ff.
AUU.SIU	Acta Universitatis Upsaliensis. Studia Indoeuropaea Upsaliensia. Uppsala–Stockholm 1, 1969 ff.
AW	Antike Welt. Zeitschrift für Archäologie und Urgeschichte. Zürich 1, 1970 ff.
BCdNH.T	Bibliothèque copte de Nag Hammadi, Textes. Québec/Louvain 1, 1977 ff.

BCESS	Bibliothèque des Centres d'Études supérieures spécialisés. Paris 1, 1956 ff.
BYUS	Brigham Young University Studies. Provo, Utah 1, 1959 ff.
CEM	Collection d'études mythologiques, Paris 1, 1974 ff.
CG	Codex Gnosticus. Cf. NHC *infra*.
CSA	Cahiers de la Société asiatique. Paris 1, 1933 ff.
CStL	Cambridge Studies in Linguistics, Cambridge 1, 1969 ff.
CTbL	Cambridge Textbooks in Linguistics, Cambridge 1, 1974 ff.
CTL	Current Trends in Linguistics. The Hague 1, 1963 ff.
EHiRel	Études d'histoire des religions. Paris 1, 1973 ff.
FbIdS	Forschungsberichte des Instituts für deutsche Sprache, Tübingen 1, 1968 ff.
FGrHist	Fragmente der griechischen Historiker. Berlin 1, 1923 ff.
FRW	Forum Religionswissenschaft. München 1, 1979 ff.
HDR	Harvard Dissertations in Religion. Missoula, Mont. 1, 1975 ff.
HNTC	Harper's New Testament Commentaries. New York 1, 1957 ff.
HRR	Historicorum Romanorum Reliquiae, ed. H. Peter, 2 Bände. Leipzig 1883/1906, Band I ²1914.
IDBSup	Interpreter's Dictionary of the Bible. Supplementary Volume. Nashville, Tenn. 1976.
ISMEO	Istituto Italiano per il Medio et Estremo Oriente. Roma.
IUO.SMin	Istituto Universitario Orientale Seminario di Studi Asiatici. Series Minor. Napoli 1, 1974 ff.
JAbSP	Journal of Abnormal and Social Psychology. Lancaster, Penn. 1, 1921 ff.
KVHAAH.FFS	Kungl. Vitterhets Historie och Antikvitets Akademiens Handlingar. Filologisk-filosofiska serien, Stockholm 1, 1954 ff.
LSJ	Greek English Lexicon, eds. H. G. Liddell/R. Scott/H. Stuart Jones, Oxford ⁹1940 and later reprints.
LSJSup	Greek English Lexicon. A Supplement, ed. E. A. Barber, Oxford 1968.
NHC	Nag Hammadi Codices. Cf. CG *supra*.
NHS	Nag Hammadi Studies. Leiden 1, 1971 ff.
NLH	New Literary History. Charlottesville, Va. 1, 1969 ff.
NumenSup	Supplements to Numen. Leiden 1, 1954 ff.
PDRI	Publications of the Diaspora Research Institute. Tel Aviv.

PMAPA   Philological Monographs of the American Philological
            Association. Cleveland, Ohio 1, 1931 ff.
RelStR   Religious Studies Review. Waterloo, Ont. 1, 1975 ff.
RTT   Research in Text Theory/Untersuchungen in Texttheo-
            rie. Berlin–New York 1, 1977 ff.
SBL   Society of Biblical Literature [Chico, Calif.].
SEG   Supplementum Epigraphicum Graecum. Leiden 1,
            1923–25, 1971; Alphen aan den Rijn/Germantown, Md.
            26, 1976 ff.
StAeg   Studia Aegyptiaca. Budapest 1, 1974 ff.
StIr   Studia Iranica. Paris 1, 1972 ff.
TAPA   Transactions of the American Philological Association.
            Boston 1, 1869 ff.; Cleveland, Ohio 104, 1974 ff.
WBMLUHW.K   Wissenschaftliche Beiträge der Martin-Luther-Universi-
            tät Halle–Wittenberg. Reihe K: Byzantinistische Bei-
            träge. Halle 1, 1968 ff.

Supplementary Bibliography
(1979–1988)

DAVID HELLHOLM

This Supplementary Bibliography does not claim to be complete, only representative. Literature up to 1983 referred to in the 1st edition is not repeated here. A few titles published before 1979 have been included. For abbreviations used in the Supplement, see above pp. 791 ff.

I. Texts and Editions

ALEXANDER, P. J.: *The Byzantine Apocalyptic Tradition,* ed. with an Introduction by D. deF. Abrahamse, Berkeley/Los Angeles/London 1985, 13–147 (Part One: Texts)

BARNSTONE, W.: *The Other Bible.* Ancient Esoteric Texts from the Pseudepigrapha, The Dead Sea Scrolls, the Nag Hammadi Library, and Other Sources, San Francisco 1984.

BERGER, K.: "Das Buch der Jubiläen", in: *JSHRZ,* Band II: Unterweisung in erzählender Form, Gütersloh 1981.

BERTRAND, D. A.: *La vie grecque d'Adam et Ève.* Introduction, texte, traduction et commentaire (Recherches intertestamentaires 1), Paris 1987.

BETZ, H. D. (ED.): *The Greek Magical Papyri in Translation.* Including the Demotic Spells, Vol. I: Texts, Chicago/London 1985.

BEYER, K.: *Die aramäischen Texte vom Toten Meer* samt den Inschriften aus Palästina, dem Testament Levi aus der Kairoer Genisa, der Fastenrolle und den alten talmudischen Zitaten; Aramaistische Einleitung, Text, Übersetzung, Deutung, Grammatik/Wörterbuch, Deutsch-aramäische Wortliste, Register, 2nd ed. Göttingen 1986.

BLACK, M. in Consultation with J. C. VANDERKAM: *The Book of Enoch or I Enoch.* A New English Edition with Commentary and Textual Notes. With an Appendix on the 'Astronomical' Chapters (72–82) by O. NEUGEBAUER (SVTP 7), Leiden 1985.

BOYCE, M.: *Zoroastrianism* (Textual Sources for the Study of Religion), Manchester 1984.

CHARLESWORTH, J. H. (ED.): *The Old Testament Pseudepigrapha.* Vol. I: Apocalyptic Literature and Testaments, Garden City, N. Y. 1983.

– Vol. II: Expansions of the 'Old Testament' and Other Legends, Wisdom and Philosophical Literature, Prayers, Psalms, and Odes, Fragments of Lost Judeo-Hellenistic Works, Garden City, N. Y. 1985.

CHARLESWORTH, J. H.: *The New Testament Apocrypha and Pseudepigrapha:* a Guide to Publications, with Excurses on Apocalypses, Metuchen, N. J./London 1987.

DÍEZ MACHO, A.: *Apocrifos de Antiguo Testamento,* I–IV, Madrid 1982–1984.

DUPONT-SOMMER, A./PHILONENKO, M.: *La Bible. Écrits intertestamentaires* (Bibliothèque de la Pléiade, tome III), Paris 1987.

GUILLAUMONT, A.: "Textes de Nag Hammadi: «L'Apocalypse de Pierre»", in: *Annuaire du Collège de France 1979–1980* 80 (1980) 471–473.

HENRICHS, A./KOENEN, L.: "Der Kölner Mani-Kodex", in: *ZPE* 19 (1975) 1–85; 32 (1978) 87–199; 44 (1981) 201–318; 48 (1982) 1–59.

HOFMANN, H.: *Das sogenannte hebräische Henochbuch (3 Henoch).* Nach dem von HUGO ODEBERG vorgelegten Material zum erstenmal ins Deutsche übersetzt (BBB 58), 2nd ed. Bonn 1984.

HOLLADAY, C. R.: *Fragments from Hellenistic Jewish Authors,* Vol. II: Poets – The Ethic Poets, Philo and Theodotus, and Ezekiel the Tragedian (SBL Texts and Translations, Pseudepigrapha Series), Atlanta, GA 1989 (forthcoming).

JACOBSON, H.: *The Exagoge of Ezekiel,* Cambridge 1983.

JEANSONNE, S. P.: *The Old Greek Translation of Daniel 7–12* (CBQ.MS 19), Washington, D. C. 1988.

DE JONGE, M./HOLLANDER, H. W./DE JONGE, H. J./KORTEWEG, TH.: *The Testaments of the Twelve Patriarchs.* A Critical Edition of the Greek Text (PVTG 1.2), Leiden 1978.

KAISER, O. (ED.): *Texte aus der Umwelt des Alten Testaments.* Band II, Lieferung 1: Deutungen der Zukunft in Briefen, Orakeln und Omina, Gütersloh 1986.

KESSELS, A. H. M./VAN DER HORST, P. W.: "The Vision of Dorotheus (Pap. Bodmer 29): Edited with Introduction, Translation and Notes", in: *VigChr* 41 (1987) 313–359.

KIRK, G. S./RAVEN, J. E./SCHOFIELD, M.: *The Presocratic Philosophers.* A Critical History with a Selection of Texts, Cambridge 2nd ed. 1983.

KLIJN, A. F. J.: *Der lateinische Text der Apokalypse des Esra.* Mit einem Index grammaticus von G. MUSSIES (TU 131), Berlin 1983.

– *Die Esra-Apokalypse (IV. Esra).* Nach dem lateinischen Text unter Benutzung der anderen Versionen übersetzt und herausgegeben (GCS), Berlin 1988.

KLOPPENBORG, J. S.: *Q Parallels: Synopsis, Critical Notes & Concordance* (Foundation & Facets), Sonoma, CA 1988.

KNIBB, M. A.: *The Ethiopic Book of Enoch.* 2 Vol. (I: Text, Apparatus; II: Introduction, Translation, Commentary), Oxford 1978.

KOENEN, L./RÖMER, C.: *Der Kölner Mani-Kodex.* Abbildungen und Diplomatischer Text, Bonn 1985.

LAYTON, B.: *The Gnostic Scriptures,* A New Translation with Annotations and Introductions, Garden City, N. Y. 1987.

LEEMHUIS, F./KLIJN, A. F. J./VAN GELDER, G. J. H.: *The Arabic Text of the Apocalypse of Baruch,* Edition and Translation with a Parallel Translation of the Syriac Text, Leiden 1986.

MAHÉ, J.-P.: *Hermès en Haute Egypte; Tome II: Le fragment du Discours Parfait et les Définitions hermétiques arméniennes (NH VI, 8.8a)* (BCdNH.T 7), Québec/Louvain 1982.

McGINN, B.: *Apocalyptic Spirituality.* Treatises and Letters of Lactantius, Adso of Montier-en-der, Joachim of Fiore, The Spiritual Franciscans, Savonarola. Translation and Introduction (The Classics of Western Spirituality), New York/Ramsay/Toronto 1979.

MORARD, F.:*L'Apocalypse d'Adam (NH V,5):* Texte établi et présenté (BCdNH.T 15), Québec/Louvain 1985.

NEUGEBAUER, O.: *The 'Astronomical' Chapters of the Ethiopic Book of Enoch (72–82).* Translation and Commentary. With Additional Notes on the Aramaic Fragments by M. BLACK (Det Kongelige Danske Videnskaberness Selskab, Matematisk-fysiske Meddelelser 40:10), Copenhagen 1981 [=Appendix A in M. Black 1985].

NEWSOM, C.: *Songs of the Sabbath Sacrifice: A Critical Edition, Translation and Commentary* (HSS 27), Atlanta, GA 1985.

NICKELSBURG, G. W. E./STONE, M. E.: *Faith an Piety in Early Judaism: Texts and Documents,* Philadelphia, PA 1983, esp. 117–201.

"Der Orphische Papyrus von Derveni", in: *ZPE* 47 (1982) 1–12 *(Appendix, no editor).*

PHILONENKO, M./PHILONENKO-SAYAR, B.: *L'Apocalypse d'Abraham.* Introduction, texte slave, traduction et notes *(Semitica* 31), Paris 1981.

– "Die Apokalypse Abrahams", in: *JSHRZ,* Band V: Apokalypsen, Gütersloh 1982.

PIETERSMA, A./TURNER COMSTOCK, S./ATTRIDGE, H.: *The Apocalypse of Elijah [Coptic] based on P. Chester Beatty 2018* (SBL Texts and Translations 19: Pseudepigraphia Series 9), Chico, CA [now Atlanta, GA] 1981.

SCHÄFER, P. (ED.): *Synopse zur Hekhalot-Literatur* (TSAJ 2), Tübingen 1981.

– *Konkordanz zur Hekhalot-Literatur.* Band 1 (TSAJ 12), Tübingen 1986.
– *Konkordanz zur Hekhalot-Literatur.* Band 2 (TSAJ 13), Tübingen 1987.
– *Übersetzung der Hekhalot-Literatur.* Band 2 (TSAJ 17), Tübingen 1987.
SCHMIDT, F.: *Le Testament Grec d'Abraham. Introduction, édition critique des deux recensions grecques, traduction* (TSAJ 11), Tübingen 1986.
SCHNEEMELCHER, W. (ED.): *Neutestamentliche Apokryphen in deutscher Übersetzung,* Band I: Evangelien, 5. Auflage, Tübingen 1987.
– Band II: Apostolisches, Apokalypsen und Verwandtes, 5. Auflage, Tübingen: in preparation for 1989.
SPARKS, H. F. D. (ED.): *The Apocryphal Old Testament,* Oxford 1984.
SCHRAGE, W.: "Die Elia-Apokalypse", in: *JSHRZ,* Band V: Apokalypsen, Gütersloh 1980.
STONE, M. E./STRUGNELL, J.: *The Books of Elijah. Parts 1 and 2* (SBL Texts and Translations 18: Pseudepigrapha Series 1), Missoula, MT [now Atlanta, GA] 1979.
STONE, M. E.: *The Armenian Version of IV Ezra.* Edition and Translation (University of Pennsylvania Armenian Texts and Studies 1), Missoula, MT [now Atlanta, GA] 1979.
– *Armenian Apocrypha.* Relating to the Patriarchs and Prophets, with Introduction, Translation and Commentary, Jerusalem 1982.
UHLIG, S.: "Das äthiopische Henochbuch", in: *JSHRZ,* Band V: Apokalypsen, Gütersloh 1984.
WENGST, K.: *Didache (Apostellehre), Barnabasbrief, Zweiter Klemensbrief, Schrift an Diognet.* Eingeleitet, herausgegeben, übertragen und erläutert (SUC II), Darmstadt 1984.

II. General Works on Apocalypticism

AUNE, D.: *Prophecy in Early Christianity and the Ancient Mediterranean World,* Grand Rapids, MI 1983.
BOUSSET, W.: *Der Antichrist in der Überlieferung des Judentums, des Neuen Testaments und der alten Kirche.* Ein Beitrag zur Auslegung der Apokalypse [1st ed. 1895], Hildesheim/Zürich/New York 1983.
COHEN, S. J. D.: *From the Maccabees to the Mishnah,* Philadelphia, PA 1987.
COLLINS, J. J.: *The Apocalyptic Imagination.* An Introduction to the Jewish Matrix of Christianity, New York 1984.
– *Daniel,* with an Introduction to Apocalyptic Literature (FOTL 20), Grand Rapids, MI 1984, 1–24 ("Introduction to Apocalyptic Literature"; Lit!).
– "Apocalyptic Literature", in: R. A. Kraft/G. W. E. Nickelsburg (edd.): *Early Judaism and its Modern interpreters* (The Bible and Its Modern Interpreters), Atlanta, GA/Philadelphia, PA 1986, 345–370.
– "The Place of Apocalypticism in the Religion of Israel", in: P. D. Miller, Jr./P. D. Hanson/ S. D. McBride (edd.): *Ancient Israelite Religion.* Essays in Honor of Frank Moore Cross, Philadelphia, PA 1987, 539–558.
– "The Apocalyptic Context of Christian Origins", in: M. P. O'Connor/D. N. Freedman (edd.): *Background of the Bible,* Winona Lake, IN 1987, 257–271.
COLLINS, J. J./GRUENWALD, I./FINE, L.: "Apocalypse", in: M. Eliade (ed.): *The Encyclopedia of Religion,* Vol. I, New York/London 1987, 334–344.
CULIANU, I. P.: *Iter in silvis. Saggi scelti sulla gnosi e altri studi,* Vol. I ("Gnosis" II), Messina 1981.
DEAN-OTTING, M.: *Heavenly Journeys: A Study of the Motif in Hellenistic Jewish Literature* (Judentum und Umwelt 8), Frankfurt am Main/Bern/New York 1984.
GAMMIE, J. G.: "Recent Books and Emerging Issues in the Study of Apocalyptic", in: *Quarterly Review* 5 (1985) 9–108.
GARCÍA MARTÍNEZ, F.: "Encore l'Apocalyptique", in: *JSJ* 17 (1986) 224–232.

GLASSON, T. F.: "What is Apocalyptic?", in: *NTS* 27 (1980/81) 98–105.

HANSON, P. D.: "Apocalyptic Literature", in: D. A. Knight/M. Tucker (edd.), *The Hebrew Bible and Its Modern Interpreters,* Philadelphia, PA/Chico, CA [now Atlanta, GA] 1985, 465–488.

– *Old Testament Apocalyptic* (Interpreting Biblical Texts), Nashville, TN 1987.

HIMMELFARB, M.: *Tours of Hell.* An Apocalyptic Form in Jewish and Christian Literature, Philadelphia, PA 1983/1985.

HORSLEY, R. A./HANSON, J. S.: *Bandits, Prophets and Messiahs: Popular Movements at the Time of Jesus,* Minneapolis, MN 1985.

KIPPENBERG, H. G.: "'Dann wird der Orient herrschen und der Okzident dienen.' Zur Begründung eines gesamtvorderasiatischen Standpunktes im Kampf gegen Rom", in: N. W. Bolz/ W. Hübener (edd.): *Spiegel und Gleichnis.* FS für J. Taubes, Würzburg 1983, 40–48.

KÖRTNER, U. H. J.: *Weltangst und Weltende.* Eine Theologische Interpretation der Apokalyptik, Göttingen 1988.

KOCH, K.: "Apokalyptik", in: *EKL* I, Göttingen 3rd ed. 1986, 192–199.

LAMBERT, W. G.: *The Background of Jewish Apocalyptic,* London 1978.

MCGINN, B.: *Visions of the End. Apocalyptic Tradition in the Middle Ages,* New York 1979.

MÜLLER, U. B.: "Apokalyptische Strömungen", in: J. Becker et alii, *Die Anfänge des Christentums.* Alte Welt und neue Hoffnung, Stuttgart/Berlin/Köln/Mainz 1987, 217–254.

NICHOLSON, E. W.: "Apocalyptic", in: G. W. Anderson (ed.): *Tradition and Interpretation.* Essays by Members of the Society for Old Testament Study, Oxford 1979, 189–213.

PÖHLMANN, W.: "Apokalyptische Geschichtsdeutung und geistiger Widerstand", in: *KuD* 34 (1988) 60–75.

ROWLAND, CH.: *The Open Heaven.* A Study of Apocalyptic in Judaism and Early Christianity, New York 1982.

SCHMIDT, F.: "'Traqué comme un loup.' A propos du débat actuel sur l'Apocalyptique juive", in: *ASSR* 53 (1982) 5–21.

SCHÜRER, E.: *The History of the Jewish People in the Age of Jesus Christ,* A New English Version Revised and Edited by G. Vermes, F. Millar, M. Goodman, Vol. III:1, Edinburgh 1986, 240–306.

– Vol. III:2, Edinburgh 1987, 746–756, 757–760, 787–808.

SMITH, J. Z.: *Map is not Territory.* Studies in the History of Religions (SJLA 23), Leiden 1978.

– *Imagining Religion,* Chicago 1982.

STECK, O. H.: "Überlegungen zur Eigenart der spätisraelitischen Apokalyptik", in: J. Jeremias/ L. Perlitt (edd.): *Die Botschaft und die Boten.* FS für H. W. Wolff, Neukirchen-Vluyn 1981, 301–315.

STONE, M. E.: "Apocalyptic Literature", in: M. E. Stone (ed.): *Jewish Writings of the Second Temple Period* (CRI II), Assen/Philadelphia, PA 1984, 383–441.

SULLIVAN, L. E.: *Icanchu's Drum: An Orientation to Meaning in South American Religions,* New York 1988, 549–614 with endnotes 867–885.

TIGCHELAAR, E. J. C.: "More on Apocalyptic and Apocalypses", in: *JSJ* 18 (1987) 137–144.

VANDERKAM, J. C.: "Recent Studies in 'Apocalyptic'", in: *Word World* 4 (1984) 70–77.

III. Collections of Essays

ALTHAUS, H. (ED.): *Apokalyptik und Eschatologie.* Sinn und Ziel der Geschichte, Freiburg i. Br. 1987 with contributions by:

MERKLEIN, H.: "Eschatologie im Neuen Testament", 11–42;

MAIER, J.: "Apokalyptik im Judentum", 43–72;

SCHAEFFLER, R.: "Vollendung der Welt oder Weltgericht. Zwei Vorstellungen vom Ziel der Geschichte in Religion und Philosophie", 73–104;

HÜNERMANN, P.: "Reich Gottes – Sinn und Ziel der Geschichte", 105–142.

CAQUOT, A./HADAS-LEBEL, M./RIAUD, J. (EDD.): *Hellenica et Judaica.* Hommage à Valentin Nikiprowetzky, Leuven/Paris 1986 with contributions pertaining to Apocalypticism by:

DIMANT, D.: *"4QFlorilegium* and the Idea of the Community as Temple", 165–189;

BOGAERT, P.-M.: "La chronologie dans la dernière vision de Daniel (*DN* 10,4 et 12,11–12)", 207–211;

CHARLESWORTH, J. H.: "Greek, Persian, Roman, Syrian, and Egyptian Influences in Early Jewish Theology", 219–243;

HILGERT, E.: "«By the Sea of Jamnia», *TNaph* 6:1", 245–255;

RIAUD, J.: "«Le puissant t'emportera dans la tente.» La destinée ultime du juste selon les *Paralipomena Jeremiae Prophetae*", 257–265;

HADAS-LEBEL, M.: "Rome «quatrième empire» et le symbole du porc", 297–312.

CIRILLO, L./ROSELLI, A. (EDD.): *Codex Manichaicus Coloniensis.* Atti del Simposio Internazionale (Rende-Amantea 3–7 settembre 1984), Cosenca 1986 with the contributions by:

CIRILLO, L.: "Elchasaiti e Battisti di Mani", 97–140;

KLIJN, A. F. J.: "Alchasoios et CMC", 141–152;

KOENEN, L.: "Manichaean Apocalypticism at the Crossroads of Iranian, Egyptian, Jewish and Christian Thought", 285–332;

ROSENSTIEHL, J. M.: "C.M.C. 60,13–62,9: contribution à l'étude de l'Apocalypse apocryphe de Paul", 345–354.

COLLINS, A. Y. (ED.): *Early Christian Apocalypticism: Genre and Social Setting (SEMEIA* 36), Atlanta, GA 1986 with contributions by:

COLLINS, A. Y.: "Introduction: Early Christian Apocalypticism", 1–11;

HELLHOLM, D.: "The Problem of Apocalyptic Genre and the Apocalypse of John", 13–64;

AUNE, D.: "The Apocalypse of John and the Problem of Genre", 65–96;

HIMMELFARB, M.: "The Experience of the Visionary and Genre in the Ascension of Isaiah 6–11 and the Apocalypse of Paul", 97–111;

OSIEK, C.: "The Genre and Function of the Shepherd of Hermas", 113–121;

SCHÜSSLER FIORENZA, E.: "The Followers of the Lamb: Visionary Rhetoric and Social-Political Situation", 123–146;

THOMPSON, L.: "A Sociological Analysis of Tribulation in the Apocalypse of John", 147–174.

HANSON, P. D. (ED.): *Visionaries and Their Apocalypses* (Issues in Religion and Theology 2), Philadelphia, PA 1983 with a new 'Introduction' by the editor and reprints of contributions from 1971–80 by:

HANSON, D.: "Introduction", 1–15;

KOCH, K.: "What is Apocalyptic? An Attempt at a Preliminary Definition", 16–36;

HANSON, P. D.: "Old Testament Apocalyptic Reexamined", 37–60;

COLLINS, J. J.: "Apocalyptic Eschatology as the Transcendence of Death", 61–64;

STONE, M.: "New Light on the Third Century", 85–91;

STONE, M.: "Enoch and Apocalyptic Origins", 92–100;

SMITH, J. Z.: "Wisdom and Apocalyptic", 101–120;

PERRIN, N.: "Apocalyptic Christianity", 121–145;

GAGER, J. G.: "The Attainment of Millennial Bliss Through Myth: The Book of Revelation", 146–155.

VAN HENTEN, J. W./DE JONGE, H. J./VAN ROODEN, P. T./WESSELIUS, J. W. (EDD.): *Tradition and Re-Interpretation in Jewish and Early Christian Literature.* Essays in Honour of J. C. H. Lebram (StPB 36), Leiden 1986 with contributions pertaining to Apocalypticism by:

VAN D. KOOIJ, A.: "A Case of Reinterpretation in the Old Greek of Daniel 11", 72–80;

DEHANDSCHUTTER, B.: "Pseudo-Cyprian, Jude and Enoch. Some Notes on 1 Enoch 1:9", 114–120;

BERGER, K.: "Streit um Gottes Vorsehung. Zur Position der Gegner im 2. Petrusbrief", 121–135;

DE JONGE, M.: "Two Messiahs in the Testaments of the Twelve Patriarchs?", 150–162;
VAN UCHELEN, N. A.: "Ethical Terminology in Heykhalot-texts", 250–258.
Interpretation 39 (1985) April issue devoted to the Book of Daniel with contributions by:
KOCH, K.: "Is Daniel also Among the Prophets?", 117–130;
COLLINS, J. J.: "Daniel and His Social World", 131–143;
GAMMIE, J. G.: "A Journey Through Danielic Spaces", 144–156.
Interpretation 40 (1986) July issue devoted to the Book of Revelation with contributions by:
COLLINS, A. Y.: "Reading the Book of Revelation in the Twentieth Century", 229–242;
BARR, D. L.: "The Apocalypse of John as Oral Enactment", 243–256;
BORING, M. E.: "The Theology of Revelation", 257–269.
KAPPLER, C. ET COLLABORATEURS (EDD.): *Apocalypses et voyages dans l'au-delà*, Paris 1987 with
contributions by:
KAPPLER, C.: "Introduction général", 15–48;
BOTTÉRO, J.: "Le «Pays-sans-retour»", 55–82;
XELLA, P.: "Baal et la mort", 83–100;
RIBICHINI, S.: "Traditions phéniciennes chez Philon de Byblos: une vie éternelle pour des
dieux mortels", 101–118;
BÉRARD, C.: "Apocalypses éleusiennes", 127–156;
PIÑERO-SAÉNZ, A.: "Les traditions de l'inspiration dans l'apocalyptique juive et chrétienne
(VIe s. av. J.C. – IIIe s. ap. J.C.)", 157–184;
GARCÍA-MARTÍNEZ, F.: "Les traditions apocalyptiques à Qumrân", 201–236;
KAPPLER, C.: "L'apocalypse latine de Paul", 237–266;
RENAUD, E.: "Le récit du *mi'râj:* une version arabe de l'ascension du Prophète dans le *Tafsîr* de
Tabarî", 267–292;
PIEMONTESE, A. M.: "Le voyage de Mahomet au paradis et en enfer: une version persane du
mi'râj", 293–320;
SCOPELLO, M.: "Contes apocalyptiques et apocalypses philosophiques dans la bibliothèque
de Nag Hammadi", 321–350;
GIGNOUX, P.: "Apocalypses et voyages extra-terrestres dans l'Iran mazdéen", 351–376;
TEIXIDOR, J.: "L'apôtre marchand d'âmes dans la première littérature syriaque. Voies com-
merciales et voies de l'Evangile au Proche Orient, 379–398;
BRAET, H.: "Les visions de l'Invisible (VIe–XIIIe siècle)", 405–420;
CARDINI, F.: "Note sur la tradition apocalyptique dans l'Italie médiéval (XIIe–XVe siècle)",
421–444;
VERNANT, J.: "L'Apocalypse et le nucléaire", 445–472;
FERRAROTTI, F.: "Elle lui dit alors, la Gabrielle . . .", 473–480.
KLIMKEIT, H.-J. (ED.): *Tod und Jenseits im Glauben der Völker* (Sammlung Harrassowitz),
Wiesbaden 1978 with contributions by:
OZOLS, J.: "Über die Jenseitsvorstellungen des vorgeschichtlichen Menschen", 14–39;
THIEL, J. F.: "Tod und Jenseitsglaube in Bantu-Afrika", 40–47;
SCHÜTZINGER, H.: "Tod und ewiges Leben im Glauben des Alten Zweistromlandes", 48–61;
KLIMKEIT, H.-J.: "Der iranische Auferstehungsglaube", 62–76;
PLÖGER, O.: "Tod und Jenseits im Alten Testament", 77–85;
ZIMMERMANN, H.: "Tod und Auferstehung im neutestamentlichen Frühchristentum",
86–96;
HOHEISEL, K.: "Tod und Jenseits im außerbiblischen Judentum des Orients", 97–109;
GABELMANN, H.: "Tod und Apotheose in der römischen Grabkunst", 111–129;
NAGEL, T.: "Das Leben nach dem Tod in islamischer Sicht", 130–144;
VOGEL, C.: "Tod und Jenseits nach der Lehre des Buddha", 145–157;
FISCHER, K.: "Darstellungen vom Tode auf einigen buddhistischen Kunstwerken", 158–174;
SAGASTER, K.: "Grundgedanken des tibetischen Totenbuches", 175–189.

La Littérature Intertestamentaire. Colloque de Strasbourg (17–19 octobre 1983) (BCESS), Paris 1985 with contributions by:
CAQUOT, A.: "Avant-propos", 5–9;
CHARLESWORTH, J. H.: "The Significance of the New Edition of the Old Testament Pseudepigrapha", 11–28;
PIÑERO-SAÉNZ, A.: "Les conceptions de l'inspiration dans les Pseudépigraphes de l'Ancien Testament", 29–41;
HULTGÅRD, A.: "Théophanie et présence divine dans le judaïsme antique: Quelques remarques à partir des textes «intertestamentaires»", 43–55;
CAQUOT, A.: "Éléments aggadiques dans le livre des «Jubilés»", 57–68;
LAPERROUSAZ, E.-M.: "Le classement chronologique des passages messianiques des «Manuscrits de la mer Morte»", 69–88;
PHILONENKO-SAYAR, B.: "La version slave de l'«Apocalypse de Baruch»", 89–97;
ROSENSTIEHL, J.-M.: "Les révélations d'Élie. Élie et les tourments des damnés", 99–107;
BERTRAND, D. A.: "Le destin «post mortem» des protoplastes selon la «Vie grecque d'Adam et Ève»", 109–118;
PETIT, M.: "La cachette de l'Arche d'Alliance: à partir de la «Vie de Jérémie» 9–15 dans les «Vitae Prophetarum»", 119–131;
RIAUD, J.: "Les samaritains dans les «Paralipomena Jeremiae»", 133–152;
HADOT, J.: "Le milieu d'origine du «Liber Antiquitatum Biblicarum»", 153–171;
ANDERSON, H.: "Third and Fourth Maccabees and Jewish Apologetics", 173–179;
SÄNGER, D.: "Erwägungen zur historischen Einordnung und zur Datierung von «Joseph und Aseneth»", 181–202;
SCHMIDT, F.: "L'autorité du «Quatrième Livre d'Esdras» dans la discussion sur la parenté des Juifs et des Indiens d'Amerique (1540–1661)", 203–220;
PHILONENKO, M.: "Prière au soleil et liturgie angélique", 221–228.
LAMBRECHT, J. (ED.): *L'Apocalypse johannique et l'Apocalyptique dans le Nouveau Testament* (BEThL 53), Paris-Gembloux/Leuven 1980 with contributions by:
VANNI, U.: "L'Apocalypse johannique. État de la question", 21–46;
BOGAERT, P.-M.: "Les apocalypses contemporaines de Baruch, d'Esdras et de Jean", 47–68;
JANNSENS, Y.: "Apocalypses de Nag Hammadi", 69–75;
LAMBRECHT, J.: "A Structuration of Revelation 4,1–22,5", 77–104;
SCHÜSSLER FIORENZA, E.: "Apocalypsis and Propheteia. The Book of Revelation in the Context of Early Christian Prophecy", 105–128;
HARTMAN, L.: "Form and Message. A Preliminary Discussion of «Partial Texts» in Rev 1–3 and 22,6 ff.", 129–149;
DELOBEL, J.: "Le texte de l'Apocalypse: Problèmes de méthode", 151–166;
MUSSIES, G.: "The Greek of the Book of Revelation", 167–177;
LUST, J.: "The Order of the Final Events in Revelation and Ezekiel", 179–183;
YARBRO COLLINS, A.: "Revelation 18: Taunt-Song or Dirge?", 185–204;
WILCOX, M.: "Tradition and Redaction of Rev 21,9–22,5", 205–215;
VAN SCHAIK, A. P.: "Ἄλλος ἄγγελος in Apk 14", 217–228;
COPPENS, J.: "La mention d'un Fils d'homme angélique en Ap 14,14", 229;
PRIGENT, P.: "Le temps et le Royaume dans l'Apocalypse", 231–245;
HOLTZ, T.: "Gott in der Apokalypse", 247–265;
DE JONGE, M.: "The Use of the Expression ὁ χριστός in the Apocalypse of John", 267–281;
DEHANDSCHUTTER, B.: "The Meaning of Witness in the Apocalypse", 283–288;
BÖCHER, O.: "Das Verhältnis der Apokalypse des Johannes zum Evangelium des Johannes", 289–301;
GEYSER, A. S.: "Some Salient New Testament Passages on the Restoration of the Twelve Tribes of Israel", 305–310;

RESE, M.: "Die Rolle Israels im apokalyptischen Denken des Paulus", 311–318;

MAYEDA, G.: "Apocalyptic in the Epistle to the Romans – An Outline", 319–323;

COLLINS, R. F.: "Tradition, Redaction, and Exhortation in I Th 4,13–5,11", 325–343;

COPPENS, J.: "Le *katechon* et le *katechôn*: derniers obstacles à la parousie du Seigneur Jésus", 345–348;

KORTEWEG, T.: "«You will seek me and you will not find me» (Jn 7,34). An Apocalyptic Pattern in Johannine Theology", 349–354;

PESCH, R.: "Markus 13", 355–368;

NEIRYNCK, F.: "Marc 13. Examen critique de l'interprétation de R. Pesch", 369–401;

LÖVESTAM, E.: "The ἡ γενεὰ αὕτη in Mk 13,30 parr.", 403–413;

BEASLEY-MURRAY, G. R.: "Jesus and Apocalyptic: With Special Reference to Mark 14,62", 415–429.

MARCUS, J./SOARDS, M. L. (EDD.): *Apocalyptic and the New Testament*. Essays in Honor of J. Louis Martyn (JSNT.SS 24), Sheffield 1988 (forthcoming), with contributions by:

STURM, R. E.: "Defining the Word 'Apocalyptic': A Problem in Biblical Criticism";

MARCUS, J.: "'The Time Has Been Fulfilled!' (Mark 1.15)";

SCHABERG, J.: "Mark 14.62: Early Christian Merkabah Imagery?";

BROOKS, S. H.: "Apocalyptic Paraenesis in Matthew 6.19–34";

COPE, O. L.: "'To the Close of the Age': The Role of Apocalyptic Thought in the Gospel of Matthew";

SCROGGS, R.: "Eschatological Existence in Matthew and Paul: *Coincidentia Oppositorum*";

BOOMERSHINE, T. E.: "'Epistemology at the Turn of the Ages' in Paul, Jesus, and Mark";

DE BOER, M. C.: "Paul and Jewish Apocalyptic Eschatology";

HAYS, R. B.: "'The Righteous One' as Eschatological Deliverer: A Case Study in Paul's Apocalyptic Hermeneutics";

KOVACS, J. L.: "The Archons, the Spirit, and the Death of Christ: Do We Need the Hypothesis of Gnostic Opponents to Explain 1 Corinthians 2.2–26?";

SOARDS, M. L.: "*Seeking* and *Sinning* according to Galatians 2.17";

ANDERSON, C. P.: "Who Are the Heirs of the New Age in the Epistle to the Hebrews?";

DUFF, N. J.: "The Significance of Pauline Apocalyptic for Theological Ethics";

LEHMANN, P.: "Barmen and the Church's Call to Faithfulness and Social Responsibility";

MARTYN, D. W.: "A Child and Adam: A Parable of the Two Ages".

MAUSER, U. (ED.): *Horizons in Biblical Theology* 7/2 (1985) with contributions by:

HANSON, P. D.: "Biblical Apocalypticism: The Theological Dimension", 1–20;

KEE, H. C.: "New Rule of God, New People of God", 21–51;

HAGNER, D. A.: "Apocalyptic Motifs in the Gospel of Matthew: Continuity and Discontinuity", 53–82;

GOWAN, D. E.: "The Fall and Redemption of the Material World in Apocalyptic Literature", 83–103;

BEKER, J. C.: "Suffering and Triumph in Paul's Letter to the Romans", 105–119.

Neotestamentica (Journal of the New Testament Society of South Africa [NTSSA]) 17 (1983) with contributions by:

VORSTER, W. S.: "1 Enoch and the Jewish Literary Setting of the New Testament. A Study in Text Types", 1–14;

HARTMAN, L.: "An Early Example of Jewish Exegesis: 1 Enoch 10:16–11:2", 16–27;

LE ROUX, J. H.: "The Use of Scripture in 1 Enoch 10:16–11:2", 28–38;

THOM, J. C.: "Aspects of the Form, Meaning and Function of the Book of Watchers", 40–48;

DE VILLIERS, P. G. R.: "Revealing the Secrets. Wisdom and the World in the Similitudes of Enoch", 50–68;

DECOOK, P. B.: "Holy Ones, Sons of God, and the Transcendent Future of the Righteous in 1 Enoch and the New Testament", 70–82;

MALAN, J. C.: "Enochic (Apocalyptic) and Christian Perspectives on Relationships", 94–96.

NEUSNER, J./GREEN, W. S./FRERICHS, E. (EDD.): *Judaism and their Messiahs at the Turn of the Christian Era,* Cambridge 1987, with contributions by:

GREEN, W. S.: "Introduction: Messiah in Judaism: Rethinking the Question", 1–13;

MACK, B. L.: "Wisdom Makes a Difference: Alternatives to 'Messianic' Configurations", 15–48;

NICKELSBURG, G. W. E.: "Salvation without and with a Messiah: Developing Beliefs in Writings Ascribed to Enoch", 49–68;

GOLDSTEIN, J. A.: "How the Authors of 1 and 2 Maccabees Treated the 'Messianic' Promises", 69–96;

COLLINS, J. J.: "Messianism in the Maccabean Period", 97–109;

TALMON, S.: "Waiting for the Messiah: The Spiritual Universe of the Qumran Covenanters", 111–137;

HECHT, R. D.: "Philo and Messiah", 139–168;

MACREA, G.: "Messiah and Gospel", 169–185;

KEE, H. C.: "Christology in Mark's Gospel", 187–208;

STONE, M. E.: "The Question of the Messiah in 4 Ezra", 209–224;

CHARLESWORTH, J. H.: "From Jewish Messianology to Christian Christology: Some Caveats and Perspectives", 225–264;

NEUSNER, J.: "Mishna and Messiah", 265–282.

PESCE, M. (ED.): *Isaia, il diletto e la chiesa: Visione ed esegesi profetica cristiano-primitiva nell'*Ascensione di Isaia. Atti del Convegno di Roma 9–10 aprile 1981 (Testi e Ricerche di Scienze religiose 20), Brescia 1983 with contributions by:

PESCE, M.: "Presupposti per l'utilizzazione storica dell'*Ascensione di Isaia.* Formazione e tradizione del testo; genere letterario; cosmologia angelica", 13–76;

PERRONE, L.: "Note critiche (e «autocritiche») sull'edizione del testo etiopico dell'*Ascensione di Isaia*", 77–93;

CULIANU, I. P.: "La *Visione di Isaia* e la tematica della *Himmelsreise*", 95–116;

GNOLI, G.: "Questioni comparative sull'*Ascensione* d'Isaia: la tradizione iranica", 117–132;

BORI, P. C.: "L'esperienza profetica nell'*Ascensione di Isaia*", 133–154;

BIANCHI, U.: "L'*Ascensione di Isaia.* Tematiche soteriologiche di *descensus/ascensus*", 155–183;

SIMONETTI, M.: "Note sulla cristologia dell'*Ascensione di Isaia*", 185–209;

NORELLI, E.: "Sulla pneumatologia dell'*Ascensione di Isaia*", 211–276;

ACERBI, A.: "L'*Ascensione di Isaia* nelle testimonianze del IV e V secolo. Ambiti di presenza e ipotesi ricostruttive", 277–298.

PHILONENKO, M. (ED.): *Apocalyptique iranienne et dualisme juif: questions actuelles,* Stockholm 1989 (forthcoming) with contributions by:

WIDENGREN, G.: "Avant-propos";

– "Les quatre âges du monde";

HULTGÅRD, A.: "Le Bahman Yasht – structure et genèse";

PHILONENKO, M.: "Le dualisme juif".

STUIP, R. E. V./VELLEKOOP, C. (EDD.): *Visioenen* (Utrechtse bijdragen tot de mediëvistiek 6), Utrecht 1986 with contributions by:

BODEWITZ, H. W.: "Oudindische visionaire literatuur", 9–23;

KESSELS, A. H. M.: "Visioenen in de Griekse traditie: Er en Thespesios", 24–53;

NELSON, H. L. W.: "De twee vermaardste 'visioenen' van de Latijnse literatuur: Cicero's *Droom van Scipio* en Boek VI van Vergilius' *Aeneis*", 54–77;

DE NIE, G.: "*Een ontzagwekkende man.* Beelden van de heilige in visioen en maatschappij in zesde-eeuws Gallië", 78–97;

EDEL, D.: "De Keltische traditie: de verkenning van de Andere Wereld", 98–121;

VAN RUN, A. J.: "*Imaginaria visione.* Over kunst en visioenen in de Meddeleeuwen", 122–150;

VELLEKOOP, C.: "Het visioen van boer Gottschalk", 151–168;

ALINEI, M.: "Dantes visies en Dantes visioenen", 169–192;

MOMMAERS, P.: "Het visioen bij de mystica Hadewijch", 193–204;

VEKEMAN, H. W. J.: "Het visioen als middeleeuws genre", 205–225;

VERGOTE, A.: "Psychologische interpretatie van visioenen", 226–239.

TEMPORINI, H./HAASE, W. (EDD.): *Aufstieg und Niedergang der römischen Welt,* Berlin/New York. 1979–1987 with contributions pertaining to Apocalypticism by:

Volume 17,4 (1984):

BLANCO, A. G.: "A Bibliographical Approach", 2241–2281 (4. Nag Hammadi, *ibid.* 2247–2252; 5. The Version of the Asclepius, *ibid.* 2253);

WIGTIL, D. N.: "Incorrect Apocalyptic: The Hermetic 'Asclepius' as an Improvement on the Greek Original", 2282–2297.

Volume 19,2 (1979):

RUBINKIEWICZ, R.: "La vision de l'histoire dans l'Apocalypse d'Abraham", 137–151.

Volume 20,1 (1987):

COLLINS, J. J.: "The development of the Sibylline Tradition", 421–459.

Volume 20,2 (1987):

STROBEL, A.: "Weltenjahr, große Konjunktion und Messiasstern. Ein thematischer Überblick", 988–1187.

Volume 21,2 (1984):

COLLINS, A. Y.: "Numerical Symbolism in Jewish and Early Christian Apocalyptic Literature", 1221–1287.

Volume 23,2 (1980):

SEGAL, A. F.: "Heavenly Ascent in Hellenistic Judaism, Early Christianity and their Environment", 1333–1394;

HANSON, J. S.: "Dreams and Visions in the Graeco-Roman World and Early Christianity", 1395–1427;

BERGER, K.: "Hellenistisch-heidnische Prodigien und die Vorzeichen jüdischer und christlicher Apokalyptik", 1428–1469;

AUNE, D. E.: "Magic in Early Christianity", 1507–1557.

Volume 25,2 (1984):

BERGER, K.: "Hellenistische Gattungen im Neuen Testament", 1031–1432, therein 1316–1325.

TUCKER, G. (ED.): *Focus on Apocalypticism* [= *Quarterly Review* 4 (1984) 9–84] with contributions by:

JEWETT, R.: "Coming to Terms with the Doom Boom", 9–22;

HANSON, P. D.: "The Apocalyptic Consciousness", 23–39;

NEWSOM, C.: "The Past as Revelation: History in Apocalyptic Literature", 40–53;

JENNINGS, JR., T. W.: "Apocalyptic and Contemporary Theology", 54–68;

COLLINS, A. Y.: "'What the Spirit Says to the Churches': Preaching the Apocalypse", 69–84.

WILLIS, W. (ED.): *The Kingdom of God in 20th-Century Interpretation,* Peabody, MA 1987 with contributions pertaining to Apocalypticism by:

PATRICK, D.: "The Kingdom of God in the Old Testament", 67–79;

COLLINS, J. J.: "The Kingdom of God in the Apocrypha and Pseudepigrapha", 81–95;

VIVIANO, B. T.: "The Kingdom of God in the Qumran Literature", 97–107;

MICHAELS, J. R.: "The Kingdom of God and the Historical Jesus", 109–118;

FARMER, R.: "The Kingdom of God in the Gospel of Matthew", 119–130;

BORING, M. E.: "The Kingdom of God in Mark", 131–145;

O'TOOLE, R.: "The Kingdom of God in Luke-Acts", 147–162;

HODGSON, JR., R.: "The Kingdom of God in the School of St. John", 163–174;

DONFRIED, K. P.: "The Kingdom of God in Paul", 175–190;

FURGESON, E.: "The Kingdom of God in Early Patristic Literature", 191–208.

IV. Works Related to Specific Topics and Texts

ABUSCH, I. T.: *"Alaktu* and *Halakhah.* Oracular Decision, Divine Revelation", in: *HThR* 80 (1987) 15–42.

ACERBI, A.: *Serra lignea.* Studi sulla fortuna della Ascensione di Isaia, Roma 1984.

ADLER, W.: "Berossus, Manetho and 1 Enoch in the World Chronicle of Pandorus", in: *HThR* 76 (1983) 419–442.

AEJMELAEUS, L.: *Wachen vor dem Ende.* Die traditionsgeschichtlichen Wurzeln von 1. Thess. 5:1–11 und Luk 21:34–36 (Schriften der Finnischen Exegetischen Gesellschaft 44), Helsinki 1985.

AGUS, J. B.: "The Messianic Ideal and the Apocalyptic Vision", in: *Judaism* 32 (1983) 205–214.

ALAND, K.: "Noch einmal: Das Problem der Anonymität und Pseudonymität in der christlichen Literatur der ersten beiden Jahrhunderte", in: E. Dassmann/K. S. Frank (edd.): *Pietas.* FS für B. Kötting (JAC.E8), Münster/Westf. 1980, 121–139.

ALEXANDER, P. J.: *The Byzantine Apocalyptic Tradition,* ed. with an Introduction by D. deF. Abrahamse, Berkeley/Los Angeles/London 1985, 151–225 (Part Two: Themes).

ALEXANDER, P. S.: "Notes on the 'Imago mundi' of the Book of Jubilees", in: *JJS* 33 ([= G. Vermes/J. Neusner (edd.): *Essays in Honour of Y. Yadin,* Oxford] 1982) 197–213.

– "Comparing Merkavah Mysticism and Gnosticism: An Essay in Method", in: *JJS* 35 (1984) 1–18.

– "3 Enoch and the Talmud", in: *JSJ* 13 (1986) 40–68.

ANDERSON, B. W.: "The Apocalyptic Rendering of the Isaiah Tradition", in: J. Neusner/ P. Borgen/R. Horsley (edd.): *The Social World of Formative Christianity and Judaism:* Essays in Tribute to Howard Clark Kee, Philadelphia, PA 1988, 17–38.

ARANA, G.: "Ideas escatológicas judías en el Apocalipsis copto de Elias", in: N. Fernández Marcos et alii (edd.): *Simposio Bíblico Español, Salamanca 1982,* Madrid 1984, 663–679.

ARTHUR, R. L.: "On the Origin of the World (II, 5)", in: R. L. Arthur, *The Wisdom Goddess: Feminine Motifs in Eight Nag Hammadi Documents.* With Critical Translations of On the Origin of the World and The Thunder by R. L. Arthur, Lanham, MD/New York/London 1984, 187–217.

ASENSIO, F.: "El protagonismo del 'Hombre-Hijo de Hombre' del Salmo 8", in *EstB* 41 (1983) 17–51.

ASMUSSEN, H. G.: *Daniel, Prophet oder Fälscher?* Eine historisch-kritische und literarhistorische Untersuchung, Heidelberg 1981.

AUNE, D. E.: "The Social Matrix of the Apocalypse of John", in: *BR* 26 (1981) 16–32.

– "The Influence of Roman Imperial Court Ceremonial on the Apocalypse of John", in: *BR* 28 (1983) 5–26.

– "Oracles", in: M. Eliade (ed.): *The Encyclopedia of Religion,* Vol. XI, New York/London 1987, 81–87.

– "The Apocalypse of John and Graeco-Roman Revelatory Magic", in: *NTS* 33 (1987) 481–501.

BACCHIOCCHI, S.: "Sabbatical Typologies of Messianic Redemption" in: *JSJ* 17 (1986) 153–176.

BAIRD, W.: "Visions, Revelation, and Ministry: Reflections on 2 Cor 12:1–5 and Gal 1:11–17", in: *JBL* 104(1985) 651–662.

BAMPFYLDE, G.: "The Prince of the Host in the Book of Daniel and the Dead Sea Scrolls", in: *JSJ* 14 (1983) 129–134.

– "The Similitudes of Enoch. Historical Allusions", in: *JSJ* 15 (1984) 9–13.

BARABÁS, A. M.: "Movimientos étnicos religiosos y seculares en América Latina", in: *América Indígena* 46 (1986) 495–529.

BARKER, M.: *The Older Testament. The Survival of Themes from the Ancient Royal Cult in Sectarian Judaism and Early Christianity,* London 1987.

BARR, D.: "The Apocalypse as a Symbolic Transformation of the World: A Literary Analysis", in: *Int* 38 (1984) 39–50.
- "Elephants and Holograms: From Metaphor to Methodology in the Study of John's Apocalypse", in: K. H. Richards (ed.): *SBL Seminar Papers 25, 1986,* Atlanta, GA 1986, 400–411.
BARRETT, C. K.: "Gnosis and the Apocalypse of John", in: A. H. B. Logan/A. J. M. Wedderburn (edd.): *New Testament and Gnosis.* Essays in Honour of Robert McL. Wilson, Edinburgh 1983, 125–137.
BAUCKHAM, R. J.: "A Note on a Problem in the Greek Version of 1 Enoch 1:9", in: *JThS* 31 (1980) 136–138.
- "The Worship of Jesus in Apocalyptic Christianity", in: *NTS* 27 (1980/81) 322–341.
- "The Son of Man: 'a man in any position' or 'someone'", in: *JSNT* 19 (1983) 23–33.
- "Enoch and Eliah in the Coptic Apocalypse of Eliah", in: E. A. Livingstone (ed.): *Studia Patristica XVI.* Papers presented to the Seventh International Conference on Patristic Studies (TU 129), Berlin 1985, 69–76.
- "The Two Fig Tree Parables in the Apocalypse of Peter", in: *JBL* 104 (1985) 269–287.
BAUMGARTEN, J.: "Some Problems of the Jubilees Calendar in Current Research", in: *VT* 32 (1982) 485–489.
- "The Book of Elkesai and Merkabah Mysticism", in: *JSJ* 17 (1986) 212–223.
- "The Calendars of the Book of Jubilees and the Temple Scroll", in: *VT* 37 (1987) 71–78.
BEAGLEY, A. J.: *The 'Sitz im Leben' of the Apocalypse with Particular Reference to the Role of the Church's Enemies* (BZNW 50), Berlin/New York 1987.
BEALE, G. K.: "The Danielic Background for Revelation 13:18 and 17:9", in: *TynB* 31 (1980) 163–170.
- "The Problem of the Man from the Sea in IV Ezra 13 and its Relation to the Messianic Concept in John's Apocalypse", in: *NT* 25 (1983) 182–188.
- *The Use of Daniel in Jewish Apocalyptic Literature and in the Revelation of St. John,* Lanham, MD/New York/London 1984.
- "The Origin of the Title 'King of Kings and Lord of Lords' in Revelation 17.14", in: *NTS* 31 (1985) 618–620.
- "A Reconsideration of the Text of Daniel in the Apocalypse", in: *Bib.* 67 (1986) 539–543.
BEASLEY-MURRAY, G. R.: "The Interpretation of Daniel 7", in: *CBQ* 45 (1983) 44–58.
BEAUVERY, R.: "L'Apocalypse au Risque de la Numismatique: Babylone, la Grand Prostituée et le Sixième Roi Vespasien et la Déesse Rome", in: *RB* 90 (1983) 243–260.
BECKWITH, R. T.: "The Earliest Enoch Literature and its Calendar: Marks of their Origin, Date and Motivation", in: *RdQ* 10 (1981) 365–403.
- "Daniel 9 and the Date of Messiah's Coming in Essene, Hellenistic, Pharisaic, Zealot and Early Christian Computation", in: *ibid.,* 521–542.
BEKER, J. C.: *Paul the Apostle. The Triumph of God in Life and Thought,* Philadelphia, PA 1980, 2nd ed. with a new preface by the author 1984.
- *Paul's Apocalyptic Gospel.* The Coming Triumph of God, Philadelphia, PA 1982.
BELL, A. A., JR.: "The Date of John's Apocalypse. The Evidence of Some Roman Historians Reconsidered", in: *NTS* 25 (1979) 93–102.
BELLET, P.: "An Orthodox Source for the Tractate 'On the Origin of the World' (CG II 103.2–28)", in: *Le Muséon* 97 (1984) 5–24.
BERGER, K.: *Formgeschichte des Neuen Testaments,* Heidelberg 1984, 280–305.
- "Henoch", in: *RAC* 14 [Lief. 107–108/109 1988] 473–545.
BERGER, P.-R.: "Kollyrium für die blinden Augen, Apk 3:18", in: *NT* 27 (1985) 174–195.
BERGMAN, J.: "Ancient Egyptian Theogony in a Greek Magical Papyrus (PGM VII, 11.516–521)", in: M. Heerma van Voss et alii (edd.), *Studies in Egyptian Religion Dedicated to Professor Jan Zandee* (SHR 63), Leiden 1982, 28–37.

- "Nephthys decouverte dans un papyrus magique", in: *Mélanges Adolphe Gutbub* (Publication de la recherche – Université Montpellier), Montpellier 1984, 1–11.
- BERGMEYER, R.: "Altes und Neues zur 'Sonnenfrau am Himmel (Apk 12). Religionsgeschichtliche und quellenkritische Beobachtungen zu Apk 12,1–17", in: *ZNW* 73 (1982) 97–109.
- "Jerusalem, du hochgebaute Stadt", in: *ZNW* 74 (1983) 86–106.
- "Die Buchrolle und das Lamm (Apk 5 und 10)", in: *ZNW* 76 (1985) 225–242.
- BETHGE, H.-G.: "Introduction": H.-G. Bethge/O. S. Wintermute (Translation): "On the Origin of the World", in: W. Barnstone (ed.), *The Other Bible,* San Francisco 1984, 62–74.
- BETZ, O.: "Vision and Recognition in Jewish Apocalypticism", in: *The Eighth World Congress of Jewish Studies. Division A: The Period of the Bible,* Jerusalem 1982, 111–117.
- BEYLOT, R.: "Sur deux textes apocalyptiques éthiopiens", in: *Semitica* 30 (1980) 89–92.
- BLACK, M.: "The Twenty Angel Dekadarchs at 1 Enoch 6.7 and 69.2", in: *JJS* 33 ([= G. Vermes/J. Neusner (edd.): *Essays in Honour of Y. Yadin,* Oxford] 1982) 227–235.
- "Aramaic barnasha and the 'Son of Man'", in: *ET* 95 (1983–84) 200–206.
- "Two Unusual Nomina Dei in the Second Vision of Enoch", in: W. C. Weinrich (ed.): *The New Testament Age.* Essays in Honour of Bo Reicke, Vol. I, Macon, GA 1984, 53–59.
- "The Composition, Character, and Date of the 'Second Vision of Enoch'", in: M. Brecht (ed.): *Text – Wort – Glaube.* Studien zur Überlieferung, Interpretation und Autorisierung biblischer Texte. Kurt Aland gewidmet (AKG 50), Berlin 1980, 19–30.
- BLENKINSOPP, J.: "Interpretation and the Tendency to Sectarianism: An Aspect of Second Temple History", in: E. P. Sanders/A. I. Baumgarten/A. Mendelson (edd.): *Jewish and Christian Self-Definition.* Vol. 2: Aspects of Judaism in the Graeco-Roman Period, Philadelphia, PA/London 1981, 1–26, 299–309.
- BLEVINS, J. L.: "The Genre of Revelation", in: *RExp* 77 (1980) 393–408.
- BÖCHER, O.: "Johanneisches in der Apokalypse des Johannes", in: *NTS* 27 (1980/81) 310–121.
- *Kirche in Zeit und Endzeit. Aufsätze zur Offenbarung des Johannes,* Neukirchen-Vluyn 1983.
- BODENMANN, R.: *Naissance d'une Exégèse. Daniel dans l'Eglise ancienne des trois premiers siècles* (Beiträge zur Geschichte der biblischen Exegese 28), Tübingen 1986.
- DE BOER, M. C.: *The Defeat of Death.* Apocalyptic Eschatology in 1 Corinthians 15 and Romans 5 (JSNT.SS 22), Sheffield 1988.
- BÖHL, F.: "'Askese' vor dem Offenbarungsempfang im apokalyptischen und rabbinischen Schrifttum", in: *Frankfurter Judaistische Beiträge* 12 (1984) 83–104.
- BOGAERT, P. M.: "Relecture et reforme historisantes du livre Daniel attestées par la première version greque (Papyrus 967)", in: R. Kuntzmann/J. Schlosser (edd.): *Études sur le judaisme hellénistique.* Congrès de Strasbourg (1983) (LeDiv 119), Paris 1984, 197–224.
- "Une version longue inéditée de Visio beati Esdrae dans le légendier de Teano (Barb. lat. 2318)", in: *RBen* 94 (1984) 50–70.
- BORGEN, P.: "The Son of Man – Saying in John 3:13–14", in: idem, *Philo, John and Paul.* New Perspectives on Judaism and Early Christianity (Brown Judaic Studies 131), Atlanta, GA 1987, 103–120.
- BOYCE, M.: "On the antiquity of Zoroastrian apocalyptic", in: *BSOAS* 47 (1984) 57–75.
- BRANDENBURGER, E.: *Das Recht des Weltenrichters.* Untersuchung zu Matthäus 25,31–46 (SBS 99), Stuttgart 1980.
- *Markus 13 und die Apokalyptik* (FRLANT 134), Göttingen 1984.
- BRANICK, V. P.: "Apocalyptic Paul?", in: *CBQ* 47 (1985) 664–675.
- BRASHLER, J./DIRKSE, P. A./PARROT, D. M.: "Hermes Trismegistus: Asclepius" (Introduction and Translation), in: W. Barnstone (ed.), *The Other Bible,* San Francisco 1984, 575–580.
- BREYTENBACH, C.: *Nachfolge und Zukunfterwartung nach Markus.* Eine methodenkritische Studie (AThANT 71), Zürich 1984.
- BROWNLEE, W. H.: "'The Anointed Ones of Aaron and Israel' – Thesis, Antithesis, Synthesis", in: A. Caquot et alii (edd.): *Mélanges bibliques et orientaux en l'honneur de M. Mathias Delcor* (AOAT 215), Kevelaer/Neukirchen-Vluyn 1985, 37–44.

BRUNNER, H.: "Weltende", in: *LÄ* VI, Wiesbaden 1986, 1213–1214.

BRUNNER-TRAUT, E.: *Gelebte Mythen*. Beiträge zum altägyptischen Mythos, Darmstadt 1981.

BÜCHLI, J.: *Der Poimandres – ein paganisiertes Evangelium*. Sprachliche und begriffliche Untersuchungen zum 1. Traktat des Corpus Hermeticum (WUNT 27), Tübingen 1987.

BURKERT, W.: *Greek Religion*. Archaic and Classical. Transl. J. Raffan, Oxford/Cambridge, MA 1985.

BURGMANN, H.: *Zwei lösbare Qumranprobleme: Die Person des Lügenmannes; Die Interkalation im Kalender*, Frankfurt am Main 1986.

BUSTO SAIZ, R.: "El texto teodonico de Daniel y la tradución de Simaco", in: *Sefarad* 40 (1980) 41–55.

BURCHARD, C.: "1 Korinther 15, 39–41", in: *ZNW* 75 (1984) 233–258.

CALLAWAY, P. R.: *The History of the Qumran Community*. An Investigation (Journal for the Study of the Pseudepigrapha [JSP]. Supplement Series 3) Sheffield/Winona Lake, IN 1987.

CAQUOT, A.: "Le livre des Jubilées, Melkisedeq et les dîmes", in: *JJS* 33 ([= G. Vermes/J. Neusner (edd.): *Essays in Honour of Y. Yadin*, Oxford] 1982) 257–264.

CAMPONOVO, O.: *Königtum, Königherrschaft und Reich Gottes in den frühjüdischen Schriften* (OBO 58), Fribourg/Göttingen 1984.

CANCIK, HUB.: "Der Eingang in die Unterwelt. Ein religionswissenschaftlicher Versuch zu Vergil, Aeneis 6, 236–272", in: *Der altsprachliche Unterricht*, Stuttgart 1983, 55–69.

CARAGOUNIS, C. C.: *The Son of Man*. Vision and Interpretation (WUNT 38), Tübingen 1986.

– "The Interpretation of the Ten Horns of Daniel 7", in: *EThL* 63 (1987) 106–113.

CARLINI, A.: "P Michigan 130 (Inv. 44-H) e il problema dell'unicità di redazione del Pastore di Erma", in: *ParPass* 38 (1983) 29–37.

– La tradizione manoscritta del Pastor di Herma e il problema dell'unità di composizione dell'opera", in: *FS zum 100jährigen Bestehen der Papyrussammlung der Österreichischen National-bibliothek. Textband*, Wien 1983, 97–100.

– "Papiri e stratificazione testuale nei Patres Apostolici", in: *Atti del XVII Congr. Intern. di Papirologia 2*, Napoli 1984, 367–372.

– "Due estratti del Pastori di Erma nella versione Palatina in Par. lat. 3182", in: *SCO* 35 (1985) 311–312.

– "Uno nuovo testimone delle Visione di Erma", in: *AeR* 30 (1985) 197–202.

– "Le passeggiate di Erma verso Cuma (su due luoghi controversi del *Pastore*)", in: S. F. Bondì/ S. Pernigotti/F. Serra/A. Vivian (edd.): *Studi in onore di E. Bresciani*, Pisa 1986, 105–109.

– "La tradizione testuale de Pastore di Erma e i nuovi papiri", in: G. Cavallo (ed.): *Le strade del testo*, Bari 1987, 23–43.

CARLSON, D. C.: "Vengeance and Angelic Mediation in Testament of Moses 9 and 10", in: *JBL* 101 (1982) 85–95.

CARNEGIE, D. R.: "Worthy is the Lamb: The Hymns in Revelation", in: H. H. Rewdon (ed.): *Christ the Lord*. Studies in Christology presented to Donald Guthrie, Leicester 1982, 243–256.

CARREZ, M.: "De la prophétie à l'apocalypse", in: *Le Monde de la Bible* 42 (1986) 37–38.

CASEY, M.: *Son of Man. The Interpretation and influence of Daniel 7*, London 1979.

CHADWICK, H.: "Oracles of the End in the Conflict of Paganism and Christianity in the Fourth Century", in: E. Lucchesi/H. D. Saffrey (edd.): *Mémorial André-Jean Festugière. Antiquité paienne et chrétienne* (Cahiers d'Orientalisme 10), Genève 1984, 125–129.

CHARLESWORTH, J. H.: "The Triumphant Majority as Seen by a Dwindled Minority: The Outsider According to the Insider of the Jewish Apocalypses, 70–130", in: J. Neusner/E. S. Frerichs (edd.): *To See Ourselves as Others See Us: Christian, Jews, 'Others' in Late Antiquity* (Studies in the Humanities), Atlanta, GA 1985, 285–316.

CHERIX, P.: *Le concept de notre Grande Puissance (CG VI, 4):* Texte, remarques philologiques, traduction et notes (OBO 47), Fribourg/Göttingen 1982.

CHESTER, A.: *Divine Revelation and Divine Titles in the Pentateuchal Targumim* (TSAJ 14), Tübingen 1986.

CIRILLO, L.: "Erma e il problema dell'apocalittica a Roma", in: *Cristianesimo nella storia* 4 (1983) 1–31.

COHEN, S. J. D.: "Yavneh Revisited: Pharisees, Rabbis and the End of Jewish Sectarianism", in: K. H. Richards (ed.): *SBL Seminar Papers 21, 1982,* Chico, CA [now Atlanta, GA] 1982, 45–61.

COLLINS, A. Y.: *Crisis & Catharsis.* The Power of the Apocalypse, Philadelphia, PA 1984.

– "Insiders and Outsiders in the Book of Revelation and its Social Context", in: J. Neusner/E. S. Frerichs (edd.): *To See Ourselves as Others See Us: Christian, Jews, 'Others' in Late Antiquity* (Studies in the Humanities), Atlanta, GA 1985, 187–218.

– "Vilification and Self-Definition in the Book of Revelation", in: G. W. E. Nickelsburg/G. W. MacRae (edd.): *Christians among Jews and Gentiles.* Essays in Honor of Krister Stendahl, Philadelphia, PA 1986, 308–320.

– "The Origin of the Designation of Jesus as 'Son of Man'", in: *HThR* 80 (1987) 391–407.

COLLINS, J. J.: "Patterns of Eschatology at Qumran", in: B. Halpern/J. D. Levenson (edd.): *Traditions in Transformation.* Turning Points in Biblical Faith. FS for F. M. Cross, Vinona Lake, IN 1981, 351–375.

– "Apocalyptic Genre and Mythic Allusions in Daniel", in: *JSOT* 21 (1981) 83–100.

– "Testaments", in: M. E. Stone (ed.): *Jewish Writings of the Second Temple Period* (CRI II), Assen/Philadelphia, PA 1984, 325–355.

– "The Sibylline Oracles", in: *ibid.,* 357–382.

– "Was the Dead Sea Sect an Apocalyptic Community?", in: L. H. Schiffmann (ed.), *Essays in Memory of Yigael Yadin,* New York, *in press.*

COLPE, C.: "Development of Religious Thought", in: E. Yarshater (ed.): *The Cambridge History of Iran,* Vol. 3(2): The Seleucid, Parthian and Sasanian Periods, Cambridge etc. 1983, 819–865, esp. 831–836.

COPPENS, J.: *La relève apocalyptique du Messianisme royal.* Vol. 2: Le Fils d'homme vétéro- et intertestamentaire, Leuven 1983.

COUGHENOUR, R. A.: "The Wisdom Stance of Enoch's Redactor", in: *JSJ* 13 (1982) 47–55.

COURT, J. M.: *Myth and History in the Book of Revelation,* London 1979.

COUTURIER, G.: "La vision du conseil divine: étude d'une forme commune au prophétisme et à l'apocalyptique", in: *ScEs* 36 (1984) 5–43.

CROTTY, R. B.: "Eschatological Ambiguity in Pre-Christian Judaism", in: *Colloquium* 16 (1984) 1–10.

CULIANU, I. P.: *"Iatroi kai manteis.* Sulle strutture dell'estatismo greco", in: *Studi Storico-Religiosi,* N. S. 4 (1980) 287–303.

– *"Inter lunam terrasque . . .* Incubazione, catalessi ed estasi in Plutarco", in: *Perennitas.* Studi in onore di A. Brelich (Edizioni dell'Ateneo), Roma 1980, 149–172.

– "Le vol magique dans l'Antiquité tardive", in: *RHR* 98 (1981) 57–66.

– "The Angels of the Nations and the Origins of Gnostic Dualism", in: R. van den Broek/ M. J. Vermaseren (edd.): *Studies in Gnosticism and Hellenistic Religions* presented to Gilles Quispel on the Occasion of his 65th Birthday (EPRO 91), Leiden 1981, 78–91.

– "L'«Ascension de l'âme» dans les mystères et hors des mystéres", in: U. Bianchi/M. J. Vermaseren (edd.): *La soteriologia dei Culti orientali nell'impero Romano.* Atti del colloquio internazionale su la soteriologia dei culti orientali nell'Impero Romano, Roma 24–28 Settembre 1979 (EPRO 92), Leiden 1982, 276–302.

– *Psychanodia* I: A Survey of the Evidence concerning the Ascension of the Soul and its Relevance (EPRO 99), Leiden 1983.

– *Expériences de l'extase.* Extase, ascension et récit visionaire de l'Hellénisme au Moyen-Age (BH), Paris 1984.

– "Ascension", in: M. Eliade (ed.): *The Encyclopedia of Religion,* Vol. I, New York/London 1987, 435–441.

– "Sky", in: M. Eliade (ed.): *The Encyclopedia of Religion,* Vol. XIII, New York/London 1987, 343–345.

DALEY, B. with SCHREINER, J. and LONA, H. E.: *Eschatologie in der Schrift und Patristik* (Handbuch der Dogmengeschichte, Faszikel 7a), Freiburg/Basel/Wien 1986.

DAVIES, W. D.: "From Schweitzer to Scholem: Reflections on Sabbatai Svi", in: idem, *Jewish and Pauline Studies,* Philadelphia, PA 1984, 257–277.

DAVIES, P. R.: "Eschatology in the Book of Daniel", in: *JSOT* 17 (1980) 33–53.

– *The Damascus Covenent.* An Interpretation of the 'Damascus Document' (JSOT.SS 25), Scheffield 1983.

– "Calendrical Change and Qumran Origins: An Assessment of VanderKam's Theory", in: *CBQ* 45 (1983) 80–89.

– "Eschatology at Qumran", in: *JBL* 104 (1985) 39–55.

– "Qumran Beginnings", in: K. H. Richards (ed.): *SBL Seminar Papers 25, 1986,* Atlanta, GA 1986, 361–368.

– "The Social World of Apocalyptic Writings", in: R. E. Clements (ed.): *The Social World of the Old Testament,* Cambridge in preparation for 1989.

DAY, J. A.: "The Daniel of Ugarit and Ezekiel and the Hero of the Book of Daniel", in: *VT* 30 (1980) 174–184.

– "A Case of Inner Scriptural Interpretation. The Dependence of Isaiah XXV.13–XXVII.11 on Hosea XIII.4–XIV.10 (Eng. 9) and its Relevance to Some Theories of the Redaction of the 'Isaiah Apocalypse'", in: *JThS* 31 (1980) 309–319.

DELCOR, M.: "Le livre des paraboles d'Henoch Etiopien: le problème de son origine à la lumière des découvertes récentes", in: *EstB* 38 (1979–80) 5–33.

DESJARDINS, M.: "Law in 2 Baruch and 4 Ezra", in: *SR* 14 (1985) 25–37.

DEUTSCH, C.: "Transformation of Symbols: The New Jerusalem in Rv 21:1–22:5", in: *ZNW* 78 (1987) 106–126.

DEXINGER, F.: "Die frühesten samaritanischen Belege der Taheb-Vorstellung", in: *Kairos* 26 (1984) 224–252.

– "Der 'Prophet wie Moses' in Qumran und bei den Samaritanern", in: A. Caquot el alii (edd.): *Mélanges bibliques et orientaux en l'honneur de M. Mathias Delcor* (AOAT 215), Kevelaer/Neukirchen-Vluyn 1985, 97–111.

DÍEZ MACHO, A.: "La Christologia del Hijo de Homre y el uso de la tercera persona en vez de la primera", in: *ScrTh* 14 (1982) 189–201.

DÍEZ MERINO, L.: "Los 'vigilantes' en la literatura intertestamentaria", in: N. Fernández Marcos et alii (edd.): *Simposio Biblico Español, Salamanca 1982,* Madrid 1984, 575–609.

DIMANT, D.: "Jerusalem and the Temple According to the Animal Apocalypse (1 Enoch 85–90) in the Light of the Dead Sea Scrolls' Thought", in: *Shnaton. An Annual for Biblical and Ancient Near Eastern Studies* 5–6 (1981/82) 177–183 (Hebrew).

– "The Biography of Enoch and the Books of Enoch", in: *VT* 33 (1983) 14–29.

– "Qumran Sectarian Literature", in: M. E. Stone (ed.): *Jewish Writings of the Second Temple Period* (CRI II), Assen/Philadelphia, PA 1984, 483–550.

DONAHUE, J. R.: "Recent Studies on the Origin of 'Son of Man' in the Gospels", in: *CBQ* 48 (1986) 484–498.

DONALDSON, T. L.: "Levitical Messianology in Late Judaism. Origins, Development and Decline", in: *JRTS* 23 (1980) 193–207.

DUBOIS, J.-D.: "Le préambule de l'Apocalypse de Pierre (Nag Hammadi VII, 70,14–20)", in: J. Ries/Y. Janssens/J.-M. Sevrin (edd.): *Gnosticisme et monde hellénistique.* Actes du Colloque de Louvain-la-Neuve (11–14 mars 1980) (Publications de l'Institut Orientaliste de Louvain 27), Louvain-la-Neuve 1982, 384–392.

DUCHESNE-GUILLEMIN, J.: „Apocalypse juive et apocalypse iranienne", in: U. Bianchi/M. J. Vermaseren (edd.): *La soteriologia dei Culti orientali nell'impero Romano.* Atti del colloquio internazionale su la soteriologia dei culti otientali nell'Impero Romano, Roma 24–28 Settembre 1979 (EPRO 92), Leiden 1982, 753–761.

DUHAIME, J.: "La règle de la guerre de Qumrân et l'apocalyptique", in: *ScEs* 36 (1984) 67–88.

– "La doctrine des Esséeniens de Qumrân sur l'aprèsmort", in: G. Couturier/A. Charrou/ G. Durand (edd.): *Essais sur la mort*. Travaux d'un séminaire de recherche sur la mort. Faculté de Théologie, Université de Montréal (Héritage et projet 29), Montréal 1985, 99–121.

– "Dualistic Reworking in the Scrolls of Qumran", in: *CBQ* 49 (1987) 32–56.

EDWARDS, S. A.: "Christological Perspectives in the Book of Revelation", in: R. F. Berkey/S. A. Edwards (edd.): *Christological Perspectives*. FS H. K. McArthur, New York 1982, 139–154, 281–286.

EHRLICH, E. L.: "'In der Heilsgeschichte liegt die Heilszukunft': messianische und endzeitliche Vorstellungen des Judentums", in: *IKaZ* 13 (1984) 321–332.

ETCHEVERRÍA, R. T.: "'El discurso profético de este libro' (Apoc 22,7.10.18–19)", in: *Salm.* 29 (1982) 283–308.

EVANS, C. A.: "On the Prologue of John and the Trimorphic Protennoia", in: *NTS* 27 (1980–81) 395–401.

FARBER, P.: *Wesen, Aufgabe und Hierarchie der Engel in den drei Henochbüchern* (Diss. Graz Universität), Graz 1984.

FERCH, A. J.: "Daniel 7 and Ugarit.: A Reconsideration", in: *JBL* 99 (1980) 75–86.

– "The Book of Daniel and the 'Maccabean Thesis'", in: *AUSS* 21 (1983) 129–141.

FISCHER, K. M.: "Die Christlichkeit der Offenbarung Johannes", in: *ThLZ* 106 (1981) 165–172.

FITZMYER, J. A.: "Another View of the 'Son of Man' Debate", in: *JSNT* 4 (1979) 58–68.

FLUSSER, D.: "The Hubris of the Antichrist in a Fragment from Qumran", in: *Immanuel* 10 (1980) 31–37.

FRANKLYN, P. N.: "The Cultic and Pious Climax of Eschatology in the Psalms of Salomon", in: *JSJ* 18 (1987) 1–18.

FUHS, H. F.: "Die äthiopische Übersetzung des Henoch. Ein Beitrag zur Apokalyptikforschung der Gegenwart", in: *Biblische Notizen* 8 (1979) 336–356.

FUNK, W.-P.: "Notizen zur weiteren Textkonstitution der zweiten Apokalypse des Jakobus", in: P. O. Scholz/R. Stempel (edd.): *Nubia et Oriens Christianus*. FS für C. D. G. Müller zum 60. Geburtstag (Bibliotheca Nubica I), Köln 1987, 107–114.

GAMMIE, J. G.: "On the Intention and Sources of Daniel I–VI", in: *VT* 31 (1981) 282–292.

GARCÍA-MARTÍNEZ, F.: "4QOrNab. Nueva sintesis", in: *Sefarad* 40 (1980) 5–25.

– "4QMes. Aram. y el Libro de Neò", in: *Salm.* 28 (1981) 195–232.

– "Notas al margen de 4QpsDaniel arameo", in: *Aula Orientalis* 1 (1983) 193–208.

– "Orígenes apocalípticos del movimiento esenio y orígenes de la secta qumránica", in: *Communio* 18 (1985) 353–368.

GARBINI, G.: "Proverbi per un anno. Il libro dei Proverbi e il calendario", in: *Henoch* 6 (1984) 139–146.

GAROFALO, S.: "Sette monti, su cuisiede la donna (Apoc. 17,9)", in: Professoren der Phil.- Theol. Hochschule Fulda (edd.): *Kirche und Bibel*. FS E. Schick, Paderborn etc. 1979, 97–104.

GAYLORD, H. E.: "How Satanael Lost his 'El'?", in: *JJC* 33 (1982) 303–309.

– "The Slavonic Version of III Baruch", in: *Polata Knigopisnja* VII (1983) 49–56.

GEORGI, D.: "Die Visionen vom himmlischen Jerusalem in Apk 21 und 22", in: D. Lührmann/ G. Strecker (edd.): *Kirche*. FS für Günther Bornkamm zum 75. Geburtstag, Tübingen 1980, 351–372.

– "Who ist the true Prophet?", in: G. W. E. Nickelsburg/G. W. MacRae (edd.): *Christians among Jews and Gentiles*. Essays in Honor of Krister Stendahl, Philadelphia, PA 1986, 100–126.

GERLEMANN, G.: *Der Menschensohn* (Studia Biblica 1), Leiden 1983.

GERO, S.: "Henoch und die Sibylle", in: *ZNW* 73 (1982) 148–150.

GESE, H.: "Die Weisheit, der Menschensohn und die Ursprünge der Christologie als konsequente Entfaltung der biblischen Theologie", in: *SEÅ* 44 (1979) 77–114.

– "Die Bedeutung der Krise unter Antiochus IV. Epiphanes für die Apokalyptik des Danielbuches", in: *ZThK* 80 (1983) 373–388.

– "Das Geschichtsbild des Danielbuches und Ägypten", in: M. Görg (ed.): *Fontes atque pontes*. Eine Festgabe für H. Brunner (Ägypten und Altes Testament 5), Wiesbaden 1983, 139–154.

GEYSER, A.: "The Twelve Tribes in Revelation: Judean and Judeo-Christian Apocalypticism", in: *NTS* 28 (1982) 388–399.

GIANOTTO, C.: "La figura di Melchisedek nella tradizioni giudaica, cristiana e gnostica (sec. II a. C–III d. C.)", in: *Annali di storia dell'esegesi* 1 (1984) 137–152.

GIBLIN, C. H.: "Revelation 11.1–13: Its Form, Function, and Contextual Integration", in: *NTS* 30 (1984) 433–459.

GIGNOUX, P.: "Nouveaux regards sur l'apocalyptique iranienne", in: *Comptes rendus de l'Académie des inscriptions et belles lettres,* Paris 1986, 334–346.

GILHUS, I. S.: *The Nature of the Archons.* A Study in the Soteriology of a Gnostic Treatise from Nag Hammadi (CG II,4) (Studies in Oriental Religions 12), Wiesbaden 1985.

GLESSMER, U.: "Das astronomische Henoch-Buch als Studienobjekt", in: *Biblische Notizen* 36 (1987) 69–129.

LE GOFF, J.: *The Birth of Purgatory* (tr. A. Goldhammer), London 1984.

GOOD, E. M.: "Apocalyptic as Comedy: The Book of Daniel", in: *Semeia* 32 (1984) 41–70.

GOODING, D. W.: "The Literary Structure of the Book of Daniel and its Implications", in: *TynB* 32 (1981) 43–79.

GOURGUES, M.: "The Thousand-Year Reign (Rev. 20:1–6): Terrestrial or Celestial?", in: *CBQ* 47 (1985) 676–681.

GRABBE, L. L.: "Chronography in 4 Ezra and 2 Baruch", in: K. H. Richards (ed.): *SBL Seminar Papers 20, 1981,* Chico, CA [now Atlanta, GA] 1981, 49–63.

GREENSPOON, L.: "The Origin of the Idea of Resurrection", in: B. Halpern/J. D. Levenson (edd.): *Traditions in Transformation.* Turning Points in Biblical Faith. FS for F. M. Cross, Vinona Lake, IN 1981, 247–321.

GRUENWALD, I.: "Manichaeism und Judaism in the Light of the Cologne Mani Codex", *ZPE* 50 (1983) 29–45.

GÜTTGEMANNS, E.: "Die Semiotik des Traums in apokalyptischen Texten am Beispiel von Apokalypse 1", in: *LingBibl* 59 (1987) 7–54.

GUNDRY, R. H.: "The New Jerusalem: People as Place not Place for People", in: *NT* 29 (1987) 254–264.

– "The Hellenization of Dominical Tradition and the Christianization of Jewish Traditions in the Eschatology of 1–2 Thessalonians", in: *NTS* 33 (1987) 161–178.

GWYN GRIFFITHS, J.: "The Great Egyptian Cults of Oecumenical Spiritual Significance", in: A. H. Armstrong (ed.): *Classical Mediterranean Spirituality: Egyptian, Greek, Roman,* New York 1986, 39–65.

– "Hellenistic Religions", in: M Eliade (ed.): *The Encyclopedia of Religion,* Vol. VI, New York/London 1987, 252–266.

– "The Idea of Posthumous Judgement in Israel and Egypt", in: M. Görg (ed.): *Fontes atque pontes.* Eine Festgabe für H. Brunner (Ägypten und Altes Testament 5), Wiesbaden 1983, 186–204.

HALL, R. G.: "The 'Christian Interpolation' in the Apocalypse of Abraham", in: *JBL* 107 (1988) 107–110.

HALPERIN, D. J.: "Origen, Ezechiel's 'Merkabah' and the Ascension of Moses", in: *ChH* 50 (1981) 261–275.

– "Heavenly Ascension in Ancient Judaism. The Nature of the Experience", in: K. H. Richards (ed.): *SBL Seminar Papers 26, 1987,* Atlanta, GA 1987, 218–232.

– *Faces of the Chariot. Early Jewish Responses to Ezekiel's Vision* (TSAJ 16), Tübingen 1988.

HARNISCH, W.: "Die Ironie der Offenbarung. Exegetische Erwägungen zur Zionvision im 4. Buch Esra", in: *ZAW* 95 (1983) 75–95.

HARRELSON, W.: "Ezra among the Wicked in 2 Esdras 3–10", in: J. L. Crenshaw/S. Sandmel (edd.): *The Divine Helmsman: Studies on God's Control of Human Events, Presented to Lou H. Silberman,* New York 1980, 21–39.

HARTMAN, L.: *Asking for a Meaning.* A Study of 1 Enoch 1–5 (CB.NS 12), Lund 1979.

– "Zur Hermeneutik neutestamentlicher eschatologischer Texte", in: H.-J. Zobel (ed.): *Hermeneutik eschatologischer biblischer Texte,* Greifswald 1983, 30–48.

– "Vad säger Sibyllan? Byggnad och budskap i de sibyllinska oraklens fjärde bok", in: P. W. Bøckman/R. E. Kristiansen (edd.): *Context.* Essays in Honour of Peder J. Borgen («Relieff» 24), Trondheim 1987, 61–74.

HASEL, G. F.: "The Four World Empires of Daniel 2 Against Its Near Eastern Environment", in: *JSOT* 12 (1979) 17–30.

– "Resurrection in the Theology of Old Testament Apocalyptic", in: *ZAW* 92 (1980) 267–284.

– "The Book of Daniel: Evidences Relating to Persons and Chronology", in: *AUSS* 19 (1981) 37–49.

– "The Book of Daniel and Matters of Language: Evidences Relating to Names, Words, and the Aramaic Language, in: *ibid.,* 211–225.

HELLHOLM, D.: *Genre-specific differentiae specificae of Apocalyptic Texts: A Generic Investigation of Lucian's Icaromenippos* (SO.SS), Oslo 1989 (forthcoming).

HEMER, C. J.: *The Letters to the Seven Churches of Asia in Their Local Setting* (JSNTS 11), Sheffield 1986.

HENGEL, M.: "Entstehungszeit und Situation des Markusevangeliums", in: Hub. Cancik (ed.): *Markus-Philologie.* Historische, literarische und stilistische Untersuchungen zum zweiten Evangelium (WUNT 33), Tübingen 1984, 1–45.

– "Hadrians Politik gegenüber Juden und Christen", to be published in: *E. Bickermann Memorial Volume* (JAOS), Baltimore, MD 1988.

HILHORST, A.: "Hermas", in: *RAC* 14 [Lief. 108/109 1988] 682–701.

HILLS, J.: "The *Epistula Apostolorum* and the Genre 'Apocalypse'", in: K. H. Richards (ed.): *SBL Seminar Papers 25, 1986,* Atlanta, GA 1986, 581–595.

HIMMELFARB, M.: "From Prophecy to Apocalypse: The Book of Watchers and Tours of Heaven", in: A. Green (ed.): *Jewish Spirituality: From the Bible to the Middle Ages,* New York 1986, 149–153.

– "Apocalyptic Ascent and the Heavenly Temple", in: K. H. Richards (ed.): *SBL Seminar Papers 26, 1987,* Atlanta, GA 1987, 210–217.

HOLLAND, G. S.: *The Tradition that You Received from Us: 2 Thessalonians in the Pauline Tradition* (HUTh 24), Tübingen 1988.

HOLLANDER, H. W./DE JONGE, M. (EDD.): *The Testament of the Twelve Patriarchs.* A Commentary (SVTP 8), Leiden 1985.

HOLTZ, T.: *Der Erste Brief an die Thessalonicher* (EKK XIII), Zürich/Neukirchen-Vluyn 1986, 182–239.

HORBURY, W.: "The Messianic Association of the 'Son of Man'", in: *JThS* 36 (1985) 34–55.

HORSLEY, R. A.: "Popular Messianic Movements around the Time of Jesus", in: *CBQ* 46 (1984) 471–495.

– "Menachem in Jerusalem. A Brief Messianic Episode among the Sicarii – not 'Zealot Messianism'", in: *NT* 27 (1985) 334–348.

– "Popular Prophetic Movements at the Time of Jesus: Their Principle Features and Social Origins", in: *JSNT* 26 (1986) 3–27.

VAN DER HORST, P.: "Moses' Throne Vision in Ezekiel the Dramatist", in: *JJS* 34 (1983) 21–29.

– "Some Notes on the *Exagoge* of Ezekiel", in: *Mn* 37 (1984) 354–375.

HULTGÅRD, A.: *L'eschatologie des Testaments des Douze Patriarches.* I: Interprétation des textes (AUU. HR 6), Uppsala 1977.
- *L'eschatologie des Testaments des Douze Patriarches.* II: Composition de l'ouvrage, textes et traductions (AUU. HR 7), Uppsala 1982.
HURTADO, L. W.: "Revelation 4–5 in the Light of Jewish Apocalyptic Analogies", in: *JSOT* 25 (1985) 105–124.
HUTTER, M.: "'Halte diese Worte geheim!' – Eine Notiz zu einem apokalyptischen Brauch", in: *Biblische Notizen* 25 (1984) 14–18.
HYLDAHL, N.: "Auferstehung Christi – Auferstehung der Toten (1 Thess. 4,13–18)", in: S. Pedersen (ed.): *Die Paulinische Literatur und Theologie* (Theologiske studier 7), Århus/Göttingen 1980, 119–135.
IOVINO, P.: *Chiesa e tribolazione.* Il tema della *thlipsis* nelle Lettere di S. Paolo (Facoltà Theologica di Sicilia Studi 1), Palermo 1985.
ISAAC, E.: "New Light Upon the Book of Enoch from Newly-Found Ethiopic Manuscript", in: *JAOS* 103 (1983) 399–411.
JACOBSON, H.: "Mysticism and Apocalyptic in Ezekiel's *Esagoge*", in: *Illinois Classical Studies* 6 (1981) 272–293.
JANKO, R.: "Forgetfulness in the Golden Tablets of Memory", in: *CQ* 34 (1984) 89–100.
JANOWSKI, B./LICHTENBERGER, H.: "Enderwartung und Reinheitsidee: Zur eschatologischen Deutung von Reinheit und Sühne in der Qumrangemeinde", in: *JJS* 34 (1983) 31–62.
JANSSENS, Y.: "The Trimorphic Protennoia and the Fourth Gospel", in: A. H. B. Logan/A. J. M. Wedderburn (edd.): *The New Testament and Gnosis.* Essays in Honour of Robert McL. Wilson, Edinburgh 1983, 229–244.
JESKE, R. L.: "Spirit and Community in the Johannine Apocalypse", in: *NTS* 31 (1985) 452–466.
JEWETT, R.: *The Thessalonian Correspondence.* Pauline Rhetoric and Millenarian Piety (Foundations and Facets), Philadelphia, PA 1986.
JOHANSON, B. C.: *To All the Brethren.* A Text-Linguistic and Rhetorical Approach to I Thessalonians (CB.NT 16), Stockholm 1987, 118–140.
DE JONGE, H. J.: "ΒΟΤΡΥΣ ΒΟΗΣΕΙ: The Age of Kronos and the Millennium in Papias of Hierapolis", in: M. J. Vermaseren (ed.): *Studies in Hellenistic Religions* (EPRO 78), Leiden 1979, 37–49.
DE JONGE, M.: "Two Interesting Interpretations of the Rending of the Temple-Veil in the Testaments of the Twelve Patriarchs", in: *Bijdr.* 46 (1985) 350–362.
- "The Future of Israel in the Testaments of the Twelve Patriarchs", in: *JSJ* 17 (1986) 196–211.
KARRER, M.: *Die Johannesoffenbarung als Brief.* Studien zu ihrem literarischen, historischen und theologischen Ort (FRLANT 140), Göttingen 1986.
KEARNS, R.: *Vorfragen zur Christologie II.* Überlieferungsgeschichtliche und Rezeptionsgeschichtliche Studien zur Vorgeschichte eines Christologischen Hoheitstitels, Tübingen 1980.
- *Das Traditionsgefüge um den Menschensohn.* Ursprünglicher Gehalt und älteste Veränderung im Urchristentum, Tübingen 1986.
- *Die Endchristologisierung des Menschensohnes,* Tübingen 1988.
KEE, H. C.: "The Man' in Fourth Ezra: Growth of a Tradition", in: K. H. Richards (ed.): *SBL Seminar Papers 20, 1981,* Chico, CA [now Atlanta, GA] 1981, 199–208.
- "Pauline Eschatology: Relationships with Apocalyptic and Stoic Thought", in: E. Gräßer/O. Merk (edd.): *Glaube und Eschatologie.* FS für W. G. Kümmel, Tübingen 1985, 135–158.
KIPPENBERG, H. G.: "Das Gentilcharisma der Davividen in der jüdischen, frühchristlichen und gnostischen Religionsgeschichte Palestinas", in: J. Taubes (ed.): *Theokratie* (Religionsgeschichte und Politische Theologie 3), Paderborn/München/Wien/Zürich 1987, 127–147.
KIRSCHNER, R.: "Apocalyptic and Rabbinic Responses to the Destruction of 70", in: *HThR* 78 (1985) 27–46.
KLAUCK, H.-J.: "Die Himmelfahrt des Paulus (2 Kor 12,2–4) in der koptischen Paulusapokalyp-

se aus Nag Hammadi (NHC V/2)", in: *Studien zum Neuen Testament und seiner Umwelt* 10 (1985) 151–190.

KLIJN, A. F. J.: "An Analysis of the Use of the Story of the Flood in the Apocalypse of Adam", in: R. van den Broek/M. J. Vermaseren (edd.): *Studies in Gnosticism and Hellenistic Religions* presented to Gilles Quispel on the Occasion of his 65th Birthday (EPRO 91), Leiden 1981, 218–226.

KLOPPENBORG, J. S.: "The Function of Apocalyptic Language in Q", in: K. H. Richards (ed.): *SBL Seminar Papers 25, 1986,* Atlanta, GA 1986, 224–235.

– "Symbolic Eschatology and the Apocalypticism of Q", in: *HThR* 80 (1987) 287–306.

KNIBB, M.: "Prophecy and the Emergence of the Jewish Apocalypses", in: R. Coggins/A. Phillips/M. Knibb (edd.): *Israel's Prophetic Tradition.* Essays in Honour of Peter Ackroyd, Cambridge 1982, 155–180.

– "Apocalyptic and Wisdom in 4 Ezra", in: *JSJ* 13 (1982) 56–75.

– "Exile in the Damascus Document", in: *JSOT* 25 (1983) 99–117.

– *The Qumran Community* (Cambridge Commentaries on Writings of the Jewish and Christian World 200 BC to AD 200, Vol. 2), Cambridge 1987.

KOBELSKI, P. J.: *Melchizedek and Melchireša'* (CMQ.MS 10), Washington, D.C. 1981.

KOCH, K./NIEWITSCH, T./TUBACH, J.: *Das Buch Daniel* (EdF 144), Darmstadt 1980.

KOCH, K.: "'Adam, was hast du getan?' Erkenntnis und Fall in der zwischentestamentlichen Literatur", in: T. Rendtorff (ed.): *Glaube und Toleranz.* Das theologische Erbe der Aufklärung, Gütersloh 1982, 211–242.

– "Sabbatstruktur der Geschichte. Die sogenannte Zehn-Wochen-Apokalypse (1 Hen 93,1–10; 91,11–17) und das Ringen um die alttestamentlichen Chronologien im späten Israelitentum", in: *ZAW* 95 (1983) 403–430.

– "Dareios, der Meder", in: C. L. Mayers/M. O'Connor (edd.): *The Word of the Lord Shall Go Forth.* Essays in Honor of D. N. Freedman in Celebration of his 60th Birthday (American Schools of Oriental Research. Special Volume Series 1), Winona Lake, IN 1983, 287–299.

– *Daniel* (BK 22,1; Lieferung 1), Neukirchen-Vluyn 1986 ff.

– "Die Bedeutung der Apokalyptik für die Interpretation der Schrift", in: M. Klopfenstein/ U. Luz/S. Talmon/E. Tov (edd.): *Mitte der Schrift?* Ein christlich-jüdisches Gespräch. Texte des Berner Symposions vom 6.–12. Januar 1985 (Judaica et Christiana 11), Bern/Frankfurt Main/New York/Paris 1987, 185–215.

– *Studien zur alttestamentlichen und altorientalischen Religionsgeschichte,* Göttingen 1987.

KOLENKOW, A. B.: "The Fall of the Temple and the Coming of the End: The Spectrum and Process of Apocalyptic Argument in 2 Baruch and other Authors", in: K. H. Richards (ed.): *SBL Seminar Papers 21, 1982,* Chico, CA [now Atlanta, GA] 1982, 243–250.

– "Asceticism, Apocalypticism and Alternatives – Hypotheses für Spectra of Occurrences: Studies and Summaries of Three Times in Early Church History", in: K. H. Richards (ed.): *SBL Seminar Papers 23, 1984,* Chico, CA [now Atlanta, GA] 1984, 241–245.

KREITZER, L.: "Hadrian and the Nero *Redivivus* Myth", in: *ZNW* 79 (1988) 92–115.

KRETSCHMAR, G.: *Die Offenbarung des Johannes.* Die Geschichte ihrer Auslegung im 1. Jahrtausend (CThM 9), Stuttgart 1985.

KRIEG, M.: "MO'ED NAQAM – ein Kultdrama aus Qumran", in: *ThZ* 41 (1985) 3–30.

KÜCHLER, M.: *Frühjüdische Weisheitstraditionen.* Zum Fortgang weisheitlichen Denkens im Bereich des frühjüdischen Jahweglaubens (OBO 26), Freiburg (Schweiz)/Göttingen 1979, 62–87.

– *Schweigen, Schmuck und Schleier.* Drei neutestamentliche Vorschriften zur Verdrängung der Frauen auf dem Hintergrund einer frauenfeindlichen Exegese des Alten Testaments im antiken Judentum (NTOA 1), Freiburg (Schweiz)/Göttingen 1986, 220–460.

KVANVIG, H. S.: "An Akkadian Vision as Background for Dan. 7?", in: *StTh* 35 (1981) 85–89.

– "Henoch und der Menschensohn. Das Verhältnis von Hen 14 zu Dan 7", in: *StTh* 38 (1984) 101–133.

– *Roots of Apocalyptic.* The Mesopotamian Background of the Enoch Figure and the Son of Man (WMANT 61), Neukirchen-Vluyn 1987.

LACOCQUE, A.: "The Vision of the Eagle in 4 Esdras. A Rereading of Daniel 7 in the First Century C. E.", in: K. H. Richards (ed.): *SBL Seminar Papers 20, 1981,* Chico, CA [now Atlanta, GA] 1981, 237–257.

– "Apocalyptic Symbolism: A Ricoeurian Hermeneutical Approach", in: *BR* 26 (1981) 6–15.

– *Daniel et son temps.* Recherches sur le mouvement apocalyptique juif au II siècle avant Jesus-Christ (Le Monde de la Bible), Geneva 1983.

– *Daniel and His Time* (Studies on Personalities of the Old Testament), Columbia, SC 1988.

LAMPE, P.: "Die Apokalyptiker – ihre Situation und ihr Handeln", in: H. Merklein/E. Zenger (edd.): *Eschatologie und Friedenshandeln* (SBS 101), Stuttgart 2nd ed. 1982, 59–114.

LANDMAN, A.: *Messias-interpretaties in de Targumim,* Kampen (NL) 1986.

LANE FOX, R.: *Pagans and Christians,* New York 1986, 375–418, 741–749.

LANG, B.: "Street Theater: Raising the Dead, and the Zoroastrian Connection in Ezekiel's Prophecy", in: J. Lust (ed.): *Ezekiel and His Book.* Textual and Literary Criticism and Their Interrelation (BEThL 74), Leuven 1986, 317–321.

LEBRAM, J. C. H.: "Zwei Danielprobleme (Review K. Koch, Das Buch Daniel, Darmstadt 1980)", in: *BiOr* 39 (1982) 510–517.

– *Das Buch Daniel* (ZBK. AT 23), Zürich 1984.

LEIVESTAD, R.: "Betydningen av uttrykket 'menneskesønnen'", in: *DTT* 48 (1985) 51–64.

LEVINE, B. A.: "From the Aramaic Enoch Fragments: The Semantics of Cosmography", in: *JJS* 33 ([= G. Vermes/J. Neusner (edd.): *Essays in Honour of Y. Yadin,* Oxford] 1982) 311–326.

LEUTZSCH, M.: *Die Wahrnehmung sozialer Wirklichkeit im 'Hirten' des Hermas* (Diss. Bochum) 1986.

LICHT, J.: "An Analysis of Baruch's Prayer (syr. Bar. 21)", in: *JJS* 33 ([=G. Vermes/J. Neusner (edd.): *Essays in Honour of Y. Yadin,* Oxford] 1982) 327–332.

LICHTENBERGER, H.: "Zu Vorkommen und Bedeutung von jasar im Jubiläenbuch", in: *JSJ* 14 (1983) 1–10.

LICHTHEIM, M.: *Late Egyptian Wisdom Literature in the International Context* (OBO 32), Freiburg (Schweiz)/Göttingen 1983.

LINCOLN, A. T.: *Paradise Now and Not Yet.* Studies in the Role of the Heavenly Dimension in Paul's Thought with Special Reference to His Eschatology (SNTS. MS 43), Cambridge 1981.

LINDARS, B.: "Response to Richard Bauckham: The Idiomatic Use of Barnasha", in: *JSNT* 19 (1983) 35–41.

LÖVESTAM, E.: "Eschatologie und Tradition im 2. Petrusbrief", in: W. C. Weinrich (ed.): *The New Testament Age.* Essays in Honor of Bo Reicke, Vol. II, Macon, GA 1984, 287–300.

LONA, H. E.: *Die Eschatologie im Kolosser- und Epheserbrief* (FzB 48), Würzburg 1984.

LOPRIENO, A.: "Il pensiero egizio e l'Apocalittica Giudaica", in: *Henoch* 3 (1981) 289–320.

LUCIANI, F.: "Le vicende di Enoch nell'interpretazione di Filone Alessandrino", in: *RivBib* 31 (1983) 43–68.

LÜHRMANN, D.: *Das Markusevangelium* (HNT 3), Tübingen 1987, 213–226.

LUTTIKHUIZEN, G. P.: *The Revelation of Elchasai.* Investigations into the Evidence for a Mesopotamian Jewish Apocalypse of the Second Century and its Reception by Judeo-Christian-Propagandists (TSAJ 8), Tübingen 1985.

– "The Evaluation of the Teaching of Jesus in Christian Gnostic Dialogues", in: *NT* 30 (1988) 158–168.

MAHÉ, J.-P.: "Le fragment du *Discours Parfait* dans la bibliothèque Nag Hammadi", in: B. Barc (ed.): *Colloque International sur les Textes de Nag Hammadi (Québec, 22–25 août 1978)* (BCdNH.E 1), Québec/Louvain 1981, 304–327.

– "Le *Discours Parfait* d'après l'*Asclépius* latin: Utilisation des sources et cohérence rédactionelle", in: *ibid.,* 405–434.

MALHERBE, A. J.: *Paul and the Thessalonians. The Philosophic Tradition of Pastoral Care*, Philadelphia, PA 1987.

MAIER, G.: *Die Johannesoffenbarung und die Kirche* (WUNT 12), Tübingen 1981.

MANNS, F.: "Traces d'une Haggadah pascale chrétienne dans l'Apocalypse de Jean?", in: *Antonianum* 56 (1981) 265–295.

MANSFELD, J.: "Providence and the Destruction of the Universe in Early Stoic Thought. With Some Remarks on the 'Mysteries of Philosophy'", in: M. J. Vermaseren (ed.): *Studies in Hellenistic Religions* (EPRO 78), Leiden 1979, 129–188.

– "Hesiod and Parmenides in Nag Hammadi", in: *VigChr* 35 (1981) 174–182.

MARBÖCK, J.: "Henoch – Adam – der Thronwagen. Zu frühjüdischen Traditionen bei Ben Sira", in: *BZ* 25 (1981) 103–111.

MARSHALL, I. H.: "Is Apocalyptic the Mother of Christian Theology?", in: G. F. Hawthorne/ O. Betz (edd.): *Tradition and Interpretation in the New Testament. Essays in Honor of E. Earle Ellis*, Grand Rapids/Tübingen 1987, 33–42.

MARTOLA, N.: The Priest Annointed for Battle", in: *Nordisk Judaistik* 4 (1983) 21–40.

MARTYN, J. L.: "Apocalyptic Antinomies in Paul's Letter to the Galatians", in: *NTS* 31 (1985) 410–424.

MATTER, E. A.: "The 'Revelatio Esdrae' in Latin and English Traditions", in: *RBen* 92 (1982) 376–392.

McCOMISKEY, TH. E.: "The Seventy 'Weeks' of Daniel Against the Background of Ancient Near Eastern Literature", in: *WThJ* 47 (1985) 18–45.

McGINN, B.: "Revelation", in: R. Alter/F. Kermode (edd.): *The Literary Guide to the Bible*, London 1987, 523–541.

McNICOL, A. J.: "The Heavenly Sanctuary in Judaism: A Model for Tracing the Origin of an Apocalypse", in: *JRSt* 13 (1987) 66–94.

MICHAELS, J. R.: "Jewish and Christian Apocalyptic Letters: 1 Peter, Revelation, and 2 Baruch 78–87", in: K. H. Richards (ed.): *SBL Seminar Papers 26, 1987*, Atlanta, GA 1987, 268–275.

MINEAR, P. S.: *New Testament Apocalyptic* (Interpreting Biblical Texts), Nashville, TN 1981.

MOLENBERG, C.: "A Study of the Roles of Shemihaza and Asael in Enoch 6–11", in: *JJS* 35 (1984) 136–146.

MOMIGLIANO, A.: "Indicazioni preliminari su apocalissi ed Esodo nella tradizione Giudaica", in: *RSIt* 97 (1986) 353–366.

MOOR, M. S.: "Jesus Christ: 'Superstar' (Revelation XXII, 16b)", in: *NT* 24 (1982) 82–91.

MORALDI, L.: *Testi gnostici* (Classici della Religioni, Sezione guinta: Le altre confessioni cristiane), Turin 1982.

MORARD, F.: "Thématique de l'*Apocalypse d'Adam* du Codex V de Nag Hammadi", in: B. Barc (ed.): *Colloque International sur les Textes de Nag Hammadi (Québec, 22–25 août 1978)* (BCdNH.E 1), Québec/Louvain 1981, 288–294.

MOSCA, P. G.: "Ugarit and Daniel 7. A Missing Link", in: *Bibl.* 67 (1986) 496–517.

MÜLLER, H.-P.: "Die aramäische Inschrift von Deir 'Alla und die älteren Bileamsprüche", in: *ZAW* 94 (1982) 214–244.

MUELLER, J. R.: "The Apocalypse of Abraham and the Destruction of the Second Temple", in: K. H. Richards (ed.): *SBL Seminar Papers 21, 1982*, Chico, CA [now Atlanta, GA] 1982, 341–349.

MÜLLER, K.: "'Die Propheten sind schlafen gegangen' (syrBar 85,3). Nachbemerkungen zur überlieferungsgeschichtlichen Reputation der Pseudepigraphie im Schrifttum der frühjüdischen Apokalyptik", in: *BZ* 26 (1982) 179–207.

– *Das Judentum in der religionsgeschichtlichen Arbeit am Neuen Testament*. Eine kritische Rückschau auf die Entwicklung einer Methodik bis zu den Qumranfunden (Judentum und Umwelt 6), Frankfurt/Bern 1983.

MÜLLER, M.: "Jesu brug af udtrykket 'menneskesønnen'", in: *DTT* 46 (1983) 201–220.

– Der Ausdruck "Menschensohn" in den Evangelien (AThD 17), Leiden 1984.
– "The Expression 'the Son of Man' as Used by Jesus", in: StTh 38 (1984) 47–64.
– "Betydningen av בר אנש i Dan. 7,13", in: DTT 47 (1984) 177–186.
MÜLLER, U. B.: Die Offenbarung des Johannes (ÖTK 19), Gütersloh/Würzburg 1984.
MÜNCHOW, CH.: Ethik und Eschatologie. Ein Beitrag zum Verständnis der frühjüdischen Apokalyptik mit einem Ausblick auf das Neue Testament, Göttingen 1981.
MUÑOZ LEÓN, D.: "El IV de Esdras y el Targum Palestinense. Las cuatro últimas visiones (9,26–14,48)", in: EstB 42 (1984) 5–20.
– "La estructura del Apocalipsis de Juan. Una approximación a la luz de la composición del 4.° de Esdras y del 2.° del Baruc", in: EstB 43 (1985) 125–172.
MURPHY, F. J.: The Structure and Meaning of Second Baruch (SBL.DS 78), Atlanta, GA 1985.
– "2 Baruch and the Romans", in: JBL 104 (1985) 663–669.
– "Sapiential Elements in the Syriac Apocalypse of Baruch", in: JQR 76 (1986) 311–327.
– "The Temple in the Syriac Apocalypse of Baruch", in: JBL 106 (1987) 671–683.
MURPHY-O'CONNOR, J.: "The Damascus Document Revisited", in: RB 92 (1985) 223–246 [= K. H. Richards (ed.): SBL Seminar Papers 25, 1986, Atlanta, GA 1986, 369–383].
MUSSIES, G.: "Catalogues of Sins and Virtues Personified (NHC II,5)", in: R. van den Broek/ M. J. Vermaseren (edd.): Studies in Gnosticism and Hellenistic Religions presented to Gilles Quispel on the Occasion of his 65th Birthday (EPRO 91), Leiden 1981, 315–353.
MUSSNER, F.: "'Weltherrschaft' als eschatologisches Thema der Johannesapokalypse", in: E. Gräßer/O. Merk (edd.): Glaube und Eschatologie. FS für W. G. Kümmel, Tübingen 1985, 209–227.
NEBE, G.: 'Hoffnung' bei Paulus. Elpis und ihre Synonyme im Zusammenhang der Eschatologie (StUNT 16), Göttingen 1983.
NEUGEBAUER, O.: Ethiopic Astronomy and Computus (SÖAW.PH 347), Wien 1979.
NEUSNER, J.: "Judaism in a Time of Crisis: Four Responses to the Destruction of the Second Temple", in: Judaism 21 (1972) 313–327.
– "One Theme, Two Settings: The Messiah in the Literature of the Synagogue and in the Rabbis' Canon of Late Antiqutiy", in: Henoch 7 (1985) 257–269.
– "Beyond Myth, after Apocalypse: The Mishnaic Conception of History", in: J. Neusner/P. Borgen/R. Horsley (edd.): The Social World of Formative Christianity and Judaism: Essays in Tribute to Howard Clark Kee, Philadelphia, PA 1988, 92–107.
NEWSOM, C. A.: "The Development of 1 Enoch 6–19: Cosmogony and Judgment", in: CBQ 42 (1980) 310–329.
– "The Past as Revelation: History in Apocalyptic Literature", in: Quarterly Review 4 (1984) 40–53.
– "Merkabah Exegesis in the Qumran Sabbath Shirot", in: JSJ 38 (1987) 11–30.
NICKELSBURG, G. W. E.: "Apocalypse and Myth in 1 Enoch 6–11", in: JBL 96 (1977) 383–405.
– "The Books of Enoch in Recent Research", in: RelStR 7 (1981) 210–217.
– "Some Related Traditions in the Apocalypse of Adam, The Books of Adam and Eve, and 1 Enoch", in: B. Layton (ed.): The Rediscovery of Gnosticism: Proceedings of the International Conference on Gnosticism at Yale, New Haven, Connecticut, March 28–31, 1979. Volume Two: Sethian Gnosticism (SHR 41), Leiden 1981, 515–539.
– "Enoch, Levi, and Peter: Recipients of Revelation in Upper Galilee", in: JBL 100 (1981) 575–600.
– "The Epistle of Enoch and the Qumran Literature", in: JJS 33 ([= G. Vermes/J. Neusner (edd.): Essays in Honour of Y. Yadin, Oxford] 1982) 333–348.
– "Stories of Biblical and Early Post-Biblical Times", in: M. E. Stone (ed.): Jewish Writings of the Second Temple Period (CRI II), Assen/Philadelphia, PA 1984, 33–87.
– "The Bible Rewritten and Expanded", in: ibid., 89–156.
– "Revealed Wisdom as a Criterion for Inclusion and Exclusion: From Jewish Sectarianism to

Early Christianity", in: J. Neusner/E. S. Frerichs (edd.): *To See Ourselves as Others See Us: Christian, Jews, 'Others' in Late Antiqutiy* (Studies in the Humanities), Atlanta, GA 1985, 73–91.

- "1 Enoch and Qumran Origins: The State of the Question and Some Prospects for Answers", in: K. H. Richards (ed.): *SBL Seminar Papers 25, 1986,* Atlanta, GA 1986, 341–360.

- "Salvation Without and With a Messiah: Developing Beliefs in Writings Ascribed to Enoch", in: J. Neusner/W. S. Green/E. S. Frerichs (edd.): *Judaisms and Their Messiahs at the Turn of the Christian Era,* Cambridge/New York 1987, 49–68.

NICOL, B.: "Isaiah's Vision and the Visions of Daniel", in: *VT* 29 (1979) 501–504.

NIDITCH, S.: "The Visionary", in: J. J. Collins/G. W. Nickelsburg (edd.): *Ideal Figures in Ancient Judaism,* Chico, CA [now Atlanta, GA] 1980, 153–179.

- *The Symbolic Vision in Biblical Tradition* (HSM 30), Chico, CA [now Atlanta, GA] 1983.

- "Ezekiel 40–48 in a Visionary Context", in: *CBQ* 48 (1986) 208–224.

NIJENDIJK, L. W.: *Die Christologie des Hirten des Hermas. Exegetisch, religions- und dogmengeschichtlich untersucht* (Diss. Utrecht) 1986.

NODET, E.: "La Dédicace, les Maccabées et le Messie", in: *RB* 93 (1986) 321–375.

VON NORDHEIM, E.: *Die Lehre der Alten.* II: Das Testament als Literaturgattung im Alten Testament und im Alten Vorderen Orient (ALGHJ 18), Leiden 1985.

OBERWEIS, M.: "Die Bedeutung der neutestamentlichen Rätselzahlen 666 (Apk 13,18) und 153 (Joh 21,11)", in: *ZNW* 77 (1986) 226–241.

ORTON, D. E.: *The Understanding Scribe.* Matthew and the Apocalyptic Ideal (JSNT.SS 25), Sheffield 1988.

OSBURN, C. D.: "1 Enoch 80:2–8 (67:5–7) and Jude 12–13", in: *CBQ* 47 (1985) 296–303.

OSIEK, C.: *Rich and Poor in the Shepherd of Hermas.* An Exegetical-Social Investigation (CBQ.MS 15), Washington, D.C. 1983.

OSSIO, J. M. (ED.): *Ideología mesiánica del mundo andino,* Lima 1973.

OSWALD, J.: "Recent Studies in Old Testament Eschatology and Apocalyptic", in: *JETS* 24 (1981) 289–301.

OTZEN, B.: "Heavenly Visions in Early Judaism: Origin and Function", in: W. B. Barrick/J. R. Spencer (edd.): *In the Shelter of Elyon.* Essays on Ancient Palestinian Life and Literature in Honor of G. W. Ahlström (JSOT.SS 31), Sheffield 1984, 199–215.

PACE, S.: "The Stratigraphy of the Text of Daniel and the Question of Theological Tendenz (!) in the Old Greek", in: *Bulletin of the International Organization for Septuagint and Cognate Studies* 17 (1984) 15–35.

PAINCHAUD, L.: "Deux citations vétéro-testamentaires dans l'Écrit sans titre (*NH* II,5): *Ps* 22,7–92,13 et *Is* 41,25", in: *Le Muséon* 98 (1985) 83–94.

PARKE, H. W.: *The Oracles of Apollo in Asia Minor,* London/Sidney/Dover 1985.

- *Sibylls and Sibylline Prophecy in Classical Antiquity,* ed. by B. C. McGing, London 1988.

PAUL, SH.: "Dan 6,8: An Aramaic Reflex of Assyrian Legal Terminology", in: *Bibl.* 65 (1984) 106–110.

PEARSON, B. A.: "Jewish Sources in Gnostic Literature", in: M. E. Stone (ed.): *Jewish Writings of the Second Temple Period* (CRI II), Assen/Philadelphia, PA 1984, 443–481 [= K. H. Richards (ed.): *SBL Seminar Papers 25, 1986,* Atlanta, GA 1986, 422–454].

- "The Problem of 'Jewish Gnostic' Literature", in: C. W. Hedrick/R. Hodgson, Jr. (edd.): *Nag Hammadi, Gnosticism, and Early Christianity,* Peabody, MA 1986, 15–35.

PERENTIDIS, S.: "La jonction de l'*Apocalypse de Sedrach* avec l'*Homélie sur l'Amour* d'Éphrem", in: *JThS* 36 (1985) 393–396.

PLEYNIK, J.: "The Taking up of the Faithful and the Resurrection of the Dead in 1 Thessalonians 4:13–18", in: *CBQ* 46 (1984) 274–283.

POIRIER, P.-H.: "La Prôtennoia trimorphe (NH XIII,1) et le vocabulaire du Descensus ad inferos", in: *Le Muséon* 96 (1983) 193–204.

Popkes, W.: "Die Funktion der Sendschreiben in der Johannes-Apokalypse. Zugleich ein Beitrag zur Spätgeschichte der neutestamentlichen Gleichnisse", in: *ZNW* 74 (1983) 90–107.

Porter, P. A.: *Metaphors and Monsters*. A literary-critical study of Daniel 7 and 8 (CB.OT 20), Lund 1984.

Prigent, P.: "Pour une théologie de l'image: Les visions de l'Apocalypse", in: *RHPhR* 59 (1979) 373–378.

– "L'Apocalypse. Exégèse Historique et Analyse Structural", in: *NTS* 26 (1980) 127–137.

– *L'Apocalypse de Saint Jean* (CNT(N) 14), Lausanne/Paris 1981.

Pucci, M.: "Some Historical Remarks on Rufinus' Historia Ecclesiastica (H. E. IV, 2,1–5)", in: *Rivista Storica dell'Antichita* 9 (1981) 123–128.

– *La rivolta Ebraica al tempo di Traiano*, Pisa 1981.

– "Sullo sfondo politico dei moti insurrezionali ebraici dell' 116–117 D.C.", in: *AIVS* 141 (1982/83) 265–277.

– "C. P. J. II 158,435 e la rivolta Ebraica al tempo di Traiano", in: *ZPE* 51 (1983) 95–103.

Raabe, P. R.: "Daniel 7: Its Structure and Role in the Book", in: R. Ahroni (ed.): *Biblical and Other Studies in Memory of S. D. Goitein* (=*Hebrew Annual Review* 9 [1985]), Columbus, OH 1986, 267–276.

Reddish, M. G.: "Martyr Christology in the Apocalypse", in: *JSNT* 33 (1988) 85–95.

Reid, S. B.: *The Sociological Setting of the Historical Apocalypses of 1 Enoch and the Book of Daniel* (Diss. Emory University, Atlanta, GA 1981).

– "1 Enoch: the Rising Elite of the Apocalyptic Movement", in: K. H. Richards (ed.): *SBL Seminar Papers 22, 1983*, Chico CA [now Atlanta, GA] 1983, 147–156.

– "The Structure of the Ten Week Apocalypse and the Book of Dream Visions", in: *JSJ* 16 (1985) 189–201.

Rikvin, E.: "The Book of Jubilees – An Anti-Pharisaic Pseudepigraph", in: *Eretz Israel* 16 (1982) 193–198.

Ringgren, H.: "Judgment of the Dead", in: M. Eliade (ed.): *The Encyclopedia of Religion*, Vol. VIII, New York/London 1987, 205–208.

Roberge, M.: "Le rôle du *Noûs* dans la *Paraphrase de Sem*", in: B. Barc (ed.): *Colloque International sur les Textes de Nag Hammadi (Québec, 22–25 août 1978)* (BCdNH.E 1), Québec/Louvain 1981, 328–339.

Robinson, J. M.: "Sethians and Johannine Thought: The Trimorphic Protennoia and the Prologue of the Gospel of John", in: B. Layton (ed.): *The Rediscovery of Gnosticism:* Proceedings of the International Conference on Gnosticism at Yale, New Haven, Connecticut, March 28–31, 1979. Volume Two: Sethian Gnosticism (SHR 41), Leiden 1981, 643–662, Discussion 662–670.

Robinson, S. W.: *The Testament of Adam: An Examination of the Syriac and Greek Traditions* (SBL.DS 52), Chico, CA [now Atlanta, GA] 1982.

Rochais, G.: "Qu'est-ce que l'apocalyptique?", in: *ScEs* 36 (1984) 273–286.

Rordorf, W.: "Die Neronische Christenverfolgung im Spiegel der Apokryphen Paulusakten", in: *NTS* 28 (1981) 365–374.

Roloff, J.: *Die Offenbarung des Johannes* (ZBK.NT 18), Zürich 1984.

Rook, J. T.: "A Twenty-Eight-Day Month Tradition in the Book of Jubilees", in: *VT* 31 (1981) 83–87.

Rosso Ubigli, L.: "Qohelet di frone all'Apocalittica", in: *Henoch* 5 (1983) 209–234.

– "La fortuna di Enoch nel giudaismo antico: valenza e problemi", in: *Annali di storia dell'esegesi* 1 (1984) 153–163.

Rowland, C.: "The Visions of God in Apocalyptic Literature", in: *JSJ* 10 (1979) 137–154.

– "The Vision of the Risen Christ in Rev. I: 13 ff.: The Debt of an Early Christology to an Aspect of Jewish Angelology", in: *JThS* 31 (1980) 1–11.

– "Apocalyptic Visions and the Exaltation of Christ in the Letter to the Colossians", in: *JSNT* 19 (1983) 73–83.

- "John 1:15. Jewish Apocalyptic and Targumic Tradition", in: *NTS* 30 (1983) 498–507.
- "A Man Clothed in Linen. Dan 10.6 ff. and Jewish Angelology", in: *JSNT* 24 (1985) 99–110.
RUBINKIEWICZ, R.: "Les sémitismes dans l'Apocalypse d'Abraham", in: *FolOr* 21 (1980) 141–148.
- *Die Eschatologie von Henoch 9–11 und das Neue Testament* (Österreichische Biblische Studien 6), Klosterneuburg 1984.
SABOURIN, L.: "Traits Apocalyptiques dans l'Évangile de Matthieu", in: *ScEs* 33 (1981) 357–372.
SACCHI, P.: "Ordine cosmico e prospettiva ultraterrena nel postesilio", in: *RivBib* 30 (1982) 11–33.
- "Riflessioni sull'essenza dell'apocalittica: Peccato d'origine e libertà dell'uomo", in: *Henoch* 5 (1983) 31–61.
- "Enoc Ethiopico 91,15 ed il problema della Medizione", in: *Henoch* 7 (1985) 257–269.
SAHLIN, H.: "Wie wurde ursprünglich die Benennung 'Der Menschensohn' verstanden?", in: *StTh* 37 (1983) 147–179.
SALDARINI, A. J.: "Varieties of Rabbinic Responses to the Destruction of the Temple", in: K. H. Richards (ed.): *SBL Seminar Papers 21, 1982,* Chico, CA [now Atlanta, GA] 1982, 437–458.
SANDERS, E. P.: *Jesus and Judaism,* London 1985.
SATAKE, A.: "Kirche und feindliche Welt. Zur dualistischen Auffassung der Menschenwelt in der Johannesapokalypse", in: D. Lührmann/G. Strecker (edd.): *Kirche.* FS für Günther Bornkamm zum 75. Geburtstag, Tübingen 1980, 329–349.
SAYLER, G. B.: "2 Baruch: A Story of Grief and Consolation", in: K. H. Richards (ed.): *SBL Seminar Papers 21, 1982,* Chico, CA [now Atlanta, GA] 1982, 485–500.
- *Have the Promises Failed?* A Literary Analysis of 2 Baruch (SBL.DS 72), Chico, CA [now Atlanta, GA] 1984.
SCHADE, H.-H.: *Apokalyptische Christologie bei Paulus.* Studien zum Zusammenhang von Christologie und Eschatologie in den Paulusbriefen (GTA 18), Göttingen 2nd ed. 1984.
SCHALIT, A.: *Assumptio Mosis* (ALGHJ 17), Leiden 1987.
SCHABERG, J.: "Daniel 7–12 and the New Testament Passion-Resurrection-Predictions", in: *NTS* 31 (1985) 208–222.
SCHÄFER, P.: "New Testament and Hekhaloth Literature: The Journey into Heaven in Paul and in Merkavah Mysticism", in: *JJS* 35 (1984) 19–35.
SCHENKE, G.: "Anthropologische Implikationen der Erlösungsvorstellung in der Schrift 'Die dreigestaltige Protennoia' (NHC XIII)", in: P. Nagel (ed.): *Studien zum Menschenbild in Gnosis und Manichäismus* (WBMLUHW.K 5), Halle/Saale 1979, 173–179.
- *Die dreigestaltige Protennoia* (Nag Hammadi Codex XIII): Herausgegeben, übersetzt und kommentiert (TU 132), Berlin 1984.
SCHERRER, S. J.: *Revelation 13 as an Historical Source for the Imperial Cult under Domitian* (Diss. Harvard University, Cambridge, MA 1979).
SCHIFFMAN, L. H.: "The Eschatological Community of the Serek-ha-'Edah", in: *PAAJR* 51 (1984) 105–125.
SCHNELLE, U.: "Der erste Thessalonicherbrief und die Entstehung der paulinischen Anthropologie", in: *NTS* 32 (1986) 207–224.
SCHOLER, D. M.: Bibliographia gnostica
    1982 Supplementum XI, in: *NT* 24 (1982) 340–368.
    1983 Supplementum XII, in: *NT* 25 (1983) 356–381.
    1984 Supplementum XIII, in: *NT* 26 (1984) 341–373.
    1985 Supplementum XIV, in: *NT* 27 (1985) 349–378.
    1986 Supplementum XV, in: *NT* 28 (1986) 356–380.
    1987 Supplementum XVI, in: *NT* 29 (1987) 353–381.
- *Nag Hammadi Bibliography* 1970–1985, Leiden 1988/89.

Schüssler Fiorenza, E.: *The Book of Revelation: Justice and Judgment,* Philadelphia, PA 1985.

Schunck, K.-D.: "Die Attribute des eschatologischen Messias. Strukturlinien in der Ausprägung des alttestamentlichen Messiasbildes", in: *ThLZ* 110 (1985) 331–348.

Schwartz, D. R.: "The Tribes of As. Mos. 4:7–9", in: *JBL* 99 (1980) 217–223.

Schwartz, J.: "Note sur la 'petite apocalypse' de l'Asclepius", in: *RHPhR* 62 (1982) 165–169.

Schwarz, J.: "Jubilees, Bethel and the Temple of Jacob", in: *HUCA* 56 (1985) 63–85.

Seaford, R.: "Immortality, Salvation, and the Elements", in: *HSCP* 90 (1986) 1–26.

Seeber, C.: "Jenseitigkeit", in: *LÄ* III, Wiesbaden 1980, 249–252.

Segal, A. F.: "Paul and Ecstacy", in: K. H. Richards (ed.): *SBL Seminar Papers 25, 1986,* Atlanta, GA 1986, 555–580.

Segal, R.: *The Myth of Poimandres,* Paris 1986.

Sellin, G.: *Der Streit um die Auferstehung der Toten.* Eine religionsgeschichtliche und exegetische Untersuchung von 1. Korinther 15 (FRLANT 138), Göttingen 1986.

Shaked, S.: "Iranian Influences on Judaism: First Century B. C. E. to Second Century C. E.", in: W. D. Davies/L. Finkelstein (edd.): *The Cambridge History of Judaism,* Vol. 1, Cambridge 1984, 308–325.

– "First Man, First King. Notes on Semitic-Iranian Syncretism and Iranian Mythological Transformations", in: S. Shaked/D. Shulman/G. G. Stroumsa (edd.): *Gilgul. Essays on Transformation, Revolution and Permanence in the History of Religions.* Dedicated to R. J. Zwi Werblowski (SHR 50), Leiden 1987, 238–256.

Shea, W. H.: "Daniel 3: Extra-Biblical Texts and the Convocation on the Plain of Dura", in: *AUSS* 20 (1982) 29–52.

– "The Covenantal Form of the Letters to the Seven Churches", in: *AUSS* 21 (1983) 71–84.

– "A Further Note on Daniel 6: Daniel as Governor", in: *AUSS* 21 (1983) 169–171.

– "Wrestling with the Prince of Persia", in: *AUSS* 21 (1983) 225–250.

– "Further Literary Structures in Daniel 2–7", in: *AUSS* 22 (1984) 193–202; 277–295.

Shellrude, G. M.: "The Apocalypse of Adam: Evidence for a Christian Gnostic Provenance", in: M. Krause (ed.): *Gnosis and Gnosticism.* Papers read at the Eighth International Conference on Patristic Studies (Oxford September 3rd-8th, 1979). (NHS 17), Leiden 1981, 82–91.

– *Nag Hammadi Apocalypses: A Study of the Relation of Selected Texts to the Traditional Apocalypse* (Ph.D. diss., St. Andrews University, 1986).

Smalley, S. S.: "John's Revelation and John's Community", in: *BJRL* 69 (1987) 549–571.

Smith, M.: "Ascent to the Heavens and the Beginning of Christianity", in: *Eranos* 50 (1981) 403–429.

Soggin, J. A.: "Profezia ed Apocalittica nel Giudaismo Postesilico", in: *RivBib* 30 (1982) 161–173.

Staats, R.: "Hermas", in: *TRE* 15 (1986) 100–108.

Stanley, J. E.: "The Apocalypse and Contemporary Sect Analysis", in: K. H. Richards (ed.): *SBL Seminar Papers 25, 1986,* Atlanta, GA 1986, 412–421.

– *The Use of the Symbol of Four World Empires in Daniel 2, Daniel 7, 4 Ezra 11–12, Revelation 13, and 'Antiquities of the Jews' to Inspire Resistance to or Acceptance of Hellenism: Insights from the Sociology of Knowledge and Sect Analysis* (Diss. Iliff School of Theology, Denver, CO 1986).

Starcky, J.: "La signification du messianisme; IV. Les Hasmonéens", in: *Le Monde de la Bible* 42 (1986) 39–40.

Steck, O. H.: "Weltgeschehen und Gottesvolk im Buch Daniel", in: D. Lührmann/G. Strecker (edd.): *Kirche.* FS für Günther Bornkamm zum 75. Geburtstag, Tübingen 1980, 53–78.

Stegemann, H.: "Die 'Mitte der Schrift' aus der Sicht der Gemeinde von Qumran", in: M. Klopfenstein/U. Luz/S. Talmon/E. Tov (edd.): *Mitte der Schrift?* Ein jüdisch-christliches Gespräch. Texte des Berner Symposions vom 6.–12. Januar 1985 (Judaica et Christiana 11), Bern/Frankfurt Main/New York/Paris 1987, 149–184.

Stone, M.: "Reactions to the Destructions of the Second Temple", in: *JSJ* 12 (1981) 195–204.

- "The Metamorphosis of Ezra: Jewish Apocalypse and Medieval Vision", in: *JThS* 33 (1982) 1–18.
- "Coherence and Inconsistency in the Apocalypses: The Case of 'the End' in 4 Ezra", in: *JBL* 102 (1983) 229–243.
- "The Armenian Vision of Ezekiel", in: G. W. E. Nickelsburg/G. W. MacRae (edd.): *Christians among Jews and Gentiles*. Essays in Honor of Krister Stendahl, Philadelphia, PA 1986, 261–269.
- "Categorization and Classification of the Apocrypha and Pseudepigrapha", in: *Abr-Nahrain* 24 (1986) 167–177.
- "The Parabolic Use of Natural Order in Judaism of the Second Temple Age", in: S. Shaked/ D. Shulman/G. G. Stroumsa (edd.): *Gilgul. Essays on Transformation, Revolution and Permanence in the History of Religions*. Dedicated to R. J. Zwi Werblowski (SHR 50), Leiden 1987, 298–308.

STUHLMANN, R.: *Das eschatologische Maß im Neuen Testament* (FRLANT 132), Göttingen 1983.

SURIN, K.: *Theology and the Problem of Evil*, Oxford 1986.

SUTER, D. W.: *Tradition and Composition in the Parables of Enoch* (SBL.DS 47), Missoula, MT [now Atlanta, GA] 1979.
- "Māšāl in the Similitudes of Enoch", in: *JBL* 100 (1981) 193–212.
- "Weighed in the Balance: The Similitudes of Enoch in Recent Discussion", in: *RelStR* 7 (1981) 217–221.
- "The Measure of Redemption: The Similitudes of Enoch, Nonviolence and National Integrity", in: K. H. Richards (ed.): *SBL Seminar Papers 22, 1983*, Chico, CA [now Atlanta, GA] 1983, 167–176.

SVEDLUND, G.: "Notes on *bar nash* and the Detrimental Effects on Its Transformation into the Title 'The Son of Man'", in: T. Kronholm/E. Riad (edd.): *On the Dignity of Man*. Oriental and Classical Studies in Honour of Frithiof Rundgren (= *OrSuec* 33–35 [1984–86]), Stockholm 1986, 401–413.

TABOR, J. D.: *Things Unutterable: Paul's Ascent to Paradise in Its Greco-Roman, Judaic and Early Christian Contexts* (Studies in Judaism), Lanham, MD/New York/London 1986.

TAEGER, J.-W.: "Einige neue Veröffentlichungen zur Apokalypse des Johannes", in: *VF* 29 (1984) 50–75.

TEIXIDOR, J.: "Contexto epigráfico y literario de Esdras y Daniel", in: N. Fernández Marcos et alii (edd.): *Simposio Biblico Español, Salamanca 1982*, Madrid 1984, 128–140.

THIERING, B. E.: "The Three and a Half Years of Elijah", in: *NT* 23 (1981) 41–55.

THOMPSON, S.: *The Apocalypse and Semitic Syntax* (MSSNTS 52), Cambridge 1985.

TOLL, C.: "Zur Bedeutung des aramäischen Ausdruckes *bar nāš*", in: T. Kronholm/E. Riad (edd.): *On the Dignity of Man*. Oriental and Classical Studies in Honour of Frithiof Rundgren (= *OrSuec* 33–35 [1984–86]), Stockholm 1986, 421–428.

TRAVIS, S. H.: *Christ and the Judgment of God* (Foundations for Faith), Basingstoke 1986.

TREVER, J. C.: "The Book of Daniel and the Origin of the Qumran Community", in: *BA* 48 (1985) 89–102.
- "The Spiritual Odyssey of the Qumran Teacher", in: K. H. Richards (ed.): *SBL Seminar Papers 25, 1986*, Atlanta, GA 1986, 384–399.

TREVÈS, M.: "Remarques sur l'Apocalypse", in: *CCER* 33 (1985) 33–42.

TUBACH, J.: "Spuren des astronomischen Henochbuches bei den Manichäern Mittelasiens", in: P. O. Scholz/R. Stempel (edd.): *Nubia et Oriens Christianus*. FS für C. D. G. Müller zum 60. Geburtstag (Bibliotheca Nubica I), Köln 1987, 73–95.

TURNER, J. D.: "Trimorphic Protennoia" (Introduction and Translation), in: W. Barnstone, *The Other Bible*, San Francisco 1984, 588–593.
- "Sethian Gnosticism: A Literary History", in: C. W. Hedrick/R. Hodgson, Jr. (edd.): *Nag Hammadi, Gnosticism, and Early Christianity*, Peabody, MA 1986, 55–86.

UHLIG, S.: "Zur Überlieferungsgeschichte des äthiopischen Henochsbuches", in: *OrChr* 69 (1985) 184–193.

ULLMANN, W.: "Apokalyptik und Magie im gnostischen Mythos", in: K.-W. Tröger (ed.): *Altes Testament – Frühjudentum – Gnosis*. Neue Studien zu "Gnosis und Bibel", Berlin/ Gütersloh 1980, 169–194.

ULRICHSEN, J. H.: "Die sieben Häupter und die zehn Hörner. Zur Datierung der Offenbarung des Johannes", in: *StTh* 39 (1985) 1–20.

VANDERKAM, J. C.: "Enoch Traditions in Jubilees and other Second-Century Sources", in: P. J. Achtemeyer (ed.): *SBL Seminar Papers 17, 1978,* Missoula, MT [now Atlanta, GA] 1978, 229–251.

– "The Origin, Character and Early History of the 364-Day Calendar: A Reassessment of Jaubert's Hypotheses", in: *CBQ* 41 (1979) 390–411.

– "The Putative Author of the Book of Jubilees", in: *JSSt* 26 (1981) 209–217.

– "Some Major Issues in the Contemporary Study of 1 Enoch: Reflections on J. T. Milik's The Book of Enoch: Aramaic Fragments at Qumran Cave 4", in: *MAARAV* 3 (1982) 115–118.

– "A Twenty-Eight-Day Month Tradition in the Book of Jubilees?", in: *VT* 32 (1982) 504–506.

– "The 364-Day Calendar in the Enochic Literature", in: K. H. Richards (ed.): *SBL Seminar Papers 22, 1983,* Chico, CA [now Atlanta, GA] 1983, 157–165.

– "1 Enoch 77,3 and a Babylonian Map of the World", in: *RdQ* 11 (1983) 271–278.

– *Enoch and the Growth of an Apocalyptic Tradition* (CBQ.MS 16), Washington, D.C. 1984.

– "Studies in the Apocalypse of Weeks (1 Enoch 93:1–10; 91:11–17)", in: *CBQ* 46 (1984) 511–523.

– "The Prophetic-Sapiential Origins of Apocalyptical Thought", in: J. D. Martin/P. R. Davies (edd.): *A Word in Season*. Essays of Honor of W. McKane (JSOT.SS 42), Sheffield 1986, 163–176.

VANNI, U.: *L'Apocalisse: ermeneutica, esegesi, teologia* (Associazione Biblica Italiana. Supplementi alla Rivista Biblica 17), Bologna 1988.

VASHOLZ, R. I.: "An Additional Note on the 4Q Enoch Fragments and 11Q Tg Job", in: *MAARAV* 3 (1982) 115–118.

VERMES, G.: *Jesus and the World of Judaism,* London 1983.

DE VILLIERS, P. G. R.: "Understanding the Way of God: Form, Function and Message of the Historical Review in 4 Ezra 3:4–27", in: K. H. Richards (ed.): *SBL Seminar Papers 20, 1981,* Chico, CA [now Atlanta, GA] 1981, 357–378.

– "The Interpretation of a Text in the Light of its Socio-cultural Setting", in: *Neotestamentica* 18 (1984) 66–79.

VÖGTLE, A.: *Das Buch mit den sieben Siegeln*. Die Offenbarung des Johannes in Auswahl gedeutet, Freiburg i. Br. etc. 1981.

– "«Dann sah ich einen neuen Himmel und eine neue Erde . . .» (Apk 21,1)", in: E. Gräßer/O. Merk (edd.): *Glaube und Eschatologie*. FS für W. G. Kümmel, Tübingen 1985, 303–333.

VORSTER, W. S.: "'Genre' and the Revelation of John: A study in text, context and intertext", in: *Neotestamentica* 22 (1988) forthcoming.

WACHOLDER, B. Z.: *The Dawn of Qumran: The Sectarian Torah and the Teacher of Righteousness* (MHUC), Cincinnati, OH/New York, NY 1983.

– "The Date of the Eschaton in the Book of Jubilees: A Commentary on Jub. 49:22–50:5, CD 1:1–20 and 16:2–3", in: *HUCA* 56 (1985) 87–101.

WACKER, M.-T.: *Weltordnung und Gericht: Studien zu 1 Henoch 22,* Würzburg 1982.

WALTER, N.: "«Hellenistische» Eschatologie im Neuen Testament", in: E. Grässer/O. Merk (edd.): *Glaube und Eschatologie*. FS für W. G. Kümmel, Tübingen 1985, 335–356.

– "«Hellenistische» Eschatologie im Frühjudentum – ein Beitrag zur «Biblischen Theologie»", in: *ThLZ* 110 (1985) 331–348.

Wesselius, J. W.: "Language and Style in Biblical Aramaic: Observations on the Unity of Daniel II–VI", in: *VT* 38 (1988) 194–209.

West, M. L.: *The Orphic Poems,* Oxford 1983.

Whealon, J. F.: "New Patches on an Old Garment: The Book of Revelation", in: *BTB* 11 (1981) 54–59.

Wilken, R. L.: "Early Christian Chiliasm, Jewish Messianism, and the Idea of the Holy Land", in: G. W. E. Nickelsburg/G. W. MacRae (edd.): *Christians among Jews and Gentiles.* Essays in Honor of Krister Stendahl, Philadelphia, PA 1986, 298–307.

Willett, T. W.: *Eschatology in the Theodicies of 2 Baruch and 4 Ezra* (JSP.SS 4), Sheffield 1988.

Williams, R. J.: "The Sages of Ancient Egypt in the Light of Recent Scholarship", in: *JAOS* 101 (1981) 1–19.

Wilson, G. H.: "Wisdom in Daniel and the Origin of Apocalyptic", in: R. Ahroni (ed.): *Biblical and Other Studies in Memory of S. D. Goitein* (=*Hebrew Annual Review* 9 [1985]), Columbus, OH 1986, 373–381.

Wilson, R. R.: "From Prophecy to Apocalyptic: Reflections on the Shape of Israelite Religion", in: R. C. Culley/T. W. Overholt (edd.): *Anthropological Perspectives on Old Testament Prophecy* (*SEMEIA* 21), Chico, CA [now Atlanta, GA] 1982, 79–95.

Widengren, G.: "La rencontre avec la *DAĒNA,* qui représente les actions de l'homme", in: G. Gnoli (ed.): *Orientalia Romana.* Essays and Lectures 5: Iranian Studies (Serie Orientale Roma 52), Roma 1983, 41–79.

Wisse, F.: "The Paraphrase of Shem" (Introduction and Translation), in: W. Barnstone (ed.): *The Other Bible,* San Francisco 1984, 101–115.

Wissmann, H./Smend, R./Uffenheimer, B./Klein, G./May, G.: "Eschatologie I–V", in: *TRE* 10 (1982) 254–305.

Wolff, C.: "Die Gemeinde des Christus in der Apokalypse des Johannes", in: *NTS* 27 (1980/81) 186–197.

Wolter, M.: *Rechtfertigung und zukünftiges Heil.* Untersuchungen zu Röm 5,1–11 (BZNW 43), Berlin/New York 1978.

Wright, R. M./Hill, J. D.: "History, Ritual, and Myth: Nineteenth Century Millenarian Movements in the Northwest Amazon", in: *Ethnohistory* 33 (1986) 31–54.

Wyller, E. A.: "Die Offenbarung des Johannes in henologischer Sicht", in: K. Gloy/E. Rudolph (edd.): *Einheit und Grundlagen der Philosophie,* Darmstadt 1985, 46–72.

Yamauchi, I.: "Hermeneutical Issues in the Book of Daniel", in: *JRTS* 23 (1980) 13–22.

– "Jewish Gnosticism? The Prologue of John, Mandaean Parallels, and the Trimorphic Protennoia", in: R. van den Broek/M. J. Vermaseren (edd.): *Studies in Gnosticism and Hellenistic Religions* presented to Gilles Quispel on the Occasion of his 65th Birthday (EPRO 91), Leiden 1981, 467–497.

In view of future projects the editor would greatly appreciate, if the scholarly community would provide him with information about new releases pertaining to the field of Apocalyptic studies.

Index of Modern Authors

Pagenumbers are devided by the periods (55. 670. = 55 and 670); footnote references follow immediately upon the colons (33:50. 88:29,31–32. = footnote 50 on page 33 and footnotes 29, 31–32 on page 88).

Index of Passages

Pagenumbers are devided by the periods (55. 670. = 55 and 670); footnote references follow immediately upon the colons (33:50. 88:29,31–32. = footnote 50 on page 33 and footnotes 29, 31–32 on page 88).

I. Israelite and Jewish Texts

A. Old Testament

Genesis			22,28ff.	285
1	613		22,31	12
1,3	613		23,7–10	167
14	216		23,18–24	167
17,7	696		24	669:54. 680
18,1–19,3	168		24,3–9	167
28,12–15	169		24,7	675. 680
32,25–32	168		24,7f.	679
37,5–11	169		24,15–24	167
40,5–41,36	169		24,17	675. 680
40,12	427		24,17ff.	679
40,18	427		24,24	669:54
49,1–27	167			
49,10	696		Deuteronomy	
				282
Exodus			3,2	653
	550:4		6,20ff.	483:53
3,4	470		21,23	696
7,8–10,29	612		26,5	182:38
7,21	349:17		28,62	182:38
9,22	612:37		31,25ff.	605
10,12	612:37		32,1–43	167
10,21	612:37		32,21	540:40
19,10–25	167		33	191
24,9–11	168		33,2–29	167
24,15–18	168			
34	492		Joshua	
			5,14	422
Numbers			8,1–2	653
21,29	285			
21,34	653			

B. Apocrypha, Pseudepigrapha and Other Early Jewish Texts

C. Qumran and Related Texts

D. Rabbinic Texts and Jewish Mysticism

E. Published Compilations and Inscriptions

II. Early Christian Texts

A. New Testament

B. Apostolic Fathers and Other Early Christian Texts

C. Syriac Texts

III. Iranian Texts

A. Avesta

B. Pahlavi-Texts and Inscriptions

C. New Persian Texts

D. Other Texts

Armenian:
Ara et
Semiramis 238

Eznik of Kolb
De Deo
II, IX, 190 130. 130:273

Greek and Latin:
Oracles of
Hystaspes

(See further II.C. 26. 87. 119. 121–127. 131
under Lactantius) 131:286. 132. 146. 150.
154. 234:27. 398. 398:32.
400–402. 565. 657. 671:59.
786 f.

Plutarchos, *De Iside et Osiride* 46–47:
see under VII. A.

Syriac: see under II.D.

IV. Mesopotamian Texts

According to Editions:

[ed. Biggs 1967]
Text: Biggs II 383. 384 f.

[ed. Grayson 1975]
Dynastic
Prophecy 382 f. 385

[eds. Grayson-Lambert 1964]
Text A 379 f. 383. 385
Text B 383 f.
Text C
(Shulgi Prophecy) 382 f. 385
Text D (Marduk
Prophecy) 381–383. 385

[eds. Hunger-Kaufman 1975]
Uruk Prophecy 380 f. 383. 385
r 3–10 380 f.
r 11–19 380 f.

Akkadian Oracles and
Prophecies
[Texts:
ANET 449 f.] 245:40

Atrahasis Epos
[eds. Lambert-Millard 1969;
von Soden 1978] 250 f.

Vision of the Nether World
[Text:
ANET 109 f.] 240. 240:14

V. Aramaic and Hettite Texts

Aramaic Papyri of the
Fifth Century B. C.
[ed. Cowley 1923]
97 ff. Nr. 27 195:92

The Bileam Inscription from
Deir ʿAlla
240. 246. 386. 780

Hettite Text
on Kingship
in Heaven
[Text:
ANET 120 f.] 250. 250:54

VI. Egyptian Texts

A. Documents from Ancient Egypt (Urk)

B. Funerary Texts

C. Literary Texts, Papyri and Ostraca

VII. Classical Texts
Cf. also section I.E.

A. Greek Texts

B. Latin Texts

VIII. Gnostic Texts

A. Manichaean Texts

B. Mandaean Texts

C. Nag Hammadi Texts

IX. Varia

C. Arabic Texts

D. Aztec Texts

E. Annamite Texts

List of Committee Members and Authors
(1988)

Prof. Dr. Jan Assmann, Ägyptologisches Institut, Marstallhof 4, D-6900 Heidelberg, Germany, BRD

Prof. Dr. Jan Bergman Uppsala universitet, Teologiska institutionen, Box 1604, S-751 46 Uppsala, Sweden

Prof. Dr. Hans Dieter Betz, The Divinity School, Swift Hall, The University of Chicago, Chicago, Ill. 60637, USA

Prof. Dr. Walter Burkert, Wildsbergstraße 8, CH-8610 Uster-Zürich, Switzerland

Prof. Dr. Hubert Cancik, Haußerstraße 89, D-7400 Tübingen, Germany, BRD

Prof. Dr. Jean Carmignac †

Prof. Dr. Adela Yarbro Collins, Dept. of Theology, University of Notre Dame, Notre Dame, IN 46556, USA

Prof. Dr. John J. Collins, Dept. of Theology, University of Notre Dame, Notre Dame, IN 46556, USA

Prof. Dr. Burkhard Gladigow, Abteilung für Religionswissenschaft, Universität Tübingen, Reutlinger Straße 2, D-7400 Tübingen, Germany, BRD

Prof. Dr. J. Gwyn Griffiths, Dept. of Classics and Ancient History, University College of Swansea, Swansea SA2 8PP, Wales, Great Britain

Prof. Dr. Wolfgang Harnisch, Am Vogelherd 16, D-3550 Marburg-Cappel, Germany, BRD

Prof. Dr. Lars Hartman, Uppsala universitet, Teologiska institutionen, Box 1604, S-751 46 Uppsala, Sweden

Prof. Dr. Sven S. Hartman †

Doc. Dr. David Hellholm, Dept. of Christian Studies, University of Bergen, Sydnesplass 9, N-5007 Bergen, Norway

Prof. Dr. Martin Hengel, Schwabstraße 51, D-7400 Tübingen, Germany, BRD

Prof. Dr. Anders Hultgård, Dept. of History of Religions, University of Bergen, Sydnesplass 9, N-5007 Bergen, Norway

Prof. Dr. Thorvald Källstad, Uppsala universitet, Teologiska institutionen, Box 1604, S-751 46 Uppsala, Sweden

Prof. Dr. Hans G. Kippenberg, Nieuwe Kijk in't Jatstraat 104, NL-Groningen, The Netherlands

Prof. Dr. Klaus Koch, Universität Hamburg, Alttestamentliches Seminar, Sedanstraße 19, D-2000 Hamburg 13, Germany, BRD

Prof. Dr. Dr. Martin Krause, Melcherstraße 30, D-4400 Münster/Westf., Germany, BRD

Prof. Dr. Jürgen C. H. Lebram, Rich. Wagnerstraße 60, D-7410 Reutlingen, Germany, BRD

Prof. Dr. Evald Lövestam, Lunds universitet, Theologicum, Sandgatan 1, S-223 50 Lund, Sweden

Prof. Dr. George W. MacRae †

Prof. Dr. Wayne A. Meeks, Dept. of Religious Studies, Yale University, P. O. Box 2160, New Haven, CT 06520, USA

Prof. Dr. Ulrich B. Müller, Philosophische Fakultät, Universität des Saarlandes, D-6600 Saarbrücken 11, Germany, BRD

Prof. Dr. George W. E. Nickelsburg, School of Religion, University of Iowa, Iowa City, Iowa 52242, USA

Prof. Dr. Tord Olsson, Lunds universitet, Theologicum, Sandgatan 1, S-223 50 Lund, Sweden

Prof. Dr. Marc Philonenko, 32 rue de l'Université, F-67000 Strasbourg, France

Prof. Dr. Helmer Ringgren, Uppsala universitet, Teologiska institutionen, Box 1604, S-751 46 Uppsala, Sweden

Prof. Dr. Dr. Kurt Rudolph, Holderstrauch 7, D-3550 Marburg/Lahn, Germany, BRD

Prof. Dr. Torgny Säve-Söderbergh, Kyrkogårdsgatan 27, S-752 35 Uppsala, Sweden

Prof. Dr. E. P. Sanders, The Queen's College, Oxford OX1 4AW, England

Prof. Dr. Luise Schottroff, Im Rosental 6, D-3500 Kassel, Germany, BRD

Prof. Dr. Elisabeth Schüssler Fiorenza, Harvard Divinity School, 45 Francis Avenue, Cambridge, MA 02138, USA

Prof. Dr. Marcel Simon †

Prof. Dr. Morton Smith, Dept. of History, Columbia University, New York, NY 10027, USA

Prof. Dr. Dr. Hartmut Stegemann, Nikolausberger Weg 5b, D-3400 Göttingen, Germany, BRD

Prof. Dr. Dr. Geo Widengren, Karlavägen 95, S-115 22 Stockholm, Sweden